The NEW

DICTIONARY OF THOUGHTS

A Cyclopedia of Quotations

*From the Best Authors of the World,
Both Ancient and Modern,
Alphabetically Arranged by Subjects*

ORIGINALLY COMPILED BY
TRYON EDWARDS, D.D.
REVISED AND ENLARGED BY
C. N. CATREVAS, A.B.
AND
JONATHAN EDWARDS, A.M.

PREFACE

The first English *Dictionary of Words* was issued in 1552, but it was not until 1877 that the first *Dictionary of Thoughts* was published by Tryon Edwards. Such a compilation of the condensed and striking thoughts of the world's best thinkers on important and interesting subjects, arranged in alphabetical order of topics for ready reference, is a daily necessity.

Tillotson has said, speaking of the brief and noticeably striking sayings of wise and good men: "They are of great value, like the dust of gold, or the sparks of diamonds." Johnson counts him a benefactor of mankind who "condenses the great thoughts and rules of life into short sentences that are easily impressed on the memory, and recur promptly to the mind." Swift compares such thoughts to "burning glasses, as they collect the diffused rays of wit and learning in authors, and make them point with warmth and quickness on the reader's imagination."

A carefully compiled, intelligently edited, and properly arranged *Dictionary of Thoughts* finds eager users wherever there exists among writers, speakers, and readers an inclination to develop and broaden their scope of knowledge and to know the thoughts of the world's greatest minds from ancient to modern times. In this twentieth century, with the radio and the improvements in modern publishing greatly enlarging the field for speakers and writers, it is more valuable from the purely practical point of view than ever before.

THE NEW DICTIONARY OF THOUGHTS was originally compiled during more than fifty years of active literary effort by Tryon Edwards, son of the famous New England divine of the same name, who is represented in the volume by several quotations. It has been revised by C. N. Catrevas with the assistance of C. A. Bender and of Jonathan Edwards, a descendant of the great preacher and educator of the same name, and now includes hundreds of quotations from modern writers, both in the main body of the work and in a supplement (p. 725 ff.) which brings together representative quotations from modern writers for ready reference.

Another recent addition is a section of *Familiar Phrases* (p. 735 ff.) and special compilations of *Familar Expressions from the Bible* (p. 48b ff.) and *Familiar Phrases from Shakespeare* (p. 589b ff.)

The *Subject Finder*, which precedes the text (p. iv ff.), makes it possible to find all the quotations on associated subjects with a minimum of effort, and the *Authors' Reference Index*, at the end of the volume, includes biographical information about the authors quoted as well as page references to quotations.

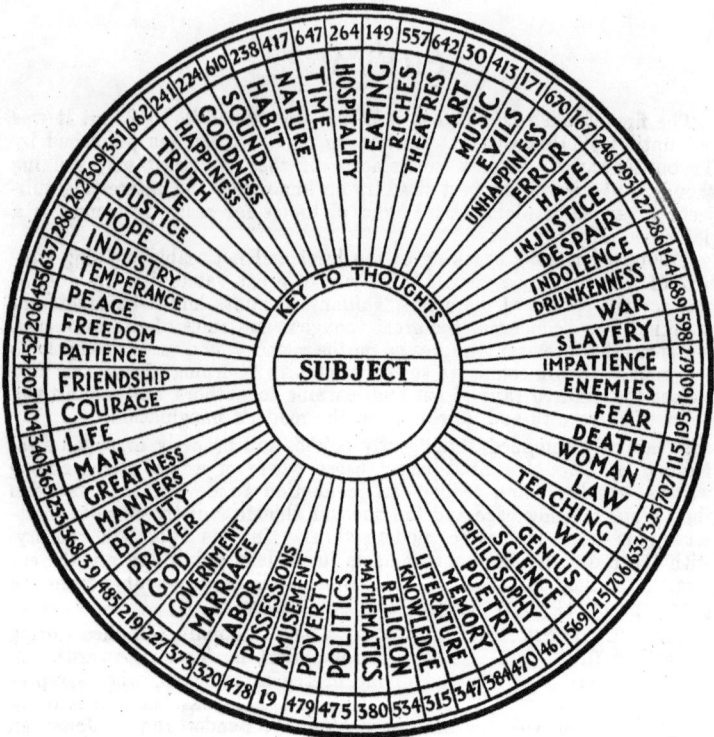

A QUICK GUIDE TO MAJOR SUBJECTS

The subjects will be found along the radii of the circle and the page references along the circumference. For other subjects see *Subject Finder with Cross References*, p. v.

SUBJECT FINDER WITH CROSS REFERENCES

A THESAURUS INDEX

NOTE—Names printed in italic capital letters refer to subjects which are included under different headings, the proper title in each case being given below in small letters. An asterisk (*) after a title refers to the supplement of quotations from recent writers at the end of the book. Cross references in italic small letters have an antonymous relation to the main heading. The rest are synonyms or other closely associated ideas.

v

BELIEF
Doubt
Credulity
Creed
Doctrine
Expectation
Faith
Hope
Opinion
Prejudice
Religion
Sects
Theories
Trust
BELONGINGS
Possessions
BENEFICENCE
Meanness
Benevolence
Charity
Doing well
Generosity
Gifts
Goodness
Help
Kindness
Liberality
Magnanimity
Philanthropy
Well-doing
BENEVOLENCE
See Beneficence
BENIGNITY
Beneficence
BENT
Inclination
BEREAVEMENT
Death
BEST THINGS
Evils
Blessedness
Excellence
Goodness
Ideals
Merit
Perfection
BETROTHAL
Courtship
BETTERMENT
Improvement
BIAS
Prejudice
BIBLE
Christianity
Gospel
Theology
BICKERING
Contention
BIGOTRY
See Intolerance
BILLS
Debt
BIOGRAPHY
Anecdotes
Books
History
Letters
Life
Writing

BIRTH
Death
Ancestry
Babe
Children
Family
Infancy
Mother
Parents
Posterity
BITTERNESS
Resentment
BLAME
Censure
BLANDISHMENT
Flattery
BLARNEY
Flattery
BLASPHEMY
Profanity
BLESSEDNESS
Misery
Delight
Glory
Happiness
Holiness
Joy
Perfection
BLINDNESS
Eye
BLISS
Happiness
BLOCKHEAD
See Dulness
BLOOD
Ancestry
BLOODSHED
Murder
BLUFF
Affectation
BLUNDER
Mistake
BLUNTNESS
Candor
BLUSH
Bashfulness
Delicacy
Diffidence
Innocence
Modesty
Purity
Shame
BLUSTERING
Equanimity
Arrogance
Boasting
Ill nature
Threats
BOASTING
Modesty
Blustering
Conceit
Egotism
Ostentation
Self-conceit
Self-praise
Snobs
Vain-glory
Vanity

BODY
Soul
Health
Mortality
BOLDNESS
Cowardice
Bravery
Confidence
Courage
Heroism
Impudence
Rashness
Recklessness
Valor
BOMBAST
Blustering
BONDAGE
Slavery
BOOKS
Allegories
Authorship
Ballads
Biography
Fables
Fiction
History
Ink
Learning
Letters
Libraries
Literature
Novels
Pen
Poetry
Reading
Rhetoric
Romance
Study
Style
Tragedy
Words
Writing
BORES
See Dulness
BORROWING
Lending
Credit
Debt
Plagiarism
Suretyship
BOYS
Children
BRAGGING
Boasting
BRAIN
Mind
BRAVADO
Blustering
BRAVERY
See Courage
BREAD
Diet
BREADTH
Broadmindedness*
BREEDING
Good breeding
BREVITY
Verbosity
Simplicity

BRIBERY
Honesty
Conspiracy
Corruption
Dishonesty
Knavery
Roguery
Treachery
Villainy
BRIDE
Wife
BROADMINDED-
NESS*
Bigotry
Openmindedness*
Toleration
BROTHERHOOD
Selfishness
Christianity
Communism
Companionship
Equality
Friendship
Humanity
Man
Society
BRUTALITY
Cruelty
BUFFOONERY
Jesting
BUILDING
Architecture
BURIAL
Death
BURLESQUE
Satire
BUSINESS
Idleness
Commerce
Employment
Executives*
Industry
Occupation
Salesmen*
Trade
BUSYBODIES
See Babblers
BUT
Contradiction
Contrast

CABAL
Conspiracy
CAJOLERY
Flattery
CALAMITY
See Adversity
CALCULATION
Cunning
CALMNESS
Equanimity
CALUMNY
See Abuse
Babblers
CALVINISM
Christianity
Protestantism
CANDOR
See Truth

DECISION
  Indecision
  Firmness
  Positiveness
  Resolution
DECLAMATION
  Oratory
DECORATION
  Ornament
DECORUM
  Decency
DEDUCTION
  Logic
DEEDS
  Inactivity
  Action
  Doing well
  Well-doing
DEFAMATION
  Calumny
DEFEAT
  Victory
  Failure
DEFECTS
  Failings
DEFERENCE
  See Civility
DEFIANCE
  Rebellion
DEFICIENCIES
  Failings
DEFINITION
  Obscurity
  Accuracy
DEFORMITY
  Beauty
DEGENERACY
  Depravity
DEGRADATION
  Depravity
DEJECTION
  Despondency
DELAY
  Haste
  Procrastination
  Time
DELIBERATION
  Thought
DELICACY
  Insensibility
  Cultivation
  Decency
  Modesty
  Purity
  Refinement
  Sensibility
  Sensitiveness
  Tact
  Taste
DELIGHT
  See Enjoyment
DELINQUENCY
  Crime
DELUSION
  Truth
  Error
  Mistake
  Self-deception
  Superstition

DEMEANOR
  Behavior
DEMOCRACY
  Tyranny
  America
  Equality
  Levelers
  Liberty
  Republic
DENIAL
  Contradiction
DENUNCIATION
  Abuse
DEPARTURE
  Farewell
DEPENDENCE
  Independence
  Poverty
  Servants
  Slavery
  Weakness
DEPORTMENT
  Behavior
DEPRAVITY
  See Baseness
DEPRESSION*
  Prosperity
  Adversity
  Panic
  Poverty
DEPRIVATION
  Poverty
DEPTH
  Wisdom
DERANGEMENT
  Insanity
DERISION
  Ridicule
DEROGATION
  Detraction
DESIRE
  Indifference
  Ambition
  Appetite
  Covetousness
  Inclination
  Love
  Lust
  Wants
  Wishes
  Yearnings
DESOLATION
  Conviviality
  Emptiness
  Loneliness*
  Misery
  Poverty
  Ruins
DESPAIR
  Hope
  Despondency
  Disappointment
  Melancholy
  Sadness
  Sorrow
DESPATCH
  Dispatch
DESPERATION
  Recklessness

DESPONDENCY
  See Despair
DESPOTISM
  Democracy
  Dictatorship*
  Oppression
  Tyranny
DESTINY
  Choice
  Fate
  Fortune
  God
DESTITUTION
  Poverty
DETACHMENT
  Disinterestedness
DETECTION
  Discovery
DETERMINATION
  Decision
DETRACTION
  See Babblers
DEVELOPMENT
  Progress
DEVIATION
  Constancy
  Compromise
  Inconstancy
  Instability
DEVIL
  God
  Hell
DEVOTION
  Hate
  Affection
  Constancy
  Fidelity
  Love
  Piety
DEVOUTNESS
  Devotion
DEW
DEXTERITY
  Ability
DIALECT
  Accent
DIALOGUE
  Conversation
DICE
  See Cards
DICTATORSHIP*
  See Despotism
DICTION
  Language
DIET
  *Cooking**
  Dinner
  Eating
  Feasting
  Gluttony
  Indigestion
  Vegetarianism*
DIFFERENCE
  See Contention
DIFFICULTY
  Simplicity
  Adversity
  Hardship
  Trouble

DIFFIDENCE
  See Bashfulness
DIGESTION
  Diet
DIGNITY
  Humility
  Eminence
  Glory
  Gravity
  Honor
  Pride
  Self-respect
DIGRESSION
  Deviation
DILIGENCE
  Sloth
  Effort
  Industry
  Labor
  Perseverance
  Work
DIN
  Noise
DINNER
  See Diet
DIPLOMACY
  Tact
DIRECTION
  Purpose
DIRT
  Cleanliness
  Impurity
  Scandal
DISAGREEMENT
  Difference
DISAPPOINTMENT
  Delight
  Defeat
  Despondency
  Failure
DISAPPROVAL
  Censure
DISARMAMENT
  Peace
DISASTER
  Calamity
DISBELIEF
  Doubt
DISCERNMENT
  See Intelligence
DISCIPLINE
  Indulgence
  Education
  Order
  Punishment
  Self-improvement
  Study
DISCOMFITURE
  Defeat
DISCONTENT
  Contentment
  Complaining
  Despondency
  Fretfulness
  Grumbling
  Moroseness
  Murmuring
  Rebellion
  Restlessness

DISCORD
Contention
DISCOURAGEMENT
Despondency
DISCOURSE
Speech
DISCOURTESY
Impudence
DISCOVERY
  Familiarity
Innovation
Invention
Novelty
Originality
DISCRETION
  Indiscretion
Caution
Common sense
Consideration
Judgment
Prudence
Reflection
Sense
DISCRIMINATION
Discernment
DISCUSSION
  Silence
Agitation
Argument
Assertions
Controversy
Conversation
DISDAIN
Contempt
DISEASE
  Health
Indigestion
Sickness
DISESTEEM
Disgrace
DISFAVOR
Disgrace
DISFIGUREMENT
Deformity
DISGRACE
  Honor
Defeat
Infamy
Shame
DISGUISE
Concealment
Deceit
Dissimulation
Hypocrisy
DISHONESTY
  Honesty
Bribery
Corruption
Crime
Deceit
Dissimulation
Equivocation*
Falsehood
Fraud
Hypocrisy
Liars
Lying
DISHONOR
Disgrace

DISILLUSION-
  MENT*
Delusion
Cynics
Knowledge
Wisdom
DISINTERESTED-
  NESS
Interest
Benevolence
Generosity
Justice
Magnanimity
Philanthropy
DISLOYALTY
Treachery
DISMAY
Fear
DISOBEDIENCE
  Obedience
Obstinacy
Perverseness
Rebellion
DISORDER
Anarchy
DISPARAGEMENT
Detraction
DISPATCH
  Delay
Haste
Promptness
Punctuality
DISPLAY
Ostentation
DISPOSITION
Character
Inclination
Temper
DISPUTATION
Controversy
DISREPUTE
Disgrace
DISRESPECT
Impudence
DISSATISFACTION
Discontent
DISSENSION
Contention
DISSIMULATION
  See Disguise
DISSIPATION
  Moderation
Drinking
Drunkenness
Excess
Indulgence
Intemperance
Licentiousness
Waste
Wine
DISTANCE
  Familiarity
Absence
Reserve
DISTINCTION
  Mediocrity
Eminence
Fame
Glory

DISTRESS
Affliction
DISTRUST
  Trust
Doubt
Suspicion
DIVERSION
  Work
Amusements
Pleasure
Recreation
DIVERSITY
Variety
DIVINITY
God
DOCILITY
  Obstinacy
Deference
Humility
Meekness
Obedience
Submission
DOCTRINE
  See Belief
DOGMATISM
  *Openmindedness**
Bigotry
Fanaticism
Pedantry
Zeal
DOING WELL
  See Beneficence
DOLE*
Charity
DOLOR
Sadness
DOMESTIC
  Travel
Family
Home
Servants
DOMINION
Empire
DOOM
Destiny
DOUBT
  See Unbelief
DREAD
Fear
DREAMS
  Facts
Castles in the air
Fancy
Imagination
Reverie
DRESS
  See Dandy
DRINKING
  Abstinence
Dissipation
Drunkenness
Intemperance
Wine
DRONES
Sloth
DRUDGERY
Work
DRUGS
Medicine

DRUNKENNESS
  See Drinking
DUELS
  Friendship
Murder
Violence
DULNESS
  Wit
Blockhead
Bores
Coxcomb
Ennui
Fools
Ignorance
Insensibility
Loquacity
Mediocrity
Monotony*
Obscurity
Verbosity
DUPLICITY
Deceit
DUSK
Twilight
DUTY
  Choice
Obligation
Responsibility
Right
Trust

EARLY RISING
  Sloth
Morning
Sunrise
Time
EARNESTNESS
  Indifference
Effort
Enthusiasm
Sincerity
EARTH
  Heaven
Agriculture
Country
Farming*
Nature
World
EASE
Idleness
EATING
  See Diet
ECCENTRICITY
  *Standardization**
Deviation
Individuality
Originality
Singularity
ECONOMISTS*
ECONOMY
  See Frugality
ECSTASY
Joy
EDIFICATION
Education
EDUCATION
Cultivation
Discipline
Improvement

EXAMPLE
  Precept
  Emulation
  Influence
  Precedent
EXCELLENCE
  Mediocrity
  Eminence
  Goodness
  Greatness
  Merit
  Perfection
  Worth
EXCELSIOR
  See Aims
EXCESS
  See Dissipation
EXCITEMENT
  Repose
  Action
  Adventure*
  Agitation
  Emotion
  Passion
EXCUSES
  See Apologies
EXECUTIVES*
  *Employees**
  Business
  Commanders
  Committees*
  Master
EXERCISE
  Rest
  Exertion
  Gymnastics
  Work
EXERTION
  See Effort
EXHORTATION
  Advice
EXISTENCE
  Life
EXPECTATION
  Despair
  Anticipation
  Hope
  Pursuit
EXPEDIENCY
  Principles
  Compromise
  Interest
  Means
  Opportunity
EXPEDITION
  Dispatch
EXPENSE
  Gifts
  Bargain
  Cost *
  Extravagance
EXPERIENCE
  Ignorance
  Age
  Disillusionment*
  Observation
  Suffering
  Wisdom

EXPERIMENT
  Science
EXPIATION
  Retribution
EXPLANATION
  Teaching
EXPLETIVES
  Profanity
EXPRESSION
  Face
  Language
EXTRAVAGANCE
  See Prodigality
EXTREMES
  Moderation
  Excess
  Intemperance
EYE
  Countenance
  Face
  Looks
  Observation
  Physiognomy

FABLES
  Facts
  Allegory
  Literature
  Mythology
FACE
  See Countenance
FACTION
  Union and unity
  Contention
  Creed
  Party
  Sects
FACTS
  See Truth
FAILINGS
  Virtue
  Error
  Faults
  Imperfection
  Sin
  Weakness
FAILURE
  Success
  Defeat
FAIRNESS
  Justice
FAITH
  See Belief
FALLACY
  Error
FALSEHOOD
  See Dishonesty
FAME
  Oblivion
  Glory
  Honor
  Reputation
FAMILIARITY
  Distance
  Acquaintance
  Companionship
  Friendship
  Knowledge

FAMILY
  Guests
  Ancestry
  Birth
  Children
  Domestic
FANATICISM
  See Intolerance
FANCY
  Facts
  Castles in the air
  Dreams
  Imagination
  Reverie
  Speculation
  Wonder
FAREWELL
  Welcome
  Death
  Parting
FARMING*
  See Agriculture
FASCINATION
  Charm*
FASHION
  Eccentricity
  Appearances
  Custom
  Dandy
  Dress
  Foppery
  Imitation
  Vanity
FASTIDIOUSNESS
  Indifference
  Cleanliness
  Dandy
  Delicacy
  Dress
  Foppery
  Taste
FATE
  See Destiny
FATHER
  Parents
FAULTS
  See Failings
FAWNING
  Flattery
FEALTY
  Fidelity
FEAR
  Courage
  Anxiety
  Cowardice
  Panic
  Superstition
FEASTING
  See Diet
FEELINGS
  Insensibility
  Emotion
  Heart
  Sensibility
  Sensitiveness
  Sentiment
FELICITY
  Happiness

FEMININITY
  Woman
FEROCITY
  Cruelty
FERVOR
  Enthusiasm
FESTIVITY
  Conviviality
FICKLENESS
  Constancy
  Change
  Coquette
  Inconstancy
  Indecision
  Instability
  Irresolution
  Mutability
FICTION
  See Books
FIDELITY
  Treachery
  Constancy
  Devotion
  Faith
FIGHTING
  Contention
FILTH
  Dirt
FINANCE
  Money
FINERY
  Ornament
FIRMNESS
  Indecision
  Constancy
  Decision
  Positiveness
  Purpose
  Resolution
FLATTERY
  Censure
  Compliments
  Courts and
    courtiers
  Praise
FLIPPANCY
  Levity
FLOWERS
  Nature
FLUENCY
  Eloquence
FOLLY
  Wisdom
  Indiscretion
  Rashness
  Recklessness
FOOLS
  Blockhead
  Bores
  Coxcomb
FOPPERY
  See Dandy
FORBEARANCE
  Intolerance
  Gentleness
  Lenity
  Patience
  Toleration

FORCE
Gentleness
Energy
Oppression
Persecution
Power
Revolution
Strength
Violence
War
FOREBODING
See Anxiety
FORETHOUGHT
Rashness
Caution
Providence
Prudence
Wisdom
FORGETFULNESS
Remembrance
Neglect
Oblivion
Past
FORGIVENESS
See Clemency
FORMALISM
Simplicity
Ceremony
Custom
Etiquette
Forms
Tradition
FORMS
See Formalism
FORTITUDE
Cowardice
Bravery
Courage
Endurance
Firmness
Patience
Resignation
Resolution
Stoicism
Strength
FORTUNE
Misfortune
Accident
Chance
Destiny
Fate
Luck
Wealth
FOUNDATIONS
Beginnings
FRAILTIES
Failings
FRANKNESS
Candor
FRATERNITY
Brotherhood
FRAUD
See Dishonesty
FREEDOM
Slavery
Democracy
Independence
Liberty
Republic

FRETFULNESS
Good nature
Complaining
Discontent
Grumbling
Ill nature
Moroseness
Murmuring
FRICTION
Contention
FRIENDSHIP
Enemies
Acquaintance
Associates
Brotherhood
Companionship
Society
FRIGHT
Fear
FRIVOLITY
Levity
FROWNS
Ill nature
FRUGALITY
Extravagance
Abstinence
Bargain
Caution
Economy
Forethought
Miser
Providence
Prudence
Self-denial
Temperance
Thrift*
FRUSTRATION
Defeat
FUN
Pleasure
FURY
Rage
FUTURITY
See Future state
FUTURE STATE
Past
Eternity
Futurity
Heaven
Hell
Immortality

GAIN
See Avarice
GALL
Malice
GALLANTRY
Devotion
Compliments
Courts and courtiers
Courtship
Deference
Flattery
Kisses
Vows
GAMBLING
See Cards
GARRULITY
Loquacity

GASCONADE
Blustering
GAYETY
Moroseness
Cheerfulness
Conviviality
Good humor
Happiness
Laughter
Mirth
Smiles
Vivacity
GEMS
Ornament
Riches
Wealth
GENERALIZATION*
Facts
Assertions
Reason
Speculation
Theories
GENEROSITY
See Beneficence
GENIALITY
Amiability
GENIUS
Mediocrity
Ability
Art
Inspiration
Originality
Talent
GENTILITY*
Vulgarity
Ancestry
Aristocracy
GENTLEMAN
See Gentility
GENTLENESS
Cruelty
Clemency
Compassion
Gentility
Humanity
Kindness
Lenity
Mercy
GEOLOGY
Earth
Science
GIFTS
See Beneficence
GLADNESS
Joy
GLOOM
Melancholy
GLORY
Infamy
Distinction
Eminence
Fame
Honor
GLUTTONY
Abstinence
Eating
Excess
Feasting
Intemperance

GOD
Devil
Omnipotence
Omniscience
Omnipresence
GOLD
See Avarice
GOOD BREEDING
Vulgarity
Civility
Etiquette
Manners
Politeness
Refinement
GOOD HUMOR
See Cheerfulness
GOOD NATURE
Ill nature
Amiability
Benevolence
Complacency
Equanimity
Kindness
Lenity
Patience
GOODNESS
See Virtue
GOODS
Property
GOOD SENSE
Common sense
GORGING
Gluttony
GOSPEL
Bible
GOSSIP
See Babblers
GOVERNMENT
Anarchy
Law
Party
Politics
Statesmanship
GRACE
Awkwardness
Disgrace
Beauty
Blessedness
Charm*
Delicacy
Forgiveness
Goodness
Gracefulness
Holiness
GRACEFULNESS
See Grace
GRATITUDE
Ingratitude
Appreciation
Obligation
Thankfulness
GRAVE
Life
Death
End
Epitaphs
Monuments
Mortality
Oblivion

GRAVITY
  Levity
  Earnestness
  Sadness
  Sobriety
GREATNESS
  Mediocrity
  Distinction
  Eminence
  Fame
  Glory
  Honor
GREED
  Avarice
GREETING
  Welcome
GRIEF
  Joy
  Sadness
  Sorrow
  Tears
GRIT
  Courage
GRUMBLING
  See Fretfulness
GUESTS
  Family
  Hospitality
  Visitors
GUIDANCE
  Opposition
  Advice
  Counsel
  Example
  Instruction
  Precept
  Teaching
GUILE
  Deceit
GUILT
  Innocence
  Conscience
  Crime
  Remorse
  Sin
GULLIBILITY
  Credulity
GYMNASTICS
  See Exercise

HABIT
  Innovation
  Custom
  Fashion
  Tradition
HAIR
  Beard
HALLUCINATION
  Delusion
HAND
  Mind
  Deeds
HAPPINESS
  Unhappiness
  Contentment
  Delight
  Enjoyment
  Joy
  Pleasure

HARDSHIP
  See Adversity
HARLOT
  See Licentiousness
HARM
  Injury
HARMONY
  Music
  Peace
HASTE
  Delay
  Dispatch
  Impulse
  Indiscretion
  Promptness
  Rashness
  Recklessness
HATRED
  Love
  Enemies
  Jealousy
  Malevolence
  Malice
  Resentment
  Revenge
HAUTEUR
  Pride
HAZARD
  Danger
HEAD
  Body
  Heart
  Intellect
  Mind
  Reason
  Understanding
HEALTH
  Disease
  Body
  Strength
HEARING
  Sound
HEARSAY
  Rumor
HEART
  Head
  Emotion
  Feelings
  Love
  Sensibility
  Soul
HEAVEN
  Hell
  Eternity
  Future state
  Paradise
HEIRS
  Children
  Inheritance
HELL
  Heaven
  Devil
  Punishment
HELP
  See Beneficence
HEREDITY
  Ancestry
HEROISM
  See Courage

HESITATION
  Indecision
HISTORY
  Fiction
  Biography
  Past
HOARDING
  Miser
HOLIDAYS
  Sabbath
HOLINESS
  Infamy
  Grace
  Piety
  Purity
  Religion
  Reverence
HOLLOWNESS
  Insincerity
HOLLYWOOD*
  Actors
  Theatres
HOME
  Travel
  Domestic
  Family
  House
  Mother
HONESTY
  See Truth
HONOR
  Disgrace
  Distinction
  Esteem
  Fame
  Glory
  Honesty
  Integrity
HOPE
  Despair
  Anticipation
  Confidence
  Expectation
  Faith
  Trust
HOSPITALITY
  Meanness
  Guests
  Inns
  Visitors
HOTELS
  Inns
HOUSE
  Building
  Home
HUMANITY
  Cruelty
  Brotherhood
  Life
  Man
  Society
  Sympathy
HUMILITY
  Pride
  Docility
  Meekness
  Modesty
  Resignation
  Submission

HUMOR
  See Wit
HUNGER
  Appetite
HURRY
  Haste
HUSBANDS*
  Bachelor
  Marriage
  Men
HYPOCRISY
  See Affectation

IDEALS
  See Aims
IDEAS
  See Thought
IDIOSYNCRASY
  Eccentricity
IDLENESS
  Occupation
  Inactivity
  Indolence
  Leisure
  Rest]
  Sloth
IGNOMINY
  Disgrace
IGNORANCE
  Knowledge
  Blockhead
  Coxcomb
  Dulness
  Fools
  Innocence
ILL NATURE
  Good nature
  Complaining
  Fretfulness
  Malevolence
  Malice
  Moroseness
  Murmuring
  Perverseness
ILLS
  See Adversity
ILLUSION
  Delusion
IMAGINATION
  Facts
  Castles in the air
  Dreams
  Fancy
  Fiction
IMITATION
  Originality
  Emulation
  Example
  Hypocrisy
  Plagiarism
IMMODESTY
  Impurity
IMMORALITY
  Depravity
IMMORTALITY
  Mortality
  Eternity
  Heaven
  Soul

IMPARTIALITY
Disinterestedness
IMPATIENCE
Patience
Fretfulness
Haste
Restlessness
IMPERFECTION
See Failings
IMPERTINENCE
Politeness
Arrogance
Boldness
Impudence
Insult
IMPETUOSITY
Rashness
IMPIETY
Profanity
IMPOLITENESS
Impudence
IMPORTUNITY
Asking
IMPOSSIBILITY
Facts
Absurdities
Perfection
IMPRESSIONS
Facts
Appearances
Belief
Feelings
IMPROPRIETY
Vulgarity
IMPROVEMENT
Progress
Self-improvement
Study
IMPROVIDENCE
See Prodigality
IMPRUDENCE
Indiscretion
IMPUDENCE
See Impertinence
IMPULSE
Reason
Inclination
Instinct
IMPURITY
Purity
Vulgarity
INACCURACY
Error
INACTIVITY
See Idleness
INANITY
Bores
INATTENTION
Neglect
INCENTIVES
Motives
INCIVILITY
Impertinence
INCLINATION
Duty
Desire
Impulse
Instinct
Wishes

INCONSISTENCY
Consistency
Change
Fickleness
Inconstancy
Instability
Mutability
INCONSTANCY
Constancy
Change
Fickleness
Mutability
INCONTINENCE
Licentiousness
INCREDULITY
See Unbelief
INDECENCY
Impurity
INDECISION
Decision
Irresolution
Weakness
INDELICACY
Impurity
INDEPENDENCE
Dependence
Freedom
Liberty
Self-reliance
INDEXES
Interest
Insensibility
Neglect
INDIGENCE
Poverty
INDIGESTION
Health
Feasting
Gluttony
Sickness
INDIGNITY
Insult
INDISCRETION
Discretion
Folly
Mistake
Rashness
INDIVIDUALITY
Imitation
Character
Distinction
Eccentricity
Singularity
INDOLENCE
See Idleness
INDULGENCE
Abstinence
Firmness
Drinking
Eating
Lenity
Licentiousness
INDUSTRY
See Diligence
INELEGANCE
Vulgarity
INEQUALITY
Slavery

INERTIA
Indolence
INEXPERIENCE
Innocence
INFAMY
Honor
Baseness
Depravity
Disgrace
INFANCY
Old age
Babe
Children
INFIDELITY
See Unbelief
INFLUENCE
Example
Guidance
Power
INFORMATION
Knowledge
INGENUITY
Ability
INGENUOUSNESS
Candor
INGRATITUDE
Gratitude
Insensibility
INHERITANCE
Eugenics*
Wills
INHUMANITY
Cruelty
INIQUITY
Sin
INJURY
See Abuse
INJUSTICE
Justice
Oppression
Persecution
Tyranny
INK
See Authorship
INNOCENCE
Experience
Guilt
Ignorance
Purity
Virtue
INNOVATION
Tradition
Change
Discovery
Invention
Novelty
Originality
INNS
Home
Hospitality
INQUIRY
Indifference
Curiosity
Inquisitiveness
Question
Science
Study
INQUISITIVENESS
See Babblers

INSANITY
*Normality**
Delusion
Madness
INSECURITY
Uncertainty
INSENSIBILITY
Sensibility
Dulness
Indifference
INSIGHT
Discernment
INSINCERITY
Sincerity
Deceit
Dishonesty
Dissimulation
Hypocrisy
Pretension
Treachery
INSOLENCE
Impertinence
INSPIRATION
Enthusiasm
Genius
God
Influence
INSTABILITY
Firmness
Change
Fickleness
Inconstancy
Indecision
Irresolution
Mutability
INSTINCT
Reason
Impulse
Inclination
Motives
INSTRUCTION
Education
Guidance
Teaching
**INSUBORDI-
   NATION**
Disobedience
INSULT
Courtesy
Abuse
Arrogance
Impertinence
Impudence
Offence
Ridicule
Sneering
INSURRECTION
Rebellion
INTEGRITY
Dishonesty
Honesty
Honor
Rectitude
INTELLECT
Body
Soul
Mind
Reason
Understanding

INTELLIGENCE
Dulness
Ignorance
Common sense
Discernment
Discretion
Judgment
Knowledge
Perception
Prudence
Sense
Understanding
Wisdom

INTEMPERANCE
Temperance
Dissipation
Drinking
Drunkenness
Excess
Extremes
Indulgence

INTENTIONS
Deeds
Aims
Motives
Purpose

INTEREST
Disinterestedness
Indifference
Attention
Lending
Selfishness

INTERFERING
Busybodies

INTIMACY
Familiarity

INTOLERANCE
Toleration
Bigotry
Dogmatism
Fanaticism
Persecution
Tyranny
Zeal

INTOXICATION
Drunkenness

INTRIGUE
Conspiracy

INTRODUCTION
Preface

INTUITION
Perception

INVECTIVE
Abuse

INVENTION
See Innovation

INVESTIGATION
Inquiry

IRE
Anger

IRELAND*

IRONY
Humor
Jeering
Ridicule
Sarcasm
Satire
Sneering
Wit

IRRESOLUTION
Resolution
Indecision
Instability
Weakness

IRREVERENCE
Levity

IRRITABILITY
Ill nature

ISOLATION
Solitude

JAZZ*
Dancing
Music

JEALOUSY
Contentment
Covetousness
Distrust
Envy
Rivalry
Suspicion

JEERING
See Irony

JESTING
Gravity
Humor
Levity
Nonsense
Raillery
Repartee
Wag
Wit

JESUS
Christ

JEWELS
Gems

JEWS

JOKING
Jesting

JOLLITY
Mirth

JOURNALISM
See Authorship

JOY
See Happiness

JUDGMENT
See Intelligence

JURISPRUDENCE
See Justice

JUSTICE
Injustice
Equity
Jurisprudence
Law
Lawyers
Punishment
Recompense
Reward
Right

JUSTIFICATION
Excuses

KILLING
Murder

KIN
Family

KINDNESS
See Beneficence

KINGS
Courts and courtiers
Despotism
Government
Power

KISSES
See Courtship

KNAVERY
Virtue
Baseness
Cunning
Deceit
Depravity
Dishonesty
Fraud
Malevolence
Mischief
Roguery
Villainy
Wickedness

KNOWLEDGE
Ignorance
Discovery
Education
Facts
Learning
Science
Statistics*
Truth
Understanding
Wisdom

LABOR
See Work

LANGUAGE
See Words

LANGUOR
Sloth

LARGESS
Generosity

LAUDATION
Praise

LAUGHTER
Sobriety
Gayety
Jesting
Levity
Mirth
Smiles
Vivacity

LAW
Anarchy
Equity
Government
Jurisprudence
Justice
Lawyers
Order
Punishment
Statesmanship

LAWYERS
See Law

LAXITY
Licentiousness
Neglect

LAZINESS
Sloth

LEADERSHIP
Statesmanship

LEARNING
Ignorance
Education
Instruction
Knowledge
Self-improvement
Study
Teaching
Wisdom

LECHERY
Licentiousness

LEGENDS
Mythology

LEISURE
Work
Idleness
Indolence
Recreation
Rest
Sloth

LENDING
Borrowing
Credit
Help
Money
Suretyship
Usurer

LENITY
Cruelty
Clemency
Compassion
Forbearance
Forgiveness
Gentleness
Kindness
Mercy
Moderation
Patience
Toleration

LETHARGY
Indifference

LETTERS
Absence
Ink
Pen
Writing

LEVELLERS
Aristocracy
Agrarianism
Anarchists
Communism
Democracy
Equality
Republic

LEVITY
Gravity
Inconstancy
Jeering
Jesting
Raillery
Ridicule
Sneering
Wag

LEWDNESS
Licentiousness

LIARS
See Dishonesty

LIBEL
Calumny

LIBERALITY
  See Beneficence
LIBERTINES
  Licentiousness
LIBERTY
  Slavery
  Democracy
  Freedom
  Independence
  Republic
LIBRARIES
  See Books
LICENTIOUSNESS
  Abstinence
  Anarchy
  Harlot
  Impurity
  Indiscretion
  Indulgence
  Sensuality
  Vice
  Voluptuousness
LIFE
  Death
  Action
  Biography
  Birth
  Energy
  Humanity
  Man
  Soul
  Spirit
  Vivacity
LIGHT
  Night
  Day
  Knowledge
  Sun
  Understanding
LIKING
  Affection
LINEAGE
  Ancestry
LINGERING
  Delay
LIQUOR
  Drinking
LISTLESSNESS
  Ennui
LITERATURE
  See Books
LITIGATION
  Contention
LITTLE THINGS
  Best Things
  Trifles
LIVELINESS
  Vivacity
LOAFING
  Idleness
LOATHING
  Hatred
LOGIC
  Sophistry
  Argument
  Metaphysics
  Method
  Mind
  Philosophy

LOGIC (*cont.*)
  Reason
  Rhetoric
  Science
  Thought
  Truth
LOITERING
  Idleness
LONELINESS*
  Companionship
  Absence
  Desolation
  Farewell
  Parting
  Retirement
  Solitude
LONGING
  Yearnings
LOOKS
  Character
  Appearances
  Beauty
  Body
  Countenance
  Dandy
  Dress
  Eye
  Face
  Fashion
  Foppery
  Impressions
  Manners
  Ornament
  Ostentation
  Physiognomy
LOQUACITY
  Silence
  Bores
  Eloquence
  Language
  Oratory
  Rhetoric
  Speech
  Talking
  Tongue
  Verbosity
  Words
LORD
  God
LOSSES
  Gain
  Adversity
  Waste
LOVE
  Hatred
  Affection
  Courtship
  Desire
  Devotion
  Esteem
  Lust
  Marriage
  Romance
  Sexes
  Tenderness
LOWLINESS
  Humility
LOYALTY
  Constancy

LUCK
  Purpose
  Accident
  Cards
  Chance
  Destiny
  Dice
  Fate
  Fortune
  Gambling
  Wagers
LUCRE
  Money
LUNACY
  Insanity
LUST
  Indifference
  Appetite
  Covetousness
  Desire
  Harlot
  Impurity
  Indulgence
  Licentiousness
  Sexes
  Yearnings
LUXURY
  Poverty
  Elegance
  Extravagance
  Gems
  Indulgence
  Intemperance
  Money
  Ornament
  Ostentation
  Pleasure
  Prodigality
  Prosperity
  Riches
  Sensuality
  Voluptuousness
  Wealth
LYING
  See Dishonesty

MADNESS
  Normality
  Anger
  Insanity
  Psychoanalysis*
  Rage
  Rashness
  Recklessness
MAGAZINES
  Journalism
MAGIC
  Alchemy
  Miracles
MAGNANIMITY
  Meanness
  Beneficence
  Benevolence
  Chivalry
  Clemency
  Disinterestedness
  Forbearance
  Forgiveness
  Generosity

MAGNANIMITY
  (*cont.*)
  Kindness
  Lenity
  Mercy
  Moderation
  Patience
  Toleration
MAGNET
MAIDENHOOD
  Mother
  Chastity
  Children
  Daughters
  Innocence
  Modesty
  Purity
  Youth
MAJESTY
  Dignity
MAJORITY
  Minorities
  Democracy
  Equality
  Government
  Mob
  Politics
  Populace
  Republic
MALEVOLENCE
  See Malice
MALICE
  Kindness
  Abuse
  Anger
  Calumny
  Cruelty
  Enemies
  Evil-speaking
  Hatred
  Meanness
  Mischief
  Rage
  Resentment
  Revenge
  Slander
  Vengeance
  Villainy
MAMMON
  Riches
MAN
  Woman
  Bachelor
  Beard
  Humanity
  Husbands*
  Life
  Men
  Sexes
MANAGEMENT
  Executives*
MANKIND
  Man
MANLINESS
  Courage
MANNERS
  Address
  Behavior
  Ceremony

NAGGING
  Criticism
NAÏVETÉ
  Innocence
NAMES
  Honor
  Language
  Nicknames
  Reputation
  Slang*
  Speech
  Titles
  Words
NATIONS
  Empire
  Government
  Patriotism
  People
  Populace
  Society
  State
NATURE
  Art
  Autumn
  Clouds
  Country
  Day
  Dew
  Earth
  Evening
  Flowers
  Life
  Morning
  Night
  Rain
  Rainbow
  Sea
  Spring
  Stars
  Sun
  Sunrise
  Sunset
  Trees
  Twilight
  Wind
  World
NEATNESS
  Dress
NECESSITY
  Choice
  Destiny
  Fate
  Force
  Law
  Obligation
  Poverty
  Wants
NEGLECT
  Diligence
  Delay
  Forgetting
  Idleness
  Indifference
  Procrastination
  Sloth
NEIGHBORS
  Acquaintance
NERVE
  Boldness

NERVOUSNESS
  Restlessness
NEUTRALITY
  Fanaticism
  Broadmindedness*
  Disinterestedness
  Indecision
  Indifference
  Openmindedness*
  Toleration
NEWS
  Secrecy
  Facts
  Ink
  Journalism
  Newspaper
  Pen
  Press
  Writing
NEWSPAPER
  See News
NICETY
  Delicacy
NICKNAMES
  See Names
NIGGARDLINESS
  Miser
NIGHT
  Day
  Evening
  Midnight
  Obscurity
  Stars
  Sunset
  Twilight
NOBILITY
  Baseness
  Aristocracy
  Dignity
  Distinction
  Eminence
  Greatness
  Place
  Position
  Rank
  Station
  Titles
NOISE
  Music
  Blustering
  Loquacity
  Sound
  Speech
NONCHALANCE
  Equanimity
NONSENSE
  Sense
  Absurdities
  Folly
  Humor
  Jesting
  Levity
  Raillery
NORMALITY*
  Deformity
  Disease
  Insanity
  Health
  Standardization*

NOVELS
  Books
  Fiction
  Literature
  Reading
  Romance
  Writing
NOVELTY
  Antiquity
  Discovery
  Innovation
  Invention
  Modernity*
  Originality
  Variety
NUTRITION
  Diet

OATHS
  Assertions
  Curses
  Positiveness
  Profanity
  Promise
  Threats
  Vows
OBDURACY
  Obstinacy
OBEDIENCE
  Disobedience
  Deference
  Docility
  Duty
  Humility
  Meekness
  Submission
OBJECTIVES
  Aims
OBLIGATION
  Freedom
  Borrowing
  Debt
  Duty
  Gratitude
  Necessity
  Responsibility
  Thankfulness
OBLIVION
  Fame
  Death
  Forgetting
  Grave
  Night
  Obscurity
OBLOQUY
  Abuse
OBSCENITY
  Impurity
OBSCURITY
  Fame
  Simplicity
  Concealment
  Mystery
  Oblivion
  Poverty
  Secrecy
  Style
OBSEQUIOUSNESS
  Flattery

OBSERVATION
  Dulness
  Attention
  Experience
  Eye
  Impressions
  Perception
  Vigilance
  Watchfulness
OBSTACLES
  Difficulty
OBSTINACY
  Docility
  Firmness
  Independence
  Perseverance
  Perverseness
  Rebellion
  Resolution
  Self-will
OBTUSENESS
  Dulness
OCCUPATION
  Idleness
  Business
  Employment
  Labor
  Trade
  Work
OCEAN
  Sea
ODDITY
  Eccentricity
ODDS
  Chance
ODIUM
  Censure
OFFENCE
  Right
  Crime
  Impertinence
  Impudence
  Injury
  Injustice
  Insult
  Resentment
  Sin
  Vice
  Wrong
OFFICE
  Authority
  Duty
  Executives*
  Government
  Place
  Politics
  Position
  Power
  Statesmanship
  Station
  Trust
OFFICIOUSNESS
  Busybodies
OLD AGE
  See Age
OMNIPOTENCE
  Weakness
  God
  Power

PRACTICALITY
Usefulness
PRACTICE
Experience
PRAISE
Censure
Applause
Compliments
Encouragement
Flattery
Popularity
PRATTLE
Babblers
PRAYER
Self-reliance
Asking
Devotion
Piety
Worship
PREACHING
Advice
Eloquence
Instruction
Ministers
Missionaries*
Oratory
Teaching
PREAMBLE
Preface
PRECAUTION
Forethought
PRECEDENT
Innovation
Authority
Custom
History
Law
Tradition
PRECEPT
Example
Advice
Counsel
Creed
Doctrine
Law
Maxims
Principles
Proverbs
PRECISION
Accuracy
PRECOCITY
Genius
PREDESTINATION
Destiny
PREDILECTION
Inclination
PREFACE
End
Books
Literature
Writing
PREFERENCE
Choice
PREFERMENT
Office
PREJUDICE
Justice
Bigotry
Fanaticism

PREJUDICE (*cont.*)
Intolerance
Opinion
Party
Sentiment
PRELUDE
Preface
PREPAREDNESS
War
*PRESBYTERIAN
ISM*
Calvinism
PRESENT
Futurity
Past
Gifts
Modernity*
Time
PRESS
See News
PRESUMPTION
Impudence
PRETENSION
Modesty
Affectation
Boasting
Conceit
Dishonesty
Falsehood
Fraud
Lying
Ostentation
Vanity
PREVARICATION
Dishonesty
PREVENTION
Help
Caution
Forethought
Opposition
Prudence
PRICE
Cost*
PRIDE
Humility
Arrogance
Boasting
Conceit
Dignity
Egotism
Self-conceit
Self-praise
Self-respect
Snobs
Vain-glory
Vanity
PRINCIPLES
Expediency
Belief
Creed
Doctrine
Law
Maxims
Opinion
Precedent
Precept
Theories
PRINTING
Press

PRIVACY
Solitude
PRIVATION
Poverty
PRIVILEGE
Aristocracy
PROBITY
Integrity
PROCEDURE
Method
PROCLIVITY
Inclination
PROCRASTI-
NATION
See Delay
PRODIGALITY
Economy
Extravagance
Gambling
Improvidence
Rashness
Recklessness
Waste
PROFANITY
Reverence
Curses
Impurity
Oaths
PROFICIENCY
Ability
PROFIT
Gain
PROFLIGACY
Depravity
PROGRESS
Improvement
Reform
Self-improvement
PROHIBITION
Temperance
PROLETARIAT
Populace
PROLIXITY
Verbosity
PROLOGUE
Preface
PROMINENCE
Eminence
PROMISCUITY
Licentiousness
PROMISE
Forgetting
Debt
Intentions
Oaths
Obligation
Threats
Vows
PROMPTNESS
Delay
Dispatch
Haste
Punctuality
PROOF
Evidence
PROPAGANDA
Publicity*
PROPENSITY
Inclination

PROPERTY
Poverty
Money
Possessions
Riches
Wealth
PROPINQUITY
Familiarity
PROPOSAL
Courtship
PROPRIETY
Etiquette
PROSE
Literature
PROSPERITY
Poverty
Money
Possessions
Property
Riches
Wealth
PROSTITUTE
Harlot
PROTEST
Agitation
PROTESTANTISM
Calvinism
Christianity
Church
Creed
Ministers
Religion
Sects
Worship
PROVERBS
Apothegms
Maxims
Quotations
Truisms
PROVIDENCE
Improvidence
Economy
Forethought
Frugality
God
Prudence
Thrift*
PROWESS
Ability
PROXIMITY
Familiarity
PRUDENCE
Indiscretion
Caution
Common sense
Consideration
Discretion
Economy
Expediency
Forethought
Frugality
Intelligence
Policy
Providence
Sense
Thrift*
Wisdom
PRUDERY
Modesty

SLAVERY
Independence
Dependence
Despotism
Dictatorship*
Oppression
Persecution
Tyranny

SLEEP
Action
Bed
Night
Quiet
Peace
Repose
Rest

SLOTH
Industry
Idleness
Inactivity
Indolence
Neglect
Procrastination

SLUMBER
Sleep

SMILES
Gravity
Amiability
Cheerfulness
Complacency
Delight
Good humor
Good nature
Happiness
Humor
Jesting
Joy
Laughter
Mirth
Nonsense
Pleasure
Wit

SMUGNESS
Self-righteousness

SMUT
Impurity

SNEERING
Admiration
Contempt
Cynics
Irony
Jeering
Misanthropy
Ridicule
Sarcasm
Satire

SNOBS
Democracy
Affectation
Aristocracy
Arrogance
Conceit
Egotism
Pretension
Pride
Self-conceit
Vanity

SNUBS
Insult

SOBRIETY
Intemperance
Abstinence
Gravity
Moderation
Self-control
Temperance

SOCIABILITY
Conviviality

SOCIETY
Solitude
Associates
Companionship
Conviviality
Humanity
Man
People
Populace

SOLACE
Consolation

SOLDIER
See War

SOLECISM
Absurdities

SOLEMNITY
Gravity

SOLIDARITY
Union and unity

SOLITUDE
Companionship
Absence
Desolation
Loneliness*
Quiet
Rest
Retirement

SONG
Ballads
Jazz*
Poetry
Music
Voice

SOPHISTICATION
Disillusionment*

SOPHISTRY
Truth
Error
Falsehood
Pedantry
Subtlety

SORROW
Joy
Affliction
Grief
Sadness
Suffering
Tears
Unhappiness

SOUL
Body
Conscience
Emotion
Eternity
Feelings
Heart
Immortality
Intellect
Mind
Spirit

SOUND
Silence
Music
Noise
Voice

SOUVENIRS
Remembrance

SPECIALTY
Occupation
Trade

SPECULATION
Facts
Fancy
Imagination
Philosophy
Reverie
Theories
Thought
Wonder

SPEECH
See Talking

SPEED
Dispatch

SPENDING
Extravagance

SPIRIT
Body
Courage
Emotion
Energy
Enterprise
Enthusiasm
Feelings
Life
Soul
Vivacity
Zeal

SPITE
Malice

SPLEEN
Malice

SPORT
Recreation

SPRIGHTLINESS
Vivacity

SPRING
Autumn
Flowers
Love
Nature

SQUABBLES
Quarrels

SQUANDERING
Prodigality

STABILITY
Character

STAGE
Theatres

STAGNATION
Sloth

STAMINA
Strength

**STANDARDI-
ZATION***
Variety
Efficiency*
Method
Monotony*
Order

STARS
Sun
Evening
Night

STATE
See Nations

STATESMANSHIP
Commanders
Government
Kings
Law
Politics

STATION
See Rank

STATISTICS*
Theories
Economists*
Facts
Knowledge
Science

STEADFASTNESS
Constancy

STEALING
Crime

STERNNESS
Firmness

STEWARDSHIP
Master
Debt
Duty
Obligation
Responsibility
Servants

STIMULANTS
Drinking

STOICISM
Complaining
Endurance
Equanimity
Fortitude
Indifference
Patience
Philosophy
Resignation
Self-control

STOLIDITY
Insensibility

STOMACH
Eating

STORY-TELLING
Anecdotes
Conversation
Fiction
Literature
Novels
Talking
Writing

**STRAIGHT-FOR-
WARDNESS**
Sincerity

STRATAGEM
Artifice

STRENGTH
Weakness
Endurance
Energy
Force
Health
Power

TEMPERAMENT*
  See Temper
TEMPERANCE
  See Abstinence
TEMPTATION
  Indifference
  Desire
  Devil
  Lust
  Opportunity
  Passion
TENACITY
  Perseverance
TENDENCY
  Inclination
TENDERNESS
  Cruelty
  Affection
  Compassion
  Gentleness
  Kindness
  Love
  Sensitiveness
  Sympathy
TENETS
  Doctrine
TERMAGANTS
  Ill nature
TERROR
  Fear
TERSENESS
  Brevity
TESTIMONY
  Evidence
TESTINESS
  Ill nature
THANKFULNESS
  See Gratitude
THEATRES
  Actors
  Amusements
  Hollywood*
  Literature
  Showmanship*
  Tragedy
THEFT
  Dishonesty
THEOLOGY
  Science
  Bible
  Christianity
  Church
  Creed
  Doctrine
  Ministers
  Preaching
  Religion
  Sects
THEORIES
  See Thought
THOROUGHNESS
  Industry
THOUGHT
  Action
  Association
  Belief
  Consideration
  Contemplation
  Ideas

THOUGHT (cont.)
  Logic
  Meditation
  Opinion
  Reason
  Reflection
  Retrospection
  Reverie
  Speculation
  Study
  Theories
THREATS
  Promise
  Blustering
  Curses
  Oaths
  Quarrels
THRIFT*
  See Frugality
THRILLS
  Excitement
TIDINESS
  Cleanliness
  Order
TILLAGE
  Agriculture
TIME
  Eternity
  Age
  Antiquity
  Delay
  Futurity
  Past
  Present
  Procrastination
TIMIDITY
  Diffidence
TITLES
  See Aristocracy
TOIL
  Labor
TOLERATION
  Intolerance
  Broadmindedness*
  Disinterestedness
  Forbearance
  Neutrality
  Openmindedness*
TOMORROW
  Futurity
TONGUE
  See Talking
TORMENT
  Pain
TORTURE
  Persecution
TOUCHINESS
  Ill nature
TRACTABILITY
  Docility
TRADE
  Bargain
  Business
  Commerce
  Specialty
TRADITION
  Innovation
  Custom
  Precedent

TRADUCTION
  Calumny
TRAGEDY
  Humor
  Adversity
  Literature
  Theatres
TRAINING
  Education
TRAMP
  Vagrant
TRANQUILLITY
  Repose
TRANSGRESSION
  Sin
TRAVEL
  Home
  Adventure*
  Experience
  Observation
  Walking
TRAVESTY
  Caricature
TREACHERY
  Constancy
  Conspiracy
  Deceit
  Inconstancy
  Treason
TREASON
  Patriotism
  Conspiracy
  Deceit
  Rebellion
  Treachery
TREES
  Flowers
  Nature
TREPIDATION
  Fear
TRESPASS
  Sin
TRIALS
  See Adversity
TRIBULATION
  Trials
TRICKERY
  Artifice
TRIFLES
  Best things
  Little things
TRIUMPH
  Victory
TROUBLE
  See Adversity
TRUCULENCE
  Contention
TRUISMS
  See Apothegms
TRUST
  Distrust
  Belief
  Confidence
  Duty
  Expectation
  Faith
  Hope
  Responsibility
  Stewardship

TRUTH
  Error
  Accuracy
  Candor
  Confession
  Facts
  Honesty
  Integrity
  Knowledge
  Realism*
  Science
  Sincerity
  Statistics*
TURBULENCE
  Contention
TURMOIL
  Contention
TURPITUDE
  Depravity
TWILIGHT
  Sunrise
  Evening
  Sunset
TYRANNY
  See Despotism

UMBRAGE
  Resentment
UNBELIEF
  Belief
  Agnosticism
  Atheism
  Cynics
  Distrust
  Doubt
  Incredulity
  Infidelity
  Scepticism
  Suspicion
  Uncertainty
UNCERTAINTY
  Knowledge
  Doubt
  Indecision
  Instability
  Irresolution
  Mystery
  Suspense
UNDERSTANDING
  See Intelligence
UNFAIRNESS
  Injustice
UNFAITHFULNESS
  Treachery
UNGAINLINESS
  Awkwardness
UNHAPPINESS
  Happiness
  Affliction
  Discontent
  Grief
  Misery
  Misfortune
  Pain
  Sadness
  Sorrow
  Suffering
UNIFORMITY
  Standardization *

THE THINKER

—Rodin

The NEW
DICTIONARY *of* THOUGHTS
BEING
A CYCLOPEDIA OF QUOTATIONS

A

ABASEMENT.—Ambition can creep as well as soar.—*Burke.*

ABILITY.—Ability involves responsibility; power, to its last particle, is duty.—*A. Maclaren.*

A dwarf is small, even if he stands on a mountain; a colossus keeps his height, even if he stands in a well.—*Seneca.*

A traveller at Sparta, standing long upon one leg, said to a Lacedæmonian, "I do not believe you can do as much." "True," said he, "but every goose can."—*Plutarch.*

There is something that is much more scarce, something finer far, something rarer than ability. It is the ability to recognize ability.—*Elbert Hubbard.*

To know how to hide one's ability is great skill.—*Rochefoucauld.*

The abilities of man must fall short on one side or the other, like too scanty a blanket when you are abed.—If you pull it upon your shoulders, your feet are left bare; if you thrust it down to your feet, your shoulders are uncovered.—*Sir William Temple.*

Every person is responsible for all the good within the scope of his abilities, and for no more, and none can tell whose sphere is the largest.—*Gail Hamilton.*

We should be on our guard against the temptation to argue directly from skill to capacity, and to assume when a man displays skill in some feat, his capacity is therefore considerable.—*Tom H. Pear.*

Without the assistance of natural capacity, rules and precepts are of no efficacy.—*Quintilian.*

The winds and waves are always on the side of the ablest navigators.—*Gibbon.*

What we do upon some great occasion will probably depend on what we already are; and what we are will be the result of previous years of self-discipline.—*H. P. Liddon.*

The ablest men in all walks of modern life are men of faith. Most of them have much more faith than they themselves realize.—*Bruce Barton.*

Men are often capable of greater things than they perform.—They are sent into the world with bills of credit, and seldom draw to their full extent.—*Horace Walpole.*

A genius can't be forced; nor can you make an ape an alderman.—*Thomas Somerville.*

Ability doth hit the mark where presumption over-shooteth and diffidence falleth short.—*Nicholas Cusa.*

A pint can't hold a quart—if it holds a pint it is doing all that can be expected of it.—*Margaret Deland.*

Faith in the ability of a leader is of slight service unless it be united with faith in his justice.—*General George W. Goethals.*

The question "Who ought to be boss?" is like asking "Who ought to be the tenor in the quartet?" Obviously, the man who can sing tenor.—*Henry Ford.*

Ability is a poor man's wealth.—*M. Wren.*

There may be luck in getting a good job—but there's no luck in keeping it.—*J. Ogden Armour.*

ABODES.—A castle after all is but a house—the dullest one when lacking company.—*James Sheridan Knowles.*

ABSENCE.—Absence from those we love is self from self—a deadly banishment.—*Shakespeare.*

Wives in their husbands' absences grow subtler, and daughters sometimes run off with the butler.—*Byron.*

1

Love reckons hours for months, and days for years; and every little absence is an age.—*Dryden.*

Absence in love is like water upon fire; a little quickens, but much extinguishes it.—*Hannah More.*

The absent are like children, helpless to defend themselves.—*Charles Reade.*

Absence makes the heart grow fonder. —*Thomas Haynes Bayly.*

Absence lessens moderate passions and increases great ones; as the wind extinguishes the taper, but fans a fire.— *Rochefoucauld.*

Distance of time and place generally cure what they seem to aggravate; and taking leave of our friends resembles taking leave of the world, of which it has been said, that it is not death, but dying, which is terrible.—*Fielding.*

Absence, like death, sets a seal on the image of those we love: we cannot realize the intervening changes which time may have effected.—*Goldsmith.*

The absent are never without fault, nor the present without excuse.— *Franklin.*

The joy of meeting pays the pangs of absence; else who could bear it?—*Rowe.*

As the presence of those we love is as a double life, so absence, in its anxious longing and sense of vacancy, is as a foretaste of death.—*Mrs. Jameson.*

ABSTINENCE.—(See "TEMPERANCE.")

Abstinence is whereby a man refraineth from anything which he may lawfully claim.—*Eliot.*

Always rise from the table with an appetite, and you will never sit down without one.—*Penn.*

Against diseases the strongest fence is the defensive virtue, abstinence.—*Herrick.*

Abstinence is as easy to me as temperance would be difficult.—*Samuel Johnson.*

Refrain to-night, and that shall lend a hand of easiness to the next abstinence; the next more easy; for use can almost change the stamp of nature, and either curb the devil, or throw him out with wondrous potency.—*Shakespeare.*

The stomach begs and clamors, and listens to no precepts. And yet it is not

an obdurate creditor; for it is dismissed with small payment if you give it only what you owe, and not as much as you can.—*Seneca.*

To set the mind above the appetites is the end of abstinence, which if not a virtue, is the groundwork of a virtue.— *Johnson.*

It is continued temperance which sustains the body for the longest period of time, and which most surely preserves it free from sickness.—*W. Humboldt.*

ABSURDITIES.—There is nothing so absurd or ridiculous that has not at some time been said by some philosopher. Fontenelle says he would undertake to persuade the whole republic of readers to believe that the sun was neither the cause of light or heat, if he could only get six philosophers on his side.—*Goldsmith.*

To pardon those absurdities in ourselves which we condemn in others, is neither better nor worse than to be more willing to be fools ourselves than to have others so.—*Pope.*

ABUSE.—Abuse is often of service. —*Johnson.*

It is the wit and policy of sin to hate those we have abused.—*Davenant.*

I never yet heard man or woman much abused that I was not inclined to think the better of them, and to transfer the suspicion or dislike to the one who found pleasure in pointing out the defects of another.—*Jane Porter.*

Abuse of any one generally shows that he has marked traits of character. The stupid and indifferent are passed by in silence.—*Tryon Edwards.*

It is not he who gives abuse that affronts, but the view that we take of it as insulting; so that when one provokes you it is your own opinion which is provoking.—*Epictetus.*

Abuse me as much as you will; it is often a benefit rather than an injury. —*E. Nott.*

The difference between coarse and refined abuse is the difference between being bruised by a club and wounded by a poisoned arrow.—*Johnson.*

Cato, being scurrilously treated by a low and vicious fellow, quietly said to him, "A contest between us is very unequal, for thou canst bear ill language with ease, and return it with pleasure; but to me it is unusual to hear, and disagreeable to speak it."

There are none more abusive to others than they that lie most open to it themselves; but the humor goes round, and he that laughs at me to-day will have somebody to laugh at him to-morrow.—*Seneca.*

ACCENT.—Accent is the soul of language; it gives to it both feeling and truth.—*Rousseau.*

ACCIDENT.—Nothing is or can be accidental with God.—*Longfellow.*

No accidents are so unlucky but that the wise may draw some advantage from them; nor are there any so lucky but that the foolish may turn them to their own prejudice.—*Rochefoucauld.*

What reason, like the careful ant, draws laboriously together, the wind of accident sometimes collects in a moment.—*Schiller.*

What men call accident is the doing of God's providence.—*Bailey.*

ACCURACY.—Accuracy is the twin brother of honesty; inaccuracy, of dishonesty.—*C. Simmons.*

Accuracy of statement is one of the first elements of truth; inaccuracy is a near kin to falsehood.—*Tryon Edwards.*

ACQUAINTANCE.—If a man does not make new acquaintances as he advances through life, he will soon find himself left alone; one should keep his friendships in constant repair.—*Johnson.*

It is good discretion not to make too much of any man at the first; because one cannot hold out that proportion.—*Bacon.*

It is expedient to have acquaintance with those who have looked into the world, who know men, understand business, and can give you good intelligence and good advice when they are wanted.—*Bp. Horne.*

I love the acquaintance of young people; because, in the first place, I don't like to think myself growing old. In the next place, young acquaintances must last longest, if they do last; and then young men have more virtue than old men; they have more generous sentiments in every respect.—*Johnson.*

Three days of uninterrupted company

in a vehicle will make you better acquainted with another, than one hour's conversation with him every day for three years.—*Lavater.*

Never say you know a man till you have divided an inheritance with him.—*Lavater.*

If a man is worth knowing at all, he is worth knowing well.—*Alexander Smith.*

ACQUIREMENT.—That which we acquire with most difficulty we retain the longest; as those who have earned a fortune are commonly more careful of it than those by whom it may have been inherited.—*Colton.*

Every noble acquisition is attended with its risks; he who fears to encounter the one must not expect to obtain the other.—*Metastasio.*

An unjust acquisition is like a barbed arrow, which must be drawn backward with horrible anguish, or else will be your destruction.—*Jeremy Taylor.*

ACTION.— Heaven never helps the man who will not act.—*Sophocles.*

Action may not always bring happiness; but there is no happiness without action.—*Disraeli.*

Remember you have not a sinew whose law of strength is not action; not a faculty of body, mind, or soul, whose law of improvement is not energy.—*E. B. Hall.*

Our grand business is not to see what lies dimly at a distance, but to do what lies clearly at hand.—*Carlyle.*

Only actions give to life its strength, as only moderation gives it its charm.—*Richter.*

Every noble activity makes room for itself.—*Emerson.*

Mark this well, ye proud men of action! ye are, after all, nothing but unconscious instruments of the men of thought.—*Heine.*

The actions of men are like the index of a book; they point out what is most remarkable in them.

Happiness is in action, and every power is intended for action; human happiness, therefore, can only be complete as all the powers have their full and legitimate play.—*Thomas.*

Great actions, the lustre of which dazzles us, are represented by politicians as the effects of deep design; whereas they are commonly the effects of caprice and passion. Thus the war between Augustus and Antony, supposed to be owing to their ambition to give a master to the world, arose probably from jealousy.—*Rochefoucauld.*

A right act strikes a chord that extends through the whole universe, touches all moral intelligence, visits every world, vibrates along its whole extent, and conveys its vibrations to the very bosom of God!—*T. Binney.*

Good thoughts, though God accept them, yet toward men are little better than good dreams except they be put in action.—*Bacon.*

Doing is the great thing. For if, resolutely, people do what is right, in time they come to like doing it.—*Ruskin.*

Activity is God's medicine; the highest genius is willingness and ability to do hard work. Any other conception of genius makes it a doubtful, if not a dangerous possession.—*R. S. MacArthur.*

That action is not warrantable which either fears to ask the divine blessing on its performance, or having succeeded, does not come with thanksgiving to God for its success.—*Quarles.*

A holy act strengthens the inward holiness. It is a seed of life growing into more life.—*F. W. Robertson.*

If you have no friends to share or rejoice in your success in life—if you cannot look back to those to whom you owe gratitude, or forward to those to whom you ought to afford protection, still it is no less incumbent on you to move steadily in the path of duty: for your active exertions are due not only to society; but in humble gratitude to the Being who made you a member of it, with powers to serve yourself and others.—*Walter Scott.*

The actions of men are the best interpreters of their thoughts.—*Locke.*

Act well at the moment, and you have performed a good action for all eternity.—*Lavater.*

In activity we must find our joy as well as glory; and labor, like everything else that is good, is its own reward.—*E. P. Whipple.*

To do an evil act is base. To do a good one without incurring danger, is common enough. But it is the part of a good man to do great and noble deeds though he risks everything in doing them.—*Plutarch.*

All our actions take their hue from the complexion of the heart, as landscapes do their variety from light.—*W. T. Bacon.*

Life was not given for indolent contemplation and study of self, nor for brooding over emotions of piety: actions and actions only determine the worth.—*Fichte.*

A good action is never lost; it is a treasure laid up and guarded for the doer's need.—*Calderon.*

Deliberate with caution, but act with decision; and yield with graciousness, or oppose with firmness.—*Colton.*

Existence was given us for action. Our worth is determined by the good deeds we do, rather than by the fine emotions we feel.—*E. L. Magoon.*

I have never heard anything about the resolutions of the apostles, but a great deal about their acts.—*H. Mann.*

Think that day lost whose slow descending sun views from thy hand no noble action done.—*J. Bobart.*

The more we do, the more we can do; the more busy we are the more leisure we have.—*Hazlitt.*

To will and not to do when there is opportunity, is in reality not to will; and to love what is good and not to do it, when it is possible, is in reality not to love it.—*Swedenborg.*

Life though a short, is a working day. —Activity may lead to evil; but inactivity cannot be led to good.—*Hannah More.*

Unselfish and noble actions are the most radiant pages in the biography of souls.—*Thomas.*

It is vain to expect any advantage from our profession of the truth if we be not sincerely just and honest in our actions.—*Sharpe.*

We should not be so taken up in the search for truth, as to neglect the needful duties of active life; for it is only action that gives a true value and commendation to virtue.—*Cicero.*

Be great in act, as you have been in thought.—Suit the action to the word, and the word to the action.—*Shakespeare.*

We must be doing something to be happy.—Action is no less necessary to us than thought.—*Hazlitt.*

Active natures are rarely melancholy.—Activity and sadness are incompatible.—*Bovee.*

In all exigencies or miseries, lamentation becomes fools, and action wise folk.—*Sir P. Sidney.*

Nothing, says Goethe, is so terrible as activity without insight.—Look before you leap is a maxim for the world.—*E. P. Whipple.*

Actions are ours; their consequences belong to heaven.—*Sir P. Francis.*

The flighty purpose never is o'ertook unless the deed go with it.—*Shakespeare.*

The end of man is action, and not thought, though it be of the noblest.—*Carlyle.*

The firefly only shines when on the wing; so it is with the mind; when we rest we darken.—*Bailey.*

Thought and theory must precede all salutary action; yet action is nobler in itself than either thought or theory.—*Wordsworth.*

What man knows should find expression in what he does.—The chief value of superior knowledge is that it leads to a performing manhood.—*Bovee.*

Life, in all ranks and situations, is an outward occupation, an actual and active work.—*W. Humboldt.*

Every action of our lives touches on some chord that will vibrate in eternity.—*E. H. Chapin.*

Nothing ever happens but once in this world. What I do now I do once for all. It is over and gone, with all its eternity of solemn meaning.—*Carlyle.*

Only the actions of the just smell sweet and blossom in the dust.—*Shirley.*

Action is eloquence; the eyes of the ignorant are more learned than their ears.—*Shakespeare.*

The acts of this life are the destiny of the next.—*Eastern Proverb.*

ACTORS.—The profession of the player, like that of the painter, is one of the imitative arts, whose means are pleasure, and whose end should be virtue.—*Shenstone.*

Actors are the only honest hypocrites. Their life is a voluntary dream; and the height of their ambition is to be beside themselves. They wear the livery of other men's fortunes: their very thoughts are not their own.—*Hazlitt.*

All the world's a stage, and all the men and women in it merely players. They have their exits and their entrances; and one man in his time plays many parts.—*Shakespeare.*

An actor should take lessons from the painter and the sculptor. Not only should he make attitude his study, but he should highly develop his mind by an assiduous study of the best writers, ancient and modern, which will enable him not only to understand his parts, but to communicate a nobler coloring to his manners and mien.—*Goethe.*

It is with some violence to the imagination that we conceive of an actor belonging to the relations of private life, so closely do we identify these persons in our mind with the characters they assume upon the stage.—*Lamb.*

A young girl must not be taken to the theatre, let us say it once for all. It is not only the drama which is immoral, but the place.—*Alex. Dumas.*

The most difficult character in comedy is that of the fool, and he must be no simpleton that plays that part.—*Cervantes.*

ADDRESS.—Brahma once asked of Force, "Who is stronger than thou?" She replied, "Address."—*Victor Hugo.*

Address makes opportunities; the want of it gives them.—*Bovee.*

Give a boy address and accomplishments and you give him the mastery of palaces and fortunes where he goes. He has not the trouble of earning to own them: they solicit him to enter and possess.—*Emerson.*

The tear that is wiped with a little address may be followed, perhaps, by a smile.—*Cowper.*

A man who knows the world will not only make the most of everything he does know, but of many things he does not know; and will gain more credit by his adroit mode of hiding his ignorance, than the pedant by his awkward attempt to exhibit his erudition.—*Colton.*

There is a certain artificial polish and

address acquired by mingling in the *beau monde*, which, in the commerce of the world, supplies the place of natural suavity and good humor; but it is too often purchased at the expense of all original and sterling traits of character. —*Washington Irving*.

ADMIRATION. — Admiration is the daughter of ignorance.—*Franklin*.

Admiration is a very short-lived passion that decays on growing familiar with its object unless it be still fed with fresh discoveries and kept alive by perpetual miracles rising up to its view.—*Addison*.

Those who are formed to win general admiration are seldom calculated to bestow individual happiness.—*Lady Blessington*.

Few men are admired by their servants.—*Montaigne*.

We always like those who admire us, but we do not always like those whom we admire.—*Rochefoucauld*.

To cultivate sympathy you must be among living beings and thinking about them; to cultivate admiration, among beautiful things and looking at them.—*Ruskin*.

Admiration must be kept up by the novelty that at first produced it; and how much soever is given, there must always be the impression that more remains.—*Johnson*.

No nobler feeling than this, of admiration for one higher than himself, dwells in the breast of man.—It is to this hour, and at all hours, the vivifying influence in man's life.—*Carlyle*.

It is a good thing to believe; it is a good thing to admire. By continually looking upwards, our minds will themselves grow upwards; as a man, by indulging in habits of scorn and contempt for others, is sure to descend to the level of those he despises.

It is better in some respects to be admired by those with whom you live, than to be loved by them. And this is not on account of any gratification of vanity, but because admiration is so much more tolerant than love.—*A. Helps*.

There is a pleasure in admiration; and this it is which properly causeth admiration, when we discover a great deal in an object which we understand to be excellent; and yet we see more beyond that, which our understandings cannot fully reach and comprehend.—*Tillotson*.

There is a wide difference between admiration and love. The sublime, which is the cause of the former, always dwells on great objects and terrible; the latter on small ones and pleasing; we submit to what we admire, but we love what submits to us: in one case we are forced, in the other we are flattered, into compliance.—*Burke*.

ADVERSITY.—(See "AFFLICTION.")

Adversity is the trial of principle.— Without it a man hardly knows whether he is honest or not.—*Fielding*.

Adversity is the first path to truth.— *Byron*.

No man is more unhappy than the one who is never in adversity; the greatest affliction of life is never to be afflicted.—*Anon*.

Adversity is like the period of the former and of the latter rain,—cold, comfortless, unfriendly to man and to animal; yet from that season have their birth the flower and the fruit, the date, the rose, and the pomegranate.—*Walter Scott*.

Adversity has ever been considered the state in which a man most easily becomes acquainted with himself, then, especially, being free from flatterers.— *Johnson*.

Prosperity is no just scale; adversity is the only balance to weigh friends.— *Plutarch*.

Who hath not known ill fortune, never knew himself, or his own virtue.—*Mallet*.

Stars may be seen from the bottom of a deep well, when they cannot be discerned from the top of a mountain. So are many things learned in adversity which the prosperous man dreams not of.—*Spurgeon*.

Adversity is the diamond dust Heaven polishes its jewels with.—*Leighton*.

I never met with a single instance of adversity which I have not in the end seen was for my good.—I have never heard of a Christian on his deathbed complaining of his afflictions.—*A. Proudfit*.

We ought as much to pray for a

blessing upon our daily rod as upon our daily bread.—*John Owen.*

Heaven often smites in mercy, even when the blow is severest.—*Joanna Baillie.*

Adversity has the effect of eliciting talents which in prosperous circumstances would have lain dormant.—*Horace.*

Prosperity is a great teacher; adversity is a greater. Possession pampers the mind; privation trains and strengthens it.—*Hazlitt.*

The flower that follows the sun does so even in cloudy days.—*Leighton.*

The good things of prosperity are to be wished; but the good things that belong to adversity are to be admired.—*Seneca.*

Adversity, sage useful guest, severe instructor, but the best; it is from thee alone we know justly to value things below.—*Somerville.*

Prosperity has this property: It puffs up narrow souls, makes them imagine themselves high and mighty, and leads them to look down upon the world with contempt; but a truly noble spirit appears greatest in distress; and then becomes more bright and conspicuous.—*Plutarch.*

In the adversity of our best friends we often find something that does not displease us.—*Rochefoucauld.*

Prosperity is too apt to prevent us from examining our conduct; but adversity leads us to think properly of our state, and so is most beneficial to us.—*Johnson.*

Sweet are the uses of adversity, which, like a toad, though ugly and venomous, wears yet a precious jewel in its head.—*Shakespeare.*

The truly great and good, in affliction, bear a countenance more princely than they are wont; for it is the temper of the highest hearts, like the palm tree, to strive most upwards when it is most burdened.—*Sir P. Sidney.*

In this wild world, the fondest and the best are the most tried, most troubled, and distrest.—*Crabbe.*

Prosperity is the blessing of the Old Testament; adversity of the New, which carrieth the greater benediction and the clearer revelation of God's favor. Pros-

perity is not without many fears and distastes; adversity not without many comforts and hopes.—*Bacon.*

The sharpest sting of adversity it borrows from our own impatience.—*Bp. Horne.*

The brightest crowns that are worn in heaven have been tried, and smelted, and polished, and glorified through the furnace of tribulation.—*E. H. Chapin.*

He that can heroically endure adversity will bear prosperity with equal greatness of soul; for the mind that cannot be dejected by the former is not likely to be transported with the latter.—*Fielding.*

He that has no cross will have no crown.—*Quarles.*

Adversity is a severe instructor, set over us by one who knows us better than we do ourselves, as he loves us better too. He that wrestles with us strengthens our nerves and sharpens our skill. Our antagonist is our helper. This conflict with difficulty makes us acquainted with our object, and compels us to consider it in all its relations. It will not suffer us to be superficial.—*Burke.*

Genuine morality is preserved only in the school of adversity; a state of continuous prosperity may easily prove a quicksand to virtue.—*Schiller.*

Those who have suffered much are like those who know many languages; they have learned to understand and be understood by all.—*Mad. Swetchine.*

Though losses and crosses be lessons right severe, there's wit there ye'll get there, ye'll find no other where.—*Burns.*

A smooth sea never made a skilful mariner, neither do uninterrupted prosperity and success qualify for usefulness and happiness. The storms of adversity, like those of the ocean, rouse the faculties, and excite the invention, prudence, skill, and fortitude of the voyager. The martyrs of ancient times, in bracing their minds to outward calamities, acquired a loftiness of purpose and a moral heroism worth a lifetime of softness and security.—*Anon.*

A noble heart, like the sun, showeth its greatest countenance in its lowest estate.—*Sir P. Sidney.*

Adversity exasperates fools, dejects

cowards, draws out the faculties of the wise and industrious, puts the modest to the necessity of trying their skill, awes the opulent, and makes the idle industrious.—*Anon.*

No life is so hard that you can't make it easier by the way you take it.—*Ellen Glasgow.*

You can bear anything if it isn't your own fault.—*Katharine Fullerton Gerould.*

The real test in golf and in life is not in keeping out of the rough, but in getting out after we are in.—*Rev. John H. Moore.*

It's a different song when everything's wrong, when you're feeling infernally mortal; when it's ten against one, and hope there is none, buck up, little soldier, and chortle!—*Robert W. Service.*

Alas, how scant the sheaves for all the trouble, the toil, the pain and the resolve sublime—a few full ears; the rest but weeds and stubble, and withered wild flowers plucked before their time.— *A. B. Bragdon.*

ADVERTISING.—The great art in writing advertisements is the finding out of a proper method to catch the reader's eye; without which, a good thing may pass over unobserved, or lost among commissions of bankrupt.—*Addison.*

The business that considers itself immune to the necessity for advertising sooner or later finds itself immune to business.—*Derby Brown.*

As a profession advertising is young; as a force it is as old as the world. The first four words ever uttered, "Let there be light," constitute its charter. All nature is vibrant with its impulse.— *Bruce Barton.*

Business to-day consists in persuading crowds.—*Gerald Stanley Lee.*

Advertising is the life of trade.— *Calvin Coolidge.*

Sanely applied advertising could remake the world.—*Stuart Chase.*

Advertising is the genie which is transforming America into a place of comfort, luxury and ease for millions. *William Allen White.*

If a fellow wants to be a nobody in the business world, let him neglect sending the mail man to somebody on his behalf.—*C. F. Kettering.*

Advertising is the key to world prosperity; without it to-day modern business would be paralyzed.—*Julius Klein.*

Advertising is the principle of mass production applied to selling.—*Dr. J. T. Dorrance.*

Advertising is the essence of public contact.—*Cyrus H. K. Curtis.*

Advertising ministers to the spiritual side of trade.—*Calvin Coolidge.*

The advertising man is a liaison between the products of business and the mind of the nation. He must know both before he can serve either.—*Glenn Frank.*

I would rather pay ten million dollars for trademark-goodwill without property than one million dollars for property without trademark-goodwill.—*George K. Morrow.*

ADVICE.—When a man seeks your advice he generally wants your praise.— *Chesterfield.*

Many a man wins glory for prudence by seeking advice, then seeking advice as to what advice would be best to take, and finally following appetite.—*Austin O'Malley.*

He that gives good advice, builds with one hand; he that gives good counsel and example, builds with both; but he that gives good admonition and bad example, builds with one hand and pulls down with the other.—*Bacon.*

When a man has been guilty of any vice of folly, the best atonement he can make for it is to warn others not to fall into the like.—*Addison.*

It is a good divine that follows his own instructions. I can easier teach twenty what were good to be done, than be one of twenty to follow mine own teaching.—*Shakespeare.*

He who calls in the aid of an equal understanding doubles his own; and he who profits by a superior understanding raises his powers to a level with the heights of the superior understanding he unites with.—*Burke.*

It is easy when we are in prosperity to give advice to the afflicted.—*Æschylus.*

The worst men often give the best advice.—*Bailey.*

Advice is like snow; the softer it falls

the longer it dwells upon, and the deeper it sinks into the mind.—*Coleridge*.

Let no man value at a little price a virtuous woman's counsel.—*G. Chapman*.

Men give away nothing so liberally as their advice.—*Rochefoucauld*.

To accept good advice is but to increase one's own ability.—*Goethe*.

Good counsels observed are chains of grace.—*Fuller*.

Wait for the season when to cast good counsels upon subsiding passion.—*Shakespeare*.

Nothing is less sincere than our mode of asking and giving advice. He who asks seems to have deference for the opinion of his friend, while he only aims to get approval of his own and make his friend responsible for his action. And he who gives repays the confidence supposed to be placed in him by a seemingly disinterested zeal, while he seldom means anything by his advice but his own interest or reputation.—*Rochefoucauld*.

No man is so foolish but he may sometimes give another good counsel, and no man so wise that he may not easily err if he takes no other counsel than his own.—He that is taught only by himself has a fool for a master.—*Ben Jonson*.

Advice is seldom welcome. Those who need it most, like it least.—*Johnson*.

Every man, however wise, needs the advice of some sagacious friend in the affairs of life.—*Plautus*.

Those who school others, oft should school themselves.—*Shakespeare*.

We give advice by the bucket, but take it by the grain.—*W. R. Alger*.

They that will not be counselled, cannot be helped. It you do not hear reason she will rap you on the knuckles.—*Franklin*.

It takes nearly as much ability to know how to profit by good advice as to know how to act for one's self.—*Rochefoucauld*.

How is it possible to expect mankind to take advice when they will not so much as take warning?—*Swift*.

Do not give to your friends the most agreeable counsels, but the most advantageous.—*Tuckerman*.

Harsh counsels have no effect: they are like hammers which are always repulsed by the anvil.—*Helvetius*.

The advice of friends must be received with a judicious reserve: we must not give ourselves up to it and follow it blindly, whether right or wrong.—*Charron*.

Advice and reprehension require the utmost delicacy; painful truths should be delivered in the softest terms, and expressed no farther than is necessary to produce their due effect. A courteous man will mix what is conciliating with what is offensive; praise with censure; deference and respect with the authority of admonition, so far as can be done in consistence with probity and honor. The mind revolts against all censorian power which displays pride or pleasure in finding fault; but advice, divested of the harshness, and yet retaining the honest warmth of truth, is like honey put round the brim of a vessel full of wormwood.—Even this, however, is sometimes insufficient to conceal the bitterness of the draught.—*Percival*.

Give every man thine ear, but few thy voice; take each man's censure, but reserve thy judgment.—*Shakespeare*.

Giving advice is sometimes only showing our wisdom at the expense of another.—*Shaftesbury*.

AFFECTATION.—Affectation in any part of our carriage is but the lighting up of a candle to show our defects, and never fails to make us taken notice of, either as wanting in sense or sincerity.—*Locke*.

All affectation is the vain and ridiculous attempt of poverty to appear rich.—*Lavater*.

Affectation is a greater enemy to the face than the small-pox.—*St. Evremond*.

All affectation proceeds from the supposition of possessing something better than the rest of the world possesses. Nobody is vain of possessing two legs and two arms, because that is the precise quantity of either sort of limb which everybody possesses.—*Sydney Smith*.

Among the numerous stratagems by which pride endeavors to recommend folly to regard, scarcely one meets with less success than affectation, which is a perpetual disguise of the real character by false appearances.—*Johnson*.

Great vices are the proper objects of

our detestation, and smaller faults of our pity, but affectation appears to be the only true source of the ridiculous.—*Fielding.*

We are never so ridiculous by the qualities we have, as by those we affect to have.—*Rochefoucauld.*

Affectation is certain deformity.—By forming themselves on fantastic models the young begin with being ridiculous, and often end in being vicious.—*Blair.*

Affectation differs from hypocrisy in being the art of counterfeiting qualities which we might with innocence and safety be known to want.—Hypocrisy is the necessary burden of villainy; affectation, a part of the chosen trappings of folly.—*Johnson.*

Affectation proceeds either from vanity or hypocrisy; for as vanity puts us on affecting false characters to gain applause, so hypocrisy sets us on the endeavor to avoid censures by concealing our vices under the appearance of their opposite virtues.—*Fielding.*

Avoid all singularity and affectation.— What is according to nature is best, while what is contrary to it is always distasteful. Nothing is graceful that is not our own.—*Collier.*

Hearts may be attracted by assumed qualities, but the affections can only be fixed and retained by those that are real.—*De Moy.*

Affectation naturally counterfeits those excellencies which are farthest from our attainment, because knowing our defects we eagerly endeavor to supply them with artificial excellence.—*Johnson.*

Paltry affectation and strained allusions are easily attained by those who choose to wear them; but they are but the badges of ignorance or stupidity when it would endeavor to please.—*Goldsmith.*

All false practices and affectations of knowledge are more odious than any want or defect of knowledge can be.—*Sprat.*

Be yourself. Ape no greatness. Be willing to pass for what you are. A good farthing is better than a bad sovereign. Affect no oddness; but dare to be right, though you have to be singular.—*S. Coley.*

Affectation lights a candle to our de-fects, and though it may gratify ourselves, it disgusts all others.—*Lavater.*

AFFECTION. — There is so little to redeem the dry mass of follies and errors that make up so much of life, that anything to love or reverence becomes, as it were, a sabbath to the soul.—*Bulwer.*

How often a new affection makes a new man. The sordid becomes liberal; the cowering, heroic; the frivolous girl, the steadfast martyr of patience and ministration, transfigured by deathless love.—*E. H. Chapin.*

Mature affection, homage, devotion, does not easily express itself. Its voice is low. It is modest and retiring, it lays in ambush and waits. Such is the mature fruit. Sometimes a life glides away, and finds it still ripening in the shade. The light inclinations of very young people are as dust compared to rocks.—*Dickens.*

Our affections are our life.—We live by them; they supply our warmth.—*Channing.*

The affections are like lightning: you cannot tell where they will strike till they have fallen.—*Lacordaire.*

How sacred and beautiful is the feeling of affection in the pure and guileless soul! The proud may sneer at it, the fashionable call it a fable, the selfish and dissipated affect to despise it, but the holy passion is surely from heaven, and is made evil only by the corruptions of those it was sent to preserve and bless.—*Mordaunt.*

Of all earthly music that which reaches farthest into heaven is the beating of a truly loving heart.—*H. W. Beecher.*

If there is any thing that keeps the mind open to angel visits, and repels the ministry of evil, it is a pure human love.—*N. P. Willis.*

Our sweetest experiences of affection are meant to point us to that realm which is the real and endless home of the heart.—*H. W. Beecher.*

The affections, like conscience, are rather to be led than driven.—Those who marry where they do not love, will be likely to love where they do not marry. —*Fuller.*

Affection, like melancholy, magnifies trifles; but the magnifying of the one is like looking through a telescope at heavenly objects, that of the other, like

enlarging monsters with a microscope.—
Leigh Hunt.

The heart will commonly govern the
head; and any strong passion, set the
wrong way, will soon infatuate even
the wisest of men; therefore the first
part of wisdom is to watch the affections.—*Waterland.*

There is in life no blessing like affection; it soothes, it hallows, elevates,
subdues, and bringeth down to earth its
native heaven: life has nought else that
may supply its place.—*L. E. Landon.*

I'd rather than that crowds should
sigh for me, that from some kindred eye
the trickling tear should steal.—*H. K.
White.*

AFFLICTION.—(See ADVERSITY.)

Affliction is a school of virtue; it corrects levity, and interrupts the confidence of sinning.—*Atterbury.*

As threshing separates the wheat from
the chaff, so does affliction purify virtue.
—*Burton.*

Though all afflictions are evils in
themselves, yet they are good for us,
because they discover to us our disease
and tend to our cure.—*Tillotson.*

Affliction is the good man's shining
scene; prosperity conceals his brightest
ray; as night to stars, woe lustre gives
to man.—*Young.*

Many secrets of religion are not perceived till they be felt, and are not felt
but in the day of a great calamity.—
Jeremy Taylor.

The lord gets his best soldiers out of
the highlands of affliction.—*Spurgeon.*

That which thou dost not understand
when thou readest, thou shalt understand in the day of thy visitation; for
many secrets of religion are not perceived till they be felt, and are not felt
but in the day of calamity.—*Jeremy
Taylor.*

It has done me good to be somewhat
parched by the heat and drenched by
the rain of life.—*Longfellow.*

Affliction is the wholesome soil of virtue, where patience, honor, sweet humility, and calm fortitude, take root
and strongly flourish.—*Mallet.*

God sometimes washes the eyes of his
children with tears that they may read
aright his providence and his commandments.—*T. L. Cuyler.*

If your cup seems too bitter, if your
burden seems too heavy, be sure that it
is the wounded hand that is holding the
cup, and that it is He who carries the
cross that is carrying the burden.—*S. I.
Prime.*

I have learned more of experimental
religion since my little boy died than in
all my life before.—*Horace Bushnell.*

Paradoxical as it may seem, God
means not only to make us good, but
to make us also happy, by sickness,
disaster and disappointment.—*C. A.
Bartol.*

The hiding places of men are discovered by affliction.—As one has aptly
said, "Our refuges are like the nests of
birds; in summer they are hidden away
among the green leaves, but in winter
they are seen among the naked
branches."—*J. W. Alexander.*

Sanctified afflictions are like so many
artificers working on a pious man's
crown to make it more bright and massive.—*Cudworth.*

Heaven but tries our virtue by affliction, and oft the cloud that wraps the
present hour serves but to brighten all
our future days.—*J. Brown.*

If you would not have affliction visit
you twice, listen at once to what it
teaches.—*Burgh.*

Affliction is not sent in vain from the
good God who chastens those that he
loves.—*Southey.*

Nothing can occur beyond the strength
of faith to sustain, or transcending the
resources of religion to relieve.—*T.
Binney.*

As in nature, as in art, so in grace; it
is rough treatment that gives souls, as
well as stones, their lustre. The more
the diamond is cut the brighter it
sparkles; and in what seems hard dealing, there God has no end in view but
to perfect his people.—*Guthrie.*

It is not from the tall, crowded work-
house of prosperity that men first or
clearest see the eternal stars of heaven.
—*Theodore Parker.*

Ah! if you only knew the peace there
is in an accepted sorrow.—*Mde. Guion.*

It is not until we have passed through
the furnace that we are made to know
how much dross there is in our composition.—*Colton.*

It is a great thing, when the cup of bitterness is pressed to our lips, to feel that it is not fate or necessity, but divine love working upon us for good ends.—*E. H. Chapin.*

Afflictions sent by providence melt the constancy of the noble minded, but confirm the obduracy of the vile, as the same furnace that liquifies the gold, hardens the clay.—*Colton.*

The soul that suffers is stronger than the soul that rejoices.—*E. Shepard.*

There is such a difference between coming out of sorrow merely thankful for belief, and coming out of sorrow full of sympathy with, and trust in, Him who has released us.—*Phillips Brooks.*

Tears are often the telescope by which men see far into heaven.—*H. W. Beecher.*

Affliction comes to us all not to make us sad, but sober, not to make us sorry, but wise; not to make us despondent, but by its darkness to refresh us, as the night refreshes the day; not to impoverish, but to enrich us, as the plough enriches the field; to multiply our joy, as the seed, by planting, is multiplied a thousand-fold.—*H. W. Beecher.*

Strength is born in the deep silence of long-suffering hearts; not amid joy.—*Mrs. Hemans.*

By afflictions God is spoiling us of what otherwise might have spoiled us.—When he makes the world too hot for us to hold, we let it go.—*Powell.*

No Christian but has his Gethsemane; but every praying Christian will find there is no Gethsemane without its angel.—*T. Binney.*

With the wind of tribulation God separates, in the floor of the soul, the wheat from the chaff.—*Molinos.*

We are apt to overlook the hand and heart of God in our afflictions, and to consider them as mere accidents, and unavoidable evils.—This view makes them absolute and positive evils which admit of no remedy or relief.—If we view our troubles and trials aside from the divine design and agency in them, we cannot be comforted.—*Emmons.*

Amid my list of blessings infinite, stands this the foremost, " that my heart has bled."—*Young.*

Affliction is a divine diet which though it be not pleasing to mankind, yet Almighty God hath often imposed it as a good, though bitter, physic, to those children whose souls are dearest to him.—*Isaak Walton.*

The very afflictions of our earthly pilgrimage are presages of our future glory, as shadows indicate the sun.—*Richter.*

How fast we learn in a day of sorrow! Scripture shines out in a new effulgence; every verse seems to contain a sunbeam, every promise stands out in illuminated splendor; things hard to be understood become in a moment plain.—*H. Bonar.*

The most generous vine, if not pruned, runs out into many superfluous stems and grows at last weak and fruitless: so doth the best man if he be not cut short in his desires, and pruned with afflictions.—*Bp. Hall.*

Extraordinary afflictions are not always the punishment of extraordinary sins, but sometimes the trial of extraordinary graces.—Sanctified afflictions are spiritual promotions.—*M. Henry.*

The only way to meet affliction is to pass through it solemnly, slowly, with humility and faith, as the Israelites passed through the sea. Then its very waves of misery will divide, and become to us a wall, on the right side and on the left, until the gulf narrows before our eyes, and we land safe on the opposite shore.—*Miss Mulock.*

We should always record our thoughts in affliction: set up way-marks, that we may recur to them in health; for then we are in other circumstances, and can never recover our sick-bed views.

The good are better made by ill, as odors crushed are sweeter still.—*Rogers.*

What seem to us but dim funereal tapers, may be heaven's distant lamps.—*Longfellow.*

It is from the remembrance of joys we have lost that the arrows of affliction are pointed.—*Mackensie.*

The gem cannot be polished without friction, nor man perfected without trials.—*Chinese Proverb.*

Never on earth calamity so great, as not to leave to us, if rightly weighed, what would console 'mid what we sorrow for.—*Shakespeare.*

The lessons we learn in sadness and

from loss are those that abide.—Sorrow clarifies the mind, steadies it, forces it to weigh things correctly.—The soil moist with tears best feeds the seeds of truth.—*T. T. Munger*.

Never was there a man of deep piety, who has not been brought into extremities—who has not been put into fire—who has not been taught to say, " Though he slay me, yet will I trust in him."—*Cecil*.

As sure as God puts his children into the furnace of affliction, he will be with them in it.—*Spurgeon*.

Heaven tries our virtue by afflictions; as oft the cloud that wraps the present hour, serves but to lighten all our future days.—*J. Brown*.

Come then, affliction, if my Father wills, and be my frowning friend. A friend that frowns is better than a smiling enemy.—*Anon*.

AGE.—It is not by the gray of the hair that one knows the age of the heart.—*Bulwer*.

A graceful and honorable old age is the childhood of immortality.—*Pindar*.

How beautiful can time with goodness make an old man look.—*Jerrold*.

Old age adds to the respect due to virtue, but it takes nothing from the contempt inspired by vice; it whitens only the hair.—*J. P. Senn*.

Age does not depend upon years, but upon temperament and health.—Some men are born old, and some never grow so.—*Tryon Edwards*.

A person is always startled when he hears himself seriously called old for the first time.—*O. W. Holmes*.

The vices of old age have the stiffness of it too; and as it is the unfittest time to learn in, so the unfitness of it to unlearn will be found much greater.—*South*.

Let us repect gray hairs, especially our own.—*J. P. Senn*.

Our youth and manhood are due to our country, but our declining years are due to ourselves.—*Pliny*.

When we are young, we are slavishly employed in procuring something whereby we may live comfortably when we grow old; and when we are old, we perceive it is too late to live as we proposed.—*Pope*.

Old men's eyes are like old men's memories; they are strongest for things a long way off.—*George Eliot*.

No wise man ever wished to be younger.—*Swift*.

To be happy, we must be true to nature, and carry our age along with us.—*Hazlitt*.

Years do not make sages; they only make old men.—*Mad. Swetchine*.

Every one desires to live long, but no one would be old.—*Swift*.

Nothing is more disgraceful than that an old man should have nothing to show to prove that he has lived long, except his years.—*Seneca*.

How many fancy they have experience simply because they have grown old.—*Stanislaus*.

Men of age object too much, consult too little, adventure too little, repent too soon, and seldom drive business home to the full period, but content themselves with a mediocrity of success.—*Bacon*.

As we grow old we become both more foolish and more wise.—*Rochefoucauld*.

Age that lessens the enjoyment of life, increases our desire of living.—*Goldsmith*.

Childhood itself is scarcely more lovely than a cheerful, kindly, sunshiny old age.—*L. M. Child*.

When one becomes indifferent to women, to children, and to young people, he may know that he is superannuated, and has withdrawn from what is sweetest and purest in human existence.—*A. B. Alcott*.

Old age is a blessed time. It gives us leisure to put off our earthly garments one by one, and dress ourselves for heaven. " Blessed are they that are home-sick, for they shall get home."

A comfortable old age is the reward of a well-spent youth.—Instead of its bringing sad and melancholy prospects of decay, it should give us hopes of eternal youth in a better world.—*R. Palmer*.

No snow falls lighter than the snow of age; but none lies heavier, for it never melts.

It is a rare and difficult attainment to grow old gracefully and happily.—*L. M. Child*

Old age is a tryant, which forbids the pleasures of youth on pain of death.—*Rochefoucauld.*

Old age has deformities enough of its own.—It should never add to them the deformity of vice.—*Cato.*

We should so provide for old age that it may have no urgent wants of this world to absorb it from meditation on the next.—It is awful to see the lean hands of dotage making a coffer of the grave.—*Bulwer.*

To resist the frigidity of old age one must combine the body, the mind, and the heart.—And to keep these in parallel vigor one must exercise, study, and love.—*Bonstettin.*

When a noble life has prepared old age, it is not decline that it reveals, but the first days of immortality.—*Mad. de Staël.*

The evening of a well-spent life brings its lamps with it.—*Joubert.*

Age does not make us childish, as some say; it finds us true children.—*Goethe.*

Age is rarely despised but when it is contemptible.—*Johnson.*

As winter strips the leaves from around us, so that we may see the distant regions they formerly concealed, so old age takes away our enjoyments only to enlarge the prospect of the coming eternity.—*Richter.*

He who would pass his declining years with honor and comfort, should, when young, consider that he may one day become old, and remember when he is old, that he has once been young.—*Addison.*

That man never grows old who keeps a child in his heart.

A healthy old fellow, who is not a fool, is the happiest creature living.—*Steele.*

In old age life's shadows are meeting eternity's day.—*Clarke.*

The Grecian ladies counted their age from their marriage, not from their birth.—*Homer.*

The golden age is before us, not behind us.—*St. Simon.*

The tendency of old age to the body, say the physiologists, is to form bone.—It is as rare as it is pleasant to meet with an old man whose opinions are not ossified.—*J. F. Boyse.*

That old man dies prematurely whose memory records no benefits conferred.—They only have lived long who have lived virtuously.—*Sheridan.*

I venerate old age; and I love not the man who can look without emotion upon the sunset of life, when the dusk of evening begins to gather over the watery eye, and the shadows of twilight grow broader and deeper upon the understanding.—*Longfellow.*

While one finds company in himself and his pursuits, he cannot feel old, no matter what his years may be.—*A. B. Alcott.*

It is only necessary to grow old to become more charitable and even indulgent.—I see no fault committed by others that I have not committed myself.—*Goethe.*

An aged Christian, with the snow of time upon his head, may remind us that those points of earth are whitest which are nearest to heaven.—*E. H. Chapin.*

There are three classes into which all the women past seventy years of age I have ever known, were divided: that dear old soul; that old woman; that old witch.—*Coleridge.*

That which is called dotage, is not the weak point of all old men, but only of such as are distinguished by their levity and weakness.—*Cicero.*

There cannot live a more unhappy creature than an ill-natured old man, who is neither capable of receiving pleasures, nor sensible of conferring them on others.—*Sir W. Temple.*

As we advance in life the circle of our pains enlarges, while that of our pleasures contracts.—*Mad. Swetchine.*

Gray hairs seem to my fancy like the soft light of the moon, silvering over the evening of life.—*Richter.*

One's age should be tranquil, as childhood should be playful.—Hard work at either extremity of life seems out of place.—At mid-day the sun may burn, and men labor under it; but the morning and evening should be alike calm and cheerful.—*Arnold.*

When we are out of sympathy with the young, then I think our work in this world is over.—*G. Macdonald.*

At twenty. the will reigns; at thirty, the wit; at forty, the judgment; afterward, proportion of character.—*Grattan.*

It is often the case with fine natures, that when the fire of the spirit dies out with increasing age, the power of intellect is unaltered or increased, and an originally educated judgment grows broader and gentler as the river of life widens out to the everlasting sea.—*Mrs. Gatty.*

Some men never seem to grow old. Always active in thought, always ready to adopt new ideas, they are never chargeable with fogyism. Satisfied, yet ever dissatisfied, settled, yet ever unsettled, they always enjoy the best of what is, and are the first to find the best of what will be.

Though I look old, yet I am strong and lusty; for in my youth I never did apply hot and rebellious liquors in my blood; and did not, with unbashful forehead, woo the means of weakness and debility: therefore my age is as a lusty winter, frosty but kindly.—*Shakespeare.*

When men grow virtuous in their old age, they are merely making a sacrifice to God of the devil's leavings.—*Swift.*

Age sits with decent grace upon his visage, and worthily becomes his silver locks, who wears the marks of many years well spent, of virtue, truth well tried, and wise experience.—*Rowe.*

Toward old age both men and women hang to life by their habits.—*Charles Reade.*

Probably the happiest period in life most frequently is in middle age, when the eager passions of youth are cooled, and the infirmities of age not yet begun; as we see that the shadows, which are at morning and evening so large, almost entirely disappear at mid-day.—*T. Arnold.*

Like a morning dream, life becomes more and more bright the longer we live, and the reason of everything appears more clear. What has puzzled us before seems less mysterious, and the crooked paths look straighter as we approach the end.—*Richter.*

Ye who are old, remember youth with thought of like affection.—*Shakespeare.*

Age should fly concourse, cover in retreat defects of judgment, and the will subdue; walk thoughtful on the silent, solemn shore of that vast ocean it must sail so soon.—*Young.*

Cautious age suspects the flattering form, and only credits what experience tells.—*Johnson.*

If reverence is due from others to the old, they ought also to respect themselves; and by grave, prudent, and holy actions, put a crown of glory upon their own gray heads.—*Bp. Hopkins.*

These are the effects of doting age; vain doubts, and idle cares, and over-caution.—*Dryden.*

There are two things which grow stronger in the breast of man, in proportion as he advances in years: the love of country and religion. Let them be never so much forgotten in youth, they sooner or later present themselves to us arrayed in all their charms, and excite in the recesses of our hearts an attachment justly due to their beauty.—*Chateaubriand.*

Thirst of power and of riches now bear sway, the passion and infirmity of age.—*Froude.*

Youth changes its tastes by the warmth of its blood; age retains its tastes by habit.—*Rochefoucauld.*

There is not a more repulsive spectacle than an old man who will not forsake the world, which has already forsaken him.—*Tholuck.*

AGITATION.—Agitation is the marshalling of the conscience of a nation to mould its laws.—*Sir R. Peel.*

Agitation prevents rebellion, keeps the peace, and secures progress. Every step she gains is gained forever. Muskets are the weapons of animals. Agitation is the atmosphere of the brains.—*Wendell Phillips.*

Those who mistake the excitement and agitation of reform for the source of danger, must have overlooked all history.

We believe in excitement when the theme is great; in agitation when huge evils are to be reformed. It is thus that a state or nation clears itself of great moral wrongs, and effects important changes. Still waters gather to themselves poisonous ingredients, and scatter epidemics and death. The noisy, tumbling brook, and the rolling and roaring ocean, are pure and healthful. The moral and political elements need the rockings and heavings of free discussion, for their own purification. The nation feels a healthier pulsation, and breathes a more invigorating atmosphere, than if pulpit, platform, and press, were all silent as the tomb, leaving misrule and oppression unwatched and unscathed.—*P. Cooke.*

Agitation, under pretence of reform, with a view to overturn revealed truth and order, is the worst kind of mischief. —*C. Simmons.*

Agitation is the method that plants the school by the side of the ballot-box. —*Wendell Phillips.*

AGNOSTICISM.—There is only one greater folly than that of the fool who says in his heart there is no God, and that is the folly of the people that says with its head that it does not know whether there is a God or not.—*Bismarck.*

An agnostic is a man who doesn't know whether there is a God or not, doesn't know whether he has a soul or not, doesn't know whether there is a future life or not, doesn't believe that any one else knows any more about these matters than he does, and thinks it a waste of time to try to find out.—*Dana.*

The term "agnostic" is only the Greek equivalent of the Latin and English "Ignoramus"—a name one would think scientists would be slow to apply to themselves.

Agnosticism is the philosophical, ethical, and religious dry-rot of the modern world.—*F. E. Abbot.*

AGRARIANISM.—The agrarian would divide all the property in the community equally among its members. —But if so divided to-day, industry on the one hand, and idleness on the other, would make it unequal on the morrow.—There is no agrarianism in the providence of God.—*Tryon Edwards.*

The agrarian, like the communist, would bring all above him down to his own level, or raise himself to theirs, but is not anxious to bring those below him up to himself.—*C. Simmons.*

AGRICULTURE.—Agriculture is the foundation of manufactures, since the productions of nature are the materials of art.—*Gibbon.*

Agriculture not only gives riches to a nation, but the only riches she can call her own.—*Johnson.*

Let the farmer forevermore be honored in his calling, for they who labor in the earth are the chosen people of God.—*Jefferson.*

Agriculture for an honorable and high-minded man, is the best of all occupations or arts by which men procure the means of living.—*Xenophon.*

Trade increases the wealth and glory of a country; but its real strength and stamina are to be looked for among the cultivators of the land.—*Lord Chatham.*

The farmers are the founders of civilization and prosperity.—*Daniel Webster.*

He that would look with contempt on the pursuits of the farmer, is not worthy the name of a man.—*H. W. Beecher.*

There seem to be but three ways for a nation to acquire wealth: the first is by war, as the Romans did, in plundering their conquered neighbors—this is robbery; the second by commerce, which is generally cheating; the third by agriculture, the only honest way, wherein man receives a real increase of the seed thrown into the ground, in a kind of continual miracle, wrought by the hand of God in his favor, as a reward for his innocent life and his virtuous industry. —*Franklin.*

In the age of acorns, before the times of Ceres, a single barley-corn had been of more value to mankind than all the diamonds of the mines of India.—*H. Brooke.*

The first three men in the world were a gardener, a ploughman, and a grasier; and if any object that the second of these was a murderer, I desire him to consider that as soon as he was so, he quitted our profession, and turned builder.—*Cowley.*

In a moral point of view, the life of the agriculturist is the most pure and holy of any class of men; pure, because it is the most healthful, and vice can hardly find time to contaminate it; and holy, because it brings the Deity perpetually before his view, giving him thereby the most exalted notions of supreme power, and the most endearing view of the divine benignity.—*Lord John Russell.*

Command large fields, but cultivate small ones.—*Virgil.*

Whoever makes two ears of corn, or two blades of grass to grow where only one grew before, deserves better of mankind, and does more essential service to his country than the whole race of politicians put together.—*Swift.*

The frost is God's plough which he drives through every inch of ground in the world, opening each clod, and pulverizing the whole.—*Fuller.*

We may talk as we please of lilies, and lions rampant, and spread eagles in fields of d'or or d'argent, but if heraldry were guided by reason, a plough in the field arable would be the most noble and ancient arms.—*Cowley.*

AIMS.—(See "ASPIRATION.")

High aims form high characters, and great objects bring out great minds.—*Tryon Edwards.*

Have a purpose in life, and having it, throw into your work such strength of mind and muscle as God has given you. —*Carlyle.*

The man who seeks one, and but one, thing in life may hope to achieve it; but he who seeks all things, wherever he goes, only reaps, from the hopes which he sows, a harvest of barren regrets.— *Bulwer.*

Not failure, but low aim, is crime.— *J. R. Lowell.*

Aim at perfection in everything, though in most things it is unattainable; however, they who aim at it, and persevere, will come much nearer to it, than those whose laziness and despondency make them give it up as unattainable. —*Chesterfield.*

Aim at the sun, and you may not reach it; but your arrow will fly far higher than if aimed at an object on a level with yourself.—*J. Hawes.*

Resolved to live with all my might while I do live, and as I shall wish I had done ten thousand ages hence.—*Jonathan Edwards.*

It is a sad thing to begin life with low conceptions of it. It may not be possible for a young man to measure life; but it is possible to say, I am resolved to put life to its noblest and best use.—*T. T. Munger.*

Dream manfully and nobly, and thy dreams shall be prophets.—*Bulwer.*

In great attempts it is glorious even to fail.—*Longinus.*

We want an aim that can never grow vile, and which cannot disappoint our hope. There is but one such on earth, and it is that of being like God. He who strives after union with perfect love must grow out of selfishness, and his success is secured in the omnipotent holiness of God.—*S. Brooke.*

What are the aims which are at the same time duties?—they are the perfecting of ourselves, and the happiness of others.—*Kant.*

High aims and loftly purposes are the wings of the soul aiding it to mount to heaven. In God's word we have a perfect standard both of duty and character, that by the influence of both, appealing to the best principles of our nature, we may be roused to the noblest and best efforts.—*S. Spring.*

Providence has nothing good or high in store for one who does not resolutely aim at something high or good.—A purpose is the eternal condition of success. —*T. T. Munger.*

ALCHEMY.—Alchemy may be compared to the man who told his sons of gold buried somewhere in his vineyard, where they by digging found no gold, but by turning up the mould about the roots of their vines, procured a plentiful vintage. So the search and endeavors to make gold have brought many useful inventions and instructive experiments to light.—*Bacon.*

I have always looked upon alchemy in natural philosophy, to be like over enthusiasm in divinity, and to have troubled the world much to the same purpose.—*Sir W. Temple.*

ALLEGORIES.—Allegories, when well chosen, are like so many tracks of light in a discourse, that make everything about them clear and beautiful.—*Addison.*

The allegory of a sophist is always screwed; it crouches and bows like a snake, which is never straight, whether she go, creep, or lie still; only when she is dead, she is straight enough.—*Luther.*

A man conversing in earnest, if he watch his intellectual process, will find that a material image, more or less luminous, arises in his mind with every thought which furnishes the vestment of the thought.—Hence good writing and brilliant discourse are perpetual allegories.—*Emerson.*

Allegories are fine ornaments and good illustrations, but not proof.—*Luther.*

AMBASSADOR.— An ambassador is an honest man sent to lie and intrigue abroad for the benefit of his country—*Sir H. Wotton.*

AMBITION.—Ambition is the germ from which all growth of nobleness proceeds.—*T. D. English.*

Ambition is the spur that makes man struggle with destiny. It is heaven's own incentive to make purpose great and achievement greater.—*Donald G. Mitchell.*

A noble man compares and estimates himself by an idea which is higher than himself; and a mean man, by one lower than himself.—The one produces aspiration; the other ambition, which is the way in which a vulgar man aspires.—*H. W. Beecher.*

Fling away ambition. By that sin angels fell. How then can man, the image of his Maker, hope to win by it? —*Shakespeare.*

Ambition often puts men upon doing the meanest offices: so climbing is performed in the same posture as creeping. —*Swift.*

As dogs in a wheel, or squirrels in a cage, ambitious men still climb and climb, with great labor and incessant anxiety, but never reach the top.—*Burton.*

Ambition is a lust that is never quenched, but grows more inflamed and madder by enjoyment.—*Otway.*

The noblest spirit is most strongly attracted by the love of glory.—*Cicero.*

It is the nature of ambition to make men liars and cheats who hide the truth in their hearts, and like jugglers, show another thing in their mouths; to cut all friendships and enmities to the measure of their interest, and put on a good face where there is no corresponding good will.—*Sallust.*

Ambition is the avarice of power; and happiness herself is soon sacrificed to that very lust of dominion which was first

encouraged only as the best means of obtaining it.—*Colton.*

To be ambitious of true honor and of the real glory and perfection of our nature is the very principle and incentive of virtue; but to be ambitious of titles, place, ceremonial respects, and civil pageantry, is as vain and little as the things are which we court.—*Sir. P. Sidney.*

Vaulting ambition, which o'erleaps itself.—*Shakespeare.*

Say what we will, we may be sure that ambition is an error. Its wear and tear of heart are never recompensed; it steals away the freshness of life; it deadens our vivid and social enjoyments; it shuts our souls to our youth; and we are old ere we remember that we have made a fever and a labor of our raciest years.—*Bulwer.*

Ambition is but the evil shadow of aspiration.—*G. Macdonald.*

Ambition is an idol on whose wings great minds are carried to extremes, to be sublimely great, or to be nothing.—*Southern.*

Ambition is not a vice of little people. —*Montaigne.*

Ambition is not a weakness unless it be disproportioned to the capacity. To have more ambition than ability is to be at once weak and unhappy.—*G. S. Hillard.*

It is by attempting to reach the top at a single leap, that so much misery is caused in the world.—*Cobbett.*

Ambition has one heel nailed in well, though she stretch her fingers to touch the heavens.—*Lilly.*

Ambition thinks no face so beautiful, as that which looks from under a crown. —*Sir P. Sidney.*

It is the constant fault and inseparable evil quality of ambition, that it never looks behind it.—*Seneca.*

Ambition makes the same mistake concerning power, that avarice makes as to wealth. She begins by accumulating it as a means to happiness, and finishes by continuing to accumulate it as an end. —*Colton.*

High seats are never but uneasy, and crowns are always stuffed with thorns.—*Brooks.*

The tallest trees are most in the

power of the winds, and ambitious men of the blasts of fortune.—*Penn.*

Ambition is like love, impatient both of delays and rivals.—*Denham.*

Most people would succeed in small things if they were not troubled by great ambitions.—*Longfellow.*

He who surpasses or subdues mankind, must look down on the hate of those below.—*Byron.*

Where ambition can cover its enterprises, even to the person himself, under the appearance of principle, it is the most incurable and inflexible of passions.—*Hume.*

The slave has but one master, the ambitious man has as many as there are persons whose aid may contribute to the advancement of his fortunes.—*Bruyère.*

Ambition is so powerful a passion in the human breast, that however high we reach we are never satisfied.—*Machiavelli.*

Nothing is too high for the daring of mortals: we storm heaven itself in our folly.—*Horace.*

The very substance of the ambitious is merely the shadow of a dream.—*Shakespeare.*

How like a mounting devil in the heart rules the unreined ambition.—*N. P. Willis.*

Too often those who entertain ambition, expel remorse and nature.—*Shakespeare.*

Too low they build who build below the skies.—*Young.*

Great souls, by nature half divine, soar to the stars, and hold a near acquaintance with the gods.—*Rowe.*

AMERICA.—America is another name for opportunity. Our whole history appears like a last effort of divine Providence in behalf of the human race.—*Emerson.*

America is rising with a giant's strength. Its bones are yet but cartilages.—*Fisher Ames.*

America is a fortunate country; she grows by the follies of our European nations.—*Napoleon.*

America—half-brother of the world.—*Bailey.*

The home of the homeless all over the earth.—*Street.*

If all Europe were to become a prison, America would still present a loop-hole of escape; and, God be praised! that loop-hole is larger than the dungeon itself.—*Heine.*

The home of freedom, and the hope of the down-trodden and oppressed among the nations of the earth.—*Daniel Webster.*

This is what I call the American idea, a government of the people, by the people, and for the people—a government of the principles of eternal justice, the unchanging law of God.—*Theodore Parker.*

America has proved that it is practicable to elevate the mass of mankind—the laboring or lower class—to raise them to self-respect, to make them competent to act a part in the great right and the great duty of self-government; and she has proved that this may be done by education and the diffusion of knowledge. She holds out an example a thousand times more encouraging than ever was presented before to those nine-tenths of the human race who are born without hereditary fortune or hereditary rank.—*Daniel Webster.*

AMIABILITY.—The constant desire of pleasing which is the peculiar quality of some, may be called the happiest of all desires in this, that it rarely fails of attaining its end when not disgraced by affectation.—*Fielding.*

To be amiable is most certainly a duty, but it is not to be exercised at the expense of any virtue.—He who seeks to do the amiable always, can at times be successful only by the sacrifice of his manhood.—*Simms.*

How easy to be amiable in the midst of happiness and success.—*Mad. Swetchine.*

Amiable people, though often subject to imposition in their contact with the world, yet radiate so much of sunshine that they are reflected in all appreciative hearts.—*Deulzy.*

AMUSEMENTS.—It is doing some service to humanity, to amuse innocently. They know but little of society who think we can bear to be always employed, either in duties or meditation, without relaxation.—*H. More.*

The mind ought sometimes to be diverted, that it may return the better to thinking.—*Phædrus.*

Amusement is the waking sleep of labor. When it absorbs thought, patience, and strength that might have been seriously employed, it loses its distinctive character and becomes the taskmaster of idleness.—*Willmott.*

Let the world have whatever sports and recreations please them best, provided they be followed with discretion. —*Burton.*

Amusement that is excessive and followed only for its own sake, allures and deceives us, and leads us down imperceptibly in thoughtlessness to the grave. —*Pascal.*

The habit of dissipating every serious thought by a succession of agreeable sensations is as fatal to happiness as to virtue; for when amusement is uniformly substituted for objects of moral and mental interest, we lose all that elevates our enjoyments above the scale of childish pleasures.—*Anna Maria Porter.*

Amusements are to religion like breezes of air to the flame,—gentle ones will fan it, but strong ones will put it out.—*Thomas.*

Innocent amusements are such as excite moderately, and such as produce a cheerful frame of mind, not boisterous mirth; such as refresh, instead of exhausting, the system; such as recur frequently, rather than continue long; such as send us back to our daily duties invigorated in body and spirit; such as we can partake of in the presence and society of respectable friends; such as consist with and are favorable to a grateful piety; such as are chastened by self-respect, and are accompanied with the consciousness that life has a higher end than to be amused.—*Channing.*

If those who are the enemies of innocent amusements had the direction of the world, they would take away the spring and youth, the former from the year, the latter from human life.—*Balzac.*

It is a sober truth that people who live only to amuse themselves, work harder at the task than most people do in earning their daily bread.—*H. More.*

It is exceedingly deleterious to withdraw the sanction of religion from amusement. If we feel that it is all injurious we should strip the earth of its flowers and blot out its pleasant sunshine.—*E. H. Chapin.*

Dwell not too long upon sports; for as they refresh a man that is weary, so they weary a man that is refreshed.—*Fuller.*

If you are animated by right principles, and are fully awakened to the true dignity of life, the subject of amusements may be left to settle itself.—*T. T. Munger.*

Christian discipleship does not involve the abandonment of any innocent enjoyment. Any diversion or amusement which we can use so as to receive pleasure and enjoyment to ourselves, and do no harm to others, we are perfectly free to use; and any that we cannot use without injury to ourselves or harm to others, we have no right to use, whether we are Christians or not.—*W. Gladden.*

I am a great friend to public amusements, for they keep people from vice. —*Johnson.*

Amusement to an observing mind is study.—*Disraeli.*

It is doing some service to humanity to amuse innocently; and they know very little of society who think we can bear to be always employed, either in duties or meditations, without any relaxation.—*Sir P. Sidney.*

All amusements to which virtuous women are not admitted, are, rely upon it, deleterious in their nature.—*Thackeray.*

Joining in the amusements of others is, in our social state, the next thing to sympathy in their distresses, and even the slenderest bond that holds society together should rather be strengthened than snapt.—*Landor.*

The church has been so fearful of amusements that the devil has had the charge of them; the chaplet of flowers has been snatched from the brow of Christ, and given to Mammon.—*H. W. Beecher.*

ANALOGY.—Analogy, although it is not infallible, is yet that telescope of the mind by which it is marvelously assisted in the discovery of both physical and moral truth.—*Colton.*

Those who reason only by analogies, rarely reason by logic, and are generally slaves to imagination.—*C. Simmons.*

ANARCHY.—Anarchy is the choking, sweltering, deadly, and killing rule of no rule; the consecration of cupidity and braying of folly and dim stupidity and baseness, in most of the affairs of men. Slop-shirts attainable three half-pence cheaper by the ruin of living bodies and immortal souls.—*Carlyle.*

Burke talked of "that digest of anarchy called the Rights of Man."—*Alison.*

Anarchy is hatred of human authority; atheism of divine authority—two sides of the same whole.—*Macpherson.*

ANCESTRY. — (See "BIRTH," and "GENEALOGY.")

The happiest lot for a man, as far as birth is concerned, is that it should be such as to give him but little occasion to think much about it.—*Whately.*

I will not borrow merit from the dead, myself an undeserver.—*Rowe.*

Every man is his own ancestor, and every man is his own heir. He devises his own future, and he inherits his own past.—*H. F. Hedge.*

It is the highest of earthly honors to be descended from the great and good. —They alone cry out against a noble ancestry who have none of their own. —*Ben Jonson.*

Good blood—descent from the great and good, is a high honor and privilege. —He that lives worthily of it is deserving of the highest esteem; he that does not, of the deeper disgrace.—*Colton.*

They that on glorious ancestors enlarge, produce their debt, instead of their discharge.—*Young.*

We take rank by descent. Such of us as have the longest pedigree, and are therefore the furthest removed from the first who made the fortune and founded the family, we are the noblest.—*Froude.*

Breed is stronger than pasture.—*George Eliot.*

It is, indeed, a blessing, when the virtues of noble races are hereditary.—*Nabb.*

How poor are all hereditary honors, those poor possessions from another's deeds, unless our own just virtues form our title, and give a sanction to our fond assumption.—*Shirley.*

It is a noble faculty of our nature which enables us to connect our thoughts, sympathies, and happiness, with what is distant in place or time; and looking before and after, to hold communion at once with our ancestors and our posterity. There is a moral and philosophical respect for our ancestors, which elevates the character and improves the heart. Next to the sense of religious duty and moral feeling, I hardly know what should bear with stronger obligation on a liberal and enlightened mind, than a consciousness of an alliance with excellence which is departed; and a consciousness, too, that in its acts and conduct, and even in its sentiments and thoughts, it may be actively operating on the happiness of those that come after it.—*Daniel Webster.*

A grandfather is no longer a social institution.—Men do not live in the past.—They merely look back.—Forward is the universal cry.

What can we see in the longest kingly line in Europe, save that it runs back to a successful soldier?—*Walter Scott.*

Some decent, regulated pre-eminence, some preference given to birth, is neither unnatural nor unjust nor impolitic.—*Burke.*

It is with antiquity as with ancestry, nations are proud of the one, and individuals of the other; but if they are nothing in themselves, that which is their pride ought to be their humiliation.—*Colton.*

The origin of all mankind was the same: it is only a clear and a good conscience that makes a man noble, for that is derived from heaven itself.—*Seneca.*

It is of no consequence of what parents a man is born, so he be a man of merit. —*Horace.*

The glory of ancestors sheds a light around posterity; it allows neither their good or bad qualities to remain in obscurity.—*Sallust.*

Consider whether we ought not to be more in the habit of seeking honor from our descendants than from our ancestors; thinking it better to be nobly remembered than nobly born; and striving so to live, that our sons, and our sons' sons, for ages to come, might still lead their children reverently to the doors out of which we had been carried to the grave, saying, "Look, this was his house, this was his chamber."—*Ruskin.*

Mere family never made a man great. —Thought and deed, not pedigree, are the passports to enduring fame.—*Skobeleff.*

It is fortunate to come of distinguished ancestry.—It is not less so to be such that people do not care to inquire whether you are of high descent or not. —*Bruyere.*

Few people disparage a distinguished ancestry except those who have none of their own.—*J. Hawes.*

Title and ancestry render a good man more illustrious, but an ill one more contemptible.—*Addison.*

It is a shame for a man to desire honor only because of his noble progenitors, and not to deserve it by his own virtue. —*Chrysostom.*

Philosophy does not regard pedigree. —She did not receive Plato as a noble, but made him so.—*Seneca.*

I am no herald to inquire after men's pedigrees: it sufficeth me if I know of their virtues.—*Sir P. Sidney.*

Nothing is more disgraceful than for a man who is nothing, to hold himself honored on account of his forefathers; and yet hereditary honors are a noble and splendid treasure to descendants.— *Plato.*

Some men by ancestry are only the shadow of a mighty name.—*Lucan.*

Pride in boasting of family antiquity, makes duration stand for merit.—*Zimmerman.*

The man of the true quality is not he who labels himself with genealogical tables, and lives on the reputation of his fathers, but he in whose conversation and behavior there are references and characteristics positively unaccountable except on the hypothesis that his descent is pure and illustrious.—*Theodore Parker.*

The inheritance of a distinguished and noble name is a proud inheritance to him who lives worthily of it.—*Colton.*

Honorable descent is, in all nations, greatly esteemed. It is to be expected that the children of men of worth will be like their progenitors; for nobility is the virtue of a family.—*Aristotle.*

The glory of ancestors sheds a light around posterity; it allows neither their good nor their bad qualities to remain in obscurity.—*Sallust.*

It would be more honorable to our distinguished ancestors to praise them in words less, but in deeds to imitate them more.—*H. Mann.*

They who depend on the merits of ancestors, search in the roots of the tree for the fruits which the branches ought to produce.—*Barrow.*

The man who has nothing to boast of but his illustrious ancestry, is like the potato—the best part under ground.— *Overbury.*

Distinguished birth is like a cipher: it has no power in itself like wealth, or talent, or personal excellence, but it tells, with all the power of a cipher, when added to either of the others.—*Boyes.*

The pride of blood has a most important and beneficial influence.—It is much to feel that the high and honorable belong to a name that is pledged to the present by the recollections of the past.—*L. E. Landon.*

When real nobleness accompanies the imaginary one of birth, the imaginary mixes with the real and becomes real too.—*Greville.*

We inherit nothing truly, but what our actions make us worthy of.—*Chapman.*

He that can only boast of a distinguished lineage, boasts of that which does not belong to himself; but he that lives worthily of it is always held in the highest honor.—*Junius.*

All history shows the power of blood over circumstances, as agriculture shows the power of the seeds over the soil.— *E. P. Whipple.*

Birth is nothing where virtue is not.— *Molière.*

Nobility of birth does not always insure a corresponding nobility of mind; if it did, it would always act as a stimulus to noble actions; but it sometimes acts as a clog rather than a spur. —*Colton.*

ANECDOTES.—Anecdotes and maxims are rich treasures to the man of the world, for he knows how to introduce the former at fit places in conversation, and to recollect the latter on proper occasions.—*Goethe.*

Some people exclaim, "Give me no anecdotes of an author, but give me his works"; and yet I have often found that the anecdotes are more interesting than the works.—*Disraeli.*

Anecdotes are sometimes the best vehicles of truth, and if striking and appropriate are often more impressive and powerful than argument.—*Tryon Edwards.*

Occasionally a single anecdote opens a character; biography has its comparative anatomy, and a saying or a sentiment enables the skillful hand to construct the skeleton.—*Willmott.*

Story-telling is subject to two unavoidable defects: frequent repetition and being soon exhausted; so that whoever values this gift in himself, has need of a good memory, and ought frequently to shift his company.—*Swift.*

ANGELS.—Millions of spiritual creatures walk the earth unseen, both when we sleep and when we wake.—*Milton.*

We are never like angels till our passion dies.—*Decker.*

The guardian angels of life sometimes fly so high as to be beyond our sight, but they are always looking down upon us.—*Richter.*

The angels may have wider spheres of action and nobler forms of duty than ourselves, but truth and right to them and to us are one and the same thing.—*E. H. Chapin.*

ANGER.—Anger begins in folly, and ends in repentance.—*Pythagoras.*

The fire you kindle for your enemy often burns yourself more than him.—*Chinese Proverb.*

Anger is the most impotent of passions.—It effects nothing it goes about, and hurts the one who is possessed by it more than the one against whom it is directed.—*Clarendon.*

He that would be angry and sin not, must not be angry with anything but sin.—*Secker.*

To be angry is to revenge the faults of others on ourselves.—*Pope.*

Anger is one of the sinews of the soul.—*Fuller.*

Rancour will out.—*Shakespeare.*

Anger is an expensive luxury in which only men of a certain income can indulge.—*G. W. Curtis.*

Temperate anger well becomes the wise.—*Philemon.*

When anger rushes, unrestrained, to action, like a hot steed, it stumbles in its way.—*Savage.*

When thou art above measure angry, bethink thee how momentary is man's life.—*Marcus Aurelius.*

Act nothing in a furious passion. It's putting to sea in a storm.—*Thomas Fuller.*

Anger ventilated often hurries towards forgiveness; anger concealed often hardens into revenge.—*Bulwer.*

Keep cool and you command everybody.—*St. Just.*

Anger may be kindled in the noblest breasts; but in these the slow droppings of an unforgiving temper never take the shape and consistency of enduring hatred.—*G. S. Hillard.*

Frequent fits of anger produce in the soul a propensity to be angry; which ofttimes ends in choler, bitterness, and morosity, when the mind becomes ulcerated, peevish, and querulous, and is wounded by the least occurrence.—*Plutarch.*

Beware of the fury of a patient man.—*Dryden.*

The flame of anger, bright and brief, sharpens the barb of love.—*W. S. Landor.*

A man . . . makes his inferiors his superiors by heat.—*R. W. Emerson.*

There is not in nature a thing that makes man so deformed, so beastly, as doth intemperate anger.—*John Webster.*

To be angry about trifles is mean and childish; to rage and be furious is brutish; and to maintain perpetual wrath is akin to the practice and temper of devils; but to prevent and suppress rising resentment is wise and glorious, is manly and divine.—*Watts.*

Men often make up in wrath what they want in reason.—*Alger.*

Life appears to me too short to be spent in nursing animosity or registering wrong.—*Charlotte Brontë.*

Consider how much more you often suffer from your anger and grief, than from those very things for which you are angry and grieved.—*Marcus Antoninus.*

The greatest remedy for anger is delay.—*Seneca.*

Wise anger is like fire from the flint; there is a great ado to bring it out; and when it does come, it is out again immediately.—*M. Henry.*

Anger is as a stone cast into a wasp's nest.—*Malabar Proverb.*

When a man is wrong and won't admit it, he always gets angry.—*Haliburton.*

When one is in a good sound rage, it is astonishing how calm one can be.—*Bulwer.*

He who can suppress a moment's anger may prevent a day of sorrow.

To rule one's anger is well; to prevent it is still better.—*Tryon Edwards.*

Anger is a noble infirmity; the generous failing of the just; the one degree that riseth above zeal, asserting the prerogative of virtue.—*Tupper.*

The intoxication of anger, like that of the grape, shows us to others, but hides us from ourselves.—We injure our own cause in the opinion of the world when we too passionately defend it.—*Colton.*

When angry, count ten before you speak; if very angry, count a hundred.—*Jefferson.*

Consider, when you are enraged at any one, what you would probably think if he should die during the dispute.—*Shenstone.*

Violence in the voice is often only the death rattle of reason in the throat.—*Boyes.*

All anger is not sinful, because some degree of it, and on some occasions, is inevitable.—But it becomes sinful and contradicts the rule of Scripture when it is conceived upon slight and inadequate provocation, and when it continues long.—*Paley.*

When passion is on the throne reason is out of doors.—*M. Henry.*

An angry man is again angry with himself when he returns to reason.—*Publius Syrus.*

Anger, if not restrained, is frequently more hurtful to us than the injury that provokes it.—*Seneca.*

He best keeps from anger who remembers that God is always looking upon him.—*Plato.*

When anger rises, think of the consequences.—*Confucius.*

Beware of him that is slow to anger;

for when it is long coming, it is the stronger when it comes, and the longer kept.—Abused patience turns to fury.—*Quarles.*

ANTICIPATION. — All earthly delights are sweeter in expectation than in enjoyment; but all spiritual pleasures more in fruition than in expectation.—*Feltham.*

He who foresees calamities, suffers them twice over.—*Porteous.*

All things that are, are with more spirit chased than enjoyed.—*Shakespeare.*

Among so many sad realities we can but ill endure to rob anticipation of its pleasant visions.—*Giles.*

The hours we pass with happy prospects in view are more pleasant than those crowned with fruition. In the first case we cook the dish to our own appetite; in the last it is cooked for us.—*Goldsmith.*

We often tremble at an empty terror, yet the false fancy brings a real misery.—*Schiller.*

Suffering itself does less afflict the senses than the anticipation of suffering.—*Quintilian.*

Sorrow itself is not so hard to bear as the thought of sorrow coming. Airy ghosts that work no harm do terrify us more than men in steel with bloody purposes.—*T. B. Aldrich.*

In all worldly things that a man pursues with the greatest eagerness he finds not half the pleasure in the possession that he proposed to himself in the expectation.—*South.*

The worst evils are those that never arrive.

Few enterprises of great labor or hazard would be undertaken if we had not the power of magnifying the advantages we expect from them.—*Johnson.*

Be not looking for evil.—Often thou drainest the gall of fear while evil is passing by thy dwelling.—*Tupper.*

To tremble before anticipated evils, is to bemoan what thou hast never lost.—*Goethe.*

We part more easily with what we possess than with our expectations of what we hope for: expectation always goes beyond enjoyment.—*Home.*

Our desires always disappoint us; for

though we meet with something that gives us satisfaction, yet it never thoroughly answers our expectation.—*Rochefoucauld.*

Nothing is so good as it seems beforehand.—*George Eliot.*

Nothing is so wretched or foolish as to anticipate misfortunes.—What madness is it to be expecting evil before it comes.—*Seneca.*

Why need a man forestall his date of grief, and run to meet that he would most avoid?—*Milton.*

The joys we expect are not so bright, nor the troubles so dark as we fancy they will be.—*Charles Reade.*

It is expectation makes blessings dear.—Heaven were not heaven if we knew what it were.—*Suckling.*

It is worse to apprehend than to suffer.—*Bruyere.*

It has been well said that no man ever sank under the burden of the day. It is when to-morrow's burden is added to the burden of to-day that the weight is more than a man can bear.—*G. Macdonald.*

ANTIQUITY.—All the transactions of the past differ very little from those of the present.—*M. Antoninus.*

Those we call the ancients were really new in everything.—*Pascal.*

The earliest and oldest and longest has still the mastery of us.—*George Eliot.*

All things now held to be old were once new.—What to-day we hold up by example, will rank hereafter as precedent.—*Tacitus.*

It is one proof of a good education, and of a true refinement of feeling, to respect antiquity.—*Mrs. Sigourney.*

When ancient opinions and rules of life are taken away, the loss cannot possibly be estimated.—From that moment we have no compass to govern us, nor can we know distinctly to what port to steer.—*Burke.*

I do by no means advise you to throw away your time in ransacking, like a dull antiquarian, the minute and unimportant parts of remote and fabulous times. Let blockheads read, what blockheads wrote.—*Chesterfield.*

Antiquity!—I like its ruins better than its reconstructions.—*Joubert.*

Time consecrates and what is gray with age becomes religion.—*Schiller.*

Antiquity is enjoyed not by the ancients who lived in the infancy of things, but by us who live in their maturity.—*Colton.*

What subsists to-day by violence, continues to-morrow by acquiescence, and is perpetuated by tradition, till at last the hoary abuse shakes the gray hairs of antiquity at us, and gives itself out as the wisdom of ages.—*Everett.*

Those old ages are like the landscape that shows best in the purple distance, all verdant and smooth, and bathed in mellow light.—*E. H. Chapin.*

ANXIETY.—Anxiety is the rust of life, destroying its brightness and weakening its power.—A childlike and abiding trust in Providence is its best preventive and remedy.—*Tryon Edwards.*

Do not anticipate trouble, or worry about what may never happen. Keep in the sunlight.—*Franklin.*

Better be despised for too anxious apprehensions, than ruined by too confident security.—*Burke.*

How much have cost us the evils that never happened!—*Jefferson.*

Don't be forecasting evil unless it is what you can guard against. Anxiety is good for nothing if we can't turn it into a defense.—*Meyrick.*

It is not the cares of to-day, but the cares of to-morrow that weigh a man down. For the needs of to-day we have corresponding strength given.—For the morrow we are told to trust.—It is not ours yet.—*G. Macdonald.*

When we borrow trouble, and look forward into the future and see what storms are coming, and distress ourselves before they come, as to how we shall avert them if they ever do come, we lose our proper trustfulness in God. When we torment ourselves with imaginary dangers, or trials, or reverses, we have already parted with that perfect love which casteth out fear.—*H. W. Beecher.*

Anxiety is a word of unbelief or unreasoning dread.—We have no right to allow it. Full faith in God puts it to rest.—*Horace Bushnell.*

He is well along the road to perfect manhood who does not allow the thousand little worries of life to embitter his temper, or disturb his equanimity.

An undivided heart which worships God alone, and trusts him as it should, is raised above anxiety for earthly wants.—*Geikie.*

One of the most useless of all things is to take a deal of trouble in providing against dangers that never come. How many toil to lay up riches which they never enjoy; to provide for exigencies that never happen; to prevent troubles that never come; sacrificing present comfort and enjoyment in guarding against the wants of a period they may never live to see.—*W. Jay.*

Where everything is bad it must be good to know the worst.—*F. H. Bradley.*

Never meet trouble half-way.—*John Ray.*

Borrow trouble for yourself, if that's your nature, but don't lend it to your neighbors.—*Rudyard Kipling.*

Never trouble trouble till trouble troubles you.—*Anon.*

If pleasures are greatest in anticipation, just remember that this is also true of trouble.—*Elbert Hubbard.*

Let us be of good cheer, remembering that the misfortunes hardest to bear are those which never come.—*J. R. Lowell.*

Anxiety is the poison of human life; the parent of many sins and of more miseries.—In a world where everything is doubtful, and where we may be disappointed, and be blessed in disappointment, why this restless stir and commotion of mind?—Can it alter the cause, or unravel the mystery of human events?—*Blair.*

Sufficient to each day are the duties to be done and the trials to be endured. God never built a Christian strong enough to carry to-day's duties and to-morrow's anxieties piled on the top of them.—*T. L. Cuyler.*

APOLOGIES. — Apologies only account for the evil which they cannot alter.—*Disraeli.*

Apology is only egotism wrong side out.—Nine times out of ten the first thing a man's companion knows of his short-comings, is from his apology.—*O. W. Holmes.*

No sensible person ever made an apology.—*Emerson.*

I do not trouble my spirit to vindicate itself . . . , I see the elementary laws never apologize.—*Whitman.*

APOTHEGMS.—(See "PROVERBS.")

The short sayings of wise and good men are of great value, like the dust of gold, or the sparks of diamonds.—*Tillotson.*

Apothegms to thinking minds are the seeds from which spring vast fields of new thought, that may be further cultivated, beautified, and enlarged.—*Ramsay.*

Apothegms are in history, the same as pearls in the sand, or gold in the mine.—*Erasmus.*

Aphorisms are portable wisdom, the quintessential extracts of thought and feeling.—*R. W. Alger.*

He is a benefactor of mankind who contracts the great rules of life into short sentences, that may be easily impressed on the memory, and so recur habitually to the mind.—*Johnson.*

Nothing hits harder, or sticks longer in the memory, than an apothegm.—*J. A. Murray.*

A maxim is the exact and noble expression of an important and indisputable truth.— Sound maxims are the germs of good; strongly imprinted on the memory they fortify and strengthen the will.—*Joubert.*

The excellence of aphorisms consists not so much in the expression of some rare or abstruse sentiment, as in the comprehension of some useful truth in few words.—*Johnson.*

Nor do apothegms only serve for ornament and delight, but also for action and civil use, as being the edge tools of speech, which cut and penetrate the knots of business and affairs.—*Bacon.*

Exclusively of the abstract sciences, the largest and worthiest portion of our knowledge consists of aphorisms, and the greatest and best of men is but an aphorism.—*Coleridge.*

Under the veil of these curious sentences are hid those germs of morals which the masters of philosophy have afterwards developed into so many volumes.—*Plutarch.*

A man of maxims only, is like a cyclops with one eye, and that in the back of his head.—*Coleridge.*

There are but few proverbial sayings that are not true, for they are all drawn from experience itself, which is the mother of all sciences.—*Cervantes.*

Sensible men show their sense by saying much in few words.—If noble actions are the substance of life, good sayings are its ornament and guide.—*C. Simmons.*

Few of the many wise apothegms which have been uttered from the time of the seven sages of Greece to that of poor Richard, have prevented a single foolish action.—*Macaulay.*

APPEARANCES. — There are no greater wretches in the world than many of those whom people in general take to be happy.—*Seneca.*

Do not judge from mere appearances; for the light laughter that bubbles on the lip often mantles over the depths of sadness, and the serious look may be the sober veil that covers a divine peace and joy.—The bosom can ache beneath diamond brooches; and many a blithe heart dances under coarse wool.—*E. H. Chapin.*

Foolish men mistake transitory semblances for eternal fact, and go astray more and more.—*Carlyle.*

Half the work that is done in this world is to make things appear what they are not.—*E. R. Beadle.*

How little do they see what is, who frame their hasty judgments upon that which seems.—*Southey.*

A man of the world must seem to be what he wishes to be thought.—*Bruyere.*

Beware, so long as you live, of judging men by their outward appearance.—*La Fontaine.*

The world is governed more by appearances than by realities, so that it is fully as necessary to seem to know something as to know it.—*Daniel Webster.*

The shortest and surest way to live with honor in the world, is to be in reality what we would appear to be.—*Socrates.*

APPETITE. — Reason should direct, and appetite obey.—*Cicero.*

Good cheer is no hindrance to a good life.—*Aristippus.*

Choose rather to punish your appetites than to be punished by them.—*Tyrius Maximus.*

Animals feed; man eats.—Only the man of intellect and judgment knows how to eat.—*Savarin.*

Let not thy table exceed the fourth part of thy revenue: let thy provision be solid, and not far fetched, fuller of substance than art: be wisely frugal in thy preparation, and freely cheerful in thy entertainment: if thy guests be right, it is enough; if not, it is too much: too much is a vanity; enough is a feast.—*Quarles.*

There are so few that resist the allurements and luxuries of the table, that the usual civilities at a meal are very like being politely assisted to the grave.—*N. P. Willis.*

Now good digestion wait on appetite, and health on both.—*Shakespeare.*

Temperance and labor are the two best physicians of man; labor sharpens the appetite, and temperance prevents from indulging to excess.—*Rousseau.*

A well-governed appetite is a great part of liberty.—*Seneca.*

The lower your senses are kept, the better you may govern them.—Appetite and reason are like two buckets—when one is up, the other is down.—Of the two, I would rather have the reason-bucket uppermost.—*Collier.*

For the sake of health, medicines are taken by weight and measure; so ought food to be, or by some similar rule.—*Skelton.*

APPLAUSE.—Applause is the spur of noble minds; the end and aim of weak ones.—*Colton.*

Neither human applause nor human censure is to be taken as the test of truth; but either should set us upon testing ourselves.—*Whately.*

When the million applaud you, seriously ask what harm you have done; when they censure you, what good!—*Colton.*

Applause waits on success.—The fickle multitude, like the light straw that floats on the stream, glide with the current still, and follow fortune.—*Franklin.*

Praise from the common people is generally false, and rather follows the vain than the virtuous.—*Bacon.*

A slowness to applaud betrays a cold temper or an envious spirit.—*H. More.*

O popular applause!—What heart of

man is proof against thy sweet, seducing charms!—*Cowper.*

Great minds had rather deserve contemporaneous applause without obtaining it, than obtain without deserving it. —If it follow them it is well, but they will not deviate to follow it.—*Colton.*

Man's first care should be to avoid the reproaches of his own heart, and next to escape the censures of the world.—If the last interfere with the first it should be entirely neglected.—But if not, there cannot be a greater satisfaction to an honest mind than to see its own approbation seconded by the applauses of the public.—*Addison.*

APPRECIATION. — (See "INFLUENCE.")

Next to excellence is the appreciation of it.—*Thackeray.*

To love one that is great, is almost to be great one's self.—*Mad. Neckar.*

You may fail to shine in the opinion of others, both in your conversation and actions, from being superior, as well as inferior, to them.—*Greville.*

We must never undervalue any person.—The workman loves not to have his work despised in his presence. Now God is present everywhere, and every person is his work.—*De Sales.*

Contemporaries appreciate the man rather than the merit; but posterity will regard the merit rather than the man.—*Colton.*

We should allow others' excellences, to preserve a modest opinion of our own.—*Barrow.*

Appreciation, whether of nature, or books, or art, or men, depends very much on temperament.—What is beauty or genius or greatness to one, is far from being so to another.—*Tryon Edwards.*

One of the Godlike things of this world is the veneration done to human worth by the hearts of men.—*Carlyle.*

When a nation gives birth to a man who is able to produce a great thought, another is born who is able to understand and admire it.—*Joubert.*

No story is the same to us after a lapse of time; or rather we who read it are no longer the same interpreters.—*George Eliot.*

Next to invention is the power of interpreting invention; next to beauty the power of appreciating beauty.—*Margaret Fuller.*

You will find poetry nowhere unless you bring some with you.—*Joubert.*

It is with certain good qualities as with the senses; those who have them not can neither appreciate nor comprehend them in others.—*Rochefoucauld.*

We never know a greater character unless there is in ourselves something congenial to it.—*Channing.*

He is incapable of a truly good action who finds not a pleasure in contemplating the good actions of others.—*Lavater.*

In proportion as our own mind is enlarged we discover a greater number of men of originality. — Commonplace people see no difference between one man and another.—*Pascal.*

Whatever are the benefits of fortune, they yet require a palate fit to relish and taste them.—*Montaigne.*

Every man is valued in this world as he shows by his conduct that he wishes to be valued.—*Bruyere.*

In an audience of rough people a generous sentiment always brings down the house.—In the tumult of war both sides applaud a heroic deed.—*T. W. Higginson.*

We are very much what others think of us.—The reception our observations meet with gives us courage to proceed, or damps our efforts.—*Hazlitt.*

A work of real merit finds favor at last.—*A. B. Alcott.*

To feel exquisitely is the lot of very many; but to appreciate belongs to the few.—Only one or two, here and there, have the blended passion and understanding which, in its essence, constitute worship.—*C. Auchester.*

ARCHITECTURE — Architecture is the printing press of all ages, and gives a history of the state of society in which the structure was erected, from the cromlachs of the Druids to the toyshops of bad taste.—The Tower and Westminster Abbey are glorious pages in the history of time, and tell the story of an iron despotism, and of the cowardice of an unlimited power.—*Lady Morgan.*

The architecture of a nation is great only when it is as universal and established as its language, and when provincial differences are nothing more than so many dialects.—*Ruskin.*

Architecture is frozen music.—*De Staël.*

Greek architecture is the flowering of geometry.—*Emerson.*

Architecture is a handmaid of devotion. A beautiful church is a sermon in stone, and its spire a finger pointing to heaven.—*Schaff.*

A Gothic church is a petrified religion. —*Coleridge.*

If cities were built by the sound of music, then some edifices would appear to be constructed by grave, solemn tones, and others to have danced forth to light fantastic airs.—*Hawthorne.*

Architecture is the art which so disposes and adorns the edifices raised by man, that the sight of them may contribute to his mental health, power, and pleasure.—*Ruskin.*

Houses are built to live in, more than to look on; therefore let use be preferred before uniformity, except where both may be had.—*Bacon.*

ARGUMENT.—Argument, as usually managed, is the worst sort of conversation, as in books it is generally the worst sort of reading.—*Swift.*

Be calm in arguing; for fierceness makes error a fault, and truth discourtesy.—*Herbert.*

In argument similes are like songs in love; they describe much, but prove nothing.—*Prior.*

Wise men argue causes; fools decide them.—*Anacharsis.*

He who establishes his argument by noise and command, shows that his reason is weak.—*Montaigne.*

Nothing is more certain than that much of the force as well as grace of arguments, as well as of instructions, depends on their conciseness.—*Pope.*

When a man argues for victory and not for truth, he is sure of just one ally, that is the devil.—Not the defeat of the intellect, but the acceptance of the heart is the only true object in fighting with the sword of the spirit.—*G. Macdonald.*

Men's arguments often prove nothing but their wishes.—*Colton.*

Prejudices are rarely overcome by argument; not being founded in reason they cannot be destroyed by logic.— *Tryon Edwards.*

Clear statement is argument.—*W. G. T. Shedd.*

If I were to deliver up my whole self to the arbitrament of special pleaders, to-day I might be argued into an atheist, and to-morrow into a pickpocket.—*Bulwer.*

Never argue at the dinner table, for the one who is not hungry always gets the best of the argument.

Weak arguments are often thrust before my path; but although they are most unsubstantial, it is not easy to destroy them. There is not a more difficult feat known than to cut through a cushion with a sword.—*Whately.*

The soundest argument will produce no more conviction in an empty head than the most superficial declamation; a feather and a guinea fall with equal velocity in a vacuum.—*Colton.*

An ill argument introduced with deference will procure more credit than the profoundest science with a rough, insolent, and noisy management.—*Locke.*

Heat and animosity, contest and conflict, may sharpen the wits, although they rarely do; they never strengthen the understanding, clear the perspicacity, guide the judgment, or improve the heart.—*Landor.*

Be calm in arguing: for fierceness makes error a fault, and truth discourtesy; calmness is a great advantage. —*Herbert.*

There is no good in arguing with the inevitable. The only argument available with an east wind is to put on your greatcoat.—*J. R. Lowell.*

The first duty of a wise advocate is to convince his opponents that he understands their arguments, and sympathises with their just feelings.—*Coleridge.*

There is no dispute managed without passion, and yet there is scarce a dispute worth a passion.—*Sherlock.*

Testimony is like an arrow shot from a long-bow; its force depends on the strength of the hand that draws it.— But argument is like an arrow from a cross-bow, which has equal force if drawn by a child or a man.—*Boyle.*

ARISTOCRACY.— And lords, whose

parents were the Lord knows who.—*De Foe.*

Some will always be above others.—Destroy the inequality to-day, and it will appear again to-morrow.—*Emerson.*

A social life that worships money or makes social distinction its aim, is, in spirit, an attempted aristocracy.

Among the masses, even in revolutions, aristocracy must ever exist.—Destroy it in the nobility, and it becomes centred in the rich and powerful Houses of Commons.—Pull them down, and it still survives in the master and foreman of the workshop.—*Guizot.*

I never could believe that Providence had sent a few men into the world, ready booted and spurred to ride, and millions ready saddled and bridled to be ridden.—*Richard Rumbold.*

Aristocracy has three successive ages: the age of superiorities, that of privileges, and that of vanities.—Having passed out of the first, it degenerates in the second, and dies away in the third.—*Chateaubriand.*

ARMY.—The army is a school where obedience is taught, and discipline is enforced; where bravery becomes a habit and morals too often are neglected; where chivalry is exalted, and religion undervalued; where virtue is rather understood in the classic sense of fortitude and courage, than in the modern and Christian sense of true moral excellence.—*Ladd.*

Armies, though always the supporters and tools of absolute power for the time being, are always its destroyers too, by frequently changing the hands in which they think proper to lodge it.—*Chesterfield.*

The army is a good book in which to study human life.—One learns there to put his hand to everything.—The most delicate and rich are forced to see poverty and live with it; to understand distress; and to know how rapid and great are the revolutions and changes of life.—*De Vigny.*

The best armor is to keep out of gunshot.—*Bacon.*

ARROGANCE.—When men are most sure and arrogant they are commonly most mistaken, giving views to passion without that proper deliberation which

alone can secure them from the grossest absurdities.—*Hume.*

Nothing is more hateful to a poor man than the purse-proud arrogance of the rich.—But let the poor man become rich and he runs at once into the vice against which he so feelingly declaimed.—There are strange contradictions in human character.—*Cumberland.*

The arrogant man does but blast the blessings of life and swagger away his own enjoyments.—To say nothing of the folly and injustice of such behavior, it is always the sign of a little and unbenevolent temper, having no more greatness in it than the swelling of the dropsy.—*Collier.*

ART.—True art is reverent imitation of God.—*Tryon Edwards.*

All great art is the expression of man's delight in God's work, not his own.—*Ruskin.*

The highest problem of any art is to cause by appearance the illusion of a higher reality.—*Goethe.*

The true work of art is but a shadow of the divine perfection. — *Michael Angelo.*

All that is good in art is the expression of one soul talking to another, and is precious according to the greatness of the soul that utters it.—*Ruskin.*

Art, as far as it has the ability, follows nature, as a pupil imitates his master, so that art must be, as it were, a descendant of God.—*Dante.*

The perfection of art is to conceal art.—*Quintilian.*

Never judge a work of art by its defects.—*Washington Allston.*

There is no more potent antidote to low sensuality than admiration of the beautiful.—All the higher arts of design are essentially chaste, without respect to the object.—They purify the thoughts, as tragedy purifies the passions.—Their accidental effects are not worth consideration; for there are souls to whom even a vestal is not holy.—*Schlegel.*

The artist is the child in the popular fable, every one of whose tears was a pearl. Ah! the world, that cruel stepmother, beats the poor child the harder to make him shed more pearls.—*Heine.*

The highest triumph of art, is the truest presentation of nature.—*N. P. Willis.*

The names of great painters are like passing bells.—In Velasquez you hear sounded the fall of Spain; in Titian, that of Venice; in Leonardo, that of Milan; in Raphael, that of Rome.—And there is profound justice in this; for in proportion to the nobleness of power is the guilt of its use for purposes vain or vile; and hitherto the greater the art the more surely has it been used, and used solely, for the decoration of pride, or the provoking of sensuality.—*Ruskin.*

The mission of art is to represent nature; not to imitate her.—*W. M. Hunt.*

The real truthfulness of all works of imagination,—sculpture, painting, and written fiction, is so purely in the imagination, that the artist never seeks to represent positive truth, but the idealized image of a truth.—*Bulwer.*

The ordinary true, or purely real, cannot be the object of the arts.—Illusion on a ground of truth, that is the secret of the fine arts.—*Joubert.*

Art does not imitate nature, but founds itself on the study of nature—takes from nature the selections which best accord with its own intention, and then bestows on them that which nature does not possess, viz.: the mind and soul of man.—*Bulwer.*

The object of art is to crystallize emotion into thought, and then fix it in form.—*Delsarte.*

The learned understand the reason of art; the unlearned feel the pleasure.—*Quintilian.*

The highest problem of every art is, by means of appearances, to produce the illusion of a loftier reality.—*Goethe.*

The mother of the useful art, is necessity; that of the fine arts, is luxury.—The former have intellect for their father; the latter, genius, which itself is a kind of luxury.—*Schopenhauer.*

The painter is, as to the execution of his work, a mechanic; but as to his conception and spirit and design he is hardly below even the poet.—*Schiller.*

In the art of design, color is to form what verse is to prose, a more harmonious and luminous vehicle of thought.—*Mrs. Jameson.*

Very sacred is the vocation of the artist, who has to do directly with the works of God, and interpret the teaching of creation to mankind. All honor to the man who treats it sacredly; who studies, as in God's presence, the thoughts of God which are expressed to him; and makes all things according to the pattern which he is ever ready to show to earnest and reverent genius on the mount.—*Brown.*

Art employs method for the symmetrical formation of beauty, as science employs it for the logical exposition of truth; but the mechanical process is, in the last, ever kept visibly distinct, while in the first it escapes from sight amid the shows of color and the shapes of grace.—*Bulwer.*

Would that we could at once paint with the eyes!—In the long way from the eye through the arm to the pencil, how much is lost!—*Lessing.*

The artist ought never to perpetuate a temporary expression.

In sculpture did any one ever call the Apollo a fancy piece; or say of the Laocoön how it might be made different?—A masterpiece of art has, to the mind, a fixed place in the chain of being, as much as a plant or a crystal.—*Emerson.*

Art does not lie in copying nature.—Nature furnishes the material by means of which to express a beauty still unexpressed in nature.—The artist beholds in nature more than she herself is conscious of.—*H. James.*

The highest art is always the most religious, and the greatest artist is always a devout man.—A scoffing Raphael, or an irreverent Michael Angelo, is not conceivable.—*Blaikie.*

Artists are nearest God. Into their souls he breathes his life, and from their hands it comes in fair, articulate forms to bless the world.—*J. G. Holland.*

Since I have known God in a saving manner, painting, poetry, and music have had charms unknown to me before.—I have either received what I suppose is a taste for them, or religion has refined my mind, and made it susceptible of new impressions from the sublime and beautiful.—O, how religion secures the heightened enjoyment of those pleasures which keep so many from God by their being a source of pride!—*Henry Martyn.*

ARTIFICE.—The ordinary employment of artifice, is the mark of a petty mind; and it almost always happens that he who uses it to cover himself in one place, uncovers himself in another.—*Rochefoucauld.*

To know how to dissemble is the knowledge of kings.—*Richelieu.*

Artifice is weak; it is the work of mere man, in the imbecility and self distrust of his mimic understanding.—*Hare.*

ASCETICISM.—Three forms of asceticism have existed in this weak world.—Religious asceticism, being the refusal of pleasure and knowledge for the sake, as supposed, of religion; seen chiefly in the middle ages.—Military asceticism, being the refusal of pleasure and knowledge for the sake of power; seen chiefly in the early days of Sparta and Rome.—And monetary asceticism, consisting in the refusal of pleasure and knowledge for the sake of money; seen in the present days of London and Manchester.—*Ruskin.*

I recommend no sour ascetic life. I believe not only in the thorns on the rosebush, but in the roses which the thorns defend. Asceticism is the child of sensuality and superstition. She is the secret mother of many a secret sin. God, when he made man's body, did not give us a fibre too much, nor a passion too many.—*Theodore Parker.*

ASKING.—I am prejudiced in favor of him who, without impudence, can ask boldly.—He has faith in humanity, and faith in himself.—No one who is not accustomed to give grandly can ask nobly and with boldness.—*Lavater.*

ASPIRATION.—(See "Aims," and "Ambition.")

It is not for man to rest in absolute contentment.—He is born to hopes and aspirations as the sparks fly upward, unless he has brutified his nature and quenched the spirit of immortality which is his portion.—*Southey.*

'Tis not what man does which exalts him, but what man would do!—*Browning.*

You cannot demonstrate an emotion or prove an aspiration.—*John Morley.*

No bird soars too high if he soars with his own wings.—*W. Blake.*

Man ought always to have something that he prefers to life; otherwise life itself will seem to him tiresome and void.—*Seume.*

They build too low who build beneath the skies.—*Young.*

Be always displeased with what thou art if thou desire to attain to what thou art not, for where thou hast pleased thyself, there thou abidest.—*Quarles.*

There is no sorrow I have thought more about than that—to love what is great, and try to reach it, and yet to fail.—*George Eliot.*

The heart is a small thing, but desireth great matters. It is not sufficient for a kite's dinner, yet the whole world is not sufficient for it.—*Quarles.*

We are not to make the ideas of contentment and aspiration quarrel, for God made them fast friends.—A man may aspire, and yet be quite content until it is time to rise; and both flying and resting are but parts of one contentment. The very fruit of the gospel is aspiration. It is to the heart what spring is to the earth, making every root, and bud, and bough desire to be more.—*H. W. Beecher.*

It seems to me we can never give up longing and wishing while we are thoroughly alive. There are certain things we feel to be beautiful and good, and we must hunger after them.—*George Eliot.*

What we truly and earnestly aspire to be, that in some sense we are. The mere aspiration, by changing the frame of the mind, for the moment realizes itself.—*Mrs. Jameson.*

God has never ceased to be the one true aim of all right human aspirations.—*Vinet.*

Aspirations after the holy—the only aspirations in which the soul can be assured it will never meet with disappointment.—*Maria McIntosh.*

Man can climb to the highest summits but he cannot dwell there long.—*G. B Shaw.*

There are glimpses of heaven to us in every act, or thought, or word, that raises us above ourselves.—*A. P. Stanley.*

ASSERTIONS.—Weigh not so much what men assert, as what they prove.—Truth is simple and naked, and needs not invention to apparel her comeliness.—*Sir P. Sidney.*

Assertion, unsupported by fact, is

nugatory.—Surmise and general abuse, in however elegant language, ought not to pass for truth.—*Junius.*

It is an impudent kind of sorcery to attempt to blind us with the smoke, without convincing us that the fire has existed.—*Junius.*

ASSOCIATES. — (See " COMPANION-SHIP.")

Tell me with whom thou art found, and I will tell thee who thou art.—*Goethe.*

If you wish to be held in esteem, you must associate only with those who are estimable.—*Bruyere.*

Evil communications corrupt good manners.—*Menander.*

We gain nothing by being with such as ourselves: we encourage each other in mediocrity.—I am always longing to be with men more excellent than myself.—*Lamb.*

You may depend upon it that he is a good man whose intimate friends are all good, and whose enemies are decidedly bad.—*Lavater.*

When one associates with vice, it is but one step from companionship to slavery.

Be very circumspect in the choice of thy company. In the society of thine equals thou shalt enjoy more pleasure; in the society of thy superiors thou shalt find more profit. To be the best in the company is the way to grow worse; the best means to grow better is to be the worst there.—*Quarles.*

No company is far preferable to bad, because we are more apt to catch the vices of others than their virtues, as disease is more contagious than health.—*Colton.*

Choose the company of your superiors whenever you can have it; that is the right and true pride.—*Chesterfield.*

No man can be provident of his time, who is not prudent in the choice of his company.—*Jeremy Taylor.*

A man should live with his superiors as he does with his fire: not too near, lest he burn; nor too far off, lest he freeze.—*Diogenes.*

Company, villainous company hath been the ruin of me.—*Shakespeare.*

It is best to be with those in time, that we hope to be with in eternity.—*Fuller.*

It is certain that either wise bearing or ignorant carriage is caught, as men take diseases, one of another; therefore let men take heed of their company.—*Shakespeare.*

Frequent intercourse and intimate connection between two persons, make them so alike, that not only their dispositions are moulded like each other, but their very faces and tones of voice contract a similarity.—*Lavater.*

It is no smal happiness to attend those from whom we may receive precepts and examples of virtue.—*Bp. Hall.*

When we live habitually with the wicked, we become necessarily their victims or their disciples; on the contrary, when we associate with the virtuous we form ourselves in imitation of their virtues, or at least lose, every day, something of our faults.—*Agapet.*

In all societies it is advisable to associate if possible with the highest; not that they are always the best, but because, if disgusted there, we can always descend; but if we begin with the lowest to ascend is impossible.—*Colton.*

It is only when men associate with the wicked with the desire and purpose of doing them good, that they can rely upon the protection of God to preserve them from contamination.—*C. Hodge.*

It is meet that noble minds keep ever with their likes; for who so firm that cannot be seduced.—*Shakespeare.*

People will in a great degree, and not without reason, form their opinion of you by that they have of your friends, as, says the Spanish proverb, " Tell me with whom you live and I will tell you who you are."

Those unacquainted with the world take pleasure in intimacy with great men; those who are wiser fear the consequences.—*Horace.*

ASSOCIATION.—I have only to take up this or that to flood my soul with memories.—*Madame Deluzy.*

There is no man who has not some interesting associations with particular scenes, or airs, or books, and who does not feel their beauty or sublimity enhanced to him by such connections.—*Alison.*

That man is little to be envied whose

patriotism would not gain force on the plain of Marathon, or whose piety would not grow warmer amid the ruins of Iona.—*Johnson.*

He whose heart is not excited on the spot which a martyr has sanctified by his sufferings, or at the grave of one who has greatly benefited mankind, must be more inferior to the multitude in his moral, than he possibly can be above them in his intellectual nature. — *Southey.*

ASTRONOMY.—Astronomy is one of the sublimest fields of human investigation. The mind that grasps its facts and principles receives something of the enlargement and grandeur belonging to the science itself.—It is a quickener of devotion.—*H. Mann.*

No one can contemplate the great facts of astronomy without feeling his own littleness and the wonderful sweep of the power and providence of God.— *Tryon Edwards.*

An undevout astronomer is mad.— *Young.*

The contemplation of celestial things will make a man both speak and think more sublimely and magnificently when he comes down to human affairs.— *Cicero.*

ATHEISM.—The three great apostles of practical atheism that make converts without persecuting, and retain them without preaching, are health, wealth, and power.—*Colton.*

Atheism is rather in the life than in the heart of man.—*Bacon.*

To be an atheist requires an infinitely greater measure of faith than to receive all the great truths which atheism would deny.—*Addison.*

Atheism, if it exists, is the result of ignorance and pride, of strong sense and feeble reason, of good eating and ill living.—It is the plague of society, the corrupter of morals, and the underminer of property.—*Jeremy Collier.*

If a man of sober habits, moderate, chaste, and just in all his dealings should assert there is no God, he would at least speak without interested motives; but such a man is not to be found.—*Bruyere.*

No one is so thoroughly superstitious as the godless man. Life and death to him are haunted grounds filled with

goblin forms of vague and shadowy dread.—*Mrs. Stowe.*

Atheism is the death of hope, the suicide of the soul.

The footprint of the savage in the sand is sufficient to prove the presence of man to the atheist who will not recognize God though his hand is impressed on the entire universe.—*Hugh Miller.*

Few men are so obstinate in their atheism, that a pressing danger will not compel them to the acknowledgment of a divine power.—*Plato.*

A little philosophy inclineth men's minds to atheism; but depth in philosophy bringeth men's minds to religion; for while the mind of man looketh upon second causes scattered, it may sometimes rest in them, and go no further.— But when it beholdeth the chain of them, confederate and linked together, it must needs fly to Providence and Deity.—*Bacon.*

Virtue in distress, and vice in triumph, make atheists of mankind.—*Dryden.*

Atheism is the folly of the metaphysician, not the folly of human nature.— *George Bancroft.*

In agony or danger, no nature is atheist.—The mind that knows not what to fly to, flies to God.—*H. More.*

The atheist is one who fain would pull God from his throne, and in the place of heaven's eternal king set up the phantom chance.—*Glynn.*

Plato was right in calling atheism a disease.—The human intellect in its healthy action, holds it for certain that there is a Great Being over us, invisible, infinite, ineffable, but of real, solid personality, who made and governs us, and who made and governs all things.—*R. D. Hitchcock.*

An irreligious man, a speculative or a practical atheist, is as a sovereign, who voluntarily takes off his crown and declares himself unworthy to reign.— *Blackie.*

Atheism is never the error of society, in any stage or circumstance whatever. —In the belief of a Deity savage and sage have alike agreed.—The great error has been, not the denial of one God, but the belief of many; but polytheism has been a popular and poetical, rather than a philosophical error.—*Henry Fergus.*

Atheism is a disease of the soul, before it becomes an error of the understanding.—*Plato.*

God never wrought miracles to convince atheism, because His ordinary works convince it.—*Bacon.*

There are innumerable souls that would resent the charge of the fool's atheism, yet daily deny God in very deed.

The atheist is one of the most daring beings in creation—a contemner of God who explodes his laws by denying his existence.—*John Foster.*

What can be more foolish than to think that all this rare fabric of heaven and earth could come by chance, when all the skill of art is not able to make an oyster? To see rare effects, and no cause; a motion, without a mover; a circle, without a centre; a time, without an eternity; a second, without a first: these are things so against philosophy and natural reason, that he must be a beast in understanding who can believe in them. The thing formed, says that nothing formed it; and that which is made, is, while that which made it is not! This folly is infinite.—*Jeremy Taylor.*

A traveller amid the scenery of the Alps, surrounded by the sublimest demonstrations of God's power, had the hardihood to write against his name, in an album kept for visitors, "An atheist." Another who followed, shocked and indignant at the inscription, wrote beneath it, "If an atheist, a fool; if not, a liar!"—*G. B. Cheever.*

Atheists put on a false courage in the midst of their darkness and misapprehensions, like children who when they fear to go in the dark, will sing or whistle to keep up their courage.—*Pope.*

Whoever considers the study of anatomy can never be an atheist.—*Lord Herbert.*

ATTENTION.—The power of applying attention, steady and undissipated, to a single object, is the sure mark of a superior genius.—*Chesterfield.*

Few things are impracticable in themselves: and it is for want of application, rather than of means, that men fail of success.—*Rochefoucauld.*

Attention makes the genius; all learning, fancy, science, and skill depend upon it.—Newton traced his great discoveries to it.—It builds bridges, opens new worlds, heals diseases, carries on the business of the world.—Without it taste is useless, and the beauties of literature unobserved.—*Willmott.*

If I have made any improvement in the sciences, it is owing more to patient attention than to anything beside.—*Sir I. Newton.*

If there be anything that can be called genius, it consists chiefly in ability to give that attention to a subject which keeps it steadily in the mind, till we have surveyed it accurately on all sides.—*Reid.*

It is attention, more than any difference between minds and men.—In this is the source of poetic genius, and of the genius of discovery in science.—It was this that led Newton to the invention of fluxions, and the discovery of gravitation, and Harvey to find out the circulation of the blood, and Davy to those views which laid the foundation of modern chemistry.—*Brodie.*

AUTHORITY.—(See "OFFICE.")

Nothing is more gratifying to the mind of man than power or dominion.—*Addison.*

Nothing sooner overthrows a weak head than opinion of authority; like too strong liquor for a frail glass.—*Sir P. Sidney.*

Nothing more impairs authority than a too frequent or indiscreet use of it. If thunder itself was to be continual, it would excite no more terror than the noise of a mill.

Man, proud man! dressed in a little brief authority, plays such fantastic tricks before high heaven as make the angels weep.—*Shakespeare.*

They that govern make least noise, as they that row the barge do work and puff and sweat, while he that governs sits quietly at the stern, and scarce is seen to stir.—*Selden.*

He who is firmly seated in authority soon learns to think security, and not progress, the highest lesson of statecraft.—*J. R. Lowell.*

AUTHORSHIP.—Authorship, according to the spirit in which it is pursued, is an infancy, a pastime, a labor, a handicraft, an art, a science, or a virtue.—*Schlegel.*

The two most engaging powers of an author, are, to make new things familiar, and familiar things new.—*Johnson.*

It is quite as much of a trade to make a book, as to make a clock.—It requires more than mere genius to be an author.—*Bruyere.*

No author is so poor that he cannot be of some service, if only as a witness of his time.—*Fauchet.*

To write well is to think well, to feel well, and to render well; it is to possess at once intellect, soul, and taste.—*Buffon.*

He who purposes to be an author, should first be a student.—*Dryden.*

Never write on a subject without first having read yourself full on it; and never read on a subject till you have thought yourself hungry on it.—*Richter.*

Clear writers, like clear fountains, do not seem so deep as they are; the turbid seem the most profound.—*Landor.*

No fathers or mothers think their own children ugly; and this self-deceit is yet stronger with respect to the offspring of the mind.—*Cervantes.*

The most original authors are not so because they advance what is new, but because they put what they have to say as if it had never been said before.—*Goethe.*

The chief glory of a country, says Johnson, arises from its authors.—But this is only when they are oracles of wisdom.—Unless they teach virtue they are more worthy of a halter than of the laurel.—*Jane Porter.*

Next to doing things that deserve to be written, nothing gets a man more credit, or gives him more pleasure than to write things that deserve to be read.—*Chesterfield.*

There are three difficulties in authorship:—to write anything worth publishing—to find honest men to publish it—and to get sensible men to read it.—*Colton.*

Talent alone cannot make a writer; there must be a man behind the book.—*Emerson.*

Every author in some degree portrays himself in his works, even if it be against his will.—*Goethe.*

Writers are the main landmarks of the past.—*Bulwer.*

A great writer is the friend and benefactor of his readers.—*Macaulay.*

Satire lies about men of letters during their lives, and eulogy after their death.—*Voltaire.*

It is doubtful whether mankind are most indebted to those who like Bacon and Butler dig the gold from the mine of literature, or to those who, like Paley, purify it, stamp it, fix its real value, and give it currency and utility.—*Colton.*

Authorship is a royal priesthood; but woe to him who rashly lays unhallowed hands on the ark or altar, professing a zeal for the welfare of the race, only to secure his own selfish ends.—*Horace Greeley.*

AUTUMN.—The melancholy days are come, the saddest of the year.—*Bryant.*

A moral character is attached to autumnal scenes.—The flowers fading like our hopes, the leaves falling like our years, the clouds fleeting like our illusions, the light diminishing like our intelligence, the sun growing colder like our affections, the rivers becoming frozen like our lives—all bear secret relations to our destinies.—*Chateaubriand.*

Season of mist and mellow fruitfulness.—*Keats.*

The Sabbath of the year.—*Logan.*

Magnificent autumn! He comes not like a pilgrim, clad in russet weeds; not like a hermit, clad in gray; but like a warrior with the stain of blood on his brazen mail.—His crimson scarf is rent; his scarlet banner dripping with gore; his step like a flail on the threshing floor.—*Longfellow.*

The leaves in autumn do not change color from the blighting touch of frost, but from the process of natural decay.—They fall when the fruit is ripened, and their work is done.—And their splendid coloring is but their graceful and beautiful surrender of life when they have finished their summer offering of service to God and man. And one of the great lessons the fall of the leaf teaches, is this: Do your work well, and then be ready to depart when God shall call.—*Tryon Edwards.*

The tints of autumn—a mighty flower garden, blossoming under the spell of the enchanter, frost.—*Whittier.*

Who at this season does not feel im-

pressed with a sentiment of melancholy?
—*A. Alison.*

O, it sets my heart a clickin' like the
tickin' of a clock, when the frost is on
the punkin and the fodder's in the shock.
—*James Whitcomb Riley.*

AVARICE.—Avarice is the vice of declining years.—*Bancroft.*

The lust of avarice has so totally
seized upon mankind that their wealth
seems rather to possess them, than they
to possess their wealth.—*Pliny.*

We are but stewards of what we
falsely call our own; yet avarice is so
insatiable that it is not in the power of
abundance to content it.—*Seneca.*

Poverty wants some things, luxury
many, avarice all things.—*Cowley.*

Avarice is wider than injustice, and
all fallen nations lost liberty through
avarice which engendered injustice.—
Austin O'Malley.

Avarice increases with the increasing
pile of gold.—*Juvenal.*

Avarice is to the intellect and heart,
what sensuality is to the morals.—*Mrs.
Jameson.*

The lust of gold, unfeeling and remorseless, the last corruption of degenerate man.—*Johnson.*

The avaricious man is like the barren
sandy ground of the desert which sucks
in all the rain and dew with greediness,
but yields no fruitful herbs or plants for
the benefit of others.—*Zeno.*

All the good things of the world are
no further good to us than as they are
of use; and of all we may heap up we
enjoy only as much as we can use, and
no more.—*DeFoe.*

Avarice, in old age, is foolish; for
what can be more absurd than to increase our provisions for the road the
nearer we approach to our journey's end?
—*Cicero.*

How vilely has he lost himself who
has become a slave to his servant, and
exalts him to the dignity of his Maker!
—*Penn.*

AVIATION.—Lindbergh Flies Alone.
—Alone? Is he alone at whose right
side rides Courage, with Skill within the
cockpit and Faith upon his left? Does
solitude surround the brave when Adventure leads the way and Ambition
reads the dials? Is there no company
with him for whom the air is cleft by
Daring and the darkness is made light
by Emprise? True, the fragile bodies
of his weaker fellows do not weigh down
his plane; true, the fretful minds of
weaker men are lacking from his
crowded cabin; but as his airship keeps
her course he holds communion with
those rarer spirits that inspire to intrepidity and by their sustaining potency give strength to arm, resource to
mind, content to soul. Alone? With
what other companions would that man
fly to whom the choice is given?—
Editorial in the New York "Sun."

For I dipt into the future far as human
   eye can see,
Saw the vision of the world, and all the
   wonder that would be;

Saw the heavens filled with commerce,
   argosies of magic sails,
Pilots of the purple twilight, dropping
   down with costly bales;

Heard the heavens filled with shouting,
   and there rained a ghastly dew
From the nations' airy navies, grappling
   in the central blue.—*Tennyson.*

In aeronautics one finds new things
only by looking for them.—*Cierva.*

A bird is an instrument working
according to mathematical law, which
instrument it is within the capacity of
man to reproduce with all its movements.—*Leonardo Da Vinci.*

Armies do not protect against the
aerial way.—*Alexander Graham Bell.*

In a few years the young man and
even the young woman who has not
learned to fly will be regarded as natural
phenomena as to-day are those who cannot drive automobiles.—*F. A. Tichenor.*

In the development of no other branch
of engineering has scientific work been
so intensive or so rapid as in aeronautics.
—*Alexander Klemin.*

All except very short distance, high
class, passenger travel will be by air in
the days to come.—*Anthony H. G.
Fokker.*

AWKWARDNESS.—Awkwardness is
a more real disadvantage than it is generally thought to be: it often occasions
ridicule, and always lessens dignity.—
Chesterfield.

An awkward man never does justice to himself; to his intelligence, to his intentions, or to his actual merit.—A fine person, or a beauteous face are in vain without the grace of deportment.—*Churchill.*

B

BABBLERS.—(See " Gossip.")
They always talk who never think.—*Prior.*

Fire and sword are but slow engines of destruction in comparison with the babbler.—*Steele.*

Talkers are no good doers, be assured. —We go to use our hands and not our tongues.—*Shakespeare.*

BABE.—Of all the joys that lighten suffering earth, what joy is welcomed like a new-born child?—*Mrs. Norton.*

A babe in the house is a well-spring of pleasure, a messenger of peace and love, a resting place for innocence on earth, a link between angels and men.—*Tupper.*

A sweet new blossom of humanity, fresh fallen from God's own home, to flower on earth.—*Massey.*

Some wonder that children should be given to young mothers.—But what instruction does the babe bring to the mother!—She learns patience, self-control, endurance; her very arm grows strong so that she holds the dear burden longer than the father can.—*T. W. Higginson.*

Living jewels, dropped unstained from heaven.—*Pollock.*

A rose with all its sweetest leaves yet folded.—*Byron.*

The coarsest father gains a new impulse to labor from the moment of his baby's birth.—Every stroke he strikes is for his child.—New social aims, and new moral motives come vaguely up to him. —*T. W. Higginson.*

Good Christian people, here is for you an inestimable loan.—Take all heed thereof, and in all carefulness employ it. —With high recompense, or else with heavy penalty, will it one day be required back.—*Carlyle.*

Could we understand half what mothers say and do to us when infants, we should be filled with such conceit of our own importance as would make us insupportable through life.—Happy the child whose mother is tired of talking nonsense to him before he is old enough to know the sense of it.—*Hare.*

BACHELOR.—I have no wife or children, good or bad, to provide for; a mere spectator of other men's fortunes and adventures, and how they play their parts; which, methinks, are diversely presented unto me, as from a common theatre or scene.—*Burton.*

Because I will not do the wrong to mistrust any, I will do myself the right to trust none; I will live a bachelor.—*Shakespeare.*

A man unattached, and without a wife, if he have any genius at all, may raise himself above his original position, may mingle with the world of fashion, and hold himself on a level with the highest; but this is less easy for him who is engaged.—It seems as if marriage put the whole world in their proper rank.—*Bruyere.*

A bachelor's life is a splendid breakfast; a tolerably flat dinner; and a most miserable supper.

BALLADS. — Ballads are the vocal portraits of the national mind.—*Lamb.*

Ballads are the gipsy children of song, born under green hedge-rows, in the leafy lanes and by-paths of literature, in the genial summer time.—*Longfellow.*

Let me write the ballads of a nation, and I care not who may make its laws. —*Fletcher of Saltoun.*

A well composed song or ballad strikes the mind, and softens the feelings, and produces a greater effect than a moral work, which convinces our reason but does not warm our feelings or effect the slightest alteration of our habits.—*Napoleon.*

Ballads and popular songs are both the cause and effect of general morals; they are first formed, and then re-act.— In both points of view they are an index of public morals.—*H. Martineau.*

BARGAIN.—I will give thrice so much land to any well-deserving friend; but in the way of bargain, mark me, I will cavil on the ninth part of a hair.—*Shakespeare.*

A dear bargain is always disagreeable, particularly as it is a reflection on the buyer's judgment.

Whenever you buy or sell, let or hire, make a definite bargain, and never trust to the flattering lie, " We shan't disagree about trifles."

There are many things in which one gains and the other loses; but if it is essential to any transaction that only one side shall gain, the thing is not of God.—*G. Macdonald.*

BASENESS.—Every base occupation makes one sharp in its practice, and dull in every other.—*Sir P. Sidney.*

There is a law of forces which hinders bodies from sinking beyond a certain depth in the sea; but in the ocean of baseness the deeper we get the easier the sinking.—*J. R. Lowell.*

Baseness of character or conduct not only sears the conscience, but deranges the intellect.—Right conduct is connected with right views of truth.—*Colton.*

BASHFULNESS. — There are two kinds of bashfulness: one, the awkwardness of the booby, which a few steps into the world will convert into the pertness of a coxcomb; the other, a consciousness, which the most delicate feelings produce, and the most extensive knowledge cannot always remove.—*Mackenzie.*

Bashfulness is more frequently connected with good sense than with over-assurance; and impudence, on the other hand, is often the effect of downright stupidity.—*Shenstone.*

Bashfulness is a great hindrance to a man, both in uttering his sentiments and in understanding what is proposed to him; it is therefore good to press forward with discretion, both in discourse and company of the better sort.—*Bacon.*

Conceit not so high an opinion of any one as to be bashful and impotent in their presence.—*Fuller.*

Bashfulness is an ornament to youth, but a reproach to old age.—*Aristotle.*

Bashfulness may sometimes exclude pleasure, but seldom opens any avenue to sorrow or remorse.—*Johnson.*

We do not accept as genuine the person not characterized by this blushing bashfulness, this youthfulness of heart, this sensibility to the sentiment of suavity and self-respect. Modesty is bred of self-reverence.—Fine manners are the mantle of fair minds.—None are truly great without this ornament.—*A. B. Alcott.*

We must prune it with care, so as only to remove the redundant branches, and not injure the stem, which has its root in a generous sensitiveness to shame. —*Plutarch.*

BEARD.—He that hath a beard is more than a youth, and he that hath none is less than a man.—*Shakespeare.*

Beard was never the true standard of brains.—*Fuller.*

BEAUTY.—Socrates called beauty a short-lived tyranny; Plato, a privilege of nature; Theophrastus, a silent cheat; Theocritus, a delightful prejudice; Carneades, a solitary kingdom; Aristotle, that it was better than all the letters of recommendation in the world; Homer, that it was a glorious gift of nature, and Ovid, that it was a favor bestowed by the gods.

The fountain of beauty is the heart, and every generous thought illustrates the walls of your chamber.

If virtue accompanies beauty it is the heart's paradise; if vice be associate with it, it is the soul's purgatory.—It is the wise man's bonfire, and the fool's furnace.—*Quarles.*

The best part of beauty is that which no picture can express.—*Bacon.*

Beauty hath so many charms one knows not how to speak against it; and when a graceful figure is the habitation of a virtuous soul—when the beauty of the face speaks out the modesty and humility of the mind, it raises our thoughts up to the great Creator; but after all, beauty, like truth, is never so glorious as when it goes the plainest.—*Sterne.*

The beauty seen, is partly in him who sees it.—*Bovee.*

After all, it is the divinity within that makes the divinity without; and I have been more fascinated by a woman of talent and intelligence, though deficient in personal charms, than I have been by the most regular beauty.—*Washington Irving.*

There is no more potent antidote to low sensuality than the adoration of beauty.—All the higher arts of design are essentially chaste.—They purify the thoughts, as tragedy, according to Aristotle, purifies the passions.—*Schlegel.*

There is no beautifier of complexion, or form, or behavior, like the wish to scatter joy and not pain around us.

Even virtue is more fair when it appears in a beautiful person.—*Virgil.*

Beauty is but the sensible image of the Infinite.—Like truth and justice it lives within us; like virtue and the moral law it is a companion of the soul.—*Bancroft.*

That which is striking and beautiful is not always good; but that which is good is always beautiful.—*Ninon de l'Enclos.*

If either man or woman would realize the full power of personal beauty, it must be by cherishing noble thoughts and hopes and purposes; by having something to do and something to live for that is worthy of humanity, and which, by expanding the capacities of the soul, gives expansion and symmetry to the body which contains it.—*Upham.*

Every trait of beauty may be referred to some virtue, as to innocence, candor, generosity, modesty, or heroism.—*St. Pierre.*

To cultivate the sense of the beautiful, is one of the most effectual ways of cultivating an appreciation of the divine goodness.—*Bovee.*

No man receives the full culture of a man in whom the sensibility to the beautiful is not cherished; and there is no condition of life from which it should be excluded.—Of all luxuries this is the cheapest, and the most at hand, and most important to those conditions where coarse labor tends to give grossness to the mind.—*Channing.*

To give pain is the tyranny; to make happy, the true empire of beauty.—*Steele.*

If the nose of Cleopatra had been a little shorter, it would have changed the history of the world.—*Pascal.*

Beauty in a modest woman is like fire at a distance, or a sharp sword beyond reach.—The one does not burn, or the other wound those that come not too near them.—*Cervantes.*

Beauty is often worse than wine; intoxicating both the holder and beholder.—*Zimmerman.*

The most natural beauty in the world is honesty and moral truth.—For all beauty is truth.—True features make the beauty of the face; true proportions, the beauty of architecture; true measures, the beauty of harmony and music.—*Shaftesbury.*

How goodness heightens beauty!—*Hannah More.*

Beauty is the mark God sets on virtue.—Every natural action is graceful; every heroic act is also decent, and causes the place and the bystanders to shine.—*Emerson.*

The soul, by an instinct stronger than reason, ever associates beauty with truth.—*Tuckerman.*

No woman can be handsome by the force of features alone, any more than she can be witty by only the help of speech.—*Hughes.*

Beauty is like an almanack: if it last a year it is well.—*T. Adams.*

There are no better cosmetics than a severe temperance and purity, modesty and humility, a gracious temper and calmness of spirit; and there is no true beauty without the signatures of these graces in the very countenance.—*Ray.*

The common foible of women who have been handsome is to forget that they are no longer so.—*Rochefoucauld.*

How much wit, good-nature, indulgences, how many good offices and civilities, are required among friends to accomplish in some years what a lovely face or a fine hand does in a minute!—*Bruyere.*

Beauty is as summer fruits, which are easy to corrupt and cannot last; and for the most part it makes a dissolute youth, and an age a little out of countenance; but if it light well, it makes virtues shine and vice blush.—*Bacon.*

Beauty is an outward gift which is seldom despised, except by those to whom it has been refused.—*Gibbon.*

A woman who could always love would never grow old; and the love of mother and wife would often give or preserve many charms if it were not too often combined with parental and conjugal anger. There remains in the faces of women who are naturally serene and peaceful, and of those rendered so by religion, an after-spring, and later an after-summer, the reflex of their most beautiful bloom.—*Richter.*

Beauty is the first present nature gives

t'o women and the first it takes away.—*Méré.*

If you tell a woman she is beautiful, whisper it softly; for if the devil hears it he will echo it many times.—*Durivage.*

An appearance of delicacy, and even of fragility, is almost essential to beauty.—*Burke.*

Beauty is but a vain and doubtful good; a shining gloss that fadeth suddenly; a flower that dies when it begins to bud; a doubtful good, a gloss, a glass, a flower, lost, faded, broken, dead within an hour.—*Shakespeare.*

What tender force, what dignity divine, what virtue consecrating every feature; around that neck what dross are gold and pearl!—*Young.*

Beauty, unaccompanied by virtue, is as a flower without perfume.—*From the French.*

Loveliness needs not the aid of foreign ornament, but is, when unadorned, adorned the most.—*Thomson.*

I pray thee, O God, that I may be beautiful within.—*Socrates.*

All beauty does not inspire love; some beauties please the sign without captivating the affections.—*Cervantes.*

The criterion of true beauty is, that it increases on examination; if false, that it lessens.—There is therefore, something in true beauty that corresponds with right reason, and is not the mere creation of fancy.—*Greville.*

Every year of my life I grow more convinced that it is wisest and best to fix our attention on the beautiful and the good, and dwell as little as possible on the evil and the false.—*Cecil.*

By cultivating the beautiful we scatter the seeds of heavenly flowers, as by doing good we cultivate those that belong to humanity.—*Howard.*

In all ranks of life the human heart yearns for the beautiful; and the beautiful things that God makes are his gift to all alike.—*H. B. Stowe.*

Beauty attracts us men; but if, like an armed magnet it is pointed, beside, with gold or silver, it attracts with tenfold power.—*Richter.*

There should be as little merit in loving a woman for her beauty, as a man for his prosperity, both being equally subject to change.—*Pope.*

Never lose an opportunity of seeing anything that is beautiful; for beauty is God's handwriting—a wayside sacrament. Welcome it in every fair face, in every fair sky, in every fair flower, and thank God for it as a cup of blessing.—*Emerson.*

Beauty of form affects the mind, but then it must not be the mere shell that we admire, but the thought that this shell is only the beautiful case adjusted to the shape and value of a still more beautiful pearl within.—The perfection of outward loveliness is the soul shining through its crystalline covering.—*Jane Porter.*

O! how much more doth beauty beauteous seem, by that sweet ornament which truth doth give!—*Shakespeare.*

BED.—(See "SLEEP.")

The bed is a bundle of paradoxes: we go to it with reluctance, yet we quit it with regret; we make up our minds every night to leave it early, but we make up our bodies every morning to keep it late.—*Colton.*

What a delightful thing rest is!—The bed has become a place of luxury to me. —I would not exchange it for all the thrones in the world.—*Napoleon.*

In bed we laugh; in bed we cry; in bed are born; in bed we die; the near approach the bed doth show, of human bliss to human woe.—*Benserade.*

Early to bed, and early to rise, makes a man healthy, wealthy, and wise.—*Franklin.*

Night is the time for rest; how sweet when labors close, to gather round an aching heart the curtain of repose; stretch the tired limbs, and lay the weary head down on our own delightful bed.—*J. Montgomery.*

BEGINNINGS.—Let us watch well our beginnings, and results will manage themselves.—*Alex. Clark.*

When the ancients said a work well begun was half done, they meant to impress the importance of always endeavoring to make a good beginning.—*Polybius.*

Meet the first beginnings; look to the budding mischief before it has time to ripen to maturity.—*Shakespeare.*

BEHAVIOR.—Behavior is a mirror in

which every one displays his image.—*Goethe.*

What is becoming in behavior is honorable, and what is honorable is becoming.—*Cicero.*

A consciousness of inward knowledge gives confidence to the outward behavior, which, of all things, is the best to grace a man in his carriage.—*Feltham.*

Levity of behavior is the bane of all that is good and virtuous.—*Seneca.*

Oddities and singularities of behavior may attend genius, but when they do, they are its misfortunes and blemishes.—The man of true genius will be ashamed of them; at least he will never affect to distinguish himself by whimsical peculiarities.—*Sir W. Temple.*

BELIEF.—(See "RELIGION.")

Nothing is so easy as to deceive one's self; for what we wish, that we readily believe.—*Demosthenes.*

There are many great truths which we do not deny, and which nevertheless we do not fully believe.—*J. W. Alexander.*

He that will believe only what he can fully comprehend, must have a very long head or a very short creed.—*Colton.*

There are three means of believing, by inspiration, by reason, and by custom.—Christianity, which is the only rational system, admits none for its sons who do not believe according to inspiration.—*Pascal.*

A man may be a heretic in the truth; and if he believes things, only on the authority of others without other reason, then, though his belief be true, yet the very truth he holds becomes heresy.—*Milton.*

Remember that what you believe will depend very much upon what you are.—*Noah Porter.*

Orthodoxy is my doxy; heterodoxy is another man's doxy.—*Bp. Warburton.*

We are slow to believe that which if believed would hurt our feelings.—*Ovid.*

The practical effect of a belief is the real test of its soundness.—*Froude.*

You believe easily what you hope for earnestly.—*Terence.*

Some believe all that parents, tutors, and kindred believe.—They take their principles by inheritance, and defend them as they would their estates, because they are born heirs to them.—*Watts.*

In belief lies the secret of all valuable exertion.—*Bulwer.*

A skeptical young man one day, conversing with the celebrated Dr. Parr, observed, that he would believe nothing which he could not understand. "Then, young man, your creed will be the shortest of any man's I know."

I am not afraid of those tender and scrupulous consciences who are ever cautious of professing and believing too much; if they are sincerely wrong, I forgive their errors and respect their integrity.—The men I am afraid of are those who believe everything, subscribe to everything, and vote for everything.—*Shipley.*

He who expects men to be always as good as their beliefs, indulges a groundless hope; and he who expects men to be always as bad as their beliefs, vexes himself with a needless fear.—*J. S. Kieffer.*

It is a singular fact that many men of action incline to the theory of fatalism, while the greater part of men of thought believe in a divine providence.—*Balzac.*

Newton, Pascal, Bossuet, Racine, Fenelon, that is to say some of the most enlightened men on earth, in the most philosophical of all ages, have been believers in Jesus Christ; and the great Condé, when dying, repeated these noble words, "Yes, I shall see God as he is, face to face!"—*Vauvenargues.*

BENEFICENCE. — Christian beneficence takes a large sweep; that circumference cannot be small of which God is the centre.—*Hannah More.*

Doing good is the only certainly happy action of a man's life.—*Sir P. Sidney.*

To pity distress is but human; to relieve it is Godlike.—*A. Mann.*

We should give as we would receive, cheerfully, quickly, and without hesitation; for there is no grace in a benefit that sticks to the fingers.—*Seneca.*

We enjoy thoroughly only the pleasure that we give.—*Dumas.*

The luxury of doing good surpasses every other personal enjoyment.—*Gay.*

He that does good to another, does good also to himself, not only in the consequences, but in the very act: for the consciousness of well doing is, in itself, ample reward.—*Seneca.*

God has so constituted our nature that we cannot be happy unless we are, or think we are, the means of good to others.—We can scarcely conceive of greater wretchedness than must be felt by him who knows he is wholly useless in the world.—*Erskine Mason.*

Men resemble the gods in nothing so much as in doing good to their fellow creatures.—*Cicero.*

Rich people should consider that they are only trustees for what they possess, and should show their wealth to be more in doing good than merely in having it. —They should not reserve their benevolence for purposes after they are dead, for those who give not of their property till they die show that they would not then if they could keep it any longer.—*Bp. Hall.*

It is another's fault if he be ungrateful; but it is mine if I do not give.—To find one thankful man, I will oblige a great many that are not so.—I had rather never receive a kindness than never bestow one.—Not to return a benefit is a great sin; but not to confer one is a greater.—*Seneca.*

For his bounty there was no winter to it; an autumn it was that grew more by reaping.—*Shakespeare.*

There is no use of money equal to that of beneficence; here the enjoyment grows on reflection; and our money is most truly ours when it ceases to be in our possession.—*Mackenzie.*

Time is short;—your obligations are infinite.—Are your houses regulated, your children instructed, the afflicted relieved, the poor visited, the work of piety accomplished?—*Massillon.*

I never knew a child of God being bankrupted by his benevolence. What we keep we may lose, but what we give to Christ we are sure to keep.—*T. L. Cuyler.*

Be charitable before wealth makes thee covetous.—*Sir T. Browne.*

Of all the virtues necessary to the completion of the perfect man, there is none to be more delicately implied and less ostentatiously vaunted than that of exquisite feeling or universal benevolence.—*Bulwer.*

Money spent on ourselves may be a millstone about the neck; spent on others it may give us wings like eagles. —*R. D. Hitchcock.*

You are so to give, and to sacrifice to give, as to earn the eulogium pronounced on the woman, "She hath done what she could."—Do it now.—It is not safe to leave a generous feeling to the cooling influences of a cold world.—*Guthrie.*

The greatest pleasure I know is to do a good action by stealth, and to have it found out by accident.—*Lamb.*

Beneficence is a duty; and he who frequently practises it, and sees his benevolent intentions realized comes, at length, really to love him to whom he has done good.—*Kant.*

Time, which gnaws and diminishes all things else, augments and increaseth benefits; because a noble action of liberality doth grow continually by our generously thinking of it and remembering it.—*Rabelais.*

BENEVOLENCE. — (See "KINDNESS.")

To feel much for others, and little for ourselves; to restrain our selfish, and exercise our benevolent affections, constitutes the perfection of human nature. —*Adam Smith.*

Benevolent feeling ennobles the most trifling actions.—*Thackeray.*

There cannot be a more glorious object in creation than a human being replete with benevolence, meditating in what manner he may render himself most acceptable to the Creator by doing good to his creatures.—*Fielding.*

Benevolence is allied to few vices; selfishness to fewer virtues.—*Home.*

In this world it is not what we take up, but what we give up, that makes us rich.—*H. W. Beecher.*

He who will not give some portion of his ease, his blood, his wealth, for others' good, is a poor frozen churl.—*Joanna Baillie.*

He only does not live in vain, who employs his wealth, his thought, his speech to advance the good of others.—*Hindoo Maxim.*

I truly enjoy no more of the world's good things than what I willingly distribute to the needy.—*Seneca.*

It is good for us to think that no grace

or blessing is truly ours till we are aware that God has blessed some one else with it through us.—*Phillips Brooks.*

They who scatter with one hand, gather with two, not always in coin, but in kind. Nothing multiplies so much as kindness.—*Wray.*

Genuine benevolence is not stationary, but peripatetic; it goes about doing good.—*W. Nevins.*

Do not wait for extraordinary circumstances to do good actions: try to use ordinary situations.—*Richter.*

The best way to do good to ourselves, is to do it to others; the right way to gather, is to scatter.

This is the law of benefits between men; the one ought to forget at once what he has given, and the other ought never to forget what he has received.—*Seneca.*

Never did any soul do good, but it came readier to do the same again, with more enjoyment. Never was love, or gratitude, or bounty practised, but with increasing joy, which made the practiser still more in love with the fair act.—*Shaftesbury.*

The one who will be found in trial capable of great acts of love is ever the one who is always doing considerate small ones.—*F. W. Robertson.*

It is the glory of the true religion that it inculcates and inspires a spirit of benevolence.—It is a religion of charity, which none other ever was.—Christ went about doing good; he set the example to his disciples, and they abounded in it.—*Fuller.*

Rare benevolence! the minister of God.—*Carlyle.*

When Fenelon's library was on fire, "God be praised," he said, "that it is not the dwelling of some poor man."

The conqueror is regarded with awe; the wise man commands our respect; but it is only the benevolent man that wins our affection.

The disposition to give a cup of cold water to a disciple, is a far nobler property than the finest intellect.—*Howells.*

He who wishes to secure the good of others, has already secured his own.—*Confucius.*

Just in proportion as a man becomes good, divine, Christ-like, he passes out

of the region of theorizing into the region of benevolent activities.—It is good to think well; it is divine to act well.—*H. Mann.*

It is no great part of a good man's lot to enjoy himself.—To be good and to do good are his ends, and the glory is to be revealed hereafter.—*S. I. Prime.*

BEST THINGS.—A firm faith is the best divinity; a good life, the best philosophy; a clear conscience, the best law; honesty, the best policy; and temperance the best physic;—living for both worlds is the wisest and best life.

BIBLE.—The Bible is the only source of all Christian truth;—the only rule for the Christian life;—the only book that unfolds to us the realities of eternity.

There is no book like the Bible for excellent wisdom and use.—*Sir M. Hale.*

The philosophers, as Varro tells us, counted up three hundred and twenty answers to the question, "What is the supreme good?" How needful, then, is a divine revelation, to make plain what is the true end of our being.—*Tryon Edwards.*

There never was found, in any age of the world, either religion or law that did so highly exalt the public good as the Bible.—*Bacon.*

The Bible is a window in this prison of hope, through which we look into eternity.—*Dwight.*

The Bible is the light of my understanding, the joy of my heart, the fullness of my hope, the clarifier of my affections, the mirror of my thoughts, the consoler of my sorrows, the guide of my soul through this gloomy labyrinth of time, the telescope sent from heaven to reveal to the eye of man the amazing glories of the far distant world.

The Bible contains more true sublimity, more exquisite beauty, more pure morality, more important history, and finer strains of poetry and eloquence, than can be collected from all other books, in whatever age or language they may have been written.—*Sir Wm. Jones.*

In what light soever we regard the Bible, whether with reference to revelation, to history, or to morality, it is an invaluable and inexhaustible mine of knowledge and virtue.—*J. Q. Adams.*

Bad men or devils would not have

written the Bible, for it condemns them and their works,—good men or angels could not have written it, for in saying it was from God when it was but their own invention, they would have been guilty of falsehood, and thus could not have been good. The only remaining being who could have written it, is God —its real author.

The Scriptures teach us the best way of living, the noblest way of suffering, and the most comfortable way of dying. —*Flavel.*

There are no songs comparable to the songs of Zion; no orations equal to those of the prophets; and no politics like those which the Scriptures teach.— *Milton.*

It is a belief in the Bible, the fruit of deep meditation, which has served me as the guide of my moral and literary life.—I have found it a capital safely invested, and richly productive of interest.—*Goethe.*

The longer you read the Bible, the more you will like it; it will grow sweeter and sweeter; and the more you get into the spirit of it, the more you will get into the spirit of Christ.— *Romaine.*

I have always said, I always will say, that the studious perusal of the sacred volume will make better citizens, better fathers, and better husbands.—*Jefferson.*

Men cannot be well educated without the Bible. It ought, therefore, to hold the chief place in every seat of learning throughout Christendom; and I do not know of a higher service that could be rendered to this republic than the bringing about this desirable result.—*E. Nott.*

The general diffusion of the Bible is the most effectual way to civilize and humanize mankind; to purify and exalt the general system of public morals; to give efficacy to the just precepts of international and municipal law; to enforce the observance of prudence, temperance, justice and fortitude; and to improve all the relations of social and domestic life.—*Chancellor Kent.*

Scholars may quote Plato in their studies, but the hearts of millions will quote the Bible at their daily toil, and draw strength from its inspiration, as the meadows draw it from the brook.— *Conway.*

The Bible goes equally to the cottage of the peasant, and the palace of the king.—It is woven into literature, and colors the talk of the street.—The bark of the merchant cannot sail without it; and no ship of war goes to the conflict but it is there.—It enters men's closets; directs their conduct, and mingles in all the grief and cheerfulness of life.—*Theodore Parker.*

The Bible is one of the greatest blessings bestowed by God on the children of men.—It has God for its author; salvation for its end, and truth without any mixture for its matter.—It is all pure, all sincere; nothing too much; nothing wanting.—*Locke.*

The man of one book is always formidable; but when that book is the Bible he is irresistible.—*W. M. Taylor.*

To say nothing of its holiness or authority, the Bible contains more specimens of genius and taste than any other volume in existence.—*Landor.*

So great is my veneration for the Bible, that the earlier my children begin to read it the more confident will be my hopes that they will prove useful citizens to their country and respectable members of society.—*J. Q. Adams.*

The incongruity of the Bible with the age of its birth; its freedom from earthly mixtures; its original, unborrowed, solitary greatness; the suddenness with which it broke forth amidst the general gloom; these, to me, are strong indications of its Divine descent: I cannot reconcile them with a human origin.— *Channing.*

I believe that the Bible is to be understood and received in the plain and obvious meaning of its passages; for I cannot persuade myself that a book intended for the instruction and conversion of the whole world should cover its true meaning in any such mystery and doubt that none but critics and philosophers can discover it.—*Daniel Webster.*

The Gospel is not merely a book—it is a living power—a book surpassing all others.—I never omit to read it, and every day with the same pleasure. Nowhere is to be found such a series of beautiful ideas, and admirable moral maxims, which pass before us like the battalions of a celestial army . . . The soul can never go astray with this book for its guide.—*Napoleon on St. Helena.*

In this little book (the New Testament), is contained all the wisdom of the world.—*Ewald.*

All the distinctive features and superiority of our republican institutions are derived from the teachings of Scripture. —*Everett.*

Just as all things upon earth represent and image forth all the realities of another world, so the Bible is one mighty representative of the whole spiritual life of humanity.—*Helen Keller.*

Voltaire spoke of the Bible as a short-lived book. He said that within a hundred years it would pass from common use. Not many people read Voltaire to-day, but his house has been packed with Bibles as a depot of a Bible society. —*Bruce Barton.*

I cannot too greatly emphasize the importance and value of Bible study— more important than ever before in these days of uncertainties, when men and women are apt to decide questions from the standpoint of expediency rather than on the eternal principles laid down by God, Himself.—*John Wanamaker.*

When you have read the Bible, you will know it is the word of God, because you will have found it the key to your own heart, your own happiness and your own duty.—*Woodrow Wilson.*

No lawyer can afford to be ignorant of the Bible.—*Rufus Choate.*

I believe a knowledge of the Bible without a college course is more valuable than a college course without a Bible.—*William Lyon Phelps.*

The Bible remained for me a book of books, still divine—but divine in the sense that all great books are divine which teach men how to live righteously.—*Sir Arthur Keith.*

All that I am I owe to Jesus Christ, revealed to me in His divine Book.— *David Livingstone.*

I have always believed in the inspiration of the Holy Scriptures, whereby they have become the expression to man of the Word and Will of God.—*Warren G. Harding.*

The Holy Bible is not only great but high explosive literature. It works in strange ways and no living man can tell

or know how that book in its journeyings through the world has started an individual soul 10,000 different places into a new life, a new belief, a new conception and a new faith.—*Stanley Baldwin.*

It has been truly said that any translation of the masterpiece (the Bible) must be a failure.—*Dr. E. J. Goodspeed.*

To my early knowledge of the Bible I owe the best part of my taste in literature, and the most precious, and on the whole, the one essential part of my education.—*Ruskin.*

Peruse the works of our philosophers; with all their pomp of diction, how mean, how contemptible, are they, compared with the Scriptures! Is it possible that a book at once so simple and sublime should be merely the work of man? The Jewish authors were incapable of the diction, and strangers to the morality contained in the Gospel, the marks of whose truths are so striking and inimitable that the inventor would be a more astonishing character than the hero.—*Rousseau.*

The morality of the Bible is, after all, the safety of society.—*F. C. Monfort.*

The Bible rose to the place it now occupies because it deserved to rise to that place, and not because God sent anybody with a box of tricks to prove its divine authority.—*Bruce Barton.*

The Bible, thoroughly known, is literature in itself—the rarest and richest in all departments of thought and imagination which exists.—*James Anthony Froude.*

That the truths of the Bible have the power of awakening an intense moral feeling in every human being; that they make bad men good, and send a pulse of healthful feeling through all the domestic, civil, and social relations; that they teach men to love right, and hate wrong, and seek each other's welfare as children of a common parent; that they control the baleful passions of the heart, and thus make men proficient in self-government; and finally that they teach man to aspire after conformity to a being of infinite holiness, and fill him with hopes more purifying, exalted, and suited to his nature than any other book the world has ever known—these are facts as incontrovertible as the laws of philoso ·

phy, or the demonstrations of mathematics.—*F. Wayland.*

We account the Scriptures of God to be the most sublime philosophy. I find more sure marks of authenticity in the Bible than in any profane history whatever.—*Isaac Newton.*

Of the Bible, says Garibaldi, " This is the cannon that will make Italy free."

Sink the Bible to the bottom of the ocean, and still man's obligations to God would be unchanged.—He would have the same path to tread, only his lamp and his guide would be gone;—the same voyage to make, but his chart and compass would be overboard. — *H. W. Beecher.*

I know the Bible is inspired because it finds me at greater depths of my being than any other book.—*Coleridge.*

The highest earthly enjoyments are but a shadow of the joy I find in reading God's word.—*Lady Jane Grey.*

They who are not induced to believe and live as they ought by those discoveries which God hath made in Scripture, would stand out against any evidence whatever; even that of a messenger sent express from the other world. —*Atterbury.*

Do you know a book that you are willing to put under your head for a pillow when you lie dying? That is the book you want to study while you are living. There is but one such book in the world.—*Joseph Cook.*

Hold fast to the Bible as the sheet-anchor of your liberties; write its precepts in your hearts, and practice them in your lives. To the influence of this book we are indebted for all the progress made in true civilization, and to this we must look as our guide in the future. " Righteousness exalteth a nation; but sin is a reproach to any people."—*U. S. Grant.*

The most learned, acute, and diligent student cannot, in the longest life, obtain an entire knowledge of this one volume. The more deeply he works the mine, the richer and more abundant he finds the ore; new light continually beams from this source of heavenly knowledge, to direct the conduct, and illustrate the work of God and the ways of men; and he will at last leave the world confessing, that the more he studied

the Scriptures, the fuller conviction he had of his own ignorance, and of their inestimable value.—*Walter Scott.*

Philosophical argument, especially that drawn from the vastness of the universe, in comparison with the apparent insignificance of this globe, has sometimes shaken my reason for the faith that is in me; but my heart has always assured and reassured me that the gospel of Jesus Christ must be a divine reality.—*Daniel Webster.*

Cities fall, empires come to nothing, kingdoms fade away as smoke. Where is Numa, Minos, Lycurgus? Where are their books? and what has become of their laws? But that this book no tyrant should have been able to consume, no tradition to choke, no heretic maliciously to corrupt; that it should stand unto this day, amid the wreck of all that was human, without the alteration of one sentence so as to change the doctrine taught therein,—surely there is a very singular providence, claiming our attention in a most remarkable manner. —*Bp. Jewell.*

A noble book! All men's book! It is our first, oldest statement of the never-ending problem,—man's destiny, and God's ways with him here on earth; and all in such free-flowing outlines,— grand in its sincerity; in its simplicity and its epic melody.—*Carlyle.*

One monarch to obey, one creed to own; that monarch God; that creed his word alone.

If there is any one fact or doctrine, or command, or promise in the Bible which has produced no practical effect on your temper, or heart, or conduct, be assured you do not truly believe it.—*Payson.*

There is a Book worth all other books which were ever printed.—*Patrick Henry.*

The Bible furnishes the only fitting vehicle to express the thoughts that overwhelm us when contemplating the stellar universe.—*O. M. Mitchell.*

The grand old Book of God still stands, and this old earth, the more its leaves are turned over and pondered, the more it will sustain and illustrate the sacred Word.—*Prof. Dana.*

In my investigation of natural science, I have always found that, whenever I can meet with anything in the Bible on my subjects, it always affords me a firm platform on which to stand.—*Lieutenant Maury.*

It is impossible to mentally or socially enslave a Bible-reading people. The principles of the Bible are the groundwork of human freedom.—*Horace Greeley.*

I speak as a man of the world to men of the world; and I say to you, Search the Scriptures! The Bible is the book of all others, to be read at all ages, and in all conditions of human life; not to be read once or twice or thrice through, and then laid aside, but to be read in small portions of one or two chapters every day, and never to be intermitted, unless by some overruling necessity.—*J. Q. Adams.*

Give to the people who toil and suffer, for whom this world is hard and bad, the belief that there is a better made for them. Scatter Gospels among the villages, a Bible for every cottage.—*Victor Hugo.*

The word of God will stand a thousand readings; and he who has gone over it most frequently is the surest of finding new wonders there.—*J. Hamilton.*

Holy Scripture is a stream of running water, where alike the elephant may swim, and the lamb walk without losing its feet.—*Gregory the Great.*

A Bible and a newspaper in every house, a good school in every district—all studied and appreciated as they merit—are the principal support of virtue, morality, and civil liberty.—*Franklin.*

As the profoundest philosophy of ancient Rome and Greece lighted her taper at Israel's altar, so the sweetest strains of the pagan muse were swept from harps attuned on Zion's hill.—*Bp. Thomson.*

The whole hope of human progress is suspended on the ever-growing influence of the Bible.—*William H. Seward.*

The Bible is the only cement of nations, and the only cement that can bind religious hearts together.—*Bunsen.*

All human discoveries seem to be made only for the purpose of confirming more and more strongly the truths that come from on high and are contained in the sacred writings.—*Herschel.*

After all, the Bible must be its own

argument and defence. The power of it can never be proved unless it is felt. The authority of it can never be supported unless it is manifest. The light of it can never be demonstrated unless it shines.—*H. J. Van Dyke.*

You never get to the end of Christ's words. There is something in them always behind. They pass into proverbs, into laws, into doctrines, into consolations; but they never pass away, and after all the use that is made of them they are still not exhausted.—*A. P. Stanley.*

Nobody ever outgrows Scripture; the book widens and deepens with our years.—*Spurgeon.*

After reading the doctrines of Plato, Socrates, or Aristotle, we feel that the specific difference between their words and Christ's is the difference between an inquiry and a revelation.—*Joseph Parker.*

A loving trust in the Author of the Bible is the best preparation for a wise and profitable study of the Bible itself.—*H. C. Trumbull.*

I have read the Bible through many times, and now make it a practice to read it through once every year.—It is a book of all others for lawyers, as well as divines; and I pity the man who cannot find in it a rich supply of thought and of rules for conduct.—*Daniel Webster.*

So far as I have observed God's dealings with my soul, the flights of preachers sometimes entertained me, but it was Scripture expressions which did penetrate my heart, and in a way peculiar to themselves.—*John Brown of Haddington.*

A man may read the figures on the dial, but he cannot tell how the day goes unless the sun is shining on it; so we may read the Bible over, but we cannot learn to purpose till the spirit of God shine upon it and into our hearts.—*T. Watson.*

There is no book on which we can rest in a dying moment but the Bible.—*Selden.*

The Bible is to us what the star was to the wise men; but if we spend all our time in gazing upon it, observing its motions, and admiring its splendor, without being led to Christ by it, the use of it will be lost to us.—*Thomas Adams.*

MOSES

—*Michelangelo*

48a

FAMILIAR EXPRESSIONS *from* THE BIBLE

Arranged Alphabetically According to Key Words

A

Unto every one that hath shall be given, and he shall have abundance; but from him that hath not shall be taken away even that which he hath.—*N. T., Matthew, xxv, 29; Mark, iv, 25.*

They are like the deaf adder that stoppeth her ear.—*O. T., Psalms, lviii, 4.*

The furnace of affliction.—*O. T., Isaiah, xlviii, 10.*

He that is not with me is against me. —*N. T., Matthew, xii, 30.*

I am Alpha and Omega, the beginning and the ending, saith the Lord.—*N. T., Revelation, i, 8.*

But Peter said, Ananias . . . thou hast not lied unto men, but unto God.— *N. T., Acts, v, 3–5.*

Let him be Anathema, Maranatha.— *N. T., I Corinthians, xvi, 22.*

The ancient and honourable.—*O. T., Isaiah, ix, 15.*

He that is slow to anger is better than the mighty; and he that ruleth his spirit than he that taketh a city.—*O. T., Proverbs, xvi, 32.*

Touch not mine anointed.—*O. T., I Chronicles, xvi, 22; Psalms, cv, 15.* This text was the basis of benefit of clergy—the theory that one dedicated to the church must not be put to death.

A soft answer turneth away wrath.— *O. T., Proverbs, xv, 1.*

Go to the ant, thou sluggard; consider her ways, and be wise.—*O. T., Proverbs, vi, 6.*

He kept him as the apple of his eye.— *O. T., Deuteronomy, xxxii, 10.*

And he gathereth them together into a place called in the Hebrew tongue Armageddon.—*N. T., Revelation, xvi, 16.*

Terrible as an army with banners.— *O. T., Song of Solomon, vi, 4, 10.*

Ask, and it shall be given you; seek, and ye shall find; knock, and it shall be opened unto you.—*N. T., Matthew, vii, 7.*

B

Out of the mouths of babes and sucklings hast thou ordained strength.— *O. T., Psalms, viii, 2.*

Refrain your tongue from backbiting. —*Apocrypha, Wisdom of Solomon, i, 11.*

Thou art weighed in the balances, and art found wanting.—*O. T., Daniel, v, 27.*

Is there no balm in Gilead?—*O. T., Jeremiah, viii, 22.*

Now Barabbas was a robber.—*N. T., John, xviii, 40.*

So fight I, not as one that beateth the air.—*N. T., I Corinthians, ix, 26.*

Whose God is their belly.—*N. T., Philippians, iii, 19.*

A bird of the air shall carry thy voice, and that which hath wings shall tell the matter.—*O. T., Ecclesiastes, x, 20.*

Blind leaders of the blind.—*N. T., Matthew, xv, 14.*

The blood is the life.—*O. T., Deuteronomy, xii, 23.*

His blood shall be on us and on our children.—*N. T., Matthew, xxvii, 25.*

Whoso sheddeth man's blood, by man shall his blood be shed.—*O. T., Genesis, ix, 6.*

Bone of my bones.—*O. T., Genesis, ii, 23.*

Of making many books there is no end. —*O. T., Ecclesiastes, xii, 12.*

Ye shall know my breach of promise.— *O. T., Numbers, xiv, 34.*

Give us this day our daily bread.— *N. T., Matthew, vi, 11.*

Man shall not live by bread alone.— *N. T., Matthew, iv, 4.*

Cast thy bread upon the waters: for thou shalt find it after many days.— *O. T., Ecclesiastes, xi, 1.*

As the bridegroom rejoiceth over the bride.—*O. T., Isaiah, lxii, 5.*

Am I my brother's keeper?—*O. T., Genesis, iv, 9.*

And that ye study to be quiet, and to do your own business.—*N. T., I Thessalonians, iv, 11.*

Tattlers also, and busybodies, speaking things which they ought not.—*N. T., I Timothy, v, 13.*

Thou shalt become an astonishment, a proverb, and a byword, among all nations.—*O. T., Deuteronomy, xxviii, 37.*

C

Render therefore unto Caesar the things which are Caesar's, and unto God the things that are God's.—*N. T., Matthew, xxii, 21.*

And bring hither the fatted calf, and kill it.—*N. T., Luke, xv, 23.*

Neither do men light a candle, and put it under a bushel, but on a candlestick.—*N. T., Matthew, v, 15.*

Woe unto them that draw iniquity with cords of vanity, and sin as it were with a cart rope!—*O. T., Isaiah, v, 18.*

The cattle upon a thousand hills.— *O. T., Psalms, l, 10.*

They are as stubble before the wind, and as chaff that the storm carrieth away.—*O. T., Job, xxi, 18.*

Charity shall cover the multitude of sins.—*N. T., I Peter, iv, 8.*

Whosoever shall smite thee on thy right cheek, turn to him the other also. —*N. T., Matthew, v, 39; Luke, vi, 29.*

48b

Be of good cheer.—*N. T., Matthew, xiv, 27.*

Suffer the little children to come unto me, and forbid them not; for of such is the kingdom of God.—*N. T., Mark, x, 14; Luke, xviii, 16.*

Many are called but few are chosen.—*N. T., Matthew, xxii, 14.*

Shall the clay say to him that fashioneth it, What makest thou?—*O. T., Isaiah, xiv, 9.*

Our fathers were under the cloud.—*N. T., I Corinthians, x, 1.*

Compassed about with so great a cloud of witnesses.—*N. T., Hebrews, xii, 1.*

If thine enemy hunger, feed him; if he thirst, give him drink: for in so doing thou shalt heap coals of fire on his head.—*N. T., Romans, xii, 20.*

I know thy works, that thou art neither cold nor hot: I would thou wert cold or hot.—*N. T., Revelation, iii, 15.*

Miserable comforters are ye all.—*O. T., Job, xvi, 2.*

Wiser in his own conceit than seven men that can render a reason.—*O. T., Proverbs, xxvi, 16.*

For this thing was not done in a corner.—*N. T., Acts, xxvi, 26.*

Served the creature more than the Creator.—*N. T., Romans, i, 25.*

Then came Jesus forth wearing the crown of thorns and the purple robe.—*N. T., John, xix, 5.*

As a lodge in a garden of cucumbers.—*O. T., Isaiah, i, 8.* Hence, "Cool as a cucumber."

My cup runneth over.—*O. T., Psalms, xxiii, 5.*

D

We have piped unto you, and ye have not danced.—*N. T., Matthew, xi, 17; Luke, vii, 32.*

Darkness which may be felt.—*O. T., Exodus, x, 21.*

Men loved darkness rather than light, because their deeds were evil.—*N. T., John, iii, 19.*

Let the dead bury their dead.—*N. T., Matthew, viii, 22; Luke, ix, 60.*

We have made a covenant with death.—*O. T., Isaiah, xxviii, 15.*

At the point of death.—*N. T., Mark, v, 23.*

Passed from death unto life.—*N. T., John, v, 24.*

The valley of the shadow of death.—*O. T., Psalms, xxiii, 4.*

O death, where is thy sting? O grave, where is thy victory?—*N. T., I Corinthians, xv, 55.*

Whither thou goest, I will go; and where thou lodgest, I will lodge: thy people shall be my people, and thy God my God: Where thou diest will I die, and there will I be buried: the Lord do so to me, and more also, if aught but death part thee and me.—*O. T., Ruth, i, 16, 17.*

Forgive us our debts, as we forgive our debtors.—*N. T., Matthew, vi, 12.*

The valley of decision.—*O. T., Joel, iii, 14.*

Deep calleth unto deep.—*O. T., Psalms, xlii, 7.*

Out of the depths [de profundis] have I cried unto thee, O Lord.—*O. T., Psalms, cxxx, 1.*

The desert shall rejoice, and blossom as the rose.—*O. T., Isaiah, xxxv, 1.*

Your adversary, the devil, as a roaring lion, walketh about, seeking whom he may devour.—*N. T., I Peter, v, 8.*

All things whatsoever ye would that men should do to you, do ye even so to them: for this is the law and the prophets.—*N. T., Matthew, vii, 12.*

Inasmuch as ye have done it unto one of the least of these my brethren, ye have done it unto me.—*N. T., Matthew, xxv, 40.*

Carried about with every wind of doctrine.—*N. T., Ephesians, iv, 14.*

A living dog is better than a dead lion.—*O. T., Ecclesiastes, ix, 4.*

I had rather be a door-keeper in the house of my God, than to dwell in the tents of wickedness.—*O. T., Psalms, lxxxiv, 10.*

Oh that I had wings like a dove! for then would I fly away and be at rest.—*O. T., Psalms, lv, 6.*

Behold, this dreamer cometh.—*O. T., Genesis, xxxvii, 19.*

The nations are as a drop of a bucket, and are counted as the small dust of the balance.—*O. T., Isaiah, xl, 15.*

For dust thou art, and unto dust shalt thou return.—*O. T., Genesis, iii, 19.*

When ye go out of that city, shake off the very dust from your feet for a testimony against them.—*N. T., Luke, ix, 5.*

His enemies shall lick the dust.—*O. T., Psalms, lxxii, 9.*

E

The hearing ear, and the seeing eye.—*O. T., Proverbs, xx, 12.*

He that blesseth his friend with a loud voice, rising early in the morning, it shall be counted a curse to him.—*O. T., Proverbs, xxvii, 14.*

Of the earth, earthy.—*N. T., I Corinthians, xv, 47.*

Take thine ease, eat, drink, and be merry.—*N. T., Luke, xii, 19.*

Let us eat and drink; for tomorrow we die.—*N. T., I Corinthians, xv, 32.*

The end is not yet.—*N. T., Matthew, xxiv, 6.*

The eyes of a fool are in the ends of the earth.—*O. T., Proverbs, xvii, 24.*

Can the Ethiopian change his skin, or the leopard his spots?—*O. T., Jeremiah, xiii, 23.*

Sufficient unto the day is the evil thereof.—*N. T., Matthew, vi, 34.*

Eye for eye, tooth for tooth, hand for hand, foot for foot.—*O. T., Deuteronomy, xix, 21.*

I was eyes to the blind, and feet was I to the lame.—*O. T., Job, xxix, 15.*

Servants, be obedient to them that are your masters . . . not with eyeservice, as menpleasers; but as the servants of Christ.—*N. T., Ephesians, vi, 5.*

F

The face of the earth.—*O. T., Numbers, xii, 3.*

I have kept the faith.—*N. T., II Timothy, iv, 7.*

The shield of faith.—*N. T., Ephesians, vi, 16.*

We walk by faith, not by sight.—*N. T., II Corinthians, v, 7.*

Faithful unto death.—*N. T., Revelation, ii, 10.*

Till thou hast paid the uttermost farthing.—*N. T., Matthew, v, 26; Luke, xii, 59.*

He . . . was gathered to his fathers.—*Apocrypha, I Maccabees, ii, 69.*

Fear came upon me, and trembling; . . . the hair of my flesh stood up.—*O. T., Job, iv, 14, 15.*

I am fearfully and wonderfully made.—*O. T., Psalms, cxxxix, 14.*

This image's head was of fine gold, his breast and his arms of silver, his belly and his thighs of brass, his legs of iron, his feet part of iron and part of clay.—*O. T., Daniel, ii, 32, 33.*

Fight the good fight of faith.—*N. T., I Timothy, vi, 12.*

They sewed fig-leaves together and made themselves aprons.—*O. T., Genesis, iii, 7.*

As a firebrand plucked from the burning.—*O. T., Amos, iv, 11.*

Many that are first shall be last; and the last shall be first.—*N. T., Matthew, xix, 30.*

The spirit indeed is willing, but the flesh is weak.—*N. T., Matthew, xxvi, 41.*

Flesh of my flesh.—*O. T., Genesis, ii, 23.*

The land of Egypt, when we sat by the fleshpots, and when we did eat bread to the full.—*O. T., Exodus, xvi, 3.*

Dead flies cause the ointment of the apothecary to send forth a stinking savour.—*O. T., Ecclesiastes, x, 1.*

There shall be one fold and one shepherd.—*N. T., John, x, 16.*

For ever and ever.—*N. T., Galatians, i, 5.*

Father, forgive them; for they know not what they do.—*N. T., Luke, xxiii, 34.*

Ye shall know them by their fruits. Do men gather grapes of thorns, or figs of thistles?—*N. T., Matthew, vii, 16.*

And he died in a good old age, full of days, riches, and honour.—*O. T., I Chronicles, xxix, 28.*

Full of good works.—*N. T., Acts, ix, 36.*

G

Mine afflictions and my misery, the wormwood and the gall.—*O. T., Lamentations, iii, 19.*

Empty, swept, and garnished.—*N. T., Matthew, xii, 44.*

Wide is the gate and broad is the way that leadeth to destruction, and many there be which go in thereat: Because strait is the gate and narrow is the way which leadeth unto life, and few there be that find it.—*N. T., Matthew, vii, 13, 14.*

Tell it not in Gath, publish it not in Askalon, lest the daughters of the Philistines rejoice.—*O. T., II Samuel, i, 20.*

He said, It is finished, and he bowed his head and gave up the ghost.—*N. T., John, xix, 30.*

There were giants in the earth in those days.—*O. T., Genesis, vi, 4.*

It is more blessed to give than to receive.—*N. T., Acts, xx, 35.*

Give, and it shall be given unto you.—*N. T., Luke, vi, 38.*

God loveth a cheerful giver.—*N. T., II Corinthians, ix, 7.*

We see through a glass, darkly.—*N. T., I Corinthians, xiii, 12.*

Ye blind guides, which strain at a gnat, and swallow a camel.—*N. T., Matthew, xxiii, 24.*

And Aaron shall lay both his hands upon the head of the live goat [scapegoat], and confess over him all the iniquities of the children of Israel, and all their transgressions in all their sins, putting them on the head of the goat, and shall send him away by the hand of a fit man into the wilderness.—*O. T., Leviticus, xvi, 21.*

God forbid!—*N. T., Romans, iii, 31.*

God will provide.—*O. T., Genesis, xxii, 8.*

Fallen from grace.—*N. T., Galatians, v, 4.*

The fathers have eaten sour grapes, and the children's teeth are set on edge.—*O. T., Ezekiel, xviii, 2.*

H

Then shall ye bring down my grey hairs with sorrow to the grave.—*O. T., Genesis, xlii, 38.*

The very hairs of your head are all numbered.—*N. T., Matthew, x, 30.*

And Jesus said unto him, No man, having put his hand to the plow, and looking back, is fit for the kingdom of God.—*N. T., Luke, ix, 62.*

His hand will be against every man, and every man's hand against him.—*O. T., Genesis, xvi, 12.*

And should not I spare Nineveh, that great city, wherein are more than six score thousand persons that cannot discern between their right hand, and their left?—*O. T., Jonah, iv, 11.*

When thou doest alms, let not thy left hand know what thy right hand doeth.—*N. T., Matthew, vi, 3.*

If I forget thee, O Jerusalem, let my right hand forget her cunning.—*O. T., Psalms, cxxxvii, 5.*

The right hands of fellowship.—*N. T., Galatians, ii, 9.*

When Pilate saw that he could prevail nothing, but that rather a tumult

St. Matthew   St. Luke

St. Mark   St. John

THE PROPHETS

480

was made, he took water, and washed his hands before the multitude, saying, I am innocent of the blood of this just person: see ye to it.—*N. T., Matthew, xxvii, 24.*

As the hart panteth after the water-brooks, so panteth my soul after Thee, O God.—*O. T., Psalms, xlii, 1.*

The Son of man hath not where to lay his head.—*N. T., Matthew, viii, 20.*

A man after his own heart.—*O. T., I Samuel, xiii, 14.*

The whole head is sick, and the whole heart faint.—*O. T., Isaiah, i, 5.*

Hope deferred maketh the heart sick.—*O. T., Proverbs, xiii, 12.*

Let us lift up our heart with our hands unto God in the heavens.—*O. T., Lamentations, iii, 41.*

Open not thine heart to every man.—*Apocrypha, Ecclesiasticus, viii, 19.*

The heaven is my throne, and the earth is my footstool.—*O. T., Isaiah, lxvi, 1.*

I will make him an help meet for him.—*O. T., Genesis, ii, 18.*

He smote them hip and thigh with a great slaughter.—*O. T., Judges, xv, 8.*

Man goeth to his long home.—*O. T., Ecclesiastes, xii, 5.*

Let them first show piety at home.—*N. T., I Timothy, v, 4.*

Sweeter also than honey and the honeycomb.—*O. T., Psalms, xix, 10.*

Who against hope believed in hope.—*N. T., Romans, iv, 18.*

Prisoners of hope.—*O. T., Zechariah, ix, 12.*

If a house be divided against itself, that house cannot stand.—*N. T., Mark, iii, 25.*

In my father's' house are many mansions.—*N. T., John, xiv, 2.*

And that which you have spoken in the ear in closets shall be proclaimed upon the housetops.—*N. T., Luke, xii, 3.*

Thou hypocrite, first cast out the beam out of thine own eye; and then shalt thou see clearly to cast out the mote out of thy brother's eye.—*N. T., Matthew, vii, 5.*

Woe unto you, scribes and Pharisees, hypocrites! for ye make clean the outside of the cup and of the platter, but within they are full of extortion and excess.—*N. T., Matthew, xxiii, 25.*

I

She looketh well to the ways of her household, and eateth not the bread of idleness.—*O. T., Proverbs, xxxi, 27.*

J

I the Lord thy God am a jealous God, visiting the iniquity of the fathers upon the children unto the third and fourth generation of them that hate me.—*O. T., Exodus, xx, 5.*

And while yet he spake, lo, Judas, one of the twelve, came. . . . And forthwith he came to Jesus, and said, Hail, Master; and kissed him.—*N. T., Matthew, xxvi, 47, 49.*

Judge not, that ye be not judged.—*N. T., Matthew, vii, 1; Luke, vi, 37.*

Judge not according to the appearance.—*N. T., John, vii, 24.*

K

The king of terrors [death].—*O. T., Job, xviii, 14.*

Fear God, Honour the King.—*N. T., I Peter, ii, 17.*

All knees shall be weak as water.—*O. T., Ezekiel, vii, 17.*

Knowledge puffeth up, but charity edifieth.—*N. T., I Corinthians, viii, 1.*

He that increaseth knowledge increaseth sorrow.—*O. T., Ecclesiastes, i, 18.*

L

Come unto me, all ye that labour and are heavy laden.—*N. T., Matthew, xi, 28.*

Labour of love.—*N. T., I Thessalonians, i, 3.*

The labourer is worthy of his hire.—*N. T., Luke, x, 7.*

The sleep of a labouring man is sweet.—*O. T., Ecclesiastes, v, 12.*

Behold the Lamb of God.—*N. T., John, i, 29.*

He is brought as a lamb to the slaughter.—*O. T., Isaiah, liii, 7.*

Thy word is a lamp unto my feet, and a light unto my path.—*O. T., Psalms, cxix, 105.*

The land of the living.—*O. T., Job, xxviii, 13.*

A land flowing with milk and honey.—*O. T., Exodus, iii, 8; Jeremiah, xxxii, 22.*

He will laugh thee to scorn.—*Apocrypha, Ecclesiasticus, xiii, 7.*

We all do fade as a leaf.—*O. T., Isaiah, lxiv, 6.*

Much learning doth make thee mad.—*N. T., Acts, xxvi, 24.*

A little leaven leaveneth the whole lump.—*N. T., I Corinthians, v, 6; Galatians, v, 9.*

My name is Legion: for we are many.—*N. T., Mark, v, 9.*

The letter [of the law] killeth, but the spirit giveth life.—*N. T., II Corinthians, iii, 6.*

The liberal deviseth liberal things.—*O. T., Isaiah, xxxii, 8.*

Stand fast therefore in the liberty wherewith Christ hath made us free.—*N. T., Galatians, v, 1.*

Man's life on earth is a warfare.—*Vulgate, O. T., Job, vii, 1.*

For what is your life? It is even a vapour, that appeareth for a little time, and then vanisheth away.—*N. T., James, iv, 14.*

He was a burning and a shining light.—*N. T., John, v, 35.*

They made light of it.—*N. T., Matthew, xxii, 5.*

And God said, Let there be light: and there was light.—*O. T., Genesis, i, 3.*

I am the light of the world.—*N. T., John, viii, 12.*

Consider the lilies of the field, how they grow; they toil not, neither do they spin: And yet I say unto you, That even Solomon in all his glory was not arrayed like one of these.—*N. T., Matthew, vi, 28, 29; Luke, xii, 27.*

As a lily among thorns, so is my love among thy daughters.—*O. T., Song of Solomon, ii, 2.*

Bold as a lion.—*O. T., Proverbs, xxviii, 1.*

A man of unclean lips.—*O. T., Isaiah, vi, 5.*

Let your loins be girded about, and your lights burning.—*N. T., Luke, xii, 35.*

Greater love hath no man than this, that a man lay down his life for his friends.—*N. T., John, xv, 13.*

Many waters can not quench love, neither can the floods drown it.—*O. T., Song of Solomon, viii, 7.*

Perfect love casteth out fear.—*N. T., John, iv, 18.*

Love is strong as death.—*O. T., Song of Solomon, viii, 6.*

Not greedy of filthy lucre.—*N. T., I Timothy, iii, 3.*

M

Ye cannot serve God and mammon.—*N. T., Matthew, vi, 24; Luke, xvi, 13.*

God created man in his own image, in the image of God created he him.—*O. T., Genesis, i, 27.*

Cease ye from man, whose breath is in his nostrils.—*O. T., Isaiah, ii, 22.*

Man being in honour abideth not: he is like the beasts that perish.—*O. T., Psalms, xlix, 12, 20.*

As for man his days are as grass: as a flower of the field, so he flourisheth. The wind passeth over it, and it is gone; and the place thereof shall know it no more.—*O. T., Psalms, ciii, 15, 16.*

Man that is born of a woman is of few days, and full of trouble. He cometh forth like a flower, and is cut down: he fleeth also as a shadow, and continueth not.—*O. T., Job, xiv, 1, 2.*

It is not good that man should be alone.—*O. T., Genesis, ii, 18.*

What . . . God hath joined together, let not man put asunder.—*N. T., Matthew, xix, 6.*

It is better to marry than to burn.—*N. T., I Corinthians, vii, 9.*

No man can serve two masters.—*N. T., Matthew, vi, 24.*

Be strong, and quit yourselves like men.—*O. T., I Samuel, iv, 9.*

Is any merry? let him sing psalms.—*N. T., James, v, 13.*

How are the mighty fallen.—*O. T., II Samuel, i, 19.*

His heart is . . . as hard as a piece of the nether millstone.—*O. T., Job, xli, 24.*

Clothed, and in his right mind.—*N. T., Mark, v, 15; Luke, viii, 35.*

All of one mind.—*N. T., I Peter, iii, 8.*

The love of money is the root of all evil.—*N. T., I Timothy, vi, 10.*

As is the mother, so is her daughter.—*O. T., Ezekiel, xvi, 44.*

Out of thine own mouth will I judge thee.—*N. T., Luke, xix, 22.*

N

And they were both naked, the man and his wife, and were not ashamed.—*O. T., Genesis, ii, 25.*

Naked came I out of my mother's womb, and naked shall I return thither: the Lord gave and the Lord hath taken away; blessed be the name of the Lord.—*O. T., Job, i, 21.*

The thing that hath been, it is that which shall be, and that which is done is that which shall be done: and there is no new thing under the sun.—*O. T., Ecclesiastes, i, 9.*

The night cometh when no man can work.—*N. T., John, ix, 9.*

Nimrod the mighty hunter before the Lord.—*O. T., Genesis, x, 9.*

Clearer than the noonday.—*O. T., Job, xi, 17.*

O

The people arose as one man.—*O. T., Judges, xx, 8.*

Set thine house in order.—*O. T., Isaiah, xxxviii, 1.*

P

The parting of the way.—*O. T., Ezekiel, xxi, 21.*

Thou shalt not pass.—*O. T., Numbers, xx, 18.*

He maketh me to lie down in green pastures.—*O. T., Psalms, xxiii, 2.*

Peace be to you [Pax vobiscum].—*O. T., Genesis, xliii, 23, etc.*

The peace of God, which passeth all understanding.—*N. T., Philippians, iv, 7.*

Glory to God in the highest, and on earth peace, good will toward men.—*N. T., Luke, ii, 14.*

Peace, peace; when there is no peace.—*O. T., Jeremiah, vi, 14; viii, 11.*

Her ways are the ways of pleasantness, and all her paths are peace.—*O. T., Proverbs, iii, 17.*

Give not that which is holy unto the dogs, neither cast ye your pearls before swine, lest they trample them under their feet, and turn again and rend you.—*N. T., Matthew, vii, 6.*

Written with a pen of iron, and with the point of a diamond.—*O. T., Jeremiah, xvii, 1.*

Physician, heal thyself.—*N. T., Luke, iv, 23.*

They were strangers and pilgrims on the earth.—*N. T., Hebrews, xi, 13.*

The Lord went before them by day in a pillar of cloud, to lead them the way; and by night in a pillar of fire.—*O. T., Exodus, xiii, 21.*

He that diggeth a pit shall fall into it.—*O. T., Ecclesiastes, x, 8.*

Ye have the poor always with you.—*N. T., Matthew, xxvi, 11; Mark, xiv, 7; John, xii, 8.*

He that hath pity upon the poor lendeth unto the Lord.—*O. T., Proverbs, xix, 17.*

What mean ye that ye beat my people to pieces and grind the faces of the poor?—*O. T., Isaiah, iii, 15.*

How agree the kettle and the earthen pot together?—*Apocrypha, Ecclesiasticus, xiii, 2.*

There is death in the pot.—*O. T., II Kings, iv, 40.*

Esau selleth his birthright for a mess of pottage.—*O. T., Genesis, heading of Chapter xxv in Genevan version, published in 1537.*

Hath not the potter power over the clay, of the same lump to make one vessel unto honour and another unto dishonour?—*N. T., Romans, ix, 21.*

The powers that be are ordained of God.—*N. T., Romans, xiii, 1.*

It is hard for thee to kick against the pricks.—*N. T., Acts, xxvi, 14.*

Pride goeth before destruction, and a haughty spirit before a fall.—*O. T., Proverbs, xvi, 18.*

A prophet is not without honour, save in his own country, and in his own house.—*N. T., Matthew, xiii, 57; Mark, vi, 4; Luke, iv, 24; John, iv, 44.*

And the publican, standing afar off, would not lift up so much as his eyes unto heaven, but smote upon his breast, saying, God be merciful to me a sinner.—*N. T., Luke, xviii, 13.*

Q

Simon Peter said unto him, Lord, whither goest thou [Quo vadis, Domine]?—*N. T., John, xiii, 36.*

R

The race is not to the swift, nor the battle to the strong.—*O. T., Ecclesiastes, ix, 11.*

He maketh the sun to rise on the evil and on the good, and sendeth rain on the just and on the unjust.—*N. T., Matthew, v, 45.*

Thou trusteth in the staff of this broken reed.—*O. T., Isaiah, xxxvi, 6.*

Joy shall be in heaven over one sinner that repenteth, more than over ninety and nine just persons, which need no repentance.—*N. T., Luke, xv, 7.*

God is no respecter of persons.—*N. T., Acts, x, 34.*

It is easier for a camel to go through the eye of a needle, than for a rich man to enter into the kingdom of God.—*N. T., Matthew, xix, 24.*

Riches certainly make themselves wings; they fly away as an eagle toward heaven.—*O. T., Proverbs, xxiii, 5.*

It was founded upon a rock.—*N. T., Matthew, vii, 25; Luke, vi, 48.*

He that spareth his rod hateth his son.—*O. T., Proverbs, xiii, 24.*

Let us crown ourselves with rosebuds before they be withered.—*Apocrypha, Wisdom of Solomon, ii, 8.*

Make it plain upon the tables, that he may run that readeth it.—*O. T., Habakkuk, ii, 2.*

S

Let your speech be always with grace, seasoned with salt.—*N. T., Colossians, iv, 6.*

Ye are the salt of the earth: but if the salt have lost his savour, wherewith shall it be salted?—*N. T., Matthew, v, 13.*

His [Lot's] wife looked back from behind him, and she became a pillar of salt.—*O. T., Genesis, xix, 26.*

And every one that heareth these sayings of mine and doeth them not, shall be likened unto a foolish man, which built his house upon the sand: And the rain descended, and the floods came, and the winds blew, and beat upon that house; and it fell: and great was the fall of it.—*N. T., Matthew, vii, 26, 27.*

Get thee behind me, Satan.—*N. T., Matthew, xvi, 23.*

Vain babblings, and oppositions of science falsely so called.—*N. T., I Timothy, vi, 20.*

My father hath chastised you with whips, but I will chastise you with scorpions.—*O. T., I Kings, xii, 11; II Chronicles, x, 14.*

The sea gave up the dead which were in it.—*N. T., Revelation, xx, 13.*

They that go down to the sea in ships.—*O. T., Psalms, cvii, 23.*

In season, out of season.—*N. T., II Timothy, iv, 2.*

The seat of the scornful.—*O. T., Psalms, i, 1.*

Stolen waters are sweet, and bread eaten in secret is pleasant.—*O. T., Proverbs, ix, 17.*

Now the serpent was more subtle than any beast of the field.—*O. T., Genesis, iii, 1.*

Well done, thou good and faithful servant.—*N. T., Matthew, xxv, 21.*

He that is greatest among you shall be your servant.—*N. T., Matthew, xxiii, 11.*

As sheep that have not a shepherd.—*O. T., I Kings, xxii, 17.*

He shall separate them one from another, as a shepherd divideth his sheep from the goats.—*N. T., Matthew, xxv, 32.*

The men of Gilead said unto him, Art thou an Ephraimite? If he said Nay; then said they unto him, Say now Shibboleth: and he said Sibboleth: for he could not frame to pronounce it right. Then they took him, and slew him.—*O. T., Judges, xii, 5, 6.*

Whose shoe's latchet I am not worthy to unloose.—*N. T., John, i, 27.*

My days are swifter than a weaver's shuttle.—*O. T., Job, ix, 25.*

Signs of the times.—*N. T., Matthew, xvi, 3.*

Your sin will find you out.—*O. T., Numbers, xxxii, 23.*

Skin for skin, yea, all that a man hath will he give for his life.—*O. T., Job, ii, 4.*

He saith among the trumpets, Ha, ha; and he smelleth the battle afar off, the thunder of the captains and the shouting.—*O. T., Job, xxxix, 25.*

He is despised and rejected of men: a man of sorrows, and acquainted with grief.—*O. T., Isaiah, liii, 3.*

What is a man profited, if he shall gain the whole world and lose his own soul?—*N. T., Matthew, xvi, 26.*

Whatsoever a man soweth, that shall he also reap.—*N. T., Galatians, vi, 7.*

Man is born unto trouble, as the sparks fly upward.—*O. T., Job, v, 7.*

Are not two sparrows sold for a farthing? and one of them shall not fall to the ground without your Father.—*N. T., Matthew, xi, 29.*

A spectacle unto the world, and to angels.—*N. T., I Corinthians, iv, 9.*

A wounded spirit who can bear?—*O. T., Proverbs, xviii, 14.*

The ornament of a meek and quiet spirit.—*N. T., Peter, iii, 4.*

I have broken the staff of your bread.—*O. T., Leviticus, xxvi, 26.*

Leave not a stain in thine honour.—*Apocrypha, Ecclesiasticus, xxxiii, 22*

When the morning stars sang together, and all the sons of God shouted for joy.—*O. T., Job, xxxviii, 7.*

A stiff-necked people.—*O. T., Exodus, xxxiii, 3.*

Use a little wine for thy stomach's sake.—*N. T., Timothy, v, 23.*

He that is without sin among you, let him cast the first stone.—*N. T., John, viii, 7.*

I was a stranger, and ye took me in.—*N. T., Matthew, xxv, 35.*

My strength is made perfect in weakness.—*N. T., II Corinthians, xii, 9.*

A man of strife and a man of contention.—*O. T., Jeremiah, xv, 10.*

Stumbling-block.—*N. T., Romans, xiv, 13.*

In the sweat of thy face shalt thou eat bread.—*O. T., Genesis, iii, 19.*

They shall beat their swords into ploughshares, and their spears into pruning-hooks: nation shall not lift up sword against nation, neither shall they learn war any more.—*O. T., Isaiah, ii, 4; Joel, iii, 10; Micah, iv, 3.*

T

The earthy tabernacle weigheth down the mind that museth upon many things.—*Apocrypha, Wisdom of Solomon, ix, 15.*

We spend our years as a tale that is told.—*O. T., Psalms, xc, 9.*

Their words seemed to them as idle tales.—*N. T., Luke, xxiv, 11.*

I was afraid, and went and hid thy talent in the earth.—*N. T., Matthew, xxv, 25.*

O that my head were waters, and mine eyes a fountain of tears.—*O. T., Jeremiah, ix, 1.*

Weeping and gnashing of teeth.—*N. T., Matthew, xxii, 13.*

I am escaped with the skin of my teeth.—*O. T., Job, xix, 20.*

A thorn in the flesh.—*N. T., II Corinthians, xii, 7.*

Which of you with taking thought can add to his stature one cubit?—*N. T., Luke, xii, 25.*

Hast thou given the horse strength? hast thou clothed his neck with thunder?—*O. T., Job, xxxix, 19.*

How beautiful upon the mountains are the feet of him that bringeth good tidings.—*O. T., Isaiah, lii, 7.*

To every thing there is a season, and a time to every purpose under heaven.—*O. T., Ecclesiastes, iii, 1.*

The tongue can no man tame; it is an unruly evil.—*N. T., James, iii, 8.*

If I do not remember thee, let my tongue cleave to the roof of my mouth.—*O. T., Psalms, cxxxvii, 6.*

The strife of tongues.—*O. T., Psalms, xxxi, 20.*

Touch not; taste not; handle not.—*N. T., Colossians, ii, 21.*

The name of the Lord is a strong tower.—*O. T., Proverbs, xviii, 10.*

The way of transgressors is hard.—*O. T., Proverbs, xiii, 15.*

Lay up for yourselves treasures in heaven, where neither moth nor rust doth corrupt and where thieves do not break through nor steal.—*N. T., Matthew, vi, 20.*

The tree of life.—*O. T., Genesis, ii, 9; Proverbs, xiii, 12; xv, 4.*

Spreading himself like a green bay tree.—*O. T., Psalms, xxxvii, 35.*

The righteous shall flourish like the palm tree: he shall grow like a cedar of Lebanon.—*O. T., Psalms, xcii, 12.*

If the trumpet give an uncertain sound, who shall prepare himself to the battle?—*N. T., I Corinthians, xiv, 8.*

The truth shall make you free.—*N. T., John, viii, 32.*

In the twinkling of an eye.—*N. T., I Corinthians, xv, 52.*

V

All is vanity and vexation of spirit.—*O. T., Ecclesiastes, i, 14.*

We preach not ourselves, but Christ Jesus the Lord. . . . But we have this treasure in earthen vessels, that the excellency of the power may be of God, and not of us.—*N. T., II Corinthians, iv, 5, 7.*

A still small voice.—*O. T., Kings, xix, 12.*

His voice is as the sound of many waters.—*N. T., Revelation, i, 15.*

The voice of him that crieth in the wilderness.—*O. T., Isaiah, xl, 3.*

W

The wages of sin is death.—*N. T., Romans, vi, 23.*

Wars and rumours of wars.—*N. T., Matthew, xxiv, 6.*

Watch and pray.—*N. T., Matthew, xxvi, 41; Mark, xiii, 33; xiv, 33; Luke, xxii, 40, 46.*

Watchman, what of the night?—*O. T., Isaiah, xxi, 11.*

The younger son gathered all together, and took his journey into a far country, and there wasted his substance with riotous living.—*N. T., Luke, xv, 13.*

Unstable as water.—*O. T., Genesis, xlix, 4.*

As water spilt on the ground, which cannot be gathered up again.—*O. T., II Samuel, xiv, 14.*

The waters wear the stones.—*O. T., Job, xiv, 19.*

He leadeth me beside the still waters. —*O. T., Psalms, xxiii, 2.*

I am going the way of all the earth. —*O. T., Joshua, xxiii, 14.*

I shall go the way whence I shall not return.—*O. T., Job, xvi, 22.*

There be three things which are too wonderful for me, yea, four which I know not: the way of an eagle in the air; the way of a serpent upon a rock; the way of a ship in the midst of the sea; and the way of a man with a maid. —*O. T., Proverbs, xxx, 18, 19.*

For my thoughts are not your thoughts, neither are your ways my ways.—*O. T., Isaiah, lv, 8.*

Be not weary in well-doing.—*N. T., II Thessalonians, iii, 13.*

Their appearance and their work were as it were a wheel in the middle of a wheel.—*O. T., Ezekiel, i, 16.*

They have sown the wind, and they shall reap the whirlwind.—*O. T., Hosea, viii, 7.*

The wife of thy bosom.—*O. T., Deuteronomy, xiii, 6.*

Giving honour unto the wife, as unto the weaker vessel.—*N. T., I Peter, iii, 7.*

Therefore shall a man leave his father and his mother, and shall cleave unto his wife: and they shall be one flesh.— *O. T., Genesis, ii, 24.*

Whoso findeth a wife findeth a good thing.—*O. T., Proverbs, xviii, 22.*

The wind bloweth where it listeth.— *N. T., John, iii, 8.*

The speeches of one that is desperate, which are as wind.—*O. T., Job, vi, 26.*

Neither do men put new wine into old bottles: else the bottles break, and the wine runneth out, and the bottles perish.—*N. T., Matthew, ix, 17.*

Unto you that fear my name shall the Sun of righteousness arise with healing in his wings.—*O. T., Malachi, iv, 2.*

If I take the wings of the morning, and dwell in the uttermost parts of the sea.—*O. T., Psalms, cxxxix, 9.*

He did fly upon the wings of the wind. —*O. T., Psalms, xviii, 10.*

The price of wisdom is above rubies. —*O. T., Job, xxviii, 18.*

Wisdom crieth without; she uttereth her voice in the streets.—*O. T., Proverbs, i, 20.*

Wisdom is the gray hair unto men, and an unspotted life is old age.— *Apocrypha, Wisdom of Solomon, iv, 9.*

They . . . are at their wit's end.— *O. T., Psalms, cvii, 27.*

The wolf also shall dwell with the lamb, and the leopard shall lie down with the kid.—*O. T., Isaiah, xi, 6.*

Beware of false prophets, which come to you in sheep's clothing, but inwardly they are ravening wolves.—*N. T., Matthew, vii, 15.*

A virtuous woman is a crown to her husband.—*O. T., Proverbs, xii, 4.*

It is better to dwell in the corner of a housetop than with a brawling woman in a wide house.—*O. T., Proverbs, xxi, 9.*

One man among a thousand have I found; but a woman among all those have I not found.—*O. T., Ecclesiastes, vii, 28.*

A continual dropping in a very rainy day and a contentious woman are alike. —*O. T., Proverbs, xxvii, 15.*

As a jewel of gold in a swine's snout, so is a fair woman which is without discretion.—*O. T., Proverbs, xi, 22.*

Seek me a woman that hath a familiar spirit.—*O. T., I Samuel, xxviii, 7.*

Let your women keep silence in the churches.—*N. T., I Corinthians, xiv, 34.*

The words of his mouth were smoother than butter, but war was in his heart: his words were softer than oil, yet were they drawn swords.—*O. T., Psalms, lv, 21.*

The words of the wise are as goads.— *O. T., Ecclesiastes, xii, 11.*

If any would not work, neither should he eat.—*N. T., II Thessalonians, iii, 10.*

Their works do follow them.—*N. T., Revelation, xiv, 13.*

World without end.—*O. T., Isaiah, xlv, 17.*

Unspotted from the world.—*N. T., James, i, 27.*

The children of this world are in their generation wiser than the children of light.—*N. T., Luke, xvi, 8.*

Her end is bitter as wormwood.— *O. T., Proverbs, v, 4.*

Flee from the wrath to come.—*N. T., Matthew, iii, 7.*

In the same hour came forth fingers of a man's hand, and wrote over against the candlestick upon the plaister of the wall of the king's palace. . . . And this is the writing that was written, MENE, MENE, TEKEL, UPHARSIN.—*O. T., Daniel, v, 5, 25.*

What I have written I have written. —*N. T., John, xix, 22.*

Y

Let your yea be yea; and your nay, nay.—*N. T., James, v, 12.*

The days of our years are three-score years and ten.—*O. T., Psalms, xc, 10.*

From the womb of the morning: thou hast the dew of thy youth.—*O. T., Psalms, cx, 3.*

BIGOTRY.—The mind of the bigot is like the pupil of the eye; the more light you pour upon it, the more it will contract.—*O. W. Holmes.*

The bigot sees religion, not as a sphere, but a line; and it is the line in which he is moving. He is like an African buffalo—sees right forward, but nothing on the right or the left. He would not perceive a legion of angels or devils at the distance of ten yards, on the one side or the other.—*John Foster.*

Bigotry has no head, and cannot think; no heart, and cannot feel. When she moves, it is in wrath; when she pauses it is amidst ruin; her prayers are curses—her God is a demon—her communion is death.—*O'Connell.*

There is no bigotry like that of "free thought" run to seed.—*Horace Greeley.*

Bigotry murders religion to frighten fools with her ghost.—*Colton.*

There is no tariff so injurious as that with which sectarian bigotry guards its commodities.—It dwarfs the soul by shutting out truths from other continents of thought, and checks the circulation of its own.—*E. H. Chapin.*

When once a man is determined to believe, the very absurdity of the doctrine does but confirm him in his faith.—*Junius.*

A man must be both stupid and uncharitable who believes there is no virtue or truth but on his own side.—*Addison.*

The bigot for the most part clings to opinions adopted without investigation, and defended without argument, while he is intolerant of the opinions of others.—*Buck.*

BIOGRAPHY.—Biography is the personal and home aspect of history.—*Wilmott.*

One of the new terrors of death.—*John Arbuthnot* (referring to catchpenny lives of eminent men issued immediately after the subjects' death by Edmund Curll).

The poor dear dead have been laid out in vain; turned into cash, they are laid out again.—*Thomas Hood.*

Now the Poet cannot die, nor leave his music as of old, but round him ere he scarce be cold begins the scandal and the cry.—*Alfred Lord Tennyson.*

The best teachers of humanity are the lives of great men.—*Orson Squire Fowler.*

Great men have often the shortest biographies.—Their real life is in their books or deeds.

There is properly no history, only biography.—*Emerson.*

One anecdote of a man is worth a volume of biography.—*William Ellery Channing.*

The remains of great and good men, like Elijah's mantle, ought to be gathered up and preserved by their survivors; that as their works follow them in the reward of them, they may stay behind in their benefit.—*M. Henry.*

Most biographies are of little worth. —They are panegyrics, not lives.—The object is, not to let down the hero; and consequently what is most human, most genuine, most characteristic in his history, is excluded.—No department of literature is so false as biography.—*William Ellery Channing.*

Rich as we are in biography, a well-written life is almost as rare as a well-spent one; and there are certainly many more men whose history deserves to be recorded than persons able and willing to furnish the record.—*Carlyle.*

To be ignorant of the lives of the most celebrated men of antiquity is to continue in a state of childhood all our days.—*Plutarch.*

A life that is worth writing at all, is worth writing minutely and truthfully. —*Longfellow.*

Biography, especially of the great and good, who have risen by their own exertions to eminence and usefulness, is an inspiring and ennobling study.—Its direct tendency is to reproduce the excellence it records.—*H. Mann.*

Of all studies, the most delightful and useful is biography.—The seeds of great events lie near the surface; historians delve too deep for them.—No history was ever true; but lives which I have read, if they were not, had the appearance, the interest, the utility of truth.—*Landor.*

Biography is the most universally pleasant and profitable of all reading.—*Carlyle.*

Those only who live with a man can

write his life with any genuine exactness and discrimination, and few people who have lived with a man know what to remark about him.—*Johnson.*

Biographies of great, but especially of good men, are most instructive and useful as helps, guides, and incentives to others. Some of the best are almost equivalent to gospels—teaching high living, high thinking, and energetic actions for their own and the world's good.—*S. Smiles.*

History can be formed from permanent monuments and records; but lives can only be written from personal knowledge, which is growing every day less, and in a short time is lost forever.—*Johnson.*

My advice is, to consult the lives of other men as we would a looking-glass, and from thence fetch examples for our own imitation.—*Terence.*

BIRTH. — (See "ANCESTRY," and "GENEALOGY.")

Our birth is nothing but our death begun, as tapers waste the moment they take fire.—*Young.*

Custom forms us all; our thoughts, our morals, our most fixed belief, are consequences of the place of our birth. —*Hill.*

What is birth to a man if it be a stain to his dead ancestors to have left such an offspring?—*Sir P. Sidney.*

A noble birth and fortune, though they make not a bad man good, yet they are a real advantage to a worthy one, and place his virtues in the fairest light.—*Lillo.*

High birth is a gift of fortune which should never challenge esteem toward those who receive it, since it costs them neither study nor labor.—*Bruyere.*

Of all vanities and fopperies, the vanity of high birth is the greatest. True nobility is derived from virtue, not from birth. Titles, indeed, may be purchased; but virtue is the only coin that makes the bargain valid.—*Burton.*

Distinguished birth is indeed an honor to him who lives worthily of the virtue of his progenitors. If, as Seneca says, "Virtue is the only nobility," he is doubly a nobleman who is not only descended from a virtuous ancestry, but is himself virtuous.

When real nobleness accompanies the imaginary one of birth, the imaginary seems to mix with the real and become real too.—*Greville.*

Those who have nothing else to recommend them to the respect of others but only their blood, cry it up at a great rate, and have their mouths perpetually full of it.—By this mark they commonly distinguish themselves; but you may depend upon it there is no good bottom, nothing of the true worth of their own when they insist so much and set their credit on that of others.—*Charron.*

I have learned to judge of men by their own deeds, and not to make the accident of birth the standard of their merit.—*Mrs. Hale.*

Features alone do not run in the blood; vices and virtues, genius and folly, are transmitted through the same sure but unseen channel.—*Hazlitt.*

BLESSEDNESS. — True blessedness consisteth in a good life and a happy death.—*Solon.*

Nothing raises the price of a blessing like its removal; whereas, it was its continuance which should have taught us its value.—*H. Moore.*

Blessings we enjoy daily, and for the most of them, because they be so common, men forget to pay their praises.— But let not us, because it is a sacrifice so pleasing to him who still protects us, and gives us flowers, and showers, and meat, and content.—*Izaak Walton.*

Reflect upon your present blessings, of which every man has many: not on your past misfortunes, of which all men have some.—*Dickens.*

The beloved of the Almighty are the rich who have the humility of the poor, and the poor who have the magnanimity of the rich.—*Saadi.*

Let me tell you that every misery I miss is a new blessing.—*Izaak Walton.*

There are three requisites to the proper enjoyment of earthly blessings: a thankful reflection, on the goodness of the giver; a deep sense of our own unworthiness; and a recollection of the uncertainty of our long possessing them. —The first will make us grateful; the second, humble; and the third, moderate.—*Hannah More.*

Blessings ever wait on virtuous deeds,

and though a late, a sure reward succeeds.—*Congreve.*

It is generally true that all that is required to make men unmindful of what they owe to God for any blessing, is, that they should receive that blessing often and regularly.—*Whately.*

How blessings brighten as they take their flight!—*Young.*

Health, beauty, vigor, riches, and all the other things called goods, operate equally as evils to the vicious and unjust, as they do as benefits to the just.—*Plato.*

The good things of life are not to be had singly, but come to us with a mixture; like a schoolboy's holiday, with a task affixed to the tail of it.—*Charles Lamb.*

Blessedness consists in the acomplishment of our desires, and in our having only regular desires.—*Augustine.*

BLOCKHEAD. — (See "COMMON SENSE.")

A blockhead cannot come in, nor go away, nor sit, nor rise, nor stand, like a man of sense.—*Bruyere.*

There never was any party, faction, sect, or cabal whatsoever, in which the most ignorant were not the most violent; for a bee is not a busier animal than a blockhead.—*Pope.*

Heaven and earth fight in vain against a dunce.—*Schiller.*

BLUSH.—A blush is the color of virtue.—*Diogenes.*

Whoever blushes seems to be good.—*Menander.*

Whoever blushes, is already guilty; true innocence is ashamed of nothing.—*Rousseau.*

The ambiguous livery worn alike by modesty and shame.—*Balfour.*

When a girl ceases to blush, she has lost the most powerful charm of her beauty.—*Gregory.*

A blush is beautiful, but often inconvenient.—*Goldoni.*

A blush is a sign that nature hangs out, to show where chastity and honor dwell.—*Gotthold.*

Better a blush on the face than a blot on the heart.—*Cervantes.*

The man that blushes is not quite a brute.—*Young.*

Men blush less for their crimes, than for their weaknesses and vanity.—*Bruyere.*

Blushing is the livery of virtue, though it may sometimes proceed from guilt.—*Bacon.*

It is better for a young man to blush, than to turn pale.—*Cicero.*

The blush is nature's alarm at the approach of sin, and her testimony to the dignity of virtue.—*Fuller.*

The troubled blood through his pale face was seen to come and go with tidings from his heart, as it a running messenger had been.—*Spenser.*

The inconvenience, or the beauty of the blush, which is the greater? — *Madame Neckar.*

Playful blushes, that seem but luminous escapes of thought.—*Moore.*

BLUSTERING. — A killing tongue, but a quiet sword.—*Shakespeare.*

A brave man is sometimes a desperado; but a bully is always a coward.—*Haliburton.*

It is with narrow souled people as with narrow necked bottles; the less they have in them, the more noise they make in pouring it out.—*Pope.*

There are braying men in the world as well as braying asses; for what is loud and senseless talking other than a way of braying.—*L'Estrange.*

They that are loudest in their threats are the weakest in the execution of them.—It is probable that he who is killed by lightning hears no noise; but the thunder-clap which follows, and which most alarms the ignorant, is the surest proof of their safety.—*Colton.*

Commonly they whose tongue is their weapon, use their feet for defense.—*Sir P. Sidney.*

BOASTING.—We wound our modesty and make foul the clearness of our deservings, when of ourselves we publish them.—*Shakespeare.*

Where boasting ends, there dignity begins.—*Young.*

Where there is much pretension, much has been borrowed; nature never pretends.—*Lavater.*

There is this benefit in brag, that the speaker is unconsciously expressing his own ideal.—Humor him by all means;

draw it all out, and hold him to it.—*Emerson.*

Who knows himself a braggart, let him fear this; for it will come to pass that every braggart shall be found an ass.—*Shakespeare.*

Men of real merit, whose noble and glorious deeds we are ready to acknowledge are not yet to be endured when they vaunt their own actions.—*Æschines.*

Usually the greatest boasters are the smallest workers. The deep rivers pay a larger tribute to the sea than shallow brooks, and yet empty themselves with less noise.—*W. Secker.*

With all his tumid boasts, he's like the sword-fish, who only wears his weapon in his mouth.—*Madden.*

Conceit, more rich in matter than in words, brags of his substance: they are but beggars who can count their worth.—*Shakespeare.*

A gentleman that loves to hear himself talk, will speak more in a minute than he will stand to in a month.—*Shakespeare.*

Self-laudation abounds among the unpolished, but nothing can stamp a man more sharply as ill-bred.—*Charles Buxton.*

Lord Bacon told Sir Edward Coke when he was boasting, "The less you speak of your greatness, the more shall I think of it."

The empty vessel makes the greatest sound.—*Shakespeare.*

BODY.—Our bodies are but dust, but they can bring praise to him that formed them.—Dull and tuneless in themselves, they can become glorious harps on which the music of piety may be struck to heaven.—*Punshon.*

Can any honor exceed that which has been conferred on the human body?—Can any powers exceed the powers—any glory exceed the glory with which it is invested?—No wonder the apostle should beseech men to present their bodies a living sacrifice to God.—*Pulsford.*

Our body is a well-set clock, which keeps good time, but if it be too much or indiscreetly tampered with, the alarum runs out before the hour.—*Bp. Hall.*

It is shameful for a man to rest in ignorance of the structure of his own body, especially when the knowledge of it mainly conduces to his welfare, and directs his application of his own powers.—*Melancthon.*

God made the human body, and it is the most exquisite and wonderful organization which has come to us from the divine hand.—It is a study for one's whole life.—If an undevout astronomer is mad, an undevout physiologist is madder.—*H. W. Beecher.*

If there be anything common to us by nature, it is the members of our corporeal frame; yet the apostle taught that these, guided by the spirit as its instruments, and obeying a holy will, become transfigured, so that, in his language, the body becomes a temple of the Holy Ghost, and the meanest faculties, the lowest appetites, the humblest organs are ennobled by the spirit mind which guides them.—*F. W. Robertson.*

BOLDNESS.—We make way for the man who boldly pushes past us.—*Bovee.*

Boldness is ever blind, for it sees not dangers and inconveniences; whence it is bad in council though good in execution.—The right use of the bold, therefore, is, that they never command in chief, but serve as seconds under the direction of others.—For in council it is good to see dangers, and in execution not to see them unless they be very great.—*Bacon.*

Fools rush in where angels fear to tread.—*Pope.*

Who bravely dares must sometimes risk a fall.—*Smollett.*

Carried away by the irresistible influence which is always exercised over men's minds by a bold resolution in critical circumstances.—*Guizot.*

Fortune befriends the bold.—*Dryden.*

It is wonderful what strength of purpose and boldness and energy of will are roused by the assurance that we are doing our duty.—*Scott.*

BOOKS.—A book is the only immortality.—*R. Choate.*

Books are lighthouses erected in the great sea of time.—*E. P. Whipple.*

Books are embalmed minds.—*Bovee.*

A good book is the very essence of a

good man.—His virtues survive in it, while the foibles and faults of his actual life are forgotten.—All the goodly company of the excellent and great sit around my table, or look down on me from yonder shelves, waiting patiently to answer my questions and enrich me with their wisdom.—A precious book is a foretaste of immortality.—*T. L. Cuyler.*

Books are immortal sons deifying their sires.—*Plato.*

I love to lose myself in other men's minds. When I am not walking, I am reading. I cannot sit and think; books think for me.—*Charles Lamb.*

God be thanked for books; they are the voices of the distant and the dead, and make us heirs of the spiritual life of past ages.—*Channing.*

If a book come from the heart it will contrive to reach other hearts.—All art and authorcraft are of small account to that.—*Carlyle.*

Tradition is but a meteor, which, if it once falls, cannot be rekindled.—Memory, once interrupted, is not to be recalled.—But written learning is a fixed luminary, which, after the cloud that had hidden it has passed away, is again bright in its proper station.—So books are faithful repositories, which may be awhile neglected or forgotten, but when opened again, will again impart instruction.—*Johnson.*

Books are the metempsychosis; the symbol and presage of immortality.—The dead are scattered, and none shall find them; but behold they are here.—*H. W. Beecher.*

Books are standing counselors and preachers, always at hand, and always disinterested; having this advantage over oral instructors, that they are ready to repeat their lesson as often as we please.—*Chambers.*

Books are masters who instruct us without rods or ferules, without words or anger, without bread or money. If you approach them, they are not asleep; if you seek them, they do not hide; if you blunder, they do not scold; if you are ignorant, they do not laugh at you.—*Richard de Bury.*

Some books are to be tasted; others swallowed; and some few to be chewed and digested.—*Bacon.*

Except a living man there is nothing more wonderful than a book! a message to us from the dead—from human souls we never saw, who lived, perhaps, thousands of miles away. And yet these, in those little sheets of paper, speak to us, arouse us, terrify us, teach us, comfort us, open their hearts to us as brothers.—*Charles Kingsley.*

Books are those faithful mirrors that reflect to our mind the minds of sages and heroes.—*Gibbon.*

Books, like friends, should be few and well chosen. Like friends, too, we should return to them again and again—for, like true friends, they will never fail us—never cease to instruct—never cloy—

Next to acquiring good friends, the best acquisition is that of good books.—*Colton.*

A good book is the best of friends, the same to-day and forever.—*Tupper.*

Without books, God is silent, justice dormant, natural science at a stand, philosophy lame, letters dumb, and all things involved in darkness.—*Bartholini.*

Books are not absolutely dead things, but do contain a certain potency of life in them, to be as active as the soul whose progeny they are; they preserve, as in a vial, the purest efficacy and extraction of the living intellect that bred them.—*Milton.*

My books kept me from the ring, the dog-pit, the tavern, and the saloon.—The associate of Pope and Addison, the mind accustomed to the noble though silent discourse of Shakespeare and Milton, will hardly seek or put up with low or evil company and slaves.—*Thomas Hood.*

A book may be compared to your neighbor: if it be good, it cannot last too long; if bad, you cannot get rid of it too early.—*Brooke.*

Books are the legacies that genius leaves to mankind, to be delivered down from generation to generation, as presents to those that are yet unborn.—*Addison.*

There is no book so poor that it would not be a prodigy if wholly wrought out by a single mind, without the aid of prior investigators.—*Johnson.*

The past but lives in written words: a thousand ages were blank if books had not evoked their ghosts, and kept the pale unbodied shades to warn us from fleshless lips.—*Bulwer*.

There is no book so bad but something valuable may ,be derived from it,—*Pliny*.

If all the crowns of Europe were placed at my disposal on condition that I should abandon my books and studies, I should spurn the crowns away and stand by the books.—*Fenelon*.

Books are a guide in youth, and an entertainment for age. They support us under solitude, and keep us from becoming a burden to ourselves. They help us to forget the crossness of men and things, compose our cares and our passions, and lay our disappointments asleep. When we are weary of the living, we may repair to the dead, who have nothing of peevishness, pride, or design in their conversation.—*Jeremy Collier*.

Books are but waste paper unless we spend in action the wisdom we get from thought.—*Bulwer*.

The books we read should be chosen with great care, that they may be, as an Egyptian king wrote over his library, " The medicines of the soul."

Be as careful of the books you read, as of the company you keep; for your habits and character will be as much influenced by the former as by the latter. —*Paxton Hood*.

When I get a little money, I buy books; and if any is left, I buy food and clothes.—*Erasmus*.

The silent influence of books, is a mighty power in the world; and there is a joy in reading them known only to those who read them with desire and enthusiasm.—Silent, passive, and noiseless though they be, they yet set in action countless multitudes, and change the order of nations.—*Giles*.

Books, like proverbs, receive their chief value from the stamp and esteem of the ages through which they have passed.—*Sir W. Temple*.

It is books that teach us to refine our pleasures when young, and to recall them with satisfaction when we are old.—*Leigh Hunt*.

A good book is the precious life-blood of a master-spirit, embalmed and treasured up on purpose for a life beyond.—*Milton*.

Books, to judicious compilers, are useful; to particular arts and professions, they are absolutely necessary; to men of real science, they are tools: but more are tools to them.—*Johnson*.

Books are the true levellers.—They give to all who faithfully use them, the society, the spiritual presence of the greatest and best of our race.—*Channing*.

Books that you may carry to the fireside, and hold readily in your hand, are the most useful after all.—*Johnson*.

There is no worse robber than a bad book.—*Italian Proverb*.

We are as liable to be corrupted by books, as by companions.—*Fielding*.

Some books, like the City of London, fare the better for being burned.—*Tom Brown*.

Few are sufficiently sensible of the importance of that economy in reading which selects, almost exclusively, the very first order of books. Why, except for some special reason, read an inferior book, at the very time you might be reading one of the highest order?—*John Foster*.

A bad book is the worse that it cannot repent.—It has not been the devil's policy to keep the masses of mankind in ignorance; but finding that they will read, he is doing all in his power to poison their books.—*E. N. Kirk*.

A good book, in the language of the book-sellers, is a salable one; in that of the curious, a scarce one; in that of men of sense, a useful and instructive one.—*Chambers*.

Bad books are like intoxicating drinks; they furnish neither nourishment, nor medicine.—Both improperly excite; the one the mind; the other the body.—The desire for each increases by being fed.—Both ruin; one the intellect; the other the health; and together, the soul.—The safeguard against each is the same—total abstinence from all that intoxicates either mind or body.—*Tryon Edwards*.

In good books is one of the best safeguards from evil.—Life's first danger has been said to be an empty mind which, like an unoccupied room, is open for base spirits to enter.—The taste for reading provides a pleasant and elevating preoccupation.—*H. W. Grout*.

When a book raises your spirit, and inspires you with noble and manly thoughts, seek for no other test of its excellence.—It is good, and made by a good workman.—*Bruyere.*

Choose an author as you choose a friend.—*Roscommon.*

In books, it is the chief of all perfections to be plain and brief.—*Butler.*

To use books rightly, is to go to them for help; to appeal to them when our own knowledge and power fail; to be led by them into wider sight and purer conception than our own, and to receive from them the united sentence of the judges and councils of all time, against our solitary and unstable opinions.—*Ruskin.*

The best books for a man are not always those which the wise recommend, but often those which meet the peculiar wants, the natural thirst of his mind, and therefore awaken interest and rivet thought.—*Channing.*

Books (says Bacon) can never teach the use of books; the student must learn by commerce with mankind to reduce his speculations to practice. No man should think so highly of himself as to suppose he can receive but little light from books, nor so meanly as to believe he can discover nothing but what is to be learned from them.—*Johnson.*

If religious books are not widely circulated among the masses in this country, and the people do not become religious, I do not know what is to become of us as a nation. And the thought is one to cause solemn reflection on the part of every patriot and Christian. If truth be not diffused, error will be; if God and his word are not known and received, the devil and his works will gain the ascendancy; if the evangelical volume does not reach every hamlet, the pages of a corrupt and licentious literature will; if the power of the gospel is not felt through the length and breadth of the land, anarchy and misrule, degradation and misery, corruption and darkness, will reign without mitigation or end.—*Daniel Webster.*

Dead counsellors are the most instructive, because they are heard with patience and reverence.—*Johnson.*

A house without books is like a room without windows. No man has a right to bring up his children without surrounding them with books, if he has the means to buy them. It is a wrong to his family. Children learn to read by being in the presence of books. The love of knowledge comes with reading and grows upon it. And the love of knowledge, in a young mind, is almost a warrant against the inferior excitement of passions and vices.—*H. Mann.*

The constant habit of perusing devout books is so indispensable, that it has been termed the oil of the lamp of prayer. Too much reading, however, and too little meditation, may produce the effect of a lamp inverted; which is extinguished by the very excess of that aliment, whose property is to feed it. —*H. More.*

The books that help you most, are those which make you think the most. —The hardest way of learning is that of easy reading; but a great book that comes from a great thinker is a ship of thought, deep freighted with truth and beauty.—*Theodore Parker.*

There was a time when the world acted on books; now books act on the world.—*Joubert.*

To buy books only because they were published by an eminent printer, is much as if a man should buy clothes that did not fit him, only because made by some famous tailor.—*Pope.*

If a secret history of books could be written, and the author's private thoughts and meanings noted down alongside of his story, how many insipid volumes would become interesting, and dull tales excite the reader!—*Thackeray.*

The book to read is not the one which thinks for you, but the one which makes you think. No book in the world equals the Bible for that.—*McCosh.*

The best of a book is not the thought which it contains, but the thought which it suggests; just as the charm of music dwells not in the tones but in the echoes of our hearts.—*O. W. Holmes.*

There is a kind of physiognomy in the titles of books no less than in the faces of men, by which a skillful observer will know as well what to expect from the one as the other.—*Bp. Butler.*

Every man is a volume if you know how to read him.—*Channing.*

When a new book comes out I read an old one.—*Rogers.*

Thou mayst as well expect to grow stronger by always eating as wiser by always reading. Too much overcharges Nature, and turns more into disease than nourishment. 'Tis thought and digestion which make books serviceable, and give health and vigor to the mind. —*Fuller.*

That is a good book which is opened with expectation, and closed with delight and profit.—*A. B. Alcott.*

The most foolish kind of a book is a kind of leaky boat on the sea of wisdom; some of the wisdom will get in anyhow.—*O. W. Holmes.*

The books of Nature and of Revelation equally elevate our conceptions and invite our piety; they are both written by the finger of the one eternal, incomprehensible God.—*T. Watson.*

Books are men of higher stature; the only men that speak aloud for future times to hear.—*Barrett.*

The society of dead authors has this advantage over that of the living: they never flatter us to our faces, nor slander us behind our backs, nor intrude upon our privacy, nor quit their shelves until we take them down.—*Colton.*

A man who writes an immoral but immortal book may be tracked into eternity by a procession of lost souls from every generation, every one to be a witness against him at the judgment, to show to him and to the universe the immeasurableness of his iniquity.—*G. B. Cheever.*

Master books, but do not let them master you.—Read to live, not live to read.—*Bulwer.*

A book is a garden, an orchard, a storehouse, a party, a company by the way, a counsellor, a multitude of counsellors.—*H. W. Beecher.*

Most books, like their authors, are born to die; of only a few books can it be said that death hath no dominion over them; they live, and their influence lives forever.—*J. Swartz.*

Books should to one of these fours ends conduce, for wisdom, piety, delight, or use.—*Denham.*

Deep versed in books, but shallow in himself.—*Milton.*

We ought to reverence books; to look on them as useful and mighty things.—If they are good and true, whether they are about religion, politics, farming, trade, law, or medicine, they are the message of Christ, the maker of all things—the teacher of all truth.— *C. Kingsley.*

Books are the best of things if well used; if abused, among the worst.— They are good for nothing but to inspire.—I had better never see a book than be warped by its attraction clean out of my own orbit, and made a satellite instead of a system.—*Emerson.*

The colleges, while they provide us with libraries, furnish no professors of books; and I think no chair is so much needed.—*Emerson.*

The books that help you most are those that make you think the most.— *Theodore Parker.*

The last thing that we discover in writing a book, is to know what to put at the beginning.—*Pascal.*

After all manner of professors have done their best for us, the place we are to get knowledge is in books.—The true university of these days is a collection of books.—*Carlyle.*

Many books require no thought from those who read them, and for a very simple reason; they made no such demand upon those who wrote them. Those works, therefore, are the most valuable, that set our thinking faculties in the fullest operation.—*Colton.*

He that loves not books before he comes to thirty years of age, will hardly love them enough afterward to understand them.—*Clarendon.*

As well almost kill a man, as kill a good book; for the life of the one is but a few short years, while that of the other may be for ages.—Who kills a man kills a reasonable creature, God's image; but he who destroys a good book, kills reason itself; kills as it were, the image of God.—*Milton.*

No book can be so good as to be profitable when negligently read.— *Seneca.*

Upon books the collective education of the race depends; they are the sole instruments of registering, perpetuating, and transmitting thought.—*H. Rogers.*

BORES.—Few men are more to be shunned than those who have time, but know not how to improve it, and so spend it in wasting the time of their neighbors, talking forever though they have nothing to say.—*Tryon Edwards.*

The secret of making one's self tiresome, is, not to know when to stop.—*Voltaire.*

There are some kinds of men who cannot pass their time alone; they are the flails of occupied people.—*Bonald.*

There are few wild beasts more to be dreaded than a talking man having nothing to say.—*Swift.*

O, he is as tedious as is a tired horse, or a railing wife; worse than a smoky house.—*Shakespeare.*

It is hoped that, with all modern improvements, a way will be discovered of getting rid of bores; for it is too bad that a poor wretch can be punished for stealing your handkerchief or gloves, and that no punishment can be inflicted on those who steal your time, and with it your temper and patience, as well as the bright thoughts that might have entered your mind, if they had not been frightened away by the bore.—*Byron.*

We are almost always wearied in the company of persons with whom we are not permitted to be weary.—*Rochefoucauld.*

BORROWING. — Borrowing is not much better than begging.—*Lessing.*

If you would know the value of money, go and try to borrow some.—He that goes a-borrowing goes a-sorrowing. —*Franklin.*

Neither a borrower, nor a lender be; for loan oft loses both itself and friend; and borrowing dulls the edge of husbandry.—*Shakespeare.*

Getting into debt, is getting into a tanglesome net.—*Franklin.*

The borrower runs in his own debt.—*Emerson.*

He that would have a short Lent, let him borrow money to be repaid at Easter.—*Franklin.*

No remedy against this consumption of the purse; borrowing only lingers it out, but the disease is incurable.—*Shakespeare.*

BRAVERY.—The best hearts are ever the bravest.—*Sterne.*

No man can be brave who considers pain the greatest evil of life; or temperate, who regards pleasure as the highest good.—*Cicero.*

A true knight is fuller of bravery in the midst, than in the beginning of danger.—*Sir P. Sidney.*

Some one praising a man for his foolhardy bravery, Cato, the elder, said, "There is a wide difference between true courage and a mere contempt of life." —*Plutarch.*

At the bottom of not a little of the bravery that appears in the world, there lurks a miserable cowardice. Men will face powder and steel because they have not the courage to face public opinion. —*E. H. Chapin.*

True bravery is shown by performing without witnesses what one might be capable of doing before all the world.— *Rochefoucauld.*

Nature often enshrines gallant and noble hearts in weak bosoms; oftenest, God bless her, in woman's breast.— *Dickens.*

The bravery founded on hope of recompense, fear of punishment, experience of success, on rage, or on ignorance of danger, is but common bravery, and does not deserve the name.—True bravery proposes a just end; measures the dangers, and meets the result with calmness and unyielding decision.—*La None.*

All brave men love; for he only is brave who has affections to fight for, whether in the daily battle of life, or in physical contests.—*Hawthorne.*

BREVITY. — Brevity is the soul of wit.—*Shakespeare.*

Have something to say; say it, and stop when you've done.—*Tryon Edwards.*

Genuine good taste consists in saying much in few words, in choosing among our thoughts, in having order and arrangement in what we say, and in speaking with composure.—*Fenelon.*

When one has no design but to speak plain truth, he may say a great deal in a very narrow compass.—*Steele.*

The one prudence of life is concentration.—*Emerson.*

One rare, strange virtue in speeches,

and the secret of their mastery, is, that they are short.—*Halleck.*

Brevity is the best recommendation of speech, whether in a senator or an orator.—*Cicero.*

Talk to the point, and stop when you have reached it.—Be comprehensive in all you say or write.—To fill a volume about nothing is a credit to nobody.—*John Neal.*

The fewer the words, the better the prayer.—*Luther.*

Words are like leaves, and where they most abound, much fruit of sense beneath is rarely found.—*Pope.*

If you would be pungent, be brief; for it is with words as with sunbeams—the more they are condensed, the deeper they burn.—*Southey.*

Say all you have to say in the fewest possible words, or your reader will be sure to skip them; and in the plainest possible words, or he will certainly misunderstand them.—*Ruskin.*

I saw one excellency within my reach —it was brevity, and I determined to obtain it.—*Jay.*

Brevity to writing is what charity is to all other virtues; righteousness is nothing without the one, nor authorship without the other.—*Sydney Smith.*

When you introduce a moral lesson let it be brief.—*Horace.*

Never be so brief as to become obscure.—*Tryon Edwards.*

BRIBERY.—Judges and senators have been bought with gold.—*Pope.*

The universe is not rich enough to buy the vote of an honest man.—*Gregory.*

Though authority be a stubborn bear, yet he is oft led by the nose with gold. —*Shakespeare.*

Petitions not sweetened with gold, are but unsavory, and often refused; or if received, are pocketed, not read.—*Massinger.*

Who thinketh to buy villainy with gold, shall find such faith so bought, so sold.—*Marston.*

A man who is furnished with arguments from the mint, will convince his antagonist much sooner than one who draws them from reason and philosophy. —Gold is a wonderful clearer of the understanding; it dissipates every doubt

and scruple in an instant; accommodates itself to the meanest capacities; silences the loud and clamorous, and cringes over the most obstinate and inflexible.— Philip of Macedon was a man of most invincible reason this way. He refuted by it all the wisdom of Athens; confounded their statesmen; struck their orators dumb; and at length argued them out of all their liberties.—*Addison.*

BROTHERHOOD.—To live is not to live for one's self alone; let us help one another.—*Menander.*

The sixteenth century said, "Responsibility to God."—The present nineteennth says, "The brotherhood of man." —*C. L. Thompson.*

Whoever in prayer can say, "Our Father," acknowledges and should feel the brotherhood of the whole race of mankind.—*Tryon Edwards.*

There is no brotherhood of man without the fatherhood of God.—*H. M. Field.*

We must love men ere they will seem to us worthy of our love.—*Shakespeare.*

If God is thy father, man is thy brother.—*Lamartine.*

The brotherhood of man is an integral part of Christianity no less than the Fatherhood of God; and to deny the one is no less infidel than to deny the other.—*Lyman Abbott.*

We are members of one great body, planted by nature in a mutual love, and fitted for a social life.—We must consider that we were born for the good of the whole.—*Seneca.*

The race of mankind would perish did they cease to aid each other.—We cannot exist without mutual help. All therefore that need aid have a right to ask it from their fellow-men; and no one who has the power of granting can refuse it without guilt.—*Walter Scott.*

The universe is but one great city, full of beloved ones, divine and human, by nature endeared to each other.— *Epictetus.*

However degraded or wretched a fellow mortal may be, he is still a member of our common species.—*Seneca.*

Jesus throws down the dividing prejudices of nationality, and teaches universal love, without distinction of race, merit, or rank.—A man's neighbor is every one that needs help.—*J. C. Geikie.*

Our doctrine of equality and liberty and humanity comes from our belief in the brotherhood of man, through the fatherhood of God.—*Calvin Coolidge.*

The crest and crowning of all good, life's final star, is Brotherhood.—*Edwin Markham.*

BUILDING.—He that is fond of building will soon ruin himself without the help of enemies.—*Plutarch.*

Never build after you are five-and-forty; have five years' income in hand before you lay a brick; and always calculate the expense at double the estimate.—*Kett.*

They go to the forest for palm or pine, the stuff for the humbler homes; the mountain gives up its valued gifts, for the stately spires and domes; but whether they work with marble or sod, the builder is hand in hand with God. —*William Dunbar.*

BUSINESS.—An excellent monument might be erected to the Unknown Stockholder. It might take the form of a solid stone ark of faith apparently floating in a pool of water.—*Felix Riesenberg.*

Business may not be the noblest pursuit, but it is true that men are bringing to it some of the qualities which actuate the explorer, scientist, artist: the zest, the open-mindedness, even the disinterestedness, with which the scientific investigator explores some field of pure research.—*Earnest Elmo Calkins.*

After all, what the worker does is buy back from those who finance him the goods that he himself produces. Pay him a wage that enables him to buy, and you fill your market with ready consumers.—*James J. Davis.*

We demand that big business give people a square deal; in return we must insist that when anyone engaged in big business honestly endeavours to do right, he shall himself be given a square deal.—*Theodore Roosevelt.*

The man who is above his business may one day find his business above him.—*Drew.*

Not because of any extraordinary talents did he succeed, but because he had a capacity on a level for business and not above it.—*Tacitus.*

To business that we love, we rise betimes, and go to it with delight.—*Shakespeare.*

Business without profit is not business any more than a pickle is candy.—*Charles F. Abbott.*

Markets as well as mobs respond to human emotions; markets as well as mobs can be inflamed to their own destruction.—*Owen D. Young.*

The art of winning in business is in working hard—not taking things too seriously.—*Elbert Hubbard.*

To manage a business successfully requires as much courage as that possessed by the soldier who goes to war. Business courage is the more natural because all the benefits which the public has in material wealth come from it.—*Charles F. Abbott.*

The way to stop financial "joy-riding" is to arrest the chauffeur, not the automobile.—*Woodrow Wilson.*

The manufacturer who waits in the woods for the world to beat a path to his door, is a great optimist. But the manufacturer who shows his "mouse-traps" to the world keeps the smoke coming out of his chimney.—*O. B. Winters.*

The best mental effort in the game of business is concentrated on the major problem of securing the consumer's dollar before the other fellow gets it.—*Stuart Chase.*

All business proceeds on beliefs, or judgments of probabilities, and not on certainties.—*Charles W. Eliot.*

The lawyer and the doctor and other professional men have often a touch of civilization. The banker and the merchant seldom.—*Jim Tully.*

The old days of caveat emptor—let the buyer beware—are gone.—*Alvan Macauley.*

Formerly when great fortunes were only made in war, war was a business; but now when great fortunes are only made by business, business is war.—*Bovee.*

Men of great parts are often unfortunate in the management of public business, because they are apt to go out of the common road by the quickness of their imagination.—*Swift.*

Anybody can cut prices, but it takes brains to make a better article.—*Alice Hubbard.*

If the Golden Rule is to be preached at all in these modern days, when so much of our life is devoted to business, it must be preached specially in its application to the conduct of business.—*Ferdinand S. Schenck.*

Business is never so healthy as when, like a chicken, it must do a certain amount of scratching for what it gets.—*Henry Ford.*

The musician, the painter, the poet, are, in a larger sense, no greater artists than the man of commerce.—*W. S. Maverick.*

Success or failure in business is caused more by the mental attitude even than by mental capacities.—*Walter Dill Scott.*

That I should make him that steals my coat a present of my cloak—what would become of business?—*Katharine Lee Bates.*

There are two times in a man's life when he should not speculate; when he can't afford it and when he can.—*Samuel Clemens.*

BUSYBODIES.—(See "Bores.")

I never knew any one to interfere with other people's disputes, but that he heartily repented of it.—*Lord Carlisle.*

One who is too wise an observer of the business of others, like one who is too curious in observing the labor of bees, will often be stung for his curiosity.—*Pope.*

Nobody ever pries into another man's concerns, but with a design to do, or to be able to do him a mischief.—*South.*

BUT.—"But" is a word that cools many a warm impulse, stifles many a kindly thought, puts a dead stop to many a brotherly deed.—No one would ever love his neighbor as himself if he listened to all the "buts" that could be said.—*Bulwer.*

Oh, now comes that bitter word—but, which makes all nothing that was said before, that smoothes and wounds, that strikes and dashes more than flat denial, or a plain disgrace.—*Daniel.*

The meanest, most contemptible kind of praise is that which first speaks well of a man, and then qualifies it with a " but."—*H. W. Beecher.*

I know of no manner of speaking so offensive as that of giving praise, and closing it with an exception.—*Steele.*

I do not like "But yet."—It does allay the good precedence.—Fie upon "but yet."—"But yet" is as a jailer, to bring forth some monstrous malefactor. —*Shakespeare.*

C

CALAMITY.—Calamity is man's true touchstone.—*Beaumont and Fletcher.*

Calamity is the perfect glass wherein we truly see and know ourselves.—*Davenant.*

When any calamity has been suffered, the first thing to be remembered, is, how much has been escaped.—*Johnson.*

It is only from the belief of the goodness and wisdom of a supreme being, that our calamities can be borne in the manner which becomes a man.—*Mackenzie.*

He who foresees calamities, suffers them twice over.—*Porteus.*

A trouble is a trouble, and the general idea, in the country, is to treat it as such, rather than to snatch the knotted cords from the hand of God and deal out murderous blows.—*William McFee.*

If we take sinful means to avoid calamity, that very often brings it upon us.—*Wall.*

CALUMNY.—(See "Scandal," and " Slander.")

Be thou chaste as ice, and pure as snow, thou shalt not escape calumny.—*Shakespeare.*

Back-wounding calumny the whitest virtue strikes.—*Shakespeare.*

When conscience is pure it triumphs o'er bitter malice, o'er dark calumny; but if there be in it one single stain, reproaches beat like hammers in the ears.—*Alexander Pushkin.*

Opposition and calumny are often the brightest tribute that vice and folly can pay to virtue and wisdom.—*Rutherford B. Hayes.*

Who stabs my name would stab my person too, did not the hangman's axe lie in the way.—*Crown.*

To persevere in one's duty, and be silent, is the best answer to calumny.—*Cecil.*

The calumniator inflicts wrong by

slandering the absent; and he who gives credit to the calumny before he knows it is true, is equally guilty.—The person traduced is doubly injured; by him who propagates, and by him who credits the slander.—*Herodotus.*

Neglected calumny soon expires; show that you are hurt, and you give it the appearance of truth.—*Tacitus.*

Close thine ear against him that opens his mouth against another.—If thou receive not his words, they fly back and wound him.—If thou receive them, they flee forward and wound thee.—*Quarles.*

There are calumnies against which even innocence loses courage.—*Napoleon.*

Those who ought to be most secure against calumny, are generally those who least escape it.—*Stanislaus.*

I never think it needful to regard calumnies; they are sparks, which, if you do not blow them, will go out of themselves.—*Boerhave.*

Calumny crosses oceans, scales mountains, and traverses deserts with greater ease than the Scythian Abaris, and, like him, rides upon a poisoned arrow.—*Colton.*

Never chase a lie; if you let it alone, it will soon run itself to death.—You can work out a good character faster than calumny can destroy it.—*E. Nott.*

I am beholden to calumny, that she hath so endeavored to belie me.—It shall make me set a surer guard on myself, and keep a better watch upon my actions.—*Ben Jonson.*

I never listen to calumnies; because, if they are untrue, I run the risk of being deceived; and if they are true, of hating persons not worth thinking about.—*Montesquieu.*

Calumny is like the wasp that worries you, which it is not best to try to get rid of unless you are sure of slaying it; for otherwise it returns to the charge more furious than ever.—*Chamfort.*

To persevere in one's duty and be silent, is the best answer to calumny.—*Washington.*

He that lends an easy and credulous ear to calumny, is either a man of very ill morals, or he has no more sense and understanding than a child.—*Menander.*

No might nor greatness in mortality

can censure 'scape; back wounding calumny the whitest virtue strikes: What king so strong, can tie the gall up in the slanderous tongue?—*Shakespeare.*

The upright man, if he suffer calumny to move him, fears the tongue of man more than the eye of God.—*Colton.*

False praise can please, and calumny affright, none but the vicious and the hypocrite.—*Horace.*

We cannot control the evil tongues of others, but a good life enables us to despise them.—*Cato.*

To seem disturbed at calumny, is the way to make it believed, and stabbing your defamer, will not prove you innocent.—Live an exemplary life, and then your good character will overcome and refute the calumny.—*Blair.*

Calumny would soon starve and die of itself if nobody took it in and gave it a lodging.—*Leighton.*

Believe nothing against another but on good authority; and never report what may hurt another, unless it be a greater hurt to some other to conceal it.—*Penn.*

CALVINISM. — Calvinism is a term used to designate, not the opinions of an individual, but a mode of religious thought, or a system of religious doctrine, of which the person whose name it bears was an eminent expounder.—*A. A. Hodge.*

There is no system which equals Calvinism in intensifying, to the last degree, ideas of moral excellence and purity of character.—It has always worked for liberty.—There never was a system since the world began, which puts upon man such motives to holiness, or builds batteries which sweep the whole ground of sin with such horrible artillery.—*H. W. Beecher.*

Calvinism has produced characters nobler and grander than any which republican Rome ever produced.—*Froude.*

Calvinism is a democratic and republican religion.—*De Tocqueville.*

Wherever Calvinism was established, it brought with it not only truth but liberty, and all the great developments which these two fertile principles carry with them.—*D'Aubigne.*

To the Calvinists, more than to any other class of men, the political liberties of Holland, England, and America are due.—*Motley.*

There was not a reformer in Europe so resolute as Calvin to exorcise, tear out, and destroy what was seen to be false—so resolute to establish what was true in its place, and to make truth, to the last fibre of it, the rule of practical life.—*Froude.*

He that will not honor the memory, and respect the influence of Calvin, knows but little of the origin of American independence.—*Bancroft.*

Calvin's Institutes, in spite of its imperfections, is, on the whole, one of the noblest edifices ever erected by the mind of man, and one of the mightiest codes of moral law which ever guided him.—*Guizot.*

"In the centuries after the Reformation," says Froude, "Calvinism numbered among its adherents nearly every man in Europe who abhorred a lie.—It made men haters of sin and intolerant of evil and loathing all wrong.—Some of its adherents may have been deficient in the graces of society and the amenities of life, but their sternness and intolerance was born of profound convictions, and their ideal of social life was lofty, and made up in part from the Bible views of heaven."

The promulgation of Calvin's theology was one of the longest steps that mankind has taken toward personal freedom.—*John Fiske.*

Bancroft, speaking of the great Calvinistic doctrines embodied in the "Confession of Faith," says: "They infused enduring elements into the institutions of Geneva, and made it for the modern world, the impregnable fortress of popular liberty—the fertile seed-plot of Democracy."

CANDOR. — The diligent fostering of a candid habit of mind, even in trifles, is a matter of high moment both to character and opinions.—*Howson.*

I can promise to be candid, though I may not be impartial.—*Goethe.*

Candor is the brightest gem of criticism.—*Disraeli.*

Candor is the seal of a noble mind, the ornament and pride of man, the sweetest charm of women, the scorn of

rascals, and the rarest virtue of sociability.—*Sternac.*

It is great and manly to disdain disguise; it shows our spirit, and proves our strength.—*Young.*

Making my breast transparent as pure crystal, that the world, jealous of me, may see the foulest thought my heart doth hold.—*Buckingham.*

Examine what is said, not him who speaks.—*Arabian Proverb.*

I make it my rule, to lay hold of light and embrace it, wherever I see it, though held forth by a child or an enemy.—*President Edwards.*

In reasoning upon moral subjects, we have great occasion for candor, in order to compare circumstances, and weigh arguments with impartiality.—*Emmons.*

CANT.—Cant is the voluntary overcharging or prolongation of a real sentiment; hypocrisy is the setting up pretence to a feeling you never had, and have no wish for.—*Hazlitt.*

Cant is itself properly a double-distilled lie, the materia prima of the devil, from which all falsehoods, imbecilities, and abominations body themselves, and from which no true thing can come.—*Carlyle.*

Of all the cants in this canting world, though the cant of hypocrites may be the worst, the cant of criticism is the most tormenting.—*Sterne.*

Cant is good to provoke common sense.—*Emerson.*

The affectation of some late authors to introduce and multiply cant words is the most ruinous corruption in any language.—*Swift.*

CARDS.—It is very wonderful to see persons of the best sense passing hours together in shuffling and dividing a pack of cards with no conversation but what is made up of a few game-phrases, and no other ideas but those of black or red spots ranged together in different figures. Would not a man laugh to hear any one of his species complaining that life is short?—*Addison.*

It is quite right that there should be a heavy duty on cards; not only on moral grounds; not only because they act on a social party like a torpedo, silencing the merry voice and numbing the play of the features; not only to fill the hunger of the public purse, which is always empty, however much you may put into it; but also because every pack of cards is a malicious libel on courts, and on the world, seeing that the trumpery with number one at the head is the best part of them; and that it gives kings and queens no other companions than knaves.—*Southey.*

CARE. — Care admitted as a guest, quickly turns to be master.—*Bovee.*

Care is no cure, but rather a corrosive for things that are not to be remedied.—*Shakespeare.*

Cares are often more difficult to throw off than sorrows; the latter die with time; the former grow upon it.—*Richter.*

They lose the world who buy it, with much care.—*Shakespeare.*

Our cares are the mothers not only of our charities and virtues, but of our best joys, and most cheering and enduring pleasures.—*Simms.*

Put off thy cares with thy clothes; so shall thy rest strengthen thy labor, and so thy labor sweeten thy rest.—*Quarles.*

To carry care to bed, is to sleep with a pack on your back.—*Haliburton.*

Providence has given us hope and sleep as a compensation for the many cares of life.—*Voltaire.*

The cares of to-day are seldom those of to-morrow; and when we lie down at night we may safely say to most of our troubles, " Ye have done your worst, and we shall see you no more."—*Cowper.*

Only man clogs his happiness with care, destroying what is, with thoughts of what may be.—*Dryden.*

Life's cares are comforts; such by heaven design'd; he that hath none must make them, or be wretched; cares are employments; and without employ the soul is on the rack; the rack of rest, to souls most adverse; action all their joy.—*Young.*

This world has cares enough to plague us; but he who meditates on others' woe, shall, in that meditation, lose his own.—*Cumberland.*

We can easily manage, if we will only take, each day, the burden appointed for it.—But the load will be too heavy for us if we carry yesterday's burden over again to-day, and then add the burden of the morrow to the weight before we

are required to bear it.—*John Newton.*

" Many of our cares," says Scott, " are but a morbid way of looking at our privileges."—We let our blessings get mouldy, and then call them curses.— *H. W. Beecher.*

The every-day cares and duties, which men call drudgery, are the weights and counterpoises of the clock of time, giving its pendulum a true vibration, and its hands a regular motion; and when they cease to hang upon the wheels, the pendulum no longer swings, the hands no longer move, and the clock stands still.—*Longfellow.*

Anxious care rests on a basis of heathen worldly-mindedness, and of heathen misunderstanding of the character of God.—*A. Maclaren.*

He that takes his cares on himself loads himself in vain with an uneasy burden.—I will cast my cares on God; he has bidden me; they cannot burden him.—*Bp. Hall.*

Care keeps his watch in every old man's eye; and where care lodges sleep will never lie.—*Shakespeare.*

Men do not avail themselves of the riches of God's grace.—They love to nurse their cares, and seem as uneasy without some fret as an old friar would be without his hair girdle.—They are commanded to cast their cares on the Lord; but even when they attempt it, they do not fail to catch them up again, and think it meritorious to walk burdened.—*H. W. Beecher.*

CARICATURE. — Nothing conveys a more inaccurate idea of a whole truth than a part of a truth so prominently brought forth as to throw the other parts into shadow.—This is the art of caricature, by the happy use of which you might caricature the Apollo Belvidere.—*Bulver.*

Take my advice, and never draw caricature.—By the long practice of it I have lost the enjoyment of beauty.—I never see a face but distorted, and never have the satisfaction to behold the human face divine.—*Hogarth.*

CASTLES IN THE AIR.—Charming Alnaschar visions! It is the happy privilege of youth to construct you!—*Thackeray.*

If you have built castles in the air,

your work need not be lost; there is where they should be. Now put foundations under them.—*Thoreau.*

We build on the ice, and write on the waves of the sea.—The waves roaring, pass away; the ice melts, and away goes our palace, like our thoughts.—*Herder.*

Ever building to the clouds, and never reflecting that the poor narrow basis cannot sustain the giddy, tottering column.—*Schiller.*

CAUTION.—It is well to learn caution by the misfortunes of others.—*Publius Syrus.*

All is to be feared where all is to be lost.—*Byron.*

Caution is crediting, and reserve in speaking, and in revealing one's self to but very few, are the best securities both of a good understanding with the world, and of the inward peace of our own minds.—*Thomas à Kempis.*

When using a needle you move your fingers delicately, and with a wise caution.—Use the same precaution with the inevitable dullness of life.—Give attention; keep yourself from imprudent precipitation; and do not take things by the point.—*Rance.*

Look before you leap; see before you go.—*Tusser.*

When clouds are seen wise men put on their cloaks.—*Shakespeare.*

None pities him that's in the snare, who warned before, would not beware. —*Herrick.*

Open your mouth and purse cautiously, and your stock of wealth and reputation shall, at least in repute, be great.—*Zimmerman.*

Whenever our neighbor's house is on fire, it cannot be amiss for the engines to play a little on our own. Better to be despised for too anxious apprehensions, than ruined by too confident security.—*Burke.*

Trust not him that hath once broken faith; he who betrayed thee once, will betray thee again.—*Shakespeare.*

He that is over-cautious will accomplish but very little.—*Schiller.*

Take warning by the misfortunes of others, that others may not take example from you.—*Saadi.*

More firm and sure the hand of cour-

age strikes, when it obeys the watchful eye of caution.—*Thomson.*

Things done well and with a care, exempt themselves from fear.—*Shakespeare.*

I don't like these cold, precise, perfect people, who, in order not to speak wrong, never speak at all, and in order not to do wrong, never do anything.— *H. W. Beecher.*

CENSURE.—Censure is the tax a man pays to the public for being eminent.— *Swift.*

The censure of those who are opposed to us, is the highest commendation that can be given us.—*St. Evremond.*

He that well and rightly considereth his own works will find little cause to judge hardly of another.—*Thos. à Kempis.*

There are but three ways for a man to revenge himself for the censure of the world: to despise it; to return the like; or to live so as to avoid it.—The first of these is usually pretended; the last is almost impossible; the universal practice is for the second.—*Swift.*

Forbear to judge, for we are sinners all.—*Shakespeare.*

The readiest and surest way to get rid of censure, is to correct ourselves.— *Demosthenes.*

It is folly for an eminent person to think of escaping censure, and a weakness to be affected by it.—All the illustrious persons of antiquity, and indeed of every age, have passed through this fiery persecution.—There is no defence against reproach but obscurity; it is a kind of concomitant to greatness, as satires and invectives were an essential part of a Roman triumph.—*Addison.*

Censure pardons the ravens, but rebukes the doves.—*Juvenal.*

Few persons have sufficient wisdom to prefer censure, which is useful, to praise which deceives them.—*Rochefoucauld.*

Horace appears in good humor while he censures, and therefore his censure has the more weight, as supposed to proceed from judgment and not from passion.—*Young.*

If any one speak ill of thee, consider whether he hath truth on his side; and if so, reform thyself, that his censures may not affect thee.—*Epictetus.*

The villain's censure is extorted praise.
—*Pope.*

It is harder to avoid censure than to gain applause, for this may be done by one great or wise action in an age; but to escape censure a man must pass his whole life without sayir¬ or doing one ill or foolish thing.—*Hume.*

He is always the severest censor on the merits of others who has the least worth of his own.—*E. L. Magoon.*

It is impossible to indulge in habitual severity of opinion upon our fellow-men without injuring the tenderness and delicacy of our own feelings.—*H. W. Beecher.*

Most of our censure of others is only oblique praise of self, uttered to show the wisdom and superiority of the speaker.—It has all the invidiousness of self-praise, and all the ill-desert of falsehood.—*Tryon Edwards.*

We hand folks over to God's mercy, and show none ourselves.—*George Eliot.*

The most censorious are generally the least judicious, or deserving, who, having nothing to recommend themselves, will be finding fault with others.—No man envies the merit of another who has enough of his own.—*Rule of Life.*

Our censure of our fellow-men, which we are prone to think a proof of our superior wisdom, is too often only the evidence of the conceit that would magnify self, or of the malignity or envy that would detract from others.—*Tryon Edwards.*

CEREMONY.—All ceremonies are, in themselves, very silly things; but yet a man of the world should know them.—They are the outworks of manners and decency, which would too often be broken in upon, if it were not for that defence which keeps the enemy at a proper distance.—*Chesterfield.*

Ceremony is the invention of wise men to keep fools at a distance; as good breeding is an expedient to make fools and wise men equals.—*Steele.*

To dispense with ceremony is the most delicate mode of conferring a compliment.—*Bulwer.*

To repose our confidence in forms and ceremonies, is superstition; but not to submit to them is pride or self-conceit. —*Pascal.*

Ceremonies differ in every country; they are only artificial helps which ignorance assumes to imitate politeness, which is the result of good sense and good-nature.—*Goldsmith.*

If we use no ceremony toward others, we shall be treated without any.—People are soon tired of paying trifling attentions to those who receive them with coldness, and return them with neglect. —*Hazlitt.*

Ceremony resembles that base coin which circulates through a country by royal mandate; it serves every purpose of real money at home, but is entirely useless if carried abroad.—A person who should attempt to circulate his native trash in another country would be thought either ridiculous or culpable.— *Goldsmith.*

Ceremony was devised at first, to set a gloss on faint deeds, hollow welcomes, and recanting goodness; but where there is true friendship, there needs none.— *Shakespeare.*

To divest either politics or religion of ceremony, is the most certain method of bringing either into contempt.—The weak must have their inducements to admiration as well as the wise; and it is the business of a sensible government to impress all ranks with a sense of subordination, whether this be effected by a diamond buckle, a virtuous edict, a sumptuary law, or a glass necklace.— *Goldsmith.*

CHANCE.—(See "ACCIDENT.") There is no such thing as chance; and what seems to us the merest accident springs from the deepest source of destiny.— *Schiller.*

By the word chance we merely express our ignorance of the cause of any fact or effect—not that we think that chance was itself the cause.—*Henry Fergus.*

The doctrine of chances is the bible of the fool.

There is no doubt such a thing as chance; but I see no reason why Providence should not make use of it.— *Simms.*

What can be more foolish than to think that all this rare fabric of heaven and earth could come by chance, when all the skill of art is not able to make an oyster!—*Jeremy Taylor.*

Chance is but the pseudonym of God for those particular cases which he does not choose to subscribe openly with his own sign-manual.—*Coleridge.*

The mines of knowledge are often laid bare by the hazel-wand of chance.—*Tupper.*

Many shining actions owe their success to chance, though the general or statesman runs away with the applause.—*Home.*

Be not too presumptuously sure in any business; for things of this world depend on such a train of unseen chances that if it were in man's hands to set the tables, still he would not be certain to win the game.—*Herbert.*

How often events, by chance, and unexpectedly, come to pass, which you had not dared even to hope for!—*Terence.*

Chance never writ a legible book; never built a fair house; never drew a neat picture; never did any of these things, nor ever will; nor can it, without absurdity, be supposed to do them, which are yet works very gross and rude, and very easy and feasible, as it were, in comparison to the production of a flower or a tree.—*Barrow.*

Chance is always powerful.—Let your hook be always cast; in the pool where you least expect it, there will be a fish.—*Ovid.*

Chance is a word void of sense; nothing can exist without a cause.—*Voltaire.*

He who distrusts the security of chance takes more pains to effect the safety which results from labor. To find what you seek in the road of life, the best proverb of all is that which says: "Leave no stone unturned."—*Bulwer.*

There is no such thing as chance or accident, the words merely signify our ignorance of some real and immediate cause.—*Adam Clarke.*

Chance generally favors the prudent.—*Joubert.*

CHANGE.—The world is a scene of changes; to be constant in nature were inconstancy.—*Cowley.*

The circumstances of the world are so variable, that an irrevocable purpose or opinion is almost synonymous with a foolish one.—*W. H. Seward.*

Perfection is immutable, but for things imperfect, to change is the way

to perfect them.—Constancy without knowledge cannot be always good; and in things ill, it is not virtue but an absolute vice.—*Feltham.*

What I possess I would gladly retain.—Change amuses the mind, yet scarcely profits.—*Goethe.*

If a great change is to be made in human affairs, the minds of men will be fitted to it; the general opinions and feelings will draw that way. Every fear and hope will forward it; and they who persist in opposing this mighty current will appear rather to resist the decrees of Providence itself, than the mere designs of men.—They will not be so much resolute and firm as perverse and obstinate.—*Burke.*

He that will not apply new remedies must expect new evils.—*Bacon.*

To-day is not yesterday.—We ourselves change.—How then, can our works and thoughts, if they are always to be the fittest, continue always the same.—Change, indeed, is painful, yet ever needful; and if memory have its force and worth, so also has hope.—*Carlyle.*

History fades into fable; fact becomes clouded with doubt and controversy; the inscription moulders from the tablet; the statue falls from the pedestal.—Columns, arches, pyramids, what are they but heaps of sand, and their epitaphs but characters written in the dust?—*Washington Irving.*

Remember the wheel of Providence is always in motion; and the spoke that is uppermost will be under; and therefore mix trembling always with your joy.—*Philip Henry.*

It is not strange that even our loves should change with our fortunes.—*Shakespeare.*

In this world of change naught which comes stays, and naught which goes is lost.—*Mad. Swetchine.*

CHARACTER.—(See "Talents.")

Character is perfectly educated will.—*Novalis.*

The noblest contribution which any man can make for the benefit of posterity, is that of a good character. The richest bequest which any man can leave to the youth of his native land, is that of a shining, spotless example.—*R. C. Winthrop.*

Let us not say, Every man is the architect of his own fortune; but let us say, Every man is the architect of his own character.—*G. D. Boardman.*

Give us a character on which we can thoroughly depend, which we know to be based on principle and on the fear of God, and it is wonderful how many brilliant and popular and splendid qualities we can safely and gladly dispense with.—*A. P. Stanley.*

Talents are best nurtured in solitude; character is best formed in the stormy billows of the world.—*Goethe.*

There is not a man or woman, however poor they may be, but have it in their power, by the grace of God, to leave behind them the grandest thing on earth, character; and their children might rise up after them and thank God that their mother was a pious woman, or their father a pious man.—*N. Macleod.*

Only what we have wrought into our character during life can we take away with us.—*Humboldt.*

It is not what a man gets, but what a man is, that he should think of.—He should think first of his character, and then of his condition: for if he have the former, he need have no fears about the latter.—Character will draw condition after it.—Circumstances obey principles.—*H. W. Beecher.*

Men best show their character in trifles, where they are not on their guard.—It is in insignificant matters, and in the simplest habits, that we often see the boundless egotism which pays no regard to the feelings of others, and denies nothing to itself.—*Schopenhauer.*

He who acts wickedly in private life, can never be expected to show himself noble in public conduct. He that is base at home, will not acquit himself with honor abroad; for it is not the man, but only the place that is changed.—*Æschines.*

Character is a diamond that scratches every other stone.—*Bartol.*

Character and personal force are the only investments that are worth anything.—*Whitman.*

Actions, looks, words, steps, form the alphabet by which you may spell characters: some are mere letters, some contain entire words, lines, pages, which at once decipher the life of a man. One such genuine uninterrupted page may be your key to all the rest; but first be certain that he wrote it all alone, and without thinking of publisher or reader.—*Lavater.*

A man's character is the reality of himself.—His reputation is the opinion others have formed of him.—Character is in him;—reputation is from other people—that is the substance, this is the shadow.—*H. W. Beecher.*

The best characters are made by vigorous and persistent resistance to evil tendencies; whose amiability has been built upon the ruins of ill-temper, and whose generosity springs from an overmastered and transformed selfishness. Such a character, built up in the presence of enemies, has far more attraction than one which is natively pleasing.—*Dexter.*

A good character is, in all cases, the fruit of personal exertion. It is not inherited from parents; it is not created by external advantages; it is no necessary appendage of birth, wealth, talents, or station; but it is the result of one's own endeavors—the fruit and reward of good principles manifested in a course of virtuous and honorable action.—*J. Hawes.*

As the sun is best seen at his rising and setting, so men's native dispositions are clearest seen when they are children, and when they are dying.—*Boyle.*

As there is much beast and some devil in man, so is there some angel and some God in him. The beast and the devil may be conquered, but in this life never destroyed.—*Coleridge.*

Every man, as to character, is the creature of the age in which he lives.—Very few are able to raise themselves above the ideas of their times.—*Voltaire.*

The great hope of society is in individual character.—*Channing.*

The Duc de Chartres used to say, that no man could less value character than himself, and yet he would gladly give twenty thousand pounds for a good character, because, he could, at once, make double that sum by it.—*Colton.*

Characters do not change.—Opinions alter, but characters are only developed.—*Disraeli.*

The character is like white paper; if

once blotted, it can hardly ever be made to appear white as before.—*J. Hawes.*

As they, who for every slight infirmity take physic to repair their health, do rather impair it; so they, who for every trifle are eager to vindicate their character, do rather weaken it.—*J. Mason.*

Our character is but the stamp on our souls of the free choices of good and evil we have made through life.—*Geikie.*

Truthfulness is a corner-stone in character, and if it be not firmly laid in youth, there will ever after be a weak spot in the foundation.—*J. Davis.*

A Persian carpet or piece of Sheraton makes a distinguished end and bears itself with dignity to the last—as aristocrats before the guillotine. But a Brussels or bit of mid-Victorian will be found to grovel, show its unlovely wounds and scream for pity.—*Eden Phillpotts.*

Character is the result of two things: Mental attitude and the way we spend our time.—*Elbert Hubbard.*

When the late J. P. Morgan was asked what he considered the best bank collateral, he replied, "Character."

I would like to see a state of society in which every man and woman preferred the old Scottish Sunday to the modern French one. We should then find solid and eternal foundations of character and self-command.—*Ramsey MacDonald.*

The miracle, or the power, that elevates the few is to be found in their industry, application, and perseverance under the promptings of a brave, determined spirit.—*Mark Twain.*

We want the spirit of America to be efficient; we want American character to be efficient; we want American character to display itself in what I may, perhaps, be allowed to call spiritual efficiency—clear disinterested thinking and fearless action along the right lines of thought.—*Woodrow Wilson.*

Most people are other people. Their thoughts are someone else's opinions, their lives a mimicry, their passions a quotation.—*Oscar Wilde.*

Character building begins in our infancy and continues until death.—*Mrs. Franklin D. Roosevelt.*

A tree will not only lie as it falls, but it will fall as it leans.—*J. J. Gurney.*

The harder you throw down a football and a good character, the higher they rebound; but a thrown reputation is like an egg.—*Austin O'Malley.*

Character is built out of circumstances.—From exactly the same materials one man builds palaces, while another builds hovels.—*G. H. Lewes.*

The shortest and surest way to live with honor in the world, is to be in reality what we would appear to be; all human virtues increase and strengthen themselves by the practice and experience of them.—*Socrates.*

The character that needs law to mend it, is hardly worth the tinkering.—*Jerrold.*

If you would create something, you must be something.—*Goethe.*

Not education, but character, is man's greatest need and man's greatest safeguard.—*Spencer.*

If you can talk with crowds and keep your virtue, or walk with kings—nor lose the common touch, if neither foes nor loving friends can hurt you, if all men count with you, but none too much: if you can fill the unforgiving minute with sixty seconds' worth of distance run, yours is the earth and everything that's in it, and—which is more—you'll be a man, my son.—*Kipling.*

What others say of me matters little, what I myself say and do matters much. —*Elbert Hubbard.*

No amount of ability is of the slightest avail without honor.—*Andrew Carnegie.*

The most important thing for a young man is to establish a credit—a reputation, character.—*John D. Rockefeller.*

There is nothing so fatal to character as half-finished tasks.—*David Lloyd George.*

There is no single royal road to character—a variety of routes will always need to be used. The development of right character in youth is too important to risk disregarding any promising line of attack.—*Frank Cody.*

Taste and habits change progressively. In the old days the lady with a past repented and died; to-day she repents and lives happily ever after.—*Daniel Frohman.*

If I take care of my character, my

reputation will take care of itself.—*D. L. Moody.*

There is a broad distinction between character and reputation, for one may be destroyed by slander, while the other can never be harmed save by its possessor. Reputation is in no man's keeping. You and I cannot determine what other men shall think and say about us. We can only determine what they *ought* to think of us and say about us.—*J. G. Holland.*

A man may be outwardly successful all his life long, and die hollow and worthless as a puff-ball; and he may be externally defeated all his life long, and die in the royalty of a kingdom established within him.—A man's true estate of power and riches, is to be in himself; not in his dwelling, or position, or external relations, but in his own essential character.—That is the realm in which he is to live, if he is to live as a Christian man.—*H. W. Beecher.*

It is not money, nor is it mere intellect, that governs the world; it is moral character, and intellect associated with moral excellence.—*T. D. Woolsey.*

Character is higher than intellect. . . . A great soul will be strong to live as well to think.—*Emerson.*

Character must stand behind and back up everything—the sermon, the poem, the picture, the play. None of them is worth a straw without it.—*J. G. Holland.*

To judge human character rightly a man may sometimes have very small experience provided he has a very large heart.—*Bulwer.*

Make but few explanations. The character that cannot defend itself is not worth vindicating.—*F. W. Robertson.*

No more fatal error can be cherished than that any character can be complete without the religious element. The essential factors in character building are religion, morality, and knowledge.—*J. L. Pickard.*

In the destiny of every moral being there is an object more worthy of God than happiness.—It is character.—And the grand aim of man's creation is the development of a grand character—and grand character is, by its very nature, the product of probationary discipline. —*Austin Phelps.*

To be worth anything, character must be capable of standing firm upon its feet in the world of daily work, temptation, and trial; and able to bear the wear and tear of actual life. Cloistered virtues do not count for much.—*S. Smiles.*

The great thing in this world is not so much where we are, but in what direction we are moving.—*O. W. Holmes.*

Do what you know and perception is converted into character.—*Emerson.*

We shall never wander from Christ while we make character the end and aim of all our intellectual discipline; and we shall never misconceive character while we hold fast to Christ, and keep him first in our motto and our hearts.— *S. F. Scovel.*

Nothing can work me damage, except myself.—The harm that I sustain I carry about me, and never am a real sufferer but by my own fault.—*St. Bernard.*

Good character is human nature in its best form.—It is moral order embodied in the individual.—Men of character are not only the conscience of society, but in every well governed state they are its best motive power; for it is moral qualities which, in the main, rule the world. —*S. Smiles.*

Never does a man portray his own character more vividly, than in his manner of portraying another.—*Richter.*

Should one tell you that a mountain had changed its place, you are at liberty to doubt it; but if any one tells you that a man has changed his character, do not believe it.—*Mahomet.*

A good heart, benevolent feelings, and a balanced mind, lie at the foundation of character. Other things may be deemed fortuitous; they may come and go; but character is that which lives and abides, and is admired long after its possessor has left the earth.—*John Todd.*

You cannot dream yourself into a character; you must hammer and forge one for yourself.—*Froude.*

CHARITY.— First daughter to the love of God, is charity to man.—*Drennan.*

The word "alms" has no singular, as if to teach us that a solitary act of charity scarcely deserves the name.

Charity gives itself rich; covetousness hoards itself poor.—*German Proverb.*

Charity is never lost: it may meet with ingratitude, or be of no service to those on whom it was bestowed, yet it ever does a work of beauty and grace upon the heart of the giver.

The deeds of charity we have done shall stay with us forever.—Only the wealth we have so bestowed do we keep; the other is not ours.—*Middleton.*

Defer not charities till death. He that does so is rather liberal of another man's substance than his own.—*Stretch.*

Posthumous charities are the very essence of selfishness when bequeathed by those who, even alive, would part with nothing.—*Colton.*

I would have none of that rigid and circumspect charity which is never exercised without scrutiny, and which always mistrusts the reality of the necessities laid open to it.—*Massillon.*

Beneficence is a duty; and he who frequently practices it and sees his benevolent intentions realized, at length comes to love him to whom he has done good.—*Kant.*

How often it is difficult to be wisely charitable—to do good without multiplying the sources of evil. To give alms is nothing unless you give thought also. It is written, not "blessed is he that feedeth the poor," but "blessed is he that considereth the poor." A little thought and a little kindness are often worth more than a great deal of money.—*Ruskin.*

The charities that soothe, and heal, and bless, lie scattered at the feet of men like flowers.—*Wordsworth.*

Every good act is charity. Your smiling in your brother's face, is charity; an exhortation of your fellow-man to virtuous deeds, is equal to alms-giving; your putting a wanderer in the right road, is charity; your assisting the blind, is charity; your removing stones, and thorns, and other obstructions from the road, is charity; your giving water to the thirsty, is charity. A man's true wealth hereafter, is the good he does in this world to his fellow-man. When he dies, people will say, "What property has he left behind him?" But the angels will ask, "What good deeds has he sent before him."—*Mahomet.*

The charity that hastens to proclaim its good deeds, ceases to be charity, and

is only pride and ostentation.—*Hutton.*

It is an old saying, that charity begins at home; but this is no reason that it should not go abroad: a man should live with the world as a citizen of the world; he may have a preference for the particular quarter or square, or even alley in which he lives, but he should have a generous feeling for the welfare of the whole.—*Cumberland.*

A man should fear when he enjoys only the good he does publicly.—Is it not publicity rather than charity, which he loves? Is it not vanity, rather than benevolence, that gives such charities?—*H. W. Beecher.*

In my youth I thought of writing a satire on mankind, but now in my age I think I should write an apology for them.—*Walpole.*

When faith and hope fail, as they do sometimes, we must try charity, which is love in action. We must speculate no more on our duty, but simply do it. When we have done it, however blindly, perhaps Heaven will show us why.—*Mulock.*

Pity, forbearance, long-sufferance, fair interpretation, excusing our brother, and taking in the best sense, and passing the gentlest sentence, are certainly our duty; and he that does not so is an unjust person.—*Jeremy Taylor.*

Give work rather than alms to the poor. The former drives out indolence, the latter industry.

There are two kinds of charity, remedial and preventive.—The former is often injurious in its tendency; the latter is always praiseworthy and beneficial.—*Tryon Edwards.*

To pity distress is but human; to relieve it is Godlike.—*H. Mann.*

Prayer carries us half-way to God, fasting brings us to the door of his palace, and alms-giving procures us admission.—*Koran.*

We are rich only through what we give; and poor only through what we refuse and keep.—*Mad. Swetchine.*

Public charities and benevolent associations for the gratuitous relief of every species of distress, are peculiar to Christianity; no other system of civil or religious policy has originated them;

they form its highest praise and characteristic feature.—*Colton*.

The spirit of the world has four kinds of spirits diametrically opposed to charity, resentment, aversion, jealousy, and indifferences.—*Bossuet*.

The place of charity, like that of God, is everywhere.

Proportion thy charity to the strength of thine estate, lest God proportion thine estate to the weakness of thy charity.— Let the lips of the poor be the trumpet of thy gift, lest in seeking applause, thou lose thy reward.—Nothing is more pleasing to God than an open hand, and a closed mouth.—*Quarles*.

A rich man without charity is a rogue; and perhaps it would be no difficult matter to prove that he is also a fool.—*Fielding*.

Our true acquisitions lie only in our charities, we gain only as we give.— *Simms*.

My poor are my best patients.—God pays for them.—*Boerhaave*.

We should give as we would receive, cheerfully, quickly, and without hesitation, for there is no grace in a benefit that sticks to the fingers.—*Seneca*.

That charity is bad which takes from independence its proper pride, and from mendicity its proper shame.—*Southey*.

In giving of thine alms inquire not so much into the person, as his necessity.— God looks not so much on the merits of him that requires, as to the manner of him that relieves.—If the man deserve not, thou hast given to humanity.— *Quarles*.

He who has never denied himself for the sake of giving, has but glanced at the joys of charity.—*Mad. Swetchine*.

Be charitable and indulgent to every one but thyself.—*Joubert*.

The last, best fruit that comes late to perfection, even in the kindliest soul, is tenderness toward the hard, forbearance toward the unforbearing, warmth of heart toward the cold, and philanthropy toward the misanthropic.—*Richter*.

The truly generous is truly wise, and he who loves not others, lives unblest. —*Home*.

Great minds, like heaven, are pleased in doing good, though the ungrateful subjects of their favors are barren in return.—*Rowe*.

Nothing truly can be termed my own, but what I make my own by using well; those deeds of charity which we have done, shall stay forever with us; and that wealth which we have so bestowed, we only keep; the other is not ours.— *Middleton*.

While actions are always to be judged by the immutable standard of right and wrong, the judgment we pass upon men must be qualified by considerations of age, country, situation, and other incidental circumstances; and it will then be found, that he who is most charitable in his judgment, is generally the least unjust.—*Southey*.

Let him who neglects to raise the fallen, fear lest, when he falls, no one will stretch out his hand to lift him up. —*Saadi*.

I will chide no heathen in the world but myself, against whom I know most faults.—*Shakespeare*.

Loving kindness is greater than laws; and the charities of life are more than all ceremonies.—*Talmud*.

CHASTITY.—A pure mind in a chaste body is the mother of wisdom and deliberation; sober counsels and ingenuous actions; open deportment and sweet carriage; sincere principles and unprejudiced understanding; love of God and self-denial; peace and confidence; holy prayers and spiritual comfort; and a pleasure of spirit infinitely greater than the sottish pleasure of unchastity.— *Jeremy Taylor*.

Chastity enables the soul to breathe a pure air in the foulest places.—Continence makes her strong, no matter in what condition the body may be.—Her sway over the senses makes her queenly: her light and peace render her beautiful. —*Joubert*.

A man defines his standing at the court of chastity, by his views of women. —He cannot be any man's friend, nor his own, if not hers.—*A. B. Alcott*.

There needs not strength to be added to inviolate chastity; the excellency of the mind makes the body impregnable. —*Sir P. Sidney*.

That chastity of honor, which feels a stain like a wound.—*Burke*.

CHEERFULNESS. — I had rather have a fool make me merry, than experience make me sad. — *Shakespeare.*

What sunshine is to flowers, smiles are to humanity. They are but trifles, to be sure; but, scattered along life's pathway, the good they do is inconceivable.

A cheerful temper joined with innocence will make beauty attractive, knowledge delightful, and wit good-natured. It will lighten sickness, poverty, and affliction; convert ignorance into an amiable simplicity, and render deformity itself agreeable. — *Addison.*

Oh, give us the man who sings at his work. — *Carlyle.*

The highest wisdom is continual cheerfulness; such a state, like the region above the moon, is always clear and serene. — *Montaigne.*

Wondrous is the strength of cheerfulness, and its power of endurance — the cheerful man will do more in the same time, will do it better, will persevere in it longer, than the sad or sullen. — *Carlyle.*

Honest good humor is the oil and wine of a merry meeting, and there is no jovial companionship equal to that where the jokes are rather small and the laughter abundant. — *Washington Irving.*

Cheerfulness is as natural to the heart of a man in strong health, as color to his cheek; and wherever there is habitual gloom, there must be either bad air, unwholesome food, improperly severe labor, or erring habits of life. — *Ruskin.*

Be cheerful always. There is no path but will be easier traveled, no load but will be lighter, no shadow on heart and brain but will lift sooner for a person of determined cheerfulness.

Get into the habit of looking for the silver lining of the cloud, and, when you have found it, continue to look at it, rather than at the leaden gray in the middle. It will help you over many hard places. — *Willitts.*

To be free-minded and cheerfully disposed at hours of meals, and of sleep, and of exercise, is one of the best precepts of long-lasting. — *Bacon.*

A light heart lives long. — *Shakespeare.*

Cheerfulness is health; its opposite, melancholy, is disease. — *Haliburton.*

If my heart were not light, I would die. — *Joanna Baillie.*

If the soul be happily disposed everything becomes capable of affording entertainment, and distress will almost want a name. — *Goldsmith.*

The true source of cheerfulness is benevolence. — The soul that perpetually overflows with kindness and sympathy will always be cheerful. — *P. Godwin.*

Climate has much to do with cheerfulness, but nourishing food, a good digestion, and good health much more. — *A. Rhodes.*

If good people would but make their goodness agreeable, and smile instead of frowning in their virtue, how many would they win to the good cause. — *Usher.*

An ounce of cheerfulness is worth a pound of sadness to serve God with. — *Fuller.*

God is glorified, not by our groans but by our thanksgivings; and all good thought and good action claim a natural alliance with good cheer. — *E. P. Whipple.*

I have always preferred cheerfulness to mirth. The former is an act, the latter a habit of the mind. Mirth is short and transient; cheerfulness, fixed and permanent. Mirth is like a flash of lightning, that breaks through a gloom of clouds, and glitters for a moment. Cheerfulness keeps up a kind of daylight in the mind, filling it with a steady and perpetual serenity. — *Addison.*

You have not fulfilled every duty unless you have fulfilled that of being cheerful and pleasant. — *C. Buxton.*

If I can put one touch of a rosy sunset into the life of any man or woman, I shall feel that I have worked with God. — *G. Macdonald.*

Be cheerful: do not brood over fond hopes unrealized until a chain is fastened on each thought and wound around the heart. Nature intended you to be the fountain-spring of cheerfulness and social life, and not the monument of despair and melancholy. — *A. Helps.*

Burdens become light when cheerfully borne. — *Ovid.*

The habit of looking on the best side of every event is worth more than a thousand pounds a year. — *Johnson.*

The cheerful live longest in years,

and afterwards in our regards. Cheerfulness is the offshoot of goodness.—*Bovee.*

The mind that is cheerful at present will have no solicitude for the future, and will meet the bitter occurrences of life with a smile.—*Horace.*

Cheerful looks make every dish a feast; and it is that which crowns a welcome.—*Massinger.*

Every one must have felt that a cheerful friend is like a sunny day, which sheds its brightness on all around; and most of us can, as we choose, make of this world either a palace or a prison.—*Sir J. Lubbock.*

There is no greater every-day virtue than cheerfulness. This quality in man among men is like sunshine to the day, or gentle renewing moisture to parched herbs. The light of a cheerful face diffuses itself, and communicates the happy spirit that inspires it. The sourest temper must sweeten in the atmosphere of continuous good humor.

Wondrous is the strength of cheerfulness, altogether past calculation its powers of endurance. Efforts, to be permanently useful, must be uniformly joyous,—a spirit all sunshine, graceful from very gladness, beautiful because bright.—*Carlyle.*

You find yourself refreshed by the presence of cheerful people.—Why not make earnest effort to confer that pleasure on others?—Half the battle is gained if you never allow yourself to say anything gloomy.—*L. M. Child.*

To be happy, the temperament must be cheerful and gay, not gloomy and melancholy.—A propensity to hope and joy, is real riches; one to fear and sorrow, is real poverty.—*Hume.*

To make knowledge valuable, you must have the cheerfulness of wisdom. Goodness smiles to the last.—*Emerson.*

Every time a man smiles, and much more when he laughs, it adds something to his fragment of life.—*Sterne.*

Not having enough sunshine is what ails the world.—Make people happy, and there will not be half the quarreling, or a tenth part of the wickedness there now is.—*L. M. Child.*

Cheerfulness is a friend to grace; it puts the heart in tune to praise God, and so honors religion by proclaiming to the world that we serve a good master.—Be serious, yet cheerful.—Rejoice in the Lord always.—*Watson.*

Always look out for the sunlight the Lord sends into your days.—*Hope Campbell.*

CHILDREN. — Many children, many cares; no children, no felicity.—*Bovee.*

Childhood shows the man, as morning shows the day.—*Milton.*

The child is father of the man.—*Wordsworth.*

·I love these little people; and it is not a slight thing, when they, who are so fresh from God, love us.—*Dickens.*

The clew of our destiny, wander where we will, lies at the foot of the cradle.—*Richter.*

The interests of childhood and youth are the interests of mankind.—*Janes.*

Never fear spoiling children by making them too happy. Happiness is the atmosphere in which all good affections grow—the wholesome warmth necessary to make the heart-blood circulate healthily and freely; unhappiness—the chilling pressure which produces here an inflammation, there an excrescence, and, worst of all, "the mind's green and yellow sickness"—ill temper.—*Bray.*

Children have more need of models than of critics.—*Joubert.*

If I were asked what single qualification was necessary for one who has the care of children, I should say patience—patience with their tempers, with their understandings, with their progress. It is not brilliant parts or great acquirements which are necessary for teachers, but patience to go over first principles again and again; steadily to add a little every day; never to be irritated by wilful or accidental hinderance.

Beware of fatiguing them by illjudged exactness.—If virtue offers itself to the child under a melancholy and constrained aspect, while liberty and license present themselves under an agreeable form, all is lost, and your labor is in vain.—*Fenelon.*

Children sweeten labors, but they make misfortunes more bitter.—They increase the cares of life, but they mitigate the remembrance of death.—*Bacon.*

In bringing up a child, think of its old age.—*Joubert.*

Some one says, "Boys will be boys"; he forgot to add, "Boys will be men."

The future destiny of the child is always the work of the mother.—*Bonaparte.*

The interests of childhood and youth are the interests of mankind.—*Janes.*

When parents spoil their children, it is less to please them than to please themselves. It is the egotism of parental love.

Good Christian people, here lies for you an inestimable loan;—take all heed thereof, in all carefulness employ it. With high recompense, or else with heavy penalty, will it one day be required back.—*Carlyle.*

Your little child is your only true democrat.—*Mrs. Stowe.*

Call not that man wretched, who, whatever ills he suffers, has a child to love.—*Southey.*

I have often thought what a melancholy world this would be without children; and what an inhuman world, without the aged.—*Coleridge.*

What gift has Providence bestowed on man that is so dear to him as his children?—*Cicero.*

God sends children for another purpose than merely to keep up the race—to enlarge our hearts; and to make us unselfish and full of kindly sympathies and affections; to give our souls higher aims; to call out all our faculties to extended enterprise and exertion; and to bring round our firesides bright faces, happy smiles, and loving, tender hearts. —My soul blesses the great Father, every day, that he has gladdened the earth with little children.—*Mary Howitt.*

Be ever gentle with the children God has given you.—Watch over them constantly; reprove them earnestly, but not in anger.—In the forcible language of Scripture, "Be not bitter against them." —"Yes—they are good boys," said a kind father. "I talk to them much, but I do not beat my children: the world will beat them."—It was a beautiful thought, though not elegantly expressed. —*Burritt.*

Childhood has no forebodings; but then it is soothed by no memories of outlived sorrow.—*George Eliot.*

Children are God's apostles, sent forth, day by day, to preach of love, and hope and peace.—*J. R. Lowell.*

A torn jacket is soon mended, but hard words bruise the heart of a child.— *Longfellow.*

Blessed be the hand that prepares a pleasure for a child, for there is no saying when and where it may bloom forth. —*Jerrold.*

You cannot teach a child to take care of himself unless you will let him try to take care of himself. He will make mistakes; and out of these mistakes will come his wisdom.—*H. W. Beecher.*

Of nineteen out of twenty things in children, take no special notice; but if, as to the twentieth, you give a direction or command, see that you are obeyed.— *Tryon Edwards.*

An infallible way to make your child miserable, is to satisfy all his demands. —Passion swells by gratification; and the impossibility of satisfying every one of his wishes will oblige you to stop short at last after he has become headstrong.—*Home.*

With children we must mix gentleness with firmness.—They must not always have their own way, but they must not always be thwarted.—If we never have headaches through rebuking them, we shall have plenty of heartaches when they grow up.—Be obeyed at all costs; for if you yield up your authority once, you will hardly get it again.—*Spurgeon.*

Children generally hate to be idle.— All the care then should be, that their busy humor should be constantly employed in something that is of use to them.—*Locke.*

Who is not attracted by bright and pleasant children, to prattle, to creep, and to play with them?—*Epictetus.*

The child's grief throbs against its little heart as heavily as the man's sorrow; and the one finds as much delight in his kite or drum, as the other in striking the springs of enterprise, or soaring on the wings of fame.—*E. H. Chapin.*

Children are very nice observers, and will often perceive your slightest defects.—In general, those who govern children, forgive nothing in them, but everything in themselves.—*Fenelon.*

Childhood and genius have the same master-organ in common—inquisitiveness.—Let childhood have its way, and as it began where genius begins, it may find what genius finds.—*Bulwer.*

Who feels injustice; who shrinks before a slight; who has a sense of wrong so acute, and so glowing a gratitude for kindness, as a generous boy?—*Thackeray.*

The first duty to children is to make them happy.—If you have not made them so, you have wronged them.—No other good they may get can make up for that.—*Buxton.*

In the man whose childhood has known caresses and kindness, there is always a fibre of memory that can be touched to gentle issues.—*George Eliot.*

When a child can be brought to tears, not from fear of punishment, but from repentance for its offence, he needs no chastisement.—When the tears begin to flow from grief at one's own conduct, be sure there is an angel nestling in the bosom.—*A. Mann.*

You save an old man and you save a unit; but you save a boy, and you save a multiplication table.—*"Gipsy" Smith.*

The only way on God's earth you will ever solve the problem of reaching the masses, is by getting hold of the Children. You get boys and girls started right and the devil will hang crêpe on his door.—*Rev. William A. Sunday.*

What the best and wisest parent wants for his own child that must the community want for all its children.—*John Dewey.*

Before you beat a child, be sure you yourself are not the cause of the offense. —*Austin O'Malley.*

Lord, give to men who are old and rougher the things that little children suffer, and let men keep bright and undefiled the young years of the little child.— *John Masefield.*

Infancy isn't what it is cracked up to be. Children, not knowing that they are having an easy time, have a good many hard times. Growing and learning and obeying the rules of their elders, or fighting against them, are not easy things to do.—*Don Marquis.*

Man, a dunce uncouth, errs in age and youth: babies know the truth.—*Swinburne.*

Every child born into the world is a new thought of God, an ever-fresh and radiant possibility.—*Kate Douglas Wiggin.*

The child's heart curseth deeper in the silence than the strong man in his wrath.—*E. B. Browning.*

The sweetest roamer is a boy's young heart.—*George Edward Woodberry.*

I think that saving a little child and bringing him into his own, is a derned sight better business than loafing around the throne.—*John Hay.*

Those lives are, indeed, narrow and confined which are not blessed with several children.—*John Burroughs.*

There should be no enforced respect for grown-ups. We cannot prevent children from thinking us fools by merely forbidding them to utter their thoughts; in fact, they are more likely to think ill of us if they dare not say so.—*Bertrand Russell.*

It always grieves me to contemplate the initiation of children into the ways of life when they are scarcely more than infants.—It checks their confidence and simplicity, two of the best qualities that heaven gives them, and demands that they share our sorrows before they are capable of entering into our enjoyments. —*Dickens.*

All the gestures of children are graceful; the reign of distortion and unnatural attitudes commences with the introduction of the dancing master.—*Sir J. Reynolds.*

In praising or loving a child, we love and praise not that which is, but that which we hope for.—*Goethe.*

The smallest children are nearest to God, as the smallest planets are nearest the sun.—*Richter.*

Above all things endeavor to breed them up in the love of virtue, and that holy plain way of it which we have lived in, that the world in no part of it get into my family. I had rather they were homely, than finely bred as to outward behavior; yet I love sweetness mixed with gravity, and cheerfulness tempered with sobriety.—*Penn to his wife.*

The true idea of self-restraint is to

let a child venture.—The mistakes of children are often better than their no-mistakes.—*H. W. Beecher*.

Just as the twig is bent, the tree is inclined.—*Pope*.

The training of children is a profession, where we must know how to lose time in order to gain it.—*Rousseau*.

The tasks set to children should be moderate. Over-exertion is hurtful both physically and intellectually, and even morally. But it is of the utmost importance that they should be made to fulfil all their tasks correctly and punctually. This will train them for an exact and conscientious discharge of their duties in after life.—*Hare*.

Heaven lies about us in our infancy.—*Wordsworth*.

The plays of natural lively children are the infancy of art.—Children live in a world of imagination and feeling.—They invest the most insignificant object with any form they please, and see in it whatever they wish to see.—*Oehlenschlager*.

As the vexations men receive from their children hasten the approach of age, and double the force of years, so the comforts they reap from them are balm to all their sorrows, and disappoint the injuries of time. Parents repeat their lives in their offspring; and their esteem for them is so great, that they feel their sufferings and taste their enjoyments as much as if they were their own.—*R. Palmer*.

Childhood has no forebodings; but then it is soothed by no memories of outlived sorrow.—*George Eliot*.

Children are excellent physiognomists, and soon discover their real friends.—Luttrell calls them all lunatics, and so in fact they are.—What is childhood but a series of happy delusions?—*Sydney Smith*.

Let all children remember, if ever they are weary of laboring for their parents, that Christ labored for his; if impatient of their commands, that Christ cheerfully obeyed; if reluctant to provide for their parents, that Christ forgot himself and provided for his mother amid the agonies of the crucifixion. The affectionate language of this divine example to every child is, " Go thou and do likewise."—*Dwight*.

They who have to educate children should keep in mind that boys are to become men, and that girls are to become women. The neglect of this momentous consideration gives us a race of moral hermaphrodites.—*Hare*.

In the long course of my legal profession, I have met with several sons who had, in circumstance of difficulty, abandoned their fathers; but never did I meet with a father that would not cheerfully part with his last shilling to save or bless his son.—*David Daggett*.

Whether it be for good or evil, the education of the child is principally derived from its own observation of the actions, words, voice, and looks of those with whom it lives.—The friends of the young, then, cannot be too circumspect in their presence to avoid every and the least appearance of evil.—*Jebb*.

Children do not know how their parents love them, and they never will till the grave closes over those parents, or till they have children of their own.—*Cooke*.

Where children are, there is the golden age.—*Novalis*.

Childhood sometimes does pay a second visit to a man; youth never.—*Mrs. Jameson*.

CHIVALRY.—The age of chivalry has gone, and one of calculators and economists has succeeded.—*Burke*.

The age of chivlary is never past, so long as there is a wrong left unredressed on earth.—*Charles Kingsley*.

Collision is as necessary to produce virtue in men, as it is to elicit fire in inanimate matter; and so chivalry is of the essence of virtue.—*Russell*.

CHOICE.—The measure of choosing well, is, whether a man likes and finds good in what he has chosen.—*Lamb*.

Be ignorance thy choice where knowledge leads to woe.—*Beattie*.

Life often presents us with a choice of evils rather than of good.—*Colton*.

God offers to every mind its choice between truth and repose.—*Emerson*.

Choose always the way that seems the best, however rough it may be; custom will soon render it easy and agreeable.—*Pythagoras*.

Between two evils, choose neither; between two goods, choose both.—*Tryon Edwards.*

CHRIST.—All history is incomprehensible without Christ.—*Renan.*

Jesus Christ, the condescension of divinity, and the exaltation of humanity.—*Phillips Brooks.*

In his life, Christ is an example, showing us how to live; in his death, he is a sacrifice, satisfying for our sins; in his resurrection, a conqueror; in his ascension, a king; in his intercession, a high priest.—*Luther.*

The nature of Christ's existence is mysterious, I admit; but this mystery meets the wants of man.—Reject it and the world is an inexplicable riddle; believe it, and the history of our race is satisfactorily explained.—*Napoleon.*

Jesus Christ is a God to whom we can approach without pride, and before whom we may abase ourselves without despair.—*Pascal.*

I believe Plato and Socrates. I believe in Jesus Christ.—*Coleridge.*

As little as humanity will ever be without religion, as little will it be without Christ.—*Strauss.*

Every step toward Christ kills a doubt. Every thought, word, and deed for Him carries you away from discouragement.—*T. L. Cuyler.*

The name of Christ—the one great word—well worth all languages in earth or heaven.—*Bailey.*

God never gave a man a thing to do, concerning which it were irreverent to ponder how the Son of God would have done it.—*G. Macdonald.*

This is part of the glory of Christ as compared with the chiefest of His servants that He alone stands at the absolute center of humanity, the one completely harmonious man, unfolding all which was in humanity, equally and fully on all sides, the only one in whom the real and ideal met and were absolutely one.—He is the absolute and perfect truth, the highest that humanity can reach; at once its perfect image and supreme Lord.—*French.*

As the print of the seal on the wax is the express image of the seal itself, so Christ is the express image—the perfect representation of God.—*Ambrose.*

The difference between Socrates and Jesus Christ? The great Conscious; the immeasurably great Unconscious.—*Carlyle.*

An era in human history is the life of Jesus, and its immense influence for good leaves all the perversion and superstition that has accrued almost harmless.—*R. W. Emerson.*

CHRISTIAN.—A Christian is the highest style of man.—*Young.*

Though a great man may, by a rare possibility, be an infidel, yet an intellect of the highest order must build upon Christianity.—*De Quincey.*

The only truly happy men I have ever known, were Christians.—*John Randolph.*

Christians have burned each other, quite persuaded that all the Apostles would have done as they did.—*Byron.*

The only way to realize that we are God's children is to let Christ lead us to our Father.—*Phillips Brooks.*

A man can no more be a Christian without facing evil and conquering it, than he can be a soldier without going to battle, facing the cannon's mouth, and encountering the enemy in the field.—*E. H. Chapin.*

The devotion to the person of Christ that steers clear of the doctrines and precepts of Christ, is but sentimental rhapsody.—*Herrick Johnson.*

Scratch the Christian and you find the pagan—spoiled.—*I. Zangwill.*

Christians and camels receive their burdens kneeling.—*Ambrose Bierce.*

He who was foretold and foreshadowed by the holy religion of Judea, which was designed to free the universal aspiration of mankind from every impure element, he has come to instruct, to obey, to love, to die, and by dying to save mankind.—*Pressense.*

Every occupation, plan, and work of man, to be truly successful, must be done under the direction of Christ, in union with his will, from love to him, and in dependence on his power.—*Müller.*

Christ is the great central fact in the world's history; to him everything looks forward or backward. All the lines of history converge upon him. All the march of providence is guided by him.

All the great purposes of God culminate in him. The greatest and most momentous fact which the history of the world records is the fact of his birth.—*Spurgeon.*

The Christian faith reposes in a person rather than a creed.—Christ is the personal, living center of theology, around which the whole Christian system is ensphered.—Christ is the personal source of the individual Christian life; the personal head of the whole Christian church; the personal sovereign of the kingdom of grace.—*R. B. Welch.*

That there should be a Christ, and that I should be Christless; that there should be a cleansing, and that I should remain foul; that there should be a Father's love, and I should be an alien; that there should be a heaven, and I should be cast into hell, is grief embittered, sorrow aggravated.—*Spurgeon.*

Let it not be imagined that the life of a good Christian must be a life of melancholy and gloominess; for he only resigns some pleasures to enjoy others infinitely better.—*Pascal.*

One truly Christian life will do more to prove the divine origin of Christianity than many lectures. It is of much greater importance to develop Christian character, than to exhibit Christian evidences.—*J. M. Gibson.*

It is a truth that stands out with startling distinctness on the pages of the New Testament, that God has no sons who are not servants.—*H. D. Ward.*

The Christian life is not merely knowing or hearing, but doing the will of Christ.—*F. W. Robertson.*

I have known what the enjoyments and advantages of this life are, and what are the more refined pleasures which learning and intellectual power can bestow; and with all the experience that more than three-score years can give, I now, on the eve of my departure, declare to you, that health is a great blessing; competence obtained by honorable industry is a great blessing; and a great blessing it is, to have kind, faithful, and loving friends and relatives; but that the greatest of all blessings, as it is the most ennobling of all privileges, is to be indeed a Christian.—*Coleridge.*

It is more to the honor of a Christian by faith to overcome the world, than by monastical vows to retreat from it; more for the honor of Christ to serve him in the city, than to serve him in the cell.—*M. Henry.*

He is no good Christian who thinks he can be safe without God, or not safe with him.—*Henshaw.*

It does not require great learning to be a Christian and be convinced of the truth of the Bible. It requires only an honest heart and a willingness to obey God.—*Barnes.*

No man is so happy as the real Christian; none so rational, so virtuous, so amiable. How little vanity does he feel, though he believes himself united to God! How far is he from abjectness, though he ranks himself with the worms of the earth.—*Pascal.*

To be good and to do good are the two great objects set before the Christian; to develop a perfect character by rendering a perfect service. True Christian culture leads to and expresses itself in service, while faithful and loving service is the best means of Christian culture.—*Washington Gladden.*

A child of God should be a visible beatitude for joy and happiness, and a living doxology for gratitude and adoration.— *Spurgeon.*

The Christian has greatly the advantage of the unbeliever, having everything to gain and nothing to lose.—*Byron.*

Faith makes, life proves, trials confirm, and death crowns the Christian.—*Hopfner.*

A Christian is nothing but a sinful man who has put himself to school to Christ for the honest purpose of becoming better.—*H. W. Beecher.*

A Christian in this world is but gold in the ore; at death, the pure gold is melted out and separated, and the dross cast away and consumed.—*Flavel.*

The Christian needs a reminder every hour; some defeat, surprise, adversity, peril; to be agitated, mortified, beaten out of his course, so that all remains of self will be sifted out.—*Horace Bushnell.*

The best advertisement of a workshop is first-class work. The strongest attraction to Christianity is a well-made Christian character.—*T. L. Cuyler.*

CHRISTIANITY. — Christianity is more than history. It is also a system of truths. Every event which its history records, either is a truth, or suggests or expresses a truth, which man needs assent to or to put into practice. —*Noah Porter.*

Heathenism was the seeking religion; Judaism, the hoping religion; Christianity is the reality of what heathenism sought and Judaism hoped for.— *Luthardt.*

Christianity is not a theory or speculation, but a life; not a philosophy of life, but a life and a living process.— *Coleridge.*

The distinction between Christianity and all other systems of religion consists largely in this, that in these others men are found seeking after God, while Christianity is God seeking after men.— *T. Arnold.*

He who shall introduce into public affairs the principles of primitive Christianity, will revolutionize the world.— *Franklin.*

Christianity did not come from Heaven to be the amusement of an idle hour, or the food of mere imagination; to be " as a very lovely song of one that hath a pleasant voice, and playeth well upon an instrument." It is intended to be the guide and companion of all our hours—the serious occupation of our whole existence.—*Bp. Jebb.*

Christianity is the good man's text; his life, the illustration.

Where science speaks of improvement, Christianity speaks of renovation; where science speaks of development, Christianity speaks of sanctification; where science speaks of progress, Christianity speaks of perfection. — *J. P. Thompson.*

So comprehensive are the doctrines of the Gospel, that they involve all moral truth known by man; so extensive are the precepts, that they require every virtue, and forbid every sin. Nothing has been added either by the labors of philosophy or the progress of human knowledge.

Christianity everywhere gives dignity to labor, sanctity to marriage, and brotherhood to man.—Where it may not convince, it enlightens; where it does not convert it restrains; where it does not renew, it refines; where it does not sanctify, it subdues and elevates.— It is profitable alike for this world, and for the world that is to come.—*Lord Lawrence.*

Christianity is not a religion of transcendental abstraction, or brilliant speculation; its children are neither monks, mystics, epicureans, nor stoics.—It is the religion of loving, speaking, and doing, as well as believing.—It is a life as well as a creed.—It has a rest for the heart, a word for the tongue, a way for the feet, and a work for the hand. The same Lord who is the foundation of our hopes, the object of our faith, and the subject of our love, is also the model of our conduct, for " He went about doing good, leaving us an example that we should follow his steps." —*Cumming.*

It matters little whether or no Christianity makes men richer. But it does make them truer, purer, nobler. It is not more wealth that the world wants, a thousandth part as much as it is more character; not more investments, but more integrity; not money, but manhood; not regal palaces, but regal souls. —*E. G. Beckwith.*

Give Christianity a common law trial; submit the evidence pro and con to an impartial jury under the direction of a competent court, and the verdict will assuredly be in its favor.—*Chief Justice Gibson.*

Christianity is the companion of liberty in all its conflicts—the cradle of its infancy, and the divine source of its claims.—*De Tocqueville.*

The religion of Christ has made a Republic like ours possible; and the more we have of this religion the better the Republic.—*H. M. Field.*

However much the priestlings of science may prate against the Bible, the high priests of science are in accord with Christianity.—*Prof. Simpson.*

Independent of its connection with human destiny hereafter, the fate of republican government is indissolubly bound up with the fate of the Christian religion, and a people who reject its holy faith will find themselves the slaves of their own evil passions and of arbitrary power.—*Lewis Cass.*

Christianity is the basis of republican

government, its bond of cohesion, and its life-giving law.—More than the Magna Charta itself the Gospels are the roots of English liberty.—That Magna Charta, and the Petition of Right, with our completing Declaration, was possible only because the Gospels had been before them.—*R. S. Storrs.*

There is no leveler like Christianity, but it levels by lifting all who receive it to the lofty table-land of a true character and of undying hope both for this world and the next.

Prophecy and miracles argue the imperfection of the state of the church, rather than its perfection. For they are means designed by God as a stay or support, or as a leading string to the church in its infancy, rather than as means adapted to it in its full growth.—*Jonathan Edwards.*

Christianity will gain by every step that is taken in the knowledge of man.—*Spurzheim.*

There never was found in any age of the world, either philosophy, or sect, or religion, or law, or discipline, which did so highly exalt the good of the community, and increase private and particular good as the holy Christian faith.—Hence, it clearly appears that it was one and the same God that gave the Christian law to men, who gave the laws of nature to the creatures.—*Bacon.*

Christianity has no ceremonial.—It has forms, for forms are essential to order; but it disdains the folly of attempting to reinforce the religion of the heart by the antics of the body or mind.—*Croly.*

Christianity requires two things from every man who believes in it: first, to acquire property by just and righteous means, and second, to look not only on his own things, but also on the things of others.—*H. J. Van Dyke.*

With Christianity came a new civilization, and a new order of ideas.—Tastes were cultivated, manners refined, views broadened, and natures spiritualized.—*Azarias.*

Whatever may be said of the philosophy of Coleridge, his proof of the truth of Christianity was most simple and conclusive.—It consisted in the words, "Try it for yourself."

Christianity proves itself, as the sun is seen by its own light.—Its evidence is involved in its excellence.—*Coleridge.*

The moral and religious system which Jesus Christ has transmitted to us, is the best the world has ever seen, or can see.—*Franklin.*

When a man is opposed to Christianity, it is because Christianity is opposed to him. Your infidel is usually a person who resents the opposition of Christianity to that in his nature and life which Jesus came to rebuke and destroy.—*Robert Hall.*

Christianity is intended to be the guide, the guardian, the companion of all our hours: to be the food of our immortal spirits; to be the serious occupation of our whole existence.—*Jebb.*

The task and triumph of Christianity is to make men and nations true and just and upright in all their dealings, and to bring all law, as well as all conduct, into subjection and conformity to the law of God.—*H. J. Van Dyke.*

Christianity works while infidelity talks. She feeds the hungry, clothes the naked, visits and cheers the sick, and seeks the lost, while infidelity abuses her and babbles nonsense and profanity. "By their fruits ye shall know them."—*H. W. Beecher.*

Had the doctrines of Jesus been preached always as pure as they came from his lips, the whole civilized world would now have been Christians.—*Jefferson.*

After reading the doctrines of Plato, Socrates, or Aristotle, we feel that the specific difference between their words and Christ's. is the difference between an inquiry and a revelation.—*Joseph Parker.*

Through its whole history the Christion religion has developed supreme affinities for best things. For the noblest culture, for purest morals, for magnificent literatures, for most finished civilizations, for most energetic national temperaments, for most enterprising races, for most virile and progressive stock of mind, it has manifested irresistible sympathies. Judging its future by its past, no other system of human thought has so splendid a destiny. It is the only system which possesses undying youth.—*A. Phelps.*

There's not much practical Christianity in the man who lives on better terms with angels and seraphs, than with his children, servants, and neighbors.—*H. W. Beecher.*

Whatever men may think of religion, the historic fact is, that in proportion as the institutions of Christianity lose their hold upon the multitudes, the fabric of society is in peril.—*A. T. Pierson.*

The tendency of Christian ideas is to mental growth.—The mind must expand that takes them in with cordial sympathy. The conversion of Saul of Tarsus wrought in him an intellectual as well as a moral revolution.—*A. Phelps.*

Christianity has its best exponents in the lives of the saints.—It is only when our creeds pass into the iron of the blood that they become vital and organic.—Faith if not transmuted into character, has lost its power.—*C. L. Thompson.*

"Learn of me," says the philosopher, "and ye shall find restlessness." "Learn of me," says Christ, "and ye shall find rest."—*Drummond.*

Christianity is the only system of faith which combines religious beliefs with corresponding principles of morality.—It builds ethics on religion.—*A. Phelps.*

Christianity as an idea begins with thinking of God in the same way that a true son thinks of his father; Christianity as a life, begins with feeling and acting toward God as a true son feels and acts toward his father.—*C. H. Parkhurst.*

Christ built no church, wrote no book, left no money, and erected no monuments; yet show me ten square miles in the whole earth without Christianity, where the life of man and the purity of women are respected, and I will give up Christianity.—*Drummond.*

Christendom is accounted for only by Christianity; and Christianity burst too suddenly into the world to be of the world.—*F. D. Huntington.*

Christianity always suits us well enough so long as we suit it. A mere mental difficulty is not hard to deal with. With most of us it is not reason that makes faith hard, but life.—*Jean Ingelow.*

Christianity is a missionary religion, converting, advancing, aggressive, encompassing the world; a non-missionary church is in the bands of death.—*Max Müller.*

If ever Christianity appears in its power it is when it erects its trophies upon the tomb; when it takes up its votaries where the world leaves them; and fills the breast with immortal hope in dying moments.—*Robert Hall.*

The real security of Christianity is to be found in its benevolent morality; in its exquisite adaption to the human heart; in the facility with which it accommodates itself to the capacity of every human intellect; in the consolation which it bears to every house of mourning; and in the light with which it brightens the great mystery of the grave.—*Macaulay.*

There was never law, or sect, or opinion did so much magnify goodness, as the Christian religion doth.—*Bacon.*

Christianity ruined emperors, but saved peoples.—It opened the palaces of Constantinople to the barbarians, but it opened the doors of cottages to the consoling angels of Christ.—*Musset.*

Christianity is intensely practical.—She has no trait more striking than her common sense.—*Buxton.*

Christianity is the record of a pure and holy soul, humble, absolutely disinterested, a truth-speaker, and bent on serving, teaching, and uplifting men.—It teaches that to love the All-perfect is happiness.—*Emerson.*

Christianity, rightly understood, is identical with the highest philosophy; the essential doctrines of Christianity are necessary and eternal truths of reason.—*Coleridge.*

The true social reformer is the faithful preacher of Christianity; and the only organization truly potent for the perfection of Society, is the Christian Church.—I know of nothing which, as a thought, is more superficial, or which, as a feeling, is better entitled to be called hatred of men, than that which disregards the influence of the gospel in its efforts for social good, or attempts to break its hold on mankind by destroying their faith in its living power.—*J. H. Seelye.*

The true Christian is the true citizen, lofty of purpose, resolute in endeavor, ready for a hero's deeds, but never looking down on his task because it is cast in the day of small things; scornful of baseness, awake to his own duties as well as to his rights, following the higher law with reverence, and in this world doing all that in his power lies, so that when death comes he may feel that mankind is in some degree better because he lived.—*Theodore Roosevelt.*

The steady discipline of intimate friendship with Jesus results in men becoming like Him.—*Dr. Harry Emerson Fosdick.*

We not only can be, but we must be Christians; only, however, if we recognize that Christianity is progressive historical development still in the making.—*Rudolph Eucken.*

The way to preserve the peace of the church is to preserve its purity.—*M. Henry.*

Surely the church is a place where one day's truce ought to be allowed to the dissensions and animosities of mankind.—*Burke.*

The Church of Christ is the world's only social hope and the sole promise of Peace.—*General Sir Douglas Haig.*

Going to church doesn't make you a Christian any more than going to a garage makes you an automobile.—*W. A. "Billy" Sunday.*

American Catholics rejoice in our separation of Church and State; and I can conceive no combination of circumstances likely to arise which should make a union desirable either to Church or State.—*James Cardinal Gibbons.*

Business checks up on itself frequently to be sure that it still is headed for its original goals. Is there not need for a similar check-up on the part of the church?—*Bruce Barton.*

Man is not yet so transfigured that he has ceased to keep the window of his mind and heart open towards Jerusalem, Galilee, Mecca, Canterbury, or Plymouth. The abstract proposal that we worship at any place where God lets down the ladder is not yet an adequate substitute for the deep desire to go up to some central sanctuary where the religious artist vindicates a concrete universal in the realm of the spirit.—*Willard L. Sperry.*

I never weary of great churches. It is my favorite kind of mountain scenery. Mankind was never so happily inspired as when it made a cathedral.—*Robert Louis Stevenson.*

I belong to the Great Church which holds the world within its starlit aisles; that claims the great and good of every race and clime; that finds with joy the grain of gold in every creed, and floods with light and love the germs of good in every soul.—*Robert G. Ingersoll.*

Religion is a process of turning your skull into a tabernacle, not of going up to Jerusalem once a year.—*Austin O'Malley.*

If the growth of modern science has taught anything to religion and to the modern world, it is that the method of progress is the method of evolution, not the method of revolution. Let every man reflect well on these things before he assists in stabbing to death, or in allowing to starve to death, organized religion in the United States.—*Robert Andrews Millikan.*

CIRCUMSTANCES.—He is happy whose circumstances suit his temper; but he is more excellent who can suit his temper to any circumstances.—*Hume.*

Men are the sport of circumstances, when the circumstances seem the sport of men.—*Byron.*

It is our relation to circumstances that determines their influence over us. —*The same wind that carries one vessel into port may blow another off shore.—Bovee.*

A man is what the winds and tides have made him.—*Jim Tully.*

One must follow circumstances, use the forces about us, do in a word what we find to do.—*Anatole France.*

Most men and women have to take the way in life which happens to be open to them. They have neither the leisure nor the inclination to mark and digest the experiences which come their way. Only a few are free to select their paths and choose those which yield the richest harvests of experience.—*Sir Arthur Keith.*

Circumstances are the rulers of the weak; they are but the instruments of the wise.—*Samuel Lover.*

Circumstances form the character; but like petrifying waters they harden while they form.—*L. E. Landon.*

Men are not altered by their circumstances, but as they give them opportunities of exerting what they are in themselves; and a powerful clown is a tyrant in the most ugly form in which he can possibly appear.—*Steele.*

Occasions do not make a man either strong or weak, but they show what he is.—*Thomas à Kempis.*

Circumstances!—I make circumstances!—*Napoleon.*

CITIES.—The city is an epitome of the social world.—All the belts of civilization intersect along its avenues.—It contains the products of every moral zone and is cosmopolitan, not only in a national, but in a moral and spiritual sense.—*E. H. Chapin.*

Cities force growth, and make men talkative and entertaining, but they make them artificial.—*Emerson.*

The union of men in large masses is indispensable to the development and rapid growth of their higher faculties.— Cities have always been the fireplaces of civilization, whence light and heat radiated out into the dark, cold world. —*Theodore Parker.*

God the first garden made, and Cain the first city.—*Cowley.*

I have found by experience, that they who have spent all their lives in cities, contract not only an effeminacy of habit, but of thinking.—*Goldsmith.*

If you suppress the exorbitant love of pleasure and money, idle curiosity, iniquitous purpose, and wanton mirth, what a stillness would there be in the greatest cities.—*Bruyère.*

The city has always been the decisive battle ground of civilization and religion. It intensifies all the natural tendencies of man. From its fomented energies, as well as from its greater weight of numbers, the city controls. Ancient civilizations rose and fell with their leading cities. In modern times, it is hardly too much to say, " as goes the city so goes the world."—*S. J. Mc-Pherson.*

I bless God for cities.—They have been as lamps of life along the pathways of humanity and religion.—Within them, science has given birth to her noblest discoveries.—Behind their walls, freedom has fought her noblest battles. —They have stood on the surface of the earth like great breakwaters, rolling back or turning aside the swelling tide of oppression.—Cities, indeed, have been the cradles of human liberty.— They have been the active sentries of almost all Church and state reformation. —*Guthrie.*

If you would know and not be known, live in a city.—*Colton.*

Men, by associating in large masses, as in camps and cities, improve their talents, but impair their virtues; and strengthen their minds, but weaken their morals.—*Colton.*

The conditions of city life may be made healthy, so far as the physical constitution is concerned.—But there is connected with the business of the city so much competition, so much rivalry, so much necessity for industry, that I think it is a perpetual, chronic, wholesale violation of natural law.—There are ten men that can succeed in the country, where there is one that can succeed in the city.—*H. W. Beecher.*

Whatever makes men good Christians, makes them good citizens.— *Daniel Webster.*

There is no solitude more dreadful for a stranger, an isolated man, than a great city.—So many thousands of men, and not one friend.—*Boiste.*

In the country, a man's mind is free and easy, and at his own disposal; but in the city, the persons of friends and acquaintance, one's own and other people's business, foolish quarrels, ceremonies, visits, impertinent discourses, and a thousand other fopperies and diversions steal away the greatest part of our time, and leave no leisure for better and more necessary employment. Great towns are but a larger sort of prison to the soul, like cages to birds, or pounds to beasts.—*Charron.*

CIVILITY. — (See " COURTESY.") Civility is a charm that attracts the love of all men; and too much is better than to show too little.—*Bp. Horne.*

The general principles of urbanity,

politeness, or civility, have been the same in all nations; but the mode in which they are dressed is continually varying. The general idea of showing respect is by making yourself less; but the manner, whether by bowing the body, kneeling, prostration, pulling off the upper part of our dress, or taking away the lower, is a matter of custom. —*Sir J. Reynolds.*

While thou livest, keep a good tongue in thy head.—*Shakespeare.*

The insolent civility of a proud man is, if possible, more shocking than his rudeness could be; because he shows you by his manner, that he thinks it mere condescension in him, and that his goodness alone bestows upon you what you have no pretence to claim.—*Chesterfield.*

Nothing costs less, nor is cheaper, than the compliments of civility.—*Cervantes.*

When a great merchant of Liverpool was asked by what means he had contrived to realize the large fortune he possessed, his reply was, "By one article alone, in which thou mayest deal too, if thou pleasest—it is civility."—*Bentley.*

If a civil word or two will render a man happy, he must be a wretch, indeed, who will not give them to him.—Such a disposition is like lighting another man's candle by one's own, which loses none of its brilliancy by what the other gains.—*Penn.*

CIVILIZATION.—All that is best in the civilization of to-day, is the fruit of Christ's appearance among men.—*Daniel Webster.*

More than one of the strong nations may shortly have to choose between a selfish secular civilization, whose God is science, and an unselfish civilization whose God is Christ.—*R. D. Hitchcock.*

If you would civilize a man, begin with his grandmother.—*Victor Hugo.*

Here is the element or power of conduct, of intellect and knowledge, of beauty, and of social life and manners, and all needful to build up a complete human life.—We have instincts responding to them all, and requiring them all, and we are perfectly civilized only when all these instincts of our nature—all these elements in our civilization have

been adequately recognized and satisfied.—*Matthew Arnold.*

In order to civilize a people, it is necessary first to fix it, and this cannot be done without inducing it to cultivate the soil.—*De Tocqueville.*

The most civilized people are as near to barbarism, as the most polished steel is to rust.—Nations, like metals, have only a superficial brilliancy.—*Rivarol.*

The true test of civilization is, not the census, nor the size of cities, nor the crops, but the kind of man that the country turns out.—*Emerson.*

A sufficient and sure method of civilization is the influence of good women. —*Emerson.*

The ultimate tendency of civilization is toward barbarism.—*Hare.*

The ease, the luxury, and the abundance of the highest state of civilization, are as productive of selfishness as the difficulties, the privations, and the sterilities of the lowest.—*Colton.*

It is the triumph of civilization that at last communities have obtained such a mastery over natural laws that they drive and control them. The winds, the water, electricity, all aliens that in their wild form were dangerous, are now controlled by human will, and are made useful servants.—*H. W. Beecher.*

Civilization is the upward struggle of mankind, in which millions are trampled to death that thousands may mount on their bodies.—*Balfour.*

Nations, like individuals, live or die, but civilization cannot perish.—*Mazzini.*

The old Hindoo saw, in his dream, the human race led out to its various fortunes.—First, men were in chains, that went back to an iron hand—then he saw them led by threads from the brain, which went upward to an unseen hand. The first was despotism, iron, and ruling by force.—The last was civilization, ruling by ideas.—*Wendell Phillips.*

No civilization other than that which is Christian, is worth seeking or possessing.—*Bismarck.*

The post office, with its educating energy, augmented by cheapness, and guarded by a certain religious sentiment in mankind, so that the power of a wafer, or a drop of wax guards a letter as it flies over sea and land, and bears it to its address as if a battalion of artillery had brought it, I look upon as a first measure of civilization.—*Emerson.*

With Christianity came a new civilization and a new order of ideas.— Tastes were cultivated, manners refined, views broadened, and natures spiritualized.—*Azarias.*

Christianity has carried civilization along with it, whithersoever it has gone. —And as if to show that the latter does not depend on physical causes, some of the countries, the most civilized in the days of Augustus, are now in a state of hopeless barbarism.—*Hare.*

No true civilization can be expected permanently to continue which is not based on the great principles of Christianity.—*Tryon Edwards.*

CLEANLINESS. — Cleanliness of body was ever esteemed to proceed from a due reverence to God.—*Bacon.*

Certainly, this is a duty—not a sin.— Cleanliness is, indeed, next to Godliness. —*John Wesley.*

Let thy mind's sweetness have its operation upon thy body, thy clothes, and thy habitation.—*Herbert.*

The consciousness of clean linen is, in, and of itself, a source of moral strength, second only to that of a clean conscience.—A well-ironed collar or a fresh glove has carried many a man through an emergency in which a wrinkle or a rip would have defeated him.—*E. S. Phelps.*

Even from the body's purity the mind receives a secret sympathetic aid. —*Thomson.*

So great is the effect of cleanliness upon man, that it extends even to his moral character.—Virtue never dwelt long with filth; nor do I believe there ever was a person scrupulously attentive to cleanliness who was a consummate villain.—*Rumford.*

Beauty commonly produces love, but cleanliness preserves it.—Age itself is not unamiable while it is preserved clean and unsullied—like a piece of metal constantly kept smooth and bright, which we look on with more pleasure than on a new vessel cankered with rust.—*Addison.*

Cleanliness may be recommended as a mark of politeness, as it produces affection, and as it bears analogy to purity of mind.—As it renders us agreeable to others, so it makes us easy to ourselves.—It is an excellent preservative of health; and several vices, destructive both to body and mind, are inconsistent with the habit of it.— *Addison.*

CLEMENCY.—Clemency is not only the privilege, the honor, and the duty of a prince, but it is also his security, and better than all his garrisons, forts, and guards to preserve himself and his dominions in safety.—It is the brightest jewel in a monarch's crown.—*Stretch.*

Lenity will operate with greater force, in some instances, than rigor.—It is, therefore, my first wish, to have my whole conduct distinguished by it.— *Washington.*

Clemency, which we make a virtue of, proceeds sometimes from vanity, sometimes from indolence, often from fear, and almost always from a mixture of all three.—*Rochefoucauld.*

As meekness moderates anger, so clemency moderates punishment.— *Stretch.*

In general, indulgence for those we know, is rarer than pity for those we know not.—*Rivarol.*

Clemency is profitable for all; mischiefs contemned lose their force.— *Stretch.*

CLOUDS. — Those playful fancies of the mighty sky.—*Albert Smith.*

That looked as though an angel, in his upward flight, had left his mantle floating in mid-air.—*Joanna Baillie.*

My God, there go the chariots in which thou ridest forth to inspect thy fields, gardens, meadows, forests, and plains.—They are the curtains, which, at thy good pleasure, thou drawest as a covering over the plants, that they may not be withered and destroyed by the heat; and not seldom are they the arsenal in which thou keepest thine artillery of thunder and lightning, at times to strike the children of men with reverential awe, or inflict on them some great punishment.—*Gotthold.*

COMFORT.—Of all created comforts, God is the leader; you are the borrower, not the owner.—*Rutherford.*

It is a little thing to speak a phrase of common comfort, which by daily use has almost lost its sense; and yet, on the ear of him who thought to die unmourned, it will fall like the choicest music.—*Talfourd.*

I have enjoyed many of the comforts of life, none of which I wish to esteem lightly; yet I confess I know not any joy that is so dear to me, that so fully satisfies the inmost desires of my mind, that so enlivens, refines, and elevates my whole nature, as that which I derive from religion—from faith in God.—May this God be thy God, thy refuge, thy comfort, as he has been mine.—*Lavater.*

Most of our comforts grow up between our crosses.—*Young.*

The comforts we enjoy here below, are not like the anchor in the bottom of the sea, that holds fast in a storm, but like the flag upon the top of the mast, that turns with every wind.—*C. Love.*

Giving comfort under affliction requires that penetration into the human mind, joined to that experience which knows how to soothe, how to reason, and how to ridicule, taking the utmost care not to apply those arts improperly.—*Fielding.*

COMMANDERS. — He who rules must humor full as much as he commands.—*George Eliot.*

It is better to have a lion at the head of an army of sheep, than a sheep at the head of an army of lions.—*De Foe.*

The right of commanding is no longer an advantage transmitted by nature; like an inheritance, it is the fruit of labors, the price of courage.—*Voltaire.*

A brave captain is as a root, out of which, as branches, the courage of his soldiers doth spring.—*Sir P. Sidney.*

A man must require just and reasonable things if he would see the scales of obedience properly trimmed.—From orders which are improper, springs resistance which is not easily overcome.—*Basil.*

COMMERCE.—I am wonderfully delighted to see a body of men thriving in their own fortunes, and at the same time promoting the public stock; or, in other words, raising estates for their own families by bringing into their country whatever is wanting, and carrying out of it whatever is superfluous.—*Addison.*

Perfect freedom is as necessary to the health and vigor of commerce, as it is to the health and vigor of citizenship.—*Patrick Henry.*

Commerce tends to wear off those prejudices which maintain destruction and animosity between nations.—It softens and polishes the manners of men.—It unites them by one of the strongest of all ties—the desire of supplying their mutual wants.—It disposes them to peace by establishing in every state an order of citizens bound by their interest to be the guardians of public tranquillity.—*F. W. Robertson.*

Commerce has made all winds her messengers; all climes her tributaries; all people her servants.—*Tryon Edwards.*

Commerce may well be termed the younger sister, for, in all emergencies, she looks to agriculture both for defence and for supply.—*Colton.*

Every dollar spent for missions has added hundreds to the commerce of the world.—*N. G. Clark.*

It may almost be held that the hope of commercial gain has done nearly as much for the cause of truth, as even the love of truth itself.—*Bovee.*

A well regulated commerce is not like law, physic, or divinity, to be overstocked with hands; but, on the contrary, flourishes by multitudes, and gives employment to all its professors.—*Addison.*

A statesman may do much for commerce—most, by leaving it alone.—A river never flows so smoothly as when it follows its own course, without either aid or check.—Let it make its own bed; it will do so better than you can.

Commerce defies every wind, outrides every tempest and invades every zone.—*Bancroft.*

Commerce is no missionary to carry more or better than you have at home. —But what you have at home, be it gospel, or be it drunkenness, commerce carries the world over.—*E. E. Hale.*

COMMON SENSE.—(See "SENSE.")

Common sense is, of all kinds, the most uncommon.—It implies good judgment, sound discretion, and true and practical wisdom applied to common life.—*Tryon Edwards.*

Fine sense, and exalted sense, are not half as useful as common sense.—There are forty men of wit to one man of sense.—He that will carry nothing about him but gold, will be every day at a loss for readier change.—*Pope.*

To act with common sense according to the moment, is the best wisdom I know; and the best philosophy is to do one's duties, take the world as it comes, submit respectfully to one's lot; bless the goodness that has given us so much happiness with it, whatever it is; and despise affectation.—*Walpole.*

Common sense is the knack of seeing things as they are, and doing things as they ought to be done.—*C. E. Stowe.*

"Knowledge, without common sense," says Lee, is "folly; without method, it is waste; without kindness, it is fanaticism; without religion, it is death." But with common sense, it is wisdom; with method, it is power; with charity, it is beneficence; with religion, it is virtue, and life, and peace.—*Farrar.*

If a man can have only one kind of sense, let him have common sense.—If he has that and uncommon sense too, he is not far from genius.—*H. W. Beecher.*

He was one of those men who possess almost every gift, except the gift of the power to use them.—*C. Kingsley.*

The crown of all faculties is common sense.—It is not enough to do the right thing, it must be done at the right time and place.—Talent knows what to do; tact knows when and how to do it.—*W. Matthews.*

The figure which a man makes in life, the reception which he meets with in company, the esteem paid him by his acquaintance—all these depend as much upon his good sense and judgment, as upon any other part of his character. A man of the best intentions, and farthest removed from all injustice and violence, would never be able to make himself much regarded, without a moderate share of parts and understanding.—*Hume.*

Common sense is only a modification of talent.—Genius is an exaltation of it.

—The difference is, therefore, in degree, not nature.—*Bulwer.*

No man is quite sane. Each has a vein of folly in his composition—a slight determination of blood to the head, to make sure of holding him hard to some one point which he has taken to heart.—*Emerson.*

If common sense has not the brilliancy of the sun, it has the fixity of the stars.—*Caballero.*

One pound of learning requires ten pounds of common sense to apply it.—*Persian Proverb.*

If you haven't grace, the Lord can give it to you.—If you haven't learning, I'll help you to get it.—But if you haven't common sense, neither I, nor the Lord can give it to you.—*John Brown* (of Haddington, to his students).

COMMUNISM.—What is a communist?—One who has yearnings for equal division of unequal earnings.—Idler or bungler, he is willing to fork out his penny and pocket your shilling.—*Ebenezer Elliott.*

Your levelers wish to level down as far as themselves.—But they cannot bear leveling up to themselves.—They would all have some people under them.—Why not then have some people above them?—*Johnson.*

Communism possesses a language which every people can understand.—Its elements are hunger, envy, and death.—*Heine.*

COMPANIONSHIP.— (See "Associates.")

Good company, and good discourse are the very sinews of virtue.—*Izaak Walton.*

It is good discretion not to make too much of any man at the first, because one cannot hold out in that proportion.—*Bacon.*

It is expedient to have an acquaintance with those who have looked into the world; who know men, understand business, and can give you good intelligence and good advice when they are wanted.—*Bp. Horne.*

Be cautious with whom you associate, and never give your company or your confidence to those of whose good principles you are not sure.—*Bp. Coleridge.*

No company is preferable to bad, because we are more apt to catch the vices of others than their virtues, as disease is far more contagious than health.—*Colton.*

What is companionship where nothing that improves the intellect is communicated, and where the larger heart contracts itself to the model and dimension of the smaller?—*Landor.*

Wicked companions invite and lure us to hell.—*Fielding.*

No man can possibly improve in any company for which he has not respect enough to be under some degree of restraint.—*Chesterfield.*

No man can be provident of his time, who is not prudent in the choice of his company.—*Jeremy Taylor.*

Evil companions are the devil's agents whom he sends abroad into the world to debauch virtue, and to advance his kingdom; and by these ambassadors he effects more than he could in his own person.—*Anthony Horneck.*

Take rather than give the tone of the company you are in.—If you have parts, you will show them, more or less, upon every subject; and if you have not, you had better talk sillily upon a subject of other people's choosing than of your own.—*Chesterfield.*

The most agreeable of all companions is a simple, frank man, without any high pretensions to an oppressive greatness; one who loves life, and understands the use of it; obliging, alike, at all hours; above all, of a golden temper, and steadfast as an anchor.—For such an one we gladly exchange the greatest genius, the most brilliant wit, the profoundest thinker.—*Lessing.*

COMPARISON.—If we rightly estimate what we call good and evil, we shall find it lies much in comparison.—*Locke.*

The superiority of some men is merely local.—They are great because their associates are little.—*Johnson.*

When the moon shone we did not see the candle: so doth the greater glory dim the less.—A substitute shines lightly as a king until a king be by, and then his state empties itself, as doth an inland brook into the main of waters.—*Shakespeare.*

COMPASSION. — There never was any heart truly great and generous, that was not also tender and compassionate. —*South.*

It is the crown of justice and the glory, where it may kill with right, to save with pity.—*Beaumont and Fletcher.*

The dew of compassion is a tear.— *Byron.*

Compassion to an offender who has grossly violated the laws, is, in effect, a cruelty to the peaceable subject who has observed them.—*Junius.*

Man may dismiss compassion from his heart, but God will never.—*Cowper.*

COMPENSATION.—There is wisdom in the saying of Feltham, that the whole creation is kept in order by discord, and that vicissitude maintains the world.—Many evils bring many blessings.—Manna drops in the wilderness. —Corn grows in Canaan.—*Willmott.*

All advantages are attended with disadvantages.—A universal compensation prevails in all conditions of being and existence.—*Hume.*

No evil is without its compensation. —The less money, the less trouble.— The less favor, the less envy.—Even in those cases which put us out of wits, it is not the loss itself, but the estimate of the loss that troubles us.—*Seneca.*

Whatever difference may appear in the fortunes of mankind, there is, nevertheless, a certain compensation of good and evil which makes them equal.—*W. Rochefoucauld.*

If the poor man cannot always get meat, the rich man cannot always digest it.—*Giles.*

If poverty makes man groan, he yawns in opulence.—When fortune exempts us from labor, nature overwhelms us with time.—*Rivarol.*

When you are disposed to be vain of your mental acquirements, look up to those who are more accomplished than yourself, that you may be fired with emulation; but when you feel dissatisfied with your circumstances, look down on those beneath you, that you may learn contentment—*H. More.*

When fate has allowed to any man more than one great gift, accident or necessity seems usually to contrive that one shall encumber and impede the other.—*Swinburne.*

As there is no worldly gain without some loss, so there is no worldly loss without some gain.—If thou hast lost thy wealth, thou hast lost some trouble with it.—If thou art degraded from thy honor, thou art likewise freed from the stroke of envy.—If sickness hath blurred thy beauty, it hath delivered thee from pride.—Set the allowance against the loss and thou shalt find no loss great.—He loses little or nothing who reserves himself.—*Quarles.*

COMPLACENCY. — Complaisance renders a superior amiable, an equal agreeable, and an inferior acceptable. It smooths distinction, sweetens conversation, and makes every one in the company pleased with himself. It produces good nature and mutual benevolence, encourages the timorous, soothes the turbulent, humanizes the fierce, and distinguishes a society of civilized persons from a confusion of savages.—*Addison.*

Complacency is a coin by the aid of which all the world can, for want of essential means, pay its club bill in society. —It is necessary, however, that it may lose nothing of its merits, to associate judgment and prudence with it.—*Voltaire.*

Complaisance, though in itself it be scarce reckoned in the number of moral virtues, is that which gives a luster to every talent a man can be possessed of. —I would advise every man of learning, who would not appear a mere scholar or philosopher, to make himself master of this social virtue.—*Addison.*

Complaisance pleases all; prejudices none; adorns wit; renders humor agreeable; augments friendship; redoubles love; and united with justice and generosity, becomes the secret chain of the society of mankind.—*M. de Scuderi.*

COMPLAINING.—We do not wisely when we vent complaint and censure.— We cry out for a little pain, when we do but smile for a great deal of contentment.—*Feltham.*

Every one must see daily instances of people who complain from a mere habit of complaining; and make their friends uneasy, and strangers merry, by murmuring at evils that do not exist, and repin-

ing at grievances which they do not really feel.—*Graves.*

I will chide no brother in the world but myself, against whom I know most faults.—*Shakespeare.*

The man who is fond of complaining, likes to remain amid the objects of his vexation.—It is at the moment that he declares them insupportable that he will most strongly revolt against every means proposed for his deliverance.—This is what suits him.—He asks nothing better than to sigh over his position and to remain in it.—*Guizot.*

I will not be as those who spend the day in complaining of headache, and the night in drinking the wine that gives it.—*Goethe.*

Murmur at nothing: if our ills are irreparable, it is ungrateful; if remediless, it is vain. A Christian builds his fortitude on a better foundation than stoicism; he is pleased with everything that happens, because he knows it could not happen unless it had first pleased God and that which pleases Him must be the best.—*Colton.*

The usual fortune of complaint is to excite contempt more than pity.—*Johnson.*

I have always despised the whining yelp of complaint, and the cowardly feeble resolve.—*Burns.*

COMPLIMENTS.—Compliments are only lies in court clothes.—*Sterling.*

A deserved and discriminating compliment is often one of the strongest encouragements and incentives to the diffident and self-distrustful.—*Tryon Edwards.*

A compliment is usually accompanied with a bow, as if to beg pardon for paying it.—*Hare.*

Compliments of congratulation are always kindly taken, and cost nothing but pen, ink, and paper. I consider them as draughts upon good breeding, where the exchange is always greatly in favor of the drawer.—*Chesterfield.*

Compliments which we think are deserved, we accept only as debts, with indifference; but those which conscience informs us we do not merit, we receive with the same gratitude that we do favors given away.—*Goldsmith.*

COMPROMISE.—Compromise is but

the sacrifice of one right or good in the hope of retaining another,—too often ending in the loss of both.—*Tryon Edwards.*

From the beginning of our history the country has been afflicted with compromise. It is by compromise that human rights have been abandoned. I insist that this shall cease. The country needs repose after all its trials; it deserves repose. And repose can only be found in everlasting principles.—*Charles Sumner.*

CONCEALMENT. — (See "CRIME.") To conceal anything from those to whom I am attached, is not in my nature.—I can never close my lips where I have opened my heart.—*Dickens.*

He who can conceal his joys, is greater than he who can hide his griefs.—*Lavater.*

It is great cleverness to know how to conceal our cleverness.—*Rochefoucauld.*

"Thou shalt not get found out" is not one of God's commandments; and no man can be saved by trying to keep it.—*Leonard Bacon.*

CONCEIT. — (See "SELF-CONCEIT.") Conceit is the most contemptible, and one of the most odious qualities in the world.—It is vanity driven from all other shifts, and forced to appeal to itself for admiration.—*Hazlitt.*

It is wonderful how near conceit is to insanity!—*Jerrold.*

Wind puffs up empty bladders; opinion, fools.—*Socrates.*

He who gives himself airs of importance, exhibits the credentials of impotence.—*Lavater.*

The overweening self-respect of conceited men relieves others from the duty of respecting them at all.—*H. W. Beecher.*

Conceit is to nature, what paint is to beauty; it is not only needless, but it impairs what it would improve.—*Pope.*

The more one speaks of himself, the less he likes to hear another talked of. —*Lavater.*

They say that every one of us believes in his heart, or would like to have others believe, that he is something which he is not.—*Thackeray.*

Conceit and confidence are both of them cheats.—The first always imposes

on itself; the second frequently deceives others.—*Zimmerman.*

A man—poet, prophet, or whatever he may be—readily persuades himself of his right to all the worship that is voluntarily tendered.—*Hawthorne.*

None are so seldom found alone, or are so soon tired of their own company, as those coxcombs who are on the best terms with themselves.—*Colton.*

No man was ever so much deceived by another, as by himself.—*Greville.*

Every man, however little, makes a figure in his own eyes.—*Home.*

It is the admirer of himself, and not the admirer of virtue, that thinks himself superior to others.—*Plutarch.*

The weakest spot in every man is where he thinks himself to be the wisest. —*Emmons.*

The best of lessons, for a good many people, would be, to listen at a key-hole. —It is a pity for such that the practice is dishonorable.—*Mad. Swetchine.*

If he could only see how small a vacancy his death would leave, the proud man would think less of the place he occupies in his life-time.—*Legouve.*

One's self-satisfaction is an untaxed kind of property, which it is very unpleasant to find depreciated.—*George Eliot.*

If its colors were but fast colors, self-conceit would be a most comfortable quality.—But life is so humbling, mortifying, disappointing to vanity, that a great man's idea of himself gets washed out of him by the time he is forty.—*C. Buxton.*

I've never any pity for conceited people, because I think they carry their comfort about with them.—*George Eliot.*

Conceit may puff a man up, but can never prop him up.—*Ruskin.*

We uniformly think too well of ourselves. But self-conceit is specially the mark of a small and narrow mind. Great and noble natures are most free from it.

CONDUCT. — Conduct is the great profession. Behavior is the perpetual revealing of us. What a man does, tells us what he is.—*F. D. Huntington.*

If we do not weigh and consider to what end life is given us, and thereupon order and dispose it aright, pretend what we will as to arithmetic, we do not, and cannot number our days in the narrowest and most limited signification.—*Clarendon*.

It is not enough that you form, and even follow the most excellent rules for conducting yourself in the world; you must, also, know when to deviate from them, and where lies the exception.—*Greville*.

Fools measure actions, after they are done, by the event; wise men beforehand, by the rules of reason and right. The former look to the end, to judge of the act. Let me look to the act, and leave the end with God.—*Bp. Hall*.

The integrity of men is to be measured by their conduct, not by their professions.—*Junius*.

I will govern my life and my thoughts as if the whole world were to see the one and read the other.—For what does it signify to make anything a secret to my neighbor, when to God, who is the searcher of our hearts, all our privacies are open.—*Seneca*.

Every one of us, whatever our speculative opinions, knows better than he practices, and recognizes a better law than he obeys.—*Froude*.

In all the affairs of life let it be your great care, not to hurt your mind, or offend your judgment.—And this rule, if observed carefully in all your deportment, will be a mighty security to you in your undertakings.—*Epictetus*.

All the while that thou livest ill, thou hast the trouble, distraction, and inconveniences of life, but not the sweet and true use of it.—*Fuller*.

CONFESSION.—A man should never be ashamed to own he has been in the wrong, which is but saying, in other words, that he is wiser to-day than he was yesterday.—*Pope*.

The confession of evil works is the first beginning of good works.—*Augustine*.

Why does no man confess his vices?—because he is yet in them.—It is for a waking man to tell his dream.—*Seneca*.

Be not ashamed to confess that you have been in the wrong. It is but owning what you need not be ashamed of—that you now have more sense than you

had before, to see your error; more humility to acknowledge it, more grace to correct it.—*Seed*.

If thou wouldst be justified, acknowledge thine injustice.—He that confesses his sin, begins his journey toward salvation.—He that is sorry for it, mends his pace.—He that forsakes it, is at his journey's end.—*Quarles*.

It is not our wrong actions which it requires courage to confess, so much as those which are ridiculous and foolish.—*Rousseau*.

Confession of sin comes from the offer of mercy.—Mercy displayed causes confession to flow, and confession flowing opens the way for mercy.—If I have not a contrite heart, God's mercy will never be mine; but if God had not manifested his mercy in Christ, I could never have had a contrite heart.—*Arnot*.

CONFIDENCE. — Trust men and they will be true to you; treat them greatly and they will show themselves great.—*Emerson*.

I think I have learned, in some degree at least, to disregard the old maxim "Do not get others to do what you can do yourself." My motto on the other hand is, "do not do that which others can do as well."—*Booker T. Washington*.

Trust not him that hath once broken faith.—*Shakespeare*.

He that does not respect confidence will never find happiness in his path.—The belief in virtue vanishes from his heart; the source of nobler actions becomes extinct in him.—*Auffenberg*.

Confidence is a plant of slow growth; especially in an aged bosom.—*Johnson*.

Trust him with little, who, without proofs, trusts you with everything, or when he has proved you, with nothing.—*Lavater*.

When young, we trust ourselves too much; and we trust others too little when old.—Rashness is the error of youth; timid caution of age.—Manhood is the isthmus between the two extremes—the ripe and fertile season of action when, only, we can hope to find the head to contrive, united with the hand to execute.—*Colton*.

Society is built upon trust, and trust

upon confidence in one another's integrity.—*South*.

All confidence is dangerous, if it is not entire; we ought on most occasions to speak all, or conceal all. We have already too much disclosed our secrets to a man, from whom we think any one single circumstance is to be concealed.—*Bruyère*.

Let us have a care not to disclose our hearts to those who shut up theirs against us.—*Beaumont*.

Fields are won by those who believe in winning.—*T. W. Higginson*.

They can conquer who believe they can.—*Dryden*.

Confidence imparts a wondrous inspiration to its possessor.—It bears him on in security, either to meet no danger, or to find matter of glorious trial.—*Milton*.

The human heart, at whatever age, opens only to the heart that opens in return.—*Maria Edgeworth*.

Confidence in one's self, though the chief nurse of magnanimity, doth not leave the care of necessary furniture for it; of all the Grecians, Homer doth make Achilles the best armed.—*Sir P. Sidney*.

I could never pour out my inmost soul without reserve to any human being, without danger of one day repenting my confidence.—*Burns*.

There are cases in which a man would be ashamed not to have been imposed upon. There is a confidence necessary to human intercourse, and without which men are often more injured by their own suspicions, than they could be by the perfidy of others.—*Burke*.

Self-trust is the essence of heroism.—*Emerson*.

Confidence, in conversation, has a greater share than wit.—*Rochefoucauld*.

Confidence in another man's virtue, is no slight evidence of one's own.—*Montaigne*.

If we are truly prudent we shall cherish those noblest and happiest of our tendencies—to love and to confide.—*Bulwer*.

Trust him little who praises all; him less who censures all; and him least who is indifferent to all.—*Lavater*.

To confide, even though to be betrayed, is much better than to learn only to conceal.—In the one case your neighbor wrongs you;—but in the other you are perpetually doing injustice to yourself.—*Simms*.

Never put much confidence in such as put no confidence in others. A man prone to suspect evil is mostly looking in his neighbor for what he sees in himself. As to the pure all things are pure, even so to the impure all things are impure.—*Hare*.

All confidence which is not absolute and entire, is dangerous.—There are few occasions but where a man ought either to say all, or conceal all; for, how little soever you have revealed of your secret to a friend, you have already said too much if you think it not safe to make him privy to all particulars.—*Beaumont*.

CONSCIENCE. — Conscience! conscience! man's most faithful friend!—*Crabbe*.

Man's conscience is the oracle of God.—*Byron*.

Conscience is the reason, employed about questions of right and wrong, and accompanied with the sentiments of approbation or condemnation.—*Whewell*.

A tender conscience is an inestimable blessing; that is, a conscience not only quick to discern what is evil, but instantly to shun it, as the eyelid closes itself against the mote.—*N. Adams*.

The truth is not so much that man has conscience, as that conscience has man.—*Dorner*.

It is far more important to me to preserve an unblemished conscience than to compass any object however great.—*Channing*.

He will easily be content and at peace, whose conscience is pure.—*Thomas à Kempis*.

Conscience is God's vicegerent on earth, and, within the limited jurisdiction given to it, it partakes of his infinite wisdom and speaks in his tone of absolute command. It is a revelation of the being of a God, a divine voice in the human soul, making known the presence of its rightful sovereign, the author of the law of holiness and truth.—*Bowen*.

I feel within me a peace above all

earthly dignities, a still and quiet conscience.—*Shakespeare.*

If conscience smite thee once, it is an admonition; if twice, it is a condemnation.

What other dungeon is so dark as one's own heart! What jailer so inexorable as one's self!—*Hawthorne.*

A good conscience is a continual Christmas.—*Franklin.*

Conscience is merely our own judgment of the right or wrong of our actions, and so can never be a safe guide unless enlightened by the word of God. —*Tryon Edwards.*

We cannot live better than in seeking to become better, nor more agreeably than in having a clear conscience.—*Socrates.*

The voice of conscience is so delicate that it is easy to stifle it; but it is also so clear that it is impossible to mistake it.—*Mad. de Staël.*

Conscience is the voice of the soul, as the passions are the voice of the body.— No wonder they often contradict each other.—*Rousseau.*

A conscience void of offence, before God and man, is an inheritance for eternity.—*Daniel Webster.*

A good conscience is the palace of Christ; the temple of the Holy Ghost; the paradise of delight; the standing Sabbath of the saints.—*Augustine.*

To endeavor to domineer over conscience, is to invade the citadel of heaven.—*Charles V.*

Conscience is the true vicar of Christ in the soul; a prophet in its information; a monarch in its peremptoriness; a priest in its blessings or anathemas, according as we obey or disobey it.—*J. Newman.*

Conscience, in most men, is but the anticipation of the opinions of others.— *Taylor.*

No man ever offended his own conscience, but first or last it was revenged upon him for it.—*South.*

Conscience, honor, and credit, are all in our interest; and without the concurrence of the former, the latter are but impositions upon ourselves and others. —*Steele.*

There is no future pang can deal that justice on the self-condemned, he deals on his own soul.—*Byron.*

If any speak ill of thee, flee home to thine own conscience, and examine thine heart; if thou be guilty, it is a just correction; if not guilty, it is a fair instruction. Make use of both—so shalt thou distil honey out of gall, and out of an open enemy make a secret friend.— *Quarles.*

We never do evil so thoroughly and heartily as when led to it by an honest but perverted, because mistaken, conscience.—*Tryon Edwards.*

Conscience is a great ledger book in which all our offences are written and registered, and which time reveals to the sense and feeling of the offender.— *Burton.*

Our conscience is a fire within us, and our sins as the fuel; instead of warming, it will scorch us, unless the fuel be removed, or the heat of it be allayed by penitential tears.—*J. M. Mason.*

There is no witness so terrible—no accuser so powerful as conscience which dwells within us.—*Sophocles.*

Conscience, true as the needle to the pole points steadily to the pole-star of God's eternal justice, reminding the soul of the fearful realities of the life to come.—*E. H. Gillett.*

He that is conscious of crime, however bold by nature, becomes a coward.— *Menander.*

Conscience warns us as a friend before it punishes as a judge.—*Stanislaus.*

Conscience tells us that we ought to do right, but it does not tell us what right is—that we are taught by God's word.—*H. C. Trumbull.*

That conscience approves of any given course of action, is, of itself, an obligation.—*Bp. Butler.*

Conscience has nothing to do as lawgiver or judge, but is a witness against me if I do wrong, and which approves if I do right.—To act against conscience is to act against reason and God's law.

Conscience is not law.—No.—God has made and reason recognizes the law, and conscience is placed within us to prompt to the right, and warn against the wrong

A disciplined conscience is a man's best friend.—It may not be his most amiable, but it is his most faithful monitor.—*A. Phelps.*

What conscience dictates to be done, or warns me not to do, this teach me more than hell to shun, that more than heaven pursue.—*Pope.*

A good conscience is to the soul what health is to the body; it preserves constant ease and serenity within us, and more than countervails all the calamities and afflictions which can befall us without.—*Addison.*

Labor to keep alive in your heart that little spark of celestial fire called conscience.—*Washington.*

There is no class of men so difficult to be managed in a state as those whose intentions are honest, but whose consciences are bewitched.—*Napoleon.*

Preserve your conscience always soft and sensitive. If but one sin force its way into that tender part of the soul and is suffered to dwell there, the road is paved for a thousand iniquities.—*Watts.*

Tenderness of conscience is always to be distinguished from scrupulousness. The conscience cannot be kept too sensitive and tender; but scrupulousness arises from bodily or mental infirmity, and discovers itself in a multitude of ridiculous, superstitious, and painful feelings.—*Cecil.*

The men who succeed best in public life are those who take the risk of standing by their own convictions.—*J. A. Garfield.*

Cowardice asks, Is it safe? Expediency asks, Is it politic? Vanity asks, Is it popular? but Conscience asks, Is it right?—*Punshon.*

A wounded conscience is able to unparadise paradise itself.—*Fuller.*

Were conscience always clear and decided in its awards, we could scarcely remain unconsoled for the resignation of any delight, however delightful.—It is doubt in all cases, that is the real malicious devil.—*Mrs. Alexander.*

The torture of a bad conscience is the hell of a living soul.—*Calvin.*

Keep your conduct abreast of your conscience, and very soon your conscience will be illumined by the radiance of God.—*W. M. Taylor.*

A man of integrity will never listen to any reason against conscience.—*Home.*

In the commission of evil, fear no man so much as thyself.—Another is but one witness against thee; thou art a thousand.—Another thou mayst avoid, thyself thou canst not.—Wickedness is its own punishment.—*Quarles.*

My dominion ends where that of conscience begins.—*Napoleon.*

Many a lash in the dark, doth conscience give the wicked.—*Boston.*

Trust that man in nothing who has not a conscience in everything.—*Sterne.*

He who commits a wrong will himself inevitably see the writing on the wall, though the world may not count him guilty.—*Tupper.*

Some persons follow the dictates of their conscience, only in the same sense in which a coachman may be said to follow the horses he is driving.—*Whately.*

Conscience doth make cowards of us all.—*Shakespeare.*

The foundation of true joy is in the conscience.—*Seneca.*

A quiet conscience makes one so serene.—*Byron.*

A clean and sensitive conscience, a steadfast and scrupulous integrity in small things as well as great, is the most valuable of all possessions, to a nation as to an individual.—*H. J. Van Dyke.*

Conscience—that vicegerent of God in the human heart, whose still, small voice the loudest revelry cannot drown.—*W. H. Harrison.*

A good conscience fears no witness, but a guilty conscience is solicitous even in solitude.—If we do nothing but what is honest, let all the world know it.—But if otherwise, what does it signify to have nobody else know it, so long as I know it myself?—Miserable is he who slights that witness.—*Seneca.*

Conscience is not given to a man to instruct him in the right, but to prompt him to choose the right instead of the wrong when he is instructed as to what is right. It tells a man that he ought to do right, but does not tell him what is right. And if a man has made up his mind that a certain wrong course is the right one, the more he follows his conscience the more hopeless he is as a wrongdoer. One is pretty far gone in an evil way when he serves the devil conscientiously.—*H. C. Trumbull.*

What we call conscience, is, in many instances, only a wholesome fear of the constable.—*Bovee.*

Conscience, though ever so small a worm while we live, grows suddenly into a serpent on our deathbed.—*Jerrold.*

I am more afraid of my own heart, than of the Pope and all his cardinals.— I have within me the great Pope, self.— *Luther.*

Be fearful only of thyself, and stand in awe of none more than of thine own conscience.—There is a Cato in every man—a severe censor of his manners.— And he that reverences this judge will seldom do anything he need repent of. —*Burton.*

Conscience is justice's best minister. It threatens, promises, rewards, and punishes, and keeps all under its control. —The busy must attend to its remonstrances; the most powerful submit to its reproof, and the angry endure its upbraidings.—While conscience is our friend, all is peace; but if once offended, farewell to the tranquil mind.—*Mary Wortley Montague.*

It is astonishing how soon the whole conscience begins to unravel if a single stitch drops.—One single sin indulged in makes a hole you could put your head through.—*C. Buxton.*

CONSERVATISM.—A conservative is a man who will not look at the new moon, out of respect for that "ancient institution," the old one.—*Jerrold.*

We are reformers in spring and summer.—In autumn and winter we stand by the old.—Reformers in the morning; conservatives at night.—Reform is affirmative; conservatism, negative.—Conservatism goes for comfort; reform for truth.—*Emerson.*

Generally young men are regarded as radicals. This is a popular misconception. The most conservative persons I ever met are college undergraduates.— *Woodrow Wilson.*

A conservative is a man who is too cowardly to fight and too fat to run.— *E. Hubbard.*

The highest function of conservatism is to keep what progressiveness has accomplished.—*R. H. Fulton.*

I often think it's comical how nature always does contrive that every boy and every gal, that's born into this world alive, is either a little Liberal, or else a little Conservative.—*Sir William S. Gilbert.*

The conservative may clamor against reform, but he might as well clamor against the centrifugal force.—He sighs for "the good old times."—He might as well wish the oak back into the acorn. —*E. H. Chapin.*

CONSIDERATION.—Better it is to the right conduct of life to consider what will be the end of a thing, than what is the beginning of it; for what promises fair at first, may prove ill, and what seems at first a disadvantage, may prove very advantageous.—*William V. Wells.*

Consideration is the soil in which wisdom may be expected to grow, and strength be given to every upspringing plant of duty.—*Emerson.*

CONSISTENCY.—(See "INCONSISTENCY.")

With consistency a great soul has simply nothing to do.—He may as well concern himself with his shadow on the wall.—*Emerson.*

Intellectual consistency is far from being the first want of our nature, and is seldom a primary want in minds of great persuasive, as distinguished from convincing power.—*Strahan.*

Do I contradict myself? Very well then I contradict myself. (I am large, I contain multitudes.)—*Walt Whitman.*

Those who honestly mean to be true contradict themselves more rarely than those who try to be consistent.—*O. W. Holmes.*

Without consistency there is no moral strength.—*Owen.*

Either take Christ into your lives, or cast him out of your lips.—Either be what thou seemest, or else be what thou art.—*Dyer.*

He who prays as he ought, will endeavor to live as he prays.—*Owen.*

CONSOLATION.—Before an affliction is digested, consolation comes too soon; and after it is digested, it comes too late; but there is a mark between these two, as fine almost as a hair, for a comforter to take aim at.—*Sterne.*

God has commanded time to console the unhappy.—*Joubert.*

For every bad there might be a worse; and when one breaks his leg let him be thankful it was not his neck.—*Bp. Hall.*

Consolation, indiscreetly pressed upon us when we are suffering under affliction, only serves to increase our pain and to render our grief more poignant.—*Rousseau.*

Nothing does so establish the mind amidst the rollings and turbulences of present things, as to look above them and beyond them—above them, to the steady and good hand by which they are ruled, and beyond them, to the sweet and beautiful end to which, by that hand, they will be brought.—*Jeremy Taylor.*

Quiet and sincere sympathy is often the most welcome and efficient consolation to the afflicted.—Said a wise man to one in deep sorrow, "I did not come to comfort you; God only can do that; but I did come to say how deeply and tenderly I feel for you in your affliction."—*Tryon Edwards.*

The powers of Time as a comforter can hardly be overstated; but the agency by which he works is exhaustion. —*L. E. Landon.*

CONSPIRACY.—Conspiracy—a game invented for the amusement of unoccupied men of rank.

Conspiracies no sooner should be formed than executed.—*Addison.*

Combinations of wickedness would overwhelm the world by the advantage which licentious principles afford, did not those who have long practiced perfidy grow faithless to each other.—*Johnson.*

Conspiracies, like thunder clouds, should in a moment form and strike like lightning, ere the sound is heard.—*Dow.*

CONSTANCY. — Constancy is the complement of all other human virtues. —*Mazzini.*

The secret of success is constancy of purpose.—*Disraeli.*

A good man it is not mine to see. Could I see a man possessed of constancy, that would satisfy me.—*Confucius.*

It is often constancy to change the mind.—*Hoole.*

Without constancy there is neither love, friendship, nor virtue in the world. —*Addison.*

I am constant as the Northern star, of whose true-fixed and resting quality there is no fellow in the firmament.—*Shakespeare.*

Constancy to truth and principle may sometimes lead to what the world calls inconstancy in conduct.—*Tryon Edwards.*

O heaven! were man but constant, he were perfect.—*Shakespeare.*

CONTEMPLATION. — There is a sweet pleasure in contemplation; and when a man hath run through a set of vanities in the declension of his age, he knows not what to do with himself if he cannot think.—*Blount.*

In order to improve the mind, we ought less to learn, than to contemplate. —*Descartes.*

Contemplation is to knowledge, what digestion is to food—the way to get life out of it.—*Tryon Edwards.*

A contemplative life has more the appearance of piety than any other; but the divine plan is to bring faith into activity and exercise.—*Cecil.*

Let us unite contemplation with action.—In the harmony of the two, lies the perfection of character.—They are not contradictory and incompatible, but mutually helpful to each other.—Contemplation will strengthen for action, and action sends us back to contemplation, and thus the inner and outer life will be harmoniously developed.—*Foote.*

CONTEMPT.—There is not in human nature a more odious disposition than a proneness to contempt, which is a mixture of pride and ill-nature.—Nor is there any which more certainly denotes a bad disposition; for in a good and benign temper, there can be no room for it.—It is the truest symptom of a base and bad heart.—*Fielding.*

It is often more necessary to conceal contempt than resentment, the former being never forgiven, but the latter sometimes forgot. Wrongs are often forgiven; contempt never.—*Chesterfield.*

None but the contemptible are apprehensive of contempt.—*Rochefoucauld.*

Contempt is the only way to triumph over calumny.—*Mad. de Maintenon.*

I have unlearned contempt.—It is a sin that is engendered earliest in the soul, and doth beset it like a poison-worm, feeding on all its beauty.—*N. P. Willis.*

Contempt naturally implies a man's esteeming himself greater than the person whom he contemns.—He, therefore, that slights and contemns an affront, is properly superior to it.—Socrates, being kicked by an ass, did not think it a revenge proper for him to kick the ass again.—*South.*

Speak with contempt of no man.—Every one hath a tender sense of reputation.—And every man hath a sting, which he may, if provoked too far, dart out at one time or another.—*Burton.*

Despise not any man, and do not spurn anything; for there is no man that hath not his hour, nor is there anything that hath not its place.—*Rabbi Ben Azai.*

The basest and meanest of all human beings are generally the most forward to despise others.—So that the most contemptible are generally the most contemptuous.—*Fielding.*

Contempt is commonly taken by the young for an evidence of understanding; but it is neither difficult to acquire, nor meritorious when acquired. To discover the imperfections of others is penetration; to hate them for their faults is contempt. We may be clearsighted without being malevolent, and make use of the errors we discover, to learn caution, not to gratify satire.—*Sydney Smith.*

Christ saw much in this world to weep over, and much to pray over; but he saw nothing in it to look upon with contempt.—*E. H. Chapin.*

CONTENTION. — Weakness on both sides, is, as we know, the trait of all quarrels.—*Voltaire.*

Contention is like fire, for both burn so long as there is any exhaustible matter to contend within.—Only herein it transcends fire, for fire begets not matter, but consumes it; debates beget matter, but consume it not.—*T. Adams.*

It is as hard a thing to maintain a sound understanding, a tender conscience, a lively, gracious, heavenly spirit, and an upright life in the midst of contention, as to keep your candle lighted in the greatest storms.—*Baxter.*

Religious contention is the devil's harvest.—*Fontaine.*

Never contend with one that is foolish, proud, positive, testy, or with a superior, or a clown, in matter of argument.—*Fuller.*

Where two discourse, if the anger of one rises, he is the wise man who lets the contest fall.—*Plutarch.*

I never love those salamanders that are never well but when they are in the fire of contention.—I will rather suffer a thousand wrongs than offer one.—I have always found that to strive with a superior, is injurious; with an equal, doubtful; with an inferior, sordid and base; with any, full of unquietness.—*Bp. Hall.*

CONTENTMENT. — A contented mind is the greatest blessing a man can enjoy in this world; and if, in the present life, his happiness arises from the subduing of his desires, it will arise in the next from the gratification of them —*Addison.*

Submission is the only reasoning between a creature and its maker and contentment in his will is the best remedy we can apply to misfortunes.—*Sir W. Temple.*

It is right to be contented with what we have, never with what we are.—*Mackintosh.*

If we fasten our attention on what we have, rather than on what we lack, a very little wealth is sufficient.—*F. Johnson.*

A wise man will always be contented with his condition, and will live rather according to the precepts of virtue, than according to the customs of his country—*Antisthenes.*

I never complained of my condition but once, said an old man—when my feet were bare, and I had no money to buy shoes; but I met a man without feet, and became contented.

Content can soothe, where'er by fortune placed; can rear a garden in the desert waste.—*H. K. White.*

Great is he who enjoys his earthenware as if it were plate, and not less great is the man to whom all his plate is no more than earthenware.—*Leighton.*

Want of desire is the greatest riches. —*Vigée.*

The contented man is never poor; the discontented never rich.

Whether happiness may come or not, one should try and prepare one's self to do without it.—*George Eliot.*

An ounce of contentment is worth a pound of sadness, to serve God with.—*Fuller.*

If you are but content you have enough to live upon with comfort.—*Plautus.*

Since we cannot get what we like, let us like what we can get.—*Spanish Proverb.*

He who is not contented with what he has, would not be contented with what he would like to have.

Contentment is natural wealth, luxury is artificial poverty.—*Socrates.*

Resign every forbidden joy; restrain every wish that is not referred to God's will; banish all eager desires, all anxiety; desire only the will of God; seek him alone and supremely, and you will find peace.—*Fenelon.*

There is a sense in which a man looking at the present in the light of the future, and taking his whole being into account, may be contented with his lot: that is Christian contentment.—But if a man has come to that point where he is so content that he says, "I do not want to know any more, or do any more, or be any more," he is in a state in which he ought to be changed into a mummy! —Of all hideous things a mummy is the most hideous; and of mummies, the most hideous are those that are running about the streets and talking.—*H. W. Beecher.*

One who is contented with what he has done will never become famous for what he will do.—He has lain down to die, and the grass is already growing over him.—*Bovee.*

I am always content with what happens; for I know that what God chooses is better than what I choose.—*Epictetus.*

The fountain of content must spring up in the mind; and he who has so little knowledge of human nature as to see happiness by changing anything but his own disposition, will waste his life in fruitless efforts, and multiply the griefs which he proposes to remove.—*Johnson.*

That happy state of mind, so rarely possessed, in which we can say, "I have enough," is the highest attainment of philosophy. Happiness consists, not in possessing much, but in being content with what we possess. He who wants little always has enough.—*Zimmermann.*

My God, give me neither poverty nor riches, but whatsoever it may be thy will to give, give me, with it, a heart that knows humbly to acquiesce in what is thy will.—*Gotthold.*

Contentment gives a crown, where fortune hath denied it.—*Ford.*

What though we quit all glittering pomp and greatness, we may enjoy content; in that alone is greatness, power, wealth, honor, all summed up.—*Powell.*

If two angels were sent down from heaven, one to conduct an empire, and the other to sweep a street, they would feel no inclination to change employments.—*John Newton.*

To be content with even the best people, we must be contented with little and bear a great deal. Those who are most perfect have many imperfections, and we have great faults; between the two, mutual toleration becomes very difficult.—*Fenelon.*

True contentment depends not upon what we have; a tub was large enough for Diogenes, but a world was too little for Alexander.—*Colton.*

Learn to be pleased with everything; with wealth, so far as it makes us beneficial to others; with poverty, for not having much to care for; and with obscurity, for being unenvied.—*Plutarch.*

They that deserve nothing should be content with anything. Bless God for what you have, and trust God for what you want. If we cannot bring our condition to our mind, we must bring our mind to our condition; if a man is not content in the state he is in, he will not be content in the state he would be in.—*Erskine Mason.*

You traverse the world in search of happiness, which is within the reach of every man; a contented mind confers it all.—*Horace.*

Contentment is a pearl of great price, and whoever procures it at the expense of ten thousand desires makes a wise and a happy purchase.—*Balguy.*

It is a great blessing to possess what one wishes, said one to an ancient philosopher.—It is a greater still, was the reply, not to desire what one does not possess.

Contentment with the divine will is the best remedy we can apply to misfortunes.—*Sir W. Temple.*

Contentment produces, in some measure, all those effects which the alchymist ascribes to what he calls the philosopher's stone; and if it does not bring riches, it does the same thing by banishing the desire of them. If it cannot remove the disquietudes arising from a man's mind, body, or fortune, it makes him easy under them.—*Addison.*

He that is never satisfied with anything, satisfies no one.

A man who finds no satisfaction in himself, seeks for it in vain elsewhere.—*Rochefoucauld.*

Content has a kindly influence on the soul of man, in respect of every being to whom he stands related. It extinguishes all murmuring, repining, and ingratitude toward that Being who has allotted us our part to act in the world. It destroys all inordinate ambition; gives sweetness to the conversation, and serenity to all the thoughts; and if it does not bring riches, it does the same thing by banishing the desire of them.—*Addison.*

The noblest mind the best contentment has.—*Spenser.*

CONTRADICTION. — We must not contradict, but instruct him that contradicts us; for a madman is not cured by another running mad also.—*Antisthenes.*

We take contradiction more easily than is supposed, if not violently given, even though it is well founded.—Hearts are like flowers; they remain open to the softly falling dew, but shut up in the violent downpour of rain.—*Richter.*

Assertion is not argument; to contradict the statement of an opponent is not proof that you are correct.—*Johnson.*

CONTRAST. — The lustre of diamonds is invigorated by the interposition of darker bodies; the lights of a picture are created by the shades; the highest pleasure which nature has in-

dulged to sensitive perception is that of rest after fatigue.—*Johnson.*

The rose and the thorn, and sorrow and gladness are linked together.—*Saadi.*

Where there is much light, the shadow is deep.—*Goethe.*

If there be light, then there is darkness; if cold, then heat; if height, depth also; if solid, then fluid; hardness and softness; roughness and smoothness; calm and tempest; prosperity and adversity; life and death.—*Pythagoras.*

Joy and grief are never far apart.—In the same street the shutters of one house are closed, while the curtains of the next are brushed by the shadows of the dance. —A wedding party returns from the church; and a funeral winds to its door. —The smiles and sadness of life are the tragi-comedy of Shakespeare.—Gladness and sighs brighten and dim the mirror he beholds.—*Willmott.*

It is a very poor, though common pretence to merit, to make it appear by the faults of other men; a mean wit or beauty may pass in a room where the rest of the company are allowed to have none; it is something to sparkle among diamonds; but to shine among pebbles is neither credit nor value worth the pretending.—*Sir W. Temple.*

CONTROVERSY. — There is no learned man but will confess he hath much profited by reading controversies; his senses awakened, his judgment sharpened, and the truth which he holds more firmly established. In logic they teach that contraries laid together more evidently appear; and controversy being permitted, falsehood will appear more false, and truth more true.—*Milton.*

Most controversies would soon be ended, if those engaged in them would first accurately define their terms, and then adhere to their definitions.—*Tryon Edwards.*

Disagreement is refreshing when two men lovingly desire to compare their views to find out truth.—Controversy is wretched when it is only an attempt to prove another wrong.—Religious controversy does only harm.—It destroys humble inquiry after truth, and throws all the energies into an attempt to prove ourselves right—a spirit in which no man gets at truth.—*F. W. Robertson.*

The evils of controversy are transitory, while its benefits are permanent. —*Robert Hall.*

What Cicero says of war may be applied to disputing,—it should always be so managed as to remember that the only true end of it is peace.—But generally, disputants are like sportsmen—their whole delight is in the pursuit; and a disputant no more cares for the truth, than the sportsman for the hare.—*Pope.*

CONVERSATION. — It is good to rub and polish our brain against that of others.—*Montaigne.*

The first ingredient in conversation is truth; the next, good sense; the third, good humor; and the fourth, wit.—*Sir W. Temple.*

One of the best rules in conversation is, never to say a thing which any of the company can reasonably wish had been left unsaid.—*Swift.*

Among well-bred people, a mutual deference is affected; contempt of others disguised; authority concealed; attention given to each in his turn; and an easy stream of conversation is maintained, without vehemence, without interruption, without eagerness for victory, and without any airs of superiority.— *Hume.*

To listen well, is as powerful a means of influence as to talk well, and is as essential to all true conversation.

A single conversation across the table with a wise man is worth a month's study of books.—*Chinese Proverb.*

Know how to listen, and you will profit even from those who talk badly. —*Plutarch.*

Great talent for conversation should be accompanied with great politeness. He who eclipses others owes them great civilities; and, whatever mistaken vanity may tell us, it is better to please in conversation than to shine in it.

The art of conversation consists as much in listening politely, as in talking agreeably.—*Atwell.*

No one will ever shine in conversation who thinks of saying fine things; to please, one must say many things indifferent, and many very bad.—*Francis Lockier.*

The reason why so few people are agreeable in conversation, is, that each

is thinking more of what he is intending to say, than of what others are saying; and we never listen when we are planning to speak.—*Rochefoucauld.*

I don't like to talk much with people who always agree with me. It is amusing to coquette with an echo for a little while, but one soon tires of it.—*Carlyle.*

He who sedulously attends, pointedly asks, calmly speaks, coolly answers, and ceases when he has no more to say, is in possession of some of the best requisites of conversation.—*Lavater.*

Never hold any one by the button, or the hand, in order to be heard out; for if people are unwilling to hear you, you had better hold your tongue than them. —*Chesterfield.*

Silence is one great art of conversation.—*Hazlitt.*

Conversation is an art in which a man has all mankind for competitors.—*Emerson.*

In conversation, humor is more than wit, and easiness more than knowledge. —Few desire to learn, or think they need it.—All desire to be pleased, or at least to be easy.—*Sir W. Temple.*

The tone of good conversation is brilliant and natural.—It is neither tedious nor frivolous.—It is instructive without pedantry; gay, without tumultuousness; polished, without affectation; gallant, without insipidity; waggish, without equivocation.—*Rousseau.*

As it is the characteristic of great wits to say much in few words, so it is of small wits to talk much, and say nothing.—*Rochefoucauld.*

Not only to say the right thing in the right place, but far more difficult, to leave unsaid the wrong thing at the tempting moment.—*Sala.*

It is a secret known to but few, yet of no small use in the conduct of life, that when you fall into a man's conversation, the first thing you should consider, is, whether he has a greater inclination to hear you, or that you should hear him. —*Steele.*

Our companions please us less from the charms we find in their conversation, than from those they find in ours.—*Greville.*

There cannot be a greater rudeness

than to interrupt another in the current of his discourse.—*Locke.*

The less men think, the more they talk.—*Montesquieu.*

He kept up with the current literature, and distilled from it a polite essence, with which he knew how to perfume his conversation.—*William Dean Howells.*

There's lots of people—this town wouldn't hold them; who don't know much excepting what's told them.— *Will Carleton.*

All bitter feelings are avoided, or at least greatly reduced by prompt, face-to-face discussion.—*Walter B. Pitkin.*

Good talk is like good scenery—continuous, yet constantly varying, and full of the charm of novelty and surprise.— *Randolph S. Bourne.*

Were we to talk less about the problems which faced us, and thought more about facing those problems, the evasive corner which obscured prosperity would certainly be more accessible.—*Lowell Gilmore.*

Inject a few raisins of conversation into the tasteless dough of existence.— *O. Henry.*

Speak well of every one if you speak of them at all—none of us are so very good.—*Elbert Hubbard.*

Be sincere. Be simple in words, manners and gestures. Amuse as well as instruct. If you can make a man laugh, you can make him think and make him like and believe you.—*Alfred E. Smith.*

Next to family affection, health, and the love of work, does anything contribute so much to the pleasantness of life, restoring and raising our self-esteem, as the traffic in kind speeches? —*Lucy Elliot Keeler.*

My observation is that, generally speaking, poverty of speech is the outward evidence of poverty of mind.— *Bruce Barton.*

Conversation is the laboratory and workshop of the student.—*Ralph Waldo Emerson.*

On their own merits modest men are dumb.—*George Coleman (the younger).*

When in the company of sensible men, we ought to be doubly cautious of talking too much, lest we lose two good things—their good opinion and our own

improvement; for what we have to say we know, but what they have to say we know not.—*Colton.*

Take as many half minutes as you can get, but never talk more than half a minute without pausing and giving others an opportunity to strike in.— *Swift.*

For good or ill, your conversation is your advertisement. Every time you open your mouth you let men look into your mind. Do they see it well clothed, neat, businesslike?—*Bruce Barton.*

Patrick Henry was more impressed by Washington's quiet conversation than by the fervid oratory of others. When asked whom he considered the greatest man in Congress, he answered: "Rutledge, if you speak of eloquence, is by far the greatest orator, but Colonel Washington, who has no pretensions to eloquence, is a man of more solid judgment and information than any man on that floor."—*Rupert Hughes.*

It were endless to dispute upon everything that is disputable.—*William Penn.*

We sometimes disputed, and very fond we were of argument, and very desirous of confuting one another, which is apt to become a very bad habit. I had caught it by reading my father's books of dispute about religion. Persons of good sense, I have since observed, seldom fall into it, except lawyers, university men, and men of all sorts that have been bred at Edinburgh.—*Benjamin Franklin.*

Conversation opens our views, and gives our faculties a more vigorous play; it puts us upon turning our notions on every side, and holds them up to a light that discovers those latent flaws which would probably have lain concealed in the gloom of unagitated abstraction.— *Melmoth.*

The pith of conversation does not consist in exhibiting your own superior knowledge on matters of small importance, but in enlarging, improving, and correcting the information you possess, by the authority of others.—*Walter Scott.*

Repose is as necessary in conversation as in a picture.—*Hazlitt.*

In private conversation between intimate friends the wisest men very often talk like the weakest; for, indeed, the talking with a friend is nothing else but thinking aloud.—*Addison.*

Conversation should be pleasant without scurrility, witty without affectation, free without indecency, learned without conceitedness, novel without falsehood. —*Shakespeare.*

One would think that the larger the company is, the greater variety of thoughts and subjects would be started in discourse; but instead of this, we find that conversation is never so much straitened and confined as in large assemblies. —*Addison.*

In company it is a very great fault to be more forward in setting off one's self, and talking to show one's parts, than to learn the worth, and be truly acquainted with the abilities of men.—*He that makes it his business not to know, but to be known, is like a foolish tradesman, who makes all the haste he can to sell off his old stock, but takes no thought of laying in any new.—Charron.*

Conversation warms the mind, enlivens the imagination, and is continually starting fresh game that is immediately pursued and taken, which would never have occurred in the duller intercourse of epistolary correspondence.—*Franklin.*

It is not necessary to be garrulous in order to be entertaining.—To be a judicious and sympathetic listener will go far toward making you an agreeable companion, self-forgetful, self-possessed, but not selfish enough to monopolize the conversation.—*A. L. Jack.*

It is wonderful that so many shall entertain those with whom they converse by giving them the history of their pains and aches; and imagine such narrations their quota of the conversation. This is, of all other, the meanest help to discourse, and a man must not think at all, or think himself very insignificant when he finds an account of his headache answered by another's asking what is the news in the last mail.—*Steele.*

CONVERSION.—As to the value of conversions, God only can judge.—He alone can know how wide are the steps which the soul has to take before it can approach to a community with him, to the dwelling of the perfect, or to the intercourse and friendship of higher natures.—*Goethe.*

In what way, or by what manner of working God changes a soul from evil to good—how he impregnates the barren rock with priceless gems and gold—is, to the human mind, an impenetrable mystery.—*Coleridge.*

Conversion is not implanting eyes, for they exist already; but giving them a right direction, which they have not.—*Plato.*

Conversion is but the first step in the divine life.—As long as we live we should more and more be turning from all that is evil, and to all that is good.—*Tryon Edwards.*

We are born with our backs upon God and heaven, and our faces upon sin and hell, till grace comes, and that converts —turns us.—*Philip Henry.*

Conversion is a deep work—a heart-work.—It goes throughout the man, throughout the mind, throughout the members, throughout the entire life.—*Alleine.*

Where there is a sound conversion, then a man is wholly given unto God, body, soul, and spirit. He regards not sin in his heart, but hath a respect to all God's commandments.—*Bolton.*

The time when I was converted was when religion became no longer a mere duty, but a pleasure.—*Prof. Lincoln.*

Conversion is no repairing of the old building; but it takes all down and erects a new structure. The sincere Christian is quite a new fabric, from the foundation to the top-stone all new.—*Alleine.*

CONVIVIALITY.—There are few tables where convivial talents will not pass in payment, especially where the host wants brains, or the guest has money.—*Zimmerman.*

The dangers of a convivial spirit are, that it may lead to excess in that which, in moderation, is good.—Excessive indulgence has made many a young man prematurely old, and changed a noble nature to that of the beast.—*Armstrong.*

COQUETTE.—A coquette is a young lady of more beauty than sense, more accomplishments than learning, more charms of person than graces of mind, more admirers than friends, more fools than wise men for attendants.—*Longfellow.*

A coquette is a woman without any heart, who makes a fool of a man that hasn't got any head.

Heartlessness and fascination, in about equal quantities, constitute the receipt for forming the character of a court coquette.—*Mad. Deluzy.*

An accomplished coquette excites the passions of others, in proportion as she feels none herself.—*Hazlitt.*

The characteristic of coquettes is affectation governed by whim.—Their life is one constant lie; and the only rule by which you can form any judgment of them, is, that they are never what they seem.—*Fielding.*

A coquette is like a recruiting sergeant, always on the lookout for fresh victims.—*Jerrold.*

There is one antidote only for coquetry, and that is true love.—*Mad. Deluzy.*

The adoration of his heart had been to her only as the perfume of a wild flower, which she had carelessly crushed with her foot in passing.—*Longfellow.*

The most effective coquetry is innocence.—*Lamartine.*

She who only finds her self-esteem in admiration, depends on others for her daily food and is the very servant of her slaves.—Over men she may exert a childish power, which not ennobles, but degrades her state.—*Joanna Baillie.*

A coquette is one that is never to be persuaded out of the passion she has to please, nor out of a good opinion of her own beauty.—Time and years she regards as things that wrinkle and decay only other women; forgets that age is written in the face; and that the same dress which became her when young, now only makes her look the older.—Affectation cleaves to her even in sickness and pain, and she dies in a high head and colored ribbons.—*Fielding.*

God created the coquette as soon as he had made the fool.—*Victor Hugo.*

CORRUPTION.—O that estates, degrees, and offices were not derived corruptly, and that clear honor were purchased by the merit of the wearer.—*Shakespeare.*

Corrupt influence is itself the perennial spring of all prodigality, and of all disorder; it loads us more than millions of debt; takes away vigor from our arms, wisdom from our councils, and every shadow of authority and credit from the most venerable parts of our constitution.—*Burke.*

The corruptions of the country are closely allied to those of the town, with no difference but what is made by another mode of thought and living.—*Swift.*

COUNSEL.—Consult your friend on all things, especially on those which respect yourself.—His counsel may then be useful where your own self-love might impair your judgment.—*Seneca.*

The kingdom of Israel was first rent and broken by ill counsel; upon which there are set, for our instruction, the two marks whereby bad counsel is ever best discerned—that it was young counsel for the persons, and violent counsel for the matter.—*Bacon.*

In counsel it is good to see dangers; but in execution, not to see them unless they be very great.—*Bacon.*

There is as much difference between the counsel that a friend giveth, and that a man giveth himself, as there is between the counsel of a friend and a flatterer.—*Bacon.*

Good counsels observed, are chains to grace, which, neglected, prove halters to strange, undutiful children.—*Fuller.*

Counsel and conversation are a second education, which improve all the virtue, and correct all the vice of the first, and of nature itself.—*Clarendon.*

Whoever is wise is apt to suspect and be diffident of himself, and upon that account is willing to hearken unto counsel; whereas the foolish man, being, in proportion to his folly, full of himself, and swallowed up in conceit, will seldom take any counsel but his own, and for the very reason that it is his own.—*Balguy.*

COUNTENANCE.—(See "FACE.")

It is hard for the face to conceal the thoughts of the heart—the true character of the soul.—The look without is an index of what is within.

The cheek is apter than the tongue to tell an errand.—*Shakespeare.*

A cheerful, easy, open countenance will make fools think you a good-natured man, and make designing men think you an undesigning one.—*Chester-field.*

Alas! how few of nature's faces there are to gladden us with their beauty!—The cares, and sorrows, and hungerings of the world change them, as they change hearts; and it is only when the passions sleep and have lost their hold forever that the troubled clouds pass off, and leave heaven's surface clear.—It is a common thing for the countenances of the dead, even in that fixed and rigid state, to subside into the long forgotten expression of infancy, and settle into the very look of early life.—So calm, so peaceful do they grow again, that those who knew them in their happy childhood, kneel by the coffin's side in awe, and see the angels even upon earth.—*Dickens.*

COUNTRY.—If you would be known and not know, vegetate in a village.—If you would know and not be known, live in a city.—*Colton.*

The country is both the philosopher's garden and his library, in which he reads and contemplates the power, wisdom, and goodness of God.—*Penn.*

Not rural sights alone, but rural sounds, exhilarate the spirit, and restore the tone of languid nature.—*Cowper.*

There is virtue in country houses, in gardens and orchards, in fields, streams, and groves, in rustic recreations and plain manners, that neither cities nor universities enjoy.—*A. B. Alcott.*

Men are taught virtue and a love of independence, by living in the country.—*Menander.*

If country life be healthful to the body, it is no less so to the mind.—*Ruffini.*

In those vernal seasons of the year when the air is calm and pleasant, it were an injury and sullenness against nature not to go out and see her riches, and partake in her rejoicing with heaven and earth.—*Milton.*

I consider it the best part of an education to have been born and brought up in the country.—*A. B. Alcott.*

God made the country, and man made the town.—What wonder, then, that health and virtue should most abound, and least be threatened in the fields and groves.—*Cowper.*

I fancy the proper means for increasing the love we bear to our native country, is, to reside some time in a foreign one.—*Shenstone.*

Let our object be our country, our whole country, and nothing but our country.—*Daniel Webster.*

Our country, however bounded or described—still our country, to be cherished in all our hearts—to be defended by all our hands.—*R. C. Winthrop.*

COURAGE.—Courage consists, not in blindly overlooking danger, but in seeing and conquering it.—*Richter.*

True courage is cool and calm.—The bravest of men have the least of a brutal, bullying insolence, and in the very time of danger are found the most serene and free.—*Shaftsbury.*

The truest courage is always mixed with circumspection; this being the quality which distinguishes the courage of the wise from the hardiness of the rash and foolish.—*Jones of Nayland.*

It is an error to suppose that courage means courage in everything.—Most people are brave only in the dangers to which they accustom themselves, either in imagination or practice.—*Bulwer.*

Courage that grows from constitution, often forsakes a man when he has occasion for it; courage which arises from a sense of duty, acts in a uniform manner.—*Addison.*

Courage from hearts and not from numbers grows.—*Dryden.*

Courage is, on all hands, considered as an essential of high character.—*Froude.*

Conscience is the root of all true courage; if a man would be brave let him obey his conscience.—*J. F. Clarke.*

Courage in danger is half the battle.—*Plautus.*

True courage is not the brutal force of vulgar heroes, but the firm resolve of virtue and reason.—*Whitehead.*

No man can answer for his courage who has never been in danger.—*Rochefoucauld.*

Moral courage is a virtue of higher cast and nobler origin than physical.—It springs from a consciousness of virtue, and renders a man, in the pursuit or defence of right, superior to the fear of reproach, opposition, or contempt.—*S. G. Goodrich.*

Physical courage which despises all danger, will make a man brave in one way; and moral courage, which despises all opinion, will make a man brave in another.—The former would seem most necessary for the camp; the latter for the council; but to constitute a great man both are necessary.—*Colton.*

To see what is right and not to do it, is want of courage.—*Confucius.*

True courage is the result of reasoning.—Resolution lies more in the head than in the veins; and a just sense of honor and of infamy, of duty and of religion, will carry us farther than all the force of mechanism.—*Collier.*

If we survive danger it steels our courage more than anything else.—*Niebuhr.*

A great deal of talent is lost in this world for the want of a little courage.—*Sydney Smith.*

Women and men of retiring timidity are cowardly only in dangers which affect themselves, but are the first to rescue when others are endangered.—*Richter.*

Courage ought to be guided by skill, and skill armed by courage.—Hardiness should not darken wit, nor wit cool hardiness.—Be valiant as men despising death, but confident as unwonted to be overcome.—*Sir P. Sidney.*

Courage consists not in hazarding without fear, but being resolutely minded in a just cause.—*Plutarch.*

That courage is poorly housed which dwells in numbers.—The lion never counts the herd that is about him, nor weighs how many flocks he has to scatter.—*Hill.*

By how much unexpected, by so much we must awake, and endeavor for defence; for courage mounteth with occasion.—*Shakespeare.*

The brave man is not he who feels no fear, for that were stupid and irrational; but he whose noble soul subdues its fear, and bravely dares the danger nature shrinks from.—*Joanna Baillie.*

COURTESY. — (See "CIVILITY.") When saluted with a salutation, salute the person with a better salutation, or at least return the same, for God taketh account of all things.—*Koran.*

The small courtesies sweeten life; the greater, ennoble it.—*Bovee.*

Hail! ye small sweet courtesies of life; for smooth do ye make the road of it, like grace and beauty, which beget inclinations to love at first sight; it is ye who open the door and let the stranger in.—*Sterne.*

There is a courtesy of the heart; it is allied to love.—From it springs the purest courtesy in the outward behavior.—*Goethe.*

Life is not so short but that there is always time for courtesy.—*Emerson.*

As the sword of the best tempered metal is most flexible, so the truly generous are most pliant and courteous in their behavior to their inferiors.—*Fuller.*

Small kindnesses, small courtesies, small considerations, habitually practised · in our social intercourse, give a greater charm to the character than the display of great talents and accomplishments.—*M. A. Kelty.*

There is no outward sign of true courtesy that does not rest on a deep moral foundation.—*Goethe.*

A churlish courtesy rarely comes but either for gain or falsehood.—*Sir P. Sidney.*

We should be as courteous to a man as we are to a picture, which we are willing to give the advantage of the best light.—*Emerson.*

Courtesy is a science of the highest importance.—It is like grace and beauty in the body, which charm at first sight, and lead on to further intimacy and friendship.—*Montaigne.*

The whole of heraldry and chivalry is in courtesy.—A man of fine manners shall pronounce your name with all the ornament that titles of nobility could add.—*Emerson.*

The courtesies of a small and trivial character are the ones which strike deepest to the grateful and appreciating heart. It is the picayune compliments which are the most appreciated; far more than the double ones we sometimes pay.—*Henry Clay.*

Approved valor is made precious by natural courtesy.—*Sir P. Sidney.*

COURTS AND COURTIERS. — A court is an assemblage of noble and distinguished beggars.—*Talleyrand.*

The court is a golden, but fatal circle, upon whose magic skirts a thousand devils sit tempting innocence, and beckon early virtue from its center.—*N. Lee.*

An old courtier, with veracity, good sense, and a faithful memory, is an inestimable treasure; he is full of transactions and maxims; in him one may find the history of the age, enriched with a great many curious circumstances which we never meet with in books; from him we may learn rules for our conduct and manners, of the more weight, because founded on facts, and illustrated by striking examples.—*Bruyère.*

Bred in camps, trained in the gallant openness of truth that best becomes a soldier, thou art happily a stranger to the baseness and infamy of courts.—*Mallet.*

The court is like a palace built of marble—made up of very hard, and very polished materials.—*Bruyère.*

The chief requisites for a courtier are a flexible conscience and an inflexible politeness.—*Lady Blessington.*

With the people of courts the tongue is the artery of their withered life, the spiral spring and flag-feather of their souls.—*Richter.*

See how he sets his countenance for deceit, and promises a lie before he speaks.—*Dryden.*

Poor wretches, that depend on greatness's favor, dream, as I have done, and wake and find nothing.—*Shakespeare.*

COURTSHIP. — Courtship consists in a number of quiet attentions, not so pointed as to alarm, nor so vague as not to be understood.—*Sterne.*

The pleasantest part of a man's life is generally that which passes in courtship, provided his passion be sincere, and the party beloved, kind, with discretion. Love, desire, hope, all the pleasing motions of the soul, rise in the pursuit. —*Addison.*

She half consents, who silently denies. —*Ovid.*

She is a woman, therefore may be wooed; she is a woman, therefore may be won.—*Shakespeare.*

If you cannot inspire a woman with love of yourself, fill her above the brim with love of herself; all that runs over will be yours.—*Colton.*

Men are April when they woo; December when they wed.—*Shakespeare.*

With women worth being won, the softest lover ever best succeeds.—*A. Hill.*

I profess not to know how women's hearts are wooed and won.—To me they have always been matters of riddle and admiration.—*Washington Irving.*

The man that has a tongue, I say, is no man, if with his tongue he cannot win a woman.—*Shakespeare.*

Let a woman once give you a task and you are hers, heart and soul; all your care and trouble lend new charms to her for whose sake they are taken.— To rescue, to revenge, to instruct, or to protect a woman, is all the same as to love her.—*Richter.*

COVETOUSNESS.—Desire of having is the sin of covetousness.—*Shakespeare.*

If money be not thy servant, it will be thy master. The covetous man cannot so properly be said to possess wealth, as that may be said to possess him.— *Bacon.*

Covetousness, by a greediness of getting more, deprives itself of the true end of getting; it loses the enjoyment of what it had got.—*Sprat.*

The only gratification a covetous man gives his neighbors, is, to let them see that he himself is as little better for what he has, as they are.—*Penn.*

Covetous men are fools, miserable wretches, buzzards, madmen, who live by themselves, in perpetual slavery, fear, suspicion, sorrow, discontent, with more of gall than honey in their enjoyments; who are rather possessed by their money than possessors of it; bound 'prentices to their property; mean slaves and drudges to their substance.—*Burton.*

The covetous person lives as if the world were made altogether for him, and not he for the world; to take in everything and part with nothing.—*South.*

Covetousness swells the principal to no purpose, and lessens the use to all purposes.—*Jeremy Taylor.*

A man may as easily fill a chest with grace as the heart with gold.—The air fills not the body, neither does money the covetous heart of man.—*Spenser.*

When all sins are old in us and go upon crutches, covetousness does but then lie in her cradle.—*Decker.*

Covetousness is both the beginning and end of the devil's alphabet—the first vice in corrupt nature that moves, and the last which dies.—*South.*

Why are we so blind?—That which we improve, we have; that which we hoard, is not for ourselves.—*Mad. Deluzy.*

The covetous man heaps up riches, not to enjoy, but to have them; he starves himself in the midst of plenty; cheats and robs himself of that which is his own, and makes a hard shift to be as poor and miserable with a great estate as any man can be without it.—*Tillotson.*

Refrain from covetousness, and thy estate shall prosper.—*Plato.*

The covetous man pines in plenty, like Tantalus up to the chin in water, and yet thirsty.—*T. Adams.*

After hypocrites, the greatest dupes the devil has are those who exhaust an anxious existence in the disappointments and vexations of business, and live miserably and meanly only to die magnificently and rich.—They serve the devil without receiving his wages, and for the empty foolery of dying rich, pay down their health, happiness, and integrity.—*Colton.*

COWARDICE.—The craven's fear is but selfishness, like his merriment.—*Whittier.*

Cowardice is not synonymous with prudence.—It often happens that the better part of discretion is valor.—*Hazlitt.*

It is the coward who fawns upon those above him.—It is the coward who is insolent whenever he dares be so.—*Junius.*

Cowards falter, but danger is often overcome by those who nobly dare.—*Queen Elizabeth.*

Peace and plenty breed cowards; hardness ever of hardiness is the mother.—*Shakespeare.*

At the bottom of a good deal of the bravery that appears in the world there lurks a miserable cowardice.—Men will face powder and steel because they cannot face public opinion.—*E. H. Chapin.*

Cowards die many times before their death; the valiant never taste of death but once.—*Shakespeare.*

COXCOMB.—(See "Foppery.")

A coxcomb begins by determining that his own profession is the first; and he finishes by deciding that he is the first in his profession.—*Colton.*

Nature has sometimes made a fool; but a coxcomb is always of a man's own making.—*Addison.*

Foppery is never cured.—It is the bad stamina of the mind, which, like those of the body, are never rectified.—Once a coxcomb, always a coxcomb.—*Johnson.*

None are so seldom found alone, and are so soon tired of their own company as those coxcombs who are on the best terms with themselves.—*Colton.*

A coxcomb is ugly all over with the affectation of the fine gentleman.—*Johnson.*

CREDIT. — Credit is like a looking-glass, which, when once sullied by a breath, may be wiped clear again; but if once cracked can never be repaired.—*Walter Scott.*

The most trifling actions that affect a man's credit are to be regarded. The sound of your hammer at five in the morning, or nine at night, heard by a creditor, makes him easier six months longer; but if he sees you at a billiard table, or hears your voice at a tavern when you should be at work, he sends for his money the next day.—*Franklin.*

Too large a credit has made many a bankrupt; taking even less than a man can answer with ease, is a sure fund for extending it whenever his occasions require.—*The Guardian.*

Nothing so cements and holds together all the parts of a society as faith or credit, which can never be kept up unless men are under some force or necessity of honestly paying what they owe to one another.—*Cicero.*

CREDITOR. — Creditors have better memories than debtors; they are a superstitious sect, great observers of set days and times.—*Franklin.*

The creditor whose appearance gladdens the heart of a debtor may hold his head in sunbeams, and his foot on storms.—*Lavater.*

CREDULITY.—O credulity, thou hast as many ears as fame has tongues, open to every sound of truth, as falsehood.—*Harvard.*

Credulity is belief on slight evidence, with no evidence, or against evidence. In this sense it is the infidel, not the believer, who is credulous. "The simple," says Solomon, "believeth every word." —*Tryon Edwards.*

The more gross the fraud, the more glibly will it go down and the more greedily will it be swallowed, since folly will always find faith wherever impostors will find impudence.—*Bovee.*

The only disadvantage of an honest heart is credulity.—*Sir P. Sidney.*

Credulity is the common failing of inexperienced virtue; and he who is spontaneously suspicious may justly be charged with radical corruption.—*Johnson.*

Credulity is perhaps a weakness, almost inseparable from eminently truthful characters.—*Tuckerman.*

As credulity is a more peaceful possession of the mind than curiosity, so preferable is that wisdom which converses about the surface, to that pretended philosophy which enters into the depth of things, and then comes back gravely with the informations and discoveries that in the inside they are good for nothing.—*Swift.*

I cannot spare the luxury of believing that all things beautiful are what they seem.—*Halleck.*

The general goodness which is nourished in noble hearts, makes every one think that strength of virtue to be in another whereof they find assured foundation in themselves.—*Sir P. Sidney.*

It is a curious paradox that precisely in proportion to our own intellectual weakness, will be our credulity as to the mysterious powers assumed by others. —*Colton.*

You believe easily that which you hope for earnestly.—*Terence.*

The most positive men are the most credulous, since they most believe themselves, and advise most with their falsest flatterer and worst enemy,—their own self-love.—*Pope.*

Generous souls are still most subject to credulity.—*Davenant.*

Some men are bigoted in politics, who are infidels in religion.—Ridiculous credulity!—*Junius.*

We believe at once in evil, we only believe in good upon reflection.—Is not this sad?—*Mad. Deluzy.*

More persons, on the whole, are humbugged by believing in nothing, than by believing too much.—*P. T. Barnum.*

Your noblest natures are most credulous.—*Chapman.*

To take for granted as truth all that is alleged against the fame of others, is a species of credulity that men would blush at on any other subject.—*Jane Porter.*

Beyond all credulity is the credulousness of atheists, who believe that chance could make the world, when it cannot build a house.—*Clarke.*

The remedy for the present threatened decay of faith is not a more stalwart creed or a more unflinching acceptance of it, but a profoundly spiritual life.—*Lyman Abbott.*

Charles the Second, hearing Vossius, a celebrated free-thinker, repeating some incredible stories about the Chinese, said, "This is a very strange man. He believes everything but the Bible!"

CREED.—(See "BELIEF.")

A good creed is a gate to the city that hath foundations; a misleading creed may be a road to destruction, or if both misleading and alluring it may become what Shakespeare calls a primrose path to the eternal bonfire.—*Jospeh Cook.*

In politics, as in religion, we have less charity for those who believe the half of our creed, than for those who deny the whole of it.—*Colton.*

If you have a Bible creed, it is well; but is it filled out and inspired by Christian love?—*J. F. Brodie.*

Though I do not like creeds in religious matters, I verily believe that creeds had something to do with our Revolution.—In their religious controversies the people of New England had always been accustomed to stand on points; and when Lord North undertook to tax them, then they stood on points also.—It so happened, fortunately, that their opposition to Lord North was a point on which they were all united.— *Daniel Webster.*

The weakest part of a man's creed is that which he holds for himself alone; the strongest is that which he holds in common with all Christendom.—*Mc-Vickar.*

CRIME.—(See "CONCEALMENT.")

Society prepares the crime; the criminal commits it.

Heaven will permit no man to secure happiness by crime.—*Alfieri.*

Whenever man commits a crime heaven finds a witness.—*Bulwer.*

Of all the adult male criminals in London, not two in a hundred have entered upon a course of crime who have lived an honest life up to the age of twenty.—Almost all who enter on a course of crime do so between the ages of eight and sixteen.—*Shaftesbury.*

Crimes sometimes shock us too much; vices almost always too little.—*Hare.*

Small crimes always precede great ones. Never have we seen timid innocence pass suddenly to extreme licentiousness.—*Racine.*

Fear follows crime, and is its punishment.—*Voltaire.*

The contagion of crime is like that of the plague.—Criminals collected together corrupt each other.—They are worse than ever when, at the termination of their punishment, they return to society.—*Napoleon.*

Those who are themselves incapable of great crimes, are ever backward to suspect others.—*Rochefoucauld.*

It is supposable that in the eyes of angels, a struggle down a dark lane and a battle of Leipsic differ in nothing but in degree of wickedness.—*Willmott.*

There is no den in the wide world to hide a rogue.—Commit a crime and the earth is made of glass.—Commit a crime, and it seems as if a coat of snow fell on the ground, such as reveals in the woods the track of every partridge, and fox, and squirrel.—*Emerson.*

If poverty is the mother of crimes, want of sense is the father of them.—*Bruyère.*

Man's crimes are his worst enemies, following him like shadows, till they drive his steps into the pit he dug.—*Creon.*

We easily forget crimes that are known only to ourselves.—*Rochefoucauld.*

Crimes lead into one another.—They

who are capable of being forgers, are capable of being incendiaries.—*Burke.*

Crime is not punished as an offence against God, but as prejudicial to society.—*Froude.*

The villainy you teach me I will execute; and it shall go hard but I will better the instruction.—*Shakespeare.*

For the credit of virtue it must be admitted that the greatest evils which befall mankind are caused by their crimes.—*Rochefoucauld.*

CRITICISM. — Criticism, as it was first instituted by Aristotle, was meant as a standard of judging well.—*Johnson.*

Criticism is the child and handmaid of reflection.—It works by censure, and censure implies a standard.—*R. G. White.*

It is ridiculous for any man to criticise the works of another if he has not distinguished himself by his own performances.—*Addison.*

Criticism is as often a trade as a science; requiring more health than wit, more labor than capacity, more practice than genius.—*Bruyère.*

Criticism often takes from the tree caterpillars and blossoms together.—*Richter.*

It is easy to criticise an author, but difficult to appreciate him.—*Vauvenargues.*

Ten censure wrong, for one that writes amiss.—*Pope.*

Silence is sometimes the severest criticism.—*Charles Buxton.*

Neither praise nor blame is the object of true criticism.—Justly to discriminate, firmly to establish, wisely to prescribe, and honestly to award—these are the true aims and duties of criticism.—*Simms.*

It is a maxim with me, that no man was ever written out of a reputation but by himself.—*Bentley.*

Of all the cants in this canting world, deliver me from the cant of criticism.—*Sterne.*

Doubtless criticism was originally benignant, pointing out the beauties of a work rather than its defects.—The passions of men have made it malignant, as the bad heart of Procrustes turned the bed, the symbol of repose, into an instrument of torture.—*Longfellow*.

The most noble criticism is that in which the critic is not the antagonist so much as the rival of the author.—*Disraeli*.

It is quite cruel that a poet cannot wander through his regions of enchantment without having a critic, forever, like the old man of the sea, upon his back.—*Moore*.

Get your enemies to read your works in order to mend them; for your friend is so much your second self that he will judge too much like you.—*Pope*.

Is it in destroying and pulling down that skill is displayed?—The shallowest understanding, the rudest hand, is more than equal to that task.—*Burke*.

The pleasure of criticism takes from us that of being deeply moved by very beautiful things.—*Bruyère*.

It is a barren kind of criticism which tells you what a thing is not.—*R. W. Griswold*.

The legitimate aim of criticism is to direct attention to the excellent.—The bad will dig its own grave, and the imperfect may safely be left to that final neglect from which no amount of present undeserved popularity can rescue it.—*Bovee*.

The opinion of the great body of the reading public, is very materially influenced even by the unsupported assertions of those who assume a right to criticise.—*Macaulay*.

The strength of criticism lies only in the weakness of the thing criticised.—*Longfellow*.

CRITICS.—Critics are sentinels in the grand army of letters, stationed at the corners of newspapers and reviews, to challenge every new author.—*Longfellow*.

There is scarcely a good critic of books born in our age, and yet every fool thinks himself justified in criticising persons.—*Bulwer*.

Critics must excuse me if I compare them to certain animals called asses, who, by gnawing vines, originally taught the great advantage of pruning them.—*Shenstone*.

The eyes of critics, whether in commending or carping. are both on one side, like those of a turbot.—*Landor*.

A spirit of criticism, if indulged in, leads to a censoriousness of disposition that is destructive of all nobler feeling. The man who lives to find faults has a miserable mission.

Some critics are like chimney-sweepers; they put out the fire below, and frighten the swallows from their nests above; they scrape a long time in the chimney, cover themselves with soot, and bring nothing away but a bag of cinders, and then sing out from the top of the house, as if they had built it.—*Longfellow*.

The critical faculty has its value in correcting errors, reforming abuses, and demolishing superstitions.—But the constructive faculty is much nobler in itself, and immeasurably more valuable in its results, for the obvious reason that it is a much nobler and better thing to build up than to pull down.—It requires skill and labor to erect a building, but any idle tramp can burn it down.—Only God can form and paint a flower, but any foolish child can pull it to pieces.—*J. M. Gibson*.

It behooves the minor critic, who hunts for blemishes, to be a little distrustful of his own sagacity.—*Junius*.

To be a mere verbal critic is what no man of genius would be if he could; but to be a critic of true taste and feeling, is what no man without genius could be if he would.—*Colton*.

Critics are a kind of freebooters in the republic of letters, who, like deer, goats, and diverse other graminivorous animals, gain subsistence by gorging upon buds and leaves of the young shrubs of the forest, thereby robbing them of their verdure and retarding their progress to maturity.—*Washington Irving*.

He, whose first emotion on the view of an excellent production is to undervalue it, will never have one of his own to show.—*Aikin*.

The severest critics are always those who have either never attempted, or who have failed in original composition.—*Hazlitt*.

Of all mortals a critic is the silliest; for, inuring himself to examine all things, whether they are of consequence or not, he never looks upon anything but with a design of passing sentence upon it; by which means he is never a companion, but always a censor.—*Steele.*

There are some critics who change everything that comes under their hands to gold; but to this privilege of Midas they join sometimes his ears.—*J. P. Senn.*

CROSS.—The cross is the only ladder high enough to touch Heaven's threshold.—*G. D. Boardman.*

The greatest of all crosses is self.—If we die in part every day, we shall have but little to do on the last.—These little daily deaths will destroy the power of the final dying.—*Fenelon.*

Carry the cross patiently, and with perfect submission; and in the end it shall carry you.—*Thomas à Kempis.*

While to the reluctant the cross is too heavy to be borne, it grows light to the heart of willing trust.

The cross of Christ, on which he was extended, points, in the length of it, to heaven and earth, reconciling them together; and in the breadth of it, to former and following ages, as being equally salvation to both.

The cross of Christ is the sweetest burden that I ever bore; it is such a burden as wings are to a bird, or sails to a ship, to carry me forward to my harbor.—*Rutherford.*

CRUELTY.—All cruelty springs from hard-heartedness and weakness.—*Seneca.*

I would not enter on my list of friends the man who needlessly sets foot upon a worm.—*Cowper.*

Cruelty and fear shake hands together.—*Balzac.*

Man's inhumanity to man, makes countless thousands mourn.—*Burns.*

Cruelty, like every other vice, requires no motive outside of itself; it only requires opportunity.—*George Eliot.*

One of the ill effects of cruelty is that it makes the by-standers cruel.—*Buxton.*

Cruelty to dumb animals is one of the distinguishing vices of the lowest and basest of the people.—Wherever it is found, it is a certain mark of ignorance and meanness.—*Jones of Nayland.*

Detested sport, that owes its pleasures to another's pain.—*Cowper.*

CULTIVATION.—The highest purpose of intellectual cultivation is, to give a man a perfect knowledge and mastery of his own inner self.—*Novalis.*

Virtue and talents, though allowed their due consideration, yet are not enough to procure a man a welcome wherever he comes. Nobody contents himself with rough diamonds, or wears them so. When polished and set, then they give a lustre.—*Locke.*

It matters little whether a man be mathematically, or philologically, or artistically cultivated, so he be but cultivated.—*Goethe.*

Partial culture runs to the ornate; extreme culture to simplicity.—*Bovee.*

It is very rare to find ground which produces nothing.—If it is not covered with flowers, fruit trees, and grains, it produces briars and pines.—It is the same with man; if he is not virtuous, he becomes vicious.—*Bruyère.*

Cultivation to the mind, is as necessary as food to the body.—*Cicero.*

That is true cultivation which gives us sympathy with every form of human life, and enables us to work most successfully for its advancement. Refinement that carries us away from our fellow-men is not God's refinement.—*H. W. Beecher.*

As the soil, however rich it may be, cannot be productive without culture, so the mind, without cultivation, can never produce good fruit.—*Seneca.*

I am very sure that any man of common understanding may, by culture, care, attention, and labor, make himself whatever he pleases, except a great poet.—*Chesterfield.*

Whatever expands the affections, or enlarges the sphere of our sympathies—whatever makes us feel our relation to the universe and all that it inherits in time and in eternity, and to the great and beneficent cause of all, must unquestionably refine our nature, and elevate us in the scale of being.—*Channing.*

CUNNING.—(See "KNAVERY.")

Cunning is the ape of wisdom.—*Locke.*

Cunning signifies, especially, a habit or gift of overreaching, accompanied with enjoyment and a sense of superiority.—It is associated with small and dull conceit, and with an absolute want of sympathy or affection.—It is the intensest rendering of vulgarity, absolute and utter.—*Ruskin.*

Cleverness and cunning are incompatible.—I never saw them united.—The latter is the resource of the weak, and is only natural to them.—Children and fools are always cunning, but clever people never.—*Byron.*

Cunning is none of the best nor worst qualities; it floats between virtue and vice: there is scarce any exigence where it may not, and perhaps ought not to be supplied by prudence.—*Bruyère.*

Cunning pays no regard to virtue, and is but the low mimic of wisdom.—*Bolingbroke.*

The greatest of all cunning is to seem blind to the snares which we know are laid for us; men are never so easily deceived as while they are endeavoring to deceive others.—*Rochefoucauld.*

The certain way to be cheated is to fancy one's self more cunning than others.—*Charron.*

A cunning man is never a firm man; but an honest man is; a double-minded man is always unstable; a man of faith is firm as a rock. There is a sacred connection between honesty and faith; honesty is faith applied to worldly things, and faith is honesty quickened by the Spirit to the use of heavenly things.—*Edward Irving.*

Cunning has effect from the credulity of others. It requires no extraordinary talents to lie and deceive.—*Johnson.*

We should do by our cunning as we do by our courage,—always have it ready to defend ourselves, never to offend others.—*Greville.*

Cunning is only the mimic of discretion, and may pass upon weak men, as vivacity is often mistaken for wit, and gravity for wisdom.—*Addison.*

Cunning leads to knavery.—It is but a step from one to the other, and that very slippery.—Only lying makes the difference; add that to cunning, and it is knavery.—*Bruyère.*

We take cunning for a sinister or crooked wisdom, and certainly there is a great difference between a cunning man and a wise man, not only in point of honesty, but in point of ability.—*Bacon.*

The common practice of cunning is the sign of a small genius.—It almost always happens that those who use it to cover themselves in one place, lay themselves open in another.—*Rochefoucauld.*

In a great business there is nothing so fatal as cunning management.—*Junius.*

The very cunning conceal their cunning; the indifferently shrewd boast of it.—*Bovee.*

A cunning man overreaches no one half as much as himself.—*H. W. Beecher.*

The most sure way of subjecting yourself to be deceived, is to consider yourself more cunning than others.—*Rochefoucauld.*

Discretion is the perfection of reason, and a guide to us in the duties of life; cunning is a kind of instinct, that only looks out after our immediate interests and welfare. Discretion is only found in men of strong sense and good understanding; cunning is often to be met with in brutes themselves, and in persons who are but the fewest removes from them.—*Bruyère.*

All my own experience of life teaches me the contempt of cunning, not the fear. The phrase "profound cunning" has always seemed to me a contradiction in terms. I never knew a cunning mind which was not either shallow, or, on some points, diseased.—*Mrs. Jameson.*

CURIOSITY.—The first and simplest emotion which we discover in the human mind, is curiosity.—*Burke.*

Seize the moment of excited curiosity on any subject, to solve your doubts; for if you let it pass, the desire may never return, and you may remain in ignorance.—*W. Wirt.*

Curiosity in children is but an appetite for knowledge. One great reason why children abandon themselves wholly to silly pursuits and trifle away their time insipidly is, because they find their curiosity balked, and their inquiries neglected.—*Locke.*

Men are more inclined to ask curious questions, than to obtain necessary instruction.—*Quesnel.*

The over curious are not over wise.—*Massinger.*

Curiosity is as much the parent of attention, as attention is of memory.—*Whately.*

No heart is empty of the humor of curiosity, the beggar being as attentive, in his station, to an increase of knowledge, as the prince.—*Osborn.*

How many a noble art, now widely known, owes its young impulse to this power alone.—*Sprague.*

Eve, with all the fruits of Eden blest, save only one, rather than leave that one unknown, lost all the rest.—*Moore.*

Avoid him who, for mere curiosity, asks three questions running about a thing that cannot interest him.—*Lavater.*

Curiosity is a kernel of the forbidden fruit which still sticketh in the throat of a natural man, sometimes to the danger of his choking.—*Fuller.*

There are different kinds of curiosity; one of interest, which causes us to learn that which would be useful to us; and the other of pride, which springs from a desire to know that of which others are ignorant.—*Rochefoucauld.*

Curiosity is one of the permanent and certain characteristics of a vigorous intellect.—Every advance into knowledge opens new prospects and produces new incitements to further progress.—*Johnson.*

The curiosity of an honorable mind willingly rests where the love of truth does not urge it further onward and the love of its neighbor bids it stop.—In other words, it willingly stops at the point where the interests of truth do not beckon it onward, and charity cries " Halt."—*Coleridge.*

Inquisitive people are the funnels of conversation; they do not take anything for their own use, but merely to pass it on to others.—*Steele.*

The gratification of curiosity rather frees us from uneasiness, than confers pleasure.—We are more pained by ignorance, than delighted by instruction.—Curiosity is the thirst of the soul.—*Johnson.*

A person who is too nice an observer of the business of the crowd, like one who is too curious in observing the labor of bees, will often be stung for his curiosity.—*Pope.*

I loathe that low vice, curiosity.—*Byron.*

Curiosity is looking over other people's affairs, and overlooking our own.—*H. L. Wayland.*

What a vast deal of time and ease that man gains who is not troubled with the spirit of impertinent curiosity about others; who lets his neighbor's thoughts and behavior alone; who confines his inspections to himself, and cares chiefly for his own duty and conscience.

CURSES.— Dinna curse him, sir; I have heard it said that a curse was like a stone flung up to the heavens, and most likely to return on the head of him that sent it.—*Walter Scott.*

Curses are like young chickens, and still come home to roost.—*Bulver.*

CUSTOM.—(See " FASHION.")

Custom is the universal sovereign.—*Pindar.*

The way of the world is to make laws, but follow customs.—*Montaigne.*

Custom is often only the antiquity of error.—*Cyprian.*

Custom may lead a man into many errors, but it justifies none.—*Fielding.*

Custom is the law of fools.—*Vanbrugh.*

Choose always the way that seems best, however rough it may be, and custom will soon render it easy and agreeable.—*Pythagoras.*

Custom doth make dotards of us all. —*Carlyle.*

There is no tyrant like custom, and no freedom where its edicts are not resisted.—*Bovee.*

As the world leads, we follow.—*Seneca.*

Men commonly think according to their inclinations, speak according to their learning and imbibed opinions, but generally act according to custom.—*Bacon.*

In this great society wide lying around us, a critical analysis would find very few spontaneous actions. It is almost all custom and gross sense.—*Emerson.*

The influence of custom is incalculable; dress a boy as a man, and he will at once change his conception of himself.—*B. St. John.*

New customs, though they be never so ridiculous, nay, let them be unmanly, yet are followed.—*Shakespeare.*

There are not unfrequently substantial reasons underneath for customs that appear to us absurd.—*C. Brontë.*

Custom is the law of one description

of fools, and fashion of another; but the two parties often clash, for precedent is the legislator of the first, and novelty of the last.—*Colton.*

Be not so bigoted to any custom as to worship it at the expense of truth.—*Zimmerman.*

The custom and fashion of to-day will be the awkwardness and outrage of to-morrow—so arbitrary are these transient laws.—*Dumas.*

Custom governs the world; it is the tyrant of our feelings and our manners and rules the world with the hand of a despot.—*J. Bartlett.*

To follow foolish precedents, and wink with both our eyes, is easier than to think.—*Cowper.*

Immemorial custom is transcendent law.—*Menu.*

The despotism of custom is on the wane.—We are not content to know that things are; we ask whether they ought to be.—*J. S. Mill.*

Man yields to custom, as he bows to fate—in all things ruled, mind, body, and estate.—*Crabbe.*

CYNICS.—It will generally be found that those who sneer habitually at human nature, and affect to despise it, are among its worst and least pleasant samples.—*Dickens.*

Don't be a cynic, and bewail and bemoan.—Omit the negative propositions. —Don't waste yourself in rejection, nor bark against the bad, but chant the beauty of the good.—Set down nothing that will help somebody.—*Emerson.*

The cynic is one who never sees a good quality in a man, and never fails to see a bad one.—He is the human owl, vigilant in darkness and blind to light, mousing for vermin, and never seeing noble game.—*H. W. Beecher.*

To admire nothing is the motto which men of the world always affect.—They think it vulgar to wonder or be enthusiastic.—They have so much corruption and charlatanism, that they think the credit of all high qualities must be delusive.—*Brydges.*

D

DANCING.—The gymnasium of running, walking on stilts, climbing, etc., steels and makes hardy single powers and muscles, but dancing, like a corporeal poesy, embellishes, exercises, and equalizes all the muscles at once.—*Richter.*

Those move easiest, who have learned to dance.—*Pope.*

A merry, dancing, drinking, laughing, quaffing, and unthinking time.—*Dryden.*

Dancing is an amusement which has been discouraged in our country by many of the best people, and not without some reason.—It is associated in their mind with balls; and this is one of the worst forms of social pleasure.—The time consumed in preparing for a ball, the waste of thought upon it, the extravagance of dress, the late hours, the exhaustion of strength, the exposure of health, and the languor of the succeeding day—these and other evils connected with this amusement, are strong reasons for banishing it from the community.—But dancing ought not, therefore, to be proscribed.—On the contrary, balls should be discouraged for this among other reasons, that dancing, instead of being a rare pleasure, requiring elaborate preparation, may become an every-day amusement, and mix with our common intercourse. — This exercise is among the most healthful.—The body as well as the mind feels its gladdening influence.—No amusement seems more to have a foundation in our nature.—The animation of youth overflows spontaneously in harmonious movements.—The true idea of dancing entitles it to favor.—Its end is to realize perfect grace in motion; and who does not know that a sense of the graceful is one of the higher faculties of our nature.—*Channing.*

The chief benefit of dancing is to learn one how to sit still.—*Johnson.*

Learn to dance, not so much for the sake of dancing, as for coming into a room and presenting yourself genteelly and gracefully.—Women, whom you ought to endeavor to please, cannot forgive a vulgar and awkward air and gestures.—*Chesterfield.*

In ancient times dancing, as a religious service, was before and to the Lord; in modern days it is too often a dissipating amusement for and to the devil.

A ballroom is nothing more or less than a great market place of beauty.—

For my part, were I a buyer, I should like making my purchases in a less public mart.—*Bulwer*.

You may be invited to a ball or dinner because you dance or tell a good story; but no one since the time of Queen Elizabeth has been made a cabinet minister or a lord chancellor for such reasons.—*E. Pierrepont*.

Well was it said, by a man of sagacity, that dancing was a sort of privileged and reputable folly, and that the best way to be convinced of this was to close the ears and judge of it by the eyes alone.—*Gotthold*.

For children and youth, dancing in the parlor or on the green may be a very pleasant and healthful amusement, but when we see older people dancing we are ready to ask with the Chinese, " Why don't you have your servants do it for you? "

All the gestures of children are graceful; the reign of distortion and unnatural attitudes commences with the introduction of the dancing master.—*Sir Joshua Reynolds*.

Where wildness and disorder are visible in the dance, there Satan, death, and all kinds of mischief are likewise on the floor.—*Gotthold*.

DANDY.—A dandy is a clothes-wearing man,—a man whose trade, office, and existence consist in the wearing of clothes.—Every faculty of his soul, spirit, person, and purse is heroically consecrated to this one object—the wearing of clothes wisely and well; so that as others dress to live, he lives to dress.—*Carlyle*.

A fool may have his coat embroidered with gold, but it is a fool's coat still.—*Rivarol*.

Dandies, when first-rate, are generally very agreeable men.—*Bulwer*.

The all-importance of clothes has sprung up in the intellect of the dandy, without effort, like an instinct of genius: he is inspired with cloth—a poet of clothing.—*Carlyle*.

DANGER. — Danger levels man and brute, and all are fellows in their need. —*Byron*.

We should never so entirely avoid danger as to appear irresolute and cowardly; but, at the same time, we should avoid unnecessarily exposing ourselves to danger, than which nothing can be more foolish.—*Cicero*.

A timid person is frightened before a danger; a coward during the time; and a courageous person afterward.—*Richter*.

Let the fear of a danger be a spur to prevent it; he that fears not, gives advantage to the danger.—*Quarles*.

It is better to meet danger than to wait for it.—He that is on a lee shore, and foresees a hurricane, stands out to sea and encounters a storm to avoid a shipwreck.—*Colton*.

A man's opinion of danger varies at different times according to his animal spirits, and he is actuated by considerations which he dares not avow.—*Smollett*.

DAUGHTERS.—To a father waxing old nothing is dearer than a daughter. —Sons have spirits of higher pitch, but less inclined to sweet, endearing fondness.—*Euripides*.

A daughter is an embarrassing and ticklish possession.—*Menander*.

Fathers, I think, are most apt to appreciate the excellence and attainments of their daughters; mothers, those of their sons.

DAY.—There is nothing more universally commended than a fine day; the reason is, that people can commend it without envy.—*Shenstone*.

Every day is a little life, and our whole life is but a day repeated. Therefore live every day as if it would be the last. Those that dare lose a day, are dangerously prodigal; those that dare misspend it are desperate.—*Bp. Hall*.

Count that day lost, whose low descending sun views from thy hand no worthy action done.—*Stanford*.

" I've lost a day "—the prince who nobly cried, had been an emperor without his crown.—*Young*.

Enjoy the blessings of the day if God sends them: and the evils bear patiently and sweetly; for this day only is ours: we are dead to yesterday, and not born to to-morrow.—*Jeremy Taylor*.

DEATH.—It is not death, it is dying that alarms me.—*Montaigne*.

Death is as the foreshadowing of life. We die that we may die no more.— *Herman Hooker*.

This world is the land of the dying; the next is the land of the living.—*Tryon Edwards.*

Men fear death, as if unquestionably the greatest evil, and yet no man knows that it may not be the greatest good.—*W. Mitford.*

We call it death to leave this world, but were we once out of it, and enstated into the happiness of the next, we should think it were dying indeed to come back to it again.—*Sherlock.*

Death has nothing terrible which life has not made so. A faithful Christian life in this world is the best preparation for the next.—*Tryon Edwards.*

It is impossible that anything so natural, so necessary, and so universal as death, should ever have been designed by Providence as an evil to mankind.—*Swift.*

We understand death for the first time when he puts his hand upon one whom we love.—*Mad. De Staël.*

Death is like thunder in two particulars: we are alarmed at the sound of it, and it is formidable only from that which preceded it.—*Colton.*

Death, to a good man, is but passing through a dark entry, out of one little dusky room of his father's house, into another that is fair and large, lightsome and glorious, and divinely entertaining.—*Clarke.*

Death is not, to the Christian, what it has often been called, "Paying the debt of nature." No, it is not paying a debt; it is rather like bringing a note to a bank to obtain solid gold in exchange for it. You bring a cumbrous body which is nothing worth, and which you could not wish to retain long; you lay it down, and receive for it, from the eternal treasures, liberty, victory, knowledge, and rapture.—*John Foster.*

We picture death as coming to destroy; let us rather picture Christ as coming to save. We think of death as ending; let us rather think of life as beginning, and that more abundantly. We think of losing; let us think of gaining. We think of parting, let us think of meeting. We think of going away; let us think of arriving. And as the voice of death whispers "You must go from earth," let us hear the voice of Christ saying, "You are but coming to Me!"—*N. Macleod.*

No man who is fit to live need fear to die. To us here, death is the most terrible thing we know. But when we have tasted its reality it will mean to us birth, deliverance, a new creation of ourselves. It will be what health is to the sick man; what home is to the exile; what the loved one given back is to the bereaved. As we draw near to it a solemn gladness should fill our hearts. It is God's great morning lighting up the sky. Our fears are the terror of children in the night. The night with its terrors, its darkness, its feverish dreams, is passing away; and when we awake it will be into the sunlight of God.—*Fuller.*

The gods conceal from men the happiness of death, that they may endure life.—*Lucan.*

A wise and due consideration of our latter end, is neither to render us sad, melancholy, disconsolate, or unfit for the business and offices of life; but to make us more watchful, vigilant, industrious, sober, cheerful, and thankful to that God who hath been pleased thus to make us serviceable to him, comfortable to ourselves, and profitable to others; and after all this, to take away the bitterness and sting of death, through Jesus Christ our Lord.—*Sir M. Hale.*

One may live as a conqueror, a king, or a magistrate; but he must die a man. The bed of death brings every human being to his pure individuality, to the intense contemplation of that deepest and most solemn of all relations—the relation between the creature and his Creator.—*Daniel Webster.*

If thou expect death as a friend, prepare to entertain him; if as an enemy, prepare to overcome him.—Death has no advantage except when he comes as a stranger.—*Quarles.*

What a superlatively grand and consoling idea is that of death! Without this radiant idea—this delightful morning star, indicating that the luminary of eternity is going to rise, life would, to my view, darken into midnight melancholy. The expectation of living here, and living thus always, would be indeed a prospect of overwhelming despair. But thanks to that fatal decree that dooms us to die; thanks to that gospel which opens the visions of an endless life; and thanks above all to that Saviour friend who has promised to conduct the faithful through the sacred trance of death, into scenes of Paradise and everlasting delight.—*John Foster.*

Death is the golden key that opens the palace of eternity.—*Milton.*

Death expecteth thee everywhere; be wise, therefore, and expect death everywhere.—*Quarles.*

The ancients feared death; we, thanks to Christianity, fear only dying.—*Guesses at Truth.*

Death is the crown of life.—Were death denied, poor man would live in vain; to live would not be life; even fools would wish to die.—*Young.*

Death opens the gate of fame, and shuts the gate of envy after it.—It unloosens the chain of the captive, and puts the bondsman's task in another's hands.—*Sterne.*

Be still prepared for death: and death or life shall thereby be the sweeter.—*Shakespeare.*

To neglect, at any time, preparation for death, is to sleep on our post at a siege; to omit it in old age, is to sleep at an attack.—*Johnson.*

One of the fathers says, "There is but this difference between the death of old men and young; that old men go to death, and death comes to the young."

He who should teach men to die, would, at the same time, teach them to live.—*Montaigne.*

A dislike of death is no proof of the want of religion. The instincts of nature shrink from it, for no creature can like its own dissolution.—But though death is not desired, the result of it may be, for dying to the Christian is the way to life eternal.—*W. Jay.*

A good man, when dying, once said, "Formerly death appeared to me like a wide river, but now it has dwindled to a little rill; and my comforts, which were as the rill, have become the broad and deep river."

He whom the gods love, dies young.—*Menander.*

Is death the last sleep? No, it is the last and final awakening.—*Walter Scott.*

The air is full of farewells to the dying, and mournings for the dead.—*Longfellow.*

The good die first; and they whose hearts are dry as summer dust burn to the socket.—*Wordsworth.*

Cullen, in his last moments, whispered, "I wish I had the power of writing or speaking, for then I would describe to you how pleasant a thing it is to die."—*Derby.*

The darkness of death is like the evening twilight; it makes all objects appear more lovely to the dying.—*Richter.*

Men may live fools, but fools they cannot die.—*Young.*

Death is the liberator of him whom freedom cannot release; the physician of him whom medicine cannot cure; the comforter of him whom time cannot console.—*Colton.*

Let death be daily before your eyes, and you will never entertain any abject thought, nor too eagerly covet anything.—*Epictetus.*

On death and judgment, heaven and hell, who oft doth think, must needs die well.—*Sir W. Raleigh.*

It matters not at what hour the righteous fall asleep.—Death cannot come untimely to him who is fit to die.—The less of this cold world the more of heaven; the briefer life, the earlier immortality.—*Milman.*

There is no better armor against the shafts of death than to be busied in God's service.—*Fuller.*

He who always waits upon God, is ready whensoever he calls.—He is a happy man who so lives that death at all times may find him at leisure to die.—*Feltham.*

Let dissolution come when it will, it can do the Christian no harm, for it will be but a passage out of a prison into a palace; out of a sea of troubles into a haven of rest; out of a crowd of enemies, to an innumerable company of true, loving, and faithful friends; out of shame, reproach, and contempt, into exceeding great and eternal glory.—*Bunyan.*

We sometimes congratulate ourselves at the moment of waking from a troubled dream; it may be so the moment after death.—*Hawthorne.*

Death and love are the two wings

that bear the good man to heaven.— *Michael Angelo.*

If Socrates died like a philosopher, Jesus Christ died like a God.—*Rousseau.*

Each departed friend is a magnet that attracts us to the next world.—*Richter.*

Living is death; dying is life.—On this side of the grave we are exiles, on that, citizens; on this side, orphans; on that, children; on this side, captives; on that, freemen; on this side disguised, unknown; on that, disclosed and proclaimed as the sons of God.— *H. W. Beecher.*

It is as natural to man to die, as to be born; and to a little infant, perhaps the one is as painful as the other.— *Bacon.*

Death stamps the characters and conditions of men for eternity.—As death finds them in this world, so will they be in the next.—*Emmons.*

Ah! what a sign it is of evil life, when death's approach is seen so terrible!— *Shakespeare.*

How shocking must thy summons be, O death, to him that is at ease in his possessions! who, counting on long years of pleasure here, is quite unfurnished for the world to come.—*Blair.*

I love to think of my little children whom God has called to himself as away at school—at the best school in the universe, under the best teachers, learning the best things, in the best possible manner.

Readiness for death is that of character, rather than of occupation. It is right living which prepares for safe or even joyous dying.

O death! We thank thee for the light that thou wilt shed upon our ignorance. —*Bossuet.*

I believe that a family lives but a half life until it has sent its forerunners into the heavenly world, until those who linger here can cross the river, and fold transfigured a glorious form in the embrace of an endless life.—*Bridgman.*

I never think he is quite ready for another world who is altogether weary of this.—*H. A. Hamilton.*

There is no death! What seems so is transition; this life of mortal breath is but a suburb of the life elysian, whose portal we call death.—*Longfellow.*

When I am dying I want to know that I have a similarity to God, so that my will is the same as his will, and that I love and hate and wish what he does. —*J. Cook.*

The bad man's death is horror; but the just does but ascend to glory from the dust.—*Habbington.*

Whom the Gods love die young no matter how long they live.—*E. Hubbard.*

Every minute dies a man, every minute one is born.—*Tennyson.*

Every minute dies a man, and one and one-sixteenth is born.—*Anon.*

Tom's no more—and so no more of Tom.—*Byron.*

Each person is born to one possession which outvalues all the others—his last breath.—*Mark Twain.*

Alexander the Great, seeing Diogenes looking attentively at a parcel of human bones, asked the philosopher what he was looking for. "That which I cannot find," was the reply. "the difference between your father's bones and those of his slaves."

A good man being asked during his last illness, whether he thought himself dying, "Really, friend, I care not whether I am or not; for if I die I shall be with God; if I live, He will be with me."

Not by lamentations and mournful chants ought we to celebrate the funeral of a good man, but by hymns, for in ceasing to be numbered with mortals he enters upon the heritage of a diviner life.—*Plutarch.*

Leaves have their time to fall, and flowers to wither at the North-wind's breath, and stars to set—but all, thou hast all seasons for thine own, O death! —*Mrs. Hemans.*

The sense of death is most in apprehension, and the poor beetle that we tread upon feels a pang as great as when a giant dies.—*Shakespeare.*

The chamber where the good man meets his fate is privileged beyond the common walk of virtuous life, quite on the verge of heaven.—*Young.*

As long as we are living, God will give us living grace, and he wont give us dying grace till it's time to die. What's the use of trying to feel like dying when you aint dying, nor anywhere near it?—*H. W. Beecher.*

I know of but one remedy against the fear of death that is effectual and that will stand the test either of a sick-bed, or of a sound mind—that is, a good life, a clear conscience, an honest heart, and a well-ordered conversation; to carry the thoughts of dying men about us, and so to live before we die as we shall wish we had when we come to it. —*Norris.*

Man's highest triumph, man's profoundest fall, the death-bed of the just is yet undrawn by mortal hand; it merits a divine: angels should paint it, angels ever there; there, on a post of honor and of joy.—*Young.*

Be of good cheer about death, and know this of a truth, that no evil can happen to a good man, either in life' or after death.—*Socrates.*

Death did not first strike Adam, the first sinful man, nor Cain, the first hypocrite, but Abel, the innocent and righteous.—The first soul that met death overcame death; the first soul parted from earth went to heaven.—Death argues not displeasure, because he whom God loved best dies first, and the murderer is punished with living.—*Bp. Hall.*

DEBT.—I have discovered the philosopher's stone, that turns everything into gold: it is, "Pay as you go."—*John Randolph.*

Debt is the secret foe of thrift, as vice and idleness are its open foes.—The debt-habit is the twin brother of poverty.—*T. T. Munger.*

Run not into debt, either for wares sold, or money borrowed; be content to want things that are not of absolute necessity, rather than to run up the score: such a man pays, at the latter end, a third part more than the principal, and is in perpetual servitude to his creditors; lives uncomfortably; is necessitated to increase his debts to stop his creditors' mouths; and many times falls into desperate courses.—*Sir M. Hale.*

Do not accustom yourself to consider debt only as an inconvenience; you will find it a calamity.—*Johnson.*

Poverty is hard, but debt is horrible. —A man might as well have a smoky house and a scolding wife. which are said to be the two worst evils of our life.—*Spurgeon.*

Think what you do when you run in debt; you give to another power over your liberty. If you cannot pay at the time, you will be ashamed ,to see your creditor; will be in fear when you speak to him; will make poor, pitiful, sneaking excuses, and by degrees come to lose your veracity, and sink into base, downright lying; for the second vice is lying, the first is running in debt. A freeborn man ought not to be ashamed nor afraid to see or speak to any man living, but poverty often deprives a man of all spirit and virtue. It is hard for an empty bag to stand upright.—*Franklin.*

The first step in debt is like the first step in falsehood, involving the necessity of going on in the same course, debt following debt, as lie follows lie.—*S. Smiles.*

Youth is in danger until it learns to look upon debts as furies.—*Bulwer.*

Paying of debts is, next to the grace of God, the best means of delivering you from a thousand temptations to vanity and sin.—Pay your debts, and you will not have wherewithal to buy costly toys or pernicious pleasures.— Pay your debts, and you will not have what to lose to a gamester.—Pay your debts, and you will of necessity abstain from, many indulgences that war against the spirit and bring you into captivity to sin, and cannot fail to end in your utter destruction, both of soul and body. —*Delany.*

"Out of debt, out of danger," is, like many other proverbs, full of wisdom; but the word danger does not sufficiently express all that the warning demands.— For a state of debt and embarrassment is a state of positive misery, and the sufferer is as one haunted by an evil spirit, and his heart can know neither rest nor peace till it is cast out.— *Bridges.*

A man who owes a little can clear it off in a little time, and, if he is prudent, he will: whereas a man, who, by long negligence, owes a great deal, despairs of ever being able to pay, and therefore never looks into his accounts at all. —*Chesterfield.*

A small debt produces a debtor; a large one, an enemy.—*Publius Syrus.*

Debt is to a man what the serpent is to the bird; its eye fascinates, its breath poisons, its coil crushes sinew and bone, its jaw is the pitiless grave.—*Bulwer.*

DECEIT.—There is no wickedness so desperate or deceptive—we can never foresee its consequences.

Of all the evil spirits abroad in the world, insincerity is the most dangerous.—*Froude.*

Deceivers are the most dangerous members of society.—They trifle with the best affections of our nature, and violate the most sacred obligations.—*Crabbe.*

No man, for any considerable period, can wear one face to himself and another to the multitude, without finally getting bewildered as to which may be true.—*Hawthorne.*

Idiots only may be cozened twice.—*Dryden.*

There is less misery in being cheated than in that kind of wisdom which perceives, or thinks it perceives, that all mankind are cheats.—*E. H. Chapin.*

It is as easy to deceive one's self without perceiving it, as it is difficult to deceive others without their finding it out.—*Rochefoucauld.*

We never deceive for a good purpose; knavery adds malice to falsehood.—*Bruyère.*

Our double dealing generally comes down upon ourselves.—To speak or act a lie is alike contemptible in the sight of God and man.—*Everton.*

The surest way of making a dupe is to let your victim suppose you are his.—*Bulwer.*

No man was ever so much deceived by another as by himself.—*Greville.*

Deceit is the false road to happiness; and all the joys we travel through to vice, like fairy banquets, vanish when we touch them.—*A. Hill.*

Who dares think one thing and another tell, my heart detests him as the gates of hell.—*Pope.*

The first and worst of all frauds is to cheat one's self.—All sin is easy after that.—*Bailey.*

He that has no real esteem for any of the virtues, can best assume the appearance of them all.—*Colton.*

When once a concealment or a deceit has been practiced in matters where all should be fair and open as day, confidence can never be restored, any more than you can restore the white bloom to the grape or plum that you once pressed in your hand.—*H. W. Beecher.*

O, what a tangled web we weave, when first we practice to deceive.—*Walter Scott.*

Many an honest man practices on himself an amount of deceit, sufficient, if practiced on another, and in a little different way, to send him to the State prison.—*Bovee.*

Mankind, in the gross, is a gaping monster, that loves to be deceived, and has seldom been disappointed.—*Mackenzie.*

All deception in the course of life is indeed nothing else but a lie reduced to practice, and falsehood passing from words into things.—*South.*

There are three persons you should never deceive: your physician, your confessor, and your lawyer.—*Walpole.*

Were we to take as much pains to be what we ought, as we do to disguise what we are, we might appear like ourselves without being at the trouble of any disguise at all.—*Rochefoucauld.*

It many times falls out that we deem ourselves much deceived in others, because we first deceived ourselves.—*Sir P. Sidney.*

DECENCY.—Virtue and decency are so nearly related that it is difficult to separate them from each other but in our imagination.—*Cicero.*

Want of decency is want of sense.—*Roscommon.*

Decency of behavior in our lives obtains the approbation of all with whom we converse, from the order, consistency, and moderation of our words and actions.—*Steele.*

Decency is the least of all laws, but yet it is the law which is most strictly observed.—*Rochefoucauld.*

DECISION.—There is nothing more to be esteemed than a manly firmness and decision of character.—I like a person who knows his own mind and sticks to it; who sees at once what, in given circumstances, is to be done, and does it.—*Hazlitt.*

When we can say "no," not only to things that are wrong and sinful, but also to things pleasant, profitable, and good which would hinder and clog our grand duties and our chief work, we shall understand more fully what life is worth, and how to make the most of it.—*C. A. Stoddard.*

I hate to see things done by halves.— If it be right, do it boldly,—if it be wrong leave it undone.—*Gilpin.*

Decision of character will often give to an inferior mind command over a superior.—*W. Wirt.*

When desperate ills demand a speedy cure, distrust is cowardice, and prudence folly.—*Johnson.*

Men must be decided on what they will not do, and then they are able to act with vigor in what they ought to do.—*Mencius.*

The block of granite which was an obstacle in the pathway of the weak becomes a stepping-stone in the pathway of the strong.—*Carlyle.*

All the world over it is true that a double-minded man is unstable in all his ways, like a wave on the streamlet, tossed hither and thither with every eddy of its tide.—A determinate purpose in life and a steady adhesion to it through all disadvantages, are indispensable conditions of success.—*W. M. Punshon.*

The souls of men of undecided and feeble purpose are the graveyards of good intentions.

It is a poor and disgraceful thing not to be able to reply, with some degree of certainty, to the simple questions, "What will you be? What will you do?"—*John Foster.*

He that cannot decidedly say "No," when tempted to evil, is on the highway to ruin.—He loses the respect even of those who would tempt him, and becomes but the pliant tool and victim of their evil designs.—*J. Hawes.*

The man who has not learned to say "No" will be a weak if not a wretched man as long as he lives.—*A. Maclaren.*

DEEDS.—Our deeds determine us, as much as we determine our deeds.— *George Eliot.*

We are our own fates.—Our deeds are our own doomsmen.—Man's life was made not for creeds, but actions.— *Meredith.*

How oft the sight of means to do ill deeds makes ill deeds done!—*Shakespeare.*

Our deeds are seeds of fate, sown here on earth, but bringing forth their harvest in eternity.—*G. D. Boardman.*

The flighty purpose never is o'ertook, unless the deed go with it.—*Shakespeare.*

Our deeds follow us, and what we have been makes us what we are.

It is our own past which has made us what we are. We are the children of our own deeds. Conduct has created character; acts have grown into habits, each year has pressed into us a deeper moral print; the lives we have led have left us such as we are to-day.—*Dykes.*

A word that has been said may be unsaid—it is but air.—But when a deed is done, it cannot be undone, nor can our thoughts reach out to all the mischiefs that may follow.—*Longfellow.*

Look on little deeds as great, on account of Christ, who dwells in us, and watches our life; look on great deeds as easy, on account of His great power.— *Pascal.*

Good actions ennoble us, and we are the sons of our own deeds.—*Cervantes.*

We should believe only in deeds; words go for nothing everywhere.— *Rojas.*

No matter what a man's aims, or resolutions, or professions may be, it is by one's deeds that he is to be judged, both by God and man.—*H. W. Beecher.*

Blessings ever wait on virtuous deeds, and though a late, a sure reward succeeds.—*Congreve.*

Foul deeds will rise, though all the earth o'erwhelm them, to men's eyes.— *Shakespeare.*

Good deeds ring clear through heaven like a bell.—*Richter.*

A noble deed is a step toward God.— *J. G. Holland.*

A life spent worthily should be measured by deeds, not years.—*Sheridan.*

DEFEAT.—What is defeat?—Nothing but education; nothing but the first step to something better.—*Wendell Phillips.*

Defeat is a school in which truth always grows strong.—*H. W. Beecher.*

No man is defeated without some resentment, which will be continued with obstinacy while he believes himself in the right, and asserted with bitterness, if even to his own conscience he is detected in the wrong.—*Johnson.*

It is defeat that turns bone to flint, and gristle to muscle, and makes men invincible, and formed those heroic natures that are now in ascendency in the world.—Do not then be afraid of defeat. —You are never so near to victory as when defeated in a good cause.—*H. W. Beecher.*

DEFERENCE. — Deference is the most delicate, the most indirect, and the most elegant of all compliments, and before company is the genteelest kind of flattery.—*Shenstone.*

Deference is the instinctive respect which we pay to the great and good.— The unconscious acknowledgment of the superiority or excellence of others.— *Tryon Edwards.*

Deference often shrinks and withers as much upon the approach of intimacy, as the sensitive plant does upon the touch of one's finger.—*Shenstone.*

DEFINITION.—All arts acknowledge that then only we know certainly, when we can define; for definition is that which refines the pure essence of things from the circumstance.—*Milton.*

Just definitions either prevent or put an end to disputes.—*Emons.*

A large part of the discussions of disputants come from the want of accurate definition.—Let one define his terms and then stick to the definition, and half the differences in philosophy and theology would come to an end, and be seen to have no real foundation.—*Tryon Edwards.*

I am apt to think that men find their simple ideas agree, though in discourse they confound one another with different names.—*Locke.*

DEFORMITY. — Many a man has risen to eminence under the powerful reaction of his mind against the scorn of the unworthy, daily evoked by his personal defects, who, with a handsome person, would have sunk into the luxury of a careless life under the tranquilizing smiles of continual admiration.—*De Quincey.*

Do you suppose we owe nothing to Pope's deformity?—He said to himself, "If my person be crooked, my verses shall be straight."—*Hazlitt.*

Deformity is daring; it is its essence to overtake mankind by heart and soul and make itself the equal, aye, the superior of others.—*Byron.*

Deformity of heart I call the worst deformity of all; for what is form, or face, but the soul's index, or its case?—*Colton.*

DELAY.— (See "PROCRASTINATION" and "INACTIVITY.")

Delay has always been injurious to those who are prepared.—*Lucan.*

Defer no time; delays have dangerous ends.—*Shakespeare.*

It is one of the illusions, that the present hour is not the critical, decisive hour.—Write it on your heart that every day is the best day in the year. —No man has learned anything rightly until he knows and feels that every day is doomsday.—*Carlyle.*

O, how many deeds of deathless virtue and immortal crime the world had wanted had the actor said, "I will do this to-morrow!"—*Lord John Russell.*

God keep you from "It is too late." When the fool has made up his mind the market has gone by.—*Spanish Proverb.*

No man ever served God by doing things to-morrow. If we honor Christ, and are blessed, it is by the things which we do to-day.

Procrastination is the thief of time; year after year it steals till all are fled, and to the mercies of a moment leaves the vast concerns of an eternal scene.— *Young.*

He that takes time to resolve, gives leisure to deny, and warning to prepare. —*Quarles.*

The procrastinator is not only indolent and weak but commonly false too; most of the weak are false.—*Lavater.*

In delay we waste our lights in vain; like lamps by day.—*Shakespeare.*

To-morrow, didst thou say? Go to —I will not hear of it—To-morrow! 'tis a sharper who stakes his penury against thy plenty—who takes thy ready cash, and pays thee nought but wishes, hopes, and promises, the currency of idiots. To-morrow! it is a period nowhere to be found in all the hoary registers of time, unless perchance in the fool's calendar. Wisdom disclaims the word, nor holds society with those that own it. 'Tis fancy's child, and folly is its father: wrought on such stuff as dreams are; and baseless as the fantastic visions of the evening.—*Cotton.*

To-morrow I will live, the fool does say: to-day itself's too late; the wise lived yesterday.—*Martial.*

To-morrow, and to-morrow, and to-morrow, creeps in this petty pace from day to day, to the last syllable of recorded time; and all our yesterdays have lighted fools the way to dusty death.—*Shakespeare.*

Every delay is hateful, but it gives wisdom.—*Publius Syrus.*

Some one speaks admirably of the well-ripened fruit of sage delay.—*Balzac.*

Shun delays, they breed remorse; take thy time while time is lent thee.—Creeping snails have weakest force; fly their fault, lest thou repent thee.—*Good* is best when soonest wrought; lingering labors come to nought.—*Southwell.*

Where duty is plain delay is both foolish and hazardous; where it is not, delay may be both wisdom and safety.—*Tryon Edwards.*

Time drinketh up the essence of every great and noble action which ought to be performed but is delayed in the execution.—*Veeshnoo Sarma.*

The surest method of arriving at a knowledge of God's eternal purposes about us is to be found in the right use of the present moment. Each hour comes with some little fagot of God's will fastened upon its back.—*F. W. Faber.*

DELICACY.—Delicacy is to the affections what grace is to beauty.—*Degerando.*

True delicacy, that most beautiful heart-leaf of humanity, exhibits itself most significantly in little things.—*Mary Howitt.*

The finest qualities of our nature, like the bloom on fruits, can be preserved only by the most delicate handling.—*Thoreau.*

If you destroy delicacy and a sense of shame in a young girl you deprave her very fast.—*Mrs. Stowe.*

Weak men, often, from the very principle of their weakness, derive a certain susceptibility, delicacy, and taste, which render them, in these particulars, much superior to men of stronger and more consistent minds, who laugh at them.—*Greville.*

Friendship, love, and piety, ought to be handled with a sort of mysterious secrecy.—They ought to be spoken of only in the rare moments of perfect confidence—to be mutually understood in silence.—Many things are too delicate to be thought; many more to be spoken.—*Novalis.*

An appearance of delicacy, and even of fragility, is almost essential to beauty.—*Burke.*

Delicacy is to the mind what fragrance is to the fruit.—*A. Poincelot.*

DELIGHT.—What more felicity can fall to man than to enjoy delight with liberty?—*Spenser.*

As high as we have mounted in delight, in our dejection do we sing as low.—*Wordsworth.*

These violent delights have violent ends, and in their triumph die, like fire and powder, which, as they kiss, consume.—*Shakespeare.*

I am convinced that we have a degree of delight, and that no small one, in the real misfortunes and pains of others.—*Burke.*

Sensual delights soon end in loathing, quickly bring a glutting surfeit, and degenerate into torments when they are continued and unintermitted.—*John Howe.*

DELUSION.—No man is happy without a delusion of some kind.—Delusions are as necessary to our happiness as realities.—*Bovee.*

The worst deluded are the self-deluded.—*Bovee.*

Were we perfectly acquainted with the object, we should never passionately desire it.—*Rochefoucauld.*

We strive as hard to hide our hearts from ourselves as from others, and always with more success; for in deciding upon our own case we are both judge, jury, and executioner, and where sophistry cannot overcome the first, or flattery the second, self-love is always ready to

defeat the sentence by bribing the third.
—*Colton.*

You think a man to be your dupe.—
If he pretends to be so, who is the
greatest dupe—he or you?—*Bruyère.*

It many times falls out that we deem
ourselves much deceived in others, because we are first deceived ourselves.—
Sir P. Sidney.

When our vices quit us, we flatter
ourselves with the belief that it is we
who quit them.—*Rochefoucauld.*

O thoughts of men accurst.—Past and
to come seem best; things present,
worst.—*Shakespeare.*

This is the excellent foppery of the
world! that, when we are sick in fortune, we make guilty of our disasters,
the sun, the moon, and the stars: as if
we were villains by necessity; fools, by
heavenly compulsion; knaves, thieves,
and treachers, by spherical predominance; drunkards, liars, and adulterers,
by an enforced obedience of planetary
influence; and all that we are evil in, by
a divine thrusting on.—*Shakespeare.*

Mankind in the gross is a gaping monster, that loves to be deceived, and has
seldom been disappointed.—*Mackenzie.*

Hope tells a flattering tale, delusive,
vain, and hollow.—*Wrother.*

The disappointment of manhood succeeds the delusion of youth.—*Disraeli.*

DEMOCRACY.—The love of democracy is that of equality.—*Montesquieu.*

In every village there will arise some
miscreant, to establish the most grinding tyranny by calling himself the people.—*Sir Robert Peel.*

The history of the gospel has been
the history of the development and
growth of Christian democratic ideas.—
H. W. Beecher.

Your little child is your only true
democrat.—*Mrs. Stowe.*

It is the most beautiful truth in
morals that we have no such thing as a
distinct or divided interest from our
race.—In their welfare is ours; and by
choosing the broadest paths to effect
their happiness, we choose the surest and
shortest to our own.—*Bulwer.*

Knowledge and goodness—these make
degrees in heaven, and they must be the
graduating scale of a true democracy.—
Miss Sedgwick.

Lycurgus being asked why he, who
in other respects appeared to be so zealous for the equal rights of men, did not
make his government democratic rather
than an oligarchy, replied, " Go you,
and try a democracy in your own
house."—*Plutarch.*

If there were a people consisting of
gods, they would be governed demo-
cratically; so perfect a government is
not suitable to men.—*Rousseau.*

Intellectual superiority is so far from
conciliating confidence that it is the
very spirit of a democracy, as in France,
to proscribe the aristocracy of talents.
To be the favorite of an ignorant multitude, a man must descend to their
level; he must desire what they desire,
and detest all they do not approve: he
must yield to their prejudices, and substitute them for principles. Instead of
enlightening their errors, he must adopt
them, and must furnish the sophistry
that will propagate and defend them.—
Fisher Ames.

Democracy will itself accomplish the
salutary universal change from the delusive to the real, and make a new
blessed world of us bye and bye.—
Carlyle.

The progress of democracy seems irresistible, because it is the most uniform,
the most ancient, and the most permanent tendency which is to be found in
history.—*De Tocqueville.*

The devil was the first democrat.—
Byron.

" It is a great blessing," says Pascal,
" to be born a man of quality, since it
brings a man as far forward at eighteen
or twenty as another would be at fifty,
which is a clear gain of thirty years."—
These thirty years are commonly wanting to the ambitious characters of de-
mocracies.—The principle of equality,
which allows every man to arrive at
everything, prevents all men from rapid
advancement.—*De Tocqueville.*

The real democratic American idea is,
not that every man shall be on a level
with every other, but that every one
shall have liberty, without hindrance, to
be what God made him.—*H. W. Beecher*

DEPENDENCE. — There is none so
great but he may both need the help
and service, and stand in fear of the

power and unkindness, even of the meanest of mortals.—*Seneca.*

God has made no one absolute.— The rich depend on the poor, as well as the poor on the rich.—The world is but a magnificent building; all the stones are gradually cemented together.—No one subsists by himself alone.—*Feltham.*

No degree of knowledge attainable by man is able to set him above the want of hourly assistance.—*Johnson.*

Dependence is a perpetual call upon humanity, and a greater incitement to tenderness and pity than any other motive whatever.—*Thackeray.*

The greatest man living may stand in need of the meanest, as much as the meanest does of him.—*Fuller.*

Heaven's eternal wisdom has decreed, that man should ever stand in need of man.—*Theocritus.*

Dependence goes somewhat against the grain of a generous mind; and it is no wonder that it should do so, considering the unreasonable advantage which is often taken of the inequality of fortune.—*Jeremy Collier.*

In an arch, each single stone, which, if severed from the rest, would be perhaps defenceless, is sufficiently secured by the solidity and entireness of the whole fabric of which it is a part.— *Boyle.*

How beautifully is it ordered, that as many thousands work for one, so must every individual bring his labor to make the whole.—The highest is not to despise the lowest, nor the lowest to envy the highest; each must live in all and by all. —So God has ordered, that men, being in need of each other, should learn to love each other, and to bear each other's burdens.—*G. A. Sala.*

The acknowledgment of weakness which we make in imploring to be relieved from hunger and from temptation, is surely wisely put in our prayer. —Think of it, you who are rich, and take heed how you turn a beggar away. —*Thackeray.*

The beautiful must ever rest in the arms of the sublime.—The gentle need the strong to sustain it, as much as the rock-flowers need rocks to grow on, or the ivy the rugged wall which it embraces.—*Mrs. Stowe.*

Depend on no man, on no friend but him who can depend on himself.—He only who acts conscientiously toward himself, will act so toward others.— *Lavater.*

DEPRAVITY.—(See " SIN.")

We are all sinful; and whatever one of us blames in another each one will find in his own heart.—*Seneca.*

Men sometimes affect to deny the depravity of our race; but it is as clearly taught in the lawyers' office and in courts of justice, as in the Bible itself. —Every prison, and fetter, and scaffold, and bolt, and bar, and chain is evidence that man believes in the depravity of man.—*Tryon Edwards.*

Controlled depravity is not innocence; and it is not the labor of delinquency in chains that will correct abuses. Never did a serious plan of amending any old tyrannical establishment propose the authors and abettors of the abuses as the reformers of them.—*Burke.*

Every man has his devilish moments. —*Lavater.*

Original sin is in us, like the beard. —We are shaved to-day and look clean, and have a smooth chin; to-morrow our beard has grown again, nor does it cease growing while we remain on earth.— In like manner original sin cannot be extirpated from us; it springs up in us as long as we live.—Nevertheless we are bound to resist it to our utmost strength, and to cut it down unceasingly.—*Luther.*

We have such an habitual persuasion of the general depravity of human nature, that in falling in with strangers we almost always reckon on their being irreligious, till we discover some specific indication of the contrary.—*J. Foster.*

It is not occasionally that the human soul is under the influence of depravity; but this is its habit and state till the soul is renewed by grace.—*Dick.*

DESIRE. — Desires are the pulses of the soul;—as physicians judge by the appetite, so may you by desires.—*Manton.*

The thirst of desire is never filled, nor fully satisfied.—*Cicero.*

It is much easier to suppress a first desire than to satisfy those that follow.— *Rochefoucauld.*

The reason that so many want their

desires is that their desires want reason. —He may do what he will, who will do but what he may.—*Warwick.*

Everyone would have something, such perhaps as we are ashamed to utter. The proud man would have honor; the covetous man, wealth and abundance; the malicious, revenge on his enemies; the epicure, pleasure and long life; the barren, children; the wanton, beauty; each would be humored in his own desire, though in opposition both to God's will, and his own good.—*Bp. Hall.*

Some desire is necessary to keep life in motion; he whose real wants are supplied, must admit those of fancy.— *Johnson.*

Those things that are not practicable are not desirable. There is nothing in the world really beneficial that does not lie within the reach of an informed understanding and a well-protected pursuit. There is nothing that God has judged good for us that he has not given us the means to accomplish, both in the natural and the moral world. If we cry, like children, for the moon, like children we must cry on.—*Burke.*

Where necessity ends, desire and curiosity begin; no sooner are we supplied with everything nature can demand, than we sit down to contrive artificial appetites.—*Johnson.*

The stoical schemes of supplying our wants by lopping off our desires, is like cutting off our feet when we want shoes. —*Swift.*

A wise man will desire no more than he may get justly, use soberly, distribute cheerfully, and leave contentedly.

The passions and desires, like the two twists of a rope, mutually mix one with the other, and twine inextricably round the heart; producing good, if moderately indulged; but certain destruction, if suffered to become inordinate.—*Burton.*

By annihilating the desires, you annihilate the mind.—Every man without passions has within him no principle of action, nor motive to act.—*Helvetius.*

Every desire bears its death in its very gratification.—Curiosity languishes under repeated stimulants, and novelties cease to excite surprise, until at length we do not wonder even at a miracle.—*Washington Irving.*

We trifle when we assign limits to our desires, since nature hath set none.— *Bovee.*

Inordinate desires commonly produce irregular endeavors. If our wishes be not kept in submission to God's providence, our pursuits will scarcely be kept under the restraints of his precepts.— *M. Henry.*

Our nature is inseparable from desires, and the very word desire—the craving for something not possessed— implies that our present felicity is not complete.—*Hobbes.*

However rich or elevated we may be, a nameless something is always wanting to our imperfect fortune.—*Horace.*

Unlawful desires are punished after the effect of enjoying; but impossible desires are punished in the desire itself. —*Sir P. Sidney.*

Before we passionately desire anything which another enjoys, we should examine as to the happiness of its possessor.—*Rochefoucauld.*

He who can wait for what he desires takes the course not to be exceedingly grieved if he fails of it; he on the contrary who labors after a thing too impatiently thinks the success when it comes is not a recompense equal to all the pains he has been at about it.— *Bruyère.*

There is nothing capricious in nature; and the implanting of a desire indicates that its gratification is in the constitution of the creature that feels it.—*Emerson.*

In moderating, not in satisfying desires, lies peace.—*Heber.*

The soul of man is infinite in what it covets.—*Ben Jonson.*

When a man's desires are boundless, his labors are endless.—They will set him a task he can never go through, and cut him out work he can never finish.— The satisfaction he seeks is always absent, and the happiness he aims at is ever at a distance.—*Balguy.*

It should be an indispensable rule in life to contract our desires to our present condition, and whatever may be our expectations to live within the compass of what we actually possess.—It will be time enough to enjoy an estate when it comes into our hands; but if we anticipate our good fortune we shall lose the pleasure of it when it arrives, and may possibly never possess what we have so foolishly counted on.—*Addison*.

DESOLATION.—No one is so utterly desolate, but some heart, though unknown, responds unto his own.—*Longfellow*.

None are so desolate but something dear,—dearer than self,—possesses or is possessed.—*Byron*.

No soul is desolate as long as there is a human being for whom it can feel trust and reverence.—*George Eliot*.

My desolation begins to make a better life.—*Shakespeare*.

What is the worst of woes that wait on age? What stamps the wrinkle deeper on the brow?—To view each loved one blotted from life's page, and be alone on earth.—*Byron*.

Unhappy he, who from the first of joys—society—cut off, is left alone, amid this world of death!—*Thomson*.

DESPAIR.—What we call despair is often only the painful eagerness of unfed hope.—*George Eliot*.

He that despairs measures Providence by his own little contracted model and limits infinite power to finite apprehensions.—*South*.

Considering the unforeseen events of this world, we should be taught that no human condition should inspire men with absolute despair.—*Fielding*.

It is impossible for that man to despair who remembers that his Helper is omnipotent.—*Jeremy Taylor*.

Despair is like froward children, who, when you take away one of their playthings, throw the rest into the fire for madness. It grows angry with itself, turns its own executioner, and revenges its misfortunes on its own head.—*Charron*.

Despair is the offspring of fear, of laziness, and impatience; it argues a defect of spirit and resolution, and often of honesty too. I would not despair unless I saw my misfortune recorded in the book of fate, and signed and sealed by necessity.—*Collier*.

Despair gives courage to the weak.— Resolved to die, he fears no more, but

rushes on his foes, and deals his deaths around.—*Somerville*.

Beware of desperate steps.—The darkest day, live till to-morrow, will have passed away.—*Cowper*.

He that despairs degrades the Deity, and seems to intimate that He is insufficient, or not just to his word; in vain hath he read the Scriptures, the world, and man.—*Feltham*.

He who despairs wants love and faith, for faith, hope, and love are three torches which blend their light together, nor does the one shine without the other. —*Metastasio*.

Despair gives the shocking ease to the mind that mortification gives to the body.—*Greville*.

Despair is the damp of hell, as joy is the serenity of heaven.—*Donne*.

The fact that God has prohibited despair gives misfortune the right to hope all things, and leaves hope free to dare all things.—*Mad. Swetchine*.

Religion converts despair, which destroys, into resignation, which submits —*Lady Blessington*.

DESPONDENCY.—To despond is to be ungrateful beforehand.—Be not looking for evil.—Often thou drainest the gall of fear while evil is passing by thy dwelling.—*Tupper*.

Life is a warfare; and he who easily desponds deserts a double duty—he betrays the noblest property of man, which is dauntless resolution; and he rejects the providence of that all-gracious Being who guides and rules the universe.— *Jane Porter*.

To believe a business impossible is the way to make it so.—How many feasible projects have miscarried through despondency, and been strangled in their birth by a cowardly imagination.— *Collier*.

In the lottery of life there are more prizes drawn than blanks, and to one misfortune there are fifty advantages. Despondency is the most unprofitable feeling a man can indulge in.—*De Witt Talmage*.

Despondency is not a state of humility.—On the contrary, it is the vexation and despair of a cowardly pride; nothing is worse.—Whether we stumble, or whether we fall, we must only think of

rising again and going on in our course.
—*Fenelon.*

Despondency is ingratitude; hope is
God's worship.—*H. W. Beecher.*

Some persons depress their own minds,
despond at the first difficulty, and conclude that making any progress in
knowledge, further than serves their
ordinary business, is above their capacity.—*Locke.*

As to feel that we can do a thing is
often success, so to doubt and despond
is a sure step to failure.

DESPOTISM.—I will believe in the
right of one man to govern a nation des-
potically when I find a man born into
the world with boots and spurs, and a
nation born with saddles on their backs.
—*Algernon Sidney.*

Despotism can no more exist in a
nation until the liberty of the press be
destroyed, than the night can happen
before the sun is set.—*Colton.*

It is odd to consider the connection
between despotism and barbarity, and
how the making one person more than
man makes the rest less.—*Addison.*

In times of anarchy one may seem a
despot in order to be a savior.—*Mirabeau.*

Despots govern by terror.—They know
that he who fears God fears nothing else,
and therefore they eradicate from the
mind, through their Voltaire and Helvetius, and the rest of that infamous
gang, that only sort of fear which generates true courage.—*Burke.*

As virtue is necessary in a republic,
and honor in a monarchy, fear is what
is required in a despotism.—As for virtue, it is not at all necessary, and honor
would be dangerous there.—*Montesquieu.*

All despotism is bad; but the worst is
that which works with the machinery of
freedom.—*Junius.*

It is difficult for power to avoid
despotism.—The possessors of rude
health—the characters never strained by
a doubt—the minds that no questions
disturb and no aspirations put out of
breath—there, the strong, are also the
tyrants.—*Gasparin.*

When the savages wish to have fruit
they cut down the tree and gather it.—

That is exactly a despotic government.
—*Montesquieu.*

There is something among men more
capable of shaking despotic power than
lightning, whirlwind, or earthquake;
that is the threatened indignation of the
whole civilized world.—*Daniel Webster.*

DESTINY.—Man proposes, but God
disposes.—*Thomas à Kempis.*

We are but the instruments of heaven;
our work is not design, but destiny.—
Owen Meredith.

No man of woman born, coward or
brave, can shun his destiny.—*Homer.*

Destiny is the scapegoat which we
make responsible for all our crimes and
follies; a necessity which we set down
for invincible when we have no wish to
strive against it.—*Balfour.*

The acts of this life are the destiny of
the next.—*Eastern Proverb.*

That which God writes on thy forehead, thou wilt come to it.—*Koran.*

Destiny is but a phrase of the weak
human heart—the dark apology for
every error.—The strong and virtuous
admit no destiny.—On earth conscience
guides; in heaven God watches.—And
destiny is but the phantom we invoke
to silence the one and dethrone the
other.—*Bulwer.*

Philosophers never stood in need of
Homer or the Pharisees to be convinced
that everything is done by immutable
laws; that everything is settled; that
everything is the necessary effect of
some previous cause.—*Voltaire.*

The clew of our destiny, wander where
we will, lies at the cradle foot.—*Richter.*

Nothing comes to pass but what God
appoints.—Our fate is decreed, and
things do not happen by chance, but
every man's portion of joy or sorrow is
predetermined.—*Seneca.*

That which is not allotted the hand
cannot reach; and what is allotted you
will find wherever you may be.—*Saadi.*

Man supposes that he directs his life
and governs his actions, when his existence is irretrievably under the control
of destiny.—*Goethe.*

If the course of human affairs be considered, it will be seen that many things
arise against which heaven does not allow us to guard.—*Machiavelli.*

Death and life have their determined

appointments; riches and honors depend upon heaven.—*Confucius.*

The wheels of nature are not made to roll backward: everything presses on toward eternity: from the birth of time an impetuous current has set in, which bears all the sons of men toward that interminable ocean. Meanwhile heaven is attracting to itself whatever is congenial to its nature, is enriching itself by the spoils of earth, and collecting within its capacious bosom whatever is pure, permanent, and divine.—*Robert Hall.*

I do not mean to expose my ideas to ingenious ridicule by maintaining that everything happens to every man for the best; but I will contend, that he who makes the best use of it, fulfills the part of a wise and good man.—*Cumberland.*

Thoughts lead on to purposes; purposes go forth in action; actions form habits; habits decide character; and character fixes our destiny.—*Tryon Edwards.*

DETRACTION.—(See "SLANDER.")

The detractor may, and often does, pull down others, but by so doing he never, as he seems to suppose, elevates himself to their position.—The most he can do is, maliciously to tear from them the blessings which he cannot enjoy himself.

To be traduced by ignorant tongues, is the rough brake that virtue must go through.—*Shakespeare.*

Those who propagate evil reports frequently invent them; and it is no breach of charity to suppose this to be always the case, because no man who spreads detraction would have scrupled to produce it, as he who should diffuse poison in a brook would scarce be acquitted of a malicious design, though he should allege that he received it of another who is doing the same elsewhere.—*Adventurer.*

To make beads of the faults of others, and tell them over every day, is infernal.—If you want to know how devils feel, you do know if you are such an one.—*H. W. Beecher.*

Happy are they that hear their detractions, and can put them to mending.—*Shakespeare.*

In some dispositions there is such an envious kind of pride that they cannot endure that any but themselves should be set forth for excellent; so that when they hear one justly praised, they will either seek to dismount his virtues, or, if they be like a clear light, they will stab him with a "but" of detraction.—*Feltham.*

Much depends upon a man's courage when he is slandered and traduced. Weak men are crushed by detraction; but the brave hold on and succeed.

He whose first emotion, on the view of an excellent work, is to undervalue or depreciate it, will never have one of his own to show.—*Aikin.*

Base natures joy to see hard hap happen to them they deem happy.—*Sir P. Sidney.*

Whoever feels pain in hearing a good character of his neighbor, will feel pleasure in the reverse; and those who despair to rise to distinction by their virtues are happy if others can be depressed to a level with themselves.—*J. Barker.*

The man that makes a character, makes foes.—*Young.*

If we considered detraction to be bred of envy, and nested only in deficient minds, we should find that the applauding of virtue would win us far more honor than seeking to disparage it.— That would show we loved what we commended, while this tells the world we grudge at what we want ourselves.—*Feltham.*

There is no readier way for a man to bring his own worth into question, than by endeavoring to detract from the worth of other men.—*Tillotson.*

Unjustifiable detraction always proves the weakness as well as meanness of the one who employs it.—To be constantly carping at, and exaggerating petty blemishes in the characters of others, putting an unfavorable construction on their language, or "damning with faint praise" their deeds, betrays, on the part of the detractor, a conscious inability to maintain a reputable standing on legitimate and honorable ground.—*E. L. Magoon.*

DEVIATION.—When people once begin to deviate, they do not know where to stop.—*George III.*

Ah! to what gulfs a single deviation from the track of human duties leads!—*Byron.*

Deviation from either truth or duty

is a downward path, and none can say where the descent will end.—"He that despiseth small things shall fall by little and little."—*Tryon Edwards.*

DEVIL.—The devil is no idle spirit, but a vagrant, runagate walker, that never rests in one place.—The motive, cause, and main intention of his walking is to ruin man.—*T. Adams.*

No sooner is a temple built to God, but the devil builds a chapel hard by.—*Herbert.*

As no good is done, or spoken, or thought by any man without the assistance of God, working in and with those that believe in him, so there is no evil done, or spoken, or thought without the assistance of the devil, who worketh with strong though secret power in the children of unbelief.—All the works of our evil nature are the work of the devil.—*J. Wesley.*

What, man! Defy the devil! Consider he's an enemy to mankind.—*Shakespeare.*

He who would fight the devil with his own weapons, must not wonder if he finds him an overmatch.—*South.*

The devil knoweth his own, and is a particularly bad paymaster.—*F. M. Crawford.*

The devil has at least one good quality, that he will flee if we resist him.—Though cowardly in him, it is safety for us.—*Tryon Edwards.*

Talk of devils being confined to hell, or hidden by invisibility!—We have them by shoals in the crowded towns and cities of the world.—Talk of raising the devil!—What need for that, when he is constantly walking to and fro in our streets, seeking whom he may devour.—*Anon.*

DEVOTION.—All is holy where devotion kneels.—*O. W. Holmes.*

The most illiterate man who is touched with devotion, and uses frequent exercises of it, contracts a certain greatness of mind, mingled with a noble simplicity, that raises him above others of the same condition. By this, a man in the lowest condition will not appear mean, or in the most splendid fortune insolent.—*Johnson.*

The private devotions and secret offices of religion are like the refreshing of a garden with the distilling and petty drops of a waterpot; but addressed from the temple, they are like rain from heaven.—*Jeremy Taylor.*

Satan rocks the cradle when we sleep at our devotions.—*Bp. Hall.*

It is of the utmost importance to season the passions of the young with devotion, which seldom dies in the mind that has received an early tincture of it. Though it may seem extinguished for a while by the cares of the world, the heats of youth, or the allurements of vice, it generally breaks out and discovers itself again as soon as discretion, consideration, age, or misfortunes have brought the man to himself. The fire may be covered and overlaid but cannot be entirely quenched and smothered.—*Addison.*

All the duties of religion are eminently solemn and venerable in the eyes of children. But none will so strongly prove the sincerity of the parent; none so powerfully awaken the reverence of the child; none so happily recommend the instruction he receives, as family devotions, particularly those in which petitions for the children occupy a distinguished place.—*Dwight.*

The secret heart is devotion's temple; there the saint lights the flame of purest sacrifice, which burns unseen but not unaccepted.—*Hannah More.*

The inward sighs of humble penitence rise to the ear of heaven, when pealed hymns are scattered to the common air.—*Joanna Baillie.*

Solid devotions resemble the rivers which run under the earth—they steal from the eyes of the world to seek the eyes of God; and it often happens that those of whom we speak least on earth, are best known in heaven.—*Caussin.*

The best and sweetest flowers in paradise, God gives to his people when they are on their knees in the closet.—Prayer, if not the very gate of heaven, is the key to let us into its holiness and joys.—*T. Brooks.*

Once I sought a time and place for solitude and prayer; but now where'er I find thy face I find a closet there.

DEW.—The dews of evening—those tears of the sky for the loss of the sun.—*Chesterfield.*

Stars of the morning—dew-drops—which the sun impearls on every leaf and flower.—*Milton.*

Dew-drops—nature's tears, which she sheds on her own breast for the fair which die.—The sun insists on gladness; but at night, when he is gone, poor nature loves to weep.—*Bailey.*

Dew-drops are the gems of morning, but the tears of mournful eve.—*Coleridge.*

Earth's liquid jewelry, wrought of the air.—*Bailey.*

DICE.—I look upon every man as a suicide from the moment he takes the dice-box desperately in his hand; all that follows in his career from that fatal time is only sharpening the dagger before he strikes it to his heart.—*Cumberland.*

I never hear the rattling of dice that it does not sound to me like the funeral bell of the whole family.—*Jerrold.*

The best throw with the dice, is to throw them away.—*Old Proverb.*

DIET. — Regimen is better than physic. Every one should be his own physician.—We should assist, not force nature.—Eat with moderation what you know by experience agrees with your constitution.—Nothing is good for the body but what we can digest.—What can procure digestion?—Exercise.—What will recruit strength?—Sleep.—What will alleviate incurable evils?—Patience.—*Voltaire.*

In general, mankind, since the improvement of cookery, eat twice as much as nature requires.—*Franklin.*

All courageous animals are carnivorous, and greater courage is to be expected in a people whose food is strong and hearty, than in the half-starved of other countries.—*Sir W. Temple.*

Food improperly taken, not only produces diseases, but affords those that are already engendered both matter and sustenance; so that, let the father of disease be what it may, intemperance is its mother.—*Burton.*

Simple diet is best; for many dishes bring many diseases; and rich sauces are worse than even heaping several meats upon each other.—*Pliny.*

The chief pleasure in eating does not consist in costly seasoning, or exquisite flavor, but in yourself. Do you seek for sauce by labor?—*Horace.*

If thou wouldst preserve a sound body, use fasting and walking; if a healthful soul, fasting and praying.—Walking exercises the body; praying exercises the soul; fasting cleanses both.—*Quarles.*

One meal a day is enough for a lion, and it ought to be for a man.—*G. Fordyce.*

A fig for your bill of fare; show me your bill of company.—*Swift.*

DIFFERENCE. — It is remarkable that men, when they differ in what they think considerable, are apt to differ in almost everything else. Their difference begets contradiction; contradiction begets heat; heat rises into resentment, rage, and ill-will.—Thus they differ in affection, as they differ in judgment, and the contention which began in pride, ends in anger.—*Cato.*

In all differences consider that both you and your opponent or enemy are mortal, and that ere long your very memories will be extinguished.—*Aurel.*

If men would consider not so much wherein they differ, as wherein they agree, there would be far less of uncharitableness and angry feeling in the world.—*Addison.*

DIFFICULTY.—What is difficulty? Only a word indicating the degree of strength requisite for accomplishing particular objects; a mere notice of the necessity for exertion; a bugbear to children and fools; only a stimulus to men.—*Samuel Warren.*

It has been the glory of the great masters in all arts to confront and to overcome; and when they had overcome the first difficulty, to turn it into an instrument for new conquests over new difficulties; thus to enable them to extend the empire of science.

Difficulty is a severe instructor, set over us by the Supreme guardian and legislator, who knows us better than we know ourselves, and loves us better too. —He that wrestles with us strengthens our nerves and sharpens our skill.—Our antagonist is our helper.—*Burke.*

The greatest difficulties lie where we are not looking for them.—*Goethe.*

The weak sinews become strong by their conflict with difficulties.—Hope is born in the long night of watching and tears.—Faith visits us in defeat and disappointment, amid the consciousness of earthly frailty and the crumbling tombstones of mortality.—*E. H. Chapin.*

It is not every calamity that is a curse, and early adversity is often a blessing.—Surmounted difficulties not only teach, but hearten us in our future struggles.—*Sharp.*

Difficulty is the soil in which all manly and womanly qualities best flourish; and the true worker, in any sphere, is continually coping with difficulties. His very failures, throwing him upon his own resources, cultivate energy and resolution; his hardships teach him fortitude; his successes inspire self-reliance.

It cannot be too often repeated that it is not helps, but obstacles, not facilities, but difficulties that make men.—*W. Mathews.*

Difficulties are God's errands; and when we are sent upon them we should esteem it a proof of God's confidence—as a compliment from him.—*H. W. Beecher.*

Difficulties strengthen the mind, as labor does the body.—*Seneca.*

There is no merit where there is no trial; and till experience stamps the mark of strength, cowards may pass for heroes, and faith for falsehood.—*A. Hill.*

The greater the obstacle, the more glory we have in overcoming it; the difficulties with which we are met are the maids of honor which set off virtue.—*Moliere.*

Difficulties show men what they are.—In case of any difficulty God has pitted you against a rough antagonist that you may be a conqueror, and this cannot be without toil.—*Epictetus.*

Our energy is in proportion to the resistance it meets.—We attempt nothing great but from a sense of the difficulties we have to encounter; we persevere in nothing great but from a pride in overcoming them.—*Hazlitt.*

There are difficulties in your path.—Be thankful for them.—They will test your capabilities of resistance; you will be impelled to persevere from the very energy of the opposition.—But what of him that fails?—What does he gain?—Strength for life.—The real merit is not in the success. but in the endeavor; and

win or lose, he will be honored and crowned.—*W. M. Punshon.*

DIFFIDENCE — Persons extremely reserved and diffident are like the old enamelled watches, which had painted covers that hindered you from seeing what time it was.—*Walpole.*

We are as often duped by diffidence as by confidence.—*Chesterfield.*

Diffidence may check resolution, and obstruct performance, but it compensates its embarrassments by more important advantages.—It conciliates the proud, and softens the severe; averts envy from excellence, and censure from miscarriage.—*Johnson.*

Nothing sinks a young man into low company, both of men and women, so surely as timidity and diffidence of himself.—If he thinks he shall not please, he may depend upon it that he will not.—But with proper endeavors to please, and a degree of persuasion that he shall, it is almost certain that he will.—*Chesterfield.*

One with more of soul in his face than words on his tongue.—*Wordsworth.*

Have a proper self-respect and think less of what others may think of you, and it will aid you to overcome diffidence, and help you to self-possession and self-reliance.

DIGNITY. — True dignity is never gained by place, and never lost when honors are withdrawn.—*Massinger.*

Dignity of position adds to dignity of character, as well as to dignity of carriage.—Give us a proud position, and we are impelled to act up to it.—*Bovee.*

Dignity consists not in possessing honors, but in the consciousness that we deserve them.—*Aristotle.*

Lord Chatham and Napoleon were as much actors as Garrick or Talma.—An imposing air should always be taken as evidence of imposition.—Dignity is often a veil between us and the real truth of things.—*E. P. Whipple.*

Dignity and love do not blend well, nor do they continue long together.—*Ovid.*

Most of the men of dignity, who awe or bore their more genial brethren, are simply men who possess the art of passing off their insensibility for wisdom.

their dullness for depth, and of concealing imbecility of intellect under haughtiness of manner.—*E. P. Whipple.*

DILIGENCE.—What we hope ever to do with ease, we must learn first to do with diligence.—*Johnson.*

The expectations of life depend upon diligence; the mechanic that would perfect his work must first sharpen his tools.—*Confucius.*

Diligence is the mother of good luck, and God gives all things to industry. Work while it is called to-day, for you know not how much you may be hindered to-morrow. One to-day is worth two to-morrows; never leave that till to-morrow which you can do to-day.—*Franklin.*

Who makes quick use of the moment, is a genius of prudence.—*Lavater.*

He who labors diligently need never despair; for all things are accomplished by diligence and labor.—*Menander.*

In all departments of activity, to have one thing to do, and then to do it, is the secret of success.

DINNER.—A dinner lubricates business.—*Stowell.*

Before dinner, men meet with great inequality of understanding, and those who are conscious of their inferiority have the modesty not to talk: when they have drunk wine, every man feels himself happy, and loses that modesty, and grows impudent and vociferous; but he is not improved; he is only not sensible of his defects.—*Johnson.*

A good dinner sharpens wit, while it softens the heart.—*Doran.*

The pleasant talk of the dinner table promotes digestion, and prevents the mind from dwelling on the grinding of the digestive mill that is going on within us. The satisfaction and repose that follow a full meal tend to check a disposition to splenetic argument, or too much zeal in supporting an opinion, while the freedom and abandon of the intercourse kept up is eminently conducive to the feelings of general benevolence.—*Jerdan.*

DIRT.—"Ignorance," says Ajax, "is a painless evil."—So, I should think, is dirt, considering the merry faces that go along with it.—*George Eliot.*

Dirt is not dirt, but only something

in the wrong place.—*Lord Palmerston.*

DISAPPOINTMENT. — The disappointment of manhood succeeds to the delusion of youth.—*Disraeli.*

No man, with a man's heart in him, gets far on his way without some bitter, soul-searching disappointment.—Happy he who is brave enough to push on another stage of the journey, and rest where there are "living springs of water, and three-score and ten palms."—*Brown.*

The best enjoyment is half disappointment to what we intend or would have in this world.—*Bailey.*

Oft expectation fails, and most oft where most it promises; and oft it hits where hope is coldest, and despair most sits.—*Shakespeare.*

How disappointment tracks the steps of hope.—*L. E. Landon.*

He who expects much will be often disappointed; yet disappointment seldom cures us of expectation, or has any other effect than that of producing a moral sentence or peevish exclamation.—*Johnson.*

In the light of eternity we shall see that what we desired would have been fatal to us, and that what we would have avoided was essential to our well-being.—*Fenelon.*

Man must be disappointed with the lesser things of life before he can comprehend the full value of the greater.—*Bulwer.*

There is many a thing which the world calls disappointment, but there is no such a word in the dictionary of faith. What to others are disappointments are to believers intimations of the way of God.—*John Newton.*

Mean spirits under disappointment, like small beer in a thunder-storm, always turn sour.—*John Randolph.*

An old man once said, "When I was young, I was poor; when old, I became rich; but in each condition I found disappointment.—When I had the faculties for enjoyment, I had not the means; when the means came, the faculties were gone."—*Mad. Gasparin.*

We mount to heaven mostly on the ruins of our cherished schemes, finding our failures were successes.—*A. B. Alcott.*

It is sometimes of God's mercy that men in the eager pursuit of worldly aggrandizement are baffled; for they are very like a train going down an inclined plane—putting on the brake is not pleasant, but it keeps the car on the track and from ruin.—*H. W. Beecher.*

Life often seems like a long shipwreck of which the débris are friendship, glory, and love.—The shores of existence are strewn with them.—*Mad. de Staël.*

DISCERNMENT.—After a spirit of discernment, the next rarest things in the world are diamonds and pearls.—*Bruyère.*

To succeed in the world, it is much more necessary to possess the penetration to discern who is a fool, than to discover who is a clever man.—*Talleyrand.*

Penetration or discernment has an air of divination; it pleases our vanity more than any other quality of the mind.—*Rochefoucauld.*

The idiot, the Indian, the child, and the unschooled farmer's boy stand nearer to the light by which nature is to be read, than the dissector or the antiquary. —*Emerson.*

DISCIPLINE.—A stern discipline pervades all nature, which is a little cruel that it may be very kind.—*Spenser.*

No pain, no palm; no thorns, no throne; no gall, no glory; no cross, no crown.—*Penn.*

A man in old age is like a sword in a shop window.—Men that look upon the perfect blade do not imagine the process by which it was completed.—Man is a sword; daily life is the workshop; and God is the artificer; and those cares which beat upon the anvil, and file the edge, and eat in, acid-like, the inscription on the hilt—those are the very things that fashion the man.—*H. W. Beecher.*

The discipline which corrects the baseness of worldly passions, fortifies the heart with virtuous principles, enlightens the mind with useful knowledge, and furnishes it with enjoyment from within itself, is of more consequence to real felicity, than all the provisions we can make of the goods of fortune.—*Blair.*

DISCONTENT. — Discontent is the want of self-reliance; it is infirmity of will.—*Emerson.*

Our condition never satisfies us; the present is always the worst.—Though Jupiter should grant his request to each, we should continue to importune him.—*Fontaine.*

Noble discontent is the path to heaven.—*T. W. Higginson.*

Discontent is like ink poured into water, which fills the whole fountain full of blackness. It casts a cloud over the mind, and renders it more occupied about the evil which disquiets than about the means of removing it.—*Feltham.*

The root of all discontent is self-love. —*J. F. Clarke.*

The more self is indulged the more it demands, and, therefore, of all men the selfish are the most discontented.

All human situations have their inconveniences.—We feel those of the present, but neither see nor feel those of the future; and hence we often make troublesome changes without amendment, and frequently for the worse.—*Franklin.*

The best remedy for our discontent is to count our mercies. By the time we have reckoned up a part of these, we shall be on our knees praising the Lord for His great mercy and love.—*The Quiver.*

We love in others what we lack ourselves, and would be everything but what we are.—*Stoddard.*

One thing only has been lent to youth and age in common—discontent.—*M. Arnold.*

A perverse and fretful disposition makes any state of life unhappy.—*Cicero.*

The splendid discontent of God with Chaos, made the world; and from the discontent of man the world's best progress springs.—*E. W. Wilcox.*

Poor in abundance, famished at a feast.—*Young.*

There are two kinds of discontent in this world: the discontent that works, and the discontent that wrings its hands. The first gets what it wants, and the second loses what it had. There is no cure for the first but success, and there is no cure at all for the second.—*Gordon Graham.*

Our discontent is from comparison: were better states unseen, each man would like his own.—*John Norris.*

That which makes people dissatisfied

with their condition, is the chimerical idea they form of the happiness of others.—*Thomson.*

Discontents are sometimes the better part of our life.—I know not which is the most useful.—Joy I may choose for pleasure; but adversities are the best for profit; and sometimes these do so far help me, that I should, without them, want much of the joy I have.—*Feltham.*

A good man and a wise man may, at times, be angry with the world, and at times grieved for it; but no man was ever discontented with the world if he did his duty in it.—*Southey.*

Save me from impious discontent at aught thy wisdom has denied or thy goodness has lent.—*Pope.*

DISCOVERY.—A new principle is an inexhaustible source of new views.—*Vauvenargues.*

It is a mortifying truth, and ought to teach the wisest of us humility, that many of the most valuable discoveries have been the result of chance rather than of contemplation, and of accident rather than of design.—*Colton.*

If I have ever made any valuable discoveries, it has been owing more to patient attention, than to any other talent.—*Sir Isaac Newton.*

It is a profound mistake to think that everything has been discovered; as well think the horizon the boundary of the world.—*Lemierre.*

He who sins against men, may fear discovery; but he who sins against God is sure of it.

Through every rift of discovery some seeming anomaly drops out of the darkness, and falls, as a golden link, into the great chain of order.—*E. H. Chapin.*

It is the modest, not the presumptuous inquirer, who makes a real and safe progress in the discovery of divine truths.—He follows God in his works and in his word.—*Bolingbroke.*

DISCRETION. — The greatest parts, without discretion, may be fatal to their owner.—Polyphemus, deprived of his eye, was only the more exposed on account of his enormous strength and stature.—*Hume.*

Be discreet in all things, and so render it unnecessary to be mysterious about any.—*Wellington.*

There are many shining qualities in the mind of man; but none so useful as discretion. It is this which gives a value to all the rest, and sets them at work in their proper places, and turns them to the advantage of their possessor. Without it, learning is pedantry; wit, impertinence; virtue itself looks like weakness; and the best parts only qualify a man to be more sprightly in errors, and active to his own prejudice. Though a man has all other perfections and wants discretion, he will be of no great consequence in the world; but if he has this single talent in perfection, and but a common share of others, he may do what he pleases in his station of life.—*Addison.*

Discretion in speech, is more than eloquence.—*Bacon.*

Open your mouth and purse cautiously, and your stock of wealth and reputation shall, at least in repute, be great.—*Zimmerman.*

A sound discretion is not so much indicated by never making a mistake, as by never repeating it.—*Bovee.*

The better part of valor is discretion, in the which better part I have saved my life.—*Shakespeare.*

Discretion is the perfection of reason, and a guide to us in all the duties of life.—It is only found in men of sound sense and good understanding.—*Bruyère.*

Discretion is the salt, and fancy the sugar of life; the one preserves, the other sweetens it.—*Bovee.*

If thou art a master, be sometimes blind, if a servant, sometimes deaf.—*Fuller.*

DISCUSSION.—Free and fair discussion will ever be found the firmest friend to truth.—*G. Campbell.*

It is an excellent rule to be observed in all discussions, that men should give soft words and hard arguments; that they should not so much strive to silence or vex, as to convince their opponents.—*Wilkins.*

He who knows only his own side of the case, knows little of that.—*J. Stuart Mill.*

He that is not open to conviction, is not qualified for discussion.—*Whately.*

Whosoever is afraid of submitting any question, civil or religious, to the test of free discussion, is more in love with his own opinion than with truth.—*T. Watson.*

Understand your antagonist before you answer him.

The more discussion the better, if passion and personality be eschewed.— Discussion, even if stormy, often winnows truth from error—a good never to be expected in an uninquiring age.— *Channing.*

There is no dispute managed without passion, and yet there is scarce a dispute worth a passion.—*Sherlock.*

There is nothing displays the quickness of genius more than a dispute—as two diamonds, encountering, contribute to each other's lustre.—But perhaps the odds is against the man of taste in this particular.—*Shenstone.*

The pain of dispute exceeds, by much, its utility.—All disputation makes the mind deaf, and when people are deaf I am dumb.—*Joubert.*

Gratuitous violence in argument betrays a conscious weakness of the cause, and is usually a signal of despair.— *Junius.*

Men are never so likely to settle a question rightly, as when they discuss it freely.—*Macaulay.*

In debate, rather pull to pieces the argument of thine antagonist, than offer him any of thine own; for thus thou will fight him in his own country.— *Fielding.*

If thou take delight in idle argumentation, thou mayest be qualified to combat with the sophists, but will never know how to live with men.—*Socrates.*

Reply with wit to gravity, and with gravity to wit.—Make a full concession to your adversary; give him every credit for the arguments you know you can answer, and slur over those you feel you cannot.—But above all, if he have the privilege of making his reply, take especial care that the strongest thing you have to urge be the last.—*Colton.*

Do not use thyself to dispute against thine own judgment to show thy wit, lest it prepare thee to be indifferent about what is right; nor against another man to vex him, or for mere trial of skill, since to inform or be informed ought to be the end of all conferences. —*Penn.*

It is in disputes, as in armies, where the weaker side sets up false lights, and makes a great noise to make the enemy believe them more numerous and strong than they really are.—*Swift.*

DISEASE.—The disease and its medicine are like two factions in a besieged town; they tear one another to pieces, but both unite against their common enemy—Nature.—*Jeffrey.*

Diseases are the penalties we pay for over indulgence, or for our neglect of the means of health.

In these days half our diseases come from the neglect of the body, and the over work of the brain.—In this railway age the wear and tear of labor and intellect go on without pause or self-pity. —We live longer than our forefathers; but we suffer more, from a thousand artificial anxieties and cares.—They fatigued only the muscles; we exhaust the finer strength of the nerves.—*Bulwer.*

Taking medicine is often only making a new disease to cure or hide the old one.

It is with disease of the mind, as with those of the body; we are half dead before we understand our disorder, and half cured when we do.—*Colton.*

Sickness and disease are in weak minds the sources of melancholy; but that which is painful to the body, may be profitable to the soul. Sickness puts us in mind of our mortality, and, while we drive on heedlessly in the full career of worldly pomp and jollity, kindly pulls us by the ear, and brings us to a proper sense of our duty.—*Burton.*

DISGRACE.—Disgrace is not in the punishment, but in the crime.—*Alfieri.*

Among the numberless contradictions in our nature hardly any is more glaring than this, between our sensitiveness to the slightest disgrace which we fancy cast upon us from without and our callousness to the grossest which we bring down on ourselves. In truth, they who are most sensitive to the one are often the most callous to the other.— *Guesses at Truth.*

Do not talk about disgrace from a thing being known, when the disgrace is, that the thing should exist.—*Falconer.*

Whatever disgrace we may have deserved or incurred, it is almost always in our power to re-establish our character. —*Rochefoucauld.*

DISGUISE. — Men would not live long in society, were they not the mutual dupes of each other.—*Rochefoucauld.*

Disguise yourself as you may to your fellow-men, if you are honest with yourself conscience will make known your real character, and the heart-searching one always knows it.—*Payson.*

Were we to take as much pains to be what we ought to be, as we do to disguise what we really are, we might appear like ourselves without being at the trouble of any disguise whatever.— *Rochefoucauld.*

DISHONESTY. — Dishonesty is a forsaking of permanent for temporary advantages.—*Bovee.*

I have known a vast quantity of nonsense talked about bad men not looking you in the face.—Don't trust that idea. —Dishonesty will stare honesty out of countenance any day in the week, if there is anything to be got by it.— *Dickens.*

He who purposely cheats his friend, would cheat his God.—*Lavater.*

Every man takes care that his neighbor shall not cheat him. But a day comes when he begins to care that he do not cheat his neighbor. Then all goes well. He has changed his market-cart into a chariot of the sun.—*Emerson.*

That which is won ill, will never wear well, for there is a curse attends it which will waste it.—The same corrupt dispositions which incline men to sinful ways of getting, will incline them to the like sinful ways of spending.—*M. Henry.*

If you attempt to beat a man down and so get his goods for less than a fair price, you are attempting to commit burglary as much as though you broke into his shop to take the things without paying for them.—There is cheating on both sides of the counter, and generally less behind it than before.—*H. W. Beecher.*

So grasping is dishonesty, that it is no respecter of persons; it will cheat friends as well as foes; and were it possible, would cheat even God himself.—*Bancroft.*

I could never draw the line between

meanness and dishonesty.—What is mean, so far as I can see, slides by indistinguishable gradations into what is dishonest.—*G. Macdonald.*

DISINTERESTEDNESS. — Men of the world hold that it is impossible to do a benevolent action, except from an interested motive; for the sake of admiration, if for no grosser and more tangible gain. Doubtless they are also convinced, that, when the sun is showering light from the sky, he is only standing there to be stared at.—*Anon.*

The slightest emotion of disinterested kindness that passes through the mind improves and refreshes it, producing generous thought and noble feeling.— We should cherish kind wishes, for a time may come when we may be able to put them in practice.—*Miss Mitford.*

Love thyself last.—Cherish the hearts that hate thee.—Be just and fear not.— Let all the ends thou aimest at be thy country's, thy God's, and truth's; then if thou fallest, thou fallest a blessed martyr.—*Shakespeare.*

DISOBEDIENCE. — Wherever there is authority, there is a natural inclination to disobedience.—*Haliburton.*

Rogues differ little. Each begun first as a disobedient son.—*Chinese Proverb.*

That men so universally disobey God bespeaks alienation and enmity of mind, for as obedience proceeds from love so disobedience proceeds from enmity.— *John Howe.*

Disobedient children, if preserved from the gallows, are reserved for the rack, to be tortured by their own posterity.— One complaining,. that never father had so undutiful a child as he had, yes, said his son, with less grace than truth, my grandfather had.—*Fuller.*

DISPATCH.—Dispatch is the soul of business.—*Chesterfield.*

True dispatch is a rich thing, for time is the measure of business, as money is of wares; and business is bought at a dear hand where there is small dispatch. —*Bacon.*

Use dispatch.—Remember that the world only took six days for its creation. —Ask me for whatever you please except time; that is the only thing which is beyond my power.—*Napoleon.*

To choose time is to save time.—

There be three parts of business—the preparation, the debate or examination, and the perfection; whereof if you look for dispatch let the middle only be the work of many and the first and last the work of few.—*Bacon.*

If it were done when it is done then it were well it were done quickly.—*Shakespeare.*

Our only safe rule is, " Whatsoever our hand findeth to do, to do it with all our might."—Let it be a subject of daily prayer, as well as an object of daily endeavor, to do our right work at the right time.—*N. Macleod.*

Measure not dispatch by the times of sitting, but by the advancement of business.—*Bacon.*

DISPOSITION.—A good disposition is more valuable than gold; for the latter is the gift of fortune, but the former is the dower of nature.—*Addison.*

The most phlegmatic dispositions often contain the most inflammable spirits, as fire is struck from the hardest flints.—*Hazlitt.*

The man who has so little knowledge of human nature as to seek happiness by changing anything but his own dispositions, will waste his life in fruitless efforts, and multiply the griefs which he proposes to remove.—*Colton.*

Envy's memory is nothing but a row of hooks to hang up grudges on. Some people's sensibility is a mere bundle of aversions; and you hear them display and parade it, not in recounting the things they are attached to, but in telling you how many things and persons " they cannot bear."—*John Foster.*

A tender-hearted, compassionate disposition, which inclines men to pity and to feel the misfortunes of others, and which is incapable of involving any man in ruin and misery, is, of all tempers of mind, the most amiable; and though it seldom receives much honor, is worthy of the highest.—*Fielding.*

There is no security in a good disposition if the support of good principles, that is to say, of religion—of Christian faith, be wanting.—It may be soured by misfortune, corrupted by wealth, blighted by neediness, and lose all its original brightness, if destitute of that support.—*Southey.*

DISSIMULATION.—Dissimulation is but a faint kind of policy or wisdom, for it asketh a strong wit and a strong heart to know when to tell the truth, and to do it: therefore it is the weaker of politicians that are the greatest dissemblers.—*Bacon.*

Dissimulation in youth is the forerunner of perfidy in old age.—It degrades parts and learning, obscures the luster of every accomplishment, and sinks us into contempt.—The path of falsehood is a perplexing maze.—One artifice leads on to another, till, as the intricacy of the labyrinth increases, we are left entangled in our own snare.—*Blair.*

Dissimulation is often humble, often polished, grave, smooth, decorous; but it is rarely gay and jovial, a hearty laugher, or a merry, cordial, boon companion.—*Bulwer.*

Dissimulation is ever productive of embarrassment; whether the design is evil or not, artifice is always dangerous and almost inevitably disgraceful. The best and safest policy is never to have recourse to deception, to avail yourself of quirks, or to practice low cunning, but to prove yourself in every circumstance of life upright and sincere. This system is that which noble minds will adopt, and the dictates of an enlightened and superior understanding would be sufficient to insure its adoption.—*Bruyère.*

DISSIPATION.—Dissipation is absolutely a labor when the round of Vanity fair has been once made; but fashion makes us think lightly of the toil, and we describe the circle as mechanically as a horse in a mill.—*Zimmerman.*

There is a dissipation of thought and feeling, as well of bodily energies; and the latter is as wasteful and ruinous to the mind and heart, as the former is to the health and strength of the body.—Dreamy reveries, desultory reading, unregulated and scattering thought, plans formed without reason, or never carried out to wise results, are as truly dissipation of the soul as the wildest revelries and indulgences are of the body.

DISTANCE.—Distance lends enchantment to the view.—*Campbell.*

Distance sometimes endears friendship, and absence sweeteneth it—for separation from those we love shows us, by the

loss, their real value and dearness to us.
—*Howell.*

Wishes, like painted landscapes, best delight while distance recommends them. —Afar off they appear beautiful; but near, they show their coarse and ordinary colors.—*Yalden.*

Sweetest melodies are those that are by distance made more sweet.—*Wordsworth.*

Glories, like glow-worms afar off, shine bright, but looked at near have neither heat nor light.—*J. Webster.*

Distance in truth produces in idea the same effect as in real perspective.—Objects are softened, rounded, and rendered doubly graceful.—The harsher and more ordinary points of character are melted down, and those by which it is remembered are the more striking outlines that mark sublimity, grace, or beauty.—There are mists, too, as in the natural horizon, to conceal what is less pleasing in distant objects; and there are happy lights, to stream in full glory upon those points which can profit by brilliant illumination.—*Walter Scott.*

DISTINCTION. — You may fail to shine in the opinion of others, both in your conversation and actions, from being superior, as well as inferior to them. —*Greville.*

Talent and worth are the only eternal grounds of distinction.—To these the Almighty has affixed his everlasting patent of nobility, and these it is which make the bright immortal names to which our children, as well as others, may aspire. —*Miss Sedgwick.*

All our distinctions are accidental.— Beauty and deformity, though personal qualities, are neither entitled to praise or censure; yet it so happens that they color our opinion of those qualities to which mankind have attached importance.—*Zimmerman.*

How men long for celebrity!—Some would willingly sacrifice their lives for fame, and not a few would rather be known by their crimes than not known at all.—*Sinclair.*

DISTRUST.—A certain amount of distrust is wholesome, but not so much of others as of ourselves.—Neither vanity nor conceit can exist in the same atmosphere with it.—*Mad. Neckar.*

Excessive distrust of others is not less

hurtful than its opposite.—Most men become useless to him who is unwilling to risk being deceived.—*Vauvenargues.*

The feeling of distrust is always the last which a great mind acquires.— *Racine.*

Nothing is more certain of destroying any good feelings that may be cherished toward us than to show distrust.—On the contrary confidence leads us naturally to act kindly; we are affected by the good opinion others entertain of us, and are not easily induced to lose it.— *Mad. Sevingé.*

As health lies in labor, and there is no royal road to it but through toil, so there is no republican road to safety but in constant distrust.—*Wendell Phillips.*

What loneliness is more lonely than distrust?—*George Eliot.*

Self-distrust is the cause of most of our failures. In the assurance of strength, there is strength, and they are the weakest, however strong, who have no faith in themselves or their own powers.—*Bovee.*

To think and feel we are able, is often to be so.—*J. Hawes.*

DIVERSION.—(See "AMUSEMENT.")

Diversions are most properly applied to ease and relieve those who are oppressed by being too much employed. Those that are idle have no need of them, and yet they, above all others, give themselves up to them.—To unbend our thoughts when they are too much stretched by our cares is not more natural than it is necessary; but to turn our whole life into a holiday is not only ridiculous, but destroys pleasure instead of increasing it.—*Saville.*

Let the world have whatever sports and recreations please them best, provided they be followed with discretion. —*Burton.*

DOCILITY.—A docile disposition will, with application, surmount every difficulty.—*Manilius.*

Willingness to be taught what we do not know, is the sure pledge of growth both in knowledge and wisdom.—*Blair.*

DOCTRINE.—Doctrine is the necessary foundation of duty; if the theory is not correct, the practice cannot be right. —Tell me what a man believes, and I will tell you what he will do.—*Tryon Edwards.*

Say what men may, it is doctrine that moves the world. He who takes no position will not sway the human intellect.—*W. G. T. Shedd.*

The question is not whether a doctrine is beautiful but whether it is true.—When we wish to go to a place, we do not ask whether the road leads through a pretty country, but whether it is the right road.—*Hare.*

Doctrine is the framework of life—the skeleton of truth, to be clothed and rounded out by the living grace of a holy life.—*A. J. Gordon.*

The doctrine that rectifies the conscience, purifies the heart, and produces love to God and man, is necessarily true, whether men can comprehend all its depths and relations or not.—If it destroys sin, and makes happiness grow out of right living and right loving, it is the truth of God.—*J. B. Walker.*

Pure doctrine always bears fruit in pure benefits.—*Emerson.*

He that shall broach any doctrine that cometh not from God, whatsoever he say for it, or what gloss soever he set upon it, is a traitor to God though he were an angel from heaven.—*Boston.*

DOGMATISM.—Nothing can be more unphilosophical than to be positive or dogmatical on any subject.—When men are the most sure and arrogant, they are commonly the most mistaken and have there given reins to passion without that proper deliberation and suspense which alone can secure them from the grossest absurdities.—*Hume.*

A dogmatical spirit inclines a man to be censorious of his neighbors.—Every one of his opinions appears to him written as with sunbeams, and he grows angry that his neighbors do not see it in the same light.—He is tempted to disdain his correspondents as men of low and dark understanding because they do not believe what he does.—*Watts.*

It has been said of dogmatism, that it is only puppyism come to its full growth, and certainly the worst form this quality can assume is that of opinionativeness and arrogance.—*S. Smiles.*

Those who differ most from the opinions of their fellow-men are the most confident of the truth of their own.—*Mackintosh.*

Those who refuse the long drudgery of thought, and think with the heart rather than the head, are ever most fiercely dogmatic.—*Bayne.*

DOING WELL.— Whatever is worth doing at all, is worth doing well.—*Chesterfield.*

We do not choose our own parts in life, and have nothing to do with those parts.—Our duty is confined to playing them well.—*Epictetus.*

Rest satisfied with doing well, and leave others to talk of you as they please.—*Pythagoras.*

Thinking well is wise; planning well, wiser; doing well wisest and best of all.—*Persian Proverb.*

DOMESTIC. — Domestic happiness—thou only bliss of paradise that has survived the fall.—*Cowper.*

Domestic happiness is the end of almost all our pursuits, and the common reward of all our pains.—When men find themselves forever barred from this delightful fruition they are lost to all industry, and grow careless of their worldly affairs.—Thus they become bad subjects, bad relations, bad friends, and bad men.—*Fielding.*

A prince wants only the pleasures of private life to complete his happiness.—*Bruyère.*

Domestic worth—that shuns too strong a light.—*Lyttleton.*

Our notion of the perfect society embraces the family as its center and ornament.—Nor is there a paradise planted till the children appear in the foreground to animate and complete the picture.—*A. B. Alcott.*

No money is better spent than what is laid out for domestic satisfaction.—A man is pleased that his wife is dressed as well as other people, and the wife is pleased that she is so dressed.—*Johnson.*

DOUBT. — A bitter and perplexed, "What shall I do?" is worse to man than worse necessity.—*Coleridge.*

Modest doubt is called the beacon of the wise—the tent that searches to the bottom of the worst.—*Shakespeare.*

In contemplation, if a man begins with certainties he shall end in doubts;

but if he be content to begin with doubts, he shall end in certainties.—*Bacon.*

Doubt, indulged and cherished, is in danger of becoming denial; but if honest, and bent on thorough investigation, it may soon lead to full establishment in the truth.—*Tryon Edwards.*

When you doubt, abstain.—*Zoroaster.*

Human knowledge is the parent of doubt.—*Greville.*

Man was not made to question, but adore.—*Young.*

We know accurately only when we know little; with knowledge doubt increases.—*Goethe.*

When a doubt is propounded, learn to distinguish, and show wherein a thing holds, and wherein it doth not hold. The not distinguishing where things should be distinguished, and the not confounding, where things should be confounded, is the cause of all the mistakes in the world.—*Selden.*

The doubter's dissatisfaction with his doubt is as great and widespread as the doubt itself.—*J. Dewitt.*

Doubt is the disease of this inquisitive, restless age.—It is the price we pay for our advanced intelligence and civilization—the dim night of our resplendent day.—But as the most beautiful light is born of darkness, so the faith that springs from conflict is often the strongest and best.—*R. Turnbull.*

There is no moral power in doubt, or in the denial of truth, and any human soul that tries to live on it will die, both morally and spiritually.—It is negative, and there is no life in it.

The vain man is generally a doubter.—It is Newton who sees himself as a child on the seashore, and his discoveries in the colored shells.—*Willmott.*

Our doubts are traitors, and make us lose the good we oft might win by fearing to attempt.—*Shakespeare.*

Doubt is an incentive to search for truth, and patient inquiry leads the way to it.

Who never doubted, never half believed.—Where doubt is, there truth is —it is her shadow.—*Bailey.*

In the hands of unbelief half-truths are made to do the work of whole falsehoods.—The sowing of doubts is the sowing of dragon's teeth, which ere long will sprout up into armed and hostile men.—*E. B. Burr.*

There is no weariness like that which rises from doubting—from the perpetual jogging of unfixed reason.—The torment of suspense is very great; but as soon as the wavering, perplexed mind begins to determine, be the determination which way soever it may be, it will find itself at ease.—*South.*

Beware of doubt—faith is the subtle chain that binds us to the infinite.—*E. O. Smith.*

Misgive, that you may not mistake.—*Whately.*

Doubt is almost a natural phase of life; but as certainly as it is natural, it is also temporary, unless it is unwisely wrought into conduct.—*T. T. Munger.*

Doubt comes in at the window when inquiry is denied at the door.—*Jowett.*

Uncertain ways unsafest are, and doubt a greater mischief than despair.—*Denham.*

It is never worth while to suggest doubts in order to show how cleverly we can answer them.—*Whately.*

The man who speaks his positive convictions is worth a regiment of men who are always proclaiming their doubts and suspicions.

Never do anything concerning the rectitude of which you have a doubt.—*Pliny.*

Doubt is the vestibule which all must pass before they can enter the temple of wisdom.—When we are in doubt and puzzle out the truth by our own exertions, we have gained something that will stay by us and will serve us again.—But if to avoid the trouble of the search we avail ourselves of the superior information of a friend, such knowledge will not remain with us; we have not bought, but borrowed it.—*Colton.*

Doubt is brother devil to despair.—*O'Reilly.*

"If you are in doubt," says Talleyrand, "whether to write a letter or not —don't!"—And the advice applies to many doubts in life besides that of letter writing.—*Bulwer.*

Knowledge and personality make doubt possible, but knowledge is also the cure of doubt; and when we get a full and adequate sense of personality we are lifted into a region where doubt is almost impossible, for no man can know himself as he is, and all the fulness of his nature, without also knowing God. —*T. T. Munger.*

Give me the benefit of your convictions, if you have any, but keep your doubts to yourself, for I have enough of my own.—*Goethe.*

The doubts of an honest man contain more moral truth than the profession of faith of people under a worldly yoke.—*Doudan.*

The end of doubt is the beginning of repose.—*Petrarch.*

Doubt is hell in the human soul.—*Gasparin.*

DREAMS.—Children of the night, of indigestion bred.—*Churchill.*

A world of the dead in the hues of life.—*Mrs. Hemans.*

Dreams full oft are found of real events the forms and shadows.—*Joanna Baillie.*

We have in dreams no true perception of time—a strange property of mind!—for if such be also its property when entered into the eternal disembodied state, time will appear to us eternity!—The relations of space as well as of time are also annihilated, so that while almost an eternity is compressed into a moment, infinite space is traversed more swiftly than by real thought.—*Winslow.*

We are somewhat more than ourselves in our sleeps, and the slumber of the body seems to be but the waking of the soul.—It is the litigation of sense, but the liberty of reason; and our waking conceptions do not match the fancies of our sleeps.—*Sir. J. Browne.*

As dreams are the fancies of those that sleep, so fancies are but the dreams of those awake.—*Blount.*

Dreaming is an act of pure imagination, attesting in all men a creative power, which, if it were available in waking, would make every man a Dante or a Shakespeare.—*Hedge.*

Let not our babbling dreams affright our souls.—*Shakespeare.*

Nothing so much convinces me of the boundlessness of the human mind as its operations in dreaming.—*Clulow.*

DRESS.—Dress has a moral effect upon the conduct of mankind.—Let any gentleman find himself with dirty boots, old surtout, soiled neckcloth, and a general negligence of dress, and he will, in all probability, find a corresponding disposition in negligence of address.—*Sir J. Barrington.*

As you treat your body, so your house, your domestics, your enemies, your friends.—Dress is the table of your contents.—*Lavater.*

Out of clothes, out of countenance; out of countenance, out of wit.—*Ben Jonson.*

A becoming decency of exterior may not be necessary for ourselves, but is agreeable to others; and while it may render a fool more contemptible, it serves to embellish inherent worth.—It is like the polish of the diamond, taking something perhaps from its weight, but adding much to its brilliancy.—*David Paul Brown.*

The body is the shell of the soul, and dress the husk of that shell; but the husk often tells what the kernel is.—*Anon.*

Eat to please thyself, but dress to please others.—*Franklin.*

An emperor in his night-cap would not meet with half the respect of an emperor with a crown.—*Goldsmith.*

If honor be your clothing, the suit will last a lifetime; but if clothing be your honor, it will soon be worn threadbare. —*Arnot.*

Had Cicero himself pronounced one of his orations with a blanket about his shoulders, more people would have laughed at his dress than admired his eloquence.—*Addison.*

As the index tells the contents of the book, and directs to the particular chapter, even so do the outward habit and garments, in man or woman, give us a taste of the spirit, and point to the internal quality of the soul; and there cannot be a more evident and gross manifestation of poor, degenerate, dunghilly blood and breeding, than a rude, unpolished, disordered, and slovenly outside.—*Massinger.*

As to matters of dress, I would recommend one never to be first in the fashion nor the last out of it.—*J. Wesley.*

The medium between a fop and a sloven is what a man of sense would endeavor to keep; yet one well advises his son to appear, in his habit, rather above than below his fortune; and tells him he will find a handsome suit of clothes always procures some additional respect. My banker ever bows lowest to me when I wear my full-bottomed wig; and writes me "Mr." or "Esq." according as he sees me dressed.—*Budgell.*

The perfection of dress is in the union of three requisites—in its being comfortable, cheap, and tasteful.—*Bovee.*

Next to clothes being fine, they should be well made, and worn easily: for a man is only the less genteel for a fine coat, if, in wearing it, he shows a regard for it, and is not as easy in it as if it were a plain one.—*Chesterfield.*

Costly thy habit as thy purse can buy, but not expressed in fancy; rich, but not gaudy, for the apparel oft proclaims the man.—*Shakespeare.*

The plainer the dress with greater luster does beauty appear.—Virtue is the greatest ornament, and good sense the best equipage.—*G. Saville.*

Beauty gains little, and homeliness and deformity lose much by gaudy attire.—*Zimmerman.*

A fine coat is but a livery when the person who wears it discovers no higher sense than that of a footman.—*Addison.*

No man is esteemed for gay garments, but by fools and women.—*Sir W. Raleigh.*

The vanity of loving fine clothes and new fashions, and valuing ourselves by them, is one of the most childish pieces of folly.—*Sir M. Hale.*

Be neither too early in the fashion, nor too long out of it, nor too precisely in it.—What custom hath civilized is become decent; till then, ridiculous.—Where the eye is the jury, thine apparel is the evidence.—*Quarles.*

Dress yourself fine, where others are fine, and plain, where others are plain; but take care always that your clothes are well made and fit you, for otherwise they will give you a very awkward air.—*Chesterfield.*

A gentleman's taste in dress is, upon principle, the avoidance of all things ex-

travagant.—It consists in the quiet simplicity of exquisite neatness; but as the neatness must be a neatness in fashion, employ the best tailor; pay him ready money; and on the whole you will find him the cheapest.—*Bulwer.*

A rich dress adds but little to the beauty of a person; it may possibly create a deference, but that is rather an enemy to love.—*Shenstone.*

It is not every man that can afford to wear a shabby coat; and worldly wisdom dictates the propriety of dressing somewhat beyond one's means, but of living within them, for every one sees how we dress, but none see how we live unless we choose to let them.—*Colton.*

We sacrifice to dress till household joys and comforts cease. Dress drains our cellar dry, and keeps our larder clean; puts out our fires, and introduces hunger, frost, and woe, where peace and hospitality might reign.—*Cowper.*

In clothes clean and fresh there is a kind of youth with which age should surround itself.—*Joubert.*

Too great carelessness, equally with excess in dress, multiplies the wrinkles of old age, and makes its decay more conspicuous.—*Bruyère.*

In the indications of female poverty there can be no disguise.—No woman dresses below herself from caprice.—*Lamb.*

In civilized society external advantages make us more respected.—A man with a good coat on his back meets with a better reception than he who has a bad one.—You may analyze this and say, what is there in it?—But that will avail you nothing, for it is a part of a general system.—*Johnson.*

Persons are often misled in regard to their choice of dress by attending to the beauty of colors, rather than selecting such colors as may increase their own beauty.—*Shenstone.*

The only medicine which does women more good than harm, is dress.—*Richter.*

Those who think that in order to dress well it is necessary to dress extravagantly or grandly, make a great mistake.—Nothing so well becomes true feminine beauty as simplicity.—*G. D. Prentice.*

Two things in my apparel I will chiefly aim at—commodiousness and decency;

more than these is not commendable; yet I hate an effeminate spruceness, as much as a fantastic disorder.—A neglected comeliness is the best ornament. —*Anon.*

A loose and easy dress contributes much to give to both sexes those fine proportions of body that are observable in the Grecian statues, and which serve as models to our present artists.—*Rousseau.*

The consciousness of clean linen is, in and of itself, a source of moral strength, second only to that of a clean conscience.

DRINKING.—(See "INTEMPERANCE" and "WINE.")

The first draught serveth for health, the second for pleasure, the third for shame, and the fourth for madness.— *Anacharsis.*

The Japanese say: "A man takes a drink, then the drink takes a drink, and the next drink takes the man."

Some one commending Philip of Macedon for drinking freely, "That," said Demosthenes, "is a good quality in a sponge, but not in a king."

The maxim, "in vino veritas—that a man who is well warmed with wine will speak truth," may be an argument for drinking, if you suppose men in general to be liars; but, sir, I would not keep company with a fellow, who lies as long as he is sober, and whom you must make drunk before you can get a word of truth out of him.—*Johnson.*

The barroom as a bank: You deposit your money—and lose it; your time— and lose it; your character—and lose it; your manly independence—and lose it; your home comfort—and lose it; your self-control—and lose it; your children's happiness—and lose it; your own soul—and lose it.

Every moderate drinker could abandon the intoxicating cup, if he would; every inebriate would if he could.—*J. B. Gough.*

Whisky is a good thing in its place. There is nothing like it for preserving a man when he is dead. If you want to keep a dead man, put him in whisky; if you want to kill a live man put whisky in him.—*Guthrie.*

In the bottle, discontent seeks for comfort; cowardice, for courage; bashfulness, for confidence; sadness, for joy; and all find ruin!

Strong drink is not only the devil's way into a man, but man's way to the devil.—*Adam Clarke.*

DRUNKENNESS.—(See "INTEMPERANCE.")

Drunkenness is nothing else but a voluntary madness.—*Seneca.*

All excess is ill; but drunkenness is of the worst sort. It spoils health, dismounts the mind, and unmans men. It reveals secrets, is quarrelsome, lascivious, impudent, dangerous, and mad. He that is drunk is not a man, because he is void of reason that distinguishes a man from a beast.—*Penn.*

Drunkenness is a flattering devil, a sweet poison, a pleasant sin, which whosoever hath, hath not himself, which whosoever doth commit, doth not commit sin, but he himself is wholly sin.— *Augustine.*

Intoxicating drinks have produced evils more deadly, because more continuous, than all those caused to mankind by the great historic scourges of war, famine, and pestilence combined.—*Gladstone.*

Drunkenness is the vice of a good constitution, or a bad memory; of a constitution so treacherously good, that it never bends till it breaks, or of a memory that recollects the pleasures of getting intoxicated, but forgets the pains of getting sober.—*Colton.*

Some of the domestic evils of drunkenness are houses without windows, gardens without fences, fields without tillage, barns without roofs, children without clothing, principles, morals, or manners.—*Franklin.*

All the armies on earth do not destroy so many of the human race, nor alienate so much property, as drunkenness.—*Bacon.*

Habitual intoxication is the epitome of every crime.—*Jerrold.*

Let there be an entire abstinence from intoxicating drinks throughout this country during the period of a single generation, and a mob would be as impossible as combustion without oxygen.—*Horace Mann.*

A drunkard is the annoyance of modesty; the trouble of civility; the spoil of wealth; the distraction of reason. He is the brewer's agent; the tavern and ale-house benefactor; the beggar's companion; the constable's trouble; his wife's woe; his children's sorrow; his neighbor's scoff; his own shame. In short he is a tub of swill, a spirit of unrest, a thing below a beast, and a monster of a man.—*T. Adams.*

Drunkenness places man as much below the level of the brutes, as reason elevates him above them.—*Sinclair.*

Beware of drunkenness, lest all good men beware of thee.—Where drunkenness reigns, there reason is an exile, virtue a stranger, and God an enemy; blasphemy is wit, oaths are rhetoric, and secrets are proclamations.—*Quarles.*

Troops of furies march in the drunkard's triumph.—*Zimmerman.*

There is scarcely a crime before me that is not, directly or indirectly, caused by strong drink.—*Judge Coleridge.*

Call things by their right names.— "Glass of brandy and water!" That is the current but not the appropriate name; ask for, "A glass of liquid fire and distilled damnation."—*Robert Hall.*

It were better for a man to be subject to any vice, than to drunkenness; for all other vanities and sins are recovered, but a drunkard will never shake off the delight of beastliness; for the longer it possesseth a man, the more he will delight in it, and the older he groweth the more he shall be subject to it; for it dulleth the spirits, and destroyeth the body as ivy doth the old tree; or as the worm that engendereth in the kernel of the nut.—*Sir W. Raleigh.*

What is a drunken man like? Like a drown'd man, a fool, and a madman; one draught above heat makes him a fool; the second mads him; and a third drowns him.—*Shakespeare.*

The sight of a drunkard is a better sermon against that vice than the best that was ever preached on that subject. —*Saville.*

Of all vices take heed of drunkenness. —Other vices are but the fruits of disordered affections; this disorders, nay banishes, reason.—Other vices but impair the soul; this demolishes her two chief faculties, the understanding and the will. —Other vices make their own way; this makes way for all vices.—He that is a drunkard is qualified for all vice.— *Quarles.*

DUELS.—A duellist is only a Cain in high life.—*Jerrold.*

Duelling makes a virtue of pride and revenge; and, in defiance of the laws, both of God and man, assumes itself the right of avenging its own wrongs, and even exults in the blood of its murdered victim.—*J. Hawes.*

If all seconds were as averse to duels as their principals, very little blood would be shed in that way.—*Colton.*

Duelling, though barbarous in civilized, is a highly civilizing institution among barbarous people; and when compared to assassination is a prodigious victory gained over human passions.— *Sydney Smith.*

Duelling, as a punishment, is absurd, because it is an equal chance whether the punishment falls upon the offender, or the person offended.—Nor is it much better as a reparation, it being difficult to explain in what the satisfaction consists, or how it tends to undo an injury, or to afford a compensation for the damage already sustained.—*Paley.*

DULNESS.—A dull man is so near a dead man that he is hardly to be ranked in the list of the living; and as he is not to be buried whilst half alive, so he is as little to be employed whilst he is half dead.—*Saville.*

There are some heads that have no windows, and the day can never strike from above; nothing enters from heavenward.—*Joubert.*

What a comfort a dull but kindly man is, to be sure, at times! A ground glass shade over a gas-light does not bring more solace to our dazzled eyes than such an one to our minds.—*O. W. Holmes.*

DUTY.—There is not a moment without some duty.—*Cicero.*

Duty is carrying on promptly and faithfully the affairs now before you.— It is to fulfill the claims of to-day.— *Goethe.*

Do the duty which lieth nearest to thee! Thy second duty will already have become clearer.—*Thomas Carlyle.*

Duty is a power that rises with us in the morning, and goes to rest with us at night. It is co-extensive with the action of our intelligence. It is the shadow that cleaves to us, go where we will.—*Gladstone.*

Every duty which we omit, obscures some truth which we should have known.—*Ruskin.*

Duties are ours, events are God's. This removes an infinite burden from the shoulders of a miserable, tempted, dying creature. On this consideration only can he securely lay down his head and close his eyes.—*Cecil.*

Duty performed gives clearness and firmness to faith, and faith thus strengthened through duty becomes the more assured and satisfying to the soul.—*Tryon Edwards.*

Duty is the grandest of ideas, because it implies the idea of God, of the soul, of liberty, of responsibility, of immortality.—*Lacordaire.*

"We do not choose our own parts in life, and have nothing to do with selecting those parts. Our simple duty is confined to playing them well."—*Epictetus.*

The brave man wants no charms to encourage him to duty, and the good man scorns all warnings that would deter him from doing it.—*Bulwer.*

Do to-day's duty, fight to-day's temptation, and do not weaken and distract yourself by looking forward to things which you cannot see, and could not understand if you saw them.—*Charles Kingsley.*

The reward of one duty done is the power to fulfill another.—*George Eliot.*

Know thyself and do thine own work, says Plato; and each includes the other and covers the whole duty of man.—*Montaigne.*

The best things are nearest: light in your eyes, flowers at your feet, duties at your hand, the path of God just before you. Then do not grasp at the stars, but do life's common work as it comes, certain that daily duties and daily bread are the sweetest things of life.

God always has an angel of help for those who are willing to do their duty.—*T. L. Cuyler.*

The truth is, one's vocation is never some far-off possibility.—It is always the simple round of duties which the passing hour brings.—*J. W. Dulles.*

Let us never forget that every station in life is necessary; that each deserves our respect; that not the station itself, but the worthy fulfillment of its duties does honor to man.

There is nothing in the universe that I fear, but that I shall not know all my duty, or shall fail to do it.—*Mary Lyon.*

We are apt to mistake our vocation by looking out of the way for occasions to exercise great and rare virtues, and by stepping over the ordinary ones that lie directly in the road before us.—*H. More.*

Duties in general, like that class of them called debts, give more trouble the longer they remain undischarged.

Let men laugh, if they will, when you sacrifice desire to duty.—You have time and eternity to rejoice in.—*Theodore Parker.*

Do the duty that lies nearest to thee.—*Goethe.*

I find the doing of the will of God leaves me no time for disputing about His plans.—*G. Macdonald.*

To what gulfs a single deviation from the path of human duties leads!—*Byron.*

Who escapes a duty, avoids a gain.—*Theodore Parker.*

I believe that we are conforming to the divine order and the will of Providence when we are doing even indifferent things that belong to our condition.—*Fenelon.*

Whether your time calls you to live or die do both like a prince.—*Sir P. Sidney.*

Exactness in little duties is a wonderful source of cheerfulness.—*Faber.*

There is no evil we cannot face or fly from, but the consciousness of duty disregarded.—*Daniel Webster.*

Men do less than they ought, unless they do all that they can.—*Carlyle.*

Be not diverted from your duty by any idle reflections the silly world may make upon you, for their censures are not in your power and should not be at all your concern.—*Epictetus.*

It is one of the worst of errors to suppose that there is any path of safety except that of duty.—*Wm. Nevins.*

Every duty that is bidden to wait

comes back with seven fresh duties at its back.—*Charles Kingsley.*

There is no mean work, save that which is sordidly selfish; no irreligious work, save that which is morally wrong; in every sphere of life the post of honor is the post of duty.—*E. H. Chapin.*

Perish discretion when it interferes with duty.—*H. More.*

No man's spirits were ever hurt by doing his duty.—On the contrary, one good action, one temptation resisted and overcome, one sacrifice of desire or interest purely for conscience's sake, will prove a cordial for weak and low spirits far beyond what either indulgence, or diversion, or company can do for them.—*Paley.*

Duty performed is a moral tonic; if neglected, the tone and strength of both mind and heart are weakened, and the spiritual health undermined.—*Tryon Edwards.*

Do right, and God's recompense to you will be the power of doing more right.—*F. W. Robertson.*

Practice in life whatever thou prayest for, and God will give it thee more abundantly.—*F. D. Huntington.*

Try to put well in practice what you already know; and in so doing, you will, in good time, discover the hidden things which you now inquire about. Practice what you know, and it will help to make clear what now you do not know.—*Rembrandt.*

So nigh is grandeur to our dust, so near is God to man, when duty whispers low, "Thou must," the youth replies, "I can."—*Emerson.*

Do thy duty; that is best; leave unto the Lord the rest.—*Longfellow.*

All that any one of us has to do in this world is his simple duty. And an archangel could not do more than that to advantage.—*H. C. Trumbull.*

When the soul resolves to perform every duty, immediately it is conscious of the presence of God.—*Bacon.*

Every day remember that to-day you have a God to glorify; a Saviour to imitate; a soul to save; your body to mortify; virtue to acquire; heaven to seek; eternity to meditate upon; temptations to resist; the world to guard against; and perhaps death to meet.

By doing our duty, we learn to do it.—*E. B. Pusey.*

If I am faithful to the duties of the present, God will provide for the future.—*Bedell.*

Every hour comes with some little fagot of God's will fastened upon its back.—*Faber.*

Can any man or woman choose duties? No more than they can choose their birthplace, or their father and mother.—*George Eliot.*

It is wonderful what strength and boldness of purpose and energy will come from the feeling that we are in the way of duty.—*John Foster.*

Let us do our duty in our shop or our kitchen; in the market, the street, the office, the school, the home, just as faithfully as if we stood in the front rank of some great battle, and knew that victory for mankind depended on our bravery, strength, and skill.—When we do that, the humblest of us will be serving in that great army which achieves the welfare of the world.—*Theodore Parker.*

Do the truth ye know, and you shall learn the truth you need to know.—*G. Macdonald.*

Reverence the highest; have patience with the lowest; let this day's performance of the meanest duty be thy religion.—*Margaret Fuller.*

The consideration that human happiness and moral duty are inseparably connected, will always continue to prompt me to promote the former by inculcating the practice of the latter.—*Washington.*

There are not good things enough in life, to indemnify us for the neglect of a single duty.—*Mad. Swetchine.*

The best preparation for the future is the present well seen to, the last duty well done.—*G. Macdonald.*

The duty of man is plain and simple, and consists but of two points; his duty to God, which every man must feel; and his duty to his neighbor, to do as he would be done by.—*Thomas Paine.*

The path of duty lies in what is near, and men seek for it in what is remote.—The work of duty lies in what is easy, and men seek for it in what is difficult.—*Mencius.*

Duty by habit is to pleasure turned.
—*Brydges.*

This is the feeling that gives a man true courage—the feeling that he has a work to do at all costs; the sense of duty.—*C. Kingsley.*

Man is not born to solve the problem of the universe, but to find out what he has to do; and to restrain himself within the limits of his comprehension.—*Goethe.*

Duty is above all consequences, and often, at a crisis of difficulty, commands us to throw them overboard. It commands us to look neither to the right, nor to the left, but straight onward. Hence every act of duty is an act of faith. It is performed in the assurance that God will take care of the consequences, and will so order the course of the world, that, whatever the immediate results may be, his word shall not return to him void.

This span of life was lent for lofty duties, not for selfishness; not to be whiled away in aimless dreams, but to improve ourselves and serve mankind.—*Aubrey De Vere.*

No human being, man or woman, can act up to a sublime standard without giving offence.—*Channing.*

It is surprising how practical duty enriches the fancy and the heart, and action clears and deepens the affections.—*Martineau.*

Our grand business is not to see what lies dimly in the distance, but to do what lies clearly at hand.—*Carlyle.*

E

EARLY RISING. — Whoever has tasted the breath of morning, knows that the most invigorating and delightful hours of the day are commonly spent in bed, though it is the evident intention of nature that we should profit by them.—*Southey.*

When one begins to turn in bed, it is time to turn out.—*Wellington.*

The difference between rising at five and seven o'clock in the morning, for forty years, supposing a man to go to bed at the same hour at night, is nearly equivalent to the addition of ten years to a man's life.—*Doddridge.*

It is well to be up before daybreak, for such habits contribute to health, wealth, and wisdom.—*Aristotle.*

Early rising not only gives us more life in the same number of years, but adds, likewise, to their number; and not only enables us to enjoy more of existence in the same time, but increases also the measure.—*Colton.*

The early morning hath gold in its mouth.—*Franklin.*

Next to temperance, a quiet conscience, a cheerful mind, and active habits, I place early rising as a means of health and happiness.—*Flint.*

Few ever lived to old age, and fewer still ever became distinguished, who were not in the habit of early rising.—*J. Todd.*

Is there aught in sleep can charm the wise to lie in dead oblivion, losing half the fleeting moments of too short a life?—*Thomson.*

I would have it inscribed on the curtains of your bed and the walls of your chamber: "If you do not rise early you can make progress in nothing."—*Lord Chatham.*

He who rises late may trot all day, and not overtake his business at night.—*Franklin.*

I never knew a man come to greatness or eminence who lay abed late in the morning.—*Swift.*

Every night I make up my mind to rise early the next morning, but every morning make up my body to lie still.

Better to get up late and be wide awake then, than to get up early and be asleep all day.

Those who would bring great things to pass must rise early.—Love not sleep, lest thou come to poverty.—*M. Henry.*

EARNESTNESS.—Earnestness is enthusiasm tempered by reason.—*Pascal.*

There is no substitute for thoroughgoing, ardent, and sincere earnestness.—*Dickens.*

A man in earnest finds means, or if he cannot find, creates them.—*Channing.*

Do you wish to become rich?—You may become so if you desire it in no half-way, but thoroughly.—Do you wish to master any science or accomplishment?—Give yourself to it and it lies beneath your feet.—This world is given as the prize for the men in earnest; and that which is true of this world, is truer still of the world to come.—*F. W. Robertson.*

Earnestness is the devotion of all the faculties.—It is the cause of patience; gives endurance; overcomes pain; strengthens weakness; braves dangers; sustains hope; makes light of difficulties, and lessens the sense of weariness in overcoming them.—*Bovee.*

Earnestness commands the respect of mankind. A wavering, vacillating, dead-and-alive Christian does not get the respect of the Church or of the world.—*John Hall.*

There are important cases in which the difference between half a heart and a whole heart makes just the difference between signal defeat and a splendid victory.—*A. H. K. Boyd.*

Without earnestness no man is ever great or does really great things. He may be the cleverest of men; he may be brilliant, entertaining, popular; but he will want weight.—*Bayne.*

To impress others we must be earnest; to amuse them, it is only necessary to be kindly and fanciful.—*Tuckerman.*

The superior man is slow in his words and earnest in his conduct.—*Confucius.*

"Earnestness gives intellect," says a maxim of the Jesuits; and so says Solomon, in various expressions in the book of Proverbs.—And says Bulwer, "Earnestness is the best source of mental power; and deficiency of heart is the cause of many men never becoming great."

Man should trust in God as if God did all, and yet labor as earnestly as if he himself did all.—*Chalmers.*

EARTH. — The waters deluge man with rain, oppress him with hail, and drown him with inundations; the air rushes in storms, prepares the tempest, or lights up the volcano; but the earth, gentle and indulgent, ever subservient to the wants of man, spreads his walks with flowers, and his table with plenty; returns, with interest, every good committed to her care; and though she produces the poison, she still supplies the antidote; though constantly teased more to furnish the luxuries of man than his necessities, yet even to the last she continues her kind indulgence, and, when life is over, she piously covers his remains in her bosom.—*Pliny.*

The earth, that is nature's mother, is her tomb.—*Shakespeare.*

I believe the earth on which we stand is but the vestibule to glorious mansions, to which a moving crowd is forever pressing.—*Joanna Baillie.*

Where is the dust that has not been alive?—The spade and the plough disturb our ancestors.—From human mold we reap our daily bread.—*Young.*

The earth's a stage which God and nature do with actors fill.—*Heywood.*

Earth, with her thousand voices, praises God.—*Coleridge.*

Earth, thou great footstool of our God, who reigns on high; thou fruitful source of all our raiment, life, and food; our house, our parent, and our nurse.—*Watts.*

EATING.—The chief pleasure in eating does not consist in costly seasoning or exquisite flavor, but in yourself.—Do you seek sauce by labor?—*Horace.*

The turnpike road to most people's hearts, I find, lies through their mouths, or I mistake mankind.—*Wolcott.*

Simple diet is best, for many dishes bring many diseases, and rich sauces are worse than even heaping several meats upon each other.—*Pliny.*

Go to your banquet, then, but use delight, so as to rise still with an appetite. —*Herrick.*

For the sake of health medicines are taken by weight and measure; so ought food to be, or by some similar rule.— *Skelton.*

The difference between a rich man and a poor man, is this—the former eats when he pleases, and the latter when he can get it.—*Sir W. Raleigh.*

One should eat to live, not live to eat. —*Franklin.*

By eating what is sufficient man is enabled to work; he is hindered from working and becomes heavy, idle, and stupid if he takes too much.—As to bodily distempers occasioned by excess, there is no end of them.—*Jones.*

They are as sick that surfeit with too much, as they that starve with nothing.—*Shakespeare.*

ECCENTRICITY.—Oddities and singularities of behavior may attend genius, but when they do, they are its misfortunes and blemishes.—The man of true genius will be ashamed of them, or, at least, will never affect to be distinguished by them.—*Sir W. Temple.*

Even beauty cannot palliate eccentricity.—*Balzac.*

Eccentricity has always abounded when and where strength of character has abounded.—And the amount of eccentricity in a society has been proportional to the amount of genius, mental vigor, and moral courage it contained.—*J. S. Mill.*

He that will keep a monkey, should pay for the glasses he breaks.—*Selden.*

ECHO. — That tuneful nymph, the babbling echo, who has not learned to conceal what is told her, nor yet is able to speak till another speaks.—*Ovid.*

The shadow of a sound; a voice without a mouth, and words without a tongue.—*Horace Smith.*

The babbling gossip of the air.—*Shakespeare.*

Where we find echoes we generally find emptiness and hollowness; it is the contrary with the echoes of the heart.—*Boyes.*

ECONOMY.—If you know how to spend less than you get, you have the philosopher's stone.—*Franklin.*

Economy is the parent of integrity, of liberty, and of ease; and the beauteous sister of temperance, of cheerfulness, and health; and profuseness is a cruel and crafty demon, that gradually involves her followers in dependence and debts, and so fetters them with irons that enter into their inmost souls.—*Hawkesworth.*

Economy is in itself a source of great revenue.—*Seneca.*

Large enterprises make the few rich, but the majority prosper only through the carefulness and detail of thrift. He is already poverty-stricken whose habits are not thrifty.—*T. T. Munger.*

A sound economy is a sound understanding brought into action. It is calculation realized; it is the doctrine of proportion reduced to practice; it is foreseeing contingencies and providing against them; it is expecting contingencies and being prepared for them.—*Hannah More.*

To make three guineas do the work of five.—*Burns.*

Men talk in raptures of youth and beauty, wit and sprightliness; but after seven years of union, not one of them is to be compared to good family management, which is seen at every meal, and felt every hour in the husband's purse.—*Witherspoon.*

The regard one shows economy, is like that we show an old aunt, who is to leave us something at last.—*Shenstone.*

Waste cannot be accurately told, though we are sensible how destructive it is. Economy on the one hand, by which a certain income is made to maintain a man genteelly; and waste on the other, by which, on the same income, another man lives shabbily, cannot be defined. It is a very nice thing; as one man wears his coat out much sooner than another, we cannot tell how.—*Johnson.*

Without economy none can be rich, and with it few will be poor.—*Johnson.*

It is no small commendation to manage a little well.—To live well in abundance is the praise of the estate, not of the person.—I will study more how to give a good account of my little, than how to make it more.—*Bp. Hall.*

There is no gain so certain as that which arises from sparing what you have.—*Publius Syrus.*

No man is rich whose expenditures exceed his means; and no one is poor whose incomings exceed his outgoings.—*Haliburton.*

Economy, whether public or private, means the wise management of labor, mainly in three senses; applying labor rationally, preserving its produce carefully, and distributing its produce seasonably.—*Ruskin.*

A man's ordinary expenses ought to be but to the half of his receipts, and if he think to wax rich, but to the third part.—*Bacon.*

Economy before competence is meanness after it; therefore economy is for the poor; the rich may dispense with it.—*Bovee.*

He who is taught to live upon little

owes more to his father's wisdom than he that has a great deal left him does to his father's care.—*Penn.*

Nothing is cheap which is superfluous, for what one does not need, is dear at a penny.—*Plutarch.*

The art of living easily as to money is to pitch your scale of living one degree below your means.—*H. Taylor.*

Take care to be an economist in prosperity; there is no fear of your not being one in adversity.—*Zimmerman.*

The habit of saving is itself an education; it fosters every virtue, teaches self-denial, cultivates the sense of order, trains to forethought, and so broadens the mind.—*T. T. Munger.*

Not to be covetous, is money; not to be a purchaser, is a revenue.—*Cicero.*

Let honesty and industry be thy constant companions, and spend one penny less than thy clear gains; then shall thy pocket begin to thrive; creditors will not insult, nor want oppress, nor hunger bite, nor nakedness freeze thee.—*Franklin.*

Proportion and propriety are among the best secrets of domestic wisdom; and there is no surer test of integrity than a well-proportioned expenditure.—*Hannah More.*

The man who will live above his present circumstances, is in great danger of soon living much beneath them; or as the Italian proverb says, "The man that lives by hope, will die by despair."—*Addison.*

A man may, if he knows not how to save as he gets, keep his nose all his life to the grindstone and die not worth a groat after all.—*Franklin.*

Economy is half the battle of life; it is not so hard to earn money, as to spend it well.—*Spurgeon.*

Ere you consult fancy, consult your purse.—*Franklin.*

The world abhors closeness, and all but admires extravagance; yet a slack hand shows weakness, and a tight hand strength.—*Buxton.*

The back door robs the house.—*Herbert.*

Take care of the pence, and the pounds will take care of themselves.—*Franklin.*

There are but two ways of paying a debt; increase of industry in raising income, or increase of thrift in laying out. —*Carlyle.*

EDUCATION.—(See "TEACHING.")

Education is the apprenticeship of life.—*Willmott.*

A human being is not, in any proper sense, a human being till he is educated.—*H. Mann.*

What sculpture is to a block of marble, education is to the human soul. The philosopher, the saint, the hero, the wise, and the good, or the great, very often lie hid and concealed in a plebeian, which a proper education might have disinterred and brought to light.—*Addison.*

The great end of education is, to discipline rather than to furnish the mind; to train it to the use of its own powers, rather than fill it with the accumulations of others.—*Tryon Edwards.*

The aim of education should be to teach us rather how to think, than what to think—rather to improve our minds, so as to enable us to think for ourselves, than to load the memory with the thoughts of other men.—*Beattie.*

Education does not mean teaching people to know what they do not know; it means teaching them to behave as they do not behave.—*Ruskin.*

Education begins with life. Before we are aware the foundations of character are laid, and subsequent teaching avails but little to remove or alter them.

If a man empties his purse into his head, no man can take it away from him. An investment in knowledge always pays the best interest.—*Franklin.*

Educate your children to self-control, to the habit of holding passion and prejudice and evil tendencies subject to an upright and reasoning will, and you have done much to abolish misery from their future lives and crimes from society.

Knowledge does not comprise all which is contained in the large term of education. The feelings are to be disciplined; the passions are to be restrained; true and worthy motives are to be inspired; a profound religious feeling is to be instilled, and pure morality inculcated under all circumstances. All this is comprised in education.—*Daniel Webster.*

The standards of a genuinely liberal education, as they have been understood, more or less from the time of Aristotle, are being progressively undermined by the utilitarians and the sentimentalists.—*Irving Babbitt.*

Education is the only cure for certain diseases the modern world has engendered, but if you don't find the disease, the remedy is superfluous—*John Buchan.*

The more purely intellectual aim of education should be the endeavor to make us see and imagine the world in an objective manner as far as possible as it really is in itself, and not merely through the distorting medium of personal desires.—*Bertrand Russell.*

Educational institutions will become, more and more purely, institutions for educating people; and, as they become this, they will cease to be seats of scientific inquiry save on the very lowest level.—*Walter B. Pitkin.*

First we shall want the pupil to understand, speak, read, and write his mother tongue well.—*H. G. Wells.*

Education should be a conscious, methodical application of the best means in the wisdom of the ages to the end that youth may know how to live completely.—*Austin O'Malley.*

Character development is the great, if not the sole, aim of education.—*O'Shea.*

States should spend money and effort on this great all-underlying matter of spiritual education as they have hitherto spent them on beating and destroying each other.—*John Galsworthy.*

Dull boys are more likely than others to get into difficulties, largely because they want, and need, more work with their hands and less intellectual work, but do not get it.—*E. H. Johnson.*

There can be but a single goal of education, and that—education to courage.—*Dr. Alfred Adler.*

Observation more than books, experience rather than persons, are the prime educators.—*A. B. Alcott.*

I may safely predict that the education of the future will be inventive-minded. It will believe so profoundly in the high value of the inventive or creative spirit that it will set itself to develop that spirit by all means within its power.—*Harry Overstreet.*

Education is a companion which no misfortune can depress—no crime destroy—no enemy alienate—no despotism enslave. At home, a friend; abroad, an introduction; in solitude, a solace; and in society, an ornament. Without it, what is man?—a splendid slave, a reasoning savage.—*Varle.*

He is to be educated not because he is to make shoes, nails, and pins, but because he is a man.—*Channing.*

To know the laws of God in nature and revelation, and then to fashion the affections and will into harmony with those laws—this is education.—*S. F. Scovel.*

Modern education too often covers the fingers with rings, and at the same time cuts the sinews at the wrists.—*Sterling.*

Universal suffrage, without universal education, would be a curse.—*H. L. Wayland.*

There are five tests of the evidence of education—correctness and precision in the use of the mother tongue; refined and gentle manners, the result of fixed habits of thought and action; sound standards of appreciation of beauty and of worth, and a character based on those standards; power and habit of reflection; efficiency or the power to do.—*Nicholas Murray Butler.*

The problem of education is twofold: first to know, and then to utter. Everyone who lives any semblance of an inner life thinks more nobly and profoundly than he speaks.—*R. L. Stevenson.*

Today toys are recognized by educators and welfare workers as a vital part of child development comparable with the need for nourishing food and instruction in the three Rs.—*Dr. Paul T. Cherington.*

We have in America the largest public school system on earth, the most expensive college buildings, the most extensive curriculum, but nowhere else is education so blind to its objectives, so indifferent to any specific outcome as in America. One trouble has been its negative character. It has aimed at the repression of faults rather than the creation of virtues.—*William P. Faunce.*

I care not what subject is taught if only it be taught well.—*Thomas H. Huxley.*

The whole object of education is, or should be, to develop mind. The mind should be a thing that works. It should be able to pass judgment on events as they arise, make decisions.—*Sherwood Anderson.*

Boys and girls should be taught to think first of others in material things; they should be infected with the wisdom to know that in making smooth the way of all lies the road to their own health and happiness.—*John Galsworthy.*

The youth of Italy shall be trained so that in this country there shall be a place for every person and every person shall be in that place. I am here today and gone tomorrow; but let no one think fascism goes with me.—*Mussolini.*

Very few can be trusted with an education.—*Louise Imogen Guiney.*

In the degree in which I have been privileged to know the intimate secrets of hearts, I ever more realize how great a part is played in the lives of men and women by some little concealed germ of abnormality. For the most part they are occupied in the task of stifling and crushing those germs, treating them like weeds in their gardens. There is another and better way, even though more difficult and more perilous. Instead of trying to suppress the weeds that can never be killed, they may be cultivated into useful or beautiful flowers. For it is impossible to conceive any impulse in a human heart which cannot be transformed into Truth or into Beauty or into Love.—*Havelock Ellis.*

I wish every immigrant could know that Lincoln spent only one year in school under the tutelage of five different teachers, and that that man still could be the author of the Gettysburg address.—*Dr. John H. Finley.*

The secret of education lies in respecting the pupil.—*Emerson.*

He that has found a way to keep a child's spirit easy, active, and free, and yet at the same time to restrain him from many things he has a mind to, and to draw him to things that are uneasy to him, has, in my opinion, got the true secret of education.—*Locke.*

Of ten infants, destined for different vocations, I should prefer that the one who is to study through life should be

the least learned at the age of twelve.—*Tissot.*

Education is the cheap defense of nations.—*Burke.*

Too much attention has been paid to making education attractive by smoothing the path as compared with inducing strenuous voluntary effort.—*A. L. Lowell.*

The man who strives to educate himself—and no one else can educate him—must win a certain victory over his own nature. He must learn to smile at his dear idols, analyze his every prejudice, scrap if necessary his fondest and most consoling belief, question his presuppositions, and take his chances with the truth.—*Everett Dean Martin.*

Look out for the boy who has to plunge into work direct from the common school and who begins by sweeping out the office. He is probably the dark horse you had better watch.—*Andrew Carnegie.*

We can advance and develop democracy but little faster than we can advance and develop the average level of intelligence and knowledge within the democracy. That is the problem that confronts modern educators.—*Samuel Gompers.*

Liberal education develops a sense of right, duty and honor; and more and more in the modern world, large business rests on rectitude and honor as well as on good judgment.—*Charles W. Eliot.*

Give vocational training to the manually minded, and the children's courts of the future will have less to do.—*Lawes.*

"Reeling and writhing, of course to begin with," Mock Turtle replied, "and the different branches of arithmetic—ambition, distraction, uglification and derision."—*Lewis Carroll.*

The development of desirable traits and characteristics — that intangible something which we style personality— is the chief work of the school.—*Dr. Frank Cody.*

Experience demonstrates that of any number of children of equal intellectual powers, those who receive no particular care in infancy, and who do not begin to study till the constitution begins to be consolidated, but who enjoy the benefit of a good physical education, very soon surpass in their studies those who commenced earlier, and who read numerous books when very young.—*Spurzheim.*

Instruction ends in the schoolroom, but education ends only with life. A child is given to the universe to be educated.—*F. W. Robertson.*

Neither piety, virtue, nor liberty can long flourish in a community where the education of youth is neglected.—*Cooper.*

Education is the knowledge of how to use the whole of oneself. Many men use but one or two faculties out of the score with which they are endowed. A man is educated who knows how to make a tool of every faculty—how to open it, how to keep it sharp, and how to apply it to all practical purposes.—*H. W. Beecher.*

The worst education that teaches self-denial is better than the best that teaches everything else and not that.—*J. Sterling.*

The best education in the world is that got by struggling to get a living.—*Wendell Phillips.*

He has seen but little of life who does not discern everywhere the effect of early education on men's opinions and habits of thinking. Children bring out of the nursery that which displays itself throughout their lives.—*Cecil.*

The poorest education that teaches self-control, is better than the best that neglects it.—*Anon.*

It makes little difference what the trade, business, or branch of learning, in mechanical labor, or intellectual effort, the educated man is always superior to the common laborer. One who is in the habit of applying his powers in the right way will carry system into any occupation, and it will help him as much to handle a rope as to write a poem.—*F. M. Crawford.*

The sure foundations of the State are laid in knowledge, not in ignorance; and every sneer at education, at culture, and at book-learning which is the recorded wisdom of the experience of mankind, is the demagogue's sneer at intelligent liberty, inviting national degeneracy and ruin.—*G. W. Curtis.*

You demand universal suffrage,—I demand universal education to go with it. —*W. E. Forster.*

Education in its widest sense includes everything that exerts a formative influence, and causes a young person to be, at a given point, what he is.—*Mark Hopkins.*

Education is a debt due from the present to future generations.—*George Peabody.*

The education of the human mind commences in the cradle.—*T. Cogan.*

Education is not learning; it is the exercise and development of the powers of the mind; and the two great methods by which this end may be accomplished are in the halls of learning, or in the conflicts of life.—*Princeton Review.*

Don't fall into the vulgar idea that mind is a warehouse, and education but a process of stuffing it full of goods.

The aim of education should be to convert the mind into a living fountain, and not a reservoir. That which is filled by merely pumping in, will be emptied by pumping out.—*John M. Mason.*

Every day's experience shows how much more actively education goes on out of the schoolroom, than in it.

Men are every day saying and doing, from the power of education, habit, and imitation, what has no root whatever in their serious convictions.—*Channing.*

The best school of discipline is home —family life is God's own method of training the young; and homes are very much what women make them.—*S. Smiles.*

There is a moral as well as an intellectual objection to the custom, frequent in these times, of making education consist in a mere smattering of twenty different things, instead of in the mastery of five or six.—*Chadwick.*

It depends on education to open the gates which lead to virtue or to vice, to happiness or to misery.—*Jane Porter.*

That call not education, which decries God and his truth, content the seed to strew of moral maxims, and the mind imbue with elements which form the worldly wise; so call the training, which can duly prize such lighter lore, but chiefly holds to view what God requires us to believe and do, and notes man's end, and shapes him for the skies.—*Bp. Mant.*

The true order of learning should be,

first, what is necessary; second, what is useful; and third, what is ornamental.—To reverse this arrangement, is like beginning to build at the top of the edifice.—*Mrs. Sigourney.*

Education commences at the mother's knee, and every word spoken in the hearing of little children tends toward the formation of character.—Let parents always bear this in mind.—*H. Ballou.*

That which we are we are all the while teaching, not voluntarily, but involuntarily.—*Emerson.*

The wisest man may always learn something from the humblest peasant.—*J. P. Senn.*

Public instruction should be the first object of government.—*Napoleon.*

No woman is educated who is not equal to the successful management of a family.—*Burnap.*

The schoolmaster deserves to be beaten himself who beats nature in a boy for a fault. And I question whether all the whippings in the world can make their parts which are naturally sluggish rise one minute before the hour nature hath appointed.—*Fuller.*

All who have meditated on the art of governing mankind have been convinced that the fate of empires depends on the education of youth.—*Aristotle.*

It is by education I learn to do by choice, what other men do by the constraint of fear.—*Aristotle.*

Jails and prisons are the complement of schools; so many less as you have of the latter, so many more must you have of the former.—*H. Mann.*

The schoolmaster is abroad, and I trust him, armed with his primer, against the soldier in full military array.—*Brougham.*

Schoolhouses are the republican line of fortifications.—*Horace Mann.*

The education of the present race of females is not very favorable to domestic happiness.—For my own part, I call education, not that which smothers a woman with accomplishments, but that which tends to consolidate a firm and regular system of character.—That which tends to form a friend, a companion, and a wife.—*Hannah More.*

Do not ask if a man has been through college; ask if a college has been through him—if he is a walking university.—*E. H. Chapin.*

An intelligent class can scarce ever be, as a class, vicious, and never, as a class, indolent.—The excited mental activity operates as a counterpoise to the stimulus of sense and appetite.—*Everett.*

Early instruction in truth will best keep out error. Some one has well said, "Fill the bushel with wheat, and you may defy the devil to fill it with tares."—*Tryon Edwards.*

Education gives fecundity of thought, copiousness of illustration, quickness, vigor, fancy, words, images, and illustrations; it decorates every common thing, and gives the power of trifling without being undignified and absurd.—*Sydney Smith.*

If we work upon marble, it will perish; if on brass, time will efface it; if we rear temples, they will crumble into dust; but if we work upon immortal minds, and imbue them with principles, with the just fear of God and love of our fellow-men, we engrave on those tablets something that will brighten to all eternity.—*Daniel Webster.*

Never educate a child to be a gentleman or lady only, but to be a man, a woman.—*Herbert Spencer.*

It is on the sound education of the people that the security and destiny of every nation chiefly rest.—*Kossuth.*

Nothing so good as a university education, nor worse than a university without its education.—*Bulwer.*

Family education and order are some of the chief means of grace; if these are duly maintained, all the means of grace are likely to prosper and become effectual.—*Jonathan Edwards.*

A college education shows a man how little other people know.—*Haliburton.*

'Tis education forms the common mind; just as the twig is bent the tree is inclined.—*Pope.*

Education does not consist in mastering languages, but is found in that moral training which extends beyond the schoolroom to the playground and the street, and which teaches that a meaner thing can be done than to fail in recitation.—*Chadbourne.*

No part of education is more important to young woman than the society of the other sex of her own age.—It is only by this association that they acquire that insight into character which is almost their only defence.—*Burnap.*

Education does not commence with the alphabet; it begins with a mother's look, with a father's nod of approbation, or a sign of reproof; with a sister's gentle pressure of the hand, or a brother's noble act of forbearance; with handfuls of flowers in green dells, on hills, and daisy meadows; with birds' nests admired, but not touched; with creeping ants, and almost imperceptible emmets; with humming-bees and glass beehives; with pleasant walks in shady lanes, and with thoughts directed in sweet and kindly tones and words to nature, to beauty, to acts of benevolence, to deeds of virtue, and to the source of all good —to God Himself!—*Anon.*

Thelwall thought it very unfair to influence a child's mind by inculcating any opinions before it had come to years of discretion to choose for itself.—I showed him my garden, and I told him it was my botanical garden.—" How so? " said he; " it is covered with weeds."—" O," I replied, " that is only because it has not yet come to its age of discretion and choice.—The weeds, you see, have taken the liberty to grow, and I thought it unfair in me to prejudice the soil toward roses and strawberries."—*Coleridge.*

Education is our only political safety. —Outside of this ark all is deluge.—*H. Mann.*

EFFORT.—(See "LABOR.")

Things don't turn up in this world until somebody turns them up.—*Garfield.*

The fact is, nothing comes; at least, nothing good. All has to be fetched.— *Charles Buxton.*

If you would relish food, labor for it before you take it; if enjoy clothing, pay for it before you wear it; if you would sleep soundly, take a clear conscience to bed with you.—*Franklin.*

EGOTISM.—Egotism is the tongue of vanity.—*Chamfort.*

It is never permissible to say " I say." —*Mad. Neckar.*

The more you speak of yourself, the more you are likely to lie.—*Zimmerman.*

An egotist is a man who talks so much about himself that he gives me no time to talk about myself.—*H. L. Wayland.*

The more any one speaks of himself, the less he likes to hear another talked of.—*Lavater.*

Egotism is more like an offence than a crime, though 'tis allowable to speak of yourself provided nothing is advanced in your own favor; but I cannot help suspecting that those who abuse themselves are, in reality, angling for approbation.—*Zimmerman.*

Do you wish men to speak well of you? Then never speak well of yourself.—*Pascal.*

There is not one wise man in twenty that will praise himself.—*Shakespeare.*

When all is summed up, a man never speaks of himself without loss; his accusations of himself are always believed; his praises never.—*Montaigne.*

Christian piety annihilates the egotism of the heart; worldly politeness veils and represses it.—*Pascal.*

The personal pronoun " I," might well be the coat of arms of some individuals. —*Rivarol.*

I shall never apologize to you for egotism.—I think very few men in writing to their friends have enough of it.— *Sidney Smith.*

It is a false principle, that because we are entirely occupied with ourselves, we must equally occupy the thoughts of others.—The contrary inference is the fair one.—*Hazlitt.*

The reason why lovers are never weary of one another is this—they are ever talking of themselves.—*Rochefoucauld.*

What hypocrites we seem to be whenever we talk of ourselves!—Our words sound so humble while our hearts are so proud.—*Hare.*

An egotist will always speak of himself, either in praise or censure; but a modest man ever shuns making himself the subject of his conversation.—*Bruyère.*

We often boast that we are never bored; but we are so conceited that we do not perceive how often we bore others.—*Rochefoucauld.*

ELEGANCE. — When the mind loses

its feeling for elegance, it grows corrupt and grovelling, and seeks in the crowd what ought to be found at home.—*Landor.*

Elegance is something more than ease —more than a freedom from awkwardness and restraint.—It implies a precision, a polish, and a sparkling which is spirited, yet delicate.—*Hazlitt.*

Taste and elegance, though they are reckoned only among the smaller and secondary morals, are of no mean importance in the regulations of life.—A moral taste is not of force to turn vice into virtue; but it recommends virtue with something like the blandishments of pleasure, and it infinitely abates the evils of vice.—*Burke.*

ELOQUENCE.—True eloquence consists in saying all that is proper, and nothing more.—*Rochefoucauld.*

Brevity is a great charm of eloquence. —*Cicero.*

Action is eloquence; the eyes of the ignorant are more learned than their ears.—*Shakespeare.*

The clear conception, outrunning the deductions of logic, the high purpose, the firm resolve, the dauntless spirit, speaking on the tongue, beaming from the eye, informing every feature, and urging the whole man onward, right onward to his object,—this, this is eloquence; or rather it is something greater and higher than all eloquence; it is action, noble, sublime, godlike action.— *Daniel Webster.*

It is but a poor eloquence which only shows that the orator can talk.—*Sir Joshua Reynolds.*

Eloquence is relative.—One can no more pronounce on the eloquence of any composition, than on the wholesomeness of a medicine without knowing for whom it is intended.—*Whately.*

The truest eloquence is that which holds us too mute for applause.—*Bulwer.*

Those who would make us feel, must feel themselves.—*Churchill.*

No man ever did, or ever will become most truly eloquent without being a constant reader of the Bible, and an admirer of the purity and sublimity of its language.—*Fisher Ames.*

It is of eloquence as of a flame; it requires matter to feed it, and motion to excite it; and it brightens as it burns.— *Tacitus.*

Eloquence is in the assembly, not merely in the speaker.—*William Pitt.*

Eloquence is logic on fire.—*Lyman Beecher.*

Eloquence is vehement simplicity.— *Cecil.*

There is no eloquence without a man behind it.—*Emerson.*

Eloquence is the transference of thought and emotion from one heart to another, no matter how it is done.— *John B. Gough.*

There is not less eloquence in the voice, the eye, the gesture, than in words. —*Rochefoucauld.*

If any thing I have ever said or written deserves the feeblest encomiums of my fellow countrymen, I have no hesitation in declaring that for their partiality I am indebted, solely indebted, to the daily and attentive perusal of the Sacred Scriptures, the source of all true poetry and eloquence, as well as of all good and all comfort.—*Daniel Webster.*

Speech is the body; thought, the soul, and suitable action the life of eloquence. —*C. Simmons.*

Talking and eloquence are not the same.—To speak and to speak well are two things.—A fool may talk, but a wise man speaks.—*Ben. Jonson.*

True eloquence does not consist in speech.—It cannot be brought from far. —Labor and learning may toil for it in vain.—Words and phrases may be marshalled in every way, but they cannot compass it.—It must consist in the man, in the subject, and in the occasion.— *Daniel Webster.*

The manner of speaking is full as important as the matter, as more people have ears to be tickled than understandings to judge.—*Chesterfield.*

The pleasure of eloquence is, in greatest part, owing often to the stimulus of the occasion which produces it—to the magic of sympathy which exalts the feeling of each, by radiating on him the feeling of all.—*Emerson.*

Great is the power of eloquence; but never is it so great as when it pleads along with nature, and the culprit is a child strayed from his duty, and returned to it again with tears.—*Sterne*

Honesty is one part of eloquence. We persuade others by being in earnest ourselves.—*Hazlitt.*

EMINENCE.—Every man ought to aim at eminence, not by pulling others down, but by raising himself; and enjoy the pleasures of his own superiority, whether imaginary or real, without interrupting others in the same felicity.—*Johnson.*

The road to eminence and power from obscure condition ought not to be made too easy, nor a thing too much of course. If rare merit be the rarest of all rare things, it ought to pass through some sort of probation. The temple of honor ought to be seated on an eminence. If it be open through virtue, let it be remembered, too, that virtue is never tried but by some difficulty and some struggle.—*Burke.*

It is folly for an eminent man to think of escaping censure, and a weakness for him to be affected by it.—All the illustrious persons of antiquity, and indeed of every age in the world, have passed through this fiery persecution.—*Addison.*

EMOTION.—All loving emotions, like plants, shoot up most rapidly in the tempestuous atmosphere of life.—*Richter.*

The taste for emotion may become a dangerous taste; we should be very cautious how we attempt to squeeze out of human life more ecstasy and paroxysm than it can well afford.—*Sydney Smith.*

Emotion has no value in the Christian system save as it is connected with right conduct.—It is the bud, not the flower, and is of no value until it expands into the flower.—Every religious sentiment, every act of devotion which does not produce a corresponding elevation of life, is worse than useless; it is absolutely pernicious, because it ministers to self-deception, and tends to lower the tone of personal morals.—*Murray.*

Emotion turning back on itself, and not leading on to thought or action, is the element of madness.—*J. Sterling.*

Emotion, whether of ridicule, anger, or sorrow, whether raised at a puppet-show, a funeral, or a battle, is your grandest of levelers.—The man who would be always superior should be always apathetic.—*Bulwer.*

Emotion which does not lead to and flow out in right action is not only useless, but it weakens character, and becomes an excuse for neglect of effort.—*Tryon Edwards.*

EMPIRE.—As a general truth, nothing is more opposed to the well-being and freedom of men, than vast empires.—*De Tocqueville.*

Extended empire, like expanded gold, exchanges solid strength for feeble splendor.—*Johnson.*

It is not their long reigns, nor their frequent changes which occasion the fall of empires, but their abuse of power.—*Crabbe.*

EMPLOYMENT. — (See "Occupation," and "Time.")

Employment is nature's physician, and is essential to human happiness.—*Galen.*

Be always employed about some rational thing, that the devil find thee not idle.—*Jerome.*

Life is hardly respectable if it has no generous task, no duties or affections that constitute a necessity of existing.—Every man's task is his life-preserver.—*G. B. Emerson.*

"I have," says Richter, "fire-proof, perennial enjoyments, called employments"; and says Burton, "So essential to human happiness is employment, that indolence is justly considered the mother of misery."

He that does not bring up his son to some honest calling and employment, brings him up to be a thief.—*Jewish Maxim.*

Employment gives health, sobriety, and morals.—Constant employment and well-paid labor produce, in a country like ours, general prosperity, content, and cheerfulness.—*Daniel Webster.*

The devil never tempted a man whom he found judiciously employed.—*Spurgeon.*

The safe and general antidote against sorrow, is employment. It is commonly observed, that among soldiers and seamen, though there is much kindness, there is little grief; they see their friend fall without that lamentation which is indulged in security and idleness, because they have no leisure to spare from the care of themselves; and whoever shall keep his thoughts equally busy, will find himself equally unaffected by irretrievable losses.—*Johnson.*

Not to enjoy life, but to employ life, ought to be our aim and inspiration.—*Macduff.*

Employment and ennui are simply incompatible.—*Mad. Deluzy.*

We have employments assigned to us for every circumstance in life. When we are alone, we have our thoughts to watch; in the family, our tempers; and in company, our tongues.—*Hannah More.*

The wise prove, and the foolish confess, by their conduct, that a life of employment is the only life worth leading.—*Paley.*

Life's cares are comforts, such by heaven designed; he that has none must make them or be wretched.—Cares are employments, and without employ the soul is on a rack—the rack of rest to souls most adverse:—action all their joy.—*Young.*

Occupation is one great source of enjoyment. No man, properly occupied, was ever miserable.—*L. E. Landon.*

EMPTINESS.—Four things are grievously empty: a head without brains, a wit without judgment, a heart without honesty, and a purse without money.—*Earle.*

EMULATION.—Emulation is a noble passion.—It is enterprising, but just withal.—It keeps within the terms of honor, and makes the contest for glory just and generous; striving to excel, not by depressing others, but by raising itself.—*Beaumont.*

Emulation admires and strives to imitate great actions; envy is only moved to malice.—*Balzac.*

Emulation is the devil-shadow of aspiration.—To excite it is worthy only of the commonplace vulgar schoolmaster, whose ambition is to show what fine scholars he can turn out, that he may get the more pupils.—*G. Macdonald.*

Emulation, in the sense of a laudable ambition, is founded on humility, for it implies that we have a low opinion of our present, and think it necessary to advance and make improvement.—*Bp. Hall.*

Where there is emulation, there will be vanity; where there is vanity, there will be folly.—*Johnson.*

The emulation of a man of genius is seldom with his contemporaries. The competitors with whom his secret ambition seeks to vie are the dead.—*Bulwer.*

Emulation has been termed a spur to virtue, and assumes to be a spur of gold. —But it is a spur composed of baser materials, and if tried in the furnace will be found wanting.—*Colton.*

Emulation looks out for merits, that she may exalt herself by a victory; envy spies out blemishes, that she may have another by a defeat.—*Colton.*

There is a long and wearisome step between admiration and imitation.—*Richter.*

Without emulation we sink into meanness, or mediocrity, for nothing great or excellent can be done without it.—*Beaumont.*

ENCOURAGEMENT. — Faint not; the miles to heaven are but few and short.—*Rutherford.*

Correction does much, but encouragement does more.—Encouragement after censure is as the sun after a shower.—*Goethe.*

We ought not to raise expectations which it is not in our power to satisfy. —It is more pleasing to see smoke brightening into flame, than flame sinking into smoke.—*Johnson.*

All may do what has by man been done.—*Young.*

I believe that any man's life will be filled with constant and unexpected encouragement, if he makes up his mind to do his level best each day, and as nearly as possible reaching the highwater mark of pure and useful living.—*Booker T. Washington.*

END.—Let the end try the man.—*Shakespeare.*

If well thou hast begun, go on; it is the end that crowns us, not the fight.—*Herrick.*

The end crowns all, and that old common arbitrator, time, will one day end it.—*Shakespeare.*

All's well that ends well; still the finis is the crown.—*Shakespeare.*

ENDURANCE.—Not in the achievement, but in the endurance of the human soul, does it show its divine grandeur, and its alliance with the infinite God.—*E. H. Chapin.*

The greater the difficulty, the more glory in surmounting it.—*Skilful* pilots gain their reputation from storms and tempests.—*Epicurus.*

The palm-tree grows best beneath a ponderous weight, and even so the character of man.—The petty pangs of small daily cares have often bent the character of men, but great misfortunes seldom.—*Kossuth.*

There is nothing in the world so much admired as a man who knows how to bear unhappiness with courage.—*Seneca*

Our strength often increases in proportion to the obstacles imposed upon it.—It is thus we enter upon the most perilous plans after having had the shame of failing in more simple ones.—*Rapin.*

He conquers who endures.—*Persius.*

By bravely enduring, an evil which cannot be avoided is overcome.—*Old Proverb.*

ENEMIES.—Make no enemies. — He is insignificant indeed who can do thee no harm.—*Colton.*

Have you fifty friends?—it is not enough.—Have you one enemy?—it is too much.—*Italian Proverb.*

If we could read the secret history of our enemies, we should find in each man's life sorrow and suffering enough to disarm all hostility.—*Longfellow.*

There is no little enemy.—*Franklin.*

Those who get through the world without enemies are commonly of three classes: the supple, the adroit, the phlegmatic. The leaden rule surmounts obstacles by yielding to them; the oiled wheel escapes friction; the cotton sack escapes damage by its impenetrable elasticity.—*Whately.*

It is much safer to reconcile an enemy than to conquer him; victory may deprive him of his poison, but reconciliation of his will.—*Feltham.*

However rich or powerful a man may be it is the height of folly to make personal enemies; for one unguarded moment may yield you to the revenge of the most despicable of mankind.—*Lyttleton.*

We should never make enemies, if for no other reason, because it is so hard to behave toward them as we ought.—*Palmer.*

Some men are more beholden to their bitterest enemies than to friends who appear to be sweetness itself. The former frequently tell the truth, but the latter never.—*Cato.*

Observe your enemies, for they first find out your faults.—*Antisthenes.*

To love an enemy is the distinguished characteristic of a religion which is not of man but of God. It could be delivered as a precept, only by him who lived and died to establish it by his example.

It is the enemy whom we do not suspect who is the most dangerous.—*Rojas.*

Our worst enemies are those we carry about with us in our own hearts. Adam fell in Paradise and Lucifer in heaven, while Lot continued righteous in Sodom.

Let us carefully observe those good qualities wherein our enemies excel us, and endeavor to excel them by avoiding what is faulty, and imitating what is excellent in them.—*Plutarch.*

I am persuaded that he who is capable of being a bitter enemy can never possess the necessary virtues that constitute a true friend.—*Fitzosborne.*

Men of sense often learn from their enemies.—It is from their foes, not their friends, that cities learn the lesson of building high walls and ships of war; and this lesson saves their children, their homes, and their properties.—*Aristophanes.*

Be assured those will be thy worst enemies, not to whom thou hast done evil, but who have done evil to thee.— And those will be thy best friends, not to whom thou hast done good, but who have done good to thee.—*Lavater.*

Did a person but know the value of an enemy, he would purchase him with pure gold.—*Raunci.*

Plutarch has written an essay on the benefits which a man may receive from his enemies; and among the good fruits of enmity, mentions this in particular, that by the reproaches which it casts upon us we see the worst side of ourselves.—*Addison.*

Our enemies are our outward consciences.—*Shakespeare.*

In order to have an enemy, one must be somebody.—One must be a force before he can be resisted by another force.—A malicious enemy is better than a clumsy friend.—*Mad. Swetchine.*

A merely fallen enemy may rise again, but the reconciled one is truly vanquished.—*Schiller.*

Whatever the number of a man's friends, there will be times in his life when he has one too few; but if he has only one enemy, he is lucky indeed if he has not one too many.—*Bulwer.*

Heat not a furnace for your foe so hot that it do singe yourself.—*Shakespeare.*

If you want enemies, excel others; if friends, let others excel you.—*Colton.*

Though all things do to harm him what they can, no greater enemy to himself than man.—*Earl of Stirling.*

Our enemies come nearer the truth in the opinions they form of us than we do in our opinion of ourselves.—*Rochefoucauld.*

The fine and noble way to destroy a foe, is not to kill him; with kindness you may so change him that he shall cease to be so; then he's slain.—*Aleyn.*

There is no enemy can hurt us but by our own hands.—Satan could not hurt us, if our own corruption betrayed us not.—Afflictions cannot hurt us without our own impatience.—Temptations cannot hurt us, without our own yieldance. —Death could not hurt us, without the sting of our own sins.—Sins could not hurt us, without our own impenitence.— *Bp. Hall.*

O wise man, wash your hands of that friend who associates with your enemies. —*Saadi.*

"No one's enemy but his own," is generally the enemy of everybody with whom he is in relation.—His leading quality is a reckless imprudence, and a selfish pursuit of selfish enjoyments, independent of all consequences.—He runs rapidly through his means; calls, in a friendly way, on his friends, for bonds, bail, and securities; involves his nearest kin; leaves his wife a beggar, and quarters his orphans on the public; and after enjoying himself to his last guinea, entails a life of dependence upon his progeny, and dies in the ill-understood reputation of harmless folly which is more injurious to society than some positive crimes.—*Mrs. Jameson.*

ENERGY. — The longer I live, the more deeply am I convinced that that which makes the difference between one man and another—between the weak and powerful, the great and insignificant, is energy—invisible determination—a purpose once formed, and then death or victory.—This quality will do anything that is to be done in the world; and no talents, no circumstances, no opportunities will make one a man without it.— *Buxton.*

This world belongs to the energetic.— *Emerson.*

Energy will do anything that can be done in the world; and no talents, no circumstances, no opportunities will make a two-legged animal a man without it.—*Goethe.*

To think we are able, is almost to be so; to determine on attainment, is frequently attainment itself.—Earnest resolution has often seemed to have about it almost a savor of omnipotence. —*S. Smiles.*

Our remedies oft in ourselves do lie, which we ascribe to heaven; the fated sky gives us free scope; only, doth backward pull our slow designs, when we ourselves are dull.—*Shakespeare.*

The truest wisdom, in general, is a resolute determination.—*Napoleon.*

The wise and active conquer difficulties by daring to attempt them.—Sloth and folly shiver and shrink at sight of toil and hazard, and make the impossibility they fear.—*Rowe.*

He alone has energy who cannot be deprived of it.—*Lavater.*

Toil, feel, think, hope; you will be sure to dream enough before you die, without arranging for it. *J. Sterling.*

There is no genius in life like the genius of energy and activity.—*D. G. Mitchell.*

Resolution is omnipotent.—Determine to be something in the world, and you will be something.—Aim at excellence, and excellence will be attained.—This is the great secret of effort and eminence. —"I cannot do it," never accomplished anything; "I will try," has wrought wonders.—*J. Hawes.*

The reward of a thing well done, is to have done it.—*Emerson.*

ENJOYMENT. — Those who would enjoyment gain must find it in the purpose they pursue.—*Mrs. Hale.*

No enjoyment, however inconsiderable, is confined to the present moment. A man is the happier for life from having made once an agreeable tour, or lived for any length of time with pleasant people, or enjoyed any considerable interval of innocent pleasure.—*Sydney Smith.*

Gratitude is the memory of the heart; therefore forget not to say often, I have all I have ever enjoyed.—*Mrs. L. M. Child.*

Restraint is the golden rule of enjoyment.—*L. E. Landon.*

He scatters enjoyment, says Lavater, who enjoys much; and it is equally true that he will enjoy much who scatters enjoyments to others.

Temper your enjoyments with prudence, lest there be written on your heart that fearful word "satiety."—*Quarles.*

True enjoyment comes from activity of the mind and exercise of the body; the two are ever united.—*Humboldt.*

Imperfect enjoyment is attended with regret; a surfeit of pleasure with disgust. There is a certain nick of time, a certain medium to be observed, with which few people are acquainted.—*Evremond.*

Only mediocrity of enjoyment is allowed to man.—*Blair.*

I have told you of the Spaniard who always put on his spectacles when about to eat cherries, that they might look bigger and more tempting. In like manner I make the most of my enjoyments; and though I do not cast my cares away, I pack them in as little compass as I can, and carry them as conveniently as I can for myself, and never let them annoy others.—*Southey.*

Whatever can lead an intelligent being to the exercise or habit of mental enjoyment, contributes more to his happiness than the highest sensual or mere bodily pleasures. The one feeds the soul, while the other, for the most part, only exhausts the frame, and too often injures the immortal part.

Let all seen enjoyments lead to the unseen fountain from whence they flow. —*Haliburton.*

The less you can enjoy, the poorer and scantier yourself; the more you can enjoy, the richer and more vigorous.—*Lavater.*

All solitary enjoyments quickly pall, or become painful.—*Sharp.*

Whatever advantage or enjoyment we snatch beyond the certain portion allotted us by nature, is like money spent before it is due, which at the time of regular payment will be missed and regretted.—*Johnson.*

The enjoyments of this present short life, which are indeed but puerile amusements, must disappear when placed in competition with the greatness and durability of the glory which is to come.—*Haller.*

Sleep, riches, health, and so every blessing, are not truly and fully enjoyed till after they have been interrupted.—*Richter.*

What we have, we prize, not to the worth while we enjoy it; but being lacked and lost, why then we rack the value; then we find the virtue that possession would not show us while it was ours.—*Shakespeare.*

ENNUI.—Ennui is the desire of activity without the fit means of gratifying the desire.—*Bancroft.*

Ennui is one of our greatest enemies; remunerative labor, our most lasting friend.—*Moser.*

I do pity unlearned gentlemen on a rainy day.—*Falkland.*

The victims of ennui paralyze all the grosser feelings by excess, and torpify all the finer by disuse and inactivity. Disgusted with this world and indifferent about another, they at last lay violent hands upon themselves, and assume no small credit for the sangfroid with which they meet death. But alas! such beings can scarcely be said to die, for they have never truly lived.—*Colton.*

Ennui has, perhaps, made more gamblers than avarice; more drunkards than thirst; and perhaps as many suicides as despair.—*Colton.*

Ennui is a word which the French invented, though of all nations in Europe they know the least of it.—*Bancroft.*

That which renders life burdensome to us, generally arises from the abuse of it. —*Rousseau.*

As gout seems privileged to attack the

bodies of the wealthy, so ennui seems to exert a similar prerogative over their minds.—*Colton.*

Ambition itself is not so reckless of human life as ennui.—*Clemency* is a favorite attribute of the former, but ennui has the taste of a cannibal.—*Bancroft.*

There is nothing so insupportable to man as to be in entire repose, without passion, occupation, amusement, or application. Then it is that he feels his own nothingness, isolation, insignificance, dependent nature, powerlessness, emptiness. Immediately there issue from his soul ennui, sadness, chagrin, vexation, despair.—*Pascal.*

ENTERPRISE.—The method of the enterprising is to plan with audacity, and execute with vigor; to sketch out a map of possibilities, and then to treat them as probabilities.—*Bovee.*

To do anything in this world worth doing, we must not stand back shivering and thinking of the cold and danger, but jump in, and scramble through as well as we can.—*Sydney Smith.*

Before undertaking any design weigh the story of thy action with the danger of the attempt.—If the glory outweigh the danger it is cowardice to neglect it; if the danger exceed the glory, it is rashness to attempt it; if the balances stand poised, let thine own genius cast them. —*Quarles.*

Kites rise against, not with the wind. —No man ever worked his passage anywhere in a dead calm.—*John Neal.*

Attempt the end, and never stand to doubt; nothing so hard but search will find it out.—*Herrick.*

ENTHUSIASM. — Every great and commanding movement in the annals of the world is the triumph of enthusiasm. —Nothing great was ever achieved without it.—*Emerson.*

Enthusiasm is a virtue rarely to be met with in seasons of calm and unruffled prosperity.—It flourishes in adversity, kindles in the hour of danger, and awakens to deeds of renown.—The terrors of persecution only serve to quicken the energy of its purposes.—It swells in proud integrity, and, great in the purity of its cause, it can scatter defiance amidst hosts of enemies.—*Chalmers.*

The sense of this word among the Greeks affords the noblest definition of it; enthusiasm signifies "God in us."— *Mad. De Staël.*

Opposition always inflames the enthusiast, never converts him.—*Schiller.*

No virtue is safe that is not enthusiastic.—*Seeley.*

An excess of excitement, and a deficiency of enthusiasm, may easily characterize the same person or period. Enthusiasm is grave, inward, self-controlled; mere excitement is outward, fantastic, hysterical, and passing in a moment from tears to laughter; from one aim to its very opposite.—*J. Sterling.*

Truth is never to be expected from authors whose understandings are warped with enthusiasm; for they judge all actions and their causes by their own perverse principles, and a crooked line can never be the measure of a straight one. —*Dryden.*

Nothing is so contagious as enthusiasm.—It is the real allegory of the tale of Orpheus; it moves stones, and charms brutes.—It is the genius of sincerity, and truth accomplishes no victories without it.—*Bulwer.*

Enlist the interests of stern morality and religious enthusiasm in the cause of political liberty, as in the time of the old Puritans, and it will be irresistible.— *Coleridge.*

All noble enthusiasms pass through a feverish stage, and grow wiser and more serene.—*Channing.*

Every production of genius must be the production of enthusiasm.—*Disraeli.*

Let us recognize the beauty and power of true enthusiasm; and whatever we may do to enlighten ourselves or others, guard against checking or chilling a single earnest sentiment.—*Tuckerman.*

The enthusiasm of old men is singularly like that of infancy.—*Nerval.*

Great designs are not accomplished without enthusiasm of some sort.—It is the inspiration of everything great.— Without it no man is to be feared, and with it none despised.—*Bovee.*

Enthusiasm is an evil much less to be dreaded than superstition.—Superstition is the disease of nations; enthusiasm, that of individuals.—The former grows inveterate by time; the latter is cured by it.—*Robert Hall.*

Enthusiasts soon understand each other.—*Irving*.

No wild enthusiast ever yet could rest, till half mankind were, like himself, possest.—*Cowper*.

ENVY.—Envy has no other quality but that of detracting from virtue.—*Livy*.

Envy is a passion so full of cowardice and shame, that nobody ever had the confidence to own it.—*Rochester*.

A man that hath no virtue in himself ever envieth virtue in others; for men's minds will either feed upon their own good, or upon others' evil; and who wanteth the one will prey upon the other; and whoso is out of hope to attain to another's virtue, will seek to come at even hand by depressing another's fortune.—*Bacon*.

Whoever feels pain in hearing a good character of his neighbor, will feel a pleasure in the reverse. And those who despair to rise in distinction by their virtues, are happy if others can be depressed to a level with themselves.—*Franklin*.

Envy sets the stronger seal on desert; if he have no enemies, I should esteem his fortune most wretched.—*Ben Jonson*.

Fools may our scorn, not envy raise, for envy is a kind of praise.—*Gay*.

If our credit be so well built, so firm that it is not easy to be shaken by calumny or insinuation, envy then commends us, and extols us beyond reason to those upon whom we depend, till they grow jealous, and so blow us up when they cannot throw us down.—*Clarendon*.

All envy is proportionate to desire; we are uneasy at the attainments of another, according as we think our own happiness would be advanced by the addition of that which he withhol from us; and therefore whatever depresses immoderate wishes, will, at the same time, set the heart free from the corrosion of envy, and exempt us from that vice which is, above most others, tormenting to ourselves, hateful to the world, and productive of mean artifices and sordid projects.—*Johnson*.

If we did but know how little some enjoy of the great things that they possess, there would not be much envy in the world.—*Young*.

The truest mark of being born with great qualities, is being born without envy.—*Rochefoucauld*.

Every other sin hath some pleasure annexed to it, or will admit of some excuse, but envy wants both.—We should strive against it, for if indulged in it will be to us as a foretaste of hell upon earth.—*Burton*.

Envy will merit, as its shade, pursue but, like a shadow, proves the substance true.—*Pope*.

Many men profess to hate another, but no man owns envy, as being an enmity or displeasure for no cause but another's goodness or felicity.—*Jeremy Taylor*.

Emulation looks out for merits, that she may exalt herself by a victory; envy spies out blemishes, that she may lower another by a defeat.—*Colton*.

Envy is like a fly that passes all a body's sounder parts, and dwells upon the sores.—*Chapman*.

Envy feels not its own happiness but when it may be compared with the misery of others.—*Johnson*.

Other passions have objects to flatter them, and which seem to content and satisfy them for a while.—There is power in ambition, pleasure in luxury, and pelf in covetousness; but envy can gain nothing but vexation.—*Montaigne*.

There is no surer mark of the absence of the highest moral and intellectual qualities than a cold reception of excellence.—*Bailey*.

Base rivals, who true wit and merit hate, maliciously aspire to gain renown, by standing up, and pulling others down.—*Dryden*.

Base envy withers at another's joy, and hates the excellence it cannot reach.—*Thomson*.

Envy, like the worm, never runs but to the fairest fruit; like a cunning bloodhound, it singles out the fattest deer in the flock.—Abraham's riches were the Philistines' envy, and Jacob's blessings had Esau's hatred.—*Beaumont*.

Envy is but the smoke of low estate, ascending still against the fortunate.—*Brooke*.

Envy always implies conscious inferiority wherever it resides.—*Pliny*.

No crime is so great to envy as daring to excel.—*Churchill.*

We are often vain of even the most criminal of our passions; but envy is so shameful a passion that we never dare to acknowledge it.—*Rochefoucauld.*

The envious praise only that which they can surpass; that which surpasses them they censure.—*Colton.*

Men of noble birth are noted to be envious toward new men when they rise; for the distance is altered; it is like a deceit of the eye, that when others come on they think themselves go back.—*Bacon.*

Envy ought to have no place allowed it in the heart of man; for the goods of this present world are so vile and low that they are beneath it; and those of the future world are so vast and exalted that they are above it.—*Colton.*

If envy, like anger, did not burn itself in its own fire, and consume and destroy those persons it possesses before it can destroy those it wishes worst to, it would set the whole world on fire, and leave the most excellent persons the most miserable.—*Clarendon.*

Envy, if surrounded on all sides by the brightness of another's prosperity, like the scorpion confined within a circle of fire, will sting itself to death.—*Colton.*

Envy makes us see what will serve to accuse others, and not perceive what may justify them.—*Bp. Wilson.*

As a moth gnaws a garment, so doth envy consume a man.—*Chrysostom.*

The envious man grows lean at the success of his neighbor.—*Horace.*

The benevolent have the advantage of the envious, even in this present life; for the envious man is tormented not only by all the ill that befalls himself, but by all the good that happens to another; whereas the benevolent man is the better prepared to bear his own calamities unruffled, from the complacency and serenity he has secured from contemplating the prosperity of all around him.—*Colton.*

EPITAPHS.—They are the abstract and brief chronicles of the time; after your death you were better have a bad epitaph than their ill report while you live.—*Shakespeare.*

Some persons make their own epitaphs, and bespeak the reader's goodwill. It were, indeed, to be wished, that every man would early learn in this manner to make his own, and that he would draw it up in terms as flattering as possible, and that he would make it the employment of his whole life to deserve it.—*Goldsmith.*

Do ye not laugh, O, listening friends, when men praise those dead whose virtues they discovered not when living?—It takes much marble to build the sepulchre.—How little of lath and plaster would have repaired the garret!—*Bulwer.*

If all would speak as kindly of the living as in epitaphs they do of the dead, slander and censorious gossip would soon be strangers in the world.

EQUALITY.—All men are by nature equal, made, all, of the same earth by the same Creator, and however we deceive ourselves, as dear to God is the poor peasant as the mighty prince.—*Plato.*

By the law of God, given by him to humanity, all men are free, are brothers, and are equals.—*Mazzini.*

In the gates of eternity the black hand and the white hold each other with an equal clasp.—*Mrs. Stowe.*

Equality is the share of every one at their advent upon earth; and equality is also theirs when placed beneath it.—*Enclos.*

Liberty, equality—bad principles! The only true principle for humanity is justice; and justice to the feeble is protection and kindness.—*Amiel.*

Your fat king, and your lean beggar, is but variable service; two dishes, but to one table; that is the end.—*Shakespeare.*

Kings and their subjects, masters and slaves, find a common level in two places —at the foot of the cross and in the grave.—*Colton.*

It is not true that equality is a law of nature.—Nature has no equality.—Its sovereign law is subordination and dependence.—*Vauvenargues.*

If by saying that all men are born free and equal, you mean that they are all equally born, it is true, but true in no other sense; birth, talent, labor, vir tue, and providence, are forever making differences.—*Eugene Edwards.*

Let them ease their hearts with prate of equal rights, which man never knew.—*Byron.*

So far is it from being true that men are naturally equal, that no two people can be half an hour together but one shall acquire an evident superiority over the other.—*Johnson.*

Society is a more level surface than we imagine. Wise men or absolute fools are hard to be met with; and there are few giants or dwarfs.—*Hazlitt.*

They who say all men are equal speak an undoubted truth, if they mean that all have an equal right to liberty, to their property, and to their protection of the laws.—But they are mistaken if they think men are equal in their station and employments, since they are not so by their talents.—*Voltaire.*

Equality is one of the most consummate scoundrels that ever crept from the brain of a political juggler—a fellow who thrusts his hand into the pocket of honest industry or enterprising talent, and squanders their hard-earned profits on profligate idleness or indolent stupidity.—*Paulding.*

Men are by nature unequal.—It is vain, therefore, to treat them as if they were equal.—*Froude.*

Some must follow, and some command, though all are made of clay.—*Longfellow.*

The equality of conditions is more complete in the Christian countries of the present day, than it has been at any time, or in any part of the world.—Its gradual development is a providential fact, and it possesses all the characteristics of a divine decree; it is universal, it is durable, and it constantly eludes all human interference; and all events, as well as all men, contribute to its progress.—*De Tocqueville.*

Whatever difference there may appear to be in men's fortunes, there is still a certain compensation of good and ill in all, that makes them equal.—*Charron.*

When the political power of the clergy was founded and began to exert itself, and they opened their ranks to all classes, to the poor and the rich, the villain and the lord, equality penetrated into the government through the church; and the being who as a serf must have vegetated in perpetual bondage, took his place, as a priest, in the midst of nobles, and not unfrequently above the head of kings.—*De Tocqueville.*

EQUANIMITY.—In this thing one man is superior to another, that he is better able to bear prosperity or adversity.—*Philemon.*

The excellence of equanimity is beyond all praise.—One of this disposition is not dejected in adversity, nor elated in prosperity: he is affable to others, and contented in himself.—*Buck.*

EQUITY.—Equity is a roguish thing.—For law we have a measure, and know what to trust to; equity is according to the conscience of him that is chancellor, and as that is larger or narrower, so is equity.—It is all one as if they should make the standard for the measure we call a foot, a chancellor's foot.—What an uncertain measure would this be!—One chancellor has a long foot; another, a short foot; a third, an indifferent foot.—It is the same thing with the chancellor's conscience.—*Selden.*

Equity is that exact rule of righteousness or justice which is to be observed between man and man.—It is beautifully and comprehensively expressed in the words of the Saviour, " All things whatsoever ye would that men should do to you, do ye even so to them, for this is the law and the prophets."—*Buck.*

Equity in law is the same that the spirit is in religion, what every one pleases to make it: sometimes they go according to conscience, sometimes according to law, sometimes according to the rule of court.—*Selden.*

EQUIVOCATION. — I doubt the equivocation of the fiend that lies like truth.—*Shakespeare.*

A sudden lie may sometimes be only manslaughter upon truth; but by a carefully constructed equivocation truth is always, with malice aforethought, deliberately murdered.—*Morley.*

Be these juggling fiends no more believed, that palter with us in a double sense; that keep the word of promise to our ear, and break it to our hope.—*Shakespeare.*

When thou art obliged to speak, be sure to speak the truth; for equivocation is half way to lying, and lying is the whole way to hell.—*Penn.*

He who is guilty of equivocation, may well be suspected of hypocrisy.—*Maunder.*

We must speak by the card, or equivocation will undo us.—*Shakespeare.*

There is no possible excuse for a guarded lie.—Enthusiastic and impulsive people will sometimes falsify thoughtlessly, but equivocation is malice prepense.—*H. Ballou.*

The lie indirect is often as bad, and always meaner and more cowardly than the lie direct.

ERROR.—(See "TRUTH.")

Find earth where grows no weed, and you may find a heart wherein no error grows.—*Knowles.*

Men err from selfishness; women because they are weak.—*Mad. De Staël.*

There are errors which no wise man will treat with rudeness, while there is a probability that they may be the refraction of some great truth still below the horizon.—*Coleridge.*

Our understandings are always liable to error.—Nature and certainty are very hard to come at, and infallibility is mere vanity and pretence.—*Marcus Antoninus.*

Men are apt to prefer a prosperous error to an afflicted truth.—*Jeremy Taylor.*

A man should never be ashamed to own he has been in the wrong, which is but saying, in other words, that he is wiser to-day than he was yesterday.—*Pope.*

The copy-books tell us that "to err is human." That is wrong. To err is inhuman, to be holy is to live in the straight line of duty and of truth to God's life in every intrinsic existence.—*Phillips Brooks.*

My principal method for defeating error and heresy, is, by establishing the truth. One purposes to fill a bushel with tares; but if I can fill it first with wheat, I may defy his attempts.—*John Newton.*

Wrong conduct is far more powerful to produce erroneous thinking, than erroneous thinking to produce wrong conduct.—*J. S. Kieffer.*

Error commonly has some truth in what it affirms, is wrong generally in what it denies.—*F. L. Patton.*

Half the truth will very often amount to absolute falsehood.—*Whately.*

No tempting form of error is without some latent charm derived from truth. —*Keith.*

It is only an error of judgment to make a mistake, but it argues an infirmity of character to adhere to it when discovered. The Chinese say, "The glory is not in never falling, but in rising every time you fall."—*Bovee.*

It is almost as difficult to make a man unlearn his errors as his knowledge. Malinformation is more hopeless than non-information; for error is always more busy than ignorance. Ignorance is a blank sheet, on which we may write; but error is a scribbled one, from which we must first erase. Ignorance is contented to stand still with her back to the truth; but error is more presumptuous, and proceeds in the wrong direction. Ignorance has no light, but error follows a false one. The consequence is, that error, when she retraces her steps, has farther to go before she can arrive at truth, than ignorance.—*Colton.*

Few practical errors in the world are embraced on conviction, but on inclination; for though the judgment may err on account of weakness, yet, where one error enters at this door, ten are let into it through the will; that, for the most part, being set upon those things which truth is a direct obstacle to the enjoyment of; and where both cannot be had, a man will be sure to buy his enjoyment, though he pays down truth for the purchase.—*South.*

In all science error precedes the truth, and it is better it should go first than last.—*Walpole.*

Errors to be dangerous must have a great deal of truth mingled with them. —It is only from this alliance that they can ever obtain an extensive circulation. —From pure extravagance, and genuine, unmingled falsehood, the world never has, and never can sustain any mischief. —*Sydney Smith.*

Our greatest glory is not in never falling, but in rising every time we fall.—*Confucius.*

If any one sincerely, candidly, unselfishly tries to understand and to obey the voice of divine wisdom, he will not go fatally astray.—*H. L. Wayland.*

There is no error so crooked but it hath in it some lines of truth, nor is any poison so deadly that it serveth not some wholesome use.—Spurn not a seeming error, but dig below its surface for the truth.—*Tupper.*

Error is sometimes so nearly allied to truth that it blends with it as imperceptibly as the colors of the rainbow fade into each other.—*Clulow.*

Error of opinion may be tolerated where reason is left free to combat it.—*Jefferson.*

Error is not a fault of our knowledge, but a mistake of our judgment giving assent to that which is not true.—*Locke.*

Sometimes we may learn more from a man's errors, than from his virtues.—*Longfellow.*

From the errors of others a wise man corrects his own.—*Publius Syrus.*

False doctrine does not necessarily make the man a heretic, but an evil heart can make any doctrine heretical.—*Coleridge.*

To make no mistakes is not in the power of man; but from their errors and mistakes the wise and good learn wisdom for the future.—*Plutarch.*

The least error should humble, but we should never permit even the greatest to discourage us.—*Potter.*

Honest error is to be pitied, not ridiculed.—*Chesterfield.*

Errors of theory or doctrine are not so much false statements, as partial statements.—Half a truth received, while the corresponding half is unknown or rejected, is a practical falsehood.—*Tryon Edwards.*

There is nothing so true that the damps of error have not warped it.—*Tupper.*

The consistency of great error with great virtue, is one of the lessons of universal history.—But error is not made harmless by such associations.—False theories, though held by the greatest and best of men, and though not thoroughly believed, have wrought much evil.—*Channing.*

All errors spring up in the neighborhood of some truth; they grow round about it, and, for the most part, derive

their strength from such contiguity.—*T. Binney.*

Whatever is only almost true is quite false, and among the most dangerous of errors, because being so near truth, it is the more likely to lead astray.—Precise knowledge is the only true knowledge, and he who does not teach exactly, does not teach at all.—*H. W. Beecher.*

In its influence on the soul, error has been compared to a magnet concealed near the ship's compass.—As in the latter case, the more favorable the winds, and the greater the diligence and skill in working the ship, the more rapidly will it be speeded on in a wrong course; and so in the former, the greater the struggle for safety, the more speedy the progress to ruin.—*Tryon Edwards.*

There will be mistakes in divinity while men preach, and errors in governments while men govern.—*Dudley Carleton.*

The little I have seen of the world teaches me to look upon the errors of others in sorrow, not in anger. When I take the history of one poor heart that has sinned and suffered, and think of the struggles and temptations it has passed through, the brief pulsations of joy, the feverish inquietude of hope and fear, the pressure of want, the desertion of friends, I would fain leave the erring soul of my fellow-man with Him from whose hands it came.—*Longfellow.*

ESTEEM.—The chief ingredients in the composition of those qualities that gain esteem and praise, are good nature, truth, good sense, and good breeding.—*Addison.*

The esteem of wise and good men is the greatest of all temporal encouragements to virtue; and it is a mark of an abandoned spirit to have no regard to it.—*Burke.*

Esteem has more engaging charms than friendship and even love.—It captivates hearts better, and never makes ingrates.—*Rochefoucauld.*

Esteem cannot be where there is no confidence; and there can be no confidence where there is no respect.—*Giles.*

We have so exalted a notion of the human soul that we cannot bear to be despised, or even not to be esteemed by it.—Man, in fact, places all his happiness in this esteem.—*Pascal.*

All true love is founded on esteem.—*Buckingham.*

ESTIMATION.—A life spent worthily should be measured by deeds, not years.—*Sheridan.*

To judge of the real importance of an individual, we should think of the effect his death would produce.—*Levis.*

It is seldom that a man labors well in his minor department unless he overrates it.—It is lucky for us that the bee does not look upon the honeycomb in the same light we do.—*Whately.*

Men judge us by the success of our efforts. God looks at the efforts themselves.—*Charlotte Elizabeth.*

ETERNITY.—(See "FUTURE STATE.")

What is eternity? was asked of a deaf and dumb pupil, and the beautiful and striking answer was, "It is the lifetime of the Almighty."

Eternity is a negative idea clothed with a positive name.—It supposes, in that to which it is applied, a present existence, and is the negation of a beginning or an end of that existence.—*Paley.*

No man can pass into eternity, for he is already in it.—*Farrar.*

This is the world of seeds, of causes, and of tendencies; the other is the world of harvests and results and of perfected and eternal consequences.

Eternity, thou pleasing dreadful thought! through what variety of untried being! through what new scenes and changes must we pass! The wide, the unbounded prospect lies before me; but shadows, clouds, and darkness rest upon it.—*Addison.*

He that will often put eternity and the world before him, and will dare to look steadfastly at both of them, will find that the more he contemplates them, the former will grow greater and the latter less.—*Colton.*

The wish falls often, warm upon my heart, that I may learn nothing here that I cannot continue in the other world; that I may do nothing here but deeds that will bear fruit in heaven.—*Richter.*

The most momentous concern of man is the state he shall enter upon after this short and transitory life is ended; and in proportion as eternity is of greater importance than time, so ought men to be solicitous upon what grounds their expectations with regard to that durable state are built, and on what assurances their hopes or their fears stand.—*Clarke.*

How vast is eternity!—It will swallow up all the human race; it will collect all the intelligent universe; it will open scenes and prospects wide enough, great enough, and various enough to fix the attention, and absorb the minds of all intelligent beings forever.—*Emmons.*

Every natural longing has its natural satisfaction. If we thirst, God has created liquids to gratify thirst. If we are susceptible of attachment, there are beings to gratify that love. If we thirst for life and love eternal, it is likely that there are an eternal life and an eternal love to satisfy that craving.—*F. W. Robertson.*

Eternity invests every state, whether of bliss or suffering, with a mysterious and awful importance entirely its own.—It gives weight and moment to whatever it attaches, compared to which all interests that know a period fade into absolute insignificance.—*Robert Hall.*

The sum and substance of the preparation needed for a coming eternity is, that we believe what the Bible tells us, and do what the Bible bids us.—*Chalmers.*

There is, I know not how, in the minds of men, a certain presage, as it were, of a future existence, and this takes the deepest root, and is most discoverable in the greatest geniuses and most exalted souls.—*Cicero.*

Eternity looks grander and kinder if time grows meaner and more hostile.—*Carlyle.*

All great natures delight in stability; all great men find eternity affirmed in the very promise of their faculties.—*Emerson.*

The grand difficulty is so to feel the reality of both worlds as to give each its due place in our thoughts and feelings—to keep our mind's eye, and our heart's eye, ever fixed on the land of Promise, without looking away from the road along which we are to travel toward it.—*Hare.*

The eternal world is not merely a world beyond time and the grave. It embraces time; it is ready to realize itself under all the forms of temporal things. Its light and power are latent everywhere, waiting for human souls to welcome it, ready to break through the transparent veil of earthly things and to suffuse with its ineffable radiance the common life of man.—*John Caird.*

The thought of eternity consoles for the shortness of life.—*Malesherbes.*

The disappointed man turns his thoughts toward a state of existence where his wiser desires may be fixed with the certainty of faith.—The successful man feels that the objects he has ardently pursued fail to satisfy the craving of an immortal spirit. The wicked man turneth away from his wickedness, that he may save his soul alive.—*Southey.*

Eternity stands always fronting God; a stern colossal image, with blind eyes, and grand dim lips, that murmur evermore, "God — God — God!"—*E. B Browning.*

Our object in life should be to accumulate a great number of grand questions to be asked and resolved in eternity.—Now we ask the sage, the genius, the philosopher, the divine, but none can tell; but we will open our queries to other respondents—we will ask angels, redeemed spirits, and God.—*Foster.*

What we call eternity may be but an endless series of the transitions which men call deaths, abandonments of home, going ever to fairer scenes and loftier heights.—Age after age, the spirit—that glorious nomad—may shift its tent, carrying with it evermore its elements, activity and desire.—*Bulwer.*

Let me dream that love goes with us to the shore unknown.—*Mrs. Hemans.*

ETIQUETTE. — A man may with more impunity be guilty of an actual breach, either of real good breeding or good morals, than appear ignorant of the most minute points of fashionable etiquette.—*Walter Scott.*

We must conform, to a certain extent, to the conventionalities of society, for they are the ripened results of a varied and long experience.—*A. A. Hodge.*

Good taste rejects excessive nicety; it treats little things as little things, and is not hurt by them.—*Fenelon.*

EVASION. — Evasions are the common shelter of the hard-hearted, the false, and the impotent when called upon to assist; the real great, alone plan instantaneous help, even when their looks or words presage difficulties.—*Lavater.*

Evasion is unworthy of us, and is always the intimate of equivocation.—*Balzac.*

Evasion, like equivocation, comes generally from a cowardly or a deceiving spirit, or from both; afraid to speak out its sentiments, or from guile concealing them.

EVENING.—Now came still evening on, and twilight gray had in her sober livery all things clad.—*Milton.*

A paler shadow strews its mantle over the mountains; parting day dies like the dolphin, whom each pang imbues with a new color as it gasps away.—*Byron.*

The evening came.—The setting sun stretched his celestial rods of light across the level landscape, and like the miracle in Egypt, smote the rivers, the brooks, and the ponds, and they became as blood.—*Longfellow.*

Evening is the delight of virtuous age; it seems an emblem of the tranquil close of a busy life—serene, placid, and mild, with the impress of the great Creator stamped upon it; it spreads its quiet wings over the grave, and seems to promise that all shall be peace beyond it.—*Bulwer.*

There is an evening twilight of the heart, when its wild passion waves are lulled to rest.—*Halleck.*

EVENTS.—Events of all sorts creep or fly exactly as God pleases.—*Cowper.*

Coming events cast their shadows before.—*Campbell.*

Often do the spirits of great events stride on before the events, and in to-day already walks to-morrow. — *Coleridge.*

There is little peace or comfort in life if we are always anxious as to future events.—He that worries himself with the dread of possible contingencies will never be at rest.—*Johnson.*

EVIDENCE.—Upon any given point, contradictory evidence seldom puzzles the man who has mastered the laws of evidence, but he knows little of the laws of evidence who has not studied the unwritten law of the human heart; and without this last knowledge a man of action will not attain to the practical, nor will a poet achieve the ideal.—*Bulwer.*

Hear one side and you will be in the dark; hear both sides, and all will be clear.—*Haliburton.*

EVILS.—Evil is in antagonism with the entire creation.—*Zschokke.*

If we rightly estimate what we call good and evil, we shall find it lies much in comparison.—*Locke.*

Physical evils destroy themselves, or they destroy us.—*Rousseau.*

By the very constitution of our nature, moral evil is its own curse.—*Chalmers.*

This is the course of every evil deed, that, propagating still it brings forth evil.—*Coleridge.*

There is this good in real evils,—they deliver us, while they last, from the petty despotism of all that were imaginary.—*Colton.*

Even in evil, that dark cloud that hangs over creation, we discern rays of light and hope, and gradually come to see, in suffering and temptation, proofs and instruments of the sublimest purposes of wisdom and love.—*Channing.*

To be free from evil thoughts is God's best gift.—*Æschylus.*

It is some compensation for great evils, that they enforce great lessons.—*Bovee.*

All physical evils are so many beacon lights to warn us from vice.—*Bowen.*

The existence of evil, as Whately well says, is the great theological difficulty; and the apparent want of success of good men in overcoming it, is but one branch of this difficulty.—*Bristed.*

The first lesson of history, is, that evil is good.—*Emerson.*

Many have puzzled themselves about the origin of evil. I am content to observe that there is evil, and that there is a way to escape from it, and with this I begin and end.—*John Newton.*

Good has but one enemy, the evil; but the evil has two enemies, the good and itself.—*J. Von Muller.*

Evil is but the shadow, that, in this world, always accompanies good.—You may have a world without shadow, but it will be a world without light—a mere dim, twilight world. If you would deepen the intensity of the light, you must be content to bring into deeper blackness and more distinct and definite outline, the shade that accompanies it. —*F. W. Robertson.*

He who does evil that good may come, pays a toll to the devil to let him into heaven.—*Hare.*

There is nothing truly evil, but what is within us; the rest is either natural or accidental.—*Sir P. Sidney.*

We sometimes learn more from the sight of evil than from an example of good; and it is well to accustom ourselves to profit by the evil which is so common, while that which is good is so rare.—*Pascal.*

If we could annihilate evil we should annihilate hope, and hope is the avenue of faith.—*Bulwer.*

Imaginary evils soon become real by indulging our reflections on them; as he who in a melancholy fancy sees something like a face on the wall or the wainscot, can, by two or three touches with a lead pencil, make it look visible, and agreeing with what he fancied.—*Swift.*

It is a great evil not to be able to bear an evil.—*Bion.*

As it is the chief concern of wise men to retrench the evils of life by the reasonings of philosophy, it is the employment of fools to multiply them by the sentiments of superstition.—*Addison.*

The lives of the best of us are spent in choosing between evils.—*Junius.*

If you do what you should not, you must bear what you would not. —*Franklin.*

We cannot do evil to others without doing it to ourselves.—*Desmahis.*

The first evil choice or act is linked to the second; and each one to the one that follows, both by the tendency of our evil nature and by the power of habit, which holds us as by a destiny.— As Lessing says, " Let the devil catch you but by a single hair, and you are his forever."—*Tryon Edwards.*

He who is in evil, is also in the punishment of evil.—*Swedenborg.*

As there is much beast and some devil in man, so there is some angel and some God in him.—*The* beast and devil may be conquered, but in this life are never destroyed.—*Coleridge.*

Much that we call evil is really good in disguise; and we should not quarrel rashly with adversities not yet understood, nor overlook the mercies often bound up in them.—*Sir T. Browne.*

It is a proof of our natural bias to evil, that in all things good, gain is harder and slower than loss; but in all things bad or evil, getting is quicker and easier than getting rid of them.—*Hare.*

All evil, in fact the very existence of evil, is inexplicable till we refer to the fatherhood of God.—It hangs a huge blot in the universe till the orb of divine love rises behind it.—In that we detect its meaning.—It appears to us but a finite shadow, as it passes across the disk of infinite light.—*E. H. Chapin.*

The evil that men do lives after them; the good is oft interred with their bones. —*Shakespeare.*

Never let a man imagine that he can pursue a good end by evil means, without sinning against his own soul.—The evil effect on himself is certain.— *Southey.*

The truest definition of evil is that which represents it as something contrary to nature.—Evil is evil because it is unnatural.—A vine which should bear olive-berries—an eye to which blue seems yellow, would be diseased.—An unnatural mother, an unnatural son, an unnatural act, are the strongest terms of condemnation.—*F. W. Robertson.*

Evils in the journey of life are like the hills which alarm travelers on their road.—Both appear great at a distance, but when we approach them we find they are far less insurmountable than we had conceived.—*Colton.*

There is some soul of goodness in things evil, would men observantly distil it out.—*Shakespeare.*

For every evil there is a remedy, or there is not; if there is one I try to find it; and if there is not, I never mind it. —*Miss Mulock.*

Every evil to which we do not succumb is a benefactor.—As the Sandwich Islander believes that the strength and valor of the enemy he kills passes into himself, so we gain the strength of the temptation we resist.—*Emerson.*

There are thousands hacking at the branches of evil to one who is striking at the root.—*Thoreau.*

There are three modes of bearing the ills of life: by indifference, which is the most common; by philosophy, which is the most ostentatious; and by religion, which is the most effectual.—*Colton.*

With every exertion the best of men can do but a moderate amount of good; but it seems in the power of the most contemptible individual to do incalculable mischief.—*Washington Irving.*

All evils natural, are moral goods; all discipline, indulgence on the whole.— *Young.*

In the history of man it has been very generally the case, that when evils have grown insufferable they have touched the point of cure.—*E. H. Chapin.*

Evil is wrought by want of thought, as well as by want of heart.—*Hood.*

As surely as God is good, so surely there is no such thing as necessary evil. —*Southey.*

Not to return one good office for another is inhuman; but to return evil for good is diabolical. There are too many even of this sort, who, the more they owe, the more they hate.—*Seneca.*

EVIL SPEAKING.—A good word is an easy obligation; but not to speak ill, requires only our silence, which costs us nothing.—*Tillotson.*

It is safer to affront some people than to oblige them: for the better a man deserves the worse they will speak of him; as if the possessing of open hatred to their benefactors were an argument that they lie under no obligation.— *Seneca.*

Ill deeds are doubled with an evil word.—*Shakespeare.*

How much better it is that he should speak ill of me to all the world, than all the world speak ill of me to him.— *Tasso.*

It may be asked,—whether the inconveniences and ill-effects which the world feels from the licentiousness of this practice, are not sufficiently counterbalanced by the real influence it has upon men's lives and conduct?—for if there was no evil-speaking in the world, thousands would be encouraged to do ills, and would rush into many indecorums, like a horse into the battle, were they sure to escape the tongues of men.—*Sterne.*

Evil report, like the Italian stiletto, is an assassin's weapon.—*Mad. de Maintenon.*

It is not good to speak evil of all whom we know to be bad; it is worse to judge evil of any who may prove good. —To speak ill upon knowledge shows a want of charity; to speak ill upon suspicion shows a want of honesty.—To know evil of others and not speak it is sometimes discretion; to speak evil of others and not know it, is always dishonesty.—*A. Warwick.*

Where the speech is corrupted, the mind is also.—*Seneca.*

When will talkers refrain from evil speaking?—When listeners refrain from evil hearing.—*Hare.*

EXAGGERATION. — Some persons are exaggerators by temperament.— They do not mean untruth, but their feelings are strong, and their imaginations vivid, so that their statements are largely discounted by those of calm judgment and cooler temperament.— They do not realize that "we always weaken what we exaggerate."—*Tryon Edwards.*

Exaggeration is a blood relation to falsehood, and nearly as blameable.— *H. Ballou.*

Exaggeration, as to rhetoric, is using a vast force to lift a feather; as to morals and character, it is using falsehood to lift one's self out of the confidence of his fellowmen.

There are some persons who would not for their lives tell a direct and wilful lie, but who so exaggerate that it seems as if for their lives they could not tell the exact truth.—*Paget.*

Never speak by superlatives; for in so doing you will be likely to wound either truth or prudence. Exaggeration is neither thoughtful, wise, nor safe. It is a proof of the weakness of the understanding, or the want of discernment of him that utters it, so that even when he speaks the truth, he soon finds it is received with partial, or even utter unbelief.

There is a sort of harmless liars, frequently to be met with in company, who

deal much in the marvellous. Their usual intention is to please and entertain: but as men are most delighted with what they conceive to be truth, these people mistake the means of pleasing, and incur universal blame.—*Hume.*

The habit of exaggeration becomes, in time, a slavish necessity, and they who practise it pass their lives in a kind of mental telescope through whose magnifying medium they look upon themselves, and everything around them.— *J. B. Owen.*

Perfectly truthful men of vivid imagination and great force of sentiment often feel so warmly, and express themselves so strongly, as to give what they say a disagreeable air of exaggeration and almost of falsehood.—*J. F. Boyes.*

Exaggerated language employed on trivial occasions spoils that simplicity and singleness of mind so necessary to a right judgment of ourselves and others.

Those who exaggerate in their statements belittle themselves.—*C. Simmons.*

Some men can never state an ordinary fact in ordinary terms.—All their geese are swans, till you see the birds.—*J. B. Owen.*

There is no strength in exaggeration; even the truth is weakened by being expressed too strongly.

EXAMPLE.—There is a transcendent power in example. We reform others unconsciously, when we walk uprightly. —*Mad. Swetchine.*

Men trust rather to their eyes than to their ears.—The effect of precepts is, therefore, slow and tedious, while that of examples is summary and effectual. —*Seneca.*

Example is more forcible than precept.—People look at my six days in the week to see what I mean on the seventh.—*Cecil.*

People seldom improve when they have no model but themselves to copy after.—*Goldsmith.*

Nothing is so infectious as example.— *Charles Kingsley.*

We can do more good by being good, than in any other way.—*Rowland Hill.*

Though "the words of the wise be as nails fastened by the masters of assemblies," yet their examples are the hammer to drive them in to take the

EXAMPLE 174 EXAMPLE

deeper hold. A father that whipped his son for swearing, and swore himself whilst he whipped him, did more harm by his example than good by his correction.—*Fuller.*

Example is the school of mankind; they will learn at no other.—*Burke.*

Noble examples stir us up to noble actions, and the very history of large and public souls inspires a man with generous thoughts.—*Seneca.*

I am satisfied that we are less convinced by what we hear than by what we see.—*Herodotus.*

The first great gift we can bestow on others is a good example.—*Morell.*

So act that your principle of action might safely be made a law for the whole world.—*Kant.*

It is certain, that either wise bearing or ignorant carriage is caught, as men take diseases one of another; therefore, let them take heed of their company.—*Shakespeare.*

No man is so insignificant as to be sure his example can do no hurt.—*Lord Clarendon.*

The innocence of the intention abates nothing of the mischief of the example.—*Robert Hall.*

One watch set right will do to set many by; one that goes wrong may be the means of misleading a whole neighborhood; and the same may be said of example.—*Dilwin.*

Be a pattern to others, and then all will go well; for as a whole city is infected by the licentious passions and vices of great men, so it is likewise reformed by their moderation.—*Cicero.*

Alexander received more bravery of mind by the pattern of Achilles, than by hearing the definition of fortitude.—*Sir P. Sidney.*

A wise and good man will turn examples of all sorts to his own advantage. The good he will make his patterns, and strive to equal or excel them. The bad he will by all means avoid.—*Thomas à Kempis.*

In early life I had nearly been betrayed into the principles of infidelity; but there was one argument in favor of Christianity that I could not refute, and that was the consistent character and example of my own father.

Thou canst not rebuke in children what they see practised in thee.—Till reason be ripe, examples direct more than precepts.—Such as is thy behavior before thy children's faces, such is theirs behind thy back.—*Quarles.*

Live with wolves, and you will learn to howl.—*Spanish Proverb.*

My advice is to consult the lives of other men, as one would a looking-glass, and from thence fetch examples for imitation.—*Terence.*

Example has more followers than reason.—We unconsciously imitate what pleases us, and approximate to the characters we most admire.—A generous habit of thought and action carries with it an incalculable influence.—*Bovee.*

You can preach a better sermon with your life than with your lips.

Allured to brighter worlds and led the way.—*Goldsmith.*

Our lives, by acts exemplary, not only win ourselves good names, but do to others give matter for virtuous deeds, by which we live.—*Chapman.*

The conscience of children is formed by the influences that surround them; their notions of good and evil are the result of the moral atmosphere they breathe.—*Richter.*

Of all commentaries upon the Scriptures, good examples are the best and the liveliest.—*Donne.*

None preaches better than the ant, and she says nothing.—*Franklin.*

Precept is instruction written in the sand.—The tide flows over it, and the record is gone.—Example is graven on the rock, and the lesson is not soon lost.—*Channing.*

A world of mischief may be done by a single example of avarice or luxury.—One voluptuous palate makes many more.—*Seneca.*

Whatever parent gives his children good instruction, and sets them at the same time a bad example, may be considered as bringing them food in one hand, and poison in the other.—*Balguy.*

There are bad examples that are worse than crimes; and more states have perished from the violation of morality, than from the violation of law.—*Montesquieu.*

Not the cry, but the flight of the wild

EXAMPLE 175 EXCELSIOR

duck, leads the flock to fly and follow. —*Chinese Proverb.*

It is a good divine that follows his own instructions. I can easier teach twenty men what were good to be done, than to be one of twenty to follow mine own teaching.—*Shakespeare.*

The pulpit teaches to be honest, the market-place trains to overreaching and fraud.—*Teaching has not a tithe of the efficacy of example and training.—H. Mann.*

Example is a dangerous lure; where the wasp got through, the gnat sticks fast.—*Fontaine.*

Example teaches better than precept. It is the best modeler of the character of men and women. To set a lofty example is the richest bequest a man can leave behind him.—*S. Smiles.*

There is no part of history which seems capable of either more instruction or entertainment, than that which offers to us the lives of great and virtuous men who have made an eminent figure on the public stage of the world. In these we see what the annals of a whole age can afford that is worthy of notice; and in the wide field of universal history gather all its flowers, and possess ourselves of all that is good in it.—*Middleton.*

Preaching is of much avail, but practise is far more effective.—*A godly life is the strongest argument you can offer to the skeptic.—No reproof or denunciation is so potent as the silent influence of a good example.—M. Ballou.*

Nothing is so contagious as example. —*Never was any considerable good or evil done without producing its like.— We imitate good actions through emulation; and bad ones through the evil of our nature, which shame conceals, but example sets at liberty.—Rochefoucauld.*

We are all of us more or less echoes, repeating involuntarily the virtues, the defects, the movements, and the characters of those among whom we live.— *Joubert.*

Every great example takes hold of us with the authority of a miracle, and says to us, "If ye had but faith, ye, also, could do the same things."—*Jacobi.*

Examples of vicious courses, practised in a domestic circle, corrupt more readily and more deeply, when we behold them in persons of authority.—*Juvenal.*

No life can be pure in its purpose, and strong in its strife, and all life not be purer and stronger thereby.—*Owen Meredith.*

Much more gracious and profitable is doctrine by ensample, than by rule.— *Spenser.*

EXCELLENCE.—One that desires to excel should endeavor it in those things that are in themselves most excellent.— *Epictetus.*

Virtue and genuine graces in themselves speak what no words can utter.— *Shakespeare.*

Human excellence, apart from God, is like the fabled flower which, according to the Rabbis, Eve plucked when passing out of paradise; severed from its native root it is only the touching memorial of a lost Eden—sad while charming and beautiful, but dead.—*Stanford.*

Those who attain to any excellence commonly spend life in some one single pursuit, for excellence is not often gained upon easier terms.—*Johnson.*

Nothing is such an obstacle to the production of excellence as the power of producing what is good with ease and rapidity.—*Aikin.*

There is a moral excellence attainable by all who have the will to strive for it; but there is an intellectual and physical superiority which is above the reach of our wishes, and is granted to only a few.—*Crabbe.*

Excellence is never granted to man but as the reward of labor. It argues no small strength of mind to persevere in habits of industry without the pleasure of perceiving those advances, which, like the hand of a clock, whilst they make hourly approaches to their point, yet proceed so slowly as to escape observation.—*Sir J. Reynolds.*

EXCELSIOR.—People never improve unless they look to some standard or example higher and better than themselves.—*Tryon Edwards.*

What we truly and earnestly aspire to be, that in some sense we are.—The mere aspiration, by changing the frame and spirit of the mind, for the moment realizes itself.—*Mrs. Jameson.*

It is but a base, ignoble mind that

mounts no higher than a bird can soar.—
Shakespeare.

While we converse with what is above
us, we do not grow old, but grow young.
—*Emerson.*

Who shoots at the midday sun, though
sure he shall never hit the mark, yet
sure he is that he shall shoot higher
than he who aims but at a bush.—*Sir P.
Sidney.*

Lift up thyself, look around, and see
something higher and brighter than
earth, earth worms, and earthly darkness.—*Richter.*

Fearless minds climb soonest unto
crowns.—*Shakespeare.*

Beside the pleasure derived from acquired knowledge, there lurks in the
mind of man, and tinged with a shade of
sadness, an unsatisfactory longing for
something beyond the present—a striving toward regions yet unknown and
unopened.—*Humboldt.*

Happy those who here on earth have
dreamt of a higher vision! They will
the sooner be able to endure the glories
of the world to come.—*Novalis.*

The little done vanishes from the sight
of him who looks forward to what is
still to do.—*Goethe.*

Too low they build who build beneath
the stars.—*Young.*

O sacred hunger of ambitious minds!
—*Spenser.*

The hunger and thirst of immortality
is upon the human soul, filling it with
aspirations and desires for higher and
better things than the world can give.
—We can never be fully satisfied but
in God.—*Tryon Edwards.*

As plants take hold, not for the sake
of staying, but only that they may climb
higher, so it is with men.—By every
part of our nature we clasp things above
us, one after another, not for the sake
of remaining where we take hold, but
that we may go higher.—*H. W. Beecher.*

Desires and inspirations after the holy
are the only ones as to which the human soul can ever be assured that they
will never meet with disappointment.—
Miss Macintosh.

EXCESS.—Let us teach ourselves that
honorable step, not to outdo discretion.
—*Shakespeare.*

All things that are pernicious in their

progress must be evil in their birth, for
no sooner is the government of reason
thrown off, than they rush forward of
their own accord; weakness takes a
pleasure to indulge itself; and having
imperceptibly launched out into the
main ocean, can find no place where to
stop.—*Cicero.*

He who indulges his sense in any excesses, renders himself obnoxious to his
own reason; and to gratify the brute in
him, displeases the man, and sets his
two natures at variance.—*W. Scott.*

The body oppressed by excesses, bears
down the mind, and depresses to the
earth any portion of the divine Spirit we
had been endowed with.—*Horace.*

The excesses of our youth are drafts
upon our old age, payable with interest,
about thirty years after date.—*Colton.*

Pleasures bring effeminacy, and effeminacy foreruns ruin; such conquests,
without blood or sweat, do sufficiently
revenge themselves upon their intemperate conquerors.—*Quarles.*

Violent delights have violent ends, and
in their triumph die; like fire and
powder, which, as they kiss, consume.—
They are as sick that surfeit with too
much, as they that starve with nothing.
—*Shakespeare.*

Pliability and liberality, when not restrained within due bounds, must ever
turn to the ruin of their possessor.—
Tacitus.

The best principles, if pushed to excess, degenerate into fatal vices.—Generosity is nearly allied to extravagance;
charity itself may lead to ruin; and the
sternness of justice is but one step removed from the severity of oppression.
—*Alison.*

The desire of power in excess caused
angels to fall; the desire of knowledge in
excess caused man to fall; but in charity
is no excess, neither can man or angels
come into danger by it.—*Bacon.*

Let pleasure be ever so innocent the
excess is always criminal.—*Evremond.*

There can be no excess to love, to
knowledge, to beauty, when these attributes are considered in the purest
sense.—*Emerson.*

All excess brings on its own punishment, even here.—By certain fixed,
settled, and established laws of him who

is the God of nature, excess of every kind destroys that constitution which temperance would preserve.—The debauchee offers up his body a living sacrifice to sin.—*Colton.*

Too much noise deafens us; too much light blinds us; too great a distance, or too much of promixity equally prevents us from being able to see; too long or too short a discourse obscures our knowledge of a subject; too much of truth stuns us.—*Pascal.*

Excess generally causes reaction and produces a change in the opposite direction, whether it be in the seasons, or in individuals, or in government.—*Plato.*

EXCITEMENT. — Excitement is so engraven on our nature that it may be regarded as an appetite; and like all other appetites it is not sinful unless indulged unlawfully, or to excess.—*Guthrie.*

It is the passions that wear—the appetites that grind out the force of life. —Excitement in the higher realm of thought and feeling does not wear out or waste men.—The moral sentiments nourish and feed us.—*H. W. Beecher.*

Violent excitement exhausts the mind, and leaves it withered and sterile.—*Fenelon.*

The language of excitement is at best but picturesque merely.—You must be calm before you can utter oracles.—*Thoreau.*

Never be afraid because the community teems with excitement.—Silence and death are dreadful.—The rush of life, the vigor of earnest men, and the conflict of realities, invigorate, cleanse, and establish the truth.—*H. W. Beecher.*

Religious excitement is to the steady influence of Christian principle as is the flush of fever to the uniform glow of health.—*N. Murray.*

Excitement is of impulse, while earnestness is of principle; the one a glow, the other a fire; the one common, the other rare; the one theorizes, the other acts; the one needs company, the other can live alone.—The two are oftener found in separation than in union, though neither is incompatible with the other.—*Merry.*

EXCUSES. — Of all vain things excuses are the vainest.—*Buxton.*

He that is good for making excuses, is seldom good for anything else.—*Franklin.*

Uncalled for excuses are practical confessions.—*C. Simmons.*

Oftentimes excusing of a fault, doth make a fault the worse by the excuse. —*Shakespeare.*

EXERCISE. — Health is the vital principle of bliss; and exercise, of health. —*Thomson.*

Inactivity, supineness, and effeminacy have ruined more constitutions than were ever destroyed by excessive labors. Moderate exercise and toil, so far from prejudicing, strengthen and consolidate the body.—*Dr. Rush.*

Why do strong arms fatigue themselves with silly dumb-bells? Trenching a vineyard is worthier exercise for men. —*Martial.*

Games played with the ball, and others of that nature, are too violent for the body and stamp no character on the mind.—*T. Jefferson.*

I take the true definition of exercise to be, labor without weariness.—*Johnson.*

The only way for a rich man to be healthy is by exercise and abstinence, to live as if he was poor; which are esteemed the worst parts of poverty.—*Sir W. Temple.*

The wise, for cure, on exercise depend. —Better to hunt in fields for health unbought than fee the doctor for a nauseous draught.—*Dryden.*

Such is the constitution of man, that labor may be styled its own reward.— Nor will any external incitements be requisite if it be considered how much happiness is gained, and how much misery escaped, by frequent and violent agitation of the body.—*Johnson.*

EXERTION.—Every man's task is his life-preserver.—*Emerson.*

Never live in hope or expectation, while your arms are folded. God helps those that help themselves. Providence smiles on those who put their shoulders to the wheel that propels to wealth and happiness.

It is only the constant exertion and working of our sensitive, intellectual, moral, and physical machinery that keeps us from rusting, and so becoming useless.—*C. Simmons.*

Experience shows that success is due less to ability than to zeal. The winner is he who gives himself to his work, body and soul.—*Charles Buxton.*

EXPECTATION.—In our pursuit of the things of this world, we usually prevent enjoyment by expectation; we anticipate our happiness, and eat out the heart and sweetness of worldly pleasures by delightful forethoughts of them; so that when we come to possess them, they do not answer the expectation, nor satisfy the desires which were raised about them, and they vanish into nothing.—*Tillotson.*

By expectation every day beguiled; dupe of to-morrow even from a child.—*Goldsmith.*

We part more easily with what we possess, than with the expectation of what we wish for: and the reason of it is, that what we expect is always greater than what we enjoy.

Oft expectation fails, and most oft there where most it promises.—*Shakespeare.*

Nothing is so good as it seems beforehand.—*George Eliot.*

'Tis expectation makes a blessing dear; heaven were not heaven if we knew what it were.—*Suckling.*

Uncertainty and expectation are the joys of life. Security is an insipid thing, though the overtaking and possessing of a wish discovers the folly of the chase.—*Congreve.*

We love to expect, and when expectation is either disappointed or gratified, we want to be again expecting.—*Johnson.*

Our ancestors have travelled the iron age; the golden is before us.—*St. Pierre.*

With what a heavy and retarding weight does expectation load the wing of time.—*W. Mason.*

EXPEDIENCY.—Many things lawful are not expedient, but nothing can be truly expedient which is unlawful or sinful.—*C. Simmons.*

Expedients are for an hour, but principles are for the ages.—Just because the rains descend, and the winds blow, we cannot afford to build on the shifting sands.—*H. W. Beecher.*

When private virtue is hazarded on the perilous cast of expediency, the pillars of the republic, however apparent their stability, are infected with decay at the very centre.—*E. H. Chapin.*

EXPENSE.— (See "EXTRAVAGANCE.")

What maintains one vice would bring up two children. You may think, perhaps, that a little tea, or a little punch now and then, diet a little more costly, clothes a little finer, and a little entertainment now and then, can be no great matter; but remember, "Many a little makes a mickle." Beware of little expenses. A small leak will sink a great ship.—*Franklin.*

Riches are for spending, and spending for honor and good actions; therefore extraordinary expense must be limited by the worth of the occasion.—*Bacon.*

Buy what thou hast no need of, and ere long thou shalt sell thy necessaries.—*Franklin.*

No money is better spent than what is laid out for domestic satisfaction. A man is pleased that his wife is dressed as well as other people, and the wife is pleased that she is so dressed.—*Johnson.*

Gain may be temporary and uncertain; but ever while you live, expense is constant and certain: and it is easier to build two chimneys than to keep one in fuel.—*Franklin.*

The vices, and follies, and sins of men, cost more than everything else; and the useless and abominable expenditures of nations are a weight on their prosperity, and crush the spirits, benight the minds, and well-nigh enslave the bodies of their people.—*C. Simmons.*

He that buys what he does not want, will soon want what he cannot buy.

EXPERIENCE. — Experience is the extract of suffering.—*A. Helps.*

Experience is the name men give to their follies or their sorrows.—*Musset.*

All is but lip-wisdom which wants experience.—*Sir P. Sidney.*

Experience is the successive disenchantment of the things of life.—It is reason enriched by the spoils of the heart.—*J. P. Senn.*

Experience is the shroud of illusions.—*Finod.*

This is one of the sad conditions of life, that experience is not transmissible. No man will learn from the suffering of another; he must suffer himself.

To most men experience is like the stern lights of a ship, which illumine only the track it has passed.—*Coleridge.*

However learned or eloquent, man knows nothing truly that he has not learned from experience.—*Wieland.*

Experience is the Lord's school, and they who are taught by Him usually learn by the mistakes they make that in themselves they have no wisdom; and by their slips and falls, that they have no strength.—*John Newton.*

Experience keeps a dear school; but fools will learn in no other, and scarce in that; for it is true, we may give advice, but we cannot give conduct.—*Franklin.*

No man was ever so completely skilled in the conduct of life, as not to receive new information from age and experience.—*Terence.*

The rules which experience suggests are better than those which theorists elaborate in their libraries.—*R. S. Storrs.*

Experience joined with common sense, to mortals is a providence.—*Green.*

He cannot be a perfect man, not being tried and tutored in the world.—Experience is by industry achieved, and perfected by the swift course of time.—*Shakespeare.*

No man was ever endowed with a judgment so correct and judicious, but that circumstances, time, and experience, would teach him something new, and apprise him that of those things with which he thought himself the best acquainted, he knew nothing; and that those ideas which in theory appeared the most advantageous were found, when brought into practice, to be altogether impracticable.—*Terence.*

When I was young I was sure of everything; in a few years, having been mistaken a thousand times, I was not half so sure of most things as I was before; at present, I am hardly sure of anything but what God has revealed to me.—*John Wesley.*

To wilful men, the injuries that they themselves procure must be their schoolmasters.—*Shakespeare.*

Adversity is the first path to truth. He who hath proved war, storm, or woman's rage, whether his winters be eighteen or eighty, hath won the experience which is deemed so weighty.—*Byron.*

It is foolish to try to live on past experience. It is a very dangerous, if not a fatal habit to judge ourselves to be safe because of something that we felt or did twenty years ago.—*Spurgeon.*

It may serve as a comfort to us in all our calamities and afflictions, that he who loses anything and gets wisdom by it, is a gainer by the loss.—*L'Estrange.*

Nobody will use other people's experience, nor has any of his own till it is too late to use it.—*Hawthorne.*

That man is wise to some purpose who gains his wisdom at the expense and from the experience of another.—*Plautus.*

Experience is a jewel, and it had need be so, for it is often purchased at an infinite rate.—*Shakespeare.*

Each succeeding day is the scholar of that which went before it.—*Publius Syrus.*

Experience, if wisdom's friend, her best; if not, her foe.—*Young.*

Every man's experience of to-day, is that he was a fool yesterday and the day before yesterday.—To-morrow he will most likely be of exactly the same opinion.—*Mackay.*

Experience takes dreadfully high school-wages, but he teaches like no other.—*Carlyle.*

He hazardeth much who depends for his learning on experience.—An unhappy master is he who is made wise only by many shipwrecks; a miserable merchant, who is neither rich nor wise till he has been bankrupt.—By experience we find out a short way by long wandering.—*Roger Ascham.*

Experience is the common schoolhouse of fools and ill men.—Men of wit and honesty are otherwise instructed.—*Erasmus.*

We are often prophets to others, only because we are our own historians.—*Mad. Swetchine.*

In all instances where our experience of the past has been extensive and uniform, our judgment as to the future amounts to moral certainty.—*Beattie.*

Experience, that chill touchstone whose sad proof reduces all things from their false hue.—*Byron.*

Life consists in the alternate process of learning and unlearning, but it is often wiser to unlearn than to learn.—*Bulwer.*

Experience teaches slowly, and at the cost of mistakes.—*Froude.*

I know the past, and thence will assay to glean a warning for the future, so that man may profit by his errors, and derive experience from his folly—*Shelley.*

Experience is a safe light to walk by, and he is not a rash man who expects success in the future by the same means which secured it in the past.—*Wendell Phillips.*

Experience—making all futures, fruits of all the pasts.—*Arnold.*

EXTRAVAGANCE. — (See "Expense," and "Economy.")

He that is extravagant will soon become poor, and poverty will enforce dependence, and invite corruption.—*Johnson.*

The passion of acquiring riches in order to support a vain expense, corrupts the purest souls.—*Fenelon.*

Waste of time is the most extravagant and costly of all expenses.—*Theophrastus.*

Prodigality is the vice of a weak nature, as avarice is of a strong one.—It comes of a weak craving for those blandishments of the world which are easily had for money.—*H. Taylor.*

That is suitable to a man, in point of ornamental expense, not which he can afford to have, but which he can afford to lose.—*Whately.*

The man who builds, and lacks wherewith to pay, provides a home from which to run away.—*Young.*

The covetous man never has money; the prodigal will have none shortly.—*Ben Jonson.*

Laws cannot prevent extravagance; and this perhaps is not always an evil to the public. A shilling spent idly by a fool may be picked up by a wiser person, who knows better what to do with it; it is, therefore, not lost.—*Franklin.*

EXTREMES.—Extremes are dangerous.—A middle estate is safest, as a middle temper of the sea, between a still calm and a violent tempest, is most hopeful to bear the mariner to his haven.—*Swinnock.*

All extremes are error.—The reverse of error is not truth, but error still.—Truth lies between these extremes.—*Cecil.*

The man who can be nothing but serious, or nothing but merry, is but half a man.—*Leigh Hunt.*

There is a mean in everything.—Even virtue itself hath its stated limits, which, not being strictly observed, it ceases to be virtue.—*Horace.*

Extremes meet in almost everything: it is hard to tell whether the statesman at the top of the world, or the ploughman at the bottom, labors hardest.

Extreme views are never just; something always turns up which disturbs the calculations founded on their data.—*Tancred.*

That extremes beget extremes, is an apothegm built on the most profound observation of the human mind.—*Colton.*

The blast that blows loudest is soonest overblown.—*Smollett.*

Extremes, though contrary, have the like effects.—Extreme heat kills, and so extreme cold; extreme love breeds satiety, and so extreme hatred; and too violent rigor tempts chastity, as does too much license.—*Chapman.*

Mistrust the man who finds everything good; the man who finds everything evil; and still more the man who is indifferent to everything.—*Lavater.*

We must remember how apt man is to extremes—rushing from credulity and weakness, to suspicion and distrust.—*Bulwer.*

The greatest flood has soonest ebb; the sorest tempest, the most sudden calm; the hottest love, the coldest end; and from the deepest desire often ensues the deadliest hate.—*Socrates.*

It is a hard but good law of fate, that as every evil, so every excessive power wears itself out.—*Herder.*

Neither great poverty, nor great riches will hear reason.—*Fielding.*

Both in individuals, and in masses, violent excitement is always followed by remission, and often by reaction. We are all inclined to depreciate what we have over-praised, and, on the other hand, to show undue indulgence where we have shown undue rigor.—*Macaulay.*

Too austere a philosophy makes few wise men; too rigorous politics, few good subjects; too hard a religion, few persons whose devotion is of long continuance.—*St. Evremond.*

No violent extremes endure; a sober moderation stands secure.—*Aleyn.*

Extremes are vicious and proceed from men; compensation is just, and proceeds from God.—*Bruyère.*

EYE.—That fine part of our constitution, the eye, seems as much the receptacle and seat of our passions, appetites, and inclinations, as the mind itself; at least it is the outward portal to introduce them to the house within, or rather the common thoroughfare to let our affections pass in and out. Love, anger, pride, and avarice, all visibly move in those little orbs.—*Addison.*

One of the most wonderful things in nature is a glance of the eye; it transcends speech; it is the bodily symbol of identity.—*Emerson.*

It is the eyes of other people that ruin us. If all but myself were blind I should neither want a fine house nor fine furniture.—*Franklin.*

The balls of sight are so formed, that one man's eyes are spectacles to another, to read his heart with.—*Johnson.*

The curious questioning eye, that plucks the heart of every mystery.—*Mellen.*

Men are born with two eyes, but only one tongue, in order that they should see twice as much as they say.—*Colton.*

The eyes are the pioneers that first announce the soft tale of love.—*Propertius.*

The eye speaks with an eloquence and truthfulness surpassing speech.—It is the window out of which the winged thoughts often fly unwittingly.—It is the tiny magic mirror on whose crystal surface the moods of feeling fitfully play, like the sunlight and shadow on a quiet stream.—*Tuckerman.*

The eye is the pulse of the soul; as physicians judge the heart by the pulse, so we by the eye.—*T. Adams.*

Who has a daring eye, tells downright truths and downright lies.—*Lavater.*

Where is any author in the world teaches such beauty as a woman's eye? —*Shakespeare.*

The eye is the window of the soul; the intellect and will are seen in it.— The animals look for man's intentions right into his eyes.—Even a rat, when you hunt and bring him to bay, looks you in the eye.—*Hiram Powers.*

A beautiful eye makes silence eloquent; a kind eye makes contradiction an assent; an enraged eye makes beauty deformed.—This little member gives life to every other part about us.— *Addison.*

The eye of the master will do more work than both his hands.—*Franklin.*

Lovers are angry, reconciled, entreat, thank, appoint, and finally speak all things by their eyes.—*Montaigne.*

The dearest things in the world are our neighbor's eyes; they cost everybody more than anything else in housekeeping.—*Smith.*

Our eyes, when gazing on sinful objects, are out of their calling, and out of God's keeping.—*Fuller.*

A wanton eye is the messenger of an unchaste heart.—*Augustine.*

The eye observes only what the mind, the heart, the imagination are gifted to see; and sight must be reinforced by insight before souls can be discerned as well as manners; ideas as well as objects; realities and relations as well as appearances and accidental connections. —*E. P. Whipple.*

Eyes are bold as lions, roving, running, leaping, here and there, far and near.—They speak all languages; wait for no introduction; ask no leave of age or rank; respect neither poverty nor riches, neither learning nor power, nor virtue, nor sex, but intrude, and come again, and go through and through you in a moment of time.—What inundation of life and thought is discharged from one soul into another through them!— *Emerson.*

Men of cold passions have quick eyes. —*Hawthorne.*

'Twas but for a moment—and yet in that time she crowded the impressions of many an hour; her eye had a glow, like the sun of her clime, which waked every feeling at once into flower!—*Moore.*

The eyes of women are Promethean fires.—*Shakespeare.*

Eyes will not see when the heart wishes them to be blind.—Desire conceals truth, as darkness does the earth. —*Seneca.*

Faster than his tongue did make offence, his eye did heal it up.—*Shakespeare.*

The heart's hushed secret in the soft dark eye.—*L. E. Landon.*

The intelligence of affection is carried on by the eye only.—Good breeding has made the tongue falsify the heart and act a part of continued restraint, while Nature has preserved the eyes to herself, that she may not be disguised or misrepresented.—*Addison.*

Eyes raised toward heaven are always beautiful, whatever they may be.—*Joubert.*

Sweet, silent rhetoric of persuading eyes.—*Davenant.*

An eye can threaten like a loaded and levelled pistol, or can insult, like hissing or kicking; or in its altered mood, can, by beams of kindness, make the heart dance with joy.—Some eyes have no more expression than blueberries, while others are as deep as a well which you can fall into.—*Emerson.*

Her eyes are homes of silent prayer. —*Tennyson.*

A lover's eyes will gaze an eagle blind. —*Shakespeare.*

Whatever of goodness emanates from the soul gathers its soft halo in the eyes; and if the heart be a lurking place of crime, the eyes are sure to betray the secret.—*F. Saunders.*

Language is slow; the mastery of wants doth teach it to the infant, drop by drop, as brooklets gather.—Yet there is a love, simple and sure, that asks no discipline of weary years, the language of the soul, told through the eye.—The stammering lip oft mars the perfect thought; but the heart's lightning hath no obstacle.—Quick glances, like the thrilling wires, transfuse the telegraphic look.—*Mrs. Sigourney.*

F

FABLES.—Fables, like parables, are more ancient than formal arguments and are often the most effective means of presenting and impressing both truth and duty.—*Tryon Edwards.*

Fables take off from the severity of instruction, and enforce at the same time that they conceal it.—*Addison.*

The fable is allegorical; its actions are natural, but its agents imaginary.—The tale is fictitious, but not imaginary, for both its agents and actions are drawn from the passing scenes of life.—Tales are written mainly for amusement : fables for instruction.—*Crabbe.*

The virtue which we gather from a fable or an allegory, is like the health we get by hunting, as we are engaged in an agreeable pursuit that draws us on with pleasure, and makes us insensible of the fatigues that accompany it.—*Addison.*

FACE.—(See "PHYSIOGNOMY" and " EYE.")

There is in every human countenance, either a history or a prophecy, which must sadden, or at least soften, every reflecting observer.—*Coleridge.*

A good face is the best letter of recommendation.—*Queen Elizabeth.*

Look in the face of the person to whom you are speaking if you wish to know his real sentiments, for he can command his words more easily than his countenance.—*Chesterfield.*

A cheerful face is nearly as good for an invalid as healthy weather.—*Franklin.*

Your face is a book, where men may read strange matters.—*Shakespeare.*

We are all sculptors and painters, and our material is our own flesh and blood and bones.—Any nobleness begins, at once, to refine a man's features; any meanness or sensuality to imbrute them. —*Thoreau.*

The cheek is apter than the tongue to tell an errand.—*Shakespeare.*

I am persuaded that there is not a single sentiment, whether tending to good or evil in the human soul, that has not its distinct interpreter in the glance of the eye, and in the muscling of the countenance. When nature is permitted to express herself by this language of the face, she is understood by all people, and those who were never taught a letter can instantly read her signatures and impressions, whether they be of wrath, hatred, envy, pride, jealousy, vexation, contempt, pain, fear, horror, and dismay; or of attention, respect, wonder, surprise, pleasure, transport, complacence, affection, desire, peace, lowliness, and love.—*Brooke.*

All men's faces are true, whatsoever their hands are.—*Shakespeare.*

Truth makes the face of that person shine who speaks and owns it.—*South.*

There are faces so fluid with expression, so flushed and rippled by the play of thought, that we can hardly find what the mere features really are.—When the delicious beauty of lineaments loses its power, it is because a more delicious beauty has appeared—that an interior and durable form has been disclosed.—*Emerson.*

Faces are as legible as books, with this in their favor, that they may be perused in much less time, and are less liable to be misunderstood.—*F. Saunders.*

The faces which have charmed us the most escape us the soonest.—*Walter Scott.*

The countenance is the title-page which heralds the contents of the human volume, but like other title-pages it sometimes puzzles, often misleads, and often says nothing to the purpose.—*W. Matthews.*

Features are the visible expression of the soul.—the outward manifestation of the feeling and character within.—*Tryon Edwards.*

I more and more see this, that we judge men's abilities less from what they say or do, than from what they look. 'Tis the man's face that gives him weight. His doings help, but not more than his brow.—*Charles Buxton.*

I never knew a genius yet who did not carry about him, either in face or person, or in a certain inexplicable grace of manner, the patent of nobility which heaven has bestowed upon him.—*The Ogilvies.*

There is a garden in her face, where roses and white lillies show—a heavenly paradise wherein all pleasant fruits do grow.—*R. Alison.*

In thy face I see the map of honor, truth, and loyalty.—*Shakespeare.*

A beautiful face is a silent commendation.—*Bacon.*

That same face of yours looks like the title-page to a whole volume of roguery.—*Cibber.*

The loveliest faces are to be seen by moonlight, when one sees half with the eye, and half with the fancy.—*Bovee.*

A countenance habitually under the influence of amiable feelings acquires a beauty of the highest order from the frequency with which such feelings stamp their character upon it.—*Mrs. S. C. Hale.*

He had a face like a benediction.—*Cervantes.*

If we could but read it, every human being carries his life in his face, and is good-looking, or the reverse, as that life has been good or evil. On our features the fine chisels of thought and emotion are eternally at work.—*Alexander Smith.*

In the faces of women who are naturally serene and peaceful, and of those rendered so by religion, there remains an after-spring, and later, an after-summer, the reflex of their most beautiful bloom. —*Richter.*

As the language of the face is universal, so it is very comprehensive.—It is the shorthand of the mind, and crowds a great deal in a little room.—A man may look a sentence as soon as speak a word.—*Collier.*

FACTION.—Faction is the demon of discord armed with power to do endless mischief, and intent only on destroying whatever opposes its progress.—Woe to that state in which it has found an entrance.—*Crabbe.*

A feeble government produces more factions than an oppressive one.—*Fisher Ames.*

Faction is the excess and abuse of party.—It begins when the first idea of private interest, preferred to public good, gets footing in the heart.—It is always dangerous, yet always contemptible.—*Chenevix.*

Seldom is faction's ire in haughty minds extinguished but by death; it oft, like flame suppressed, breaks forth again, and blazes higher.—*May.*

FACTS.— Any fact is better established by two or three good testimonies.

than by a thousand arguments.—*Emmons.*

Facts are to the mind, what food is to the body.—On the due digestion of the former depend the strength and wisdom of the one, just as vigor and health depend on the other.—The wisest in council, the ablest in debate, and the most agreeable companion in the commerce of human life, is that man who has assimilated to his understanding the greatest number of facts.—*Burke.*

From principles is derived probability, but truth or certainty is obtained only from facts.

Every day of my life makes me feel more and more how seldom a fact is accurately stated; how almost invariably when a story has passed through the mind of a third person it becomes, so far as regards the impression it makes in further repetitions, little better than a falsehood; and this, too, though the narrator be the most truth-seeking person in existence.—*Hawthorne.*

There should always be some foundation of fact for the most airy fabric; pure invention is but the talent of a deceiver.—*Byron.*

Facts are God's arguments; we should be careful never to misunderstand or pervert them.—*Tryon Edwards.*

FAILINGS. — The finest composition of human nature, as well as the finest china, may have flaws in it, though the pattern may be of the highest value.

Every one has a wallet behind for his own failings, and one before for the failings of others.—*La Fontaine.*

If we had no failings ourselves we should not take so much pleasure in finding out those of others.—*Rochefoucauld.*

Such is the force of envy and ill-nature, that the failings of good men are more published to the world than their good deeds; and one fault of a well-deserving man shall meet with more reproaches than all his virtues will with praise.—*N. P. Willis.*

FAILURE. — We mount to heaven mostly on the ruins of our cherished schemes, finding our failures were successes.—*A. B. Alcott.*

Every failure is a step to success; every detection of what is false directs us toward what is true; every trial exhausts some tempting form of error. Not only so, but scarcely any attempt is entirely a failure; scarcely any theory, the result of steady thought, is altogether false; no tempting form of error is without some latent charm derived from truth.—*Whewell.*

Sometimes a noble failure serves the world as faithfully as a distinguished success.—*Dowden.*

Failure is often God's own tool for carving some of the finest outlines in the character of his children; and, even in this life, bitter and crushing failures have often in them the germs of new and quite unimagined happiness.—*T. Hodgkin.*

He only is exempt from failures who makes no efforts.—*Whately.*

Failure is, in a sense, the highway to success, inasmuch as every discovery of what is false leads us to seek earnestly after what is true, and every fresh experience points out some form of error which we shall afterward carefully avoid.—*Keats.*

It is an awful condemnation for a man to be brought by God's providence face to face with a great possibility of service and of blessing, and then to show himself such that God has to put him aside, and look for other instruments.—*McLaren.*

In the lexicon of youth, which fate reserves for a bright manhood, there is no such word as fail.—*Bulwer.*

They never fail who die in a great cause.—*Byron.*

There is only one real failure in life that is possible, and that is, not to be true to the best one knows.—*Farrar.*

Only the astrologer and the empyric never fail.—*Willmott.*

A failure establishes only this, that our determination to succeed was not strong enough.—*Bovee.*

FAITH. — Faith affirms many things respecting which the senses are silent, but nothing which they deny.—It is superior to their testimony, but never opposed to it.—*Pascal.*

Faith is a certain image of eternity. All things are present to it—things past, and things to come; it converses with angels, and antedates the hymns of glory. Every man that hath this grace is as certain there are glories for him, if he perseveres in duty, as if he had heard and sung the thanksgiving song for the blessed sentence of doomsday.—*Jeremy Taylor.*

Never yet did there exist a full faith in the divine word which did not expand the intellect while it purified the heart; which did not multiply the aims and objects of the understanding, while it fixed and simplified those of the desires and passions.—*Coleridge.*

All the scholastic scaffolding falls, as a ruined edifice, before one single word—faith.—*Napoleon.*

There is a limit where the intellect fails and breaks down, and this limit is where the questions concerning God, and freewill, and immortality arise.—*Kant.*

Faith marches at the head of the army of progress.—It is found beside the most refined life, the freest government, the profoundest philosophy, the noblest poetry, the purest humanity.—*T. T. Munger.*

Faith must have adequate evidence, else it is mere superstition.—*A. A. Hodge.*

Under the influence of the blessed Spirit, faith produces holiness, and holiness strengthens faith. Faith, like a fruitful parent, is plenteous in all good works; and good works, like dutiful children, confirm and add to the support of faith.

Faith in an all-seeing and personal God, elevates the soul, purifies the emotions, sustains human dignity, and lends poetry, nobility, and holiness to the commonest state, condition, and manner of life.—*Juan Valera.*

We cannot live on probabilities. The faith in which we can live bravely and die in peace must be a certainty, so far as it professes to be a faith at all, or it is nothing.—*Froude.*

Some wish they did, but no man disbelieves.—*Young.*

Christian faith is a grand cathedral, with divinely pictured windows.—Standing without, you can see no glory, nor can imagine any, but standing within every ray of light reveals a harmony of unspeakable splendors.—*Hawthorne.*

Epochs of faith, are epochs of fruitfulness; but epochs of unbelief, however glittering, are barren of all permanent good.—*Goethe.*

In actual life every great enterprise begins with and takes its first forward step in faith.—*Schlegel.*

Faith is not only a means of obeying, but a principal act of obedience; not only an altar on which to sacrifice, but a sacrifice itself, and perhaps, of all, the greatest. It is a submission of our understandings; an oblation of our idolized reason to God, which he requires so indispensably, that our whole will and affections, though seemingly a larger sacrifice, will not, without it, be received at his hands.—*Young.*

The saddest thing that can befall a soul is when it loses faith in God and woman.—*Alexander Smith.*

The Calvinistic people of Scotland, Switzerland, Holland, and New England, have been more moral than the same classes among other nations. Those who preached faith, or in other words a pure mind, have always produced more popu-lar virtue than those who preached good acts, or the mere regulation of outward works.—*Sir James Macintosh.*

Things of God that are marvellous are to be believed on a principle of faith, not to be pried into by reason. For if reason set them open before our eyes, they would no longer be marvellous.—*S. Gregory.*

Man is not made to question, but adore.—*Young.*

Naturally, men are prone to spin themselves a web of opinions out of their own brain, and to have a religion that may be called their own. They are far readier to make themselves a faith, than to receive that which God hath formed to their hands; are far readier to receive a doctrine that tends to their carnal commodity, or honor, or delight, than one that tends to self-denial.—*Baxter.*

Faith and works are as necessary to our spiritual life as Christians, as soul and body are to our life as men; for faith is the soul of religion, and works, the body.—*Colton.*

Faith is not reason's labor, but repose.—*Young.*

Flatter not thyself in thy faith in God, if thou hast not charity for thy neighbor; I think not thou hast charity for thy neighbor, if thou wantest faith in God.—Where they are not both together, they are both wanting; they are both dead if once divided.—*Quarles.*

There never was found in any age of the world, either philosopher or sect, or law, or discipline which did so highly exalt the public good as the Christian faith.—*Bacon.*

Faith makes the discords of the present the harmonies of the future.—*Collyer.*

Despotism may govern without faith, but Liberty cannot.—*De Tocqueville.*

Faith is the eye that sees Him, the hand that clings to Him, the receiving power that appropriates Him.—*Woodbridge.*

Faith is to believe, on the word of God, what we do not see, and its reward is to see and enjoy what we believe.—*Augustine.*

Faith evermore looks upward and describes objects remote; but reason can discover things only near—sees nothing that's above her.—*Quarles.*

Faith makes all evil good to us, and all good better; unbelief makes all good evil, and all evil worse. Faith laughs at the shaking of the spear; unbelief trembles at the shaking of a leaf, unbelief starves the soul; faith finds food in famine, and a table in the wilderness. In the greatest danger, faith says, "I have a great God." When outward strength is broken, faith rests on the promises. In the midst of sorrow, faith draws the sting out of every trouble, and takes out the bitterness from every affliction.—*Cecil.*

Faith in order, which is the basis of science, cannot reasonably be separated from faith in an ordainer, which is the basis of religion.—*Asa Gray.*

Science has sometimes been said to be opposed to faith, and inconsistent with it.—But all science, in fact, rests on a basis of faith, for it assumes the permanence and uniformity of natural laws—a thing which can never be demonstrated.—*Tryon Edwards.*

The steps of faith fall on the seeming void, but find the rock beneath.—*Whittier.*

When men cease to be faithful to their

God, he who expects to find them so to each other will be much disappointed.—*Bp. Horne.*

To believe is to be strong. Doubt cramps energy. Belief is power.—*F. W. Robertson.*

Faith is the root of all good works; a root that produces nothing is dead.—*Bp. Wilson.*

As the flower is before the fruit, so is faith before good works.—*Whately.*

Faith and works are like the light and heat of a candle; they cannot be separated.

Faith without works is like a bird without wings; though she may hop about on earth, she will never fly to heaven.—But when both are joined together, then doth the soul mount up to her eternal rest.—*Beaumont.*

What I admire in Columbus is not his having discovered a world, but his having gone to search for it on the faith of an opinion.—*Turgot.*

Faith is the pencil of the soul that pictures heavenly things.—*T. Burbridge.*

All I have seen teaches me to trust the Creator for all I have not seen.—*Emerson.*

The errors of faith are better than the best thoughts of unbelief.—*Thomas Russell.*

The experience of life nearly always works toward the confirmation of faith. —It is the total significance of life that it reveals God to man; and life only can do this; neither thought, nor demonstration, nor miracle, but only life, weaving its threads of daily toil and trial and joy into a pattern on which, at last, is inscribed the name of "God."—*T. T. Munger.*

All the strength and force of man comes from his faith in things unseen. He who believes is strong; he who doubts is weak. Strong convictions precede great actions.—*J. F. Clarke.*

Faith lights us through the dark to Deity; faith builds a bridge across the gulf of death, to break the shock that nature cannot shun, and lands thought smoothly on the further shore.—*Young.*

Christian faith is nothing else but the soul's venture. It ventures to Christ, in opposition to all legal terrors. It ventures on Christ in opposition to our guiltiness. It ventures for Christ, in opposition to all difficulties and discouragements.—*W. Bridges.*

While reason is puzzling herself about the mystery, faith is turning it into her daily bread and feeding on it thankfully in her heart of hearts.—*F. D. Huntington.*

Strike from mankind the principle of faith, and men would have no more history than a flock of sheep.—*Bulwer.*

It is faith among men that holds the moral elements of society together, as it is faith in God that binds the world to his throne.—*W. M. Evarts.*

There is one sure criterion of judgment as to religious faith in doctrinal matters; can you reduce it to practice?—If not, have none of it.—*H. Ballou.*

Ignorance as to unrevealed mysteries is the mother of a saving faith; and understanding in revealed truths is the mother of a sacred knowledge.—Understand not therefore that thou mayest believe, but believe that thou mayest understand.—Understanding is the wages of a lively faith, and faith is the reward of an humble ignorance.—*Quarles.*

Faith is the root of all blessings. Believe, and you shall be saved; believe, and you must needs be satisfied; believe, and you cannot but be comforted and happy.—*Jeremy Taylor.*

Faith does nothing alone—nothing of itself, but everything under God, by God, through God.—*Stoughton.*

Much knowledge of divine things is lost to us through want of faith.—*Heraclitus.*

I prefer a firm religious faith to every other blessing.—For it makes life a discipline of goodness; creates new hopes, when those of the world vanish; throws over the decay of life the most gorgeous of all lights; and awakens life even in death.—*Sir H. Davy.*

Faith is like love: it cannot be forced.—As trying to force love begets hatred, so trying to compel religious belief leads to unbelief.—*Schopenhauer.*

FALSEHOOD.—(See "LIARS.")

Dishonor waits on perfidy.—A man should blush to think a falsehood; it is the crime of cowards.—*C. Johnson.*

Dare to be true; nothing can need a lie.—*Herbert.*

The lie of fear is the refuge of cowardice, and the lie of fraud the device of the cheat.—The inequalities of men and the lust of acquisition are a constant premium on lying.—*Edward Bellamy.*

A lie has always a certain amount of weight with those who wish to believe it.—*E. W. Rice.*

If falsehood had, like truth, but one face only, we should be upon better terms; for we should then take the contrary to what the liar says for certain truth; but the reverse of truth hath a hundred figures, and is a field indefinite without bound or limit.—*Montaigne.*

Falsehoods not only disagree with truths, but usually quarrel among themselves.—*Daniel Webster.*

The gain of lying is nothing else but not to be trusted of any, nor to be believed when we say the truth.—*Sir W. Raleigh.*

Some men relate what they think, as what they know; some men of confused memories, and habitual inaccuracy, ascribe to one man what belongs to another; and some talk on without thought or care. A few men are sufficient to broach falsehoods, which are afterwards innocently diffused by successive relaters.—*Johnson.*

A liar begins with making falsehood appear like truth, and ends with making truth itself appear like falsehood.—*Shenstone.*

None but cowards lie.—*Murphy.*

He who tells a lie is not sensible how great a task he undertakes; for he must invent twenty more to maintain that one.—*Pope.*

No species of falsehood is more frequent than flattery; to which the coward is betrayed by fear, the dependent by interest, and the friend by tenderness.

Falsehood is never so successful as when she baits her hook with truth, and no opinions so fatally mislead us, as those that are not wholly wrong; as no watches so effectually deceive the wearer as those that are sometimes right.—*Colton.*

It is more from carelessness about the truth, than from intention of lying, that there is so much falsehood in the world. —*Johnson.*

Falsehood, like the dry rot, flourishes the more in proportion as air and light are excluded.—*Whately.*

When Aristotle was asked what a man could gain by telling a falsehood, he replied "Never to be credited when he speaks the truth."

Although the devil be the father of lies, he seems, like other great inventors, to have lost much of his reputation by the continual improvements that have been made upon him.—*Swift.*

The telling of a falsehood is like the cut of a sabre; for though the wound may heal, the scar of it will remain.—*Saadi.*

Falsehood is so easy, truth so difficult! Examine your words well and you will find that even when you have no motive to be false it is very hard to say the exact truth, even about your own immediate feelings—much harder than to say something fine about them which is not the exact truth.—*George Eliot.*

Not the least misfortune in a prominent falsehood is the fact that tradition is apt to repeat it for truth.—*H. Ballou.*

Falsehood, like poison, will generally be rejected when administered alone; but when blended with wholesome ingredients, may be swallowed unperceived.—*Whately.*

O, what a goodly outside falsehood hath; a goodly apple rotten at the heart!—*Shakespeare.*

Falsehood has an infinity of combinations, but truth has only one mode of being.—*Rousseau.*

Do not let us lie at all. Do not think of one falsity as harmless, and another as slight, and another as unintended. Cast them all aside; they may be light and accidental, but they are ugly soot from the smoke of the pit, and it is better that our hearts should be swept clean of them, without one care as to which is largest or blackest.—*Ruskin.*

Round dealing is the honor of man's nature; and a mixture of falsehood is like alloy in gold and silver, which may make the metal work the better, but it embaseth it.—*Bacon.*

Nothing gives such a blow to friendship as detecting another in an untruth.

—It strikes at the root of our confidence ever after.—*Hazlitt.*

Falsehood often lurks upon the tongue of him, who, by self-praise, seeks to enhance his value in the eyes of others.—*G. J. Bennett.*

Let falsehood be a stranger to thy lips.—Shame on the policy that first began to tamper with the heart, to hide its thoughts,—And doubly shame on that inglorious tongue that sold its honesty, and told a lie.—*Havard.*

Half a fact is a whole falsehood.—He who gives the truth a false coloring by his false manner of telling it, is the worst of liars.—*E. L. Magoon.*

Every lie, great or small, is the brink of a precipice, the depth of which nothing but Omniscience can fathom.—*C. Reade.*

This above all; to thine own self be true; and it must follow, as the night the day, thou canst not then be false to any man.—*Shakespeare.*

FAME.—What is fame?—The advantage of being known by people of whom you yourself know nothing, and for whom you care as little.—*Stanislaus.*

The way to fame is like the way to heaven, through much tribulation.—*Sterne.*

Fame, to the ambitious, is like salt water to the thirsty—the more one gets, the more he wants.—*Ebers.*

Human life is too short to recompense the cares which attend the most private condition: therefore it is, that our souls are made, as it were, too big for it; and extend themselves in the prospect of a longer existence, in good fame, and memory of worthy actions, after our decease.—*Steele.*

Fame is no sure test of merit, but only a probability of such, it is an accident, not a property of man.—*Carlyle.*

That fame is the universal passion is by nothing more discovered than by epitaphs. The generality of mankind are not content to sink ingloriously into the grave, but wish to be paid that tribute after their deaths, which in many cases may not be due to the virtues of their lives.—*Kett.*

Fame is the perfume of heroic deeds.—*Socrates.*

I courted fame but as a spur to brave

and honest deeds; who despises fame wil soon renounce the virtues that deserve it.—*Mallet.*

Of present fame think little, and of future less; the praises that we receive after we are buried, like the flowers that are strewed over our grave, may be gratifying to the living, but they are nothing to the dead; the dead are gone, either to a place where they hear them not, or where, if they do, they will despise them.—*Colton.*

There is not in the world so toilsome a trade as the pursuit of fame: life concludes before you have so much as sketched your work.—*Bruyère.*

He that pursues fame with just claims, trusts his happiness to the winds; but he that endeavors after it by false merit, has to fear, not only the violence of the storm, but the leaks of his vessel.—*Johnson.*

The temple of fame stands upon the grave; the flame upon its altars is kindled from the ashes of the dead.—*Hazlitt.*

It often happens that those of whom we speak least on earth are best known in heaven.—*Caussin.*

Men think highly of those who rise rapidly in the world, whereas nothing rises quicker than dust, straw, and feathers.—*Hare.*

Fame, like the river, is narrowest where it is bred, and broadest afar off.—*Davenant.*

Much of reputation depends on the period in which it rises.—In dark periods, when talents appear, they shine like the sun through a small hole in the window-shutter, and the strong beam dazzles amid the surrounding gloom.—open the shutter, and the general diffusion of light attracts no notice.—*Walpole.*

Few people make much noise after their deaths who did not do so while living.—*Hazlitt.*

Let us satisfy our own consciences, and trouble not ourselves by looking for fame. If we deserve it, we shall attain it: if we deserve it not we cannot force it. The praise bad actions obtain dies soon away; if good deeds are at first unworthily received, they are after-ward more properly appreciated.—*Seneca.*

Our admiration of a famous man lessens upon our nearer acquaintance with him; and we seldom hear of a celebrated person without a catalogue of some of his weaknesses and infirmities.—*Addison.*

Even the best things are not equal to their fame.—*Thoreau.*

An earthly immortality belongs to a great and good character.—History embalms it; it lives in its moral influence, in its authority, in its example, in the memory of its words and deeds.—*E. Everett.*

A man who cannot win fame in his own age, will have a very small chance of winning it from posterity.—There may be some half dozen exceptions to this truth among myriads that attest it; but what man of common sense would invest any large amount of hope in so unpromising a lottery?—*Bulwer.*

It is the penalty of fame that a man must ever keep rising.—"Get a reputation, and then go to bed," is the absurdest of all maxims.—"Keep up a reputation or go to bed," would be nearer the truth.—*E. H. Chapin.*

What a heavy burden is a name that has too soon become famous.—*Voltaire.*

Fame is an undertaker that pays but little attention to the living, but bedizens the dead, furnishes out their funerals, and follows them to the grave.—*Colton.*

Worldly fame is but a breath of wind that blows now this way, and now that, and changes name as it changes direction.—*Dante.*

In fame's temple there is always to be found a niche for rich dunces, importunate scoundrels, or successful butchers of the human race.—*Zimmerman.*

I am not covetous for gold; but if it be a sin to covet honor, I am the most offending soul alive.—*Shakespeare.*

Fame is a flower upon a dead man's heart.—*Motherwell.*

Fame—a few words upon a tombstone, and the truth of those not to be depended on.—*Bovee.*

If fame is only to come after death, I am in no hurry for it.—*Martial.*

As the pearl ripens in the obscurity

of its shell, so ripens in the tomb all the fame that is truly precious.—*Landor.*

Suppose your candidate for fame pursues unremittingly the object of his love, through every difficulty and over every obstacle, till at last he overtakes her ladyship, and is permitted to kiss the hem of her garment on mount immortality, what will the dear-bought damsel boot him? If he take her to his bosom, she has no flesh and blood to warm it. If he taste of her lip, there is no more nectar in it than there are sunbeams in a cucumber.—Every rascal who has been bold and fearless enough, Nimrod, Cataline, and Tom Paine, all have had a smack at her before him: They have all more or less become famous, and will be remembered much longer than better men.—*Daniel Webster.*

Milton neither aspired to present fame, nor even expected it.—His high ambition was (to use his own words), "To leave something so written, to after ages, that they should not willingly let it die."—And Cato finally observed, he would much rather posterity should ask why no statues were erected to him, than why they were.—*Colton.*

Those who despise fame seldom deserve it.—We are apt to undervalue the purchase we cannot reach, to conceal our poverty the better.—It is a spark that kindles upon the best fuel, and burns brightest in the bravest breast.—*Jeremy Collier.*

It is an indiscreet and troublesome ambition that cares so much about fame; about what the world says of us; to be always looking in the faces of others for approval; to be always anxious about the effect of what we do or say; to be always shouting to hear the echoes of our own voices.—*Longfellow.*

Good fame is like fire; when you have kindled you may easily preserve it; but if you extinguish it, you will not easily kindle it again.—*Bacon.*

He who would acquire fame must not show himself afraid of censure.—The dread of censure is the death of genius.—*Simms.*

Men's fame is like their hair, which grows after they are dead, and with just as little use to them.—*Villiers.*

Fame is a revenue payable only to our ghosts; and to deny ourselves all present satisfaction, or to expose ourselves to so much hazard for this, were as great madness as to starve ourselves or fight desperately for food to be laid on our tombs after our death.—*Mackenzie.*

Common fame is the only liar that deserves to have some respect.—Though she tells many an untruth, she often hits right, and most especially when she speaks ill of men.—*Saville.*

Of all the possessions of this life fame is the noblest: when the body has sunk into the dust the great name still lives.—*Schiller.*

To get a name can happen but to few: it is one of the few things that cannot be bought.—It is the free gift of mankind, which must be deserved before it will be granted, and is at last unwillingly bestowed.—*Johnson.*

Time has a doomsday book, on whose pages he is continually recording illustrious names.—But as often as a new name is written there, an old one disappears.—Only a few stand in illuminated characters never to be effaced.—*Longfellow.*

Only the actions of the just smell sweet and blossom in the dust.—*Shirley.*

Men's evil manners live in brass; their virtues we write in water.—*Shakespeare.*

No true and permanent fame can be founded except in labors which promote the happiness of mankind.—*Charles Sumner.*

FAMILIARITY.—All objects lose by too familiar a view.—*Dryden.*

Make not thy friends too cheap to thee, nor thyself to thy friend.—*Fuller.*

Though familiarity may not breed contempt, it takes off the edge of admiration.—*Hazlitt.*

The confidant of my vices is my master, though he were my valet.—*Goethe.*

Vice is a monster of such frightful mien as to be hated, needs but to be seen; but seen too oft, familiar with her face, we first endure, then pity, then embrace.—*Pope.*

Be not too familiar with thy servants. —At first it may beget love, but in the end it will breed contempt.—*Fuller.*

Familiarities are the aphides that imperceptibly suck out the juices intended for the germ of love.—*Landor.*

When a man becomes familiar with his goddess, she quickly sinks into a woman.—*Addison.*

FAMILY.—The family was ordained of God that children might be trained up for himself; it was before the church, or rather the first form of the church on earth.

Civilization varies with the family, and the family with civilization.—Its highest and most complete realization is found where enlightened Christianity prevails; where woman is exalted to her true and lofty place as equal with the man; where husband and wife are one in honor, influence, and affection, and where children are a common bond of care and love.—This is the idea of a perfect family.—*W. Aikman.*

Happy are the families where the government of parents is the reign of affection, and obedience of the children the submission of love.

If I might control the literature of the household, I would guarantee the well-being of the church and state.—*Bacon.*

If God has taught us all truth in teaching us to love, then he has given us an interpretation of our whole duty to our households.—We are not born as the partridge in the wood, or the ostrich of the desert, to be scattered everywhere; but we are to be grouped together, and brooded by love, and reared day by day in that first of churches, the family.—*H. W. Beecher.*

As are families, so is society.—If well ordered, well instructed, and well governed, they are the springs from which go forth the streams of national greatness and prosperity—of civil order and public happiness.—*Thayer.*

The ties of family and of country were never intended to circumscribe the soul. —If allowed to become exclusive, engrossing, clannish, so as to shut out the general claims of the human race, the highest end of Providence is frustrated, and home, instead of being the nursery, becomes the grave of the heart.—*Channing.*

A happy family is but an earlier heaven.—*Bowring.*

A house without a roof would scarcely be a more different home, than a family unsheltered by God's friendship, and the sense of being always rested in His providential care and guidance.—*Horace Bushnell.*

"The last word" is the most dangerous of infernal machines, and the husband and wife should no more fight to get it than they would struggle for the possession of a lighted bombshell.—*Douglas Jerrold.*

"A family without government," says Matthew Henry, "is like a house without a roof, exposed to every wind that blows."—He might better have said, like a house in flames, a scene of confusion, and commonly too hot to live in.

Woman is the salvation or the destruction of the family.—She carries its destiny in the folds of her mantle.—*Amiel.*

FANATICISM.—Fanaticism is the child of false zeal and superstition, the father of intolerance and persecution.—*Fletcher.*

What is fanaticism to-day is the fashionable creed to-morrow, and trite as the multiplication table a week after.—*Wendell Phillips.*

Fanaticism is such an overwhelming impression of the ideas relating to the future world as disqualifies for the duties of this.—*Robert Hall.*

The downright fanatic is nearer to the heart of things than the cool and slippery disputant.—*E. H. Chapin.*

Fanaticism, the false fire of an overheated mind.—*Cowper.*

Everybody knows that fanaticism is religion caricatured, and yet, with many, contempt of fanaticism is regarded as a sign of hostility to religion.—*E. P. Whipple.*

The blind fanaticism of one foolish honest man may cause more evil than the united efforts of twenty rogues.—*Grimm.*

The weakness of human nature has always appeared in times of great revivals of religion, by a disposition to run into extremes, especially in these three things: enthusiasm, superstition, and intemperate zeal.—*Jonathan Edwards.*

Fanatic faith, once wedded fast to some dear falsehood, hugs it to the last.—*Moore.*

Of all things wisdom is the most terrified with epidemical fanaticism, because, of all enemies, it is that against which she is the least able to furnish any kind of resource.—*Burke.*

We often excuse our own want of philanthropy by giving the name of fanaticism to the more ardent zeal of others.—*Longfellow.*

FANCY.—Fancy rules over two thirds of the universe, the past and future, while reality is confined to the present.—*Richter.*

Fancy and humor, early and constantly indulged, may expect an old age overrun with follies.—*Watts.*

Most marvellous and enviable is that fecundity of fancy which can adorn whatever it touches, which can invest naked fact and dry reasoning with unlooked for beauty, make flowers bloom even on the brow of the precipice, and turn even the rock itself into moss and lichens.—This faculty is most important for the vivid and attractive exhibition of truth to the minds of men.—*Fuller.*

Fancy has an extensive influence in morals.—Some of the most powerful and dangerous feelings, as ambition and envy, derive their principal nourishment from a source so trivial.—Its effects on the common affairs of life is greater than might be supposed. — Naked reality would scarcely keep the world in motion.—*Clulow.*

Fancy, when once brought into religion, knows not where to stop,—it is like one of those fiends in old stories which any one could raise, but which, when raised, could never be kept within the magic circle.—*Whately.*

Every fancy that we would substitute for a reality, is, if we saw aright, and saw the whole, not only false, but every way less beautiful and excellent than that which we sacrifice to it.—*J. Sterling.*

FAREWELL.—In that fatal word,—howe'er we promise, hope, believe, there breathes despair.—*Byron.*

I never spoke that word " farewell," but with an utterance faint and broken; a heart-sick yearning for the time when it should never more be spoken.—*Caroline Bowles.*

That bitter word, which closed all earthly friendships, and finished every feast of love—farewell!—*Pollok.*

Pass-word of memory—of by-gone days—thou everlasting epitaph—is there a land in which thou hast no dwelling place?—There is, O God, a world where human lips may say " Farewell! " no more!

Like some low and mournful spell, we whisper that sad word, " farewell."—*P. Benjamin.*

FASHION.—(See "CUSTOM.")

It is the rule of rules, and the general law of all laws, that every person should observe the fashions of the place where he is.—*Montaigne.*

Fashion is the science of appearances, and it inspires one with the desire to seem rather than to be.—*E. H. Chapin.*

Every generation laughs at the old fashions, but follows religiously the new.—*Thoreau.*

Fashion is, for the most part, nothing but the ostentation of riches.—*Locke.*

Without depth of thought, or earnestness of feeling, or strength of purpose, living an unreal life, sacrificing substance to show, substituting the fictitious for the natural, mistaking a crowd for society, finding its chief pleasure in ridicule, and exhausting its ingenuity in expedients for killing time, fashion is among the last influences under which a human being who respects himself, or who comprehends the great end of life, would desire to be placed.—*Channing.*

A fop of fashion is the mercer's friend, the tailor's fool, and his own foe.—*Lavater.*

Change of fashions is the tax which industry imposes on the vanity of the rich.—*Chamfort.*

Fashion is gentility running away from vulgarity, and afraid of being overtaken by it.—It is a sign the two things are not far asunder.—*Hazlitt.*

Fashion is a word which knaves and fools may use to excuse their knavery and folly.—*Churchill.*

The mere leader of fashion has no genuine claim to supremacy; at least, no abiding assurance of it. He has embroidered his title upon his waistcoat, and carries his worth in his watch chain; and if he is allowed any real precedence for this, it is almost a moral swindle—a way of obtaining goods under false pretences.—*E. H. Chapin.*

Fashion is a tyrant from which nothing frees us.—We must suit ourselves to its fantastic tastes.—But being compelled to live under its foolish laws, the wise man is never the first to follow, nor the last to keep them.—*Pascal.*

Fashion seldom interferes with nature without diminishing her grace and efficiency.—*Tuckerman.*

Thus grows up fashion, an equivocal semblance; the most puissant, the most fantastic and frivolous, the most feared and followed, and which morals and violence assault in vain.—*Emerson.*

The fashion doth wear out more apparel than the man.—*Shakespeare.*

He alone is a man, who can resist the genius of the age, the tone of fashion, with vigorous simplicity and modest courage.—*Lavater.*

Avoid singularity.—There may often be less vanity in following the new modes, than in adhering to the old ones. —It is true that the foolish invent them, but the wise may conform to, instead of contradicting them.—*Joubert.*

Those who seem to lead the public taste, are, in general, merely outrunning it in the direction it is spontaneously pursuing.—*Macaulay.*

Fashion is only the attempt to realize art in living forms and social intercourse.—*O. W. Holmes.*

Fashion is the great governor of the world.—It presides not only in matters of dress and amusement, but in law, physic, politics, religion, and all other things of the gravest kind.—Indeed, the wisest men would be puzzled to give any better reason why particular forms in all these have been at certain times universally received, and at other times universally rejected, than that they were in, or out of fashion.—*Fielding.*

It is as absurd to suppose that everything fashionable is bad, as it would be to suppose that everything unfashionable is good.—*Momerie.*

To be happy is of far less consequence to the worshippers of fashion than to appear so; even pleasure itself they sacrifice to parade, and enjoyment to ostentation.—*Colton.*

Fashion must be forever new, or she becomes insipid.—*J. R. Lowell.*

Cast an eye on the gay and fashionable world, and what see we for the most part, but a set of querulous, emaciated, fluttering fantastical beings, worn out in the keen pursuit of pleasure—creatures that know, own, condemn, deplore, and yet pursue their own infelicity? The decayed monuments of error! The thin remains of what is called delight!—*Young.*

We should conform to the manners of the greater number, and so behave as not to draw attention to ourselves.—Excess either way shocks, and every wise man should attend to this in his dress as well as language; never be affected in anything, but follow, without being in too great haste, the changes of fashion.—*Moliere.*

Be not too early in the fashion, nor too long out of it; nor at any time in the extremes of it.—*Lavater.*

Custom is the law of one description of fools, and fashion of another; but the two parties often clash, for precedent is the legislator of the first, and novelty of the last!—*Colton.*

FASTIDIOUSNESS.—Fastidiousness is only another form of egotism; and all men who know not where to look for truth, save in the narrow well of self, will find their own image at the bottom, and mistake it for what they are seeking. —*J. R. Lowell.*

Fastidiousness is the envelope of indelicacy.—*Haliburton.*

Like other spurious things, fastidiousness is often inconsistent with itself, the coarsest things are done, and the cruelest things said by the most fastidious people.—*Mrs. Kirkland.*

FATE. — There is a divinity that shapes our ends, rough-hew them as we will.—*Shakespeare.*

Fate is not the ruler, but the servant of Providence.—*Bulwer.*

What must be shall be; and that which is a necessity to him that struggles, is little more than choice to him that is willing.—*Seneca.*

All things are by fate, but poor blind man sees but a part of the chain, the nearest link, his eyes not reaching to that equal beam which poises all above. —*Dryden.*

Whatever may happen to thee, it was prepared for thee from all eternity; and the implication of causes was, from eternity, spinning the thread of thy being, and of that which is incident to it.—*Marcus Antoninus.*

God overrules all mutinous accidents, brings them under his laws of fate, and makes them all serviceable to his purpose.—*Marcus Antoninus.*

"Whosoever quarrels with his fate does not understand it," says Bettine; and among all her sayings she spoke none wiser.—*Mrs. L. M. Child.*

Heaven from all creatures hides the book of fate.—*Shakespeare.*

If you believe in fate, believe in it, at least, for your good.—*Emerson.*

Fate is the friend of the good, the guide of the wise, the tyrant of the foolish, the enemy of the bad.—*W. R. Alger.*

A strict belief in fate is the worst kind of slavery; on the other hand there is comfort in the thought that God will be moved by our prayers.—*Epicurus.*

Thought presides over all.—Fate, that dead phantom, shall vanish from action, and providence alone be visible in heaven and on earth.—*Bulwer.*

All things are ordered by God, but his providence takes in our free agency, as well as his own sovereignty.—*Tryon Edwards.*

All is created and goes according to order, yet o'er our lifetime rules an uncertain fate.—*Goethe.*

Our wills and fates do so contrary run, that our devices still are overthrown; our thoughts are ours, their ends none of our own.—*Shakespeare.*

Fate! there is no fate.—Between the thought and the success God is the only agent.—*Bulwer.*

FAULTS.—(See "IMPERFECTIONS.")

He will be immortal who liveth till he be stoned by one without fault.—*Fuller.*

If the best man's faults were written on his forehead, he would draw his hat over his eyes.—*Gray.*

We should correct our own faults by seeing how uncomely they appear in others.—*Beaumont.*

This I always religiously observed, as a rule, never to chide my husband before company nor to prattle abroad of miscarriages at home. What passes between two people is much easier made up than when once it has taken air.

We confess small faults, in order to insinuate that we have no great ones.—*Rochefoucauld.*

You will find it less easy to uproot faults, than to choke them by gaining virtues.—*Ruskin.*

No one sees the wallet on his own back, though every one carries two packs, one before, stuffed with the faults of his neighbors; the other behind, filled with his own.—*Old Proverb.*

To reprove small faults with undue vehemence, is as absurd as if a man should take a great hammer to kill a fly on his friend's forehead.—*Anon.*

People are commonly so employed in pointing out faults in those before them, as to forget that some behind may at the same time be descanting on their own.—*Dilwyn.*

It is not so much the being exempt from faults, as having overcome them, that is an advantage to us; it being with the follies of the mind as with the weeds of a field, which if destroyed and consumed upon the place of their birth, enrich and improve it more than if none had ever sprung there.—*Pope.*

If thou wouldst bear thy neighbor's faults, cast thine eyes upon thine own. —*Molinos.*

He who exhibits no faults is a fool or a hypocrite whom we should distrust.—*Joubert.*

We easily forget our faults when they are known only to ourselves.—*Rochefoucauld.*

Observe your enemies for they first find out your faults.—*Antisthenes.*

If we were faultless we should not be so much annoyed by the defects of those with whom we associate.—*Fenelon.*

Every one is eagle-eyed to see another's faults and deformity.—*Dryden.*

To acknowledge our faults when we are blamed, is modesty; to discover them to one's friends, in ingenuousness, is confidence; but to proclaim them to the world, if one does not take care, is pride. —*Confucius.*

Endeavor to be always patient of the faults and imperfections of others; for thou hast many faults and imperfections of thine own that require forbearance. If thou art not able to make thyself that which thou wishest, how canst thou expect to mold another in conformity to thy will?—*Thomas à Kempis.*

The wise man has his foibles as well as the fool.—Those of the one are known to himself, and concealed from the world; while those of the other are known to the world, and concealed from himself.—*J. Mason.*

Think of your own faults the first part of the night when you are awake, and of the faults of others the latter part of the night when you are asleep.—*Chinese Proverb.*

Men are almost always cruel on their neighbors' faults, and make the overthrow of others the badge of their own ill-masked virtue.—*Sir P. Sidney.*

Faults of the head are punished in this world, those of the heart in another; but as most of our vices are compound, so also is their punishment.—*Colton.*

The greatest of faults is to be conscious of none.—*Carlyle.*

If you are pleased at finding faults, you are displeased at finding perfections. —*Lavater.*

Bad men excuse their faults; good men will leave them.—*Ben Jonson.*

The fault-finder—it is his nature's plague to spy into abuses; and oft his jealousy shapes faults that are not.—*Shakespeare.*

Ten thousand of the greatest faults in our neighbors are of less consequence to us than one of the smallest in ourselves. —*Whately.*

The lowest people are generally the first to find fault with show or equipage; especially that of a person lately emerged from his obscurity. They never once consider that he is breaking the ice for themselves.—*Shenstone.*

To find fault is easy; to do better may be difficult.—*Plutarch.*

FEAR. — Fear is the tax that conscience pays to guilt.—*Sewell.*

Fear is implanted in us as a preservative from evil; but its duty, like that of other passions, is not to overbear reason, but to assist it.—It should not be suffered to tyrannize in the imagination, to raise phantoms of horror, or to beset life with supernumerary distresses.— *Johnson.*

Present fears are less than horrible imaginings.—*Shakespeare.*

We often pretend to fear what we really despise, and more often to despise what we really fear.—*Colton.*

Fear guides more to duty than gratitude.—For one man who is virtuous from the love of virtue, or from the obligation he thinks he lies under to the giver of all, there are thousands who are good only from their apprehension of punishment.—*Goldsmith.*

In time we hate that which we often fear.—*Shakespeare.*

God planted fear in the soul as truly as he planted hope or courage.—It is a kind of bell or gong which rings the mind into quick life and avoidance on the approach of danger.—It is the soul's signal for rallying.—*H. W. Beecher.*

Fear on guilt attends, and deeds of darkness; the virtuous breast ne'er knows it.—*Havard.*

Fear nothing but what thine industry may prevent, and be confident of nothing but what fortune cannot defeat.—It is no less folly to fear what cannot be avoided than to be secure when there is a possibility of preventing.—*Quarles.*

Fear is the mother of foresight.—*H. Taylor.*

Nothing is so rash as fear; its counsels very rarely put off, whilst they are always sure to aggravate the evils from which it would fly—*Burke.*

Fear is more painful to cowardice than death to true courage.—*Sir P. Sidney.*

All fear is painful, and when it conduces not to safety, is painful without use.—Every consideration, therefore, by which groundless terrors may be removed, adds something to human happiness.—*Johnson.*

Good men have the fewest fears.—He who fears to do wrong has but one great fear; he has a thousand who has overcome it.—*Bovee.*

He who fears being conquered is sure of defeat.—*Napoleon.*

Early and provident fear is the mother of safety.—*Burke.*

Fear manifested invites danger; concealed cowards insult known ones.—*Chesterfield.*

It is only the fear of God that can deliver us from the fear of man.—*Witherspoon.*

There is great beauty in going through life without anxiety or fear.—Half our fears are baseless, and the other half discreditable.—*Bovee.*

There is a virtuous fear which is the effect of faith, and a vicious fear which is the product of doubt and distrust.— The former leads to hope as relying on God, in whom we believe; the latter inclines to despair, as not relying upon God, in whom we do not believe.—Persons of the one character fear to lose God; those of the other character fear to find him.—*Pascal.*

In morals, what begins in fear usually ends in wickedness; in religion, what begins in fear usually ends in fanaticism. Fear, either as a principle or a motive, is the beginning of all evil.—*Mrs. Jameson.*

Fear is two-fold; a fear of solicitous anxiety, such as makes us let go our confidence in God's providence, and a fear of prudential caution, whereby, from a due estimate of approaching evil, we endeavor our own security.—The former is wrong and forbidden; the latter not only lawful, but laudable.—*South.*

Desponding fear, of feeble fancies full, weak and unmanly, loosens every power. —*Thomson.*

No one loves the man whom he fears. —*Aristotle.*

FEASTING.—(See "HOSPITALITY.")

It is not the quantity of the meat, but the cheerfulness of the guests, which makes the feast.—*Clarendon.*

He who feasts every day, feasts no day.—*C. Simmons.*

The turnpike road to people's hearts, I find, lies through their mouths, or I mistake mankind.—*Peter Pindar.*

To pamper the body is a miserable expression of kindness and courtesy; the most sumptuous repast is "the feast of reason and the flow of soul"—an intellectual and moral treat.—*C. Simmons.*

He that feasts his body with banquets and delicate fare, and starves his soul for want of spiritual food, is like him that feasts his slave and starves his wife.

When I behold a fashionable table set out in all its magnificence, I fancy that I see gouts and dropsies, fevers and lethargies, with other innumerable distempers, lying in ambuscade among the dishes. Nature delights in the most plain and simple diet. Every animal, but man, keeps to one dish. Herbs are the food of this species, fish of that, and flesh of a third. Man falls upon everything that comes in his way; not the smallest fruit or excrescence of the earth, scarce a berry or a mushroom can escape him.—*Addison.*

FEELINGS.—(See "SENSIBILITY.")

Our feelings were given us to excite to action, and when they end in themselves, they are cherished to no good purpose.—*Sandford.*

Feeling in the young precedes philosophy, and often acts with a better and more certain aim.—*Carleton.*

Strong feelings do not necessarily make a strong character. The strength of a man is to be measured by the power of the feelings he subdues, not by the power of those which subdue him.

Cultivate consideration for the feelings of other people if you would not have your own injured. Those who complain most of ill-usage are those who abuse others the oftenest.

The last, best fruit which comes to late perfection, even in the kindliest soul, is, tenderness toward the hard, forbearance toward the unforbearing, warmth of heart toward the cold, philanthropy toward the misanthropic.—*Richter.*

The heart of man is older than his head. The first-born is sensitive, but blind—his younger brother has a cold, but all-comprehensive glance. The blind must consent to be led by the clear-sighted, if he would avoid falling.— *Ziegler.*

Some people carry their hearts in their heads; very many carry their heads in their hearts. The difficulty is to keep them apart, and yet both actively working together.

A word—a look, which at one time would make no impression—at another time wounds the heart; and like a shaft flying with the wind, pierces deep, which, with its own natural force, would scarce

have reached the object aimed at.—
Sterne.

Every human feeling is greater and
larger than its exciting cause—a proof, I
think, that man is designed for a higher
state of existence.—*Coleridge.*

The heart that is soonest awake to the
flowers is always the first to be touched
by the thorns.—*Moore.*

Feelings come and go, like light troops
following the victory of the present; but
principles, like troops of the line, are undisturbed and stand fast.—*Richter.*

Feeling does not become stronger in
the religious life by waiting, but by using it.—*H. W. Beecher.*

He who looks upon Christ through
frames and feelings is like one who sees
the sun on the water, and so sees it
quivering and moving as the water
moves.—But he that looks upon him in
the glass of his word by faith, sees him
forever the same.—*Nottidge.*

Thought is deeper than all speech;
feeling deeper than all thought; soul to
souls can never teach what unto themselves was taught.—*Cranch.*

Feeling hearts, touch them but rightly,
pour a thousand melodies unheard before.—*Rogers.*

Our higher feelings move our animal
nature; and our animal nature, irritated,
may call back a semblance of those emotions; but the whole difference between
nobleness and baseness lies in the question, whether the feeling begins from below or above.—*F. W. Robertson.*

In religion faith does not spring out of
feeling, but feeling out of faith.—The
less we feel the more we should trust.—
We cannot feel right till we have believed.—*Bonar.*

The heart has often been compared to
the needle of the compass for its constancy; has it ever been so for its variations?—Yet were any man to keep minutes of his feelings from youth to age,
what a table of variations would they
present—how numerous, how diverse,
how strange!—*Hare.*

FICKLENESS. — Fickleness has its
rise in our experience of the fallacious-
ness of present pleasure, and in our ignorance of the vanity of that which is
absent.—*Pascal.*

The uncertain glory of an April day.
—*Shakespeare.*

They are the weakest-minded and the
hardest-hearted men that most love
change.—*Ruskin.*

Everything by starts, and nothing
long.—*Dryden.*

He wears his faith but as the fashion
of his hat; it ever changes with the next
block.—*Shakespeare.*

A fickle memory is bad; a fickle course
of conduct is worse; but a fickle heart
and purposes, worst of all.—*C. Simmons.*

FICTION.—Man is a poetical animal
and delights in fiction.—*Hazlitt.*

Fiction allures to the severe task by
a gayer preface.—Embellished truths are
the illuminated alphabet of larger children.—*Willmott.*

I have often maintained that fiction
may be much more instructive than real
history.—*John Foster.*

Every fiction that has ever laid strong
hold on human belief is the mistaken
image of some great truth.—*Martineau.*

Fiction is no longer a mere amusement; but transcendent genius, accom-
modating itself to the character of the
age, has seized upon this province of
literature, and turned fiction from a toy
into a mighty engine.—*Channing.*

The most influential books and the
truest in their influence, are works of
fiction.—They repeat, rearrange, and
clarify the lessons of life, disengage us
from ourselves, constrain us to the acquaintance of others, and show us the
web of experience, but with a single
change. — That monstrous, consuming
ego of ours struck out.—*R. L. Stevenson.*

The best histories may sometimes be
those in which a little of the exaggeration of fictitious narrative is judiciously
employed.—Something is lost in accuracy, but much is gained in effect.—The
fainter lines are neglected, but the great
characteristic features are imprinted on
the mind forever.—*Macaulay.*

Many works of fiction may be read
with safety; some even with profit; but
the constant familiarity, even with such as
are not exceptionable in themselves, relaxes the mind, which needs hardening;
dissolves the heart, which wants fortify-
ing; stirs the imagination, which wants
quieting; irritates the passions, which

want calming; and, above all, disinclines and disqualifies for active virtues and for spiritual exercises. The habitual indulgence in such reading, is a silent mining mischief. Though there is no act, and no moment, in which any open assault on the mind is made, yet the constant habit performs the work of a mental atrophy—it produces all the symptoms of decay; and the danger is not less for being more gradual, and therefore less suspected.—*H. More.*

Fiction is not falsehood, as some seem to think.—It is rather the fanciful and dramatic grouping of real traits around imaginary scenes or characters.—It may give false views of men or things, or it may, in the hands of a master, more truthfully portray life than sober history itself.—*Tryon Edwards.*

Those who delight in the study of human nature, may improve in the knowledge of it, and in the profitable application of it by the perusal of the best selected fictions.—*Whately.*

FIDELITY.—Nothing is more noble, nothing more venerable than fidelity.—Faithfulness and truth are the most sacred excellences and endowments of the human mind.—*Cicero.*

Fidelity is the sister of justice.—*Horace.*

His words are bonds; his oaths are oracles; his heart is as far from fraud as heaven from earth.—*Shakespeare.*

It goes far toward making a man faithful to let him understand that you think him so; and he that does but suspect I will deceive him, gives me a sort of right to do it.—*Seneca.*

Trust reposed in noble natures obliges them the more.—*Dryden.*

The way to fill a large sphere is to glorify a small one. There is no large sphere; you are your sphere; the man regenerate and consecrated is the lordliest thing on earth, because he makes himself so.—*Edward Braislin.*

I am constant as the Northern star, of whose true-fixed and resting quality there is no fellow in the firmament.—*Shakespeare.*

Fidelity is seven-tenths of business success.—*Parton.*

Faithful found among the faithless, his loyalty he kept, his love, his zeal,

nor number, nor example with him wrought to swerve from truth, or change his constant mind.—*Milton.*

O Heaven! were man but constant, he were perfect; that one error fills him with faults.—*Shakespeare.*

To God, thy country, and thy friend be true, then thou'lt ne'er be false to any one.—*Vaughan.*

FIRMNESS.—Firmness of purpose is one of the most necessary sinews of character, and one of the best instruments of success.—Without it genius wastes its efforts in a maze of inconsistencies.—*Chesterfield.*

When firmness is sufficient, rashness is unnecessary.—*Napoleon.*

The firm, without pliancy, and the pliant, without firmness, resemble vessels without water, and water without vessels.—*Lavater.*

The greatest firmness is the greatest mercy.—*Longfellow.*

I know no real worth but that tranquil firmness which meets dangers by duty, and braves them without rashness.—*Stanislaus.*

Steadfastness is a noble quality, but, unguided by knowledge or humility, it becomes rashness, or obstinacy.—*Swartz.*

Firmness, both in suffering and exertion, is a character which I would wish to possess.—I have always despised the whining yelp of complaint; and the cowardly feeble resolve.—*Burns.*

It is only persons of firmness that can have real gentleness.—Those who appear gentle are, in general, only a weak character, which easily changes into asperity.—*Rochefoucauld.*

That profound firmness which enables a man to regard difficulties but as evils to be surmounted, no matter what shape they may assume.—*Cockton.*

The purpose firm is equal to the deed.—*Young.*

FLATTERY.—Men find it more easy to flatter than to praise.—*Richter.*

Of all wild beasts preserve me from a tyrant; and of all tame, from a flatterer.—*Ben Jonson.*

The art of flatterers is to take advantage of the foibles of the great, to foster their errors, and never to give advice which may annoy.—*Molière.*

If we would not flatter ourselves, the flattery of others could not harm us.—*Rochefoucauld.*

Flatterers are the worst kind of traitors for they will strengthen thy imperfections, encourage thee in all evils, correct thee in nothing, but so shadow and paint all thy vices and follies as thou shalt never, by their will, discern good from evil, or vice from virtue.—*Sir W. Raleigh.*

Flattery corrupts both the receiver and the giver; and adulation is not of more service to the people than to kings.—*Burke.*

There is an oblique way of reproof, which takes off the sharpness of it, and an address in flattery, which makes it agreeable, though never so gross; but of all flatterers, the most skilful is he who can do what you like, without saying anything which argues he does it for your sake.—*Pope.*

He that is much flattered soon learns to flatter himself.—We are commonly taught our duty by fear or shame, but how can they act upon a man who hears nothing but his own praises?—*Johnson.*

Deference before company is the genteelest kind of flattery. The flattery of epistles affects one less, as they cannot be shown without an appearance of vanity. Flattery of the verbal kind is gross. In short, applause is of too coarse a nature to be swallowed in the gross, though the extract of tincture be ever so agreeable.—*Shenstone.*

To be flattered is grateful, even when we know that our praises are not believed by those who pronounce them; for they prove at least our power, and show that our favor is valued, since it is purchased by the meanness of falsehood.—*Johnson.*

Flattery is never so agreeable as to our blind side; commend a fool for his wit, or a knave for his honesty, and they will receive you into their bosom.—*Fielding.*

Flattery, though a base coin, is the necessary pocket-money at court; where, by custom and consent, it has obtained such a currency, that it is no longer a fraudulent, but a legal payment.—*Chesterfield.*

Know thyself, thine evil as well as thy good, and flattery shall not harm thee; her speech shall be a warning, a humbling, and a guide; for wherein thou lackest most, there chiefly will thy sycophant commend thee.—*Tupper.*

No man flatters the woman he truly loves.—*Tuckerman.*

Adulation is the death of virtue.—Who flatters, is, of all mankind, the lowest, save he who courts the flattery.—*H. More.*

You play the spaniel, and think with wagging of your tongue to win me.—*Shakespeare.*

Nothing is so great an instance of ill-manners as flattery. If you flatter all the company, you please none; if you flatter only one or two, you affront the rest.—*Swift.*

Flattery is a base coin which gains currency only from our vanity.—*Rochefoucauld.*

Imitation is the sincerest flattery.—*Cotton.*

It is better to fall among crows than flatterers; for those devour only the dead—these the living.—*Antisthenes.*

We sometimes think we hate flattery, when we only hate the manner in which we have been flattered.—*Rochefoucauld.*

Some there are who profess to despise all flattery, but even these are, nevertheless, to be flattered, by being told that they do despise it.—*Colton.*

The rich man despises those who flatter him too much, and hates those who do not flatter him at all.—*Talleyrand.*

A death-bed flattery is the worst of treacheries. Ceremonies of mode and compliment are mightily out of season when life and salvation come to be at stake.—*L'Estrange.*

There is scarcely any man, how much soever he may despise the character of a flatterer, but will condescend in the meanest manner to flatter himself.—*Fielding.*

Allow no man to be so free with you as to praise you to your face.—Your vanity, by this means, will want its food, but at the same time your passion for esteem will be more fully gratified; men will praise you in their actions; where you now receive one compliment, you will then receive twenty civilities.—*Steele.*

The lie that flatters I abhor the most.
—*Cowper.*

There is no detraction worse than to over-praise a man; for if his worth prove short of what report doth speak of him, his own actions are ever giving the lie to his honor.—*Feltham.*

There is no tongue that flatters like a lover's; and yet in the exaggeration of his feelings, flattery seems to him commonplace.—*Bulwer.*

There is no flattery so adroit or effectual as that of implicit assent.—*Hazlitt.*

Flatterers are the worst kind of enemies.—*Tacitus.*

The most skilful flattery is to let a person talk on, and be a listener.—*Addison.*

The most subtle flattery a woman can receive is that conveyed by actions, not by words.—*Mad. Neckar.*

Self-love is the greatest of flatterers.—*Rochefoucauld.*

A fool flatters himself; the wise man flatters the fool.—*Bulwer.*

It is a dangerous crisis when a proud heart meets with flattering lips.—*Flavel.*

When flatterers meet the devil goes to dinner.—*De Foe.*

We love flattery, even when we see through it, and are not deceived by it, for it shows that we are of importance enough to be courted.—*Emerson.*

Adroit observers will find that some who affect to dislike flattery may yet be flattered indirectly by a well-seasoned abuse and ridicule of their rivals.—*Colton.*

It has well been said that the arch-flatterer, with whom all petty flatterers have intelligence, is a man's self.—*Bacon.*

Flattery is often a traffic of mutual meanness, where, although both parties intend deception, neither are deceived.—*Colton.*

The only benefit of flattery is that by hearing what we are not, we may be instructed what we ought to be.—*Swift.*

'Tis an old maxim in the schools, that flattery is the food of fools.—Yet now and then your men of wit will condescend to take a bit.—*Swift.*

FLOWERS. — Flowers are God's thoughts of beauty taking form to gladden mortal gaze.

Lovely flowers are the smiles of God's goodness.—*Wilberforce.*

Flowers are the sweetest things that God ever made and forgot to put a soul into.—*H. W. Beecher.*

What a desolate place would be a world without flowers?—It would be a face without a smile; a feast without a welcome.—Are not flowers the stars of the earth?—And are not our stars the flowers of heaven?—*Mrs. Balfour.*

To me the meanest flower that blows can give thoughts that do often lie too deep for tears.—*Wordsworth.*

What a pity flowers can utter no sound?—A singing rose, a whispering violet, a murmuring honeysuckle,—oh, what a rare and exquisite miracle would these be!—*H. W. Beecher.*

The flowers are nature's jewels, with whose wealth she decks her summer beauty.—*Croly.*

The instinctive and universal taste of mankind selects flowers for the expression of its finest sympathies, their beauty and fleetingness serving to make them the most fitting symbols of those delicate sentiments for which language seems almost too gross a medium.—*Hillard.*

Flowers are love's truest language.—*P. Benjamin.*

To analyze the charms of flowers is like dissecting music; it is one of those things which it is far better to enjoy, than to attempt fully to understand.—*Tuckerman.*

In eastern lands they talk in flowers, and tell in a garland their loves and cares.—*Percival.*

How the universal heart of man blesses flowers!—They are wreathed round the cradle, the marriage altar, and the tomb.—They should deck the brow of the youthful bride, for they are in themselves a lovely type of marriage.—They should twine round the tomb, for their perpetually renewed beauty is a symbol of the resurrection.—They should festoon the altar, for their fragrance and beauty ascend in perpetual worship before the most high.—*Mrs. L. M. Child.*

It is with flowers as with moral qualities; the bright are sometimes poisonous, but I believe never the sweet.—*Hare.*

Your voiceless lips, O, flowers, are

living preachers—each cup a pulpit, and each leaf a book.—*Horace Smith.*

Stars of earth, these golden flowers; emblems of our own great resurrection; emblems of the bright and better land. —*Longfellow.*

Every rose is an autograph from the hand of God on his world about us.—He has inscribed his thoughts in these marvellous hieroglyphics which sense and science have, these many thousand years, been seeking to understand.—*Theodore Parker.*

A passion for flowers, is, I think, the only one which long sickness leaves untouched with its chilling influence.—*Mrs. Hemans.*

To cultivate a garden is to walk with God.—*Bovee.*

There is not the least flower but seems to hold up its head and to look pleasantly, in the secret sense of the goodness of its heavenly Maker.—*South.*

Flowers are God's thoughts of beauty, taking form to gladden mortal gaze;—bright gems of earth, in which, perchance, we see what Eden was—what Paradise may be!

FOLLY.—Folly consists in drawing of false conclusions from just principles, by which it is distinguished from madness, which draws just conclusions from false principles.—*Locke.*

There is a foolish corner even in the brain of the sage.—*Aristotle.*

This peculiar ill property has folly, that it enlarges men's desires while it lessens their capacities.—*South.*

Men of all ages have the same inclinations over which reason exercises no control. Thus wherever men are found there are follies, aye, and the same follies.—*Fontenelle.*

The wise man has his follies no less than the fool; but herein lies the difference—the follies of the fool are known to the world, but are hidden from himself; the follies of the wise man are known to himself, but hidden from the world.—*Colton.*

Want and sorrow are the wages that folly earns for itself, and they are generally paid.—*Schubart.*

He who lives without folly is not so wise as he imagines.—*Rochefoucauld.*

FOOLS.—The world is full of fools; and he who would not wish to see one, must not only shut himself up alone, but must also break his looking-glass.—*Boileau.*

What the fool does in the end, the wise man does in the beginning.—*Spanish maxim.*

A fool in a high station is like a man on the top of a high mountain—everything appears small to him and he appears small to everybody.

In all companies there are more fools than wise men, and the greater part always gets the better of the wiser.—*Rabelais.*

If any young man expects without faith, without thought, without study, without patient, persevering labor, in the midst of and in spite of discouragement, to attain anything in this world that is worth attaining, he will simply wake up, by-and-by, and find that he has been playing the part of a fool.—*M. J. Savage.*

People have no right to make fools of themselves, unless they have no relations to blush for them.—*Haliburton.*

A fool may be known by six things: anger, without cause; speech, without profit; change, without progress; inquiry, without object; putting trust in a stranger, and mistaking foes for friends. —*Arabian Proverb.*

There are many more fools in the world than there are knaves, otherwise the knaves could not exist.—*Bulwer.*

Nothing is more intolerable than a prosperous fool; and hence we see men who, at one time, were affable and agreeable, completely changed by prosperity, despising old friends and clinging to new.—*Cicero.*

A fool always finds some greater fool to admire him.—*Boileau.*

There is no greater fool than he that says, "There is no God," unless it be the one who says he does not know whether there is one or not.—*Bismarck.*

A fool at forty is a fool indeed.—*Young.*

None but a fool is always right.—*Hare.*

To be a man's own fool is bad enough; but the vain man is everybody's.—*Penn.*

The greatest of fools is he who imposes on himself, and thinks certainly he knows that which he has least studied, and of which he is most profoundly ignorant.—*Shaftesbury.*

A fool may have his coat embroidered with gold, but it is a fool's coat still.—*Rivarol.*

There are more fools than wise men; and even in wise men, more folly than wisdom.—*Chamfort.*

Men may live fools, but fools they cannot die.—*Young.*

A man may be as much a fool from the want of sensibility, as from the want of sense.—*Mrs. Jameson.*

A fool can no more see his own folly than he can see his ears.—*Thackeray.*

Young men think old men fools, and old men know young men to be so.—*Metcalf.*

Where lives the man that has not tried how mirth can into folly glide, and folly into sin!—*Walter Scott.*

Fools are often united in the strictest intimacies, as the lighter kinds of woods are the most closely glued together.—*Shenstone.*

Fools with bookish knowledge, are children with edged weapons; they hurt themselves, and put others in pain.—The half-learned is more dangerous than the simpleton.—*Zimmerman.*

To pursue trifles is the lot of humanity; and whether we bustle in a pantomime, or strut at a coronation, or shout at a bonfire, or harangue in a senate-house; whatever object we follow, it will at last conduct us to futility and disappointment. The wise bustle and laugh as they walk in the pageant, but fools bustle and are important; and this probably, is all the difference between them.—*Goldsmith.*

I am always afraid of a fool; one cannot be sure he is not a knave.—*Hazlitt.*

FOPPERY.—(See "COXCOMB.")

Foppery is the egotism of clothes.—*Victor Hugo.*

Foppery is never cured; it is of the bad stamina of the mind, which, like those of the body, are never rectified.—Once a coxcomb, always a coxcomb.—*Johnson.*

The soul of this man is in his clothes.—*Shakespeare.*

Fops take a world of pains, to prove that bodies can exist without brains; the former so fantastically drest, that the latter's absence may be safely guessed.—*Churchill.*

Puppets, who, though on idiotism's dark brink, because they've heads, dare fancy they can think!—*Wolcott.*

A shallow brain, behind a serious mask; an oracle within an empty cask—the solemn fop!—*Cowper.*

FORBEARANCE.—If thou would'st be borne with, then bear with others.—*Fuller.*

The kindest and the happiest pair, will find occasion to forbear; find something every day they live, to pity, and perhaps forgive.—*Cowper.*

Cultivate forbearance till your heart yields a fine crop of it. Pray for a short memory as to all unkindnesses.—*Spurgeon.*

It is a noble and great thing to cover the blemishes and excuse the failings of a friend; to draw a curtain before his stains, and to display his perfection; to bury his weaknesses in silence, but to proclaim his virtues on the house-top.—*South.*

Use every man after his deserts, and who shall escape whipping?—*Shakespeare.*

To bear injuries, or annoying and vexatious events, meekly, patiently, prayerfully, and with self-control, is more than taking a city.—*C. Simmons.*

There is a limit at which forbearance ceases to be a virtue.—*Burke.*

FORCE.—Who overcomes by force, hath overcome but half his foe.—*Milton.*

Force rules the world—not opinion; but opinion which makes use of force.—*Pascal.*

FOREBODING.—A heavy summons lies like lead upon me.—*Shakespeare.*

Half our forebodings of our neighbors, are but our wishes, which we are ashamed to utter in any other form.—*L. E. Landon.*

FORETHOUGHT. — To fear the worst, oft cures the worst.—*Shakespeare.*

To have too much forethought is the part of a wretch; to have too little is the part of a fool.—*Cecil.*

As a man without forethought scarcel**y**

deserves the name of man, so forethought without reflection is but a phrase for the instinct of the beast.—*Coleridge.*

It is only the surprise and newness of the thing which makes terrible that misfortune, which by premeditation might be made easy to us; for what some people make light by sufferance, others do by foresight.—*Seneca.*

Happy those who knowing they are subject to uncertain changes, are prepared and armed for either fortune; a rare principle, and with much labor learned in wisdom's school.—*Massinger.*

He that foretells his own calamity, and makes events before they come, doth twice endure the pains of evil destiny.—*Davenant.*

Human foresight often leaves its proudest possessor only a choice of evils.—*Colton.*

If a man take no thought about what is distant, he will find sorrow near at hand.—*Confucius.*

In life, as in chess, forethought wins.—*Buxton.*

Whatever is foretold by God will be done by man; but nothing will be done by man because it is foretold by God.—*Wordsworth.*

Whoever fails to turn aside the ills of life by prudent forethought, must submit to the course of destiny.—*Schiller.*

Accustom yourself to submit on every occasion to a small present evil, to obtain a greater distant good. This will give decision, tone, and energy to the mind, which, thus disciplined, will often reap victory from defeat, and honor from repulse.—*Colton.*

Few things are brought to a successful issue by impetuous desire, but most by calm and prudent forethought.—*Thucydides.*

FORGETFULNESS. — Though the past haunt me as a spirit, I do not ask to forget.—*Mrs. Hemans.*

There is a noble forgetfulness—that which does not remember injuries.—*C. Simmons.*

When out of sight, quickly also out of mind.—*Thos. à Kempis.*

FORGIVENESS.—(See "PARDON.")

To err is human; to forgive, divine.—*Pope.*

His heart was as great as the world, but there was no room in it to hold the memory of a wrong.—*Emerson.*

He that cannot forgive others, breaks the bridge over which he himself must pass if he would ever reach heaven; for every one has need to be forgiven.—*Herbert.*

Said General Oglethorpe to Wesley, "I never forgive." "Then I hope, sir," said Wesley, "you never sin."

We hand folks over to God's mercy, and show none ourselves.—*George Eliot.*

Forgiveness is the most necessary and proper work of every man; for, though, when I do not a just thing, or a charitable, or a wise, another man may do it for me, yet no man can forgive my enemy but myself.—*Lord Herbert.*

A brave man thinks no one his superior who does him an injury; for he has it then in his power to make himself superior to the other by forgiving it.—*Pope.*

Life that ever needs forgiveness has for its first duty to forgive.—*Bulwer.*

A more glorious victory cannot be gained over another man, than this, that when the injury began on his part, the kindness should begin on ours.—*Tillotson.*

It has been a maxim with me to admit of easy reconciliation with a person whose offence proceeded from no depravity of heart; but where I was convinced it did so, to forego, for my own sake, all opportunities of revenge. I have derived no small share of happiness from this principle.—*Shenstone.*

The heart has always the pardoning power.—*Mad. Swetchine.*

A wise man will make haste to forgive, because he knows the full value of time and will not suffer it to pass away in unnecessary pain.—*Rambler.*

It is hard for a haughty man ever to forgive one that has caught him in a fault, and whom he knows has reason to complain of him: his resentment never subsides till he has regained the advantage he has lost, and found means to make the other do him equal wrong.—*Bruyère.*

Never does the human soul appear so strong and noble as when it foregoes re-

venge, and dares to forgive an injury.—
E. H. Chapin.

It is more easy to forgive the weak who have injured us, than the powerful whom we have injured. That conduct will be continued by our fears which commenced in our resentment. He that has gone so far as to cut the claws of the lion will not feel himself quite secure until he has also drawn his teeth.—
Colton.

Little, vicious minds abound with anger and revenge, and are incapable of feeling the pleasure of forgiving their enemies.—*Chesterfield.*

It is easier for the generous to forgive, than for the offender to ask forgiveness.
—*Thomson.*

They never pardon who commit the wrong.—*Dryden.*

The sun should not set on our anger; neither should it rise on our confidence.
—We should forgive freely, but forget rarely.—I will not be revenged; this I owe to my enemy.—I will remember; this I owe to myself.—*Colton.*

To be able to bear provocation is an argument of great reason, and to forgive it of a great mind.—*Tillotson.*

The narrow soul knows not the god-like glory of forgiving.—*Rowe.*

Only the brave know how to forgive; it is the most refined and generous pitch of virtue human nature can arrive at.—
Sterne.

May I tell you why it seems to me a good thing for us to remember wrong that has been done us? That we may forgive it.—*Dickens.*

We pardon as long as we love.—*Roche-foucauld.*

We forgive too little; forget too much.
—*Mad. Swetchine.*

Humanity is never so beautiful as when praying for forgiveness, or else forgiving another.—*Richter.*

When thou forgivest, the man who has pierced thy heart stands to thee in the relation of the sea-worm, that perforates the shell of the mussel, which straightway closes the wound with a pearl.—*Richter.*

He who has not forgiven an enemy has never yet tasted one of the most sublime enjoyments of life.—*Lavater.*

A Christian will find it cheaper to pardon than to resent. Forgiveness saves the expense of anger, the cost of hatred, the waste of spirits.—*Hannah More.*

Hath any wronged thee?—Be bravely revenged.—Slight it, and the work is begun: forgive, and it is finished.—He is below himself that is not above an injury.—*Quarles.*

Who from crimes would pardoned be, in mercy should set others free.—*Shakespeare.*

"I can forgive, but I cannot forget," is only another way of saying, "I will not forgive."—Forgiveness ought to be like a cancelled note—torn in two, and burned up, so that it never can be shown against one.—*H. W. Beecher.*

Of him that hopes to be forgiven it is required that he forgive.—On this great duty eternity is suspended; and to him that refuses to practice it the throne of mercy is inaccessible, and the Saviour of the world has been born in vain.—
Johnson.

It is in vain for you to expect, it is impudent for you to ask of God forgiveness for yourself if you refuse to exercise this forgiving temper as to others.—*Hoadly.*

Pardon, not wrath, is God's best attribute.—*B. Taylor.*

The more we know, the better we forgive.—Whoe'er feels deeply, feels for all that live.—*Mad. de Staël.*

Forgive many things in others; nothing in yourself.—*Ausonius.*

FORMALISM.—It is the tendency, if not the essence of formalism to set the outward institutions of religion above its inward truths; to be punctilious in the round of ceremonial observances, while neglectful of those spiritual sacrifices with which God is well pleased; to substitute means in the room of ends, and to rest in the type and symbol without rising to the glorious reality.—
Pearson.

What are all the forms of religion, compared with the true and holy life of the devoted Christian?—*Bp. Thomson.*

The house of the formalist is as empty of religion as the white of an egg is of savor.—*Bunyan.*

FORMS.—Forms are but symbols; we should never rest in them, but make them the stepping stones to the good to which they point.

The more men have multiplied the forms of religion, the more vital Godliness has declined.—*Emmons.*

Of what use are forms, seeing at times they are empty?—Of the same use as barrels, which, at times, are empty too. —*Hare.*

FORTITUDE. — Fortitude I take to be the quiet possession of a man's self, and an undisturbed doing his duty whatever evils beset, or dangers lie in the way.—In itself an essential virtue, it is a guard to every other virtue.—*Locke.*

The human race are sons of sorrow born; and each must have its portion. Vulgar minds refuse, or crouch beneath their load; the brave bear theirs without repining.—*Mallet.*

True fortitude is seen in great exploits that justice warrants and that wisdom guides.—*Addison.*

There is a strength of quiet endurance as significant of courage as the most daring feats of prowess.—*Tuckerman.*

Who fights with passions and overcomes, that man is armed with the best virtue—passive fortitude.—*J. Webster.*

The fortitude of the Christian consists in patience, not in enterprises which the poets call heroic and which are commonly the effects of interest, pride, and worldly honor.—*Dryden.*

FORTUNE. — The wheel of fortune turns round incessantly, and who can say to himself, "I shall to-day be uppermost."—*Confucius.*

Fortune is ever seen accompanying industry, and is as often trundling in a wheelbarrow as lolling in a coach and six.—*Goldsmith.*

It cannot be denied that outward accidents conduce much to fortune; favor, opportunity, death of others, occasion fitting virtue: but chiefly, the mold of a man's fortune is in his own hands.— *Bacon.*

We make our fortunes, and we call them fate.—*Alroy.*

Fortune is like the market, where many times if you can stay a little the price will fall; and, again, it is sometimes like a Sibyl's offer, which at first offereth the commodity at full, then consumeth part and part, and still holdeth up the price.—*Bacon.*

May I always have a heart superior, with economy suitable, to my fortune. —*Shenstone.*

Human life is more governed by fortune than by reason.—*Hume.*

Fortune does not change men; it only unmasks them.—*Riccoboni.*

The way of fortune is like the milky-way in the sky; which is a number of small stars, not seen asunder, but giving light together: so it is a number of little and scarce discerned virtues, or rather faculties and customs, that make men fortunate.—*Bacon.*

We should manage our fortune as we do our health—enjoy it when good, be patient when it is bad, and never apply violent remedies except in an extreme necessity.—*Rochefoucauld.*

Ovid finely compares a broken fortune to a falling column; the lower it sinks, the greater weight it is obliged to sustain. When a man's circumstances are such that he has no occasion to borrow, he finds numbers willing to lend him; but should his wants be such that he sues for a trifle, it is two to one whether he will be trusted with the smallest sum.— *Goldsmith.*

There is no one, says another, whom fortune does not visit once in his life; but when she does not find him ready to receive her, she walks in at the door, and flies out at the window.—*Montesquieu.*

"Fortune knocks at every man's door once in a life," but in a good many cases the man is in a neighboring saloon and does not hear her.—*Mark Twain.*

Every man is the maker of his own fortune.—*Tattler.*

We do not know what is really good or bad fortune.—*Rousseau.*

The bad fortune of the good turns their faces up to heaven; the good fortune of the bad bows their heads down to the earth.—*Saadi.*

Fortune is the rod of the weak, and the staff of the brave.—*J. R. Lowell.*

Ill fortune never crushed that man whom good fortune deceived not.—*Ben Jonson.*

The fortunate circumstances of our lives are generally found. at last. to be of our own producing.—*Goldsmith.*

High fortune makes both our virtues and vices stand out as objects that are brought clearly to view by the light.—*Rochefoucauld.*

Fortune, to show us her power, and abate our presumption, seeing she could not make fools wise, has made them fortunate.—*Montaigne.*

Depend not on fortune, but on conduct.—*Publius Syrus.*

It requires greater virtues to support good than bad fortune.—*Rochefoucauld.*

There is nothing keeps longer than a middling fortune, and nothing melts away sooner than a great one. Poverty treads upon the heels of great and unexpected riches.—*Bruyère.*

To be thrown upon one's own resources, is to be cast into the very lap of fortune; for our faculties then undergo a development and display an energy of which they were previously unsusceptible.—*Franklin.*

Fortune gives too much to many, but to none enough.—*Martial.*

It is a madness to make fortune the mistress of events, because in herself she is nothing, but is ruled by prudence. —*Dryden.*

We are sure to get the better of fortune if we do but grapple with her.—*Seneca.*

Fortune is ever seen accompanying industry.—*Goldsmith.*

Many have been ruined by their fortunes, and many have escaped ruin by the want of fortune.—To obtain it the great have become little, and the little great.—*Zimmermann.*

The power of fortune is confessed only by the miserable, for the happy impute all their success to prudence or merit.—*Swift.*

FRAUD.—For the most part fraud in the end secures for its companions repentance and shame.—*C. Simmons.*

All frauds, like the wall daubed with untempered mortar, with which men think to buttress up an edifice, always tend to the decay of what they are devised to support.—*Whately.*

The more gross the fraud the more glibly will it go down, and the more greedily be swallowed, since folly will always find faith where impostors will find impudence.—*Colton.*

The first and worst of all frauds is to cheat oneself.—*Bailey.*

Fraud generally lights a candle for justice to get a look at it; and a rogue's pen indites the warrant for his own arrest.

FREEDOM. — To have freedom is only to have that which is absolutely necessary to enable us to be what we ought to be, and to possess what we ought to possess.—*Rahel.*

No man is free who is not master of himself.—*Epictetus.*

Countries are well cultivated, not as they are fertile, but as they are free.—*Montesquieu.*

The cause of freedom is identified with the destinies of humanity, and in whatever part of the world it gains ground, by and by it will be a common gain to all who desire it.—*Kossuth.*

The only freedom worth possessing is that which gives enlargement to a people's energy, intellect, and virtues. The savage makes his boast of freedom. But what is its worth? He is, indeed, free from what he calls the yoke of civil institutions. But other and worse chains bind him. The very privation of civil government is in effect a chain; for, by withholding protection from property it virtually shackles the arm of industry, and forbids exertion for the melioration of his lot. Progress, the growth of intelligence and power, is the end and boon of liberty; and, without this, a people may have the name, but want the substance and spirit of freedom.—*Channing.*

This is what I call the American idea of freedom—a government of all the people, by all the people, for all the people; of course, a government of the principles of eternal justice—the unchanging law of God.—*Theodore Parker.*

Void of freedom, what would virtue be?—*Lamartine.*

There is no legitimacy on earth but in a government which is the choice of the nation.—*Joseph Bonaparte.*

The greatest glory of a free-born people is to transmit that freedom to their children.—*Havard.*

None are more hopelessly enslaved

than those who falsely believe they are free.—*Goethe.*

True freedom consists with the observance of law.—Adam was as free in paradise as in the wilds to which he was banished for his transgression.—*Thornton.*

The only freedom which deserves the name is that of pursuing our own good, in our own way, so long as we do not attempt to deprive others of theirs, or impede their efforts to obtain it.—*J. S. Mill.*

Many politicians lay it down as a self-evident proposition, that no people ought to be free till they are fit to use their freedom.—The maxim is worthy of the fool in the old story, who resolved not to go into the water till he had learned to swim.—*Macaulay.*

He is the freeman whom the truth makes free, and all are slaves beside.—*Cowper.*

Freedom of religion, freedom of the press, and freedom of person under the protection of the habeas corpus, these are principles that have guided our steps through an age of revolution and reformation.—*Jefferson.*

There must be no tampering with the delicate machinery by which religious liberty and equality are secured, and no fostering of any spirit which would tend to destroy that machinery.—*James Cardinal Gibbons.*

A useful definition of liberty is obtained only by seeking the principle of liberty in the main business of human life, that is to say, in the process by which men educate their responses and learn to control their environment.—*Walter Lippman.*

Indignation boils my blood at the thought of the heritage we are throwing away; at the thought that, with few exceptions, the fight for freedom is left to the poor, forlorn and defenseless, and to the few radicals and revolutionaries who would make use of liberty to destroy, rather than to maintain, American institutions. . . .—*Arthur Garfield Hays.*

Men are free when they are in a living homeland . . . not when they are escaping to some wild west. The most unfree souls go west, and shout of freedom. Men are freest when they are most unconscious of freedom. The shout is the rattling of chains, always was.—*D. H. Lawrence.*

Real freedom comes from the mastery, through knowledge, of historic conditions and race character which makes possible a free and intelligent use of experience for the purpose of progress.—*Hamilton Wright Mabie.*

I believe in freedom—social, economical, domestic, political, mental and spiritual.—*Elbert Hubbard.*

FRETFULNESS.—Men call fretting a minor fault—a foible and not a vice. —But there is no vice except drunkenness which can so utterly destroy the peace and happiness of a home.—*Helen Hunt.*

FRIENDSHIP.—Let me live in a house by the side of the road and be a friend to man.—*Sam Walter Foss.*

I made courtiers; I never pretended to make friends, said Napoleon. . . . On a rocky little island he fretted away the last years of his life—alone.—*Bruce Barton.*

Friendships are fragile things, and require as much care in handling as any other fragile and precious thing.—*Randolph S. Bourne.*

The lintel low enough to keep out pomp and pride; the threshold high enough to turn deceit aside; the doorband strong enough from robbers to defend: this door will open at a touch to welcome every friend.—*Van Dyke.*

No one should ever go a journey with any other than him with whom one walks arm in arm, in the evening, the twilight, and agrees that if either should have a son he shall be named after the other.—*Robert Cortes Holliday.*

It is great to have friends when one is young, but indeed it is still more so when you are getting old. When we are young, friends are, like everything else, a matter of course. In the old days we know what it means to have them.—*Edvard Grieg.*

He alone has lost the art to live who cannot win new friends.—*S. Weir Mitchell.*

A friend should be one in whose understanding and virtue we can equally confide, and whose opinion we can value at once for its justness and its sincerity.

He who has made the acquisition of a judicious and sympathizing friend, may be said to have doubled his mental resources.—*Robert Hall.*

There is nothing more becoming any wise man, than to make choice of friends, for by them thou shalt be judged what thou art: let them therefore be wise and virtuous, and none of those that follow thee for gain; but make election rather of thy betters than thy inferiors, shunning always such as are poor and needy; for if thou givest twenty gifts, and refuse to do the like but once, all that thou hast done will be lost, and such men will become thy mortal enemies.—*Sir W. Raleigh.*

Friendship improves happiness, and abates misery, by doubling our joy, and dividing our grief.—*Addison.*

Old friends are best. King James used to call for his old shoes; they were the easiest for his feet.—*Selden.*

Those friends are weak and worthless, that will not use the privilege of friendship in admonishing their friends with freedom and confidence, as well of their errors as of their danger.—*Bacon.*

In poverty and other misfortunes of life, true friends are a sure refuge.— The young they keep out of mischief; to the old they are a comfort and aid in their weakness, and those in the prime of life they incite to noble deeds. —*Aristotle.*

Thou mayest be sure that he that will in private tell thee of thy faults, is thy friend, for he adventures thy dislike, and doth hazard thy hatred; there are few men that can endure it, every man for the most part delighting in self-praise, which is one of the most universal follies that bewitcheth mankind.— *Sir W. Raleigh.*

He that hath no friend, and no enemy, is one of the vulgar; and without talents, powers, or energy.—*Lavater.*

Be not the fourth friend of him who had three before and lost them.— *Lavater.*

Let friendship creep gently to a height; if it rushes to it, it may soon run itself out of breath.—*Fuller.*

If thy friends be of better quality than thyself, thou mayest be sure of two things; the first, they will be more careful to keep thy counsel, because they have more to lose than thou hast; the second, they will esteem thee for thyself, and not for that which thou dost possess.—*Sir W. Raleigh.*

It is best to live as friends with those in time with whom we would be to all eternity.—*Fuller.*

By friendship you mean the greatest love, the greatest usefulness, the most open communication, the noblest sufferings, the severest truth, the heartiest counsel, and the greatest union of minds of which brave men and women are capable.—*Jeremy Taylor.*

If a man does not make new acquaintances as he passes through life, he will soon find himself left alone. A man should keep his friendships in constant repair.—*Johnson.*

The love of man to woman is a thing common and of course, and at first partakes more of instinct and passion than of choice; but true friendship between man and man is infinite and immortal. —*Plato.*

Life has no blessing like a prudent friend.—*Euripides.*

Be more prompt to go to a friend in adversity than in prosperity.—*Chilo.*

The most powerful and the most lasting friendships are usually those of the early season of our lives, when we are most susceptible of warm and affectionate impressions. The connections into which we enter in any after-period decrease in strength as our passions abate in heat; and there is not, I believe, a single instance of a vigorous friendship that ever struck root in a bosom chilled by years.—*Fitzosborne.*

Be careful to make friendship the child and not the father of virtue, for many are rather good friends than good men; so, although they do not like the evil their friend does, yet they like him who does the evil; and though no counselors of the offence, they yet protect the offender.—*Sir P. Sidney.*

Because discretion is always predominant in true friendship, it works and prevails least upon fools. Wicked men are often reformed by it, weak men seldom. —*Clarendon.*

All men have their frailties; and whoever looks for a friend without imperfections, will never find what he seeks.

We love ourselves notwithstanding our faults, and we ought to love our friends in like manner.—*Cyrus.*

False friendship, like the ivy, decays and ruins the walls it embraces; but true friendship gives new life and animation to the object it supports.—*Burton.*

We take care of our health, we lay up money, we make our roof tight and our clothing sufficient, but who provides wisely that he shall not be wanting in the best property of all—friends?—*Emerson.*

No one can lay himself under obligation to do a wrong thing. Pericles, when one of his friends asked his services in an unjust cause, excused himself, saying, "I am a friend only as far as the altar." —*Fuller.*

Friendship is the shadow of the evening, which strengthens with the setting sun of life.—*La Fontaine.*

Purchase not friends by gifts; when thou ceasest to give, such will cease to love.—*Fuller.*

You'll find the friendship of the world mere outward show!—'Tis like the harlot's tears, the statesman's promise, or the false patriot's zeal, full of fair seeming, but delusion all.—*Savage.*

Friendship with the evil is like the shadow in the morning, decreasing every hour; but friendship with the good is like the evening shadows, increasing till the sun of life sets.—*Herder.*

The friendships of the world are oft confederacies in vice, or leagues of pleasure.—*Addison.*

Friendship must be accompanied with virtue, and always lodged in great and generous minds.—*Trap.*

Real friendship is a slow grower, and never thrives unless engrafted upon a stock of known and reciprocal merit.—*Chesterfield.*

Get not your friends by bare compliments, but by giving them sensible tokens of your love. It is well worth while to learn how to win the heart of a man the right way. Force is of no use to make or preserve a friend, who is an animal that is never caught nor tamed but by kindness and pleasure. Excite them by your civilities, and show them that you desire nothing more than their satisfaction; oblige with all your soul that friend who has made you a present of his own.—*Socrates.*

The attachments of mere mirth are but the shadows of that true friendship of which the sincere affections of the heart are the substance.—*Burton.*

The friends thou hast and their adoption tried, grapple them to thy soul with hooks of steel.—*Shakespeare.*

Make not a bosom friend of a melancholy soul: he'll be sure to aggravate thy adversity, and lessen thy prosperity. He goes always heavy loaded; and thou must bear half. He's never in a good humor; and may easily get into a bad one, and fall out with thee.—*Fuller.*

Make not thy friends too cheap to thee, nor thyself to thy friend.—*Fuller.*

Nothing more dangerous than a friend without discretion; even a prudent enemy is preferable.—*La Fontaine.*

The light of friendship is like the light of phosphorus, seen plainest when all around is dark.—*Crowell.*

False friends are like our shadow, keeping close to us while we walk in the sunshine, but leaving us the instant we cross into the shade.—*Bovee.*

The amity that wisdom knits not, folly may easily untie.—*Shakespeare.*

Kindred weaknesses induce friendships as often as kindred virtues.—*Bovee.*

Heaven gives us friends, to bless the present scene; resumes them to prepare us for the next.—*Young.*

Life is to be fortified by many friendships.—To love and to be loved is the greatest happiness of existence.—*Sydney Smith.*

He that doth a base thing in zeal for his friend burns the golden thread that ties their hearts together.—*Jeremy Taylor.*

That friendship will not continue to the end which is begun for an end.—*Quarles.*

He is our friend who loves more than admires us, and would aid us in our great work.—*Channing.*

What an argument in favor of social connections is the observation that by communicating our grief we have less, and by communicating our pleasure we have more.—*Greville.*

The firmest friendships have been

formed in mutual adversity; as iron is most strongly united by the fiercest flame.—*Colton.*

Friendship is a plant of slow growth, and must undergo and withstand the shocks of adversity before it is entitled to the appelation.—*Washington.*

Friendship hath the skill and observation of the best physician, the diligence and vigilance of the best nurse, and the tenderness and patience of the best mother.—*Clarendon.*

Friends should not be chosen to flatter. —The quality we prize is that rectitude which will shrink from no truth.—Intimacies which increase vanity destroy friendship.—*Channing.*

Be slow to fall into friendship; but when thou art in, continue firm and constant.—*Socrates.*

The loss of a friend is like that of a limb; time may heal the anguish of the wound, but the loss cannot be repaired. —*Southey.*

It is one of the severest tests of friendship to tell your friend his faults. —So to love a man that you cannot bear to see a stain upon him, and to speak painful truth through loving words, that is friendship.—*H. W. Beecher.*

One of the surest evidences of friendship that one can display to another, is telling him gently of a fault.—If any other can excel it, it is listening to such a disclosure with gratitude, and amending the error.—*Bulwer.*

There is nothing so great that I fear to do it for my friend; nothing so small that I will disdain to do it for him.— *Sir P. Sidney.*

We learn our virtues from the friends who love us; our faults from the enemy who hates us.—We cannot easily discover our real character from a friend. —He is a mirror, on which the warmth of our breath impedes the clearness of the reflection.—*Richter.*

A friend that you have to buy won't be worth what you pay for him, no matter what that may be.—*G. D. Prentice.*

Take heed how you place your good will upon any other ground than proof of virtue.—Neither length of acquaintance, mutual secrecies, nor height of benefits can bind a vicious heart; no man

being good to others who is not good in himself.—*Sir P. Sidney.*

There are three friendships which are advantageous: friendship with the upright, with the sincere, and with the man of much observation.—Friendship with the man of specious airs, with the insinuatingly soft, and with the glib-tongued, these are injurious.—*Confucius.*

A true friend is the gift of God, and he only who made hearts can unite them. —*South.*

The difficulty is not so great to die for a friend, as to find a friend worth dying for.—*Home.*

Poor is the friendless master of a world; a world in purchase of a friend is gain.—*Young.*

That is a choice friend who conceals our faults from the view of others, and discovers them to our own.—*Secker.*

Two persons cannot long be friends if they cannot forgive each other's little failings.—*Bruyère.*

Never contract friendship with a man that is not better than thyself.—*Confucius.*

No man can expect to find a friend without faults, nor can he propose himself to be so to another—Every man will have something to do for his friend, and something to bear with in him.— Only the sober man can do the first; and for the latter, patience is requisite.— It is better for a man to depend on himself than to be annoyed with either a madman or a fool.—*O. Feltham.*

The only way to have a friend is to be one.—*Emerson.*

Friendship is the privilege of private men; for wretched greatness knows no blessing so substantial.—*Tate.*

FRUGALITY. — Frugality may be termed the daughter of prudence, the sister of temperance, and the parent of liberty. He that is extravagant will quickly become poor, and poverty will enforce dependence and invite corruption.—*Johnson.*

Frugality is founded on the principle that all riches have limits.—*Burke.*

If frugality were established in the state, if our expenses were laid out rather in the necessaries than the superfluities of life, there might be fewer wants, and even fewer pleasures, but infinitely more happiness.—*Goldsmith.*

He seldom lives frugally who lives by chance. Hope is always liberal, and they that trust her promises make little scruple of revelling to-day on the profits of to-morrow.—*Johnson.*

Frugality is a fair fortune; and habits of industry a good estate.—*Franklin.*

The way to wealth is as plain as the way to market.—It depends chiefly on two words, industry and frugality; that is, waste neither time nor money, but make the best use of both.—Without industry and frugality nothing will do; with them, everything.—*Franklin.*

He that spareth in everything is an inexcusable niggard.—He that spareth in nothing is an inexcusable madman.—The mean is to spare in what is least necessary, and to lay out more liberally in what is most required.—*Halifax.*

By sowing frugality we reap liberty, a golden harvest.—*Agesilaus.*

Frugality is good if liberality be joined with it.—The first is leaving off superfluous expenses; the last is bestowing them for the benefit of those who need.—The first, without the last, begets covetousness; the last without the first begets prodigality.—*Penn.*

With parsimony a little is sufficient; without it nothing is sufficient; but frugality makes a poor man rich.—*Seneca.*

Nature is avariciously frugal.—In matter it allows no atom to elude its grasp; in mind, no thought or feeling to perish.—It gathers up the fragments that nothing be lost.—*Thomas.*

FUTURITY.— Everything that looks to the future elevates human nature; for life is never so low or so little as when occupied with the present.—*L. E. Landon.*

We are always looking to the future; the present does not satisfy us.—Our ideal, whatever it may be, lies further on.—*Gillett.*

Trust no future however pleasant; let the dead past bury its dead. Act—act in the living present, heart within, and God o'erhead.—*Longfellow.*

How narrow our souls become when absorbed in any present good or ill!—It is only the thought of the future that makes them great.—*Richter.*

The veil which covers the face of futurity is woven by the hand of mercy.—*Bulwer.*

What is already passed is not more fixed than the certainty that what is future will grow out of what has already passed, or is now passing.—*G. B. Cheever.*

The future is always a fairy land to the young.—*Sala.*

Age and sorrow have the gift of reading the future by the past.—*Farrar.*

The golden age is not in the past, but in the future; not in the origin of human experience, but in its consummate flower; not opening in Eden, but out from Gethsemane.—*E. H. Chapin.*

Look not mournfully to the past—it comes not back again; wisely improve the present—it is thine; go forth to meet the shadowy future without fear, and with a manly heart.—*Longfellow.*

God will not suffer man to have a knowledge of things to come; for if he had prescience of his prosperity, he would be careless; and if understanding of his adversity, he would be despairing and senseless.—*Augustine.*

The best preparation for the future, is the present well seen to, and the last duty done.—*G. Macdonald.*

The future, only, is our goal.—We are never living, but only hoping to live; and looking forward always to being happy, it is inevitable that we never are so.—*Pascal.*

We always live prospectively, never retrospectively, and there is no abiding moment.—*Jacobi.*

Oh, blindness to the future! kindly given, that each may fill the circle marked by heaven.—*Pope.*

Every to-morrow has two handles. We can take hold of it with the handle of anxiety or the handle of faith.

We should live for the future, and yet should find our life in the fidelities of the present; the last is the only method of the first.—*H. W. Beecher.*

FUTURE STATE. — (See "Eternity.")

There is, I know not how, in the minds of men, a certain presage, as it were, of a future existence, and this takes the deepest root, and is most discoverable, in the greatest geniuses and most exalted souls.—*Cicero.*

Why will any man be so impertinently officious as to tell me all prospect of a future state is only fancy and delusion? Is there any merit in being the messenger of ill news? If it is a dream, let me enjoy it, since it makes me both the happier and better man.—*Addison.*

If there were no future life, our souls would not thirst for it.—*Richter.*

We are born for a higher destiny than that of earth.—There is a realm where the rainbow never fades, where the stars will be spread before us like islands that slumber on the ocean, and where the beings that now pass over before us like shadows, will stay in our presence forever.—*Bulwer.*

It is the divinity that stirs within us. —'Tis heaven itself that points out an hereafter, and intimates eternity to man. —*Addison.*

Belief in a future life is the appetite of reason.—*Landor.*

I feel my immortality o'ersweep all pains, all tears, all time, all fears, and like the eternal thunders of the deep, peal in my ears this truth—" Thou livest forever."—*Byron.*

A voice within us speaks that startling word, " Man, thou shalt never die! "— Celestial voices hymn it to our souls; according harps, by angel fingers touched, do sound forth still the song of our great immortality.—*Dana.*

There's none but fears a future state; and when the most obdurate swear they do not, their trembling hearts belie their boasting tongues.—*Dryden.*

My mind can take no hold on the present world nor rest in it a moment, but my whole nature rushes onward with irresistible force toward a future and better state of being.—*Fichte.*

To me there is something thrilling and exalting in the thought that we are drifting forward into a splendid mystery— into something that no mortal eye hath yet seen, and no intelligence has yet declared.—*E. H. Chapin.*

The dead carry our thoughts to another and a nobler existence.—They teach us, and especially by all the strange and seemingly untoward circumstances of their departure from this life, that they and we shall live in a future state forever.—*O. Dewey.*

We believe that we shall know each other's forms hereafter, and, in the bright fields of the better land, shall call the lost dead to us.—*N. P. Willis.*

Divine wisdom, intending to detain us some time on earth, has done well to cover with a veil the prospect of the life to come; for if our sight could clearly distinguish the opposite bank, who would remain on this tempestuous coast of time?—*Mad. De Staël.*

The grand difficulty is to feel the reality of both worlds, so as to give each its due place in our thoughts and feelings: to keep our mind's eye and our heart's eye ever fixed on the land of promise, without looking away from the road along which we are to travel toward it.—*Hare.*

Another life, if it were not better than this, would be less a promise than a threat.—*J. P. Senn.*

What a world were this; how unendurable its weight, if they whom death had sundered did not meet again?— *Southey.*

You ask if we shall know our friends in heaven.—Do you suppose we are greater fools there than here?—*Emmons.*

G

GAIN.—The true way to gain much, is never to desire to gain too much.— He is not rich that possesses much, but he that covets no more; and he is not poor that enjoys little, but he that wants too much.—*Beaumont.*

Sometimes the best gain is to lose.— *Herbert.*

GALLANTRY.—Gallantry consists in saying the most empty things in an agreeable manner.—*Rochefoucauld.*

Gallantry to women—the sure road to their favor—is nothing but the appearance of extreme devotion to all their wants and wishes, a delight in their satisfaction, and a confidence in yourself as being able to contribute toward it.— *Hazlitt.*

Gallantry thrives most in the atmosphere of the court.—*Mad. Neckar.*

The gallantry of the mind consists in agreeable flattery.—*Rochefoucauld.*

Gallantry, though a fashionable crime, is a very detestable one.—The wretch who pilfers from us in the hour of distress is innocent compared to the plunderer who robs us of happiness and reputation.—*Kelley.*

Conscience has no more to do with gallantry, than it has with politics.—*Sheridan.*

GAMBLING.—Gambling is the child of avarice, but the parent of prodigality.—*Colton.*

Gambling is a kind of tacit confession that those engaged therein do, in general, exceed the bounds of their respective fortunes; and therefore they cast lots to determine on whom the ruin shall at present fall, that the rest may be saved a little longer.—*Blackstone.*

Gambling with cards, or dice, or stocks, is all one thing; it is getting money without giving an equivalent for it.—*H. W. Beecher.*

By gambling we lose both our time and treasure, two things most precious to the life of man.—*Feltham.*

It is possible that a wise and good man may be prevailed on to gamble; but it is impossible that a professed gamester should be a wise and good man.—*Lavater.*

Some play for gain; to pass time others play; both play the fool; who gets by play is loser in the end.—*Heath.*

I look upon every man as a suicide from the moment he takes the dice-box desperately in his hand.—All that follows in his fatal career, from that time, is only sharpening the dagger before he strikes it to his heart.—*Cumberland.*

Curst is the wretch enslaved to such a vice, who ventures life and soul upon the dice.—*Horace.*

The gamester, if he die a martyr to his profession, is doubly ruined; he adds his soul to every other loss, and by the act of suicide renounces earth to forfeit heaven.—*Colton.*

All gaming, since it implies a desire to profit at the expense of others, involves a breach of the tenth commandment.—*Whately.*

Keep flax from fire, and youth from gaming.—*Franklin.*

Gambling is the child of avarice, the brother of iniquity, and the father of mischief.—*Washington.*

Gambling houses are temples where the most sordid and turbulent passions contend; there no spectator can be indifferent. A card or a small square of ivory interests more than the loss of an empire, or the ruin of an unoffending group of infants and their nearest relatives.—*Zimmermann.*

There is nothing that wears out a fine face like the vigils of the card-table, and those cutting passions which naturally attend them. Hollow eyes, haggard looks, and pale complexions are the natural indications of a female gamester. Her morning sleeps are not able to repay her midnight watchings.—*Steele.*

Although men of eminent genius have been guilty of all other vices, none worthy of more than a secondary name has ever been a gamester. Either an excess of avarice, or a deficiency of excitability, is the cause of it; neither of which can exist in the same bosom with genius, patriotism, or virtue.—*Landor.*

An assembly of the states or a court of justice, shows nothing so serious and grave as a table of gamesters playing very high; a melancholy solicitude clouds their looks; envy and rancor agitate their minds while the meeting lasts, without regard to friendship, alliances, birth, or distinctions.—*Bruyère.*

Games of chance are traps to catch school-boy novices and gaping country squires, who begin with a guinea and end with a mortgage.—*Cumberland.*

Play not for gain, but sport; who plays for more than he can lose with pleasure stakes his heart.—*Herbert.*

If thou desire to raise thy fortunes by the casts of fortune, be wise betimes, lest thou repent too late.—What thou winnest, is prodigally spent.—What thou losest, is prodigally lost.—It is an evil trade that prodigality drives, and a bad voyage where the pilot is blind.—*Quarles.*

Gaming finds a man a cully, and leaves him a knave.—*Cumberland.*

Sports and gaming, whether pursued from a desire of gain or the love of pleasure, are as ruinous to the temper and disposition of the one addicted to them, as they are to his fame and fortune.—*Burton.*

Gambling, in all countries, is the vice of the aristocracy.—The young find it established in the best circles, and enticed by the habits of others they are ruined when the habit becomes their own.—*Bulwer.*

Bets, at the first, were fool-traps, where the wise, like spiders, lay in ambush for the flies.—*Dryden.*

The best throw with the dice is to throw them away.—*C. Simmons.*

GAYETY.—(See "GOOD HUMOR.")

Gayety is to good humor, as animal perfumes to vegetable fragrance: the one overpowers weak spirits, the other recreates and revives them.—*Johnson.*

Gayety is not a proof that the heart is at ease, for often in the midst of laughter the heart is sad.—*Mad. De Genlis.*

The gayety of the wicked is like the flowery surface of Mount Ætna, beneath which materials are gathering for an eruption that will one day reduce all its beauties to ruin and desolation.

Leaves seem light, useless, idle, wavering, and changeable—they even dance; yet God has made them part of the oak. —So he has given us a lesson, not to deny stout-heartedness within, because we see lightsomeness without.—*Leigh Hunt.*

Gayety is often the reckless ripple over depths of despair.—*E. H. Chapin.*

GEMS. — How very beautiful these gems are! It is strange how deeply colors seem to penetrate one like scent. —I suppose that is the reason why gems are used as spiritual emblems in Revelations.—They look like fragments of heaven.—*George Eliot.*

GENEROSITY.—Men of the noblest dispositions think themselves happiest when others share their happiness with them.—*Duncan.*

True generosity is a duty as indispensably necessary as those imposed on us by law.—It is a rule imposed by reason, which should be the sovereign law of a rational being.—*Goldsmith.*

Generosity, wrong placed, becometh a vice; a princely mind will undo a private family.—*Fuller.*

True generosity does not consist in obeying every impulse of humanity, in following blind passion for our guide, and impairing our circumstances by present benefactions, so as to render us incapable of future ones.—*Goldsmith.*

There is wisdom in generosity, as in everything else.—A friend to everybody

is often a friend to nobody; or else, in his simplicity, he robs his family to help strangers, and so becomes brother to a beggar.—*Spurgeon.*

For his bounty, there was no winter in't; an autumn 'twas that grew the more by reaping.—*Shakespeare.*

As the sword of the best tempered metal is most flexible, so the truly generous are most pliant and courteous in their behavior to their inferiors.—*Fuller.*

The generous who is always just, and the just who is always generous, may, unannounced, approach the throne of heaven.—*Lavater.*

He that gives all, though but little gives much; because God looks not to the quantity of the gift, but to the quality of the givers.—*Quarles.*

Generosity during life is a very different thing from generosity in the hour of death; one proceeds from genuine liberality and benevolence, the other from pride or fear.—*Horace Mann.*

A generous man places the benefits he confers beneath his feet; those he receives, nearest his heart.

One great reason why men practise generosity so little in the world is, their finding so little there: generosity is catching; and if so many men escape it, it is in a great degree from the same reason that countrymen escape the smallpox,—because they meet with no one to give it them.—*Greville.*

The truly generous is the truly wise, and he who loves not others, lives unblest.—*Home.*

Generosity is the accompaniment of high birth; pity and gratitude are its attendants.—*Corneille.*

Some are unwisely liberal, and more delight to give presents than to pay debts.—*Sir P. Sidney.*

A man there was, and they called him mad; the more he gave, the more he had.—*Bunyan.*

What I gave, I have; what I spent, I had; what I kept, I lost.—*Old Epitaph.*

When you give, take to yourself no credit for generosity, unless you deny yourself something in order that you may give.—*H. Taylor.*

The secret pleasure of a generous act is the great mind's bribe.—*Dryden.*

What seems to be generosity is often

no more than disguised ambition, which overlooks a small interest in order to secure a great one.—*Rochefoucauld*.

Almost always the most indigent are the most generous.—*Stanislaus*.

How much easier it is to be generous than just! Men are sometimes bountiful who are not honest.—*Junius*.

If there be any truer measure of a man than by what he does, it must be by what he gives.—*South*.

I would have a man generous to his country, his neighbors, his kindred, his friends, and most of all his poor friends. Not like some who are most lavish with those who are able to give most to them.—*Pliny*.

All my experience of the world teaches me that in ninety-nine cases out of a hundred, the safe and just side of a question is the generous and merciful side.—*Mrs. Jameson*.

It is not enough to help the feeble up, but to support him after.—*Shakespeare*.

He who gives what he would as readily throw away, gives without generosity; for the essence of generosity is in self-sacrifice.—*H. Taylor*.

GENIUS.—Genius is infinite painstaking.—*Longfellow*.

Genius is nothing but continued attention.—*Helvetius*.

Genius is a superior aptitude to patience.—*Buffon*.

I know no such thing as genius; it is nothing but labor and diligence.—*Hogarth*.

Genius is but a mind of large general powers accidentally determined in a particular direction.—*Johnson*.

Genius is supposed to be a power of producing excellencies which are out of the reach of the rules of art; a power which no precepts can teach, and which no industry can acquire.—*Sir Joshua Reynolds*.

A man's genius is always, in the beginning of life, as much unknown to himself as to others; and it is only after frequent trials, attended with success, that he dares think himself equal to those undertakings in which those who have succeeded have fixed the admiration of mankind.—*Hume*.

The popular notion of genius is—of one who can do almost everything—except make a living.

Genius is only a superior power of seeing.—*Ruskin*.

The greatest genius is never so great as when it is chastised and subdued by the highest reason.—*Colton*.

There is no genius in life like the genius of energy and industry.—*D. G. Mitchell*.

We meet with few utterly dull and stupid souls; the sublime and transcendent are still fewer; the generality of mankind stand between these two extremes; the interval is filled with multitudes of ordinary geniuses, but all very useful, the ornaments and supports of the commonwealth: these produce the agreeable and the profitable, and are conversant in commerce, finances, war, navigation, arts, trades, society, and conversation.—*Bruyère*.

The richest genius, like the most fertile soil, when uncultivated, shoots up into the rankest weeds; and instead of vines and olives for the pleasure and use of man, produces to its slothful owner the most abundant crop of poisons.—*Hume*.

Talent, lying in the understanding, is often inherited; genius, being the action of reason and imagination, rarely or never.—*Coleridge*.

Men of genius are often dull and inert in society; as the blazing meteor, when it descends to earth, is only a stone.—*Longfellow*.

Genius finds its own road, and carries its own lamp.—*Willmott*.

The drafts which true genius draws upon posterity, although they may not always be honored so soon as they are due, are sure to be paid with compound interest in the end.—*Colton*.

When a true genius appears in the world, you may know him by this sign, that the dunces are all in confederacy against him.—*Swift*.

Every man who observes vigilantly, and resolves steadfastly, grows unconsciously into genius.—*Bulwer*.

Genius is the gold in the mine; talent is the miner who works and brings it out.—*Lady Blessington*.

Great geniuses have the shortest biographies.—*Emerson*.

Genius must be born; it never can be taught.—*Dryden.*

The first and last thing required of genius is the love of truth.—*Goethe.*

There is no work of genius which has not been the delight of mankind; no word of genius to which the human heart and soul have not, sooner or later, responded.—*J. R. Lowell.*

The merit of great men is not understood but by those who are formed to be such themselves.—Genius speaks only to genius.—*Stanislaus.*

Genius always gives its best at first; prudence, at last.—*Lavater.*

Genius may be described as the spirit of discovery.—It is the eye of intellect, and the wing of thought.—It is always in advance of its time—the pioneer for the generation which it precedes.—*Simms.*

Genius does what it must, and talent what it can.—*Owen Meredith.*

There never appear more than five or six men of genius in an age, and if they were united the world could not stand before them.—*Swift.*

Cleverness is a sort of genius for instrumentality. It is the brain of the hand. In literature, cleverness is more frequently accompanied by wit, genius, and sense, than by humor.—*Coleridge.*

Genius, without religion, is only a lamp on the outer gate of a palace; it may serve to cast a gleam of light on those that are without, while the inhabitant is in darkness.—*H. More.*

All the means of action—the shapeless masses—the materials—lie everywhere about us.—What we need is the celestial fire to change the flint into the transparent crystal, bright and clear.—That fire is genius.—*Longfellow.*

One of the strongest characteristics of genius is the power of lighting its own fire.—*John Foster.*

Genius is entitled to respect, only when it promotes the peace and improves the happiness of mankind.—*Lord Essex.*

To carry the feelings of childhood into the powers of manhood, to combine the child's sense of wonder and novelty with the appearances which every day for years has rendered familiar, this is the character and privilege of genius, and

one of the marks which distinguish it from talent.—*Coleridge.*

Nothing will give permanent success in any enterprise of life, except native capacity cultivated by honest and persevering effort.—Genius is often but the capacity for receiving and improving by discipline.—*G. Eliot.*

GENTILITY.—There cannot be a surer proof of low origin, or of an innate meanness of disposition, than to be always talking and thinking about being genteel.—*Hazlitt.*

Gentility is neither in birth, wealth, manner, nor fashion—but in the mind. A high sense of honor, a determination never to take a mean advantage of another, an adherence to truth, delicacy, and politeness toward those with whom we have dealings, are its essential characteristics.

I would not have you stand so much on your gentility, which is an airy and mere borrowed thing from dead men's dust and bones, and none of yours, except you make and hold it.—*Ben Jonson.*

How weak a thing is gentility, if it wants virtue!—*Fuller.*

GENTLEMAN.—Whoever is open, loyal, true; of humane and affable demeanor; honorable himself, and in his judgment of others; faithful to his word as to law, and faithful alike to God and man—such a man is a true gentleman.

The flowering of civilization is the finished man—the man of sense, of grace, of accomplishment, of social power—the gentleman.—*Emerson.*

Education begins the gentleman, but reading, good company, and reflection must finish him.—*Locke.*

The taste of beauty, and the relish of what is decent, just, and amiable, perfect the character of the gentleman and the philosopher. And the study of such a taste or relish will be ever the great employment and concern of him who covets as well to be wise and good as agreeable and polite.—*Shaftesbury.*

Thoughtfulness for others, generosity, modesty, and self-respect are the qualities which make a real gentleman or lady, as distinguished from the veneered article which commonly goes by that name.—*Huxley.*

Repose and cheerfulness are the badge

of the gentleman—repose in energy.—*Emerson.*

It is a grand old name, that of gentleman, and has been recognized as a rank and power in all stages of society. To possess this character is a dignity of itself, commanding the instinctive homage of every generous mind, and those who will not bow to titular rank will yet do homage to the gentleman. His qualities depend not upon fashion or manners, but upon moral worth; not on personal possessions, but on personal qualities.—*S. Smiles.*

You may depend upon it, religion is, in its essence, the most gentlemanly thing in the world.—It will, alone, gentilize, if unmixed with cant; and I know nothing else, which, alone, will.—*Coleridge.*

Perhaps propriety is as near a word as any to denote the manners of the gentleman.—Elegance is necessary to the fine gentleman; dignity is proper to noblemen; and majesty to kings.—*Hazlitt.*

Men of courage, men of sense, and men of letters are frequent: but a true gentleman is what one seldom sees.—*Steele.*

The real gentleman should be gentle in everything, at least in everything that depends on himself,—carriage, temper, constructions, aims, desires. He ought therefore to be mild, calm, quiet, even, temperate,—not hasty in judgment, not exorbitant in ambition, not overbearing, not proud, not rapacious, not oppressive; for these things are contrary to gentleness.—*Hare.*

We sometimes meet an original gentleman, who, if manners had not existed, would have invented them.—*Emerson.*

He that can enjoy the intimacy of the great, and on no occasion disgust them by familiarity, or disgrace himself by servility, proves that he is as perfect a gentleman by nature, as his companions are by rank.—*Colton.*

Gentleman is a term that does not apply to any station, but to the mind and feelings in every station.—*Talfourd.*

It is difficult to believe that a true gentleman will ever become a gamester, a libertine, or a sot.—*E. H. Chapin.*

Perhaps a gentleman is a rarer man than some of us think for. Which of us

can point out many such in his circle; men whose aims are generous, whose truth is not only constant in its kind, but elevated in its degree; whose want of meanness makes them simple, who can look the world honestly in the face with an equal manly sympathy for the great and the small.—*Thackeray.*

To be a gentleman is to be honest, to be gentle, to be generous, to be brave, to be wise, and possessing all those qualities to exercise them in the most graceful outward manner.—*Thackeray.*

GENTLENESS.—We are indebted to Christianity for gentleness, especially toward women.—*C. Simmons.*

True gentleness is love in society, holding intercourse with those around it. —It is considerateness; it is tenderness of feeling; it is promptitude of sympathy; it is love in all its depths, and in all its delicacy.—It is everything included in that matchless grace, " the gentleness of Christ."—*J. Hamilton.*

True gentleness is founded on a sense of what we owe to him who made us, and to the common nature which we all share.—It arises from reflection on our own failings and wants, and from just views of the condition and duty of men. —It is native feeling heightened and improved by principle.—*Blair.*

Nothing is so strong as gentleness; nothing so gentle as real strength.—*Francis de Sales.*

What thou wilt thou shalt rather enforce with thy smile than hew to it with thy sword.—*Shakespeare.*

GEOLOGY.—(See "SCIENCE.")

So long as the phenomena (of geology) are simply recorded, and only the natural and obvious causes inferred from them, there can be no fear that the results of the study will prove hostile to religion.—If the representations they give of nature are the fictions of men, they cannot stand against the progress of science; and if they truly picture the works of God, they must be easily reconcilable with his revealed manifestations.—*Wiseman.*

Geology gives us a key to the patience of God.—*J. G. Holland.*

GIFTS.—It is the will, and not the gift that makes the giver.—*Lessing.*

The manner of giving shows the character of the giver, more than the gift itself.—*Lavater.*

There is a gift that is almost a blow, and there is a kind word that is munificence; so much is there in the way of doing things.—*A. Helps.*

Give what you have. To some one it may be better than you dare to think.—*Longfellow.*

We should give as we would receive, cheerfully, quickly, and without hesitation; for there is no grace in a benefit that sticks to the fingers.—*Seneca.*

To reveal its complacence by gifts, is one of the native dialects of love.—*Mrs. Sigourney.*

Serving God with our little, is the way to make it more; and we must never think that wasted with which God is honored, or men are blest.

Give according to your means, or God will make your means according to your giving.—*John Hall.*

A gift, its kind, its value, and appearance; the silence or the pomp that attends it; the style in which it reaches you, may decide the dignity or vulgarity of the giver.—*Lavater.*

Presents which our love for the donor has rendered precious are ever the most acceptable.—*Ovid.*

People do not care to give alms without some security for their money; and a wooden leg or a withered arm is a sort of draft upon heaven for those who choose to have their money placed to account there.—*Mackenzie.*

He who loves with purity considers not the gift of the lover, but the love of the giver.—*Thomas à Kempis.*

One must be poor to know the luxury of giving.—*George Eliot.*

Examples are few of men ruined by giving.—Men are heroes in spending—cravens in what they give.—*Bovee.*

When a friend asks, there is no to-morrow.—*Herbert.*

When thou makest presents, let them be of such things as will last long; to the end they may be in some sort immortal, and may frequently refresh the memory of the receiver.—*Fuller.*

The best thing to give to your enemy is forgiveness; to an opponent, tolerance; to a friend, your heart; to your child, a good example; to a father, defer-

ence; to your mother, conduct that will make her proud of you; to yourself, respect; to all men, charity.—*Balfour.*

It is a proof of boorishness to confer a favor with a bad grace.—How little does a smile cost!—*Bruyère.*

Every gift, though it be small, is in reality great if given with affection.—*Pindar.*

The secret of giving affectionately is great and rare; it requires address to do it well; otherwise we lose instead of deriving benefit from it.—*Corneille.*

Independence is of more value than any gifts; and to receive gifts is to lose it.—Men most commonly seek to oblige thee only that they may engage thee to serve them.—*Saadi.*

Rich gifts wax poor when givers prove unkind.—*Shakespeare.*

The heart of the giver makes the gift dear and precious.—*Luther.*

Gifts are as the gold which adorns the temple; grace is like the temple that sanctifies the gold.—*Burkitt.*

Who gives a trifle meanly is meaner than the trifle.—*Lavater.*

That which is given with pride and ostentation is rather an ambition than a bounty.—*Seneca.*

He gives not best who gives most; but he gives most who gives best.—If I cannot give bountifully, yet I will give freely, and what I want in my hand, I will supply by my heart.—*Warwick.*

Gifts weigh like mountains on a sensitive heart.—To me they are oftener punishments than pleasures.—*Mad. Fee.*

GLORY.—True glory consists in doing what deserves to be written; in writing what deserves to be read; and in so living as to make the world happier and better for our living in it.—*Pliny.*

True glory takes root, and even spreads; all false pretences, like flowers, fall to the ground; nor can any counterfeit last long.—*Cicero.*

It is by what we ourselves have done, and not by what others have done for us, that we shall be remembered by after ages. It is by thought that has aroused the intellect from its slumbers, which has given luster to virtue and dignity to truth, or by those examples which have inflamed the soul with the love of goodness, and not by means of sculptured marble, that I hold communion with Shakespeare and Milton, with Johnson and Burke, with Howard and Wilberforce.—*Francis Wayland.*

Real glory springs from the silent conquest of ourselves.—Without that, the conqueror is nought but the foist slave.—*Thompson.*

As to be perfectly just is an attribute of the divine nature, to be so to the utmost of our abilities is the glory of man.—*Addison.*

Our greatest glory consists not in never falling, but in rising every time we fall.—*Goldsmith.*

Glory, built on selfish principles, is shame and guilt.—*Cowper.*

Like madness is the glory of this life.—*Shakespeare.*

He that first likened glory to a shadow, did better than he was aware of; they are both vain.—Glory, also, like the shadow, goes sometimes before the body, and sometimes in length infinitely exceeds it.—*Montaigne.*

By skillful conduct and artificial means a person may make a sort of name for himself; but if the inner jewel be wanting, all is vanity, and will not last.—*Goethe.*

Two things ought to teach us to think but meanly of human glory—that the very best have had their calumniators, and the very worst their panegyrists.—*Colton.*

Let us not disdain glory too much; nothing is finer, except virtue.—The height of happiness would be to unite both in this life.—*Chateaubriand.*

The shortest way to glory is to be guided by conscience.—*Home.*

Those great actions whose luster dazzles us are represented by politicians as the effects of deep design, whereas they are commonly the effects of caprice and passion.—*Rochefoucauld.*

The glory of a people, and of an age, is always the work of a small number of great men, and disappears with them.—*Grimm.*

GLUTTONY.—Swinish gluttony ne'er looks to heaven amid his gorgeous feast, but with besotted, base ingratitude, crams and blasphemes his feeder.—*Milton.*

They whose sole bliss is eating, can give but that one brutish reason why they live.—*Juvenal.*

Some men are born to feast, and not to fight; whose sluggish minds, even in fair honor's field, still on their dinner turn.—*Joanna Baillie.*

Their kitchen is their shrine, the cook their priest, the table their altar, and their belly their God.—*Buck.*

Gluttony is the source of all our infirmities and the fountain of all our diseases. As a lamp is choked by a superabundance of oil, and a fire extinguished by excess of fuel, so is the natural health of the body destroyed by intemperate diet.—*Burton.*

I have come to the conclusion that mankind consume too much food.—*Sydney Smith.*

As houses well stored with provisions are likely to be full of mice, so the bodies of those who eat much are full of diseases.—*Diogenes.*

The pleasures of the palate deal with us like the Egyptian thieves, who strangle those whom they embrace.—*Seneca.*

He who is a slave to his belly seldom worships God.—*Saadi.*

I am a great eater of beef, and I believe that does harm to my wit.—*Shakespeare.*

GOD.—This is one of the names which we give to that eternal, infinite, and incomprehensible being, the creator of all things, who preserves and governs every thing by his almighty power and wisdom, and who is the only object of our worship.—*Cruden.*

God is a spirit, infinite, eternal, and unchangeable in his being, wisdom, power, holiness, justice, goodness, and truth.—*Catechism.*

We know God easily, if we do not constrain ourselves to define him.—*Joubert.*

The Mohammedans have ninety-nine names for God, but among them all they have not " our Father."

We should give God the same place in our hearts that he holds in the universe.

If we have God in all things while they are ours, we shall have all things in God when they are taken away.

There is something in the nature of things which the mind of man, which reason, which human power cannot effect, and certainly that which produces this must be better than man. What can this be but God?—*Cicero.*

There is a beauty in the name appropriated by the Saxon nations to the Deity, unequalled except by his most venerated Hebrew appellation. They called him "GOD," which is literally "THE GOOD." The same word thus signifying the Deity and His most endearing quality.—*Turner.*

The demand of the human understanding for causation requires but the one old and only answer, God.—*Dexter.*

Let the chain of second causes be ever so long, the first link is always in God's hand.—*Lavington.*

God is a circle whose center is everywhere, and its circumference nowhere.—*Empedocles.*

They that deny a God, destroy man's nobility; for clearly man is of kin to the beasts by his body, and if he be not of kin to God by his spirit, he is a base and ignoble creature.—*Bacon.*

The ancient hieroglyphic for God was the figure of an eye upon a sceptre, to denote that he sees and rules all things.—*Barker.*

It were better to have no opinion of God at all than such an one as is unworthy of him; for the one is only unbelief—the other is contempt.—*Plutarch.*

I had rather believe all the fables in the Talmud and the Koran, than that this universal frame is without a mind.—*Bacon.*

In all the vast and the minute, we see the unambiguous footsteps of the God, who gives its luster to the insect's wing, and wheels his throne upon the rolling worlds.—*Cowper.*

If God did not exist it would be necessary to invent him.—*Voltaire.*

Nature is too thin a screen; the glory of the omnipresent God bursts through everywhere.—*Emerson.*

The very word "God" suggests care, kindness, goodness; and the idea of God in his infinity, is infinite care, infinite kindness, infinite goodness.—We give God the name of good: it is only by shortening it that it becomes God.—*H. W. Beecher.*

At the foot of every page in the annals of nations may be written, "God reigns."

Events as they pass away proclaim their original; and if you will but listen reverently, you may hear the receding centuries, as they roll into the dim distances of departed time, perpetually chanting "Te Deum Laudamus," with all the choral voices of the countless congregations of the age.—*Bancroft.*

It is impossible to govern the world without God. He must be worse than an infidel that lacks faith, and more than wicked that has not gratitude enough to acknowledge his obligation.—*Washington.*

God is great, and therefore he will be sought: he is good, and therefore he will be found.

If in the day of sorrow we own God's presence in the cloud, we shall find him also in the pillar of fire, brightening and cheering our way as the night comes on.

In all his dispensations God is at work for our good.—In prosperity he tries our gratitude; in mediocrity, our contentment; in misfortune, our submission; in darkness, our faith; under temptation, our steadfastness, and at all times, our obedience and trust in him.

God governs the world, and we have only to do our duty wisely, and leave the issue to him.—*John Jay.*

When the mind of man looketh upon second causes scattered, it may sometimes rest in them, and go no further. But when it beholdeth the chain of them confederate and linked together, it must fly to Providence and Deity.—*Bacon.*

There is a God in science, a God in history, and a God in conscience, and these three are one.—*Joseph Cook.*

How often we look upon God as our last and feeblest resource! We go to him because we have nowhere else to go. And then we learn that the storms of life have driven us, not upon the rocks, but into the desired haven.—*Geo. Macdonald.*

I have read up many queer religions; and there is nothing like the old thing, after all. I have looked into the most philosophical systems, and have found none that will work without a God.—*J. C. Maxwell.*

An old mystic says somewhere, "God is an unutterable sigh in the innermost depths of the soul." With still greater justice, we may reverse the proposition, and say the soul is a never ending sigh after God.—*Christlieb.*

The world we inhabit must have had an origin; that origin must have consisted in a cause; that cause must have been intelligent; that intelligence must have been supreme; and that supreme, which always was and is supreme, we know by the name of God.

Two men please God—who serves Him with all his heart because he knows Him; who seeks Him with all his heart because he knows Him not.—*Panin.*

He who bridles the fury of the billows, knows also to put a stop to the secret plans of the wicked.—Submitting to His holy will, I fear God; I have no other fear.—*Racine.*

It is one of my favorite thoughts, that God manifests himself to mankind in all wise, good, humble, generous, great and magnanimous men.—*Lavater.*

There is nothing on earth worth being known but God and our own souls.—*Bailey.*

A foe to God was never a true friend to man.—*Young.*

There is something very sublime, though very fanciful in Plato's description of God—"That truth is his body, and light his shadow."—*Addison.*

If God were not a necessary being of himself, he might almost seem to be made for the use and benefit of men.—*Tillotson.*

We cannot too often think, that there is a never sleeping eye that reads the heart, and registers our thoughts.—*Bacon.*

I fear God, and next to God I chiefly fear him who fears him not.—*Saadi.*

The very impossibility which I find to prove that God is not, discovers to me his existence.—*Bruyère.*

Amid all the war and contest and variety of human opinion, you will find one consenting conviction in every land, that there is one God, the king and father of all.—*Maximus Tyrius.*

Live near to God, and so all things will appear to you little in comparison with eternal realities.—*R. M. McCheyne.*

The whole world is a phylactery, and everything we see is an item of the wisdom, power, or goodness of God.—*Sir Thomas Browne.*

As a countenance is made beautiful by the soul's shining through it, so the world is beautified by the shining through it of God.—*Jacobi.*

God's thoughts, his will, his love, his judgments are all man's home. To think his thoughts, to choose his will, to love his loves, to judge his judgments, and thus to know that he is in us, is to be at home.—*George Macdonald.*

God should be the object of all our desires, the end of all our actions, the principle of all our affections, and the governing power of our whole souls.—*Massillon.*

In all thine actions think that God sees thee, and in all his actions labor to see him.—That will make thee fear him, and this will move thee to love him.—The fear of God is the beginning of knowledge, and the knowledge of God is the perfection of love.—*Quarles.*

If we look closely at this world, where God seems so utterly forgotten, we shall find that it is he, who, after all, commands the most fidelity and the most love.—*Mad. Swetchine.*

What is there in man so worthy of honor and reverence as this, that he is capable of contemplating something higher than his own reason, more sublime than the whole universe—that Spirit which alone is self-subsistent, from which all truth proceeds, without which is no truth?—*Jacobi.*

To escape from evil we must be made, as far as possible, like God; and this resemblance consists in becoming just, and holy, and wise.—*Plato.*

GOLD.—(See "MONEY," and "MISER.")

Gold is the fool's curtain, which hides all his defects from the world.—*Feltham.*

The lust of gold, unfeeling and remorseless; the last corruption of degenerate man.—*Johnson.*

It is much better to have your gold in the hand than in the heart.—*Fuller.*

Gold, like the sun, which melts wax, but hardens clay, expands great souls and contracts bad hearts.—*Rivarol.*

It is observed of gold, in an old epigram, that to have it is to be in fear, and to want it is to be in sorrow.—*Johnson*.

To purchase heaven has gold the power? can gold remove the mortal hour? in life can love be bought with gold? are friendship's pleasures to be sold? no—all that's worth a wish—a thought, fair virtue gives unbribed, unbought. Cease then on trash thy hopes to bind, let nobler views engage thy mind.—*Johnson*.

There is no place so high that an ass laden with gold cannot reach it.—*Rojas*.

Midas longed for gold.—He got it, so that whatever he touched became gold, and he, with his long ears, was little the better for it.—*Carlyle*.

There are two metals, one of which is omnipotent in the cabinet, and the other in the camp,—gold and iron. He that knows how to apply them both, may indeed attain the highest station, but he must know something more to keep it.—*Colton*.

Give him gold enough, and marry him to a puppet, or an aglet-baby, or an old trot with ne'er a tooth in her head, though she have as many diseases as two and fifty horses; why, nothing comes amiss, so money comes withal.—*Shakespeare*.

A mask of gold hides all deformities. —*Dekker*.

How quickly nature falls to revolt when gold becomes her object.—*Shakespeare*.

O cursed lust of gold! when, for thy sake, the fool throws up his interest in both worlds, first starved in this, then damned in that to come!—*Blair*.

How few, like Daniel, have God and gold together.—*Bp. Villiers*.

Gold! in all ages the curse of mankind!—To gain thee, men yield honor, affection, and lasting renown, and for thee barter the crown of eternity.—*P. Benjamin*.

A vain man's motto is: "Win gold and wear it"; a generous, "Win gold and share it"; a miser's, "Win gold and hoard it"; a profligate's, "Win gold and spend it"; a broker's, "Win gold and lend it"; a gambler's, "Win gold and lose it"; a wise man's, "Win gold and use it."

They who worship gold in a world so corrupt as this, have at least one thing to plead in defence of their idolatry— the power of their idol.—This idol can boast of two peculiarities; it is worshipped in all climates, without a single temple, and by all classes, without a single hypocrite.—*Colton*.

Mammon has enriched his thousands, and has damned his ten thousands.—*South*.

As the touchstone tries gold, so gold tries men.—*Chilo*.

GOOD-BREEDING. — (See "MANNERS" and "POLITENESS.")

Good-breeding is benevolence in trifles, or the preference of others to ourselves in the daily occurrences of life. —*Lord Chatham*.

Good-breeding is surface Christianity. —*O. W. Holmes*.

Good-breeding is the art of showing men, by external signs, the internal regard we have for them. It arises from good sense, improved by conversing with good company.—*Cato*.

One principal point of good-breeding is to suit our behavior to the three several degrees of men—our superiors, our equals, and those below us.—*Swift*.

Nothing can constitute good-breeding which has not good nature for its foundation.—*Bulwer*.

Good-breeding is the result of much good sense, some good nature, and a little self-denial for the sake of others, and with a view to obtain the same indulgence from them.—*Chesterfield*.

A man endowed with great perfections, without good-breeding, is like one who has his pockets full of gold, but always wants change for his ordinary occasions. —*Steele*.

Good-breeding is not confined to externals, much less to any particular dress or attitude of the body; it is the art of pleasing or contributing as much as possible to the ease and happiness of those with whom you converse.—*Fielding*.

Good qualities are the substantial riches of the mind; but it is good-breeding that sets them off to advantage.— *Locke*.

The scholar, without good-breeding, is a pedant; the philosopher, a cynic; the soldier, a brute; and every man disagreeable.—*Chesterfield*.

A man's own good-breeding is the best security against other people's ill-manners. It carries along with it a dignity that is respected by the most petulant. Ill-breeding invites and authorizes the familiarity of the most timid. No man ever said a pert thing to the Duke of Marlborough. No man ever said a civil one to Sir Robert Walpole.—*Chesterfield.*

Among well-bred people, a mutual deference is affected; contempt of others disguised; authority concealed; attention given to each in his turn; and an easy stream of conversation maintained, without vehemence, without interruption, without eagerness for victory, and without any airs of superiority.—*Hume.*

Good-breeding shows itself most, where to an ordinary eye it appears the least.—*Addison.*

Virtue itself often offends, when coupled with bad manners.—*Middleton.*

The summary of good-breeding may be reduced to this rule: "Behave to all others as you would they should behave to you."—*Fielding.*

There are few defects in our nature so glaring as not to be veiled from observation by politeness and good-breeding.—*Stanislaus.*

The highest point of good-breeding is to show a very nice regard to your own dignity, and with that in your own heart, to express your value for the man above you.—*Steele.*

One may know a man that never conversed in the world, by his excess of good-breeding.—*Addison.*

As ceremony is the invention of wise men to keep fools at a distance, so good-breeding is an expedient to make fools and wise men equal.—*Steele.*

Wisdom, valor, justice, and learning, cannot keep a man in countenance that is possessed with these excellencies, if he wants that inferior art of life and behaviour, called good breeding.—*Steele.*

GOOD HUMOR.—(See "HUMOR.")

Good humor is the health of the soul; sadness is its poison.—*Stanislaus.*

Honest good humor is the oil and wine of a merry meeting, and there is no jovial companionship equal to that where the jokes are rather small, and the laughter abundant.—*Washington Irving.*

This portable quality of good humor seasons all the parts and occurrences we meet with in such a manner that there are no moments lost, but they all pass with so much satisfaction that the heaviest of loads, when it is a load, that of time, is never felt by us.—*Steele.*

Some people are commended for a giddy kind of good humor, which is no more a virtue than drunkenness.—*Pope.*

Good humor will sometimes conquer ill humor, but ill humor will conquer it oftener; and for this plain reason, good humor must operate on generosity; ill humor on meanness.—*Greville.*

GOOD NATURE. — Good nature is the very air of a good mind; the sign of a large and generous soul, and the peculiar soil in which virtue prospers.—*Goodman.*

The current of tenderness widens as it proceeds; and two men imperceptibly find their hearts filled with good nature for each other, when they were at first only in pursuit of mirth and relaxation.—*Goldsmith.*

An inexhaustible good nature is one of the most precious gifts of heaven, spreading itself like oil over the troubled sea of thought, and keeping the mind smooth and equable in the roughest weather.—*Washington Irving.*

Good nature, like a bee, collects honey from every herb. Ill nature, like the spider, sucks poison from the sweetest flower.

Good nature is one of the richest fruits of true Christianity.—*H. W. Beecher.*

Affability, mildness, tenderness, and a word which I would fain bring back to its original signification of virtue—I mean good nature—are of daily use; they are the bread of mankind and the staff of life.—*Dryden.*

Good nature is the beauty of the mind, and like personal beauty, wins almost without anything else—sometimes, indeed, in spite of positive deficiencies.—*Hanway.*

A shrewd observer once said, that in walking the streets of a slippery morning, one might see where the good natured people lived, by the ashes thrown on the ice before the doors.—*Franklin.*

Good nature is stronger than tomahawks.—*Emerson.*

Good nature is more agreeable in conversation than wit, and gives a certain air to the countenance which is more amiable than beauty.—It shows virtue in the fairest light; takes off, in some measure, from the deformity of vice; and makes even folly and impertinence supportable.—*Addison.*

Good nature is often a mere matter of health.—With good digestion we are apt to be good natured; with bad digestion, morose.—*H. W. Beecher.*

Good sense and good nature are never separated; and good nature is the product of right reason.—It makes allowance for the failings of others by considering that there is nothing perfect in mankind; and by distinguishing that which comes nearest to excellence, though not absolutely free from faults, will certainly produce candor in judging.—*Dryden.*

GOODNESS.— (See "BENEFICENCE.")

There are two perfectly good men; one dead, and the other unborn.—*Chinese Proverb.*

Be not merely good; be good for something.—*Thoreau.*

In nothing do men approach so nearly to the gods as in doing good to men.—*Cicero.*

There may be a certain pleasure in vice, but there is a higher in purity and virtue.—The most commanding of all delights is the delight in goodness.—The beauty of holiness is but one beauty, but it is the highest.—It is the loss of the sense of sin and shame that destroys both men and states.—*Independent.*

He that is a good man, is three quarters of his way toward the being a good Christian, wheresoever he lives, or whatsoever he is called.—*South.*

We may be as good as we please, if we please to be good.—*Barrow.*

Real goodness does not attach itself merely to this life—it points to another world. Political or professional reputation cannot last forever, but a conscience void of offence before God and man is an inheritance for eternity.—*Daniel Webster.*

We can do more good by being good

than in any other way.—*Rowland Hill.*

If there be a divine providence, no good man need be afraid to do right; he will only fear to do wrong.—*Haygood.*

To be doing good is man's most glorious task.—*Sophocles.*

To be good, we must do good; and by doing good we take a sure means of being good, as the use and exercise of the muscles increase their power.—*Tryon Edwards.*

It is a law of our humanity, that man must know good through evil.—No great principle ever triumphed but through much evil.—No man ever progressed to greatness and goodness but through great mistakes.—*F. W. Robertson.*

By desiring what is perfectly good, even when we do not quite know what it is, and cannot do what we would, we are part of the divine power against evil, widening the skirts of light and making the struggle with darkness narrower.—*George Eliot.*

Let a man be never so ungrateful or inhuman, he shall never destroy the satisfaction of my having done a good office.—*Seneca.*

The good are heaven's peculiar care.—*Ovid.*

All the fame which ever cheated humanity into higher notions of its own importance would never weigh in my mind against the pure and pious interest which a virtuous being may be pleased to take in my welfare.—*Byron.*

He who loves goodness harbors angels, reveres reverence, and lives with God.—*Emerson.*

He is good that does good to others. If he suffers for the good he does, he is better still; and if he suffers from them to whom he did good, he has arrived to that height of goodness that nothing but an increase of his sufferings can add to it; if it proves his death, his virtue is at its summit; it is heroism complete.—*Bruyère.*

I have known some men possessed of good qualities which were very serviceable to others, but useless to themselves; like a sun-dial on the front of a house, to inform and benefit the neighbors and passengers, but not the owner within.—*Swift.*

He that does good to another, does

also good to himself; not only in the consequence, but in the very act of doing it; for the consciousness of well-doing is an ample reward.—*Seneca.*

A good man is kinder to his enemy than bad men to their friends.—*Bp. Hall.*

The good for virtue's sake abhor to sin.—*Horace.*

Never did any soul do good, but it came readier to do the same again, with more enjoyment. Never was love, or gratitude, or bounty practised but with increasing joy, which made the practiser still more in love with the fair act.—*Shaftesbury.*

A good man is influenced by God himself, and has a kind of divinity within him; so it may be a question whether he goes to heaven, or heaven comes to him.—*Seneca.*

The best portion of a good man's life is his little, nameless, unremembered acts of kindness and of love.—*Wordsworth.*

Experience has convinced me that there is a thousand times more goodness, wisdom, and love in the world than men imagine.—*Gehles.*

Nothing can make a man truly great but being truly good and partaking of God's holiness.—*M. Henry.*

It is only great souls that know how much glory there is in being good.—*Sophocles.*

How far that little candle throws his beams! so shines a good deed in a naughty world.—*Shakespeare.*

In the heraldry of heaven goodness precedes greatness, and so on earth it is more powerful.—The lowly and lovely may often do more good in their limited sphere than the gifted.—*Bp. Horne.*

Beautiful is the activity which works for good, and beautiful the stillness which waits for good; blessed the self-sacrifice of one, and blessed the self-forgetfulness of the other.—*Collyer.*

Goodness consists not in the outward things we do, but in the inward thing we are.—To be good is the great thing.—*E. H. Chapin.*

A good man doubles the length of his existence; to have lived so as to look back with pleasure on our past life is to live twice.—*Martial.*

The soul is strong that trusts in goodness.—*Massinger.*

You are not very good if you are not better than your best friends imagine you to be.—*Lavater.*

We must first be made good, before we can do good; we must first be made just, before our works can please God—for when we are justified by faith in Christ, then come good works.—*Latimer.*

A good deed is never lost.—He who sows courtesy, reaps friendship; he who plants kindness, gathers love; pleasure bestowed upon a grateful mind was never sterile, but generally gratitude begets reward.—*Basil.*

It seems to me it is only noble to be good.—Kind hearts are more than coronets.—*Tennyson.*

There never was law, or sect, or opinion did so much magnify goodness as the Christian religion doth.—*Bacon.*

As I know more of mankind I expect less of them, and am ready to call a man a good man upon easier terms than I was formerly.—*Johnson.*

To love the public, to study universal good, and to promote the interest of the whole world, as far as it lies in our power, is the height of goodness, and makes that temper which we call divine. —*Shaftesbury.*

Goodness is love in action, love with its hand to the plow, love with the burden on its back, love following his footsteps who went about continually doing good.—*J. Hamilton.*

He is a good man whose intimate friends are all good, and whose enemies are decidedly bad.—*Lavater.*

Of all virtues and dignities of the mind, goodness is the greatest, being the character of the Deity; and without it, man is a busy, mischievous, wretched thing.—*Bacon.*

Your actions, in passing, pass not away, for every good work is a grain of seed for eternal life.—*Bernard.*

His daily prayer, far better understood in acts than in words, was simply doing good.—*Whittier.*

Live for something.—Do good, and leave behind you a monument of virtue that the storms of time can never destroy.—Write your name in kindness, love, and mercy on the hearts of thousands you come in contact with year by year, and you will never be forgotten.—Your name and your good deeds will shine as the stars of heaven.—*Chalmers.*

That is good which doth good.—*Venning.*

Do all the good you can, in all the ways you can, to all the souls you can, in every place you can, at all the times you can, with all the zeal you can, as long as ever you can.—*J. Wesley.*

Whatever mitigates the woes, or increases the happiness of others, is a just criterion of goodness; and whatever injures society at large, or any individual in it, is a criterion of iniquity.—*Goldsmith.*

Nothing is rarer than real goodness.—*Rochefoucauld.*

Goodness thinks no ill where no ill seems.—*Milton.*

To an honest mind, the best perquisites of a place are the advantages it gives for doing good.—*Addison.*

GOOD SENSE.— (See "COMMON SENSE.")

GOSPEL.—My heart has always assured and reassured me that the gospel of Christ must be a Divine reality.—The sermon on the mount cannot be merely a human production.—This belief enters into the very depth of my conscience.—The whole history of man proves it.—*Daniel Webster.*

All the gospels, in my judgment, date back to the first century, and are substantially by the authors to whom they are attributed.—*Renan.*

The shifting systems of false religion are continually changing their places; but the gospel of Christ is the same forever. While other false lights are extinguished, this true light ever shineth.—*T. L. Cuyler.*

So comprehensive are the doctrines of the gospel, that they involve all moral truth known by man; so extensive are the precepts, that they require every virtue, and forbid every sin. Nothing has been added, either by the labors of philosophy or the progress of human knowledge.

Did you ever notice that while the gospel sets before us a higher and more blessed heaven than any other religion,

its hell is also deeper and darker than any other?—*Warren.*

I search in vain in history to find the similar to Jesus Christ, or anything which can approach the gospel.—Neither history, nor humanity, nor the ages, nor nature, offer me anything with which I am able to compare or explain it.—There is nothing there which is not beyond the march of events and above the human mind.—What happiness it gives to those who believe it! What marvels there which those admire who reflect upon it!—*Napoleon.*

God writes the gospel not in the Bible alone, but on trees, and flowers, and clouds, and stars.—*Luther.*

The gospel is the fulfillment of all hopes, the perfection of all philosophy, the interpreter of all revelations, and a key to all the seeming contradictions of truth in the physical and moral world.—*Hugh Miller.*

We can learn nothing of the gospel except by feeling its truths. There are some sciences that may be learned by the head, but the science of Christ crucified can only be learned by the heart.—*Spurgeon.*

The gospel in all its doctrines and duties appears infinitely superior to any human composition.—It has no mark of human ignorance, imperfection, or sinfulness, but bears the signature of divine wisdom, authority, and importance, and is most worthy of the supreme attention and regard of all intelligent creatures.—*Emmons.*

There is not a book on earth so favorable to all the kind and to all the sublime affections, or so unfriendly to hatred, persecution, tyranny, injustice, and every sort of malevolence as the gospel.—It breathes, throughout, only mercy, benevolence, and peace.—*Beattie.*

GOSSIP.—(See "TATTLING.")

Gossip has been well defined as putting two and two together, and making it five.

I hold it to be a fact, that if all persons knew what each said of the other, there would not be four friends in the world.—*Pascal.*

News-hunters have great leisure, with little thought; much petty ambition to be thought intelligent, without any other pretension than being able to communicate what they have just learned.—*Zimmermann.*

When of a gossipping circle it was asked "What are they doing?" the answer was, "Swapping lies."

There is a set of malicious, prating, prudent gossips, both male and female, who murder characters to kill time; and will rob a young fellow of his good name before he has years to know the value of it.—*Sheridan.*

Fire and sword are but slow engines of destruction in comparison with the babbler.—*Steele.*

Truth is not exciting enough to those who depend on the characters and lives of their neighbors for all their amusement.—*Bancroft.*

An empty brain and a tattling tongue are very apt to go together; the most silly and trivial items of news or scandal fill the former and are retailed by the latter.

Gossip, pretending to have the eyes of an Argus, has all the blindness of a bat. —*Ouida.*

In private life I never knew any one interfere with other people's disputes but that he heartily repented of it.—*Carlyle.*

Let the greatest part of the news thou hearest be the least part of what thou believest, lest the greatest part of what thou believest be the least part of what is true. Where lies are easily admitted, the father of lies will not easily be kept out.—*Quarles.*

Gossip is the henchman of rumor and scandal.—*Feuillet.*

Gossip is always a personal confession either of malice or imbecility, and the young should not only shun it, but by the most thorough culture relieve themselves from all temptation to it.—It is a low, frivolous, and too often a dirty business.—*J. G. Holland.*

Tale bearers are just as bad as tale makers.—*Sheridan.*

Narrow-minded and ignorant persons talk about persons and not things; hence gossip is the bane and disgrace of so large a portion of society.

As to people saying a few idle words about us, we must not mind that any more than the old church steeple minds the rooks cawing about it.—*George Eliot.*

GOVERNMENT.—(See "STATESMAN-SHIP.")

They that govern most make least noise. In rowing a barge, they that do drudgery work, slash, puff, and sweat; but he that governs, sits quietly at the stern, and scarce is seen to stir.—*Selden.*

No matter what theory of the origin of government you adopt, if you follow it out to its legitimate conclusions it will bring you face to face with the moral law.—*H. J. Van Dyke.*

The less government we have the better—the fewer laws and the less confided power. The antidote to this abuse of formal government is the influence of private character, the growth of the individual.—*Emerson.*

Men well governed should seek after no other liberty, for there can be no greater liberty than a good government. —*Sir W. Raleigh.*

When men put their trust in God and in knowledge, the government of the majority is, in the end, the government of the wise and good.—*Spalding.*

While just government protects all in their religious rites, true religion affords government its surest support.—*Washington.*

The best of all governments is that which teaches us to govern ourselves.—*Goethe.*

No government ought to exist for the purpose of checking the prosperity of its people or to allow such a principle in its policy.—*Burke.*

The less of government the better, if society be kept in peace and prosperity.—*Channing.*

That is the most perfect government under which a wrong to the humblest is an affront to all.—*Solon.*

Government is not mere advice; it is authority, with power to enforce its laws. —*Washington.*

The principal foundation of all states is in good laws and good arms.—*Machiavelli.*

The punishment suffered by the wise who refuse to take part in the government, is to live under the government of bad men.—*Plato.*

Government is only a necessary evil, like other go-carts and crutches.—*Our* need of it shows exactly how far we are still children.—*All overmuch governing kills the self-help and energy of the governed.—Wendell Phillips.*

A man must first govern himself ere he is fit to govern a family; and his family ere he be fit to bear the government of the commonwealth.—*Sir W. Raleigh.*

A king may be a tool, a thing of straw; but if he serves to frighten our enemies, and secure our property, it is well enough; a scarecrow is a thing of straw, but it protects the corn.—*Pope.*

We settle things by a majority vote, and the psychological effect of doing that is to create the impression that the majority is probably right. Of course, on any fine issue the majority is sure to be wrong. Think of taking a majority vote on the best music. Jazz would win over Chopin. Or on the best novel. Many cheap scribblers would win over Tolstoy. And any day a prizefight will get a bigger crowd, larger gate receipts and wider newspaper publicity than any new revelation of goodness, truth or beauty could hope to achieve in a century. . . .—*Rev. Dr. Harry Emerson Fosdick.*

States are not made, nor patched; they grow: Grow slow through centuries of pain.—*John Masefield.*

Only free people can hold their purpose and their honor steady to a common end, and prefer the interest of mankind to any narrow interest of their own.—*Woodrow Wilson.*

I resent at any time or any place the attitude that the safety of this country depends on any man holding his job. No man has achieved that strength, and this country has not deteriorated to that weakness.—*Owen D. Young.*

The true strength of rulers and empires lies not in armies or emotions, but in the belief of men that they are inflexibly open and truthful and legal. As soon as a government departs from that standard it ceases to be anything more than "the gang in possession," and its days are numbered.—*H. G. Wells.*

This nation, under God, shall have a new birth of freedom, that government of the people, by the people, for the people, shall not perish from the earth.—*Abraham Lincoln.*

The actual achievement of democracy is that it gives a tolerably good time to the under-dog. Or, at least, it tries; and it is, I think, for this reason that most of us accept it as our political creed.—*Sir James Jeans.*

The world must be made safe for democracy.—*Woodrow Wilson.*

Politics resemble religion; attempting to divest either of ceremony is the most certain method of bringing either into contempt. The weak must have their inducements to admiration as well as the wise; and it is the business of a sensible government to impress all ranks with a sense of subordination, whether this be effected by a diamond, or a virtuous edict, a sumptuary law, or a glass necklace.—*Goldsmith.*

Though the people support the government, the government should not support the people.—*Grover Cleveland.*

The proper function of a government is to make it easy for the people to do good and difficult for them to do evil.—*Gladstone.*

Governments are necessarily continuing concerns. They have to keep going in good times and in bad. They therefore need a wide margin of safety. If taxes and debt are made all the people can bear when times are good, there will be certain disaster when times are bad.—*Calvin Coolidge.*

The form of government is unimportant—the spirit everything.—*General Von Schmidt.*

No man ever saw the people of whom he forms a part. No man ever saw a government. I live in the midst of the Government of the United States, but I never saw the Government of the United States.—*Woodrow Wilson.*

If we can develop a class of educated men with nothing else to do but to better government, we ought to use them; and we ought to use them by having the profession of the politician recognized as essential to the welfare of the Republic.—*William Howard Taft.*

The vigorous and growing opposition of organized labor to all schemes of government ownership in industry is one of the most hopeful and encouraging facts in American political life.—*John Spargo.*

The culminating point of administration is to know well how much power, great or small, we ought to use in all circumstances.—*Montesquieu.*

Society cannot exist unless a controlling power upon will and appetite be placed somewhere; and the less of it there is within, the more there must be without.—It is ordained in the eternal constitution of things, that men of intemperate minds cannot be free.—Their passions forge their fetters.—*Burke.*

The world is governed by three things —wisdom, authority, and appearance. Wisdom for thoughtful people, authority for rough people, and appearances for the great mass of superficial people who can look only at the outside.

Government owes its birth to the necessity of preventing and repressing the injuries which associated individuals have to fear from one another.—It is the sentinel who watches, in order that the common laborer be not disturbed.—*Raynal.*

It is to self-government, the great principle of popular representation and administration, the system that lets in all to participate in its counsels, that we owe what we are, and what we hope to be.—*Daniel Webster.*

A republican government is in a hundred points weaker than one that is autocratic; but in this one point it is the strongest that ever existed—it has educated a race of men that are men.—*H. W. Beecher.*

All good government must begin in the home.—It is useless to make good laws for bad people.—Public sentiment is more than law.—*H. R. Haweis.*

There be three sorts of government, monarchical, aristocratical, and democratical, and they are to fall three different ways into ruin: the first, by tyranny; the second, by ambition; the last, by tumults.—A commonwealth, grounded on any one of these, is not of long continuance; but wisely mingled, each guards the other and makes government exact.—*Quarles.*

Society is well governed when the people obey the magistrates, and the magistrates obey the laws.—*Solon.*

The very idea of the power and right of the people to establish government presupposes the duty of every individual to obey the established government.—*Washington.*

He that would govern others, first should be the master of himself, richly endued with depth of understanding and height of knowledge.—*Massinger.*

All government and exercise of power, no matter in what form, which is not based on love, and directed by knowledge, is tyranny.—*Mrs. Jameson.*

A government for the people must depend for its success on the intelligence, the morality, the justice, and the interest of the people themselves.—*Grover Cleveland.*

Power exercised with violence has seldom been of long duration, but temper and moderation generally produce permanence in all things.—*Seneca.*

The aggregate happiness of society, which is best promoted by the practise of a virtuous policy, is, or ought to be, the end of all government.—*Washington.*

No government is respectable which is not just.—Without unspotted purity of public faith, without sacred public principle, fidelity, and honor, no mere forms of government, no machinery of laws, can give dignity to political society.—*Daniel Webster.*

A mercantile democracy may govern long and widely; a mercantile aristocracy cannot stand.—*Landor.*

The worst of governments are always the most changeable, and cost the people dearest.—*Butler.*

The only choice which Providence has graciously left to a vicious government is either to fall by the people if they become enlightened, or with them, if they are kept enslaved and ignorant.—*Coleridge.*

The surest way of governing, both in a private family and a kingdom, is, for the husband and the prince sometimes to drop their prerogatives.—*Hughes.*

The administration of government, like a guardianship, ought to be directed to the good of those who confer, not of those who receive the trust.—*Cicero.*

It seems to me a great truth, that human things cannot stand on selfishness, mechanical utilities, economics, and law courts; that if there be not a religious element in the relations of men, such relations are miserable, and doomed to ruin.—*Carlyle.*

It is among the evils, and perhaps not the smallest, of democratic governments, that the people must feel before they will see.—When this happens, they are roused to action.—Hence it is that those kinds of government are too slow.—*Washington.*

When Tarquin the Proud was asked what was the best mode of governing a conquered city, he replied only by beating down with his staff all the tallest poppies in his garden.—*Livy.*

It is better for a city to be governed by a good man than even by good laws.—*Aristotle.*

Nothing will ruin the country if the people themselves will undertake its safety; and nothing can save it if they leave that safety in any hands but their own.—*Daniel Webster.*

For forms of government let fools contest.—That which is best administered is best.—*Pope.*

It may pass for a maxim in state, that the administration cannot be placed in too few hands, nor the legislation in too many.—*Swift.*

Few consider how much we are indebted to government, because few can represent how wretched mankind would be without it.—*Addison.*

When any of the four pillars of government, religion, justice, counsel, and treasure, are mainly shaken or weakened, men had need to pray for fair weather.—*Bacon.*

All free governments, whatever their name, are in reality governments by public opinion; and it is on the quality of this public opinion that their prosperity depends.—*J. R. Lowell.*

GRACE.—"What is grace?" was asked of an old colored man, who, for over forty years, had been a slave.—"Grace," he replied, "is what I should call giving something for nothing."

The king-becoming graces are justice, verity, temperance, stableness, bounty, perseverance, mercy, lowliness, devotion, patience, courage, fortitude. — *Shakespeare.*

Let grace and goodness be the principal loadstone of thy affections. For love which hath ends, will have an end;

whereas that which is founded on true virtue, will always continue.—*Dryden.*

Whatever is graceful is virtuous, and whatever is virtuous is graceful.—*Cice*

The Christian graces are like perfumes, the more they are pressed, the sweeter they smell; like stars that shine brightest in the dark; like trees which, the more they are shaken, the deeper root they take, and the more fruit they bear.—*Beaumont.*

That word "Grace," in an ungracious mouth, is profane.—*Shakespeare.*

Virtue, wisdom, goodness, and real worth, like the loadstone, never lose their power. These are the true graces, which are linked hand in hand, because it is by their influence that human hearts are so firmly united to each other.—*Burton.*

Grace is but glory begun, and glory is but grace perfected.—*Jonathan Edwards.*

God appoints our graces to be nurses to other men's weaknesses.—*H. W. Beecher.*

The growth of grace is like the polishing of metals. There is first an opaque surface; by and by you see a spark darting out, then a strong light; till at length it sends back a perfect image of the sun that shines upon it.—*Payson.*

There is no such way to attain to greater measure of grace as for a man to live up to the little grace he has.—*Brooks.*

Grace comes into the soul, as the morning sun into the world; first a dawning; then a light; and at last the sun in his full and excellent brightness.—*T. Adams.*

You pray for the graces of faith and hope and love; but prayer alone will not bring them.—They must be wrought in you through labor and patience and suffering.—They are not kept put up in bottles for us, to be had for the mere asking; they must be the outgrowth of the life.—Prayer for them will be answered, but God will have us work out each one in the way of duty.—*H. W. Beecher.*

The being of grace must go before the increase of it; for there is no growth without life, and no building without a foundation.—*Lavington.*

As grace is first from God, so it is continually from him, as much as light is all day long from the sun, as well as at first dawn or at sun-rising.—*Jonathan Edwards.*

As heat is opposed to cold, and light to darkness, so grace is opposed to sin. —Fire and water may as well agree in the same vessel, as grace and sin in the same heart.—*T. Brooks.*

GRACEFULNESS.—Grace is to the body, what good sense is to the mind.—*Rochefoucauld.*

A graceful and pleasing figure is a perpetual letter of recommendation.—*Bacon.*

Gracefulness has been defined to be the outward expression of the inward harmony of the soul.—*Hazlitt.*

All the actions and attitudes of children are graceful because they are the offspring of the moment, without affectation, and free from all pretense.—*Fuseli.*

How inimitably graceful children are before they learn to dance.—*Coleridge.*

It is graceful in a man to think and speak with propriety, to act with deliberation, and in every occurrence of life to find out and persevere in the truth.—*Cicero.*

GRATITUDE. — (See "THANKFULNESS.")

Gratitude is not only the memory but the homage of the heart—rendered to God for his goodness.—*N. P. Willis.*

If I only have the will to be grateful, I am so.—*Seneca.*

In noble hearts the feeling of gratitude has all the ardor of a passion.—*Poincelot.*

A grateful thought toward heaven is of itself a prayer.—*Lessing.*

Cicero calls gratitude the mother of virtues, the most capital of all duties, and uses the words grateful and good as synonymous terms, inseparably united in the same character.—*Bate.*

Gratitude to God makes even a temporal blessing a taste of heaven.—*Romaine.*

Our thanks should be as fervent for mercies received, as our petitions for mercies sought.—*C. Simmons.*

He that urges gratitude pleads the cause both of God and men, for without it we can neither be sociable nor religious.—*Seneca.*

He enjoys much who is thankful for little; a grateful mind is both a great and a happy mind.—*Secker.*

He who receives a benefit should never forget it; he who bestows should never remember it.—*Charron.*

To the generous mind the heaviest debt is that of gratitude, when it is not in our power to repay it.—*Franklin.*

He who acknowledges a kindness has it still, and he who has a grateful sense of it has requited it.—*Cicero.*

When I find a great deal of gratitude in a poor man, I take it for granted there would be as much generosity if he were rich.—*Pope.*

There is as much greatness of mind in acknowledging a good turn, as in doing it.—*Seneca.*

Those who make us happy are always thankful to us for being so; their gratitude is the reward of their benefits.—*Mad. Swetchine.*

We can be thankful to a friend for a few acres or a little money; and yet for the freedom and command of the whole earth, and for the great benefits of our being, our life, health, and reason, we look upon ourselves as under no obligation.—*Seneca.*

O Lord, who lends me life, lend me a heart replete with thankfulness.—*Shakespeare.*

From David learn to give thanks for everything.—Every furrow in the Book of Psalms is sown with the seeds of thanksgiving.—*Jeremy Taylor.*

No metaphysician ever felt the deficiency of language so much as the grateful.—*Colton.*

God is pleased with no music below so much as with the thanksgiving songs of relieved widows and supported orphans; of rejoicing, comforted, and thankful persons.—*Jeremy Taylor.*

Epicurus says, "gratitude is a virtue that has commonly profit annexed to it." And where is the virtue that has not? But still the virtue is to be valued for itself, and not for the profit that attends it.—*Seneca.*

Gratitude to God should be as habitual as the reception of mercies is constant, as ardent as the number of them is great, as devout as the riches of divine grace and goodness is incomprehensible. —*C. Simmons.*

Gratitude is a virtue most deified and yet most deserted; it is the ornament of rhetoric and the libel of practical life.— *J. W. Forney.*

It is another's fault if he be ungrateful, but it is mine if I do not give.—To find one thankful man, I will oblige a great many that are not so.—*Seneca.*

The gratitude of place-expectants is a lively sense of future favors.—*Walpole.*

He who remembers the benefits of his parents is too much occupied with his recollections to remember their faults.— *Béranger.*

If gratitude is due from children to their earthly parent, how much more is the gratitude of the great family of men due to our father in heaven.—*H. Ballou.*

GRAVE. — A grave, wherever found, preaches a short and pithy sermon to the soul.—*Hawthorne.*

Earth's highest station ends in "Here he lies;" and "Dust to dust" concludes the noblest songs.—*Young.*

The grave buries every error, covers every defect, extinguishes every resentment.—From its peaceful bosom spring none but fond regrets and tender recollections.—Who can look down upon the grave of an enemy, and not feel a compunctious throb that he should have warred with the poor handful of dust that lies moldering before him.—*Washington Irving.*

It is sadness to sense to look to the grave, but gladness to faith to look beyond it.

A Christian graveyard is a cradle, where, in the quiet motions of the globe, Jesus rocks his sleeping children.—By and by he will wake them from their slumber, and in the arms of angels they shall be translated to the skies.—*G. B. Cheever.*

An angel's arm can't snatch me from the grave; legions of angels can't confine me there.—*Young.*

The disciples found angels at the grave of him they loved, and we should always find them, too, but that our eyes are too full of tears for seeing.—*H. W. Beecher.*

All along the pathway of life are tombstones, by the side of which we have promised to strive for Heaven.

The churchyard is the market-place where all things are rated at their true value, and those who are approaching it talk of the world and its vanities with a wisdom unknown before.—*Baxter.*

When I look upon the tombs of the great, every emotion of envy dies within me; when I read the epitaphs of the beautiful, every inordinate desire goes out.—*Addison.*

We go to the grave of a friend, saying, "A man is dead," but angels throng about him, saying, "A man is born."— *H. W. Beecher.*

We weep over the graves of infants and the little ones taken from us by death; but an early grave may be the shortest way to heaven.—*Tryon Edwards.*

Of all the pulpits from which the human voice is ever sent forth, there is none from which it reaches so far as from the grave.—*Ruskin.*

O how small a portion of earth will hold us when we are dead, who ambitiously seek after the whole world while we are living.—*Philip of Macedon.*

The ancients feared death; we, thanks to Christianity, fear only dying.—*Guesses at Truth.*

I like that ancient Saxon phrase which calls the burial ground "God's acre!" It is just; it consecrates each grave within its walls, and breathes a benison over the sleeping dust.—*Longfellow.*

Only the actions of the just smell sweet and blossom in the dust.—*Shirley.*

GRAVITY.—Gravity is only the bark of wisdom; but it preserves it.—*Confucius.*

Too much gravity argues a shallow mind.—*Lavater.*

Those wanting wit affect gravity, and go by the name of solid men.—*Dryden.*

Gravity is a mysterious carriage of the body, invented to cover the defects of the mind.—*Rochefoucauld.*

The very essence of assumed gravity is design, and consequently deceit; a taught trick to gain credit with the world for more sense and knowledge than a man is worth.—*Sterne.*

There is a gravity which is not austere, nor captious, which belongs not to melancholy nor dwells in contraction of heart, but arises from tenderness and hangs on reflection.—*Landor.*

All the sobriety religion needs or requires is that which real earnestness produces.—When men say "be sober," they usually mean "be stupid."—When the Bible says "be sober," it means "rouse up to the earnestness and vivacity of life."—The old scriptural sobriety was effectual doing; ascetic sobriety is effectual dullness.—*H. W. Beecher.*

As in a man's life, so in his studies, it is the most beautiful and humane thing in the world so to mingle gravity with pleasure, that the one may not sink into melancholy, nor the other rise up into wantonness.—*Pliny.*

There is a false gravity that is a very ill symptom; and as rivers which run very slowly have always most mud at the bottom, so a solid stiffness in the constant course of a man's life, is the sign of a thick bed of mud at the bottom of his brain.—*Saville.*

Gravity is but the rind of wisdom; but it is a preservative rind.—*Joubert.*

Gravity is the very essence of imposture; it not only mistakes other things, but is apt perpetually to mistake itself.—*Shaftesbury.*

Gravity must be natural and simple; there must be urbanity and tenderness in it.—A man must not formalize on everything.—He who does so is a fool; and a grave fool is, perhaps, more injurious than a light fool.—*Cecil.*

Gravity is the ballast of the soul, which keeps the mind steady.—*Fuller.*

There is a care for trifles which proceeds from love and conscience, and which is most holy; and there is a care for trifles which comes of idleness and frivolity, and is most base.—And so, also, there is a gravity proceeding from thought, which is most noble, and a gravity proceeding from dullness and mere incapability for enjoyment, which is most base.—*Ruskin.*

Gravity—the body's wisdom to conceal the mind.—*Young.*

As in our lives, so also in our studies, it is most becoming and most wise to temper gravity with cheerfulness, that the former may not imbue our minds with melancholy, nor the latter degenerate into licentiousness.—*Pliny.*

GREATNESS.—A really great man is known by three signs—generosity in the design, humanity in the execution, moderation in success.—*Bismarck.*

The greatest man is he who chooses the right with invincible resolution; who resists the sorest temptations from within and without; who bears the heaviest burdens cheerfully; who is calmest in storms, and most fearless under menace and frowns; and whose reliance on truth, on virtue, and on God, is most unfaltering.—*Channing.*

He only is great who has the habits of greatness; who, after performing what none in ten thousand could accomplish, passes on like Samson, and "tells neither father nor mother of it."—*Lavater.*

The true test of a great man—that, at least, which must secure his place among the highest order of great men—is, his having been in advance of his age.—*Brougham.*

A contemplation of God's works, a generous concern for the good of mankind, and the unfeigned exercise of humility—these only, denominate men great and glorious.—*Addison.*

The study of God's word, for the purpose of discovering God's will, is the secret discipline which has formed the greatest characters.—*J. W. Alexander.*

Greatness lies, not in being strong, but in the right using of strength; and strength is not used rightly when it serves only to carry a man above his fellows for his own solitary glory. He is the greatest whose strength carries up the most hearts by the attraction of his own.

Difficulty is a nurse of greatness—a harsh nurse, who rocks her foster children roughly, but rocks them into strength and athletic proportions.—The mind, grappling with great aims and wrestling with mighty impediments, grows by a certain necessity to the stature of greatness.—*Bryant.*

If any man seeks for greatness, let him forget greatness and ask for truth, and he will find both.—*Horace Mann.*

There never was any heart truly great and gracious, that was not also tender and compassionate.—*South.*

The superiority of some men is merely local. They are great because their associates are little.—*Johnson.*

A nation's greatness resides not in her material resources, but in her will, faith, intelligence, and moral forces.—*J. M. Hoppin.*

Not a day passes over the earth but men and women of no note do great deeds, speak great words, and suffer noble sorrows. Of these obscure heroes, philosophers, and martyrs the greater part will never be known till that hour when many that were great shall be small, and the small great.—*Charles Reade.*

A great man may be the personification and type of the epoch for which God destines him, but he is never its creator.—*D'Aubigné.*

No man has come to true greatness who has not felt in some degree that his life belongs to his race, and that what God gives him he gives him for mankind.—*Phillips Brooks.*

The greatest men in all ages have been lovers of their kind.—*All true leaders of men have it.*—Faith in men and love to men are unfailing marks of true greatness.

If I am asked who is the greatest man? I answer the best; and if I am required to say who is the best? I reply he that has deserved most of his fellow-creatures.—*Sir William Jones.*

It is easy in the world to live after the world's opinion—it is easy in solitude to live after your own; but the great man is he who, in the midst of the world, keeps with perfect sweetness the independence of solitude.—*Emerson.*

In estimating the greatness of great men, the inverted law of the physical stands for the intellectual and spiritual nature—the former is lessened by distance, the latter increased.—*Schopenhauer.*

Great men are the commissioned guides of mankind, who rule their fellows because they are wiser.—*Carlyle.*

The theory that a great man is merely the product of his age, is rejected by the common sense and common observation of mankind.—The power that guides large masses of men, and shapes the channels in which the energies of a great people flow, is something more than a mere aggregate of derivative forces. It is a compound product, in which the genius of the man is one element, and the sphere opened to him by the character of his age and the institutions of his country, is another.—*G. S. Hillard.*

Nothing can be truly great which is not right.—*Johnson.*

Great men often obtain their ends by means beyond the grasp of vulgar intellect, and even by methods diametrically opposite to those which the multitude would pursue. But, to effect this, bespeaks as profound a knowledge of mind as that philosopher evinced of matter, who first produced ice by the agency of heat.—*Colton.*

If the title of great man ought to be reserved for him who cannot be charged with an indiscretion or a vice; who spent his life in establishing the independence, the glory, and durable prosperity of his country; who succeeded in all that he undertook, and whose successes were never won at the expense of honor, justice, integrity, or by the sacrifice of a single principle—this title will not be denied to Washington.—*Sparks.*

A great, a good, and a right mind is a kind of divinity lodged in flesh, and may be the blessing of a slave as well as of a prince: it came from heaven, and to heaven it must return; and it is a kind of heavenly felicity, which a pure and virtuous mind enjoys, in some degree, even upon earth.—*Seneca.*

In life we shall find many men that are great, and some men that are good, but very few men that are both great and good.—*Colton.*

The great men of the earth are but marking stones on the road of humanity; they are the priests of its religion.—*Mazzini.*

Subtract from the great man all that he owes to opportunity, all that he owes to chance, and all that he has gained by the wisdom of his friends and the folly of his enemies, and the giant will often be seen to be a pigmy.—*Colton.*

Distinction is the consequence, never the object, of a great mind.—*Washington Allston.*

However brilliant an action may be, it

ought not to pass for great when it is not the result of a great design.—*Rochefoucauld.*

Nothing can make a man truly great but being truly good, and partaking of God's holiness.—*M. Henry.*

Everything great is not always good, but all good things are great.—*Demosthenes.*

There is but one method, and that is hard labor; and a man who will not pay that price for greatness had better at once dedicate himself to the pursuit of the fox, or to talk of bullocks, and glory in the goad.—*Sydney Smith.*

The reason why great men meet with so little pity or attachment in adversity, would seem to be this: the friends of a great man were made by his fortune, his enemies by himself, and revenge is a much more punctual paymaster than gratitude.—*Colton.*

Great men never make bad use of their superiority; they see it, and feel it, and are not less modest. The more they have, the more they know their own deficiencies.—*Rousseau.*

He who is great when he falls is great in his prostration, and is no more an object of contempt than when men tread on the ruins of sacred buildings, which men of piety venerate no less than if they stood.—*Seneca.*

Times of general calamity and confusion have ever been productive of the greatest minds. The purest ore is produced from the hottest furnace, and the brightest thunderbolt is elicited from the darkest storm.—*Colton.*

The truly great consider first, how they may gain the approbation of God; and secondly, that of their own conscience; having done this, they would then willingly conciliate the good opinion of their fellowmen.—*Colton.*

Great souls are not those which have less passion and more virtue than common souls, but only those which have greater designs.—*Rochefoucauld.*

A great mind may change its objects, but it cannot relinquish them; it must have something to pursue; variety is its relaxation, and amusement its repose.—*Colton.*

Men in great place are thrice servants; servants of the sovereign or state, servants of fame, and servants of business; so that they have no freedom, neither in their persons, in their actions, nor in their times.—It is a strange desire to seek power over others, and to lose power over a man's self.—*Bacon.*

He is great who can do what he wishes; he is wise who wishes to do what he can.—*Ifland.*

A solemn and religious regard to spiritual and eternal things is an indispensable element of all true greatness.—*Daniel Webster.*

The difference between one man and another is by no means so great as the superstitious crowd supposes.—But the same feelings which in ancient Rome produced the apotheosis of a popular emperor, and in modern times the canonization of a devout prelate, lead men to cherish an illusion which furnishes them with something to adore.—*Macaulay.*

He is great enough that is his own master.—*Bp. Hall.*

Great minds, like heaven, are pleased in doing good, though the ungrateful subjects of their favors are barren in return.—*Rowe.*

What millions died that Cæsar might be great.—*Campbell.*

High stations tumult, not bliss create. —None think the great unhappy, but the great.—*Young.*

The most substantial glory of a country is in its virtuous great men.—Its prosperity will depend on its docility to learn from their example.—*Fisher Ames.*

Great is he who enjoys his earthenware as if it were plate, and not less great is the man to whom all his plate is no more than earthenware.—*Seneca.*

Some are born great; some achieve greatness; and some have greatness thrust upon them.—*Shakespeare.*

Since by your greatness you are nearer heaven in place be nearer it in goodness.

There never was yet a truly great man that was not at the same time truly virtuous.—*Franklin.*

It is to be lamented that great characters are seldom without a blot.—*Washington.*

The world cannot do without great

men, but great men are very trouble-some to the world.—*Goethe.*

He is not great, who is not greatly good.—*Shakespeare.*

Great men lose somewhat of their greatness by being near us; ordinary men gain much.—*Landor.*

Speaking generally, no man appears great to his contemporaries, for the same reason that no man is great to his serv-ants—both know too much of him.—*Colton.*

There never was a great institution or a great man, that did not, sooner or later, receive the reverence of mankind.—*Theodore Parker.*

Great minds must be ready not only to take opportunities, but to make them.—*Colton.*

Great men undertake great things be-cause they are great; fools, because they think them easy.—*Vauvenargues.*

He who comes up to his own idea of greatness, must always have had a very low standard of it in his mind.—*Ruskin.*

The man who does his work, any work, conscientiously, must always be in one sense a great man.—*Mulock.*

In the truly great, virtue governs with a scepter of knowledge and wisdom.—*Sir P. Sidney.*

Greatness lies not in being strong, but in the right using of strength.—*H. W. Beecher.*

GRIEF.—Never does a man know the force that is in him till some mighty affection or grief has humanized the soul.—*F. W. Robertson.*

There is no greater grief than to re-member days of joy when misery is at hand.—*Dante.*

Sorrow's crown of sorrow is remember-ing happier things.—*Tennyson.*

Great grief makes sacred those upon whom its hand is laid.—Joy may ele-vate, ambition glorify, but only sorrow can consecrate.—*Horace Greeley.*

Light griefs are plaintive, but great ones are dumb.—*Seneca.*

Every one can master a grief but he that hath it.—*Shakespeare.*

No grief is so acute but that time ameliorates it.—*Cicero.*

Time is the great comforter of grief,

but the agency by which it works is exhaustion.—*L. E. Landon.*

Moderate lamentation is the right of the dead; excessive grief the enemy of the living.—*Shakespeare.*

If the internal griefs of every man could be read, written on his forehead, how many who now excite envy, would appear to be objects of pity?—*Metas-tasio.*

Who fails to grieve when just occasion calls, or grieves too much, deserves not to be blest: inhuman, or effeminate, his heart.—*Young.*

Grief should be like joy, majestic, se-date, confirming, cleansing, equable, making free, strong to consume small troubles, to command great thoughts, grave thoughts, thoughts lasting to the end.—*De Vere.*

Well has it been said that there is no grief like the grief which does not speak.—*Longfellow.*

Some grief shows much of love; but much of grief shows still some want of wit.—*Shakespeare.*

Grief knits two hearts in closer bonds than happiness ever can; common suffer-ings are far stronger links than common joys.—*Lamartine.*

Excess of grief for the dead is mad-ness; for it is an injury to the living, and the dead know it not.—*Xenophon.*

Why destroy present happiness by a distant misery which may never come at all, or you may never live to see it?—Every substantial grief has twenty shad-ows, and most of them shadows of your own making.—*Sydney Smith.*

While grief is fresh, every attempt to divert only irritates.—You must wait till it be digested, and then amusement will dissipate the remains of it.—*John-son.*

Grief hallows hearts even while it ages heads.—*Bailey.*

Sorrow's best antidote is employment.—*Young.*

Give sorrow words.—The grief that does not speak, whispers the o'erfraught heart, and bids it break.—*Shakespeare.*

Bion, seeing a person who was tearing the hair off his head for sorrow, said, "Does this man think that baldness is a remedy for grief?"

GRUMBLING.—Every one may see daily instances of people who complain from the mere habit of complaining.—*Graves.*

There is an unfortunate disposition in man to attend much more to the faults of his companions that offend him, than to their perfections which please him.—*Greville.*

Just as you are pleased at finding faults, you are displeased at finding perfections.—*Lavater.*

Grumblers are commonly an idle set.—Having no disposition to work themselves, they spend their time in whining and complaining both about their own affairs and those of their neighbors.

Those who complain most are most to be complained of.—*M. Henry.*

There is a very large and very knowing class of misanthropes who rejoice in the name of grumblers, persons who are so sure that the world is going to ruin that they resent every attempt to comfort them as an insult to their sagacity, and accordingly seek their chief consolation in being inconsolable, and their chief pleasure in being displeased.—*E. P. Whipple.*

I pity the man who can travel from Dan to Beersheba, and cry it is all barren.—*Sterne.*

Had we not faults of our own, we should take less pleasure in complaining of others.—*Fénelon.*

GUESTS. — True friendship's laws are by this rule expressed: welcome the coming, speed the parting guest.—*Pope.*

Be bright and jovial among your guests to-night.—*Shakespeare.*

The first day, a guest; the second, a burden; the third, a pest.—*Laboulaye.*

Unbidden guests are often welcomest when they are gone.—*Shakespeare.*

Let the one you would welcome to your hospitality, be one you can welcome to your respect and esteem, if not to your personal friendship.

GUIDANCE. — A sound head, an honest heart, and an humble spirit are the three best guides through time and to eternity.

That man may safely venture on his way, who is so guided that he cannot stray.—*Walter Scott.*

He that takes truth for his guide, and duty for his end, may safely trust to God's providence to lead him aright.—*Pascal.*

If we acknowledge God in all our ways, he has promised safely to direct our steps, and in our experience we shall find the promise fulfilled.—*Payson.*

GUILT.—(See "REMORSE.")

Guilt is the very nerve of sorrow.—*Horace Bushnell.*

God hath yoked to guilt, her pale tormentor, misery.—*Bryant.*

Let no man trust the first false step of guilt: it hangs upon a precipice, whose steep descent in lost perdition ends.—*Young.*

Adversity, how blunt are all the arrows of thy quiver in comparison with those of guilt.—*Blair.*

The mind of guilt is full of scorpions.—*Shakespeare.*

It is the inevitable end of guilt that it places its own punishment on a chance which is sure to occur.—*L. E. Landon.*

From the body of one guilty deed a thousand ghostly fears and haunting thoughts proceed.—*Wordsworth.*

Better it were, that all the miseries which nature owns were ours at once, than guilt.—*Shakespeare.*

To what deep gulfs a single deviation from the track of human duties leads.—*Byron.*

He who is conscious of secret and dark designs, which, if known, would blast him, is perpetually shrinking and dodging from public observation, and is afraid of all around, and much more of all above him.—*W. Wirt.*

The guilty mind debases the great image that it wears, and levels us with brutes.—*Havard.*

They whose guilt within their bosom lies, imagine every eye beholds their blame.—*Shakespeare.*

Guilt upon the conscience, like rust upon iron, both defiles and consumes it, gnawing and creeping into it, as that does which at last eats out the very heart and substance of the metal.—*South.*

The guilt that feels not its own shame is wholly incurable.—It was the redeeming promise in the fault of Adam, that with the commission of his crime came the sense of his nakedness.—*Simms.*

Though it sleep long, the venom of great guilt, when death, or danger, or detection comes, will bite the spirit fiercely.—*Shakespeare.*

Guilt once harbored in the conscious breast, intimidates the brave, degrades the great.—*Johnson.*

Guilt is the source of sorrow, the avenging fiend, that follows us behind with whips and stings.—*Rowe.*

The guilt being great, the fear doth still exceed.—*Shakespeare.*

The greatest incitement to guilt is the hope of sinning with impunity.—*Cicero.*

Guiltiness will speak though tongues were out of use.—*Shakespeare.*

Oh, that pang, where more than madness lies, the worm that will not sleep, and never dies.—*Byron.*

Oh, what a state is guilt! how wild, how wretched, when apprehension can form nought but fears, and we distrust security itself.—*Havard.*

The consequences of our crimes long survive their commission, and, like the ghosts of the murdered, forever haunt the steps of the malefactor.—*Walter Scott.*

Suspicion always haunts the guilty mind; the thief doth fear each bush an officer.—*Shakespeare.*

Beside one deed of guilt, how blest is guileless woe!—*Bulwer.*

Let wickedness escape, as it may at the bar, it never fails of doing justice upon itself; for every guilty person is his own hangman.—*Seneca.*

Fraud and falsehood are his weak and treacherous allies, and he lurks trembling in the dark, dreading every ray of light, lest it should discover him, and give him up to shame and punishment. —*Fielding.*

They who engage in iniquitous designs miserably deceive themselves when they think they will go so far and no farther; one fault begets another; one crime renders another necessary; and thus they are impelled continually downward into a depth of guilt, which at the commencement of their career they would have died rather than have incurred.— *Southey.*

The sin lessens in the guilty one's estimation, only as the guilt increases.— *Schiller.*

GYMNASTICS.—The exercise of all the muscles of the body in their due proportion is one great secret of health and comfort as well as of strength, and the full development of manly vigor.— *W. Hall.*

Gymnastics open the chest, exercise the limbs, and give a man all the pleasure of boxing, without the blows. I could wish that learned men would lay out the time they employ in controversies and disputes about nothing, in this method of fighting with their own shadows. It might conduce very much to evaporate the spleen, which makes them uneasy to the public as well as to themselves.—*Addison.*

H

HABIT.—How use doth breed a habit in a man.—*Shakespeare.*

Any act often repeated soon forms a habit; and habit allowed, steadily gains in strength.—At first it may be but as the spider's web, easily broken through, but if not resisted it soon binds us with chains of steel.—*Tryon Edwards.*

We first make our habits, and then our habits make us.

All habits gather, by unseen degrees, as brooks make rivers, rivers run to seas.—*Dryden.*

Habit is a cable.—We weave a thread of it every day, and at last we cannot break it.—*H. Mann.*

If an idiot were to tell you the same story every day for a year, you would end by believing him.—*Burke.*

Habit is the deepest law of human nature.—*Carlyle.*

Habit is either the best of servants, or the worst of masters.—*Emmons.*

The habit of virtue cannot be formed in the closet; good habits are formed by acts of reason in a persevering struggle with temptation.—*B. Gilpin.*

In a majority of things habit is a greater plague than ever afflicted Egypt. —In religious character it is a grand felicity.—*John Foster.*

Charity should be the habit of our estimates; kindness of our feelings; benevolence of our affections; cheerfulness of our social intercourse; generosity of our living; improvement of our progress; prayer of our desires; fidelity of our self-examination; being and doing good of our entire life.

When we have practised good actions awhile, they become easy; when they are easy, we take pleasure in them; when they please us, we do them frequently; and then, by frequency of act, they grow into a habit.—*Tillotson.*

The chains of habit are generally too small to be felt until they are too strong to be broken.—*Johnson.*

As character to be used for eternity must be formed in time and in good time, so good habits to be used for happiness in this life must be formed early; and then they will be a treasure to be desired in the house of the wise, and an oil of life in their dwellings.—*G. B. Cheever.*

We are all the time following the influences which will presently be our rulers; we are making our own destiny. We are choosing our habits, our associates, our traits, our homes. In time these acquire a power over us which enslaves our will, and from them we neither will nor can break loose.—*H. L. Wayland.*

Habits are to the soul what the veins and arteries are to the blood, the courses in which it moves.—*Horace Bushnell.*

Habit, if not resisted, soon becomes necessity.—*Augustine.*

The phrases that men hear or repeat continually, end by becoming convictions and ossify the organs of intelligence.—*Goethe.*

I trust everything, under God, to habit, upon which, in all ages, the lawgiver has well as the schoolmaster has mainly placed his reliance; habit which makes everything easy, and casts all difficulties upon the deviation from the wonted course. Make sobriety a habit, and intemperance will be hateful and hard; make prudence a habit, and reckless profligacy will be as contrary to the nature of the child, grown to be an adult, as the most atrocious crimes are to any of your lordships. Give a child the habit of sacredly regarding the truth, of carefully respecting the property of others, of scrupulously abstaining from all acts of improvidence which can involve him in distress, and he will just as likely think of rushing into an element in which he cannot breathe, as of lying, or cheating, or stealing.—*Brougham.*

If we would know who is the most degraded and wretched of human beings, look for a man who has practised a vice so long that he curses it and yet clings to it; that he pursues it because he feels a great law of his nature driving him on toward it: but reaching it, knows that it will gnaw his heart, and make him roll himself in the dust with anguish.

There are habits, not only of drinking, swearing, and lying, but of every modification of action, speech, and thought. Man is a bundle of habits; in a word, there is not a quality or function, either of body or mind, which does not feel the influence of this great law of animated nature.—*Paley.*

Habit, to which all of us are more or less slaves.—*Fontaine.*

In early childhood you may lay the foundation of poverty or riches, industry or idleness, good or evil, by the habits to which you train your children. Teach them right habits then, and their future life is safe.

Habits, though in their commencement like the filmy line of the spider, trembling at every breeze, may, in the end, prove as links of tempered steel, binding a deathless being to eternal felicity or woe.—*Mrs. Sigourney.*

What a curious phenomenon it is that you can get men to die for the liberty of the world who will not make the little sacrifice that is needed to free themselves from their own individual bondage.—*Bruce Barton.*

The underlying cause of all weakness and unhappiness in man has always been, and still is, weak habit-of-thought.—*Horace Fletcher.*

Bad habits are as infectious by example as the plague itself is by contact.—*Fielding.*

Habit is ten times nature.—*Wellington.*

A large part of Christian virtue consists in good habits.—*Paley.*

Habits are the petrefaction of feelings.—*L. E. Landon.*

Habits work more constantly and with greater force than reason, which, when we have most need of it, is seldom fairly consulted, and more rarely obeyed. —*Locke.*

Refrain to-night, and that shall lend a kind of easiness to the next abstinence; the next more easy; for use almost can change the stamp of nature, and either curb the devil or throw him out with wondrous potency.—*Shakespeare.*

Habit, if wisely and skillfully formed, becomes truly a second nature; but unskillfully and unmethodically directed, it will be as it were the ape of nature, which imitates nothing to the life, but only clumsily and awkwardly.—*Bacon.*

Habit with him was all the test of truth; "it must be right, I've done it from my youth."—*Crabbe.*

I must think forever: would an eternal train of my usual thoughts be either worthy of me or useful to me? I must feel forever: would an eternal reign of my present spirit and desires please or satisfy me? I must act forever: would an eternal course of my habitual conduct bring happiness, or even bear reflection?

Habits are soon assumed; but when we endeavor to strip them off, it is being flayed alive.—*Cowper.*

Sow an act, and you reap a habit; sow a habit, and you reap a character; sow a character, and you reap a destiny. —*G. D. Boardman.*

Habit is the beneficent harness of routine which enables silly men to live respectably, and unhappy men to live calmly.—*George Eliot.*

Good habits are the best magistrates.

Like flakes of snow that fall imperceptibly upon the earth, the seemingly unimportant events of life succeed one another.—As the snow-flakes gather, so our habits are formed.—No single flake that is added to the pile produces a sensible change.—No single action creates, however it may exhibit a man's character.—But as the tempest hurls the avalanche down the mountain and overwhelms the inhabitant and his habitation, so passion, acting on the elements of mischief which pernicious habits have brought together, may overthrow the edifice of truth and virtue.—*Bentham.*

The habits of time are the soul's dress for eternity.—Habit passes with its owner beyond this world into a world where destiny is determined by character, and character is the sum and expression of all preceding habit.—*G. B. Cheever.*

Long customs are not easily broken; he that attempts to change the course of his own life very often labors in vain. —*Johnson.*

Habit is the child of impulse.—There is in human life the period of impulse, when habit is nothing; and there is the period of habit, when impulse is nothing.—Young persons are creatures of impulse; old persons are creatures of habit.—Almost everything is impulse with a little child, and nothing can be called habit; almost everything is habit in the second childhood of old age, and there is very little that can be called impulse.—Impulse is habit in formation; habit is impulse fixed.—When habit is once formed, impulse is powerless against it.—Indeed all impulse falls into it—It is like a deep and swift and resistless river, into which an opposing mountain current may pour with tremendous momentary shock and agitation, but with no effect whatever, save to increase the volume, rapidity, and fury of the tide, which is turned downward to the sea.—*G. B. Cheever.*

HAIR.—The hair is the richest ornament of women.—Of old, virgins used to wear it loose, except when they were in mourning.—*Luther.*

Her head was bare, but for her native ornament of hair, which in a simple knot was tied; sweet negligence—unheeded bait of love.—*Dryden.*

Fair tresses man's imperial race ensnare, and beauty draws us with a single hair.—*Pope.*

By common consent gray hairs are a crown of glory; the only object of respect that can never excite envy.—*Bancroft.*

How ill white hairs become a fool and jester!—*Shakespeare.*

Soft hair, on which light drops a diadem.—*Massey.*

Those curious locks, so aptly twined, whose every hair a soul doth bind.—*Carew.*

Beware of her fair locks, for when she

winds them round a young man's neck, she will not set him free again.—*Goethe*.

Her sunny locks hang on her temples like a golden fleece.—*Shakespeare*.

The hairs of age are messengers which bid us to repent and pray.—Of death they are the harbingers that do prepare the way.—*Vaux*.

Hair, 'tis the robe which curious nature weaves to hang upon the head, and to adorn our bodies.—When we were born, God doth bestow that garment.—When we die, then like a soft and silken canopy it still is over us.—In spite of death, our hair grows in the grave, and that alone looks fresh, when all our other beauty is gone.—*Decker*.

HAND.—I love a hand that meets my own with a grasp that causes some sensation.—*F. S. Osgood*.

Other parts of the body assist the speaker but the hands speak themselves.—By them we ask, promise, invoke, dismiss, threaten, entreat, deprecate.—By them we express fear, joy, grief, our doubts, assent, or penitence; we show moderation or profusion, and mark number and time.—*Quintilian*.

The hand is the mind's only perfect vassal; and when, through age or illness, the connection between them is interrupted, there are few more affecting tokens of human decay.—*Tuckerman*.

HAPPINESS.—(See " OCCUPATION.")

Happiness can be built only on virtue, and must of necessity have truth for its foundation.—*Coleridge*.

No man is happy who does not think himself so.—*Marcus Antoninus*.

Happiness is neither within us only, or without us; it is the union of ourselves with God.—*Pascal*.

The world would be both better and brighter if we would dwell on the duty of happiness, as well as on the happiness of duty.—*Sir J. Lubbock*.

Happiness consists in being perfectly satisfied with what we have got and with what we haven't got.

It is not how much we have, but how much we enjoy, that makes happiness.—*Spurgeon*.

I am more and more convinced that our happiness or unhappiness depends far more on the way we meet the events of life, than on the nature of those events themselves.—*Humboldt*.

Happiness is like manna; it is to be gathered in grains, and enjoyed every day. It will not keep; it cannot be accumulated; nor have we got to go out of ourselves or into remote places to gather it, since it has rained down from Heaven, at our very doors.

Seek happiness for its own sake, and you will not find it; seek for duty, and happiness will follow as the shadow comes with the sunshine.—*Tryon Edwards*.

In vain do they talk of happiness who never subdued an impulse in obedience to a principle. He who never sacrificed a present to a future good, or a personal to a general one, can speak of happiness only as the blind do of colors.—*Horace Mann*.

Men of the noblest dispositions think themselves happiest when others share their happiness with them.—*Jeremy Taylor*.

All who would win joy, must share it; happiness was born a twin.—*Byron*.

Happiness is a butterfly, which, when pursued, is always just beyond your grasp, but which, if you will sit down quietly, may alight upon you.

Happiness in this world, when it comes, comes incidentally.—Make it the object of pursuit, and it leads us a wild-goose chase, and is never attained.—*Hawthorne*.

If one only wished to be happy, this could be easily accomplished; but we wish to be happier than other people, and this is always difficult, for we believe others to be happier than they are.—*Montesquieu*.

Happiness consists in the attainment of our desires, and in our having only right desires.—*Augustine*.

The strength and the happiness of a man consists in finding out the way in which God is going, and going in that way, too.—*H. W. Beecher*.

Few things are needful to make the wise man happy, but nothing satisfies the fool;—and this is the reason why so many of mankind are miserable.—*Rochefoucauld*.

What happiness is, the Bible alone shows clearly and certainly, and points out the way that leads to the attainment of it.—"In Cicero and Plato, and other such writers," says Augustine, "I meet with many things acutely said, and things that excite a certain warmth of emotions, but in none of them do I find these words, 'Come unto me, all ye that labor, and are heavy laden, and I will give you rest.'"—*Coleridge.*

Call no man happy till you know the end of his life. Till then, at most, he can only be counted fortunate.—*Herodotus.*

The rays of happiness, like those of light, are colorless when unbroken.—*Longfellow.*

Happiness is dependent on the taste, and not on things.—It is by having what we like that we are made happy, not by having what others think desirable.—*Rochefoucauld.*

Human happiness seems to consist in three ingredients; action, pleasure, and indolence. And though these ingredients ought to be mixed in different proportions, according to the disposition of the person, yet no one ingredient can be entirely wanting without destroying in some measure the relish of the whole composition.—*Hume.*

Happiness is not the end of life; character is.—*H. W. Beecher.*

Happiness is like a sunbeam, which the least shadow intercepts, while adversity is often as the rain of spring.—*Chinese Proverb.*

Happiness is the legitimate fruitage of love and service. It never comes and never can come by making it an end, and it is because so many persons mistake here and seek for it directly, instead of loving and serving God, and thus obtaining it, that there is so much dissatisfaction and sorrow.

Set happiness before you as an end, no matter in what guise of wealth, or fame, or oblivion even, and you will not attain it.—But renounce it and seek the pleasure of God, and that instant is the birth of your own.—*A. S. Hardy.*

It is only a poor sort of happiness that could ever come by caring very much about our own narrow pleasures. We can only have the highest happiness, such as goes along with true greatness, by having wide thoughts and much feeling for the rest of the world as well as

ourselves; and this sort of happiness often brings so much pain with it, that we can only tell it from pain by its being what we would choose before everything else, because our souls see it is good.—*George Eliot.*

Happiness is like the statue of Isis, whose veil no mortal ever raised.—*L. E. Landon.*

If you cannot be happy in one way, be in another; this facility of disposition wants but little aid from philosophy, for health and good humor are almost the whole affair. Many run about after felicity, like an absent man hunting for his hat, while it is in his hand or on his head.—*Sharp.*

There is this difference between happiness and wisdom, that he that thinks himself the happiest man, really is so; but he that thinks himself the wisest, is generally the greatest fool.—*Colton.*

No person is either so happy or so unhappy as he imagines.—*Rochefoucauld.*

We take greater pains to persuade others that we are happy, than in endeavoring to be so ourselves.—*Goldsmith.*

I see in this world two heaps—one of happiness, and the other of misery. Now, if I can take but the smallest bit from the second, and add it to the first, I carry a point. I should be glad indeed to do great things; but I will not neglect such little ones as this.—*John Newton.*

False happiness is like false money; it passes for a time as well as the true, and serves some ordinary occasions; but when it is brought to the touch, we find the lightness and alloy, and feel the loss.—*Pope.*

Man courts happiness in a thousand shapes; and the faster he follows it the swifter it flies from him. Almost everything promiseth happiness to us at a distance, but when we come nearer, either we fall short of it, or it falls short of our expectation; and it is hard to say which of these is the greatest disappointment. Our hopes are usually bigger than the enjoyment can satisfy; and an evil long feared, besides that it may never come, is many times more painful and troublesome than the evil itself when it comes.—*Tillotson.*

The chief secret of comfort lies in not suffering trifles to vex us, and in prudently cultivating our undergrowth of small pleasures, since very few great ones, alas! are let on long leases.—*Sharp.*

If the principles of contentment are not within us, the height of station and worldly grandeur will as soon add a cubit to a man's stature as to his happiness.—*Sterne.*

The spider's most attenuated thread is cord, is cable to man's tender tie on earthly bliss—it breaks at every breeze. —*Young.*

As we are now living in an eternity, the time to be happy is today.—*Grenville Kleiser.*

Search for a single, inclusive good is doomed to failure. Such happiness as life is capable of comes from the full participation of all our powers in the endeavor to wrest from each changing situation of experience its own full and unique meaning.—*John Dewey.*

The habit of being happy enables one to be freed, or largely freed, from the domination of outward conditions.—*Robert Louis Stevenson.*

This is the true joy of life—the being used for a purpose recognized by yourself as a mighty one, the being thoroughly worn out before you are thrown to the scrap-heap; the being a force of nature instead of a feverish, selfish clod of ailments and grievances. —*G. Bernard Shaw.*

Wealth I ask not, hope nor love, nor a friend to know me; all I ask, the heavens above, and the road below me. —*Robert Louis Stevenson.*

The secret of happines is renunciation.—*Andrew Carnegie.*

The belief that youth is the happiest time of life is founded on a fallacy. The happiest person is the person who thinks the most interesting thoughts, and we grow happier as we grow older. —*William Lyon Phelps.*

What is happiness, anyhow? Is this one of its hours—so impalpable—a mere breath, an evanescent tinge? I am not sure—so let me give myself the benefit of the doubt. Hast Thou, pellucid, in Thy azure depths, medicine for case like mine?—*Walt Whitman.*

Happiness is the supreme object of existence.—*J. Gilchrist Lawson.*

Happiness is the harvest of a quiet eye.—*Austin O'Malley.*

The foolish man seeks happiness in the distance; the wise grows it under his feet.—*James Oppenheim.*

Best trust the happy moments. What they gave makes man less fearful of the certain grave and gives his work compassion and new eyes, the days that make us happy make us wise.—*John Masefield.*

Happiness, to some elation, is to others, mere stagnation.—*Amy Lowell.*

Seek not happiness too greedily, and be not fearful of unhappiness.—*Lao-Tze.*

Unhappy is the man who is not so much dissatisfied with what he has as with what the other fellow possesses. —*Chauncey M. Depew.*

The really happy man never laughs— or seldom—though he may smile. He does not need to laugh, for laughter, like weeping, is a relief of mental tension—and the happy are not overstrung.—*Prof. F. A. P. Aveling.*

To attain happiness in another world we need only to believe something, while to secure it in this world we must needs do something.—*Charlotte Perkins Gilman.*

Service to a just cause rewards the worker with more real happiness and satisfaction than any other venture of life.—*Carrie Chapman Catt.*

An act of goodness is of itself an act of happiness. No reward coming after the event can compare with the sweet reward that went with it.—*Maurice Maeterlinck.*

The Greeks said grandly in their tragic phrase, "Let no one be called happy till his death"; to which I would add, "Let no one, till his death, be called unhappy."—*E. B. Browning.*

That all who are happy are equally happy is not true. A peasant and a philosopher may be equally satisfied, but not equally happy.—*Johnson.*

The true happiness is of a retired nature, and an enemy to pomp and noise; it arises, in the first place, from the enjoyment of one's self; and in the next, from the friendship and conversation of a few select companions; it loves shade and solitude, and naturally haunts groves and fountains, fields and meadows; in short, it feels everything it wants within itself, and receives no addition from multitudes of witnesses and spectators. On the contrary, false happiness loves to be in a crowd, and to draw the eyes of the world upon her. She does not receive satisfaction from the applauses which she gives herself, but from the admiration which she raises in others. She flourishes in courts and palaces, theatres and assemblies, and has no existence but when she is looked upon.—*Addison.*

Happiness and virtue rest upon each other; the best are not only the happiest, but the happiest are usually the best. —*Bulwer.*

The sunshine of life is made up of very little beams that are bright all the time. To give up something, when giving up will prevent unhappiness; to yield, when persisting will chafe and fret others; to go a little around rather than come against another; to take an ill look or a cross word quietly, rather than resent or return it,—these are the ways in which clouds and storms are kept off, and a pleasant and steady sunshine secured.—*Aikin.*

True happiness renders men kind and sensible; and that happiness is always shared with others.—*Montesquieu.*

No thoroughly occupied man was ever yet very miserable.—*L. E. Landon.*

Silence is the perfectest herald of joy. I were but little happy if I could say how much.—*Shakespeare.*

The most happy man is he who knows how to bring into relation the end and the beginning of his life.—*Goethe.*

There is one way of attaining what we may term, if not utter, at least mortal happiness; it is by a sincere and unrelaxing activity for the happiness of others.—*Bulwer.*

The haunts of happiness are varied, but I have more often found her among little children, home firesides, and country houses than anywhere else.—*Sydney Smith.*

Happiness is a sunbeam which may pass through a thousand bosoms without losing a particle of its original ray; nay, when it strikes on a kindred heart, like

the converged light on a mirror, it reflects itself with redoubled brightness.—It is not perfected till it is shared.—*Jane Porter.*

He only is happy as well as great who needs neither to obey nor command in order to be something.—*Goethe.*

That state of life is most happy where superfluities are not required, and necessaries are not wanting.—*Plutarch.*

There is in all of us an impediment to perfect happiness, namely, weariness of what we possess, and a desire for what we have not.—*Mad. Rieux.*

It is not the place, nor the condition, but the mind alone that can make any one happy or miserable.—*L'Estrange.*

The happiest life is that which constantly exercises and educates what is best in us.—*Hamerton.*

There is little pleasure in the world that is sincere and true beside that of doing our duty and doing good.—No other is comparable to this.—*Tillotson.*

Do not speak of your happiness to one less fortunate than yourself.—*Plutarch.*

The common course of things is in favor of happiness.—Happiness is the rule, misery the exception.—Were the order reversed, our attention would be called to examples of health and competency, instead of disease and want.—*Paley.*

Objects we ardently pursue bring little happiness when gained; most of our pleasures come from unexpected sources. —*Herbert Spencer.*

To be happy is not the purpose of our being, but to deserve happiness.—*Fichte.*

The great high-road of human welfare and happiness lies along the highway of steadfast well-doing, and they who are the most persistent and work in the truest spirit, will invariably be the most successful.—*S. Smiles.*

Whether happiness may come or not, one should try and prepare one's self to do without it.—*George Eliot.*

There is but one way to tranquillity of mind and happiness; let this, therefore, be always ready at hand with thee, both when thou wakest early in the morning, and all the day long, and when thou goest late to sleep, to account no external things thine own, but commit all these to God.—*Epictetus.*

All mankind are happier for having

been happy, so that if you make them happy now, you make them happy twenty years hence by the memory of it. —*Sydney Smith.*

To be happy you must forget yourself.—Learn benevolence; it is the only cure of a morbid temper.—*Bulwer.*

Philosophical happiness is to want little; civil or vulgar happiness is to want much and enjoy much.—*Burke.*

The happiest women, like the happiest nations, have no history.—*George Eliot.*

I have now reigned above fifty years in victory or peace, beloved by my subjects, dreaded by my enemies, and respected by my allies. Riches and honors, power and pleasure, have waited on my call, nor does any earthly blessing appear to have been wanting to my felicity. In this situation, I have diligently numbered the days of pure and genuine happiness which have fallen to my lot; they amount to fourteen. O man, place not thy confidence in this present world! —*The Caliph Abdelraham.*

Human happiness has no perfect security but freedom; freedom none but virtue; virtue none but knowledge; and neither freedom, virtue, nor knowledge has any vigor or immortal hope, except in the principles of the Christian faith, and in the sanctions of the Christian religion.—*Josiah Quincy.*

If I may speak of myself, my happy hours have far exceeded, and far exceed, the scanty numbers of the Caliph of Spain; and I shall not scruple to add, that many of them are due to the pleasing labor of composing my history.—*Gibbon.*

The best advice on the art of being happy is about as easy to follow as advice to be well when one is sick.—*Mad. Swetchine.*

Happiness consists in activity.—Such is the constitution of our nature.—It is a running stream, and not a stagnant pool.—*J. M. Good.*

The question, "Which is the happiest season of life," being referred to an aged man, he replied: "When spring comes, and in the soft air the buds are breaking on the trees, and they are covered with blossoms, I think, How beautiful is Spring! And when the summer comes, and covers the trees with its heavy foli-

age, and singing birds are among the branches, I think, How beautiful is Summer! When autumn loads them with golden fruit, and their leaves bear the gorgeous tint of frost, I think, How beautiful is Autumn! And when it is sere winter, and there is neither foliage nor fruit, then I look up through the leafless branches, as I never could until now, and see the stars shine."

The world owes all its onward impulses to men ill at ease. The happy man inevitably confines himself within ancient limits.

The true felicity of life is to be free from anxieties and perturbations; to understand and do our duties to God and man, and to enjoy the present without any serious dependence on the future.—*Seneca.*

Reason's whole pleasure, all the joys of sense, lie in three words, health, peace, and competence.—*Pope.*

I questioned death—the grisly shade relaxed his brow severe—and—" I am happiness," he said, " if virtue guides thee here."—*Heber.*

HARDSHIP. — The difficulties, hardships, and trials of life, the obstacles one encounters on the road to fortune, are positive blessings.—They knit the muscles more firmly, and teach self-reliance.—Peril is the element in which power is developed.—*W. Mathews.*

Ability and necessity dwell near each other.—*Pythagoras.*

He who has battled with poverty and hard toil will be found stronger and more expert than he who could stay at home from the battle, concealed among the provision wagons, or unwatchfully abiding by the stuff.—*Carlyle.*

It is not helps, but obstacles, not facilities but difficulties, that make men. —*W. Mathews.*

Kites rise against, not with the wind. —No man ever worked his passage anywhere in a dead calm.—*John Neal.*

HARLOT.—She weaves the winding-sheet of souls, and lays them in the urn of everlasting death.—*Pollok.*

It is the strumpet's plague to beguile many, and be beguiled by one.—*Shakespeare.*

HASTE. — Though I am always in

haste, I am never in a hurry.—*John Wesley.*

The more haste ever the worse speed.—*Churchill.*

No two things differ more than hurry and despatch. Hurry is the mark of a weak mind; despatch of a strong one.—*Colton.*

Haste is of the devil.—*Koran.*

Wisely and slow;—they stumble that run fast.—*Shakespeare.*

Hurry is only good for catching flies.—*Russian Proverb.*

Haste and rashness are storms and tempests, breaking and wrecking business; but nimbleness is a full fair wind blowing it with speed to the haven.—*Fuller.*

The longest way round is the shortest way home.

Haste trips its own heels, and fetters and stops itself.—*Seneca.*

Haste is not always speed. We must learn to work and wait. This is like God, who perfects his works through beautiful gradations.

Unreasonable haste is the direct road to error.—*Molière.*

Haste usually turns upon being late, and may be avoided by a habit like that of Lord Nelson, to which he ascribed his success in life, of always being ten minutes too early.—*Bovee.*

It is of no use running; to set out betimes is the main point.—*La Fontaine.*

Rapidity does not always mean progress, and hurry is akin to waste.—The old fable of the hare and the tortoise is just as good now, and just as true, as when it was first written.—*C. A. Stoddard.*

Stay awhile to make an end the sooner.—*Paulet.*

Fraud and deceit are ever in a hurry.—Take time for all things.—Great haste makes great waste.—*Franklin.*

Whoever is in a hurry shows that the thing he is about is too big for him.—Haste and hurry are very different things.—*Chesterfield.*

Manners require time, and nothing is more vulgar than haste.—*Emerson.*

Modest wisdom plucks me from overcredulous haste.—*Shakespeare.*

Hurry and cunning are the two apprentices of despatch and skill, but neither of them ever learns the master's trade.—*Colton.*

HATRED.—Malice can always find a mark to shoot at, and a pretence to fire.—*C. Simmons.*

Hatred is the vice of narrow souls; they feed it with all their littlenesses, and make it the pretext of base tyrannies.—*Balzac.*

If I wanted to punish an enemy it should be by fastening on him the trouble of constantly hating somebody.—*H. More.*

I will tell you what to hate. Hate hypocrisy; hate cant; hate intolerance, oppression, injustice, Pharisaism; hate them as Christ hated them—with a deep, abiding, God-like hatred.—*F. W. Robertson.*

When our hatred is violent, it sinks us even beneath those we hate.—*Rochefoucauld.*

Hate no one; hate their vices, not themselves.—*J. G. C. Brainard.*

If there is any person whom you dislike, that is the one of whom you should never speak.—*Cecil.*

Hatred is the madness of the heart.—*Byron.*

Thousands are hated, while none are loved without a real cause.—*Lavater.*

Hatred is active, and envy passive dislike; there is but one step from envy to hate.—*Goethe.*

Dislike what deserves it, but never hate, for that is of the nature of malice, which is applied to persons, not to things.—*Penn.*

It is human nature to hate him whom you have injured.—*Tacitus.*

Hatred does not cease by hatred, but only by love; this is the eternal rule.—*Buddha.*

I shall never permit myself to stoop so low as to hate any man.—*Booker T. Washington.*

We hate some persons because we do not know them; and we will not know them because we hate them.—*Colton.*

The hatred of those who are most nearly connected is the most inveterate.—*Tacitus.*

Heaven has no rage like love to hatred turned.—*Congreve.*

If you hate your enemies, you will contract such a vicious habit of mind as by degrees will break out upon those who are your friends, or those who are indifferent to you.—*Plutarch.*

The passion of hatred is so durable and so inveterate, that the surest prognostic of death in a sick man is a wish for reconciliation.—*Bruyère.*

There are glances of hatred that stab, and raise no cry of murder.—*George Eliot.*

Malice and hatred are very fretting, and make our own minds sore and uneasy.—*Tillotson.*

HEAD.—The head, truly enlightened, will have a wonderful influence in purifying the heart; and the heart really affected with goodness will much conduce to the directing of the head.—*Sprat.*

Such is man's unhappy condition, that though the weakness of the heart has a prevailing power over the strength of the head, yet the strength of the head has but small force against the weakness of the heart.—*Tatler.*

A woman's head is always influenced by heart; but a man's heart by his head.—*Lady Blessington.*

HEALTH.—A sound mind in a sound body; if the former be the glory of the latter, the latter is indispensable to the former.—*Tryon Edwards.*

The building of a perfect body crowned by a perfect brain, is at once the greatest earthly problem and grandest hope of the race.—*Dio Lewis.*

A wise physician is a John Baptist, who recognizes that his only mission is to prepare the way for a greater than himself—Nature.—*A. S. Hardy.*

Half the spiritual difficulties that men and women suffer arise from a morbid state of health.—*H. W. Beecher.*

Without health life is not life; it is only a state of languor and suffering—an image of death.—*Rabelais.*

Take care of your health; you have no right to neglect it, and thus become a burden to yourself, and perhaps to others. Let your food be simple; never eat too much; take exercise enough; be systematic in all things; if unwell, starve yourself till you are well again, and you

may throw care to the winds, and physic to the dogs.—*W. Hall.*

Health is the soul that animates all the enjoyments of life, which fade and are tasteless without it.—*Sir W. Temple.*

If the mind, that rules the body, ever so far forgets itself as to trample on its slave, the slave is never generous enough to forgive the injury, but will rise and smite the oppressor.—*Longfellow.*

Regularity in the hours of rising and retiring, perseverance in exercise, adaptation of dress to the variations of climate, simple and nutritious aliment, and temperance in all things are necessary branches of the regimen of health.—*Mrs. Sigourney.*

The morality of clean blood ought to be one of the first lessons taught us by our pastors and teachers.—The physical is the substratum of the spiritual; and this fact ought to give to the food we eat, and the air we breathe, a transcendent significance.—*Tyndale.*

Wet feet are some of the most effective agents death has in the field. It has peopled more graves than all the gory engines of war. Those who neglect to keep their feet dry are suicides.—*Abernethy.*

Men that look no further than their outsides, think health an appurtenance unto life, and quarrel with their constitutions for being sick; but I that have examined the parts of man, and know upon what tender filaments that fabric hangs, do wonder that we are not always so; and considering the thousand doors that lead to death, do thank my God that we can die but once.—*Sir T. Browne.*

To preserve health is a moral and religious duty, for health is the basis of all social virtues.—We can no longer be useful when not well.—*Johnson.*

Dyspepsia is the remorse of a guilty stomach.—*A. Kerr.*

Health is certainly more valuable than money, because it is by health that money is procured; but thousands and millions are of small avail to alleviate the tortures of the gout, to repair the broken organs of sense, or resuscitate the powers of digestion. Poverty is, indeed, an evil from which we naturally fly; but let us not run from one enemy to another, nor take shelter in the arms of sickness.—*Johnson.*

If men gave three times as much attention as they now do to ventilation, ablution, and exercise in the open air, and only one third as much to eating, luxury, and late hours, the number of doctors, dentists, and apothecaries, and the amount of neuralgia, dyspepsia, gout, fever, and consumption, would be changed in a corresponding ratio.

Never hurry; take plenty of exercise; always be cheerful, and take all the sleep you need, and you may expect to be well.—*J. F. Clarke.*

Life is not to live, but to be well.—*Martial.*

There is this difference between the two temporal blessings—health and money; money is the most envied, but the least enjoyed; health is the most enjoyed, but the least envied; and this superiority of the latter is still more obvious when we reflect that the poorest man would not part with health for money, but that the richest would gladly part with all his money for health.—*Colton.*

The first wealth is health. Sickness is poor-spirited, and cannot serve any one; it must husband its recources to live. But health answers its own ends, and has to spare; runs over, and inundates the neighborhoods and creeks of other men's necessities.—*Emerson.*

To become a thoroughly good man is the best prescription for keeping a sound mind in a sound body.—*Bowen.*

The ingredients of health and long life, are great temperance, open air, easy labor, and little care.—*Sir P. Sidney.*

Youth will never live to age unless they keep themselves in health with exercise, and in heart with joyfulness.—*Sir P. Sidney.*

The only way for a rich man to be healthy is by exercise and abstinence, to live as if he were poor.—*Sir W. Temple.*

It is the opinion of those who best understand the physical system, that if the physical laws were strictly observed from generation to generation, there would be an end to the frightful diseases that cut life short, and of the long list of maladies that make life a torment or a trial, and that this wonderful machine, the body,—this "goodly temple," would gradually decay, and men would

at last die as if gently falling asleep.—*Mrs. Sedgwick.*

With stupidity and sound digestion man may fret much; but what in these dull unimaginative days are the terrors of conscience to the diseases of the liver.—*Carlyle.*

Anguish of mind has driven thousands to suicide; anguish of body, none. This proves that the health of the mind is of far more consequence to our happiness than the health of the body, although both are deserving of much more attention than either receives.—*Colton.*

People who are always taking care of their health are like misers, who are hoarding up a treasure which they have never spirit enough to enjoy.—*Sterne.*

In these days, half our diseases come from the neglect of the body in the overwork of the brain. In this railway age, the wear and tear of labor and intellect go on without pause or self-pity. We live longer than our forefathers; but we suffer more from a thousand artificial anxieties and cares. They fatigued only the muscles, we exhaust the finer strength of the nerves.—*Bulwer.*

Health is so necessary to all the duties, as well as pleasures of life, that the crime of squandering it is equal to the folly.—*Johnson.*

Health is the greatest of all possessions; a pale cobbler is better than a sick king.—*Bickerstaff.*

Regimen is better than physic. Every one should be his own physician. We ought to assist, and not to force nature. Eat with moderation what agrees with your constitution. Nothing is good for the body but what we can digest. What medicine can procure digestion? Exercise. What will recruit strength? Sleep. What will alleviate incurable evils? Patience.—*Voltaire.*

What a searching preacher of self-command is the varying phenomenon of health.—*Emerson.*

Look to your health; and if you have it, praise God and value it next to a good conscience; for health is the second blessing that we mortals are capable of—a blessing that money cannot buy; therefore value it, and be thankful for it.—*Izaak Walton.*

The first sure symptoms of a mind in

health are rest of heart and pleasure found at home.—*Young.*

There are two things in life that a sage must preserve at every sacrifice, the coats of his stomach, and the enamel of his teeth.—Some evils admit of consolations, but there are no comforters for dyspepsia and the toothache.—*Bulwer.*

Seldom shall we see in cities, courts, and rich families, where men live plentifully, and eat and drink freely, that perfect health and athletic soundness and vigor of constitution which are commonly seen in the country, where nature is the cook, and necessity the caterer, and where they have no other doctor but the sun and fresh air.—*South.*

Gold that buys health can never be ill spent; nor hours laid out in harmless merriment.—*J. Webster.*

Joy, temperance, and repose, slam the door on the doctor's nose.—*Longfellow.*

Be sober and temperate, and you will be healthy.—*Franklin.*

If you want to know if your brain is flabby feel of your legs.—*Bruce Barton.*

There is still an immense amount to be learned about health, but if what is at present known to a few were part of the general knowledge, the average expectation of life could probably be increased by about ten years.—*J. B. S. Haldane.*

As knowledge with regard to the effects of food upon man increases, it is more than conceivable that the races that first avail themselves of the new values of nutrition may decrease the handicaps of disease, lengthen their lives, and so become the leaders of the future. —*Victor G. Heiser.*

It is the superstition of medicine that is responsible for all the health cults of modern times. You have elevated the desire for health, youth and longevity to the position of a religion.—*Rabbi Stephen S. Wise.*

Some people think that doctors and nurses can put scrambled eggs back into the shell.—*Dorothy Canfield.*

Health, beauty, vigor, riches, and all the other things called good, operate equally as evils to the vicious and unjust, as they do as benefits to the just. —*Plato.*

We are beginning to recognize that amusement . . . is a commodity as essential to the physical and mental health and well-being of the human animal as lumber, wheat, oil, steel, or textiles.—*Milton Sills.*

He who has health, has hope; and he who has hope, has everything.—*Arabian Proverb.*

Few things are more important to a community than the health of its women.—If strong is the frame of the mother, says a proverb, the son will give laws to the people.—And in nations where all men give laws, all men need mothers of strong frames.—*T. W. Higginson.*

HEART.—The heart is the best logician.—*Wendell Phillips.*

If wrong our hearts, our heads are right in vain.—*Young.*

A good heart is worth gold.—*Shakespeare.*

A loving heart is the truest wisdom.— *Dickens.*

The heart has reasons that reason does not understand.—*Bossuet.*

The ways of the heart, like the ways of providence, are mysterious.—*Ware.*

Suppose that a man would advertise to take photographs of the heart; would he get many customers?—*D. L. Moody.*

If a good face is a letter of recommendation, a good heart is a letter of credit. —*Bulwer.*

All who know their own minds, do not know their own hearts.—*Rochefoucauld.*

What I am concerned about in this fast-moving world in a time of crises, both in foreign and domestic affairs, is not so much a program as a spirit of approach, not so much a mind as a heart. A program lives today and dies tomorrow. A mind, if it be open, may change with each new day, but the spirit and the heart are as unchanging as the tides.—*Owen D. Young.*

The heart of man is of it selfe but little, yet great things cannot fill it: it is not big enough at one meale to satisfie a bird, and yet the whole world cannot satisfie it.—*Thomas Dekker.*

There is no instinct like that of the heart.—*Byron.*

Every one must in a measure be alone in the world; for no heart was ever cast in the same mold as that which we bear within us.—*Berni.*

The wrinkles of the heart are more indelible than those of the brow.—*Deluzy.*

A kind heart is a fountain of gladness, making everything in its vicinity to freshen into smiles.—*Washington Irving.*

When the heart goes before, like a lamp, and illumines the pathway, many things are made clear that else lie hidden in darkness.—*Longfellow.*

When the heart speaks, glory itself is an illusion.—*Napoleon.*

Heaven's sovereign saves all beings but himself that hideous sight, a naked human heart.—*Young.*

There are many persons the brilliancy of whose minds depends on the heart.— When they open that, it is hardly possible for it not to throw out some fire.— *Desmalis.*

Memory, wit, fancy, acuteness, cannot grow young again in old age; but the heart can.—*Richter.*

All our actions take their hue from the complexion of the heart, as landscapes their variety from light.—*Bacon.*

It is much easier to pull up many weeds out of a garden, than one corruption out of the heart; to procure a hundred flowers to adorn a knot, than one grace to beautify the soul.

The heart never grows better by age; I fear rather worse; always harder. A young liar will be an old one; and a young knave will only be a greater knave as he grows older.—*Chesterfield.*

The depraved and sinful heart does not of itself grow better, but goes on from bad to worse; but the heart renewed by divine grace, grows steadily in the divine likeness; its path is that of the just, that shineth more and more to the perfect day.

To judge human character rightly, a man may sometimes have very small experience, provided he has a very large heart.—*Bulwer.*

Mind is the partial side of man; the heart is everything.—*Rivarol.*

The heart of a wise man should resemble a mirror, which reflects every object without being sullied by any.— *Confucius.*

Each heart is a world.—You find all within yourself that you find without.— To know yourself you have only to set down a true statement of those that ever loved or hated you.—*Lavater.*

What the heart has once owned and had, it shall never lose.—*H. W. Beecher.*

What sad faces one always sees in the asylum for orphans!—It is more fatal to neglect the heart than the head. —*Theodore Parker.*

Nothing is less in our power than the heart, and far from commanding we are forced to obey it.—*Rousseau.*

The nice, calm, cold thought, which in women shapes itself so rapidly that they hardly know it as thought, should always travel to the lips by way of the heart.—It does so in those women whom all love and admire.—*O. W. Holmes.*

The human heart is like the millstone in a mill; when you put wheat under it, it turns and grinds the wheat into flour. —If you put no wheat in, it still grinds on, but then it is itself it grinds and slowly wears away.—*Luther.*

Many flowers open to the sun, but only one follows him constantly.—Heart, be thou the sunflower, not only open to receive God's blessing, but constant in looking to him.—*Richter.*

The hardest trial of the heart is, whether it can bear a rival's failure without triumph.—*Aikin.*

The heart of man is a short word, a small substance, scarce enough to give a kite a meal, yet great in capacity; yea, so indefinite in desire that the round globe of the world cannot fill the three corners of it.—When it desires more and cries, "Give, give," I will set it over to the infinite good, where the more it hath, it may desire more, and see more to be desired.—*Bp. Hall.*

Want and wealth equally harden the human heart, as frost and fire are both alien to the human flesh.—Famine and gluttony alike drive away nature from the heart of man.—*Theodore Parker.*

A noble heart, like the sun, showetl its greatest countenance in its lowes estate.—*Sir P. Sidney.*

The heart of a good man is the sanc

tuary of God in this world.—*Mad. Neckar.*

You may as soon fill a bag with wisdom, a chest with virtue, or a circle with a triangle, as the heart of man with anything here below.—A man may have enough of the world to sink him, but he can never have enough to satisfy him.—*T. Brooks.*

When the heart is won, the understanding is easily convinced.—*C. Simmons.*

The heart is an astrologer that always divines the truth.—*Calderon.*

Men, as well as women, are oftener led by their hearts than their understandings.—The way to the heart is through the senses; please the eyes and ears, and the work is half done.—*Chesterfield.*

Something the heart must have to cherish; must love, and joy, and sorrow learn: something with passion clasp, or perish, and in itself to ashes burn.—*Longfellow.*

HEAVEN. — Heaven hath many tongues to talk of it, more eyes to behold it, but few hearts that rightly affect it.—*Bp. Hall.*

He that studies to know duty, and labors in all things to do it, will have two heavens—one of joy, peace, and comfort on earth, and the other of glory and happiness beyond the grave.

There is a land where everlasting suns shed everlasting brightness; where the soul drinks from the living streams of love that roll by God's high throne!—myriads of glorious ones bring their accepted offering. Oh! how blest to look from this dark prison to that shrine, to inhale one breath of Paradise divine, and enter into that eternal rest which waits the sons of God!—*Bowring.*

If I ever reach heaven I expect to find three wonders there: first, to meet some I had not thought to see there; second, to miss some I had expected to see there; and third, the greatest wonder of all, to find myself there.—*John Newton.*

There are treasures laid up in the heart,—treasures of charity, piety, temperance, and soberness. These treasures a man takes with him beyond death when he leaves this world.—*Buddhist Scriptures.*

Heaven's the perfection of all that can be said or thought—riches, delight, harmony, health, beauty; and all these not subject to the waste of time, but in their height eternal.—*Shirley.*

To that state all the pious on earth are tending. Heaven is attracting to itself whatever is congenial to its nature; is enriching itself by the spoils of the earth, and collecting within its capacious bosom whatever is pure, permanent, and divine, leaving nothing for the last fire to consume but the objects and slaves of concupiscence; while everything which grace has prepared and beautified shall be gathered and selected from the ruins of the world to adorn that eternal city "which hath no need of the sun or moon to shine in it; for the glory of God doth lighten it, and the Lamb is the light thereof."—*R. Hall.*

My gems are falling away; but it is because God is making up his jewels.—*Wolfe.*

The love of heaven makes one heavenly.—*Shakespeare.*

It is heaven upon earth to have a man's mind move in charity, rest in providence, and turn upon the poles of truth. —*Bacon.*

"Do you think we shall know each other in heaven?" said one friend to another. "Yes," was the answer. "Do you think we shall be greater fools there than here?"—*Evans.*

Where is heaven? I cannot tell. Even to the eye of faith, heaven looks much like a star to the eye of flesh. Set there on the brow of night, it shines most bright, most beautiful; but it is separated from us by so great a distance as to be raised almost as high above our investigations as above the storms and clouds of earth.—*Guthrie.*

Few, without the hope of another life, would think it worth their while to live above the allurements of sense.—*Atterbury.*

The generous who is always just, and the just who is always generous, may, unannounced, approach the throne of heaven.—*Lavater.*

There are two unalterable prerequisites to man's being happy in the world to come. His sins must be pardoned and his nature must be changed. He must have a title to heaven and a fitness for heaven. These two ideas underlie the whole of Christ's work, and without the title to, and the fitness for, no man can enter the kingdom of God.—*Seeley*.

Every saint in heaven is as a flower in the garden of God, and holy love is the fragrance and sweet odor that they all send forth, and with which they fill the bowers of that paradise above. Every soul there is as a note in some concert of delightful music, that sweetly harmonizes with every other note, and all together blend in the most rapturous strains in praising God and the Lamb forever.—*Jonathan Edwards*.

Heaven must be in me before I can be in heaven.—*Stanford*.

One sweetly solemn thought comes to me o'er and o'er; I'm nearer to my home to-day than I've ever been before; nearer my Father's house, where the many mansions be; nearer the great white throne, nearer the jasper sea; nearer the bound of life, where I lay my burden down; nearer leaving my cross; nearer wearing my crown!—*Phœbe Cary*.

If God hath made this world so fair, where sin and death abound, how beautiful, beyond compare, will paradise be found.—*Montgomery*.

Heaven to me's a fair blue stretch of sky, earth's jest a dusty road.—*John Masefield*.

Heaven, the treasury of everlasting joy.—*Shakespeare*.

Perfect purity, fulness of joy, everlasting freedom, perfect rest, health, and fruition, complete security, substantial and eternal good.—*H. More*.

Earth has no sorrow that heaven cannot heal.—*Moore*.

It is heaven only that is given away —only God may be had for the asking. —*J. R. Lowell*.

I would not give one moment of heaven for all the joy and riches of the world, even if it lasted for thousands and thousands of years.—*Luther*.

That happy sense of direct relation with Heaven is known evidently to multitudes of human souls of all faiths, and in all lands; evidently often a dream,— demonstrably, as I conceive, often a reality; in all cases dependent on resolution, patience, self-denial, prudence, obedience; of which some pure hearts

are capable without effort, and some by constancy.—*John Ruskin*.

Spend in pure converse our eternal day; think each in each, immediately wise; learn all we lacked before; hear, know, and say what this tumultuous body now denies; and feel, who have laid our groping hands away; and see, no longer blinded by our eyes.—*Rupert Brooke*.

One of the hardest lessons we have to learn in this life, and one that many persons never learn, is to see the divine, the celestial, the pure in the common, the near at hand,—to see that heaven lies about us here in this world.—*John Burroughs*.

To appreciate heaven well 'tis good for a man to have some fifteen minutes of hell.—*Will Carleton*.

Great Spirit, give to me a heaven not so large as yours but large enough for me.—*Emily Dickinson*.

That which at first seemed a curse has turned out to be a blessing. For if men believe, as I do, that this present earth is the only heaven, they will strive all the more to make heaven of it. To feel that we are mere birds of passage, only temporary probationers, is not conducive to the best conduct.—*Sir Arthur Keith*.

Heav'n is but the vision of fulfill'd desire. And hell the shadow from a soul on fire.—*Omar Khayyam*.

Better limp all the way to heaven than not get there at all.—*William A. "Billy" Sunday*.

In the spiritual world no one is permitted to think and will in one way and speak and act in another.—*Emanuel Swedenborg*.

Who seeks for heaven alone to save his soul may keep the path, but will not reach the goal; while he who walks in love may wander far, yet God will bring him where the blessed are.— *Henry Van Dyke*.

Nothing is farther · than the earth from heaven; nothing is nearer than heaven to earth.—*Hare*.

If the way to heaven be narrow, it is not long; and if the gate be strait, it opens into endless life.—*Beveridge*.

The joys of heaven will begin as soon as we attain the character of heaven and do its duties.—Try that and prove its truth.—As much goodness and piety, so much heaven.—*Theodore Parker.*

Heaven is the day of which grace is the dawn, the rich, ripe fruit of which grace is the lovely flower; the inner shrine of that most glorious temple to which grace forms the approach and outer court.—*Guthrie.*

It is not talking but walking that will bring us to heaven.—*M. Henry.*

The hope of heaven under troubles is like wind and sails to the soul.—*Rutherford.*

The city which God has prepared is as imperishable in its inhabitants as its materials. Its pearl, its jasper, its pure gold, are only immortal to frame the abode of immortals. No cry of death is in any of its dwellings. No funeral darkens along any of its ways. No sepulcher of the holiest relics gleams among the everlasting hills. "Violence is not heard in the land." "There is no more death." Its very name has perished. "Is swallowed up in victory."—*R. W. Hamilton.*

To us who are Christians, is it not a solemn, but a delightful thought, that perhaps nothing but the opaque bodily eye prevents us from beholding the gate which is open just before us; and nothing but the dull ear prevents us from hearing the ringing of those bells of joy which welcome us to the heavenly land?—*H. W. Beecher.*

No man will go to heaven when he dies who has not sent his heart thither while he lives. Our greatest security is to be derived from duty, and our only confidence from the mercy of God through Jesus Christ.—*Bp. Wilson.*

Here must be the heir, if yonder his inheritance; here the laborer, if yonder his rest; here the candidate, if yonder his reward.—As he now adds excellence to excellence, as he is now not barren nor unfruitful, so shall an entrance be ministered to him abundantly into the everlasting kingdom of our Lord and Saviour Jesus Christ.—*R. W. Hamilton.*

We are as near to heaven as we are far from self, and far from the love of a sinful world.—*Rutherford.*

HEIRS.—(See "INHERITANCE.")

HELL.—(See "INTENTIONS.")

Hell is truth seen too late—duty neglected in its season.—*Tryon Edwards.*

Hell is as ubiquitous as condemning conscience.—*F. W. Robertson.*

Hell is but the collected ruins of the moral world, and sin is the principle that has made them.

When the world dissolves, all places will be hell that are not heaven.—*Marlowe.*

In the utmost solitudes of nature the existence of hell seems to me as legibly declared, by a thousand spiritual utterances, as that of heaven.—*Ruskin.*

The mind is its own place, and in itself can make a heaven of hell, a hell of heaven.—*Milton.*

Hell is full of good meanings and wishings.—*Herbert.*

Character is not changed by passing into eternity, except in degree.—The wilfully wicked on earth will continue so in the other world.

Men might go to heaven with half the labor they put forth to go to hell, if they would but venture their industry in the right way.—*Ben Jonson.*

Hell is the full knowledge of the truth, when truth, resisted long, is sworn our foe, and calls eternity to do her right.—*Young.*

Divines and dying men may talk of hell, but in my heart her several torments dwell.—*Shakespeare.*

If there be a paradise for virtues, there must be a hell for crimes.—*Cousin.*

A guilty conscience is a hell on earth, and points to one beyond.

Tell me not of the fire and the worm, and the blackness and darkness of hell. —To my terrified conscience there is hell enough in this representation of it, that it is the common sewer of all that is abominable and abandoned and reckless as to principle, and depraved as to morals, the one common eddy where all things that are polluted and wretched and filthy are gathered together.—*Beaumont.*

HELP.—Help thyself, and God will help thee.—*Herbert.*

When a person is down in the world, an ounce of help is better than a pound of preaching.—*Bulwer.*

God helps them that help themselves.
—*Old Proverb.*

Light is the task where many share
the toil.—*Homer.*

'Tis not enough to help the feeble up,
but to support him after.—*Shakespeare.*

It is one of the most beautiful compensations of this life, that no man can sincerely try to help another without helping himself.

God be praised, who, to believing souls, gives light in darkness, comfort in despair.—*Shakespeare.*

God has so ordered that men, being in need of each other, should learn to love each other, and bear each other's burdens.—*Sala.*

HEROISM.—Nobody, they say, is a hero to his valet. Of course not; for one must be a hero to understand a hero.—The valet, I dare say, has great respect for some person of his own stamp.—*Goethe.*

Worship your heroes from afar; contact withers them.—*Mad. Neckar.*

Of two heroes, he is the greatest who esteems his rivals most.—*Beaumelle.*

Heroes in history seem to us poetic because they are there.—But if we should tell the simple truth of some of our neighbors, it would sound like poetry.—*G. W. Curtis.*

There are heroes in evil as well as in good.—*Rochefoucauld.*

The prudent see only the difficulties, the bold only the advantages, of a great enterprize; the hero sees both; diminishes the former and makes the latter preponderate, and so conquers.—*Lavater.*

In analyzing the character of heroes it is hardly possible to separate altogether the share of fortune from their own.—*Hallam.*

A light supper, a good night's sleep, and a fine morning have often made a hero of the same man who, by indigestion, a restless night, and a rainy morning, would have proved a coward.—*Chesterfield.*

We cannot think too highly of our nature, nor too humbly of ourselves. When we see the martyr to virtue, subject as he is to the infirmities of a man, yet suffering the tortures of a demon, and bearing them with the magnanimity

of a God, do we not behold a heroism that angels may indeed surpass, but which they cannot imitate, and must admire.—*Colton.*

Fear nothing so much as sin, and your moral heroism is complete.—*C. Simmons.*

Mankind is not disposed to look narrowly into the conduct of great victors when their victory is on the right side. —*George Eliot.*

Heroes are not known by the loftiness of their carriage; the greatest braggarts are generally the merest cowards. —*Rousseau.*

To live well in the quiet routine of life, to fill a little space because God wills it, to go on cheerfully with a petty round of little duties and little avocations; to smile for the joys of others when the heart is aching—who does this, his works will follow him. He is one of God's heroes.—*Farrar.*

The heroes of literary history have been no less remarkable for what they have suffered, than for what they have achieved.—*Johnson.*

However great the advantages which nature bestows on us, it is not she alone, but fortune in conjunction with her, which makes heroes.—*Rochefoucauld.*

Self-trust is the essence of heroism.— *Emerson.*

The grandest of heroic deeds are those which are performed within four walls and in domestic privacy.—*Richter.*

The man who rules his spirit, saith the voice that cannot err, is greater than the one who takes a city.—If each would have dominion of himself, would govern wisely, and thus show true courage, knowledge, power, benevolence, all the princely soul of private virtues, then each would be a prince—a hero—a man in likeness of his maker.—*Mrs. S. J. Hale.*

Every man is a hero and an oracle to somebody, and to that person, whatever he says, has an enhanced value.— *Emerson.*

Dream not that helm and harness are signs of valor true.—Peace hath higher tests of manhood than battle ever knew. —*Whittier.*

Take away ambition and vanity, and

where will be your heroes and patriots? —*Seneca.*

The greatest obstacle to being heroic is the doubt whether one may not be going to prove one's self a fool.—The truest heroism is to resist the doubt; and the profoundest wisdom to know when it ought to be resisted and when obeyed.—*Hawthorne.*

Unbounded courage and compassion joined proclaim him good and great, and make the hero and the man complete.—*Addison.*

One murder makes a villain; millions a hero.—*Bp. Porteus.*

The world's battlefields have been in the heart chiefly; more heroism has been displayed in the household and the closet, than on the most memorable battlefields of history.—*H. W. Beecher.*

The heroes of mankind are the mountains, the highlands of the moral world. —*A. P. Stanley.*

HISTORY. — History is philosophy teaching by example, and also by warning; its two eyes are geography and chronology.

History is but the unrolled scroll of prophecy.—*Garfield.*

All history is a lie.—*Sir R. Walpole.*

History is a voice forever sounding across the centuries the laws of right and wrong. Opinions alter, manners change, creeds rise and fall, but the moral law is written on the tablets of eternity.—*Froude.*

When Frederic the Great would have his secretary read history to him, he would say, " Bring me my liar."

History is little more than the register of the crimes, follies, and misfortunes of mankind.—*Gibbon.*

History is but a kind of Newgate calendar, a register of the crimes and miseries that man has inflicted on his fellow-man.—*Washington Irving.*

History is but the development and revelation of providence.—*Kossuth.*

We read history through our prejudices.—*Wendell Phillips.*

God is in the facts of history as truly as he is in the march of the seasons, the revolutions of the planets, or the architecture of the worlds.—*J. Lanahan.*

This I hold to be the chief office of history, to rescue virtuous actions from the oblivion to which a want of records would consign them, and that men should feel a dread of being considered infamous in the opinions of posterity, from their depraved expressions and base actions.—*Tacitus.*

An historian ought to be exact, sincere, and impartial; free from passion, unbiased by interest, fear, resentment, or affection; and faithful to the truth, which is the mother of history, the preserver of great actions, the enemy of oblivion, the witness of the past, the director of the future.

What is history but a fable agreed upon?—*Napoleon.*

What are all histories but God manifesting himself, shaking down and trampling under foot whatsoever he hath not planted.—*Cromwell.*

Truth is very liable to be left-handed in history.—*A. Dumas.*

History is neither more nor less than biography on a large scale.—*Lamartine.*

The best thing which we derive from history is the enthusiasm that it raises in us.—*Goethe.*

Grecian history is a poem; Latin history, a picture; modern history a chronicle.—*Chateaubriand.*

If men could learn from history, what lessons it might teach us!—But passion and party blind our eyes, and the light which experience gives is a lantern on the stern which shines only on the waves behind us.—*Coleridge.*

The men who make history, have not time to write it.—*Metternich.*

We must consider how very little history there is; I mean real, authentic history.—That certain kings reigned, and certain battles were fought, we can depend on as true; but all the coloring, all the philosophy of history is conjecture.—*Johnson.*

The impartiality of history is not that of the mirror, which merely reflects objects but of the judge who sees, listens, and decides.—*Lamartine.*

Violent natures make history.—The instruments they use almost always kill. —Religion and philosophy have their vestments covered with innocent blood. —*Doudan.*

As in every human character so in

every transaction there is a mixture of good and evil: a little exaggeration, a little suppression, a judicious use of epithets, a watchful and searching skepticism with respect to the evidence on one side, a convenient credulity with respect to every report or tradition on the other, may easily make a saint of Laud, or a tyrant of Henry the Fourth. —*Macaulay*.

An old courtier, with veracity, good sense, and a faithful memory, is an inestimable treasure; he is full of transactions and maxims; in him one may find the history of the age, enriched with a great many curious circumstances, which we never meet with in books.—*Bruyère*.

History has its foreground and its background, and it is principally in the management of its perspective that one artist differs from another. Some events must be represented on a large scale, others diminished; the great majority will be lost in the dimness of the horizon, and a general idea of their joint effect will be given by a few slight touches.—*Macaulay*.

Each generation gathers together the imperishable children of the past, and increases them by new sons of light, alike radiant with immortality.—*Bancroft*.

Out of monuments, names, words, proverbs, traditions, private records and evidences, fragments of stories, passages of books, and the like, we do save and recover somewhat from the deluge of time. —*Bacon*.

He alone reads history aright, who, observing how powerfully circumstances influence the feelings and opinions of men, how often vices pass into virtues, and paradoxes into axioms, learns to distinguish what is accidental and transitory in human nature from what is essential and immutable.—*Macaulay*.

All history is but a romance, unless it is studied as an example.—*Croly*.

To be entirely just in our estimate of other ages is not only difficult, but is impossible. Even what is passing in our presence we see but through a glass darkly. In historical inquiries the most instructed thinkers have but a limited advantage over the most illiterate. Those who know the most approach least to agreement.—*Froude*.

The more we know of history, the less shall we esteem the subjects of it; and to despise our species is the price we must too often pay for our knowledge of it.—*Colton*.

What is public history but a register of the successes and disappointments, the vices, the follies and the quarrels of those who engage in contention for power.—*Paley*.

There is nothing that solidifies and strengthens a nation like reading the nation's history, whether that history is recorded in books, or embodied in customs, institutions, and monuments.—*J. Anderson*.

It is when the hour of conflict is over, that history comes to a right understanding of the strife, and is ready to exclaim, "Lo, God is here, and we knew it not!"—*Bancroft*.

Providence conceals itself in the details of human affairs, but becomes unveiled in the generalities of history.— *Lamartine*.

Every great writer is a writer of history, let him treat on what subjects he may.—He carries with him, for thousands of years, a portion of his times.—*Landor*.

Many historians take pleasure in putting into the mouths of princes what they have neither said nor ought to have said.—*Voltaire*.

We find but few historians who have been diligent enough in their search for truth. It is their common method to take on trust what they distribute to the public; by which means, a falsehood, once received from a famed writer, becomes traditional to posterity.—*Dryden*.

The present state of things is the consequence of the past; and it is natural to inquire as to the sources of the good we enjoy or the evils we suffer. If we act only for ourselves, to neglect the study of history is not prudent; if intrusted with the care of others, it is not just.—*Johnson*.

History is not, as it was once regarded, merely a liberal pursuit in which men found wholesome food for the imagination and sympathies; but now is a department of serious scientific investigation.—We study it in the hope of giving new precision, definiteness, and solidity to the principles of political science.—*J. R. Seeley.*

The history of the past is a mere puppet show.—A little man comes out and blows a little trumpet, and goes in again. —You look for something new, and lo! another little man comes out and blows another little trumpet, and goes in again. —And it is all over.—*Longfellow.*

Not to know what has been transacted in former times is to be always a child. —If no use is made of the labors of past ages, the world must remain always in the infancy of knowledge.—*Cicero.*

Those who have employed the study of history, as they ought, for their instruction, for the regulation of their private manners, and the management of public affairs, must agree with me that it is the most pleasant school of wisdom. —*Dryden.*

History maketh a young man to be old, without wrinkles or gray hairs, privileging him with the experience of age, without either the infirmities or inconveniences thereof.—*Fuller.*

Historians give us the extraordinary events, and omit just what we want, the every-day life of each particular time and country.—*Whately.*

History needs distance, perspective. Facts and events which are too well attested cease, in some sort, to be malleable.—*Joubert.*

History is the glass through which we may behold, with ancestral eyes, not only the various deeds of past ages and the old accidents that attend them, but also discern the different humors of men. —*Howell.*

History presents the pleasantest features of poetry and fiction—the majesty of the epic, the moving accidents of the drama, and the surprises and moral of the romance.—*Willmott.*

Biography is the only true history.— *Carlyle.*

History makes us some amends for the shortness of life.—*Skelton.*

What are most of the histories of the world but lies?—Lies immortalized, and consigned over as a perpetual abuse and a flaw upon posterity.—*South.*

There is no part of history so generally useful as that which relates to the progress of the human mind, the gradual improvement of reason, the successive advances of science, the vicissitudes of learning and ignorance, the extinction and resuscitation of arts, and the revolutions of the intellectual world. —If accounts of battles and invasions are peculiarly the business of princes, the useful and elegant arts are not to be neglected, and those who have kingdoms to govern have understandings to cultivate.—*Johnson.*

History is the first distinct product of man's spiritual nature, his earliest expression of what can be called thought. —*Carlyle.*

We may gather out of history a policy no less wise than eternal, by the comparison and application of other men's forepast miseries with our own like errors and ill deservings.—*Sir W. Raleigh.*

HOLIDAYS. — Who first invented work, and bound the free and holiday-rejoicing spirit down?—*Lamb.*

If all the year were playing holidays, to sport would be as tedious as to work; but when they seldom come, the wished for come.—*Shakespeare.*

The holiest of all holidays are those kept by ourselves in silence and apart, the secret anniversaries of the heart, when the full tide of feeling overflows.— *Longfellow.*

Let your holidays be associated with great public events, and they may be the life of patriotism as well as a source of relaxation and personal employment.— *Tryon Edwards.*

Under the leaves, amid the grass, lazily the day shall pass, yet not be wasted.— From my drowsy ease I borrow health and strength to bear my boat through the great life ocean.—*Mackay.*

HOLINESS.—Holiness is the symmetry of the soul.—*Philip Henry.*

A holy life is not an ascetic, or gloomy, or solitary life, but a life regulated by divine truth and faithful in Christian duty.—It is living above the world while we are still in it.—*Tryon Edwards.*

It must be a prospect pleasing to God to see his creatures forever drawing nearer to him by greater degrees of resemblance.—*Addison.*

Blessed is the memory of those who have kept themselves unspotted from the world.—Yet more blessed and more dear the memory of those who have kept themselves unspotted in the world.— *Mrs. Jameson.*

Holiness is not the way to Christ, but Christ is the way to holiness.

Holiness is the architectural plan on which God buildeth up his living temple.—*Spurgeon.*

Our holy lives must win a new world's crown.—*Shakespeare.*

Holiness is religious principle put into action.—It is faith gone to work.—It is love coined into conduct; devotion helping human suffering, and going up in intercession to the great source of all good. —*F. D. Huntington.*

If it be the characteristic of a worldly man that he desecrates what is holy, it should be of the Christian to consecrate what is secular, and to recognize a present and presiding divinity in all things. —*Chalmers.*

Not all the pomp and pageantry of worlds reflect such glory on the eye supreme, as the meek virtues of the holy man.—*R. Montgomery.*

Everything holy is before what is unholy; guilt presupposes innocence, not the reverse.—Angels, but not fallen ones, were created.—Man does not properly rise to the highest, but first sinks down from it, and then afterward rises again.— *Richter.*

The essence of true holiness consists in conformity to the nature and will of God.—*Lucas.*

Holiness consisteth not in a cowl or in a garment of gray.—When God purifies the heart by faith, the market is sacred as well as the sanctuary; neither remaineth there any work or place which is profane.—*Luther.*

Holiness in us, is the copy or transcript of the holiness that is in Christ.— As the wax hath line for line from the seal, and the child feature for feature from the father, so is holiness in us from him.—*Philip Henry.*

What Christianity most needs in her antagonism with every form of unbelief, is holy living.—*Christlieb.*

The beauty of holiness has done more, and will do more, to regenerate the world and bring in everlasting righteousness than all the other agencies put together.—It has done more to spread

religion in the world, than all that has ever been preached or written on the evidences of Christianity.—*Chalmers.*

A holy life is a voice; it speaks when the tongue is silent, and is either a constant attraction or a perpetual reproof.— *Leighton.*

The serene, silent beauty of a holy life is the most powerful influence in the world, next to the might of the Spirit of God.—*Pascal.*

Real holiness has love for its essence, humility for its clothing, the good of others as its employment, and the honor of God as its end.—*Emmons.*

Holiness is what is loved by all the gods. It is loved because it is holy, and not holy because it is loved.—*Plato.*

There cannot be named a pursuit or enterprise of human beings, in which there is so little possibility of failure, as praying for sanctification.—*J. W. Alexander.*

HOME. — To Adam paradise was home.—To the good among his descendants, home is paradise.—*Hare.*

The first sure symptom of a mind in health, is rest of heart, and pleasure felt at home.—*Young.*

Without hearts there is no home.— *Byron.*

Our home joys are the most delightful earth affords, and the joy of parents in their children is the most holy joy of humanity. It makes their hearts pure and good, it lifts men up to their Father in heaven.—*Pestalozzi.*

The first indication of domestic happiness is the love of one's home.— *Montlosier.*

A hundred men may make an encampment, but it takes a woman to make a home.—*Chinese Proverb.*

It was the policy of the good old gentleman to make his children feel that home was the happiest place in the world; and I value this delicious home-feeling as one of the choicest gifts a parent can bestow.—*Washington Irving.*

He is the happiest, be he king or peasant, who finds peace in his home.— *Goethe.*

When home is ruled according to God's word, angels might be asked to stay with us, and they would not find themselves out of their element.—*Spurgeon.*

Households there may be, well-ordered and abounding in comfort—families there may be, whose various members live in harmony and love—but homes, in their true sense, there cannot be where there is not one whom manly choice has made a wife and infant lips have learned to honor with the name of mother.—*Dudley A. Tyng.*

Home is the resort of love, of joy, of peace, and plenty, where supporting and supported, polished friends and dearest relatives mingle into bliss.—*Thomson.*

It is indeed at home that every man must be known by those who would make a just estimate either of his virtue or felicity; for smiles and embroidery are alike occasional, and the mind is often dressed for show in painted honor and fictitious benevolence.—*Johnson.*

The strength of a nation, especially of a republican nation, is in the intelligent and well-ordered homes of the people. —*Mrs. Sigourney.*

Six things are requisite to create a "happy home." Integrity must be the architect, and tidiness the upholsterer. It must be warmed by affection, lighted up with cheerfulness; and industry must be the ventilator, renewing the atmosphere and bringing in fresh salubrity day by day; while over all, as a protecting canopy and glory, nothing will suffice except the blessing of God.—*Hamilton.*

The paternal hearth, that rallying place of the affections.—*Washington Irving.*

There is a magic in that little word, home; it is a mystic circle that surrounds comforts and virtues never known beyond its hallowed limits.—*Southey.*

Be it ever so humble, there's no place like home.—*Payne.*

Home is the seminary of all other institutions.—*E. H. Chapin.*

Eighty per cent of our criminals come from unsympathetic homes. — *Hans Christian Andersen.*

America's future will be determined by the home and the school. The child becomes largely what it is taught, hence we must watch what we teach it, and how we live before it.—*Jane Addams.*

There is no happiness in life, and there is no misery, like that growing out of the dispositions which consecrate or desecrate a home.—*E. H. Chapin.*

The most essential element in any home is God.—*Dr. Frank Crane.*

The family circle is the supreme conductor of Christianity.—*Henry Drummond.*

Many a man who pays rent all his life owns his own home; and many a family has successfully saved for a home only to find itself at last with nothing but a house.—*Bruce Barton.*

Christianity begins at home. We build our characters there, and what we become in after years is largely determined by our training and home environment.—*Tillman Hobson.*

Men are free when they are in a living homeland, not when they are straying and breaking away.—*D. H. Lawrence.*

A dining room table with children's eager, hungry faces around it, ceases to be a mere dining room table, and becomes an altar.—*Simeon Strunsky.*

If this world affords true happiness, it is to be found in a home where love and confidence increase with the years, where the necessities of life come without severe strain, where luxuries enter only after their cost has been carefully considered.—*A. Edward Newton.*

Just a wee cot—the cricket's chirr— love and the smiling face of her.— *James Whitcomb Riley.*

We have comforts that kings might consider luxuries, yet it is real punishment for us to stay at home; we have wealth and occupation, but little of that peace of mind surpassing wealth which the sage finds in meditation.—*Dr. Joseph Collins.*

Every house where love abides and friendship is a guest, is surely home, and home, sweet home; for there the heart can rest.—*Henry Van Dyke.*

Hard indeed, in a world which has come to feel that it is more important to have an automobile to get away from home with, than to have a home which you might like to stay in.—*Katharine Fullerton Gerould.*

A man is always nearest to his good

when at home, and farthest from it when away.—*J. G. Holland.*

Home, the spot of earth supremely blest, a dearer, sweeter spot than all the rest.—*Montgomery.*

Stint yourself, as you think good, in other things; but don't scruple freedom in brightening home. Gay furniture and a brilliant garden are a sight day by day, and make life blither.—*Buxton.*

To most men their early home is no more than a memory of their early years. The image is never marred. There's no disappointment in memory, and one's exaggerations are always on the good side.—*George Eliot.*

A good home implies good living, which is also a means and a token of true culture, since without good living there can be no good thinking, and—I speak it reverently—no good praying; for mind and soul must have something healthy to go upon.—*J. P. Thompson.*

This fond attachment to the well-known place whence first we started into life's long race, maintains its hold with such unfailing sway, we feel it e'en in age, and at our latest day.—*Cowper.*

To be happy at home is the ultimate aim of all ambition; the end to which every enterprise and labor tends, and of which every desire prompts the prosecution.—*Johnson.*

We need not power or splendor; wide hall or lordly dome; the good, the true, the tender, these form the wealth of home.—*S. J. Hale.*

Only the home can found a state.—*Joseph Cook.*

HONESTY. — An honest man's the noblest work of God.—*Pope.*

Honesty is the best policy.—*Franklin.*

Make yourself an honest man, and then you may be sure there is one rascal less in the world.—*Carlyle.*

It was a grand trait of the old Roman that with him one and the same word meant both honor and honesty.—*Advance.*

To be honest, as this world goes, is to be one man picked out of ten thousand.—*Shakespeare.*

The shortest and surest way to live with honor in the world, is to be in reality what we would appear to be; and if we observe, we shall find, that all human virtues increase and strengthen themselves by the practice and experience of them.—*Socrates.*

All other knowledge is hurtful to him who has not honesty and good-nature.—*Montaigne.*

Nothing more completely baffles one who is full of trick and duplicity than straightforward and simple integrity in another. A knave would rather quarrel with a brother-knave than with a fool, but he would rather avoid a quarrel with one honest man than with both. He can combat a fool by management and address, and he can conquer a knave by temptations. But the honest man is neither to be bamboozled nor bribed.—*Colton.*

He who freely praises what he means to purchase, and he who enumerates the faults of what he means to sell, may set up a partnership with honesty.—*Lavater.*

A grain of honesty and native worth is of more value than all the adventitious ornaments, estates, or preferments, for the sake of which some of the better sort so oft turn knaves.—*Shaftesbury.*

Let honesty be as the breath of thy soul; then shalt thou reach the point of happiness, and independence shall be thy shield and buckler, thy helmet and crown; then shall thy soul walk upright, nor stoop to the silken wretch because he hath riches, nor pocket an abuse because the hand which offers it wears a ring set with diamonds.—*Franklin.*

The only disadvantage of an honest heart is credulity.—*Sir P. Sidney.*

A straight line is shortest in morals as well as in geometry.—*Rahel.*

God looks only to the pure, not to the full hands.—*Laberius.*

He who says there is no such thing as an honest man, is himself a knave.—*Berkeley.*

I hope I shall always possess firmness and virtue enough to maintain what I consider the most enviable of all titles, the character of an honest man.—*Washington.*

True honesty takes into account the claims of God as well as those of man; it renders to God the things that are

God's, as well as to man the things that are man's.—*C. Simmons.*

It would be an unspeakable advantage, both to the public and private, if men would consider that great truth, that no man is wise or safe, but he that is honest.—*Sir W. Raleigh.*

To one who said, "I do not believe that there is an honest man in the world," another replied, "It is impossible that any one man should know all the world, but quite possible than one may know himself."

True honor is to honesty what the court of chancery is to common law.—*Shenstone.*

Socrates being asked the way to honest fame, said, "Study to be what you wish to seem."

The difference there is betwixt honor and honesty, seems to be chiefly the motive: the truly honest man does that from duty, which the man of honor does for the sake of character.—*Shenstone.*

The man who pauses in his honesty wants little of a villain.—*J. Martyn.*

Refined policy has ever been the parent of confusion, and ever will be so, as long as the world endures. Plain good intention, which is as easily discovered at the first view as fraud is surely detected at last, is of no mean force in the government of mankind. Genuine simplicity of heart is a healing and cementing principle.—*Burke.*

Money dishonestly acquired is never worth its cost, while a good conscience never costs as much as it is worth.—*J. P. Senn.*

If he does really think that there is no distinction between virtue and vice, when he leaves our houses let us count our spoons.—*Johnson.*

If honesty did not exist, we ought to invent it as the best means of getting rich.—*Mirabeau.*

No legacy is so rich as honesty.—*Shakespeare.*

Prefer loss before unjust gain: for that brings grief but once; this forever.—*Chilo.*

There is no terror in your threats; for I am armed so strong in honesty that they pass by me as the idle wind, which I respect not.—*Shakespeare.*

Lands mortgaged may return, but honesty once pawned is ne'er redeemed.—*Middleton.*

"Honesty is the best policy"; but he who acts only on that principle is not an honest man.—No one is habitually guided by it in practice.—An honest man is always before it, and a knave is generally behind it.—*Whately.*

Hope of ill gain is the beginning of loss.—*Democritus.*

Do not consider anything for your interest which makes you break your word, quit your modesty, or inclines you to any practice which will not bear the light, or look the world in the face.—*Marcus Antoninus.*

Honest policy is a good friend, both to our safety and to our usefulness. The serpent's head may well become a good Christian's body, especially if it have a dove's eye in it.—*M. Henry.*

Put it out of the power of truth to give you an ill character.—If anybody reports you not to be an honest man let your practice give him the lie.—*Marcus Antoninus.*

Honesty is not only the deepest policy, but the highest wisdom, since however difficult it may be for integrity to get on, it is a thousand times more difficult for knavery to get off; and no error is more fatal than that of those who think that virtue has no other reward because they have heard that she is her own.—*Colton.*

HONOR.—Honor and shame from no condition rise; act well your part, there all the honor lies.—*Pope.*

Honor's a sacred tie,—the noble mind's distinguishing perfection, that aids and strengthens virtue where it meets her, and imitates her actions where she is not.—*Addison.*

Honor is not a matter of any man's calling merely, but rather of his own actions in it.—*Dwight.*

That nation is worthless that will not, with pleasure, venture all for its honor.—*Schiller.*

Mine honor is my life; both grow in one; take honor from me and my life is done.—*Shakespeare.*

Woman's honor is nice as ermine; it will not bear a soil.—*Dryden.*

Honor is unstable, and seldom the

same; for she feeds upon opinion, and is as fickle as her food. She builds a lofty structure on the sandy foundation of the esteem of those who are of all beings the most subject to change.—*Colton.*

If it be a sin to covet honor, I am the most offensive soul alive.—*Shakespeare.*

Purity is the feminine, truth the masculine of honor.—*Hare.*

Let honor be to us as strong an obligation as necessity is to others.—*Pliny.*

Honor is most capricious in her rewards.—She feeds us with air, and often pulls down our house to build our monument.—*Colton.*

Our own heart, and not other men's opinion, forms our true honor.—*Coleridge.*

Hereditary honors are a noble and splendid treasure to descendants.—*Plato.*

Honor is like the eye, which cannot suffer the least impurity without damage.—It is a precious stone, the price of which is lessened by a single flaw.—*Bossuet.*

The giving of riches and honors to a wicked man is like giving strong wine to him that hath a fever.—*Plutarch.*

When vice prevails, and impious men bear sway, the post of honor is a private station.—*Addison.*

The chastity of honor which felt a stain like a wound.—*Burke.*

Better to die ten thousand deaths than wound my honor.—*Addison.*

Life every man holds dear; but the dear man holds honor far more precious dear than life.—*Shakespeare.*

HOPE.—Hope springs eternal in the human breast; man never is, but always to be blest.—*Pope.*

Hope is a prodigal young heir, and experience is his banker, but his drafts are seldom honored since there is often a heavy balance against him, because he draws largely on a small capital and is not yet in possession.—*Colton.*

No affliction nor temptation, no guilt nor power of sin, no wounded spirit nor terrified conscience, should induce us to despair of help and comfort from God.—*T. Scott.*

Hope calculates its schemes for a

long and durable life; presses forward to imaginary points of bliss; and grasps at impossibilities; and consequently very often ensnares men into beggary, ruin, and dishonor.—*Addison.*

The hours we pass with happy prospects in view are more pleasing than those crowded with fruition.—*Goldsmith.*

Hope, of all passions, most befriends us here; joy has her tears, and transport has her death; hope, like a cordial, innocent though strong, man's heart at once inspirits and serenes, nor makes him pay his wisdom for his joys.—*Young.*

You cannot put a great hope into a small soul.—*J. L. Jones.*

We speak of hope; but is not hope only a more gentle name for fear.—*L. E. Landon.*

Hope is a flatterer, but the most upright of all parasites; for she frequents the poor man's hut, as well as the palace of his superior.—*Shenstone.*

Man is, properly speaking, based upon hope; he has no other possession but hope; this world of his is emphatically the place of hope.—*Carlyle.*

Hope is the last thing that dies in man, and though it be exceedingly deceitful, yet it is of this good use to us, that while we are traveling through life it conducts us in an easier and more pleasant way to our journey's end.—*Rochefoucauld.*

We are never beneath hope, while above hell; nor above hope, while beneath heaven.

The miserable hath no other medicine but only hope.—*Shakespeare.*

Auspicious hope, in thy sweet garden grow wreaths for each toil, a charm for every woe.—*Campbell.*

True hope is swift, and flies with swallow's wings; kings it makes gods, and meaner creatures kings.—*Shakespeare.*

Hope is but the dream of those that wake.—*Prior.*

Hope—of all ills that men endure, the only cheap and universal cure; the captive's freedom, and the sick man's health, the lover's victory, and the beggar's wealth.—*Crowley.*

The man who lives only by hope

will die with despair.—*Italian Proverb.*

A propensity to hope and joy is real riches; one to fear and sorrow, real poverty.—*Hume.*

It is worth a thousand pounds a year to have the habit of looking on the bright side of things.—*Johnson.*

Hope is like the sun, which, as we journey toward it, casts the shadow of our burden behind us.—*S. Smiles.*

The world dares say no more for its device, than "while I live, I hope"; but the children of God can add by virtue of a living hope, "while I expire, I hope."—*Leighton.*

Had mankind nothing to expect beyond the grave, their best faculties would be a torment to them; and the more considerate and virtuous they were, the greater concern and grief they would feel from the shortness of their prospects.—*Balguy.*

He that would undermine the foundations of our hope for eternity, seeks to beat down the column which supports the feebleness of humanity.

If the mere delay of hope deferred makes the heart sick, what will the death of hope—its final and total disappointment—despair, do to it?—*W. Nevins.*

Hope is the most beneficial of all the affections, and doth much to the prolongation of life, if it be not too often frustrated; but entertaineth the fancy with an expectation of good.—*Bacon.*

Hope warps judgment in council, but quickens energy in action.—*Bulwer.*

Hope—fortune's cheating lottery, where for one prize, a hundred blanks there be.—*Cowley.*

Hope is always liberal, and they that trust her promises make little scruple of reveling to-day on the profits of to-morrow.—*Johnson.*

It is necessary to hope, though hope should be always deluded; for hope itself is happiness, and its frustrations, however frequent, are yet less dreadful than its extinction.—*Johnson.*

Hope is a delusion; no hand can grasp a wave or a shadow.—*Victor Hugo.*

The mighty hopes that make us men. —*Tennyson.*

Hope is the only good that is common to all men; those who have nothing else possess hope still.—*Thales.*

I have a knack of hoping, which is as good as an estate in reversion, if one can keep from the temptation of turning it into certainty, which may spoil all.—*George Eliot.*

Eternity is the divine treasure house, and hope is the window, by means of which mortals are permitted to see, as through a glass darkly, the things which God is preparing.—*Mountford.*

In all things it is better to hope than to despair.—*Goethe.*

For present grief there is always a remedy; however much thou sufferest, hope; hope is the greatest happiness of man.—*Schefer.*

Hope is a lover's staff; walk hence with that, and manage it against despairing thoughts.—*Shakespeare.*

Hope is brightest when it dawns from fears.—*Walter Scott.*

Hope is the chief blessing of man; and that hope only is rational of which we are sensible that it cannot deceive us.—*Johnson.*

The good man's hope is laid far—far beyond the sway of tempests, or the furious sweep of mortal desolation.—*H. K. White.*

Hope is a pleasant acquaintance, but an unsafe friend; not the man for your banker, though he may do for a traveling companion.—*Haliburton.*

Hope is the best part of our riches.— What sufficeth it that we have the wealth of the Indies in our pockets, if we have not the hope of heaven in our souls?— *Bovee.*

Where there is no hope, there can be no endeavor.—*Johnson.*

He that lives on hopes will die fasting. —*Franklin.*

Hope is the best possession.—None are completely wretched but those who are without hope, and few are reduced so low as that.—*Hazlitt.*

Hope is love's happiness, but not its life.—*L. E. Landon.*

Hope is like the cork to the net, which keeps the soul from sinking in despair; and fear, like the lead to the net, which

keeps it from floating in presumption.—
Bp. Watson.

This wonder we find in hope, that she
is both a flatterer and a true friend.—
How many would die did not hope sustain them; how many have died by hoping too much!—*Feltham.*

Whatever enlarges hope will also exalt
courage.—*Johnson.*

Hope writes the poetry of the boy,
but • memory that of the man. Man
looks forward with smiles, but backward
with sighs. Such is the wise providence
of God. The cup of life is sweetness at
the brim—the flavor is impaired as we
drink deeper, and the dregs are made
bitter that we may not struggle when it
is taken from our lips.—*Emerson.*

I live on hope, and that I think do all
who come into this world.—*Robert
Bridges.*

Under the storm and the cloud today,
and today the hard peril and pain—to-
morrow the stone shall be rolled away,
for the sunshine shall follow the rain.
—*Joaquin Miller.*

The heart bowed down by weight of
woe to weakest hope will cling.—*Alfred
Bunn.*

A man not perfect, but of heart so
high, of such heroic rage, that even his
hopes became a part of earth's eternal
heritage.—*R. W. Gilder.*

The worldly hope men set their hearts
upon turns ashes—or it prospers; and
anon, like snow upon the desert's dusty
face, lighting a little hour or two—is
gone.—*Omar Khayyam.*

We do not raise our hands to the
void for things beyond hope.—*Rabindranath Tagore.*

Hope proves a man deathless. It is
the struggle of the soul, breaking loose
from what is perishable, and attesting
her eternity.—*Henry Melville.*

Hope is life and life is hope.—*Adele
Shreve.*

Before you give up hope, turn back
and read the attacks that were made
upon Lincoln.—*Bruce Barton.*

My country owes me nothing. It
gave me, as it gives every boy and girl,
a chance. It gave me schooling, independence of action, opportunity for service and honor. In no other land could
a boy from a country village, without

inheritance or influential friends, look
forward with unbounded hope.—*Herbert
Hoover.*

It was a Spring that never came, but
we have lived enough to know what we
have never had remains. It is the things
we have that go.—*Sara Teasdale.*

Cling to the flying hours; and yet
let one pure hope, one great desire, like
song on dying lips be set—that ere we
fall in scattered fire our hearts may lift
the world's heart higher.—*Edmund W.
Gosse.*

HOSPITALITY.—(See "FEASTING.")

If a man be gracious to strangers, it
shows that he is a citizen of the world,
and his heart is no island, cut off from
other islands, but a continent that joins
them.—*Bacon.*

Like many other virtues, hospitality
is practised, in its perfection, by the
poor.—If the rich did their share, how
the woes of this world would be light-
ened!—*Mrs. Kirkland.*

HOUSE.—My precept to all who
build, is, that the owner should be an
ornament to the house, and not the
house to the owner.—*Cicero.*

Houses are built to live in, more than
to look at; therefore let use be preferred
before uniformity, except where both
may he had.—*Bacon.*

HUMANITY.—I am a man, and
whatever concerns humanity is of interest to me.—*Terence.*

When a university course convinces
like a slumbering woman and child convince, when the minted gold in the
vault smiles like the night-watchman's
daughter, when warranty deeds loafe in
chairs opposite and are my friendly companions, I intend to reach them my
hand, and make as much of them as I
do of men and women like you.—*Walt
Whitman.*

I hate Spiders—I dislike all kinds of
Insects. Their cold intelligence, their
empty, stereotyped, unremitted industry
repel me. And I am not altogether
happy about the future of the Human
Race; when I think of the slow refriger-
ation of the Earth, the Sun's waning,
and the ultimate, inevitable collapse of
the Solar System, I have grave misgiv-
ings.—*Logan Pearsall Smith.*

It will be very generally found that

those who sneer habitually at human nature, and affect to despise it, are among its worst and least pleasant samples.—*Dickens.*

A man's nature runs either to herbs or weeds; therefore let him seasonably water the one and destroy the other.—*Bacon.*

I do not know what comfort other people find in considering the weakness of great men, but 'tis always a mortification to me to observe that there is no perfection in humanity.—*S. Montague.*

The true proof of the inherent nobleness of our common nature is in the sympathy it betrays with what is noble wherever crowds are collected. Never believe the world is base; if it were so, no society could hold together for a day.—*Bulwer.*

It is only when blinded by self-love, that we can think proudly of our nature. Take away that blind, and in our judgment of others we are quicksighted enough to see there is very little in that nature to rely on.

Human nature is not so much depraved as to hinder us from respecting goodness in others, though we ourselves want it. We love truth too well to resist the charms of sincerity.—*Steele.*

There is but one temple in the world, and that is the body of man.—Nothing is holier than this high form.—We touch heaven when we lay our hand on a human body.—*Novalis.*

Our humanity were a poor thing but for the divinity that stirs within us.—*Bacon.*

Being reproached for giving to an unworthy person, Aristotle said, "I did not give it to the man, but to humanity."

Christianity is the highest perfection of humanity.—*Johnson.*

A rational nature admits of nothing which is not serviceable to the rest of mankind.—*Marcus Antoninus.*

However exquisitely human nature may have been described by writers, the true practical system can be learned only in the world.—*Fielding.*

As there is much beast and some devil in man, so there is some angel and some God in him.—The beast and devil

may be conquered, but in this life never wholly destroyed.—*Coleridge.*

A man's nature is best perceived in privateness, for there is no affectation; in passion, for that putteth a man out of his precepts; and in a new case or experiment, for there custom leaveth him.—*Bacon.*

Humanity is a duty made known and enjoined by revelation, and ever keeping pace with the progress of Christianity.—*Sydney Smith.*   •

HUMILITY. — Humility that low sweet root, from which all heavenly virtues shoot.—*Moore.*

The casting down of our spirits in true humility is but like throwing a ball to the ground, which makes it rebound the higher toward heaven.—*J. Mason.*

True humility is not an abject, groveling, self-despising spirit; it is but a right estimate of ourselves as God sees us.—*Tryon Edwards.*

Sense shines with a double luster when it is set in humility. An able and yet humble man is a jewel worth a kingdom.—*Penn.*

It is easy to look down on others; to look down on ourselves is the difficulty.—*Peterborough.*

The doctrines of grace humble man without degrading, and exalt without inflating him.—*Charles Hodge.*

It was pride that changed angels into devils; it is humility that makes men as angels.—*Augustine.*

Humility in religion, as in the world, is the avenue to glory.—*Guesses at Truth.*

Be wise; soar not too high to fall, but stoop to rise.—*Massinger.*

They that know God will be humble; they that know themselves cannot be proud.—*Flavel.*

Humility is the genuine proof of Christian virtue.—Without it we keep all our defects; and they are only crusted over by pride, which conceals them from others, and often from ourselves.—*Rochefoucauld.*

Humility is the root, mother, nurse, foundation, and bond of all virtue.—*Chrysostom.*

It is the witness still of excellence to put a strange face on its own perfection.—*Shakespeare.*

Heaven's gates are not so highly arched as princes' palaces; they that enter there must go upon their knees.—*J. Webster.*

Humanity cannot be degraded by humiliation. It is its very character to submit to such things. There is a consanguinity between benevolence and humility. They are virtues of the same stock.—*Burke.*

The sufficiency of my merit is to know that my merit is not sufficient.—*Augustine.*

Humility is to make a right estimate of one's self.—*Spurgeon.*

Humility is a virtue all preach, none practise, and yet everybody is content to hear. The master thinks it good doctrine for his servant, the laity for the clergy, and the clergy for the laity.—*Selden.*

There is but one road to lead us to God—humility; all other ways would only lead astray, even were they fenced in with all virtues.—*Boileau.*

Sense shines with a double lustre when set in humility.—*Penn.*

It is from out of the depths of our humility that the height of our destiny looks grandest. Let me truly feel that in myself I am nothing, and at once, through every inlet of my soul, God comes in, and is everything in me.—*W. Mountford.*

It is no great thing to be humble when you are brought low; but to be humble when you are praised is a great and rare attainment.—*St. Bernard.*

Epaminondas, finding himself lifted up in the day of his public triumph, the next day went drooping and hanging down his head; and being asked what was the reason of his so great dejection, made answer: "Yesterday I felt myself transported with vainglory, therefore I chastise myself for it to-day."—*Plutarch.*

The Christian is like the ripening corn; the riper he grows the more lowly he bends his head.—*Guthrie.*

Believe me, the much-praised lambs of humility would not bear themselves so meekly if they but possessed tiger's claws.—*H. Heine.*

If thou wouldst find much favor and peace with God and man, be very low in thine own eyes. Forgive thyself little and others much.—*Leighton.*

Humility is the Christian's greatest honor; and the higher men climb, the further they are from heaven.—*Jane Porter.*

Trees that, like the poplar, lift upward all their boughs, give no shade and no shelter whatever their height. Trees the most lovingly shelter and shade us when, like the willow, the higher soar their summits, the lowlier droop their boughs.—*Bulwer.*

Much misconstruction and bitterness are spared to him who thinks naturally upon what he owes to others, rather than on what he ought to expect from them.—*Mad. Guizot.*

I believe the first test of a truly great man is his humility.—*Ruskin.*

Humility, like darkness, reveals the heavenly lights.—*Thoreau.*

There is nothing so clear-sighted and sensible as a noble mind in a low estate.—*Jane Porter.*

God walks with the humble; he reveals himself to the lowly; he gives understanding to the little ones; he discloses his meaning to pure minds, but hides his grace from the curious and the proud.—*Thos. à Kempis.*

The street is full of humiliations to the proud.—*Emerson.*

There is many a wounded heart without a contrite spirit.—The ice may be broken into a thousand pieces, but it is ice still.—But expose it to the beams of the sun of righteousness, and then it will melt.—*Middleton.*

Should you ask me, What is the first thing in religion? I should reply, The first, second, and third thing therein—nay, all—is humility.—*Augustine.*

After crosses and losses men grow humbler and wiser.—*Franklin.*

Humility is the solid foundation of all the virtues.—*Confucius.*

The beloved of the Almighty are the rich who have the humility of the poor, and the poor who have the magnanimity of the rich.—*Saadi.*

Humility is the first lesson we learn from reflection, and self-distrust the first proof we give of having obtained a knowledge of ourselves.—*Zimmermann.*

It is in vain to gather virtues without humility; for the spirit of God delights to dwell in the hearts of the humble.— *Erasmus.*

Humbleness is always grace; always dignity.—*J. R. Lowell.*

To be humble to superiors, is duty; to equals, is courtesy; to inferiors, is nobleness; and to all, safety; it being a virtue that, for all its lowliness, commandeth those it stoops to.—*Sir T. More.*

True dignity abides with him only, who, in the silent hour of inward thought, can still suspect, and still revere himself, in lowliness of heart.—*Wordsworth.*

If thou desire the love of God and man, be humble, for the proud heart, as it loves none but itself, is beloved of none but itself. — Humility enforces where neither virtue, nor strength, nor reason can prevail.—*Quarles.*

Humility is not a weak and timid quality; it must be carefully distinguished from a groveling spirit.—There is such a thing as an honest pride and self-respect.—Though we may be servants of all, we should be servile to none. —*E. H. Chapin.*

The fullest and best ears of corn hang lowest toward the ground.—*Bp. Reynolds.*

Humility and love are the essence of true religion; the humble formed to adore; the loving to associate with eternal love.—*Lavater.*

Truly, this world can get on without us, if we would but think so.—*Longfellow.*

Nothing sets a person so much out of the devil's reach as humility.—*Jonathan Edwards.*

The richest pearl in the Christian's crown of graces is humility.—*Good.*

Humility is the eldest born of virtue, and claims the birth-right at the throne of heaven.—*Murphy.*

He that places himself neither higher nor lower than he ought to do, exercises the truest humility.—*Colton.*

The saint that wears heaven's brightest crown in deepest adoration bends; the weight of glory bows him down the most when most his soul ascends; nearest the throne itself must be the footstool of humility.—*J. Montgomery.*

By humility I mean not the abjectness of a base mind, but a prudent care not to overvalue ourselves.—*Crew.*

Humility is to have a right estimate of one's self—not to think less of himself than he ought.—The higher a man is in grace, the lower will he be in his own esteem.—*Spurgeon.*

Humility is the truest abstinence in the world.—It is abstinence from selflove and self-conceit, from vaunting our own praise and exploits, from ambition and avarice, the strongest propensities of our nature, and consequently is the noblest self-denial.—*Delany.*

True humility makes way for Christ, and throws the soul at his feet.—*J. Mason.*

HUMOR.—(See " Good-Humor.")

Wit may be a thing of pure imagination, but humor involves sentiment and character.—Humor is of a genial quality; dwells in the same character with pathos, and is always mingled with sensibility.—*Giles.*

I live in a constant endeavor to fence against the infirmities of ill-health, and other evils of life, by mirth. I am persuaded that every time a man smiles—but much more so when he laughs—it adds something to this fragment of life. —*Sterne.*

There is certainly no defence against adverse fortune which is, on the whole, so effectual as an habitual sense of humor.—*T. W. Higginson.*

True humor springs not more from the head than from the heart.—It is not contempt; its essence is love.—It issues not in laughter, but in still smiles, which lie far deeper.—*Carlyle.*

Good humor is one of the best articles of dress one can wear in society.— *Thackeray.*

These poor gentlemen endeavor to gain themselves the reputation of wits and humorists by such monstrous conceits as almost qualify them for bedlam; not considering that humor should always lie under the check of reason, and that it requires the direction of the nicest judgment, by so much the more as it indulges itself in the most boundless freedoms.—*Addison.*

For health and the constant enjoyment of life, give me a keen and ever present sense of humor; it is the next best thing to an abiding faith in providence.—*G. B. Cheever.*

The world is a perpetual caricature of itself; at every moment it is the mockery and the contradiction of what it is pretending to be. But as it nevertheless intends all the time to be something different and highly dignified, at the next moment it corrects and checks and tries to cover up the absurd thing it was; so that a conventional world, a world of masks, is superimposed on the reality, and passes in every sphere of human interest for the reality itself. Humor is the perception of this illusion, whilst the convention continues to be maintained, as if we had not observed its absurdity.—*George Santayana.*

He must not laugh at his own wheeze: A snuff box has no right to sneeze.—*Keith Preston.*

With the fearful strain that is on me night and day, if I did not laugh I should die.—*Abraham Lincoln.*

I do not think anyone can be taught anything about humor, but I do think that certain persons may be taught the mechanism of producing humorous copy that will sell to magazines and newspapers.—*Don Marquis.*

We love a joke that hands us a pat on the back while it kicks the other fellow down stairs.—*C. L. Edson.*

It was the saying of an ancient sage that humor was the only test of gravity, and gravity of humor.—*Shaftesbury.*

HUNGER.—(See "Appetite.")

HURRY.—(See "Haste.")

HUSBAND.—(See "Marriage.")

HYPOCRISY.—The hypocrite was a man who stole the livery of the court of heaven to serve the devil in.—*Pollock.*

As a man loves gold, in that proportion he hates to be imposed upon by counterfeits; and in proportion as a man has regard for that which is above price and better than gold, he abhors that hypocrisy which is but its counterfeit.—*Cecil.*

Don't stay away from church because there are so many hypocrites. There's always room for one more.—*A. R. Adams.*

A bad man is worse when he pretends to be a saint.—*Bacon.*

Satan was the first that practised falsehood under saintly show.—*Milton.*

If you cultivate piety as an end and not a means, you will become a hypocrite.—*Austin O'Malley.*

A man who hides behind the hypocrite is smaller than the hypocrite.—*W. E. Biederwolf.*

The worst sort of hypocrite and liar is the man who lies to himself in order to feel at ease.—*Hilaire Belloc.*

I hope you have not been leading a double life, pretending to be wicked and being really good all the time. That would be hypocrisy.—*Oscar Wilde.*

We are companions in hypocrisy.—*William Dean Howells.*

The world consists almost exclusively of people who are one sort and who behave like another sort.—*Zona Gale.*

No man is a hypocrite in his pleasures.—*Johnson.*

The devil can cite Scripture for his purpose. An evil soul, producing holy witness, is like a villain with a smiling cheek; a goodly apple rotten at the heart.—*Shakespeare.*

If the devil ever laughs, it must be at hypocrites; they are the greatest dupes he has; they serve him better than any others, but receive no wages; nay, what is still more extraordinary, they submit to greater mortifications to go to hell, than the sincerest Christian to go to heaven.—*Colton.*

Hypocrisy is the necessary burden of villainy; affectation, part of the chosen trappings of folly; the one completes a villain, the other only finishes a fop. Contempt is the proper punishment of affectation, and detestation the just consequence of hypocrisy.—*Johnson.*

But then I sigh, and, with a piece of Scripture, tell them—that God bids us do good for evil: and thus I clothe my naked villainy, with old odd ends, stolen forth of Holy Writ: and seem a saint, when most I play the devil. Why, I can smile, and murder while I smile: and cry, content, to that which grieves my heart; and wet my cheeks with artificial tears, and frame my face to all occasions.—*Shakespeare.*

Hypocrisy desires to appear rather

than to be good; honesty, to be good rather than seem so.—Fools purchase reputation by the sale of desert; wise men seek desert even at the hazard of reputation.—*Warwick.*

Some people speak as if hypocrites were confined to religion; but they are everywhere; people pretending to wealth when they have not a sixpence, assuming knowledge of which they are ignorant, shamming a culture they are far removed from, adopting opinions they do not hold.—*Albert Goodrich.*

Hypocrisy is the homage that vice pays to virtue.—*Rochefoucauld.*

An atheist is but a mad ridiculous derider of piety; but a hypocrite makes a sober jest of God and religion; he finds it easier to be upon his knees than to rise to a good action; like an impudent debtor, who goes every day to talk familiarly to his creditor, without ever paying what he owes.—*Pope.*

Hypocrisy is the necessary burden of villainy.—*Johnson.*

The most terrible of lies is not that which is uttered but that which is lived —*W. G. Clarke.*

It is hard to personate and act a part long; for where truth is not at the bottom nature will always be endeavoring to return, and will peep out and betray herself one time or another.—*Tillotson.*

Hypocrites do the devil's drudgery in Christ's livery.—*M. Henry.*

False face must hide what the false heart doth know.—*Shakespeare.*

Hypocrisy is folly.—It is much easier, safer, and pleasanter to be the thing which a man aims to appear, than to keep up the appearance of what he is not.—*Cecil.*

The hypocrite shows the excellence of virtue by the necessity he thinks himself under of seeming to be virtuous.—*Johnson.*

There is some virtue in almost every vice except hypocrisy; and even that, while it is a mockery of virtue, is, at the same time, a compliment to it.—*Hazlitt.*

The hypocrite pays tribute to God that he may impose upon man.

Hypocrisy is much more eligible than open infidelity and vice, it wears the livery of religion, and is cautious of giving scandal.—*Swift.*

Hypocrisy, detest her as we may, and no man's hatred ever wronged her yet, may claim this merit still, that she admits the worth of what she mimics with such care.—*Cowper.*

'Tis a cowardly and servile humor to hide and disguise a man's self under a visor, and not to dare to show himself what he is. By that our followers are trained up to treachery. Being brought up to speak what is not true, they make no conscience of a lie.—*Montaigne.*

Saint abroad and devil at home.— *Bunyan.*

Hypocrisy, the only evil that walks invisible, except to God alone.—*Milton.*

With devotion's visage, and pious action, we do sugar o'er the devil himself. —*Shakespeare.*

No man can, for any considerable time, wear one face to himself, and another to the multitude, without finally getting bewildered as to which is the true one.—*Hawthorne.*

One may smile and smile and be a villain still.—*Shakespeare.*

I

IDEALS.—The best and noblest lives are those which are set toward high ideals. And the highest and noblest ideal that any man can have is Jesus of Nazareth.—*Almeron.*

A large portion of human beings live not so much in themselves as in what they desire to be.—They create an ideal character the perfections of which compensate in some degree for imperfections of their own.—*E. P. Whipple.*

We never reach our ideals, whether of mental or moral improvement, but the thought of them shows us our deficiencies, and spurs us on to higher and better things.—*Tryon Edwards.*

We all have day dreams of what we wish to be, or have, or do; and the high imaginary standard, like the good resolutions we form, aids us, often, to a higher and better life.

Every life has its actual blanks which the ideal must fill up, or which else remain bare and profitless forever.—*J. W. Howe.*

Every man has, at times, in his mind the ideal of what he should be, but is not. In all men that seek to improve, it is better than the actual character.— No one is so satisfied with himself that he never wishes to be wiser, better, and more holy.—*Theodore Parker.*

Ideality is only the avant-courier of the mind, and where that, in a healthy and normal state goes, I hold it to be a prophecy that realization can follow.— *H. Mann.*

Ideals are the world's masters.—*J. G. Holland.*

What we need most, is not so much to realize the ideal as to idealize the real.—*Hedge.*

Ideal beauty is a fugitive which is never located.—*Mad. Sévigné.*

We build statues of snow, and weep to see them melt.—*Walter Scott.*

Great objects form great minds.—*Emmons.*

A man's ideal, like his horizon, is constantly receding from him as he advances toward it.—*W. G. T. Shedd.*

Nothing more powerfully argues a life beyond this than the failure of ideals here. Each gives us only fragments of humanity, of heart, of mind, of charity, of love and of virtue.

Man can never come up to his ideal standard.—It is the nature of the immortal spirit to raise that standard higher and higher as it goes from strength to strength, still upward and onward.—The wisest and greatest men are ever the most modest.—*S. M. F. Ossoli.*

IDEAS.—Ideas control the world.— *Garfield.*

A healthful hunger for a great idea is the beauty and blessedness of life.—*Jean Ingelow.*

In these days we fight for ideas, and newspapers are our fortresses. — *H. Heine.*

Old ideas are prejudices, and new ones caprices.—*Dondan.*

A great idea is usually original to more than one discoverer.—Great ideas come when the world needs them. — They surround the world's ignorance and press for admission.—*A. Phelps.*

Many ideas grow better when transplanted into another mind than in the one where they sprung up. That which

was a weed in one becomes a flower in the other, and a flower again dwindles down to a mere weed by the same change. Healthy growths may become poisonous by falling upon the wrong mental soil, and what seemed a nightshade in one mind unfolds as a morning-glory in the other.—*O. W. Holmes.*

Temples have their images; and we see what influence they have always had over a great part of mankind.—But, in truth, the ideas and images in men's minds are the invisible powers that constantly govern them; and to these they all pay universally a ready submission. —*Jonathan Edwards.*

Ideas are the great warriors of the world, and a war that has no idea behind it is simply a brutality.—*Garfield.*

Ideas are like beards; men do not have them until they grow up.—*Voltaire.*

Our ideas, like orange-plants, spread out in proportion to the size of the box which imprisons the roots.—*Bulwer.*

Ideas are the factors that lift civilization. They create revolutions. There is more dynamite in an idea than in many bombs.—*Bp. Vincent.*

By what strange law of mind is it, that an idea long overlooked, and trodden under foot as a useless stone, suddenly sparkles out in new light as a discovered diamond?—*Mrs. Stowe.*

Ideas are cosmopolitan.—They have the liberty of the world.—You have no right to take the sword and cross the bounds of other nations, and enforce on them laws or institutions they are unwilling to receive.—But there is no limit to the sphere of ideas. Your thoughts and feelings, the whole world lies open to them, and you have the right to send them into any latitude, and to give them sweep around the earth, to the mind of every human being.—*H. W. Beecher.*

Ideas go booming through the world louder than cannon. Thoughts are mightier than armies. Principles have achieved more victories than horsemen or chariots.—*W. M. Paxton.*

To the thinker, the most trifling external object often suggests ideas, which extend, link after link, from earth to heaven.—*Bulwer.*

A soul occupied with great ideas best

performs small duties.—*H. Martineau.*

If the ancients left us ideas, to our credit be it spoken, we moderns are building houses for them.—*A. B. Alcott.*

Ideas, though vivid and real, are often indefinite, and are shy of the close furniture of words.—*Tupper.*

Our land is not more the recipient of the men of all countries than of their ideas.—*Bancroft.*

To have ideas is to gather flowers; to think, is to weave them into garlands.—*Mad. Swetchine.*

An idea, like a ghost, according to the common notion of ghosts, must be spoken to a little before it will explain itself.—*Dickens.*

Events are only the shells of ideas; and often it is the fluent thought of ages that is crystallized in a moment by the stroke of a pen or the point of a bayonet.—*E. H. Chapin.*

Bred to think as well as speak by vote, we furnish our minds, as we furnish our houses, with the fancies of others, and according to the mode and age of our country.—We pick up our ideas and notions in common conversation, as in schools.—*Bolingbroke.*

Ideas make their way in silence like the waters that, filtering behind the rocks of the Alps, loosen them from the mountains on which they rest.—*D'Aubigné.*

When young men are beginning life, the most important period, it is often said, is that in which their habits are formed.—That is a very important period.—But the period in which the ideas of the young are formed and adopted is more important still.—For the ideal with which you go forth to measure things determines the nature, so far as you are concerned, of everything you meet.—*H. W. Beecher.*

Ideas in the mind are the transcript of the world; words are the transcript of ideas; and writing and printing are the transcript of words.—*Addison.*

A vague recollection fills my mind, an image dazzling, but undefined, like the memory of a gorgeous dream.—It crowds my brain confusedly, but will not stay.—It changes like the tremulous sunshine on the wave, till imagination itself is dazzled, bewildered, overpowered.—*Longfellow.*

He who wishes to fulfill his mission in the world must be a man of one idea, that is of one great overmastering purpose, overshadowing all his aims, and guiding and controlling his entire life.—*Bate.*

IDLENESS.—(See "INDOLENCE.")

Idleness is the bane of body and mind, the nurse of naughtiness, the chief author of all mischief, one of the seven deadly sins, the cushion upon which the devil chiefly reposes, and a great cause not only of melancholy, but of many other diseases; for the mind is naturally active; and if it be not occupied about some honest business, it rushes into mischief or sinks into melancholy.—*Burton.*

The idle man is the devil's cushion, on which he taketh his free ease, who, as he is incapable of any good, so he is fitly disposed for all evil motions.—*Bp. Hall.*

Idleness is the hot-bed of temptation, the cradle of disease, the waster of time, the canker-worm of felicity. To him that has no employment, life in a little while will have no novelty; and when novelty is laid in the grave, the funeral of comfort will soon follow.

Idleness is a constant sin, and labor is a duty. Idleness is the devil's home for temptation and for unprofitable, distracting musings; while labor profiteth others and ourselves.—*Baxter.*

Idleness is the key of beggary, and the root of all evil.—*Spurgeon.*

In idleness there is perpetual despair.—*Carlyle.*

From its very inaction, idleness ultimately becomes the most active cause of evil; as a palsy is more to be dreaded than a fever. The Turks have a proverb, which says, that the devil tempts all other men, but that idle men tempt the devil.—*Colton.*

If idleness do not produce vice or malevolence, it commonly produces melancholy.—*Sydney Smith.*

The first external revelations of the dry-rot in men is a tendency to lurk and lounge; to be at street corners without intelligible reason; to be going anywhere when met; to be about many places rather than any; to do nothing tangible but to have an intention of performing a number of tangible duties to-morrow or the day after.—*Dickens.*

Idleness is only the refuge of weak minds, and the holiday of fools.—*Chesterfield.*

Troubles spring from idleness, and grievous toils from needless ease: many without labor would live by their own wits only, but they break for want of stock.—*Franklin.*

Too much idleness, I have observed, fills up a man's time much more completely, and leaves him less his own master, than any sort of employment whatsoever.—*Burke.*

It is a mistake to imagine, that the violent passions only, such as ambition and love, can triumph over the rest. Idleness, languid as it is, often masters them all; she influences all our designs and actions, and insensibly consumes and destroys both passions and virtues.—*Rochefoucauld.*

If you are idle you are on the way to ruin, and there are few stopping places upon it.—It is rather a precipice than a road.—*H. W. Beecher.*

Some one saying to the famous Marquis Spinola, that a distinguished general had died of having nothing to do, he replied, "Upon my word, that is enough to kill anybody."

Life is a short day; but it is a working day. Activity may lead to evil, but inactivity cannot lead to good.—*Hannah More.*

Not only is he idle who is doing nothing, but he that might be better employed.—*Socrates.*

Laziness grows on people; it begins in cobwebs and ends in iron chains. The more business a man has to do the more he is able to accomplish, for he learns to economize his time.—*Sir M. Hale.*

I would have inscribed on the curtains of your bed, and the walls of your chamber, "If you do not rise early, you can never make progress in anything. If you do not set apart your hours of reading, if you suffer yourself or any one else to break in upon them, your days will slip through your hands unprofitably and frivolous, and really unenjoyed by yourself."—*Lord Chatham.*

To be idle and to be poor have al-

ways been reproaches; and therefore every man endeavors with his utmost care to hide his poverty from others, and his idleness from himself.—*Johnson.*

A man who is able to employ himself innocently is never miserable. It is the idle who are wretched. If I wanted to inflict the greatest punishment on a fellow-creature I would shut him alone in a dark room without employment.

Idleness among children, as among men, is the root of all evil, and leads to no other evil more certain than ill temper.—*Hannah More.*

So long as idleness is quite shut out from our lives, all the sins of wantonness, softness, and effeminacy are prevented; and there is but little room for temptation.—*Jeremy Taylor.*

It would be thought a hard government that should tax its people one-tenth part of their time, to be employed in its service; but idleness taxes many of us much more; sloth, by bringing on diseases, absolutely shortens life. Sloth, like rust, consumes faster than labor wears, while the used key is always bright. Dost thou love life, then do not squander time, for that is the stuff life is made of. How much more than is necessary do we spend in sleep, forgetting that the sleeping fox catches no poultry, and there will be sleeping enough in the grave!—*Franklin.*

By nature's laws, immutable and just, enjoyment stops where indolence begins.—*Pollok.*

I look upon indolence as a sort of suicide; for the man is efficiently destroyed, though the appetite of the brute may survive.—*Cicero.*

The idle levy a very heavy tax upon the industrious when, by frivolous visitations, they rob them of their time. Such persons beg their daily happiness from door to door, as beggars their daily bread. A mere gossip ought not to wonder if we are tired of him, seeing that we are indebted for the honor of his visit solely to the circumstance of his being tired of himself.

Much bending breaks the bow; much unbending the mind.—*Bacon.*

Employment, which Galen calls "Nature's physician," is so essential to human happiness that indolence is justly considered as the mother of misery.—*Burton.*

The way to be nothing is to do nothing.—*Howe.*

The busy man is troubled with but one devil; the idle man by a thousand. —*Spanish Proverb.*

Sloth makes all things difficult, but industry, all things easy.—He that rises late must trot all day, and shall scarce overtake his business at night, while laziness travels so slowly that poverty soon overtakes him.—*Franklin.*

Evil thoughts intrude in an unemployed mind, as naturally as worms are generated in a stagnant pool.

Idleness is an inlet to disorder, and makes way for licentiousness.—People who have nothing to do are quickly tired of their own company.—*Collier.*

Rather do what is nothing to the purpose than be idle, that the devil may find thee doing.—The bird that sits is easily shot when the fliers escape the fowler.—Idleness is the Dead Sea that swallows all the virtues, and is the self-made sepulcher of a living man.—*Quarles.*

An idle brain is the devil's workshop. —*English Proverb.*

Among those whom I never could persuade to rank themselves with idlers, and who speak with indignation of my morning sleeps and nocturnal rambles, one passes the day in catching spiders, that he may count their eyes with a microscope; another exhibits the dust of a marigold separated from the flower with a dexterity worthy of Leuwenhoeck himself. Some turn the wheel of electricity; some suspend rings to a loadstone, and find that what they did yesterday, they can do again to-day.— Some register the changes of the wind, and die fully convinced that the wind is changeable.—There are men yet more profound, who have heard that two colorless liquors may produce a color by union, and that two cold bodies will grow hot if they are mingled: they mingle them, and produce the effect expected, say it is strange, and mingle them again.—*Johnson.*

Idleness is the stupidity of the body, and stupidity is the idleness of the mind. —*Seume.*

Stagnation is something worse than death; it is corruption also.—*Simms.*

Satan selects his disciples when they are idle; but Christ chose his when they were busy at their work, either mending their nets, or casting them into the sea. —*Farrendon.*

They that do nothing are in the readiest way to do that which is worse than nothing.—*Zimmermann.*

Idleness is many gathered miseries in one name.—*Richter.*

The idle, who are neither wise for this world nor the next, are emphatically fools.—*Tillotson.*

Satan finds some mischief still for idle hands to do.—*Watts.*

Idleness is the burial of a living man. —*Jeremy Taylor.*

Absence of occupation is not rest; a mind quite vacant is a mind distressed. —*Cowper.*

Idleness travels very slowly, and poverty soon overtakes her.—*Hunter.*

Idleness is the gate of all harms.—An idle man is like a house that hath no walls; the devils may enter on every side.—*Chaucer.*

It is an undoubted truth that the less one has to do the less time one finds to do it in. One yawns, one procrastinates, one can do it when one will, and, therefore, one seldom does it at all; whereas, those who have a great deal of business must buckle to it; and then they always find time enough to do it.— *Chesterfield.*

Do not allow idleness to deceive you; for while you give him to-day he steals to-morrow from you.—*Crowquill.*

I would not waste the springtime of my youth in idle dalliance; I would plant rich seeds to blossom in my manhood, and bear fruit when I am old.— *Hillhouse.*

Go to the ant, thou sluggard, learn to live, and by her busy ways, reform thine own.—*Smart.*

Ten thousand harms more than the ills we knew, our idleness doth hatch.— *Shakespeare.*

Idleness is the sepulcher of virtue.— *Mad. Roland.*

IGNORANCE.—(See "KNOWLEDGE.")
Ignorance is a mere privation, by

which nothing can be produced; it is a vacuity in which the soul sits motionless and torpid for want of attraction. —*Johnson.*

Better be unborn than untaught, for ignorance is the root of misfortune.—*Plato.*

Have the courage to be ignorant of a great number of things, in order to avoid the calamity of being ignorant of everything.—*Sydney Smith.*

He that does not know those things which are of use and necessity for him to know, is but an ignorant man, whatever he may know besides.—*Tillotson.*

Nothing is so indicative of deepest culture as a tender consideration of the ignorant.—*Emerson.*

There never was any party, faction, sect, or cabal whatsoever, in which the most ignorant were not the most violent; for a bee is not a busier animal than a blockhead. However, such instruments are, perhaps, necessary; for it may be with states as with clocks, which must have some dead weight hanging at them, to help and regulate the motion of the finer and more useful parts.—*Pope.*

To be ignorant of one's ignorance is the malady of ignorance.—*A. B. Alcott.*

It is impossible to make people understand their ignorance; for it requires knowledge to perceive it, and therefore he that can perceive it hath it not.—*Jeremy Taylor.*

Ignorance is not so damnable as humbug, but when it prescribes pills it may happen to do more harm.—*George Eliot.*

Ages of ignorance and simplicity are thought to be ages of purity. But the direct contrary is the case. Rude periods have that grossness of manners which is as unfriendly to virtue as luxury itself. Men are less ashamed as they are less polished.—*Warton.*

By ignorance is pride increased; those most assume who know the least.—*Gay.*

Ignorance, which in behavior mitigates a fault, is, in literature, a capital offence. —*Joubert.*

The ignorant hath an eagle's wings and an owl's eyes.—*George Herbert.*

There is no slight danger from general ignorance; and the only choice

which Providence has graciously left to a vicious government is either to fall by the people, if they are suffered to become enlightened, or with them, if they are kept enslaved and ignorant.— *Coleridge.*

It is as great a point of wisdom to hide ignorance, as to discover knowledge.

'Tis sad work to be at that pass, that the best trial of truth must be the multitude of believers, in a crowd where the number of fools so much exceeds that of the wise.—*Montaigne.*

To be proud of learning is the greatest ignorance.—*Jeremy Taylor.*

It is with nations as with individuals, those who know the least of others think the highest of themselves; for the whole family of pride and ignorance are incestuous, and mutually beget each other.—*Colton.*

Ignorance, when voluntary, is criminal, and a man may be properly charged with that evil which he neglected or refused to learn how to prevent.—*Johnson.*

In the natural world ignorance is visited as sharply as willful disobedience; incapacity meets the same punishment as crime.—Nature's discipline is not even a word and a blow and the blow first, but the blow without the word.—It is left for the sufferer to find out why the blow was given. —*Huxley.*

So long as thou art ignorant be not ashamed to learn.—Ignorance is the greatest of all infirmities, and, when justified, the chiefest of all follies.— *Izaak Walton.*

Ignorance gives a sort of eternity to prejudice, and perpetuity to error.— *Robert Hall.*

If thou art wise thou knowest thine own ignorance; and thou art ignorant if thou knowest not thyself.—*Luther.*

Nothing is so good for an ignorant man as silence; and if he was sensible of this he would not be ignorant.— *Saadi.*

He that is not aware of his ignorance will be only misled by his knowledge.— *Whately.*

It is better to be a beggar than ignorant; for a beggar only wants money,

but an ignorant person wants humanity.
—*Aristippus*.

Ignorance is the curse of God; knowledge the wing wherewith we fly to heaven.—*Shakespeare*.

The ignorance that knows itself, and judges and condemns itself, is not an absolute ignorance; which to be, it must be ignorant of itself.—*Montaigne*.

Ignorance is the night of the mind, but a night without moon or star.—*Confucius*.

A wise man in the company of those who are ignorant, has been compared to a beautiful girl in the company of blind men.—*Saadi*.

As if anything were so common as ignorance! The multitude of fools is a protection to the wise.—*Cicero*.

Ignorance is a prolonged infancy, only deprived of its charm.—*Boufflers*.

A man is never astonished or ashamed that he does not know what another does; but he is surprised at the gross ignorance of the other in not knowing what he knows.—*Haliburton*.

It is not wisdom but ignorance that teaches men presumption.—Genius may sometimes be arrogant, but nothing is so diffident as knowledge.—*Bulwer*.

There are times when ignorance is bliss, indeed.—*Dickens*.

Ignorance has been said to be the mother of devotion; it is rather the mother of superstition.

Nothing is so haughty and assuming as ignorance where self-conceit sets up to be infallible.—*South*.

Ignorance lies at the bottom of all human knowledge, and the deeper we penetrate the nearer we come to it.—For what do we truly know, or what can we clearly affirm of any one of those important things upon which all our reasonings must of necessity be built—time and space, life and death, matter and mind.—*Colton*.

Too much attention cannot be bestowed on that important, yet much neglected branch of learning, the knowledge of man's ignorance.—*Whately*.

Be ignorance thy choice, where knowledge leads to woe.—*Beattie*.

Where ignorance is bliss 'tis folly to be wise.—*Gray*.

The highest reach of human science is the scientific recognition of human ignorance.—*Sir Wm. Hamilton*.

ILL-NATURE.—Ill-humor is but the inward feeling of our own want of merit; a dissatisfaction with ourselves which is always united with an envy that foolish vanity excites.—*Goethe*.

The world is so full of ill-nature, that I have lampoons sent me by people who cannot spell, and satires composed by those who scarce know how to write.—*Spectator*.

It is impossible that an ill-natured man can have a public spirit; for how should he love ten thousand men who has never loved one?—*Pope*.

An ill-humored man, is, almost of course, a selfish man, unhappy in himself, and disagreeable to others.—His chief pleasure seems to be, to be displeased, if not with himself, yet with all about him.

ILLS.—What we count the ills of life are often blessings in disguise, resulting in good to us in the end.—Though for the present not joyous but grievous, yet, if received in a right spirit, they work out fruits of righteousness for us at last.—*M. Henry*.

It is better to try to bear the ills we have, than to anticipate those which may never come.—*Rochefoucauld*.

Think of the ills from which you are exempt, and it will aid you to bear patiently those which now you may suffer.—*Cecil*.

Philosophy easily triumphs over past and future ills; but present ills triumph over philosophy.—*Rochefoucauld*.

We trust, that somehow, good will be the final goal of ill.—*Tennyson*.

We satisfied ourselves, the other day, that there was no real ill in life except severe bodily pain; everything else is the child of the imagination, and depends on our thoughts.—All other ills find a remedy either from time, or moderation, or strength of mind.—*Mad. Sévigné*.

The fear of ill exceeds the ill we fear.

IMAGINATION. — Many have no happier moments than those that they pass in solitude, abandoned to their own imagination, which sometimes puts sceptres in their hands or miters on their heads, shifts the scene of pleasure with endless variety, bids all the forms of beauty sparkle before them, and gluts them with every change of visionary luxury.—*Johnson.*

We are all of us imaginative in some form or other, for images are the brood of desire.—*George Eliot.*

No man will be found in whose mind airy notions do not sometimes tyrannize, and force him to hope or fear beyond the limits of sober probability.—*Johnson.*

A vile imagination, once indulged, gets the key of our minds, and can get in again very easily, whether we will or no, and can so return as to bring seven other spirits with it more wicked than itself; and what may follow no one knows.—*Spurgeon.*

He who has imagination without learning has wings and no feet.—*Joubert.*

Imagination rules the world.—*Napoleon.*

Do what he will, he cannot realize half he conceives.—The glorious vision flies.—Go where he may, he cannot hope to find the truth and beauty which are pictured in his mind.—*Rogers.*

The soul without imagination is what an observatory would be without a telescope.—*H. W. Beecher.*

The world of reality has its limits; the world of imagination is boundless.—Not being able to enlarge the one, let us contract the other; for it is from their difference that all the evils arise which render us unhappy.—*Rousseau.*

Whatever makes the past or future predominate over the present, exalts us in the scale of thinking beings.—*Johnson.*

Thought convinces; feeling persuades.—If imagination furnishes the fact with wings, feeling is the great, stout muscle which plies them, and lifts him from the ground.—Thought sees beauty; emotion feels it.—*Theodore Parker.*

Imagination, where it is truly creative, is a faculty, not a quality; its seat is in the higher reason, and it is efficient only as the servant of the will.—Imagination, as too often understood, is mere fantasy—the image-making power, common to all who have the gift of dreams.—*J. R. Lowell.*

Imagination is the ruler of our dreams

—a circumstance that may account for the peculiar vividness of the impressions they produce.—Let reason be the ruler of our waking thoughts.—*Clulow.*

The faculty of imagination is the great spring of human activity, and the principal source of human improvement. As it delights in presenting to the mind scenes and characters more perfect than those which we are acquainted with, it prevents us from ever being completely satisfied with our present condition, or with our past attainments, and engages us continually in the pursuit of some untried enjoyment, or of some ideal excellence. Destroy this faculty, and the condition of man will become as stationary as that of the brutes.—*Dugald Stewart.*

Imagination disposes of everything; it creates beauty, justice, and happiness, which are everything in this world.—*Pascal.*

Imagination is the eye of the soul.—*Joubert.*

Imagination ennobles appetites which in themselves are low, and spiritualizes acts which, else, are only animal.—But the pleasures which begin in the senses only sensualize.—*F. W. Robertson.*

The poet's eye, in a fine frenzy rolling, doth glance from heaven to earth, from earth to heaven; and as imagination bodies forth the forms of things unknown, the poet's pen turns them to shape, and gives to airy nothing a local habitation and a name; such tricks hath strong imagination.—*Shakespeare.*

Our griefs, as well as our joys, owe their strongest colors to our imaginations.—There is nothing so grievous to be borne that pondering upon it will not make it heavier; and there is no pleasure so vivid that the animation of fancy cannot enliven it.—*Jane Porter.*

Solitude is as needful to the imagination as society is wholesome for the character.—*J. R. Lowell.*

An uncommon degree of imagination constitutes poetical genius.—*Dugald Stewart.*

The lunatic, the lover, and the poet, are of imagination all compact.—*Shakespeare.*

It is the divine attribute of the imagination, that when the real world is shut out it can create a world for itself, and with a necromantic power can conjure up glorious shapes and forms, and brilliant visions to make solitude populous, and irradiate the gloom of a dungeon.—*Washington Irving.*

IMITATION.— Man is an imitative creature, and whoever is foremost leads the herd.—*Schiller.*

We imitate only what we believe and admire.—*Willmott.*

Insist on yourself; never imitate. Your own gift you can present every moment with the cumulative force of a whole life's cultivation; but of the adopted talent of another, you have only an extemporaneous half-possession. That which each can do best none but his Maker can teach him.—*Emerson.*

It is by imitation, far more than by precept, that we learn everything; and what we learn thus, we acquire not only more effectually, but more pleasantly.— This forms our manners, our opinions, our lives.—*Burke.*

Precepts are useful, but practice and imitation go far beyond them.—Hence the importance of watching early habits that they may be free from what is objectionable.—*Knighton.*

Imitation belittles.—*Bovee.*

He who imitates evil always goes beyond the example that is set; he who imitates what is good always falls short. —*Guicciardini.*

It is a poor wit who lives by borrowing the words, decisions, mien, inventions, and actions of others.—*Lavater.*

I hardly know so true a mark of a little mind as the servile imitation of others.—*Gréville.*

Men are so constituted that every one undertakes what he sees another successful in, whether he has aptitude for it or not.—*Goethe.*

Every kind of imitation speaks the person that imitates inferior to him whom he imitates, as the copy is to the original.—*South.*

Imitators are a servile race.—*Fontaine.*

Imitation causes us to leave natural ways to enter into artificial ones; it therefore makes slaves.—*Vinet.*

IMMODESTY.—(See "MODESTY.")

IMMORTALITY.—(See "SOUL.")

Those who hope for no other life are dead even for this.—*Goethe.*

The seed dies into a new life, and so does man.—*G. Macdonald.*

The thought of being nothing after death is a burden insupportable to a virtuous man; we naturally aim at happiness, and cannot bear to have it confined to our present being.—*Dryden.*

When I consider the wonderful activity of the mind, so great a memory of what is past, and such a capacity of penetrating into the future; when I behold such a number of arts and sciences, and such a multitude of discoveries thence arising, I believe and am firmly persuaded that a nature which contains so many things within itself cannot but be immortal.—*Cicero.*

Those who live in the Lord never see each other for the last time.—*German Motto.*

The spirit of man, which God inspired, cannot together perish with this corporeal clod.—*Milton.*

All men's souls are immortal, but the souls of the righteous are both immortal and divine.—*Socrates.*

Nothing more powerfully argues a life beyond this than the failure of our ideas here.—Each gives us only fragments of humanity; fragments of heart, of mind, of charity, of love, of virtue.—He who inspires such thoughts and hopes, will surely give a sphere for their realization.

For the great hereafter I trust in the infinite love of God as expressed in the life and death of our Lord and Saviour Jesus Christ.—*J. G. Holland.*

How happens it that the pure and holy have such firm confidence in the immortality of the soul? Do they not by a deeper instinct or intuition, recognize their spirituality, and feel that they belong more to spirit than to flesh—more to eternity than to time?—*R. Turnbull.*

The belief that we shall never die is the foundation of our dying well.—*Turretin.*

Whatsoever that be within us that feels, thinks, desires, and animates, is something celestial, divine, and, consequently, imperishable.—*Aristotle.*

To assure us of the future existence of the good in a state of glory and blessedness, and in bodies changed from mortality to immortality, each of the three great dispensations has had its instance of translations from earth to heaven; the patriarchal, in the person of Enoch; the Jewish, in the person of Elijah; and the Christian in the person of Christ.

What springs from earth dissolves to earth again, and heaven-born things fly to their native seat.—*Marcus Antoninus.*

I feel my immortality o'ersweep all pains, all tears, all time, all fears; and peal, like the eternal thunders of the deep, into my ears this truth—thou livest forever!—*Byron.*

Seems it strange that thou shouldst live forever? Is it less strange that thou shouldst live at all?—This is a miracle; and that no more.—*Young.*

Nothing short of an eternity could enable men to imagine, think, and feel, and to express all they have imagined, thought and felt.—Immortality, which is the spiritual desire, is the intellectual necessity.—*Bulwer.*

We do not believe in immortality because we have proved it, but, we forever try to prove it because we believe it.—*James Martineau.*

Our dissatisfaction with any other solution is the blazing evidence of immortality.—*Emerson.*

On the imagination God sometimes paints, by dream and symbol, the likeness of things to come.—What the foolish-wise call fanaticism, belongs to the same part of us as hope.—Each is the yearning of the soul for the great "Beyond," which attests our immortality.—*Bulwer.*

How gloomy would be the mansions of the dead to him who did not know that he should never die; that what now acts, shall continue its agency, and what now thinks, shall think on forever. —*Johnson.*

'Tis the divinity that stirs within us; 'tis heaven itself that points out an hereafter and intimates eternity to man.— *Addison.*

The date of human life is too short to recompense the cares which attend the most private condition; therefore it is that our souls are made, as it were, too big for it, and extend themselves in the prospect of a longer existence.—*Steele.*

Most of those who deny the immortality of the soul, only maintain this opin-

ion because they wish it. But in the height of their sinful pleasures, the truth which stares them in the face, begins on earth that punishment, to the fullness of which they are doomed hereafter.— *Jewish Spy.*

Can it be? matter immortal? and shall spirit die? above the nobler, shall less nobler rise? shall man alone, for whom all else revives, no resurrection know? shall man alone, imperial man! be sown in barren ground, less privileged than grain, on which he feeds?—*Young.*

The old, old fashion—death! Oh, thank God, all who see it, for that older fashion yet—of immortality!—*Dickens.*

We are born for a higher destiny than that of earth.—There is a realm where the rainbow never fades, where the stars will be spread out before us like islands that slumber on the ocean, and where the beings that pass before us like shadows, will stay in our presence forever.—*Bulwer.*

Immortality is the greatness of our being; the scene for attaining the fullness and perfection of our existence.— *C. Simmons.*

We are much better believers in immortality than we can give grounds for. —The real evidence is too subtle, or is higher than we can write down in propositions.—*Emerson.*

Without a belief in personal immortality religion is like an arch resting on one pillar, or like a bridge ending in an abyss.—*Max Müller.*

The creator made us to be the image of his own eternity, and in the desire for immortality we feel we have sure proof of our capacity for it.—*Southey.*

Not all the subtilties of metaphysics can make me doubt a moment of the immortality of the soul, and of a beneficent providence. I feel it, I believe it, I desire it, I hope it, and will defend it to my last breath.—*Rousseau.*

The dust goes to its place, and man to his own.—It is then I feel my immortality.—I look through the grave into heaven.—I ask no miracle, no proof, no reasoning, for me.—I ask no risen dust to teach me immortality.—I am conscious of eternal life.—*Theodore Parker.*

As often as I hear of some undeserved wretchedness, my thoughts rest on that world where all will be made straight, and where the labors of sorrow will end in joy.—*Fichte.*

The belief of a future state is a troublesome check on human passions, and one can never make libertines tranquil and resolute without having first made them unbelievers.—*Massillon.*

A voice within us speaks that startling word, "Man, thou shalt never die!" Celestial voices hymn to our souls; according harps, by angel fingers touched, do sound forth still the song of great immortality.—*Dana.*

Faith in the hereafter is as necessary for the intellectual, as for the moral character; and to the man of letters, as well as the Christian, the present forms but the slightest portion of his existence.—*Southey.*

A man really looking onward to an immortal life, on whatever grounds, exhibits to us the human soul in an ennobled attitude.—*Whewell.*

Man only of all earthly creatures, asks, "Can the dead die forever?"— and the instinct that urges the question is God's answer to man, for no instinct is given in vain.—*Bulwer.*

Every natural longing has its natural satisfaction.—If we thirst, God has created liquids to gratify thirst.—If we are susceptible of attachment, there are beings to gratify our love.—If we thirst for life and love eternal, it is likely that there are an eternal life and an eternal love to satisfy that craving.—*F. W. Robertson.*

Immortality is the glorious discovery of Christianity.—*Channing.*

The monuments of the nations are all protests against nothingness after death; so are statues and inscriptions; so is history.—*Lew Wallace.*

One short sleep past, we wake eternally, and death shall be no more.— *Donne.*

It is immortality, and that alone, which amid life's pains, abasements, the soul can comfort, elevate, and fill.— *Young.*

IMPATIENCE. — Impatience grasps at all, and admits of no delay, scorning to wait God's leisure, and to attend humbly and dutifully upon the issues of his wise and just providence.—*South.*

In all evils which admit a remedy,

impatience should be avoided, because it wastes that time and attention in complaints which, if properly applied, might remove the cause.—*Johnson.*

Impatience turns an ague into a fever, a fever to the plague, fear into despair, anger into rage, loss into madness, and sorrow to amazement.—*Jeremy Taylor.*

Peevishness may be considered the canker of life, that destroys its vigor, and checks its improvement; that creeps on with hourly depredations, and taints and vitiates what it cannot consume.— *Johnson.*

I have not so great a struggle with my vices, great and numerous as they are, as I have with my impatience. My efforts are not absolutely useless; yet I have never been able to conquer this ferocious wild beast.—*Calvin.*

Adversity borrows its sharpest sting from our impatience.—*Bp. Horne.*

In that worthiest of all struggles, the struggle for self-mastery and goodness, we are far less patient with ourselves than God is with us.—*J. G. Holland.*

Impatience dries the blood sooner than age or sorrow.—*Cleon.*

Whoever is out of patience is out of possession of his soul.—Men must not turn bees, and kill themselves in stinging others.—*Bacon.*

Oh! how impatience gains upon the soul, when the long promised hour of joy draws near.—How slow the tardy moments seem then to roll.—*Mrs. Tighe.*

Such is our impatience, our hatred of procrastination in everything but the amendment of our practices and the adornment of our nature, one would imagine we were dragging time along by force, and not he us.—*Landor.*

IMPERFECTION.—(See "FAULTS.")

Imperfection is in some sort essential to all that we know of life.—Nothing that lives is, or can be rigidly perfect. —The fox-glove blossom, a third part bud; a third part past, and a third part in full bloom, is a type of the life of this world.—*Ruskin.*

He censures God who quarrels with the imperfections of men.—*Burke.*

I am too conscious of mine own imperfections to rake into and dilate upon the failings of other men; and though I carry always some ill-nature about me, yet it is, I hope, no more than is in this world necessary for a preservative.— *Marvell.*

No human face is exactly the same in its lines on each side; no leaf is perfect in its lobes, and no branch in its symmetry.—All admit irregularity, as they imply change.—To banish imperfection is to destroy expression, to check exertion, to paralyze vitality.—All things are better, lovelier, and more beloved for the imperfections which have been divinely appointed, that the law of human life may be effort, and the law of human judgment may be mercy.— *Ruskin.*

It is only imperfection that complains of what is imperfect.—The more perfect we are, the more gentle and quiet we become toward the defects of others.— *Fénelon.*

The finer the nature, the more flaws will show through the clearness of it; and it is a law of this universe that the best things shall be seldomest seen in their best forms.—*Ruskin.*

What an absurd thing it is to pass over all the valuable parts of a man, and fix our attention on his infirmities. —*Addison.*

Great men are very apt to have great faults; and the faults appear the greater by their contrast with their excellencies. —*C. Simmons.*

It is not so much being free from faults and imperfections as overcoming them that is an advantage to us; it being with follies and weaknesses and errors, as with the weeds of a field, which, if destroyed on the soil where they grow, enrich and improve it, more than if they had never sprung up there.

IMPERTINENCE. — (See "IMPUDENCE" and "INSULT.")

Receive no satisfaction for premeditated impertinence; forget it, and forgive it, but keep inexorably at a distance him who offered it.—*Lavater.*

A man has no more right to say an uncivil thing than to act one; no more right to say a rude thing to another than to knock him down.—*Johnson.*

He is guilty of impertinence who considers not the circumstances of time, or engrosses the conversation, or makes himself the subject of his discourse, or

pays no regard to the company he is in. —*Cicero.*

IMPOSSIBILITY.— Few things are impossible in themselves.—It is not so much means, as perseverance, that is wanting to bring them to a successful issue.—*Rochefoucauld.*

One great difference between a wise man and a fool is, the former only wishes for what he may possibly obtain; the latter desires impossibilities. — *Democritus.*

"Impossible !" That is not good French.—*Napoleon.*

It is not a lucky word, this same "impossible"; no good comes of those who have it so often in their mouth.—*Carlyle.*

Impossible is a word only to be found in the dictionary of fools.—*Napoleon.*

Nothing is impossible; there are ways that lead to everything, and if we had sufficient will we should always have sufficient means.—It is often merely for an excuse that we say things are impossible.—*Rochefoucauld.*

"Impossible"—never let me hear that foolish word again.—*Mirabeau.*

IMPRESSIONS.—The mind unlearns with difficulty what has long been impressed on it.—*Seneca.*

If you would stand well with a great mind, leave him with a favorable impression of yourself; if with a little mind, leave him with a favorable opinion of himself.—*Coleridge.*

The least and most imperceptible impressions received in our infancy have consequences very important and of long duration.—It is with these first impressions as with a river, whose waters we can easily turn at its source; with the same facility we may turn the minds of children to what direction we please.— *Locke.*

Do not all impressions made in life continue immortal as the soul itself? May they not form the picture-gallery, upon which we shall gaze through the boundless ages of eternity?—*Bate.*

Our first impressions, whether of persons or things, have great influence on all our future estimates and opinions.

IMPROVEMENT. — Slumber not in the tents of your fathers. The world is advancing. Advance with it.—*Mazzini.*

Judge of thine improvement, not by what thou speakest or writest, but by the firmness of thy mind, and the government of thy passions and affections.—*Fuller.*

People seldom improve when they have no other model but themselves to copy after.—*Goldsmith.*

Where we cannot invent, we may at least improve; we may give somewhat of novelty to that which was old, condensation to that which was diffuse, perspicuity to that which was obscure, and currency to that which was recondite.—*Colton.*

Use your gifts faithfully, and they shall be enlarged; practice what you know, and you shall attain to higher knowledge.—*Arnold.*

Infinite toil would not enable you to sweep away a mist; but by ascending a little you may often look over it altogether. So it is with our moral improvement; we wrestle fiercely with a vicious habit, which would have no hold upon us if we ascended into a higher moral atmosphere.—*A. Helps.*

It is necessary to try to surpass one's self always; this occupation ought to last as long as life.—*Queen Christiana.*

To hear always, to think always, to learn always, it is thus that we live truly; he who aspires to nothing, and learns nothing, is not worthy of living. —*A. Helps.*

If a better system is thine, import it; if not, make use of mine.—*Horace.*

All of us, who are worth anything, spend our manhood in unlearning the follies, or expiating the mistakes of our youth.—*Shelley.*

Much of the wisdom of one age, is the folly of the next.—*C. Simmons.*

IMPROVIDENCE.—(See "Waste.")

Waste not, want not; willful waste makes woful want.—*Franklin.*

What maintains one vice, would bring up two children.—Remember, many a little makes a mickle; and further, beware of little expenses; a small leak will sink a great ship.—*Franklin.*

Hundreds would never have known want, if they had not first known waste. —*Spurgeon.*

It has always been more difficult for a man to keep than to get, for in the

one case fortune aids, as it often assists injustice; but in the other, sense is required.—Therefore we often see a person deficient in cleverness, rise in wealth; and then, from want of sense, roll head-over-heels to the bottom.— *Basil.*

There are men born under that constellation which maketh them as unapt to enrich themselves as they are ready to impoverish others.—*Hooker.*

How full or how empty our lives, depends, we say, on Providence. Suppose we say, more or less on improvidence.— *Bovee.*

IMPRUDENCE.—(See "Prudence.")

IMPUDENCE. — (See "Impertinence.")

A true and genuine impudence is ever the effect of ignorance, without the least sense of it.—*Steele.*

The man who cannot blush, and who has no feelings of fear, has reached the acme of impudence.—*Menander.*

He that knows the world will not be bashful; he who knows himself will not be impudent.—*C. Simmons.*

The way to avoid the imputation of impudence is, not to be ashamed of what we do, but never to do what we ought to be ashmed of.—*Cicero.*

IMPULSE.—Act upon your impulses, but pray that they may be directed by God.—*E. Tennent.*

Since the generality of persons act from impulse much more than from principle, men are neither so good nor so bad as we are apt to think them.— *Hare.*

A true history of human events would show that a far larger proportion of our acts are the results of sudden impulses and accident, than of that reason of which we so much boast.—*Cooper.*

Our first impulses are good, generous, heroical; reflection weakens and kills them.—*L. A. Martin.*

What persons are by starts, they are by nature—you see them at such times off their guard.—Habit may restrain vice, and virtue may be obscured by passion, but intervals best discover man. —*Sterne.*

The first impulse of conscience is apt to be right; the first impulse of appetite or passion is generally wrong.—

We should be faithful to the former, but suspicious of the latter.—*Tryon Edwards.*

IMPURITY.—The man who tells me an indelicate story, does me an injury.—*J. T. Fields.*

An impure man is every good man's enemy.—*H. W. Beecher.*

INACTIVITY.—(See "DELAY.")

The Commons, faithful to their system, remained in a wise and masterly inactivity.—*Mackintosh.*

If he had sat still, the enemy's army would have mouldered to nothing.—*Clarendon.*

Learning teaches how to carry things in suspense without prejudice till you resolve.—*Bacon.*

Of Washington it was said, he knew how to conquer by delay; and the tactics of Fabius in harassing the army of Hannibal, by countermarching and ambuscades, while avoiding an open conflict, gained him the name of "Delayer."—*Haven.*

In the meantime, our policy is a masterly inactivity.—*J. C. Calhoun.*

The mightiest powers by deepest calms are fed.—*B. W. Procter.*

There are many times and circumstances in life when "Our strength is, to sit still."—*Tryon Edwards.*

He that takes time to think and consider will act more wisely than he that acts hastily and on impulse.—*C. Simmons.*

Nature knows no pause in her progress and development, and attaches her curse on all inaction.—*Goethe.*

Doing nothing with a deal of skill.—*Cowper.*

The keenest pangs the wretched find are rapture to the dreary void,—the leafless desert of the mind—the waste of feelings unemployed.—*Byron.*

Thoughtful, disciplined, intended inaction.—*John Randolph.*

INATTENTION.—(See "ATTENTION.")

INCLINATION.—It is very pleasant to follow one's inclinations; but unfortunately, we cannot follow them all: they are like the teeth sown by Cadmus—they spring up, get in each other's way, and fight.—*L. E. Landor.*

All men that are ruined are ruined on the side of their natural propensities.—*Burke.*

A good inclination is but the first rude draught of virtue; but the finishing strokes are from the will; which, if well disposed, will, by degrees perfect; if ill disposed, will, by the superinduction of ill habits, quickly deface it.—*South.*

Almost everyone has a predominant inclination, to which his other desires and actions submit, and which governs him, though perhaps with some intervals, through the whole course of his life.—*Hume.*

No profit grows where is no pleasure taken; in brief, sir, study what you most affect.—*Shakespeare.*

God never accepts a good inclination instead of a good action, where that action may be done; nay, so much the contrary, that, if a good inclination be not seconded by a good action, the want of that action is made so much the more criminal and inexcusable.—*South.*

INCONSISTENCY.—(See "CONSISTENCY.")

Mutability of temper and inconsistency with ourselves is the greatest weakness of human nature.—*Addison.*

A conscience enlightened, and yet a heart erratic, make mankind a bundle of marvelous incongruities and inconsistencies.—*C. Simmons.*

How often in this world are the actions that we condemn the result of sentiments that we love, and opinions that we admire.—*Mrs. Jameson.*

No author ever drew a character consistent to human nature, but he was forced to ascribe to it many inconsistencies.—*Bulwer.*

We are always complaining that our days are few, and acting as though there would be no end of them.—*Seneca.*

Men talk as if they believed in God, but they live as if they thought there was none: their vows and promises are no more than words of course.—*L'Estrange.*

In religion not to do as thou sayest is to unsay thy religion in thy deeds, and to undo thyself by doing.—*Venning.*

Among the numberless contradictions in our nature, hardly any is more glaring than this, between our sensitiveness to the slightest disgrace which we fancy cast upon us from without, and our callousness to what is wrong in ourselves. In truth, they who are the most sensitive to the one are often the most callous to the other.—*Anon.*

Some persons do first, think afterward, and then repent forever.—*Secker.*

INCONSTANCY.—Nothing that is not a real crime makes a man appear so contemptible and little in the eyes of the world as inconstancy, especially when it regards religion or party. In either of these cases, though a man perhaps does but his duty in changing his side, he not only makes himself hated by those he left, but is seldom heartily esteemed by those he comes over to.—*Addison.*

Clocks will go as they are set; but man, irregular man, is never constant, never certain.—*Otway.*

Inconstancy is but a name to fright poor lovers from a better choice.—*Rutter.*

Were man but constant, he were perfect; that one error fills him with faults; makes him run through sins; inconstancy falls off ere it begins.—*Shakespeare.*

INCREDULITY.—Incredulity is not wisdom, but the worst kind of folly. It is folly, because it causes ignorance and mistake, with all the consequences of these; and it is very bad, as being accompanied with disingenuity, obstinacy, rudeness, uncharitableness, and the like bad dispositions, from which credulity itself, the other extreme sort of folly, is exempt.—*Barrow.*

The incredulous are of all men the most credulous; they believe the miracles of Vespasian, in order not to believe those of Moses.—*Pascal.*

Nothing is so contemptible as that affectation of wisdom which some display by universal incredulity.—*Goldsmith.*

Incredulity robs us of many pleasures, and gives us nothing in return.—*J. R. Lowell.*

Of all the signs of a corrupt heart and a feeble head, the tendency of incredulity is the surest.—Real philosophy seeks rather to solve than to deny.—*Bulwer.*

A sceptical young man said to Dr. Parr that he would believe nothing which he could not understand. "Then," said the Doctor, "your creed will be the shortest of any man's I know."—*A. Helps.*

Some men will believe nothing but what they can comprehend; and there are but few things that such are able to comprehend.—*Evremond.*

The amplest knowledge has the largest faith.—Ignorance is always incredulous.—*Willmott.*

INDECISION.—(See "DECISION" and "RESOLUTION.")

The wavering mind is but a base possession.—*Euripides.*

In matters of great concern, and which must be done, there is no surer argument of a weak mind than irresolution —to be undetermined where the case is plain, and the necessity urgent. To be always intending to live a new life, but never to find time to set about it, this is as if a man should put off eating, drinking, and sleeping, from one day and night to another, till he is starved and destroyed.—*Tillotson.*

It is a miserable thing to live in suspense; it is the life of a spider.—*Swift.*

It is a great evil, as well as a misfortune, to be unable to utter a prompt and decided "No."—*C. Simmons.*

There is nothing in the world more pitiable than an irresolute man, oscillating between two feelings, who would willingly unite the two, and who does not perceive that nothing can unite them.—*Goethe.*

When a man has not a good reason for doing a thing, he has one good reason for letting it alone.—*Thomas Scott.*

Nothing can be more destructive to vigor of action than protracted, anxious fluctuation, through resolutions adopted, rejected, resumed, and suspended, and nothing causes a greater expense of feeling.—A man without decision can never be said to belong to himself; he is as a wave of the sea, or a feather in the air which every breeze blows about as it listeth.—*John Foster.*

INDEPENDENCE.—It is not the greatness of a man's means that makes him independent, so much as the smallness of his wants.—*Cobbett.*

These two things, contradictory as they may seem, must go together, manly dependence and manly independence, manly reliance and manly self-reliance. —*Wordsworth.*

The greatest of all human benefits, that, at least, without which no other benefit can be truly enjoyed, is independence.—*Parke Godwin.*

Happy the man to whom heaven has given a morsel of bread without laying him under the obligation of thanking any other for it than heaven itself.— *Cervantes.*

The word independence is united to the ideas of dignity and virtue; the word dependence, to the ideas of inferiority and corruption.—*J. Bentham.*

Independency may be found in comparative as well as in absolute abundance; I mean where a person contracts his desires within the limits of his fortune.—*Shenstone.*

Be and continue poor, young man, while others around you grow rich by fraud and disloyalty; be without place or power, while others beg their way upward; bear the pain of disappointed hopes, while others gain the accomplishment of theirs by flattery; forego the gracious pressure of the hand for which others cringe and crawl. Wrap yourself in your own virtue, and seek a friend and your daily bread. If you have in such a course grown gray with unblenched honor, bless God, and die.— *Heinzelmann.*

Let all your views in life be directed to a solid, however moderate, independence; without it no man can be happy, nor even honest.—*Junius.*

The moral progression of a people can scarcely begin till they are independent. —*Martineau.*

Go to New England, and visit the domestic firesides, if you would see the secret of American Independence. — Religion has made them what they are.— *Mosquera.*

It should be the lesson of our life to grow into a holy independence. of every judgment which has not the sanction of conscience and of God.—No man can lift up his head with manly calmness and peace who is the slave of other men's judgments.—*J. W. Alexander.*

There is often as much independence in not being led, as in not being driven. —*Tryon Edwards.*

Hail! independence, hail! heaven's next best gift to that of life and an immortal soul!—*Thomson.*

INDEXES.—An index is a necessary implement, without which a large author is but a labyrinth without a clue to direct the readers within.—*Fuller.*

I certainly think the best book in the world would owe the most to a good index; and the worst book, if it had in it but a single good thought, might be kept alive by it.—*Horace Binney.*

Of many large volumes the index is the best portion and the most useful.— A glance through the casement gives whatever knowledge of the interior is needful.—An epitome is only a book shortened; and as a general rule, the worth increases as the size lessens.— *Willmott.*

A book without an index is much like a compass-box, without the needle, perplexing instead of directive to the point we would reach.—*Anon.*

Those authors who are voluminous would do well, if they would be remembered as long as possible, not to omit a duty which authors in general, and especially modern authors neglect, that of appending to their works a good index. —*Henry Rogers.*

Get thorough insight into the index, by which the whole book is governed.— *Swift.*

I have come to regard a good book as curtailed of half its value if it has not a pretty full index. It is almost impossible without such a guide to reproduce on demand the most striking thoughts or facts the book contains, whether for citation or further consideration.—*Horace Binney.*

INDIFFERENCE.—Set honor in one eye, and death in the other, and I will look on both indifferently.—*Shakespeare.*

Indifference never wrote great works, nor thought out striking inventions, nor reared the solemn architecture that awes the soul, nor breathed sublime music, nor painted glorious pictures, nor undertook heroic philanthropies.—All these grandeurs are born of enthusiasm, and are done heartily.—*Anon.*

Nothing for preserving the body like having no heart.—*J. P. Senn.*

Indifference is the invincible giant of the world.—*Ouida.*

INDIGESTION.—(See "HEALTH.")
Old friendships are destroyed by toasted cheese, and hard salted meat has led to suicide. Unpleasant feelings of the body produce correspondent sensations of the mind, and a great scene of wretchedness is sketched out by a morsel of indigestible and misguided food.—*Sydney Smith.*

How many serious family quarrels, marriages out of spite, and alterations of wills, might have been prevented by a gentle dose of blue pill!—What awful instances of chronic dyspepsia in the characters of Hamlet and Othello! Banish dyspepsia and spirituous liquors from society, and you have no crime, or at least so little that you would not consider it worth mentioning.—*C. Kingsley.*

Dyspepsia is the remorse of a guilty stomach.—*A. Kerr.*

INDISCRETION.—An indiscreet man is more hurtful than an ill-natured one; for the latter will only attack his enemies, and those he wishes ill to; the other injures indifferently both friends and foes.—*Addison.*

Indiscretion and wickedness, be it known, are first cousins.—*L'Enclos.*

For good and evil in our actions meet; wicked is not much worse than indiscreet.—*Donne.*

The generality of men expend the early part of their lives in contributing to render the latter part miserable.—*Bruyère.*

Indiscretion, rashness, falsehood, levity, and malice produce each other.—*Lavater.*

We waste our best years in distilling the sweetest flowers of life into potions, which, after all, do not immortalize, but only intoxicate.—*Longfellow.*

Three things too much, and three too little are pernicious to man; to speak much, and know little; to spend much, and have little; to presume much, and be worth little.—*Cervantes.*

We may outrun by violent swiftness that which we run at, and lose by overrunning.—*Shakespeare.*

Imprudence, silly talk, foolish vanity, and vain curiosity, are closely allied; they are children of one family.—*Fontaine.*

INDIVIDUALITY.—Every individual nature has its own beauty.—In every company, at every fireside, one is struck with the riches of nature, when he hears so many tones, all musical, sees in each person original manners which have a proper and peculiar charm, and reads new expressions of face.—He perceives that nature has laid for each the foundations of a divine building if the soul will build thereon.—*Emerson.*

There are men of convictions whose very faces will light up an era, and there are believing women in whose eyes you may almost read the whole plan of salvation.—*Fields.*

Individuality is everywhere to be spared and respected as the root of everything good.—*Richter.*

You are tried alone; alone you pass into the desert; alone you are sifted by the world.—*F. W. Robertson.*

Every great man is a unique.—The Scipionism of Scipio is precisely that part which he could not borrow.—*Emerson.*

Everything without tells the individual that he is nothing; everything within persuades him that he is everything.—*X. Doudan.*

It was perhaps ordained by Providence, to hinder us from tyrannizing over one another, that no individual should be of so much importance as to cause, by his retirement or death, any chasm in the world.—*Johnson.*

The epoch of individuality is concluded, and it is the duty of reformers to initiate the epoch of association. Collective man is omnipotent upon the earth he treads.—*Mazzini.*

The worth of a state, in the long run, is the worth of the individuals composing it.—*J. S. Mill.*

The greatest works are done by the ones.—The hundreds do not often do much—the companies never; it is the units—the single individuals, that are the power and the might.—Individual effort is, after all, the grand thing.—*Spurgeon.*

Human faculties are common, but that which converges these faculties into my identity, separates me from every other man.—That other man cannot think my thoughts, speak my words, do my works.—He cannot have my sins, and I cannot have his virtues.—*Giles.*

Individuality is everywhere to be spared and respected as the root of everything good.—*Richter.*

We live too much in platoons; we march by sections; we do not live in our individuality enough; we are slaves to fashion in mind and heart, if not to our passions and appetites.—*E. H. Chapin.*

The great political controversy of the ages has reached its end in the recognition of the individual.—The socialistic party would again sink the individual in the government, and make it possible for the government to perpetuate itself and become absolute.—*F. C. Monfort.*

If the world is ever conquered for Christ, it will be by every one doing their own work, filling their own sphere, holding their own post, and saying to Jesus, Lord, what wilt thou have me to do.—*Guthrie.*

Each mind hath its own method.—A true man never acquires after college rules.—What you have yourself aggregated in a natural manner surprises and delights when it is produced.—We cannot oversee each other's secret.—*Emerson.*

That life only is truly free which rules and suffices for itself.—*Bulwer.*

Not armies, not nations, have advanced the race; but here and there, in the course of ages, an individual has stood up and cast his shadow over the world.—*E. H. Chapin.*

It is said that if Noah's ark had had to be built by a company, they would not have laid the keel yet; and it may be so.—What is many men's business is nobody's business.—The greatest things are accomplished by individual men.—*Spurgeon.*

INDOLENCE.—(See "IDLENESS.")

Indolence is the sleep of the mind.—*Vauvenargues.*

I look upon indolence as a sort of suicide; for the man is effectually destroyed, though the appetite of the brute may survive.—*Chesterfield.*

What is often called indolence is, in fact, the unconscious consciousness of incapacity.—*H. C. Robinson.*

Indolence and stupidity are first cousins.—*Rivarol.*

Laziness grows on people; it begins in cobwebs, and ends in iron chains.—The more one has to do the more he is able to accomplish.

So long as he must fight his way, the man of genius pushes forward, conquering and to conquer. But how often is he at last overcome by a Capua! Ease and fame bring sloth and slumber.—*Buxton.*

Nothing ages like laziness.—*Bulwer.*

What men want is not talent; it is purpose; in other words, not the power to achieve, but the will to labor.—*Bulwer.*

Lives spent in indolence, and therefore sad.—*Cowper.*

If you ask me which is the real hereditary sin of human nature, do you imagine I shall answer pride, or luxury, or ambition, or egotism? No; I shall say indolence. Who conquers indolence will conquer all the rest. Indeed all good principles must stagnate without mental activity.—*Zimmermann.*

Indolence, methinks, is an intermediate state between pleasure and pain, and very much unbecoming any part of our life after we are out of the nurse's arms.—*Steele.*

Of all our faults, that which we most readily admit is indolence.—We persuade ourselves that it cherishes all the peaceful virtues, and that without destroying the others it merely suspends their functions.—*Rochefoucauld.*

The darkest hour in the history of any young man is when he sits down to study how to get money without honestly earning it.—*Horace Greeley.*

Indolence is the dry rot of even a good mind and a good character; the practical uselessness of both.—It is the waste of what might be a happy and useful life.—*Tryon Edwards.*

INDULGENCE.—Sensual indulgencies are costly at both ends.—*C. Simmons.*

Those who love dainties are likely soon to be beggars.—*Franklin.*

Too many wish to be happy before becoming wise.—*Mad. Necker.*

Live only for to-day, and you ruin to-morrow.—*C. Simmons.*

INDUSTRY.—(See "IDLENESS" and "INDOLENCE.")

Industrious wisdom often doth prevent what lazy folly thinks inevitable.

He doth allot for every exercise a several hour; for sloth, the nurse of vices and rust of action is a stranger to him.—*Massinger*.

It is better to wear out than to rust out.—*Cumberland*.

If you have great talents, industry will improve them; if moderate abilities, industry will supply their deficiencies. Nothing is denied to well-directed labor; nothing is ever to be attained without it.—*Sir Joshua Reynolds*.

Sloth makes all things difficult, but industry all things easy.—*Franklin*.

There is no art or science that is too difficult for industry to attain to; it is the gift of tongues, and makes a man understood and valued in all countries, and by all nations; it is the philosopher's stone, that turns all metals, and even stones, into gold, and suffers no want to break into its dwellings; it is the northwest passage, that brings the merchant's ships as soon to him as he can desire: in a word, it conquers all enemies, and makes fortune itself pay contribution.—*Clarendon*.

Like the bee, we should make our industry our amusement.—*Goldsmith*.

One loses all the time which he might employ to better purpose.—*Rousseau*.

Fortune may find a pot, but your own industry must make it boil.

In every rank, both great and small, it is industry that supports us all.—*Gay*.

God has so made the mind of man that a peculiar deliciousness resides in the fruits of personal industry.—*Wilberforce*.

Industry need not wish, and he that lives upon hopes will die fasting. There are no gains without pains. He that hath a trade hath an estate, and he that hath a calling hath an office of profit and honor; but then the trade must be worked at, and the calling followed, or neither the estate nor the office will enable us to pay our taxes. If we are industrious, we shall never starve; for, at the workingman's house hunger looks in, but dares not enter. Nor will the bailiff or the constable enter, for industry pays debts, while idleness and neglect increase them.—*Franklin*.

If you have great talents, industry will improve them; if but moderate abilities, industry will supply their deficiencies.—*S. Smiles*.

Many are discontented with the name of idler, who are nevertheless content to do worse than nothing.—*Zimmermann*.

There is always hope in a man who actually and earnestly works.—In idleness alone is there perpetual despair.—*Carlyle*.

The celebrated Galen said that employment was nature's physician.—It is indeed so important to happiness that indolence is justly considered the parent of misery.—*Colton*.

The more we do, the more we can do; the more busy we are, the more leisure we have.—*Hazlitt*.

Though you may have known clever men who were indolent, you never knew a great man who was so; and when I hear a young man spoken of as giving promise of great genius, the first question I ask about him always is, Does he work?—*Ruskin*.

Mankind are more indebted to industry than ingenuity; the gods set up their favors at a price, and industry is the purchaser.—*Addison*.

Industry is not only the instrument of improvement, but the foundation of pleasure.—He who is a stranger to it may possess, but cannot enjoy, for it is labor only which gives relish to pleasure.—It is the indispensable condition of possessing a sound mind in a sound body, and is the appointed vehicle of every good to man.—*Blair*.

Application is the price to be paid for mental acquisition. To have the harvest we must sow the seed.—*Bailey*.

No man is born into the world whose work is not born with him.—There is always work, and tools to work with, for those who will; and blessed are the horny hands of toil.—*J. R. Lowell*.

That man is but of the lower part of the world who is not brought up to business and affairs.—*Feltham*.

A man should inure himself to voluntary labor, and not give up to indulgence and pleasure, as they beget no good constitution of body nor knowledge of mind.—*Socrates*.

Industry keeps the body healthy, the mind clear, the heart whole, and the purse full.—*C. Simmons.*

Excellence is never granted to man, but as a reward of labor.—It argues, indeed, no small strength of mind to persevere in the habits of industry without the pleasure of perceiving those advantages, which, like the hand of a clock, while they make hourly approaches to their point, yet proceed so slowly as to escape observation.—*Sir J. Reynolds.*

Every industrious man, in every lawful calling, is a useful man.—And one principal reason why men are so often useless is, that they neglect their own profession or calling, and divide and shift their attention among a multiplicity of objects and pursuits.—*Emmons.*

An hour's industry will do more to produce cheerfulness, suppress evil humors, and retrieve one's affairs, than a month's moaning.—It sweetens enjoyments, and seasons our attainments with a delightful relish.—*Barrow.*

A man who gives his children habits of industry provides for them better than by giving them a fortune.—*Whately.*

Industry hath annexed thereto the fairest fruits and the richest rewards.—*Barrow.*

The chiefest action for a man of spirit is never to be out of action; the soul was never put into the body to stand still.—*J. Webster.*

INFAMY.—(See "SLANDER.")
What grief can there be that time doth not make less?—But infamy, time never can suppress.—*Drayton.*

The most infamous are fond of fame; and those who fear not guilt, yet start at shame.—*Churchill.*

Infamy is where it is received.—If thou art a mud wall, it will stick; if marble, it will rebound.—If thou storm, it is thine; if thou contemn it, it is his.—*Quarles.*

INFANCY.—Heaven lies about us in our infancy.—*Wordsworth.*

Of all the joys that brighten suffering earth, what joy is welcomed like a new-born child?—*Mrs. Norton.*

Joy thou bringest, but mixed with trembling; anxious joys, and tender fears; pleasing hopes, and mingled sorrows; smiles of transport dashed with tears.—*Cottle.*

They who have lost an infant are never, as it were, without an infant child. Their other children grow up to manhood and womanhood, and suffer all the changes of mortality; but this one is rendered an immortal child, for death has arrested it with his kindly harshness, and blessed it into an eternal image of youth and innocence.—*Leigh Hunt.*

Ere sin could blight, or sorrow fade, death came with friendly care; the opening but to heaven conveyed, and bade it blossom there.—*Coleridge.*

A lovely bud, so soft, so fair, called hence by early doom; just sent to show how sweet a flower in paradise would bloom.—*Legh Richmond.*

Beautiful as is the morning of day, so is the morning of life.—Fallen though we are, there remains a purity, modesty, ingenuousness and tenderness of conscience about childhood, that looks as if the glory of Eden yet lingered over it, like the light of the day on the hilltops, at even, when the sun is down.—*Guthrie.*

The glorified spirit of the infant, is as a star to guide the mother to its own blissful clime.—*Mrs. Sigourney.*

INFIDELITY.—(See "UNBELIEF.")
There is but one thing without honor, smitten with eternal barrenness, inability to do or to be,—insincerity, unbelief. He who believes no thing, who believes only the shows of things, is not in relation with nature and fact at all.—*Carlyle.*

Infidelity, indeed, is the root of all sin; for did man heartily believe the promises to obedience, and the threats to disobedience, they could hardly be so unreasonable as to forfeit the one or incur the other.—*Barrow.*

Faith in God hallows and confirms the union between parents and children, and subjects and rulers.—Infidelity relaxes every band, and nullifies every blessing.—*Pestalozzi.*

When once infidelity can persuade men that they shall die like beasts, they will soon be brought to live like beasts also.—*South.*

I would rather dwell in the dim fog

of superstition than in air rarefied to nothing by the air-pump of unbelief, in which the panting breast expires, vainly and convulsively gasping for breath.—*Richter.*

There is not a single spot between Christianity and atheism on which a man can firmly fix his foot.—*Emmons.*

If on one side there are fair proofs, and no pretense of proof on the other, and the difficulties are more pressing on that side which is destitute of proof, I desire to know whether this be not upon the matter as satisfactory to a wise man as a demonstration.—*Tillotson.*

The nurse of infidelity is sensuality. —*Cecil.*

It is always safe to follow the religious belief that our mother taught us; there never was a mother yet who taught her child to be an infidel.—*H. W. Shaw.*

Freethinkers are generally those who never think at all.—*Sterne.*

Men always grow vicious before they become unbelievers; but if you would once convince profligates by topics drawn from the view of their own quiet, reputation, and health, their infidelity would soon drop off.—*Swift.*

Infidelity gives nothing in return for what it takes away. What, then, is it worth? Everything valuable has a compensating power. Not a blade of grass that withers, or the ugliest weed that is flung away to rot or die, but reproduces something.—*Chalmers.*

There is one single fact which we may oppose to all the wit and argument of infidelity, namely, that no man ever repented of being a Christian on his death-bed.—*H. More.*

Infidelity is the joint offspring of an irreligious temper and unholy speculation, employed not in examining the evidences of Christianity, but in detecting the vices and imperfections of professing Christians.

What can be more foolish than to think that all this rare fabric of heaven and earth could come by chance, when all the skill of art is not able to make an oyster.—*Jeremy Taylor.*

Take my word for it, it is not prudent to trust yourself to any man who does not believe in a God or in a future after death.—*Sir Robert Peel.*

Infidelity and Faith look both through the same perspective-glass, but at contrary ends. Infidelity looks through the wrong end of the glass; and, therefore, sees those objects near which are afar off, and makes great things little,—diminishing the greatest spiritual blessings, and removing far from us threatened evils. Faith looks at the right end, and brings the blessings that are far off close to our eye, and multiplies God's mercies, which, in the distance, lost their greatness.—*Bp. Hall.*

Charles II. hearing Vossius, a freethinker, repeating some incredible stories of the Chinese, turned to those about him and said, "This learned divine is a very strange man; he believes everything but the Bible."—*S. Smiles.*

Infidelity grows strong under oppressive civil rule; weak under that which is just.—*Christlieb.*

They that deny God destroy a man's nobility; for certainly man is of kin to the beasts by his body, and if he is not akin to God by his spirit, he is a base and ignoble creature.—*Bacon.*

Let any of those who renounce Christianity, write fairly down in a book all the absurdities they believe instead of it, and they will find it requires more faith to reject Christianity than to embrace it.—*Colton.*

Infidelity is one of the false coinages —a mass of base money that will not pass current with any heart that loves truly, or any head that thinks correctly. —It is a fearful blindness of the soul.—*Chalmers.*

Infidelity reproves nothing that is bad. It only ridicules and denounces all that is good. It tears down, but never builds up; destroys, but never imparts life; attacks religion, but offers no adequate substitute.—*J. R. Paxton.*

Hume took unwearied pains to prove that nothing could be proved.—*Bellamy*

Infidelity is seated in the heart; its origin is not in the head.—It is the wish that Christianity might not be true, that leads to an argument to prove it.—*C. Simmons.*

A man's wickedness sets Christianity against him before he can have any temptation to set himself against Christianity.—*S. Davies.*

Man may doubt here and there, but mankind does not doubt.—The universal conscience is larger than the individual conscience, and that constantly comes in to correct and check our infidelity.—*H. R. Haweis.*

Whatever rouses the moral nature, whether it be danger, or suffering, or the approach of death, banishes unbelief in a moment.

INFLUENCE.—Influence is the exhalation of character.—*W. M. Taylor.*

We live with other men, and to other men, not exclusively with, or to ourselves.—We have no intercourse with others that does not tell on them, as they are all the while influencing us.

There is little influence where there is not great sympathy.—*S. I. Prime.*

Virtue will catch, as well as vice, by contact; and the public stock of honest manly principle will daily accumulate. —*Burke.*

No act falls fruitless; none can tell how vast its powers may be; nor what results, enfolded dwell within it silently.

A good man does good merely by living.—*Bulwer.*

It is the age that forms the man, not the man that forms the age. Great minds do indeed react on the society which has made them what they are, but they only pay with interest what they have received.—*Macaulay.*

In families well ordered there is always one firm, sweet temper, which controls without seeming to dictate. The Greeks represented Persuasion as crowned.—*Bulwer.*

The spirit of a person's life is ever shedding some power, just as a flower is steadily bestowing fragrance upon the air.—*T. Starr King.*

We cannot think or act but the soul of some one who has passed before points the way.—The dead never die.— *Bulwer.*

A word or a nod from the good, has more weight than the eloquent speeches of others.—*Plutarch.*

The great must submit to the dominion of prudence and virtue, or none will long submit to the dominion of the

great.—This is a feudal tenure which they cannot alter.—*Burke.*

The least movement is of importance to all nature. The entire ocean is affected by a pebble.—*Pascal.*

Others are affected by what I am and say and do. And these others have also these spheres of influence. So that a single act of mine may spread in widening circles through a nation of humanity.—*Channing.*

Not one false man but does unaccountable mischief.—*Carlyle.*

He who wishes to exert a useful influence must be careful to insult nothing. Let him not be troubled by what seems absurd, but consecrate his energies to the creation of what is good. He must not demolish, but build. He must raise temples where mankind may come and partake of the purest pleasures.—*Goethe.*

The blossom cannot tell what becomes of its odor, and no man can tell what becomes of his influence and example, that roll away from him, and go beyond his ken on their perilous mission.—*H. W. Beecher.*

There are nine chances in ten that every man who goes with me will lose his life in the undertaking.—But there are times when dead men are worth more than living ones.—*Old John Brown.*

You cannot be buried in obscurity: you are exposed upon a grand theater to the view of the world. If your actions are upright and benevolent, be assured they will augment your power and happiness.—*Cyrus.*

Let him that would move the world, first move himself.—*Socrates.*

Though her (Lady Elizabeth Hastings) mien carries much more invitation than command, to behold her is an immediate check to loose behavior; to love her was a liberal education.—*Steele.*

One of the most melancholy things in the world is the enormous power for evil of the dead over the living. There is hardly a great painter or writer, or a man who had achieved greatness in any direction, whose name has not been used to repress rising genius.—*Hammerton.*

Forming characters! Whose?—our own, or others?—Both.—And in that momentous fact lies the peril and responsibility of our existence.— Who is sufficient for the thought?—*Elihu Burritt*.

Men are won, not so much by being blamed, as by being encompassed with love.—*Channing*.

The words that a father speaks to his children in the privacy of home are not heard by the world, but, as in whispering galleries, they are clearly heard at the end, and by posterity.—*Richter*.

Often the elements that move and mold society, are the results of the sister's counsel, and the mother's prayer.—*E. H. Chapin*.

Planets do not govern the soul, or guide the destinies of men, but trifles, lighter than straws, are levers in the building up of character.—*Tupper*.

Good words do more than hard speeches, as the sunbeams, without any noise, will make the traveler cast off his cloak, which all the blustering winds could not do, but only make him bind it closer to him.—*Leighton*.

The career of a great man remains an enduring monument of human energy.—The man dies and disappears, but his thoughts and acts survive and leave an indelible stamp upon his race.—*S. Smiles*.

There is no action of man in this life which is not the beginning of so long a chain of consequences, as that no human providence can tell what the end will be.—*Thomas of Malmesbury*.

Race and temperament go for much in influencing opinion.—*Lady Morgan*.

Blessed is the influence of one true, loving human soul on another.—*George Eliot*.

Every thought which genius and piety throw into the world alters the world.—*Emerson*.

When a great man dies, for years the light he leaves behind him, lies on the paths of men.—*Longfellow*.

The influence of individual character extends from generation to generation.—The world is molded by it.—*Macleod*.

If you had the seeds of pestilence in your body you would not have a more active contagion than you have in your tempers, tastes, and principles.—Simply to be in this world, whatever you are,

is to exert an influence—an influence too, compared with which mere language and persuasion are feeble.—*Horace Bushnell*.

No man or woman of the humblest sort can really be strong, gentle and pure and good, without the world being better for it, without somebody being helped and comforted by the very existence of that goodness.— *Phillips Brooks*.

Always so act that the immediate motive of thy will may become a universal rule for all intelligent beings.—*Kant*.

Our gifts and attainments are not only to be light and warmth in our own dwellings, but are also to shine through the windows into the dark night, to guide and cheer bewildered travelers on the road.—*H. W. Beecher*.

To help the young soul, to add energy, inspire hope, and blow the coals into a useful flame; to redeem defeat by new thought and firm action, this, though not easy, is the work of divine men.—*Emerson*.

When men do anything for God, the very least thing, they never know where it will end, nor what amount of work it will do for Him. Love's secret, therefore, is to be always doing things for God, and not to mind because they are such very little ones.—*Faber*.

We cannot live only for ourselves. A thousand fibers connect us with our fellow-men; and along those fibers, as sympathetic threads, our actions run as causes, and they come back to us as effects.—*Melville*.

Influence never dies; every act, emotion, look and word makes influence tell for good or evil, happiness or woe, through the long future of eternity.

The life of a faithful Christian man is a guide to paradise.—*Thos. à Kempis*.

INGRATITUDE.—(See "THANKFULNESS.")

He that calls a man ungrateful, sums up all the evil of which one can be guilty.—*Swift*.

He that is ungrateful has no guilt but one; all other crimes may pass for virtues in him.—*Young*.

If there be a crime of deeper dye than all the guilty train of human vices, it is ingratitude.—*Brooke*.

Ingratitude is treason to mankind.—
Thomson.

Ingratitude is the abridgment of all
baseness; a . fault never found unat-
tended with other viciousness.—*Fuller.*

An ungrateful man is like a hog under a tree eating acorns, but never looking up to see where they come from.—
Timo. Dexter.

We can be thankful to a friend for
a few acres, or a little money; and yet
for the freedom and command of the
whole earth, and for the great benefits
of our being, our life, health, and reason, we look upon ourselves as under no
obligation.—*Seneca.*

He that forgets his friend is ungrateful to him; but he that forgets his
Saviour is unmerciful to himself.—*Bunyan.*

Ingratitude is monstrous; and for the
multitude to be ungrateful, were to
make a monster of the multitude.—
Shakespeare.

Brutes leave ingratitude to man. —
Colton.

I hate ingratitude more in man than
lying, vainness, babbling, drunkenness,
or any taint of vice, whose strong corruption inhabits our frail blood.—*Shakespeare.*

Flints may be melted—we see it daily
—but an ungrateful heart cannot be;
not by the strongest and noblest flame.
—*South.*

How sharper than a serpent's tooth it
is to have a thankless child.—*Shakespeare.*

Not to return one good office for another is inhuman; but to return evil for
good is diabolical.—*Seneca.*

One ungrateful man does an injury
to all who stand in need of aid.—*Publius Syrus.*

We seldom find people ungrateful as
long as we are in a condition to render
them services.—*Rochefoucauld.*

We often fancy we suffer from ingratitude, while in reality we suffer
from self-love.—*Landor.*

There neither is, or ever was, any
person remarkably ungrateful, who was
not also insufferably proud; nor any
one proud, who was not equally ungrateful.—*South.*

Ingratitude; thou marble-hearted
fiend, more hideous when thou showest
thee in a child, than the sea monster.—
Shakespeare.

There be three usual causes of ingratitude upon a benefit received—envy,
pride, and covetousness; envy, looking
more at other's benefits than our own;
pride, looking more at ourselves than
at the benefit; covetousness, looking
more at what we would have than at
what we have.—*Bp. Hall.*

Filial ingratitude! Is it not as this
mouth should tear this hand for lifting
food to it.—*Shakespeare.*

There never was any man so wicked
as not to approve of gratitude and to
detest ingratitude, as the two things in
the whole world, the one to be the most
esteemed, and the other the most abomi-
nated.—*Seneca.*

A grateful dog is better than an ungrateful man.—*Saadi.*

Blow, blow, thou winter wind, thou
art not so unkind as man's ingratitude.
—Freeze, freeze, thou bitter sky, thou
dost not bite so nigh, as benefits forgot.
—*Shakespeare.*

He who does a kindness to an ungrateful person, sets his seal to a flint
and sows his seed upon the sand; on the
former he makes no impression, and
from the latter finds no product.—*South.*

Ungratefulness is the very poison of
manhood.—*Sir P. Sidney.*

One great cause of our insensibility
to the goodness of our Creator is the
very extensiveness of his bounty.—
Paley.

When we would, with utmost detestation, single some monster from the
traitor herd, 'tis but to say ingratitude
is his crime.—*Froude.*

Nothing more detestable does the
earth produce than an ungrateful man.—
Ausonius.

He that doth public good for multitudes, finds few are truly grateful.—
Massinger.

What unthankfulness is it to forget
our consolations, and to look upon matters of grievance; to think so much
upon two or three crosses as to forget
an hundred blessings.—*Sibbs.*

How black and base a vice ingratitude is, may be seen in those vices with

which it is always in combination, pride and hard-heartedness, or want of compassion.—*South.*

INHERITANCE.—What madness is it for a man to starve himself to enrich his heir, and so turn a friend into an enemy!—For his joy at your death will be proportioned to what you leave him.—*Seneca.*

They who provide much wealth for their children but neglect to improve them in virtue, do like those who feed their horses high, but never train them to be useful.—*Socrates.*

Enjoy what thou hast inherited from thy sires if thou wouldst really possess it.—What we employ and use is never an oppressive burden; what the moment brings forth, that only can it profit by.—*Goethe.*

INJURY.—(See "REVENGE" and "FORGIVENESS.")

No man is hurt but by himself.—*Diogenes.*

To wilful men, the injuries they themselves procure must be their schoolmasters.—*Shakespeare.*

No man ever did a designed injury to another, but at the same time he did a greater to himself.—*Home.*

Slight small injuries, and they will become none at all.—*Fuller.*

Christianity commands us to pass by injuries; policy, to let them pass by us.—*Franklin.*

Rather wink at small injuries, than be too forward to avenge them. He that to destroy a single bee should throw down the hive, instead of one enemy, would make a thousand.

It is more easy to forgive the weak who have injured us, than the powerful whom we have injured. That conduct will be continued by our fears, which commenced in our resentment.—*Colton.*

In life it is difficult to say who do you the most mischief—enemies with the worst intentions, or friends with the best.

He who has injured thee was either stronger or weaker than thee.—If weaker, spare him; if stronger, spare thyself.—*Seneca.*

The public has more interest in the punishment of an injury than the one who receives it.—*Colton.*

The injuries of life, if rightly improved, will be to us as the strokes of the statuary on his marble, forming us to a more beautiful shape, and making us fitter to adorn the heavenly temple.—*Cotton Mather.*

An injury unanswered, in time grows weary of itself and dies away in voluntary remorse. In bad dispositions, capable of no restraint but fear, it has a different effect; the silent digestion of one wrong provokes a second.—*Sterne.*

There is no ghost so difficult to lay as the ghost of an injury.—*Alexander Smith.*

Nothing can work me damage except myself.—The harm that I sustain I carry about with me, and am never a real sufferer but by my own fault.—*St. Bernard.*

If men wound you with injuries, meet them with patience: hasty words rankle the wound, soft language dresses it, forgiveness cures it, and oblivion takes away the scar. It is more noble by silence to avoid an injury than by argument to overcome it.—*Beaumont.*

As a Christian should do no injuries to others, so he should forgive the injuries others do to him.—This is to be like God, who is a good-giving, and a sin-forgiving God.—*Venning.*

The injuries we do, and those we suffer, are seldom weighed in the same balance.—*C. Simmons.*

The purpose of an injury is to vex and trouble me.—Now, nothing can do that to him that is truly valiant.—*Johnson.*

If a bee stings you, will you go to the hive and destroy it? Would not a thousand come upon you? If you receive a trifling injury, do not go about proclaiming it, or be anxious to avenge it. Let it drop. It is wisdom to say little respecting the injuries you may have received.—*Anon.*

INJUSTICE.—If thou suffer injustice, console thyself; the true unhappiness is in doing it.—*Democritus.*

The man who wears injustice by his side, though powerful millions followed him to war, combats against the odds—against high heaven.—*Havard.*

He who commits injustice is ever

made more wretched than he who suffers it.—*Plato.*

No one will dare maintain that it is better to do injustice than to bear it.—*Aristotle.*

Of all injustice, that is the greatest which goes under the name of law; and of all sorts of tyranny the forcing of the letter of the law against the equity, is the most insupportable.—*L'Estrange.*

Injustice arises either from precipitation, or indolence, or from a mixture of both.—The rapid and slow are seldom just; the unjust wait either not at all, or wait too long.—*Lavater.*

An unjust acquisition is like a barbed arrow, which must be drawn backward with horrible anguish, or else will be your destruction.—*Jeremy Taylor.*

Fraud is the ready minister of injustice.—*Burke.*

Surely they who devour the possessions of orphans unjustly shall swallow down nothing but fire into their bellies, and shall broil in raging flames.—*Koran.*

Any one entrusted with power will abuse it if not also animated with the love of truth and virtue, no matter whether he be a prince, or one of the people.—*La Fontaine.*

Did the mass of men know the actual selfishness and injustice of their rulers, not a government would stand a year. —The world would foment with revolution.—*Theodore Parker.*

Whatever is unjust is contrary to the divine will; and from this it follows that no true and abiding happiness can be gained by those who are unjust.—*Stretch.*

He that acts unjustly, is the worst rebel to himself; and though now ambition's trumpet and the drum of power may drown the sound, yet conscience will one day speak loudly to him.—*Havard.*

Men endure the losses that befall them by mere casualty with more patience than the damages they sustain by injustice.—*Sir W. Raleigh.*

INK.—My ways are as broad as the king's high road, and my means lie in an inkstand.—*Southey.*

The colored slave that waits upon thy thought, and sends that thought,

without a voice, to the ends of the earth.—*Anon.*

Oh, she is fallen into a pit of ink that the wide sea hath drops too few to wash her clean again!—*Shakespeare.*

A drop of ink may make a million think.—*Byron.*

Let there be gall enough in thy ink; though thou write with a goose-pen, no matter.—*Shakespeare.*

INNOCENCE.—He is armed without who is innocent within, be this thy screen, and this thy wall of brass.—*Horace.*

What is a stronger breastplate than a heart untainted?—*Shakespeare.*

Innocence is but a poor substitute for experience.—*Bulwer.*

There is no courage but in innocence; no constancy but in an honest cause.—*Southern.*

To be innocent is to be not guilty; but to be virtuous is to overcome our evil inclinations.—*Penn.*

The innocent seldom find an uneasy pillow.—*Cowper.*

The innocence that feels no risk and is taught no caution, is more vulnerable than guilt, and oftener assailed.—*N. P. Willis.*

O, innocence, the sacred amulet against all the poisons of infirmity, and all misfortunes, injury, and death.—*Chapman.*

Against the head which innocence secures, insidious malice aims her darts in vain; turned backward by the powerful breath of heaven.—*Johnson.*

Innocence and mystery never dwell long together.—*Mad. Necker.*

Innocence is like polished armor; it adorns and defends.—*South.*

Unstained thoughts do seldom dream on evil.—*Shakespeare.*

Innocence and ignorance are sisters. But there are noble and vulgar sisters. Vulgar innocence and ignorance are mortal, they have pretty faces, but wholly without expression, and of a transient beauty; the noble sisters are immortal, their lofty forms are unchangeable, and their countenances are still radiant with the light of paradise. They dwell in heaven, and visit only the noblest and most severely tried of mankind.—*Novalis.*

There is no man so good, who, were he to submit all his thoughts and actions to the law, would not deserve hanging ten times in his life.—*Montaigne.*

The silence, often, of pure innocence persuades when speaking fails.—*Shakespeare.*

They that know no evil will suspect none.—*Ben Jonson.*

We have not the innocence of Eden; but by God's help and Christ's example we may have the victory of Gethsemane.—*E. H. Chavin.*

INNOVATION.—A spirit of innovation is generally the result of a selfish temper and confined views. People will not look forward to posterity, who never look backward to their ancestors. —*Burke.*

It will always do to change for the better.—*Thomson.*

The ridiculous rage for innovation, which only increases the weight of the chains it cannot break, shall never fire my blood!—*Schiller.*

Dislike of innovation proceeds sometimes from the disgust excited by false humanity, canting hypocrisy, and silly enthusiasm.—*Sydney Smith.*

INNS.—There is nothing yet contrived by man by which so much happiness is produced as by a good tavern or inn.—*Johnson.*

Though I am an inn-keeper, thank heaven I am a Christian.—*Cervantes.*

He who has not been at a tavern knows not what a paradise it is.—O holy tavern! O miraculous tavern!—holy, because no carking cares are there, nor weariness, nor pain; and miraculous, because of the spits, which, of themselves turn round and round.—*Longfellow.*

INQUIRY.—It is a shameful thing to be weary of inquiry when what we search for is excellent.—*Cicero.*

All calm inquiry conducted among those who have their main principles of judgment in common, leads, if not to an approximation of views, yet, at least, to an increase of sympathy.—*T. Arnold.*

It is error only, and not truth, that shrinks from inquiry.—*Thomas Paine.*

Let not the freedom of inquiry be shackled.—If it multiplies contentions among the wise and virtuous, it exercises the charity of those who contend. —If it shakes for a time the belief that is rested only on prejudice, it finally settles it on the broader and more solid basis of conviction.—*H. K. White.*

Free inquiry, if restrained within due bounds, and applied to proper subjects, is a most important privilege of the human mind; and if well conducted, is one of the greatest friends to truth.— But when reason knows neither its office nor its limits, and when employed on subjects foreign to its jurisdiction, it then becomes a privilege dangerous to be exercised.—*D'Aubigné.*

INQUISITIVENESS. — Inquisitive people are the funnels of conversation; they do not take in anything for their own use, but merely to pass it to another.—*Steele.*

In ancient days the most celebrated precept was, "know thyself"; in modern times it has been supplanted by the more fashionable maxim, "Know thy neighbor and everything about him."— *Johnson.*

Inquisitiveness or curiosity is a kernel of the forbidden fruit, which still sticketh in the throat of a natural man, and sometimes to the danger of his choking.—*Fuller.*

An inquisitive man is a creature naturally very vacant of thought itself, and therefore forced to apply to foreign assistance.—*Steele.*

Shun the inquisitive, for you will be sure to find him leaky.—Open ears do not keep conscientiously what has been intrusted to them, and a word once spoken flies, never to be recalled.— *Horace.*

What right have we to pry into the secrets of others?—True or false, the tale that is gabbled to us, what concern is it of ours?—*Bulwer.*

The man who is inquisitive into the secrets of your affairs, with which he has no concern, should be an object of your caution.—Men no more desire another's secrets to conceal them, than they would another's purse for the pleasure only of carrying it.—*Fielding.*

INSANITY.—(See "MADNESS.")

Insanity destroys reason, but not wit.
—*Emmons.*

Those who are insane generally reason correctly, but they reason from false assumptions and on wrong principles.

Great wits are sure to madness near allied, and thin partitions do their bounds divide.—*Dryden.*

All power of fancy over reason is a degree of insanity.—*Johnson.*

Now see that noble and most sovereign reason, like sweet bells jangled, out of time and harsh.—*Shakespeare.*

This wretched brain gave way, and I became a wreck, at random driven, without one glimpse of reason, or of heaven.—*Moore.*

O, judgment, thou art fled to brutish beasts, and men have lost their reason.—*Shakespeare.*

Insane people easily detect the nonsense of other people.—*John Hallam.*

Every sense hath been o'erstrung, and each frail fibre of the brain sent forth her thoughts all wild and wide.—*Byron.*

The difference between an insane man and a fool, Locke says, is, that a fool from right principles draws a wrong conclusion, while an insane person draws a just inference from false principles.

INSENSIBILITY.—Who can all sense of others' ills escape, is but a brute, at best, in human shape.—*Juvenal.*

A thorough and mature insensibility is rarely to be acquired but by a steady perseverance in infamy.—*Junius.*

There is a calm, viscous insensibility which will baffle even the gods, and calmly say, Try all your lightnings here, and see whether I cannot quench them.—*Carlyle.*

All feeling of futurity benumbed; all Godlike passion for externals quenched; all relish of realities expired; imbruted every faculty divine; heart buried in the rubbish of the world.—*Young.*

It is an alarming state to be past feeling, especially as to religious truth and duty.—*C. Simmons.*

INSINCERITY.—(See "SINCERITY.")
It is a shameful and unseemly thing to think one thing and speak another, but how odious to write one thing and think another.—*Seneca.*

Nothing is more disgraceful than insincerity.—*Cicero.*

Insincerity in a man's own heart must make all his enjoyments—all that concerns him, unreal; so that his whole life must seem like a merely dramatic representation.—*Hawthorne.*

INSPIRATION.—I know the Bible is inspired, because it finds me at greater depths of my being than any other book.—*Coleridge.*

Inspiration is such a divine superintendence over the books of the Bible as makes them a trustworthy, infallible and safe guide concerning the way of salvation.—*Joseph Cook.*

There is a deity within us who breathes that divine fire by which we are animated.—*Ovid.*

Poets are the hierophants of an unapprehended inspiration; the mirrors of the gigantic shadows which futurity casts upon the present.—*Shelley.*

The inspiration of the sacred Scriptures, as the very word of God, is manifest by their majesty, their purity, the consent of all their parts, by their light and power to convince and convert sinners, to edify and comfort believers, and to build them up in the character that prepares for full salvation.—*Boston.*

The best evidence that the Bible is the inspired word of God is to be found within its covers.—It proves itself.—*Charles Hodge.*

Inspiration secures the perfect infallibility of the Scriptures in every part, as a record of fact and doctrine, both in thought and verbal expression; so that, although they come to us through the instrumentality of the minds, hearts, imaginations, consciences, and wills of men, they are nevertheless in the strictest sense the Word of God.—*A. A. Hodge.*

INSTABILITY.—He who begins many things finishes nothing.—*C. Simmons.*

A rolling stone can gather no moss.—*Publius Syrus.*

Some have at first for wits, then poets passed; turned critics next, and proved plain fools at last.—*Pope.*

Everything by starts, and nothing long.—*Dryden.*

It will be found that they are the

weakest-minded and the hardest-hearted men, that most love change.—*Ruskin*.

One principal reason why men are so often useless is, that they divide and shift their attention among a multiplicity of objects and pursuits.—*Emmons*.

INSTINCT.—There is not, in my opinion, anything more mysterious in nature than this instinct in animals, which thus rise above reason, and yet fall infinitely short of it.—*Addison*.

A goose flies by a chart which the Royal Geographical Society could not mend.—*O. W. Holmes*.

Though reason is progressive, instinct is stationary. Five thousand years have added no improvement to the hive of the bee, or the house of the beaver.—*Colton*.

The active part of man consists of powerful instincts, some of which are gentle and continuous; others violent and short; some baser, some nobler, and all necessary.—*F. W. Newman*.

Beasts, birds, and insects, even to the minutest and meanest of their kind, act with the unerring providence of instinct; man, the while, who possesses a higher faculty, abuses it, and therefore goes blundering on. They, by their unconscious and unhesitating obedience to the laws of nature, fulfill the end of their existence; he, in willful neglect of the laws of God, loses sight of the end of his.—*Southey*.

Improvable reason is the distinction between man and the animal.—*T. Binney*.

Honest instinct comes a volunteer, sure never to overshoot, but just to hit, while still too wide, or short of human wit.—*Pope*.

Who taught the parrot his "Welcome"? Who taught the raven in a drought to throw pebbles into a hollow tree where she espied water, that the water might rise so as she might come to it? Who taught the bee to sail through such a vast sea of air, and to find the way from a flower in a field to her hive? Who taught the ant to bite every grain of corn that she burieth in her hill, lest it should take root and grow?—*Bacon*.

Who taught the natives of the field and wood to shun their poison, and to choose their food,—prescient, the tides and tempests to withstand; build on the wave, or arch beneath the sand?—*Pope*.

We only listen to those instincts which are our own, and only give credit to the evil when it has befallen us.—*La Fontaine*.

The instinctive feeling of a great people is often wiser than its wisest men.—*Kossuth*.

All our progress is an unfolding like the vegetable bud. You have first an instinct, then an opinion, then a knowledge, as the plant has root, bud, and fruit. Trust the instinct to the end, though you can render no reason.—*Emerson*.

By a divine instinct men's minds distrust ensuing danger, as by proof we see the waters swell before a boisterous storm.—*Shakespeare*.

The instinct of brutes and insects can be the effect of nothing else than the wisdom and skill of a powerful ever-living agent.—*Newton*.

Raise reason over instinct as you can; in this 'tis God directs; in that 'tis man.—*Pope*.

INSTRUCTION.—(See "TEACHING.")

The wise are instructed by reason; ordinary minds, by experience; the stupid, by necessity; and brutes by instinct.—*Cicero*.

A good newspaper and Bible in every house, a good schoolhouse in every district, and a church in every neighborhood, all appreciated as they deserve, are the chief support of virtue, morality, civil liberty, and religion.—*Franklin*.

Life is but one continual course of instruction,—The hand of the parent writes on the heart of the child the first faint characters which time deepens into strength so that nothing can efface them.—*R. Hill*.

The great business of the moral teacher is, to make the best moral impressions and excite the best feelings, by giving the clearest, fullest and most accurate instruction as to truth and duty.—*C. Simmons*.

In moral lessons the understanding must be addressed before the conscience, and the conscience before the heart, if we would make the deepest impressions.—*Emmons.*

The fruits of the earth do not more obviously require labor and cultivation to prepare them for our use and subsistence, than our faculties demand instruction and regulation in order to qualify us to become upright and valuable members of society, useful to others, or happy ourselves.—*Barrow.*

INSULT.—(See "IMPERTINENCE.")

Whatever be the motive of an insult it is always best to overlook it; for folly scarcely can deserve resentment, and malice is punished by neglect.—*Johnson.*

The way to procure insults is to submit to them.—A man meets with no more respect than he exacts.—*Hazlitt.*

Injuries may be atoned for and forgiven; but insults admit of no compensation; they degrade the mind in its own esteem, and force it to recover its level by revenge.—*Junius.*

The greater part of mankind are more sensitive to contemptuous language, than to unjust acts; they can less easily bear insult than wrong.—*Plutarch.*

There is an insolence which none but those who themselves deserve contempt can bestow, and those only who deserve no contempt can bear.—*Fielding.*

He who puts up with insult invites injury.—*Proverb.*

The slight that can be conveyed in a glance, in a gracious smile, in a wave of the hand, is often the ne plus ultra of art.—What insult is so keen or so keenly felt, as the polite insult which it is impossible to resent?—*Julia Kavanagh.*

Oppression is more easily borne than insult.—*Junius.*

It is the nature of some minds to insult and tyrannize over little people, this being the means they use to recompense themselves for their extreme servility and condescension to their superiors.—Slaves and flatterers exact the same taxes on all below them which they pay to all above them.—*Fielding.*

I once met a man who had forgiven an injury. I hope some day to meet the man who has forgiven an insult.—*Buxton.*

Fate never wounds more deeply the generous heart, than when a blockhead's insult points the dart.—*Johnson.*

INTEGRITY.—Integrity without knowledge is weak and useless.

In all things preserve integrity; and the consciousness of thine own uprightness will alleviate the toil of business, soften the hardness of ill-success and disappointments, and give thee an humble confidence before God, when the ingratitude of man, or the iniquity of the times may rob thee of other reward.—*Paley.*

Nothing more completely baffles one who is full of trick and duplicity, than straightforward and simple integrity in another.—*Colton.*

Nothing is at last sacred but the integrity of your own mind. Absolve you to yourself, and you shall have the suffrage of the world.—*Emerson.*

Give us the man of integrity, on whom we know we can thoroughly depend; who will stand firm when others fail; the friend, faithful and true; the adviser, honest and fearless; the adversary, just and chivalrous; such an one is a fragment of the Rock of Ages.—*J. P. Stanley.*

Integrity is the first step to true greatness.—Men love to praise, but are slow to practice it.—To maintain it in high places costs self-denial; in all places it is liable to opposition, but its end is glorious, and the universe will yet do it homage.—*C. Simmons.*

A man of integrity will never listen to any plea against conscience.—*Home.*

INTELLECT.—Intellect lies behind genius, which is intellect constructive. —Intellect is the simple power, anterior to all action or construction.—*Emerson.*

Intellect is brain force.—*Schiller.*

God has placed no limits to the exercise of the intellect he has given us, on this side of the grave.—*Bacon.*

If a man's eye is on the Eternal, his intellect will grow.—*Emerson.*

The intellect has only one failing, which, to be sure, is a very considerable one.—It has no conscience. Napoleon is the readiest instance of this. If his heart had borne any proportion to his brain, he had been one of the greatest men in all history.—*J. R. Lowell.*

Every man should use his intellect, not as he uses his lamp in the study, only for his own seeing, but as the lighthouse uses its lamps, that those afar off on the sea may see the shining, and learn their way.—*H. W. Beecher.*

The education of the intellect is a great business; but an unconsecrated intellect is the saddest sight on which the sun looks down.—*Chadwick.*

Brains well prepared are the monuments where human knowledge is most surely engraved.—*Rousseau.*

A man of intellect is lost unless he unites to it energy of character.—When we have the lantern of Diogenes we must have his staff.—*Chamfort.*

Intellect—the starlight of the brain.—*N. P. Willis.*

The march of intellect is proceeding at quick time; and if its progress be not accompanied by a corresponding improvement in morals and religion, the faster it proceeds, with the more violence will you be hurried down the road to ruin.—*Southey.*

The intellect of the wise is like glass; it admits the light of heaven and reflects it.—*Hare.*

I cannot think that any man could ever tower upward into a very great philosopher unless he should begin or end with Christianity.—A great man may, by a rare possibility, be an infidel.—An intellect of the highest order must build on Christianity.—*De Quincey.*

Intellect and industry are never incompatible. There is more wisdom, and will be more benefit, in combining them than scholars like to believe, or than the common world imagine; life has time enough for both, and its happiness will be increased by the union.—*S. Turner.*

Culture of intellect without religion in the heart, is only civilized barbarism, and disguised animalism.—*Bunsen.*

Times of general calamity and confusion have ever been productive of the greatest minds. The purest ore is produced from the hottest furnace, and the brightest thunderbolt is elicited from the darkest storm.—*Colton.*

The eye of the intellect sees in all objects what it brought with it means of seeing.—*Carlyle.*

Don't despair of a student if he has one clear idea.—*Emmons.*

Intellect, talent, and genius, like murder, "will out."—*C. Simmons.*

The commerce of intellect loves distant shores. The small retail dealer trades only with his neighbor; when the great merchant trades he links the four quarters of the globe.—*Bulwer.*

Men with intellectual light alone may make advances without moral principle, but without that moral principle which gospel faith produces, permanent progress is impossible.—*J. B. Walker.*

Great minds react on the society which has made them what they are; but they only pay with interest what they have received.—*Macaulay.*

While the world lasts, the sun will gild the mountain-tops before it shines upon the plain.—*Bulwer.*

The more we know of any one ground of knowledge, the further we see into the general domains of intellect.—*Leigh Hunt.*

Mind is the great lever of all things; human thought is the process by which human ends are answered.—*Daniel Webster.*

The men of action are, after all, only the unconscious instruments of the men of thought.—*Heine.*

There never was a man all intellect; but just in proportion as men become so they become like lofty mountains, all ice and snow the higher they rise above the warm heart of the earth.—*E. H. Chapin.*

INTELLIGENCE. — (See "KNOWLEDGE" and "THOUGHT.")

Intelligence is a luxury, sometimes useless, sometimes fatal. It is a torch or firebrand according to the use one makes of it.—*Caballero.*

If a man empties his purse into his head, no one can take it from him.—*Franklin.*

The higher feelings, when acting in harmonious combination, and directed by enlightened intellect, have a boundless scope for gratification; their least indulgence is delightful, and their highest activity is bliss.—*Combe.*

It is the mind that makes the body

rich; and as the sun breaks through the darkest clouds, so honor peereth in the meanest habit.—*Shakespeare.*

The superior man is he who develops, in harmonious proportions, his moral, intellectual, and physical nature.—This should be the end at which men of all classes should aim, and it is this only which constitutes real greatness.—*Jerrold.*

Intelligence increases mere physical ability one half.—The use of the head abridges the labor of the hands.—*H. W. Beecher.*

They who have read about everything are thought to understand everything, too, but it is not always so; reading furnishes the mind only with materials of knowledge; it is thinking that makes what we read ours. We are of the ruminating kind, and it is not enough to cram ourselves with a great load of collections—we must chew them over again.—*Channing.*

Light has spread, and even bayonets think.—*Kossuth.*

God multiplies intelligence, which communicates itself like fire, infinitely. —Light a thousand torches at one torch, and the flame of the latter remains the same.—*Joubert.*

Some men of a secluded and studious life have sent forth from their closet or cloister rays of intellectual light that have agitated courts and revolutionized kingdoms; like the moon which, though far removed from the ocean and shining upon it with a serene and sober light, is the chief cause of all those ebbings and flowings which incessantly disturb that restless world of waters.—*Colton.*

A man cannot leave a better legacy to the world than a well-educated family.—*Thomas Scott.*

It is no proof of a man's understanding to be able to confirm whatever he pleases; but to be able to discern that what is true is true, and that what is false is false; this is the mark and character of intelligence.—*Swedenborg.*

We must despise no sort of talents; they all have their separate uses and duties; all have the happiness of man for their object; they all improve, exalt, and gladden life.—*Sydney Smith.*

Human learning, with the blessing of God upon it, introduces us to divine wisdom, and while we study the works of nature, the God of nature will manifest himself to us.—*Bp. Horne.*

INTEMPERANCE.—(See "Drunkenness" and "Wine.")

I never drink.—I cannot do it on equal terms with others.—It costs them only one day; but it costs me three; the first in sinning, the second in suffering, and the third in repenting.—*Sterne.*

When the cup of any sensual pleasure is drained to the bottom, there is always poison in the dregs.—*Jane Porter.*

Wise men mingle mirth with their cares, as a help either to forget or overcome them; but to resort to intoxication for the ease of one's mind, is to cure melancholy by madness.—*Charron.*

He that is a drunkard is qualified for all vice.—*Quarles.*

In our world death deputes intemperance to do the work of age.—*Young.*

Death having occasion to choose a prime minister, summoned his illustrious courtiers, and allowed them to present their claims for the office: Fever flushed his cheeks; Palsy shook his limbs; Dropsy inflated his carcass; Gout racked his joints; Asthma half strangled himself; Stone and Colic pleaded their violence; Plague, his sudden destructions; and Consumption his certainty. Then came War, with stern confidence, alluding to his many thousands devoured at a meal. Last came Intemperance, with a face like fire, shouting, "Give way, ye sickly, ferocious band of pretenders. Am I not your parent? Does not sagacity trace your origin to me? My operations ceasing, whence your power?" The grisly monarch here gave a smile of approbation, and placed intemperance at his right hand, as his favorite and prime minister.—*Dodsley.*

He that tempts me to drink beyond my measure, civilly invites me to a fever.—*Jeremy Taylor.*

Greatness of any kind has no greater foe than the habit of drinking.—*Walter Scott.*

Every inordinate cup is unblessed, and the ingredient is a devil.—*Shakespeare.*

The drunkard, says Seneca, is a voluntary madman, and some one has added, " a necessary fool."

There is no vice in nature more debasing and destructive to men than intemperance. It robs them of their reason, reputation, and interest. It renders them unfit for human society. It degrades them below the beasts that perish, and justly exposes them to universal odium and contempt.—*Emmons.*

Those men who destroy a healthful constitution of body by intemperance and an irregular life, do as manifestly kill themselves, as those who hang, or poison, or drown themselves.—*Sherlock.*

Of all the causes of crime, intemperance stands out the unapproachable chief.—*Noah Davis.*

One drinking saloon in a community means rags and misery for some of its people, and sixty thousand saloons in the nation mean rags and misery multiplied sixty thousand times. Universal happiness and prosperity cannot exist in the same land with the saloon any more than peace and safety can exist in a sheep-fold when the wolf has entered it.—*C. A. Stoddard.*

The habit of intemperance by men in office has occasioned more injury to the public, and more trouble to me, than all other causes; and, were I to commence my administration again, the first question I would ask respecting a candidate for office, would be, " Does he use ardent spirits? "—*Jefferson.*

The body, overcharged with the excess of yesterday, weighs down the mind together with itself, and fixes to the earth that particle of the divine spirit.—*Horace.*

Touch the goblet no more; it will make thy heart sore, to its very core.—*Longfellow.*

See where the wild-blazing grog shop appears, there where the red waves of wretchedness swell; it burns on the edge of tempestuous years, the horrible lighthouse of hell.—*McDonald Clarke.*

The youth who stands with a glass of liquor in his hand would do well to consider which he had best throw away —the liquor or himself.

If we could sweep intemperance out of the country, there would be hardly poverty enough left to give healthy exercise to the charitable impulses.—*Phillips Brooks.*

Intemperance is a dangerous companion.—It throws people off their guard, betrays them to a great many indecencies, to ruinous passions, to disadvantages in fortune; makes them discover secrets, drive foolish bargains, engage in gambling, and often stagger from the tavern to the stews.—*Colton.*

In intoxication men betray their real characters.—So in prosperity there is a no less honest and truth-revealing intoxication than in wine.—The varnish of power brings forth at once the defects and the beauties of the human portrait. —*Bulwer.*

Drunkenness takes away the man, and leaves only the brute; it dethrones reason from its seat; stupefies conscience; ruins health; wastes property; covers the wretch with rags; reduces wife and children to want and beggary, and gives such power to appetite that physically, as well as morally, it is next to impossible to cure it.—*W. Jay.*

INTENTIONS. — (See " HELL," and " INDECISION.")

Good intentions are very mortal and perishable things; like very mellow and choice fruit they are difficult to keep.— *C. Simmons.*

The innocence of the intention abates nothing of the mischief of the example. —*Robert Hall.*

Many good purposes and intentions lie in the churchyard.—*Philip Henry.*

The failures of life come from resting in good intentions, which are in vain unless carried out in wise action.—*C. Simmons.*

Right intention is to the actions of a man what the soul is to the body, or the root to the tree.—*Jeremy Taylor.*

If religion might be judged of according to men's intentions, there would scarcely be any idolatry in the world.— *Bp. Hall.*

" Hell is paved with good intentions," says Johnson.—Better say the way to it is.

God takes men's hearty desires and will, instead of the deed, where they have not power to fulfill it; but he never took the bare deed instead of the will. —*Baxter.*

Good intention will no more make a truth, than a good mark will make a good shot.—*Spurstowe.*

In the works of man as in those of nature, it is the intention which is chiefly worth studying.—*Goethe.*

INTEREST.—Interest speaks all languages, and acts all parts, even that of disinterestedness itself.—*Rochefoucauld.*

Interest has the security, though not the virtue of a principle.—As the world goes, it is the surest side; for men daily leave both relations and religion to follow it.—*Penn.*

How difficult it is to persuade a man to reason against his interest, though he is convinced that equity is against him. —*Trusler.*

It is more than possible, that those who have neither character nor honor, may be wounded in a very tender part, their interest.—*Junius.*

The virtues and vices are all put in motion by interest.—*Rochefoucauld.*

Interest makes some people blind, and others quick-sighted.—*Beaumont.*

When interest is at variance with conscience, any pretence that seems to reconcile them satisfies the hollowhearted.—*Home.*

INTOLERANCE. — Intolerance has been the curse of every age and state.— *S. Davies.*

Nothing dies so hard, or rallies so often as intolerance.—*H. W. Beecher.*

Whoever attempts to suppress liberty of conscience finishes some day by wishing for the Inquisition.—*Simon.*

It were better to be of no church than to be bitter for any.—*Penn.*

The intolerant man is the real pedant. —*Richter.*

The devil loves nothing better than the intolerance of reformers, and dreads nothing so much as their charity and patience.—*J. R. Lowell.*

INVENTION.—Invention is the talent of youth, as judgment is of age.— *Swift.*

Invention, strictly speaking, is little more than a new combination of those images which have been previously gathered and deposited in the memory.

Nothing can be made of nothing; he who has laid up no materials can produce no combinations.—*Sir J. Reynolds.*

Invention is a kind of muse, which, being possessed of the other advantages common to her sisters, and being warmed by the fire of Apollo, is raised higher than the rest.—*Dryden.*

A fine invention is nothing more than a fine deviation from, or enlargement on a fine model.—Imitation, if noble and general, insures the best hope of originality.—*Bulwer.*

He that invents a machine augments the power of a man and the well-being of mankind.—*H. W. Beecher.*

The great inventor is one who has walked forth upon the industrial world, not from universities, but from hovels; not as clad in silks and decked with honors, but as clad in fustian and grimed with soot and oil.—*Isaac Taylor.*

It is frivolous to fix pedantically the date of particular inventions. They have all been invented over and over fifty times. Man is the arch machine, of which all these shifts drawn from himself are toy models. He helps himself on each emergency by copying or duplicating his own structure, just so far as the need is.—*Emer...*

Where we cannot invent, we may at least improve; we may give somewhat of novelty to that which was old, condensation to that which was diffuse, perspicuity to that which was obscure, and currency to that which was recondite.—*Colton.*

IRONY.—Irony is to the high-bred what billingsgate is to the vulgar; and when one gentleman thinks another gentleman an ass, he does not say it pointblank; he implies it in the politest terms he can invent.—*Bulwer.*

Clap an extinguisher upon your irony if you are unhappily blessed with a vein of it.—*Lamb.*

Irony is an insult conveyed in the form of a compliment; insinuating the most galling satire under the phraseology of panegyric; placing its victim naked on a bed of briers and thistles, thinly covered with rose-leaves; adorning his brow with a crown of gold, which burns into his brain; teasing and fretting, and riddling him through and through, with incessant discharges of hot shot from a masked battery; laying bare the most sensitive and shrinking nerves of his mind, and then blandly touching them with ice, or smilingly pricking them with needles.—*E. P. Whipple.*

IRRESOLUTION.—(See "INDE-CISION.")

Irresolution on the schemes of life which offer themselves to our choice, and inconstancy in pursuing them, are the greatest causes of all our unhappiness.—*Addison.*

Irresolution frames a thousand horrors, embodying each.—*J. Martyn.*

Irresolution is a worse vice than rashness. He that shoots best may sometimes miss the mark; but he that shoots not at all can never hit it. Irresolution loosens all the joints of a state; like an ague, it shakes not this nor that limb, but all the body is at once in a fit. The irresolute man is lifted from one place to another; so hatcheth nothing, but addles all his actions.—*Feltham.*

Like a man to double business bound, I stand in pause where I shall first begin, and both neglect.—*Shakespeare.*

Irresolution is a heavy stone rolled up a hill by a weak child, and moved a little up just to fall back again.—*W. Rider.*

That we would do, we should do when we would; for this "would" changes, and hath abatements and delays as many, as there are tongues, are hands, are accidents; and then, this "should" is like a spendthrift sigh, that hurts by easing.—*Shakespeare.*

J

JEALOUSY.—Of all the passions, jealousy is that which exacts the hardest service, and pays the bitterest wages. Its service is, to watch the success of our enemy; its wages to be sure of it.—*Colton.*

In jealousy there is more of self-love, than of love to another.—*Rochefoucauld.*

Trifles light as air, are to the jealous confirmations strong as proofs of holy writ.—*Shakespeare.*

What frenzy dictates, jealousy believes.—*Gay.*

Jealousy sees things always with magnifying glasses which make little things large, of dwarfs giants, of suspicions truths.—*Cervantes.*

'Tis a monster begot upon itself, born on itself.—*Shakespeare.*

Jealousy is the injured lover's hell.—*Milton.*

The jealous man poisons his own banquet, and then eats it.

Jealousy lives upon doubts.—It becomes madness or ceases entirely as soon as we pass from doubt to certainty.—*Rochefoucauld.*

Jealousy is like a polished glass held to the lips when life is in doubt; if there be breath it will catch the damp and show it.—*Dryden.*

All other passions condescend at times to accept the inexorable logic of facts; but jealousy looks facts straight in the face, and ignores them utterly, and says she knows a great deal better than they can tell her.—*A. Helps.*

Jealousy is the sister of love, as the devil is the brother of angels.—*Boufflers.*

Women detest a jealous man whom they do not love, but it angers them when a man they do love is not jealous.—*L'Enclos.*

A jealous man always finds more than he looks for.—*Mlle. Scudery.*

O, Jealousy, thou ugliest fiend of hell! thy deadly venom preys on my vitals, turns the healthful hue of my fresh cheek to haggard sallowness, and drinks my spirit up.—*H. More.*

Jealousy is said to be the offspring of love; yet unless the parent makes haste to strangle the child, the child will not rest till it has poisoned the parent.—*Hare.*

Oh, beware of jealousy; it is the green-eyed monster, which doth mock the meat it feeds on.—*Shakespeare.*

It is with jealousy as with the gout; when such distempers are in the blood there is never any security against their breaking out, and that often on the slightest occasions, and when least suspected.—*Fielding.*

Yet is there one more cursed than they all, that canker-worm, that monster, jealousy, which eats the heart and feeds upon the gall, turning all love's delight to misery, through fear of losing his felicity.—*Spenser.*

All jealousy must be strangled in its birth, or time will soon make it strong enough to overcome the truth.—*Davenant.*

Love may exist without jealousy, although this is rare; but jealousy may exist without love, and this is common; for jealousy can feed on that which is bitter, no less than on that which is sweet, and is sustained by pride as often as by affection.

It is said that jealousy is love, but I deny it; for though it may be procured by love, as ashes are by fire, yet jealousy extinguishes love, as ashes smother the flame.—*Margaret of Navarre.*

Jealousy is always born with love, but does not die with it.—*Rochefoucauld.*

Jealousy is the fear or apprehension of superiority; envy our uneasiness under it.—*Shenstone.*

To doubt is an injury; to suspect a friend is breach of friendship; jealousy is a seed sown but in vicious minds; prone to distrust, because apt to deceive.—*G. Lansdowne.*

He who is next heir to supreme power, is always suspected and hated by him who actually wields it.—*Tacitus.*

That anxious torture may I never feel, which doubtful watches o'er a wandering heart.—*Mrs. Tighe.*

We are more jealous of frivolous accomplishments with brilliant success, than of the most estimable qualities without. Johnson envied Garrick whom he despised, and ridiculed Goldsmith, whom he loved.—*Hazlitt.*

Jealousy, says Rochefoucauld, is in some sort rational and just; it aims at the preservation of a good which we think belongs to us.—It is in this sense that God is said to be a jealous God, because he is earnestly, and as it were passionately desirous of our supreme love, and reverence, and service.

JEERING.—Scoff not at the natural defects of any which are not in their power to amend. It is cruel to beat a cripple with his own crutches!—*Fuller.*

A sneer is the weapon of the weak.— Like other weapons of the devil, it is always cunningly ready to our hand,

and there is more poison in the handle than in the point.—*J. R. Lowell.*

Jeer not at others upon any occasion. If they be foolish, God hath denied them understanding; if they be vicious, you ought to pity, not revile them; if deformed, God framed their bodies; and will you scorn his workmanship? Are you wiser than your Creator? If poor, poverty was designed for a motive to charity, not to contempt; you cannot see what riches they have within.—*South.*

Who can refute a sneer?—It is independent of proof, reason, argument, or sense, and may as well be used against facts and truth, as against falsehood.— *C. Simmons.*

JESTING.—Take heed of jesting; many have been ruined by it.—It is hard to jest, and not sometimes jeer too, which often sinks deeper than we intended or expected.—*Fuller.*

The Arabians have a saying, that it is not good to jest with God, death, or the devil; for the first neither can nor will be mocked; the second mocks all men one time or another; and the third puts an eternal sarcasm on those that are too familiar with him.—*Beaumont.*

A good jest in time of misfortune, is food and drink. It is strength to the arm, digestion to the stomach, and courage to the heart. A prosperous man can afford to be melancholy; but if the miserable are so, they are worse than dead—it is sure to kill them.—*Ware.*

Laughter should dimple the cheek, not furrow the brow. A jest should be such that all shall be able to join in the laugh which it occasions; but if it bears hard upon one of the company, like the crack of a string, it makes a stop in the music.—*Feltham.*

The jest loses its point when he who makes it is the first to laugh.—*Schiller.*

Men ought to find the difference between saltness and bitterness. Certainly, he that hath a satirical vein, as he maketh others afraid of his wit, so he had need be afraid of others' memory. —*Bacon.*

It is good to make a jest, but not to make a trade of jesting.—*Fuller.*

Jesting when not used upon improper matter, in an unfit manner, with excessive measure, at undue season, or to evil purpose, may be allowed.—*I. Barrow.*

Raillery is sometimes more insupportable than wrong; we have a right to resent injuries, but it is ridiculous to be angry at a jest.—*Rochefoucauld.*

Be not affronted at a jest; if one throw ever so much salt at thee thou wilt receive no harm unless thou art raw and ulcerous.—*Junius.*

He that will lose his friend for a jest deserves to die a beggar by the bargain. —Such let thy jests be, that they may not grind the credit of thy friend; and make not jests so long that thou becomest one.—*Fuller.*

Joking often loses a friend, and never gains an enemy.—*C. Simmons.*

A joker is near akin to a buffoon; and neither of them is the least related to wit.—*Chesterfield.*

A jest's prosperity lies in the ear of him that hears it, never in the tongue of him that makes it.—*Shakespeare.*

Judge of a jest when you have done laughing.—*W. Lloyd.*

JESUS.—(See "CHRIST.")

JEWS.—The Jew is the pilgrim of commerce, trading with every nation and blending with none.—*Conybeare.*

They are a piece of stubborn antiquity, compared with which Stonehenge is in its nonage. They date beyond the Pyramids.—*Lamb.*

The Jews are among the aristocracy of every land. If a literature is called rich in the possession of a few classic tragedies, what shall we say to a national tragedy, lasting for fifteen hundred years, in which the poets and actors were also the heroes?—*George Eliot.*

When with true American enthusiasm we recall the story of our war for independence and rejoice in the indomitable courage and fortitude of our revolutionary heroes, we should not fail to remember how well the Jews of America performed their part in the struggle.—*Grover Cleveland.*

No race has ever surpassed the Jewish descriptions of either the beauties or the terrors of the nature which environs man.—*Charles W. Eliot.*

They produce, in proportion to their numbers, an unusually large number of able and successful men as any one may prove by recounting the eminent Jews of the last seventy years.—*James Bryce.*

The character of a people, like the character of a person, should not be measured by its worst, but rather by its best; and, reckoned by that rule and by that standard, Israel's rank is high.—*David H. Greer.*

If I am right the Germans will say I was a German, and the French will say I was a Jew; if I am wrong the Germans will say I was a Jew and the French will say I was a German.—*Albert Einstein.*

There is not the slightest ground for anti-Semitism among us.—*Wm. Howard Taft.*

They are not Jews in America; they are American citizens.—*Woodrow Wilson.*

The Jews cannot reasonably be denied to have contributed largely to practical and experimental science. They were diligent travelers in all parts of the known world, compiling itineraries which have proved of extensive use in later times.—*William H. Prescott.*

No individual should be subjected anywhere, by reason of the fact that he is a Jew, to a denial of any common right or opportunity enjoyed by non-Jews.—*Louis D. Brandeis.*

While the Jews of the United States have remained loyal to their faith, and their race traditions, they have become indissolubly incorporated in the great army of American Citizenship.—*Theodore Roosevelt.*

JOURNALISM.—In a great democracy such as ours the outstanding need of the hour is greater information and greater tolerance. Sincere efforts at enlightenment and education by the press are more important than self-appointed leadership.—*Roy W. Howard.*

In my opinion newspaper work offers better opportunities, aside from the accumulation of money, for real serviceable, result-getting labor than any other business a young man may choose.—*Samuel G. Blythe.*

The journalist holds up an umbrella, protecting society from the fiery hail of conscience.—*George W. Russell.*

Get your facts first, and then you can distort 'em as you please.—*Mark Twain.*

The paper which obtains a reputation for publishing authentic news and only that which is fit to print, . . . will steadily increase its influence.—*Andrew Carnegie.*

If you know many people it is impossible to conduct a newspaper impersonally, and the only way to run a newspaper is in an impersonal way.—*Lord Northcliffe.*

A news sense is really a sense of what is important, what is vital, what has color and life—what people are interested in. That's journalism.—*Burton Rascoe.*

I would sooner call myself a journalist than an author for a journalist is a journeyman.—*Gilbert K. Chesterton.*

Take away the newspaper—and this country of ours would become a scene of chaos. Without daily assurance of the exact facts—so far as we are able to know and publish them—the public imagination would run riot. Ten days without the daily newspaper and the strong pressure of worry and fear would throw the people of this country into mob hysteria—feeding upon rumors, alarms, terrified by bugbears and illusions. We have become the watchmen of the night and of a troubled day. . . . *Harry Chandler.*

All journalists are, by virtue of their handicraft, alarmists; this is their way of making themselves interesting.—*Lord Riddell.*

You cannot hope to bribe or twist, Thank God, the British journalist. But seeing what the man will do unbribed, there's no occasion to.—*James Milne.*

You will generally find that the person who doesn't give a continental what the newspapers say about 'im either one way or the other subscribes to a press clipping bureau anyway.—*Elbert Hubbard.*

Just as it is the automobile manufacturer's business to sell transportation, so it is the newspaper owner's business to sell information and not advice nor propaganda.—*Walter B. Pitkin.*

To write weekly, to write daily, to write shortly, to write for busy people catching trains in the morning or for tired people coming home in the evening, is a heartbreaking task for men

who know good writing from bad.—*Virginia Woolf.*

Journalism has become, and is becoming every day in even greater degree, the most important function in the community.—*Henry George.*

The daily newspaper sustains the same relation to the young writer as the hospital to the medical student.—*George Horace Lorimer.*

How shall I speak thee, or thy power address,

Thou God of our idolatry, the Press?

* * * * *

Like Eden's dead probationary tree, Knowledge of good and evil is from thee.—*Cowper.*

We live under a government of men and morning newspapers.—*Wendell Phillips.*

I fear three newspapers more than a hundred thousand bayonets.—*Napoleon.*

JOY.—(See "HAPPINESS.")

Man is the merriest, the most joyous of all the species of creation.—Above and below him all are serious.—*Addison.*

The most profound joy has more of gravity than of gaiety in it.—*Montaigne.*

He who can conceal his joys is greater than he who can hide his griefs.—*Lavater.*

Joys are our wings; sorrows our spurs.—*Richter.*

Those who can not feel pain are not capable, either, of feeling joy.—*Raden Adjeng Kartini.*

Poor human nature, so richly endowed with nerves of anguish, so splendidly organized for pain and sorrow, is but slenderly equipped for joy. . . . A sense of ineffable joy, attainable at will, and equal in intensity and duration to (let us say) an attack of sciatica, would go far to equalize the one-sided conditions under which we live.—*George Du Maurier.*

We lose the peace of years when we hunt after the rapture of moments.—*Bulwer.*

Tranquil pleasures last the longest; we are not fitted to bear long the burden of great joys.—*Bovee.*

Joy is more divine than sorrow, for

joy is bread and sorrow is medicine.— *H. W. Beecher.*

The highest joy to the Christian almost always comes through suffering. No flower can bloom in Paradise which is not transplanted from Gethsemane. No one can taste of the fruit of the tree of life, that has not tasted of the fruits of the tree of Calvary. The crown is after the cross.

To pursue joy is to lose it. The only way to get it is to follow steadily the path of duty, without thinking of joy, and then, like sheep, it comes most surely unsought, and we "being in the way," the angel of God, bright-haired Joy, is sure to meet us.—*A. Maclaren.*

We ask God to forgive us for our evil thoughts and evil temper, but rarely, if ever, ask him to forgive us for our sadness.—*R. W. Dale.*

The very society of joy redoubles it; so that, while it lights upon my friend it rebounds upon myself, and the brighter his candle burns the more easily will it light mine.—*South.*

The joy resulting from the diffusion of blessings to all around us is the purest and sublimest that can ever enter the human mind, and can be conceived only by those who have experienced it. Next to the consolations of divine grace, it is the most sovereign balm to the miseries of life, both in him who is the object of it, and in him who exercises it.— *Bp. Porteus.*

Great joy, especially after a sudden change of circumstances, is apt to be silent, and dwells rather in the heart than on the tongue.—*Fielding.*

Here below is not the land of happiness; it is only the land of toil; and every joy which comes to us is only to strengthen us for some greater labor that is to succeed.—*Fichte.*

We can do nothing well without joy, and a good conscience which is the ground of joy.—*Sibbes.*

There is a sweet joy that comes to us through sorrow.—*Spurgeon.*

JUDGMENT.—(See "OPINION.")
As the touchstone which tries gold, but is not itself tried by gold, such is he who has the true standard of judgment. —*Epictetus.*

In forming a judgment, lay your hearts void of fore-taken opinions; else, what-soever is done or said will be measured by a wrong rule; like them who have the jaundice, to whom everything appeareth yellow.—*Sir P. Sidney.*

Men are not to be judged by their looks, habits, and appearances; but by the character of their lives and conversations, and by their works.—It is better to be praised by one's own works than by the words of another.—*L'Estrange.*

Judge thyself with the judgment of sincerity, and thou wilt judge others with the judgment of charity.—*J. Mason.*

While actions are always to be judged by the immutable standard of right and wrong, the judgments we pass upon men must be qualified by considerations of age, country, station, and other accidental circumstances; and it will then be found that he who is most charitable in his judgment is generally the least unjust.—*Southey.*

Never be a judge between thy friends in any matter where both set their hearts upon the victory. If strangers or enemies be litigants, whatever side thou favorest, thou gettest a friend; but when friends are the parties thou losest one. —*Bp. Taylor.*

Judgment is forced upon us by experience.—*Johnson.*

The judgment is like a pair of scales, and evidences like the weights; but the will holds the balances in its hand; and even a slight jerk will be sufficient, in many cases, to make the lighter scale appear the heavier.—*Whately.*

A man has generally the good or ill qualities which he attributes to mankind.—*Shenstone.*

It is with our judgments as with our watches: no two go just alike, yet each believes his own.—*Pope.*

How little do they see what really is, who frame their hasty judgment upon that which seems.—*Southey.*

We judge ourselves by what we feel capable of doing; others judge us by what we have done.—*Longfellow.*

Men's judgments are a parcel of their fortunes; and things outward do draw the inward quality after them.—*Shakespeare.*

The most necessary talent in a man of conversation, which is what we ordinarily intend by a gentleman, is a good judgment. He that has this in perfection is master of his companion, without letting him see it; and has the same advantage over men of other qualifications, as one that can see would have over a blind man of ten times his strength.—*Steele.*

You think it a want of judgment that one changes his opinion.—Is it a proof that your scales are bad because they vibrate with every additional weight that is added to either side?—*Miss Edgeworth.*

It is a maxim received in life that, in general, we can determine more wisely for others than for ourselves.—The reason of it is so clear in argument that it hardly wants the confirmation of experience.—*Junius.*

Everyone complains of the badness of his memory, but nobody of his judgment.—*Rochefoucauld.*

The wise determine from the gravity of the case; the irritable, from sensibility to oppression; the high-minded, from disdain and indignation at abusive power in unworthy hands.—*Burke.*

Lynx-eyed to our neighbors, and moles to ourselves.—*La Fontaine.*

The seat of knowledge is in the head; of wisdom, in the heart.—We are sure to judge wrong if we do not feel right.—*Hazlitt.*

The vulgar mind fancies that good judgment is implied chiefly in the capacity to censure; and yet there is no judgment so exquisite as that which knows properly how to approve.—*Simms.*

We do not judge men by what they are in themselves, but by what they are relatively to us.—*Mad. Swetchine.*

Fools measure actions after they are done, by the event; wise men beforehand, by the rules of reason and right. The former look to the end to judge of the act. Let me look to the act, and leave the end to God.—*Bp. Hill.*

While I am ready to adopt any well-grounded opinion, my inmost heart revolts against receiving the judgments of others respecting persons, and whenever I have done so, I have bitterly repented of it.—*Niebuhr.*

Think wrongly, if you please; but in all cases think for yourself.—*Lessing.*

No man can judge another, because no man knows himself, for we censure others but as they disagree from that humor which we fancy laudable in ourselves, and commend others but for that wherein they seem to quadrate and consent with us.—*Sir Thomas Browne.*

A flippant, frivolous man may ridicule others, may controvert them, scorn them; but he who has any respect for himself seems to have renounced the right of thinking meanly of others.—*Goethe.*

In judging of others a man laboreth in vain, often erreth, and easily sinneth; but in judging and examining himself, he always laboreth fruitfully.—*Thomas à Kempis.*

The contemporary mind may in rare cases be taken by storm; but posterity never. The tribunal of the present is accessible to influence; that of the future is incorrupt.—*Gladstone.*

I mistrust the judgment of every man in a case in which his own wishes are concerned.—*Wellington.*

In our judgment of human transactions, the law of optics is reversed; we see the most indistinctly the objects which are close around us.—*Whately.*

To judge by the event, is an error all abuse and all commit; for in every instance, courage, if crowned with success, is heroism; if clouded by defeat, temerity.—*Colton.*

There are some minds like either convex or concave mirrors, which represent objects such as they receive them, but they never receive them as they are.—*Joubert.*

Human nature is so constituted, that all see and judge better in the affairs of other men than in their own.—*Terence.*

Never forget the day of judgment. Keep it always in view. Frame every action and plan with a reference to its unchanging decisions.

Foolish men imagine that because judgment for an evil thing is delayed, there is no justice, but only accident here below. Judgment for an evil thing is many times delayed some day or two, some century or two, but it is sure as life, it is sure as death!—*Carlyle.*

Human judgment, like Luther's drunken peasant, when saved from falling on one side, topples over on the other.—*Mazzini.*

JURISPRUDENCE. — The law is made to protect the innocent by punishing the guilty.—*Daniel Webster.*

The point most liable to objection in the jury system, is the power which any one or more of the twelve have to starve the rest into compliance with their opinion; so that the verdict may possibly be given by strength of constitution, not by conviction of conscience: and "wretches hang that jurymen may dine." —*Lord Orrery.*

The criminal law is not founded on the principle of vengeance; it uses evil only as the means of preventing greater evil.—*Daniel Webster.*

The institution of the jury, if confined to criminal cases, is always in danger; but when once it is introduced into civil proceedings, it defies the aggressions of time and of man.—*De Tocqueville.*

Whenever a jury, through whimsical or ill-founded scruples, suffer the guilty to escape, they become responsible for the augmented danger of the innocent. —*Daniel Webster.*

JUSTICE.—To be perfectly just is an attribute of the divine nature; to be so to the utmost of our abilities, is the glory of man.—*Addison.*

Judges ought to be more learned than witty, more reverent than plausible, and more advised than confident. Above all things, integrity is their portion and proper virtue.—*Bacon.*

If judges would make their decisions just, they should behold neither plaintiff, defendant, nor pleader, but only the cause itself.—*B. Livingston.*

Justice discards party, friendship, and kindred, and is therefore represented as blind.—*Addison.*

One man's word is no man's word; we should quietly hear both sides.—*Goethe.*

Impartiality is the life of justice, as justice is of all good government.

Justice is the constant desire and effort to render to every man his due. —*Justinian.*

Justice is itself the great standing policy of civil society; and any departure from it, under any circumstance,

lies under the suspicion of being no policy at all.—*Burke.*

Man is unjust, but God is just; and finally justice triumphs.—*Longfellow.*

Justice is as strictly due between neighbor nations, as between neighbor citizens. A highwayman is as much a robber when he plunders in a gang, as when single; and a nation that makes an unjust war is only a great gang of robbers.—*Franklin.*

Justice without wisdom is impossible. —*Froude.*

The only way to make the mass of mankind see the beauty of justice, is by showing them, in pretty plain terms, the consequence of injustice.—*Sydney Smith.*

Be just and fear not; let all the ends thou aimest at be thy country's, thy God's, and truth's.—*Shakespeare.*

To embarrass justice by a multiplicity of laws, or hazard it by a confidence in our judges, are, I grant, the opposite rocks on which legislative wisdom has ever split; in one case the client resembles that emperor who is said to have been suffocated with the bedclothes, which were only designed to keep him warm; in the other, that town which let the enemy take possession of its walls, in order to show the world how little they depended upon aught but courage for safety.—*Goldsmith.*

The just, though they hate evil, yet give men a patient hearing; hoping that they will show proofs that they are not evil.—*Sir P. Sidney.*

Of mortal justice if thou scorn the rod, believe and tremble, thou art judged of God.—*Sweetman.*

Whenever a separation is made between liberty and justice, neither, in my opinion, is safe.—*Burke.*

All are not just because they do no wrong; but he who will not wrong me when he may, he is truly just.—*Cumberland.*

Justice delayed, is justice denied.— *Gladstone.*

At present we can only reason of the divine justice from what we know of justice in man. When we are in other scenes we may have truer and nobler ideas of it; but while in this life we can only speak from the volume that is laid open before us.—*Pope.*

Justice, like lightning, ever should appear to few men's ruin, but to all men's fear.—*Sweetman.*

Justice advances with such languid steps that crime often escapes from its slowness. Its tardy and doubtful course causes many tears to be shed.—*Corneille.*

Strike if you will, but hear me.—*Themistocles.*

When Infinite Wisdom established the rule of right and honesty, He saw to it that justice should be always the highest expediency.—*Wendell Phillips.*

What is in conformity with justice should also be in conformity to the laws. —*Socrates.*

Justice shines in smoky cottages, and honors the pious. Leaving with averted eyes the gorgeous glare obtained by polluted hands, she is wont to draw nigh to holiness, not reverencing wealth when falsely stamped with praise, and assigning to each deed its righteous doom.— *Æschylus.*

God's mill grinds slow but sure.— *Herbert.*

Mankind are always found prodigal both of blood and treasure in the maintenance of public justice.—*Hume.*

Were he my brother, nay my kingdom's heir, such neighbor nearness to our sacred blood should nothing privilege him, nor partialize the unstooping firmness of my upright soul.—*Shakespeare.*

How can a people be free that has not learned to be just?—*Sieyès.*

He who is only just is cruel.—Who on earth could live were all judged justly? —*Byron.*

Justice and power must be brought together, so that whatever is just may be powerful, and whatever is powerful may be just.—*Pascal.*

Justice is to give to every man his own.—*Aristotle.*

We ought always to deal justly, not only with those who are just to us, but likewise to those who endeavor to injure us; and this, for fear lest by rendering them evil for evil, we should fall into the same vice.—*Hierocles.*

If thou desire rest unto thy soul, be just.—He that doth no injury, fears not to suffer injury; the unjust mind is always in labor; it either practises the evil it hath projected, or projects to

avoid the evil it hath deserved.—*Quarles.*

Justice without strength, or strength without justice—fearful misfortunes!— *Joubert.*

No obligation to justice does force a man to be cruel, or to use the sharpest sentence. A just man does justice to every man and to everything; and then, if he be also wise, he knows there is a debt of mercy and compassion due to the infirmities of man's nature; and that is to be paid; and he that is cruel and ungentle to a sinning person, and does the worst to him, is in his debt and is unjust.—*Jeremy Taylor.*

God gives manhood but one clue to success, utter and exact justice; that, he guarantees, shall be always expediency. —*Wendell Phillips.*

Use every man after his desert, and who should escape whipping?—*Shakespeare.*

Justice is the great and simple principle which is the secret of success in all government, as essential to the training of an infant, as to the control of a mighty nation.—*Simms.*

Justice is the first virtue of those who command, and stops the complaints of those who obey.—*Diderot.*

Justice is the idea of God; the ideal of men; the rule of conduct writ in the nature of mankind.—*Theodore Parker.*

Justice is the great interest of man on earth. It is the ligament which holds civilized beings and civilized nations together. Wherever her temple stands, and so long as it is duly honored, there is a foundation for social security, general happiness, and the improvement and progress of our race. And whoever labors on this edifice with usefulness and distinction, whoever clears its foundations, strengthens its pillars, adorns its entablatures, or contributes to raise its august dome still higher in the skies, connects himself, in name, and fame, and character, with that which is and must be as durable as the frame of human society.—*Daniel Webster.*

He who goes no further than bare justice, stops at the beginning of virtue. —*Blair.*

Justice consists in doing no injury to men; decency in giving them no offense. —*Cicero.*

Justice is the insurance we have on

our lives and property, and obedience is the premium we pay for it.—*Penn.*

Justice, when equal scales she holds, is blind; nor cruelty, nor mercy, change her mind; when some escape for that which others die, mercy to those to these is cruelty.—*Denham.*

The sentiment of justice is so natural, and so universally acquired by all mankind, that it seems to be independent of all law, all party, all religion.—*Voltaire.*

Justice is the bread of the nation; it is always hungry for it.—*Chateaubriand.*

An honest man nearly always thinks justly.—*Rousseau.*

K

KINDNESS.—Life is made up, not of great sacrifices or duties, but of little things, in which smiles, and kindnesses, and small obligations, given habitually, are what win and preserve the heart and secure comfort.—*Sir H. Davy.*

Kindness is the golden chain by which society is bound together.—*Goethe.*

The drying up a single tear, has more of honest fame, than shedding seas of gore.—*Byron.*

Kindness in women, not their beauteous looks, shall win my love.—*Shakespeare.*

I expect to pass through life but once. —If therefore, there be any kindness I can show, or any good thing I can do to any fellow-being, let me do it now, and not defer or neglect it, as I shall not pass this way again.—*Penn.*

Kind looks, kind words, kind acts, and warm handshakes—these are secondary means of grace when men are in trouble and are fighting their unseen battles.— *John Hall.*

The best portion of a good man's life is his little, nameless, unremembered acts of kindness and of love.—*Wordsworth.*

A kind heart is a fountain of gladness, making everything in its vicinity freshen into smiles.—*Washington Irving.*

It is good for us to think no grace or blessing truly ours till we are aware that God has blessed some one else with it through us.—*Phillips Brooks.*

Kindness is a language the dumb can speak, and the deaf can hear and understand.—*Bovee.*

The true and noble way to kill a foe, is not to kill him; you, with kindness, may so change him that he shall cease to be a foe, and then he's slain.—*Aleyn.*

He hath a tear for pity, and a hand open as day for melting charity.—*Shakespeare.*

You may find people ready enough to do the Samaritan without the oil and two-pence.—*Sydney Smith.*

Paradise is open to all kind hearts.— *Béranger.*

Kind words produce their own image in men's souls; and a beautiful image it is. They soothe and quiet and comfort the hearer. They shame him out of his sour, morose, unkind feelings. We have not yet begun to use kind words in such abundance as they ought to be used.—*Pascal.*

Each one of us is bound to make the little circle in which he lives better and happier. Bound to see that out of that small circle the widest good may flow. Each may have fixed in his mind the thought that out of a single household may flow influences that shall stimulate the whole commonwealth and the whole civilized world.—*A. P. Stanley.*

Kindness in ourselves is the honey that blunts the sting of unkindness in another.—*Landor.*

An effort made for the happiness of others lifts above ourselves.—*L. M. Child.*

Ask thyself, daily, to how many ill-minded persons thou hast shown a kind disposition.—*Marcus Antoninus.*

There will come a time when three words, uttered with charity and meekness, shall receive a far more blessed reward, than three thousand volumes written with disdainful sharpness of wit. But the manner of men's writing must not alienate our hearts from the truth, if it appear they have the truth.—*H. Hooker.*

When death, the great reconciler, has come, it is never our tenderness that we repent of, but our severity.—*George Eliot.*

Kindness is the only charm permitted to the aged; it is the coquetry of white hair.—*Feuillet.*

Sow good services; sweet remembrances will grow from them.—*Mad. de Staël.*

To cultivate kindness is a valuable part of the business of life.—*Johnson.*

He who confers a favor should at once forget it, if he is not to show a sordid, ungenerous spirit. To remind a man of a kindness conferred on him, and to talk of it, is little different from reproach.—*Demosthenes.*

We may scatter the seeds of courtesy and kindness about us at little expense. —Some of them will fall on good ground, and grow up into benevolence in the minds of others, and all of them will bear fruit of happiness in the bosom whence they spring.—Once blest are all the virtues; twice blest, sometimes.—*Bentham.*

I had rather never receive a kindness, than never bestow one.—Not to return a benefit is the greater sin, but not to confer it, is the earlier.—*Seneca.*

The one who will be found in trial capable of great acts of love is ever the one who is always doing considerate small ones.—*F. W. Robertson.*

Kind words prevent a good deal of that perverseness which rough and imperious usage often produces in generous minds.—*Locke.*

The happiness of life may be greatly increased by small courtesies in which there is no parade, whose voice is too still to tease, and which manifest themselves by tender and affectionate looks, and little kind acts of attention.—*Sterne.*

What we do for ours while we have them, will be precisely what will render their memory sweet to the heart when we no longer have them.—*F. Godet.*

Kind hearts are more than coronets, and simple faith than Norman blood.—*Tennyson.*

Win hearts, and you have all men's hands and purses.—*Burleigh.*

A word of kindness is seldom spoken in vain, while witty sayings are as easily lost as the pearls slipping from a broken string.—*G. D. Prentice.*

I have sped much by land, and sea, and mingled with much people, but never yet could find a spot unsunned by human kindness.—*Tupper.*

What do we live for, if it is not to make life less difficult to each other?—*George Eliot*

He that will not give some portion of his ease, his blood, his wealth, for others' good, is a poor, frozen churl.—*Joanna Baillie.*

The cheapest of all things is kindness, its exercise requiring the least possible trouble and self-sacrifice.—*Smiles.*

In the intercourse of social life, it is by little acts of watchful kindness recurring daily and hourly, by words, tones, gestures, looks, that affection is won and preserved.—*Sala.*

Kindness seems to come with a double grace and tenderness from the old.—It seems in them the hoarded and long purified benevolence of years, as if it had survived and conquered the baseness and selfishness of the ordeal it had passed —as if the winds which had broken the form, had swept in vain across the heart, and the frosts which had chilled the blood, and whitened the thin locks, had no power over the warm tide of the affections.—*Bulwer.*

The last, best fruit which comes to late perfection, even in the kindliest soul, is tenderness toward the hard, forbearance toward the unforbearing, warmth of heart toward the cold, philanthropy toward the misanthropic. — *Richter.*

The kindness of some is too much like the echo, returning the counterpart of what it receives, not more, and sometimes less.—*Bowers.*

Half the misery of human life might be extinguished if men would alleviate the general curse they lie under by mutual offices of compassion, benevolence, and humanity.—*Addison.*

Heaven in sunshine will requite the kind.—*Byron.*

How easy is it for one benevolent being to diffuse pleasure around him, and how truly is a kind heart a fountain of gladness, making everything in its vicinity to freshen into smiles.—*Washington Irving.*

Kindness is wisdom; there is none in life but needs it, and may learn.—*Bailey.*

Since trifles make the sum of human things, and half our misery from our foibles springs; since life's best joys consist in peace and ease, and few can save or serve, but all may please; let the ungentle spirit learn from thence, a small unkindness is a great offense.—*H. More.*

It is one of the beautiful compensations of life that no man can sincerely try to help another, without helping himself.

Both man and womankind belie their nature when they are not kind.—*Bailey.*

Make a rule, and pray to God to help you to keep it, never, if possible, to lie down at night without being able to say: "I have made one human being at least a little wiser, or a little happier, or at least a little better this day."—*Charles Kingsley.*

We cannot be just unless we are kind-hearted.—*Vauvenargues.*

KINGS.—Uneasy lies the head that wears a crown.—*Shakespeare.*

He who reflects attentively upon the duties of a king, trembles at the sight of a crown.—*Levis.*

Kings, in this chiefly, should imitate God; their mercy should be above all their works.—*Penn.*

One of the strongest natural proofs of the folly of hereditary right in kings is, that nature disapproves it; otherwise she would not so frequently turn it into ridicule by giving mankind an ass in place of a lion.—*Thomas Paine.*

Kings wish to be absolute, and they are sometimes told that their best way to become so is to make themselves beloved by the people. This maxim is doubtless a very admirable one, and in some respects true; but unhappily it is laughed at in court.—*Rousseau.*

Implements of war and subjugation are the last arguments to which kings resort.—*Patrick Henry.*

It is the misfortune of kings that they scarcely ever do the good they have a mind to do; and through surprise, and the insinuations of flatterers, they often do the mischief they never intended.—*Fénelon.*

He on whom Heaven confers a sceptre knows not the weight till he bears it.—*Corneille.*

Kings' titles commonly begin by force, which time wears off and mellows into right; and power which in one age is tyranny is ripened in the next to true succession.—*Dryden.*

The people are fashioned according to the example of their king; and edicts are of less power than the model which his life exhibits.—*Claudian.*

Royalty consists not in vain pomp, but in great virtues.—*Agesilaus.*

Wise kings generally have wise counsellors; and he must be a wise man himself who is capable of distinguishing one. —*Diogenes.*

The king is but a man, as I am; the violet smells to him as it doth to me; the element shows to him as it doth to me; all his senses have but human conditions; his ceremonies laid by, in his nakedness he appears but a man; and though his affections are higher mounted than ours, yet when they stoop, they stoop with the like wing.—*Shakespeare.*

Happy the kings whose thrones are founded on their people's hearts.—*Ford.*

A crown, golden in show, is but a wreath of thorns; brings danger, troubles, cares, and sleepless nights, to him who wears a regal diadem.—*Milton.*

The example of a vicious prince will corrupt an age, but that of a good one will not reform it.—*Swift.*

The king who delegates his power to other's hands but ill deserves the crown he wears.—*Brooke.*

In sovereignty it is a most happy thing not to be compelled, but so it is a most miserable thing not to be counselled.—*Ben Jonson.*

A sovereign's great example forms a people; the public breast is noble or vile as he inspires it.—*Mallett.*

Princes are never without flatterers to seduce them; ambition to deprave them; and desires to corrupt them.—*Plato.*

All precepts concerning kings are comprehended in these: remember thou art a man; remember thou art God's vicegerent.—*Bacon.*

The king will best govern his realm who reigneth over his people as a father doth over his children.—*Agesilaus.*

The kingdom of God is the only absolute monarchy that is free from despotism.—*C. Simmons.*

KISSES.—A kiss from my mother made me a painter.—*Benjamin West.*

A long, long kiss—the kiss of youth and love.—*Byron.*

It is the passion that is in a kiss that gives to it its sweetness; it is the affection in a kiss that sanctifies it.—*Bovee.*

Kisses are like grains of gold or silver found upon the ground, of no value themselves, but precious as showing that a mine is near.—*George Villiers.*

Stolen kisses are always sweetest.—*Leigh Hunt.*

It is as old as the creation, and yet as young and fresh as ever. It pre-existed, still exists, and always will exist. Depend upon it, Eve learned it in Paradise, and was taught its beauties, virtues, and varieties by an angel, there is something so transcendent in it.—*Haliburton.*

Leave but a kiss in the cup, and I'll not look for wine.—*Ben Jonson.*

Eden revives in the first kiss of love.—*Byron.*

Dear — remembered kisses after death.—*Tennyson.*

Four sweet lips, two pure souls, and one undying affection—these are love's pretty ingredients for a kiss.—*Bovee.*

And steal immortal kisses from her lips, which, even in pure and vestal modesty, still blush as thinking their own kisses sin.—*Shakespeare.*

He kissed her and promised. Such beautiful lips! Man's usual fate—he was lost upon the coral reefs.—*Douglass Jerrold.*

That farewell kiss which resembles greeting, that last glance of love which becomes the sharpest pang of sorrow.—*George Eliot.*

You would think that, if our lips were made of horn, and stuck out a foot or two from our faces, kisses at any rate would be done for. Not so. No creatures kiss each other so much as birds.—*Buxton.*

I clasp thy waist; I feel thy bosom's beat.—O, kiss me into faintness, sweet and dim.—*Alexander Smith.*

And with a velvet lip, print on his brow such language as tongue hath never spoken.—*Mrs. Sigourney.*

There is the kiss of welcome and of parting; the long, lingering, loving, present one; the stolen, or the mutual one; the kiss of love, of joy, and of sorrow; the seal of promise and receipt of fulfilment. Is it strange, therefore, that a woman is invincible whose armory consists of kisses, smiles, sighs, and tears?—*Haliburton.*

Upon thy cheek I lay this zealous kiss, as seal to the indenture of my love.—*Shakespeare.*

A soft lip would tempt you to eternity of kissing.—*Ben Jonson.*

Now by the jealous queen of heaven, that kiss I carried from thee, dear, my true lip hath virgin'd it e'er since.—*Shakespeare.*

I felt the while a pleasing kind of smart; the kiss went tingling to my panting heart.—When it was gone, the sense of it did stay; the sweetness cling'd upon my lips all day, like drops of honey, loth to fall away.—*Dryden.*

Some say kissing is a sin; but if it was na lawful, lawyers would na allow it; if it was na holy, ministers would na do it; if it was na modest, maidens would na take it; if it was na plenty, puir folk would na get it.—*Burns.*

Blush, happy maiden, when you feel the lips that press love's glowing seal.—But as the slow years darker roll, grown wiser, the experienced soul will own as dearer far than they the lips which kiss the tears away.—*Elizabeth Akers.*

His kissing is as full of sanctity as the touch of holy bread.—*Shakespeare.*

Once he drew, with one long kiss, my whole soul through my lips.—*Tennyson.*

Then he kissed me hard, as if he plucked up kisses by the roots, that grew upon my lips.—*Shakespeare.*

KNAVERY.—(See "CUNNING.")

After long experience in the world, I affirm, before God, that I never knew a rogue who was not unhappy.—*Junius.*

The worst of all knaves are those who can mimic their former honesty.—*Lavater.*

Unluckily the credulity of dupes is as inexhaustible as the invention of knaves. They never give people possession; but they always keep them in hope.—*Burke.*

By fools knaves fatten; every knave finds a gull.—*Zimmerman.*

Take heed of an ox before, an ass behind, and a knave on all sides.—*Old Proverb.*

Knaves will thrive where honest plainness knows not how to live.—*Shirley.*

A very honest man, and a very good understanding, may be deceived by a knave.—*Junius.*

There is nothing seems so like an

honest man as an artful knave.—*C. Simmons.*

A knave thinks himself a fool all the time he is not making a fool of some other person.—*Hazlitt.*

KNOWLEDGE.—(See "IGNORANCE" and "WISDOM.")

The first step to knowledge is to know that we are ignorant.—*Cecil.*

They who know the most must mourn the deepest o'er the fatal truth that the tree of knowledge is not the tree of life.

Every branch of knowledge which a good man possesses, he may apply to some good purpose.—*C. Buchanan.*

The more you practice what you know, the more shall you know what to practice.—*W. Jenkin.*

Accurate knowledge is the basis of correct opinions; the want of it makes the opinions of most people of little value.—*C. Simmons.*

We know accurately only when we know little; with knowledge doubt increases.—*Goethe.*

It is not so important to know everything as to know the exact value of everything, to appreciate what we learn, and to arrange what we know.—*H. More.*

Knowledge is not a couch whereon to rest a searching and restless spirit; or a terrace for a wandering mind to walk up and down with a fair prospect; or a tower of state for a proud mind to raise itself upon; or a sort of commanding ground for strife and contention; or a shop for profit and sale; but a rich storehouse for the glory of the Creator, and the relief of man's estate.—*Bacon.*

The essence of knowledge is, having it, to apply it; not having it, to confess your ignorance.—*Confucius.*

He fancies himself enlightened, because he sees the deficiencies of others; he is ignorant, because he has never reflected on his own.—*Bulwer.*

He that would make real progress in knowledge, must dedicate his age as well as youth, the latter growth as well as the first fruits, at the altar of truth.—*Berkeley.*

The expression, "Knowledge is power," is used by Lord Bacon; but it had its origin long before his time, in the saying of Solomon, that "a wise man is strong: yea, a man of knowledge increaseth strength."

Socrates said that a knowledge of our own ignorance is the first step toward true knowledge.—And Coleridge said, We cannot make another comprehend our knowledge until we first comprehend his ignorance.

"Knowledge," says Bacon, "is power"; but mere knowledge is not power; it is only possibility. Action is power; and its highest manifestation is when it is directed by knowledge.—*T. W. Palmer.*

The end of all learning is to know God, and out of that knowledge to love and imitate him.—*Milton.*

Knowledge is said to be power: and it is power in the same sense that wood is fuel. Wood on fire is fuel. Knowledge on fire is power. There is no more power in knowledge than there is in the stones or stars, unless there be a spirit and life in the knowledge which give it its energy. In proportion as men have this spiritual power they become strong in the world.—*A. Mackenzie.*

The wise carry their knowledge, as they do their watches, not for display, but for their own use.

I envy no man that knows more than myself, but pity them that know less.—*Sir T. Browne.*

Every increase of knowledge may possibly render depravity more depraved, as well as it may increase the strength of virtue. It is in itself only power; and its value depends on its application.—*Sydney Smith.*

What is not fully understood is not possessed.—*Goethe.*

"Know thyself" means this, that you get acquainted with what you know, and what you can do.—*Menander.*

In many things a comprehensive survey of a subject is the shortest way of getting at a precise knowledge of a particular division of it.—*Charles Hodge.*

Knowledge, like religion, must be "experienced" in order to be known.—*E. P. Whipple.*

The sure foundations of the state are laid in knowledge, not in ignorance; and every sneer at education, at culture, at book learning, which is the recorded wisdom of the experience of mankind, is the demagogue's sneer at intelligent liberty, inviting national degeneracy and ruin.—*G. W. Curtis.*

The desire of knowledge, like the thirst of riches, increases ever with the acquisition of it.—*Sterne.*

The brightest blaze of intelligence is of incalculably less value than the smallest spark of charity.—*W. Nevins.*

The pleasure and delight of knowledge far surpasseth all other in nature. We see in all other pleasures there is satiety; and after they be used, their verdure departeth, which showeth well that they be but deceits of pleasure, and not pleasures; and that it was the novelty which pleased, not the quality; and therefore we see that voluptuous men turn friars, and ambitious princes turn melancholy. But of knowledge there is no satiety, but satisfaction and appetite are perpetually interchangeable.—*Bacon.*

It is wise to get knowledge and learning from every source—from a sot, a pot, a fool, a winter-mitten, or an old slipper.—*Rabelais.*

Reading maketh a full man; conference, a ready man: histories make men wise; poets, witty; the mathematics, subtle; natural philosophy, deep; moral philosophy, grave; logic and rhetoric, able to contend.—*Bacon.*

What novelty is worth the sweet monotony where everything is known, and loved because it is known?—*George Eliot.*

The seeds of knowledge may be planted in solitude, but must be cultivated in public.—*Johnson.*

Knowledge dwells in heads replete with thoughts of other men; wisdom, in minds attentive to their own.—*Cowper.*

Whatever our intellectual calling, no kind of knowledge is antagonistic to it. —All varieties of knowledge blend with, harmonize, and enrich the one kind of knowledge to which we attach our reputation.—*Bulwer.*

Knowledge is but folly unless it is guided by grace.—*Herbert.*

Mere knowledge is comparatively worthless unless digested into practical wisdom and common sense as applied to the affairs of life.—*Tryon Edwards.*

Man is not born to solve the problem of the universe, but to find out what he has to do; and to restrain himself within the limits of his comprehension.—*Goethe.*

Knowledge is more than equivalent to force. ·The master of mechanics laughs at strength.—*Johnson.*

What a man knows should find its expression in what he does; the value of superior knowledge is chiefly in that it leads to a performing manhood.—*Bovee.*

There is no knowledge for which so great a price is paid as a knowledge of the world; and no one ever became an adept in it except at the expense of a hardened and a wounded heart. — *Countess of Blessington.*

If you would thoroughly know anything, teach it to others.—*Tryon Edwards.*

Real knowledge, like everything else of value, is not to be obtained easily. It must be worked for, studied for, thought for, and, more than all, must be prayed for.—*T. Arnold.*

Most men want knowledge, not for itself, but for the superiority which knowledge confers; and the means they employ to secure this superiority are as wrong as the ultimate object, for no man can ever end with being superior, who will not begin with being inferior.—*Sydney Smith.*

There is nothing makes a man suspect much, more than to know little; and, therefore, men should remedy suspicion by procuring to know more, and not keep their suspicions in smother.—*Bacon.*

A grain of real knowledge, of genuine uncontrollable conviction, will outweigh a bushel of adroitness; and to produce persuasion there is one golden principle of rhetoric not put down in the books —to understand what you are talking about.—*Seeley.*

"Knowledge, without common sense," says Lee, "is folly; without method, it is waste; without kindness, it is fanaticism; without religion, it is death." But with common sense, it is wisdom; with method, it is power; with charity, it is beneficence; with religion, it is virtue and life and peace.—*Farrar.*

There is nothing so minute, or inconsiderable, that I would not rather know it than not.—*Johnson.*

It was said of one of the most intelligent men who ever lived in New England, that when asked how he came to know so much about everything, he replied, By constantly realizing my own ignorance, and never being afraid or ashamed to ask questions.—*Tryon Edwards*.

It is the glorious prerogative of the empire of knowledge, that what it gains it never loses. On the contrary, it increases by the multiple of its own power; all its ends become means; all its attainments help to new conquests.—*Daniel Webster*.

To comprehend a man's life it is necessary to know not merely what he does, but also what he purposely leaves undone. There is a imit to the work that can be got out of a human body or a human brain, and e is a wise man who wastes no energy on pursuits for which he is not fitted; and he is still wiser who, from among the things that he can do well, chooses and resolutely follows the best.—*Gladstone*.

Ignorance is the curse of God; knowledge is the wing wherewith we fly to heaven.—*Shakespeare*.

The love of knowledge in a young mind is almost a warrant against the infirm excitement of passions and vices.—*H. W. Beecher*.

All the knowledge that we mortals can acquire is not knowledge positive, but knowledge comparative, and subject to the errors and passions of humanity.—*Bulwer*.

In many things it is not well to say, "Know thyself"; it is better to say, "Know others."—*Menander*.

With the gain of knowledge, connect the habit of imparting it. This increases mental wealth by putting it in circulation; and it enhances the value of our knowledge to ourselves, not only in its depth, confirmation, and readiness for use, but in that acquaintance with human nature, that self-command, and that reaction of moral training upon ourselves, which are above all price.—*Mrs. Sigourney*.

Seldom ever was any knowledge given to keep, but to impart; the grace of this rich jewel is lost in concealment.—*Bp. Hall*.

A taste of every sort of knowledge is necessary to form the mind, and is the only way to give the understanding its due improvement to the full extent of its capacity.—*Locke*.

Does your doctor know anything?—I don't mean about medicine, but about things in general?—Is he a man of information and good sense?—If he does not know anything but medicine, the chance is that he does not know much about that.

Knowledge once gained casts a light beyond its own immediate boundaries.—*Tyndall*.

To know by rote is no knowledge; it is only a retention of what is entrusted to the memory. That which a man truly knows may be disposed of without regard to the author, or reference to the book from whence he had it.—*Montaigne*.

The knowledge we have acquired ought not to resemble a great shop without order, and without an inventory; we ought to know what we possess, and be able to make it serve us in our need.—*Leibnitz*.

Properly, there is no other knowledge but that which is got by working; the rest is yet all a hypothesis of knowledge; a thing to be argued of in schools; a thing floating in the clouds, in endless logic-vortices, till we try and fix it.—*Carlyle*.

To know that which before us lies in daily life, is the prime wisdom; what is more is fume, or emptiness, or fond impertinence, and renders us, in things that most concern, unpracticed and unprepared.—*Milton*.

Knowledge has, in our time, triumphed, and is triumphing, over prejudice and over bigotry. The civilized and Christian world is fast learning the great lesson, that difference of nation does not imply necessary hostility, and that all contact need not be war. The whole world is becoming a common field for intellect to act in. Energy of mind, genius, power, wheresoever it exists, may speak out in any tongue, and the world will hear it.—*Daniel Webster*.

The more extensive a man's knowledge of what has been done, the greater will be his power of knowing what to do.—*Disraeli*.

The shortest and the surest way of arriving at real knowledge is to unlearn the lessons we have been taught, to remount the first principles, and take nobody's word about them.—*Bolingbroke.*

Fullness of knowledge always and necessarily means some understanding of the depths of our ignorance, and that is always conducive to both humility and reverence.—*Robert Andrews Millikan.*

Scientific knowledge is constantly changing. A discovery of one year receives confirmation the next or is thrown aside.—*James T. Adams.*

For the aims of my own career, I want to promote the increase of natural knowledge, and to forward the application of scientific methods of investigation to all the problems of life, in the conviction that there is no alleviation for the sufferings of mankind except veracity of thought and action, and the resolute facing of the world as it is, when the garment of make-believe is stripped off.—*Thomas H. Huxley.*

There is but one bond of peace that is both permanent and enriching: the increasing knowledge of the world in which experiment occurs.—*Walter Lippman.*

Our present knowledge of the universe is such as to leave us with a very inadequate conception of the majesty of existence.—*Oliver J. Lodge.*

Knowledge of our duties is the most essential part of the philosophy of life. If you escape duty you avoid action. The world demands results.—*George W. Goethals.*

Knowledge may not be as a courtesan, for pleasure and vanity only; or as a bondswoman, to acquire and gain for her master's use; but as a spouse, for generation, fruit, and comfort.—*Bacon.*

The profoundly wise do not declaim against superficial knowledge in others, so much as the profoundly ignorant; on the contrary, they would rather assist it with their advice than overwhelm it with their contempt; for they know that there was a period when even a Bacon or a Newton were superficial, and that he who has a little knowledge is far more likely to get more than he that has none.—*Colton.*

If you have knowledge, let others light their candles at it.—*Fuller.*

Never carry your shotgun or your knowledge at half-cock.—*Austin O'Malley.*

Nothing in this life, after health and virtue, is more estimable than knowledge,—nor is there anything so easily attained, or so cheaply purchased,—the labor, only sitting still, and the expense but time, which, if we do not spend, we cannot save.—*Sterne.*

Many of the supposed increasers of knowledge have only given a new name, and often a worse, to what was well known before.—*Hare.*

Knowledge conquered by labor becomes a possession,—a property entirely our own. A greater vividness and permanency of impression is secured, and facts thus acquired become registered in the mind in a way that mere imparted information can never produce.—*Carlyle.*

When a king asked Euclid, whether he could not explain his art to him in a more compendious manner, he was answered, that there was no royal way to geometry. Other things may be seized by might, or purchased with money; but knowledge is to be gained only by study, and study to be prosecuted only in retirement.—*Johnson.*

Knowledge and timber should not be much used until they are seasoned.—*O. W. Holmes.*

In the present state of medical knowledge a pronouncement of the sentence of "incurable" on a patient places a serious responsibility on the physician and implies a greater knowledge than he possesses.—*Dr. Ernst P. Boas.*

We face the future with a weapon in our hands that was not given to earlier rulers of the world—I mean scientific knowledge, and the capacity for increasing it indefinitely by scientific research.—*Sir James Jeans.*

The true scientist recognizes the fact that scientific knowledge is a narrow thing, it rules out the ecstasy of life. It can only speak of that which it can handle with its hands and see with its eyes.—*Dr. Robert Norwood.*

If a little knowledge is dangerous, where is the man who has so much as to be out of danger?—*Thomas H. Huxley.*

Man often acquires just so much knowledge as to discover his ignorance, and attains so much experience as to see and regret his follies, and then dies. —*Clulow.*

Knowledge is a comfortable and necessary retreat and shelter for us in advanced age, and if we do not plant it while young, it will give us no shade when we grow old.—*Chesterfield.*

Your learning, like the lunar beam, affords light but not heat; it leaves you undevout, and frozen at heart, while speculation shines.—*Young.*

Knowledge is the consequence of time, and multitude of days are fittest to teach wisdom.—*Collier.*

What we know here is very little, but what we are ignorant of is immense.— *Laplace.*

Charles V. said that a man who knew four languages was worth four men; and Alexander the Great so valued learning, that he used to say he was more indebted to Aristotle for giving him knowledge, than to his father Philip for giving him life.

Every generation enjoys the use of a vast hoard bequeathed to it by antiquity, and transmits that hoard, augmented by fresh acquisitions, to future ages.—*Macaulay.*

He that sips of many arts, drinks of none.—*Fuller.*

Knowledge will not be acquired without pains and application. It is troublesome and deep digging for pure waters; but when once you come to the spring, they rise up and meet you.— *Felton.*

The end of all knowledge should be in virtuous action.—*Sir P. Sidney.*

Real knowledge, in its progress, is the forerunner of liberality and enlightened toleration.—*Brougham.*

He who calls in the aid of an equal understanding, doubles his own; and he who profits by a superior understanding, raises his powers to a level with the height of the understanding he unites with.—*Burke.*

A great deal of knowledge, which is not capable of making a man wise, has a natural tendency to make him vain and arrogant.—*Addison.*

Every man of sound brain whom you meet knows something worth knowing better than yourself. A man, on the whole, is a better preceptor than a book. But what scholar does not allow that the dullest book can suggest to him a new and a sound idea?—*Bulwer.*

A little knowledge leads the mind from God. Unripe thinkers use their learning to authenticate their doubts. While unbelief has its own dogma, more peremptory than the inquisitor's, patient meditation brings the scholar back to humbleness. He learns that the grandest truths appear slowly.—*Willmott.*

It is in knowledge as it is in plants; if you mean to use the plant, it is no matter for the roots; if you mean it to grow, it is safer to rest upon roots than upon slips.—*Bacon.*

All wish to possess knowledge, but few, comparatively speaking, are willing to pay the price.—*Juvenal.*

Some men think that the gratification of curiosity is the end of knowledge; some the love of fame; some the pleasure of dispute; some the necessity of supporting themselves by their knowledge; but the real use of all knowledge is this, that we should dedicate that reason which was given us by God to the use and advantage of man.—*Bacon.*

As soon as a true thought has entered our mind, it gives a light which makes us see a crowd of other objects which we have never perceived before.— *Chateaubriand.*

If a man empties his purse into his head, no one can take it away from him. —An investment in knowledge always pays the best interest.—*Franklin.*

Human learning, with the blessing of God upon it, introduces us to divine wisdom; and while we study the works of nature, the God of nature will manifest himself to us; since, to a well-tutored mind, "The heavens declare his glory, and the firmament sheweth his handiwork."—*Bp. Horne.*

Knowledge always desires increase; it is like fire, which must first be kindled by some external agent, but which will afterward propagate itself.—*Johnson.*

The dangers of knowledge are not to be compared with the dangers of ignorance. Man is more likely to miss his way in darkness than in twilight; in twilight than in full sun.—*Whately*.

One part of knowledge consists in being ignorant of such things as are not worthy to be known.—*Crates*.

Imparting knowledge is only lighting other men's candle at our lamp, without depriving ourselves of any flame.—*Jane Porter*.

The best part of our knowledge is that which teaches us where knowledge leaves off and ignorance begins.—*O. W. Holmes*.

Knowledge that terminates in curiosity and speculation is inferior to that which is useful; and of all useful knowledge that is the most so which consists in a due care and just notion of ourselves.—*St. Bernard*.

People disparage knowing and the intellectual life, and urge doing. I am very content with knowing, if only I could know. That is an august entertainment, and would suffice me a great while. To know a little would be worth the expense of this world.—*Emerson*.

Those who come last enter with advantage.—They are born to the wealth of antiquity.—The materials for judging are prepared, and the foundations of knowledge are laid to their hands.—Besides, if the point was tried by antiquity, antiquity would lose it, for the present age is really the oldest, and has the largest experience to plead.—*Collier*.

Base-minded they that lack intelligence; for God himself for wisdom most is praised, and men to God thereby are highest raised.—*Spenser*.

The word knowledge, strictly employed, implies three things, viz., truth, proof, and conviction.—*Whately*.

Pleasure is a shadow, wealth is vanity, and power a pageant; but knowledge is ecstatic in enjoyment, perennial in fame, unlimited in space, and infinite in duration. In the performance of its sacred offices, it fears no danger, spares no expense, looks in the volcano, dives into the ocean, perforates the earth, wings its flight into the skies, explores sea and land, contemplates the distant, examines the minute, comprehends the great, ascends to the sublime—no place too remote for its grasp, no height too exalted for its reach.—*De Witt Clinton*.

L

LABOR.—Labor was the primal curse, but it was softened into mercy, and made the pledge of cheerful days, and nights without a groan.—*Cowper*.

Next to faith in God, is faith in labor.—*Bovee*.

Nothing is denied to well-directed labor, and nothing is ever to be attained without it.—*Sir J. Reynolds*.

Without labor nothing prospers.—*Sophocles*.

Shun no toil to make yourself remarkable by some talent or other. Yet do not devote yourself to one branch exclusively. Strive to get clear notions about all. Give up to no science entirely, for science is but one.—*Seneca*.

The fruit derived from labor is the sweetest of all pleasures.—*Vauvenargues*.

Labor is the divine law of our existence; repose is desertion and suicide.—*Mazzini*.

A man's best friends are his ten fingers.—*Robert Collyer*.

God intends no man to live in this world without working; but it seems to me no less evident that He intends every man to be happy in his work.—*Ruskin*.

Men seldom die of hard work; activity is God's medicine. The highest genius is willingness and ability to do hard work. Any other conception of genius makes it a doubtful, if not a dangerous possession.—*R. S. MacArthur*.

Labor rids us of three great evils—irksomeness, vice, and poverty.—*Voltaire*.

Labor is one of the great elements of society—the great substantial interest on which we all stand. Not feudal service, or predial toil, or the irksome drudgery by one race of mankind subjected, on account of their color, to another; but labor, intelligent, manly, independent, thinking and acting for itself, earning its own wages, accumulating those wages into capital, educating childhood, maintaining worship, claiming the right of the elective franchise, and helping to uphold the great fabric of the State—that is American labor; and all my sympathies are with it, and my voice, till I am dumb, will be for it.—*Daniel Webster*.

From labor, health; from health, contentment springs.—*Beattie*.

No race can prosper 'til it learns that there is as much dignity in tilling the field, as in writing a poem.—*Booker T. Washington*.

Blessed is the man that has found his work.—One monster there is in the world, the idle man.—*Carlyle*.

As steady application to work is the healthiest training for every individual, so is it the best discipline of a state. Honorable industry alway travels the same road with enjoyment and duty, and progress is altogether impossible without it.—*S. Smiles*.

It is only by labor that thought can be made healthy, and only by thought that labor can be made happy; and the two cannot be separated with impunity. *Ruskin*.

If you divorce capital from labor, capital is hoarded, and labor starves.—*Daniel Webster*.

Labor is rest from the sorrows that greet us; from all the petty vexations that meet us; from the sin-promptings that assail us; from the world-sirens that lure us to ill.—*F. S. Osgood*.

There is a perennial nobleness and even sacredness in work.—Were he ever so benighted and forgetful of his high calling, there is always hope in a man who actually and earnestly works.—*Carlyle*.

I find successful exertion is a powerful means of exhilaration, which discharges itself in good humor upon others.—*Chalmers*.

Nature is just toward men. It recompenses them for their sufferings; it renders them laborious, because to the greatest toils it attaches the greatest rewards.—*Montesquieu*.

The true epic of our times is not "arms and the man," but "tools and the man," an infinitely wider kind of epic.—*Carlyle*.

The labor and sweat of our brows is so far from being a curse, that without it our very bread would not be so great a blessing.—If it were not for labor, men could neither eat so much, nor relish so pleasantly, nor sleep so soundly, nor be so healthful, so useful, so strong,

so patient, so noble, nor so untempted. —*Jeremy Taylor*.

You and I toiling for earth, may at the same time be toiling for heaven, and every day's work may be a Jacob's ladder reaching up nearer to God.—*Theodore Parker*.

Work is a great blessing; after evil came into the world, it was given as an antidote, not as a punishment.—*A. S. Hardy*.

No abilities, however splendid, can command success without intense labor and persevering application.—*A. T. Stewart*.

Alexander the Great, reflecting on his friends degenerating into sloth and luxury, told them that it was a most slavish thing to luxuriate, and a most royal thing to labor.—*Barrow*.

The guard of virtue is labor, and ease her sleep.—*Tasso*.

Do what thou dost as if the earth were heaven, and thy last day the day of judgment.—*C. Kingsley*.

Labor is life; from the inmost heart of the worker rises his God-given force, the sacred celestial life-essence breathed into him by Almighty God!—*Carlyle*.

The pernicious, debilitating tendencies of bodily pleasure need to be counteracted by the invigorating exercises of bodily labor; whereas, bodily labor without bodily pleasure converts the body into a mere machine, and brutifies the soul.—*Anon*.

The labor of the body relieves us from the fatigues of the mind; and this it is which forms the happiness of the poor. —*Rochefoucauld*.

Genius begins great works; labor alone finishes them.—*Joubert*.

Toil and pleasure, in their nature opposites, are yet linked together in a kind of necessary connection.—*Livy*.

Love, therefore, labor; if thou shouldst not want it for food, thou mayest for physic. It is wholesome to the body and good for the mind; it prevents the fruit of idleness.—*Penn*.

Avoid idleness, and fill up all the spaces of thy time with severe and useful employment; for lust easily creeps in at those emptinesses where the soul is unemployed and the body is at ease; for no easy, healthful, idle person was ever chaste if he could be tempted; but of all employments, bodily labor is the most useful, and of the greatest benefit for driving away the Devil.—*Jeremy Taylor.*

What men want is not talent, it is purpose; in other words, not the power to achieve, but will to labor. I believe that labor judiciously and continuously applied becomes genius.—*Bulwer.*

There are many ways of being frivolous, only one way of being intellectually great; that is honest labor.—*Sydney Smith.*

Whatever there is of greatness in the United States, or indeed in any other country, is due to labor. The laborer is the author of all greatness and wealth. Without labor there would be no government, and no leading class, and nothing to preserve.—*U. S. Grant.*

Hard workers are usually honest; industry lifts them above temptation.—*Bovee.*

It is to labor and to labor only, that man owes everything of exchangeable value. Labor is the talisman that has raised him from the condition of the savage; that has changed the desert and the forest into cultivated fields; that has covered the earth with cities, and the ocean with ships; that has given us plenty, comfort, and elegance, instead of want, misery, and barbarism.—*J. Macculloch.*

The lottery of honest labor, drawn by time, is the only one whose prizes are worth taking up and carrying home.—*Theodore Parker.*

If we would have anything of benefit, we must earn it, and earning it become shrewd, inventive, ingenious, active, enterprising.—*H. W. Beecher.*

None so little enjoy themselves, and are such burdens to themselves, as those who have nothing to do.—Only the active have the true relish of life.—*Jay.*

Labor is the great producer of wealth; it moves all other causes.—*Daniel Webster.*

Miserable is he who slumbers on in idleness.—There is no rest from labor on earth.—Man is born to work, and he must work while it is day.—Said a great worker, "Have I not eternity to rest in?"—*Tynman.*

There is but one method of success, and that is hard labor; and a man who will not pay that price for distinction had better at once dedicate himself to the pursuit of the fox.—*Sydney Smith.*

Excellence in any department can be attained only by the labor of a lifetime; it is not to be purchased at a lesser price.—*Johnson.*

Men give me some credit for genius. All the genius I have lies just in this: When I have a subject in hand, I study it profoundly. Day and night it is before me. I explore it in all its bearings. My mind becomes pervaded with it. Then the effort which I make the people are pleased to call the fruit of genius. It is the fruit of labor and thought.—*Alexander Hamilton.*

No way has been found for making heroism easy, even for the scholar. Labor, iron labor, is for him. The world was created as an audience for him; the atoms of which it is made are opportunities.—*Emerson.*

I have no secret of success but hard work.—*E. Turner.*

The necessity of labor is a part of the primeval curse; and all the beauty, or glory, or dignity pertaining to it, depends on the ends to which it is the means.—*Bristed.*

Labor—the expenditure of vital effort in some form, is the measure, nay, it is the maker of values.—*J. G. Holland.*

Nothing is impossible to the man who can will, and then do; this is the only law of success.—*Mirabeau.*

LANGUAGE. — (See "WORDS" and "SPEECH.")

Language as well as the faculty of speech, was the immediate gift of God.—*Noah Webster.*

Language is the dress of thought.—*Johnson.*

Language is not only the vehicle of thought, it is a great and efficient instrument in thinking.—*Sir H. Davy.*

Language is the armory of the human mind, and at once contains the trophies of its past and the weapons of its future conquests.—*Coleridge.*

What would the science of language be without missions.—*Max Müller.*

Language is the amber in which a thousand precious thoughts have been safely embedded and preserved. It has arrested ten thousand lightning-flashes of genius, which, unless thus fixed and arrested, might have been as bright, but would have also been as quickly passing and perishing as the lightning. Words convey the mental treasures of one period to the generations that follow; and laden with this, their precious freight, they sail safely across gulfs of time in which empires have suffered shipwreck, and the languages of common life have sunk into oblivion.—*Trench.*

Language most shows a man; speak that I may see thee; it springs out of the most retired and inmost part of us.—*Ben Jonson.*

The common people do not accurately adapt their thoughts to objects; nor, secondly, do they accurately adapt their words to their thoughts; they do not mean to lie; but, taking no pains to be exact, they give you very false accounts. A great part of their language is proverbial; if anything rocks at all, they say it rocks like a cradle; and in this way they go on.—*Johnson.*

If the way in which men express their thoughts is slipshod and mean, it will be very difficult for their thoughts themselves to escape being the same. If it is high flown and bombastic, a character for national simplicity and truthfulness cannot long be maintained.—*Alford.*

The Creator has gifted the whole universe with language, but few are the hearts that can interpret it. Happy those to whom it is no foreign tongue, acquired imperfectly with care and pain, but rather a native language, learned unconsciously from the lips of the great mother.—*Bulwer.*

One great use of words is to hide our thoughts.—*Voltaire.*

Charles V. used to say that "the more languages a man knew, he was so many more times a man." Each new form of human speech introduces one into a new world of thought and life. So in some degree is it in traversing other continents and mingling with other races.

As a hawk flieth not high with one wing, even so a man reacheth not to excellence with one tongue.—*Roger Ascham.*

A man who is ignorant of foreign languages is ignorant of his own.—*Goethe.*

Poetry cannot be translated; and, therefore, it is the poets that preserve the languages; for we would not be at the trouble to learn a language if we could have all that is written in it just as well in a translation. But as the beauties of poetry cannot be preserved in any language except that in which it was originally written, we learn the language.—*Johnson.*

Language is like amber in its efficacy to circulate the electric spirit of truth, it is also like amber in embalming and preserving the relics of ancient wisdom, although one is not seldom puzzled to decipher its contents. Sometimes it locks up truths which were once well known, but which, in the course of ages, have passed out of sight and been forgotten. In other cases it holds the germs of truths, of which, though they were never plainly discerned, the genius of its framers caught a glimpse in a happy moment of divination.—*Sala.*

To acquire a few tongues is the task of a few years; to be eloquent in one is the labor of a life.

A countryman is as warm in fustian as a king in velvet, and a truth is as comfortable in homely language as in fine speech. As to the way of dishing up the meat, hungry men leave that to the cook, only let the meat be sweet and substantial.—*Spurgeon.*

The language denotes the man; a coarse or refined character finds its expression naturally in a coarse or refined phraseology.—*Bovee.*

In the commerce of speech use only coin of gold and silver.—*Joubert.*

Language is properly the servant of thought, but not unfrequently becomes its master. The conceptions of a feeble writer are greatly modified by his style; a man of vigorous powers makes his style bend to his conceptions—a fact compatible enough with the acknowledgment of Dryden, that a rhyme had often helped him to an idea.—*Clulow.*

Felicity, not fluency of language, is a merit.—*E. P. Whipple.*

Thinking cannot be clear till it has had expression.—We must write, or speak, or act our thoughts, or they will remain in a half torpid form.—Our feelings must have expression, or they will be as clouds, which, till they descend in rain, will never bring up fruit or flower. —So it is with all the inward feelings; expression gives them development.— Thought is the blossom; language the opening bud; action the fruit behind it. —*H. W. Beecher.*

In the intercourse of the world people should not take words as so much genuine coin of standard metal, but merely as counters that people play with.— *Jerrold.*

Language is a solemn thing: it grows out of life—out of its agonies and ecstasies, its wants and its weariness.— Every language is a temple in which the soul of those who speak it is enshrined. —*O. W. Holmes.*

There is no tracing the connection of ancient nations but by language; therefore I am always sorry when any language is lost, for languages are the pedigree of nations.—*Johnson.*

There was speech in their dumbness; language in their very gesture.—*Shakespeare.*

Language is only the instrument of science, and words are but the signs of ideas.—*Johnson.*

Language was given us that we might say pleasant things to each other. —*Bovee.*

Languages, like our bodies, are in a perpetual flux, and stand in need of recruits to supply those words which are continually falling into disuse.—*Felton.*

Words are the leaves of the tree of language, of which, if some fall away, a new succession takes their place.— *French.*

LAUGHTER. — (See "CHEERFULNESS.")

A laugh is worth a hundred groans in any market.—*Lamb.*

It is a good thing to laugh, at any rate; and if a straw can tickle a man, it is an instrument of happiness. Beasts can weep when they suffer, but they cannot laugh.—*Dryden.*

Even this vein of laughing, as I could produce out of grave authors, hath oftentimes a strong and sinewy force in teaching and comforting.—*Milton.*

Laughter is a most healthful exertion;

it is one of the greatest helps to digestion with which I am acquainted; and the custom prevalent among our forefathers, of exciting it at table by jesters and buffoons, was founded on true medical principles.—*Hufeland.*

I like the laughter that opens the lips and the heart, that shows at the same time pearls and the soul.—*Victor Hugo.*

One good, hearty laugh is a bombshell exploding in the right place, while spleen and discontent are a gun that kicks over the man who shoots it off.— *De Witt Talmage.*

Man is the only creature endowed with the power of laughter; is he not also the only one that deserves to be laughed at?—*Greville.*

Conversation never sits easier than when we now and then discharge ourselves in a symphony of laughter; which may not improperly be called the chorus of conversation.—*Steele.*

No man who has once heartily and wholly laughed can be altogether and irreclaimably depraved.—*Carlyle.*

Next to a good soul-stirring prayer is a good laugh, when it is promoted by what is pure in itself and in its grotesque application.—*Mutchmore.*

O, glorious laughter! thou man-loving spirit, that for a time doth take the burden from the weary back, that doth lay salve to the weary feet, bruised and cut by flints and shards.—*Jerrold.*

Laugh if you are wise.—*Martial.*

I am persuaded that every time a man smiles, but much more when he laughs, it adds something to this fragment of life.—*Sterne.*

God made both tears and laughter, and both for kind purposes; for as laughter enables mirth and surprise to breathe freely, so tears enable sorrow to vent itself patiently. Tears hinder sorrow from becoming despair and madness.—*Leigh Hunt.*

Beware of him who hates the laugh of a child.—*Lavater.*

If we consider the frequent reliefs we receive from laughter, and how often it breaks the gloom which is apt to depress the mind, one would take care not to grow too wise for so great a pleasure of life.—*Addison.*

The laughter of girls is, and ever was,

among the delightful sounds of earth.—*De Quincey.*

The most utterly lost of all days, is that in which you have not once laughed.—*Chamfort.*

Laughing cheerfulness throws the light of day on all the paths of life; the evil fog of gloom hovers in the distance; sorrow is more confusing and distracting than so-called giddiness.—*Richter.*

Though laughter is looked upon by philosophers as the property of reason, the excess of it has always been considered the mark of folly.—*Addison.*

Man could direct his ways by plain reason, and support his life by tasteless food, but God has given us wit, and flavor, and brightness, and laughter to enliven the days of man's pilgrimage, and to charm his pained steps o'er the burning marle.—*Sydney Smith.*

The loud laugh, that speaks the vacant mind.—*Goldsmith.*

That laughter costs too much which is purchased by the sacrifice of decency.—*Quintilian.*

How much lies in laughter: the cipher key, wherewith we decipher the whole man!—*Carlyle.*

Men show their character in nothing more clearly than by what they think laughable.—*Goethe.*

A laugh, to be joyous, must flow from a joyous heart, for without kindness there can be no true joy.—*Carlyle.*

The horse-laugh indicates coarseness or brutality of character.—*Lavater.*

Alas for the worn and heavy soul, if, whether in youth or in age, it has outlived its privilege of spring time and sprightliness.—*Hawthorne.*

The man who cannot laugh is not only fit for treasons, stratagems, and spoils; but his whole life is already a treason and a stratagem.—*Carlyle.*

Wrinkle not thy face with too much laughter, lest thou become ridiculous; neither wanton thy heart with too much mirth, lest thou become vain; the suburbs of folly is vain mirth, and profuseness of laughter is the city of fools.—*Quarles.*

Frequent and loud laughter is the characteristic of folly and ill manners;

it is the manner in which the mob express their silly joy at silly things, and which they call being merry.—In my mind there is nothing so ill-bred as audible laughter.—*Chesterfield.*

How inevitably does an immoderate laughter end in a sigh!—*South.*

Laughing, if loud, ends in a deep sigh; and all pleasures have a sting in the tail, though they carry beauty on the face.—*Jeremy Taylor.*

No one is more profoundly sad than he who laughs too much.—*Richter.*

The life that has grown up and developed without laughter, and without the sunny brightness which youth justly claims as its right, lacks buoyancy and elasticity, and becomes heavy and unsympathetic, if not harsh and morose.—*Mrs. G. S. Reany.*

Frequent and loud laughing is the characteristic of folly and ill-manners.—True wit never made a man laugh.—*Chesterfield.*

A good laugh is sunshine in a house.—*Thackeray.*

LAW.—Going to law is losing a cow for the sake of a cat.—*Chinese Proverb.*

To seek the redress of grievances by going to law, is like sheep running for shelter to a bramble bush.—*Dilwyn.*

The Jews ruin themselves at their passover; the Moors, at their marriages; and the Christians, in their lawsuits.—*Spanish Proverb.*

The plaintiff and defendant in an action at law, are like two men ducking their heads in a bucket, and daring each other to remain longest under water.—*Johnson.*

These written laws are just like spiders' webs; the small and feeble may be caught and entangled in them, but the rich and mighty force through and despise them.—*Anacharsis.*

A countryman between two lawyers is like a fish between two cats.—*Franklin.*

Law is a bottomless pit; it is a cormorant, a harpy that devours everything.—*Arbuthnot.*

In law nothing is certain but the expense.—*S. Butler.*

No people were ever better than their laws, though many have been worse.—*Priestly.*

The law is past depth to those who, without heed, do plunge into it.—*Shakespeare*.

The law is a sort of hocus-pocus science that smiles in your face while it picks your pocket; and the glorious uncertainty of it is of more use to the professors than the justice of it.—*Macklin*.

A mouse-trap: easy to enter but not easy to get out of.—*Balfour*.

Use law and physic only in cases of necessity; they that use them otherwise, abuse themselves into weak bodies and light purses: they are good remedies, bad recreations, but ruinous habits.—*Quarles*.

A natural law is a process, not a power; it is a method of operation, not an operator. A natural law, without God behind it, is no more than a glove without a hand in it.—*Joseph Cook*.

To go to law is for two persons to kindle a fire, at their own cost, to warm others and singe themselves to cinders; and because they cannot agree as to what is truth and equity, they will both agree to unplume themselves that others may be decorated with their feathers.—*Feltham*.

A law overcharged with severity, like a blunderbuss overcharged with powder, will each of them grow rusty by disuse, and neither will be resorted to, from the shock and recoil that must inevitably follow their explosion.—*Colton*.

It is a very easy thing to devise good laws; the difficulty is to make them effective. The great mistake is that of looking upon men as virtuous, or thinking that they can be made so by laws; and consequently the greatest art of a politician is to render vices serviceable to the cause of virtue.—*Bolingbroke*.

Law is never wise but when merciful, but mercy has conditions; and that which is mercy to the myriads, may seem hard to the one; and that which seems hard to the one, may be mercy when viewed by the eye that looks on through eternity.—*Bulwer*.

Laws are like cobwebs, which may catch small flies, but let wasps and hornets break through.—*Swift*.

Laws are generally found to be nets of such a texture, as the little creep through, the great break through, and the middle size are alone entangled in.—*Shenstone*.

Chancery, and certain other law courts, seem nothing; yet, in fact, they are, the worst of them, something: chimneys for the deviltry and contention of men to escape by.—*Carlyle*.

The English laws punish vice; the Chinese laws do more, they reward virtue.—*Goldsmith*.

A fish that hangs in the net, like a poor man's right in the law, will hardly come out of it.—*Shakespeare*.

The laws keep up their credit, not because they are all just, but because they are laws. This is the mystical foundation of their authority.—*Montaigne*.

A knowledge of the laws of our country is an highly useful, and I had almost said essential part of liberal and polite education.

As the laws are above magistrates, so are the magistrates above the people: and it may truly be said, that the magistrate is a speaking law, and the law a silent magistrate.—*Cicero*.

We have no right to say that the universe is governed by natural laws, but only that it is governed according to natural laws.—*Carpenter*.

Laws are commanded to hold their tongues among arms; and tribunals fall to the ground with the peace they are no longer able to uphold.—*Burke*.

The law is the standard and guardian of our liberty; it circumscribes and defends it; but to imagine liberty without a law, is to imagine every man with his sword in his hand to destroy him, who is weaker than himself; and that would be no pleasant prospect to those who cry out most for liberty.—*Clarendon*.

Whoever goes to law, goes into a glass house, where he understands little or nothing of what he is doing; where he sees a small matter blown up into fifty times the size of its intrinsic contents, and through which, if he can perceive any other objects, he perceives them all discolored and distorted.—*Skelton*.

Law is the embodiment of the moral sentiment of the people.—*Blackstone*.

True law is right reason conformably

to nature, universal, unchangeable, eternal, whose commands urge us to duty, and whose prohibitions restrain us from evil.—*Cicero.*

Good laws make it easier to do right and harder to do wrong.—*Gladstone.*

There is no country in the world in which everything can be provided for by the laws, or in which political institutions can prove a substitute for common sense and public morality.—*De Tocqueville.*

Aristotle himself has said, speaking of the laws of his own country, that jurisprudence, or the knowledge of those laws, is the principal and most perfect branch of ethics.—*Blackstone.*

The sparks of all the sciences in the world are taken up in the ashes of the law.—*Finch.*

We as a people seem to be losing all sense of respect for ourselves and our fellow men, with the result that in a thoroughly intolerant attitude we hesitate not a minute to secure an organized minority, or even a majority, to attempt by resolution or law to impose our will on a large body of people in matters where no moral wrong is involved and where liberty is curtailed.—*John J. Raskob.*

Society cannot exist without law and order, and cannot advance except through vigorous innovators.—*Bertrand Russell.*

All things come to him that waits—even justice.—*Austin O'Malley.*

When constabulary duty's to be done, a policeman's lot is not a happy one. —*W. S. Gilbert.*

A prince who falleth out with laws, breaketh with his best friends.—*Saville.*

Four out of five potential litigants will settle their disputes the first day they come together, if you will put the idea of arbitration into their heads.— *Judge Moses H. Grossman.*

The law can make you quit drinking; but it can't make you quit being the kind that needs a law to make you quit drinking.—*Don Marquis.*

A good, contented, well-breakfasted juryman is a capital thing to get hold of. Discontented jurymen always find for the plaintiff.—*Charles Dickens.*

Law never does anything constructive. We have had enough of legislators promising to do that which laws can not do.—*Henry Ford.*

Economic depression cannot be cured by legislative action or executive pronouncement. Economic wounds must be healed by the action of the cells of the economic body, the producers and consumers themselves.—*Herbert Hoover.*

The result of the attempt to deal with evil socially rather than at its source in the individual, to substitute an outer for an inner control of appetite, has been a monstrous legalism, of which the Eighteenth Amendment is only the most notable example.—*Irving Babbitt.*

The excess of sentiment, which is misleading in philanthropy and economics, grows acutely dangerous when it interferes with legislation, or with the ordinary rulings of morality.—*Agnes Repplier.*

Laws are always unstable unless they are founded on the manners of a nation; and manners are the only durable and resisting power in a people.—*De Tocqueville.*

In effect, to follow, not to force, the public inclination, to give a direction, a form, a technical dress, and a specific sanction, to the general sense of the community, is the true end of legislation.—*Burke.*

When I hear any man talk of an unalterable law, the only effect it produces on me is to convince me that he is an unalterable fool.—*Sydney Smith.*

The science of legislation is like that of medicine in one respect, viz.: that it is far more easy to point out what will do harm, than what will do good.— *Colton.*

Laws are silent in the midst of arms. —*Cicero.*

The reason of the law is the law.— *Walter Scott.*

So great is the force of laws, and of particular forms of government, and so little dependence have they on the humors and tempers of men, that consequences almost as general and certain may sometimes be deduced from them, as any which the mathematical sciences afford us.—*Hume.*

The best way to get a bad law repealed is to enforce it strictly.—*Lincoln.*

The forms of law have always been the graves of buried liberties.—*Tourgee.*

Pity is the virtue of the law, and none but tyrants use it cruelly.—*Shakespeare.*

The people's safety is the law of God. —*James Otis.*

Law and equity are two things that God hath joined together, but which man has put asunder.—*Colton.*

A law is valuable not because it is law, but because there is right in it.— *H. W. Beecher.*

When the state is most corrupt, then the laws are most multiplied.—*Tacitus.*

Law should be like death, which spares no one.—*Montesquieu.*

They are the best laws, by which the king has the greatest prerogative, and the people the best liberty.—*Bacon.*

Laws are the silent assessors of God. —*R. W. Alger.*

We should never create by law what can be accomplished by morality.— *Montesquieu.*

A multitude of laws in a country is like a great number of physicians, a sign of weakness and malady.—*Voltaire.*

The greatest of all injustice is that which goes under the name of law; and of all sorts of tyranny, the forcing the letter of the law against the equity is the most insupportable.—*L'Estrange.*

Laws grind the poor, and rich men rule the law.—*Goldsmith.*

The universal and absolute law is that natural justice which cannot be written down, but which appeals to the hearts of all. Written laws are formulas in which we endeavor to express as concisely as possible that which, under such or such determined circumstances, natural justice demands.—*Victor Cousin.*

Consider the reason of the case, for nothing is law that is not reason.—*J. Powell.*

In civil jurisprudence it too often happens that there is so much law, that there is no room for justice, and that the claimant expires of wrong in the midst of right, as mariners die of thirst in the midst of water.—*Colton.*

To make an empire durable, the magistrates must obey the laws, and the people the magistrates.—*Solon.*

Laws are the sovereigns of sovereigns. —*Louis XIV.*

Alas! how many causes that can plead well for themselves in the courts of Westminster, and yet in the general court of the universe, and free soul of man, have no word to utter!—*Carlyle.*

Laws which are in advance of public sentiment are generally but a dead letter.—*Tryon Edwards.*

Reason is the life of law; nay, the common law itself is nothing else but reason.—*Coke.*

Let but the public mind once become thoroughly corrupt, and all attempts to secure property, liberty, or life, by mere force of laws written on parchment, will be as vain as to put up printed notices in an orchard to keep off canker-worms. *Horace Mann.*

With us, law is nothing unless close behind it stands a warm, living public opinion. Let that die or grow indifferent, and statutes was waste paper, lacking all executive force.—*Wendell Phillips.*

The good need fear no law; it is his safety, and the bad man's awe.—*Massinger.*

Multitudes of laws are signs, either of much tyranny in the prince, or much rebellious disobedience in the subject.— *Marston.*

Law is often spoken of as uncertain; but the uncertainty is not so much in the law as in the evidence.—*Tryon Edwards.*

To embarrass justice by a multiplicity of laws, or to hazard it by confidence in judges, are the opposite rocks on which all civil institutions have been wrecked, and between which legislative wisdom has never yet found an open passage.—*Johnson.*

As the law dissolves all contracts which are without a valuable consideration, so a valuable consideration often dissolves the law.—*Fielding.*

There have been many laws made by men which swerve from honesty, reason, and the dictates of nature. By the law of arms he is degraded from all honor who puts up with an affront; and by the civil law, he that takes vengeance for it, incurs a capital punishment; he that seeks redress by law for an affront is disgraced; and he that seeks redress not in this way is punished by the laws.—*Montaigne*.

We must not make a scarecrow of the law, setting it up to fear the birds of prey, and letting it keep one shape till custom make it their perch, and not their terror.—*Shakespeare*.

Possession is eleven points in the law.—*Cibber*.

Where law ends, tyranny begins.—*Wm. Pitt*.

Laws are the very bulwarks of liberty; they define every man's rights, and defend the individual liberties of all men.—*J. G. Holland*.

Ignorance of the law excuses no man; not that all men know the law, but because it is an excuse every man will plead, and no man can tell how to confute him.—*Selden*.

Of all the parts of a law, the most effectual is the vindicatory; for it is but lost labor to say, "Do this, or avoid that," unless we also declare, "This shall be the consequence of your noncompliance." The main strength and force of a law consists in the penalty annexed to it.—*Blackstone*.

Every instance of a man's suffering the penalty of the law, is an instance of the failure of that penalty in effecting its purpose, which is to deter from transgression.—*Whately*.

It is impossible for men even to murder each other without statutes and maxims, and an idea of justice and honor.—War has its laws as well as peace.—*Hume*.

"I never," said Voltaire, "was ruined but twice—once when I gained a lawsuit, and once when I lost one."

Penal laws—by which every man's danger becomes every man's safety, and by which, though all are restrained, yet all are benefited.—*Johnson*.

The laws of nature are but the ways in which the great almighty lawgiver operates; they have no efficiency except as channels of his will; rightly understood they cannot but be seen to agree with his written word.—*Tryon Edwards*.

The laws of nature are not, as some modern naturalists seem to suppose, iron chains, by which the living God, so to say, is bound hand and foot, but elastic cords rather, which he can lengthen or shorten at his sovereign will.—*Philip Schaff*.

The absolute justice of the state enlightened by the perfect reason of the state, that is law.—*Rufus Choate*.

The law of God is what we must do; the gospel is what God will give.—*Luther*.

Laws were made to restrain and punish the wicked; the wise and good do not need them as a guide, but only as a shield against rapine and oppression; they can live civilly and orderly, though there were no law in the world.—*Feltham*.

Laws can discover sin, but not remove it.—*Milton*.

LAWYERS.—No man can be a sound lawyer who is not well read in the laws of Moses.—*Fisher Ames*.

As to lawyers, their profession is supported by the indiscriminate defense of right and wrong.—*Junius*.

Pettifoggers in law, and empirics in medicine, whether their patients lose or save their property or their lives, take care to be, in either case, equally remunerated; they profit by both horns of the dilemma, and press defeat no less than success into their service. They hold, from time immemorial, the fee simple of a vast estate, subject to no alienation, diminution, revolution, or tax—the folly and ignorance of mankind.—*Colton*.

There is too much reason to apprehend, that the custom of pleading for any client, without discrimination of right or wrong, must lessen the regard due to those important distinctions, and deaden the moral sensibility of the heart.—*Percival*.

In the habits of legal men every accusation appears insufficient if they do not exaggerate it even to calumny. It is thus that justice itself loses its sanctity and its respect among men.—*Lamartine*.

Accuracy and diligence are much more necessary to a lawyer than great comprehension of mind, or brilliancy of talent.—His business is to refine, define, split hairs, look into authorities, and compare cases.—A man can never gallop over the fields of law on Pegasus, nor fly across them on the wing of oratory.—If he would stand on terra firma, he must descend.—If he would be a great lawyer, he must first consent to become a great drudge.—*Daniel Webster.*

Adversaries in law strive mightily, but eat and drink as friends.—*Shakespeare.*

By birth and interest lawyers belong to the people; by habit and taste to the aristocracy; and they may be looked upon as the natural bond and connecting link of the two great classes of society.—They are attached to public order beyond every other consideration, and the best security of public order is authority.—If they prize the free institutions of their country much, they value the legality of these institutions far more.—They are less afraid of tyranny than of arbitrary power.—*De Tocqueville.*

Lawyers on opposite sides of a case are like the two parts of shears; they cut what comes between them, but not each other.

Our profession is good if practised in the spirit of it; it is damnable fraud and iniquity when its true spirit is supplied by a spirit of mischief-making and money-getting.—The love of fame is extinguished; every ardent wish for knowledge repressed; conscience put in jeopardy, and the best feelings of the heart indurated by the mean, money-catching, abominable practises, which cover with disgrace some of the modern practitioners of law.—*Daniel Webster.*

There is a great deal of law learning that is dry, dark, cold, revolting—but it is an old feudal castle, in perfect preservation, which the legal architect, who aspires to the first honors of his profession, will delight to explore, and learn all the uses to which its various parts used to be put; and he will the better understand, enjoy and relish the progressive improvements of the science in modern times.—*W. Wirt.*

LEARNING. — Learning passes for wisdom among those who want both.—*Sir W. Temple.*

I have seldom seen much ostentation and much learning met together. The sun, rising and declining, makes long shadows; and mid-day, when he is highest, none at all.—*Bp. Hall.*

Learning is wealth to the poor, an honor to the rich, an aid to the young, and a support and comfort to the aged.

He who always seeks more light the more he finds, and finds more the more he seeks, is one of the few happy mortals who take and give in every point of time. The tide and ebb of giving and receiving is the sum of human happiness, which he alone enjoys who always wishes to acquire new knowledge, and always finds it.—*Lavater.*

The end of learning is to know God, and out of that knowledge to love him, and to imitate him, as we may the nearest, by possessing our souls of true virtue.—*Milton.*

The true order of learning should be: first, what is necessary; second, what is useful; and third, what is ornamental. To reverse this arrangement is like beginning to build at the top of the edifice. *Mrs. Sigourney.*

Learning is like mercury, one of the most powerful and excellent things in the world in skillful hands; in unskillful, the most mischievous.—*Pope.*

Learning, like money, may be of so base a coin as to be utterly void of use; or, if sterling, may require good management to make it serve the purposes of sense or happiness.—*Shenstone.*

He who has no inclination to learn more will be very apt to think that he knows enough.—*Powell.*

Learning, if rightly applied, makes a young man thinking, attentive, industrious, confident, and wary; and an old man cheerful and useful. It is an ornament in prosperity, a refuge in adversity, an entertainment at all times; it cheers in solitude, and gives moderation and wisdom in all circumstances.—*Palmer.*

A heap of ill-chosen erudition is but the luggage of antiquity.—*Balzac.*

Who can tell whether learning may not even weaken invention in a man that has great advantages from nature and birth; whether the weight and number of so many men's thoughts and notions may not suppress his own or hinder the motion and agitation of them, from which all invention arises; as heaping on wood, or too many sticks, or too close together, suppresses, and sometimes quite extinguishes a little spark, that would otherwise have grown up to a noble flame.—*Sir W. Temple.*

Much learning shows how little mortals know; much wealth, how little worldlings enjoy.—*E. Young.*

No man is the wiser for his learning: it may administer matter to work in, or objects to work upon; but wit and wisdom are born with a man.—*Selden.*

Learning, though it is useful when we know how to make a right use of it, yet considered as in our own power, and to those who trust to it without seeking a superior guidance, is usually the source of perplexity, strife, skepticism, and infidelity. It is indeed like a sword in a madman's hands, which gives him the more opportunity of hurting himself than others.—*John Newton.*

He that wants good sense is unhappy in having learning, for he has thereby only more ways of exposing himself; and he that has sense knows that learning is not knowledge, but rather the art of using it.—*Steele.*

Learning by study must be won; 'twas ne'er entailed from sire to son.—*Gay.*

There are three classes of people in the world. The first learn from their own experience—these are wise; the second learn from the experience of others—these are the happy; the third neither learn from their own experience nor the experience of others—these are fools.

A man of the best parts and greatest learning, if he does not know the world by his own experience and observation, will be very absurd, and consequently very unwelcome in company. He may say very good things; but they will be probably so ill-timed, misplaced, or improperly addressed, that he had much better hold his tongue.—*Chesterfield.*

Learning once made popular is no longer learning; it has the appearance of something which we have bestowed upon ourselves, as the dew appears to rise from the field which it refreshes.—*Johnson.*

How empty learning, how vain is art, but as it mends the life and guides the heart.—*Young.*

I observe in all my travels, this custom—ever to learn something from the information of those with whom I confer, which is the best school of all others, and to put my company upon those subjects they are best able to speak of: for it often falls out, that, on the contrary, every one will rather choose to be prating of another man's province than his own, thinking it so much new reputation acquired.—*Montaigne.*

I attribute the little I know to my not having been ashamed to ask for information, and to my rule of conversing with all descriptions of men on those topics that form their own peculiar professions and pursuits.—*Locke.*

You are to consider that learning is of great use to society; and though it may not add to the stock, it is a necessary vehicle to transmit it to others. Learned men are the cisterns of knowledge, not the fountainhead.—*Northcote.*

Learning makes a man fit company for himself.—*Young.*

Ignorance of all things is an evil neither terrible nor excessive, nor yet the greatest of all; but great cleverness and much learning, if they be accompanied by a bad training, are a much greater misfortune.—*Plato.*

Learning maketh young men temperate, is the comfort of old age, standing for wealth with poverty, and serving as an ornament to riches.—*Cicero.*

The chief art of learning, as Locke has observed, is to attempt but little at a time. The widest excursions of the mind are made by short flights frequently repeated; the most lofty fabrics of science are formed by the continued accumulation of single propositions. —*Johnson.*

A little learning is a dangerous thing! drink deep, or taste not the Pierian spring; there shallow draughts intoxicate the brain, and drinking largely sobers us again.—*Pope.*

Wear your learning, like your watch, in a private pocket.—Do not pull it out merely to show that you have one.— If asked what o'clock it is, tell it; but do not proclaim it hourly and unasked, like the watchman.—*Chesterfield.*

No man can ever lack this mortification of his vanity, that what he knows is but a very little in comparison of what he is ignorant of. Consider this, and instead of boasting thy knowledge of a few things, confess and be out of countenance for the many more which thou dost not understand.—*Thomas à Kempis.*

That learning is most requisite which unlearns evil.—*Antisthenes.*

He is a learned man that understands one subject; a very learned man who understands two.—*Emmons.*

To be proud of learning, is the greatest ignorance.—*Jeremy Taylor.*

We should not ask who is the most learned, but who is the best learned.—*Montaigne.*

The great art of learning, is to undertake but little at a time.—*Locke.*

He might have been a very clever man by nature, but he had laid so many books on his head that his brain could not move.—*Robert Hall.*

All other knowledge is hurtful to him who has not the science of honesty and good nature.—*Montaigne.*

The learning and knowledge that we have, is, at the most, but little compared with that of which we are ignorant.—*Plato.*

He who knoweth not what he ought to know, is a brute beast among men; he that knoweth no more than he hath need of, is a man among brute beasts; and he that knoweth all that may be known, is as a God among men.—*Pythagoras.*

Voracious learning, often over-fed, digests not into sense her motley meal. This bookcase, with dark booty almost burst, this forager on others' wisdom, leaves her native farm, her reason, quite untill'd.—*Young.*

He who learns, and makes no use of his learning, is a beast of burden with a load of books.—Does the ass comprehend whether he carries on his back a library or a bundle of faggots?—*Saadi.*

The most learned are often the most narrow-minded men.—*Hazlitt.*

Without controversy, learning doth make the mind of men gentle, generous, amiable, and pliant to government; whereas ignorance makes them churlish, thwarting, and mutinous; and the evidence of time doth clear this assertion, considering that the most barbarous, rude, and unlearned times have been most subject to tumults, seditions, and changes.—*Bacon.*

Learning teaches how to carry things in suspense, without prejudice, till you resolve.—*Bacon.*

It is easy to learn something about everything, but difficult to learn everything about anything.—*Emmons.*

The sweetest and most inoffensive path of life leads through the avenues of science and learning; and whoever can either remove any obstruction in this way, or open up any new prospect, ought, so far, to be esteemed a benefactor to mankind.—*Hume.*

Seeing much, suffering much, and studying much, are the three pillars of learning.—*Disraeli.*

It is a little learning, and but a little, which makes men conclude hastily.—Experience and humility teach modesty and fear.—*Jeremy Taylor.*

Learning is a dangerous weapon, and apt to wound its master if it be wielded by a feeble hand, or by one not well acquainted with its use.—*Montaigne.*

"A little learning is a dangerous thing," and yet it is what all must attain before they can arrive at great learning; it is the utmost acquisition of those who know the most in comparison of what they do not know.—*Whately.*

Some will never learn anything because they understand everything too soon.—*Blount.*

Till a man can judge whether they be truths or no, his understanding is but little improved, and thus men of much reading, though greatly learned, but may be little knowing.—*Locke.*

Mere learning is only a compiler, and manages the pen as the compositor picks out the types—each sets up a book with the hand.—Stone masons collected the dome of St. Paul's, but Wren hung it in the air.—*Willmott.*

Learning gives us a fuller conviction of the imperfections of our nature; which one would think, might dispose us to modesty: for the more a man knows, the more he discovers his ignorance.—*Jeremy Collier.*

LEISURE.—The end of labor is to gain leisure.—*Aristotle.*

Employ thy time well if thou meanest to gain leisure; and since thou art not sure of a minute, throw not away an hour. Leisure is time for doing something useful, and this leisure the diligent man will obtain, but the lazy man never, for a life of leisure and a life of laziness are two things.—*Franklin.*

Leisure is a beautiful garment, but it will not do for constant wear.—*Anon.*

Leisure and solitude are the best effect of riches, because the mother of thought. Both are avoided by most rich men, who seek company and business, which are signs of being weary of themselves.—*Sir W. Temple.*

There is room enough in human life to crowd almost every art and science in it. If we pass "no day without a line"—visit no place without the company of a book—we may with ease fill libraries, or empty them of their contents. The more we do, the more busy we are, the more leisure we have.—*Hazlitt.*

"Never less idle than when idle," was the motto which the admirable Vittoria Colonna wrought upon her husband's dressing-gown. And may we not justly regard our appreciation of leisure as a test of improved character and growing resources?—*Tuckerman.*

You cannot give an instance of any man who is permitted to lay out his own time, contriving not to have tedious hours.—*Johnson.*

Leisure is gone; gone where the spinning-wheels are gone, and the pack-horses, and the slow wagons, and the peddlers who brought bargains to the door on sunny afternoons.—*George Eliot.*

In this theater of man's life, it is reserved only for God and angels to be lookers-on.—*Pythagoras.*

I am never less at leisure than when at leisure, nor less alone than when I am alone.—*Scipio Africanus.*

Days of respite are golden days.—*South.*

Leisure is pain; take off our chariot wheels and how heavily we drag the load of life.—It is our curse, like that of Cain; it makes us wander earth around to fly that tyrant, thought.—*Young.*

Leisure for men of business, and business for men of leisure, would cure many complaints.—*Mrs. Thrale.*

Spare minutes are the gold-dust of time; the portions of life most fruitful in good or evil; the gaps through which temptations enter.

LENDING.—Neither a borrower nor a lender be; for loan oft loses both itself and friend.—*Shakespeare.*

If you lend a person money it becomes lost for any purposes of your own.—When you ask for it back again, you find a friend made an enemy by your own kindness.—If you begin to press still further, either you must part with what you have lent or else you must lose your friend.—*Plautus.*

Lend not beyond thy ability, nor refuse to lend out of thy ability; especially when it will help others more than it can hurt thee. If thy debtor be honest and capable, thou hast thy money again, if not with increase, with praise. If he prove insolvent do not ruin him to get that which it will not ruin thee to lose; for thou art but a steward, and another is thy owner, master, and judge.—*Penn.*

Whatever you lend let it be your money, and not your name. Money you may get again, and, if not, you may contrive to do without it; name once lost you cannot get again, and, if you cannot contrive to do without it, you had better never have been born.—*Bulwer.*

LENITY.—It is only necessary to grow old to become more indulgent. I see no fault committed that I have not committed myself.—*Goethe.*

Lenity will operate with greater force in some instances than rigor.—It is, therefore, my first wish to have all my conduct distinguished by it.—*Washington.*

Lenity is a part of mercy, but she must not speak too loud for fear of waking justice.—*Joubert.*

When lenity and cruelty play for a kingdom, the gentler gamester is the soonest winner.—*Shakespeare.*

Man may dismiss compassion from his heart, but God will never.—*Cowper.*

Never to judge rashly; never to interpret the actions of others in an ill-sense, but to, compassionate their infirmities, bear their burdens, excuse their weaknesses, and make up for their defects—to hate their imperfections, but love themselves, this is the true spirit of charity.—*Caussin.*

LETTERS.—It is by the benefit of letters that absent friends are, in a manner, brought together.—*Seneca.*

Letters are those winged messengers that can fly from east to west on embassies of love.—*Howell.*

The best time to frame an answer to the letters of a friend is the moment you receive them; then the warmth of friendship and the intelligence received most forcibly co-operate.—*Shenstone.*

A letter shows the man it is written to as well as the man it is written by.—*Chesterfield.*

To write a good love-letter, you ought to begin without knowing what you mean to say, and to finish without knowing what you have written.—*Rousseau.*

The true character of epistolary style is playfulness and urbanity.—*Joubert.*

A profusion of fancies and quotations is out of place in a love-letter.—True feeling is always direct, and never deviates into by-ways to cull flowers of rhetoric.—*Bovee.*

Our thoughts are much alike, but female correspondence has a charm in it, of which that of the other sex is always devoid.—*Eldon.*

When the spirits sink too low, the best cordial is to read over all the letters of one's friends.—*Shenstone.*

Let your letter be written as accurately as you are able—I mean as to language, grammar, and stops; but as

to the matter of it the less trouble you give yourself the better it will be. Letters should be easy and natural, and convey to the persons to whom we send just what we should say if we were with them.—*Chesterfield.*

It is difficult to tell to what end we keep these old memorials, for their perusal affords, in most cases, but little pleasure. Many are never looked at again, and yet we could not destroy them without a struggle; others only bring forward evidences of words broken, hopes chilled, and friendships gradually dissolved; of old attachments turned away, and stubborn contradiction of all the trusting in futurity, whose promise we once clung to. One class alone of them can call up our best feelings. If the almost forgotten memorials of the once dearly loved and long departed can carry our sympathies away from the cold, hard present, over intervening years of struggling and vexatious toil, to that almost holy period of the gone and past, calling up old thoughts and old affections; or soothing, by one lonely, unsuspected burst of tears, overcharged hearts, which have long required easing of their burthen,—there is yet enough—there is more than enough—in these old letters, to plead an excuse for so sacredly preserving them.—*Albert Smith.*

LEVELLERS.—Your levellers wish to level down as far as themselves, but they cannot bear levelling up to themselves.—*Johnson.*

Those who attempt to level never equalize. In all societies some description must be uppermost. The levellers, therefore, only change and pervert the natural order of things; they load the edifice of society by setting up in the air what the solidity of the structure requires to be on the ground.—*Burke.*

Some persons are always ready to level those above them down to themselves, while they are never willing to level those below them up to their own position. But he that is under the influence of true humility will avoid both these extremes. On the one hand, he will be willing that all should rise just so far as their diligence and worth of character entitle them to; and on the other hand, he will be willing that his superiors should be known and acknowledged in their place, and have rendered to them all the honors that are their due.—*Jonathan Edwards.*

Death and the cross are the two great levellers; kings and their subjects, masters and slaves, find a common level in two places—at the foot of the cross, and in the silence of the grave.—*Colton.*

LEVITY.—Levity of behavior is the bane of all that is good and virtuous. —*Seneca.*

In infants, levity is a prettiness; in men, a shameful defect; in old age, a monstrous folly.—*Rochefoucauld.*

Frivolity, under whatever form it appears, takes from attention its strength, from thought its originality, from feeling its earnestness.—*Mad. De Staël.*

There is always some levity even in excellent minds; they have wings to rise, and also to stay.—*Joubert.*

A light and trifling mind never takes in great ideas, and never accomplishes anything great or good.—*Sprague.*

Between levity and cheerfulness there is a wide distinction; the mind that is most open to the former is frequently a stranger to the latter.—Levity may be the offspring of folly or vice; cheerfulness is the natural offspring of wisdom and virtue.—*Blair.*

LIARS.—(See "FALSEHOOD" and "LYING.")

There is no vice that doth so cover a man with shame as to be discovered in a lie; for as Montaigne saith, "A liar would be brave toward God, while he is a coward toward men; for a lie faces God, and shrinks from man."—*Bacon.*

All that one gains by falsehood is, not to be believed when he speaks the truth. —*Aristotle.*

He who tells a lie is not sensible how great a task he undertakes; for he must be forced to invent twenty more to maintain one.—*Pope.*

A willful falsehood told is a cripple, not able to stand by itself without another to support it.—It is easy to tell a lie, but hard to tell only one lie.— *Fuller.*

One ought to have a good memory when he has told a lie.—*Corneille.*

Liars—past all shame—so past all truth.—*Shakespeare.*

Thou canst not better reward a liar than in not believing whatever he speaketh.—*Aristippus.*

They begin with making falsehood appear like truth, and end with making truth itself appear like falsehood.—*Shenstone.*

I am charmed with many points of the Turkish law; when proved the authors of any notorious falsehood, they are burned on the forehead with a hot iron.—*Lady Montague.*

A lie should be trampled on and extinguished wherever found.—I am for fumigating the atmosphere when I suspect that falsehood, like pestilence, breathes around me.—*Carlyle.*

This is the liar's lot: he is accounted a pest and a nuisance, a person marked out for infamy and scorn.—*South.*

One lie must be thatched with another or it will soon rain through.— *Owĕn.*

The hell that a lie would keep a man from, is doubtless the very best place for him to go.—*G. Macdonald.*

Who dares think one thing, and another tell, my soul detests him as the gates of hell.—*Pope.*

LIBERALITY.— (See "BENEVOLENCE.")

Liberality was formerly called honesty, as if to imply that unless we are liberal we are not honest, either toward God or man.—*Tryon Edwards.*

The riches we impart are the only wealth we shall always retain.—*M. Henry.*

Be rather bountiful than expensive; do good with what thou hast, or it will do thee no good.—*Penn.*

By Jove the stranger and the poor are sent, and what to these we give to Jove is lent.—*Homer.*

No communications can exhaust genius; no gifts impoverish charity.— *Lavater.*

Proportion thy charity to the strength of thine estate, lest God in anger proportion thine estate to the weakness of thy charity.—*Quarles.*

Liberality consists rather in giving seasonably than much.—*Bruyère.*

The office of liberality consists in giving with judgment.—*Cicero.*

The way to have nothing to give, is to give nothing.

He that lays out for God lays up for himself.

Be busy in trading, receiving, and giving, for life is too good to be wasted in living.—*J. Sterling.*

Frugality is good, if liberality be joined with it. The first is leaving off superfluous expenses; the last bestowing them to the benefit of others that need. The first without the last begets covetousness; the last without the first begets prodigality. Both together make an excellent temper. Happy the place where that is found.—*Penn.*

In defiance of all the torture, the might, and the malice of the world, the liberal man will ever be rich; for God's providence is his estate, God's wisdom and power his defense, God's love and favor his reward, and God's word his security.—*Barrow.*

He who is not liberal with what he has, does but deceive himself when he thinks he would be liberal if he had more.—*W. S. Plumer.*

Some are unwisely liberal, and more delight to give presents than to pay debts.—*Sir P. Sidney.*

What we call liberality is often but the vanity of giving; we are more fond of the ostentation than of the generosity of the act.—*Rochefoucauld.*

The liberality of some men is but indifference clad in the garb of candor.—*Whately.*

Men might be better if we deemed better of them.—The worst way to improve the world is to condemn it.—*Bailey.*

'Tis hard to school the heart to be, in spite of injury and envy, generous still.—*Ellison.*

One always receiving, never giving, is like the stagnant pool, in which whatever flows remains, whatever remains corrupts.—*J. A. James.*

LIBERTY.—True liberty consists only in the power of doing what we ought to will, and in not being constrained to do what we ought not to will.—*Jonathan Edwards.*

Reason and virtue alone can bestow liberty.—*Shaftesbury.*

There is no liberty worth anything which is not a liberty under law.—*N. J. Burton.*

Personal liberty is the paramount essential to human dignity and human happiness.—*Bulwer.*

Give me the liberty to know, to think, to believe, and to utter freely, according to conscience, above all other liberties.—*Milton.*

We hold these truths to be self-evident, that all men are created equal; that they are endowed by their Creator with inalienable rights; and that among these are life, liberty, and the pursuit of happiness.—*Jefferson.*

Is life so dear, or peace so sweet as to be purchased at the price of chains and slavery?—Forbid it, Almighty God!—I know not what course others may take, but, as for me, give me liberty or give me death.—*Patrick Henry.*

In the same proportion that ignorance and vice prevail in a republic, will the government partake of despotism.—*Sprague.*

Easier were it to hurl the rooted mountain from its base, than force the yoke of slavery upon men determined to be free.—*Southey.*

Liberty is to the collective body, what health is to every individual body. Without health no pleasure can be tasted by man; without liberty, no happiness can be enjoyed by society.—*Bolingbroke.*

The liberty of a people consists in being governed by laws which they have made themselves, under whatsoever form it be of government; the liberty of a private man is being master of his own time and actions, as far as may consist with the laws of God, and of his country.—*Cowley.*

The only rational liberty is that which is born of subjection, reared in the fear of God and love of man, and made courageous in the defense of a trust, and the prosecution of a duty.—*Simms.*

What is life? It is not to stalk about, and draw fresh air, or gaze upon the sun; it is to be free.—*Addison.*

Oh, give me liberty! for even were paradise my prison, still I should long to leap the crystal walls.—*Dryden.*

There are two freedoms, the false where one is free to do what he likes, and the true where he is free to do what he ought.—*C. Kingsley.*

Bad men cannot make good citizens. It is impossible that a nation of infidels or idolaters should be a nation of freemen. It is when a people forget God, that tyrants forge their chains. A vitiated state of morals, a corrupted public conscience, is incompatible with freedom.

No free government, or the blessings of liberty can be preserved to any people but by a firm adherence to justice, moderation, temperance, frugality, and virtue, and by a frequent recurrence to fundamental principles.—*Patrick Henry.*

Personal liberty is the right to act without interference within the limits of the law.—*J. Oerter.*

It is foolish to strive with what we cannot avoid; we are born subjects, and to obey God is perfect liberty; he that does this, shall be free, safe, and quiet; all his actions shall succeed to his wishes. —*Seneca.*

If the true spark of religious and civil liberty be kindled, it will burn. Human agency cannot extinguish it. Like the earth's central fire, it may be smothered for a time; the ocean may overwhelm it; mountains may press it down; but its inherent and unconquerable force will heave both the ocean and the land, and at some time or another, in some place or another, the volcano will break out and flame to heaven.—*Daniel Webster.*

Perfect conformity to the will of God is the sole sovereign and complete liberty.—*D'Aubigné.*

No man can always do just as he chooses until he always chooses to do God's will; and that is heaven. There is no liberty in wrong-doing.—It chains and fetters its victim as surely as effect follows cause.

Safe popular freedom consists of four things, the diffusion of liberty, of intelligence, of property, and of conscientiousness, and cannot be compounded of any three out of the four.—*Joseph Cook.*

Men do things which their fathers would have deprecated, and then draw about themselves a flimsy cordon of sophistry, and talk about the advance of humanity and liberal thought, when it is nothing after all but a preference for individual license.—*John Hall.*

False notions of liberty are strangely common. People talk of it as if it meant the liberty of doing whatever one likes—whereas the only liberty that a man, worthy of the name of man, ought to ask for, is, to have all restrictions, inward and outward, removed that prevent his doing what he ought.—*F. W. Robertson.*

There is not a truth to be gathered from history more certain, or more momentous, than this: that civil liberty cannot long be separated from religious liberty without danger, and ultimately without destruction to both. Wherever religious liberty exists, it will, first or last, bring in and establish political liberty. Wherever it is suppressed, the church establishment will, first or last, become the engine of despotism, and overthrow, unless it be itself overthrown, every vestige of political right.—*Story.*

If we must accept fate, we are not less compelled to assert liberty, the significance of the individual, the grandeur of duty, the power of character.— We are sure, though we know not how, that necessity does comport with liberty, the individual with the world, my polarity with the spirit of the times.—*Emerson.*

The principle of liberty and equality, if coupled with mere selfishness, will make men only devils, each trying to be independent that he may fight only for his own interest.—And here is the need of religion and its power, to bring in the principle of benevolence and love to men.—*John Randolph.*

Christianity is the companion of liberty in all its conflicts, the cradle of its infancy, and the divine source of its claims.—*De Tocqueville.*

Free will is not the liberty to do whatever one likes, but the power of doing whatever one sees ought to be done, even in the very face of otherwise overwhelming impulse. There lies freedom, indeed.—*G. Macdonald.*

The freedom of some is the freedom of the herd of swine that ran violently down a steep place into the sea and were drowned.

The only liberty that is valuable, is a liberty connected with order; that not only exists with order and virtue, but which cannot exist at all without them. It inheres in good and steady government, as in its substance and vital principle.—*Burke.*

Liberty is the right of every human creature, as soon as he breathes the vital air; and no human law can deprive him of that right, which he derives from the law of nature.

True liberty consists in the privilege of enjoying our own rights, not in the destruction of the rights of others.—*Pinckard.*

Man's liberty ends, and it ought to end, when that liberty becomes the curse of his neighbors.—*Farrar.*

Liberty is the right to do what the laws allow; and if a citizen could do what they forbid, it would be no longer liberty, because others would have the same powers.—*Montesquieu.*

A nation may lose its liberties in a day, and not miss them in a century.—*Montesquieu.*

If liberty with law is fire on the hearth, liberty without law is fire on the floor.—*Hillard.*

Men are qualified for civil liberty in exact proportion to their disposition to put chains upon their own appetites; in proportion as their love of justice is above their rapacity; in proportion as their soundness and sobriety of understanding is above their vanity and presumption; in proportion as they are more disposed to listen to the counsels of the wise and good, in preference to the flattery of knaves. Society cannot exist unless a controlling power upon the will and appetite is placed somewhere; and the less of it there is within, the more there must be of it without. It is ordained in the eternal constitution of things, that men of intemperate habits cannot be free. Their passions forge their fetters.—*Burke.*

Liberty will not descend to a people; a people must raise themselves to liberty; it is a blessing that must be earned before it can be enjoyed.—*Colton.*

Where liberty dwells, there is my country.—*Milton.*

A country cannot subsist well without liberty, nor liberty without virtue.—*Rousseau.*

Liberty cannot be established without morality, nor morality without faith.

It is impossible to enslave, mentally or socially, a Bible-reading people. The principles of the Bible are the groundwork of human freedom.—*Horace Greeley.*

To do what we will, is natural liberty; to do what we may consistently with the interests of the community to which we belong, is civil liberty, the only liberty to be desired in a state of civil society.—*Paley.*

When I see the spirit of liberty in action, I see a strong principle at work; and this, for a while, is all I can possibly know of it. The wild gas, the fixed air, is plainly broke loose: but we ought to suspend our judgment until the first effervescence is a little subsided, till the liquor is cleared, and until we see something deeper than the agitation of a troubled and frothy surface. I must be tolerably sure, before I venture publicly to congratulate men upon a blessing, that they have really received one.—*Burke.*

The human race is in the best condition when it has the greatest degree of liberty.—*Dante.*

Liberty and union, one and inseparable, now and forever.—*Daniel Webster.*

Interwoven is the love of liberty with every ligament of the heart.—*Washington.*

The liberty of a people consists in being governed by laws which they have made themselves, under whatsoever form it be of government; the liberty of a private man, in being master of his own time and actions, as far as may consist with the laws of God and of his country.—*Cowley.*

A Bible and a newspaper in every house, a good school in every district, —all studied and appreciated as they merit,—are the principal support of virtue, morality, and civil liberty.—*Franklin.*

The greatest glory of a free-born people, is to transmit that freedom to their children.—*Havard.*

The spirit of liberty is not, as multitudes imagine, a jealousy of our own particular rights, but a respect for the rights of others, and an unwillingness that any one, whether high or low, should be wronged or trampled under foot.—*Channing.*

Liberty consists in the right which God has given us, of doing, getting, and enjoying all the good in our power, according to the laws of God, of the State, and of our conscience.—True liberty, therefore, can never interfere with the duties, rights, and interests of others.—*C. Simmons.*

What is liberty without wisdom and without virtue?—It is the greatest of all possible evils, for it is folly, vice, and madness, without tuition or restraint.—*Burke.*

O liberty, how many crimes are committed in thy name!—*Mad. Roland.*

The people never give up their liberties but under some delusion.—*Burke.*

The Protestant principle, that "God alone is Lord of the conscience," has done more to give the mind power, and to strike off its chains, than any principle of mere secular policy in the most perfect "Bill of Rights."—*G. Spring.*

The love of religious liberty is a stronger sentiment, when fully excited, than an attachment to civil freedom. Conscience, in the cause of religion, prepares the mind to act and to suffer, beyond almost all other causes. It sometimes gives an impulse so irresistible, that no fetters of power or of opinion can withstand it. History instructs us, that this love of religious liberty, made up of the clearest sense of right and the highest conviction of duty, is able to look the sternest despotism in the face, and, with means apparently inadequate, to shake principalities and powers.—*Daniel Webster.*

A day, an hour of virtuous liberty is worth a whole eternity of bondage.—*Addison.*

The true danger is, when liberty is nibbled away, for expedients, and by parts.—*Burke.*

He is the freeman whom the truth makes free, and all are slaves beside.—*Cowper.*

There is no liberty to men whose passions are stronger than their religious feelings; there is no liberty to men in whom ignorance predominates over knowledge; there is no liberty to men who know not how to govern themselves. —*H. W. Beecher.*

LIBRARIES.—Next to acquiring good friends, the best acquisition is that of good books.—*Colton.*

Libraries are as the shrines where all the relics of saints, full of true virtue, and that without delusion or imposture, are preserved and reposed.—*Bacon.*

Libraries are the wardrobes of literature, whence men, properly informed, may bring forth something for ornament, much for curiosity, and more for use.—*Dyer.*

Let us pity those poor rich men who live barrenly in great bookless houses! Let us congratulate the poor that, in our day, books are so cheap that a man may every year add a hundred volumes to his library for the price of what his tobacco and beer would cost him. Among the earliest ambitions to be excited in clerks, workmen, journeymen, and, indeed, among all that are struggling up from nothing to something, is that of owning, and constantly adding to a library of good books. A little library, growing larger every year, is an honorable part of a young man's history. It is a man's duty to have books. A library is not a luxury, but one of the necessaries of life.—*H. W. Beecher.*

What laborious days, what watchings by the midnight lamp, what rackings of the brain, what hopes and fears, what long lives of laborious study, are here sublimed into print, and condensed into the narrow compass of these surrounding shelves!—*Horace Smith.*

The student has his Rome, his Florence, his whole glowing Italy, within the four walls of his library. He has in his books the ruins of an antique world and the glories of a modern one.—*Longfellow.*

What a place to be in is an old library! It seems as though all the souls of all the writers that have bequeathed their labors to these Bodleians were reposing here, as in some dormitory or middle state. I do not want to handle, to profane the leaves, their winding-sheets. I could as soon dislodge a shade. I seem to inhale learning, walking amid their foliage; and the odor of their old moth-scented coverings is fragrant as the first bloom of those sciential apples which grew amid the happy orchard.—*Lamb.*

My library was dukedom large enough. —*Shakespeare.*

A large library is apt to distract rather than to instruct the learner; it is much better to be confined to a few authors than to wander at random over many. —*Seneca.*

Consider what you have in the smallest chosen library. A company of the wisest and wittiest men that could be picked out of all civil countries, in a thousand years, have set in best order the results of their learning and wisdom. The men themselves were hid and inaccessible, solitary, impatient of interruption, fenced by etiquette; but the thought which they did not uncover to their bosom friend is here written out in transparent words to us, the strangers of another age.—*Emerson.*

A great library contains the diary of the human race.—The great consulting room of a wise man is a library.—*G. Dawson.*

What a world of wit is here packed together!—I know not whether the sight doth more dismay or comfort me. —It dismays me to think that here is so much I cannot know; it comforts me to think that this variety yields so good helps to know what I should.—Blessed be the memory of those who have left their blood, their spirits, their lives, in these precious books, and have willingly wasted themselves into these during monuments, to give light unto others.— *Bp. Hall.*

The true university of these days is a collection of books.—*Carlyle.*

From this slender beginning I have gradually formed a numerous and select library, the foundation of all my works, and the best comfort of my life, both at home and abroad.—*Gibbon.*

No possession can surpass, or even equal a good library, to the lover of books. Here are treasured up for his daily use and delectation, riches which increase by being consumed, and pleasures which never cloy.—*J. A. Langford.*

A library may be regarded as the solemn chamber in which a man may take counsel with all who have been wise, and great, and good, and glorious among the men that have gone before him.—*G. Dawson.*

We enter our studies, and enjoy a society which we alone can bring together. We raise no jealousy by conversing with one in preference to another: we give no offense to the most illustrious by questioning him as long as we will, and leaving him as abruptly. Diversity of opinion raises no tumult in our presence; each interlocutor stands before us, speaks or is silent, and we adjourn or decide the business at our leisure.—*Landor.*

My books are my tools, and the greater their variety and perfection the greater the help to my literary work.— *Tryon Edwards.*

The gloomy recess of an ecclesiastical library is like a harbor, into which a far-traveling curiosity has sailed with its freight, and cast anchor. The ponderous tomes are bales of the mind's merchandise. Odors of distant countries and times steal from the red leaves, the swelling ridges of vellum, and the titles in tarnished gold.—*Willmott.*

LICENTIOUSNESS. — Impure thoughts waken impure feelings, lead to impure expressions, and beget impure actions, and these lead to imbecility both of body and mind, and to the ruin of all that is noble and pure in character. —*C. Simmons.*

If you would not step into the harlot's house, do not go by the harlot's door.— *Secker.*

Lewdness is a very broad way to death, ornamented with artful flowers, and begins to allure and seduce travelers at an early age.—Parental watchfulness, guarding them from early childhood, should be diligent to keep them from this way to ruin.—*C. Simmons.*

Human brutes, like other beasts, find snares and poison in the provisions of life, and are allured by their appetites to their destruction.—*Swift.*

LIFE.—Every man's life is a plan of God.—*Horace Bushnell.*

One life; a little gleam of time between two eternities; no second chance for us forever more.—*Carlyle.*

God gives to every man the virtue, temper, understanding, taste that lifts him into life, and lets him fall in just the niche he was ordained to fill.

Remember that life is neither pain nor pleasure; it is serious business, to be entered upon with courage and in a spirit of self-sacrifice.—*De Tocqueville.*

This outer world is but the pictured scroll of worlds within the soul; a colored chart, a blazoned missal-book, wherein who rightly look may spell the splendors with their mortal eyes, and steer to Paradise.—*Alfred Noyes.*

It is not necessary to live, but to carve our names beyond that point, this is necessary.—*Gabriele d'Annunzio.*

If this life be not a real fight, in which something is eternally gained for the universe by success, it is no better than a game of private theatricals from which one may withdraw at will.—*William James.*

Life is the art of drawing sufficient conclusions from insufficient premises.—*Samuel Butler.*

Every man's life is a fairy tale, written by God's fingers.—*Hans Christian Andersen.*

Life is activity, hence the deep-seated objections to negations.—*James T. Adams.*

The life of every man is a diary in which he means to write one story, and writes another; and his humblest hour is when he compares the volume as it is with what he hoped to make it.—*James M. Barrie.*

The poorest way to face life is to face it with a sneer.—*Theodore Roosevelt.*

A little work, a little sleep, a little love and it is all over.—*Mary Roberts Rinehart.*

The idea shared by many that life is a vale of tears is just as false as the idea shared by the great majority, the idea to which youth and health and riches incline you, that life is a place of entertainment.—*Tolstoi.*

Human life may be likened to the flowers on yonder tree. The wind blows down the flowers, of which some are caught by the screens and scattered on the beautifully decorated mats and cushions, while others are blown over the fence and dropped on the dung heap.—*Fan Chen.*

Life is the only real counsellor; wisdom unfiltered through personal experience does not become a part of the moral tissue.—*Edith Wharton.*

The very commonplaces of life are components of its eternal mystery.—*Gertrude Atherton.*

This life's a hollow bubble, don't you know? Just a painted piece of twouble, don't you know? We come to earth to cwy, we gwow oldeh and we sigh, oldeh still, and then we die! Don't you know?—*Edmund Vance Cooke.*

Let your life lightly dance on the edges of time like dew on the tip of a leaf.—*Rabindranath Tagore.*

It is good to be a part of life. Just as a sun-dial counts only the sunny hours, so does life know only that it is living.—*H. G. Wells.*

Life, like a dome of many-colored glass, stains the white radiance of eternity.—*Shelley.*

The Book Of Life begins with a man and woman in a garden. It ends with Revelations.—*Oscar Wilde.*

Life is like music, it must be composed by ear, feeling and instinct, not by rule. Nevertheless one had better know the rules, for they sometimes guide in doubtful cases though not often.—*Samuel Butler.*

Life will give you what you ask of her if only you ask long enough and plainly enough.—*E. Nesbit.*

There is no cure for birth and death save to enjoy the interval. The dark background which death supplies brings out the tender colours of life in all their purity.—*George Santayana.*

If you would keep your soul from spotted sight and sound, live like the velvet mole, go, burrow underground.—*Elinor Wylie.*

Life is a long lesson in humility.—*James M. Barrie.*

While we least think it he prepares his mate. Mate, and the kings pawn played, it never ceases, though all the earth is dust of taken pieces.—*John Masefield.*

In great moments life seems neither right nor wrong, but something greater, it seems inevitable.—*Margaret Sherwood.*

Fortune is a prize to be won. Adventure is the road to it. Chance is what may lurk in the shadows at the roadside.—*O. Henry.*

It is impossible to live pleasurably without living prudently, and honorably, and justly; or to live prudently, and honorably, and justly, without living pleasurably.—*Epicurus.*

The web of our life is of a mingled yarn, good and ill together; our virtues would be proud if our faults whipped them not; and our crimes would despair if they were not cherished by our virtues.—*Shakespeare.*

Life is hardly respectable if it has no generous task, no duties or affections that constitute a necessity of existence. Every man's task is his life-preserver.—*Emerson.*

A useless life is only an early death.—*Goethe.*

Why all this toil for the triumphs of an hour?—*Young.*

Life is rather a state of embryo, a preparation for life; a man is not completely born till he has passed through death.—*Franklin.*

Life is a series of surprises. We do not guess to-day the mood, the pleasure, the power of to-morrow, when we are building up our being.—*Emerson.*

Much as we deplore our condition in life, nothing would make us more satisfied with it than the changing of places, for a few days, with our neighbors.

There is not one life which the Life-giver ever loses out of His sight; not one which sins so that He casts it away; not one which is not so near to Him that whatever touches it touches Him with sorrow or with joy.—*Phillips Brooks.*

We never live; we are always in the expectation of living.—*Voltaire.*

He lives long that lives well; and time misspent is not lived, but lost. God is better than his promise if he takes from him a long lease, and gives him a freehold of a better value.—*Fuller.*

Though we seem grieved at the shortness of life in general, we are wishing every period of it at an end. The minor longs to be at age, then to be a man of business; then to make up an estate, then to arrive at honors, then to retire.—*Addison.*

There appears to exist a greater desire to live long than to live well! Measure by man's desires, he cannot live long enough; measure by his good deeds, and he has not lived long enough; measure

by his evil deeds, and he has lived too long.—*Zimmermann.*

Life is fruitful in the ratio in which it is laid out in noble action or patient perseverance.—*Liddon.*

Life, like the waters of the seas, freshens only when it ascends toward heaven.—*Richter.*

I would so live as if I knew that I received my being only for the benefit of others.—*Seneca.*

He that embarks in the voyage of life will always wish to advance rather by the impulse of the wind than the strokes of the oar; and many founder in their passage, while they lie waiting for the gale.—*Johnson.*

Measure not life by the hopes and enjoyments of this world, but by the preparation it makes for another; looking forward to what you shall be rather than backward to what you have been.

He is not dead who departs from life with a high and noble fame; but he is dead, even while living, whose brow is branded with infamy.—*Tieck.*

I am convinced that there is no man that knows life well, and remembers all the incidents of his past existence, who would accept it again.—*Campbell.*

Who would venture upon the journey of life, if compelled to begin it at the end?—*Mad. de Maintenon.*

How small a portion of our life it is that we really enjoy! In youth we are looking forward to things that are to come; in old age we are looking backward to things that are gone past; in manhood, although we appear indeed to be more occupied in things that are present, yet even that is too often absorbed in vague determinations to be vastly happy on some future day when we have time.—*Colton.*

The earnestness of life is the only passport to the satisfaction of life.—*Theodore Parker.*

If I could get the ear of every young man but for one word, it would be this; make the most and best of yourself—There is no tragedy like a wasted life—a life failing of its true end, and turned to a false end.—*T. T. Munger.*

When I reflect upon what I have seen, have heard, and have done, I can hardly persuade myself that all that frivolous hurry and bustle and pleasure of the world had any reality; and I look on what has passed as one of those wild dreams which opium occasions, and I by no means wish to repeat the nauseous dose for the sake of the fugitive illusion. —*Chesterfield.*

We never live, but we ever hope to live.—*Pascal.*

Life, according to an Arabic proverb, is composed of two parts: that which is past—a dream; and that which is to come—a wish.

Life is like a beautiful and winding lane, on either side bright flowers, beautiful butterflies, and tempting fruits, which we scarcely pause to admire and taste, so eager are we to hasten to an opening which we imagine will be more beautiful still. But by degrees, as we advance, the trees grow bleak, the flowers and butterflies fail, the fruits disappear, and we find we have arrived—to reach a desert waste.—*G. A. Sala.*

Life is the childhood of our immortality.—*Goethe.*

Life is thick sown with thorns, and I know no other remedy than to pass quickly through them. The longer we dwell on our misfortunes, the greater is their power to harm us.—*Voltaire.*

Common sense does not ask an impossible chessboard, but takes the one before it and plays the game.—*Wendell Phillips.*

The finest lives, in my opinion, are those who rank in the common model, and with the human race, but without miracle, without extravagance.—*Montaigne.*

How great a pity that we should not feel for what end we are born into this world, till just as we are leaving it.—*Walsingham.*

Though I think no man can live well once but he that could live twice, yet for my own part, I would not live over my hours past, or begin again the thread of my days: not because I have lived them well, but for fear I should live them worse.—*Sir T. Browne.*

A man should live with his superiors as he does with his fire; not too near, lest he burn; not too far off, lest he freeze.—*Diogenes.*

When I reflect, as I frequently do, upon the felicity I have enjoyed, I sometimes say to myself, that, were the offer made me, I would engage to run again, from beginning to end, the same career of life. All I would ask, should be the privilege of an author, to correct in a second edition, certain errors of the first. —*Franklin.*

He who increases the endearments of life, increases at the same time the terrors of death.—*Young.*

To complain that life has no joys while there is a single creature whom we can relieve by our bounty, assist by our counsels, or enliven by our presence, is to lament the loss of that which we possess, and is just as rational as to die of thirst with the cup in our hands.—*Fitzosborne.*

Life, if properly viewed in any aspect, is great, but mainly great when viewed in its relation to the world to come.—*Albert Barnes.*

Hope writes the poetry of the boy, but memory that of the man. Man looks forward with smiles, but backward with sighs. Such is the wise providence of God. The cup of life is sweetest at the brim, the flavor is impaired as we drink deeper, and the dregs are made bitter that we may not struggle when it is taken from our lips.

Let us love life and feel the value of it, that we may fill it with Christ.—*A. Monod.*

We never think of the main business of life till a vain repentance minds us of it at the wrong end.—*L'Estrange.*

If we do not weigh and consider to what end this life is given us, and thereupon order and dispose it right, we do not number our days in the narrowest and most limited signification.—*Clarendon.*

It is an infamy to die and not be missed.—*Carlos Wilcox.*

Would you throughout life be up to the height of your century, always in the prime of man's reason, without crudeness and without decline, live habitually, while young, with persons older, and when old with persons younger than yourself.—*Bulwer.*

Life does not count by years. Some suffer a lifetime in a day, and so grow old between the rising and the setting of the sun.—*Augusta Evans.*

The certainty that life cannot be long,

and the probability that it will be shorter than nature allows, ought to waken every man to the active prosecution of whatever he is desirous to perform. It is true that no diligence can ensure success; death may intercept the swiftest career; but he who is cut off in the execution of an honest undertaking, has at least the honor of falling in his rank, and has fought the battle though he missed the victory.—*Johnson.*

The vanity of human life is like a rivulet, constantly passing away, and yet constantly coming on.—*Pope.*

There are two lives to each of us, the life of our actions, and the life of our minds and hearts.—History reveals men's deeds and their outward characters, but not themselves.—There is a secret self that has its own life, unpenetrated and unguessed.—*Bulwer.*

We are immortal till our work is done. —*Whitefield.*

Our life cannot be pronounced happy till the last scene has closed with resignation and hope, and in the full prospect of a blessed immortality beyond the grave.

This little life has its duties that are great—that are alone great, and that go up to heaven and down to hell.—*Carlyle.*

They who are most weary of life, and yet are most unwilling to die, are such who have lived to no purpose; who have rather breathed than lived.—*Clarendon.*

Many think themselves to be truly God-fearing when they call this world a valley of tears. But I believe they would be more so, if they called it a happy valley. God is more pleased with those who think everything right in the world, than with those who think nothing right. With so many thousand joys, is it not black ingratitude to call the world a place of sorrow and torment?—*Richter.*

Life is a quarry, out of which we are to mold and chisel and complete a character.—*Goethe.*

There is nothing in life so irrational, that good sense and chance may not set it to rights; nothing so rational, that folly and chance may not utterly confound it.—*Goethe.*

What a beautiful lesson is taught in these words of Sterne: "So quickly

sometimes has the wheel of life turned round, that many a man has lived to enjoy the benefit of that charity which his own piety projected."

The meaning, the value, the truth of life can be learned only by an actual performance of its duties, and truth can be learned and the soul saved in no other way.—*T. T. Munger.*

It is the bounty of nature that we live, but of philosophy that we live well; which is, in truth, a greater benefit than life itself.—*Seneca.*

Fleeting as were the dreams of old, remembered like a tale that's told, we pass away.—*Longfellow.*

The time of life is short; to spend that shortness basely, 'twere too long.—*Shakespeare.*

Bestow thy youth so that thou mayst have comfort to remember it, when it hath forsaken thee, and not sigh and grieve at the account thereof. Whilst thou art young thou wilt think it will never have an end; but behold, the longest day hath his evening, and thou shalt enjoy it but once; it never turns again; use it therefore as the spring-time, which soon departeth, and wherein thou oughtest to plant and sow all provisions for a long and happy life.—*Sir W. Raleigh.*

We live in deeds, not years; in thoughts, not breaths; in feelings, not in figures on the dial; we should count time by heart-throbs. He most lives who thinks most, feels the noblest, acts the best.—*Bailey.*

There is nothing which must end, to be valued for its continuance. If hours, days, months, and years pass away, it is no matter what hour, day, month, or year we die. The applause of a good actor is due to him at whatever scene of the play he makes his exit. It is thus in the life of a man of sense; a short life is sufficient to manifest himself a man of honor and virtue; when he ceases to be such, he has lived too long; and while he is such, it is of no consequence to him how long he shall be so, provided he is so to his life's end.—*Steele.*

Life, like every other blessing, derives its value from its use alone. Not for itself, but for a nobler end the eternal gave it; and that end is virtue.—*Johnson.*

Nor love thy life, nor hate; but what thou livest, live well; how long or short permit to heaven.—*Milton.*

Life is a journey, not a home; a road, not a city of habitation; and the enjoyments and blessings we have are but little inns on the roadside of life, where we may be refreshed for a moment, that we may with new strength press on to the end—to the rest that remaineth for the people of God.

'Tis not for man to trifle; life is brief, and sin is here. We have no time to sport away the hours; all must be earnest in a world like ours.—*Bonar.*

I count all that part of my life lost which I spent not in communion with God, or in doing good.—*Donne.*

The end of a dissolute life is commonly a desperate death.—*Bion.*

The truest view of life has always seemed to me to be that which shows that we are here not to enjoy, but to learn.—*F. W. Robertson.*

Nothing but a good life here can fit men for a better one hereafter.

The truest end of life is to know the life that never ends.—*Penn.*

Dost thou love life?—Then do not squander time, for that is the stuff life is made of.—*Franklin.*

That man lives twice who lives the first life well.—*Herrick.*

A sacred burden is this life ye bear; look on it; lift it; bear it solemnly; fail not for sorrow; falter not for sin; but onward, upward, till the goal ye win.—*Frances Ann Kemble.*

The end of life is to be like God, and the soul following God will be like him. —*Socrates.*

Thy life is no idle dream, but a solemn reality; it is thine own, and it is all thou hast to front eternity with.—*Carlyle.*

Life's evening will take its character from the day that preceded it.—*Shuttleworth.*

The creed of the true saint is to make the most of life, and to make the best of it.—*E. H. Chapin.*

Live while you live, the epicure would say, and seize the pleasures of the passing day.—Live while you live, the sacred preacher cries, and give to God each moment as it flies.—Lord, in my views, let both united be. I live in pleasure while I live to thee.—*Doddridge.*

He that lives to live forever, never fears dying.—*Penn.*

No man enjoys the true taste of life, but he who is ready and willing to quit it.—*Seneca.*

Live virtuously, my lord, and you cannot die too soon, nor live too long.— *Lady Russell.*

The things for which life is valuable are the satisfactions which come from the improvement of knowledge and the exercise of piety.—*Boyle.*

I will govern my life and thoughts as if the whole world were to see the one and to read the other, for what does it signify to make anything a secret to my neighbor, when to God, who is the searcher of our hearts, all our privacies are open?—*Seneca.*

Our grand business in life is not to see what lies dimly at a distance, but to do what lies clearly at hand.—*Carlyle.*

We wish for more in life rather than more of it.—*Jean Ingelow.*

There is pleasure enough in this life to make us wish to live, and pain enough to reconcile us to death when we can live no longer.

The most we can get out of life is its discipline for ourselves, and its usefulness for others.—*Tryon Edwards.*

Human life is a constant want, and ought to be a constant prayer.

Live as with God; and whatever be your calling, pray for the gift that will perfectly qualify you in it.—*Horace Bushnell.*

Life is divided into three terms— that which was, which is, and which will be. Let us learn from the past to profit by the present, and from the present to live better for the future.

Oft in my way have I stood still, though but a casual passenger, so much I felt the awfulness of life.—*Wordsworth.*

Behold eighty-three years passed away! What cares! what agitation! what anxieties! what ill-will! what sad complications! and all without other result except great fatigue of body and mind, and disgust with regard to the past, and a profound sentiment of discouragement and despair with regard to the future.—*Talleyrand.*

The shaping of our own life is our own work. It is a thing of beauty, or a thing of shame, as we ourselves make it. We lay the corner and add joint to joint, we give the proportion, we set the finish. It may be a thing of beauty and of joy for ever. God forgive us if we pervert our life from putting on its appointed glory!—*Ware.*

What a death in life it must be—an existence whose sole aim is good eating and drinking, splendid houses and elegant clothes! Not that these things are bad in moderation—and with something higher beyond. But with nothing beyond?—*Mulock.*

The greatest results in life are usually attained by simple means and the exercise of ordinary qualities. These may for the most part be summed up in these two—common sense and perseverance.—*Feltham.*

To live is not merely to breathe, it is to act; it is to make use of our organs, senses, faculties, of all those parts of ourselves which give us the feeling of existence. The man who has lived longest is not the man who has counted most years, but he who has enjoyed life most. Such a one was buried a hundred years old, but he was dead from his birth. He would have gained by dying young; at least he would have lived till that time.—*Rousseau.*

To make good use of life, one should have in youth the experience of advanced years, and in old age the vigor of youth.—*Stanislaus.*

Live as if you expected to live an hundred years, but might die to-morrow.—*Ann Lee.*

Yet through all, we know this tangled skein is in the hands of One who sees the end from the beginning; he shall yet unravel all.—*Alexander Smith.*

Be such a man, and live such a life, that if every man were such as you, and every life a life like yours, this earth would be God's Paradise.—*Phillips Brooks.*

Life is made up, not of great sacrifices or duties, but of little things, in which smiles and kindness, and small

obligations given habitually, are what preserve the heart and secure comfort.—*Sir H. Davy.*

Life is the jailer of the soul in this filthy prison, and its only deliverer is death.—What we call life is a journey to death, and what we call death is a passport to life.—*Colton.*

Age and youth look upon life from the opposite ends of the telescope; to the one it is exceedingly long, to the other exceedingly short.—*H.W.Beecher.*

Man spends his life in reasoning on the past, complaining of the present, and trembling for the future.—*Rivarol.*

Life, like war, is a series of mistakes, and he is not the best Christian nor the best general who makes the fewest false steps. Poor mediocrity may secure that, but he is best who wins the most splendid victories by the retrieval of mistakes.—*F. W. Robertson.*

With most men life is like backgammon—half skill and half luck.—*O. W. Holmes.*

LIGHT.—Hail! holy light, offspring of heaven, first born!—*Milton.*

The first creation of God, in the works of the days, was the light of sense; the last was the light of reason; and his Sabbath work, ever since, is the illumination of the spirit.—*Bacon.*

Before the sun, before the heavens thou wert, and at the voice of God, as with a mantle didst invest the rising world of waters dark and deep won from the void and formless infinite.—*Milton.*

Light! Nature's resplendent robe; without whose vesting beauty all were wrapt in gloom.—*Thomson.*

Light is the symbol of truth.—*J. R. Lowell.*

The eye's light is a noble gift of heaven! All beings live from light; each fair created thing, the very plants, turn with a joyful transport to the light.—*Schiller.*

Light is the shadow of God.—*Plato.*

Moral light is the radiance of the diviner glory.—*Dick.*

The light of nature, the light of science, and the light of reason, are but as darkness, compared with the divine light which shines only from the word of God.—*J. K. Lord.*

Science and art may invent splendid

modes of illuminating the apartments of the opulent; but these are all poor and worthless compared with the light which the sun pours freely, impartially, over hill and valley, which kindles daily the eastern and western sky; and so the common lights of reason and conscience and love are of more worth and dignity than the rare endowments which give celebrity to a few.—*Channing.*

We should render thanks to God for having produced this temporal light, which is the smile of heaven and the joy of the world, spreading it like a cloth of gold over the face of the air and earth, and lighting it as a torch, by which we may behold his works.—*Caussin.*

Walk boldly and wisely in the light thou hast; there is a hand above will help thee on.—*Bailey.*

Walk in the light and thou shalt see thy path, though thorny, bright; for God, by grace, shall dwell in thee, and God himself is light.—*Barton.*

LITERATURE.—Literature is a fragment of a fragment; of all that ever happened, or has been said, but a fraction has been written, and of this but little is extant.—*Goethe.*

The literature of an age is but the mirror of its prevalent tendencies.—*Nation.*

The triumphs of the warrior are bounded by the narrow theater of his own age; but those of a Scott or a Shakespeare will be renewed with greater and greater luster in ages yet unborn, when the victorious chieftain shall be forgotten, or shall live only in the song of the minstrel and the page of the chronicler.—*Prescott.*

The literature of a people must spring from the sense of its nationality; and nationality is impossible without self-respect, and self-respect is impossible without liberty.—*Mrs. Stowe.*

A beautiful literature springs from the depth and fulness of intellectual and moral life, from an energy of thought and feeling, to which nothing, as we believe, ministers so largely as enlightened religion.—*Channing.*

Literature happens to be the only occupation in which wages are not given in proportion to the goodness of the work done.—*Froude.*

Literature is a great staff, but a sorry crutch.—*Walter Scott.*

When literature is the sole business of life, it becomes a drudgery. When we are able to resort to it only at certain hours, it is a charming relaxation. In my earlier days I was a banker's clerk, obliged to be at the desk every day from ten till five o'clock; and I shall never forget the delight with which, on returning home, I used to read and write during the evening.—*Rogers.*

Literary dissipation is no less destructive of sympathy with the living world, than sensual dissipation. Mere intellect is as hard-hearted and as heart-hardening as mere sense; and the union of the two, when uncontrolled by the conscience and without the softening, purifying influences of the moral affections, is all that is requisite to produce the diabolical ideal of our nature.—*Anon.*

Books only partially represent their authors; the writer is always greater than his work.—*Bovee.*

Literature has her quacks no less than medicine, and they are divided into two classes; those who have erudition without genius, and those who have volubility without depth; we get second-hand sense from the one, and original nonsense from the other.—*Colton.*

In the literature of the world there is not one popular book which is immoral that continues to exist two centuries after it is produced; for in the heart of nations the false does not live so long, and the true is ethical to the end of time.—*Bulwer.*

If I might control the literature of the household, I would guarantee the well-being of the church and state.—*Bacon.*

He who would understand the real spirit of literature should not select authors of any one period alone, but rather go to the fountain head, and trace the little rill as it courses along down the ages broadening and deepening into the great ocean of thought which the men of the present are exploring.—*Garfield.*

In science, read, by preference, the newest works; in literature, the oldest. The classic literature is always modern.—*Bulwer.*

A country which has no national literature, or a literature too insignificant to force its way abroad, must always be, to its neighbors at least, in every important spiritual respect, an unknown and unestimated country.—*Carlyle.*

The decline of literature indicates the decline of a nation; the two keep pace in their downward tendency.—*Goethe.*

I never knew a man of letters ashamed of his profession.—*Thackeray.*

The study of literature nourishes youth, entertains old age, adorns prosperity, solaces adversity, is delightful at home, and unobtrusive abroad.—*Cicero.*

Nothing lives in literature but that which has in it the vitality of creative art; and it would be safe advice to the young to read nothing but what is old.—*E. P. Whipple.*

In literature, to-day, there are plenty of good masons but few good architects. —*Joubert.*

The great standard of literature, as to purity and exactness of style, is the Bible.—*Blair.*

Such superiority do the pursuits of literature possess above every other occupation, that even he who attains but a mediocrity in them, merits the preeminence above those who excel the most in the common and vulgar professions.—*Hume.*

The beaten paths of literature lead safeliest to the goal, and the talent pleases us most which submits to shine with new gracefulness through old forms. —Nor is the noblest and most peculiar mind too noble or peculiar for working by prescribed laws.—*Carlyle.*

There, is first, the literature of knowledge; and, secondly, the literature of power. The function of the first is, to teach; of the second is, to move; the first is a rudder, the second an oar or a sail. The first speaks to the mere discursive understanding; the second speaks ultimately to the higher understanding or reason, but always through affections of pleasure and sympathy.—*De Quincey.*

Literary history is the great morgue where all seek the dead ones whom they love, or to whom they are related. —*Heine.*

Let your literary compositions be kept from the public eye for nine years at least.—*Horace.*

The selection of a subject is to the author what choice of position is to the general,—once skillfully determined, the battle is already half won. Of a few writers it may be said, that they are popular in despite of their subjects—but of a great many more, that they are popular because of them.—*Bovee.*

Other relaxations are peculiar to certain times, places, and stages of life, but the study of letters is the nourishment of our youth, and the joy of our old age. They throw an additional splendor on prosperity, and are the resource and consolation of adversity; they delight at home, and are no embarrassment abroad; in short, they are company to us at night, our fellow-travelers on a journey, and attendants in our rural recesses.— *Cicero.*

There is such a thing as literary fashion, and prose and verse have been regulated by the same caprice that cuts our coats and cocks our hats.—*Disraeli.*

Literature has now become a game in which the booksellers are the kings; the critics, the knaves; the public, the pack; and the poor author, the mere table or thing played upon.—*Colton.*

Literature is the immortality of speech. —*Schlegel.*

LITTLE THINGS.—(See " Trifles.")

He that despiseth small things, shall fall by little and little.—*Ecclesiasticus.*

Most of the critical things in life, which become the starting points of human destiny, are little things.—*R. Smith.*

Minute events are the hinges on which magnificent results turn.—In a watch the smallest link, chain, ratchet, cog, or crank, is as essential as the main spring itself.—If one fall out the whole will stand still.—*Cumming.*

Without mounting by degrees, a man cannot attain to high things; and the breaking of the ladder still casteth a man back, and maketh the thing wearisome, which was easy.—*Sir P. Sidney.*

The power of little things has so often been noted that we accept it as an axiom, and yet fail to see, in each beginning, the possibility of great events. —*F. P. Edwards.*

Do little things now; so shall big things come to thee by and by asking to be done.—*Persian Proverb.*

The greatest things ever done on earth have been done by little and little—little agents, little persons, little things, by every one doing his own work, filling his own sphere, holding his own post, and saying, "Lord, what wilt thou have me to do?"—*Guthrie.*

Trivial circumstances, which show the manners of the age, are often more instructive as well as entertaining, than the great transactions of wars and negotiations, which are nearly similar in all periods, and in all countries of the world.—*Hume.*

Sometimes when I consider what tremendous consequences come from little things—a chance word, a tap on the shoulder, or a penny dropped on a news-stand—I am tempted to think . . . there are no little things.—*Bruce Barton.*

A little more patience, a little more charity for all, a little more devotion, a little more love; with less bowing down to the past, and a silent ignoring of pretended authority; brave looking forward to the future with more faith in our fellows, and the race will be ripe for a great burst of light and life.—*Elbert Hubbard.*

He crossed words of which he knew nothing; and perhaps we all do as much every moment, over things of divinest meaning.—*Leigh Hunt.*

Not for the mighty world, O Lord, tonight, nations and kingdoms in their fearful might—Let me be glad the kettle gently sings, let me be glad for little things.—*Edna Jaques.*

The electric unit, whatever it may be, but certainly infinitely "small," may ultimately win man's fight against his most deadly enemy, the *invisible* enemy.—*Arthur Brisbane.*

The million little things that drop into our hands, the small opportunities each day brings He leaves us free to use or abuse and goes unchanging along His silent way.—*Helen Keller.*

The power of little things to give instruction and happiness should be the first lesson in life, and it should be inculcated deeply.—*Russell H. Conwell.*

The smallest hair throws its shadow.—*Goethe.*

Little things are great to little men.—*Goldsmith.*

In great matters men show themselves as they wish to be seen; in small matters, as they are.—*Gamaliel Bradford.*

There is nothing too little for so little a creature as man.—It is by studying little things that we attain the great art of having as little misery and as much happiness as possible.—*Johnson.*

Life is made up, not of great sacrifices or duties, but of little things, in which smiles and kindness and small obligations, given habitually, are what win and preserve the heart and secure comfort.—*Sir H. Davy.*

Alas! how easily things go wrong; a sigh too much or a kiss too long, and there follows a mist and a weeping rain, and life is never the same again.—*George Macdonald.*

Little drops of water, little grains of sand, make the mighty ocean and the pleasant land; so the little minutes, humble though they be, make the mighty ages of eternity.—*Mrs. Julia A. Fletcher Carney.*

Little things console us, because little things afflict us.—*Pascal.*

Despise not small things, either for evil or good, for a look may work thy ruin, or a word create thy wealth.—A spark is a little thing, yet it may kindle the world.—*Tupper.*

Most persons would succeed in small things if they were not troubled with great ambitions.—*Longfellow.*

LOGIC.—Logic and metaphysics make use of more tools than all the rest of the sciences put together, and they do the least work.—*Colton.*

It was a saying of the ancients, that "truth lies in a well"; and to carry on the metaphor, we may justly say, that logic supplies us with steps whereby we may go down to reach the water.—*Watts.*

Logic is the science of the laws of thought as thought, that is, of the necessary conditions to which thought, in itself considered, is subject.—*Sir W. Hamilton.*

Logical consequences are the scarecrows of fools and the beacons of wise men.—*Thomas H. Huxley.*

Logic is a large drawer, containing

some needful instruments, and many more that are superfluous.—A wise man will look into it for two purposes, to avail himself of those instruments that are really useful, and to admire the ingenuity with which those that are not so are assorted and arranged.—*Colton.*

Logic and rhetoric make men able to contend.—Logic differeth from rhetoric as the fist from the palm; the one close, the other at large.—*Bacon.*

Ethics make one's soul mannerly and wise, but logic is the armory of reason, furnished with all offensive and defensive weapons.—*Fuller.*

Logic works; metaphysics contemplates.—*Joubert.*

Syllogism is of necessary use, even to the lovers of truth, to show them the fallacies that are often concealed in florid, witty, or involved discourses.—*Locke.*

Logic is the art of convincing us of some truth.—*Bruyère.*

LOOKS.—(See "EYE" and "FACE.")

Looks are more expressive and reliable than words; they have a language which all understand, and language itself is to be interpreted by the look as well as tone with which it is uttered.—*Tryon Edwards.*

Looks kill love, and love by looks reviveth; a smile recures the wounding of a frown.—*Shakespeare.*

Their eyes but met, and then were turned aside.—It was enough.—That mystic eloquence, unheard, yet visible, is deeply felt, and tells what else were incommunicable.—*Derozier.*

Features—the great soul's apparent seat.—*Bryant.*

What brutal mischief sits upon his brow! He may be honest, but he looks damnation.—*Dryden.*

A good face is a letter of recommendation, as a good heart is a letter of credit.—*Bulwer.*

In his looks appears a wild, distracted fierceness; I can read some dreadful purpose in his face.—*Denham.*

Cheerful looks make every dish a feast, and that it is which crowns a welcome.—*Massinger.*

'Tis not my talent to conceal my thoughts, or carry smiles and sunshine in my face, when discontent sits heavy at my heart.—*Addison.*

Coldness and aversion are in your looks, and tell no pity is concealed within.—*Havard.*

His visage seemed to bear a mixture of uncertain cheerfulness, like hope corrected by some cautious fear.—*Sewell.*

How in the looks does conscious guilt appear.—*Ovid.*

O there are looks and tones that dart an instant sunshine to the heart, as if the soul that minute caught some treasure it through life had sought; as if the very lips and eyes sparkled and spoke before us.—*Moore.*

With such ardent eyes he wandered o'er me, and gazed with such intensity of love, sending his soul out to me in a look.—*Young.*

A sweet attractive kind of grace; a full assurance given by looks; continual comfort in a face, the lineaments of gospel books.—*Roydon.*

LOQUACITY.—(See "SPEECH," "NOISE," "TALKING.")

A talkative fellow may be compared to an unbraced drum, which beats a wise man out of his wits.—Loquacity is ever running, and almost incurable.—*Feltham.*

Learn to hold thy tongue; five words cost Zacharias forty weeks of silence.—*Fuller.*

Speaking much is a sign of vanity, for he that is lavish in words is a niggard in deed.—*Sir W. Raleigh.*

Of a great and wise statesman it is said, "that he can hold his tongue in ten different languages."

Gratiano speaks an infinite deal of nothing; his reasons are as two grains of wheat hid in two bushels of chaff; you shall seek all day ere you find them, and when you have them they are not worth the search.—*Shakespeare.*

Thou may'st esteem a man of many words and many lies much alike.—*Fuller.*

Nature has given us two ears, two eyes, and but one tongue, to the end that we should hear and see more than we speak.—*Socrates.*

Those who have few affairs to attend to are great speakers.—The less men think the more they talk.—*Montesquieu.*

Labor to show more wit in discourse than words, and not to pour out a flood of the one, when you can hardly wring out of your brains a drop of the other. —*Spencer.*

Every absurdity has a champion to defend it, for error is always talkative. —*Goldsmith.*

There are braying men in the world as well as braying asses; for what is loud and senseless talking and swearing other than braying.—*L'Estrange.*

You cram these words into mine ears against the stomach of my sense.— *Shakespeare.*

He loves to hear himself talk, and will speak more in a minute than he will stand to in a month.—*Shakespeare.*

Be always less willing to speak than to hear; what thou hearest, thou receivest; what thou speakest thou givest.—It is more glorious to give, but more profitable to receive.—*Quarles.*

Many a man's tongue shakes out its master's undoing.—*Shakespeare.*

They only babble who practise not reflection.—I shall think; and thought is silence.—*Sheridan.*

He draweth out the thread of his verbosity finer than the staple of his argument.—*Shakespeare.*

They always talk who never think, and who have the least to say.—*Prior.*

The tongue of a fool is the key of his counsel, which, in a wise man, wisdom hath in keeping.—*Socrates.*

No fool can be silent at a feast.— *Solon.*

Still his tongue ran on; the less weight it bore with greater ease; and with its everlasting clack, set all men's ears upon the rack.—*Samuel Butler.*

A man that speaks too much, and museth but little, wasteth his mind in words, and is counted a fool among men.—*Tupper.*

LOSSES.—(See " MISFORTUNE.")

We never seem to know what anything means till we have lost it.—The full significance of those words, property, ease, health—the wealth of meaning that lies in the fond epithets, parent, child, friend, we never know till they are taken away; till in place of the

bright, visible being, comes the awful and desolate shadow where nothing is— where we stretch out our hands in vain, and strain our eyes upon dark and dismal vacuity.—*O. Dewey.*

Humanity may endure the loss of everything; all its possessions may be torn away without infringing its true dignity—all but the possibility of improvement.—*Fichte.*

Of all our losses, those delay doth cause, are most and heaviest.—By it oft we lose the richest treasures, knowledge, wealth, and power, and oft, alas! the never dying soul.—The calls of God and duty we intend to hear, at some convenient season, which to us may never come.—And thus we madly waste probation, forfeit heaven, and heedless sink to endless death.—*Tryon Edwards.*

Wise men ne'er sit and wail their loss, but cheerily seek how to redress their harms.—*Shakespeare.*

When wealth is lost, nothing is lost; when health is lost, something is lost; when character is lost, all is lost.—*German Motto.*

Losses are comparative, imagination only makes them of any moment.— *Pascal.*

What is taken from the fortune, also, may haply be so much lifted from the soul. The greatness of a loss, as the proverb suggests, is determinable, not so much by what we have lost, as by what we have left.—*Bovee.*

LOVE.—It is a beautiful necessity of our nature to love something.—*Jerrold.*

The greatest pleasure of life is love.— *Sir W. Temple.*

There comes a time when the souls of human beings, women more even than men, begin to faint for the atmosphere of the affections they are made to breathe.—*O. W. Holmes.*

All true love is grounded on esteem. —*Buckingham.*

The heart of him who truly loves is a paradise on earth; he has God in himself, for God is love.—*Lamennais.*

Love one human being purely and warmly, and you will love all.—The heart in this heaven, like the sun in its course, sees nothing, from the dewdrop to the ocean, but a mirror which it brightens, and warms, and fills.—*Richter.*

Love gives itself; it is not bought.—*Longfellow.*

Love was to his impassioned soul, not a mere part of its existence, but the whole, the very life-breath of his heart. —*Moore.*

We are shaped and fashioned by what we love.—*Goethe.*

The poets judged like philosophers when they feigned love to be blind.— How often do we see in a woman what our judgment and taste approve, and yet feel nothing of love toward her; how often what they both condemn, and yet feel a great deal.—*Greville.*

I am not one of those who do not believe in love at first sight, but I believe in taking a second look.—*H. Vincent.*

Passion may be blind; but to say that love is, is a libel and a lie.—Nothing is more sharp-sighted or sensitive than true love, in discerning, as by an instinct, the feelings of another.—*W. H. Davis.*

That is the true season of love, when we believe that we alone can love, that no one could ever have loved so before us, and that no one will love in the same way after us.—*Goethe.*

Absence in love is like water upon fire; a little quickens, but much extinguishes it.—*Hannah More.*

Love is never lost. If not reciprocated it will flow back and soften and purify the heart.—*Washington Irving.*

The plainest man that can convince a woman that he is really in love with her, has done more to make her in love with him than the handsomest man, if he can produce no such conviction. For the love of woman is a shoot, not a seed, and flourishes most vigorously only when ingrafted on that love which is rooted in the breast of another.—*Colton.*

Man's love is of man's life a part; it is woman's whole existence.—*Byron.*

Love which is only an episode in the life of man, is the entire history of woman's life.—*Mad. de Staël.*

The soul of woman lives in love.— *Mrs. Sigourney.*

Alas! the love of women! it is known to be a lovely and a fearful thing; for all of theirs upon that die is thrown:

and if 'tis lost, life has no more to bring to them but mockeries of the past alone. —*Byron.*

Let grace and goodness be the principal loadstone of thy affections. For love which hath ends, will have an end; whereas that which is founded on true virtue, will always continue.—*Dryden.*

Affections, like the conscience, are rather to be led than drawn; and 'tis to be feared, they that marry where they do not love, will love where they do not marry.—*Fuller.*

Love is an image of God, and not a lifeless image, but the living essence of the divine nature which beams full of all goodness.—*Luther.*

The motto of chivalry is also the motto of wisdom; to serve all, but love only one.—*Balzac.*

A man loved by a beautiful and virtuous woman, carries with him a talisman that renders him invulnerable; every one feels that such a one's life has a higher value than that of others. —*Mad. Dudevant.*

I have enjoyed the happiness of the world; I have lived and loved.—*Schiller.*

Nothing more excites to all that is noble and generous, than virtuous love. —*Home.*

Man while he loves is never quite depraved.—*Lamb.*

Mutual love, the crown of all our bliss.—*Milton.*

It is better to have loved and lost, than not to have loved at all.—*Tennyson.*

It is sweet to feel by what fine spun threads our affections are drawn together.—*Sterne.*

The treasures of the deep are not so precious as are the concealed comforts of a man locked up in woman's love.— *Middleton.*

Must love be ever treated with profaneness as a mere illusion? or with coarseness as a mere impulse? or with fear as a mere disease? or with shame as a mere weakness? or with levity as a mere accident? whereas it is a great mystery and a great necessity, lying at the foundation of human existence, morality, and happiness,—mysterious, universal, inevitable as death.—*Harriet Martineau.*

Corporeal charms may indeed **gain**

admirers, but there must be mental ones to retain them.—*Colton.*

The woman that has not touched the heart of a man, before he leads her to the altar, has scarcely a chance to charm it when possession and security turn their powerful arms against her.—*Mrs. Cowley.*

There is nothing holier in this life of ours than the first consciousness of love —the first fluttering of its silken wings —the first rising sound and breath of that wind which is so soon to sweep through the soul, to purify or to destroy. —*Longfellow.*

When the heart is still agitated by the remains of a passion, we are more ready to receive a new one than when we are entirely cured.—*Rochefoucauld.*

Love is an egotism of two.—*La Salle.*

True love's the gift which God hath given, to man alone beneath the heaven. The silver link, the silver tie, which heart to heart, and mind to mind, in body and in soul can bind.—*Walter Scott.*

Love never reasons, but profusely gives; gives, like a thoughtless prodigal, its all, and trembles then lest it has done too little.—*Hannah More.*

Love looks not with the eyes, but with the mind.—*Shakespeare.*

A man reserves his greatest and deepest love not for the woman in whose company he finds himself electrified and enkindled but for that one in whose company he may feel tenderly drowsy. —*George Jean Nathan.*

The whole business of love and love-making, is painted by the novelists in a monstrous disproportion to the other relations of life.—*W. D. Howells.*

Love is a thing to be *learned.* It is a difficult, complex maintenance of individual integrity throughout the incalculable processes of inter-human polarity. —*D. H. Lawrence.*

The Bible speaks of a mysterious sin for which there is no forgiveness: this great unpardonable sin is the murder of the "love-life" in a human being.—*Ibsen.*

If you intend to use a horse a whole day and a love for a lifetime, keep the reins taut in the morning.—*Austin O'Malley.*

I never could explain *why* I love anybody, or anything.—*Walt Whitman.*

Great loves, to the last, have pulses red; all great loves that have ever died dropped dead.—*Helen Hunt Jackson.*

The days grow shorter, the nights grow longer, the headstones thicken along the way; and life grows sadder, but love grows stronger for those who walk with us day by day.—*Ella Wilcox.*

Love . . . is like a beautiful flower which I may not touch, but whose fragrance makes the garden a place of delight just the same.—*Helen Keller.*

There will always be about the same percentage of people capable of real love, and there will always be about the same percentage of people who aren't.— *John Galsworthy.*

Love really has nothing to do with wisdom or experience or logic. It is the prevailing breeze in the land of youth. —*Bruno Lessing.*

Love looks through a telescope; envy, through a microscope.—*Henry Wheeler Shaw ("Josh Billings").*

Love that has nothing but beauty to keep it in good health, is short-lived, and apt to have ague-fits.—*Erasmus.*

But love is blind, and lovers cannot see the pretty follies that themselves commit.—*Shakespeare.*

It is in love as in war, we are often more indebted for success to the weakness of the defence, than to the energy of the attack; for mere idleness has ruined more women than passion; vanity more than idleness, and credulity more than either.—*Colton.*

Love is the virtue of women.—*Mad. Dudevant.*

Love sought is good, but given unsought is better.—*Shakespeare.*

The greatest happiness of life is the conviction that we are loved, loved for ourselves, or rather loved in spite of ourselves.—*Victor Hugo.*

It is not decided that women love more than men, but it is indisputable that they love better.—*Dubay.*

The man's courage is loved by the woman, whose fortitude again is coveted by the man. His vigorous intellect is answered by her infallible tact. Can it be true, as is so constantly affirmed, that there is no sex in souls? I doubt it exceedingly.—*Coleridge.*

As love increases, prudence diminishes. —*Rochefoucauld.*

As soon go kindle fire with snow, as seek to quench the fire of love with words.—*Shakespeare.*

Love covers a multitude of sins. When a scar cannot be taken away, the next kind office is to hide it.—Love is never so blind as when it is to spy faults.—It is like the painter, who, being to draw the picture of a friend having a blemish in one eye, would picture only the other side of his face.—It is a noble and great thing to cover the blemishes and to excuse the failings of a friend; to draw a curtain before his stains, and to display his perfections; to bury his weaknesses in silence, but to proclaim his virtues upon the house-top.—*South.*

There is nothing half so sweet in life as love's young dream.—*Moore.*

Never self-possessed, or prudent, love is all abandonment.—*Emerson.*

The desire to be beloved is ever restless and unsatisfied; but the love that flows out upon others is a perpetual well-spring from on high.—*L. M. Child.*

Love is love's reward.—*Dryden.*

No cord or cable can draw so forcibly, or bind so fast, as love can do with a single thread.—*Burton.*

If a man loves a woman for her beauty, does he love her? No; for the small-pox, which destroys her beauty without killing her, causes his love to cease. And if any one loves me for my judgment or my memory, does he really love me? No; for I can lose these qualities without ceasing to be.— *Pascal.*

Those who yield their souls captive to the brief intoxication of love, if no higher and holier feeling mingle with and consecrate their dream of bliss, will shrink trembling from the pangs that attend their waking.—*Schlegel.*

A man may be a miser of his wealth; he may tie up his talent in a napkin; he may hug himself in his reputation; but he is always generous in his love. Love cannot stay at home; a man cannot keep it to himself. Like light, it is constantly traveling. A man must spend it, must give it away.—*Macleod.*

Love is the loadstone of love.—*Mrs. Osgood.*

He who is intoxicated with wine will be sober again in the course of the night, but he who is intoxicated by the cup-bearer will not recover his senses until the day of judgment.—*Saadi.*

O love! thine essence is thy purity! Breathe one unhallowed breath upon thy flame and it is gone forever, and but leaves a sullied vase,—its pure light lost in shame.—*L. E. Landon.*

Love is a canvas furnished by Nature and embroidered by imagination.—*Voltaire.*

Take away love, and not physical nature only, but the heart of the moral world would be palsied.—*Southey.*

Young love-making, that gossamer web! Even the points it clings to—the things whence its subtle interlacings are swung—are scarcely perceptible: momentary touches of finger-tips, meetings of rays from blue and dark orbs, unfinished phrases, lightest changes of cheek and lip, faintest tremors. The web itself is made of spontaneous beliefs and indefinable joys, yearnings of one life toward another, visions of completeness, indefinite trust.—*George Eliot.*

Among all the many kinds of first love, that which begins in childish companionship is the strongest and most enduring; when passion comes to unite its force to long affection, love is at its spring-tide.—*George Eliot.*

The true one of youth's love, proving a faithful help-meet in those years when the dream of life is over, and we live in its realities.—*Southey.*

Love in marriage should be the accomplishment of a beautiful dream, and not, as it too often is, the end.—*Karr.*

The heart of a woman is never so full of affection that there does not remain a little corner for flattery and love.— *Mauvaux.*

For woman's love—I mean self-love, is boundless, just like the sea, and sometimes quite as groundless.—*N. P. Willis.*

That happy minglement of hearts, where, changed as chemic compounds are, each with its own existence parts, to find a new one, happier far!—*Moore.*

Our first love, and last love is self-love.—*Bovee.*

Love reasons without reason.—*Shakespeare.*

To love one who loves you, to admire one who admires you, in a word, to be the idol of one's idol, is exceeding the limit of human joy; it is stealing fire from heaven.—*Mad. de Girardin.*

It seems to me that the coming of love is like the coming of spring—the date is not to be reckoned by the calendar. It may be slow and gradual; it may be quick and sudden. But in the morning, when we wake and recognize a change in the world without, verdure on the trees, blossoms on the sward, warmth in the sunshine, music in the air, we say spring has come.—*Bulwer.*

Love and a cough cannot be hid.—*Herbert.*

Nothing quickens the perceptions like genuine love. From the humblest professional attachment to the most chivalric devotion, what keenness of observation is born under the influence of that feeling which drives away the obscuring clouds of selfishness, as the sun consumes the vapor of the morning.—*Tuckerman.*

Nuptial love maketh mankind; friendly love perfecteth it; but wanton love corrupteth and embaseth it.—*Bacon.*

Where there is room in the heart there is always room in the house.—*Moore.*

A supreme love, a motive that gives a sublime rhythm to a woman's life, and exalts habit into partnership with the soul's highest needs, is not to be had where and how she wills: to know that high initiation, she must often tread where it is hard to tread, and feel the chill air. and watch through darkness.—*George Eliot.*

Love is the purification of the heart from self; it strengthens and ennobles the character, gives a higher motive and a nobler aim to every action of life, and makes both man and woman strong, noble, and courageous; and the power to love truly and devotedly is the noblest gift with which a human being can be endowed; but it is a sacred fire that must not be burned to idols.—*Miss Jewsbury.*

One expresses well only the love he does not feel.—*J. A. Karr.*

In love, as in war, a fortress that parleys is half taken.—*Margaret of Valois.*

Love is like the moon; when it does not increase it decreases.—*Ségur.*

Love is the most terrible, and also the most generous of the passions; it is the only one that includes in its dreams the happiness of some one else.—*J. A. Karr.*

A woman whom we truly love is a religion.—*Emile de Girardin.*

It is strange that men will talk of miracles, revelations, inspiration, and the like, as things past, while love remains.—*Thoreau.*

Life is a flower of which love is the honey.—*Victor Hugo.*

The maid that loves goes out to sea upon a shattered plank, and puts her trust in miracles for safety.—*Young.*

Love is strongest in pursuit; friendship in possession.—*Emerson.*

Base men, being in love, have then a nobility in their natures, more than is native to them.—*Shakespeare.*

The cure for all the ills and wrongs, the cares, the sorrows, and the crimes of humanity, all lie in that one word "love." It is the divine vitality that everywhere produces and restores life. To each and every one of us, it gives the power of working miracles if we will.—*Mrs. L. M. Child.*

It is astonishing how little one feels poverty when one loves.—*Bulwer.*

Love reckons hours for months, and days for years; and every little absence is an age.—*Dryden.*

Two things create love perfection and usefulness, to which answer, on our part, admiration and desire; and both these are centered in love.—*Jeremy Taylor.*

A murderous guilt shows not itself more soon than love that would seem hid; love's night is noon.—*Shakespeare.*

A man of sense may love like a madman, but not as a fool.—*Rochefoucauld.*

Love lessens woman's delicacy, and increases man's.—*Richter.*

It is possible that a man can be so changed by love as hardly to be recognized as the same person.—*Terence.*

A youth's love is the more passionate; virgin love is the more idolatrous.—*Hare.*

No disguise can long conceal love where it is, nor feign it where it is not. —*Rochefoucauld.*

In matters of love and appetite beware of surfeits. Nothing contributes so much to the duration of either as moderation in their gratification.—*Bovee.*

As every lord giveth a certain livery to his servants, love is the very livery of Christ. Our Saviour, who is the Lord above all lords, would have his servants known by their badge, which is love.—*Bp. Latimer.*

A man's want of beauty is of small account if he be not deficient in other amiable qualities, for there is no conquest without the affections, and what mole can be so blind as a woman in love.—*Ninon de l'Enclos.*

There is no permanent love but that which has duty for its eldest brother; so that if one sleeps the other watches, and honor is safe.—*Stahl.*

All loves should be simply stepping-stones to the love of God. So it was with me; and blessed be his name for his great goodness and mercy.—*Plato.*

Why is it so difficult to love wisely, so easy to love too well?—*Miss M. E. Braddon.*

Where love and wisdom drink out of the same cup, in this every-day world, it is the exception.—*Mad. Necker.*

Love makes obedience lighter than liberty.—*R. W. Alger.*

Love is to the moral nature what the sun is to the earth.—*Balzac.*

One half, the finest half of life, is hidden from the man who does not love with passion.—*Beyle.*

He who, silent, loves to be with us— he who loves us in our silence—has touched one of the keys that ravish hearts.—*Lavater.*

It is folly to pretend that one ever wholly recovers from a disappointed passion. Such wounds always leave a scar. There are faces I can never look upon without emotion; there are names I can never hear spoken without almost starting.—*Longfellow.*

A woman cannot love a man she feels to be her inferior; love without veneration and enthusiasm is only friendship. —*Mad. Dudevant.*

The heart of a young woman in love is a golden sanctuary which often enshrines an idol of clay.—*Limayrac.*

They love least, that let men know their love.—*Shakespeare.*

Love is an alliance of friendship and animalism; if the former predominate it is a passion exalted and refined; if the latter, gross and sensual.—*Colton.*

We love a girl for very different things than understanding. We love her for her beauty, her youth, her mirth, her confidingness, her character, with its faults, caprices, and God knows what other inexpressible charms; but we do not love her understanding. Her mind we esteem if it is brilliant, and it may greatly elevate her in our opinion; nay, more, it may enchain us when we already love. But her understanding is not that which awakens and inflames our passions.—*Goethe.*

The love of a delicate female is always shy and silent. Even when fortunate, she scarcely breathes it to herself; but when otherwise, she buries it in the recesses of her bosom, and there lets it cower and brood among the ruins of her peace.—*Washington Irving.*

In love we rarely think of moral qualities, and scarcely of intellectual ones.— Temperament and manner alone, with beauty, excite love.—*Hazlitt.*

First love is an instinct—at once a gift and a sacrifice.—Every other is a philosophy—a bargain.—*A. S. Hardy.*

He credited her with a number of virtues, of the existence of which her conduct and conversation had given but limited indications.—But, then, lovers have a proverbial power of balancing inverted pyramids, going to sea in sieves, and successfully performing other kindred feats impossible to a faithless and unbelieving generation.—*L. Malet.*

Faith, like light, should always be simple and unbending; while love, like warmth, should beam forth on every side, and bend to every necessity of our brethren.—*Luther.*

There is a passion of reverence, almost of pity, mingling with the love of an honest man for a pure girl, which makes it the most exquisite, perhaps, of all human sentiments.—*L. Malet.*

We love the virtues, but do not fall in love with them.—They confirm and nurture love, but after middle age they do not give it birth.—*A. S. Hardy.*

I know no better augury of a young man's future than true filial devotion. Very rarely does one go morally wrong, whose passionate love to his mother is a ruling force in his life, and whose continual desire is to gladden her heart. Next to the love of God, this is the noblest emotion. I do not remember a single instance of a young fellow going to the bad who was tenderly devoted to his parents.—*Thain Davidson.*

The accents of love are all that is left of the language of paradise.—*Bulwer.*

We never know how much one loves till we know how much he is willing to endure and suffer for us; and it is the suffering element that measures love.— The characters that are great, must, of necessity, be characters, that shall be willing, patient, and strong to endure for others.—To hold our nature in the willing service of another, is the divine idea of manhood, of the human character.—*H. W. Beecher.*

To love is to place our happiness in the happiness of another.—*Leibnitz.*

The reason why lovers are never weary of one another is this—they are always talking of themselves.—*Rochefoucauld.*

Oh, let the steps of youth be cautious how they advance into a dangerous world; our duty only can conduct us safe, our passions are seducers; and of all, the strongest is love.—*Southey.*

We attract hearts by the qualities we display: we retain them by the qualities we possess.—*Suard.*

Oh, why should man's success remove the very charms that wake his love!—*Walter Scott.*

Stimulate the heart of love and the mind to be early accurate, and all other virtues will rise of their own accord, and all vices will be thrown out.—*Coleridge.*

It is the very essence of love, of nobleness, of greatness, to be willing to suffer for the good of others.—*Spence.*

A woman is more considerate in affairs of love than a man; because love is more the study and business of her life.—*Washington Irving.*

Of all the paths leading to a woman's love, pity is the straightest.—*Beaumont.*

Love needs new leaves every summer of life, as much as your elm-tree, and new branches to grow broader and wider, and new flowers to cover the ground.—*Mrs. Stowe.*

Love with old men is as the sun upon the snow, it dazzles more than it warms them.—*J. P. Senn.*

Love's like the measles, all the worse when it comes late in life.—*Jerrold.*

The blood of youth burns not with such excess, as gravity's revolt to wantonness.—*Shakespeare.*

The worst thing an old man can be is a lover.—*Otway.*

True love is eternal, infinite, and always like itself. It is equal and pure, without violent demonstrations: it is seen with white hairs and is always young in the heart.—*Balzac.*

Love, and you shall be loved.—All love is mathematically just, as much as the two sides of an algebraic equation.—*Emerson.*

Love makes its record in deeper colors as we grow out of childhood into manhood; as the emperors signed their names in green ink when under age, but when of age, in purple.—*Longfellow.*

In peace, love tunes the shepherd's reed; in war, he mounts the warrior's steed; in halls, in gay attire is seen; in hamlets, dances on the green. Love rules the court, the camp, the grove, and men below, and saints above; for love is heaven, and heaven is love.—*Walter Scott.*

Young love is a flame; very pretty, often very hot and fierce, but still only light and flickering. The love of the older and disciplined heart is as coals, deep-burning, unquenchable.—*H. W. Beecher.*

Love sees what no eye sees; love hears what no ear hears; and what never rose in the heart of man love prepares for its object.—*Lavater.*

If nobody loves you, be sure it is your own fault.—*Doddridge.*

With thee all toils are sweet; each clime hath charms; earth—sea alike—our world within our arms!—*Byron.*

Love must shun the path where many rove; one bosom to recline upon, one heart to be his only one, are quite enough for love!—*Moore.*

Love is the purification of the heart from self; it strengthens and ennobles the character; gives higher motive and nobler aim to every action of life, and makes both man and woman strong, noble, and courageous.—The power to love truly and devotedly is the noblest gift with which a human being can be endowed; but it is a sacred fire that must not be burned to idols.—*Miss Jewsbury.*

It is the duty of men to love even those who injure them.—*Marcus Antoninus.*

The first symptom of love in a young man, is timidity; in a girl, it is boldness. —The two sexes have a tendency to approach, and each assumes the qualities of the other.—*Victor Hugo.*

True love of our friends should hardly attach us to the world; for the greater number of those we have loved most are gathered into eternity, so that it is but exile from them that we covet when we would prolong our stay here on earth.

A father's heart is tender, though the man's is made of stone.—*Young.*

If there is anything better than to be loved, it is loving.—*Anon.*

Certain it is that there is no kind of affection so purely angelic as the love of a father to a daughter. He beholds her both with and without regard to her sex.—In love to our wives, there is desire; to our sons, there is ambition; but in that to our daughters there is something which there are no words to express.—*Addison.*

If there be one thing pure, where all beside is sullied, and that can endure when all else passes away—if aught surpassing human deed, or word, or thought, it is a mother's love.—*Spadara.*

The love of man, in his mature years, is not so much a new emotion, as a

revival and concentration of all his departed affections toward others.—*Bulwer.*

One hour of love will teach a woman more of her true relations than all your philosophizing.—*Margaret Fuller.*

Not father or mother has loved you as God has, for it was that you might be happy he gave his only son.—When he bowed his head in the death hour, love solemnized its triumph; the sacrifice there was completed.—*Longfellow.*

Love, it has been said, flows downward. The love of parents for their children has always been far more powerful than that of children for their parents; and who among the sons of men ever loved God with a thousandth part of the love which God has manifested to us?—*Hare.*

Two sentiments alone suffice for man, were he to live the age of the rocks,—love, and the contemplation of the Deity.—*Watts.*

Love is the greatest thing that God can give us, for himself is love; and it is the greatest thing we can give to God, for it will also give ourselves, and carry with it all that is ours. The apostle calls it the bond of perfection; it is the old, the new, and the great commandment, and all the commandments, for it is the fulfilling of the law. It does the work of all the other graces without any instrument but its own immediate virtue.—*Jeremy Taylor.*

If thou neglectest thy love to thy neighbor, in vain thou professest thy love to God; for by thy love to God, the love to thy neighbor is begotten, and by the love to thy neighbor, thy love to God is nourished.—*Quarles.*

Love is the weapon which Omnipotence reserved to conquer rebel man when all the rest had failed. Reason he parries; fear he answers blow for blow; future interest he meets with present pleasure; but love is that sun against whose melting beams the winter cannot stand. There is not one human being in a million, nor a thousand men in all earth's huge quintillion whose clay heart is hardened against love.—*Tupper.*

Love is the hardest lesson in Christianity; but, for that reason, it should be most our care to learn it.—*Penn.*

It is ever the invisible that is the object of our profoundest worship. With the lover it is not the seen but the unseen that he muses upon.—*Bovee.*

The true measure of loving God is to love him without measure.—*St. Bernard.*

Divine love is a sacred flower, which in its early bud is happiness, and in its full bloom is heaven.—*Hervey.*

Love is indeed heaven upon earth; since heaven above would not be heaven without it; for where there is not love, there is fear; but, "Perfect love casteth out fear." And yet we naturally fear most to offend what we most love. —*Penn.*

How shall I do to love? Believe. How shall I do to believe? Love.— *Leighton.*

Humble love, and not proud science, keeps the door of heaven.—*Young.*

Love is the crowning grace of humanity, the holiest right of the soul, the golden link which binds us to duty and truth, the redeeming principle that chiefly reconciles the heart of life, and is prophetic of eternal good.—*Petrarch.*

They are the true disciples of Christ, not who know most, but who love most. —*Spanheim.*

Did a woman ever love who would not give all the years of tasteless serenity for one year, for one month, for one day of uncalculating delirium of love poured out upon the man who returned it.—*C. D. Warner.*

If the tender, profound, and sympathizing love, practised and recommended by Jesus, were paramount in every heart, the loftiest and most glorious idea of human society would be realized, and little be wanting to make this world a kingdom of heaven.—*Krummacher.*

LUCK.—There is no such thing as luck. It's a fancy name for being always at our duty, and so sure to be ready when the good time comes.

Hope nothing from luck, and the probability is that you will be so prepared, forewarned, and forearmed, that all shallow observers will call you lucky. —*Bulwer.*

I never knew an early-rising, hard-working, prudent man, careful of his earnings, and strictly honest, who complained of bad luck. A good character, good habits, and iron industry are impregnable to the assaults of all the ill-luck that fools ever dreamed of.—*Addison.*

All successful men have agreed in being causationists; they believed that things were not by luck, but by law— that there was not a weak or cracked link in the chain that joins the first and last of things—the cause and effect.— *Emerson.*

Ill-luck, is, in nine cases out of ten, the result of saying pleasure first and duty second, instead of duty first and pleasure second.—*T. T. Munger.*

Luck is ever waiting for something to turn up. Labor, with keen eyes and strong will, will turn up something. Luck lies in bed, and wishes the postman would bring him the news of a legacy. Labor turns out at six o'clock, and with busy pen or ringing hammer lays the foundation of a competence. Luck whines. Labor whistles. Luck relies on chance. Labor on character.— *Cobden.*

What helps luck is a habit of watching for opportunities, of having a patient but restless mind, of sacrificing one's ease or vanity, or uniting a love of detail to foresight, and of passing through hard times bravely and cheerfully.—*Victor Cherbuliez.*

Pitch a lucky man into the Nile, says the Arabian proverb, and he will come up with a fish in his mouth.—*N. P. Willis.*

Never have anything to do with an unlucky place, or an unlucky man. I have seen many clever men, very clever men, who had not shoes to their feet. I never act with them. Their advice sounds very well, but they cannot get on themselves; and if they cannot do good to themselves, how can they do good to me?—*Rothschild.*

Shallow men believe in luck, believe in circumstances. It was somebody's name, or he happened to be there at the time, or it was so then, and another day it would have been otherwise.— Strong men believe in cause and effect. —The man was born to do it, and his father was born to be the father of him and of this deed, and by looking narrowly, you shall see there was no luck in the matter, but it was all a problem in arithmetic, or an experiment in chemistry.—*Emerson.*

"Luck" is a very good word if you put a P before it.—*Anon.*

Shallow men believe in luck, wise and strong men in cause and effect.—*Emerson.*

There are no chances so unlucky from which clever people are not able to reap some advantage, and none so lucky that the foolish are not able to turn them to their own disadvantage.—*Rochefoucauld.*

Luck generally comes to those who look after it; and my notion is that it taps, once in a lifetime, at everybody's door, but if industry does not open it luck goes away.—*Spurgeon.*

LUST.—It is the difference betwixt lust and love, that this is fixed, that volatile. Love grows, lust wastes, by enjoyment; and the reason is, that one springs from a union of souls, and the other springs from a union of sense.—*Penn.*

Capricious, wanton, bold, and brutal lust is meanly selfish; when resisted, cruel; and, like the blast of pestilential winds, taints the sweet bloom of nature's fairest forms.—*Milton.*

It is the grand battle of life to teach lust the limits of the Divine law—to break it into the taste of the bread of heaven.—*I. B. Brown.*

Lust is an enemy to the purse, a foe to the person, a canker to the mind, a corrosive to the conscience, a weakness of the wit, a besotter of the senses, and, finally, a mortal bane to all the body.—*Pliny.*

So long as lust, whether of the world or the flesh, smells sweet in our nostrils, so long we are loathsome to God.—*Cotton.*

Short is the course of every lawless pleasure; grief, like a shade, on all its footsteps waits, scarce visible in joy's meridian height; but downward as its blaze declining speeds, the dwarfish shadow to a giant spreads.—*Milton.*

Lust is a captivity of the reason and an enraging of the passions. It hinders business and distracts counsel. It

sins against the body and weakens the soul.—*Jeremy Taylor.*

Lust is, of all the frailties of our nature, what most we ought to fear; the headstrong beast rushes along impatient of the course; nor hears the rider's call, nor feels the rein.—*Rowe.*

An enemy to whom you show kindness becomes your friend, excepting lust, the indulgence of which increases its enmity.—*Saadi.*

When lust, by unchaste looks, loose gestures, and foul talk, but most by lewd and lavish acts of sin, lets in defilement to the inward parts, the soul grows clotted by contagion, embodies and imbrutes till she quite lose the divine property of her first being.—*Milton.*

Servile inclinations and gross love, the guilty bent of vicious appetite; at first a sin, a horror ev'n in bliss, deprave the senses and lay waste the man; passions irregular, and next a loathing, quickly succeed to dash the wild desire.—*Havard.*

I know the very difference that lies 'twixt hallowed love and base unholy lust.—I know the one is as a golden spur, urging the spirit to all noble aims; the other but a foul and miry pit, o'erthrowing it in midst of its career.—*Fanny Kemble Butler.*

LUXURY.—Luxury makes a man so soft, that it is hard to please him, and easy to trouble him; so that his pleasures at last become his burden. Luxury is a nice master, hard to be pleased.—*Mackenzie.*

Fell luxury! more perilous to youth than storms or quicksands, poverty or chains.—*H. More.*

I know it is more agreeable to walk upon carpets than to lie upon dungeon floors; I know it is pleasant to have all the comforts and luxuries of civilization; but he who cares only for these things is worth no more than a butterfly contented and thoughtless upon a morning flower; and who ever thought of rearing a tombstone to a last-summer's butterfly?—*H. W. Beecher.*

Avarice and luxury, those pests which have ever been the ruin of every great state.—*Livy.*

All luxury corrupts either the morals or the state.—*Joubert*.

Sedition is bred in the lap of luxury, and its chosen emissaries are the beggared spendthrift and the impoverished libertine.—*Bancroft*.

It was a shrewd saying, whoever said it, "That the man who first brought ruin on the Roman people was he who pampered them by largesses and amusements."—*Plutarch*.

On the soft bed of luxury most kingdoms have expired.—*Young*.

Unless we are accustomed to them from early youth, splendid chambers and elegant furniture had best be left to people who neither have nor can have any thoughts.—*Goethe*.

You cannot spend money in luxury without doing good to the poor. Nay, you do more good to them by spending it in luxury than by giving; you make them exert industry, whereas, by giving it, you keep them idle.—*Johnson*.

Luxury may possibly contribute to give bread to the poor; but if there were no luxury, there would be no poor. —*Home*.

Oh, brethren, it is sickening work to think of your cushioned seats, your chants, your anthems, your choirs, your organs, your gowns, and your bands, and I know not what besides, all made to be instruments of religious luxury, if not of pious dissipation, while ye need far more to be stirred up and incited to holy ardor for the propagation of the truth as it is in Jesus.—*Spurgeon*.

O luxury! Thou curst of heaven's decree.—*Goldsmith*.

Were the labor and capital, now spent on pernicious luxuries, to be employed in the intellectual, moral, and religious culture of the whole people, how immense would be the gain, in every respect, though for a short time material products were diminished. A better age will look back with wonder and scorn on the misdirected industry of the present times.—*Channing*.

Superfluity comes sooner by white hairs, but competency lives longer.— *Shakespeare*.

Luxury is the first, second, and third cause of the ruin of republics. It is the vampire which soothes us into a fatal slumber while it sucks the life-blood of our veins.—*Payson*.

The more we accommodate ourselves to plain things, and the less we indulge in those artificial delights which gratify pride and luxury, the nearer we approach to a state of innocency.—*M. Henry*.

Where necessity ends, curiosity begins; and no sooner are we supplied with everything that nature can demand, than we sit down to contrive artificial appetites.—*Johnson*.

It is a shame that man, that has the seeds of virtue in him, springing into glory, should make his soul degenerate with sin, and slave to luxury; to drown his spirits in lees of sloth; to yield up the weak day to wine, to lust, and banquets.

Whenever vanity and gaiety, a love of pomp and dress, furniture, equipage, buildings, great company, expensive diversions, and elegant entertainments get the better of the principles and judgments of men and women, there is no knowing where they will stop, nor into what evils, natural, moral, or political, they will lead us.—*John Adams*.

He repents on thorns that sleeps in beds of roses.—*Quarles*.

War destroys men, but luxury destroys mankind; at once corrupts the body and the mind.—*Crown*.

Garrick showed Johnson his fine house, gardens, statues, pictures, etc., at Hampton Court.—"Ah! David, David," said the doctor, "these are the things that make death terrible."—*Bate*.

LYING.—(See "FALSEHOOD" and "LIARS.")

After a tongue has once got the knack of lying, 'tis not to be imagined how impossible almost it is to reclaim it. Whence it comes to pass that we see some men, who are otherwise very honest, so subject to this vice.—*Montaigne*.

He who has not a good memory should never take upon him the trade of lying.—*Montaigne*.

Falsehood and fraud grow up in every soil, the product of all climes.— *Addison*.

If a man had the art of second-sight for seeing lies as they have in Scotland for seeing spirits, how admirably he might entertain himself by observing the different shapes, sizes, and colors of those swarms of lies, which buzz about the heads of some people, like flies about a horse's ears in summer; or those legions hovering every afternoon so as to darken the air; or over a club of discontented grandees, and thence sent down in cargoes, to be scattered at elections.—*Swift.*

Lying is a hateful and accursed vice. We have no other tie upon one another, but our word. If we did but discover the horror and consequences of it, we should pursue it with fire and sword, and more justly than other crimes.—*Montaigne.*

Never chase a lie. Let it alone, and it will run itself to death. I can work out a good character much faster than any one can lie me out of it.—*Lyman Beecher.*

White lies are but the ushers to black ones.—*Marryat.*

Lies which are told out of arrogance and ostentation, a man should detect in his own defense, because he should not be triumphed over. Lies which are told out of malice he should expose, both for his own sake and that of the rest of mankind, because every man should rise against a common enemy; but the officious liar, many have argued, is to be excused, because it does some man good, and no man hurt.—*Steele.*

The most intangible, and therefore the worst kind of a lie, is a half-truth. —This is the peculiar device of the "conscientious" detractor.—*Washington Allston.*

A lie that is half a truth is ever the blackest of lies.—*Tennyson.*

Sin has many tools, but a lie is the handle that fits them all.—*O. W. Holmes.*

When thou art obliged to speak, be sure to speak the truth; for equivocation is half way to lying, and lying is whole way to hell.—*Penn.*

The gain of lying is, not to be trusted of any, nor to be believed when we speak the truth.—*Sir W. Raleigh.*

Lying is a certain mark of cowardice. —*Southern.*

There are people who lie simply for the sake of lying.—*Pascal.*

Every brave man shuns, more than death, the shame of lying.—*Corneille.*

It is a hard matter for a man to lie all over, nature having provided king's evidence in almost every member. The hand will sometimes act as a vane, to show which way the wind blows, even when every feature is set the other way; the knees smite together and sound the alarm of fear under a fierce countenance; the legs shake with anger, when all above is calm.—*Washington Allston.*

Lying is a most disgraceful vice; it first despises God, and then fears men. —*Plutarch.*

Every lie, great or small, is the brink of a precipice, the depth of which nothing but Omniscience can fathom.—*C. Reade.*

Lie not, neither to thyself, nor man, nor God.—It is for cowards to lie.—*Herbert.*

There is no vice that doth so cover a man with shame, as to be discovered in a lie; for, as Montaigne saith—" A liar would be brave toward God, while he is a coward toward men; for a lie faces God, and shrinks from man."—*Bacon.*

Lying is like trying to hide in a fog. —If you move about you are in danger of bumping your head against the truth. —And as soon as the fog blows away you are gone anyhow.

Habitual liars invent falsehoods not to gain any end, or even to deceive their hearers, but to amuse themselves. —It is partly practice and partly habit. —It requires an effort in them to speak the truth.—*Hazlitt.*

Half the vices in the world rise out of cowardice, and one who is afraid of lying is usually afraid of nothing else.— *Froude.*

Truth is always consistent with itself, and needs nothing to help it out; it is always near at hand, sits upon our lips, and is ready to drop out before we are aware; a lie is troublesome, and sets a man's invention upon the rack, and one trick needs a great many more to make it good. It is like building upon a false foundation, which continually stands in need of props to shore it up, and proves at last more chargeable than to have raised a substantial building at first upon a true and solid foundation.—*Addison.*

A wilful falsehood is a cripple, not able to stand by itself without another to support it. It is easy to tell a lie, but hard to tell only one lie.—*Fuller.*

As universal a practice as lying is, and as easy a one as it seems, I do not remember to have heard three good lies in all my conversation.—*Swift.*

When the world has once got hold of a lie, it is astonishing how hard it is to get it out of the world. You beat it about the head, till it seems to have given up the ghost, and lo! the next day it is as healthy as ever.—*Bulwer.*

A lie, though it be killed and dead, can sting sometimes,—like a dead wasp.—*Mrs. Jameson.*

Nothing is rarer than a solitary lie; for lies breed like toads; you cannot tell one but out it comes with a hundred young ones on its back.—*Washington Allston.*

One lie must be thatched with another, or it will soon rain through.—*Owen.*

A great lie is like a great fish on dry land; it may fret and fling, and make a frightful bother, but it cannot hurt you. You have only to keep still and it will die of itself.—*Crabbe.*

Let falsehood be a stranger to thy lips; shame on the policy that first began to tamper with the heart to hide its thoughts! and doubly shame on that unrighteous tongue that sold its honesty, and told a lie!—*Havard.*

Falsehoods not only disagree with truths, but they usually quarrel among themselves.—*Daniel Webster.*

One lie engenders another.—Once committed, the liar has to go on in his course of lying; it is the penalty of his transgression.—*F. Jacox.*

M

MADNESS.—(See "Insanity.")

Madness is consistent, which is more than can be said of poor reason.—Whatever may be the ruling passion at the time continues so throughout the whole delirium, though it should last for life. —Our passions and principles are steady in frenzy, but begin to shift and waver as we return to reason.—*Sterne.*

The insane, for the most part, reason correctly, but from false principles, while they do not perceive that their premises are incorrect.—*Tryon Edwards.*

The consummation of madness is, to do what, at the time of doing it, we intend to be afterward sorry for: the deliberate and intentional making of work for repentance.—*W. Nevins.*

This wretched brain gave way, and I became a wreck at random driven, without one glimpse of reason or of heaven.—*Moore.*

Locke says the distinction between a madman and a fool is that a fool is he that from right principles makes a wrong conclusion; but a madman is one who draws a just inference from false principles. Thus the fool who cut off the fellow's head that lay asleep, and hid it, and then waited to see what he would say when he awaked and missed his head-piece, was in the right in the first thought, that a man would be surprised to find such an alteration in things since he fell asleep; but he was a little mistaken to imagine he could awake at all after his head was cut off.—*Tatler.*

How pregnant, sometimes, his replies are; a happiness that often madness hits on, which reason and sanity could not so prosperously be delivered of!—*Shakespeare.*

He raves; his words are loose as heaps of sand, and scattered wide from sense. —So high he's mounted on his airy throne, that now the wind has got into his head, and turns his brains to frenzy. —*Dryden.*

Great wits are sure to madness near allied, and thin partitions do their bounds divide.—*Dryden.*

MAGNANIMITY.—Magnanimity is sufficiently defined by its name; yet we may say of it, that it is the good sense of pride, and the noblest way of acquiring applause.—*Rochefoucauld.*

A great mind will neither give an affront, nor bear it.—*Home.*

If you desire to be magnanimous, undertake nothing rashly, and fear nothing

thou undertakest.—Fear nothing but infamy; dare anything but injury; the
measure of magnanimity is to be neither
rash nor timorous.—*Quarles.*

Of all virtues magnanimity is the
rarest; there are a hundred persons of
merit for one who willingly acknowledges it in another.—*Hazlitt.*

Magnanimity is greatness of soul, exerted in contemning dangers and difficulties, in scorning temptations, and in
despising mere earthly pomp and splendor.—*Buck.*

A brave man knows no malice; but
forgets, in peace, the injuries of war,
and gives his direst foe a friend's embrace.—*Cowper.*

MAGNET.—That trembling vessel of
the pole, the feeling compass, navigation's soul.—*Byron.*

The obedient steel with living instinct
moves, and veers forever to the pole it
loves.—*Darwin.*

Instinct with life, it safely points the
way through trackless seas, which else
were never sailed.

MAIDENHOOD.—Nature has thrown
a veil of modest beauty over maidenhood and moss roses.—*N. P. Willis.*

The blushing beauties of a modest
maid.—*Dryden.*

A maiden never bold; of spirit so
still and quiet, that her motion blushed
at herself.—*Shakespeare.*

She had grown in her unstained seclusion, bright and pure as a first opening
lilac when it spreads its clear leaves to
the sweetest dawn of May.—*Percival.*

A child no more; a maiden now; a
graceful maiden, with a gentle brow,
and cheek tinged lightly, and a dove-
like eye; and all hearts bless her, as she
passes by.—*Mary Howitt.*

The honor of a maid is her name, and
no legacy is so rich as honesty.—*Shakespeare.*

No padlock, bolts, or bars can secure
a maiden so well as her own reserve.—
Cervantes.

A loving maiden grows unconsciously
more bold.—*Richter.*

Let the words of a virgin, though in
a good cause, and to as good purpose,
be neither violent, many, nor first, nor
last.—It is less shame for her to be lost

in a blushing silence, than to be found
in a bold eloquence.—*Quarles.*

MAJORITY.—The voice of the majority is no proof of justice.—*Schiller.*

There is one body that knows more
than anybody, and that is everybody.—
Talleyrand.

It never troubles the wolf how many
the sheep may be.—*Virgil.*

We go by the major vote, and if the
majority are insane, the sane must go
to the hospital.—*H. Mann.*

One and God make a majority.—
Frederick Douglass.

A man in the right, with God on his
side, is in the majority though he be
alone.—*H. W. Beecher.*

MALEVOLENCE.—Avoid an angry
man for a while; a malevolent one, forever.

Malevolence is misery; it is the mind
of Satan, the great enemy, an outcast
from all joy, and the opponent of all
goodness and happiness.—*J. Hamilton.*

The malignity that never forgets or
forgives is found only in base and ignoble natures, whose aims are selfish,
and whose means are indirect, cowardly,
and treacherous.—*G. S. Hillard.*

MALICE.—Malice is the devil's picture. Lust makes men brutish; malice
makes them devilish—it is mental murder.—*T. Watson.*

Malice drinks one half of its own
poison.—*Seneca.*

Malice sucks up the greater part of
her own venom, and poisons herself.—
Montaigne.

Malice, in its false witness, promotes
its tale with so cunning a confusion, so
mingles truths with falsehoods, surmises
with certainties, causes of no moment
with matters capital, that the accused
can absolutely neither grant nor deny,
plead innocence nor confess guilt.—*Sir
P. Sidney.*

There is no malice like the malice of
the renegade.—*Macaulay.*

Wit loses its respect with the good
when seen in company with malice; to
smile at the jest which plants a thorn
in another's breast, is to become a principal in the mischief.—*Sheridan.*

Malice scorned, puts out itself; but

argued, gives a kind of credit to a false accusation.—*Massinger*.

There is no small degree of malicious craft in fixing upon a season to give a mark of enmity and ill-will; a word— a look, which at one time would make no impression, at another time wounds the heart, and, like a shaft flying with the wind, pierces deep, which, with its own natural force would scarce have reached the object aimed at.—*Sterne*.

There is no benefit so large that malignity will not lessen it; none so narrow that a good interpretation will not enlarge it.—*Seneca*.

MAN.—(See "MEN.")

Indisputably a great, good, handsome man is the first of created things.—*C. Bronté*.

The test of every religious, political, or educational system is the man that it forms.—*Amiel*.

A man's ledger does not tell what he is, or what he is worth.—Count what is *in* man, not what is *on* him, if you would know what he is worth—whether rich or poor.—*H. W. Beecher*.

What a piece of work is man! How noble in reason! How infinite in faculties! In form and moving, how express and admirable! In action, how like an angel! In apprehension, how like a god!—*Shakespeare*.

What a chimera is man! what a confused chaos! what a subject of contradiction! a professed judge of all things, and yet a feeble worm of the earth! the great depositary and guardian of truth, and yet a mere huddle of uncertainty! the glory and the scandal of the universe!—*Pascal*.

Half dust, half deity, alike unfit to sink or soar.—*Byron*.

Man himself is the crowning wonder of creation; the study of his nature the noblest study the world affords.—*Gladstone*.

Limited in his nature, infinite in his desires.—*Lamartine*.

How little man is; yet, in his own mind, how great! He is lord and master of all things, yet scarce can command anything. He is given a freedom of his will; but wherefore? Was it but to torment and perplex him the more?

How little avails this freedom, if the objects he is to act upon be not as much disposed to obey as he is to command! —*Burke*.

Men are but children of a larger growth; our appetites are as apt to change as theirs, and full as craving, too, and full as vain.—*Dryden*.

Men, in general, are but great children.—*Napoleon*.

He is of the earth, but his thoughts are with the stars. Mean and petty his wants and desires; yet they serve a soul exalted with grand, glorious aims,—with immortal longings,—with thoughts which sweep the heavens, and wander through eternity. A pigmy standing on the outward crest of this small planet, his far-reaching spirit stretches outward to the infinite, and there alone finds rest.—*Carlyle*.

Man is to man all kinds of beasts; a fawning dog, a roaring lion, a thieving fox, a robbing wolf, a dissembling crocodile, a treacherous decoy, and a rapacious vulture.—*Cowley*.

It is not what he has, or even what he does which expresses the worth of a man, but what he is.—*Amiel*.

How poor, how rich, how abject, how august, how complicate, how wonderful is man! distinguished link in being's endless chain! midway from nothing to the Deity! dim miniature of greatness absolute! an heir of glory! a frail child of dust! helpless immortal! insect infinite! a worm! a God!—*Young*.

Since the generality of persons act from impulse much more than from principle, men are neither so good nor so bad as we are apt to think them.— *Hare*.

Man is the highest product of his own history. The discoverer finds nothing so grand or tall as himself, nothing so valuable to him. The greatest star is at the small end of the telescope, the star that is looking, not looked after nor looked at.—*Theodore Parker*.

Men are not to be judged by their looks, habits, and appearances; but by the character of their lives and conversations, and by their works. 'Tis better that a man's own works than that another man's words should praise him. —*L'Estrange*.

The superior man is he who develops in harmonious proportions, his moral, intellectual, and physical nature. This should be the end at which men of all classes should aim, and it is this only which constitutes real greatness.—*Douglas Jerrold.*

Man is an animal that makes bargains; no other animal does this,—one dog does not change a bone with another.—*Adam Smith.*

Man is an animal that cooks his victuals.—*Burke.*

Man is a reasoning rather than a reasonable animal.—*Alexander Hamilton.*

Do you know what a man is? Are not birth, beauty, good shape, discourse, manhood, learning, gentleness, virtue, youth, liberality, and such like, the spice and salt that season a man?—*Shakespeare.*

The record of life runs thus: Man creeps into childhood,—bounds into youth,—sobers into manhood,—softens into age,—totters into second childhood, and slumbers into the cradle prepared for him,—thence to be watched and cared for.—*Henry Giles.*

No man is so great as mankind.—*Theodore Parker.*

Every man is a divinity in disguise, a god playing the fool. It seems as if heaven had sent its insane angels into our world as to an asylum. And here they will break out into their native music, and utter at intervals the words they have heard in heaven; then the mad fit returns, and they mope and wallow like dogs!—*Emerson.*

In my youth I thought of writing a satire on mankind; but now in my age I think I should write an apology for them.—*Walpole.*

The way of every man is declarative of the end of every man.—*Cecil.*

It is of dangerous consequence to represent to man how near he is to the level of beasts, without showing him at the same time his greatness. It is likewise dangerous to let him see his greatness without his meanness. It is more dangerous yet to leave him ignorant of either; but very beneficial that he should be made sensible of both.—*Pascal.*

Man perfected by society is the best of all animals; he is the most terrible of all when he lives without law, and without justice.—*Aristotle.*

Man is greater than a world—than systems of worlds; there is more mystery in the union of soul with the body, than in the creation of a universe.—*Henry Giles.*

Show me the man you honor, and I will know what kind of a man you are, for it shows me what your ideal of manhood is, and what kind of a man you long to be.—*Carlyle.*

A man is like a bit of Labrador spar, which has no luster as you turn it in your hand until you come to a particular angle; then it shows deep and beautiful colors.—*Emerson.*

To despise our own species is the price we must often pay for a knowledge of it.—*Colton.*

A man is one whose body has been trained to be the ready servant of his mind; whose passions are trained to be the servants of his will; who enjoys the beautiful, loves truth, hates wrong, loves to do good, and respects others as himself.

Now the basest thought possible concerning man is, that he has no spiritual nature; and the foolish misunderstanding of him possible is, that he has, or should have, no animal nature. For his nature is nobly animal, nobly spiritual,—coherently and irrevocably so; neither part of it may, but at its peril, expel, despise, or defy the other.—*Ruskin.*

There are but three classes of men, the retrograde, the stationary, and the progressive.—*Lavater.*

Omit a few of the most abstruse sciences, and mankind's study of man occupies nearly the whole field of literature. The burden of history is what man has been; of law, what he does; of physiology, what he is; of ethics, what he ought to be; of revelation, what he shall be.—*George Finlayson.*

The proper study of mankind is man. —*Pope.*

Man is to be trained chiefly by studying and by knowing man.—*Gladstone.*

It is very sad for a man to make himself servant to a single thing; his manhood all taken out of him by the hydraulic pressure of excessive business. —*Theodore Parker*.

To have known one good old man— one man who, through the chances and mischances of a long life, has carried his heart in his hand, like a palm branch, waving all discords into peace— helps our faith in God, in ourselves, and in each other, more than many sermons.—*G. W. Curtis*.

Whoever considers the study of anatomy, I believe, will never be an atheist; the frame of man's body, and coherence of his parts, being so strange and paradoxical, that I hold it to be the greatest miracle of nature.—*Lord Herbert*.

There wouldn't be half as much fun in the world if it weren't for children and men, and there ain't a mite of difference between them under their skins.—*Ellen Glasgow*.

In men whom men pronounce as ill I find so much of goodness still. In men whom men pronounce divine, I find so much of sin and blot; I hesitate to draw the line between the two, when God has not.—*Joaquin Miller*.

Man is a wealth grubber, man is a pleasure seeker; man is a power wielder; man is a thinker, and man is a creative lover.—*Bell*.

There is so much good in the worst of us, and so much bad in the best of us, that it behooves all of us not to talk about the rest of us.—*Robert Louis Stevenson*.

Do what thy manhood bids thee do, from none but self expect applause; he noblest lives and noblest dies who makes and keeps his self-made laws. All other Life is living Death, a world where none but Phantoms dwell, a breath, a wind, a sound, a voice, a tinkling of the camel-bell.—*Sir Richard Burton*.

Sweating, slums, the sense of semislavery in labor, must go. We must cultivate a sense of manhood by treating men as men.—*David Lloyd George*.

For my part, I am not so sure at bottom that man is, as he says, the king of nature; he is far more its devastating tyrant. I believe he has many things to learn from animal societies, older than his own and of infinite variety.— *Romain Rolland*.

Oh, East is East, and West is West and never the twain shall meet. . . . But there is neither East nor West, Border, nor Breed, nor Birth when two strong men stand face to face, tho' they come from the ends of the earth.—*Kipling*.

I am an acme of things accomplished, and I am encloser of things to be.— *Walt Whitman*.

Man has been called "the representative product of the universe"; and we will do well to remember that in this position his actions represent the worst of which nature is capable as well as the best.—*L. V. Jacks*.

Man is an animal; but he is an animal plus something else. He is a mythic earth-tree, whose roots are in the ground, but whose top-most branches may blossom in the heavens.—*Henry George*.

What a deal of cold business doth a man misspend the better part of life in! In scattering compliments, tendering visits, gathering and venting news, following feasts and plays, making a little winter-love in a dark corner.—*Ben Jonson*.

Men are the Universe become conscious: the simplest man should consider himself too great to be called after any name.—*John Davidson*.

When man is a brute, he is the most sensual and loathsome of all brutes.— *Hawthorne*.

Every human soul is of infinite value, eternal, free; no human being, therefore, is so placed as not to have within his reach, in himself and others, objects adequate to infinite endeavor.—*Arthur J. Balfour*.

Bounded in his nature, infinite in his desires, man is a fallen god who has a recollection of heaven.—*Lamartine*.

Man should be ever better than he seem; and shape his acts, and discipline his mind, to walk adorning earth, with hope of heaven.—*Aubrey de Vere*.

A man must stand erect, not be kept erect by others.—*Marcus Aurelius*.

The way of a superior man is threefold: virtuous, he is free from anxieties; wise, he is free from perplexities; bold, he is free from fear.—*Confucius*.

Society is the master and man is the servant; and it is entirely according as society proves a good or bad master, whether he turns out a bad or a good servant.—*Sala.*

Surely, if all the world was made for man, then man was made for more than the world.—*Duplessis.*

Man! thou pendulum betwixt a smile and tear.—*Byron.*

In men this blunder still you find, all think their little set mankind.—*H. More.*

Contemporaries appreciate the man rather than the merit; but posterity will regard the merit rather than the man.—*Colton.*

An evil man is clay to God, and wax to the devil; a good man is God's wax, and Satan's clay.—*Bp. Hall.*

One cannot always be a hero, but one can always be a man.—*Goethe.*

In these two things the greatness of man consists, to have God so dwelling in us as to impart his character to us, and to have him so dwelling in us that we recognize his presence, and know that we are his, and he is ours.—The one is salvation: the other the assurance of it.—*F. W. Robertson.*

The older I grow—and I now stand on the brink of eternity—the more comes back to me that sentence in the Catechism which I learned when a child, and the fuller and deeper its meaning becomes: "What is the chief end of man? To glorify God and enjoy him forever."—*Carlyle.*

Every man is valued in this world as he shows by his conduct he wishes to be valued.—*Bruyère.*

Every man is a volume, if you know how to read him.—*Channing.*

To study mankind, is not learning to hate them; so far from such a malevolent end, it is learning to bear and live easily with them.

He is but the counterfeit of a man, who has not the life of a man.—*Shakespeare.*

The soul of man createth its own destiny of power; and as the trial is intenser here, his being hath a nobler strength of heaven.—*N. P. Willis.*

The highest manhood resides in disposition, not in mere intellect.—*H. W. Beecher.*

I mean to make myself a man, and if

I succeed in that, I shall succeed in everything else.—*Garfield.*

Who dares do all that may become a man, and dares no more, he is a man indeed.—*Shakespeare.*

There are depths in man that go to the lowest hell, and heights that reach the highest heaven, for are not both heaven and hell made out of him, everlasting miracle and mystery that he is. —*Carlyle.*

They that deny a God, destroy man's nobility, for man is of kin to the beasts by his body, and if he is not of kin to God by his spirit he is an ignoble creature.—*Bacon.*

He is the wisest and happiest man, who, by constant attention of thought discovers the greatest opportunity of doing good, and breaks through every opposition that he may improve these opportunities.—*Doddridge.*

It is not a question how much a man knows, but what use he makes of what he knows; not a question of what he has acquired, and how he has been trained, but of what he is, and what he can do.—*J. G. Holland.*

Let each man think himself an act of God; his mind a thought, his life a breath of God.—*Bailey.*

An honest man is the noblest work of God.—*Pope.*

When faith is lost, and honor dies, the man is dead.—*Whittier.*

The proud man hath no God; the envious man hath no neighbor; the angry man hath not himself. What good, then, in being a man, if one has neither himself nor a neighbor nor God.—*Bp. Hall.*

Government, religion, property, books, are nothing but the scaffolding to build men.—Earth holds up to her master no fruit like the finished man.—*Humboldt.*

It is not the situation which makes the man, but the man who makes the situation. The slave may be a freeman. The monarch may be a slave. Situations are noble or ignoble, as we make them.—*F. W. Robertson.*

The test of every religious, political, or educational system is the man which it forms.—*Amiel.*

MANNERS. — (See "GOOD BREEDING.")

Good manners is the art of making

those people easy with whom we converse; whoever makes the fewest persons uneasy, is the best bred man in company.—*Swift.*

Good manners are the settled medium of social, as specie is of commercial, life; returns are equally expected from both; and people will no more advance their civility to a bear than their money to a bankrupt.—*Chesterfield.*

Rules of conduct, whatever they may be, are not sufficient to produce good results unless the ends sought are good.—*Bertrand Russell.*

Always behave as if nothing had happened no matter what has happened.—*Arnold Bennett.*

No man is a true gentleman who does not inspire the affection and devotion of his servants.—*Andrew Carnegie.*

Good manners are the small coin of virtue.—*Women of England.*

Manners are the shadows of virtues; the momentary display of those qualities which our fellow-creatures love and respect. If we strive to become, then, what we strive to appear, manners may often be rendered useful guides to the performance of our duties.—*Sydney Smith.*

Manners are minor morals.—*Paley.*

Cultured and fine manners are everywhere a passport to regard.

Good manners are the blossom of good sense and good feeling. If the law of kindness be written in the heart, it will lead to that disinterestedness in both great and little things—that desire to oblige, and that attention to the gratification of others, which are the foundation of good manners.

A man, whose great qualities want the ornament of exterior attractions, is like a naked mountain with mines of gold, which will be frequented only till the treasure is exhausted.—*Johnson.*

The manner of saying or of doing anything goes a great way in the value of the thing itself. It was well said of him that called a good office, if done harshly and with an ill will, a stony piece of bread: "It is necessary for him that is hungry to receive it, but it almost chokes a man in the going down."—*Seneca.*

Defect in manners is usually the defect of fine perceptions. Elegance comes of no breeding, but of birth.—*Emerson.*

Grace is to the body, what good sense is to the mind.—*Rochefoucauld.*

Manner is everything with some people, and something with everybody.—*Bp. Middleton.*

There is not any benefit so glorious in itself, but it may yet be exceedingly sweetened and improved by the manner of conferring it. The virtue rests in the intent; the profit in the judicious application of the matter; but the beauty and ornament of an obligation lies in the manner of it.—*Seneca.*

A man ought to carry himself in the world as an orange tree would if it could walk up and down in the garden, swinging perfume from every little censer it holds up to the air.—*H. W. Beecher.*

Our manners and customs go for more in life than our qualities.—The price we pay for our civilization is the fine yet impassible differentiation of these.—*Howell.*

Good breeding carries along with it a dignity that is respected by the most petulant. Ill breeding invites and authorizes the familiarity of the most timid.—*Chesterfield.*

Good manners and good morals are sworn friends and fast allies.—*Bartol.*

Pride, ill nature, and want of sense are the three great sources of ill manners; without some one of these defects, no man will behave himself ill for want of experience, or what, in the language of fools, is called knowing the world.—*Swift.*

No manners are finer than even the most awkward manifestations of good will to others.

Good manners are made up of petty sacrifices.—*Emerson.*

Better were it to be unborn than to be ill bred.—*Sir W. Raleigh.*

Simplicity of manner is the last attainment. Men are very long afraid of being natural, from the dread of being taken for ordinary.—*Jeffrey.*

I have seen manners that make a similar impression with personal beauty, that give the like exhilaration and refine us like that; and in memorable experiences they are certainly better than beauty, and make that superfluous and ugly. But they must be marked by fine perception, and must always show control; you shall not be facile, apologetic, or leaky, but king over your word; and every gesture and action shall indicate power at rest. They must be inspired by the good heart. There is no beautifier of complexion, or form or behavior, like the wish to scatter joy, and not pain, around us.—*Emerson.*

Striking manners are bad manners.—*Robert Hall.*

Good breeding consists in having no particular mark of any profession, but a general elegance of manners.—*Johnson.*

We perhaps never detect how much of our social demeanor is made up of artificial airs, until we see a person who is at once beautiful and simple; without the beauty, we are apt to call simplicity awkwardness.—*George Eliot.*

We cannot always oblige, but we can always speak obligingly.—*Voltaire.*

Nature is the best posture-master.—*Emerson.*

Comport thyself in life as at a banquet. If a plate is offered thee, extend thy hand and take it moderately; if it is to be withdrawn, do not detain it. If it come not to thy side, make not thy desire loudly known, but wait patiently till it be offered thee.—*Epictetus.*

The person who screams, or uses the superlative degree, or converses with heat, puts whole drawing-rooms to flight. If you wish to be loved, love measure. You must have genius or a prodigious usefulness if you will hide the want of measure.—*Emerson.*

Manner is one of the greatest engines of influence ever given to man.

The over-formal often impede, and sometimes frustrate business by a dilatory, tedious, circuitous, and fussy way of conducting the simplest transactions. They have been compared to a dog which cannot lie down till he has made three circuits round the spot.—*Whately.*

Men are like wine; not good before the lees of clownishness be settled.—*Feltham.*

We are to carry manner from the hand to the heart, to improve a ceremonial nicety into a substantial duty, and the modes of civility into the realities of religion.—*South.*

Nothing is more reasonable and cheap than good manners.—*Anon.*

I could better eat with one who did not respect the truth or the laws, than with a sloven and unpresentable person. Moral qualities rule the world, but at short distances the senses are despotic.—*Emerson.*

There is certainly something of exquisite kindness and thoughtful benevolence in that rarest of gifts,—fine breeding.—*Bulwer.*

To be good and disagreeable is high treason against the royalty of virtue.—*H. More.*

Prepare yourself for the world, as the athletes used to do for their exercise; oil your mind and your manners, to give them the necessary suppleness and flexibility; strength alone will not do.—*Chesterfield.*

There is a policy in manner. I have heard one, not inexperienced in the pursuit of fame, give it his earnest support, as being the surest passport to absolute and brilliant success.—*Tuckerman.*

I don't believe in the goodness of disagreeable people.—*O. Dewey.*

Good manners are a part of good morals; and it is as much our duty as our interest to practise both.—*Hunter.*

Virtue itself offends when coupled with forbidding manners.—*Bp. Middleton.*

It is easier to polish the manners than to reform the heart, to disguise a fault than to conquer it. He who can venture to appear as he is, must be what he ought to be,—a difficult and arduous task, which often requires the sacrifice of many a darling inclination and the exertion of many a painful effort.—*Bowdler.*

Unbecoming forwardness oftener proceeds from ignorance than impudence.—*Gréville.*

There are peculiar ways in men, which discover what they are, through the most subtle feints and closest disguise. A blockhead cannot come in, nor go away, nor sit, nor rise, nor stand, like a man of sense.—*Bruyère.*

A company attitude is rarely anybody's best.—*Miss Sedgwick.*

How often have I seen the most solid merit and knowledge neglected, unwelcome, and even rejected, while flimsy parts, little knowledge, and less merit, introduced by the Graces, have been received, cherished, and admired!—*Chesterfield.*

One of the most important rules as to manners is to be for the most part silent as to yourself.—Say little or nothing about yourself, whether good, bad, or indifferent: nothing good, for that is vanity; nothing bad, for that is affectation; nothing indifferent, for that is silly.

What better school for manners than the company of virtuous women; where the mutual endeavor to please must insensibly polish the mind, where the example of female softness and modesty must communicate itself to their admirers, and where the delicacy of the sex puts every one on his guard lest he give offence?—*Hume*

Civility costs nothing, and buys everything.—*Lady M. W. Montague.*

A man's fortune is frequently decided by his first address. If pleasing, others at once conclude he has merit; but if ungraceful, they decide against him.—*Chesterfield.*

I can forgive a crime; it may have some grand motive; but never an awkwardness.—*Mad. Récamier.*

What a rare gift is that of manners! How difficult to define; how much more difficult to impart!—Better for a man to possess them, than to have wealth, beauty, or talent; they will more than supply all.—*Bulwer.*

The true art of being agreeable is to appear well pleased with all the company, and rather to seem well entertained with them than to bring entertainment to them. A man thus disposed may have not much learning, nor any wit; but if he has common sense, and something friendly in his behavior, it conciliates men's minds more than the brightest parts without this disposition.—*Addison.*

Those that are good manners at the court are as ridiculous in the country, as the behavior of the country is most mockable at the court.—*Shakespeare.*

A man's own manner and character is what most becomes him.—*Cicero.*

Knowledge of men and manners, the freedom of habitudes, and conversation with the best company of both sexes, is necessary to the perfection of good manners.—*Dryden.*

Good breeding shows itself most, where to an ordinary eye it appears least.—*Addison.*

Wisdom, valor, justice, and learning cannot keep in countenance a man that is possessed with these excellences, if he wants that inferior art of life and behavior called good breeding.—*Steele.*

Manners easily and rapidly mature into morals.—*H. Mann.*

It is certain that either wise bearing, or ignorant carriage is caught, as men take diseases, one from another; therefore let men take heed of their company.—*Shakespeare.*

Manners are the shadows of virtues, the momentary display of those qualities which our fellow-creatures love and respect.—*Sydney Smith.*

The immoral man, who invades another's property, is justly punished for it; and the ill bred man, who by his ill manners invades and disturbs the quiet and comforts of private life, is by common consent as justly banished society. For my own part, I really think, next to the consciousness of doing a good action, that of doing a civil one is the most pleasing; and the epithet which I should covet the most, next to that of Aristides (the Just), would be that of well bred.—*Chesterfield.*

An imposing air should always be taken as an evidence of imposition.—Dignity is often a veil between us and the real truth of things.—*E. P. Whipple.*

Manners are of more importance than laws. Upon them, in a great measure, the laws depend. The law can touch us here and there, now and then. Manners are what vex or soothe, corrupt or purify, exalt or debase, barbarize or refine, by a constant, steady, uniform, insensible operation, like that of the air we breathe in. They give their whole form and color to our lives. According to their quality, they aid morals, they supply them, or they totally destroy them.—*Burke.*

A well bred man is always sociable and complaisant.—*Montaigne.*

Manners must adorn knowledge and smooth its way in the world; without them it is like a great rough diamond, very well in a closet by way of curiosity, and also for its intrinsic value; but most prized when polished.—*Chesterfield.*

There is no policy like politeness; and a good manner is the best thing in the world either to get a good name, or to supply the want of it.—*Bulwer.*

In conversation use some, but not too much ceremony; it teaches others to be courteous, too. Demeanors are commonly paid back in their own coin.—*Fuller.*

With virtue, capacity, and good conduct, one still can be insupportable. The manners, which are neglected as small things, are often those which decide men for or against you. A slight attention to them would have prevented their ill judgments.—*Bruyère.*

The society of women is the element of good manners.—*Goethe.*

The distinguishing trait of people accustomed to good society is a calm, imperturbable quiet which pervades all their actions and habits, from the greatest to the least. They eat in quiet, move in quiet, live in quiet, and lose even their money in quiet; while low persons cannot take up either a spoon or an affront without making an amazing noise about it.—*Bulwer.*

Nothing, except what flows from the heart, can render even external manners truly pleasing.—*Blair.*

Nothing so much prevents our being natural as the desire of appearing so.—*Rochefoucauld.*

A man's own good breeding is the best security against other people's ill manners.—*Chesterfield.*

Manners are stronger than laws.—*A. Carlile.*

One may now know a man that never conversed in the world, by his excess of good breeding. A polite country esquire shall make you as many bows in half an hour, as would serve a courtier for a week.—*Addison.*

The happy gift of being agreeable seems to consist not in one, but in an assemblage of talents tending to communicate delight; and how many are there, who, by easy manners, sweetness of temper, and a variety of other undefinable qualities, possess the power of pleasing without any visible effort, without the aids of wit, wisdom, or learning, nay, as it should seem, in their defiance; and this without appearing even to know that they possess it.—*Cumberland.*

Let thy carriage be friendly, but not foolishly free; an unwary openness causeth contempt, but a little reservedness, respect; and handsome courtesy, kindness.—*Fuller.*

Fine manners are a stronger bond than a beautiful face. The former binds; the latter only attracts.—*Lamartine.*

Among well bred people, a mutual deference is affected; contempt of others disguised; authority concealed; attention given to each in his turn; and an easy stream of conversation maintained, without vehemence, without interruption, without eagerness for victory, and without any airs of superiority.—*Hume.*

Hail! ye small sweet courtesies of life, for smooth do ye make the road of it, like grace and beauty which beget inclinations to love at first sight; 'tis ye who open the door and let the stranger in.—*Sterne.*

Good breeding is the result of much good sense, some good nature, and a little self-denial for the sake of others, and with a view to obtain the same indulgence from them.—*Chesterfield.*

Complaisance renders a superior amiable, an equal agreeable, and an inferior acceptable. It smoothes distinction, sweetens conversation, and makes every one in the company pleased with himself. It produces good nature and mutual benevolence, encourages the timorous, soothes the turbulent, humanizes the fierce, and distinguishes a society of civilized persons from a confusion of savages.—*Addison.*

Coolness, and absence of heat and haste, indicate fine qualities. A gentleman makes no noise; a lady is serene.—*Emerson.*

Bad manners are a species of bad

morals; a conscientious man will not offend in that way.—*Bovee.*

The prince of darkness may be a gentleman, as we are told he is, but, whatever the God of earth and heaven is, he can surely be no gentleman.— *William James.*

There is a deportment which suits the figure and talents of each person; it is always lost when we quit it to assume that of another.—*Rousseau.*

The manner of a vulgar man has freedom without ease; the manner of a gentleman, ease without freedom.— *Chesterfield.*

To be always thinking about your manners is not the way to make them good; the very perfection of manners is not to think about yourself.—*Whately.*

Adorn yourself with all those graces and accomplishments which, without solidity, are frivolous; but without which, solidity is to a great degree useless.—*Chesterfield.*

In manners, tranquillity is the supreme power.—*Mad. de Maintenon.*

Good manners, which give color to life, are of greater importance than laws, which are but one of their manifestations. The law touches us here and there, but manners are about us everywhere.—*S. Smiles.*

MARRIAGE.—(See "WIFE.")

Never marry but for love; but see that thou lovest what is lovely.—*Penn.*

One of the good things that come of a true marriage is, that there is one face on which changes come without your seeing them; or rather there is one face which you can still see the same, through all the shadows which years have gathered upon it.—*G. Macdonald.*

If you would marry suitably, marry your equal.—*Ovid.*

What God hath joined together no man shall put asunder: God will take care of that.—*G. Bernard Shaw.*

Marriage! Nothing else demands so much from a man!—*Ibsen.*

The Don Juans among men and the light-o'-loves among women are afraid of marriage.—*Dr. Alfred Adler.*

Pleasant the snaffle of courtship, improving the manners and carriage; but the colt who is wise will abstain from the terrible throw bit of Marriage.— *Rudyard Kipling.*

You cannot weld cake-dough to cast iron, nor a girl to an old man.—*Austin O'Malley.*

The happy married man dies in good stile at home, surrounded by his weeping wife and children. The old bachelor don't die at all—he sort of rots away, like a pollywog's tail.—*Artemus Ward.*

Marriage is the Keeley cure for love's intoxication.—*Helen Rowland.*

Marriage is one long conversation, chequered by disputes.—*Robert L. Stevenson.*

Marriage is a very sea of calls and claims, which have but little to do with love.—*Ibsen.*

Being a parent used to be one of the most simple, natural, inevitable developments in the world. But nowadays, one has no business to be married unless, waking and sleeping, one is conscious of the responsibility.—*Abraham Flexner.*

Whether by design or accident, the fact remains that, with one small exception, no girl with a fancy Christian name has ever diverted the eye of a President of the United States to the matrimonial altar.—*George Jean Nathan.*

Marriage has a biological basis, and would be far more often a success if its biology were generally understood and the knowledge acted upon.—*J. B. S. Haldane.*

The whole world is strewn with snares, traps, gins and pitfalls for the capture of men by women.—*G. Bernard Shaw.*

I confess the combination of career and family is a problem for women that seems a bit difficult to me. Nursing schools and co-operative housekeeping may make it easier. Anyhow, many women are already practising it, by choice or by necessity—some 2,000,000 in fact—and in the future it will, I am sure, for economic, psychological reasons, be more and more usual for a woman to have a husband, children, a home and a career outside the home. —*Virginia C. Gildersleeve.*

Who loves the rain and loves his home, and looks on life with quiet eyes, him will I follow through the storm and at his hearth-fire keep me warm.— *Frances Shaw.*

I chose my wife, as she did her wedding gown, for qualities that would wear well.—*Goldsmith.*

Marriage is not a union merely between two creatures—it is a union between two spirits; and the intention of that bond is to perfect the nature of both, by supplementing their deficiencies with the force of contrast, giving to each sex those excellencies in which it is naturally deficient; to the one, strength of character and firmness of moral will; to the other, sympathy, meekness, tenderness; and just so solemn and glorious as these ends are for which the union was intended, just so terrible are the consequences if it be perverted and abused; for there is no earthly relationship which has so much power to ennoble and to exalt. There are two rocks, in this world of ours, on which the soul must either anchor or be wrecked—the one is God, and the other is the sex opposite.—*F. W. Robertson.*

Two persons who have chosen each other out of all the species, with the design to be each other's mutual comfort and entertainment, have, in that action, bound themselves to be good-humored, affable, discreet, forgiving, patient, and joyful, with respect to each other's frailties and perfections, to the end of their lives.—*Addison.*

When two persons have so good an opinion of each other as to come together for life, they will not differ in matters of importance, because they think of each other with respect; and in regard to all things of consideration that may affect them, they are prepared for mutual assistance and relief in such occurrences. For less occasions, they form no resolutions, but leave their minds unprepared.—*Tatler.*

The bloom or blight of all men's happiness.—*Byron.*

Take not too short a time, to make a world-wide bargain in.—*Shakespeare.*

Married in haste, we repent at leisure.—*Congreve.*

Marriage is the strictest tie of perpetual friendship, and there can be no friendship without confidence, and no confidence without integrity, and he must expect to be wretched, who pays to beauty, riches, or politeness that regard which only virtue and piety can claim.—*Johnson.*

The Christian religion, by confining marriage to pairs, and rendering the relation indissoluble, has by these two things done more toward the peace, happiness, settlement, and civilization of the world, than by any other part in this whole scheme of divine wisdom.—*Burke.*

That alliance may be said to have a double tie, where the minds are united as well as the body, and the union will have all its strength, when both the links are in perfection together.—*Colton.*

The happy minglement of hearts, where, changed as chemic compounds are, each with its own existence parts, to find a new one, happier far.—*Moore.*

A great proportion of the wretchedness which has embittered married life, has originated in a negligence of trifles. Connubial happiness is a thing of too fine a texture to be handled roughly. It is a sensitive plant, which will not bear even the touch of unkindness; a delicate flower, which indifference will chill and suspicion blast. It must be watered by the showers of tender affection, expanded by the cheering glow of kindness, and guarded by the impregnable barrier of unshaken confidence. Thus matured, it will bloom with fragrance in every season of life, and sweeten even the loneliness of declining years.—*Sprat.*

Of all the actions of a man's life, his marriage does least concern other people, yet of all actions of our life, 'tis most meddled with by other people.—*Selden.*

The reason why so few marriages are happy is because young ladies spend their time in making nets, not in making cages.—*Swift.*

Show me one couple unhappy merely on account of their limited circumstances, and I will show you ten who are wretched from other causes.—*Coleridge.*

Deceive not thyself by over-expecting happiness in the married state.—Look not therein for contentment greater than God will give, or a creature in this world can receive, namely, to be free from all inconveniences.—Marriage is not like the hill of Olympus, wholly clear, without clouds.—*Fuller.*

There is no earthly happiness exceeding that of a reciprocal satisfaction in the conjugal state.—*H. Giles.*

Marriage has in it less of beauty, but more of safety, than the single life; it hath not more ease, but less danger; it is more merry and more sad; it is fuller of sorrows and fuller of joys; it lies under more burdens, but is supported by all the strengths of love and charity; and those burdens are delightful. Marriage is the mother of the world, and preserves kingdoms, and fills cities and churches, and heaven itself.—*Jeremy Taylor.*

A person's character is but half formed till after wedlock.—*C. Simmons.*

Hail wedded love, mysterious law, true source of human offspring, sole propriety in Paradise of all things common else. By thee adulterous lust was driven from men among the bestial herds to range; by thee founded in reason, loyal, just, and pure, relations dear, and all the charities of father, son, and brother first were known.—*Milton.*

In choosing a wife, a nurse, or a school-teacher, look to the breed.— There is as much blood in men as in horses.—*C. Simmons.*

Men are generally more careful of the breed of their horses and dogs than of their children.—*Penn.*

The institution of marriage keeps the moral world in being, and secures it from an untimely dissolution. Without it, natural affection and amiableness would not exist, domestic education would become extinct, industry and economy be unknown, and man would be left to the precarious existence of the savage. But for this institution, learning and refinement would expire, government sink into the gulf of anarchy; and religion, hunted from earth, would hasten back to her native heavens.—*T. Dwight.*

Oh, friendly to the best pursuits of man, friendly to thought, to virtue, and to peace, domestic life in rural leisure passed! few know thy value, and few taste thy sweets.—*Cowper.*

He that hath wife and children, hath given hostages to fortune; for they are impediments to great enterprises, either of virtue or mischief. Certainly wife and children are a kind of discipline of humanity.—*Bacon.*

Humble wedlock is far better than proud virginity.—*Augustine.*

He that takes a wife, says Franklin, takes care; but as Emerson says, marriage has deep and serious benefits, and great joys.

Men marry to make an end; women to make a beginning.—*A. Dupuy.*

When it shall please God to bring thee to man's estate, use great providence and circumspection in choosing thy wife. For from thence will spring all thy future good or evil; and it is an action of life, like unto a stratagem of war, wherein a man can err but once!—*Sir P. Sidney.*

A married man falling into misfortune is more apt to retrieve his situation in the world than a single one, chiefly because his spirits are soothed and retrieved by domestic endearments, and his self-respect kept alive by finding that although all abroad be darkness and humiliation, yet there is a little world of love at home over which he is a monarch.—*Jeremy Taylor.*

The man, at the head of the house, can mar the pleasure of the household, but he cannot make it.—That must rest with the woman, and it is her greatest privilege.—*A. Helps.*

In the opinion of the world marriage ends all, as it does in a comedy.—The truth is precisely the reverse; it begins all.—*Mad. Swetchine.*

Save the love we pay to heaven, there is none purer, holier, than that a virtuous woman feels for him she would cleave to through life. Sisters part from sisters, brothers from brothers, children from their parents, but such a woman from the husband of her choice, never! —*Knowles.*

It is in vain that a man is born fortunate, if he be unfortunate in his marriage.—*Dacier.*

Have ever more care that thou be beloved of thy wife, rather than thyself besotted on her; and thou shalt judge of her love by these two observations: first, if thou perceive she have a care of thy estate, and exercise herself therein; the other, if she study to please thee, and be sweet unto thee in conversation, without thy instruction; for love needs no teaching nor precept.—*Sir W. Raleigh.*

God has set the type of marriage everywhere throughout the creation.—Every creature seeks its perfection in another.—The very heavens and earth picture it to us.—*Luther.*

One should believe in marriage as in the immortality of the soul.—*Balzac.*

As a great part of the uneasiness of matrimony arises from mere trifles, it would be wise in every young married man to enter into an agreement with his wife that in all disputes the party who was most convinced they were right should always surrender the victory. By this means both would be more forward to give up the cause.—*Fielding.*

Marriages are best made of dissimilar material.—*Theodore Parker.*

Two consorts in heaven are not two, but one angel.—*Swedenborg.*

There is no disparity in marriage like unsuitability of mind and purpose.—*Dickens.*

Husbands and wives talk of the cares of matrimony, and bachelors and spinsters bear them.—*W. Collins.*

Remember, that if thou marry for beauty, thou bindest thyself all thy life for that which perchance will neither last nor please thee one year; and when thou hast it, it will be to thee of no price at all; for the desire dieth when it is attained, and the affection perisheth when it is satisfied.—*Sir W. Raleigh.*

Hasty marriage seldom proveth well. —*Shakespeare.*

They who marry give hostages to the public that they will not attempt the ruin, or disturb the peace of it.—*Atterbury.*

O marriage! marriage! what a curse is thine, where hands alone consent, and hearts abhor!—*A. Hill.*

Fathers their children and themselves abuse, that wealth a husband for their daughters choose.—*Shirley.*

For any man to match above his rank, is but to sell his liberty.—*Massinger.*

But happy they, the happiest of their kind, whom gentle stars unite; and in one fate their hearts, their fortunes, and their beings blend!—*Thomson.*

Let still the woman take an elder than herself; so wears she to him; so sways she level in her husband's heart.—*Shakespeare.*

Early marriages are permanent moralities; deferred marriages are temptations to wickedness.—*H. W. Beecher.*

Themistocles, being asked whether he would rather marry his daughter to an indigent man of merit, or to a worthless man of estate, replied, that he should prefer a man without an estate, than to an estate without a man.

A good wife is like the ivy which beautifies the building to which it clings, twining its tendrils more lovingly as time converts the ancient edifice into a ruin.—*Johnson.*

The happiness of married life depends upon making small sacrifices with readiness and cheerfulness.—*Selden.*

When a man and woman are married their romance ceases and their history commences.—*Rochebrune.*

Marriage resembles a pair of shears, so joined that they cannot be separated; often moving in opposite directions, yet always punishing any one who comes between them.—*Sydney Smith.*

Maids want nothing but husbands, and when they have them, they want everything.—*Shakespeare.*

Wedlock's like wine, not properly judged of till the second glass.—*Jerrold.*

When we see the avaricious and crafty taking companions to their tables, and their beds, without any inquiry but after farms and money; or the giddy and thoughtless uniting themselves for life to those whom they have only seen by the light of tapers; when parents make articles for children without inquiring after their consent; when some marry for heirs to disappoint their brothers; and others throw themselves into the arms of those whom they do not love, because they have found themselves rejected where they were more solicitous to please; when some marry because their servants cheat them; some because they squander their own money; some because their houses are pestered with company; some because they will live like other people; and some because they are sick of themselves, we are not so much inclined to wonder that marriage is sometimes unhappy, as that it appears so little loaded with calamity; and cannot but conclude that society has something in itself eminently agreeable to human nature, when we find its pleasures so great, that even the ill choice of a companion can hardly overbalance them.—Those, therefore, that rail against matrimony, should be informed, that they are neither to wonder, or repine, that a contract begun on such principles has ended in disappointment. —*Johnson.*

He that marries is like the Doge who was wedded to the Adriatic. He knows not what there is in that which he marries: mayhap treasures and pearls, mayhap monsters and tempests await him.— *H. Heine.*

Not the marriage of convenience, nor the marriage of reason, but the marriage of love.—All other marriage, with vows so solemn, with intimacy so close, is but acted falsehood and varnished sin.— *Bulwer.*

I believe marriages would in general be as happy, and often more so, if they were all made by the Lord Chancellor, upon a due consideration of the characters and circumstances, without the parties having any choice in the matter.— *Johnson.*

Hanging and wiving go by destiny.— *Shakespeare.*

The married man is like the bee that fixes his hive, augments the world, benefits the republic, and by a daily diligence, without wronging any, profits all; but he who contemns wedlock, like a wasp, wanders an offence to the world, lives upon spoil and rapine, disturbs peace, steals sweets that are none of his own, and, by robbing the hives of others, meets misery as his due reward. —*Feltham.*

Few natures can preserve through years the poetry of the first passionate illusion. That can alone render wedlock the seal that confirms affection, and not the mocking ceremonial that consecrates its grave.—*Bulwer.*

A husband is a plaster that cures all the ills of girlhood.—*Molière.*

There is more of good nature than of good sense at the bottom of most marriages.—*Thoreau.*

The love of some men for their wives is like that of Alfieri for his horse. "My attachment for him," said he, "went so far as to destroy my peace every time

that he had the least ailment; but my love for him did not prevent me from fretting and chafing him whenever he did not wish to go my way."—*Bovee.*

Only so far as a man is happily married to himself, is he fit for married life to another, and for family life generally. —*Novalis.*

For a young man to marry a young woman, is of the Lord; for an old man to marry a young woman, is of man; but for a young man to marry an old woman, is of the devil!

She that hath a wise husband must entice him to an eternal dearness by the veil of modesty and the grave robes of chastity, the ornament of meekness, and the jewels of faith and charity. She must have no painting but blushings; her brightness must be purity, and she must shine round about with sweetness and friendship; and she shall be pleasant while she lives, and desired when she dies.—*Jeremy Taylor.*

All the molestations of marriage are abundantly recompensed with the other comforts which God bestoweth on them who make a wise choice of a wife.— *Fuller.*

Man and wife are equally concerned to avoid all offense of each other in the beginning of their conversation. A little thing can blast an infant blossom.— *Jeremy Taylor.*

In the career of female fame, there are few prizes to be obtained which can vie with the obscure state of a beloved wife, or a happy mother.—*Jane Porter.*

The last word is the most dangerous of infernal machines, and the husband and wife should no more fight to get it than they would struggle for the possession of a lighted bombshell.—*Jerrold.*

From my experience, not one in twenty marries the first love; we build statues of snow, and weep to see them melt.—*Walter Scott.*

Men should keep their eyes wide open before marriage, and half shut afterward. —*Mad. Scuderi.*

A man finds himself seven years older the day after his marriage.—*Bacon.*

Men dream in courtship, but in wedlock wake.—*Pope.*

A happy marriage is a new beginning of life, a new starting point for happiness and usefulness.—*A. P. Stanley.*

Celibacy, like the fly in the heart of an apple, dwells in perpetual sweetness, but sits alone, and is confined and dies in singularity; but marriage, like the useful bee, builds a house, and gathers sweetness from every flower, and labors and unites into societies and republics, and sends out colonies, and feeds the world with delicacies, and keeps order, and exercises many virtues, and promotes the interest of mankind, and is that state of good to which God hath designed the present constitution of the world.—*Jeremy Taylor.*

If you would have the nuptial union last, let virtue be the bond that ties it fast.—*Rowe.*

Marriage is a medicine which acts differently on good men and good women.—She does not love him quite enough—cure,—marriage.—He loves her a little too much—cure,—marriage.—*Charles Reade.*

Many a marriage has commenced, like the morning, red, and perished like a mushroom. Wherefore? Because the married pair neglected to be as agreeable to each other after their union as they were before it. Seek always to please each other, but in doing so keep heaven in mind. Lavish not your love to-day, remembering that marriage has a morrow and again a morrow. Bethink ye, my daughters, what the word housewife expresses. The married woman is her husband's domestic trust. On her he ought to be able to place his reliance in house and family; to her he should confide the key of his heart and the lock of his store-room. His honor and his home are under her protection, his welfare in her hands. Ponder this! And you, my sons, be true men of honor, and good fathers of your families. Act in such wise that your wives respect and love you. And what more shall I say to you, my children? Peruse diligently the word of God; that will guide you out of storm and dead calm, and bring you safe into port. And as for the rest —do your best!—*Frederika Bremer.*

The sanctity of marriage and the family relation make the corner-stone of our American society and civilization.—*Garfield.*

The treasures of the deep are not so precious as are the concealed comforts of a man locked up in woman's love: I scent the air of blessings when I come but near the house.—*T. Middleton.*

I know the sum of all that makes a man—a just man—happy, consists in the well choosing of his wife; and then well to discharge it, does require equality of years, of birth, of fortune.—*Massinger.*

Marriage enlarges the scene of our happiness and of our miseries.—A marriage of love is pleasant—of interest, easy, and where both meet, happy.—A happy marriage has in it all the pleasures of friendship, all the enjoyments of sense and reason, and, indeed, all the sweets of life.—*Addison.*

Few of either sex are ever united to their first love.—Yet married people jog on and call each other "My dear" and "My darling," all the same.—*Bulwer.*

Were a man not to marry a second time, it might be concluded that his first wife had given him a disgust to marriage; but by taking a second wife, he pays the highest compliment to the first, by showing that she made him so happy as a married man, that he wishes to be so a second time.—*Johnson.*

They that marry old people merely in expectation of burying them, hang themselves in the hope that some one will come and cut the halter.—*Fuller.*

If you wish to ruin yourself, marry a rich wife.—*Michelet.*

The kindest and the happiest pair will find occasion to forbear; and something, every day they live, to pity and perhaps forgive.—*Cowper.*

As the husband is, the wife is; if mated with a clown, the grossness of his nature will have weight to drag thee down.—*Tennyson.*

An uncertain marriage law is a national calamity.

Marriage with a good woman is a harbor in the tempest of life; with a bad woman, it is a tempest in the harbor.—*J. P. Senn.*

What greater thing is there for two human souls than to feel that they are joined for life—to strengthen each other in all labor, to rest on each other in all sorrow, to minister to each other in all pain, to be one with each other in silent, unspeakable memories at the moment of the last parting.—*George Eliot.*

MARTYRS.—It is the cause and not merely the death that makes the martyr.—*Napoleon.*

Christianity has made martyrdom sublime, and sorrow triumphant.—*E. H. Chapin.*

To die for the truth is not to die merely for one's faith, or one's country; it is to die for the world.

Their blood is shed in confirmation of the noblest claim—the claim to feed upon immortal truth, to walk with God, and be divinely free.—*Cowper.*

He that dies a martyr proves that he was not a knave, but by no means that he was not a fool; since the most absurd doctrines are not without such evidence as martyrdom can produce. A martyr, therefore, by the mere act of suffering, can prove nothing but his own faith.—*Colton.*

Those who completely sacrifice themselves are praised and admired; that is the sort of character men like to find in others.—*Rahel.*

It is admirable to die the victim of one's faith; it is sad to die the dupe of one's ambition.—*Lamartine.*

God discovers the martyr and confessor without the trial of flames and tortures, and will thereafter entitle many to the reward of actions which they never had the opportunity of performing.—*Addison.*

Even in this world they will have their judgment-day; and their names, which went down in the dust like a gallant banner trodden in the mire, shall rise again all glorious in the sight of nations.—*Mrs. Stowe.*

It is more difficult, and calls for higher energies of soul, to live a martyr than to die one.—*Horace Mann.*

For some not to be martyred is a martyrdom.—*Donne.*

The blood of the martyrs is the seed of the church.—*Jerome.*

They lived unknown, till persecution dragged them into fame, and chased them up to heaven. Their ashes flew no marble tells us whither. With their names no bard embalms and sanctifies his song: and history, so warm on meaner things, is cold on this.—*Cowper.*

The way of the world is, to praise dead saints, and persecute living ones.—*N. Howe.*

No language can fitly express the meanness, the baseness, the brutality, with which the world has ever treated its victims of one age and boasts of them in the next. Dante is worshiped at that grave to which he was hurried by persecution. Milton, in his own day, was "Mr. Milton, the blind adder, that spit his venom on the king's person"; and soon after, "the mighty orb of song." These absurd transitions from hatred to apotheosis, this recognition just at the moment when it becomes a mockery, saddens all intellectual history.—*E. P. Whipple.*

Two things are necessary to a modern martyr,—some to pity, and some to persecute, some to regret, and some to roast him. If martyrdom is now on the decline, it is not because martyrs are less zealous, but because martyr-mongers are more wise.—*Colton.*

When we read, we fancy we could be martyrs; when we come to act, we cannot bear a provoking word.—*Hannah More.*

The martyrs to vice far exceed the martyrs to virtue, both in endurance and in number. So blinded are we by our passions, that we suffer more to be damned than to be saved.—*Hannah More.*

O, how much those men are to be valued who, in the spirit with which the widow gave up her two mites, have given up themselves! How their names sparkle! How rich their very ashes are! How they will count up in Heaven!—*E. H. Chapin.*

Who falls for the love of God, shall rise a star.—*Ben. Jonson.*

Fools love the martyrdom of fame.—*Byron.*

MASTER.—It is a common law of nature, which no time will ever change, that superiors shall rule their inferiors.—*Dyonysius.*

Such it hath been, and shall be, that many still must labor for the one; it is nature's doom.—*Byron.*

It is not only paying wages, and giving commands, that constitute a master of a family; but prudence, equal behavior, with a readiness to protect and cherish them, is what entitles man to that character in their very hearts and sentiments.—*Steele.*

The eye of the master will do more work than both of his hands: not to oversee workmen, is to leave your purse open.—*Franklin.*

If thou art a master, sometimes be blind; if a servant, sometimes be deaf.—*Fuller.*

We must truly serve those whom we appear to command; we must bear with their imperfections, correct them with gentleness and patience, and lead them in the way to heaven.—*Fénelon.*

The measure of a master is his success in bringing all men round to his opinion twenty years later.—*Emerson.*

There is nothing so good to make a horse fat, as the eye of his master.—*Diogenes.*

Such master, such man.—*Tusser.*

Men, at some time, are masters of their fates.—*Shakespeare.*

MATHEMATICS.—Pure mathematics do remedy and cure many defects in the wit and faculties of individuals; for if the wit be dull, they sharpen it; if too wandering they fix it; if too inherent in the sense, they abstract it.—*Bacon.*

The study of the mathematics is like climbing up a steep and craggy mountain; when once you reach the top, it fully recompenses your trouble, by opening a fine, clear, and extensive prospect.

The study of mathematics cultivates the reason; that of the languages, at the same time, the reason and the taste. The former gives grasp and power to the mind; the latter both power and flexibility. The former, by itself, would prepare us for a state of certainties, which nowhere exists; the latter, for a state of probabilities, which is that of common life. Each, by itself, does but an imperfect work: in the union of both, is the best discipline for the mind, and the best mental training for the world as it is.—*Tryon Edwards.*

If a man's wits be wandering, let him study the mathematics; for in demonstrations, if his wit be called away ever so little, he must begin again.—*Johnson.*

MAXIMS.—(See "PROVERBS" and "APOTHEGMS.")

Maxims are the condensed good sense of nations.—*Sir J. Mackintosh.*

A maxim is a conclusion from observation of matters of fact, and is merely speculative; a principle carries knowledge within itself, and is prospective.—*Coleridge.*

Precepts and maxims are of great weight; and a few useful ones at hand, do more toward a wise and happy life, than whole volumes of cautions that we know not where to find.—*C. Simmons.*

Pithy sentences are like sharp nails which force truth upon our memory.—*Diderot.*

Precepts or maxims are of great weight; and a few useful ones at hand do more toward a happy life than whole volumes that we know not where to find.—*Seneca.*

The value of a maxim depends on four things: its intrinsic excellence or the comparative correctness of the principle it embodies; the subject to which it relates; the extent of its application; and the comparative ease with which it may be applied in practice.—*Charles Hodge.*

As a malicious censure, carefully worded and pronounced with assurance, is apt to pass with mankind for shrewd wit, so a virulent maxim in bold expressions, though without any justness of thought, is readily received for true philosophy.—*Shaftesbury.*

Maxims are to the intellect what laws are to actions: they do not enlighten, but guide and direct, and though themselves blind, are protecting.—*Joubert.*

It is hard to form a maxim against which an exception is not ready to start up: as "where the minister grows rich, the public is proportionately poor"; as "in a private family the steward always thrives the fastest when the lord is running out."—*Swift.*

All maxims have their antagonist maxims; proverbs should be sold in pairs, a single one being but a half truth.—*W. Matthews.*

I would fain coin wisdom,—mould it, I mean, into maxims, proverbs, sentences, that can easily be retained and transmitted.—*Joubert.*

The two maxims of any great man at court are, always to keep his countenance, and never to keep his word.—*Swift.*

General observations drawn from particulars are the jewels of knowledge, comprehending great store in a little room.—*Locke.*

MEANS.—There can be no end without means; and God furnishes no means that exempt us from the task and duty of joining our own best endeavors. The original stock, or wild olive tree of our natural powers, was not given us to be burnt or blighted, but to be grafted on.—*Coleridge.*

The end must justify the means.—*Prior.*

We put things in order; God does the rest. Lay an iron bar east and west, —it is not magnetized. Lay it north and south, and it is.—*Horace Mann.*

The means heaven yields must be embraced, and not neglected; else, if heaven would, and we will not; heaven's offer we refuse.—*Shakespeare.*

Mahomet hearing one of his soldiers say, "I'll turn my camel loose and trust him to God," said to him, "Tie your camel, and then trust him to God."— And Cromwell's charge to his soldiers, on the eve of battle, was, "Trust in Providence, but keep your powder dry."

Means without God cannot help.— God without means can, and often doth. —I will use good means, but not rest in them.—*Bp. Hall.*

How oft the sight of means to do ill deeds makes ill deeds done!—*Shakespeare.*

Some men possess means that are great, but fritter them away in the execution of conceptions that are little; others, who can form great conceptions, attempt to carry them into execution with little means. These two descriptions of men might succeed if united, but kept asunder, both fail. It is a rare thing to find a combination of great means and of great conceptions in one mind.—*Colton.*

All outward means of grace, if separate from the spirit of God, cannot profit, or conduce, in any degree, either to the knowledge or love of God.—All outward things, unless he work in them and by them, are in vain.—*John Wesley.*

MEANNESS.—Superior men, and yet not always virtuous, there have been; but there never has been a mean man, and at the same time virtuous.—*Confucius.*

Whoever is mean in his youth runs a great risk of becoming a scoundrel in riper years; meanness leads to villainy with fatal attraction.—*V. Cherbuliez.*

I have so great a contempt and detestation for meanness, that I could sooner make a friend of one who had committed murder, than of a person who could be capable, in any instance, of the former vice. Under meanness, I comprehend dishonesty; under dishonesty, ingratitude; under ingratitude, irreligion; and under this latter, every species of vice and immorality.—*Sterne.*

I have great hope of a wicked man; slender hope of a mean one. A wicked man may be converted and become a prominent saint. A mean man ought to be converted six or seven times, one right after the other, to give him a fair start and put him on an equality with a bold, wicked man.—*H. W. Beecher.*

To dally much with subjects mean and low, proves that the mind is weak or makes it so.—*Cowper.*

MEDICINE.—(See "Physic.")

Physic is, for the most part, only a substitute for temperance and exercise. —*Addison.*

Medicine has been defined to be the art or science of amusing a sick man with frivolous speculations about his disorder, and of tampering ingeniously, till nature either kills or cures him.

The disease and its medicine are like two factions in a besieged town; they tear one another to pieces, but both unite against their common enemy, Nature.—*Jeffrey.*

The poets did well to conjoin music and medicine, because the office of medicine is but to tune the curious harp of man's body.—*Bacon.*

The bitterness of the potion, and the abhorrence of the patient are necessary circumstances to the operation. It must be something to trouble and disturb the stomach that must purge and cure it.—*Montaigne.*

The best of all medicines are rest and fasting.—*Franklin.*

We seem ambitious God's whole work to undo.—With new diseases on ourselves we war, and with new physic, a worse engine far.—*Donne.*

Doctor, no medicine.—We are machines made to live—organized expressly for that purpose.—Such is our nature.—Do not counteract the living principle.—Leave it at liberty to defend itself, and it will do better than your drugs.—*Napoleon.*

Over the door of a library in Thebes is the inscription, "Medicine for the soul."—*Diodorus Siculus.*

MEDIOCRITY.—We meet with few utterly dull and stupid souls; the sublime and transcendent are still fewer; the generality of mankind stand between these two extremes; the interval is filled with multitudes of ordinary geniuses, but all very useful, and the ornaments and supports of the commonwealth.—*Bruyère.*

Minds of moderate caliber ordinarily condemn everything which is beyond their range.—*Rochefoucauld.*

Mediocrity is not allowed to poets, either by the gods or men.—*Horace.*

Mediocrity is now, as formerly, dangerous, commonly fatal, to the poet; but among even the successful writers of prose, those who rise sensibly above it are the very rarest exceptions.—*Gladstone.*

Mediocrity is excellent to the eyes of mediocre people.—*Joubert.*

Persevering mediocrity is much more respectable, and unspeakably more useful, than talented inconstancy.—*J. Hamilton.*

The art of putting into play mediocre qualities often begets more reputation than is achieved by true merit.—*Rochefoucauld.*

Mediocrity can talk; but it is for genius to observe.—*Disraeli.*

The highest order of mind is accused of folly, as well as the lowest. Nothing is thoroughly approved but mediocrity. The majority has established this, and it fixes its fangs on whatever gets beyond it either way.—*Pascal.*

Nothing in the world is more haughty than a man of moderate capacity when once raised to power.—*Wessenburg.*

The virtue of the soul does not consist in flying high, but walking orderly; its grandeur does not exercise itself in grandeur, but in mediocrity.—*Montaigne.*

There is a mean in all things; even virtue itself has stated limits; which not being strictly observed, it ceases to be virtue.—*Horace.*

They are as sick that surfeit with too much, as they that starve with nothing. It is no mean happiness, therefore, to be seated in the mean. Superfluity comes soonest by white hairs, but competency lives longest.

There are circumstances of peculiar difficulty and danger, where a mediocrity of talent is the most fatal quality that a man can possibly possess. Had Charles the First, and Louis the Sixteenth, been more wise or more weak, more firm or more yielding, in either case they had both of them saved their heads.—*Colton.*

There are certain things in which mediocrity is not to be endured, such as poetry, music, painting, public speaking.—*Bruyère.*

MEDITATION.—Meditation is the soul's perspective glass, whereby, in her long removes, she discerneth God, as if he were nearer at hand.—*Feltham.*

Meditation is the life of the soul; action is the soul of meditation; honor is the reward of action: so meditate, that thou mayst do; so do, that thou mayst purchase honor; for which purchase, give God the glory.—*Quarles.*

Meditation may think down hours to moments. The heart may give most useful lessons to the head, and learning wiser grow without his books.—*Cowper.*

By meditation I can converse with God, solace myself on the bosom of the Saviour, bathe myself in the rivers of divine pleasure, tread the paths of my rest, and view the mansions of eternity.—*Anon.*

A man of meditation is happy, not for an hour or a day, but quite round the circle of all his years.—*Isaac Taylor.*

One of the rarest of all acquirements is the faculty of profitable meditation. Most human beings, when they fancy they are meditating, are, in fact, doing nothing at all, and thinking of nothing.—*Boyd.*

No soul can preserve the bloom and

delicacy of its existence without lonely musings and silent prayer, and the greatness of this necessity is in proportion to the greatness of evil.—*Farrar.*

'Tis greatly wise to talk with our past hours and ask them what report they bore to heaven, and how they might have borne more welcome news.—*Young.*

Meditation is the nurse of thought, and thought the food for meditation.—*C. Simmons.*

Meditation is the tongue of the soul and the language of our spirit; and our wandering thoughts in prayer are but the neglects of meditation and recessions from that duty; according as we neglect meditation, so are our prayers imperfect,—meditation being the soul of prayer and the intention of our spirit.—*Jeremy Taylor.*

It is easier to go six miles to hear a sermon, than to spend one quarter of an hour in meditating on it when I come home.—*Philip Henry.*

It is not hasty reading, but seriously meditating upon holy and heavenly truths that makes them prove sweet and profitable to the soul. It is not the bee's touching on the flowers that gathers the honey, but her abiding for a time upon them, and drawing out the sweet. It is not he that reads most, but he that meditates most on divine truth, that will prove the choicest, wisest, strongest Christian.—*Bp. Hall.*

It is not the number of books you read, nor the variety of sermons you hear, nor the amount of religious conversation in which you mix, but it is the frequency and earnestness with which you meditate on these things till the truth in them becomes your own and part of your being, that ensures your growth.—*F. W. Robertson.*

Reading and conversation may furnish us with many ideas of men and things, yet it is our own meditation that must form our judgment.—*Watts.*

Meditation is that exercise of the mind by which it recalls a known truth, as some kind of creatures do their food, to be ruminated upon till all the valuable parts be extracted.—*Bp. Horne.*

MEEKNESS.—(See "HUMILITY.")

The flower of weakness grows on a stem of grace.—*J. Montgomery.*

Selfish men may possess the earth; it is the meek only who inherit it from the Heavenly Father, free from all defilements and perplexities of unrighteousness.—*Woolman.*

There will come a time when three words, uttered with charity and meekness, shall receive a far more blessed reward than three thousand volumes written with disdainful sharpness of wit.—*R. Hooker.*

Meekness is love at school, at the school of Christ.—It is the disciple learning to know, and fear, and distrust himself, and learning of him who is meek and lowly in heart, and so finding rest to his soul.—*J. Hamilton.*

Meekness cannot well be counterfeited.—It is not insensibility, or unmanliness, or servility; it does not cringe, or whine. It is benevolence imitating Christ in patience, forbearance, and quietness.—It feels keenly, but not malignantly; it abounds in good will, and bears all things.—*W. S. Plumer.*

The anger of a meek man is like fire struck out of steel, hard to be got out, and when got out, soon gone.—The meek enjoy almost a perpetual Sabbath.—*M. Henry.*

Meekness is imperfect if it be not both active and passive, leading us to subdue our own passions and resentments, as well as to bear patiently the passions and resentments of others.—*Foster.*

The meek are not those who are never at all angry, for such are insensible; but those who, feeling anger, control it, and are angry only when they ought to be. Meekness excludes revenge, irritability, morbid sensitiveness, but not self-defence, or a quiet and steady maintenance of right.—*Theophylact.*

MEETING.—The joy of meeting, not unmixed with pain.—*Longfellow.*

Absence, with all its pains, is, by this charming moment, wiped away.—*Thomson.*

The joys of meeting pay the pangs of absence; else who could bear it?—*Rowe.*

Ah me! the world is full of meetings such as this,—a thrill, a voiceless challenge and reply, and sudden partings after!—*N. P. Willis.*

In life there are meetings which seem like a fate.—*Owen Meredith.*

But here she comes, in the calm harbor of whose gentle breast, my tempest beaten soul may safely rest.—O, my heart's joy, whate'er my sorrows be, they cease and vanish on beholding thee.—By this one view all my past pains are paid, and all I have to come, more easy made.—*Dryden.*

I have not joyed an hour since you departed, for public miseries, and for private fears; but this blest meeting has o'erpaid them all.—*Dryden.*

MELANCHOLY.—Melancholy, or low spirits, is that hysterical passion which forces unbidden sighs and tears. It falls upon a contented life, like a drop of ink on white paper, which is none the less a stain that it carries no meaning with it.—*Lockhart.*

Melancholy is a fearful gift; what is it but the telescope of truth, which brings life near in utter darkness, making the cold reality too real?—*Byron.*

Melancholy is a kind of demon that haunts our island, and often conveys herself to us in an easterly wind.—*Addison.*

The noontide sun is dark, and music discord, when the heart is low.—*Young.*

Melancholy spreads itself betwixt heaven and earth, like envy between man and man, and is an everlasting mist.—*Byron.*

Whatever is highest and holiest is tinged with melancholy. The eye of genius has always a plaintive expression, and its natural language is pathos. A prophet is sadder than other men; and He who was greater than all the prophets was "a man of sorrows and acquainted with grief."—*Mrs. L. M. Child.*

The spirit of melancholy would often take its flight from us if only we would take up the song of praise.—*P. B. Power.*

I once gave a lady two-and-twenty receipts against melancholy; one was a bright fire; another, to remember all the pleasant things said to her; another, to keep a box of sugarplums on the chimney-piece and a kettle simmering on the hob. I thought this mere trifling at the moment, but have in after life discovered how true it is that these little pleasures often banish melancholy better

than higher and more exalted objects; and that no means ought to be thought too trifling which can oppose it either in ourselves or in others.—*Sydney Smith.*

Melancholy attends the best joys of an ideal life.—*Margaret Fuller.*

There is not a string attuned to mirth but has its chord of melancholy.—*Hood.*

It is impious in a good man to be sad.—*Young.*

Melancholy sees the worst of things—things as they might be, and not as they are.—It looks upon a beautiful face, and sees but a grinning skull.—*Bovee.*

Make not a bosom friend of a melancholy, sad soul.—He will be sure to aggravate thine adversity and to lessen thy prosperity.—He goes always heavily loaded, and thou must bear half.—*Fénelon.*

You may call it madness—folly; you shall not chase my gloom away; there is such a charm in melancholy, I would not, if I could, be gay.—*Rogers.*

People of gloomy, uncheerful imaginations, will discover their natural tincture of mind in all their thoughts, words, and actions. As the finest wines have often the taste of the soil, so even the most religious thoughts often draw something that is peculiar from the constitution of the mind in which they arise. When folly or superstition strikes in with this natural depravity of temper, it is not in the power, even of religion itself, to preserve the character from appearing highly absurd and ridiculous.—*Addison.*

My melancholy haunts me everywhere, and not one kindly gleam pierces the gloom of my dark thoughts, to give a glimpse of comfort.—*T. Southern.*

MEMORY.—Memory is the receptacle and sheath of all knowledge.—*Cicero.*

The memory is a treasurer to whom we must give funds, if we would draw the assistance we need.—*Rowe.*

Memory depends very much on the perspicuity, regularity, and order of our thoughts. Many complain of the want of memory, when the defect is in their judgment; and others, by grasping at all, retain nothing.—*Fuller.*

It is a terrible thought, that nothing

is ever forgotten; that not an oath is ever uttered that does not continue to vibrate through all time, in the wide-spreading current of sound; that not a prayer is lisped, that its record is not to be found stamped on the laws of nature by the indelible seal of the Almighty's will.—*Cooper.*

That memory is the book of judgment, from some ópium experiences of mine, I can believe. I have, indeed, seen the same thing asserted in modern books, and accompanied by a remark which I am convinced is true, namely: that the dread book of account, which the Scriptures speak of is, in fact, the mind itself of each individual. Of this, at least, I feel assured—that there is no such thing as forgetting, possible to the mind; a thousand accidents may and will interpose a veil between our present consciousness and the secret inscriptions on the mind; accidents of the same sort will also rend away this veil; but whether veiled or unveiled, the inscription remains forever; just as the stars seem to withdraw before the common light of day; whereas, in fact, we all know that it is the light which is drawn over them as a veil, and that they are waiting to be revealed, when the obscuring daylight shall have withdrawn.—*De Quincey.*

The secret of a good memory is attention, and attention to a subject depends upon our interest in it.—We rarely forget that which has made a deep impression on our minds.—*Tryon Edwards.*

We consider ourselves as defective in memory, either because we remember less than we desire, or less than we suppose others to remember.—*Johnson.*

No one is likely to remember what is entirely uninteresting to him.—*G. Macdonald.*

Joy's recollection is no longer joy, while sorrow's memory is sorrow still.—*Byron.*

Every one complains of his memory; nobody of his judgment.—*Rochefoucauld.*

The two offices of memory are collection and distribution.—*Johnson.*

Memory is not wisdom; idiots can by rote repeat volumes.—Yet what is wisdom without memory?—*Tupper.*

O, Memory, thou bitter-sweet—both a joy and a scourge.—*Mad. De Staël.*

If the memory is more flexible in childhood, it is more tenacious in mature age; if childhood has sometimes the memory of words, old age has that of things, which impress themselves according to the clearness of the conception of the thought which we wish to retain.—*Bonstetten.*

Memory, the daughter of attention, is the teeming mother of knowledge.—*Tupper.*

Memory is the treasure-house of the mind wherein the monuments thereof are kept and preserved.—*Fuller.*

Memory can glean, but never renew. —it brings us joys faint as is the perfume of the flowers, faded and dried, of the summer that is gone.—*H. W. Beecher.*

The memory of past favors, is like a rainbow, bright, vivid, and beautiful, but it soon fades away.—The memory of injuries is engraved on the heart, and remains forever.—*Haliburton.*

Memory seldom fails when its office is to show us the tombs of our buried hopes.—*Lady Blessington.*

The true art of memory is the art of attention.—*Johnson.*

It is an old saying that we forget nothing.—As people in fever begin suddenly to talk the language of their infancy, so we are stricken by memory sometimes, and old affections rush back on us as vivid as in the time when they were our daily talk, when their presence gladdened our eyes, when their accents thrilled in our ears,—when, with passionate tears and grief, we flung ourselves upon their hopeless corpses. Parting is death,—at least, as far as this life is concerned. A passion comes to an end; it is carried off in a coffin, or, weeping in a post-chaise; it drops out of life one way or another, and the earth-clods close over it, and we see it no more. But it has been part of our souls, and it is eternal.—*Thackeray.*

Memory is the cabinet of imagination, the treasury of reason, the registry of conscience, and the council chamber of thought.—*Basil.*

How can such deep-imprinted images sleep in us at times, till a word, a sound, awake them?—*Lessing.*

Of all the faculties of the mind, memory is the first that flourishes, and the first that dies.—*Colton.*

Memory in youth is active and easily impressible; in old age it is comparatively callous to new impressions, but still retains vividly those of earlier years.

A memory without blot or contamination must be an exquisite treasure, an inexhaustible source of pure refreshment.—*Charlotte Brontë.*

Recollection is the only paradise from which we cannot be turned out.—*Richter.*

Memory tempers prosperity, mitigates adversity, controls youth, and delights old age.—*Lactantius.*

Through the shadowy past, like a tomb-searcher, memory ran, lifting each shroud that time had cast o'er buried hopes.—*Moore.*

Memory is the friend of wit, but the treacherous ally of invention; there are many books that owe their success to two things,—the good memory of those who write them, and the bad memory of those who read them.—*Colton.*

What we learn with pleasure we never forget.—*Alfred Mercier.*

The joys I have possessed are ever mine; out of thy reach, behind eternity, hid in the sacred treasure of the past, but blest remembrance brings them hourly back.—*Dryden.*

Lulled in the countless chambers of the brain, our thoughts are linked by many a hidden chain; awake but one, and lo, what myriads rise!—*Pope.*

My memory is the thing I forget with.—*A child's definition.*

As dew to the blossom, and bud to the bee, as the scent to the rose, are those memories to me.—*Amelia B. Welby.*

They teach us to remember; why do not they teach us to forget? There is not a man living who has not, some time in his life, admitted that memory was as much of a curse as a blessing. —*F. A. Durivage.*

The memory has as many moods as the temper, and shifts its scenery like a diorama.—*George Eliot.*

There is a remembrance of the dead, to which we turn even from the charms

of the living. These we would not exchange for the song of pleasure or the bursts of revelry.—*Washington Irving.*

MEN.—(See " MAN.")

Men are but children, too, though they have gray hairs; they are only of a larger size.—*Seneca.*

The real difference between men is energy. A strong will, a settled purpose, an invincible determination, can accomplish almost anything; and in this lies the distinction between great men and little men.—*Fuller.*

God divided man into men, that they might help each other.—*Seneca.*

Men and statues that are admired in an elevated station, have a very different effect on us when we approach them: the first appear less than we imagined them: the last, larger.—*Rochefoucauld.*

I have visited many countries, and have been in cities without number, yet never did I enter a town which could not produce ten or twelve little great men; all fancying themselves known to the rest of the world, and complimenting each other upon their extensive reputation.—*Goldsmith.*

We may judge of men by their conversation toward God, but never by God's dispensations toward them.—*R. Palmer.*

All great men are in some degree inspired.—*Cicero.*

Great men stand like solitary towers in the city of God, and secret passages, running deep beneath external nature, give their thoughts intercourse with higher intelligence, which strengthens and consoles them, and of which the laborers on the surface do not even dream.—*Longfellow.*

It is far easier to know men than to know man.—*Rochefoucauld.*

Lives of great men all remind us, we can make our lives sublime.—*Longfellow.*

Men are the sport of circumstances, when the circumstances seem the sport of men.—*Byron.*

Men, by associating in large masses, as in camps and cities, improve their talents but impair their virtues; and strengthen their minds, but weaken their morals; thus a retrocession in the one, is too often the price they pay for a refinement of the other.—*Colton.*

We do not commonly find men of superior sense amongst those of the highest fortune.—*Juvenal.*

We must love men, ere to us they will seem worthy of our love.—*Shakespeare.*

Great men, like great cities, have many crooked arts and dark alleys in their hearts, whereby he that knows them may save himself much time and trouble.

Good men do not always have grace and favor, lest they should be puffed up, and grow insolent and proud.—*Chrysostom.*

MERCY.—The greatest attribute of heaven is mercy.—*Beaumont and Fletcher.*

We may imitate the Deity in all his moral attributes, but mercy is the only one in which we can pretend to equal him.—We cannot, indeed, give like God, but surely we may forgive like him.—*Sterne.*

Wilt thou draw near the nature of the gods? Draw near them then in being merciful; sweet mercy is nobility's true badge.—*Shakespeare.*

Mercifulness makes us equal to the gods.—*Claudian.*

Mercy among the virtues is like the moon among the stars,—not so sparkling and vivid as many, but dispensing a calm radiance that hallows the whole. It is the bow that rests upon the bosom of the cloud when the storm is past. It is the light that hovers above the judgment-seat.—*E. H. Chapin.*

Among the attributes of God, although they are all equal, mercy shines with even more brilliancy than justice.—*Cervantes.*

The quality of mercy is not strained; it droppeth, as the gentle rain from heaven upon the place beneath; it is twice blessed; it blesseth him that gives and him that takes: 'tis mightiest in the mightiest: it becomes the throned monarch better than his crown. Mercy is an attribute to God himself; and earthly power doth then show likest God's, when mercy seasons justice. Consider this,—that, in the course of justice, none of us should see salvation:

we do pray for mercy, and that same prayer doth teach us all to render the deeds of mercy.—*Shakespeare.*

Mercy turns her back to the unmerciful.—*Quarles.*

A God all mercy, were a God unjust.—*Young.*

Nothing emboldens sin so much as mercy.—*Shakespeare.*

Were there but a single mercy apportioned to each moment of our lives, the sum would rise very high; but how is our arithmetic confounded when every minute has more than we can distinctly number.—*Rowe.*

Mercy more becomes a magistrate than the vindictive wrath which men call justice.—*Longfellow.*

We hand folks over to God's mercy, and show none ourselves.—*George Eliot.*

If the end of one mercy were not the beginning of another, we were undone.—*Philip Henry.*

He that has tasted the bitterness of sin fears to commit it; and he that hath felt the sweetness of mercy will fear to offend it.

Mercy to him that shows it, is the rule.—*Cowper.*

Hate shuts her soul when dove-eyed Mercy pleads.—*Charles Sprague.*

As freely as the firmament embraces the world, or the sun pours forth impartially his beams, so mercy must encircle both friend and foe.—*Schiller.*

How would you be, if he, who is the top of judgment, should but judge you as you are?—O, think on that, and mercy then will breathe within your lips, like man new made.—*Shakespeare.*

O God, how beautiful the thought, how merciful the blest decree, that grace can always be found when sought, and nought shut out the soul from thee.—*Eliza Cook.*

Who will not mercy unto others show, how can he mercy ever hope to have?—*Spenser.*

Lenity will operate with greater force in some instances, than rigor.—It is, therefore, my great wish, to have my whole conduct distinguished by it.—*Washington.*

To sin because mercy abounds is the devil's logic; he that sins because of

God's mercy, shall have judgment without mercy.—Mercy is not for them that sin and fear not, but for them that fear and sin not.—*T. Watson.*

Mercy is like the rainbow, which God hath set in the clouds; it never shines after it is night.—If we refuse mercy here, we shall have justice in eternity. —*Jeremy Taylor.*

Teach me to feel another's woe, to hide the fault I see; that mercy I to others show, that mercy show to me.— *Pope.*

MERIT.—Nature creates merit, and fortune brings it into play.—*Rochefoucauld.*

Real merit of any kind, cannot long be concealed; it will be discovered, and nothing can depreciate it but a man exhibiting it himself. It may not always be rewarded as it ought; but it will always be known.—*Chesterfield.*

There is merit without elevation, but there is no elevation without some merit.—*Rochefoucauld.*

Charms strike the sight, but merit wins the soul.—*Pope.*

Mere bashfulness without merit, is awkward; and merit without modesty, insolent. But modest merit has a double claim to acceptance, and generally meets with as many patrons as beholders.—*Addison.*

If you wish your merit to be known, acknowledge that of other people.— *Oriental Proverb.*

True merit, like a river, the deeper it is, the less noise it makes.—*Halifax.*

There's a proud modesty in merit; averse from asking, and resolved to pay ten times the gifts it asks.—*Dryden.*

Elevation is to merit what dress is to a handsome person.—*Rochefoucauld.*

Good actions crown themselves with lasting bays; who deserves well, needs not another's praise.—*R. Heath.*

The sufficiency of my merit, is to know that my merit is not sufficient. —*Augustine.*

Merit is never so conspicuous as when coupled with an obscure origin, just as the moon never appears so lustrous as when it emerges from a cloud.—*Bovee.*

Contemporaries appreciate the man rather than his merit; posterity will regard the merit rather than the man.— *Colton.*

The mark of extraordinary merit is to see those most envious of it constrained to praise.—*Rochefoucauld.*

I am told so many ill things of a man, and I see so few in him, that I begin to suspect he has a real but troublesome merit, as being likely to eclipse that of others.—*Bruyère.*

The world more frequently recompenses the appearance of merit, than merit itself.—*Rochefoucauld.*

It never occurs to fools that merit and good fortune are closely united.— *Goethe.*

The force of his own merit makes his way, a gift that heaven gives for him.— *Shakespeare.*

The art of being able to make a good use of moderate abilities wins esteem, and often confers more reputation than real merit.—*Rochefoucauld.*

The best evidence of merit is the cordial recognition of it whenever and wherever it may be found.—*Bovee.*

I will not be concerned at other men's not knowing me; I will be concerned at my own want of ability.—*Confucius.*

O, that estates, degrees, and offices were not derived corruptly, and that clear honor were purchased by the merit of the wearer.—*Shakespeare.*

Among the sons of men how few are known, who dare be just to merit not their own!—*Churchill.*

We must not judge of a man's merits by his great qualities, but by the use he makes of them.—*Rochefoucauld.*

METAPHYSICS.—When he that speaks, and he to whom he speaks, neither of them understand what is meant, that is metaphysics.—*Voltaire.*

Metaphysicians can unsettle things, but they can erect nothing. They can pull down a church, but they cannot build a hovel.—*Cecil.*

Metaphysics is the anatomy of the soul.—*De Boufflers.*

Algebra is the metaphysics of arithmetic.—*Sterne.*

Metaphysicians have been learning their lesson for the last four thousand years; and it is now high time that they should begin to teach us something.

Can any of the tribe inform us why all the operations of the mind are carried on with undiminished strength and activity in dreams, except the judgment, which alone is suspended and dormant?—*Colton.*

We have no strict demonstration of anything, except mathematical truths, but by metaphysics. We can have no proof that is properly demonstrative, of any one position relating to the being and nature of God, his creation of the world, the dependence of all things on him, the nature of bodies and spirits, the nature of our own souls, or any of the great truths of morality and natural religion, but what is metaphysical.—*Jonathan Edwards.*

Metaphysicians are whetstones, on which to sharpen dull intellects.—*H. W. Beecher.*

If your adversary be ignorant, instruct him. If he reason erringly, detect his fallacies. But against ingenuity which you cannot equal, or demonstration which you cannot disprove, do not, if you would respect yourselves, cry out metaphysics!

METHOD.—Dispatch is the life of business, and method is the soul of dispatch.

Method and dispatch govern the world.

Method goes far to prevent trouble in business; for it makes the task easy, hinders confusion, saves abundance of time, and instructs those who have business depending, what to do and what to hope.—*Penn.*

Be methodical if you would succeed in business, or in anything.—Have a work for every moment, and mind the moment's work.—Whatever your calling, master all its bearings and details, its principles, instruments, and applications.—Method is essential if you would get through your work easily and with economy of time.—*W. Mathews.*

Irregularity and want of method are only supportable in men of great learning or genius, who are often too full to be exact, and therefore choose to throw down their pearls in heaps before the reader, rather than be at the pains of stringing them.—*Addison.*

Method is like packing things in a box; a good packer will get in half as much again as a bad one.—*Cecil.*

Methods are the masters of masters.—*Talleyrand.*

Marshall thy notions into a handsome method.—One will carry twice more weight packed up in bundles, than when it lies flapping and hanging about his shoulders.—*Fuller.*

The shortest way to do many things is to do only one thing at a time.—*Cecil.*

The first idea of method is a progressive transition from one step to another in any course.—If in the right course, it will be the true method; if in the wrong, we cannot hope to progress.—*Coleridge.*

Every great man exhibits the talent of organization or construction, whether it be in a poem, a philosophical system, a policy, or a strategy.—And without method there is no organization nor construction.—*Bulwer.*

Method will teach you to win time.—*Goethe.*

Method facilitates every kind of business, and by making it easy makes it agreeable, and also successful.—*C. Simmons.*

MIDNIGHT. — Midnight, — strange mystic hour,—when the veil between the frail present and the eternal future grows thin.—*Mrs. Stowe.*

This dead of midnight is the noon of thought, and wisdom mounts her zenith with the stars.—*Mrs. Barbauld.*

Midnight—that hour of night's black arch the keystone.—*Burns.*

Midnight brought on the dusky hour, friendliest to sleep and silence.—*Milton.*

Midnight the outpost of advancing day; the frontier town and citadel of night; the water-shed of time, from which the streams of yesterday and tomorrow take their way, one to the land of promise and of light—one to the land of darkness and of dreams.—*Longfellow.*

It is now the very witching time of night; when churchyards yawn, and hell itself breathes out contagion to this world.—Now could I drink hot blood and do such business as the bitter day would quake to look on!—*Shakespeare.*

The stifled hum of midnight, when traffic has lain down to rest, and the chariot wheels of vanity, still rolling here and there through distant streets, are bearing her to halls, roofed in and lighted for her; and only vice and misery, to prowl, or to moan like night birds, are abroad.—*Carlyle.*

Oh, wild and wondrous midnight, there is a might in thee to make the charmed body almost like spirit, and give it some faint glimpses of immortality.—*J. R. Lowell.*

MIND.—(See " SOUL.")

Whatever that be which thinks, understands, wills, and acts, it is something celestial and divine.—*Cicero.*

We may doubt the existence of matter, if we please, and like Berkeley deny it, without subjecting ourselves to the shame of a very conclusive confutation; but there is this remarkable difference between matter and mind, that he that doubts the existence of mind, by doubting proves it.—*Colton.*

The more accurately we search into the human mind, the stronger traces we everywhere find of the wisdom of Him who made it.—*Burke.*

The mind grows narrow in proportion as the soul grows corrupt.—*Rousseau.*

The human mind cannot create anything. It produces nothing until after having been fertilized by experience and meditation; its acquisitions are the germs of its production.—*Buffon.*

The mind is but a barren soil; a soil which is soon exhausted, and will produce no crop, or only one, unless it be continually fertilized and enriched with foreign matter.—*Sir J. Reynolds.*

As the fire-fly only shines when on the wing, so it is with the human mind —when at rest, it darkens.—*L. E. Landon.*

A mind too vigorous and active, serves only to consume the body to which it is joined, as the richest jewels are soonest found to wear their settings. —*Goldsmith.*

A perfectly just and sound mind is a rare and invaluable gift. But it is still more unusual to see such a mind unbiassed in all its actings. God has given this soundness of mind but to few: and a very small number of these few escape the bias of some predilection perhaps habitually operating; and none are at all times perfectly free.

An exquisite watch went irregularly, though no defect could be discovered in it. At last it was found that the balance wheel had been near a magnet; and here was all the mischief. If the soundest mind be magnetized by any predilection, it must act irregularly.— *Cecil.*

There is nothing so elastic as the human mind. Like imprisoned steam, the more it is pressed the more it rises to resist the pressure. The more we are obliged to do the more we are able to accomplish.—*Tryon Edwards.*

The best way to prove the clearness of our mind, is by showing its faults; as when a stream discovers the dirt at the bottom, it convinces us of the transparency and purity of the water.—*Pope.*

What stubbing, plowing, digging, and harrowing is to land, that thinking, reflecting, examining is to the mind. Each has its proper culture; and as the land that is suffered to lie waste and wild for a long time will be overspread with brushwood, brambles, and thorns, which have neither use nor beauty, so there will not fail to sprout up in a neglected, uncultivated mind, a great number of prejudices and absurd opinions, which owe their origin partly to the soil itself, the passions, and imperfections of the mind of man, and partly to those seeds which chance to be scattered in it by every wind of doctrine which the cunning of statesmen, the singularity of pedants, and the superstition of fools shall raise.—*Berkeley.*

Knowledge, wisdom, erudition, arts, and elegance, what are they, but the mere trappings of the mind, if they do not serve to increase the happiness of the possessor? A mind rightly instituted in the school of philosophy, acquires at once the stability of the oak, and the flexibility of the osier.—*Goldsmith.*

I find, by experience, that the mind and the body are more than married, for they are most intimately united; and when the one suffers, the other sympathizes.—*Chesterfield.*

A certain degree of solitude seems necessary to the full growth and spread of the highest mind; and therefore must a very extensive intercourse with men stifle many a holy germ, and scare away the gods, who shun the restless tumult of noisy companies and the discussion of petty interests.—*Novalis.*

Prepare yourselves for the great world, as the athletes used to do for their exercises; oil your mind and your manners, to give them the necessary suppleness and flexibility; strength alone will not do, as young people are too apt to think.—*Chesterfield.*

A well cultivated mind is made up of all the minds of preceding ages; it is only the one single mind educated by all previous time.—*Fontenelle.*

Mind unemployed is mind unenjoyed. —*Bovee.*

Mind is not as merchandise which decreaseth in the using, but like to the passions of men, which rejoice and expand in exertion.—*Tupper.*

Strength of mind is exercise, not rest. —*Pope.*

As the soil, however rich it may be, cannot be productive without culture, so the mind without cultivation can never produce good fruit.—*Seneca.*

He that has no resources of mind, is more to be pitied than he who is in want of necessaries for the body; to be obliged to beg our daily happiness from others, bespeaks a more lamentable poverty than that of him who begs his daily bread.—*Colton.*

If we work marble, it will perish; if we work upon brass, time will efface it; if we rear temples, they will crumble into dust; but if we work upon immortal minds and instill into them just principles, we are then engraving that upon tablets which no time will efface, but will brighten and brighten to all eternity.—*Daniel Webster.*

The blessing of an active mind, when it is in a good condition, is, that it not only employs itself, but is almost sure to be the means of giving wholesome employment to others.—*Anon.*

We find means to cure folly, but none to reclaim a distorted mind.—*Rochefoucauld.*

Frivolous curiosity about trifles, and laborious attention to little objects, which neither require nor deserve a moment's thought, lower a man, who from thence is thought, and not unjustly, incapable of greater matters.—*Chesterfield.*

A truly strong and sound mind is the mind that can equally embrace great things and small.—*I would have a man great in great things, and elegant in little things.—Johnson.*

To see a man fearless in dangers, untainted with lusts, happy in adversity, composed in a tumult, and laughing at all those things which are generally either coveted or feared, all men must acknowledge that this can be from nothing else but a beam of divinity that influences a mortal body.—*Seneca.*

If thou desirest ease, in the first place take care of the ease of thy mind; for that will make all other sufferings easy. But nothing can support a man whose mind is wounded.—*Fuller.*

Intrepidity is an extraordinary strength of mind, which raises it above the troubles, disorders, and emotions, which the sight of great perils is calculated to excite; it is by this strength that heroes maintain themselves in a tranquil state of mind, and preserve the free use of their reason under the most surprising and terrible circumstances.—*Rochefoucauld.*

The finite mind does not require to grasp the infinitude of truth, but only to go forward from light to light.—*P. Bayne.*

There are few who need complain of the narrowness of their minds if they will only do their best with them.—*Hobbes.*

Our minds are like our stomachs; they are whetted by the change of their food, and variety supplies both with fresh appetite.—*Quintilian.*

We in vain summon the mind to intense application, when the body is in a languid state.—*Gallus.*

The mind is chameleon-like in one respect, it receives hues from without; but it is unlike it in another respect, for it retains them.—*B. St. John.*

It is a great mistake to think anything too profound or rich for a popular audience.—No train of thought is too deep or subtle or grand; but the manner of presenting it to their untutored minds should be peculiar.—It should be presented in anecdote, or sparkling truism, or telling illustration, or stinging epithet, etc.; always in some concrete form, never in a logical, abstract, syllogistic shape.—*Rufus Choate.*

Hard, rugged, and dull natures of youth acquit themselves afterward the jewels of the country, and therefore their dulness at first is to be borne with, if they be diligent. That schoolmaster deserves to be beaten himself who beats nature in a boy for a fault. And I question whether all the whipping in the world can make their parts, which are naturally sluggish, rise one minute before the hour nature hath appointed.—*Fuller.*

Don't despair of a student if he has one clear idea.—*Emmons.*

A wise man is never less alone than when he is alone.—*Swift.*

The idea that there is a want of sympathy in the mass of the people with an educated man's mind, is much exaggerated in general belief.—Any fine thought, or rich expression is apprehended by the common mind somehow; vaguely at first; but so almost any thought is, at first, vaguely and uncertainly apprehended by any but a thoroughly trained mind.—*Rufus Choate.*

The defects of the mind, like those of the face, grow worse as we grow old.—*Rochefoucauld.*

The mind is its own place, and in itself can make a heaven of hell, and a hell of heaven.—*Milton.*

A weak mind is like a microscope, which magnifies trifling things, but cannot receive great ones.—*Chesterfield.*

He who cannot contract the sight of his mind, as well as dilate it, wants a great talent in life.—*Bacon.*

The failure of the mind in old age is often less the result of natural decay, than of disuse.—Ambition has ceased to operate; contentment brings indolence, and indolence decay of mental power, ennui, and sometimes death.—Men have been known to die, literally speaking, of disease induced by intellectual vacancy.—*Sir B. Brodie.*

Old minds are like old horses; you must exercise them if you wish to keep them in working order.—*John Adams.*

Few minds wear out; more rust out. —*Bovee.*

The end which at present calls forth our efforts will be found, when it is once gained, to be only one of the means to some remoter end. The natural flights of the human mind are not from pleasure to pleasure, but from hope to hope.—*Johnson.*

A mind once cultivated will not lie fallow for half an hour.—*Bulwer.*

Just as a particular soil wants some one element to fertilize it, just as the body in some conditions has a kind of famine for one special food, so the mind has its wants, which do not always call for what is best, but which know themselves and are as peremptory as the salt-sick sailor's call for a lemon or raw potato.—*O. W. Holmes.*

It is with diseases of the mind as with diseases of the body, we are half dead before we understand our disorder, and half cured when we do.—*Colton.*

Mind is the brightness of the body,— lights it, when strength, its proper but less subtle fire, begins to fail.—*J. S. Knowles.*

The great business of man is to improve his mind, and govern his manners; all other projects and pursuits, whether in our power to compass or not, are only amusements.—*Pliny.*

The mind itself must, like other things, sometimes be unbent; or else it will be either weakened or broken.—*Sir P. Sidney.*

Anguish of mind has driven thousands to suicide; anguish of body, none. This proves that the health of the mind is of far more consequence to our happiness than the health of the body, although both are deserving of much more attention than either of them receives.— *Colton.*

Sublime is the dominion of the mind over the body, that for a time can make flesh and nerve impregnable, and string the sinews like steel, so that the weak become so mighty.—*Mrs. Stowe.*

As the mind must govern the hands, so in every society the man of intelligence must direct the man of labor.— *Johnson.*

A great, a good, and a right mind is a kind of divinity lodged in flesh, and may be the blessing of a slave, as well as of a prince.—It came from heaven, and to heaven it must return; and it is a kind of heavenly felicity which a pure and virtuous mind enjoys, in some degree, even on earth.—*Seneca.*

My mind to me a kingdom is; such present joys therein I find, that it excels all other bliss that earth affords.—*Chaucer.*

Narrow minds think nothing right that is above their own capacity.—*Rochefoucauld.*

It is the mind that maketh good or ill, that maketh wretch or happy, rich or poor.—*Spenser.*

A narrow mind begets obstinacy; we do not easily believe what we cannot see.—*Dryden.*

Mental pleasures never clog;—unlike those of the body, they are increased by repetition, approved of by reflection, and strengthened by enjoyment.—*Colton.*

The mind ought sometimes to be diverted that it may return to better thinking.—*Phœdrus.*

A weak mind sinks under prosperity, as well as under adversity.—A strong mind has two highest tides, when the moon is at the full, and when there is no moon.—*Hare.*

MINISTERS.—The Christian ministry is the worst of all trades, but the best of all professions.—*John Newton.*

We ought to judge of preachers, not only from what they do say, but from what they do not say.—*Emmons.*

In pulpit eloquence, the grand difficulty is, to give the subject all the dignity it deserves without attaching any importance to ourselves.—*Colton.*

It requires as much reflection and wisdom to know what is not to be put into a sermon, as what is.—*Cecil.*

"Three things," says Luther, "make a Divine—prayer, meditation, and trials."—These make a Christian; but a Christian minister needs three more, talent, application, and acquirements.—*C. Simmons.*

If a minister takes one step into the world, his hearers will take two.—*Cecil.*

It was said of one who preached very well, and lived very ill, that when he was out of the pulpit, it was a pity he should ever go in; and when in the pulpit, it was a pity he should ever come out.—*Fuller.*

It is very easy to preach, but very hard to preach well.—No other profession demands half so much mental labor as the clerical.—*Emmons.*

The preaching that comes from the soul, most works on the soul.—*Fuller.*

I have heard many great orators, said Louis XIV. to Massilon, and have been highly pleased with them; but whenever I hear you, I go away displeased with myself.—This is the highest encomium that could be bestowed on a preacher.—*C. Simmons.*

If there were not a minister in every parish, you would quickly find cause to increase the number of constables; and if churches were not employed as places to hear God's law, there would be need of them to be prisons for law-breakers.—*South.*

The minister is to be a real man, a live man, a true man, a simple man, great in his love, in his life, in his work, in his simplicity, in his gentleness.—*John Hall.*

The proud he tamed; the penitent he cheered; nor to rebuke the rich offender, feared; his preaching much, but more his practice wrought, a living sermon of the truths he taught.—*Dryden.*

The life of a pious minister is visible rhetoric.—*Hooker.*

Men of God have always, from time to time, walked among men, and made their commission felt in the heart and soul of the commonest hearer.—*Emerson.*

MINORITIES.—Votes should be weighed, not counted.—*Schiller.*

A man that puts himself on the ground of moral principle, though the whole world be against him, is mightier than them all; for the orb of time becomes such a man's shield, and every step brings him nearer to the hand of omnipotence.—Take ground for truth, and justice, and rectitude, and piety, and fight well, and there can be no question as to the result.—We are to feel that right is itself a host.—Never be afraid of minorities, so that minorities are based on principles.—*H. W. Beecher.*

This minority is great and formidable. I do not know whether, if I aimed at the total overthrow of a kingdom, I should wish to be encumbered with a large body of partisans.—*Burke.*

The smallest number, with God and truth on their side, are weightier than thousands.—*C. Simmons.*

MIRACLES.—A miracle is a work exceeding the power of any created agent, consequently being an effect of the divine omnipotence.—*South.*

A miracle I take to be a sensible operation, which being above the comprehension of the spectator, and in his opinion contrary to the established course of nature, is taken by him to be divine.—*Locke.*

Every believer is God's miracle.—*Bailey.*

Miracles are ceased, and therefore we must needs admit the means how things are perfected.—*Shakespeare.*

Miracles are the swaddling clothes of infant churches.—*T. Fuller.*

A Miracle: An event described by those to whom it was told by men who did not see it.—*E. Hubbard.*

The human body, in its wonderful structure, is of itself a miracle of divine wisdom and power.

MIRTH.—(See "CHEERFULNESS" and "AMUSEMENT.")

Harmless mirth is the best cordial against the consumption of the spirit; wherefore jesting is not unlawful, if it trespasseth not in quantity, quality, or season.—*Fuller.*

There is nothing like fun, is there? I haven't any myself, but I do like it in others. We need all the counterweights we can muster to balance the sad relations of life. God has made sunny spots in the heart; why should we exclude the light from them?—*Haliburton.*

Man is the merriest species of the creation; all above or below him are serious.—*Addison.*

The gift of gaiety may itself be the greatest good fortune, and the most serious step toward maturity.—*Irwin Edman.*

To hear the addled citizens at their mirth—their lewd and lackwit innocent noble mirth.—*C. Morley.*

Old Times have bequeathed us a precept, to be merry and wise, but who has been able to observe it?—*Johnson.*

Frame your mind to mirth and merriment, which bar a thousand harms and lengthen life.—*Shakespeare.*

Merriment is always the effect of a sudden impression. The jest which is expected is already destroyed.—*Johnson.*

Who cannot make one in the circle of harmless merriment may be suspected of pride, hypocrisy, or formality.—*Lavater.*

"Let us be merry," said Mr. Pecksniff.—*Dickens.*

Mirth should be the embroidery of conversation, not the web; and wit the ornament of the mind, not the furniture.

I love such mirth as does not make friends ashamed to look upon one another next morning; or men, that cannot well bear it, to repent of the money they spent when they be warmed with drink; and take this for a rule, you may pick out such times and such companies, that you may make yourself merrier for a little than a great deal of money; for "it is the company and not the charge that makes the feast."—*Izaak Walton.*

Gaiety and a light heart, in all virtue and decorum, are the best medicine for the young, or rather for all.—Solitude and melancholy are poison; they are deadly to all, and above all to the young.—*Talfourd.*

Nothing is more hopeless than a scheme of merriment.—*Johnson.*

Mirthfulness is in the mind, and you cannot get it out. It is the blessed spirit that God has set in the mind to dust it, to enliven its dark places, and to drive asceticism, like a foul fiend, out of the back-door. It is just as good, in its place, as conscience or veneration. Praying can no more be made a substitute for smiling than smiling can for praying.—*H. W. Beecher.*

Care to our coffin adds a nail, no doubt; and every grin, so merry, draws one out.—*Wolcott.*

What more than mirth would mortals have?—The cheerful man is a king.—*I. Bickerstaff.*

Unseasonable mirth always turns to sorrow.—*Cervantes.*

An ounce of mirth is worth a pound of sorrow.—*Richard Baxter.*

Fun gives you a forcible hug, and

shakes laughter out of you, whether you will or no.—*Garrick.*

MISANTHROPY.—Man delights not me, nor woman either.—*Shakespeare.*

There cannot live a more unhappy creature than an ill-natured old man, who is neither capable of receiving pleasures, nor sensible of doing them to others.—*Sir W. Temple.*

Men possessing minds which are morose, solemn, and inflexible, enjoy, in general, a greater share of dignity than happiness.—*Bacon.*

The opinions of the misanthropical rest upon this very partial basis, that they adopt the bad faith of a few as evidence of the worthlessness of all.—*Bovee.*

Out of the ashes of misanthropy benevolence rises again; we find many virtues where we had imagined all was vice, many actions of disinterested friendship where we had fancied all was calculation and fraud,—and so gradually, from the two extremes, we pass to the proper medium; and feeling that no human being is wholly good or wholly base, we learn that true knowledge of mankind which induces us to expect little and forgive much. The world cures alike the optimist and the misanthrope.—*Bulwer.*

The misanthrope is a man who avoids society, only to free himself from the trouble of being useful to it; who considers his neighbors only on the side of their defects, not knowing the art of combining their virtues with their vices, and of rendering the imperfections of other people tolerable by reflecting on his own.—He is more employed in finding out and punishing the guilty, than in devising means to reform them; and because he thinks his talents are not sufficiently valued and employed by his fellow citizens, or rather because they know his foibles and do not choose to be subject to his caprices, he talks of quitting cities, towns, and societies, and living in dens or deserts.—*Saurin.*

MISCHIEF.—O mischief, thou art swift to enter in the thoughts of desperate men.—*Shakespeare.*

It is difficult to say who do you the most mischief, enemies with the worst intentions, or friends with the best.—*Bulwer.*

The opportunity to do mischief is found a hundred times a day, and that of doing good once a year.—*Voltaire.*

The sower of the seed is assuredly the author of the whole harvest of mischief.—*Demosthenes.*

Few men are so clever as to know all the mischief they do.—*Rochefoucauld.*

It shocks me to think how much mischief almost every man may do, who will but resolve to do all he can.—*Sterne.*

He that may hinder mischief, yet permits it, is an accessory.—*E. A. Freeman.*

MISER. — (See "GOLD" and "MONEY.")

The word "miser," so often used as expressive of one who is grossly covetous and saving, in its origin signifies one that is miserable, the very etymology of the word thus indicating the necessary unhappiness of the miser spirit.—*Tryon Edwards.*

The prodigal robs his heir; the miser robs himself.—*Bruyère.*

The miser is as much in want of that which he has, as of that which he has not.—*Publius Syrus.*

A miser grows rich by seeming poor; an extravagant man grows poor by seeming rich.—*Shenstone.*

A thorough miser must possess considerable strength of character to bear the self-denial imposed by his penuriousness.—Equal sacrifices, endured voluntarily, in a better cause, would make a saint or a martyr.—*Clulow.*

Misers mistake gold for good, whereas it is only a means of obtaining it.—*Rochefoucauld.*

Misers have been described as madmen, who in the midst of abundance banish every pleasure, and make, from imaginary wants, real necessities. But very few correspond to this exaggerated picture. Instead of this, we find the sober and industrious branded by the vain and the idle with the odious appellation; men who, by frugality and labor, raise themselves above their equals, and contribute their share of industry to the common stock. Whatever the vain or the ignorant may say, well were it for society had we more of this character. In general, these close men are found at last the true benefactors of society. With an avaricious man we seldom lose in our dealings, but we too frequently do in our commerce with prodigality.—*Goldsmith.*

Through life's dark road his sordid way he wends, an incarnation of fat dividends.—*C. Sprague.*

How vilely he has lost himself who becomes a slave to his servant, and exalts him to the dignity of his Maker! Gold is the God, the wife, the friend of the money-monger of the world.—*Penn.*

To cure us of our immoderate love of gain, we should seriously consider how many goods there are that money will not purchase, and these the best; and how many evils there are that money will not remedy, and these the worst.—*Colton.*

The miser, starving his brother's body, starves also his own soul, and at death shall creep out of his great estate of injustice, poor and naked and miserable. —*Theodore Parker.*

Money never can be well managed if sought solely through the greed of money for its own sake. In all meanness there is a defect of intellect as well as of heart. And even the cleverness of avarice is but the cunning of imbecility.—*Bulwer.*

A mere madness—to live like a wretch that he may die rich.—*Burton.*

The base miser starves amid his store, broods o'er his gold, and gripping still at more, sits sadly pining, and believes he's poor.—*Dryden.*

There is not in nature anything so remotely distant from God, or so extremely opposite to him, as a greedy and griping niggard.—*Barrow.*

There is a perpetual frost in the pockets of some rich people; as soon as they put their hands into them, they are frozen so they cannot draw out their purses.—Had I my way, I would hang all misers; but reversing the common mode, I would hang them up by the heels, that their money might run out of their pockets.—*Rowland Hill.*

Groan under gold, yet weep for want of bread.—*Young.*

MISERY.—(See "SORROW.")

Twins, even from the birth, are misery and man.—*Homer.*

The true recipe for a miserable existence is to quarrel with Providence.— *J. W. Alexander.*

Man is only miserable so far as he thinks himself so.—*Sannazaro.*

If you wish to be miserable, think about yourself; about what you want, what you like, what respect people ought to pay you, what people think of you; and then to you nothing will be pure. You will spoil everything you touch; you will make sin and misery for yourself out of everything God sends you; you will be as wretched as you choose.—*Charles Kingsley.*

No scene of life but teems with mortal woe.—*Walter Scott.*

Misery so little appertains to our nature, and happiness so much so, that we lament over that which has pained us, but leave unnoticed that which ha/ rejoiced us.—*Richter.*

There are a good many real miseries in life that we cannot help smiling at, but they are the smiles that make wrinkles and not dimples.—*O. W. Holmes.*

Small miseries, like small debts, hit us in so many places, and meet us at so many turns and corners, that what they want in weight, they make up in number, and render it less hazardous to stand the fire of one cannon ball, than a volley composed of such a shower of bullets.—*Colton.*

It is often better to have a great deal of harm happen to one than a little; a great deal may rouse you to remove what a little will only accustom you to endure.—*Gréville.*

As small letters hurt the sight, so do small matters him that is too much intent upon them: they vex and stir up anger, which begets an evil habit in him in reference to greater affairs.—*Plutarch.*

Misery is caused for the most part, not by a heavy crush of disaster, but by the corrosion of less visible evils, which canker enjoyment, and undermine security. The visit of an invader is necessarily rare, but domestic animosities allow no cessation.—*Johnson.*

Misery acquaints a man with strange bedfellows.—*Shakespeare.*

Man is so great that his greatness appears even in his consciousness of misery,

A tree does not know itself to be miserable. It is true that it is misery indeed to know one's self to be miserable; but then it is greatness also. In this way all man's miseries go to prove his greatness. They are the miseries of a mighty potentate, of a dethroned monarch.—*Pascal.*

If misery be the effect of virtue, it ought to be reverenced; if of ill-fortune, to be pitied; and if of vice, not to be insulted, because it is, perhaps, itself a punishment adequate to the crime by which it was produced; and the humanity of that man can deserve no panegyric who is capable of reproaching a criminal in the hands of the executioner.—*Johnson.*

A misery is not to be measured from the nature of the evil, but from the temper of the sufferer.—*Addison.*

The misery of human life is made up of large masses, each separated from the other by certain intervals. One year the death of a child; years after, a failure in trade; after another longer or shorter interval, a daughter may have married unhappily; in all but the singularly unfortunate, the integral parts that compose the sum total of the unhappiness of a man's life are easily counted and distinctly remembered.—*Coleridge.*

We should pass on from crime to crime, heedless and remorseless, if misery did not stand in our way, and our own pains admonish us of our folly.—*Johnson.*

Notwithstanding the sight of all the miseries which wring us and threaten our destruction, we have still an instinct that we cannot repress, which elevates us above our sorrows.—*Pascal.*

Half the misery in the world comes of want of courage to speak and to hear the truth plainly, and in a spirit of love.—*Mrs. Stowe.*

MISFORTUNE.—(See "CALAMITY.")
Who hath not known ill-fortune, never knew himself, or his own virtue.—*Mallet.*

Misfortune does not always wait on vice; nor is success the constant guest of virtue.—*Havard.*

The humor of turning every misfortune into a judgment, proceeds from wrong notions of religion, which, in its own nature, produces good will toward men, and puts the mildest construction upon every accident that befalls them. In this case, therefore, it is not religion that sours a man's temper, but it is his temper that sours his religion.—*Addison.*

If all the misfortunes of mankind were cast into a public stock, in order to be equally distributed among the whole species, those who now think themselves the most unhappy would prefer the share they are already possessed of before that which would fall to them by such a division.—*Socrates.*

I never knew a man who could not bear the misfortunes of another perfectly like a Christian.—*Pope.*

By struggling with misfortunes, we are sure to receive some wounds in the conflict; but a sure method to come off victorious is by running away.—*Goldsmith.*

A soul exasperated by its ills, falls out with everything, with its friend and itself.—*Addison.*

Misfortunes are in morals what bitters are in medicine; each is, at first, disagreeable; but as bitters may correct and strengthen the stomach, so adversity chastens and ameliorates the disposition.—*From the French.*

Rats and conquerors must expect no mercy in misfortune.—*Colton.*

Our bravest and best lessons are not learned through success, but through misadventure.—*A. B. Alcott.*

Depend upon it, that if a man talks of his misfortunes there is something in them that is not disagreeable to him: for where there is nothing but pure misery, there never is any mention of it.—*Johnson.*

He that is down needs fear no fall.—*Bunyan.*

Flowers never emit so sweet and strong a fragrance as before a storm. When a storm approaches thee, be as fragrant as a sweet-smelling flower.—*Richter.*

There is a chill air surrounding those who are down in the world, and people are glad to get away from them, as from a cold room.—*George Eliot.*

Men shut their doors against the setting sun.—*Shakespeare.*

Evil events come from evil causes; and what we suffer, springs, generally, from what we have done.—*Aristophanes.*

It will generally be found that men who are constantly lamenting their ill luck, are only reaping the consequences of their own neglect, mismanagement, and improvidence, or want of application.—*S. Smiles.*

After all, our worst misfortunes never happen, and most miseries lie in anticipation.—*Balzac.*

The less we parade our misfortunes, the more sympathy we command.—*O. Dewey.*

Most of our misfortunes are more supportable than the comments of our friends upon them.—*Colton.*

When misfortunes happen to such as dissent from us in matters of religion, we call them judgments; when to those of our own sect, we call them trials; when to persons neither way distinguished, we are content to attribute them to the settled course of things.—*Shenstone.*

Misfortune is never mournful to the soul that accepts it; for such do always see that in every cloud is an angel's face.—*Jerome.*

Every man deems that he has precisely the trials and temptations which are the hardest of all others for him to bear; but they are so, simply because they are the very ones he most needs.—*Mrs. L. M. Child.*

Little minds are tamed and subdued by misfortune; but great minds rise above it.—*Washington Irving.*

When I was happy I thought I knew men, but it was fated that I should know them only in misfortune.—*Napoleon.*

It is seldom that God sends such calamities upon man as men bring upon themselves and suffer willingly.—*Jeremy Taylor.*

Heaven sends us misfortunes as a moral tonic.—*Lady Blessington.*

We exaggerate misfortune and happiness alike. We are never either so wretched or so happy as we say we are. —*Balzac.*

The greatest misfortune of all is, not to be able to bear misfortune.—*Bias.*

What Cicero said of men, " that they are like wines, age souring the bad, and bettering the good," we can say of mis-

fortune, that it has the same effect upon them.—*H. Richer.*

Misfortune sprinkles ashes on the head of the man, but falls like dew on the head of the woman, and brings forth germs of strength of which she herself had no conscious possession.—*Anna Cora Mowatt.*

Let us be of good cheer, remembering that the misfortunes hardest to bear are those which never happen.—*J. R. Lowell.*

The injuries of life, if rightly improved, will be to us as the strokes of the statuary on his marble, forming us to a more beautiful shape, and making us fitter to adorn the heavenly temple. —*Cotton Mather.*

Ovid finely compares a man of broken fortune to a falling column; the lower it sinks, the greater weight it is obliged to sustain.—*Goldsmith.*

Misfortune makes of certain souls a vast desert through which rings the voice of God.—*Balzac.*

The effect of great and inevitable misfortune is, to elevate those souls which it does not deprive of all virtue.— *Guizot.*

We should learn, by reflecting on the misfortunes of others, that there is nothing singular in those which befall ourselves.—*Melmoth.*

Of fortune's sharp adversity, the worst kind of misfortune is this, that a man hath been in prosperity and it remembers when it passed is.—*Chaucer.*

Sorrow's crown of sorrow is remembering happier things.—*Tennyson.*

MISTAKE.—(See "Error.")

Any man may make a mistake, but none but a fool will continue in it.— *Cicero.*

No man ever became great or good except through many and great mistakes. —*Gladstone.*

When you make a mistake, don't look back at it long. Take the reason of the thing into your mind, and then look forward. Mistakes are lessons of wisdom. The past cannot be changed. The future is yet in your power.—*Hugh White.*

The only people who make no mistakes are dead people. I saw a man last week who has not made a mistake for four thousand years. He was a mummy in the Egyptian department of the British Museum.—*H. L. Wayland.*

It is only an error in judgment to make a mistake, but it shows infirmity of character to adhere to it when discovered.—*Bovee.*

We learn wisdom from failure much more than from success; we often discover what will do, by finding out what will not do; and probably he who never made a mistake never made a discovery. —*S. Smiles.*

Show us the man who never makes a mistake and we will show a man who never makes anything. The capacity for occasional blundering is inseparable from the capacity to bring things to pass. The only men who are past the danger of making mistakes are the men who sleep at Greenwood.—*H. L. Wayland.*

Some of the best lessons we ever learn we learn from our mistakes and failures. —The error of the past is the wisdom and success of the future.—*Tryon Edwards.*

There are few, very few, that will own themselves in a mistake, though all the world see them to be in downright nonsense.—*Swift.*

No persons are more frequently wrong, than those who will not admit they are wrong.—*Rochefoucauld.*

The Providence that watches over the affairs of men, works out their mistakes, at times, to a healthier issue than could have been accomplished by their wisest forethought.—*Froude.*

The young fancy that their follies are mistaken by the old for happiness; and the old fancy that their gravity is mistaken by the young for wisdom.—*Colton.*

Exemption from mistake is not the privilege of mortals; but when our mistakes are involuntary, we owe each other every candid consideration; and the man who, on discovering his errors, acknowledges and corrects them, is scarcely less entitled to our esteem than if he had not erred.—*J. Pye Smith.*

MOB.—(See "POPULACE.")

A mob is a monster, with heads enough, but no heart, and little brains.

Every numerous assembly is a mob; everything there depends on instantaneous turns.—*Cardinal de Retz.*

Get together a hundred or two men, however sensible they may be, and you are very likely to have a mob.—*Johnson.*

A mob is the scum that rises upmost when the nation boils.—*Dryden.*

A mob is a sort of bear; while your ring is through its nose, it will even dance under your cudgel; but should the ring slip, and you lose your hold, the brute will turn and rend you.—*Jane Porter.*

Inconstant, blind, deserting friends at need, and duped by foes; loud and seditious, when a chief inspired their headlong fury, but of him deprived, already slaves that lick'd the scourging hand.—*Thomson.*

The multitude unawed is insolent; once seized with fear, contemptible and vain.—*Mallet.*

The blind, unwieldy monster, which, at first, rattles its bones, threatening to swallow high and low, the near and distant, with its gaping jaws, at last stumbles over a thread.—*Schiller.*

A crowd always thinks with its sympathy, never with its reason.—*W. R. Alger.*

The mob is a monster, with the hands of Briareus, but the head of Polyphemus, strong to execute, but blind to perceive.—*Colton.*

Mankind in the gross is a gaping monster, that loves to be deceived, and has seldom been disappointed.—*Mackenzie.*

Let there be an entire abstinence from intoxicating drinks throughout this country during the period of a single generation, and a mob would be as impossible as combustion without oxygen. —*Horace Mann.*

These wide-mouthed brutes, that bellow thus for freedom; oh! how they run before the hand of power, flying for shelter into every brake!—*Otway.*

There is nothing so little to be expected or hoped for from this many-headed monster, when incensed, as humanity and good nature; it is much more capable of alarm and fear.—*Montaigne.*

The many-headed multitude, whom inconstancy only by accident doth guide to well-doing!—Who can set confidence there, where company takes away shame, and each may lay the fault upon his fellow.—*Sir P. Sidney.*

You have many enemies that know not why they are so, but, like village curs, bark when their fellows do.—*Shakespeare.*

License they mean, when they cry liberty.—*Milton.*

Human affairs are not so happily arranged that the best things please the most men.—It is the proof of a bad cause when it is applauded by the mob.—*Seneca.*

You can talk a mob into anything; its feelings may be—usually are—on the whole generous and right: but it has no foundation for them, no hold of them; you may tease or tickle it into any, at your pleasure; it thinks by infection, for the most part, catching a passion like a cold, and there is nothing so little that it will not roar itself wild about, when the fit is on; nothing so great but it will forget it in an hour, when the fit is past. But a gentleman's, or a gentle nation's passions are just, measured, and continuous.—*Ruskin.*

A mob is usually a creature of very mysterious existence, particularly in a large city. Where it comes from, or whither it goes, few men can tell. Assembling and dispersing with equal suddenness, it is as difficult to follow to its various sources as the sea itself; nor does the parallel stop here, for the ocean is not more fickle and uncertain, more terrible when roused, more unreasonable or more cruel.—*Dickens.*

The blind monster, with uncounted heads, the still discordant, wavering multitude.—*Shakespeare.*

It is an easy and vulgar thing to please the mob, and not a very arduous task to astonish them; but to benefit and improve them is a work fraught with difficulty, and teeming with danger.—*Colton.*

A mob is a society of bodies, voluntarily bereaving themselves of reason, and traversing its work.—The mob is man, voluntarily descending to the nature of the beast.—Its fit hour of activity is night; its actions are insane, like its whole constitution.—*Emerson.*

When roused to rage the maddening populace storms, their fury, like a rolling flame, bursts forth unquenchable; but give its violence ways, it spends itself, and as its force abates, learns to obey and yields it to your will.—*Euripides.*

As a goose is not alarmed by hissing, nor a sheep by bleating; so neither be you terrified by the voice of a senseless multitude.—*Maximus.*

MODERATION.—Moderation is the silken string running through the pearl-chain of all virtues.—*Bp. Hall.*

The pursuit, even of the best things, ought to be calm and tranquil.—*Cicero.*

Moderate desires constitute a character fitted to acquire all the good which the world can yield. He who has this character is prepared, in whatever situation he is, therewith to be content; has learned the science of being happy; and possesses the alchemic stone which changes every metal into gold.—*T. Dwight.*

It is certainly a very important lesson, to learn how to enjoy ordinary things, and to be able to relish your being, without the transport of some passion, or the gratification of some appetite.—*Steele.*

There is a German proverb which says that "Take it easy," and "Live long," are brothers.—*Bovee.*

To climb steep hills requires slow pace at first.—*Shakespeare.*

Moderation, which consists in an indifference about little things, and in a prudent and well-proportioned zeal about things of importance, can proceed from nothing but true knowledge, which has its foundation in self-acquaintance.—*Lord Chatham.*

To live long it is necessary to live slowly.—*Cicero.*

To go beyond the bounds of moderation is to outrage humanity. The greatness of the human soul is shown by knowing how to keep within proper bounds. So far from greatness consisting in going beyond its limits, it really consists in keeping within them.—*Pascal.*

I knew a wise man who had for a byword, when he saw men hasten to a conclusion, "stay a little, that we may come to the end sooner."—*Bacon.*

Moderation is the inseparable companion of wisdom, but with it genius has not even a nodding acquaintance.—*Colton.*

Howsoever varied the courses of our life, whatsoever the phases of pleasure and ambition through which it has swept along, still, when in memory we would revive the times that were comparatively the happiest, those times will be found to have been the calmest.—*Bulwer.*

Tranquil pleasures last the longest.—We are not fitted to bear long the burden of great joys.—*Bovee.*

I will not be a slave to myself, for it is a perpetual, a shameful, and the most heavy of all servitudes; and this end I may gain by moderate desires.—*Seneca.*

The true boundary of man is moderation.—When once we pass that pale, our guardian angel quits his charge of us.—*Feltham.*

Moderation is the center wherein all philosophies, both human and divine, meet.—*Bp. Hall.*

Moderation must not claim the merit of combating and conquering ambition; for they can never exist in the same subject. Moderation is the languor and sloth of the soul; ambition its activity and ardor.—*Rochefoucauld.*

Only actions give life strength; only moderation gives it a charm.—*Richter.*

In adversity assume the countenance of prosperity, and in prosperity moderate the temper and desires.—*Livy.*

Everything that exceeds the bounds of moderation, has an unstable foundation.—*Seneca.*

Moderation resembles temperance. We are not so unwilling to eat more, as afraid of doing ourselves harm by it.—*Rochefoucauld.*

They are as sick that surfeit with too much, as they that starve with nothing. It is no mean happiness, therefore, to be seated in the mean: superfluity comes sooner by white hairs, but competency lives longer.—*Shakespeare.*

Let a man take time enough for the most trival deed, though it be but the paring of his nails. The buds swell imperceptibly, without hurry or confusion, as if the short spring days were an eternity.—*Thoreau.*

It is a little stream which flows softly,

but it freshens everything along its course.—*Mad. Swetchine.*

The superior man wishes to be slow in his words, and earnest in his conduct.—*Confucius.*

The choicest pleasures of life lie within the ring of moderation.—*Tupper.*

MODESTY.—The first of all virtues is innocence; the next is modesty. If we banish modesty out of the world, she carries away with her half the virtue that is in it.—*Addison.*

Modesty is the lowest of the virtues, and is a confession of the deficiency it indicates. He who undervalues himself, is justly undervalued by others.—*Hazlitt.*

Modesty is the conscience of the body.—*Balzac.*

Modesty is the chastity of merit, the virginity of noble souls.—*E. de Girardin.*

There are as many kinds of modesty as there are races. To the English woman it is a duty; to the French woman a propriety.—*Taine.*

Modesty and the dew love the shade. Each shines in the open day only to be exhaled to heaven.—*J. P. Senn.*

A false modesty is the meanest species of pride.—*Gibbon.*

False modesty is the refinement of vanity. It is a lie.—*Bruyère.*

A modest person seldom fails to gain the good will of those he converses with, because nobody envies a man who does not appear to be pleased with himself.—*Steele.*

Make no display of your talents or attainments; for every one will clearly see, admire, and acknowledge them, so long as you cover them with the beautiful veil of modesty.—*Emmons.*

A just and reasonable modesty does not only recommend eloquence, but sets off every great talent which a man can be possessed of. It heightens all the virtues which it accompanies; like the shades in paintings, it raises and rounds every figure, and makes the colors more beautiful, though not so glaring as they would be without it.—*Addison.*

Hasty conclusions are the mark of a fool; a wise man doubteth; a fool rageth and is confident; the novice saith, "I am sure that it is so"; the better learned answers, "Peradventure, it may be so; but, I pray thee, inquire." It is a little learning, and but a little, which makes men conclude hastily. Experience and humility teach modesty and fear.—*Jeremy Taylor.*

Modesty is to merit, as shades to figures in a picture, giving it strength and beauty.—*Bruyère.*

In the modesty of fearful duty, I read as much as from the rattling tongue of saucy and audacious eloquence.—*Shakespeare.*

Modesty in a man is never to be allowed as a good quality, but a weakness, if it suppresses his virtue, and hides it from the world, when he has at the same time a mind to exert himself.—*Tatler.*

As lamps burn silent, with unconscious light, so modest ease in beauty shines most bright; unaiming charms with edge resistless fall, and she who means no mischief does it all.—*A. Hill.*

Modesty, when she goes, is gone forever.—*Landor.*

That modest grace subdued my soul; that chastity of look, which seems to hang a veil of purest light o'er all her beauties.—*Young.*

Virtues, like essences, lose their fragrance when exposed. They are sensitive plants, that will not bear too familiar approaches.—*Shenstone.*

Let us be careful to distinguish modesty, which is ever amiable, from reserve, which is only prudent. A man is hated sometimes for pride, when it was an excess of humility gave the occasion.—*Shenstone.*

Modesty is a shining light; it prepares the mind to receive knowledge, and the heart for truth.—*Guizot.*

Modesty seldom resides in a breast that is not enriched with nobler virtues.—*Goldsmith.*

Modesty is the color of virtue.—*Diogenes.*

On their own merits modest men are dumb.—*G. Coleman.*

Modesty is not only an ornament, but also a guard to virtue.—*Addison.*

An egotist will always speak of himself, either in praise or in censure; but a modest man ever shuns making himself the subject of his conversation.—*Bruyère.*

Modesty makes large amends for the pain it gives those who labor under it, by the prejudice it affords every worthy person in their favor.—*Shenstone.*

The greatest ornament of an illustrious life is modesty and humility, which go a great way in the character even of the most exalted princes.—*Napoleon.*

Modesty was designed by Providence as a guard to virtue, and that it might be always at hand it is wrought into the mechanism of the body. It is likewise proportioned to the occasions of life, and strongest in youth when passion is so too.—*Jeremy Collier.*

Modesty is the appendage of sobriety, and is to chastity, to temperance, and to humility as the fringes are to a garment.—*Jeremy Taylor.*

Modest expression is a beautiful setting to the diamond of talent and genius.—*E. H. Chapin.*

True modesty avoids everything that is criminal; false modesty everything that is unfashionable.—*Addison.*

Modesty and humility are the sobriety of the mind, as temperance and chastity are of the body.—*Whitecote.*

Modesty is the citadel of beauty and virtue.—*Demades.*

Modesty once extinguished knows not how to return.—*Seneca.*

You little know what you have done, when you have first broke the bounds of modesty; you have set open the door of your fancy to the devil, so that he can, almost at his pleasure ever after, represent the same sinful pleasure to you anew; he hath now access to your fancy to stir up lustful thoughts and desires, so that when you should think of your calling, of your God, or of your soul, your thoughts will be worse than swinish, upon the filth that is not fit to be named. If the devil here get in a foot, he will not easily be got out.—*Baxter.*

True modesty is a discerning grace, and only blushes in the proper place, but counterfeit is blind, and skulks through fear, where 'tis a shame to be ashamed to appear; humility the parent of the first; the last by vanity produced and nursed.—*Cowper.*

The crimson glow of modesty o'erspread her cheek, and gave new luster to her charms.—*T. Franklin.*

The modest man has everything to gain, and the arrogant man everything to lose, for modesty has always to deal with generosity, and arrogance with envy.—*Rivarol.*

MONEY.—Money is a handmaiden, if thou knowest how to use it; a mistress, if thou knowest not.—*Horace.*

Put not your trust in money, but put your money in trust.—*O. W. Holmes.*

Money is a good servant, but a poor master.—*D. Bouhours.*

A wise man should have money in his head, not in his heart.—*Swift.*

Make money your god, it will plague you like the devil.—*Fielding.*

All love has something of blindness in it, but the love of money especially.—*South.*

The value of a dollar is to buy just things; a dollar goes on increasing in value with all the genius and all the virtue of the world. A dollar in a university is worth more than a dollar in a jail; in a temperate, schooled, law-abiding community, than in some sink of crime, where dice, knives, and arsenic are in constant play.—*Emerson.*

Money is like manure, of very little use except it be spread.—*Bacon.*

Money never made a man happy yet, nor will it. There is nothing in its nature to produce happiness. The more a man has, the more he wants. Instead of its filling a vacuum, it makes one. If it satisfies one want, it doubles and trebles that want another way. That was a true proverb of the wise man, rely upon it: "Better is little with the fear of the Lord, than great treasure, and trouble therewith."—*Franklin.*

By doing good with his money, a man, as it were, stamps the image of God upon it, and makes it pass current for the merchandise of heaven.—*J. Rutledge.*

Make all you can, save all you can, give all you can.—*J. Wesley.*

Money spent on myself may be a millstone about my neck; money spent on others may give me wings like the angels.—*R. D. Hitchcock.*

When money represents so many things, not to love it would be to love nearly nothing. To forget true needs can be only a weak moderation; but to know the value of money and to sacrifice it always, maybe to duty, maybe even to delicacy,—that is real virtue.—*Senancour.*

The philosophy which affects to teach us a contempt of money does not run very deep.—*Henry Taylor.*

He that wants money, means, and content, is without three good friends.—*Shakespeare.*

Men are seldom more innocently employed than when they are honestly making money.—*Johnson.*

Covetous men need money least, yet most affect and seek it; prodigals who need it most, do least regard it.—*Theodore Parker.*

No man needs money so much as he who despises it.—*Richter.*

To possess money is very well; it may be a most valuable servant; to be possessed by it, is to be possessed by a devil, and one of the meanest and worst kind of devils.—*Tryon Edwards.*

It is not money, as is sometimes said, but the love of money—the excessive, selfish, covetous love of money, that is the root of all evil.

It is my opinion that a man's soul may be buried and perish under a dung-heap, or in a furrow of the field, just as well as under a pile of money.—*Hawthorne.*

Money is a bottomless sea, in which honor, conscience, and truth may be drowned.—*Kozlay.*

Money is not required to buy one necessity of the soul.—*Thoreau.*

The covetous man never has money; the prodigal will have none shortly.—*Ben Jonson.*

But for money and the need of it, there would not be half the friendship in the world. It is powerful for good if divinely used. Give it plenty of air and it is sweet as the hawthorn; shut it up and it cankers and breeds worms.—*G. Macdonald.*

To despise money is to dethrone a king.—*Chamfort.*

Remember that money is of a prolific, generating nature. Money can beget money, and its offspring can beget more, and so on. Five shillings turned is six; turned again it is seven; and so on till it becomes a hundred pounds.

The more there is of it, the more it produces at every turning, so that the profits rise quicker and quicker. He that murders a crown, destroys all that it might have produced, even scores of pounds.—*Franklin.*

There is a vast difference in one's respect for the man who has made himself, and the man who has only made his money.—*Mulock.*

Get money to live; then live and use it, else it is not true that thou hast gotten.—Surely use alone makes money not contemptible.—*Herbert.*

It happens a little unluckily that the persons who have the most infinite contempt of money are the same that have the strongest appetite for the pleasures it procures.—*Shenstone.*

All our money has a moral stamp. It is coined over again in an inward mint. The uses we put it to, the spirit in which we spend it, give it a character which is plainly perceptible to the eye of God.—*T. Starr King.*

Mammon is the largest slave-holder in the world.—*F. Saunders.*

Money and time are the heaviest burdens of life, and the unhappiest of all mortals are those who have more of either than they know how to use.—*Johnson.*

Oh, what a world of vile ill-favored faults looks handsome in three hundred pounds a year!—*Shakespeare.*

If you would know the value of money, go and try to borrow some; for he that goes a-borrowing goes a-sorrowing.—*Franklin.*

Ready money is Aladdin's lamp.—*Byron.*

Money is the life blood of the nation.—*Swift.*

Money does all things; for it gives and it takes away, it makes honest men and knaves, fools and philosophers; and so on to the end of the chapter.—*L'Estrange.*

The avaricious love of gain, which is so feelingly deplored, appears to us a principle which, in able hands, might be guided to the most salutary purposes. The object is to encourage the love of labor, which is best encouraged by the love of money.—*Sydney Smith.*

Wealth is a very dangerous inheritance, unless the inheritor is trained to active benevolence.—*C. Simmons.*

Money has little value to its possessor unless it also has value to others.—*L. Stanford.*

Mammon has enriched his thousands, and has damned his ten thousands.—*South.*

Gold is the fool's curtain, which hides all his defects from the world.—*Feltham.*

Money does all things for reward.—Some are pious and honest as long as they thrive upon it, but if the devil himself gives better wages, they soon change their party.—*Seneca.*

The use of money is all the advantage there is in having it.—*Franklin.*

Money was made not to command our will, but all our lawful pleasures to fulfill; shame and woe to us, if we our wealth obey—the horse doth with the horseman run away.—*Cowley.*

Alexander being asked why he did not gather and lay up money, said, "For fear, lest being the keeper thereof, I should be infected and corrupted."—*Venning.*

Our incomes are like our shoes; if too small, they gall and pinch us; but if too large, they cause us to stumble and to trip.—*Colton.*

No blister draws sharper than interest on money.—It works day and night; in fair weather and foul.—It gnaws at a man's substance with invisible teeth.—It binds industry with its film, as a fly is bound with a spider's web.—Debt rolls a man over and over, binding him hand and foot, and letting him hang on the fatal mesh, till the long-legged interest devours him.—One had better make his bed of Canada thistles, than attempt to lie at ease upon interest.—*H. W. Beecher.*

MONOMANIA.—Adhesion to one idea is monomania; to a few it is slavery.—*Bovee.*

The man with but one idea in his head, is sure to exaggerate that to top-heaviness, and thus he loses his equilibrium.—*A. Hill.*

The greatest part of mankind labor under one delirium or another; and Don Quixote differed from the rest, not in madness, but in the species of it.—The covetous, the prodigal, the superstitious, the libertine, and the coffee-house politician, are all Quixotes in their several way.—*Fielding.*

All mankind are crazy, said a man in the insane asylum, and I only am sane; but they are the majority, and out-voted me, and so put me here.

MONUMENTS.—Monuments are the grappling-irons that bind one generation to another.—*Joubert.*

No man who needs a monument ever ought to have one.—*Hawthorne.*

If I have done any deed worthy of remembrance, that deed will be my monument.—If not, no monument can preserve my memory.—*Agesilaus.*

They only deserve a monument who do not need one; that is, who have raised themselves a monument in the minds and memories of men.—*Hazlitt.*

The monument of the greatest man should be only a bust and a name.—If the name alone is insufficient to illustrate the bust, let them both perish.—*Landor.*

Tombs are the clothes of the dead; a grave is but a plain suit; a rich monument is an embroidered one.—*Fuller.*

Virtue alone outbuilds the pyramids; her monument shall last when Egypts fall.—*Young.*

MORALITY.—All sects are different, because they come from men; morality is everywhere the same, because it comes from God.—*Voltaire.*

The morality which is divorced from godliness, however specious and captivating to the eye, is superficial and deceptive. The only morality that is clear in its source, pure in its precepts, and efficacious in its influence, is the morality of the gospel. All else is, at best, but idolatry—the worship of something of man's own creation; and that imperfect and feeble, like himself, and wholly insufficient to give him support and strength.

Piety and morality are but the same spirit differently manifested.—Piety is religion with its face toward God; morality is religion with its face toward the world.—*Tryon Edwards.*

Some would divorce morality from religion; but religion is the root without which morality would die.—*C. A. Bartol.*

They talk of morals, O, thou bleeding lamb! the grand morality is love to thee!—*Young.*

Morality without religion is only a kind of dead-reckoning—an endeavor to find our place on a cloudy sea by measuring the distance we have run, but without any observation of the heavenly bodies.—*Longfellow.*

The Christian religion is the only one that puts morality on its proper, and the right basis, viz: the fear and love of God.—*Johnson.*

In the long run, morals without religion, will wither and die like seed sown upon stony ground, or among thorns.

The highest morality, if not inspired and vitalized by religion, is but as the marble statue, or the silent corpse, to the living and perfect man.—*S. I. Prime.*

Morality, taken as apart from religion, is but another name for decency in sin. It is just that negative species of virtue which consists in not doing what is scandalously depraved and wicked. But there is no heart of holy principle in it, any more than there is in the grosser sin.—*Horace Bushnell.*

The great mistake of my life has been that I tried to be moral without faith in Jesus; but I have learned that true morality can only keep pace with trust in Christ as my Saviour.—*Gerrit Smith.*

Morality is the vestibule of religion.—*E. H. Chapin.*

Morality does not make a Christian, yet no man can be a Christian without it.—*Bp. Wilson.*

Religion without morality is a superstition and a curse, and morality without religion is impossible.—The only salvation for man is in the union of the two as Christianity unites them.—*Mark Hopkins.*

Morality is religion in practice; religion is morality in principle.—*Wardlaw.*

The only morality that is clear in its source, pure in its precepts, and efficacious in its influence, is the morality of the gospel.—All else, at last, is but idolatry—the worship of something of man's own creation, and that, imperfect and feeble like himself, and wholly insufficient to give him support and strength.—*John Sergeant.*

Atheistic morality is not impossible, but it will never answer our purpose.—

The morality that holds the great masses of sinewy people together must be very firmly rooted in an honest, downright personal faith and fear.—*R. D. Hitchcock.*

Let us with caution indulge the supposition that morality can be maintained without religion. Reason and experience both forbid us to expect that national morality can prevail in exclusion of religious principle.—*Washington.*

To give a man a full knowledge of true morality, I would send him to no other book than the New Testament.—*Locke.*

Men are not made religious by performing certain actions which are externally good, but they must first have righteous principles, and then they will not fail to perform virtuous actions.—*Luther.*

The morality of an action depends upon the motive from which we act. If I fling half a crown to a beggar with intention to break his head, and he picks it up and buys victuals with it, the physical effect is good; but with respect to me, the action is very wrong.—*Johnson.*

Where social improvements originate with the clergy, and where they bear a just share of the toil, the condition of morals and manners cannot be very much depressed.—*J. Martineau.*

They that cry down moral honesty, cry down that which is a great part of my religion, my duty toward God, and my duty toward man. What care I to see a man run after a sermon, if he cozens and cheats as soon as he comes home. On the other side, morality must not be without religion; for if so, it may change, as I see convenience. Religion must govern it. He that has not religion to govern his morality, is no better than my mastiff dog; so long as you stroke him, and please him, he will play with you as finely as may be; he is a very good moral mastiff; but if you hurt him, he will fly in your face, and tear out your throat.—*Selden.*

Learn what a people glory in, and you may learn much of both the theory and practice of their morals.—*J. Martineau.*

I restrict myself within bounds in saying, that, so far as I have observed in this life, ten men have failed from defect in morals where one has failed from defect in intellect.—*Horace Mann.*

The health of a community, is an almost unfailing index of its morals.—*J. Martineau.*

Discourses on morality and reflection on human nature, are the best means we can make use of to improve our minds, gain a true knowledge of ourselves, and recover our souls out of the vice, ignorance, and prejudice which naturally cleave to them.—*Addison.*

In matters of prudence last thoughts are best; in matters of morality, first thoughts.—*Robert Hall.*

There is no religion without morality, and no morality without religion.—*G. Spring.*

Morality without religion is a tree without roots; a stream without any spring to feed it; a house built on the sand; a pleasant place to live in till the heavens grow dark, and the storm begins to beat.—*J. B. Shaw.*

The morality of the gospel is the noblest gift ever bestowed by God on man.—*Montesquieu.*

Nothing really immoral is ever permanently popular.—There does not exist in the literature of the world a single popular book that is immoral, two centuries after it is produced; for in the heart of nations the false does not live so long, and the true is ethical to the end of time.—*Bulwer.*

Heat water to the highest degree, you cannot make wine of it; it is water still; so, let morality be raised to the highest, it is nature still; it is old Adam put in a better dress.—*T. Watson.*

In Christianity there can be no divorce of religion from morality.—Justification and sanctification are forever united.—The heathen notion of religion as something apart from moral life, is forever thrust out of sight by the Gospel.—*M. Valentine.*

There is no true and abiding morality that is not founded in religion.—*H. W. Beecher.*

Morality, distinguished from and independent of Christian faith, is nothing; but Christian morality is of the very essence; it is the true fruit, the sure testimony, the faithful companion, the glory and perfection, yea. the very life and soul of true Christian faith. Let us beware, that we do not confound things so different as worldly and Christian morality; as the works of the natural man and those of the disciples of Christ.—*Bp. Mant.*

Morality without religion has no roots.—It becomes a thing of custom, changeable, transient, and optional.—*H. W. Beecher.*

There can be no high civility without a deep morality.—*Emerson.*

Christian morality assumes to itself no merit—it sets up no arrogant claim to God's favor—it pretends not to "open the gates of heaven"; it is only the handmaid in conducting the Christian believer in his road toward them.—*Bp. Mant.*

Every young man would do well to remember that all successful business stands on the foundation of morality.—*H. W. Beecher.*

There is very little virtue in any moral life which does not grow out of a sound theology; but there is absolutely no virtue in any theology which is not productive of sound moral life.

I have never found a thorough, pervading, enduring morality but in those who feared God.—*Jacobi.*

We deny the doctrine of the ancient Epicureans, that pleasure is the supreme good; of Hobbes, that moral rules are only the work of men's mutual fear; of Paley, that what is expedient is right, and that there is no difference among pleasures except their intensity and duration; and of Bentham, that the rules of human action are to be obtained by counting up the pleasures which actions produce.—And we maintain with Plato, that reason has a natural and rightful authority over desire and affection; with Butler, that there is a difference of kind in our principles of action; and with the general voice of mankind, that we must do what is right at whatever cost of pain and loss.—What we ought to do, that we should do, and that we must do, though it bring pain and loss.—And why? Because it is right.—*W. Whewell.*

All moral obligation resolves itself into the obligation of conformity to the will of God.—*Charles Hodge.*

There are many that say, "Give us the morality of the New Testament; never mind about the theology." Aye, but you cannot get the morality without the theology, unless you like to have rootless flowers and lamps without oil. And if you want to live as Paul enjoins, you will have to believe as Paul preaches.

The divorcement of morals and piety is characteristic of all pagan religions.—*D. J. Burrell.*

The true grandeur of humanity is in moral elevation, sustained, enlightened and decorated by the intellect of man.—*C. Sumner.*

MORNING.—The morning hour has gold in its mouth.—*Franklin.*

Sweet is the breath of morn; her rising sweet with charm of earliest birds.—*Milton.*

The morning steals upon the night, melting the darkness.—*Shakespeare.*

The morn is up again, the dewy morn, with breath all incense, and with cheek all bloom, laughing the clouds away with playful scorn, and glowing into day.—*Byron.*

The silent hours steal on, and flaky darkness breaks within the east.—*Shakespeare.*

Let your sleep be necessary and healthful, not idle and expensive of time beyond the needs and conveniences of nature; and sometimes be curious to see the preparation the sun makes when he is coming forth from his chambers in the east.—*Jeremy Taylor.*

The breezy call of incense-breathing morn.—*Gray.*

Night is in her wane; day's early flush glows like a hectic on her fading cheek, wasting its beauty.—*Longfellow.*

Nor is a day lived, if the dawn is left out of it, with the prospects it opens.—*A. B. Alcott.*

I was always an early riser. Happy the man who is! Every morning day comes to him with a virgin's love, full of bloom and freshness. The youth of nature is contagious, like the gladness of a happy child.—*Bulwer.*

Its brightness, mighty divinity! has a fleeting empire over the day, giving gladness to the fields, color to the flowers; the season of the loves; har-

monious hour of wakening birds.—
Calderon.

The cock, that is the trumpet of the
morn, doth with his lofty and shrill-
sounding throat awake the god of day.
—*Shakespeare.*

I see the spectacle of morning from the
hill-top over against my house, from
daybreak to sunrise, with emotions an
angel might share.—The long, slender
bars of cloud float, like fishes, in the
sea of crimson light.—From the earth,
as a shore, I look out into that silent
sea.—I seem to partake its rapid trans-
formations; the active enchantment
reaches me, and I dilate and conspire
with the morning wind.—*Emerson.*

Look, what envious streaks do lace
the severing clouds in yonder east!
Night's candles are burnt out, and
jocund day stands tip-toe on the misty
mountain-tops.—*Shakespeare.*

The glad sun, exulting in his might,
comes from the dusky-curtained tents
of night.—*Emma C. Embury.*

Morn in the white-wake of the morning star, came furrowing all the Orient
into gold.—*Tennyson.*

But mighty nature bounds as from
her birth: the sun is in the heavens, and
life on earth; flowers in the valley,
splendor in the beam, health on the
gale, and freshness in the stream.—
Byron.

The morning itself, few inhabitants of
cities know anything about. Among
all our good people, not one in a thousand sees the sun rise once in a year.
They know nothing of the morning.
Their idea of it is that it is that part
of the day which comes along after a
cup of coffee and a piece of toast. With
them, morning is not a new issuing of
light, a new bursting forth of the sun,
a new waking-up of all that has life
from a sort of temporary death, to behold again the works of God, the
heavens and the earth; it is only a part
of the domestic day, belonging to reading newspapers, answering notes, sending the children to school, and giving
orders for dinner. The first streak of
light, the earliest purpling of the east,
which the lark springs up to greet, and
the deeper and deeper coloring into
orange and red, till at length the "glorious sun is seen, regent of the day"—

this they never enjoy, for they never
see it. I never thought that Adam had
much the advantage of us from having
seen the world while it was new. The
manifestations of the power of God,
like his mercies, are "new every morning" and fresh every moment. We see
as fine risings of the sun as ever Adam
saw; and its risings are as much a
miracle now as they were in his day—
and, I think, a good deal more, because
it is now a part of the miracle, that for
thousands and thousands of years he
has come to his appointed time, without the variation of a millionth part
of a second. I know the morning—I am
acquainted with it, and I love it. I
love it fresh and sweet as it is—a
daily new creation, breaking forth and
calling all that have life and breath and
being to a new adoration, new enjoyments, and new gratitude.—*Daniel
Webster.*

Now from night's gloom the glorious
day breaks forth, and seems to kindle
from the setting stars.—*D. K. Lee.*

In saffron-colored mantle, from the
tides of ocean rose the morning to
bring light to gods and men.—*Homer.*

The morning, pouring everywhere, its
golden glory on the air.—*Longfellow.*

Darkness is fled.—Now flowers unfold their beauties to the sun, and
blushing, kiss the beam he sends to
wake them.—*Sheridan.*

The morning dawns with an unwonted
crimson; the flowers more odorous
seem; the garden birds sing louder, and
the laughing sun ascends the gaudy
earth with an unusual brightness; all
nature smiles, and the whole world is
pleased.—*D. K. Lee.*

Night wanes; the vapors round the
mountains curled, melt into morn, and
light awakes the world.—*Byron.*

Let the day have a blessed baptism
by giving your first waking thoughts
into the bosom of God.—The first hour
of the morning is the rudder of the day.
—*H. W. Beecher.*

Morn, like a maiden glancing o'er
her pearls, streamed o'er the manna-
dew, as though the ground were sown
with starseed.—*P. J. Bailey.*

MOROSENESS.—There is no mockery like the mockery of that spirit which

looks around in the world and believes that all is emptiness.—*E. H. Chapin.*

Moroseness is the evening of turbulence.—*Landor.*

Men possessing minds which are morose, solemn, and inflexible, enjoy, in general, a greater share of dignity than of happiness.—*Bacon.*

The morose man takes both narrow and selfish views of life and the world; he is either envious of the happiness of others, or denies its existence.—*C. Simmons.*

MORTALITY.—(See " DEATH.")

All men think all mortal but themselves.—*Young.*

To smell a turf of fresh earth is wholesome for the body; no less are thoughts of mortality cordial to the soul.—*Fuller.*

The good die first; and they whose hearts are dry as summer dust, burn to the socket.—*Wordsworth.*

Lo! as the wind is, so is mortal life; a moan, a sigh, a sob, or a storm, a strife.—*Edwin Arnold.*

The mortality of mankind is but a part of the process of living—a step on the way to immortality.—Dying, to the good man, is but a brief sleep, from which he wakes to a perfection and fullness of life in eternity.—*Tryon Edwards.*

I congratulate you and myself, that life is passing fast away. What a superlatively grand and consoling idea is that of death! Without this radiant idea, life would, to my view, darken into midnight melancholy. Oh, the expectation of living here and living thus always, would be indeed a prospect of overwhelming despair! But thanks be to that fatal decree that dooms us to die, and to that Gospel which opens the vision of an endless life; and thanks, above all, to that Saviour Friend who has promised to conduct all the faithful through the sacred trance of death, into scenes of paradise and everlasting delight!—*J. Foster.*

Death is the crown of life; were it denied, to live would not be life, and even fools would wish to die.—Death wounds to cure; we fall to rise and reign; spring from our fetters; fasten in the skies.—*Young.*

Death is not to the Christian, what it has often been called, " Paying the debt of nature "; it is rather bringing a note to the bank to obtain solid gold for it. —You bring a cumbrous body which is nothing worth, and lay it down, and receive for it, from the eternal treasures, liberty, victory, knowledge, and rapture. —*J. Foster.*

Man wants but little, nor that little long.—How soon must he resign his very dust, which frugal nature lent him for an hour.—*Young.*

Consider the lilies of the field, whose bloom is brief.—We are as they; like them we fade away, as doth the leaf.— *Rossetti.*

When we see our enemies and friends gliding away before us, let us not forget that we are subject to the general law of mortality, and shall soon be where our doom will be fixed forever.—*Johnson.*

The boast of heraldry, the pomp of power, and all that beauty, all that wealth e'er gave, await alike the inevitable hour; the path of glory leads but to the grave.—*Gray.*

The fear of death often proves mortal, and sets people on methods, to save their lives, which infallibly destroy them. This is a reflection made upon observing that there are more thousands killed in a flight, than in a battle; and may be applied to those multitudes of imaginary sick persons that break their constitutions by physic, and throw themselves into the arms of death, by endeavoring to escape it.—*Addison.*

MOTHER.—God could not be everywhere, and therefore he made mothers. —*Jewish saying.*

There is in all this cold and hollow world no fount of deep, strong, deathless love, save that within a mother's heart.—*Mrs. Hemans.*

When Eve was brought unto Adam, he became filled with the Holy Spirit, and gave her the most sanctified, the most glorious of appellations. He called her Eva, that is to say, the Mother of All. He did not style her wife, but simply mother,—mother of all living creatures. In this consists the glory and the most precious ornament of woman.—*Luther.*

Nature's loving proxy, the watchful mother.—*Bulwer.*

I think it must somewhere be written, that the virtues of mothers shall be visited on their children, as well as the sins of the fathers.—*Dickens.*

Children, look in those eyes, listen to that dear voice, notice the feeling of even a single touch that is bestowed upon you by that gentle hand! Make much of it while yet you have that most precious of all good gifts, a loving mother. Read the unfathomable love of those eyes; the kind anxiety of that tone and look, however slight your pain. In after life you may have friends, fond, dear friends, but never will you have again the inexpressible love and gentleness lavished upon you, which none but a mother bestows.—*Macaulay.*

The mother's yearning, that completest type of the life in another life which is the essence of real human love, feels the presence of the cherished child even in the base, degraded man.—*George Eliot.*

The future destiny of the child is always the work of the mother.—*Napoleon.*

The mother in her office holds the key of the soul; and she it is who stamps the coin of character, and makes the being who would be a savage but for her gentle cares, a Christian man! Then crown her queen of the world.—*Old Play.*

If you would reform the world from its errors and vices, begin by enlisting the mothers.—*C. Simmons.*

Children are what the mothers are; no fondest father's fondest care can so fashion the infant's heart, or so shape the life.—*Landor.*

All that I am, or hope to be, I owe to my angel mother.—*Lincoln.*

But one thing on earth is better than the wife, and that is the mother.—*L. Schafer.*

Unhappy is the man for whom his own mother has not made all other mothers venerable.—*Richter.*

The dignity, the grandeur, the tenderness, the everlasting and divine significance of motherhood.—*De Witt Talmage.*

All that I am my mother made me. —*John Quincy Adams.*

An ounce of mother is worth a pound of clergy.—*Spanish Proverb.*

The future of society is in the hands of the mothers. If the world was lost through woman, she alone can save it. —*De Beaufort.*

No joy in nature is so sublimely affecting as the joy of a mother at the good fortune of her child.—*Richter.*

It is the general rule, that all superior men inherit the elements of superiority from their mothers.—*Michelet.*

" What is wanting," said Napoleon one day to Madame Campan, " in order that the youth of France be well educated? " " Good mothers," was the reply. The Emperor was most forcibly struck with this answer. " Here," said he, " is a system in one word."—*J. S. C. Abbott.*

Men are what their mothers made them. You may as well ask a loom which weaves huckaback, why it does not make cashmere, as expect poetry from this engineer, or a chemical discovery from that jobber.—*Emerson.*

The instruction received at the mother's knee, and the paternal lessons, together with the pious and sweet souvenirs of the fireside, are never effaced entirely from the soul.—*Lamennais.*

Say to mothers, what a holy charge is theirs; with what a kingly power their love might rule the fountains of the new-born mind.—*Mrs. Sigourney.*

I would desire for a friend the son who never resisted the tears of his mother.—*Lacretelle.*

Observe how soon, and to what a degree, a mother's influence begins to operate! Her first ministration for her infant is to enter, as it were, the valley of the shadow of death, and win its life at the peril of her own! How different must an affection thus founded be from all others!—*Mrs. Sigourney.*

If there be aught surpassing human deed or word or thought, it is a mother's love!—*Marchioness de Spadara.*

The babe at first feeds upon the mother's bosom, but is always on her heart.—*H. W. Beecher.*

A man never sees all that his mother

has been to him till it's too late to let her know that he sees it.—*W. D. Howells.*

A father may turn his back on his child; brothers and sisters may become inveterate enemies; husbands may desert their wives, and wives their husbands. But a mother's love endures through all; in good repute, in bad repute, in the face of the world's condemnation, a mother still loves on, and still hopes that her child may turn from his evil ways, and repent; still she remembers the infant smiles that once filled her bosom with rapture, the merry laugh, the joyful shout of his childhood, the opening promise of his youth; and she can never be brought to think him all unworthy.—*Washington Irving.*

The loss of a mother is always severely felt: even though her health may incapacitate her from taking any active part in the care of her family, still she is a sweet rallying-point, around which affection and obedience, and a thousand tender endeavors to please, concentrate; and dreary is the blank when such a point is withdrawn.—*Lamartine.*

Oh, wondrous power! how little understood, entrusted to the mother's mind alone, to fashion genius, form the soul for good, inspire a West, or train a Washington.—*Mrs. Hale.*

The mother's heart is the child's schoolroom.—*H. W. Beecher.*

Stories first heard at a mother's knee are never wholly forgotten,—a little spring that never quite dries up in our journey through scorching years.—*Ruffini.*

A mother's love is indeed the golden link that binds youth to age; and he is still but a child, however time may have furrowed his cheek, or silvered his brow, who can yet recall, with a softened heart, the fond devotion, or the gentle chidings, of the best friend that God ever gives us.—*Bovee.*

Maternal love! thou word that sums all bliss.—*Pollock.*

It is generally admitted, and very frequently proved, that virtue and genius, and all the natural good qualities which men possess, are derived from their mothers.—*Hook.*

Let France have good mothers, and she will have good sons.—*Napoleon.*

What are Raphael's Madonnas but the shadow of a mother's love, fixed in permanent outline forever?—*T. W. Higginson.*

If the whole world were put into one scale, and my mother into the other, the world would kick the beam.—*Lord Langdale.*

Happy he with such a mother! faith in womankind beats with his blood, and trust in all things high comes easy to him, and though he trip and fall, he shall not blind his soul with clay.—*Tennyson.*

No language can express the power and beauty and heroism and majesty of a mother's love. It shrinks not where man cowers, and grows stronger where man faints, and over the wastes of worldly fortune sends the radiance of its quenchless fidelity like a star in heaven.—*E. H. Chapin.*

Even He that died for us upon the cross, in the last hour, in the unutterable agony of death, was mindful of his mother, as if to teach us that this holy love should be our last worldly thought, —the last point of earth from which the soul should take its flight for heaven. —*Longfellow.*

My mother's influence in molding my character was conspicuous. She forced me to learn daily long chapters of the Bible by heart. To that discipline and patient, accurate resolve I owe not only much of my general power of taking pains, but the best part of my taste for literature.—*Ruskin.*

MOTIVES.—Men are more accountable for their motives, than for anything else; and primarily, morality consists in the motives, that is in the affections. —*Archibald Alexander.*

We should often have reason to be ashamed of our most brilliant actions if the world could see the motives from which they spring.—*Rochefoucauld.*

Motives are better than actions. Men drift into crime. Of evil they do more than they contemplate, and of good they contemplate more than they do.— *Bovee.*

In the eye of that Supreme Being to whom our whole internal frame is uncovered, motives and dispositions hold the place of actions.—*Blair.*

The true motives of our actions, like the real pipes of an organ, are usually concealed; but the gilded and hollow pretext is pompously placed in the front for show.—*Colton.*

Many actions, like the Rhone, have two sources: one pure, the other impure.—*Hare.*

Acts are nothing except as they are fruits of a state, except as they indicate what the man is; words are nothing except as they express a mind or purpose. —*F. D. Maurice.*

Though a good motive cannot sanctify a bad action, a bad motive will always vitiate a good action.—In common and trivial matters we may act without motive, but in momentous ones the most careful deliberation is wisdom.—*W. Jay.*

The two great movers of the human mind are the desire of good, and the fear of evil.—*Johnson.*

God made man to go by motives, and he will not go without them, any more than a boat without steam, or a balloon without gas.—*H. W. Beecher.*

It is motive alone that gives character to the actions of men.—*Bruyère.*

It is not the incense, or the offering which is acceptable to God, but the purity and devotion of the worshiper. —*Seneca.*

He that does good for good's sake, seeks neither praise nor reward, but he is sure of both in the end.—*Penn.*

If a man speaks or acts with pure thought, happiness follows him like a shadow that never leaves him.—*Buddha.*

Let the motive be in the deed and not in the event. Be not one whose motive for action is the hope of reward. —*Kreeshna.*

Great actions, the luster of which dazzles us, are represented by politicians as the effects of deep design, whereas they are commonly the effects of caprice and passion.—*Rochefoucauld.*

Our best conjectures, as to the true spring of actions, are very uncertain; the actions themselves are all we know from history. That Cæsar was murdered by twenty-four conspirators, I doubt not; but I very much doubt

whether their love of liberty was the sole cause.—*Chesterfield.*

However brilliant an action, it should not be esteemed great unless the result of a great and good motive.—*Rochefoucauld.*

We must not inquire too curiously into motives. They are apt to become feeble in the utterance: the aroma is mixed with the grosser air. We must keep the germinating grain away from the light.—*George Eliot.*

Whatever touches the nerves of motive, whatever shifts man's moral position, is mightier than steam, or caloric, or lightning.—*E. H. Chapin.*

The morality of an action depends upon the motive from which we act.—*Johnson.*

Motives imply weakness, and the existence of evil and temptation.—Angelic natures would act from impulse alone.—*Coleridge.*

The noblest motive is the public good. —*Virgil.*

MURDER.—Blood, though it sleep a time, yet never dies.—*Chapman.*

One murder makes a villain; millions, a hero; numbers sanctify the crime.—*Porteus.*

To murder character is as truly a crime as to murder the body; the tongue of the slanderer is brother to the dagger of the assassin.—*Tryon Edwards.*

One to destroy, is murder by the law; to murder thousands takes a specious name—war's glorious art, and gives immortal fame.—*Young.*

Every unpunished murder takes away something from the security of every man's life.—*Daniel Webster.*

Nor cell, nor chain, nor dungeon speaks to the murderer like the voice of solitude.—*Maturin.*

Murder itself is past all expiation the greatest crime, which nature doth abhor. —*Goffe.*

MURMURING.—Murmur not at the ills you may suffer, but rather thank God for the many mercies and blessings you have received at his hands.

Murmur at nothing. If our ills are reparable, it is ungrateful; if remediless, it is vain. A Christian builds his fortune on a better foundation than stoicism; he is pleased with every thing that happens, because he knows it could not happen if it did not please God; and that which pleases God must be best.—*H. L. Wayland.*

He who murmurs against his condition, does not understand it; but he who accepts of it in peace, will soon learn to comprehend it. What one has experienced and learned in this respect, is always a stage he has made on his way to heaven.

MUSIC.—Music is the mediator between the spiritual and the sensual life. Although the spirit be not master of that which it creates through music, yet it is blessed in this creation, which, like every creation of art, is mightier than the artist.—*Beethoven.*

Music is the harmonious voice of creation; an echo of the invisible world one note of the divine concord whic the entire universe is destined one d to sound.—*Mazzini.*

There is something marvelous in music. I might a'most say it is, in itself, a marvel. Its position is somewhere between the region of thought and that of phenomena; a glimmering medium between mind and matter, related to both and yet differing from either. Spiritual, and yet requiring rhythm; material, aid yet independent of space.—*H. Heine.*

Music resembles poetry; in each are numerous graces which no methods teach, and which a master hand alone can reach.—*Pope.*

Explain it as we may, a martial strain will urge a man into the front rank of battle sooner than an argument, and a fine anthem excite his devotion more certainly than a logical discourse.—*Tuckerman.*

All musical people seem to be happy; it is to them the engrossing pursuit; almost the only innocent and unpunished passion.—*Sydney Smith.*

Where painting is weakest, namely, in the expression of the highest moral and spiritual ideas, there music is sublimely strong.—*Mrs. Stowe.*

Music can noble hints impart, engender fury, kindle love, with unsuspected eloquence can move and manage all the man with secret art.—*Addison.*

Music, in the best sense, does not require novelty; nay, the older it is, and the more we are accustomed to it, the greater its effect.—*Goethe.*

The man that hath not music in himself, and is not moved with concord of sweet sounds, is fit for treasons, stratagems, and spoils; let no man trust him.—*Shakespeare.*

Music is the fourth great material want of our nature,—first food, then iment, then shelter, then music.—ovee.

Music is the art of the prophets, the only art that can calm the agitations of the soul; it is one of the most magnificent and delightful presents God has given us.—*Luther.*

The highest graces of music flow from the feelings of the heart.—*Emmons.*

Music is the only sensual gratification in which mankind may indulge to excess without injury to their moral or religious feel ngs.—*Addison.*

Music, once admitted to the soul, becomes a sort of spirit, and never dies. It wanders perturbedly through the halls and galleri s of the memory, and is often heard ag in, distinct and living, as when it first c splaced the wavelets of the air.—*Bulwer.*

Preposterous ass! that never read so far to know the cause why music was ordained! was it not to refresh the mind of man, after his stu ies, or his usual pain?—*Shakespeare.*

Some of the fathers went so far as to esteem the love of music a sign of predestination, as a thing divine, and reserved for the felicities of heaven itself.—*Sir W. Temple.*

Among the instrumentalities of love and peace, surely there can be no sweeter, softer, more effective voice than that of gentle peace-breathing music.—*Elihu Burritt.*

It calls in my spirits, composes my thoughts, delights my ear, recreates my mind, and so not only fits me for after business, but fills my heart, at the present, with pure and useful thoughts; so that when the music sounds the sweetliest in my ears, truth commonly flows the clearest into my mind.—*Bp. Beveridge.*

Music, of all the liberal arts, has the

greatest influence over the passions, and is that to which the legislator ought to give the greatest encouragement.—*Napoleon*.

It is in learning music that many youthful hearts learn to love.—*Ricard*.

Next to theology I give to music the highest place and honor. And we see how David and all the saints have wrought their godly thoughts into verse, rhyme, and song.—*Luther*.

Music is the only one of the fine arts in which not only man, but all other animals, have a common property,—mice and elephants, spiders and birds.—*Richter*.

Music is a prophecy of what life is to be; the rainbow of promise translated out of seeing into hearing.—*Mrs. L. M. Child*.

The lines of poetry, the periods of prose, and even the texts of Scripture most frequently recollected and quoted, are those which are felt to be pre-eminently musical.—*Shenstone*.

The direct relation of music is not to ideas, but to emotions—in the works of its greatest masters, it is more marvelous, more mysterious than poetry.—*H. Giles*.

Music is the medicine of the breaking heart.—*A. Hunt*.

We love music for the buried hopes, the garnered memories, the tender feelings it can summon at a touch.—*L. E. Landon*.

Music washes away from the soul the dust of every-day life.—*Auerbach*.

Music has charms to soothe the savage breast, to soften rocks, and bend the knotted oak.—*Congreve*.

Almost all my tragedies were sketched in my mind, either in the act of hearing music, or a few hours after.—*Alfieri*.

Music is a discipline, and a mistress of order and good manners, she makes the people milder and gentler, more moral and more reasonable.—*Luther*.

In the germ, when the first trace of life begins to stir, music is the nurse of the soul; it murmurs in the ear, and the child sleeps; the tones are companions of his dreams,—they are the world in which he lives.—*Bettina*.

Music is one of the fairest and most

glorious gifts of God, to which Satan is a bitter enemy, for it removes from the heart the weight of sorrow, and the fascination of evil thoughts.—*Luther*.

Both music and painting add a spirit to devotion, and elevate the ardor.—*Sterne*.

Lord, what music hast thou provided for thy saints in heaven, when thou affordest bad men such music on earth!—*Izaak Walton*.

Music is the child of prayer, the companion of religion.—*Chateaubriand*.

The best sort of music is what it should be—sacred; the next best, the military, has fallen to the lot of the devil.—*Coleridge*.

Music moves us, and we know not why; we feel the tears, but cannot trace their source. Is it the language of some other state, born of its memory? For what can wake the soul's strong instinct of another world like music?—*L. E. Landon*.

Let me have music dying, and I seek no more delight.—*Kee s*.

Music is the language of praise; and one of the most essential preparations for eternity is delight in praising God; a higher acq iirement, I do think, than even delight and devotedness in prayer.—*Chalmers*.

Through every pulse the music stole, and held sublime communion with the soul; wrung from the coyest breast the imprisoned sigh, and kindled rapture in the coldest eye.—*Montgomery*.

When griping grief the heart doth wound, and doleful dumps the mind oppress, then music, with her silver sound, with speedy help doth lend redress.—*Shakespeare*.

A good ear for music, and a taste for music are two very different things which are often confounded; and so is comprehending and enjoying every object of sense and sentiment.—*Gréville*.

Music is well said to be the speech of angels.—*Carlyle*.

Music wakes the soul, and lifts it high, and wings it with sublime desires, and fits it to bespeak the Deity.—*Addison*.

There is no feeling, except the extremes of fear and grief, that does not find relief in music.—*George Eliot*.

Yea, music is the prophet's art: among

the gifts that God hath sent, one of the most magnificent.—*Longfellow*.

The meaning of song goes deep. Who is there that, in logical words, can express the effect music has on us? A kind of inarticulate, unfathomable speech, which leads us to the edge of the infinite, and lets us for moments gaze into that!—*Carlyle*.

Of all the arts beneath the heaven that man has found or God has given, none draws the soul so sweet away, as music's melting, mystic lay; slight emblem of the bliss above, it soothes the spirit all to love.—*Hogg*.

MUTABILITY.—What shadows we are, and what shadows we pursue!—*Burke*.

Man must be prepared for every event of life, for there is nothing that is durable.—*Menander*.

Mutability is the badge of infirmity. —It is seldom that a man continues to wish and design the same thing for two days alike.—*Charron*.

In human life there is constant change of fortune; and it is unreasonable to expect an exemption from the common fate.—Life itself decays, and all things are daily changing.—*Plutarch*.

Clocks will go as they are set; but man, irregular man, is never constant, never certain.—*Otway*.

The blessings of health and fortune, as they have a beginning, so they must also have an end.—Everything rises but to fall, and increases but to decay.— *Sallust*.

When Anaxagoras was told of the death of his son, he only said, "I knew he was mortal." So we in all casualties of life should say, "I knew my riches were uncertain, that my friend was but a man." Such considerations would soon pacify us, because all our troubles proceed from their being unexpected.— *Plutarch*.

It may serve as a comfort to us, in all our calamities and afflictions, that he that loses anything and gets wisdom by it is a gainer by the loss.—*L'Estrange*.

All our life goeth like Penelope's web, and what one hour effects, the next destroys.—*Augustine*.

MYSTERY.—Mystery is but another name for our ignorance; if we were om-

niscient, all would be perfectly plain.— *Tryon Edwards*.

A mystery is something of which we know that it is, though we do not know how it is.—*Joseph Cook*.

He had lived long enough to know that it is unwise to wish everything explained.—*Coningsby*.

I do not explain—I only state it; and this is all we can do with a large proportion of all the facts and truths that we know.—There is a point, easily reached, where the simplest facts end in mystery, even as they begin in it; just as each day lies between two nights. —*R. Turnbull*.

While reason is puzzling itself about mystery, faith is turning it to daily bread, and feeding on it thankfully in her heart of hearts.—*F. D. Huntington*.

Mystery magnifies danger, as a fog the sun; the hand that warned Belshazzar derived its horrifying influence from the want of a body.—*Colton*.

Each particle of matter is an immensity; each leaf a world; each insect an inexplicable compendium.—*Lavater*.

There are more things in heaven and earth than are dreamt of in your philosophy.—*Shakespeare*.

Like a morning dream, life becomes more and more bright the longer we live, and the reason of everything appears more clear. What has puzzled us before seems less mysterious, and the crooked paths look straighter as we approach the end.—*Richter*.

I do not know how the great loving Father will bring out light at last, but he knows, and he will do it.—*Livingstone, in Africa*.

I would fain know all that I need, and all that I may.—I leave God's secrets to himself.—It is happy for me that God makes me of his court, and not of his council.—*Bp. Hall*.

It is the dim haze of mystery that adds enchantment to pursuit.—*Rivarol*.

Happy is the man who is content to traverse this ocean to the haven of rest, without going into the wretched diving-bells of his own fancies.—There are depths; but depths are for God.— *Evans*.

Speculate not too much on the mysteries of truth or providence.—The effort to explain everything, sometimes may endanger faith.—Many things God reserves to himself, and many are reserved for the unfoldings of the future life.—*Tryon Edwards.*

Most men take least notice of what is plain, as if that was of no use, but puzzle their thoughts with those vast depths and abysses which no human understanding can fathom.—*Bp. Sherlock.*

We injure mysteries, which are matters of faith, by any attempt at explanation, in order to make them matters of reason. Could they be explained, they would cease to be mysteries; and it has been well said that a thing is not necessarily against reason, because it happens to be above it.—*Colton.*

To make anything very terrible, obscurity seems, in general, to be necessary.—When we know the full extent of any danger, and can accustom our eyes to it, a great deal of the apprehension vanishes.—*Burke.*

A proper secrecy is the only mystery of able men; mystery is the only secrecy of weak and cunning ones.—*Chesterfield.*

As defect of strength in us makes some weights to be immovable, so likewise, defect of understanding makes some truths to be mysterious.—*Bp. Sherlock.*

A religion without mystery must be a religion without God.

In dwelling on divine mysteries, keep thy heart humble, thy thoughts reverent, thy soul holy. Let not philosophy be ashamed to be confuted, nor logic to be confounded, nor reason to be surpassed. What thou canst not prove, approve; what thou canst not comprehend, believe; what thou canst believe, admire and love and obey. So shall thine ignorance be satisfied in thy faith, and thy doubt be swallowed up in thy reverence, and thy faith be as influential as sight. Put out thine own candle, and then shalt thou see clearly the sun of righteousness.—*Jeremy Taylor.*

MYTHOLOGY.—Mythology is the religious sentiment growing wild. —*Schelling.*

Mythology is not religion. It may rather be regarded as the ancient substitute, the poetical counterpart for dogmatic theology.—*Hare.*

The heathen mythology not only was not true, but it was not even supported as true; it not only deserved no faith, but it demanded none.—The very pretension to truth, the very demand of faith, were characteristics of Christianity.—*Whately.*

N

NAMES.—(See "REPUTATION.")

A name is a kind of face whereby one is known.—*Fuller.*

With the vulgar and the learned, names have great weight; the wise use a writ of inquiry into their legitimacy when they are advanced as authorities. —*Zimmermann.*

Who hath not owned, with rapture-smitten frame, the power of grace, the magic of a name.—*Cowper.*

Favor or disappointment has been often conceded, as the name of the claimant has affected us; and the accidental affinity or coincidence of a name, connected with ridicule or hatred, with pleasure or disgust, has operated like magic.—*Disraeli.*

"Names," says an old maxim, "are things."—They certainly are influences. —Impressions are left and opinions are shaped by them.—Virtue is disparaged, and vice countenanced, and so encouraged by them. The mean and selfish talk of their prudence and economy; the vain and proud prate about self-respect; obstinacy is called firmness, and dissipation the enjoyment of life; seriousness is ridiculed as cant, and strict morality and integrity, as needless scrupulosity; and so men deceive themselves, and society is led to look leniently, or with indifference, on what ought to be sharply condemned.—*Tryon Edwards.*

Some to the fascination of a name surrender judgment hoodwinked.—*Cowper.*

What is in a name? That which we call a rose, by any other name would smell as sweet.—*Shakespeare.*

Some men do as much begrudge others a good name, as they want one themselves; and perhaps that is the reason of it.—*Penn.*

A person with a bad name is already half-hanged.—*Old Proverb.*

One of the greatest artifices the devil uses to engage men in vice and debauchery, is to fasten names of contempt on certain virtues, and thus fill weak souls with a foolish fear of passing for scrupulous, should they desire to put them in practice.—*Pascal.*

A virtuous name is the precious, only good, for which queens and peasants' wives must contest together.—*Schiller.*

A man's name is not like a mantle which merely hangs about him, and which one perchance may safely twitch and pull, but a perfectly fitting garment, which, like the skin, has grown over him, at which one cannot rake and scrape without injuring the man himself.—*Goethe.*

Good name, in man or woman, is the immediate jewel of their souls.— Who steals my purse steals trash; but he that filches from me my good name, robs me of that which not enriches him, and makes me poor indeed.—*Shakespeare.*

The honors of a name 'tis just to guard; they are a trust but lent us, which we take, and should, in reverence to the donor's fame, with care transmit them down to other hands.—*Shirley.*

Great names debase, instead of raising those who know not how to use them.— *Rochefoucauld.*

A name truly good is the aroma from virtuous character; it is a spontaneous emanation from genuine excellence.— Such a name is not only remembered on earth, but it is written in heaven.—*J. Hamilton.*

A good name lost is seldom regained. —When character is gone, all is gone, and one of the richest jewels of life is lost forever.—*J. Hawes.*

No better heritage can a father bequeath to his children than a good name; nor is there in a family any richer heir-loom than the memory of a noble ancestor.—*J. Hamilton.*

NATIONS.—A State to prosper, must be built on foundations of a moral character; and this character is the principal element of its strength and the only guaranty of its permanence and prosperity.—*J. Currie.*

Individuals may form communities, but it is institutions alone that can create a nation.—*Disraeli.*

The best protection of a nation is its men; towns and cities cannot have a surer defense than the prowess and virtue of their inhabitants.—*Rabelais.*

It is written in God's word, and in all the history of the race, that nations, if they live at all, live not by felicity of position, or soil, or climate, and not by abundance of material good, but by the living word of the living God.— The commandments of God are the bread of life for the nations.—*R. D. Hitchcock.*

Territory is but the body of a nation. —The people who inhabit its hills and valleys are its soul, its spirit, its life.— *Garfield.*

No nation can be destroyed while it possesses a good home life.—*J. G. Holland.*

In the youth of a state, arms do flourish; in the middle age, learning; and then both of them together for a time; in the declining age, mechanical arts and merchandise.—*Bacon.*

A nation's character is the sum of its splendid deeds; they constitute one common patrimony, the nation's inheritance. They awe foreign powers, they arouse and animate our own people.— *Henry Clay.*

National progress is the sum of individual industry, energy, and uprightness, as national decay is of individual idleness, selfishness, and vice.—*S. Smiles.*

The true grandeur of nations is in those qualities which constitute the true greatness of the individual.—*C. Sumner.*

As for the just and noble idea, that nations, as well as individuals, are parts of one wondrous whole, it has hardly passed the lips or pen of any but religious men and poets.—It is the one great principle of the greatest religion which has ever nourished the morals of mankind.—*Harriet Martineau.*

NATURE.—Nature is but a name for an effect whose cause is God.—*Cowper.*

Nature has perfections, in order to show that she is the image of God; and defects, to show that she is only his image.—*Pascal.*

Nature does not capriciously scatter her secrets as golden gifts to lazy pets and luxurious darlings, but imposes tasks when she presents opportunities, and uplifts him whom she would inform. The apple that she drops at the feet of Newton is but a coy invitation to follow her to the stars.—*E. P. Whipple.*

Nature never deserts the wise and pure; no plot so narrow, be but nature there; no waste so vacant, but may well employ each faculty of sense, and keep the heart awake to love and beauty!—*Coleridge.*

Nature and revelation are alike God's books; each may have mysteries, but in each there are plain practical lessons for every-day duty.—*Tryon Edwards.*

The man who can really, in living union of the mind and heart, converse with God through nature, finds in the material forms around him, a source of power and happiness inexhaustible, and like the life of angels.—The highest life and glory of man is to be alive unto God; and when this grandeur of sensibility to him, and this power of communion with him is carried, as the habit of the soul, into the forms of nature, then the walls of our world are as the gates of heaven.—*G. B. Cheever.*

Nature knows no pause in progress and development, and attaches her curse on all inaction.—*Goethe.*

Read nature; nature is a friend to truth; nature is Christian, preaches to mankind, and bids dead matter aid us in our creed.—*Young.*

Sympathy with nature is a part of the good man's religion.—*F. H. Hedge.*

Looks through nature up to nature's God.—*Pope.*

Study nature as the countenance of God.—*Charles Kingsley.*

Hill and valley, seas and constellations, are but stereotypes of divine ideas appealing to, and answered by the living soul of man.—*E. H. Chapin.*

There is a signature of wisdom and power impressed on the works of God, which evidently distinguishes them from the feeble imitations of men.— Not only the splendor of the sun, but the glimmering light of the glowworm, proclaims his glory.—*John Newton.*

Natural objects themselves, even when they make no claim to beauty, excite the feelings, and occupy the imagination. Nature pleases, attracts, delights, merely because it is nature. We recognize in it an Infinite Power.— *W. Humboldt.*

There is no trifling with nature; it is always true, grave, and severe; it is always in the right, and the faults and errors fall to our share. It defies incompetency, but reveals its secrets to the competent, the truthful, and the pure.—*Goethe.*

Nature is the time-vesture of God that reveals him to the wise, and hides him from the foolish.—*Carlyle.*

Nature is beautiful, always beautiful! Every little flake of snow is a perfect crystal, and they fall together as gracefully as if fairies of the air caught water-drops and made them into artificial flowers to garland the wings of the wind!—*Mrs. L. M. Child.*

Nature is an Æolian harp, a musical instrument, whose tones are the re-echo of higher strings within us.—*Novalis.*

What profusion is there in His work! When trees blossom there is not a single breastpin, but a whole bosom-full of gems; and of leaves they have so many suits that they can throw them away to the winds all summer long. What unnumbered cathedrals has He reared in the forest shades, vast and grand, full of curious carvings, and haunted evermore by tremulous music; and in the heavens above, how do stars seem to have flown out of His hand faster than sparks out of a mighty forge! —*H. W. Beecher.*

Nature and wisdom always say the same.—*Juvenal.*

The laws of nature are just, but terrible. There is no weak mercy in them. Cause and consequence are inseparable and inevitable. The elements have no forbearance. The fire burns, the water drowns, the air consumes, the earth buries. And perhaps it would be well for our race if the punishment of crimes against the laws of man were as inevitable as the punishment of crimes against the laws of nature,—were man as unerring in his judgments as nature. —*Longfellow.*

Nature is commanded by obeying her. —*Bacon.*

Nature is the living, visible garment of God.—*Goethe.*

In contemplation of created things, by steps we may ascend to God.—*Milton.*

A man finds in the productions of nature an inexhaustible stock of material on which he can employ himself, without any temptations to envy or malevolence, and has always a certain prospect of discovering new reasons for adoring the sovereign author of the universe.—*Johnson.*

The laws of nature are the rules according to which effects are produced; but there must be a lawgiver—a cause which operates according to these rules. —The laws of navigation never steered a ship, and the law of gravity never moved a planet.—*T. Reid.*

Nature is the most thrifty thing in the world; she never wastes anything; she undergoes change, but there's no annihilation—the essence remains.—*T. Binney.*

The laws of nature are but the thoughts and agencies of God—the modes in which he works and carries out the designs of his providence and will.—*Tryon Edwards.*

Nature gives to every time and season some beauties of its own; and from morning to night, as from the cradle to the grave, is but a succession of changes so gentle and easy that we can scarcely mark their progress.—*Dickens.*

In nature, all is managed for the best with perfect frugality and just reserve, profuse to none, but bountiful to all; never employing on one thing more than enough, but with exact economy retrenching the superfluous, and adding force to what is principal in everything. —*Shaftesbury.*

Surely there is something in the unruffled calm of nature that overawes our little anxieties and doubts: the sight of the deep-blue sky, and the clustering stars above, seem to impart a quiet to the mind.—*Jonathan Edwards.*

It is truly a most Christian exercise to extract a sentiment of piety from the works and appearances of nature. Our Saviour expatiates on a flower, and draws from it the delightful argument of confidence in God. He gives us to see that taste may be combined with piety, and that the same heart may be occupied with all that is serious in the contemplations of religion, and be, at the same time, alive to the charms and loveliness of nature.—*Chalmers.*

In nature things move violently to their place, and calmly in their place.— *Bacon.*

Nature is a frugal mother, and never gives without measure. When she has work to do, she qualifies men for that and sends them equipped.—*Emerson.*

He that follows nature is never out of his way. Nature is sometimes subdued, but seldom extinguished.—*Bacon.*

If we did not take great pains to corrupt our nature, our nature would never corrupt us.—*Clarendon.*

Whatever you are by nature, keep to it; never desert your own line of talent. Be what nature intended you for, and you will succeed; be anything else and you will be ten thousand times worse than nothing.—*Sydney Smith.*

I follow nature as the surest guide, and resign myself, with implicit obedience, to her sacred ordinances.—*Cicero.*

It were happy if we studied nature more in natural things; and acted according to nature, whose rules are few, plain, and most reasonable.—*Penn.*

Epicureanism is human nature drunk, cynicism is human nature mad, and stoicism is human nature in despair.—*S. J. Wilson.*

The ignorant man marvels at the exceptional; the wise man marvels at the common; the greatest wonder of all is the regularity of nature.—*G. D. Boardman.*

Nature is the glass reflecting God, as by the sea reflected is the sun, too glorious to be gazed on in his sphere.— *Young.*

Nature is man's teacher. She unfolds her treasures to his search, unseals his eye, illumes his mind, and purifies his heart; an influence breathes from all the sights and sounds of her existence.— *Street.*

A poet ought not to pick Nature's pocket. Let him borrow, and so borrow as to repay by the very act of borrowing. Examine nature accurately, but write from recollection, and trust more

to the imagination than to the memory.
—*Coleridge.*

Nature is the armory of genius. Cities serve it poorly, books and colleges at second hand; the eye craves the spectacle of the horizon; of mountain, ocean, river and plain, the clouds and stars; actual contact with the elements, sympathy with the seasons as they rise and roll.—*A. B. Alcott.*

Nothing is rich but the inexhaustible wealth of nature. She shows us only surfaces, but she is million fathoms deep.—*Emerson.*

Nature hath nothing made so base, but can read some instruction to the wisest man.—*C. Aleyn.*

Nature—a thing which science and art never appear to see with the same eyes. If to an artist nature has a soul, why, so has a steam-engine. Art gifts with soul all matter that it contemplates; science turns all that is already gifted with soul into matter.—*Bulwer.*

Nature is too thin a screen; the glory of the One breaks in everywhere.—*Emerson.*

Nature is no sentimentalist—does not cosset or pamper us. We must see that the world is rough and surly, and will not mind drowning a man or a woman, but swallows your ships like a grain of dust. The cold, inconsiderate of persons, tingles your blood, benumbs your feet, freezes a man like an apple. The diseases, the elements, fortune, gravity, lightning, respect no persons.—*Emerson.*

All nature is a vast symbolism; every material fact has sheathed within it a spiritual truth.—*E. H. Chapin.*

Nature imitates herself. A grain thrown into good ground brings forth fruit; a principle thrown into a good mind brings forth fruit. Everything is created and conducted by the same Master,—the root, the branch, the fruits,— the principles, the consequences.—*Pascal.*

Nature is avariciously frugal; in matter, it allows no atom to elude its grasp; in mind, no thought or feeling to perish. It gathers up the fragments that nothing be lost.—*David Thomas.*

NECESSITY.—Necessity is the argument of tyrants: it is the creed of slaves. —*William Pitt.*

A people never fairly begins to prosper till necessity is treading on its heels. The growing want of room is one of the sources of civilization. Population is power, but it must be a population that, in growing, is made daily apprehensive of the morrow.—*Simms.*

The best teacher one can have is necessity.—*La None.*

There is no contending with necessity, and we should be very tender how we censure those that submit to it. 'Tis one thing to be at liberty to do what we will, and another thing to be tied up to do what we must.—*L'Estrange.*

There is no virtue like necessity.— *Shakespeare.*

Necessity is always the first stimulus to industry, and those who conduct it with prudence, perseverance, and energy will rarely fail. Viewed in this light, the necessity of labor is not a chastisement, but a blessing,—the very root and spring of all that we call progress in individuals and civilization in nations.—*S. Smiles.*

What fate imposes, men must needs abide; it boots not to resist both wind and tide.—*Shakespeare.*

Necessity, that great refuge and excuse for human frailty, breaks through all law; and he is not to be accounted in fault whose crime is not the effect of choice, but force.—*Pascal.*

And with necessity, the tyrant's plea, excused his devilish deeds.—*Milton.*

Necessity of action takes away the fear of the act, and makes bold resolution the favorite of fortune.—*Quarles.*

When God would educate a man He compels him to learn bitter lessons. He sends him to school to the necessities rather than to the graces, that, by knowing all suffering, he may know also the eternal consolation.—*Celia Burleigh.*

We cannot conquer fate and necessity, yet we can yield to them in such a manner as to be greater than if we could.— *Landor.*

Necessity may render a doubtful act innocent, but it cannot make it praiseworthy.—*Joubert.*

Necessity never made a good bargain. —*Franklin.*

It is observed in the golden verses of

Pythagoras, that power is never far from necessity. The vigor of the human mind quickly appears when there is no longer any place for doubt and hesitation, when diffidence is absorbed in the sense of danger, or overwhelmed by some resistless passion.—*Johnson.*

What was once to me mere matter of the fancy, now has grown to be the necessity of heart and life.—*Tennyson.*

Necessity is the mother of invention. —*Farquhar.*

The argument of necessity is not only the tyrant's plea, but the patriot's defense, and the safety of the state.— *James Wilson.*

NEGLECT.—(See "PUNCTUALITY.")

A little neglect may breed great mischief; for want of a nail the shoe was lost; for want of a shoe the horse was lost, and for want of a horse the rider was lost, being overtaken and slain by an enemy, all for want of a little care about a horse-shoe nail.—*Franklin.*

An experienced mother who had brought up a large family of children with eminent success, was once asked by a younger one what she would recommend in the case of some children who were too anxiously educated; and her reply was, "I think, my dear, a little wholesome neglect."

He that thinks he can afford to be negligent, is not far from being poor.— *Johnson.*

Negligence is the rust of the soul, that corrodes through all her best resolves.—*Feltham.*

The best ground, untilled and neglected, soonest runs out into rank weeds. —A man of knowledge that is either negligent or uncorrected cannot but grow wild and godless.—*Bp. Hall.*

A wise and salutary neglect.—*Burke.*

In persons grafted in a serious trust, negligence is a crime.—*Shakespeare.*

Self-love is not so vile a sin as self-neglecting.—*Shakespeare.*

NEUTRALITY.—When a spot of neutral ground is found in heaven, or earth, or hell, then let neuters take their stand; real neuters are nothing, and professed neuters on religious subjects, are always false and faithless in reality. —*Thomas Williams.*

Neutral men are the devil's allies.— *E. H. Chapin.*

Neutrality is no favorite with Providence, for we are so formed that it is scarcely possible for us to stand neuter in our hearts, although we may deem it prudent to appear so in our actions.— *Colton.*

Neutrality, as a lasting principle, is an evidence of weakness.—*Kossuth.*

A wise neuter joins with neither, but uses both as his honest interest leads him.—*Penn.*

Neutrality in things good or evil is both odious and prejudicial, but in matters of an indifferent nature, is safe and commendable.—*Bp. Hall.*

The cold neutrality of an impartial judge.—*Burke.*

There is in some men a dispassionate neutrality of mind, which, though it generally passes for good temper, can neither gratify nor warm us; it must indeed be granted that these men can only negatively offend; but then it should also be remembered that they cannot positively please.—*Gréville.*

NEWS.—A map does not exhibit a more distinct view of the situation and boundaries of every country, than its news does a picture of the genius and morals of its inhabitants.—*Goldsmith.*

Each mind is pressed, and open every ear, to hear new tidings, though they no way joy us.—*Fairfax.*

He comes, the herald of a noisy world, news from all nations lumbering at his back; a messenger of grief perhaps to thousands, and a joy to some.—*Cowper.*

The news; our morning, noon, and evening cry; day after day repeats it till we die.—*C. Sprague.*

News, the manna of a day.—*Green.*

When ill news comes too late to be serviceable to your neighbor, keep it to yourself.—*Zimmermann.*

Ill news is winged with fate, and flies apace.—*Dryden.*

News are as welcome as the morning air.—*Chapman.*

Though it be honest, it is never good to bring bad news.—Give to a gracious message a host of tongues; but let ill tidings tell themselves when they be felt.—*Shakespeare.*

Evil news rides post, while good news bates.—*Milton.*

The first bringer of unwelcome news hath but a losing office.—*Shakespeare.*

NEWSPAPER.—A newspaper is the history for one day of the world in which we live, and with which we are consequently more concerned than with those which have passed away, and exist only in remembrance.—*Bp. Horne.*

I read the newspapers to see how God governs the world.—*John Newton.*

A newspaper should be the maximum of information, and the minimum of comment.—*Cobden.*

Newspapers are the schoolmasters of the common people—a greater treasure to them than uncounted millions of gold.—*H. W. Beecher.*

The careful reader of a few good newspapers can learn more in a year than most scholars do in their great libraries.—*F. B. Sanborn.*

Newspapers are the world's cyclopædia of life; telling us everything from every quarter of the globe.—They are a universal whispering gallery for mankind, only their whispers are sometimes thunders.—*Tryon Edwards.*

Newspapers should be news-carriers, not news-makers.—There is truth and entertainment enough to print, without fiction or falsehood, and to publish the latter is to betray the former.—*C. Simmons.*

The press is good or evil according to the character of those who direct it.—It is a mill that grinds all that is put into its hopper.—Fill the hopper with poisoned grain and it will grind it to meal, but there is death in the bread.—*Bryant.*

In these times we fight for ideas, and newspapers are our fortresses.—*Heine.*

The newspaper is the great educator of the nineteenth century. There is no force compared with it. It is book, pulpit, platform, forum, all in one. And there is not an interest—religious, literary, commercial, scientific, agricultural, or mechanical—that is not within its grasp. All our churches, and schools, and colleges, and asylums, and art galleries feel the quaking of the printing press.—*Talmage.*

The follies, vices, and consequent miseries of multitudes, displayed in a newspaper, are so many admonitions and warnings, so many beacons, continually burning, to turn others from the rocks on which they have been shipwrecked. What more powerful dissuasive from suspicion, jealousy, and anger, than the story of one friend murdered by another in a duel? What caution likely to be more effectual against gambling and profligacy than the mournful relation of an execution, or the fate of a despairing suicide? What finer lecture on the necessity of economy than an auction of estates, houses, and furniture? Talk they of morals? There is no need of Hutcheson, Smith, or Paley. Only take a newspaper, and consider it well; read it, and it will instruct thee.—*Bp. Horne.*

A journalist is a grumbler, a censurer, a giver of advice, a regent of sovereigns, a tutor of nations. Four hostile newspapers are more to be feared than a thousand bayonets.—*Napoleon.*

The newspaper press is the people's university.—Half the readers of Christendom read little else.—*J. Parton.*

Before this century shall run out, journalism will be the whole press. Mankind will write their book day by day, hour by hour, page by page. Thought will spread abroad with the rapidity of light, instantly conceived, instantly written, instantly understood at the extremities of the earth, it will spread from pole to pole, suddenly burning with the fervor of soul which made it burst forth; it will be the reign of the human mind in all its plenitude; it will not have time to ripen, to accumulate in the form of a book; the book will arrive too late; the only book possible from day to day is a newspaper.—*Lamartine.*

Of all the amusements that can possibly be imagined for a hard-working man, after a day's toil, or in its intervals, there is nothing like reading an entertaining newspaper. It relieves his home of its dullness or sameness, and transports him to a gayer and livelier and more diversified and interesting scene.—It accompanies him in his next day's work, and if the paper be anything above the very idlest and lightest, it gives him something to think of besides the mechanical drudgery of his every-day occupation—something he can enjoy while absent, and look forward with pleasure to return to.—*Sir J. Herschell.*

The newspaper is one of the foremost wonders of the modern world. The family that does not take, and carefully read, at least one newspaper, is not living in the nineteenth century.—*J. A. Broadus.*

As a mental discipline the reading of newspapers is hurtful.—What can be worse for the mind than to think of forty things in ten minutes.—*T. T. Munger.*

These papers of the day have uses more adequate to the purposes of common life than more pompous and durable volumes.—*Johnson.*

This folio of four pages, what is it but a map of busy life—its fluctuations, and its vast concerns?—*Cowper.*

They are the abstract and brief chronicles of the time, to show virtue her own image; scorn, her own features; and the very age and body of the time, his form and pressure.—*Shakespeare.*

Newspapers will ultimately engross all literature—there will be nothing else published but newspapers.—*Lamartine.*

It seems really as if our newspapers were busy to spread superstition. Omens and dreams, and prodigies are recorded, as if they were worth minding. The increasing fashion for printing wonderful tales of crimes and accidents is worse than ridiculous, as it corrupts both the public taste and morals. It multiplies fables and crimes, and thus makes shocking things familiar while it withdraws popular attention from familiar truth, because it is not shocking. Surely, extraordinary events have not the best title to our studious attention. To study nature or man, we ought to know things that are in the ordinary course, not the unaccountable things that happen out of it.—*Fisher Ames.*

NICKNAMES.—A nickname is the heaviest stone the devil can throw at a man.—*Anon.*

A good name will wear out; a bad one may be turned; a nickname lasts forever.—*Zimmermann.*

Nicknames stick to people, and the most ridiculous are the most adhesive. —*Haliburton.*

Names alone mock destruction; they survive the doom of all creation.—*Trevanion.*

There is also an evil name or report, light, indeed, and easy to raise, but difficult to carry, and still more difficult to get rid of.—*Hesiod.*

NIGHT.—The day is done, and darkness falls from the wings of night.—*Longfellow.*

Earth, turning from the sun, brings night to man.—*Young.*

In her starry shade of dim and solitary loveliness, I learn the language of another world.—*Byron.*

This sacred shade and solitude, what is it?—It is the felt presence of the Deity.—Few are the faults we flatter when alone; vice sinks in her allurements, in ungilt, and looks, like other objects, black by night.—By night an atheist half believes a God.—*Young.*

The night is made for tenderness so still that the low whisper, scarcely audible, is heard like music, and so deeply pure that the fond thought is chastened as it springs and on the lip is made holy.—*N. P. Willis.*

The contemplation of night should lead to elevating rather than to depressing ideas. Who can fix his mind on transitory and earthly things, in presence of those glittering myriads of worlds; and who can dread death or solitude in the midst of this brilliant, animated universe, composed of countless suns and worlds, all full of light and life and motion?—*Richter.*

Night's silent reign had robbed the world of light, to lend, in lieu, a greater benefit, repose and sleep, when every mortal whom care or grief permitted, took their rest.—*Thomas May.*

Why does the evening, why does the night, put warmer love in our hearts?—Is it the nightly pressure of helplessness?—Or is it the exalting separation from the turmoils of life, that veiling of the world in which, for the soul, nothing remains but souls?—*Richter.*

Wisdom mounts her zenith with the stars.—*Mrs. Barbauld.*

Quiet night, that brings rest to the

laborer, is the outlaw's day, in which he rises early to do wrong, and when his work is ended, dares not sleep.—*Massinger.*

Darkness has divinity for me; it strikes thought inward; it drives back the soul to settle on herself, our point supreme! There lies our theater; there sits our judge. Darkness the curtain drops o'er life's dull scene; 'tis the kind hand of Providence stretched out 'twixt man and vanity: 'tis reason's reign, and virtue's too; these tutelary shades are man's asylum from the tainted throng. Night is the good man's friend, and guardian too; it no less rescues virtue, than inspires.—*Young.*

How absolute, and omnipotent is the silence of the night! And yet the stillness seems almost audible.—From all the measureless depths of air around us, comes a half sound, a half whisper, as if we could hear the crumbling and falling away of earth and all created things in the great miracle of nature, decay and reproduction ever beginning, never ending—the gradual lapse and running of the sand in the great hourglass of time.—*Longfellow.*

Oh, treacherous night! thou lendest thy ready veil to every treason, and teeming mischiefs thrive beneath thy shade.—*A. Hill.*

Under thy mantle black, there hidden lie, light-shunning theft, and traitorous intent, abhorred bloodshed, and vile felony, shameful deceit, and danger imminent, foul horror, and eke hellish dreriment.—*Spenser.*

How sweet and soothing is this hour of calm! I thank thee, night! for thou hast chased away these horrid bodements which, amidst the throng, I could not dissipate: and with the blessing of thy benign and quiet influence now will I to my couch, although to rest is almost wronging such a night as this.—*Byron.*

The worm of conscience is the companion of the owl.—The light is shunned by sinners and evil spirits only.—*Schiller.*

NOBILITY.—(See "RANK.")

The original of all men is the same, and virtue is the only nobility.—*Seneca.*

Nature's noblemen are everywhere, in town and out of town, gloved and rough-handed, rich and poor.—Prejudice against a lord because he is a lord, is losing the chance of finding a good fellow, as much as prejudice against a ploughman because he is a ploughman.—*N. P. Willis.*

Nobility should be elective, not hereditary.—*Zimmermann.*

Talent and worth are the only eternal grounds of distinction. To these the Almighty has affixed his everlasting patent of nobility. Knowledge and goodness—these make degrees in heaven, and they must be the graduating scale of a true democracy.—*Miss Sedgwick.*

Nobility, without virtue, is a fine setting without a gem.—*Jane Porter.*

Whoe'er amid the sons of reason, valor, liberty, and virtue, displays distinguished merit, is a noble of nature's own creating.—*Thomson.*

All nobility, in its beginnings, was somebody's natural superiority.—*Emerson.*

I can make a lord, but only the Almighty can make a gentleman.—*James I.*

Titles of honor add not to his worth, who is an honor to his title.—*Ford.*

If a man be endued with a generous mind, this is the best kind of nobility.—*Plato.*

Nobility is a graceful ornament to the civil order. It is the Corinthian capital of polished society. It is indeed one sign of a liberal and benevolent mind to incline to it with some sort of partial propensity.—*Burke.*

Fishwomen cry noble oysters. They certainly are full as noble as any family blazoned out in Collin's peerage. If not of as ancient an house, of as old a bed at least. And to show their richness too, pearls and they are congenial.—*Sterne.*

He who is lord of himself, and exists upon his own resources, is a noble but a rare being.—*Brydges.*

It is better to be nobly remembered, than nobly born.—*Ruskin.*

No man can ever be noble who thinks meanly or contemptuously of himself, and no man can ever be noble who thinks first and only of himself.—*W. H. Dollinger.*

The best school of nobility is the imitation of Christ.—*F. D. Huntington.*

We must have kings, we must have nobles; nature is always providing such in every society, only let us have the real instead of the titular. In every society, some are born to rule, and some to advise. The chief is the chief, all the world over, only not his cap and plume. It is only dislike of the pretender which makes men sometimes unjust to the true and finished man.—*Emerson.*

Nobility is a river that sets with a constant and undeviating current directly into the great Pacific Ocean of time; but, unlike all other rivers, it is more grand at its source than at its termination.—*Colton.*

Virtue is the first title of nobility.—*Molière.*

True nobility is derived from virtue, not from birth.—Title may be purchased, but virtue is the only coin that makes the bargain valid.—*Burton.*

It seems to me 'tis only noble to be good.—*Tennyson.*

It is not wealth, nor ancestry, but honorable conduct and a noble disposition that make men great.—*Ovid.*

A fool, indeed, has great need of a title; it teaches men to call him count or duke, and thus forget his proper name of fool.—*J. Crown.*

NOISE.—(See "LOQUACITY" and "SPEECH.")

It is with narrow-souled people as with narrow-necked bottles; the less they have in them, the more noise they make in pouring it out.—*Pope.*

Those orators who give us much noise and many words, but little argument, and less sense, and who are most loud when least lucid, should take a lesson from nature. She often gives us lightning without thunder, but never thunder without lightning.

When I was a child I used to think it was the thunder that killed people; as I grew older I found it was only the lightning that struck, and the noise of thunder was only noise.—*Anon.*

NONSENSE.—I find that nonsense, at times, is singularly refreshing.—*Talleyrand.*

Nonsense is to sense, as shade to light; it heightens effect.—*F. Saunders.*

A little nonsense, now and then, is relished by the wisest men.—*Anon.*

A careless song, with a little nonsense in it, now and then, does not misbecome a monarch.—*Horace Walpole.*

Nonsense and noise will oft prevail, when honor and affection fail.—*Lloyd.*

Hudibras has defined nonsense, as Cowley does wit, by negatives. Nonsense, says he, is that which is neither true nor false. These two great properties of nonsense, which are essential to it, give it such a peculiar advantage over all other writings, that it is incapable of being either answered or contradicted. If it affirms anything, you cannot lay hold of it; or if it denies, you cannot refute it. In a word, there are greater depths and obscurities, greater intricacies and perplexities in an elaborate and well-written piece of nonsense, than in the most abstruse and profound tract of school divinity.—*Addison.*

To write or talk concerning any subject, without having previously taken the pains to understand it, is a breach of the duty which we owe to ourselves, though it may be no offence against the laws of the land. The privilege of talking and even publishing nonsense is necessary in a free state; but the more sparingly we make use of it the better.—*Coleridge.*

Those who best know human nature will acknowledge most fully what a strength light hearted nonsense gives to a hard working man.

NOVELS.—The habitual indulgence in such reading, is a silent, ruining mischief.—*Hannah More.*

Three-fourths of the popular novels of the day enfeeble the intellect, impoverish the imagination, vulgarize the taste and style, give false or distorted views of life and human nature, and, which is worst of all, waste that precious time which should be given to solid mental improvement.—*Greyson Letters.*

Above all things, never let your son touch a novel of romance. How delusive, how destructive are those pictures of consummate bliss! They teach the youthful to sigh after beauty and happiness that never existed; to despise the little good that fortune has mixed in our cup, by expecting more than she ever gave; and in general—take the word of a man who has seen the world, and studied it more by experience than by precept—take my word for it, I say, that such books teach us very little of the world.—*Goldsmith.*

To the composition of novels and romances, nothing is necessary but paper, pens, and ink, with the manual capacity of using them.—*Fielding.*

Novels are sweet. All people with healthy literary appetites love them—almost all women and a vast number of clever, hard-headed men.—Judges, bishops, chancellors, mathematicians are notorious novel readers, as well as young boys and sweet girls, and their kind and tender mothers.—*Thackeray.*

A little grain of the romance is no ill ingredient to preserve and exalt the dignity of human nature, without which it is apt to degenerate into everything that is sordid, vicious, and low.—*Swift.*

Fiction is a potent agent for good in the hands of the good; and so it may be a potent agent for evil, according to its character and the character of its readers.

We must have books for recreation and entertainment, as well as for instruction and for business; the former are agreeable, the latter useful, and the human mind requires both. The canon law and the codes of Justinian shall have due honor and reign at the universities, but Homer and Virgil need not therefore be banished. We will cultivate the olive and the vine, but without eradicating the myrtle and the rose.—*Balzac.*

A good novel should be, and generally is, a magnifying or diminishing glass of life. It may lessen or enlarge what it reflects, but the general features of society are faithfully reproduced by it. If a man reads such works with intelligent interest, he may learn almost as much of the world from his library as from the clubs and drawing-rooms of St. James.—*Bulwer.*

The novel, in its best form, I regard as one of the most powerful engines of civilization ever invented.—*Sir J. Herschel.*

It cannot but be injurious to the human mind never to be called into effort; the habit of receiving pleasure without any exertion of thought, by the mere excitement of curiosity and sensibility, may be justly ranked among the worst effects of habitual novel reading. Like idle morning visitors, the brisk and breathless periods hurry in and hurry off in quick and profitless succession—each, indeed, for the moment of its stay preventing the pain of vacancy, while it indulges the love of sloth; but, altogether, they leave the mistress of the house—the soul—flat and exhausted, incapable of attending to her own concerns, and unfitted for the conversation of more rational guests.—*Coleridge.*

The importance of the romantic element does not rest upon conjecture. Pleasing testimonies abound. Hannah More traced her earliest impressions of virtue to works of fiction; and Adam Clark gives a list of tales that won his boyish admiration. Books of entertainment led him to believe in a spiritual world; and he felt sure that he would have been a coward, but for romances. He declared that he had learned more of his duty to God, his neighbor, and himself, from Robinson Crusoe than from all the books, except the Bible, that were known to his youth.—*Willmott.*

Novels may teach us as wholesome a moral as the pulpit. There are "sermons in stones," in healthy books, and "good in everything."—*Colton.*

Writers of novels and romances in general bring a double loss on their readers,—they rob them both of their time and money; representing men, manners, and things, that never have been, nor are likely to be; either confounding or perverting history and truth, inflating the mind, or committing violence upon the understanding.—*Mary Wortley Montague.*

Lessons of wisdom have never such power over us as when they are wrought into the heart through the groundwork of a story which engages the passions. Is it that we are like iron, and must first be heated before we can be wrought upon? Or is the heart so in love with deceit, that where a true report will not reach it, we must cheat it with a fable in order to come at the truth?—*Sterne.*

Legitimately produced, and truly inspired, fiction interprets humanity, informs the understanding, and quickens the affections. It reflects ourselves, warns us against prevailing social follies, adds rich specimens to our cabinets of character, dramatizes life for the unimaginative, daguerreotypes it for the unobservant, multiplies experience for the isolated or inactive, and cheers age, retirement, and invalidism with an available and harmless solace.—*Tuckerman.*

Novels do not force their readers to sin, but only instruct them how to sin.—*Zimmermann.*

We gild our medicines with sweets; why not clothe truth and morals in pleasant garments as well?—*Chamfort.*

To the romance writers of his time, Nicole gave the title of public poisoners, and the same title might well be applied to a large class of modern novels.

Novel reading tends to destroy a relish for history, philosophy, and other useful knowledge. Novels give false notions of life, which are dangerous and injurious.—*Beattie.*

No habitual reader of the common run of novels can love the Bible or any other book that demands thought, or inculcates the serious duties of life. He dwells in a region of imagination, where he is disgusted with the plainness and simplicity of truth, and with the sober realities that demand his attention as a rational and immortal being, and an accountable subject of God's government.

Novels are mean imitations of literature, and usually the poorest part of it. They devour much precious time, and, what is worse, have a bad effect upon mind and morals. Their fanciful, distorted, and exaggerated sketches of life tend to vitiate and corrupt the taste, and to excite expectations that can never be fulfilled.—*Varle.*

NOVELTY.—Novelty is the great parent of pleasure.—*South.*

It is not only old and early impressions that deceive us; the charms of novelty have the same power.—*Pascal.*

The earth was made so various, that the mind of desultory man, studious of change, and pleased with novelty, might be indulged.—*Cowper.*

The enormous influence of novelty—the way in which it quickens observation, sharpens sensation, and exalts sentiment—is not half enough taken note of by us, and is to me a very sorrowful matter. And yet, if we try to obtain perpetual change, change itself will become monotonous; and then we are reduced to that old despair, "If water chokes, what will you drink after it?" The two points of practical wisdom in the matter are, first, to be content with as little novelty as possible at a time; and secondly, to preserve, as much as possible, the sources of novelty.—*Ruskin.*

Such is the nature of novelty that where anything pleases it becomes doubly agreeable if new; but if it displeases, it is doubly displeasing on that very account.—*Hume.*

Novelty has charms that our minds can hardly withstand. The most valuable things, if they have for a long while appeared among us, do not make any impression as they are good, but give us a distaste as they are old. But when the influence of this fantastical humor is over, the same men or things will come to be admired again, by a happy return of our good taste.—*Thackeray.*

All, with one consent, praise newborn gauds, though they are made and molded of things past.—*Shakespeare.*

New customs, though they be never so ridiculous, nay, let them be unmanly, yet are followed.—*Shakespeare.*

Curiosity, from its nature, is a very active principle; it quickly runs over the greatest part of its objects, and soon exhausts the variety common to be met with in nature. Some degree of novelty must be one of the materials in almost every instrument which works upon the mind; and curiosity blends itself, more or less, with all our pleasures.—*Burke.*

Of all the passions that possess mankind, the love of novelty rules most the mind; in search of this from realm to realm we roam, our fleets come fraught with every folly home.—*Foote.*

In science, as in common life, we frequently see that a novelty in system, or in practise, cannot be duly appreciated till time has sobered the enthusiasm of its advocates.—*Maud.*

Before I translated the New Testament out of the Greek, all longed after it; when it was done, their longing lasted scarce four weeks. Then they desired the books of Moses; when I had translated these, they had enough thereof in a short time. After that, they would have the Psalms; of these they were soon weary, and desired other books. So it will be with the book of Ecclesiastes, which they now long for, and about which I have taken great pains. All is acceptable until our giddy brains be satisfied; afterwards we let familiar things lie, and seek after new. —*Luther.*

O

OATHS.—Nay, but weigh well what you presume to swear.—Oaths are of dreadful weight; and if they are false, draw down damnation.—*Overbury.*

Rash oaths, whether kept or broken, frequently lead to guilt.—*Johnson.*

Recognized probity is the surest of all oaths.—*Mad. Necker.*

It is a great sin to swear unto a sin, but greater sin to keep a sinful oath.—*Shakespeare.*

Of all men, a philosopher should be no swearer; for an oath, which is the end of controversies in law, cannot determine any here, where reason only must decide.—*Sir Thomas Browne.*

Not for all the sun sees, or the close earth wombs, or the profound sea hides in unknown fathoms, break thou thine oath.—*Shakespeare.*

OBEDIENCE.—The first law that ever God gave to man, was a law of obedience; it was a commandment pure and simple, wherein man had nothing to inquire after or to dispute, for as much as to obey is the proper office of a rational soul acknowledging a heavenly superior and benefactor.—From obedience and submission spring all other virtues, as all sin does from self-opinion and self-will.—*Montaigne.*

No principle is more noble, as there is none more holy, than that of a true obedience.—*H. Giles.*

No man doth safely rule but he that

hath learned gladly to obey.—*Thomas à Kempis.*

It is vain thought to flee from the work that God appoints us, for the sake of finding a greater blessing, instead of seeking it where alone it is to be found —in loving obedience.—*George Eliot.*

Thirty years of our Lord's life are hidden in these words of the gospel: "He was subject unto them."—*Bossuet.*

Let the ground of all religious actions be obedience; examine not why it is commanded, but observe it because it is commanded. True obedience neither procrastinates nor questions.—*Quarles.*

Obedience to truth known, is the king's highway to that which is still beyond us.

Obedience is the mother of success and is wedded to safety.—*Æschylus.*

Let them obey that know not how to rule.—*Shakespeare.*

Let thy child's first lesson be obedience, and the second may be what thou wilt.—*Fuller.*

Filial obedience is the first and greatest requisite of a state; by this we become good subjects to our rulers, capable of behaving with just subordination to our superiors, and grateful dependants on heaven. By this we become good magistrates; for early submission is the truest lesson to those who would learn to rule. By this the whole state may be said to resemble one family, of which the monarch is the protector, father, and friend.—*Goldsmith.*

Obedience to God is the most infallible evidence of sincere and supreme love to him.—*Emmons.*

We are born subjects, and to obey God is perfect liberty. He that does this shall be free, safe, and happy.—*Seneca.*

Wicked men obey from fear; good men, from love.—*Aristotle.*

To obey God in some things, and not in others, shows an unsound heart.— Childlike obedience moves toward every command of God, as the needle points where the loadstone draws.—*T. Watson.*

Doing the will of God leaves me no time for disputing about his plans.—*G. Macdonald.*

Obedience is not truly performed by

the body, if the heart is dissatisfied.—
Saadi.

One very common error misleads the
opinion of mankind, that authority is
pleasant, and submission painful. In
the general course of human affairs the
very reverse of this is nearer to the
truth.—Command is anxiety; obedience
is ease.—*Paley.*

How will you find good? It is not a
thing of choice; it is a river that flows
from the foot of the invisible throne,
and flows by the path of obedience.—
George Eliot.

OBLIGATION.—What do I owe to
my times, to my country, to my neighbors, to my friends?—Such are the
questions which a virtuous man ought
often to ask himself.—*Lavater.*

Man owes not only his services, but
himself to God.—*Secker.*

To owe an obligation to a worthy
friend, is a happiness, and can be no
disparagement.—*Charron.*

Obligation is thraldom, and thraldom
is hateful.—*Hobbes.*

To feel oppressed by obligation is
only to prove that we are incapable
of a proper sentiment of gratitude.—
To receive favors from the unworthy
is to admit that our selfishness is
superior to our pride.—*Simms.*

We are always much better pleased
to see those whom we have obliged, than
those who have obliged us.—*Rochefoucauld.*

It is safer to affront some people than
to oblige them; for the better a man
deserves, the worse they will speak of
him; as if the professing of open hatred
to their benefactors were an argument
that they lie under no obligation to
him.—*Seneca.*

Most men remember obligations, but
not often to be grateful; the proud are
made sour by the remembrance and the
vain silent.—*Simms.*

We are under solemn obligations to
the children of those who have loved
us.—*Poincelot.*

It is well known to all great men,
that by conferring an obligation they
do not always procure a friend, but are
certain of creating many enemies.—
Fielding.

An extraordinary haste to discharge
an obligation, is a sort of ingratitude.—
Rochefoucauld.

In some there is a kind of graceless
modesty that makes a man ashamed of
requiting an obligation, because it is a
confession that he has received one.—
Seneca.

OBLIVION.—What's past, and what's
to come, is strewed with husks and formless ruin of oblivion.—*Shakespeare.*

Oblivion is the flower that grows best
on graves.—*George Sand.*

In the swallowing gulf of dark forgetfulness and deep oblivion.—*Shakespeare.*

Oblivion is a second death, which
great minds dread more than the first.
—*De Boufflers.*

Fame is a vapor; popularity an accident; riches take wings; the only certainty is oblivion.—*Horace Greeley.*

Oblivion is the rule, and fame the exception of humanity.—*Rivarol.*

How soon men and events are forgotten! Each generation lives in a different world.

The oblivions of time will be the rem-
iniscences of eternity.—*C. Simmons.*

OBSCURITY.—(See "STYLE.")

The obscurity of a writer is generally
in proportion to his incapacity.—*Quintilian.*

How many people make themselves
abstract to appear profound! — The
greatest part of abstract terms are shadows that hide a vacuum.—*Joubert.*

Objects imperfectly discerned take
forms from the hope or fear of the beholder.—*Johnson.*

Unintelligible language is a lantern
without a light.

Blindness of heart beclouds the understanding, conscience, memory, and
indeed all the intellectual powers, and
throws a mischievous obscurity over
theological, moral, and even classical
science.—*C. Simmons.*

There is no defence against reproach
but obscurity; it is a kind of concomitant to greatness, as satires and invectives were an essential part of a Roman
triumph.—*Addison.*

Lost in the dreary shades of dull obscurity.—*Shenstone.*

Obscurity and innocence, twin sisters, escape temptations which would pierce their gossamer armor in contact with the world.—*Chamfort.*

Full many a gem of purest ray serene the dark unfathomed caves of ocean bear: full many a flower is born to blush unseen, and waste its sweetness on the desert air.—*Gray.*

Thus let me live, unseen, unknown; thus unlamented let me die; steal from the world, and not a stone tell where I lie.—*Pope.*

OBSERVATION.—I pity the man who can travel from Dan to Beersheba, and cry, 'tis all barren—and so it is, and so is all the world to him who will not cultivate the fruits it offers.—*Sterne.*

A right judgment draws us a profit from all things we see.—*Shakespeare.*

Perhaps there is no property in which men are more distinguished from each other, than in the various degrees in which they possess the faculty of observation. The great herd of mankind pass their lives in listless inattention and indifference as to what is going on around them, being perfectly content to satisfy the mere cravings of nature, while those who are destined to distinction have a lynx-eyed vigilance that nothing can escape. You see nothing of the Paul Pry in them; yet they know all that is passing, and keep a perfect reckoning, not only of every interesting passage, but of all the characters of the age who have any concern in them.—*William Wirt.*

He alone is an acute observer, who can observe minutely without being observed.—*Lavater.*

It is the close observation of little things which is the secret of success in business, in art, in science, and in every pursuit in life. Human knowledge is but an accumulation of small facts, made by successive generations of men,—the little bits of knowledge and experience carefully treasured up and growing at length into a mighty pyramid.—*S. Smiles.*

Observation made in the cloister or in the desert, will generally be as obscure as the one and as barren as the other; but he that would paint with his pencil must study originals, and not be over fearful of a little dust.—*Colton.*

Each one sees what he carries in his heart.—*Goethe.*

Shakespeare says, we are creatures that look before and after; the more surprising that we do not look round a little, and see what is passing under our very eyes.—*Carlyle.*

To behold is not necessarily to observe, and the power of comparing and combining is only to be obtained by education. It is much to be regretted that habits of exact observation are not cultivated in our schools; to this deficiency may be traced much of the fallacious reasoning and the false philosophy which prevails.—*W. Humboldt.*

An observant man, in all his intercourse with society and the world, constantly and unperceived marks on every person and thing the figure expressive of its value, and therefore, on meeting that person or thing, knows instantly what kind and degree of attention to give it.—This is to make something of experience.—*John Foster.*

General observations drawn from particulars are the jewels of knowledge, comprehending great store in a little room.—*Locke.*

OBSTINACY.—An obstinate man does not hold opinions, but they hold him; for when he is once possest with an error it is like a devil, only cast out with great difficulty. Whatsoever he lays hold on, like a drowning man, he never loses, though it do but help to sink him the sooner. His ignorance is abrupt and inaccessible, impregnable both by art and nature, and will hold out to the last, though it has nothing but rubbish to defend.—*Butler.*

Obstinacy is will asserting itself without being able to justify itself.—It is persistence without a reasonable motive. —It is the tenacity of self-love substituted for that of reason and conscience. —*Amiel.*

Obstinacy and contradiction are like a paper kite: they are only kept up so long as you pull against them.

Obstinacy is the strength of the weak. Firmness founded upon principle, upon truth and right, order and law, duty and generosity, is the obstinacy of sages.— *Lavater.*

Obstinacy and vehemency in opinion are the surest proofs of stupidity.—*Barton.*

Obstinacy and heat in argument are surest proofs of folly. Is there anything so stubborn, obstinate, disdainful, contemplative, grave, or serious, as an ass?—*Montaigne.*

Obstinacy is certainly a great vice; and in the changeful state of political affairs is frequently the cause of great mischief. It happens, however, very unfortunately, that almost the whole line of the great and masculine virtues—constancy, gravity, magnanimity, fortitude, fidelity, and firmness—are closely allied to this disagreeable quality, of which you have so just an abhorrence; and in their excess, all these virtues very easily fall into it.—*Burke.*

Obstinacy is ever most positive when it is most in the wrong.—*Mad. Necker.*

Firmness is adherence to truth and duty is generally most decided when most intelligent and conscientious, and is sometimes mistaken for obstinacy by those who do not comprehend its nature and motive.—*Tryon Edwards.*

Obstinacy and contention are common qualities, most appearing in, and best becoming, a mean and illiterate soul.—*Montaigne.*

There are few, very few, that will own themselves in a mistake.—*Swift.*

The slighter and more inconsistent the opinions of the obstinate man are, the faster he holds them, otherwise they would fall asunder of themselves: for opinions that are false he holds with more strictness and assurance than those that are true.—He is resolved to understand no man's reason but his own, because he finds no man can understand his but himself. His wits are like a sack, which the proverb says, is tied faster before it is full, than when it is; and his opinions are like plants that grow upon rocks, that stick fast, though they have no rooting. His understanding is hardened like Pharaoh's heart, and is proof against all sorts of judgments whatsoever.—*Butler.*

OCCUPATION.—(See *" Time."*)

Indolence is a delightful but distressing state; we must be doing something to be happy. Action is no less necessary than thought to the instinctive tendencies of the human frame.—*Hazlitt.*

The great happiness of life, I find, after all, to consist in the regular discharge of some mechanical duty.—*Schiller.*

Every Egyptian was commanded by law annually to declare by what means he maintained himself; and if he omitted to do it, or gave no satisfactory account of his way of living, he was punishable with death. This law Solon brought from Egypt to Athens, where it was inviolably observed as a most equitable regulation.—*Herodotus.*

No thoroughly occupied man was ever yet very miserable.—*L. E. Landon.*

I have lived to know that the great secret of human happiness is this: never suffer your energies to stagnate. The old adage of "too many irons in the fire," conveys an abominable lie. You cannot have too many—poker, tongs, and all—keep them all going.—*Adam Clarke.*

It was a maxim with the Jews, "that he that did not bring up his son to some honest calling, brought him up to be a thief."

Temptation rarely comes in working hours. It is in their leisure time that men are made or marred.—*W. M. Taylor.*

It is an undoubted truth, that the less one has to do the less time one finds to do it in. One yawns, one procrastinates, one can do it when one will, and, therefore, one seldom does it all; whereas those who have a great deal of business, must (to use a vulgar expression) buckle to it; and then they always find time enough to do' it in.—*Chesterfield.*

He who will not apply himself to business, evidently discovers that he means to get his bread by cheating, stealing, or begging, or else is wholly void of reason.—*Ischomachus.*

Occupation is a necessity to the young. They love to be busy about something, however trifling; and if not directed to some useful employment will soon engage in something that is evil, thus verifying the old proverb, "That idleness is the mother of mischief."

Let parents who hate their offspring

rear them to hate labor and to inherit riches, and before long they will be stung by every vice, racked by its poison, and damned by its penalty.—*H. W. Beecher.*

Nature has made occupation a necessity to us; society makes it a duty; habit may make it a pleasure.—*Capelle.*

Most of the trades, professions, and ways of living among mankind, take their original either from the love of pleasure, or the fear of want. The former, when it becomes too violent, degenerates into luxury, and the latter into avarice.—*Addison.*

We protract the career of time by employment, we lengthen the duration of our lives by wise thoughts and useful actions. Life to him who wishes not to have lived in vain is thought and action.—*Zimmermann.*

The prosperity of a people is proportionate to the number of hands and minds usefully employed. To the community, sedition is a fever, corruption is a gangrene, and idleness is an atrophy. Whatever body or society wastes more than it acquires, must gradually decay; and every being that continues to be fed, and ceases to labor, takes away something from the public stock.—*Johnson.*

The crowning fortune of a man is to be born with a bias to some pursuit which finds him in employment and happiness.—*Emerson.*

Employment, which Galen calls "nature's physician," is so essential to human happiness that indolence is justly considered as the mother of misery.—*Burton.*

You cannot give an instance of any man who is permitted to lay out his own time, contriving not to have tedious hours.—*Johnson.*

You see men of the most delicate frames engaged in active and professional pursuits who really have no time for idleness. Let them become idle,— let them take care of themselves, let them think of their health,—and they die! The rust rots the steel which use preserves.—*Bulwer.*

Occupation is the scythe of time.— *Napoleon.*

Occupation is the necessary basis of all enjoyment.—*Leigh Hunt.*

Every base occupation makes one sharp in its practice, and dull in every other.—*Sir P. Sidney.*

Care is a sad disease; despondency a sadder, and discontent the saddest of the three: if we wish to be cured of all these together, next to seeking the divine support, the prescription is occupation.

The want of occupation is no less the plague of society, than of solitude.— *Rousseau.*

The busy have no time for tears.— *Byron.*

Cheerfulness is the daughter of employment; and I have known a man come home, in high spirits, from a funeral, merely because he has had the management of it.—*Bp. Horne.*

I take it to be a principal rule of life, not to be too much addicted to any one thing.—*Terence.*

Occupation was one of the pleasures of paradise, and we cannot be happy without it.—*Mrs. Jameson.*

Let a man choose what condition he will, and let him accumulate around him all the goods and gratifications seemingly calculated to make him happy in it; if that man is left at any time without occupation or amusement, and reflects on what he is, the meagre, languid felicity of his present lot will not bear him up. He will turn necessarily to gloomy anticipations of the future; and unless his occupation calls him out of himself, he is inevitably wretched.— *Pascal.*

The highest excellence is seldom attained in more than one vocation. The roads leading to distinction in separate pursuits diverge, and the nearer we approach the one, the farther we recede from the other.—*Bovee.*

Absence of occupation is not rest; a mind quite vacant, is a mind distressed. —*Cowper.*

OFFENCE.—Who fears to offend takes the first step to please.—*Cibber.*

At every trifle scorn to take offence: that always shows great pride, or little sense.—*Pope.*

Offences ought to be pardoned, for

few offend willingly, but only as led by some excitement.—*Hegesippus.*

A very small offence may be a just cause for great resentment; it is often much less the particular instance which is obnoxious to us, than the proof it carries with it of the general tenor and disposition of the mind from whence it sprung.—*Gréville.*

When any one has offended me, I try to raise my soul so high that the offence cannot reach it.—*Descartes.*

It is pride which plies the world with so much harshness and severity.—We are as rigorous to offences as if we had never offended.—*Blair.*

All is not offence that indiscretion finds, and dotage terms so.—*Shakespeare.*

OFFICE.—(See "AUTHORITY.")

When a king creates an office, Providence at once creates a fool to buy it. —*Colbert.*

When impious men bear sway, the post of honor is a private station.—*Shakespeare.*

Five things are requisite to a good officer—ability, clean hands, despatch, patience, and impartiality.—*Penn.*

It is the curse of service that preferment goes by letter and affection, not by the old gradation where each second stood heir to the first.—*Shakespeare.*

High office is like a pyramid; only two kinds of animals reach the summit, reptiles and eagles.—*D'Alembert.*

If ever this free people, if this government itself is ever utterly demoralized, it will come from this incessant human wriggle and struggle for office, which is but a way to live without work. —*Abraham Lincoln.*

The gratitude of place to expectants is a lively sense of future favors.— *Walpole.*

OLD AGE.—(See "AGE.")

We hope to grow old, yet we fear old age; that is, we are willing to live, and afraid to die.—*Bruyère.*

A comfortable old age is the reward of a well-spent youth; instead of its introducing dismal and melancholy prospects of decay. it should give us hopes

of eternal youth in a better world.— *Palmer.*

As I approve of a youth that has something of the old man in him, so I am no less pleased with an old man that has something of the youth. He that follows this rule, may be old in body, but can never be so in mind.— *Cicero.*

Some men are born old, and some never seem so. If we keep well and cheerful we are always young, and at last die in youth, even when years would count us old.—*Tryon Edwards.*

Old age has been charged with being insensible to pleasure and to the enjoyments arising from the gratification of the senses—a most blessed and heavenly effect, truly, if it eases us of what in youth was the sorest plague of life.— *Cicero.*

An old man who has lived in the exercise of virtue, looking back without a blush on his past days, and pointing to that better state where alone he can be perfectly rewarded, is a figure the most venerable that can well be imagined.— *Mackenzie.*

Though every old man has been young, and every young one hopes to be old, there seems to be a most unnatural misunderstanding between those two stages of life. This unhappy want of commerce arises from arrogance or exultation in youth, and irrational despondence or self-pity in age.—*Steele.*

There is a peculiar beauty about godly old age—the beauty of holiness. Husband and wife who have fought the world side by side, who have made common stock of joy or sorrow, and become aged together, are not unfrequently found curiously alike in personal appearance, in pitch and tone of voice, just as twin pebbles on the beach, exposed to the same tidal influences, are each other's *alter ego.*—*Alexander Smith.*

Woe to the man who becomes old without becoming wise; woe to him if this world shuts its door without the future having opened its doors to him.— *Tholuck.*

Youthful follies growing on old age, are like the few young shoots on the bare top of an old stump of an oak.— *John Foster.*

When men grow virtuous only in old

age, they are merely making a sacrifice to God of the devil's leavings.—*Swift.*

There is not a more repulsive spectacle than an old man who will not forsake the world which has already forsaken him.—*Tholuck.*

Old age is a tyrant who forbids, at the penalty of life, all the pleasures of youth.—*Rochefoucauld.*

Old age is wise for itself, but not for the community.—It is wise in declining new enterprises, for it has not the power or the time to execute them; wise in shrinking from difficulty, for it has not the strength to overcome it; wise in avoiding danger, for it lacks the faculty of ready and swift action by which dangers are parried and converted into advantages.—But this is not wisdom for mankind at large, by whom new enterprises must be undertaken, dangers met, and difficulties surmounted.—*Bryant.*

To know how to grow old is the master-work of wisdom, and one of the most difficult chapters in the great art of living.—*Amiel.*

OMNIPOTENCE.—Who guides below and rules above, the great disposer and the mighty king; than he none greater; next him none can be, or is, or was; supreme, he singly fills the throne. —*Horace.*

God, veiled in majesty, alone gives light and life to all; bids the great systems move, and changing seasons in their turns advance, unmoved, unchanged himself.—*Somerville.*

My faith hath no bed to sleep upon but omnipotency.—*Rutherford.*

OMNIPRESENCE.—Yes, thou art ever present, power divine; not circumscribed by time, nor fixed by space, confined to altars, nor to temples bound.— In wealth, in want, in freedom, or in chains, in dungeons or on thrones, the faithful find thee.—*Hannah More.*

Where one is present, God is the second, and where there are two, God is the third.—*Mahomet.*

God is everywhere, the God who framed mankind to be one mighty family, himself our father, and the world our home.—*Coleridge.*

"Tell me." said a heathen philosopher to a Christian. "where is God."—"First

tell me," said the other, "where he is not."

God oft descends to visit men, unseen, and through their habitations walks, to mark their doings.—*Milton.*

OMNISCIENCE.—We cannot too often think there is a never-sleeping eye, which reads the heart, and registers our thoughts.—*Bacon.*

In all thy actions, think God sees thee; and in all his actions labor to see him.—*Quarles.*

What can escape the eye of God, all seeing, or deceive his heart, omniscient! —*Milton.*

OPINION.—(See "JUDGMENT.")

All power, even the most despotic, rests ultimately on opinion.—*Hume.*

A man's opinions are generally of much more value than his arguments.— *O. W. Holmes.*

I will utter what I believe to-day, if it should contradict all I said yesterday. —*Wendell Phillips.*

There is something among men more capable of shaking despotic power than lightning, whirlwind, or earthquake; that is, the threatened indignation of the whole civilized world.—*Daniel Webster.*

It is more true to say that our opinions depend upon our lives and habits, than to say that our lives and habits depend on our opinions.—*F. W. Robertson.*

No errors of opinion can possibly be dangerous in a country where opinion is left free to grapple with them.—*Simms.*

Opinions are stronger than armies.—If they are founded in truth and justice, they will, in the end, prevail against the bayonets of infantry, the fire of artillery, and the charges of cavalry.— *Lord Palmerston.*

Opinion is the main thing which does good or harm in the world. It is our false opinions of things which ruin us.— *Marcus Antoninus.*

The world is governed much more by opinion than by laws. It is not the judgment of courts, but the moral judgment of individuals and masses of men, which is the chief wall of defence around property and life. With the progress of society, this power of opinion is taking the place of arms.—*Channing*.

The greater part of men have no opinion, still fewer an opinion of their own, well reflected and founded upon reason. —*Seume*.

What I admire in Columbus is not his having discovered a world, but his having gone to search for it on the faith of an opinion.—*Turgot*.

Our system of thought and opinion, is often only the history of our heart. Men do not so much will according to their reason, as reason according to their will.—*Fichte*.

Popular opinion is the greatest lie in the world.—*Carlyle*.

The feeble tremble before opinion, the foolish defy it, the wise judge it, the skillful direct it.—*Mad. Roland*.

As our inclinations, so our opinions.— *Goethe*.

Our opinions on all subjects are more largely formed by our sympathies than by carefully sifted evidence.

He that never changes his opinions, never corrects his mistakes, and will never be wiser on the morrow than he is to-day.—*Tryon Edwards*.

Predominant opinions are generally the opinions of the generation that is vanishing.—*Disraeli*.

Conscience, in most men, is but the anticipation of the opinions of others.— *Taylor's Statesman*.

Public opinion is, with multitudes, a second conscience; with some, the only one.—*W. R. Alger*.

I do not regret having braved public opinion, when I knew it was wrong and was sure it would be merciless.—*Horace Greeley*.

No liberal man would impute a charge of unsteadiness to another for having changed his opinion.—*Cicero*.

A statesman should follow public opinion as a coachman follows his horses; having firm hold on the reins, and guiding them.—*J. C. Hare*.

It is common to men to err; but it is only a fool that perseveres in his error; a wise man alters his opinion, a fool never.

Differences of opinion give me but little concern; but it is a real pleasure to

be brought into communication with any one who is in earnest, and who really looks to God's will as his standard of right and wrong, and judges of actions according to their greater or less conformity.—*Arnold*.

It is the inclination and tendency of the heart which finally determines the opinions of the mind.—*Luthardt*.

To form a correct judgment concerning the tendency of any doctrine we should look rather at the forms it bears in the disciples, than in the teacher, for he only made it; they are made by it. —*J. C. Hare*.

Nothing so obstinately stands in the way of all sorts of progress, as pride of opinion; while nothing is so foolish and baseless.—*J. G. Holland*.

Public opinion cannot do for virtue what it does for vice. It is the essence of virtue to look above opinion. Vice is consistent with, and very often strengthened by, entire subserviency to it.

The eyes of other people are the eyes that ruin us. If all but myself were blind, I should want neither fine clothes, fine houses, nor fine furniture.—*Franklin*.

We never are satisfied with our opinions, whatever we may pretend, till they are ratified and confirmed by the suffrages of the rest of mankind. We dispute and wrangle forever; we endeavor to get men to come to us, when we do not go to them.—*Sir J. Reynolds*.

"That was excellently observed," say I, when I read a passage in an author, where his opinion agrees with mine. When we differ, then I pronounce him to be mistaken.—*Swift*.

The same enthusiasm that dignifies a butterfly or a medal to the virtuoso and the antiquary, may convert controversy into quixotism, and present to the deluded imagination of the theological knight-errant, a barber's basin as Mambrino's helmet. The real value of any doctrine can only be determined by its influence on the conduct of man, with respect to himself, to his fellow-creatures, or to God.—*Percival*.

Opinions, like showers, are generated in high places, but they invariably descend into lower ones, and ultimately flow down to the people, as rain unto the sea.—*Colton.*

Opinion is that high and mighty dame which rules the world, and in the mind doth frame distastes or likings; for in the human race, she makes the fancy various as the face.—*J. Howell.*

Do not think of knocking out another person's brains because he differs in opinion from you. It would be as rational to knock yourself on the head because you differ from yourself ten years ago.—*Horace Mann.*

The masses procure their opinions ready made in open market.—*Colton.*

He who has no opinion of his own, but depends upon the opinion and taste of others, is a slave.—*Klopstock.*

Social opinion is like a sharp knife. There are foolish people who regard it only with terror, and dare not touch or meddle with it; there are more foolish people, who, in rashness or defiance, seize it by the blade, and get cut and mangled for their pains; and there are wise people, who grasp it discreetly and boldly by the handle, and use it to carve out their own purposes.—*Mrs. Jameson.*

Common opinions often conflict with common sense; for reason in most minds is no match for prejudices, a hydra whose heads grow faster than they can be cut off.—*E. Wigglesworth.*

Wind puffs up empty bladders; opinion, fools.—*Socrates.*

The men of the past had convictions, while we moderns have only opinions.—*H. Heine.*

Private opinion is weak, but public opinion is almost omnipotent.—*H. W. Beecher.*

Public opinion is a weak tyrant, compared with our private opinion.—What a man thinks of himself, that it is which determines, or rather indicates his fate.—*Thoreau.*

A confident expectation that no argument will be adduced that will change our opinions is very different from a resolution that none ever shall. We may print but not stereotype our opinions.—*Whately.*

To maintain an opinion because it is thine, and not because it is true, is to prefer thyself above the truth.—*Venning.*

Those who never retract their opinions love themselves more than they love truth.—*Joubert.*

There never was in the world two opinions alike, no more than two hairs or two grains. The most universal quality is diversity.—*Montaigne.*

It has been shrewdly said that when men abuse us, we should suspect ourselves, and when they praise us, them. It is a rare instance of virtue to despise censure which we do not deserve, and still more rare to despise praise, which we do. But that integrity that lives only on opinion would starve without it. —*Colton.*

The history of human opinion is scarcely anything more than the history of human errors.—*Voltaire.*

If a man should register all his opinions upon love, politics, religion, learning, etc., beginning from his youth, and so go on to old age, what a bundle of inconsistencies and contradictions would appear at last.—*Swift.*

One of the mistakes in the conduct of human life is, to suppose that other men's opinions are to make us happy.—*Burton.*

It is with true opinions which one has the courage to utter, as with pawns first advanced on the chessboard; they may be beaten, but they have inaugurated a game which must be won.—*Goethe.*

He who is master of all opinions can never be the bigot of any.—*W. R. Alger.*

The ambitious man grasps at opinion as necessary to his designs; the vain man sues for it as a testimony to his merit; the honest man demands it as his due; and most men consider it as necessary to their existence.—*Beccaria.*

Correct opinions, well established on any subject, are the best preservative against the seductions of error.—*Bp. Mant.*

The free expression of opinion, as experience has taught us, is the safety-valve of passion. The noise of the rushing steam, when it escapes, alarms the timid; but it is the sign that we are safe. The concession of reasonable privilege anticipates the growth of furious appetite.—*Gladstone.*

I could never divide myself from any man upon the difference of opinion, or be angry with his judgment for not agreeing in that from which, within a few days, I might dissent myself.—*Sir Thomas Browne.*

Do not despise the opinion of the world; you might as well say you do not care for the light of the sun, because you can use a candle.

Change of opinion is often only the progress of sound thought and growing knowledge; and though sometimes regarded as an inconsistency, it is but the noble inconsistency natural to a mind ever ready for growth and expansion of thought, and that never fears to follow where truth and duty may lead the way. —*Tryon Edwards.*

We think very few people sensible, except those who are of our opinion.— *Rochefoucauld.*

Fly no opinion because it is new, but strictly search, and after careful view, reject it if false, embrace it if 'tis true. —*Lucretius.*

When men first take up an opinion, and then seek for reasons for it, they must be contented with such as the absurdity of it will afford.—*South.*

No liberal man would impute a charge of unsteadiness to another for having changed his opinion.—*Cicero.*

A man cannot utter two or three sentences without disclosing to intelligent ears precisely where he stands in life and thought, whether in the kingdom of the senses and the understanding, or in that of ideas and imagination, or in the realm of intuitions and duty.— *Emerson.*

It is not only arrogant, but profligate, for a man to disregard the world's opinion of himself.—*Cicero.*

It is easy in the world to live after the world's opinion; it is easy in solitude to live after our own; but the great man is he who, in the midst of the crowd, keeps with perfect sweetness the independence of solitude.—*Emerson.*

We are too much inclined to underrate the power of moral influence, the influence of public opinion, and the influence of the principles to which great men—the lights of the world and of the present age—have given their sanction. —*Daniel Webster.*

In all things reason should prevail; it

is quite another thing to be stiff, than to be steady in an opinion.—*Penn.*

As for the differences of opinion upon speculative questions, if we wait till they are reconciled, the action of human affairs must be suspended forever.—But neither are we to look for perfection in any one man, nor for agreement among many.—*Junius.*

That the voice of the common people is the voice of God, is as full of falsehood as of commonness.—*A. Warwick.*

Among the best men are diversities of opinions; which should no more, in true reason, breed hatred, than one that loves black should be angry with him that is clothed in white; for thoughts are the very apparel of the mind.—*Sir P. Sidney.*

Statutes are mere milestones, telling how far yesterday's thought had travelled; and the talk of the sidewalk to-day is the law of the land.—With us, law is nothing unless close behind it stands a warm, living public opinion.— *Wendell Phillips.*

Provided we look to and satisfy our consciences, no matter for opinion; let me deserve well though I hear ill.— *Seneca.*

The opinions of men who think are always growing and changing, like living children.—*Hamerton.*

It is always considered as a piece of impertinence in England, if a man of less than two or three thousand a year has any opinions at all upon important subjects.—*Sydney Smith.*

We should always keep a corner of our heads open and free, that we may make room for the opinions of our friends. Let us have heart and head hospitality.—*Joubert.*

Error of opinion may be tolerated where reason is left free to combat it.— *Jefferson.*

An obstinate man does not hold opinions—they hold him.—*Bp. Butler.*

OPPORTUNITY.—There is a tide in the affairs of men, which, taken at the flood, leads on to fortune; omitted, all the voyage of their life is bound in shallows and in miseries; and we must take the current when it serves, or lose our ventures.—*Shakespeare.*

Chance opportunities make us known

to others, and still more to ourselves.—*Rochefoucauld.*

The secret of success in life, is for a man to be ready for his opportunity when it comes.—*Disraeli.*

Opportunity is rare, and a wise man will never let it go by him.—*Bayard Taylor.*

Great opportunities come to all, but many do not know they have met them.—The only preparation to take advantage of them, is simple fidelity to what each day brings.—*A. E. Dunning.*

Vigilance in watching opportunity; tact and daring in seizing upon opportunity; force and persistence in crowding opportunity to its utmost of possible achievement—these are the martial virtues which must command success.—*Austin Phelps.*

Our opportunities to do good are our talents.—*C. Mather.*

For truth and duty it is ever the fitting time; who waits until circumstances completely favor his undertaking, will never accomplish anything.—*Luther.*

To choose time is to save time; and an unseasonable motion is but beating the air.—*Bacon.*

If you want to succeed in the world you must make your own opportunities as you go on. The man who waits for some seventh wave to toss him on dry land will find that the seventh wave is a long time a coming. You can commit no greater folly than to sit by the roadside until some one comes along and invites you to ride with him to wealth or influence.—*John B. Gough.*

The golden moments in the stream of life rush past us, and we see nothing but sand; the angels come to visit us, and we only know them when they are gone.—*George Eliot.*

Next to knowing when to seize an opportunity, the most important thing in life is to know when to forego an advantage.—*Disraeli.*

Occasion may be the bugle call that summons an army to battle, but the blast of a bugle can never make soldiers nor win battles.—*J. A. Garfield.*

If sorrow could enter heaven, if a sigh could be heard there, or a tear roll down the cheek of a saint in light, it would be for lost opportunities, for the time

spent in neglect of God which might have been spent for his glory.—*Payson.*

There are no times in life when opportunity, the chance to be and do, gathers so richly about the soul as when it has to suffer. Then everything depends on whether the man turns to the lower or the higher helps. If he resorts to mere expedients and tricks the opportunity is lost. He comes out no richer nor greater; nay, he comes out harder, poorer, smaller for his pain. But, if he turns to God, the hour of suffering is the turning hour of his life.—*Phillips Brooks.*

Opportunity has hair in front; behind she is bald; if you seize her by the forelock, you may hold her, but, if suffered to escape, not Jupiter himself can catch her again.—*From the Latin.*

The sure way to miss success is to miss the opportunity.—*Chasles.*

Who makes quick use of the moment, is a genius of prudence.—*Lavater.*

Turning, for them who pass, the common dust of servile opportunity to gold.—*Wordsworth.*

What is opportunity to the man who can't use it? An unfecundated egg, which the waves of time wash away into nonentity.—*George Eliot.*

Every one has a fair turn to be as great as he pleases.—*Jeremy Collier.*

He who has opportunities to inspect the sacred moments of elevated minds, and seizes none, is a son of dullness; but he who turns those moments into ridicule, will betray with a kiss, and in embracing, murder.—*Lavater.*

A philosopher being asked what was the first thing necessary to win the love of a woman, answered: "Opportunity."—*Moore.*

Opportunity, sooner or later, comes to all who work and wish.—*Lord Stanley.*

"You will never "find" time for anything. If you want time you must make it.—*Charles Buxton.*

No man possesses a genius so commanding that he can attain eminence, unless a subject suited to his talents should present itself, and an opportunity occur for their development.—*Pliny.*

There sometimes wants only a stroke of fortune to discover numberless latent good or bad qualities, which would otherwise have been eternally concealed; as words written with a certain liquor appear only when applied to the fire.—*Gréville.*

Take all the swift advantage of the hours.—*Shakespeare.*

It is common to overlook what is near by keeping the eye fixed on something remote. In the same manner present opportunities are neglected and attainable good is slighted by minds busied in extensive ranges, and intent upon future advantages. Life, however short, is made shorter by waste of time.—*Johnson.*

Miss not the occasion; by the forelock take that subtle power, the never-halting time.—*Wordsworth.*

If we do not watch, we lose our opportunities; if we do not make haste, we are left behind; our best hours escape us, the worst are come. The purest part of our life runs first, and leaves only the dregs at the bottom; and that time which is good for nothing else we dedicate to virtue, and only propose to begin to live at an age that very few people arrive at.—*Seneca.*

There is need of a sprightly and vigilant soul to discern and to lay hold on favorable junctures; a man must look before him, descry opportunities at a distance, keep his eye constantly upon them, observe all the motions they make toward him, make himself ready for their approach, and when he sees his time, lay fast hold, and not let go again, till he has done his business.—*Charron.*

Many do with opportunities as children do at the seashore; they fill their little hands with sand, and then let the grains fall through, one by one, till all are gone.—*T. Jones.*

I can not commend to a business house any artificial plan for making men producers—any scheme for driving them into business-building. You must lead them through their self-interest.—*Charles H. Steinway.*

How oft the sight of means to do ill deeds, makes deeds ill done!—*Shakespeare.*

When heaven half opens its arms, he who is faint-hearted deserves not anything.—It is this want of faith that often keeps heaven from bestowing its blessings; and even when they come

down, it is apt to send them away.—*Corneille.*

To be a great man it is necessary to turn to account all opportunities.—*Rochefoucauld.*

A wise man will make more opportunities than he finds.—*Bacon.*

How often do we sigh for opportunities of doing good, whilst we neglect the openings of Providence in little things, which would frequently lead to the accomplishment of most important usefulness!—*Crabbe.*

The best men are not those who have waited for chances but who have taken them; besieged the chance; conquered the chance; and made chance the servitor.—*E. H. Chapin.*

The public man needs but one patron, namely, the lucky moment.—*Bulwer.*

Opportunity to statesmen, is as the just degree of heat to chemists; it perfects all the work.—*Suckling.*

Do not wait for extraordinary circumstances to do good; try to use ordinary situations.—*Richter.*

Genius and great abilities are often wanting; sometimes, only opportunities.—Some deserve praise for what they have done; others for what they would have done.—*Bruyère.*

To improve the golden moment of opportunity and catch the good that is within our reach, is the great art of life.—*Johnson.*

A word spoken in season, at the right moment, is the matter of ages.—*Carlyle.*

The May of life blooms only once.—*Schiller.*

Who seeks, and will not take when once 'tis offered, shall never find it more.—*Shakespeare.*

There is an hour in each man's life appointed to make his happiness, if then he seize it.—*Beaumont and Fletcher.*

Unless a man has trained himself for his chance, the chance will only make him ridiculous. A great occasion is worth to a man exactly what his antecedents have enabled him to make of it.—*W. Matthews.*

OPPOSITION.—(See "RESOLUTION.")

A certain amount of opposition is a great help to a man; it is what he wants and must have to be good for anything.

—Hardship and opposition are the native soil of manhood and self-reliance.—*John Neal.*

The coldest bodies warm with opposition; the hardest sparkle in collision.—*Junius.*

He that wrestles with us, strengthens our nerves, and sharpens our skill. Our antagonist is our helper.—*Burke.*

Nature is upheld by antagonism.—Passions, resistance, danger, are educators. We acquire the strength we have overcome.—*Emerson.*

The greater the obstacle, the more glory in overcoming it; and difficulties are but the maids of honor to set off the virtue.—*Molière.*

It is not the victory that makes the joy of noble hearts, but the combat.—*Montalembert.*

The effects of opposition are wonderful. There are men who rise refreshed on hearing of a threat,—men to whom a crisis which intimidates and paralyzes the majority, comes graceful and beloved as a bride!—*Emerson.*

It is not ease but effort,—not facility, but difficulty, that makes men. There is, perhaps, no station in life in which difficulties have not to be encountered and overcome before any decided measure of success can be achieved.—*S. Smiles.*

A strenuous soul hates cheap success; it is the ardor of the assailant that makes the vigor of the defendant.—*Emerson.*

Opposition inflames the enthusiast, never converts him.—*Schiller.*

OPPRESSION.—A desire to resist oppression is implanted in the nature of man.—*Tacitus.*

The smallest worm will turn, being trodden on; and doves will peck, in safeguard of their brood.—*Shakespeare.*

There is no happiness for him who oppresses and persecutes; there can be no repose for him. For the sighs of the unfortunate cry for vengeance to heaven. —*Pestalozzi.*

Oppression makes wise men mad; but the distemper is still the madness of the wise, which is better than the sobriety of fools.—*Burke.*

I never could believe that Providence had sent a few men into the world, ready booted and spurred to ride, and millions ready saddled and bridled to be ridden. —*Richard Rumbold.*

An extreme rigor is sure to arm everything against it.—*Burke.*

Fishes live in the sea, as men do a-land; the great ones eat up the little ones.—*Shakespeare.*

When oppression stains the robe of state, and power's a whip of scorpions in the hands of heartless knaves, to lash th' o'erburthen'd back of honest industry, the loyal blood will turn to bitterest gall, and th' o'ercharged heart explode in execration.—*Shee.*

The camomile, the more it is trodden on, the faster it grows.—*Shakespeare.*

Power exercised with violence has seldom been of long duration, but temper and moderation generally produce permanence in all things.—*Seneca.*

Oppression is but another name for irresponsible power.—*W. Pinckney.*

ORATORY.—He is the eloquent man who can treat subjects of an humble nature with delicacy, lofty things impressively, and moderate things temperately.—*Cicero.*

It is the first rule in oratory that a man must appear such as he would persuade others to be; and that can be accomplished only by the force of his life.—*Swift.*

Every man should study conciseness in speaking; it is a sign of ignorance not to know that long speeches, though they may please the speaker, are the torture of the hearer.—*Feltham.*

List his discourse of war, and you shall hear a fearful battle rendered you in music.—*Shakespeare.*

What too many orators want in depth, they give you in length.—*Montesquieu.*

There is no power like that of true oratory. Cæsar controlled men by exciting their fears; Cicero, by captivating their affections and swaying their passions. The influence of the one perished with its author; that of the other continues to this day.—*Henry Clay.*

In oratory, the greatest art is to conceal art.—*Swift.*

An orator without judgment is a horse without a bridle.—*Theophrastus.*

When the Roman people had listened to the diffuse and polished discourses of

Cicero, they departed, saying one to another, "What a splendid speech our orator has made!" But when the Athenians heard Demosthenes, he so filled them with the subject-matter of his oration that they quite forgot the orator, and left him at the finish of his harangue, breathing revenge, and exclaiming, "Let us go and fight against Philip!"—*Colton.*

Orators are most vehement when they have the weakest cause, as men get on horseback when they cannot walk.—*Cicero.*

The effective public speaker receives from his audience in vapor, what he pours back on them in a flood.—*Gladstone.*

Extemporaneous speaking is, indeed, the groundwork of the orator's art; preparation is the last finish, and the most difficult of all his accomplishments. To learn by heart as a schoolboy, or to prepare as an orator, are two things, not only essentially different, but essentially antagonistic to each other; for the work most opposed to an effective oration is an elegant essay.—*Bulwer.*

Eloquence is vehement simplicity.—*Cecil.*

The passions are the only orators that always succeed. They are, as it were, nature's art of eloquence, fraught with infallible rules. Simplicity, with the aid of the passions, persuades more than the utmost eloquence without it.—*Rochefoucauld.*

Suit the action to the word, the word to the action; with this special observance, that you overstep not the modesty of nature.—*Shakespeare.*

It is not by the compositions he learns, but by the memory of the effects he has produced that an orator is to be judged.

The language of the heart which comes from the heart and goes to the heart—is always simple, graceful, and full of power, but no art of rhetoric can teach it. It is at once the easiest and most difficult language,—difficult, since it needs a heart to speak it; easy, because its periods though rounded and full of harmony, are still unstudied.—*Bovee.*

An orator or author is never successful till he has learned to make his words smaller than his ideas.—*Emerson.*

As thought supplies materials for discourse, so discourse gives precision to thought as well as often assists in its evolution. The best orators owe half their inspiration to the music of their own voice. Yet profundity of ideas is commonly an impediment to fluency of words.—*W. B. Clulow.*

In oratory, affectation must be avoided, it being better for man, by a native and clear eloquence to express himself, than by those words which may smell either of the lamp or the inkhorn.—*Lord Herbert.*

Oratory, like the drama, abhors lengthiness; like the drama, it must keep doing.—Beauties themselves, if they delay or distract the effect which should be produced on the audience, become blemishes.—*Bulwer.*

The elegance of the style, and the turn of the periods make the chief impression upon the hearers.—Most people have ears, but few have judgment; tickle those ears, and depend upon it, you will catch their judgments such as they are.—*Chesterfield.*

Oratory is the huffing and blustering spoiled child of a semi-barbarous age.— The press is the foe of rhetoric, but the friend of reason; and the art of declamation has been sinking in value from the moment that speakers were foolish enough to publish, and readers wise enough to read.—*Colton.*

ORDER.—Order is heaven's first law.—*Pope.*

A place for everything, everything in its place.—*Franklin.*

Order is the sanity of the mind, the health of the body, the peace of the city, the security of the state.—As the beams to a house, as the bones to the body, so is order to all things.—*Southey.*

We do not keep the outward form of order, where there is deep disorder in the mind.—*Shakespeare.*

He who has no taste for order, will be often wrong in his judgment, and seldom considerate or conscientious in his actions.—*Lavater.*

Have a time and place for everything, and do everything in its time and place, and you will not only accomplish more, but have far more leisure than those who are always hurrying, as if vainly attempting to overtake time that had been lost.—*Tryon Edwards.*

Order is a lovely nymph, the child of beauty and wisdom; her attendants are comfort, neatness, and activity; her abode is the valley of happiness: she is always to be found when sought for, and never appears so lovely as when contrasted with her opponent, disorder.—*Johnson.*

Desultoriness may often be the mark of a full head; connection must proceed from a thoughtful one.—*Danby.*

The heavens themselves, the planets, and this centre, observe degree, priority and place, insisture, course, proportion, season, form, office, and custom, in all line of order.—*Shakespeare.*

There are persons who are never easy unless they are putting your books and papers in order—that is according to their notions of the matter—and hiding things, lest they should be lost, where neither the owner nor anybody else can find them. If anything is left where you want it, it is called litter. There is a pedantry in housewifery, as well as in the gravest concerns. One complained that whenever his maid-servant had been in his library, he could not get comfortably to work again for several days.—*Hazlitt.*

Order means light and peace, inward liberty and free command over one's self; order is power.—*Amiel.*

Set all things in their own peculiar place, and know that order is the greatest grace.—*Dryden.*

Good order is the foundation of all good things.—*Burke.*

ORIGINALITY. — (See "PLAGIARISM.")

Originality is nothing but judicious imitation.—The most original writers borrowed one from another. The instruction we find in books is like fire. We fetch it from our neighbor's, kindle it at home, communicate it to others, and it becomes the property of all.—*Voltaire.*

One couldn't carry on life comfortably without a little blindness to the fact that everything has been said better than we can put it ourselves.—*George Eliot.*

People are always talking about originality; but what do they mean? As soon as we are born, the world begins to work upon us; and this goes on to the end. And after all, what can we call

our own, except energy, strength, and will? If I could give an account of all that I owe to great predecessors and contemporaries, there would be but a small balance in my favor.—*Goethe.*

A well cultivated mind is, so to speak, made up of all the minds of preceding ages; it is only one single mind which has been educated during all this time.—*Fontenelle.*

Originality is simply a pair of fresh eyes.—*T. W. Higginson.*

If we can advance propositions both true and new, these are our own by right of discovery; and if we can repeat what is old, more briefly and brightly than others, this also becomes our own, by right of conquest.—*Colton.*

The merit of originality is not novelty, it is sincerity.—The believing man is the original man; he believes for himself, not for another.—*Carlyle.*

They who have light in themselves, will not revolve as satellites.—*Anon.*

Every human being is intended to have a character of his own; to be what no other is, and to do what no other can do.—*Channing.*

Men of strong minds and who think for themselves, should not be discouraged on finding occasionally that some of their best ideas have been anticipated by former writers; they will neither anathematize others nor despair themselves. They will rather go on discovering things before discovered, until they are rewarded with a land hitherto unknown, an empire indisputably their own, both by right of conquest and of discovery.—*Colton.*

One of the best uses of originality is, to say common things in an uncommon way.

He who thinks for himself, and rarely imitates, is a free man.—*Klopstock.*

It is better to create than to be learned; creating is the true essence of life.—*Niebuhr.*

It is almost impossible for any one who reads much, and reflects a good deal, to be able, on every occasion, to determine whether a thought was another's or his own.—I have several times quoted sentences out of my own writings, in aid of my own arguments, in conversation, thinking that I was supporting them by some better authority. —*Sterne*.

Those writers who lie on the watch for novelty can have little hope of greatness; for great things cannot have escaped former observation.—*Johnson*.

I would rather be the author of one original thought than the conqueror of a hundred battles. Yet moral excellence is so much superior to intellectual, that I ought to esteem one virtue more valuable than a hundred original thoughts. —*W. B. Clulow*.

If you would create something, you must be something.—*Goethe*.

Every man is an original and solitary character.—None can either understand or feel the book of his own life like himself.—*Cecil*.

When will poets learn that a grass-blade of their own raising is worth a barrow-load of flowers from their neighbor's garden?—*J. R. Lowell*.

Those who are ambitious of originality, and aim at it, are necessarily led by others, since they seek to be different from them.—*Whately*.

ORNAMENT.—Plutarch has a fine expression, with regard to some woman of learning, humility and virtue,—that her ornaments were such as might be purchased without money, and would render any woman's life both glorious and happy.—*Sterne*.

The true ornament of matrons is virtue, not apparel.—*Justin*.

Ornament is but the guiled shore to a most dangerous sea; the beauteous scarf veiling an Indian beauty; in a word, the seeming truth which cunning times put on to entrap the wisest.— *Shakespeare*.

All finery is a sign of littleness. —*Lavater*.

We all originally came from the woods; it is hard to eradicate from any of us the old taste for the tattoo and the war-paint; and the moment that money gets into our pockets, it somehow or another breaks out in ornaments on our person, without always giving refinement to our manners.—*E. P. Whipple*.

Ornaments were invented by modesty. —*Joubert*.

Modern education too often covers

the fingers with rings, and at the same time cuts the sinews at the wrists.— *Sterling*.

Excess in apparel is another costly folly.—The very trimming of the vain world would clothe all the naked ones.— *Penn*.

Orators and stage-coachmen, when the one wants argument and the other a coat of arms, adorn their cause and their coaches with rhetoric and flower-pots.— *Shenstone*.

Education, indeed, has made the fondness for fine things next to natural; the corals and bells teach infants on the breasts to be delighted with sound and glitter.—*H. Brooke*.

Show is not substance; realities govern wise men.—*Penn*.

OSTENTATION.—I have seldom seen much ostentation and much learning met together. The sun, rising and declining, makes long shadows; at midday, when he is highest, none at all.— *Bp. Hall*.

An ostentatious man will rather relate a blunder or an absurdity he has committed, than be debarred from talking of his own dear person.—*Addison*.

Where there is much pretension, much has been borrowed; nature never pretends.—*Lavater*.

Whatever is done without ostentation, and without the people being witnesses of it, is, in my opinion, most praiseworthy: not that the public eye should be entirely avoided, for good actions desire to be placed in the light; but notwithstanding this, the greatest theatre for virtue is conscience.—*Cicero*.

Do what good thou canst unknown, and be not vain of what ought rather to be felt than seen.—*Penn*.

Surely half the world must be blind; they can see nothing unless it glitters.— *Hare*.

Ostentation is the signal flag of hypocrisy.—The charlatan is verbose and assumptive; the Pharisee is ostentatious, because he is a hypocrite.—Pride is the master sin of the devil, and the devil is the father of lies.—*E. H. Chapin*.

As in a pair of bellows, there is a forced breath without life, so in those that are puffed up with the wind of ostentation, there may be charitable words without works.—*Bp. Hall.*

P

PAIN.—Pain is the outcome of sin. —*Buddha.*

Pain may be said to follow pleasure, as its shadow; but the misfortune is, that the substance belongs to the shadow, and the emptiness to its cause.—*Colton.*

Alas! by some degree of woe we every bliss must gain; the heart can ne'er a transport know that never feels a pain. —*Lyttleton.*

Pain itself is not without its alleviations. It is seldom both violent and long-continued; and its pauses and intermissions become positive pleasures. It has the power of shedding a satisfaction over intervals of ease, which few enjoyments exceed.—*Paley.*

Pain adds rest unto pleasure, and teaches the luxury of health.—*Tupper.*

Nature has placed mankind under the government of two sovereign masters, pain and pleasure. It is for them to point out what we ought to do, as well as to determine what we shall do. On the one hand, the standard of right and wrong; on the other, the chain of causes and effects, are fastened to their throne. —*Bentham.*

Pain and pleasure, like light and darkness, succeed each other; and he only who knows how to accommodate himself to their returns, and can wisely extract the good from the evil, knows how to live.—*Sterne.*

The same refinement which brings us new pleasures, exposes us to new pains. —*Bulwer.*

There was never yet philosopher that could endure the toothache patiently, however they have writ the style of gods, and made a pish at chance and sufferance.—*Shakespeare.*

The most painful part of our bodily pain is that which is bodiless or immaterial, namely our impatience, and the delusion that it will last forever.— *Richter.*

A man of pleasure is a man of pains. —*Young.*

They talk of short-lived pleasures: be it so; pain dies as quickly, and lets her

weary prisoner go; the fiercest agonies have shortest reign.—*Bryant.*

Pain is the deepest thing we have in our nature, and union through pain and suffering has always seemed more real and holy than any other.—*Hallam.*

PAINTING.—Painting is silent poetry, and poetry is a speaking picture.— *Simonides.*

A picture is a poem without words.— *Horace.*

The love of gain never made a painter, but it has marred many.—*Washington Allston.*

A room hung with pictures, is a room hung with thoughts.—*Sir Joshua Reynolds.*

A picture is an intermediate something between a thought and a thing.— *Coleridge.*

Would that we could at once paint with the eyes!—In the long way from the eye, through the arm, to the pencil, how much is lost!—*Lessing.*

A room with pictures and a room without pictures, differ nearly as much as a room with windows and a room without windows; for pictures are loopholes of escape to the soul, leading it to other scenes and spheres, where the fancy for a moment may revel, refreshed and delighted. Pictures are consolers of loneliness, and a relief to the jaded mind, and windows to the imprisoned thought; they are books, histories, and sermons —which we can read without the trouble of turning over the leaves.—*John Gilbert.*

What a vanity is painting, which attracts admiration by the resemblance of things that in the original we do not admire!—*Pascal.*

Portraits, except of old people whose features are fixed, rarely give a correct idea of persons, except to those who have known them.—To those they recall the looks and features.

The best portraits are those in which there is a slight mixture of caricature.— *Macaulay.*

Fain would I Raphael's god-like art rehearse, where, from the mingled strength of shade and light, a new creation rises to my sight; such heavenly figures from his pencil flow, so warm with life his blended colors glow.—*Addison.*

Style in painting is the same as in writing,—a power over materials, whether words or colors, by which conceptions or sentiments are conveyed.—*Sir Joshua Reynolds.*

The painter who is content with the praise of the world for what does not satisfy himself, is not an artist, but an artisan; for though his reward be only praise, his pay is that of a mechanic.—*Washington Allston.*

The first merit of pictures is the effect they produce on the mind; and the first step of a sensible man should be to receive involuntary impressions from them.—Pleasure and inspiration first; analysis, afterward.—*H. W. Beecher.*

Portrait-painting may be to the painter what the practical knowledge of the world is to the poet, provided he considers it as a school by which he is to acquire the means of perfection in his art, and not as the object of that perfection.—*Burke.*

Softness of manner seems to be in painting what smoothness of syllables is in language, affecting the sense of sight or hearing, previous to any correspondent passion.—*Shenstone.*

The masters painted for joy, and knew not that virtue had gone out of them. They could not paint the like in cold blood. The masters of English lyric wrote their songs so. It was a fine efflorescence of fine powers.—*Emerson.*

The first degree of proficiency is, in painting, what grammar is in literature, —a general preparation for whatever the student may afterward choose for more particular application. The power of drawing, modelling, and using colors, is very properly called the language of the art.—*Sir Joshua Reynolds.*

PANIC.—A panic is a sudden desertion of us, and a going over to the enemy of our imagination.—*Bovee.*

A panic is the stampede of our self-possession.—*Rivarol.*

PARADISE.—(See " FORGIVENESS.")

Remembrance is the only paradise out of which we cannot be driven away. Indeed our first parents were not to be deprived of it.—*Richter.*

Every man has a paradise around him till he sins and the angel of an accusing conscience drives him from his Eden. And even then there are holy hours, when this angel sleeps, and man comes back, and with the innocent eyes of a child looks into his lost paradise again—into the broad gates and rural solitudes of nature.—*Longfellow.*

If God hath made this world so fair, where sin and death abound, how beautiful, beyond compare, will paradise be found!—*Montgomery.*

PARDON.—(See " FORGIVENESS.")

They who forgive most, shall be most forgiven.—*Bailey.*

The man who pardons easily, courts injury.—*Corneille.*

Nothing in this lost and ruined world bears the meek impress of the Son of God so surely as forgiveness.—*Alice Cary.*

To pardon those absurdities in ourselves which we cannot suffer in others, is neither better nor worse than to be more willing to be fools ourselves than to have others so.—*Pope.*

Mercy is not itself, that oft looks so; pardon is still the nurse of second woe.—*Shakespeare.*

Pardon others often, thyself never.—*Publius Syrus.*

Forgive thyself little, and others much.—*Leighton.*

Pardon is the virtue of victory.—*Mazzini.*

PARENTS.—(See " LOVE.")

Next to God, thy parents.—*Penn.*

Honor thy parents, those that gave thee birth, and watched in tenderness thine earliest days, and trained thee up in youth, and loved in all. Honor, obey, and love them; it shall fill their souls with holy joy, and shall bring down God's richest blessing on thee; and in days to come, thy children, if they're given, shall honor thee, and fill thy life with peace.—*Tryon Edwards.*

The voice of parents is the voice of gods, for to their children they are heaven's lieutenants.—*Shakespeare.*

We never know the love of the parent till we become parents ourselves. When we first bend over the cradle of our own child, God throws back the temple door, and reveals to us the sacredness and mystery of a father's and a mother's love to ourselves.—And in later years, when they have gone from us, there is always a certain sorrow, that we cannot tell them we have found it out.—One of the deepest experiences of a noble nature in reference to the loved ones that have passed beyond this world, is the thought of what he might have been to them, and done for them, if he had known, while they were living, what he has learned since they died.—*H. W. Beecher.*

There is no such penalty for error and folly as to see one's children suffer for it.—There is no such reward for a well-spent life as to see one's children well started in life, owing to their parents' good health, good principles, fixed character, good breeding, and in general the whole outfit, that enables them to fight the battle of life with success.—*W. G. Sumner.*

Parents wonder why the streams are bitter, when they themselves have poisoned the fountain.—*Locke.*

The sacred books of the ancient Persians say: If you would be holy instruct your children, because all the good acts they perform will be imputed to you.—*Montesquieu.*

Sins of the parents may be visited upon their children, but it is that the sting may strike back into the parents' hearts.

We speak of educating our children. Do we know that our children also educate us?—*Mrs. Sigourney.*

Parents who wish to train up their children in the way they should go, must go in the way in which they would have their children go.

The illiberality of parents, in allowance toward their children, is a harmful error, and makes them base; acquaints them with shifts; makes them sort with mean company; and makes them surfeit more when they come to plenty; and therefore the proof is best when men keep their authority toward their children, but not their purse.—*Bacon.*

A suspicious parent makes an artful child.—*Haliburton.*

The father and mother of an unnoticed family, who in their seclusion awaken the mind of one child to the idea and love of goodness, who awaken in him a strength of will to repel temptation, and who send him out prepared to profit by the conflicts of life, surpass in influence a Napoleon breaking the world to his sway.—*Channing.*

Children wish fathers looked but with their eyes; fathers that children with their judgment looked; and either may be wrong.—*Shakespeare.*

When thou art contemplating some base deed, let the presence of thy infant son act as a check on thy headlong course to sin.—*Juvenal.*

Plato seeing a child do mischief in the streets, went forth and corrected his father for it.—And this is the pattern of God's judicial proceedings, for he visits the iniquities of the fathers upon the children who imitate them, and the iniquities of the children upon the fathers who countenance and indulge them.—*J. Kitchen.*

When our parents are living we feel that they stand between us and death; when they are gone, we ourselves are in the forefront of the battle.

How many hopes and fears, how many ardent wishes and anxious apprehensions, are twisted together in the threads that connect the parent with the child!—*S. G. Goodrich.*

Whoever makes his father's heart to bleed, shall have a child that will revenge the deed.—*F. Randolph.*

Unblessed is the son who does not honor his parents; but if reverent and obedient to them, he will receive the same from his own children.—*Euripides.*

Parents must give good example and reverent deportment in the face of their children. And all those instances of charity which endear each other—sweetness of conversation, affability, frequent admonition—all significations of love and tenderness, care and watchfulness, must be expressed toward children; that they may look upon their parents as their friends and patrons, their defence and sanctuary, their treasure and their guide.

Partiality in a parent is commonly unlucky: for fondlings are in danger to be made fools, and the children that are least cockered make the best and wisest men.—*L'Estrange.*

PARTING.—In every parting there is an image of death.—*George Eliot.*

I have no parting sigh to give, so take my parting smile.—*L. E. Landon.*

"Good-bye "—that is, "God be with

you." Is this your earnest prayer in parting from your friends?

Never part without loving words to think of during your absence. It may be that you will not meet again in life. —*Richter.*

Could we see when and where we are to meet again, we would be more tender when we bid our friends good-by.—*Ouida.*

Adieu! I have too grieved a heart to take a tedious leave.—*Shakespeare.*

Let us not unman each other; part at once; all farewells should be sudden, when forever.—*Byron.*

What! gone without a word? Ay, so true love should do: it cannot speak; for truth hath better deeds than words to grace it.—*Shakespeare.*

To die and part is a less evil; but to part and live, there, there is the torment.—*Lansdowne.*

Parting and forgetting?—What faithful heart can do these? — Our great thoughts, our great affections, the truths of our life, never leave us.—Surely, they cannot be separate from our consciousness; will follow it whithersoever that shall go, and are, of their nature, divine and immortal.—*Thackeray.*

A chord, stronger or weaker, is snapped asunder in every parting, and time's busy fingers are not practised in re-splicing broken ties. Meet again you may; will it be in the same way? with the same sympathies? with the same sentiments? Will the souls, hurrying on in diverse paths, unite once more, as if the interval had been a dream? Rarely, rarely!—*Bulwer.*

There is such sweet pain in parting, that I could hang forever on thine arms and look away my life into thine eyes.—*Otway.*

Farewell, God knows when we shall meet again.—I have a faint cold fear thrill through my veins, that almost freezes up the heat of life.—*Shakespeare.*

PARTY.—Party is the madness of many, for the gain of a few.—*Pope.*

He knows very little of mankind, who expects, by any facts or reasoning, to convince a determined party-man.—*Lavater.*

Such is the turbulence of human passions in party disputes, when victory more than truth is contended for, that the post of honor is a private station.—*Washington.*

Nothing can be proposed so wild or so absurd as not to find a party, and often a very large party to espouse it.—*Cecil.*

One thing I certainly never was made for, and that is to put principles on and off at the dictation of a party, as a lackey changes his livery at his master's command.—*Horace Mann.*

Most modern partisans go for what they regard the seven cardinal principles, namely, the five loaves and two fishes.

The political parties that I would call great, are those which cling more to principles than to consequences; to general, and not to special cases; to ideas, and not to men.—Such parties are usually distinguished by a nobler character, more generous passions, more genuine convictions, and a more bold and open conduct than others.—*De Tocqueville.*

If we mean to support the liberty and independence which have cost us so much blood and treasure to establish, we must drive far away the demon of party spirit and local reproach.—*Washington.*

He that aspires to be the head of a party will find it more difficult to please his friends than to perplex his foes. He must often act from false reasons which are weak, because he dares not avow the true reasons which are strong.—*Colton.*

Men naturally sympathize with the calamities of individuals; but they are inclined to look on a fallen party with contempt rather than with pity.—*Macaulay.*

People who declare that they belong to no party certainly do not belong to ours.—*J. P. Senn.*

Party standards are the shadows in which patriotism is buried.—*St. Pierre.*

The tendency of party-spirit has ever been to disguise, and propagate, and support error.—*Whately.*

Of all kinds of credulity, the most obstinate is that of party-spirit; of men, who, being numbered, they know not why, in any party, resign the use of their own eyes and ears, and resolve to believe nothing that does not favor those whom they profess to follow.—*Johnson.*

Men in a party have liberty only for their motto; in reality they are greater slaves than anybody else would care to make them.—*Saville.*

Party-spirit is a lying, vociferous, reckless spirit, a stranger to candor, willing to pervert truth, and to use underhand and dishonest means, so it may gain the victory.—*C. Simmons.*

There is an opinion that parties in free countries are useful checks upon the administration of the government, and serve to keep alive the spirit of liberty. This, within certain limits, is probably true. But in governments of a popular character, and purely elective, it is a spirit not to be encouraged. From their natural tendency, there will always be enough of that spirit for every salutary purpose. And there being constant danger of excess, the effort ought to be, by force of public opinion, to mitigate and assuage it. A fire not to be quenched, it demands a uniform vigilance to prevent it bursting into a flame, lest, instead of warming, it should consume.—*Washington.*

PASSION. — (See "RAGE," — "ANGER.")

Passion may not unfitly be termed the mob of the man, that commits a riot on his reason.—*Penn.*

Passion is the great mover and spring of the soul: when men's passions are strongest, they may have great and noble effects; but they are then also apt to fall into the greatest miscarriages.—*Sprat.*

The passionate are like men standing on their heads; they see all things the wrong way.—*Plato.*

A wise man's heart is like a broad hearth that keeps the coals from burning the house. Good deeds in this life are coals raked up in embers, to make a fire next day.—*Overbury.*

Men spend their lives in the service of their passions, instead of employing their passions in the service of their life.—*Steele.*

Our passions are like convulsion fits, which, though they make us stronger for the time, leave us the weaker ever after.—*Swift.*

There are moments when our passions

speak and decide for us, and we seem to stand by and wonder. They carry in them an inspiration of crime, that in one instant does the work of long premeditation.—*George Eliot.*

The passions are unruly cattle, and therefore you must keep them chained up, and under the government of religion, reason and prudence. If thus kept under discipline, they are useful servants; but if you let them loose and give them head, they will be your masters, and unruly masters, and carry you, like wild and unbridled horses, into a thousand mischiefs and inconveniences, besides the great disturbance, disorder and discomposure they will occasion in your own mind.—*Sir M. Hale.*

The worst of slaves is he whom passion rules.—*Brooke.*

The mind by passion driven from its firm hold, becomes a feather to each wind that blows.—*Shakespeare.*

People have a custom of excusing the enormities of their conduct by talking of their passions, as if they were under the control of a blind necessity, and sinned because they could not help it.—*Cumberland.*

It is the excess and not the nature of our passions which is perishable. Like the trees which grow by the tomb of Protesilaus, the passions flourish till they reach a certain height, but no sooner is that height attained than they wither away.—*Bulwer.*

A vigorous mind is as necessarily accompanied with violent passions as a great fire with great heat.—*Burke.*

The passions may be humored till they become our masters, as a horse may be pampered till he gets the better of his rider; but early discipline will prevent mutiny, and keep the helm in the hands of reason.—*Cumberland.*

Passions makes us feel, but never see clearly.—*Montesquieu.*

The passions and desires, like the two twists of a rope, mutually mix one with the other, and twine inextricably round the heart; producing good, if moderately indulged; but certain destruction, if suffered to become inordinate.—*Burton.*

He submits to be seen through a microscope, who suffers himself to be caught in a fit of passion.—*Lavater.*

Passion makes the will lord of the reason.—*Shakespeare.*

Passions are likened best to floods and streams: the shallow murmur, but the deep are dumb.—*Sir W. Raleigh.*

Passion is the drunkenness of the mind.—*South.*

" All the passions," says an old writer, " are such near neighbors, that if one of them is on fire the others should send for the buckets." Thus love and hate being both passions, the one is never safe from the spark that sets the other ablaze.—*Bulwer.*

The passions are at once tempters and chastisers. As tempters, they come with garlands of flowers on brows of youth; as chastisers, they appear with wreaths of snakes on the forehead of deformity. They are angels of light in their delusion; they are fiends of torment in their inflictions.—*Henry Giles.*

Nothing doth so fool a man as extreme passion. This doth make them fools which otherwise are not, and show them to be fools which are so.—*Bp. Hall.*

Passion, though a bad regulator, is a powerful spring.—*Emerson.*

The only praiseworthy indifference is an acquired one; we must feel as well as control our passions.—*Richter.*

The brain may devise laws for the blood, but a hot temper leaps over a cold decree.—*Shakespeare.*

In strong natures, if resistance to temptation is of granite, so the passions that they admit are of fire.—*Bulwer.*

In all disputes, so much as there is of passion, so much there is of nothing to the purpose; for then reason, like a bad hound, spends upon a false scent, and forsakes the question first started. —*Sir Thomas Browne.*

Almost all men are born with every passion to some extent, but there is hardly a man who has not a dominant passion to which the others are subordinate. Discover this governing passion in every individual; and when you have found the master passion of a man, remember never to trust to him where that passion is concerned.—*Chesterfield.*

It is the strong passions which, rescuing us from sloth, can alone impart to us that continuous and earnest attention

necessary to great intellectual effort.— *Helvetius.*

The way to conquer men, is by their passions; catch but the ruling foible of their hearts, and all their boasted virtues shrink before you.—*Tolson.*

The passions are the winds that fill the sails of the vessel.—They sink it at times; but without them it would be impossible to make way.—Many things that are dangerous here below, are still necessary.—*Voltaire.*

It is the passions of men that both do and undo everything.—They are the winds that are necessary to put every thing in motion, though they often cause storms.—*Fontenelle.*

Passion often makes fools of the ablest men, and able men of the most foolish.—*Rochefoucauld.*

The passions and capacities of our nature are foundations of power, happiness and glory; but if we turn them into occasions and sources of self-indulgence, the structure itself falls, and buries everything in its overwhelming desolation.—*G. B. Cheever.*

The passions act as winds to propel our vessel, our reason is the pilot that steers her; without the winds she would not move; without the pilot she would be lost.—*F. Shulz.*

The passions should be purged; all may become innocent if they are well directed and moderated. Even hatred may be a commendable feeling when it is caused by a lively love of good. Whatever makes the passions purer makes them stronger, more durable, and more enjoyable.—*Joubert.*

The passions are the only orators who never fail to persuade.—They are nature's art of eloquence, the rules of which never fail; and the weakest man, moved by passion, is more eloquent than the strongest who has none.—*Rochefoucauld.*

The blossoms of passion, gay and luxuriant flowers, are bright and full of fragrance, but they beguile us and lead us astray, and their odor is deadly.— *Longfellow.*

In the history of the passions each human heart is a world in itself; its experience can profit no others.—*Bulwer.*

Chastise your passions, that they may not chastise you. No one who is a lover of money, of pleasure, or of glory, is likewise a lover of mankind. Riches are not among the number of things that are good. It is not poverty that causes sorrow, but covetous desires. Deliver yourself from appetite, and you will be free. He who is discontented with things present and allotted, is unskilled in life. —*Epictetus.*

If we resist our passions, it is more through their weakness than from our strength.—*Rochefoucauld.*

Strong passions are the life of manly virtues. But they need not necessarily be evil because they are passions, and because they are strong. They may be likened to blood horses, that need training and the curb only, to enable those whom they carry to achieve the most glorious triumphs.—*Simms.*

He only employs his passion who can make no use of his reason.—*Cicero.*

Men are not blindly betrayed into corruption, but abandon themselves to their passions with their eyes open; and lose the direction of truth, because they do not attend to her voice, not because they do not understand it.—*Johnson.*

A man is by nothing so much himself, as by his temper and the character of his passions and affections. If he loses what is manly and worthy in these, he is as much lost to himself, as when he loses his memory and understanding.—*Shaftesbury.*

Hold not conference, debate, or reasoning with any lust; 'tis but a preparatory for thy admission of it. The way is at the very first flatly to deny it.—*Fuller.*

When passion rules, how rare the hours that fall to virtue's share.—*Walter Scott.*

Even virtue itself, all perfect as it is, requires to be inspirited by passion; for duties are but coldly performed which are but philosophically fulfilled.—*Mrs. Jameson.*

What profits us, that we from heaven derive a soul immortal, and with looks erect survey the stars, if, like the brutal kind, we follow where our passions lead the way?—*Claudian.*

In doing good, we are generally cold, and languid, and sluggish; and of all things afraid of being too much in the right. But the works of malice and in-

justice are quite in another style. They are finished with a bold masterly hand, touched as they are with the spirit of those vehement passions that call forth all our energies whenever we oppress and persecute.—*Burke.*

Passion, in its first violence, controls interest, as the eddy for a while runs against the stream.—*Johnson.*

The passions of mankind are partly protective, partly beneficent, like the chaff and grain of the corn, but none without their use, none without nobleness when seen in balanced unity with the rest of the spirit which they are charged to defend.—*Ruskin.*

Passion looks not beyond the moment of its existence.—Better, it says, the kisses of love to-day, than the felicities of heaven afar off.—*Bovee.*

Exalted souls, have passions in proportion violent, resistless, and tormenting: they're a tax imposed by nature on pre-eminence, and fortitude and wisdom must support them.—*Lillo.*

Princes rule the people; and their own passions rule princes; but Providence can overrule the whole, and draw the instruments of his inscrutable purpose from the vices, no less than from the virtues of kings.—*Colton.*

All passions are good or bad, according to their objects: where the object is absolutely good, there the greatest passion is too little; where absolutely evil, there the least passion is too much; where indifferent, there a little is enough.—*Quarles.*

The passions are like fire, useful in a thousand ways and dangerous only in one, through their excess.—*Bovee.*

Give me that man that is not passion's slave, and I will wear him in my heart's core, aye, in my heart of hearts. —*Shakespeare.*

Alas! too well, too well they know the pain, the penitence, the woe, that passion brings down on the best, the wisest, and the loveliest.—*Moore.*

Our headstrong passions shut the door of our souls against God.—*Confucius.*

As rivers, when they overflow, drown those grounds and ruin those husbandmen, which, whilst they flowed calmly betwixt their banks they fertilized and enriched, so our passions, when they grow exorbitant and unruly, destroy those virtues to which they might be very serviceable whilst kept within their bounds.—*Boyle.*

The way to avoid evil is not by maiming our passions, but by compelling them to yield their vigor to our moral nature. —Thus they become, as in the ancient fable, the harnessed steeds that bear the chariot of the sun.—*H. W. Beecher.*

We use up in our passions the stuff that was given us for happiness.—*Joubert.*

The passions often engender their contraries.—Avarice sometimes produces prodigality, and prodigality, avarice; we are often resolute from weakness, and daring from timidity.—*Rochefoucauld.*

What a mistake to suppose that the passions are strongest in youth! The passions are not stronger, but the control over them is weaker! They are more easily excited, they are more violent and apparent; but they have less energy, less durability, less intense and concentrated power than in maturer life.—*Bulwer.*

Happy is he who is engaged in controversy with his own passions, and comes off superior; who makes it his endeavor that his follies and weaknesses may die before himself, and who daily meditates on mortality and immortality. —*Jortin.*

Oh, how the passions, insolent and strong, bear our weak minds their rapid course along; make us the madness of their will obey; then die, and leave us to our griefs a prey!—*Crabbe.*

The passions are like those demons with which Afrasahiab sailed down the Orus. Our only safety consists in keeping them asleep. If they wake, we are lost.—*Goethe.*

Passion costs me too much to bestow it on every trifle.—*T. Adam.*

Many persons in reasoning on the passions, make a continual appeal to common-sense. But passion is without common-sense, and we must frequently discard the one in speaking of the other. —*Hazlitt.*

The ruling passion, be it what it will, the ruling passion conquers reason still. —*Pope.*

May I govern my passions with ab-

solute sway, and grow wiser and better as life wears away.—*Walter Pope.*

PAST.—So sad, so fresh, the days that are no more.—*Tennyson.*

The past is the sepulchre of our dead emotions.—*Bovee.*

No hand can make the clock strike for me the hours that are passed.— *Byron.*

It is to live twice, when we can enjoy the recollections of our former life. —*Martial.*

The true past departs not; no truth or goodness realized by man ever dies, or can die; but all is still here, and, recognized or not, lives and works through endless changes.—*Carlyle.*

I desire no future that will break the ties of the past.—*George Eliot.*

Things without remedy, should be without regard; what is done, is done.— *Shakespeare.*

I know the past, and thence I will essay to glean a warning for the future so that man may profit by his errors, and derive experience from his folly.— *Shelley.*

We ought not to look back unless it is to derive useful lessons from past errors, and for the purpose of profiting by dear bought experience.—*Washington.*

Nor deem the irrevocable past as wholly wasted, wholly vain, if rising on its wrecks, at last to something nobler we attain.—*Longfellow.*

Study the past if you would divine the future.—*Confucius.*

Some are so very studious of learning what was done by the ancients, that they know not how to live with the moderns.—*Penn.*

What's gone and past help, should be past grief.—*Shakespeare.*

The admiration bestowed on former times is the bias of all times; the golden age never was the present age.—*Home.*

Our reverence for the past is just in proportion to our ignorance of it.—*Theodore Parker.*

That past which is so presumptuously brought forward as a precedent for the present, was itself founded on some past that went before it.—*Mad. de Staël.*

Many are always praising the by-gone

time, for it is natural that the old should extol the days of their youth; the weak, the time of their strength; the sick, the season of their vigor; and the disappointed, the spring-tide of their hopes.—*C. Bingham.*

It is delightful to transport one's self into the spirit of the past, to see how a wise man has thought before us, and to what a glorious height we have at last reached.—*Goethe.*

Age and sorrow have the gift of reading the future by the sad past.—*Farrar.*

The past is for us, but the sole terms on which it can become ours are its subordination to the present.—*Emerson.*

PATIENCE.—Everything comes if a man will only wait.—*Tancred.*

He that can have patience, can have what he will.—*Franklin.*

To know how to wait is the great secret of success.—*De Maistre.*

It is not necessary for all men to be great in action. The greatest and sublimest power is often simple patience.—*Horace Bushnell.*

Patient waiting is often the highest way of doing God's will.—*Collier.*

A phlegmatic insensibility is as different from patience, as a pool from a harbor. Into the one, indolence naturally sinks us; but if we arrive at the other it is by encountering many an adverse wind and rough wave, with a more skilful pilot at the helm than self, and a company under better command than the passions.—*Dilwyn.*

How poor are they who have not patience! What wound did ever heal but by degrees.—*Shakespeare.*

I have known twenty persevering girls to one patient one; but it is only the twenty-first one who can do her work, out and out, and enjoy it. For patience lies at the root of all pleasures as well as of all powers.—*Ruskin.*

Patience does not mean indifference. We may work and trust and wait, but we ought not to be idle or careless while waiting.

Life has such hard conditions that every dear and precious gift, every rare virtue, every genial endowment, love, hope, joy, wit, sprightliness, benevolence, must sometimes be put into the crucible

to distil the one elixir—patience.—*Gail Hamilton.*

Patience is the art of hoping.—*Vauvenargues.*

Patience is not passive: on the contrary it is active; it is concentrated strength.

There is one form of hope which is never unwise, and which certainly does not diminish with the increase of knowledge. In that form it changes its name, and we call it patience.—*Bulwer.*

Even the best must own that patience and resignation are the pillars of human peace on earth.—*Young.*

It's easy finding reasons why other folks should be patient.—*George Eliot.*

Enter into the sublime patience of the Lord. Be charitable in view of it. God can afford to wait; why cannot we, since we have Him to fall back upon? Let patience have her perfect work, and bring forth her celestial fruits.

The two powers which in my opinion constitute a wise man are those of bearing and forbearing.—*Epictetus.*

There's no music in a "rest," but there's the making of music in it. And people are always missing that part of the life melody, always talking of perseverance and courage and fortitude; but patience is the finest and worthiest part of fortitude, and the rarest, too.—*Ruskin.*

With patience bear the lot to thee assigned, nor think it chance, nor murmur at the load; for know what man calls fortune, is from God.—*Rowe.*

Patience is the key of content.—*Mahomet.*

He that is patient will persevere; and he that perseveres will often have occasion for, as well as trial of patience.—*Tryon Edwards.*

Accustom yourself to that which you bear ill, and you will bear it well.—*Seneca.*

Our real blessings often appear to us in the shape of pains, losses, and disappointments; but let us have patience, and we soon shall see them in their proper figures.—*Addison.*

They also serve who only stand and wait.—*Milton.*

There is no great achievement that is

not the result of patient working and waiting.—*J. G. Holland.*

The conflict of patience is such, that the vanquished is better than the vanquisher.—*Euripides.*

Patience and time do more than strength or passion.—*La Fontaine.*

All that I have accomplished, or expect or hope to accomplish, has been and will be by that plodding, patient, persevering process of accretion which builds the ant-heap, particle by particle, thought by thought, fact by fact.—*Elihu Burritt.*

Never think that God's delays are God's denials. Hold on; hold fast; hold out. Patience is genius.—*Buffon.*

Patience! why, it is the soul of peace; of all the virtues, it is nearest kin to heaven; it makes men look like gods. The best of men that ever wore earth about him was a sufferer,—a soft, meek, patient, humble, tranquil spirit; the first true gentleman that ever breathed.—*Decker.*

A patient, humble temper gathers blessings that are marred by the peevish, and overlooked by the aspiring.—*E. H. Chapin.*

Endurance is the crowning quality, and patience all the passion of great hearts.—*J. R. Lowell.*

That which in mean men we entitle patience, is pale, cold cowardice in noble breasts.—*Shakespeare.*

To bear is to conquer our fate.—*Campbell.*

Beware the fury of a patient man.—*Dryden.*

If we could have a little patience, we should escape much mortification; time takes away as much as it gives.—*Mad. de Sévigné.*

Patience is bitter, but its fruit is sweet.—*Rousseau.*

Patience is so like fortitude that she seems either her sister or her daughter —*Aristotle.*

There is no such thing as preaching patience into people unless the sermon is so long that they have to practice it while they hear. No man can learn patience except by going out into the hurly-burly world, and taking life just as

it blows. Patience is but lying to and riding out the gale.—*H. W. Beecher.*

Patience is the support of weakness; impatience is the ruin of strength.—*Colton.*

There is no road too long to the man who advances deliberately and without undue haste; no honors too distant to the man who prepares himself for them with patience.—*Bruyère.*

He surely is most in need of another's patience, who has none of his own.—*Lavater.*

Patience strengthens the spirit, sweetens the temper, stifles anger, extinguishes envy, subdues pride, bridles the tongue, restrains the hand, and tramples upon temptations.—*Bp. Horne.*

God may not give us the trivial things we pray for, but that which is far better —patience, and the development of faculties, and eternity for the use of the powers well schooled on earth.

Many people consider patience a commonplace virtue, not to say a tame and insipid one. But rightly appreciated it is grand and heroic. Without it the strongest character has a dangerously weak spot, which at any moment may be its ruin. With it, the otherwise weakest has an element of invincible strength.—*Congregationalist.*

There are times when God asks nothing of his children except silence, patience, and tears.—*C. S. Robinson.*

A curtain lecture is worth all the sermons in the world for teaching the virtue of patience and long suffering.—*Washington Irving.*

Trust to God to weave your thread into the great web, though the pattern shows it not yet.—*G. Macdonald.*

Be patient in little things. Learn to bear the every-day trials and annoyances of life quietly and calmly, and then, when unforeseen trouble or calamity comes, your strength will not forsake you.

There is as much difference between genuine patience and sullen endurance, as between the smile of love, and the malicious gnashing of the teeth.—*W. S. Plumer.*

Patience is the courage of the conqueror, the strength of man against destiny—of the one against the world, and of the soul against matter.—Therefore it is the courage of the gospel; and its importance, in a social view and to races and institutions, cannot be too earnestly inculcated.—*Bulwer.*

Patience is even more rarely manifested in the intellect than it is in the temper.—*A. Helps.*

Patience is power; with time and patience the mulberry leaf becomes silk.—*Chinese Proverb.*

The sincere and earnest approach of the Christian to the throne of the Almighty, teaches the best lesson of patience under affliction, since wherefore should we mock the Deity with supplications, when we insult him by murmuring under his decrees?—*Walter Scott.*

Steady, patient, persevering thinking, will generally surmount every obstacle in the search after truth.—*Emmons.*

PATRIOTISM.—The noblest motive is the public good.—*Virgil.*

Be just and fear not; let all the ends thou aimest at, be thy country's, thy God's, and truth's.—*Shakespeare.*

He was the bravest citizen of Rome that did most love and best serve his country; and he the saint among the Jews who most loved Zion.—*Baxter.*

Let our object be our country, our whole country, and nothing but our country. And, by the blessing of God, may that country itself become a vast and splendid monument, not of oppression and terror, but of wisdom, of peace, and of liberty, upon which the world may gaze with admiration forever.—*Daniel Webster.*

National enthusiasm is the great nursery of genius.—*Tuckerman.*

Had I a dozen sons,—each in my love alike,—I had rather have eleven die nobly for their country, than one voluptuously surfeit out of action.—*Shakespeare.*

There can be no affinity nearer than our country.—*Plato.*

Of the whole sum of human life no small part is that which consists of a man's relations to his country, and his feelings concerning it.—*Gladstone.*

When was public virtue to be found where private was not? Can he love the whole who loves no part? He be a nation's friend, who is, in truth, the friend of no man there? Who slights the charities for whose dear sake, that country, if at all, must be beloved?—*Cowper.*

The love of country produces good manners; and good manners, love of country.—The less we satisfy our individual passions, the more we leave to our general.—*Montesquieu.*

The proper means of increasing the love we bear to our native country, is to reside some time in a foreign one.—*Shenstone.*

After what I owe to God, nothing should be more dear or more sacred than the love and respect I owe to my country.—*De Thou.*

Whene'er our country calls, friends, sons, and sires should yield their treasure up, nor own a sense beyond the public safety.—*Brooke.*

My country claims me all, claims every passion; her liberty henceforth be all my thought; for her, my life, I'd willingly resign, and say with transport that the gain was mine.—*Martyn.*

The patriot's boast, where'er we roam, his first, best country ever is at home.—*Goldsmith.*

Millions for defence, but not one cent for tribute.—*C. C. Pinckney.*

I do love my country's good with a respect more tender, more holy and profound than mine own life.—*Shakespeare.*

Liberty and union, now and forever, one and inseparable.—*Daniel Webster.*

The age of virtuous politics is past, and we are deep in that of cold pretence.—Patriots are grown too shrewd to be sincere, and we too wise to trust them.—*Cowper.*

Our country's welfare is our first concern, and who promotes that best, best proves his duty.—*Havard.*

True patriots all, for be it understood, we left our country for our country's good.—*George Barrington.*

I have learned by much observation, that nothing will satisfy a patriot but a place.—*Junius.*

Patriotism is the last refuge of a scoundrel!—*Johnson.*

Love of country is one of the loftiest virtues; and so treason against it has been considered among the most damning sins.—*E. A. Storrs.*

Stirred up with high hopes of living to be brave men and worthy patriots, dear to God, and famous to all ages.—*Milton.*

PEACE.—Peace is the happy, natural state of man; war, his corruption, his disgrace.—*Thomson.*

Peace is the evening star of the soul, as virtue is its sun; and the two are never far apart.—*Colton.*

Peace is such a precious jewel that I would give anything for it but truth.—*M. Henry.*

'Tis death to me, to be at enmity; I hate it, and desire all good men's love.—*Shakespeare.*

Peace does not dwell in outward things, but within the soul; we may preserve it in the midst of the bitterest pain, if our will remain firm and submissive. Peace in this life springs from acquiescence, not in an exemption from suffering.—*Fénelon.*

Five great enemies to peace inhabit with us: viz., avarice, ambition, envy, anger, and pride. If those enemies were to be banished, we should infallibly enjoy perpetual peace.—*Petrarch.*

If we have not peace within ourselves, it is in vain to seek it from outward sources.—*Rochefoucauld.*

Lovely concord and most sacred peace doth nourish virtue, and fast friendship breed.—*Spenser.*

Peace is rarely denied to the peaceful.—*Schiller.*

The more quietly and peaceably we all get on, the better—the better for ourselves—the better for our neighbors. In nine cases out of ten the wisest policy is, if a man cheats you, quit dealing with him; if he is abusive, quit his company; if he slanders you, take care to live so that nobody will believe him: no matter who he is, or how he misuses you, the wisest way is generally to let him alone; for there is nothing better than this cool, calm, quiet way of dealing with the wrongs we meet with.

Peace is the proper result of the Christian temper. It is the great kindness which our religion doth us, that it brings us to a settledness of mind, and a consistency within ourselves.—*Bp. Patrick.*

Peace rules the day, where reason rules the mind.—*Collins.*

Nothing can bring you peace but yourself; nothing can bring you peace but the triumph of principles.—*Emerson.*

Peace hath her victories, no less renowned than war.—*Milton.*

Peace, dear nurse of arts, plenties, and joyful birth.—*Shakespeare.*

We love peace, but not peace at any price.—There is a peace more destructive of the manhood of living man, than war is destructive of his body.—Chains are worse than bayonets.—*Jerrold.*

To be prepared for war is one of the most effectual means of preserving peace.—*Washington.*

I am a man of peace. God knows how I love peace. But I hope I shall never be such a coward as to mistake oppression for peace.—*Kossuth.*

A peace is of the nature of a conquest; for then both parties nobly are subdued, and neither party loser.—*Shakespeare.*

There are interests by the sacrifice of which peace is too dearly purchased. One should never be at peace to the shame of his own soul,—to the violation of his integrity or of his allegiance to God.—*E. H. Chapin.*

Speak, move, act in peace, as if you were in prayer. In truth, this is prayer.—*Fénelon.*

No peace was ever won from fate by subterfuge or agreement; no peace is ever in store for any of us, but that which we shall win by victory over shame or sin,—victory over the sin that oppresses, as well as over that which corrupts.—*Ruskin.*

The man who consecrates his hours by vigorous effort, and an honest aim, at once he draws the sting of life and Death; he walks with nature; and her paths are peace.—*Young.*

PEDANTRY.—Pedantry crams our heads with learned lumber, and takes out our brains to make room for it.—*Colton.*

A well-read fool is the most pestilent of blockheads; his learning is a flail which he knows how to handle, and with which he breaks his neighbor's shins as well as his own. Keep a fellow of this description at arm's length, as you value the integrity of your bones.—*Stanislaus.*

If a strong attachment of a particular subject, a total ignorance of every other; an eagerness to introduce that subject upon all occasions, and a confirmed habit of declaiming upon it without either wit or discretion, be the marks of a pedantic character, as they certainly are, it belongs to the illiterate as well as the learned; and St. James's itself may boast of producing as arrant pedants as were ever sent forth from a college.—*B. Thornton.*

Pedantry, in the common acceptation of the word, means an absurd ostentation of learning, and stiffness of phraseology, proceeding from a misguided knowledge of books, and a total ignorance of men.—*Mackenzie.*

There is a pedantry in manners, as in all arts and sciences, and sometimes in trades. Pedantry is properly the overrating any kind of knowledge we pretend to, and if that kind of knowledge be a trifle in itself, the pedantry is the greater.—*Swift.*

It is not a circumscribed situation so much as a narrow vision that creates pedants; not having a pet study or science, but a narrow, vulgar soul, which prevents a man from seeing all sides and hearing all things; in short, the intolerant man is the real pedant.—*Richter.*

The vacant skull of a pedant generally furnishes out a throne and temple for vanity.—*Shenstone.*

Deep versed in books, and shallow in himself.—*Milton.*

As pedantry is an ostentatious obtrusion of knowledge, in which those who hear us cannot sympathize, it is a fault of which soldiers, sailors, sportsmen, gamesters, cultivators, and all men engaged in a particular occupation, are quite as guilty as scholars; but they have the good fortune to have the vice only of pedantry, while scholars have both the vice and the name for it too. —*S. Smith.*

With loads of learned lumber in his head.—*Pope.*

Pedantry prides herself on being wrong by rules; while common sense is contented to be right without them. The former would rather stumble in following the dead, than walk upright by the profane assistance of the living.—*Colton.*

We only toil and labor to stuff the memory, and in the mean time leave the conscience and understanding unfurnished and void. As old birds who fly abroad to forage for grain, bring it home in their beak, without tasting it themselves, to feed their young, so our pedants go picking knowledge here and there, out of several authors, and hold it at their tongues' end, only to distribute it among their pupils.—*Montaigne.*

Pedantry and taste are as inconsistent as gayety and melancholy.—*Lavater.*

A man who has been brought up among books, and is able to talk of nothing else, is a very indifferent companion, and what we call a pedant. But we should enlarge the title, and give it to every one that does not know how to think out of his profession and particular way of life.—*Addison.*

Pedantry and bigotry are millstones, able to sink the best book which carries the least part of their dead weight. The temper of the pedagogue suits not with the age; and the world, however it may be taught, will not be tutored.—*Shaftesbury.*

Brimful of learning, see the pedant stride, bristling with horrid Greek, and puffed with pride!—A thousand authors he in vain has read, and with their maxims stuffed his empty head; and thinks that without Aristotle's rules, reason is blind, and common sense a fool!—*Boileau.*

PEDIGREE.—(See "ANCESTRY.")

PEN.—There are only two powers in the world, the sword and the pen; and in the end the former is always conquered by the latter.—*Napoleon.*

The strokes of the pen need deliberation, as much as those of the sword need swiftness.—*Julia Ward Howe.*

Scholars are men of peace; they bear no arms, but their tongues are sharper than the sword; their pens carry further and give a louder report than thunder. I had rather stand in the shock of a basilisk than in the fury of a merciless pen.—*Sir Thomas Browne.*

Oh, nature's noblest gift,—my gray goose-quill!—*Byron.*

Take away the sword; states can be saved without it; bring the pen!—*Bulwer.*

PEOPLE.—What people are depends not a little on who and what their progenitors were.—Ascribe what influences you please to education, examples, habits, etc., and after all a great deal depends upon the breed.—*Mills.*

From the time when the exercise of the intellect became the source of strength and wealth, every addition to science, every fresh truth, and every new idea became a germ of power placed within reach of the people.—*De Tocqueville.*

There are three kinds of people in the world, the wills, the wont's and the can'ts. The first accomplish everything; the second oppose everything; the third fail in everything.—*Eclectic Magazine.*

The world may be divided into people that read, people that write, people that think, and fox-hunters.—*Shenstone.*

You may deceive all the people part of the time, and part of the people all the time, but not all the people all the time.—*Lincoln.*

Most people judge others either by the company they keep, or by their fortune.—*Rochefoucauld.*

Local assemblies of the people constitute the strength of free nations.—Municipal institutions are to liberty, what primary schools are to science: they bring it within the people's reach, and teach them how to use and enjoy it.—A nation may establish a system of free government, but without the spirit of municipal institutions it cannot have the spirit of liberty.—*De Tocqueville.*

PERCEPTION.—Make a point never so clear, and it is great odds that a man whose habits, and the bent of whose mind lie a contrary way shall be unable to comprehend it;—so weak a thing is reason in competition with inclination.—*Bp. Berkeley.*

We like to divine others, but do not like to be divined ourselves.—*Rochefoucauld.*

Simple creatures, whose thoughts are not taken up, like those of educated people, with the care of a great museum of dead phrases, are very quick to see the live facts which are going on about them.—*O. W. Holmes.*

Penetration seems a kind of inspiration; it gives me an idea of prophecy.—*Greville.*

The heart has eyes that the brain knows nothing of.—*C. H. Parkhurst.*

To see what is right, and not do it, is want of courage, or of principle.—*Confucius.*

PERFECTION.—Among the other excellencies of man, this is one, that he can form the image of perfection much beyond what he has experience of in himself, and is not limited in his conception of wisdom and virtue.—*Hume.*

Perfection is attained by slow degrees; it requires the hand of time.—*Voltaire.*

To arrive at perfection, a man should have very sincere friends or inveterate enemies; because he would be made sensible of his good or ill conduct, either by the censures of the one or the admonitions of the other.—*Diogenes.*

Bachelor's wives and old maid's children are always perfect.—*Chamfort.*

We are what we are; we cannot be truly other than ourselves. We reach perfection not by copying, much less by aiming at originality, but by constantly and steadily working out the life which is common to all, according to the character which God has given us.

The more perfect the sight is the more delightful the beautiful object. The more perfect the appetite, the sweeter the food. The more musical the ear, the more pleasant the melody. The more perfect the soul, the more joyous the joys of heaven and the more glorious that glory.—*Baxter.*

Perfection consists not in doing extraordinary things, but in doing ordinary things extraordinarily well. Neglect nothing; the most trivial action may be performed to God.—*Angelique Arnauld.*

Aim at perfection in everything, though in most things it is unattainable. —However, they who aim at it, and persevere, will come much nearer to it than those whose laziness and despondency make them give it up as unattainable.—*Chesterfield.*

The Stoic philosophy insults human nature, and discourages all our attempts, by enjoining and promising a perfection in this life, of which we feel ourselves incapable. The Christian religion shows compassion to our weakness, by prescribing to us only the practical task of aiming continually at further improvements and animates our endeavors, by the promise of divine aid, equal to our trial.

It is reasonable to have perfection in our eye that we may always advance toward it, though we know it can never be reached.—*Johnson.*

He who boasts of being perfect is perfect in folly. I never saw a perfect man. Every rose has its thorns, and every day its night. Even the sun shows spots, and the skies are darkened with clouds. And faults of some kind nestle in every bosom.—*Spurgeon.*

If we pretend to have reached either perfection or satisfaction, we have degraded ourselves and our work. God's work only may express that, but ours may never have that sentence written upon it, "Behold it was very good."—*Ruskin.*

Perfection does not exist; to understand it is the triumph of human intelligence; to expect to possess it is the most dangerous kind of madness.—*Alfred de Musset.*

Faultily faultless, icily regular, splendidly null, dead perfection; no more.—*Tennyson.*

Whoever thinks a faultless piece to see, thinks what ne'er was, nor is, nor ever shall be.—*Pope.*

The acorn does not become an oak in a day; the ripened scholar is not made by a single lesson; the well-trained soldier was not the raw recruit of yesterday; there are always months between the seed-time and harvest. So the path of the just is like the shining light, which shineth more and more unto the perfect day.—*R. B. Nichol.*

This is the very perfection of a man, to find out his own imperfection.—*Augustine.*

He that seeks perfection on earth leaves nothing new for the saints to find in heaven; as long as men teach, there will be mistakes in divinity; and as long as they govern, errors in state.—*F. Osborn.*

PERSECUTION.—Persecution is not wrong because it is cruel, but cruel because it is wrong.—*Whately.*

The history of persecution is a history of endeavors to cheat nature, to make water run uphill, to twist a rope of sand. It makes no difference whether the actors be many or one, a tyrant or a mob.—*Emerson.*

For belief or practice in religion no man ought to be punished or molested by any outward force whatever.—*Milton.*

The resource of bigotry and intolerance, when convicted of error, is always the same; silenced by argument, it endeavors to silence by persecution, in old times by fire and sword, in modern days by the tongue.—*C. Simmons.*

Persecution often does in this life, what the last great day will do completely, separate the wheat from the tares.—*Milner.*

In all places, and in all times, those religionists who have believed too much, have been more inclined to violence and persecution than those who have believed too little.—*Colton.*

Wherever you see persecution, there is more than a probability that truth is on the persecuted side.—*Bp. Latimer.*

The blood of the martyrs is the seed of the church.—*Jerome.*

The way of the world is, to praise dead saints, and persecute living ones.—*N. Howe.*

Of all persecutions, that of calumny is the most intolerable. Any other kind of persecution can affect our outward circumstances only, our properties, our lives; but this may affect our characters forever.—*Hazlitt.*

To banish, imprison, plunder, starve, hang, and burn men for religion, is not the gospel of Christ, but the policy of the devil.—Christ never used anything that looked like force or violence but once, and that was to drive bad men out of the temple, not to drive them in. —*Jortin.*

There is nothing more unreasonable, more inconsistent with the rights of human nature, more contrary to the spirit and precepts of the Christian religion, more iniquitous and unjust, more impolitic, than persecution.—It is against natural religion, against revealed religion, and against sound policy.— *Lord Mansfield.*

PERSEVERANCE.—The falling drops at last will wear the stone.— *Lucretius.*

Great works· are performed, not by strength, but Ly perseverance.—He that shall walk, with vigor, three hours a day, will pass, in seven years, a space equal to the circumference of the globe. —*Johnson.*

Perseverance is a Roman virtue, that wins each godlike act, and plucks success even from the spear-proof crests of rugged danger.—*Havard.*

I'm proof against that word failure. I've seen behind it. The only failure a man ought to fear is failure in cleaving to the purpose he sees to be best.— *George Eliot.*

If a man has any brains at all, let him hold on to his calling, and, in the grand sweep of things, his turn will come at last.—*W. McCune.*

An enterprise, when fairly once begun, should not be left till all that ought is won.—*Shakespeare.*

Great effects come of industry and perseverance; for audacity doth almost bind and mate the weaker sort of minds.—*Bacon.*

All the performances of human art, at which we look with praise or wonder, are instances of the resistless force of perseverance: it is by this that the quarry becomes a pyramid, and that distant countries are united with canals. If a man was to compare the effect of a single stroke of the pick-ax, or of one impression of the spade with the general design and last result, he would be overwhelmed by the sense of their disproportion; yet those petty operations, incessantly continued, in time surmount the greatest difficulties, and mountains are levelled, and oceans

bounded, by the slender force of human beings.—*Johnson.*

Much rain wears the marble.—*Shakespeare.*

Perpetual pushing and assurance put a difficulty out of countenance, and make a seeming impossibility give way. —*Jeremy Collier.*

See first that the design is wise and just: that ascertained, pursue it resolutely; do not for one repulse forego the purpose that you resolved to effect. —*Shakespeare.*

Let us only suffer any person to tell us his story, morning and evening, but for one twelve-month, and he will become our master.—*Burke.*

It is all very well to tell me that a young man has distinguished himself by a brilliant first speech. He may go on, or he may be satisfied with his first triumph; but show me a young man who has not succeeded at first, and nevertheless has gone on, and I will back that young man to do better than most of those who have succeeded at the first trial.—*C. J. Fox.*

Every man who observes vigilantly, and resolves steadfastly, grows unconsciously into genius.—*Bulwer.*

Nothing is so hard, but search will find it out.—*Herrick.*

No road is too long to the man who advances deliberately and without undue haste; and no honors are too distant for the man who prepares himself for them with patience.—*Bruyère.*

The virtue lies in the struggle, not in the prize.—*Milnes.*

Perseverance and audacity generally win.—*Mad. Deluzy.*

By gnawing through a dyke, even a rat may drown a nation.—*Burke.*

I argue not against heaven's hand or will, nor bate a jot of heart or hope, but still bear up, and steer right onward. —*Milton.*

There is no royal road to anything. —One thing at a time, and all things in succession. That which grows slowly endures.—*J. G. Holland.*

Perseverance, dear my lord, keeps honor bright. To have none, is to hang quite out of fashion, like a rusty nail in monumental mockery.—*Shakespeare.*

It is with many enterprises as with striking fire; we do not meet with success except by reiterated efforts, and often at the instant when we despaired of success.—*Mad. de Maintenon.*

Every noble work is at first impossible.—*Carlyle.*

There are two ways of attaining an important end—force and perseverance. Force falls to the lot only of the privileged few, but austere and sustained perseverance can be practised by the most insignificant. Its silent power grows irresistible with time.—*Mad. Swetchine.*

The conditions of conquest are always easy. We have but to toil awhile, endure awhile, believe always, and never turn back.—*Simms.*

I hold a doctrine, to which I owe not much, indeed, but all the little I ever had, namely, that with ordinary talent and extraordinary perseverance, all things are attainable.—*T. F. Buxton.*

The nerve that never relaxes, the eye that never blenches, the thought that never wanders,—these are the masters of victory.—*Burke.*

Hasten slowly, and without losing heart put your work twenty times upon the anvil.—*Boileau.*

Few things are impracticable in themselves; and it is for want of application, rather than of means, that men fail of success.—*Rochefoucauld.*

Victory belongs to the most persevering.—*Napoleon.*

Never despair; but if you do, work on in despair.—*Burke.*

Some men give up their designs when they have almost reached the goal; while others, on the contrary, obtain a victory by exerting, at the last moment, more vigorous efforts than before.—*Polybius.*

Hard pounding, gentlemen; but we will see who can pound the longest.—*Wellington at Waterloo.*

Perseverance gives power to weakness, and opens to poverty the world's wealth. It spreads fertility over the barren landscape, and bids the choicest fruits and flowers spring up and flourish in the desert abode of thorns and briers.—*S. G. Goodrich.*

In the lexicon of youth, which fate reserves for a bright manhood, there is no such word as fail.—*Bulwer.*

Even in social life, it is persistency which attracts confidence more than talents and accomplishments.—*E. P. Whipple.*

No rock so hard but that a little wave may beat admission in a thousand years. —*Tennyson.*

Persistent people begin their success where others end in failure.—*Edward Eggleston.*

The divine insanity of noble minds, that never falters nor abates, but labors, endures, and waits, till all that it foresees it finds, or what it cannot find, creates.—*Longfellow.*

Whoever perseveres will be crowned. —*Herder.*

The difference between perseverance and obstinacy is, that one often comes from a strong will, and the other from a strong won't.—*H. W. Beecher.*

PERVERSENESS.—Some men put me in mind of half-bred horses, which often grow worse in proportion as you feed and exercise them for improvement. —*Gréville.*

Stiff in opinion; always in the wrong. —*Dryden.*

To willful men, the injuries that they themselves procure, must be their schoolmasters.—*Shakespeare.*

So remarkably perverse is the nature of man, that he despises those that court him, and admires whoever will not bend before him.—*Thucydides.*

Some men, like spaniels, will only fawn the more when repulsed, but will pay little heed to a friendly caress.— *Abd-el-Kader.*

The worst things are the perversions of good things. Abused intellectual gifts make the dangerous villain; abused sensibilities make the accomplished tempter; abused affections engender the keenest of all misery.—*James McCosh.*

The strength of the donkey mind lies in adopting a course inversely as the arguments urged, which, well considered, requires as great a mental force as the direct sequence.—*George Eliot.*

When once a man is determined to believe, the very absurdity of the doctrine confirms him in his faith.—*Junius*.

We have all a propensity to grasp at forbidden fruit.—*From the Latin*.

PHILANTHROPY.—It is an old saying, that charity begins at home; but this is no reason it should not go abroad; a man should live with the world as a citizen of the world; he may have a preference for the particular quarter or square, or even alley in which he lives, but he should have a generous feeling for the welfare of the whole.—*Cumberland*.

Who will not give some portion of his ease, his blood, his wealth, for others' good, is a poor, frozen churl.—*Joanna Baillie*.

Not for himself, but for the world he lives.—*Lucan*.

There is no philanthropy equal to that which the gospel plants in the human heart.—It turns the severest sacrifices for Christ and humanity into pleasures, and enriches the soul with impulses and aspirations that grow only in the soil of love.—*Independent*.

This is true philanthropy, that buries not its gold in ostentatious charity, but builds its hospital in the human heart. —*Harley*.

Philanthropy, like charity, must begin at home; from this centre our sympathies should extend in an ever widening circle.—*Lamb*.

Where there is the most love to God, there will be there the truest and most enlarged philanthropy.—*Southey*.

PHILOSOPHY.—To be a philosopher is not merely to have subtle thoughts; but so to love wisdom as to live according to its dictates.—*Thoreau*.

Philosophy is the art and law of life, and it teaches us what to do in all cases, and, like good marksmen, to hit the white at any distance.—*Seneca*.

When men comfort themselves with philosophy, 'tis not because they have got two or three sentences, but because they have digested those sentences, and made them their own: philosophy is nothing but discretion.—*Selden*.

Philosophy hath given us several plausible rules for attaining peace and tranquillity of mind, but they fall very much short of bringing men to it.—*Tillotson*.

To be a husbandman, is but a retreat from the city; to be a philosopher, from the world; or rather a retreat from the world as it is man's, into the world as it is God's.—*Cowley*.

The modern sceptical philosophy consists in believing everything but the truth, and exactly in proportion to the want of evidence; in making windows that shut out the light, and passages that lead to nothing.—*Nisbet*.

True philosophy invents nothing; it merely establishes and describes what is.—*Cousin*.

Philosophy can add to our happiness in no other manner but by diminishing our misery; it should not pretend to increase our present stock, but make us economists of what we are possessed of. Happy were we all born philosophers; all born with a talent of thus dissipating our own cares by spreading them upon all mankind.—*Goldsmith*.

The discovery of what is true, and the practice of that which is good, are the two most important objects of philosophy.—*Voltaire*.

To philosophize in a just sense, is but to carry good breeding a step higher. For the accomplishment of breeding is, to learn what is decent in company or beautiful in arts; and the sum of philosophy is to learn what is just in society, and beautiful in nature and the order of the world.—*Shaftesbury*.

Philosophy is the art of living.—*Plutarch*.

Philosophy consists not in airy schemes or idle speculations; the rule and conduct of all social life is her great province.—*Thomson*.

Philosophy triumphs easily over past and over future evils, but present evils triumph over philosophy.—*Rochefoucauld*.

Philosophy is a bully that talks very loud, when the danger is at a distance; but the moment she is hard pressed by the enemy, she is not to be found at her post, but leaves the brunt of the battle to be borne by her humbler but steadier comrade, religion.—*Colton*.

Adversity's sweet milk, philosophy.—*Shakespeare*.

It is a maxim received among philosophers themselves, from the days of Aristotle down to those of Sir William Hamilton, that philosophy ceases where truth is acknowledged.—*Bulwer.*

It is not a head merely, but a heart and resolution, which complete the real philosopher.—*Shaftesbury.*

Philosophy has been called the knowledge of our knowledge; it might more truly be called the knowledge of our ignorance, or in the language of Kant, the knowledge of the limits of our knowledge.—*Max Müller.*

Philosophy is the science which considers truth.—*Aristotle.*

Christianity is a philosophy of principles rather than of rules and so is fitted for universal extension and acceptance.—*Tryon Edwards.*

Real philosophy seeks rather to solve than to deny. While we hear, every day, the small pretenders to science talk of the absurdities of alchemy, and the dream of the Philosopher's Stone, a more erudite knowledge is aware that by alchemists the greatest discoveries in science have been made, and much which still seems abstruse, had we the key to the mystic phraseology they were compelled to adopt, might open the way to yet more noble acquisitions.—*Bulwer.*

It is the bounty of nature that we live, but of philosophy, that we live well; which is, in truth, a greater benefit than life itself.—*Seneca.*

Philosophy is as far separated from impiety as religion is from fanaticism. —*Diderot.*

True philosophy is that which makes us to ourselves and to all about us, better; and at the same time, more content, patient, calm, and more ready for all decent and pure enjoyment.—*Lavater.*

All philosophy lies in two words, sustain and abstain.—*Epictetus.*

Philosophy is to poetry, what old age is to youth; and the stern truths of philosophy are as fatal to the fictions of the one, as the chilling testimonies of experience are to the hopes of the other. —*Colton.*

In wonder all philosophy began; in wonder it ends; and admiration fills up the interspace.— But the first is the wonder of ignorance; the last is the parent of adoration.—*Coleridge.*

The idea of philosophy is truth; the idea of religion is life.—*Peter Bayne.*

Philosophy is one thing, and Christianity quite another.—The former seeks to cure the vices of human nature by working upon the head; the latter by educating the heart.—Both endeavor to lead men to what is right; but philosophy only explains what it is right to do, while Christianity undertakes to make men disposed to do it.—*Ecce Homo.*

Philosophy is a proud, sullen detector of the poverty and misery of man. It may turn him from the world with a proud, sturdy contempt; but it cannot come forward and say, here are rest, grace, pardon, peace, strength, and consolation.—*Cecil.*

To study philosophy is nothing but to prepare one's self to die.—*Cicero.*

Make philosophy thy journey, theology thy journey's end: philosophy is a pleasant way, but dangerous to him that either tires or retires; in this journey it is safe neither to loiter nor to rest, till thou hast attained thy journey's end; he that sits down a philosopher rises up an atheist.—*Quarles.*

The first business of a philosopher is, to part with self-conceit.—*Epictetus.*

Philosophy, when superficially studied, excites doubt; when thoroughly explored, it dispels it.—*Bacon.*

Philosophy alone makes the mind invincible, and places us out of the reach of fortune, so that all her arrows fall short of us.—*Seneca.*

There are more things in heaven and earth, Horatio, than are dreamed of in your philosophy.—*Shakespeare."*

Be a philosopher; but amid all your philosophy, be still a man.—*Hume.*

Philosophical studies are beset by one peril, that a person easily brings himself to think that he thinks; and a smattering of science encourages conceit. Moreover, the vain man is generally a doubter. It is Newton who sees himself in a child on the seashore, and his discoveries in the colored shells.—*Willmott.*

Sublime philosophy! thou art the patriarch's ladder, reaching heaven and bright with beckoning angels; but, alas! we see thee, like the patriarch, but in dreams, by the first step, dull slumbering on the earth.—*Bulwer*.

Philosophy, if rightly defined, is nothing but the love of wisdom.—*Cicero*.

It is easy for men to write and talk like philosophers, but to act with wisdom, there is the rub!—*Rivarol*.

Admiration is the foundation of all philosophy; investigation the progress; and ignorance the end.—*Montaigne*.

Philosophy is a goddess, whose head indeed is in heaven, but whose feet are upon earth; she attempts more than she accomplishes, and promises more than she performs.—*Colton*.

Philosophy is of two kinds: that which relates to conduct, and that which relates to knowledge. The first teaches us to value all things at their real worth, to be contented with little, modest in prosperity, patient in trouble, equal-minded at all times. It teaches us our duty to our neighbor and ourselves. But it is he who possesses both that is the true philosopher. The more he knows, the more he is desirous of knowing; and yet the farther he advances in knowledge, the better he understands how little he can attain, and the more deeply he feels that God alone can satisfy the infinite desires of an immortal soul. To understand this is the height and perfection of philosophy.—*Southey*.

Philosophy goes no further than probabilities, and in every assertion keeps a doubt in reserve.—*Froude*.

The world cannot show us a more exalted character than that of a truly religious philosopher, who delights to turn all things to the glory of God; who, in the objects of his sight, derives improvement to his mind; and in the glass of things temporal, sees the image of things spiritual.—*Venning*.

He who seeks philosophy in divinity, seeks the dead among the living; and he that seeks divinity in philosophy, seeks the living among the dead.—*Venning*.

Every system of philosophy is little in comparison with Christianity.—Philosophy may expand our ideas of creation, but it neither inspires love to the moral character of the Creator, nor a well-groomed hope of eternal life.—At most, it can only place us on the top of Pisgah, and there, like Moses, we must die; it gives us no possession of the good land.—It is the province of Christianity to add, "All is yours."—*Anon*.

Divine philosophy! by whose pure light, we first distinguish, then pursue the right; thy power the breast from every error frees, and weeds out all its vices by degrees.—*Gifford*.

PHYSIC.—(See "MEDICINE.")

Physic is of little use to a temperate person, for a man's own observation on what he finds does him good, and what hurts him, is the best physic to preserve health.—*Bacon*.

We have not only multiplied diseases, but we have made them more fatal.—*Dr. R. Rush*.

Use three physicians: first, Doctor Quiet; then, Doctor Merryman; and then, Doctor Diet.

Whoever has lived twenty years ought to know what is hurtful and what wholesome to him, and know how to order himself without physic.—*Tiberius*.

Every one is a physician or a fool at forty.—*Old Maxim*.

God heals, and the doctor takes the fee.—*Franklin*.

Exercise, temperance, fresh air, and needful rest are the best of all physicians.

A wise physician, skilled our ills to heal, is more than armies to the public weal.—*Pope*.

Physicians mend or end us; but though in health we sneer, when sick we call them to attend us, without the least propensity to jeer.—*Byron*.

PHYSIOGNOMY.—(See "FACE.")

There is nothing truer than physiognomy, taken in connection with manner.—*Dickens*.

When I see a man with a sour, shriveled face, I cannot forbear pitying his wife; and when I meet with an open, ingenuous countenance, I think on the happiness of his friends, his family, and his relations.—*Addison*.

Trust not too much to an enchanting face.—*Virgil*.

It is a point of cunning to wait upon him with whom you speak with your eye, as the Jesuits give it in precept; for there be many wise men that have secret hearts and transparent countenances.—*Bacon*.

As the language of the face is universal, so 'tis very comprehensive; 'tis the shorthand of the mind, and crowds a great deal in a little room.—*Jeremy Collier.*

The features come insensibly to be formed and assume their shape from the frequent and habitual expression of certain affections of the soul. These affections are marked on the countenance; nothing is more certain than this; and when they turn into habits, they must leave on it durable impressions.—*Rousseau.*

He who observes the speaker more than the sound of his words, will seldom meet with disappointments.—*Lavater.*

Spite of Lavater, faces are often great lies.—They are the paper money of society, for which, on demand, there frequently proves to be no gold in the human coffer.—*F. G. Trafford.*

Pickpockets and beggars are the best practical physiognomists, without having read a line of Lavater, who, it is notorious, mistook a philosopher for a highwayman.—*Colton.*

The distinguishing characters of the face, and the lineaments of the body, grow more plain and visible with time and age; but the peculiar physiognomy of the mind is most discernible in children.—*Locke.*

The countenance may be defined as the title-page which heralds the contents of the human volume, but like other title-pages, it sometimes puzzles, often misleads, and often says nothing to the purpose.—*W. Matthews.*

PICTURES.—(See "PAINTING.")

PIETY.—(See "RELIGION.")

Let us learn upon earth, those things which can prepare us for heaven.—*Jerome.*

All is vanity which is not honest, and there is no solid wisdom but in true piety.—*Evelyn.*

True piety hath in it nothing weak, nothing sad, nothing constrained. It enlarges the heart; it is simple, free, and attractive.—*Fénelon.*

I do not doubt but that genuine piety is the spring of peace of mind; it enables us to bear the sorrows of life, and lessens the pangs of death: the same cannot be said of irreligion.—*Bruyère.*

Our piety must be weak and imperfect if it do not conquer the fear of death. —*Fénelon.*

Piety is a silver chain uniting heaven and earth, temporal and spiritual, God and man together.—*Caussin.*

Piety is the only proper and adequate relief of decaying man. He that grows old without religious hopes, as he declines into imbecility, and feels pains and sorrows crowding upon him, falls into a gulf of bottomless misery, in which every reflection must plunge him deeper and deeper.—*Johnson.*

A mind full of piety and knowledge is always rich; it is a bank that never fails; it yields a perpetual dividend of happiness.

Among the many strange servilities mistaken for pieties one of the least lovely is that which hopes to flatter God by despising the world and vilifying human nature.—*G. H. Lewes.*

Growth in piety will be manifest in more usefulness and less noise; more tenderness of conscience and less scrupulosity; more steadfastness, peace, humility; more resignation under God's chastisements, and more patience under man's injuries. When the corn is full in the ear, it bends down because it is full.

We are surrounded by motives to piety and devotion, if we would but mind them. The poor are designed to excite our liberality: the miserable, our pity; the sick, our assistance; the ignorant, our instruction; those that are fallen, our helping hand. In those who are vain, we see the vanity of the world; in those who are wicked, our own frailty. When we see good men rewarded, it confirms our hope; and when evil men are punished, it excites our fear.—*Bp. Wilson.*

PITY.—Pity is not natural to man. Children and savages are always cruel. Pity is acquired and improved by the cultivation of reason. We may have uneasy sensations from seeing a creature in distress, without pity; but we have not pity unless we wish to relieve him. When I am on my way to dine with a friend, and, finding it late, bid the coachman make haste, when he whips his horses I may feel unpleasantly that the animals are put to pain, but I do not wish him to desist; no, sir; I wish him to drive on.—*Johnson.*

Pity is sworn servant unto love, and this be sure, wherever it begin to make the way, it lets the master in.—*Daniel.*

Pity is akin to love; and every thought of that soft kind is welcome to my soul.—*Southern.*

Pity is the virtue of the law, and none but tyrants use it cruelly.—*Shakespeare.*

The truly brave are soft of heart and eyes, and feel for what their duty bids them do.—*Byron.*

Oh, brother man, fold to thy heart thy brother; where pity dwells, the peace of God is there.—*Whittier.*

Pity is best taught by fellowship in woe.—*Coleridge.*

Pity swells the tide of love.—*Young.*

Of all the paths that lead to a woman's love, pity is the straightest.— *Beaumont and Fletcher.*

Nothing but infinite pity is sufficient for the infinite pathos of human life.— *John Inglesant.*

PLACE.—Where you are is of no moment, but only what you are doing there. It is not the place that ennobles you, but you the place; and this only by doing that which is great and noble. —*Petrarch.*

It is not the place that maketh the person, but the person that maketh the place honorable.—*Cicero.*

Whatever the place allotted to us by Providence, that for us is the post of honor and duty. God estimates us not by the position we are in, but by the way in which we fill it.—*Tryon Edwards.*

A true man never frets about his place in the world, but just slides into it by the gravitation of his nature, and swings there as easily as a star.—*E. H. Chapin.*

To an honest mind the best perquisites of a place are the advantages it gives a man of doing good.—*Addison.*

He who thinks his place below him, will certainly be below his place.— *Saville.*

The place is dignified by the doer's deed.—*Shakespeare.*

PLAGIARISM. — (See "ORIGINALITY.")

Nothing is sillier than this charge of plagiarism. There is no sixth commandment in art. The poet dare help himself wherever he lists—wherever he finds material suited to his work. He may even appropriate entire columns with their carved capitals, if the temple he thus supports be a beautiful one. Goethe understood this very well, and so did Shakespeare before him.—*Heine.*

It is not strange that remembered ideas should often take advantage of the crowd of thoughts and smuggle themselves in as original.—Honest thinkers are always stealing unconsciously from each other.—Our minds are full of waifs and estrays which we think our own.— Innocent plagiarism turns up everywhere.—*O. W. Holmes.*

No earnest thinker is a plagiarist pure and simple. He will never borrow from others that which he has not already, more or less, thought out for himself.— *Charles Kingsley.*

Keep your hands from literary picking and stealing. But if you cannot refrain from this kind of stealth, abstain from murdering what you steal.—*Toplady.*

Plagiarists are always suspicious of being stolen from.—*Coleridge.*

It has come to be practically a sort of rule in literature, that a man, having once shown himself capable of original writing, is entitled, thenceforth, to steal from the writings of others at discretion. Thought is the property of him who can entertain it and of him who can adequately place it.—A certain awkwardness marks the use of borrowed thoughts; but as soon as we have learned what to do with them, they become our own.—*Emerson.*

Literature is full of coincidences, which some love to believe are plagiarisms.—There are thoughts always abroad in the air which it takes more wit to avoid than to hit upon.—*O. W. Holmes.*

Horace or Boileau have said such a thing, before.—I take your word for it, but I said it as my own; and may I not have the same just thoughts after them, as others may have after me?—*Bruyere.*

Plagiarists have, at least, the merit of preservation.—*Disraeli.*

Steal! to be sure they may, and, egad, serve your best thoughts as gipsies do stolen children—disfigure them to make them pass for their own.—*Sheridan.*

Most plagiarists, like the drone, have not the taste to select, the industry to acquire, nor the skill to improve, but impudently pilfer the honey ready prepared, from the hive.—*Colton.*

All the makers of dictionaries, and all compilers who do nothing else than repeat backwards and forwards the opinions, the errors, the impostures, and the truths already printed, we may term plagiarists; but they are honest plagiarists, who do not arrogate the merit of invention.—Call them, if you please, book-makers, not authors; rather second-hand dealers than plagiarists.—*Voltaire.*

Borrowed thoughts, like borrowed money, only show the poverty of the borrower.—*Lady Blessington.*

As monarchs have a right to call in the specie of a state, and raise its value by their own impression; so are there certain prerogative geniuses, who are above plagiaries, who cannot be said to steal, but, from their improvement of a thought, rather to borrow it, and repay the commonwealth of letters with interest; and may more properly be said to adopt than to kidnap a sentiment, by leaving it heir to their own fame.—*Sterne.*

It is a special trick of low cunning to squeeze out knowledge from a modest man who is eminent in any science, and then to use it as legally acquired, and pass the source in total silence.—*Horace Walpole.*

Touching plagiarism in general, it is to be remembered that all men who have sense and feeling are being continually helped; they are taught by every person whom they meet and enriched by everything that falls in their way. The greatest is he who has been oftenest aided; and, if the attainments of all human minds could be traced to their real sources, it would be found that the world had been laid most under contribution by the men of most original power, and that every day of their existence deepened their debt to their

race, while it enlarged their gifts to it. —*Ruskin.*

If we steal thoughts from the moderns, it will be cried down as plagiarism; if from the ancients, it will be cried up as erudition.—But in this respect every author is a Spartan, more ashamed of the discovery than of the depredation.—*Colton.*

There is a very pretty Eastern tale, of which the fate of plagiarists often reminds us. The slave of a magician saw his master wave his wand, and heard him give orders to the spirits who arose at the summons. The slave stole the wand, and waved it himself in the air; but he had not observed that his master used the left hand for that purpose. The spirits thus irregularly summoned, tore the thief to pieces instead of obeying his orders.—*Macaulay.*

Borrowed garments never keep one warm. A curse goes with them, as with Harry Gill's blankets. Nor can one get smuggled goods safely into kingdom come. How lank and pitiful does one of these gentry look, after posterity's customs-officers have had the plucking of him!—*J. R. Lowell.*

PLEASING.—The art of pleasing consists in being pleased. To be amiable is to be satisfied with one's self and others. —*Hazlitt.*

The happy gift of being agreeable seems to consist not in one, but in an assemblage of talents tending to communicate delight; and how many are there, who, by easy manners, sweetness of temper, and a variety of other undefinable qualities, possess the power of pleasing without any visible effort, without the aids of wit, wisdom, or learning, nay, as it should seem, in their defiance; and this without appearing even to know that they possess it.—*Cumberland.*

Most arts require long study and application; but the most useful art of all, that of pleasing, requires only the desire.

We all live in the hope of pleasing somebody; and the pleasure of pleasing ought to be greatest, and always will be greatest, when our endeavors are exerted in consequence of our duty.—*Johnson.*

People who make a point of pleasing everybody, seldom have a heart for any one. The love of self is the secret of their desire to please; and their temper is generally fickle and insincere.

If you wish to please people, you must begin by understanding them.—*Charles Reade.*

PLEASURE.—(See " HAPPINESS.")

Pleasure must first have the warrant that it is without sin; then the measure, that it is without excess.—*H. G. J. Adam.*

There is little pleasure in the world that is true and sincere beside the pleasure of doing our duty and doing good. I am sure no other is comparable to this.—*Tillotson.*

Enjoy present pleasures in such a way as not to injure future ones.—*Seneca.*

Pleasure, when it is a man's chief purpose, disappoints itself; and the constant application to it palls the faculty of enjoying it, and leaves the sense of our inability for that we wish, with a disrelish of everything else. Thus the intermediate seasons of the man of pleasure are more heavy than one would impose upon the vilest criminal.—*Steele.*

The seeds of repentance are sown in youth by pleasure, but the harvest is reaped in age by suffering.—*Colton.*

When pleasure rules the life, mind, sensibility, and health shrivel and waste, till at last, and not tardily, no joy in earth or heaven can move the worn-out heart to response.—*T. T. Munger.*

A man that knows how to mix pleasures with business, is never entirely possessed by them; he either quits or resumes them at his will; and in the use he makes of them he rather finds a relaxation of mind than a dangerous charm that might corrupt him.—*St. Evremond.*

Fly the pleasure that bites to-morrow. —*Herbert.*

The public pleasures of far the greater part of mankind are counterfeit. Very few carry their philosophy to places of diversion, or are very careful to analyze their enjoyments. The general condition of life is so full of misery, that we are glad to catch delight without inquiring whence it comes, or by what power it is bestowed.—*Johnson.*

Let your pleasures be taken as Daniel took his prayer, with his windows open —pleasures which need not cause a single blush on an ingenuous cheek.—*Theodore Parker.*

The most delicate, the most sensible of all pleasures, consists in promoting the pleasure of others.—*Bruyère.*

Pleasure is one of those commodities which are sold at a thousand shops, and bought by a thousand customers, but of which nobody ever fairly finds possession. Either they know not well how to use, or the commodity will not keep, for no one has ever yet appeared to be satisfied with his bargain. It is too subtle for transition, though sufficiently solid for sale.—*Simms.*

The worst of enemies are flatterers, and the worst of flatterers are pleasures. —*Bossuet.*

Would you judge of the lawfulness or unlawfulness of pleasure, take this rule: whatever weakens your reason, impairs the tenderness of your conscience, obscures your sense of God, or takes off the relish of spiritual things; in short, whatever increases the strength and authority of your body over your mind, that is sin to you, however innocent it may be in itself.—*Southey.*

A life merely of pleasure, or chiefly of pleasure, is always a poor and worthless life, not worth the living; always unsatisfactory in its course, always miserable in its end.—*Theodore Parker.*

The man of pleasure should more properly be termed the man of pain; like Diogenes, he purchases repentance at the highest price, and sells the richest reversion for the poorest reality.—*Colton.*

A life of pleasure makes even the strongest mind frivolous at last.—*Bulwer.*

None has more frequent conversations with disagreeable self than the man of pleasure; his enthusiasms are but few and transient; his appetites, like angry creditors, are continually making fruitless demands for what he is unable to pay; and the greater his former pleasures, the more strong his regret, the more impatient his expectations. A life of pleasure is, therefore, the most unpleasing life.—*Goldsmith.*

Pleasure is a necessary reciprocal: no one feels, who does not at the same time give it. To be pleased, one must please. What pleases you in others, will in general please them in you.—*Chesterfield.*

The greatest pleasure I know, is to do a good action by stealth, and have it found out by accident.—*Lamb.*

Centers, or wooden frames are put under the arches of a bridge, to remain no longer than till the latter are consolidated, and then are thrown away or cast into the fire. Even so, sinful pleasures are the devil's scaffolding to build a habit upon; and once formed and fixed, the pleasures are sent for firewood, and hell begins in this life.—*Coleridge.*

Mental pleasures never cloy; unlike those of the body, they are increased by repetition, approved by reflection, and strengthened by enjoyment.—*Colton.*

There is no greater fool than he who deliberately goes searching for pleasures. For every pleasure to which he habituates himself beyond those which God has put in the natural course of life, is a new fire kindled in his bones, which will burn his life-substance for fuel.—*J. M. Ludlow.*

No state can be more destitute than that of a person, who, when the delights of sense forsake him, has no pleasures of the mind.—*Burgh.*

If all the year were playing holidays, to sport would be as tedious as to work: but when they seldom come, they wished for come, and nothing pleaseth but rare accidents.—*Shakespeare.*

Pleasure and pain, beauty and deformity, good and ill, seemed to me everywhere interwoven; and one with another made a pretty mixture, agreeable enough in the main. 'Twas the same, I fancied, as in some of those rich stuffs where the flowers and ground were oddly put together, with such irregular work and contrary colors, as looked ill in the pattern, but natural and well in the piece.—*Shaftesbury.*

The roses of pleasure seldom last long enough to adorn the brow of him who plucks them, and they are the only roses which do not retain their sweetness after they have lost their beauty.—*Blair.*

Choose such pleasures as recreate much and cost little.—*Fuller.*

Pleasure, like quicksilver, is bright and coy; we strive to grasp it with our utmost skill, still it eludes us, and it glitters still: if seized at last, compute your mighty gains; what is it, but rank poison in your veins?—*Young.*

Violent delights have violent ends, and in their triumph die; like fire and powder, which, as they kiss, consume: the sweetest honey is loathsome in his own deliciousness, and in the taste confounds the appetite.—*Shakespeare.*

Consider pleasures as they depart, not as they come.—*Aristotle.*

Look upon pleasures not upon that side that is next the sun, or where they look beauteously, that is, as they come toward you to be enjoyed, for then they paint and smile, and dress themselves up in tinsel, and glass gems, and counterfeit imagery.—*Jeremy Taylor.*

Pleasure is very seldom found where it is sought. Our brightest blazes of gladness are commonly kindled by unexpected sparks.—*Johnson.*

All fits of pleasure are balanced by an equal degree of pain or languor; 'tis like spending this year, part of the next year's revenue.—*Swift.*

We have not an hour of life in which our pleasures relish not some pain, our sours, some sweetness.—*Massinger.*

Pleasure and revenge have ears more deaf than adders to the voice of any true decision.—*Shakespeare.*

The pursuit in which we cannot ask God's protection must be criminal: the pleasure for which we dare not thank him cannot be innocent.

Worldly and sensual pleasures, for the most part, are short, false, and deceitful. Like drunkenness, they revenge the jolly madness of one hour with the sad repentance of many.

He who spends all his life in sport is like one who wears nothing but fringes, and eats nothing but sauces.—*Richard Fuller.*

The purest pleasures lie within the circle of useful occupation.—Mere pleasure, sought outside of usefulness, is fraught with poison.—*H. W. Beecher.*

Let us be sure that our delights exclude not the presence of God: we may please ourselves so long as we do not displease Him.—*T. Adams.*

He buys honey too dear who licks it from thorns.—*Old Proverb.*

We smile at the ignorance of the savage who cuts down the tree in order to reach its fruit; but the same blunder is made by every person who is over eager and impatient in the pursuit of pleasure. —*Channing.*

Sinful and forbidden pleasures are like poisoned bread; they may satisfy appetite for the moment, but there is death in them at the end.—*Tryon Edwards.*

Mistake not. Those pleasures are not pleasures that trouble the quiet and tranquillity of thy life.—*Jeremy Taylor.*

If I give way to pleasure, I must also yield to grief, to poverty, to labor, to ambition, to anger until I am torn to pieces by my misfortunes and my lust. —*Seneca.*

People should be guarded against temptation to unlawful pleasures by furnishing them the means of innocent ones. In every community there must be pleasures, relaxations, and means of agreeable excitement; and if innocent are not furnished, resort will be had to criminal. Man was made to enjoy as well as labor, and the state of society should be adapted to this principle of human nature.—*Channing.*

The sweetest pleasures are those which do not exhaust hope.—*De Lévis.*

All pleasure must be bought at the price of pain.—The difference between false and true pleasure is this: for the true, the price is paid before you enjoy it; for the false, after you enjoy it.— *John Foster.*

To make pleasures pleasant shorten them.—*Charles Buxton.*

The pleasures of the world are deceitful; they promise more than they give. They trouble us in seeking them, they do not satisfy us when possessing them, and they make us despair in losing them. —*Mad. de Lambert.*

He that is violent in the pursuit of pleasure will not mind turning villain for the purchase.—*Marcus Antoninus.*

Pleasure's couch is virtue's grave.— *Duganne.*

All worldly pleasure is correspondent to a like measure of anxiety.—*F. Osborn.*

In diving to the bottom of pleasures we bring up more gravel than pearls.— *Balzac.*

There is no sterner moralist than pleasure.—*Byron.*

Venture not to the utmost bounds of even lawful pleasures; the limits of good and evil join.—*Fuller.*

What leads to unhappiness, is making pleasure the chief aim.—*Shenstone.*

Pleasure is in general, dangerous and pernicious to virtue.—To be able, therefore, to furnish pleasure that is harmless and pure and unalloyed, is as great a power as man can possess.—*Johnson.*

The man of pleasure little knows the perfect joy he loses for the disappointing gratifications which he pursues.— *Addison.*

No enjoyment is transitory; the impression which it leaves is lasting, and what is done with diligence and toil imparts to the spectator a secret force, of which one cannot say how far the effect may reach.—*Goethe.*

Often and often to me, and instinctively, has an innocent pleasure felt like a foretaste of infinite delight, an antepast of heaven. Nor can I believe otherwise than that pure happiness is of a purifying effect; like the manna from heaven, no doubt it is meant to invigorate as well as to gratify.—*Mountford.*

He who can at all times sacrifice pleasure to duty approaches sublimity.—*Lavater.*

Pleasures, riches, honor, and joy are sure to have care, disgrace, adversity, and affliction in their train. There is no pleasure without pain, no joy without sorrow. O the folly of expecting lasting felicity in a vale of tears, or a paradise in a ruined world!—*Gotthold.*

If the soul be happily disposed, everything becomes capable of affording entertainment, and distress will almost want a name.—*Goldsmith.*

Put this restriction on your pleasures; be cautious that they injure no being that lives.—*Zimmermann.*

Most pleasures, like flowers, when gathered, die.—*Young.*

All earthly delights are sweeter in expectation than enjoyment; but all spiritual pleasures more in fruition than expectation.—*Feltham.*

Pleasure and pain spring not so much from the nature of things, as from our manner of considering them.—*Pleasure* especially, is never an invariable effect of particular circumstances.—Largely that is pleasure which is thought to be so.—*Bovee.*

It is sad to think how few our pleasures really are, and for which we risk eternal good.—*Bailey.*

I look upon it as an equal injustice to loath natural pleasures as to be too much in love with them.—*Montaigne.*

What if a body might have all the pleasures in the world for asking? Who would so unman himself as, by accepting them, to desert his soul, and become a perpetual slave to his senses?—*Seneca.*

Though a taste of pleasure may quicken the relish of life, an unrestrained indulgence leads to inevitable destruction.—*Dodsley.*

The slave of pleasure soon sinks in a kind of voluptuous dotage; intoxicated with present delights, and careless of everything else, his days and nights glide away in luxury or vice, and he has no care, but to keep thought away: for thought is troublesome to him, who lives without his own approbation.—*Johnson.*

Pleasure is to woman what the sun is to the flower; if moderately enjoyed, it beautifies, refreshes and improves; but if immoderately, it withers, deteriorates and destroys.—*Colton.*

POETRY.—Poetry is the art of substantiating shadows, and of lending existence to nothing.—*Burke.*

Poetry is music in words: and music is poetry in sound: both excellent sauce, but those have lived and died poor, who made them their meat.—*Fuller.*

The office of poetry is not to make us think accurately, but feel truly.—*F. W. Robertson.*

Poetry is the music of thought, conveyed to us in the music of language.—*Chatfield.*

Words become luminous when the poet's finger has passed over them its phosphorescence.—*Joubert.*

The greatest poem is not that which is most skillfully constructed, but that in which there is the most poetry.—*L. Schefer.*

You will find poetry nowhere, unless you bring some with you.—*Joubert.*

A poet must needs be before his own age, to be even with posterity.—*J. R. Lowell.*

Sad is his lot, who, once at least in his life, has not been a poet.—*Lamartine.*

Poetry is not made out of the understanding. The question of common sense is always: "What is it good for?" a question which would abolish the rose, and be triumphantly answered by the cabbage.—*J. R. Lowell.*

The poet's eye in a fine frenzy rolling, doth glance from heaven to earth, from earth to heaven; and, as imagination bodies forth the forms of things unknown, the poet's pen turns them to shapes, and gives to airy nothing a local habitation and a name.—*Shakespeare.*

Of all kinds of ambition, that which pursues poetical fame is the wildest.—*Goldsmith.*

If the grain were separated from the chaff which fills the works of our national poets, what is truly valuable would be to what is useless in the proportion of a mole-hill to a mountain.—*Burke.*

By poetry we mean the art of employing words in such a manner as to produce an illusion on the imagination; the art of doing by means of words, what the painter does by means of colors.—*Macaulay.*

Truth shines the brighter clad in verse.—*Pope.*

Poetry reveals to us the loveliness of nature, brings back the freshness of youthful feeling, revives the relish of simple pleasures, keeps unquenched the enthusiasm which warmed the springtime of our being, refines youthful love, strengthens our interest in human nature, by vivid delineations of its tenderest and softest feelings, and, through the brightness of its prophetic visions, helps faith to lay hold on the future life.—*Channing.*

Poetry is the sister of sorrow; every man that suffers and weeps, is a poet; every tear is a verse; and every heart a poem.—*Andre.*

It is shallow criticism that would define poetry as confined to literary productions in rhyme and metre. The written poem is only poetry talking, and the statue, the picture, and the musical composition are poetry acting. Milton and Goethe, at their desks, were not more truly poets than Phidias with his chisel, Raphael at his easel, or deaf Beethoven bending over his piano, inventing and producing strains which he himself could never hope to hear.—*Ruskin.*

Poetry, good sir, in my opinion, is like a tender virgin, very young, and extremely beautiful, whom divers others virgins—namely, all the other sciences—make it their business to enrich, polish and adorn; and to her it belongs to make use of them all, and on her part to give a lustre to them all.—*Cervantes.*

Poetry and consumption are the most flattering of diseases.—*Shenstone.*

A poet ought not to pick nature's pocket. Let him borrow, and so borrow as to repay by the very act of borrowing. Examine nature accurately, but write from recollection, and trust more to the imagination than the memory.—*Coleridge.*

Poets utter great and wise things which they do not themselves understand.—*Plato.*

An artist that works in marble or colors has them all to himself and his tribe, but the man who moulds his thoughts in verse has to employ the materials vulgarized by everybody's use, and glorify them by his handling.—*O. W. Holmes.*

Poetry has been to me its own exceeding great reward: it has given me the habit of wishing to discover the good and beautiful in all that meets and surrounds me.—*Coleridge.*

There are so many tender and holy emotions flying about in our inward world, which, like angels, can never assume the body of an outward act; so many rich and lovely flowers spring up which bear no seed, that it is a happiness poetry was invented, which receives into its limbus all those incorporeal spirits, and the perfume of all these flowers.—*Richter.*

Perhaps there are no warmer lovers of the muse than those who are only permitted occasionally to gain her favors. The shrine is more reverently approached by the pilgrim from afar than the familiar worshipper. Poetry is often most beloved by one whose daily vocation is amid the bustle of the world.—*Tuckerman.*

Poetry is the utterance of deep and heart-felt truth.—The true poet is very near the oracle.—*E. H. Chapin.*

Superstition is the poetry of life, so that it does not injure the poet to be superstitious.—*Goethe.*

Some scrap of a childish song hath often been a truer alms than all the benevolent societies could give. This is the best missionary, knowing when she may knock at the door of the most curmudgeonly hearts, without being turned away unheard. For poesy is love's chosen apostle, and the very almoner of God. She is the home of the outcast, and the wealth of the needy.—*J. R. Lowell.*

You arrive at truth through poetry; I arrive at poetry through truth.—*Joubert.*

As nightingales feed on glow-worms, so poets live upon the living light of nature and beauty.—*Bailey.*

The poet, whether in prose or verse, the creator, can only stamp his images forcibly on the page, in proportion as he has forcibly felt, ardently nursed, and long brooded over them.—*Bulwer.*

Poetry is in itself strength and joy, whether it be crowned by all mankind, or left alone in its own magic hermitage.—*Sterling.*

Poets are never young in one sense. Their delicate ear hears the far-off whispers of eternity, which coarser souls must travel toward for scores of years before their dull sense is touched by them.—*O. W. Holmes.*

In poetry, which is all fable, truth still is the perfection.—*Shaftesbury.*

Whatever the poets pretend, it is plain they give immortality to none but themselves: it is Homer and Virgil we reverence and admire, not Achilles or Æneas.—*Swift.*

I have met with most poetry on trunks; so that I am apt to consider the trunk-maker as the sexton of authorship.—*Byron.*

We have more poets than judges and interpreters of poetry.—It is easier to write an indifferent poem than to understand a good one.—*Montaigne.*

In the hands of genius, the driest stick becomes an Aaron's rod, and buds and blossoms out in poetry. Is he a Burns? the sight of a mountain daisy unseals the fountains of his nature, and he embalms the "bonny gem" in the beauty of his spirit. Is he a Wordsworth? at his touch all nature is instinct with feeling; the spirit of beauty springs up in the footsteps of his going, and the darkest, nakedest grave becomes a sun-lit bank empurpled with blossoms of life. —*H. N. Hudson.*

Poetry is itself a thing of God.—He made his prophets poets; and the more we feel of poesie do we become like God in love and power.—*Bailey.*

All poets pretend to write for im-mortality, but the whole tribe have no objection to present pay and present praise. Lord Burleigh is not the only statesman who has thought one hundred pounds too much for a song, though sung by Spenser; although Oliver Goldsmith is the only poet who ever considered himself to have been overpaid.—*Colton.*

How different is the poet from the mystic.—The former uses symbols, know-ing they are symbols; the latter mistakes them for realities.—*F. W. Robertson.*

Poetry is the record of the best and happiest moments of the happiest and best minds.—*Shelley.*

Poesy is of so subtle a spirit, that in the pouring out of one language into another it will evaporate.—*Denham.*

Poetry is the art of substituting shad-ows, and of lending existence to nothing. —*Burke.*

The best of poetry is ever in alliance with real uncorrupted Christianity; and with the degeneracy of the one always comes the decline of the other: for it is to Christianity that we owe the fullest inspirations of the celestial spirit of charity.—*J. A. St. John.*

The world is full of poetry.—The air is living with its spirit; and the waves dance to the music of its melodies, and sparkle in its brightness.—*Percival.*

Poetry is most just to its divine origin, when it administers the comforts and breathes the thoughts of religion.—*Wordsworth.*

Poetry is the intellect colored by feel-ings.—*Prof. Wilson.*

Thoughts that breathe, and words that burn.—*Gray.*

He who finds elevated and lofty pleasure in the feeling of poetry is a true poet, though he never composed a line of verse in his entire lifetime.—*Mad. Dudevant.*

Poets are all who love and feel great truths, and tell them.—*Bailey.*

Poetry is something to make us wiser and better, by continually revealing those types of beauty and truth which God has set in all men's souls.—*J. R. Lowell.*

Poetry, with all its obscurity, has a more general as well as a more powerful dominion over the passions than the art of painting.—*Burke.*

All that is best in the great poets of all countries, is not what is national in them, but what is universal.—*Longfel-low.*

Poetry begotten of passion is ever de-basing; poetry born of real heartfulness, always ennobles and uplifts.—*A. A. Hop-kins.*

Poetry comes nearer to vital truth than history.—*Plato.*

One merit of poetry few persons will deny; it says more, and in fewer words, than prose.—*Voltaire.*

He who, in an enlightened and literary society, aspires to be a great poet, must first become a little child.—*Macaulay.*

They learn in suffering what they teach in song.—*Shelley.*

POLICY.—Policy consists in serving God in such a manner as not to offend the devil.—*Fuller.*

To manage men one ought to have a sharp mind in a velvet sheath.—*George Eliot.*

A statesman makes the occasion, but the occasion makes the politician.—*G. S. Hillard.*

The devil knew not what he did when he made man politic; he crossed himself by it.—*Shakespeare.*

A politician, Proteus like, must alter his face and habit, and like water seem of the same color that the vessel is that doth contain it, varying his form with the chameleon at each object's change. —*Mason.*

Let go thy hold when a great wheel runs down the hill, lest it break thy neck with following it; but the great one that goes up the hill, let him draw thee after.—*Shakespeare.*

At court one becomes a sort of human

ant-eater, and learns to catch one's prey by one's tongue.—*Bulwer.*

Measures, not men, have always been my mark.—*Goldsmith.*

Turn him to any cause of policy, the Gordian knot of it he will unloose, familiar as his garter.—*Shakespeare.*

It is not juggling that is to be blamed, but much juggling; for the world cannot be governed without it.—*Selden.*

By a kind of fashionable discipline, the eye is taught to brighten, the lip to smile, and the whole countenance to emanate with the semblance of friendly welcome, while the bosom is unwarmed by a single spark of genuine kindness and good-will.—*Washington Irving.*

Were the king at noonday to say, "This day is night," it would behoove us to reply, "Lo! there are the moon and seven stars!"—*Saadi.*

An thou canst not smile as the wind sets, thou wilt catch cold shortly.—*Shakespeare.*

A few drops of oil will set the political machine at work, when a ton of vinegar would only corrode the wheels and canker the movements.—*Colton.*

If thou be strong enough to encounter with the times, keep thy station; if not, shift a foot to gain advantage of the times. He that acts a beggar to prevent a thief is never the poorer; it is a great part of wisdom sometimes to seem a fool.—*Quarles.*

Men must learn now with pity to dispense, for policy sits above conscience. —*Shakespeare.*

POLITENESS.—(See "GOOD-BREEDING" and "MANNERS.")

There is no policy like politeness; and a good manner is the best thing in the world, either to get a good name, or supply the want of it.—*Bulwer.*

As charity covers a multitude of sins before God, so does politeness before men.—*Gréville.*

True politeness is perfect ease and freedom. It simply consists in treating others just as you love to be treated yourself.—*Chesterfield.*

"Politeness," says Witherspoon, "is real kindness kindly expressed"; an admirable definition, and so brief that all may easily remember it. This is the sum and substance of all true politeness.

Put it in practice, and all will be charmed with your manners.—*Mrs. Sigourney.*

The polite of every country seem to have but one character. A gentleman of Sweden differs but little, except in trifles, from one of any other country. It is among the vulgar we are to find those distinctions which characterize a people. —*Goldsmith.*

Politeness is like an air-cushion; there may be nothing in it, but it eases our jolts wonderfully.

Politeness is fictitious benevolence. It supplies the place of it among those who see each other only in public, or but little. The want of it never fails to produce something disagreeable to one or other.—*Johnson.*

Self-command is the main elegance.— *Emerson.*

True politeness requires humility, good sense, and benevolence. To think more highly of ourselves than we ought to think, destroys its quickening principle. —*Mrs. Sigourney.*

Politeness smoothes wrinkles.—*Joubert.*

Politeness is as natural to delicate natures as perfume is to flowers.—*De Finod.*

Discourtesy does not spring merely from one bad quality, but from several —from foolish vanity, from ignorance of what is due to others, from indolence, from stupidity, from distraction of thought, from contempt of others, from jealousy.—*Bruyère.*

Politeness is but kind feeling toward others, acted out in our intercourse with them. We are always polite to those we respect and esteem.

Good-breeding is the result of much good sense, some good nature, and a little self-denial for the sake of others. —*Chesterfield.*

Do not press your young children into book learning; but teach them politeness, including the whole circle of charities which spring from the consciousness of what is due to their fellow-beings.— *Spurzheim.*

Politeness is the result of good sense and good nature. A person possessed of these qualities, though he has never seen a court, is truly agreeable; and if without them, would continue a clown, though he had been all his lifetime a gentleman usher.—*Goldsmith.*

There is no policy like politeness, since a good manner often succeeds where the best tongue has failed.—*Magoon.*

Mutual complaisances, attentions, and sacrifices of little conveniences, are as natural an implied compact between civilized people, as protection and obedience are between kings and subjects; whoever, in either case, violates that compact, justly forfeits all advantages arising from it.—*Chesterfield.*

Politeness comes from within, from the heart: but if the forms of politeness are dispensed with, the spirit and the thing itself soon die away.—*John Hall.*

Politeness is good nature regulated by good sense.—*Sydney Smith.*

Politeness has been well defined as benevolence in small things.—*Macaulay.*

A polite man is one who listens with interest to things he knows all about, when they are told him by a person who knows nothing about them.—*De Morny.*

There is no outward sign of politeness which has not a deep, moral reason. Behavior is a mirror in which every one shows his own image. There is a politeness of the heart akin to love, from which springs the easiest politeness of outward behavior.

Politeness is not always the sign of wisdom, but the want of it always leaves room for the suspicion of folly.—*Landor.*

There are two kinds of politeness; one says, "See how polite I am"; the other, "I would make you happy."—*Tomlinson.*

The true effect of genuine politeness seems to be rather ease than pleasure.—*Johnson.*

Bowing, ceremonious, formal compliments, stiff civilities, will never be politeness; that must be easy, natural, unstudied; and what will give this but a mind benevolent and attentive to exert that amiable disposition in trifles to all you converse and live with?—*Chatham.*

The only true source of politeness is consideration,—that vigilant moral sense which never loses sight of the rights, the claims, and the sensibilities of others.

This is the one quality, over all others, necessary to make a gentleman.—*Simms.*

Men, like bullets, go farthest when they are smoothest.—*Richter.*

Not to perceive the little weaknesses and the idle but innocent affectations of the company may be allowable as a sort of polite duty. The company will be pleased with you if you do, and most probably will not be reformed by you if you do not.—*Chesterfield.*

Politeness is nothing more than an elegant and concealed species of flattery, tending to put the person to whom it is addressed in good-humor and respect with himself: but if there is a parade and display affected in it, if a man seems to say—look how condescending and gracious I am!—whilst he has only the common offices of civility to perform, such politeness seems founded in mistake, and this mistake I have observed frequently to occur in French manners.—*Cumberland.*

To the acquisition of the rare quality of politeness, so much of an enlightened understanding is necessary that I cannot but consider every book in every science, which tends to make us wiser, and of course better men, as a treatise on a more enlarged system of politeness.—*Monro.*

In all the affairs of life, social as well as political, courtesies of a small and trivial character are the ones which strike deepest in the grateful and appreciating heart.—*Henry Clay.*

Politeness does not always evince goodness, equity, complaisance, or gratitude, but it gives at least the appearance of these qualities, and makes man appear outwardly as he should be within.—*Bruyère.*

Politeness is to goodness what words are to thought. It tells not only on the manners, but on the mind and the heart; it renders the feelings, the opinions, the words, moderate and gentle.—*Joubert.*

Politeness is a mixture of discretion, civility, complaisance, and circumspection spread over all we do and say.—*St. Evremond.*

The spirit of politeness is a desire to bring about by our words and manners, that others may be pleased with us and with themselves.—*Montesquieu.*

Whoever pays you more court than he is accustomed to pay, either intends to deceive you or finds you necessary to him.—*Courtenay.*

To be over-polite is to be rude.—*Japanese Proverb.*

POLITICS.—(See "PARTY.")

If ever this free people—if this government itself is ever utterly demoralized, it will come from this incessant human wriggle and struggle for office, which is but a way to live without work. —*Abraham Lincoln.*

There is no gambling like politics.—*Disraeli.*

People vote their resentment, not their appreciation. The average man does not vote *for* anything, but *against* something.—*William Bennett Munro.*

I resent at any time or at any place the attitude that the safety of this country depends on any man holding his job. No man has achieved that strength, and this country has not deteriorated to that weakness.—*Owen D. Young.*

A politician is like quick-silver: if you try to put your finger on him, you find nothing under it.—*Austin O'Malley.*

I wonder if there is anyone in the world who can really direct the affairs of the world, or of his country, with any assurance of the result his actions would have.—*Montagu C. Norman.*

We shall have to fight the politician, who remembers only that the unborn have no votes and that since posterity has done nothing for us we need do nothing for posterity.—*Dean Inge.*

Nothing is more deceitful than the statements that what we need in politics is the business man. Politics are a business—at least they are a field in which experience tells for usefulness and effectiveness—and a man who has devoted his entire life to the successful establishment of a business is generally not the man who will be useful to the public in the administration of public business.— *William Howard Taft.*

There is among you the man who is not bound by party lines. You vote according to your common sense and your calm judgment after hearing each party set forth its program. To you I say that the strength of this independent thought is the great contribution of

the American political system.—*Franklin D. Roosevelt.*

To let politics become a cesspool, and then avoid it because it is a cesspool, is a double crime.—*Howard Crosby.*

Nothing is politically right which is morally wrong.—*Daniel O'Connell.*

It is the misfortune of all miscellaneous political combinations, that with the purest motives of their more generous members are ever mixed the most sordid interests and the fiercest passions of mean confederates.—*Bulwer.*

How little do politics affect the life, the moral life of a nation. One single good book influences the people a vast deal more.—*Gladstone.*

There is an infinity of political errors which, being once adopted, become principles.—*Abbé Raynal.*

He serves his party best who serves the country best.—*Rutherford B. Hayes.*

Politics I conceive to be nothing more than the science of the ordered progress of society along the lines of greatest usefulness and convenience to itself.— *Woodrow Wilson.*

Party honesty is party expediency.— *Grover Cleveland.*

Our Government is a government by political parties under the guiding influence of public opinion. There does not seem to be any other method by which a republic can function.—*Calvin Coolidge.*

The whole history of reparations has been a fight by the politicians to get paid, and a fight by the industrialists to prevent themselves being paid.—*Sir Joseph Stamp.*

Cicero was in politics a moderate of the most violent description.—*Anatole France.*

By discharging our duty thoroughly and well, subordinating personal desires to principle, and personal ambition to an exalted love of country, we will not only receive the endorsement of the people, but, what is far better, we will deserve their endorsement.—*Champ Clark.*

The humblest in all the land, when clad in the armor of a righteous cause, is stronger than all the hosts of error.— *William Jennings Bryan.*

A politician—one that would circumvent God.—*Shakespeare.*

To be a chemist you must study chemistry; to be a lawyer or a physician you must study law or medicine; but to be a politician you need only to study your own interests.—*Max O'Rell.*

The man who can make two ears of corn, or two blades of grass, grow on the spot where only one grew before, would deserve better of mankind, and render more essential service to the country, than the whole race of politicians put together.—*Swift.*

I hate all bungling as I do sin, but particularly bungling in politics, which leads to the misery and ruin of many thousands and millions of people.—*Goethe.*

Politics is the science of exigencies.—*Theodore Parker.*

Some have said that it is not the business of private men to meddle with government,—a bold and dishonest saying, which is fit to come from no mouth but that of a tyrant or a slave. To say that private men have nothing to do with government is to say that private men have nothing to do with their own happiness or misery; that people ought not to concern themselves whether they be naked or clothed, fed or starved, deceived or instructed, protected or destroyed.—*Cato.*

The politics of courts are so mean that private people would be ashamed to act in the same way; all is trick and finesse, to which the common cause is sacrificed.—*Lord Nelson.*

Two kinds of men generally best succeed in political life: men of no principle, but of great talent: and men of no talent, but of one principle—that of obedience to their superiors.

Great political questions stir the deepest nature of one half the nation, but they pass far above and over the heads of the other half.—*Wendell Phillips.*

A politician weakly and amiably in the right, is no match for a politician tenaciously and pugnaciously in the wrong. —You cannot, by tying an opinion to a man's tongue, make him the representative of that opinion; and at the close of any battle for principles, his name will be found neither among the dead,

nor the wounded, but among the missing. —*E. P. Whipple.*

Real political issues cannot be manufactured by the leaders of parties, and cannot be evaded by them.—They declare themselves, and come out of the depths of that deep which we call public opinion.—*Garfield.*

I know not where to look for any single work which is so full of the great principles of political wisdom, as the laws of Moses and the history of the kings of Israel and Judah.—*G. Spring.*

The violation of party faith, is, of itself, too common to excite surprise or indignation.—Political friendships are so well understood that we can hardly pity the simplicity they deceive.—*Junius.*

Every political question is becoming a social question, and every social question is becoming a religious question.—*R. T. Ely.*

A politician thinks of the next election; a statesman of the next generation.—A politician looks for the success of his party; a statesman for that of his country.—The statesman wishes to steer, while the politician is satisfied to drift.—*J. F. Clarke.*

Jarring interests of themselves create the according music of a well-mixed state.—*Pope.*

For my part, though I like the investigation of particular questions, I give up what is called "the science of political economy."—There is no such science.—There are no rules on these subjects, so fixed and invariable, that their aggregate constitutes a science.—I have recently run over twenty volumes, from Adam Smith to Professor Dew, and from the whole if I were to pick out with one hand all the mere truisms, and with the other all the doubtful propositions, little would be left.—*Daniel Webster.*

In politics, merit is rewarded by the possessor being raised, like a target, to a position to be fired at.—*Bovee.*

A mercantile deputation from Bordeaux, being asked by Louis XIV what should be done to advance their interests, replied, "Sire, let us alone."

There is no Canaan in politics.—As health lies in labor, and there is no royal road to it but through toil, so there is no republican road to safety but in constant distrust.—*Wendell Phillips.*

The strife of politics tends to unsettle the calmest understanding, and ulcerate the most benevolent heart.—There are no bigotries or absurdities too gross for parties to create or adopt under the stimulus of political passions.—*E. P. Whipple.*

There is scarcely anything more harmless than political or party malice. It is best to leave it to itself. Opposition and contradiction are the only means of giving it life or duration.—*Witherspoon.*

POPULACE.—(See "Mob.")

Nothing is so uncertain as the minds of the multitude.—*Leiz.*

You common cry of curs! whose breath I hate as reek o' the rotten fens, whose loves I prize as the dead carcasses of unburied men that do corrupt the air.—*Shakespeare.*

There have been many great men that have flattered the people, who never loved them; and there may be many that they have loved, they know not wherefore: so that, if they love they know not why, they hate upon no better ground.—*Shakespeare.*

What is the people but a herd confused, a miscellaneous rabble, who extol things vulgar, and well weigh'd, scarce worth the praise? they praise and they admire they know not what, and know not whom, but as one leads the other.—*Milton.*

The multitude which is not brought to act as unity, is confusion. That unity which has not its origin in the multitude is tyranny.—*Pascal.*

I will not choose what many men desire, because I will not jump with common spirits, and rank me with the barbarous multitude.—*Shakespeare.*

The rabble gather round the man of news, and listen with their mouths wide open; some tell, some hear, some judge of news, some make it, and he that lies most loud, is most believed.—*Dryden.*

The multitude is always in the wrong.—*Roscommon.*

There are occasions when the general belief of the people, even though it be groundless, works its effect as sure as truth itself.—*Schiller.*

The proverbial wisdom of the populace at gates, on roads, and in markets,

instructs the attentive ear of him who studies man more fully than a thousand rules ostentatiously arranged.—*Lavater.*

This gives force to the strong, that the multitude have no habit of self-reliance or original action.—*Emerson.*

The public sense is in advance of private practice.—*E. H. Chapin.*

POPULARITY.—Popular opinion is the greatest lie in the world.—*Carlyle.*

Whatever is popular deserves attention.—*Mackintosh.*

Avoid popularity; it has many snares, and no real benefit.—*Penn.*

A popular man soon becomes more powerful than power itself.

The great secrets of being courted, are, to shun others and to seem delighted with yourself.—*Bulwer.*

A generous nation is grateful even for the preservation of its rights, and willingly extends the respect due to the office of a good prince into an affection for his person.—*Junius.*

Seek not the favor of the multitude; it is seldom got by honest and lawful means. But seek the testimony of the few: and number not voices, but weigh them.—*Kant.*

True popularity is not the popularity which is followed after, but the popularity which follows after.—*Lord Mansfield.*

The vulgar and common esteem is seldom happy in hitting right; and I am much mistaken, if, amongst the writings of my time, the worst are not those which have most gained the popular applause.—*Montaigne.*

Applause waits on success; the fickle multitude, like the light straw that floats along the stream, glides with the current still, and follows fortune.—*Franklin.*

Be as far from desiring the popular love as fearful to deserve the popular hate; ruin dwells in both; the one will hug thee to death; the other will crush thee to destruction: to escape the first, be not ambitious; avoid the second, be not seditious.—*Quarles.*

Those who are commended by everybody must be very extraordinary men, or, which is more probable, very inconsiderable men.—*Gréville.*

I put no account on him who esteems

himself just as the popular breath may chance to raise him.—*Goethe*.

It is not so difficult a task to plant new truths as to root out old errors; for there is this paradox in men,—they run after that which is new, but are prejudiced in favor of that which is old.—*Colton*.

A habitation giddy and unsure hath he that buildeth on the vulgar heart.—*Shakespeare*.

The greatness of a popular character is less according to the ratio of his genius than the sympathy he shows with the prejudices and even the absurdities of his time. Fanatics do not select the cleverest, but the most fanatical leaders; as was evidenced in the choice of Robespierre by the French Jacobins, and in that of Cromwell by the English Puritans.—*Lamartine*.

The common people are but ill judges of a man's merits; they are slaves to fame, and their eyes are dazzled with the pomp of titles and large retinue. No wonder, then, that they bestow their honors on those who least deserve them. —*Horace*.

Glory is safe when it is deserved; it is not so with popularity; one lasts like a mosaic; the other is effaced like a crayon drawing.—*Boufflers*.

As inclination changes, thus ebbs and flows the unstable tide of public judgment.—*Schiller*.

The love of popularity seems little else than the love of being beloved; and is only blamable when a person aims at the affections of a people by means in appearance honest, but in their end pernicious and destructive.—*Shenstone*.

O popular applause! what heart of man is proof against thy sweet seducing charms? The wisest and the best feel urgent need of all their caution in thy gentlest gales; but swell'd into a gust—who then, alas! with all his canvas set, and inexpert, and therefore heedless, can withstand thy power?—*Cowper*.

The only popularity worth aspiring after, is the popularity of the heart—the popularity that is won in the bosom of families, and at the side of death beds.—There is another,—a high and far sounding popularity, which is, indeed, a most worthless article—a popularity which with its head among storms, and its feet on treacherous quicksands, has nothing to lull the agonies of its tottering existence but the hosannas of a drivelling generation.—*Chalmers*.

POSITION.—In general, it is not very difficult for little minds to attain splendid situations. It is much more difficult for great minds to attain the place to which their merit fully entitles them.—*Baron de Grimm*.

The higher we rise, the more isolated we become; all elevations are cold.—*De Boufflers*.

A great many men—some comparatively small men now—if put in the right position, would be Luthers and Columbuses.—*E. H. Chapin*.

From lowest place, when virtuous things proceed, the place is dignified by the doer's deed.—*Shakespeare*.

POSITIVENESS.—Give me a positive character, with a positive faith, positive opinions and positive actions, though frequently in error, rather than a negative character, with a doubting faith, wavering opinions, undecided actions and faintness of heart. Something is better than nothing.—*C. Simmons*.

Positive views of truth and duty are those that impress the mind and lead to action; negation dwells mostly in cavil and denial.—*Whately*.

The most positive men are the most credulous, since they most believe themselves, and advise most with their falsest flatterer and worst enemy, their own self-love.—*Pope*.

Positiveness is a most absurd foible. If you are in the right, it lessens your triumph; if in the wrong, it adds shame to your defeat.—*Sterne*.

Every one of his opinions appears to himself to be written with sunbeams.—*Watts*.

Positiveness is a good quality for preachers and orators, because whoever would obtrude his thoughts and reasons upon a multitude will convince others the more, as he appears convinced himself.—*Swift*.

POSSESSIONS.—No possessions are good, but by the good use we make of them; without which wealth, power, friends, and servants, do but help to make our lives more unhappy.—*Sir W. Temple*.

It so falls out that what we have we prize not to the worth whiles we enjoy it; but being lacked and lost, why then we rack the value; then we find the virtue that possession would not show us whiles it was ours.—*Shakespeare.*

In life, as in chess, one's own pawns block one's way. A man's very wealth, ease, leisure, children, books, which should help him to win, more often checkmate him.—*Charles Buxton.*

Attainment is followed by neglect, and possession by disgust. The malicious remark of the Greek epigrammatist on marriage may apply to every other course of life—that its two days of happiness are the first and the last.—*Johnson.*

Possession, why more tasteless than pursuit? Why is a wish far dearer than a crown? That wish accomplished, why the grave of bliss? Because, in the great future buried deep, beyond our plans, lies all that man with ardor should pursue.—*Young.*

In all worldly things that a man pursues with the greatest eagerness and intention of mind, he finds not half the pleasure in the actual possession of them as he proposed to himself in the expectation.—*South.*

One's own—what a charm there is in the words! how long it takes boy and man to find out their worth! how fast most of us hold on to them! faster and more jealously, the nearer we are to the general home into which we can take nothing, but must go naked as we came into the world. When shall we learn that he who multiplieth possessions, multiplieth troubles, and that the one single use of things which we call our own, is that they may be his who hath need of them?—*Hughes.*

POSTERITY.—We are too careless of posterity, not considering that as they are so the next generation will be.—*Penn.*

It is pleasant to observe how free the present age is in laying taxes on the next. "Future ages shall talk of this; they shall be famous to all posterity"; whereas their time and thoughts will be taken up about present things, as ours are now.—*Swift.*

Posterity preserves only what will pack into small compass. Jewels are handed down from age to age; less portable valuables disappear. — *Lord Stanley.*

With respect to the authority of great names, it should be remembered, that he alone deserves to have any weight or influence with posterity, who has shown himself superior to the particular and predominant error of his own times.—*Colton.*

I would much rather that posterity should inquire why no statues were erected to me, than why they were.—*Cato.*

Of this our ancestors complained, we ourselves do so and our posterity will equally lament because goodness has vanished and evil habits prevail while human affairs grow worse and worse sinking into an abyss of wickedness.—*Seneca.*

The drafts which true genius draws upon posterity although they may not always be honored so soon as they are due are sure to be paid with compound interest in the end.—*Colton.*

If we would amend the world we should mend ourselves and teach our children to be not what we are but what they should be.—*Penn.*

Time will unveil all things to posterity; it is a chatterer and speaks to those who do not question it.—*Euripides.*

A foreign nation is a contemporaneous posterity.—*A. P. Stanley.*

POVERTY.—Poverty is no disgrace to a man but it is confoundedly inconvenient.—*Sydney Smith.*

Poverty is the wicked man's tempter, the good man's perdition, the proud man's curse, the melancholy man's halter.—*Bulwer.*

Poverty is not dishonorable in itself, but only when it comes from idleness, intemperance, extravagance, and folly.—*Plutarch.*

Who can confess his poverty and look it in the face, destroys its sting: but a proud poor man, he is poor, indeed.—*L. E. Landon.*

When it is not despicable to be poor, we want fewer things to live in poverty with satisfaction, than to live magnificently with riches.—*St. Evremond.*

Poverty is the sixth sense.—*German Proverb.*

Of all the advantages which come to any young man, I believe it to be demonstrably true that poverty is the greatest.—*J. G. Holland.*

An avowal of poverty is no disgrace to any man; to make no effort to escape it is indeed disgraceful.—*Thucydides.*

Poverty eclipses the brightest virtues, and is the very sepulchre of brave designs, depriving a man of the means to accomplish what nature has fitted him for, and stifling the noblest thoughts in their embryo. Many illustrious souls may be said to have been dead among the living, or buried alive in the obscurity of their condition, whose perfections have rendered them the darlings of Providence, and companions of angels. —*Turkish Spy.*

An English judge being asked what contributed most to success at the bar, replied, " Some succeed by great talent, some by the influence of friends, some by a miracle, but the majority by commencing without a shilling."

Poverty is uncomfortable, as I can testify: but nine times out of ten the best thing that can happen to a young man is to be tossed overboard and compelled to sink or swim for himself.—*Garfield.*

He is not poor that has little, but he that desires much.—*Daniel.*

Poverty is very terrible, and sometimes kills the very soul within us; but it is the north wind that lashes men into Vikings; it is the soft, luscious, south wind, which lulls them to lotus dreams. —*Ouida.*

Want is a bitter and a hateful good, because its virtues are not understood; yet many things, impossible to thought, have been by need to full perfection brought; the daring of the soul proceeds from thence, sharpness of wit and active diligence; prudence at once, and fortitude it gives; and, if in patience taken, mends our lives.—*Dryden.*

Poor and content is rich, and rich enough; but riches endless is as poor as winter to him that ever fears he shall be poor.—*Shakespeare.*

Poverty is not always of the nature of an affliction or judgment, but is rather merely a state of life, appointed by God for the proper trial and exercise of the virtues of contentment, patience, and

resignation; and for one man to murmur against God, because he possesses not the riches he has given to another, is " the wrath that killeth the foolish man, and the envy that slayeth the silly one."—*Burgh.*

He travels safe and not unpleasantly, who is guarded by poverty and guided by love.—*Sir P. Sidney.*

In proportion as nations get more corrupt, more disgrace will attach to poverty, and more respect to wealth. There are two questions that would completely reverse this order of things: " What keeps some persons poor? and what has made some others rich?" The true answer to these queries would often make the poor man more proud of his poverty than the rich man is of his wealth, and the rich man more justly ashamed of his wealth, than the poor man unjustly is of his poverty.—*Colton.*

A wise man poor is like a sacred book that's never read; to himself he lives and to all else seems dead.—*Decker.*

Many good qualities are not sufficient to balance a single want—the want of money.—*Zimmermann.*

As pauperism, in distinction from poverty, is dependence on other people for existence, and not on our own exertions, so there is a moral pauperism in the man who is dependent on others for that support of the moral life—self respect.—*Bulwer.*

Few save the poor feel for the poor.— *L. E. Landon.*

A poor man resembles a fiddler, whose music, though liked, is not much praised, because he lives by it; while a gentleman performer, though the most wretched scraper alive, throws the audience into rapture.—*Goldsmith.*

Only experience can show how salt the savor is of others' bread, and how sad a path it is to climb and descend another's stairs.—*Dante.*

Poverty possesses this disease, that through want it teaches man to do evil. —*Euripides.*

We should not so much esteem our poverty as a misfortune, were it not that the world treats it so.—*Bovee.*

It is the great privilege of poverty to be happy and yet unenvied, to be healthy without physic, secure without a guard, and to obtain from the bounty of nature what the great and wealthy are compelled to procure by the help of art.—*Johnson.*

If poverty is the mother of crimes, want of sense is the father of them.—*Bruyère.*

It is only luxury and avarice that make poverty grievous to us; for it is a very small matter that does our business; and when we have provided against cold, hunger, and thirst, all the rest is but vanity and excess.—*Seneca.*

Poverty, in large cities, has very different appearances. It is often concealed in splendor, and often in extravagance. It is the care of a great part of mankind to conceal their indigence from the rest. They support themselves by temporary expedients, and every day is lost in contriving for to-morrow.—*Johnson.*

Want of prudence is too frequently the want of virtue; nor is there on earth a more powerful advocate for vice than poverty.—*Goldsmith.*

Poverty often deprives a man of all spirit and virtue; it is hard for an empty bag to stand upright.—*Franklin.*

Not to be able to bear poverty is a shameful thing; but not to know how to chase it away by work is a more shameful thing yet.—*Pericles.*

To be poor, and seem to be poor, is a certain way never to rise.—*Goldsmith.*

The real wants of nature are the measure of enjoyments, as the foot is the measure of the shoe. We can call only the want of what is necessary, poverty. —*St. Clement.*

Lord God, I thank thee that thou hast been pleased to make me a poor and indigent man upon earth. I have neither house nor land nor money to leave behind me.—*Luther.*

Poverty is only contemptible when it is felt to be so. Doubtless the best way to make our poverty respectable is to seem never to feel it as an evil.—*Bovee.*

Through tattered clothes small vices do appear; robes and furred gowns hide all.—*Shakespeare.*

That man is to be accounted poor, of whatever rank he be, and suffers the pains of poverty, whose expenses exceed his resources; and no man is, properly speaking, poor, but he.—*Paley.*

He is poor whose expenses exceed his income.—*Bruyère.*

Poverty palls the most generous spirits; it cows industry, and casts resolution itself into despair.—*Addison.*

Poverty is, except where there is an actual want of food and raiment, a thing much more imaginary than real. The shame of being thought poor is a great and fatal weakness, though arising in this country from the fashion of the times themselves.—*Cobbett.*

There is nothing keeps longer than a middling fortune, and nothing melts away sooner than a great one.—Poverty treads on the heels of great and unexpected riches.—*Bruyère.*

If riches are, as Bacon says, the baggage (" impedimenta ") of virtue, impeding its onward progress—poverty is famine in its commissary department, starving it into weakness for the great conflict of life.—*Tryon Edwards.*

If rich, it is easy enough to conceal our wealth; but if poor, it is not quite so easy to conceal our poverty. We shall find that it is less difficult to hide a thousand guineas than one hole in our coat.—*Colton.*

Chill penury weighs down the heart itself; and though it sometimes be endured with calmness, it is but the calmness of despair.—*Mrs. Jameson.*

It would be a considerable consolation to the poor and discontented, could they but see the means whereby the wealth they covet has been acquired, or the misery that it entails.—*Zimmermann.*

Poverty is the test of civility and the touchstone of friendship.—*Hazlitt.*

In one important respect a man is fortunate in being poor. His responsibility to God is so much the less.—*Bovee.*

It is not poverty so much as pretence, that harasses a ruined man—the struggle between a proud mind and an empty purse,—the keeping up of a hollow show that must soon come to an end. Have the courage to appear poor, and you disarm poverty of its sharpest sting.— *Mrs. Jameson.*

Poverty, labor, and calamity are not without their luxuries, which the rich, the indolent, and the fortunate in vain seek for.—*Hazlitt.*

When we have only a little we should

be satisfied; for this reason, that those best enjoy abundance who are contented with the least.—*Epicurus*.

A single solitary philosopher may be great, virtuous, and happy in the depth of poverty, but not a whole people.—*Iselin*.

Poverty is the only load which is the heavier the more loved ones there are to assist in bearing it.—*Richter*.

The cure for "Materialism" is to have enough for everybody and to spare. When people are sure of having what they need they cease to think about it. —*Henry Ford*.

As you say, I am honoured and famous and rich. But as I have to do all the hard work, and suffer an increasing multitude of fools gladly, it does not feel any better than being reviled, infamous and poor, as I used to be.—*George Bernard Shaw*.

Nations like men, can be healthy and happy, though comparatively poor. . . . Wealth is a means to an end, not the end itself. As a synonym for health and happiness, it has had a fair trial and failed dismally.—*John Galsworthy*.

Spinoza, greatest abstract philosopher, left his sister a bed and a small silver pen knife, no money, no land, no house, but his thought has taught the world's greatest thinking men.—*Arthur Brisbane*.

Thank God for poverty that makes and keeps us free, and lets us go our unobtrusive way, glad of the sun and rain, upright, serene, humane, contented with the fortunes of the day.—*Bliss Carman*.

Rattle his bones over the stones! He's only a pauper whom nobody owns! —*Thomas Noel*.

They did not break the padlock or clear the wall away. The men in debt that drank of old still drink in debt today. Chained to the rich by ruin. Cheerful in chains as then, when old unbroken Pickwick walked among the broken men.—*James Milne*.

A man forget not, though in rags he lies, and know the mortal through the crown's disguise.—*Akenside*.

The more progress we have the more we suffer from poverty—that is, some of us. Great riches seem nearly always to bring extreme poverty.—*Henry George*.

In a terrible crisis there is only one element more helpless than the poor, and that is the rich.—*Clarence Darrow*.

In America today we are nearer a final triumph over poverty than in any land. The poorhouse has vanished from amongst us.—*Herbert Hoover*.

POWER.—(See "AUTHORITY.")

I know of nothing sublime which is not some modification of power.—*Burke*.

Even in war moral power is to physical as three parts out of four.—*Napoleon*.

Power, to its last particle, is duty.— *John Foster*.

Responsibilities gravitate to the person who can shoulder them; power flows to the man who knows how.—*Elbert Hubbard*.

The basis of international anarchy is men's proneness to fear and hatred. This is also the basis of economic disputes; for the love of power, which is at their root, is generally an embodiment of fear. Men desire to be in control because they are afraid that the control of others will be used unjustly to their detriment.—*Bertrand Russell*.

Since nothing is settled until it is settled right, no matter how unlimited power a man may have, unless he exercises it fairly and justly his actions will return to plague him.—*Frank A. Vanderlip*.

It is patent in our days that not alone is wealth accumulated, but immense power and despotic economic domination are concentrated in the hands of a few, and that those few are frequently not the owners but only the trustees and directors of invested funds which they administer at their good pleasure.— *Pope Pius X*.

All human power is a compound of time and patience.—*Balzac*.

Power and liberty are like heat and moisture; where they are well mixt, everything prospers; where they are single, they are destructive.—*Saville*.

Power is so characteristically calm, that calmness in itself has the aspect of power, and forbearance implies strength. —*Bulwer*.

Arbitrary power is the natural object of temptation to a prince; as wine or women to a young fellow, or a bribe to a judge, or avarice to old age, or vanity to a woman.—*Swift.*

Power acquired by guilt has seldom been directed to any good end or useful purpose.—*Tacitus.*

It is an observation no less just than common, that there is no stronger test of a man's real character than power and authority, exciting as they do every passion, and discovering every latent vice. —*Plutarch.*

Nothing destroys authority so much as the unequal and untimely interchange of power, pressed too far and relaxed too much.—*Bacon.*

Power will intoxicate the best hearts, as wine the strongest heads. No man is wise enough, nor good enough, to be trusted with unlimited power.—*Colton.*

Power, like the diamond, dazzles the beholder, and also the wearer; it dignifies meanness; it magnifies littleness; to what is contemptible, it gives authority; to what is low, exaltation.—*Colton.*

Nothing, indeed, but the possession of some power can with any certainty discover what at the bottom is the true character of any man.—*Burke.*

We have more power than will; and it is often by way of excuse to ourselves that we fancy things are impossible.—*Rochefoucauld.*

Justice without power is inefficient; power without justice is tyranny. Justice without power is opposed, because there are always wicked men. Power without justice is soon questioned. Justice and power must therefore be brought together, so that whatever is just may be powerful, and whatever is powerful may be just.—*Pascal.*

It is not possible to found a lasting power upon injustice, perjury, and treachery.—*Demosthenes.*

Beware of dissipating your powers; strive constantly to concentrate them. Genius thinks it can do whatever it sees others doing, but it is sure to repent of every ill-judged outlay.—*Goethe.*

Power is ever stealing from the many to the few. The manna of popular liberty must be gathered each day, or it is rotten.—*Wendell Phillips.*

There is always room for a man of force, and he makes room for many. Society is a troop of thinkers, and the best heads among them take the best places.—*Emerson.*

By moral power we mean the power of a life and a character, the power of good and great purposes, the power which comes at length to reside in a man distinguished in some course of estimable or great conduct.—No other power of man compares with this, and there is no individual who may not be measurably invested with it.—*Horace Bushnell.*

To know the pains of power, we must go to those who have it; to know its pleasures, we must go to those who are seeking it.—The pains of power are real; its pleasures imaginary.—*Colton.*

PRAISE.—The real satisfaction which praise can afford, is when what is repeated aloud agrees with the whispers of conscience, by showing us that we have not endeavored to deserve well in vain.—*Johnson.*

We are all excited by the love of praise, and it is the noblest spirits that feel it most.—*Cicero.*

Praise is the best auxiliary to prayer. —He who most bears in mind what has been done for him by God will be most emboldened to ask for fresh gifts from above.—*H. Melville.*

Praise undeserved is satire in disguise. —*Broadhurst.*

No ashes are lighter than those of incense, and few things burn out sooner.— *Landor.*

Be not too great a niggard in the commendations of him that professes thy own quality; if he deserve thy praise, thou hast discovered thy judgment; if not, thy modesty; honor either returns or reflects to the giver.—*Quarles.*

What a person praises is perhaps a surer standard, even, than what he condemns, of his character, information, and abilities. No wonder, then, that most people are so shy of praising anything. —*Hare.*

Praise is a debt we owe to the virtues of others, and is due to our own from all whom malice has not made mutes, or envy struck dumb.—*Sir Thomas Browne.*

I should entertain a mean opinion of

myself if all men, or the most part, praised and admired me; it would prove me to be somewhat like them.—*Landor.*

Among the smaller duties of life, I hardly know any one more important than that of not praising where praise is not due. Reputation is one of the prizes for which men contend: it produces more labor and more talent than twice the wealth of a country could ever rear up. It is the coin of genius, and it is the imperious duty of every man to bestow it with the most scrupulous justice and the wisest economy.—*Sydney Smith.*

Praise, like gold and diamonds, owes its value only to its scarcity. It becomes cheap as it becomes vulgar, and will no longer raise expectation or animate enterprise.—*Johnson.*

It is not he that searches for praise that finds it.—*Rivarol.*

Praise follows truth afar off, and only overtakes her at the grave; plausibility clings to her skirts and holds her back till then.—*J. R. Lowell.*

It is a great happiness to be praised of them who are most praiseworthy.—*Sir P. Sidney.*

Words of praise, indeed, are almost as necessary to warm a child into a congenial life as acts of kindness and affection. Judicious praise is to children what the sun is to flowers.—*Bovee.*

Praise is but virtue's shadow; who courts her, doth more the hand-maid, than the dame admire.—*Heath.*

Praise in the beginning is agreeable enough, and we receive it as a favor; but when it comes in great quantities, we regard it only as a debt, which nothing but our merit could extort.—*Goldsmith.*

Those who are greedy of praise prove that they are poor in merit.—*Plutarch.*

Praise is the reflection doth from virtue rise; its fair encomiums do virtue raise to higher acts.—*Aleyn.*

The villain's censure is extorted praise. —*Pope.*

The most agreeable recompense which we can receive for things which we have done is to see them known, to have them applauded with praises which honor us. —*Molière.*

Praise is sometimes a good thing for the diffident and despondent. It teaches

them properly to rely on the kindness of others.—*L. E. Landon.*

How a little praise warms out of a man the good that is in him, as the sneer of contempt which he feels is unjust chills the ardor to excel.—*Bulwer.*

Expect not praise without envy until you are dead. Honors bestowed on the illustrious dead have in them no admixture of envy; for the living pity the dead; and pity and envy, like oil and vinegar, assimilate not.—*Colton.*

Damn with faint praise.—*Pope.*

Desert being the essential condition of praise, there can be no reality in the one without the other.—*Washington Allston.*

One good deed, dying tongueless, slaughters a thousand waiting upon that. Our praises are our wages.—*Shakespeare.*

There is not a person we employ who does not, like ourselves, desire recognition, praise, gentleness, forbearance, patience.—*H. W. Beecher.*

Praise never gives us much pleasure unless it concur with our own opinion, and extol us for those qualities in which we chiefly excel.—*Hume.*

Every one that has been long dead has a due proportion of praise allotted him, in which, whilst he lived, his friends were too profuse and his enemies too sparing.—*Addison.*

The love of praise, howe'er conceal'd by art, reigns more or less, and glows in every heart: the proud, to gain it, toils on toils endure, the modest shun it but to make it sure.—*Young.*

Praise not people to their faces, to the end that they may pay thee in the same coin. This is so thin a cobweb, that it may with little difficulty be seen through; 'tis rarely strong enough to catch flies of any considerable magnitude.—*Fuller.*

Allow no man to be so free with you as to praise you to your face. Your vanity by this means will want its food. At the same time your passion for esteem will be more fully gratified; men will praise you in their actions: where you now receive one compliment, you will then receive twenty civilities.— *Steele.*

Half uttered praise is to the curious mind, as to the eye half veiled beauty is more precious than the whole.—*J. Baillie.*

Praise of the wise and good! it is a meed for which I would long years of toil endure; which many a peril, many a grief would cure.—*Brydges.*

Praise has different effects, according to the mind it meets with; it makes a wise man modest, but a fool more arrogant, turning his weak brain giddy.—*Feltham.*

True praise is frequently the lot of the humble; false praise is always confined to the great.—*Home.*

We are not fond of praising, and never praise any one except from interested motives. Praise is a clever, concealed, and delicate flattery, which gratifies in different ways the giver and the receiver. The one takes it as a recompense of his merit, and the other bestows it to display his equity and discernment.—*Rochefoucauld.*

One of the most essential preparations for eternity is delight in praising God; a higher acquirement, I do think, than even delight and devotedness in prayer. —*Chalmers.*

They are the most frivolous and superficial of mankind, who can be much delighted with that praise which they themselves know to be altogether unmerited.—*Adam Smith.*

As the Greek said, many men know how to flatter; few know to praise.—*Wendell Phillips.*

It is no flattery to give a friend a due character; for commendation is as much the duty of a friend as reprehension.—*Plutarch.*

The praises of others may be of use in teaching us, not what we are, but what we ought to be.—*Hare.*

Praise no man too liberally before his face, nor censure him too lavishly behind his back: the one savors of flattery; the other of malice; and both are reprehensible; the true way to advance another's virtue is to follow it; and the best means to cry down another's vice is to decline it.—*Quarles.*

We should not be too niggardly in our praise, for men will do more to support a character than to raise one.—*Colton.*

It takes a great deal of grace to be able to bear praise. Censure seldom

does us much hurt. A man struggles up against slander, and the discouragement which comes of it may not be an unmixed evil; but praise soon suggests pride, and is therefore not an unmixed good.—*Spurgeon.*

Whenever you commend, add your reasons for doing so; it is this which distinguishes the approbation of a man of sense from the flattery of sycophants and admiration of fools.—*Steele.*

The more you speak of yourself, the more you are likely to lie.—*Zimmermann.*

Think not those faithful who praise all thy words and actions, but those who kindly reprove thy faults.—*Socrates.*

There's not one wise man among twenty will praise himself.—*Shakespeare.*

His praise is lost who waits till all commend.—*Pope.*

Praising what is lost makes the remembrance dear.—*Shakespeare.*

I will not much commend others to themselves, I will not at all commend myself to others. So to praise any to their faces is a kind of flattery, but to praise myself to any is the height of folly. He that boasts his own praises speaks ill of himself, and much derogates from his true deserts. It is worthy of blame to affect commendation.—*Arthur Warwick.*

A truly worthy man should avoid naming himself; Christian piety annihilates the worldly me; worldly civility hides and suppresses it.—*Pascal.*

Praise, more divine than prayer; prayer points our ready path to heaven; praise is already there.—*Young.*

PRAYER.—Prayer is a sincere, sensible, affectionate pouring out of the soul to God, through Christ, in the strength and assistance of the Spirit, for such things as God has promised.—*Bunyan.*

Prayer is not overcoming God's reluctance; it is laying hold of His highest willingness.—*Trench.*

The body of our prayer is the sum of our duty; and as we must ask of God whatsoever we need, so we must watch and labor for all that we ask.—*Jeremy Taylor.*

Heaven is never deaf but when man's heart is dumb.—*Quarles.*

Certain thoughts are prayers. There

are moments when, whatever be the attitude of the body, the soul is on its knees.—*Victor Hugo.*

Let not him who prays, suffer his tongue to outstrip his heart; nor presume to carry a message to the throne of grace, while that stays behind.—*South.*

Every good and holy desire, though it lack the form, hath in itself the substance and force of a prayer with God, who regardeth the very moanings, groans, and sighings of the heart.—*Hooker.*

Prayer is not eloquence, but earnestness; not the definition of helplessness, but the feeling of it; not figures of speech, but earnestness of soul.—*H. More.*

The prayer that begins with trustfulness, and passes on into waiting, will always end in thankfulness, triumph, and praise.—*A. Maclaren.*

I believe I should have been swept away by the flood of French infidelity, if it had not been for one thing, the remembrance of the time when my sainted mother used to make me kneel by her side, taking my little hands in hers, and caused me to repeat the Lord's Prayer.—*John Randolph.*

I know no blessing so small as to be reasonably expected without prayer, nor any so great but may be attained by it.—*South.*

I have been driven many times to my knees by the overwhelming conviction that I had nowhere else to go. My own wisdom, and that of all about me, seemed insufficient for the day. — *Abraham Lincoln.*

A prayer in its simplest definition is merely a wish turned God-ward.—*Phillips Brooks.*

Holy, humble, penitent, believing, earnest, persevering prayer is never lost; it always prevails to the accomplishment of the thing sought, or that with which the suppliant will be better satisfied in the end, according to the superior wisdom of his heavenly father, in which he trusts.—*Weeks.*

God's way of answering the Christian's prayer for more patience, experience, hope, and love, often is to put him into the furnace of affliction.—*Cecil.*

Our prayers should be for blessings in general, for God knows best what is good for us.—*Socrates.*

Whatsoever we beg of God, let us also work for it.—*Jeremy Taylor.*

Prayer is as much the instinct of my nature as a Christian, as it is a duty enjoined by the command of God. It is my language of worship, as a man; of dependence, as a creature; of submission, as a subject; of confession, as a sinner; of thankfulness, as the recipient of mercies; of supplication, as a needy being.—*Tryon Edwards.*

God dwells far off from us, but prayer brings him down to our earth, and links his power with our efforts.—*Mad. de Gasparin.*

I have lived to thank God that all my prayers have not been answered.—*Jean Ingelow.*

I desire no other evidence of the truth of Christianity, than the Lord's prayer.—*Mad. de Staël.*

The fewer words the better prayer.—*Luther.*

Good prayers never come creeping home. I am sure I shall receive either what I ask, or what I should ask.—*Bp. Hall.*

Prayer and provender hinder no man's journey.—*Old Proverb.*

He who runs from God in the morning will scarcely find Him the rest of the day.—*Bunyan.*

Trouble and perplexity drive me to prayer, and prayer drives away perplexity and trouble.—*Melanchthon.*

Practise in life whatever you pray for, and God will give it to you more abundantly.—*Pusey.*

Prayer covers the whole of a man's life. There is no thought, feeling, yearning, or desire, however low, trifling, or vulgar we may deem it, which, if it affects our real interest or happiness, we may not lay before God and be sure of his sympathy. His nature is such that our often coming does not tire him. The whole burden of the whole life of every man may be rolled on to God and not weary him, though it has wearied the man.—*H. W. Beecher.*

The end of our prayers is often gained by an answer very different from what we expect. "Lord, what wilt thou have me to do?" was the question of Paul; and a large part of the answer was, "I will show him how great things he must suffer."—*Tryon Edwards.*

Any heart turned God-ward, feels more joy in one short hour of prayer, than e'er was raised by all the feasts on earth since its foundation.—*Bailey.*

Mount upward, heaven is won by prayer; be sober, for thou art not there!

We, ignorant of ourselves, beg often our own harms, which the wise powers deny us for our good; so we find profit by losing of our prayers.—*Shakespeare.*

The deepest wishes of the heart find expression in secret prayer.—*Geo. E. Rees.*

Prayer ardent opens heaven, lets down a stream of glory on the consecrated hour of man, in audience with the Deity; who worships the great God, that instant joins the first in heaven, and sets his foot on hell.—*Young.*

We should pray with as much earnestness as those who expect everything from God; and should act with as much energy as those who expect everything from themselves.—*Colton.*

Our prayer and God's mercy are like two buckets in a well; while the one ascends, the other descends.—*Hopkins.*

A good man's prayers will from the deepest dungeon climb heaven's height, and bring a blessing down.—*Joanna Baillie.*

If you cannot pray over a thing, and cannot ask God to bless you in it, don't do that thing. A secret that you would keep from God is a secret that you should keep from your own heart.

Open thy heart to God, if he be there, the outspread world will be thy book of prayer.—*Tholuck.*

I have been benefited by praying for others; for by making an errand to God for them I have gotten something for myself.—*Rutherford.*

Prayer is the preface to the book of Christian living; the text of the new life sermon; the girding on of the armor for battle; the pilgrim's preparation for his journey. It must be supplemented by action or it amounts to nothing.—*A. Phelps.*

All the duties of religion are eminently solemn and venerable in the eyes of children. But none will so strongly prove the sincerity of the parent; none so powerfully awaken the reverence of the child; none so happily recommend the instruction he receives, as family devotions, particularly those in which petitions for the children occupy a distinguished place.—*T. Dwight.*

The only instance of praying to saints, mentioned in the Bible, is that of the rich man in torment calling upon Abraham; and let it be remembered, that it was practised only by a lost soul and without success.—*Cecil.*

In the morning, prayer is the key that opens to us the treasure of God's mercies and blessings; in the evening, it is the key that shuts us up under his protection and safeguard.

Prayer, as the first, second, and third element of the Christian life, should open, prolong, and conclude each day. The first act of the soul in early morning should be a draught at the heavenly fountain. It will sweeten the taste for the day. A few moments with God at that calm and tranquil season, are of more value than much fine gold. And if you tarry long so sweetly at the throne, you will come out of the closet as the high priest of Israel came from the awful ministry at the altar of incense, suffused all over with the heavenly fragrance of that communion.—*H. W. Beecher.*

Leave not off praying to God: for either praying will make thee leave off sinning; or continuing in sin will make thee desist from praying.—*Fuller.*

As my greatest business is for God, to serve him, so my daily business is with God, to ask him for strength to do it.

It is as natural and reasonable for a dependent creature to apply to its Creator for what it needs, as for a child to solicit the aid of a parent who is believed to have the disposition and ability to bestow what it needs.—*Archibald Alexander.*

The Lord's Prayer contains the sum total of religion and morals.—*Wellington.*

'Tis heaven alone that is given away;

it is only God may be had for the asking.—*J. R. Lowell.*

To pray as God would have us, with all the heart and strength and reason and will, and to believe that God will listen to our voice through Christ, and verily do the thing he pleaseth thereon, this is the last, the greatest achievement of the Christian's warfare on earth.—*Coleridge.*

Let our prayers, like the ancient sacrifices, ascend morning and evening. Let our days begin and end with God.—*Channing.*

God is infinitely great in himself; we should recognize it in humble adoration: always good; we should acknowledge it by grateful thanksgiving: we have constant need of his blessings; it becomes us to ask them at his hand.—*Tryon Edwards.*

More things are wrought by prayer than the world dreams of. What are men better than sheep or goats, that nourish a blind life within the brain, if, knowing God, they lift no hands of prayer both for themselves and those who call them friends!—*Tennyson.*

The best answer to all objections urged against prayer is the fact that man cannot help praying; for we may be sure that that which is so spontaneous and ineradicable in human nature has its fitting objects and methods in the arrangements of a boundless Providence. —*E. H. Chapin.*

He prayeth best who loveth best.—*Coleridge.*

Faith builds in the dungeon and the lazarhouse its sublimest shrines; and up, through roofs of stone, that shut out the eye of heaven, ascends the ladder where the angels glide to and fro—prayer.—*Bulwer.*

"Prayer," says St. Jerome, "is a groan." Ah! our groans are prayers as well. The very cry of distress is an involuntary appeal to that invisible Power whose aid the soul invokes.—*Mad. Swetchine.*

Prayer among men is supposed a means to change the person to whom we pray; but prayer to God doth not change him, but fits us to receive the things prayed for.—*Stillingfleet.*

The greatest prayer is patience.—*Buddha.*

Each time thou wishest to decide upon performing some enterprise, raise the eyes to heaven, pray God to bless thy project; if thou canst make that prayer, accomplish thy work.—*Leopold Schefer.*

The first petition that we are to make to Almighty God is for a good conscience, the next for health of mind, and then of body.—*Seneca.*

So weak is man, so ignorant and blind, that did not God sometimes withhold in mercy what we ask, we should be ruined at our own request.—*Hannah More.*

Human life is a constant want, and ought to be a constant prayer.—*S. Osgood.*

No man can hinder our private addresses to God; every man can build a chapel in his breast, himself the priest, his heart the sacrifice, and the earth he treads on, the altar.—*Jeremy Taylor.*

The simple heart that freely asks in love, obtains.—*Whittier.*

Is not prayer a study of truth, a sally of the soul into the unfound infinite?— No man ever prayed heartily without learning something.—*Emerson.*

Prayer is the wing wherewith the soul flies to heaven, and meditation the eye wherewith we see God.—*Ambrose.*

Trouble and perplexity drive me to prayer, and prayer drives away perplexity and trouble.—*Fénelon.*

"Never think that God's delays are God's denials."—True prayer always receives what it asks, or something better. —*Tryon Edwards.*

I never was deeply interested in any subject, I never prayed sincerely for any thing, but it came. At some time, no matter at how distant a day, somehow, in some shape—probably the last I should devise—it came.—*A. Judson.*

Remember, whatever warrant you have for praying, you have the same warrant to believe your prayers will be answered. —*J. Phillips.*

If one draw near to God with praise and prayer even half a cubit foot, God will go twenty leagues to meet him.— *E. Arnold.*

What men usually ask for when they

pray to God is, that two and two may not make four.—*Russian Proverb*.

Every prayer that is really such—that is, which flows from the inward necessity of the soul—God answers.—*Olshausen*.

As well might we expect vegetation to spring from the earth without the sunshine and the dew, as the Christian to unfold his grace and advance in his course without patient, persevering, ardent prayer.—*J. Abbott*.

The Lord's Prayer is not, as some fancy, the easiest, the most natural of all devout utterances. It may be committed to memory quickly, but it is slowly learned by heart.—*Maurice*.

No man prays in faith who thinks he knows better than God; or who, not knowing, wishes that his ignorance may overrule God's wisdom.

Sometimes, perhaps, thou hearest another pray with much freedom and fluency, whilst thou canst hardly **get** out a few broken words. Hence thou art ready to accuse thyself and admire him, as if the gilding of the key made it open the door the better.—*Gurnall*.

It is good for us to keep some account of our prayers, that we may not unsay them in our practice.—*M. Henry*.

To him who hearkens to the gods, the gods give ear.—*Homer*.

God denies a Christian nothing but with a design to give him something better.—*Cecil*.

If you would have God hear you when you pray, you must hear him when he speaks.—He stops his ears against the prayers of those who stop their ears against his laws.

God hears no more than the heart speaks; and if the heart be dumb, God will certainly be deaf.—*T. Brooks*.

In prayer it is better to have a heart without words, than words without a heart.—*Bunyan*.

The Ediles among the Romans had their doors always standing open, that all who had petitions might have free access to them.—The door of heaven is always open for the prayers of God's people.—*T. Watson*.

When we pray for any virtue, we should cultivate the virtue as well as pray for it; the form of your prayer should be the rule of your life; every petition to God is a precept to man. Look not, therefore, upon your prayers as a method of good and salvation only, but as a perpetual monition of duty. By what we require of God we see what he requires of us.—*Jeremy Taylor*.

He who prays as he ought will endeavor to live as he prays.—*Owen*.

We need not perplex ourselves as to the precise mode in which prayer is answered.—It is enough for us to know and feel that it is the most natural, the most powerful, and the most elevated expression of our thoughts and wishes in all great emergencies.—*A. P. Stanley*.

Premeditation of thought and brevity of expression are the great ingredients of that reverence that is required to a pious and acceptable prayer.—*South*.

The best and sweetest flowers of paradise God gives to his people when they are on their knees.—Prayer is the gate of heaven—the key to let us into paradise.—*T. Brooks*.

Lord Ashley, before he charged at the battle of Edge Hill, made this short prayer:—"O Lord! Thou knowest how busy I must be this day; if I forget Thee, do not Thou forget me."

Prayer without watching is hypocrisy; and watching without prayer is presumption.—*W. Jay*.

The greater thy business is, by so much the more thou hast need to pray for God's good-speed and blessing upon it, seeing it is certain nothing can prosper without his blessing. The time spent in prayer never hinders, but furthers and prospers a man's journey and business: therefore, though thy haste be never so much, or thy business never so great, yet go not about it, nor out of thy doors, till thou hast prayed.—*Bp. Bayley*.

Prayer is a virtue that prevaileth against all temptations.—*Bernard*.

True prayer never comes weeping home: I am sure that I shall get either what I ask, or what I ought to have asked.—*Leighton*.

Prayer crowns God with the honor and glory due to his name, and God crowns prayer with assurance and comfort.—The most praying souls are the most assured souls.—*T. Brooks*.

Blessed be God, I not only begin praying when I kneel down, but I do not leave off praying when I rise up.— *T. Adam.*

Never was faithful prayer lost.—Some prayers have a longer voyage than others, but then they return with their richer lading at last, so that the praying soul is a gainer by waiting for an answer.—*Gurnall.*

The Christian will find his parentheses for prayer even in the busiest hours of life.—*Cecil.*

God looks not at the oratory of your prayers, how elegant they may be; nor at the geometry of your prayers, how long they may be; nor at the arithmetic of your prayers, how many they may be; not at logic of your prayers, how methodical they may be; but the sincerity of them he looks at.—*T. Brooks.*

They never sought in vain that sought the Lord aright.—*Burns.*

The Lord's Prayer, for a succession of solemn thoughts, for fixing the attention upon a few great points, for suitableness to every condition, for sufficiency for conciseness without obscurity, for the weight and real importance of its petition, is without an equal or a rival.—*Paley.*

The Lord's Prayer is short and mysterious, and, like the treasures of the Spirit, full of wisdom and latent senses: it is not improper to draw forth those excellencies which are intended and signified by every petition, that by so excellent an authority we may know what it is lawful to beg of God.— *Jeremy Taylor.*

To a certain extent, God gives to the prayerful control of Himself, and becomes their willing agent; and when the time comes when all mysteries are solved, and the record of all lives is truthfully revealed, it will probably be seen that not those who astonished the world with their own powers, but those who quietly, through prayer, used God's power, were the ones who made the world move forward.—*E. P. Roe.*

Pray to God, at the beginning of all thy works, that so thou mayest bring them all to a good ending.—*Xenophon.*

PREACHING.—Though we live in a reading age and in a reading community,

yet the preaching of the Gospel is the form in which human agency has been and still is most efficaciously employed for the spiritual improvement of men. —*Daniel Webster.*

A strong and faithful pulpit is no mean safeguard of a nation's life.—*John Hall.*

The object of preaching, is, constantly to remind mankind of what they are constantly forgetting; not to supply the defects of human intelligence, but to fortify the feebleness of human resolutions; to recall mankind from the by-paths where they turn into that broad path of salvation which all know, but few tread.—*Sydney Smith.*

Send your audience away with a desire for, and an impulse toward spiritual improvement, or your preaching will be a failure.—*Goulburn.*

It requires as much reflection and wisdom to know what is not to be put into a sermon, as what is.—*Cecil.*

The Christian ministry is the worst of all trades, but the best of all professions.—*John Newton.*

Men of God have always, from time to time, walked among men, and made their commission felt in the heart and soul of the commonest hearer.—*Emerson.*

For years I have attended the ministrations of the house of God on the Sabbath, and though my pursuits are literary, I tell you I have received, through all these years, more intellectual nourishment and stimulus from the pulpit, than from all other sources combined.—*J. G. Holland.*

It is not a minister's wisdom but his conviction which imparts itself to others. Nothing gives life but life. Real flame alone kindles other flame; this was the power of the apostles: " We believe and therefore speak." Firm faith in what they spoke, that was the basis of the apostles' strength.—*F. W. Robertson.*

A popular preacher once said of his pulpit efforts, " I always roar when I have nothing to say."

A preacher should have the skill to teach the unlearned simply, roundly, and plainly; for teaching is of more importance than exhorting.—*Luther.*

I don't like those mighty fine preachers who round off their sentences so beautifully that they are sure to roll off the sinner's conscience.—*Rowland Hill.*

As the great test of medical practice is that it heals the patient, so the great test of preaching is that it converts and builds up the hearers.—*H. L. Wayland.*

That is not the best sermon which makes the hearers go away talking to one another, and praising the speaker, but which makes them go away thoughtful and serious, and hastening to be alone.—*Bp. Burnet.*

I would have every minister of the Gospel address his audience with the zeal of a friend, with the generous energy of a father, and with the exuberant affection of a mother.—*Fénelon.*

The preacher should be positive, but not dogmatic; earnest, but not denunciatory; tender, but not sentimental; scholarly, but not pedantic; simple, but not commonplace; impassioned, but yet graceful; popular, but not vulgar. Believing with all his heart in the reality and deadly power of sin, in the peril of the ungodly, and in the Gospel as the only adequate remedy for a ruined race, he should try to make his fellow-men believe the same; and by his tremendous earnestness, by the contagion of his own faith, he would succeed.

Reasons are the pillars of the fabric of a sermon, but similitudes are the windows which give the best light. The faithful minister avoids such stories as may suggest bad thoughts to the auditors, and will not use a light comparison to make thereof a grave application, for fear lest his poison go further than his antidote.—*Fuller.*

Some plague the people with too long sermons; for the faculty of listening is a tender thing, and soon becomes weary and satiated.—*Luther.*

To preach more than half an hour, a man should be an angel himself or have angels for hearers.—*Whitefield.*

The meanness of the earthen vessel which conveys to others the Gospel treasure, takes nothing from the value of the treasure. A dying hand may sign a deed of gift of incalculable value. A shepherd's boy may point out the way to a philosopher. A beggar may be the bearer of an invaluable present.—*Cecil.*

Many a meandering discourse one hears, in which the preacher aims at nothing, and—hits it.—*Whately.*

Grant that I may never rack a Scripture simile beyond the true intent thereof, lest, instead of sucking milk, I squeeze blood out of it.—*Fuller.*

Let your sermon grow out of your text, and aim only to develop and impress its thought.—Of a discourse that did not do this it was once wittily said, "If the text had the small-pox, the sermon would never catch it."—*Tryon Edwards.*

I love a serious preacher, who speaks for my sake and not for his own; who seeks my salvation, and not his own vainglory. He best deserves to be heard who uses speech only to clothe his thoughts, and his thoughts only to promote truth and virtue. Nothing is more detestable than a professed declaimer, who retails his discourses as a quack does his medicine.—*Massillon.*

The life of a pious minister is visible rhetoric.—*Hooker.*

He who the sword of heaven will bear, should be as holy as severe.—*Shakespeare.*

It was said of one who preached very well, and lived very ill, "that when he was out of the pulpit it was pity he should ever go into it; and when he was in the pulpit, it was pity he should ever come out of it."—*Fuller.*

The world looks at ministers out of the pulpit to know what they mean when in it.—*Cecil.*

The defects of a preacher are soon spied. Let him be endued with ten virtues, and have but one fault, and that one fault will eclipse and darken all his virtues and gifts, so evil is the world in these times.—*Luther.*

It is a good divine that follows his own instructions.—*Shakespeare.*

In pulpit eloquence, the grand difficulty lies here; to give the subject all the dignity it so fully deserves, without attaching any importance to ourselves. The Christian messenger cannot think too highly of his Prince, or too humbly of himself.—*Colton.*

All things with which we deal preach to us. What is a farm but a mute Gospel? The chaff and the wheat, weeds and plants, blight, rain, insects, sun,—it is a sacred emblem from the first furrow of spring to the last stack which the snow of winter overtakes in the fields.—*Emerson.*

It is in vain for the preacher to hope to please all alike. Let a man stand with his face in what direction he will, he must necessarily turn his back on one-half of the world.—*Anon.*

A good discourse is that from which one can take nothing without taking the life.—*Fénelon.*

Oh, that our prelates would be as diligent to sow the corn of good doctrine, as Satan is to sow cockle and darnel.—*Latimer.*

Pulpit discourses have insensibly dwindled from speaking to reading; a practice of itself sufficient to stifle every germ of eloquence.—*Sydney Smith.*

A minister, without boldness, is like a smooth file, a knife without an edge, a sentinel that is afraid to let off his gun. If men will be bold in sin, ministers must be bold to reprove.—*Gurnall.*

Evil ministers of good things, says Hooker, are like torches, a light to others, but not to themselves; or, as Cox says, like Noah's carpenters, building an ark for others, while they themselves are not saved by it.

The pulpit is the clergyman's parade; the parish is his field of active service.—*Southey.*

I preached as never sure to preach again, and as a dying man to dying men.—*Baxter.*

First, in your sermons, use your logic, and then your rhetoric; rhetoric without logic is like a tree with leaves and blossoms, but no root.—*Selden.*

To preach practical sermons, as they are called, that is sermons upon virtues and vices, without inculcating those great Scripture truths of redemption which alone can incite and enable us to forsake sin and follow righteousness, is but to put together the wheels, and set the hands of the watch, forgetting the

spring which is to make them all move.—*Bp. Horne.*

My grand point in preaching is to break the hard heart, and to heal the broken one.—*John Newton.*

Of Bradford's preaching, Foxe says, "Sharply he opened and reproved sin; sweetly he preached Christ crucified; pithily he impugned heresy and error; and earnestly he persuaded to a godly life."

To love to preach is one thing—to love those to whom we preach, quite another.—*Cecil.*

No sermon is of any value, or likely to be useful, which has not the three R's in it; ruin by the fall, redemption by Christ, and regeneration by the Holy Spirit.—My aim in every sermon, is loudly to call sinners, to quicken saints, and to be made a blessing to all.—*Ryland.*

Genius is not essential to good preaching, but a live man is.—*A. Phelps.*

The world is dying for want, not of good preaching, but of good hearing.—*G. D. Boardman.*

PRECEDENT.—A precedent embalms a principle.—*Disraeli.*

The lawless science of the law, that codeless myriad of precedent, that wilderness of single instances.—*Tennyson.*

One precedent creates another.—They soon accumulate, and constitute law.—What yesterday was fact, to-day is doctrine.—Examples are supposed to justify the most dangerous measures; and where they do not suit exactly, the defect is supplied by analogy.—*Junius.*

Precedents are the band and disgrace of legislation.—They are not wanted to justify right measures, and are absolutely insufficient to excuse wrong ones. They can only be useful to heralds, dancing-masters, and gentlemen ushers.—*Sterne.*

PRECEPT.—The practices of good men are more subject to error than their speculations. I will, then, honor good examples, but endeavor to live according to good precepts.—*Bp. Hall.*

He that lays down precepts for the government of our lives and moderating our passions, obliges human nature not only in the present but in all succeeding generations.—*Seneca.*

Too many follow example rather than precept; but it is safer to learn rather from precept than example.—Many a wise teacher does not follow his own teaching; for it is easier to say, do this, than to do it.—If then I see good doctrine with an evil life, though I pity the last, I will follow the first.—Good sayings belong to all; evil actions only to their authors.—*Warwick.*

Most precepts that are given are so general that they cannot be applied, except by an exercise of as much discretion as would be sufficient to frame them.—*Whately.*

Precepts are the rules by which we ought to square our lives. When they are contracted into sentences, they strike the affections; whereas admonition is only blowing of the coal.—*Seneca.*

It was observed of the Jesuits, that they constantly inculcated a thorough contempt of worldly things in their doctrines, but eagerly grasped at them in their lives. They were wise in their generation, for they cried down worldly things, because they wanted to obtain them, and cried up spiritual things, because they wanted to dispose of them. —*Colton.*

If to do were as easy as to know what were good to do, chapels had been churches, and poor men's cottages princes' palaces. It is a good divine that follows his own instructions; I can easier teach twenty what were good to be done, than be one of the twenty to follow mine own teaching.—*Shakespeare.*

Nothing is more unjust, however common, than to charge with hypocrisy him that expresses zeal for those virtues which he neglects to practise; since he may be sincerely convinced of the advantages of conquering his passions, without having yet obtained the victory; as a man may be confident of the advantages of a voyage or a journey, without having courage or industry to undertake it, and may honestly recommend to others those attempts which he neglects himself.—*Johnson.*

PREFACE.—A preface, being the entrance of a book, should invite by its beauty. An elegant porch announces the splendor of the interior.—*Disraeli.*

A good preface is as essential to put the reader into good humor, as a good prologue is to a play, or a fine symphony to an opera, containing something analogous to the work itself; so that we may feel its want as a desire not elsewhere to be gratified. The Italians call the preface "the sauce of the book;" and, if well-seasoned, it creates an appetite in the reader to devour the book itself.—*Disraeli.*

There's no want of meat, sir; portly and curious viands are prepared to please all kinds of appetites.—*Massinger.*

Reader, now I send thee, like a bee, to gather honey out of flowers and weeds; every garden is furnished with either, and so is ours. Read and meditate.—*H. Smith.*

Go, little book; God send thee good passage, and specially let this be thy prayer, unto them all that thee will read or hear, where thou art wrong, after their help to call, thee to correct in any part, or all.—*Chaucer.*

PREJUDICE.—He that is possessed with a prejudice is possessed with a devil, and one of the worst kind of devils, for it shuts out the truth, and often leads to ruinous error.—*Tryon Edwards.*

Prejudice is a mist, which, in our journey through the world, often dims the brightest, and obscures the best of all the good and glorious objects that meet us on our way.—*Tales of Passions.*

He who knows only his own side of the case knows little of that.—*J. Stuart Mill.*

Prejudice may be considered as a continual false medium of viewing things, for prejudiced persons not only never speak well, but also never think well of those whom they dislike, and the whole character and conduct is considered with an eye to that particular thing which offends them.—*Bp. Butler.*

Prejudice, which sees what it pleases, cannot see what is plain.—*Aubrey de Vere.*

Never try to reason the prejudice out of a man.—It was not reasoned into him, and cannot be reasoned out.—*Sydney Smith.*

All looks yellow to the jaundiced eye. —*Pope.*

Prejudice is the reason of fools.— *Voltaire.*

Ignorance is less remote from the truth than prejudice.—*Diderot.*

There is nothing stronger than human prejudice. A crazy sentimentalism, like that of Peter the Hermit, hurled half of Europe upon Asia, and changed the destinies of kingdoms.—*Wendell Phillips.*

Reasoning against a prejudice is like fighting against a shadow; it exhausts the reasoner, without visibly affecting the prejudice. Argument cannot do the work of instruction any more than blows can take the place of sunlight.—*Charles Mildmay.*

Prejudice is the child of ignorance.—*Hazlitt.*

The prejudices of ignorance are more easily removed than the prejudices of interest; the first are all blindly adopted, the second willfully preferred.—*Bancroft.*

The confirmed prejudices of a thoughtful life, are as hard to change as the confirmed habits of an indolent life: and as some must trifle away age, because they trifled away youth, others must labor on in a maze of error, because they have wandered there too long to find their way out.—*Bolingbroke.*

Beware of prejudices. They are like rats, and men's minds are like traps; prejudices get in easily, but it is doubtful if they ever get out.

There is nothing respecting which a man may be so long unconscious, as of the extent and strength of his prejudices.

Opinions grounded on prejudice are always sustained with the greatest violence.—*Jeffrey.*

The prejudiced and obstinate man does not so much hold opinions, as his opinions hold him.—*Tryon Edwards.*

When the judgment is weak the prejudice is strong.—*O'Hara.*

Every one is forward to complain of the prejudices that mislead other men and parties, as if he were free, and had none of his own. What now is the cure? No other but this, that every man should let alone others' prejudices and examine his own.—*Locke.*

Prejudice and self-sufficiency, naturally proceed from inexperience of the world, and ignorance of mankind.—*Addison.*

Even when we fancy we have grown wiser, it is only, it may be, that new prejudices have displaced old ones.—*Bovee.*

In forming a judgment, lay your hearts void of foretaken opinions; else, whatsoever is done or said, will be measured by a wrong rule: like them who have the jaundice, to whom everything appeareth yellow.—*Sir P. Sidney.*

Some prejudices are to the mind what the atmosphere is to the body; we cannot feel without the one, nor breathe without the other.—*Gréville.*

Every period of life has its peculiar prejudice; whoever saw old age that did not applaud the past, and condemn the present times?—*Montaigne.*

Prejudices may be intense, but their lives are limited.—To discover when they are dead and to bury them, is an important matter, and no unseemly tears should be shed at their funerals.

Human nature is so constituted, that all see, and judge better, in the affairs of other men, than in their own.—*Terence.*

He that never leaves his own country is full of prejudices.—*Goldoni.*

To divest one's self of some prejudices, would be like taking off the skin to feel the better.—*Gréville.*

Prejudice is the conjuror of imaginary wrongs, strangling truth, overpowering reason, making strong men weak and weak men weaker. God give us the large-hearted charity which "beareth all things, believeth all things, hopeth all things, endureth all things," which "thinketh no evil."—*Macduff.*

Prejudice is a mist, which in our journey through the world often dims the brightest and obscures the best of all the good and glorious objects that meet us on our way.—*Shaftesbury.*

Instead of casting away our old prejudices, we cherish them to a very considerable degree, and, more shame to ourselves, we cherish them because they are prejudices; and the longer they have lasted the more we cherish them. We are afraid to put men to live and trade each on his own private stock of reason, because we suspect that this stock in each man is small, and that the individuals would do better to avail themselves of the general bank and capital of nations and of ages.—*Burke.*

Never suffer the prejudice of the eye to determine the heart.—*Zimmermann.*

No wise man can have a contempt for the prejudices of others; and he should even stand in a certain awe of his own, as if they were aged parents and monitors. They may in the end prove wiser than he.—*Hazlitt.*

National antipathy is the basest, because the most illiberal and illiterate of all prejudices.—*Jane Porter.*

Because a total eclipse of the sun is above my own head, I will not therefore insist that there must be an eclipse in America also; and because snowflakes fall before my own nose, I need not believe that the Gold Coast is also snowed up.—*Richter.*

Prejudices, it is well known, are most difficult to eradicate from the heart whose soil has never been loosened or fertilized by education; they grow there, firm as weeds among rocks.—*Charlotte Brontë.*

To lay aside all prejudices, is to lay aside all principles.—He who is destitute of principles is governed by whims. —*Jacobi.*

When we destroy an old prejudice we have need of a new virtue.—*Mad. de Staël.*

None are too wise to be mistaken, but few are so wisely just as to acknowledge and correct their mistakes, and especially the mistakes of prejudice.—*Barrow.*

Prejudices are what rule the vulgar crowd.—*Voltaire.*

Moral prejudices are the stop-gaps of virtue; and as is the case with other stop-gaps, it is often more difficult to get either out or in through them, than through any other part of the fence.—*Hare.*

A man who thinks he is guarding himself against prejudices by resisting the authority of others, leaves open every avenue to singularity, vanity, self-conceit, obstinacy, and many other vices, all tending to warp the judgment, and prevent the natural operation of his faculties. We are not satisfied with our own opinions, whatever we may pretend, till they are ratified and confirmed by

suffrage of the rest of mankind. We dispute and wrangle forever; we endeavor to get men to come to us when we do not go to them.—*Sir Joshua Reynolds.*

Prejudice is never easy unless it can pass itself off for reason.—*Hazlitt.*

The great obstacle to progress is prejudice.—*Bovee.*

In whatever mind prejudice dwells, it acts, in relation to truth, as alkali does in relation to acids, neutralizing its power.—Arguments the most cogent, discourse the most powerful, can be neutralized at once by some prejudice in the mind.—*Thomas.*

Prejudice squints when it looks, and lies when it talks.—*Duchess de Abrantes.*

When prejudices arise from a generous though mistaken source, they are hugged closer to the bosom; and the kindest and most compassionate natures feel a pleasure in fostering a blind and unjust resentment.—*Erskine.*

Opinions adopted and approved by the wise and good in the past, usually have a solid foundation, and though adherence to them is sometimes counted as prejudice, they are not to be lightly disapproved or laid aside.

Men are often warned against old prejudices: I would rather warn them against new conceits. The novelty of an opinion, on most moral subjects, is a presumption against it. Generally speaking, it is only the half-thinker, who in matters concerning the feelings and ancestral opinions of men, stumbles on new conclusions. The true philosopher searches out something else—the propriety of the feeling, the wisdom of the opinion, the deep and living roots of whatever is fair and enduring. For on such points, our first and third thoughts will be apt to coincide.

PRESENT.—(See "Time.")

Every man's life lies within the present; for the past is spent and done with, and the future is uncertain.—*Marcus Antoninus.*

Devote each day to the object then in time, and every evening will find something done.—*Goethe.*

Live this day as if it were the last.— *Bp. Kerr.*

If I am faithful to the duties of the present, God will provide for the future.—*Bedell.*

Let us enjoy the fugitive hour. Man has no harbor, time has no shore, it rushes on and carries us with it.—*Lamartine.*

Man, living, feeling man, is the easy sport of the over-mastering present.—*Schiller.*

Since Time is not a person we can overtake when he is gone, let us honor him with mirth and cheerfulness of heart while he is passing.—*Goethe.*

Busy not yourself in looking forward to the events of to-morrow, but those of the days which Providence may assign you neglect not to turn to advantage.—*Horace.*

Enjoy the blessings of this day, if God sends them; and the evils bear patiently and sweetly; for only this day is ours; we are dead to yesterday, and not born to-morrow.—*Jeremy Taylor.*

Try to be happy in this very present moment; and put not off being so to a time to come; as though that time should be of another make from this, which is already come, and is ours.—*Fuller.*

In the midst of hopes and cares, of apprehensions and of disquietude, regard every day that dawns upon you as if it was to be your last; then superadded hours, to the enjoyment of which you had not looked forward, will prove an acceptable boon.—*Horace.*

Men spend their lives in anticipations, in determining to be vastly happy at some period when they have time. But the present time has one advantage over every other—it is our own. Past opportunities are gone, future are not come. We may lay in a stock of pleasures, as we would lay in a stock of wine; but if we defer the tasting of them too long, we shall find that both are soured by age.—*Colton.*

Do to-day's duty, fight to-day's temptation; do not weaken and distract yourself by looking forward to things you cannot see, and could not understand if you saw them.—*Charles Kingsley.*

Abridge your hopes in proportion to the shortness of the span of human life;

for while we converse, the hours, as if envious of our pleasure, fly away; enjoy therefore the present time, and trust not too much to what to-morrow may produce.—*Horace.*

Look upon every day as the whole of life, not merely as a section; and enjoy and improve the present without wishing, through haste, to rush on to another.—*Richter.*

To eternity itself there is no other handle than the present moment.

Let any man examine his thoughts, and he will find them ever occupied with the past or the future. We scarcely think at all of the present; or if we do, it is only to borrow the light which it gives for regulating the future. The present is never our object; the past and the present we use as means; the future only is our end. Thus, we never live, we only hope to live.—*Pascal.*

Duty and to-day are ours, results and futurity belong to God.—*Horace Greeley.*

Every day is a gift I receive from Heaven; let us enjoy to-day that which it bestows on me. It belongs not more to the young than to me, and to-morrow belongs to no one.—*Mancroix.*

We think very little of time present; we anticipate the future, as being too slow, and with a view to hasten it onward, we recall the past to stay it as too swiftly gone. We are so thoughtless, that we thus wander through the hours which are not here, regardless only of the moment that is actually our own.—*Pascal.*

Each present joy or sorrow seems the chief.—*Shakespeare.*

The future is purchased by the present.—*Johnson.*

PRESS.—The press is the foe of rhetoric, but the friend of reason.—*Colton.*

What gunpowder did for war, the printing-press has done for the mind; the statesman is no longer clad in the steel of special education, but every reading man is his judge.—*Wendell Phillips.*

In former days superstitious rites were used to exorcise evil spirits; but in our times the same object is attained, and beyond comparison more effectually, by the common newspaper. Before this talisman, ghosts, witches, and all their kindred tribes are driven from the land, never to return again. The touch of "holy water," is not so intolerable to them as the smell of printing ink.—*J. Bentham.*

When the press is the echo of sages and reformers, it works well; when it is the echo of turbulent cynics, it merely feeds political excitement.—*Lamartine.*

If by the liberty of the press, we understand merely the liberty of discussing the propriety of public measures and political opinions, let us have as much of it as you please; but, if it means the liberty of affronting, calumniating, and defaming one another, I own myself willing to part with my share of it whenever our legislators shall please to alter the law; and shall cheerfully consent to exchange my liberty of abusing others for the privilege of not being abused myself.—*Franklin.*

An enslaved press is doubly fatal; it not only takes away the true light, for in that case we might stand still, but it sets up a false one that decoys us to our destruction.—*Colton.*

This country is not priest-ridden, but press-ridden.—*Longfellow.*

The liberty of the press is a blessing when we are inclined to write against others, and a calamity when we find ourselves overborne by the multitude of our assailants.—*Johnson.*

The invention of printing added a new element of power to the race. From that hour the brain and not the arm, the thinker and not the soldier, books and not kings, were to rule the world; and weapons, forged in the mind, keen-edged and brighter than the sunbeam, were to supplant the sword and the battle-ax.—*E. P. Whipple.*

The Reformation was cradled in the printing-press, and established by no other instrument.—*Agnes Strickland.*

Let it be impressed upon your minds, let it be instilled into your children, that the liberty of the press is the palladium of all the civil, political, and religious rights.—*Junius.*

Much has been accomplished; more than people are aware—so gradual has been the advance. How noiseless is the growth of corn! Watch it night and day for a week, and you will never see it growing; but return after two months, and you will find it all whitening for the harvest. Such, and so imperceptible in the stages of their motion are the victories of the press.—*De Quincey.*

The press is not only free, it is powerful. That power is ours. It is the proudest that man can enjoy. It was not granted by monarchs; it was not gained for us by aristocracies; but it sprang from the people, and, with an immortal instinct, it has always worked for the people.—*Disraeli.*

PRETENSION.—He who gives himself airs of importance exhibits the credentials of impotence.—*Lavater.*

It is no disgrace not to be able to do everything; but to undertake or pretend to do what you are not made for, is not only shameful, but extremely troublesome and vexatious.—*Plutarch.*

The desire of appearing clever often prevents our becoming so.—*Rochefoucauld.*

Who makes the fairest show, means most deceit.—*Shakespeare.*

We are only vulnerable and ridiculous through our pretensions.—*Mad. de Girardin.*

There is a false modesty, which is vanity; a false glory, which is levity; a false grandeur, which is meanness; a false virtue, which is hypocrisy, and a false wisdom, which is prudery.—*Bruyère.*

When you see a man with a great deal of religion displayed in his shop window, you may depend upon it he keeps a very small stock of it within.—*Spurgeon.*

The more honesty a man has, the less he affects the air of a saint.—*Lavater.*

Hearts may be attracted by assumed qualities, but the affections are not to be fixed but by those that are real.—*De Moy.*

The higher the character or rank, the less the pretence, because there is less to pretend to.—*Bulwer.*

True glory strikes root, and even extends itself; all false pretensions fall as do flowers, nor can any feigned thing be lasting.—*Cicero.*

The more accomplished way of using books at present, is to serve them as some do lords—learn their titles, and then boast of their acquaintance.—*Swift.*

Where there is much pretension, much has been borrowed; nature never pretends.—*Lavater.*

As a general rule, people who flagrantly pretend to anything are the reverse of that which they pretend to. A man who sets up for a saint is sure to be a sinner, and a man who boasts that he is a sinner is sure to have some feeble, maudlin, snivelling bit of saintship about him which is enough to make him a humbug.—*Bulwer.*

Pretences go a great way with men that take fair words and magisterial looks for current payment.—*L'Estrange.*

PREVENTION.—Prevention is the best bridle.—*Feltham.*

Laws act after crimes have been committed; prevention goes before them both.—*Zimmermann.*

Who would not give a trifle to prevent what he would give a thousand worlds to cure?—*Young.*

Preventives of evil are far better than remedies; cheaper and easier of application, and surer in result.—*Tryon Edwards.*

PRIDE.—Pride the first peer and president of hell.—*Defoe.*

'Tis the most nonsensical thing in the world for a man to be proud, since 'tis in the meanest wretch's power to mortify him. How uneasy have I seen my Lord All-Pride in the park, when the company turned their eyes from him and his gaudy equipage!—*I. B. Brown.*

Pride brake the angels in heaven, and spoils all the heads we find cracked here.—*Osborn.*

Pride, like the magnet, constantly points to one object, self; but unlike the magnet, it has no attractive pole, but at all points repels.—*Colton.*

Pride is to the character, like the attic to the house—the highest part, and generally the most empty.

Pride is increased by ignorance; those assume the most who know the least.—*Gay.*

Though Diogenes lived in a tub, there might have been, for aught I know, as much pride under his rags, as in the fine-spun garments of the divine Plato. —*Swift.*

The seat of pride is in the heart, and only there; and if it be not there, it is neither in the look, nor in the clothes.—*Lord Clarendon.*

If a proud man makes me keep my distance, the comfort is that he keeps his at the same time.—*Swift.*

As thou desirest the love of God and man, beware of pride. It is a tumor in the mind, that breaks and ruins all thine actions; a worm in thy treasury, that eats and ruins thine estate. It loves no man, and is beloved of none; it disparages another's virtues by detraction, and thine own by vainglory. It is the friend of the flatterer, the mother of envy, the nurse of fury, the sin of devils, the devil of mankind. It hates superiors, scorns inferiors, and owns no equal. In short, till thou hate it, God hates thee.

Pride defeats its own end, by bringing the man who seeks esteem and reverence into contempt.—*Bolingbroke.*

We hear much of a decent pride, a becoming pride, a noble pride, a laudable pride. Can that be decent, of which we ought to be ashamed? Can that be becoming, of which God has set forth the deformity? Can that be noble which God resists and is determined to abase? Can that be laudable, which God calls abominable?—*Cecil.*

Pride is seldom delicate; it will please itself with very mean advantages.—*Johnson.*

I have been more and more convinced, the more I think of it, that, in general, pride is at the bottom of all great mistakes. All the other passions do occasional good; but whenever pride puts in its word, everything goes wrong; and what it might really be desirable to do, quietly and innocently, it is mortally dangerous to do proudly.—*Ruskin.*

Pride, like laudanum and other poisonous medicines, is beneficial in small, though injurious in large, quantities. No man who is not pleased with himself, even in a personal sense, can please others.—*Frederick Saunders.*

Pride may be allowed to this or that degree, else a man cannot keep up his dignity. In gluttony there must be eating, in drunkenness there must be drinking; 'tis not the eating, and 'tis not the drinking that must be blamed, but the excess. So in pride.—*Selden.*

Pride, as it is compounded of the vanity and ill nature that dispose men to admire themselves, and contemn other men, retains its vigor longer than any other vice, and rarely expires but with life itself. Without the sovereign influence of God's grace, men very rarely put off all the trappings of their pride till they who are about them put on their winding-sheet.—*Clarendon.*

Pride is a vice, which pride itself inclines every man to find in others, and to overlook in himself.—*Johnson.*

Pride is as loud a beggar as want, and a great deal more saucy. When you have bought one fine thing, you must buy ten more, that your appearance may be all of a piece; but it is easier to suppress the first desire than to satisfy all that follow it.—*Franklin.*

He that is proud eats up himself; pride is his glass, his trumpet, his chronicle; and whatever praises itself but in the deed, devours the deed in the praise.—*Shakespeare.*

"Pride was not made for man"; a conscious sense of guilt and folly, and their consequence, destroys the claim, and to beholders tells, here nothing but the shape of manhood dwells.—*Waller.*

Pride, like ambition, is sometimes virtuous and sometimes vicious, according to the character in which it is found, and the object to which it is directed. As a principle, it is the parent of almost every virtue and every vice—everything that pleases and displeases in mankind; and as the effects are so very different, nothing is more easy than to discover, even to ourselves, whether the pride that produces them is virtuous or vicious: the first object of virtuous pride is rectitude, and the next independence.—*Gréville.*

Of all the causes which conspire to blind man's erring judgment, and mislead the mind, what the weak head with strongest bias rules, is pride—that never failing vice of fools.—*Pope.*

There is a diabolical trio existing in the natural man, implacable, inextinguishable, co-operative and consentaneous, pride, envy, and hate; pride that makes us fancy we deserve all the goods that others possess; envy that some should be admired while we are overlooked; and hate, because all that is bestowed on others, diminishes the sum we think due to ourselves.—*Colton.*

If a man has a right to be proud of anything, it is of a good action done as it ought to be, without any base interest lurking at the bottom of it.—*Sterne.*

We mortals, men and women, devour many a disappointment between breakfast and dinner-time; keep back the tears and look a little pale about the lips, and in answer to inquiries say, "Oh, nothing!" Pride helps us; and pride is not a bad thing when it only urges us to hide our own hurts—not to hurt others.—*George Eliot.*

There is this paradox in pride—it makes some men ridiculous, but prevents others from becoming so.—*Colton.*

Men are sometimes accused of pride merely because their accusers would be proud themselves if they were in their places.—*Shenstone.*

Of all marvellous things, perhaps there is nothing that angels behold with such supreme astonishment as a proud man.—*Colton.*

I frankly confess I have a respect for family pride.—If it be a prejudice, it is prejudice in its most picturesque shape.—But I hold it is connected with some of the noblest feelings in our nature.—*L. E. Landon.*

Pride is the master sin of the devil.—*E. H. Chapin.*

There is a certain noble pride, through which merits shine brighter than through modesty.—*Richter.*

As Plato entertained some friends in a room where there was a couch richly ornamented, Diogenes came in very dirty, as usual, and getting upon the couch, and trampling on it, said, "I trample upon the pride of Plato." Plato mildly answered, "But with greater pride, Diogenes!"—*Erasmus.*

None have more pride than those who dream that they have none. You may labor against vainglory till you conceive that you are humble, and the fond conceit of your humility will prove to be pride in full bloom.—*Spurgeon*

The mind of a proud man is like a mushroom, which starts up in a night: his business is first to forget himself, and then his friends.—*South.*

A proud man never shows his pride so much as when he is civil.—*Gréville.*

There is no greater pride than in seeking to humiliate ourselves beyond measure; and sometimes there is no truer humility than to attempt great works for God.—*St. Cyran.*

To be proud of learning is the greatest ignorance.—*Bp. Taylor.*

Pride is never more offensive than when it condescends to be civil; whereas vanity, whenever it forgets itself, naturally assumes good humor.—*Cumberland.*

Pride breakfasted with plenty, dined with poverty, and supped with infamy.—*Franklin.*

Infidelity, alas! is not always built upon doubt, for this is diffident, nor philosophy always upon wisdom, for this is meek; but pride is neither.—*Colton.*

The proud never have friends; not in prosperity, for then they know nobody; and not in adversity, for then nobody knows them.

Pride is not the heritage of man; humility should dwell with frailty, and atone for ignorance, error, and imperfection.—*Sydney Smith.*

To be proud and inaccessible is to be timid and weak.—*Massillon.*

When flowers are full of heaven-descended dews, they always hang their heads; but men hold theirs the higher the more they receive, getting proud as they get full.—*H. W. Beecher.*

Pride is the common forerunner of a fall. It was the devil's sin, and the devil's ruin; and has been, ever since, the devil's stratagem, who, like an expert wrestler, usually gives a man a lift before he gives him a throw.—*South.*

Pride often defeats its own end, by bringing the man who seeks esteem and reverence, into contempt.—*Bolingbroke.*

The proud are ever most provoked by pride.—*Cowper.*

We rise in glory as we sink in pride.—*Young.*

A beggar's rags may cover as much pride as an alderman's gown.—*Spurgeon.*

Pride counterbalances all our miseries, for it either hides them, or if it discloses them, boasts of that disclosure. Pride has such a thorough possession of us, even in the midst of our miseries and faults, that we are prepared to sacrifice life with joy, if it may but be talked of.—*Pascal.*

Nature has given us pride to spare us the pain of being conscious of our imperfections.—*Rochefoucauld.*

We have some cases of the pride of learning, but a multitude of the pride of ignorance.—*W. M. Taylor.*

To acknowledge our faults when we are blamed is modesty; to discover them to one's friends, in ingenuousness, is confidence; but to preach them to all the world, if one does not take care, is pride.—*Confucius.*

This life will not admit of equality; but surely that man who thinks he derives consequence and respect from keeping others at a distance, is as baseminded as the coward who shuns the enemy from the fear of an attack.—*Goethe.*

Haughty people seem to me to have, like the dwarfs, the statures of a child and the face of a man.—*Joubert.*

When pride and presumption walk before, shame and loss follow very closely.—*Louis the Eleventh.*

Pride fills the world with harshness and severity; we are rigorous to offences as if we had never offended.—*Blair.*

The disesteem and contempt of others is inseparable from pride. It is hardly possible to overvalue ourselves but by undervaluing our neighbors.—*Clarendon.*

You who are ashamed of your poverty, and blush for your calling, are a snob; as are you who boast of your pedigree, or are proud of your wealth.—*Thackeray.*

O world, how apt the poor are to be proud!—*Shakespeare.*

Deep is the sea, and deep is hell, but pride mineth deeper; it is coiled as a poisonous worm about the foundations of the soul.—*Tupper.*

It is with nations as with individuals, those who know the least of others think the highest of themselves; for the whole family of pride and ignorance are incestuous, and mutually beget each other.—*Colton.*

In beginning the world, if you don't wish to get chafed at every turn, fold up your pride carefully, and put it under lock and key, and only let it out to air on grand occasions.—It is a garment all stiff brocade outside, and all grating sackcloth on the side next to the skin.—Even kings do not wear the dalmaticum except at a coronation.—*Bulwer.*

There are proud men of so much delicacy that it almost conceals their pride, and perfectly excuses it.—*Landor.*

Pride, which inspires us with so much envy, serves also to moderate it.—*Rochefoucauld.*

A proud man is seldom a grateful man, for he never thinks he gets as much as he deserves.—*H. W. Beecher.*

Pride either finds a desert or makes one; submission cannot tame its ferocity, nor satiety fill its voracity, and it requires very costly food—its keeper's happiness.—*Colton.*

Pride is the ape of charity, in show not much unlike, but somewhat fuller of action. They are two parallels, never but asunder; charity feeds the poor, so does pride; charity builds an hospital, so does pride. In this they differ: charity gives her glory to God; pride takes her glory from man.—*Quarles.*

The infinitely little have a pride infinitely great.—*Voltaire.*

John Bunyan had a great dread of spiritual pride; and once, after he had preached a very fine sermon, and his friends crowded round to shake him by the hand, while they expressed the utmost admiration of his eloquence, he interrupted them, saying: "Ay! you need not remind me of that, for the Devil told me of it before I was out of the pulpit!"—*Southey.*

In pride, unreasoning pride, our error lies; all quit their sphere, and rush into the skies; pride still is aiming at the blest abodes; men would be angels; angels would be gods.—*Pope.*

Pride, the most dangerous of all faults, proceeds from want of sense, or want of thought.—*Dillon.*

The devil did grin, for his darling sin is pride that apes humility.—*Coleridge.*

It is oftener from pride, than from want of understanding that we oppose the opinions adopted by the world.—We find the first places are taken in a good cause, and are unwilling to come in as second.—*Rochefoucauld.*

Pride thrust Nebuchadnezzar out of men's society, Saul out of his kingdom, Adam out of paradise, Haman out of court, and Lucifer out of heaven.—*T. Adam.*

Let me give you the history of pride in three small chapters. The beginning of pride was in heaven. The continuance of pride is on earth. The end of pride is in hell. This history shows how unprofitable it is.—*R. Newton.*

PRINCIPLES.—Our principles are the springs of our actions; our actions, the springs of our happiness or misery. Too much care, therefore, cannot be taken in forming our principles.—*Skelton.*

What is the essence and the life of character? Principle, integrity, independence, or, as one of our great old writers has it, "That inbred loyalty unto virtue which can serve her without a livery."—*Bulwer.*

Better be poisoned in one's blood, than to be poisoned in one's principles.

He who merely knows right principles is not equal to him who loves them.—*Confucius.*

The change we personally experience from time to time, we obstinately deny to our principles.—*Zimmermann.*

Principle is a passion for truth and right.—*Hazlitt.*

A principle is one thing; a maxim or rule is another.—A principle requires liberality; a rule says, "one tenth."—A principle says, "forgive"; a rule defines "seven times."—*F. W. Robertson.*

Expedients are for the hour; principles for the ages.—*H. W. Beecher.*

The principles now implanted in thy bosom will grow, and one day reach maturity; and in that maturity thou wilt find thy heaven or thy hell.—*Thomas.*

Many men do not allow their principles to take root, but pull them up every now and then, as children do the flowers they have planted, to see if they are growing.—*Longfellow.*

Always vote for a principle, though you vote alone, and you may cherish the sweet reflection that your vote is never lost.—*John Quincy Adams.*

Principles, like troops of the line, are undisturbed, and stand fast.—*Richter.*

Principles last forever; but special rules pass away with the things and conditions to which they refer.—*Seeley.*

I have all reverence for principles which grow out of sentiments; but as to sentiments which grow out of principles, you shall scarcely build a house of cards thereon.—*Jacobi.*

The restless mind of man cannot but press a principle to the real limit of its application, even though centuries should intervene between the premises and the conclusion.—*Liddon.*

The value of a principle is the number of things it will explain; and there is no good theory of a disease which does not at once suggest a cure.—*Emerson.*

PROCRASTINATION. — (See "DE-LAY.")

By the streets of "by and by," one arrives at the house of "never."—*Cervantes.*

When a fool has made up his mind the market has gone by.—*Spanish Proverb.*

Never put off till to-morrow that which you can do to-day.—*Franklin.*

Never do to-day what you can put off till to-morrow.—Delay may give clearer light as to what is best to be done.—*Aaron Burr.*

Undue procrastination indicates that a man does not see his way clearly; undue precipitation, that he does not see it at all.

Waste no vain words on the consumed time, but take the instant by the forward top; for on man's best resolved, best urged decrees, the inaudible and viewless foot of time steals, ere he can effect.—*Shakespeare.*

We pass our life in deliberation, and we die upon it.—*Quesnel.*

Procrastination says, "The next advantage we will take thoroughly."—*Shakespeare.*

He who prorogues the honesty of to-day till to-morrow, will probably prorogue his to-morrows to eternity.—*Lavater.*

Indulge in procrastination, and in time you will come to this, that because a thing ought to be done, therefore you can't do it.—*Charles Buxton.*

The man who procrastinates struggles with ruin.—*Hesiod.*

How mankind defers from day to day the best it can do, and the most beautiful things it can enjoy, without thinking that every day may be the last one, and that lost time is lost eternity!—*Max Müller.*

There is, by God's grace, an immeasurable distance between late and too late.—*Mad. Swetchine.*

To be always intending to live a new life, but never to find time to set about it; this is as if a man should put off eating and drinking and sleeping from one day and night to another, till he is starved and destroyed.—*Tillotson.*

Faith in to-morrow, instead of Christ, is Satan's nurse for man's perdition.—*G. B. Cheever.*

Be wise to-day; 'tis madness to defer; next day the fatal precedent will plead; thus on, till wisdom is push'd out of life.—*Young.*

That we would do, we should do when we would; for this would changes, and hath abatements and delays as many, as there are tongues, are hands, are accidents; and then this should is like a spendthrift sigh, that hurts by easing.—*Shakespeare.*

Unhappy he who does his work adjourn, and to to-morrow would the search delay: his lazy morrow will be like to-day.—*Persius.*

To-morrow is the day when idlers work, and fools reform, and mortal men lay hold on heaven.

Procrastination is the thief of time; year after year it steals, till all are fled, and to the mercies of a moment leaves the vast concerns of an eternal state. At thirty, man suspects himself a fool; knows it at forty, and reforms his plan; at fifty chides his infamous delay, pushes his prudent purpose to resolve; in all the magnanimity of thought, resolves,

and re-resolves, then dies the same.—
Young.

Delay not till to-morrow to be wise;
to-morrow's sun to thee may never rise.
—*Congreve.*

Is not he imprudent, who, seeing the
tide making toward him apace, will
sleep till the sea overwhelms him?—
Tillotson.

To-morrow! It is a period nowhere
to be found in all the hoary registers
of time, unless, perchance, in the fool's
calendar.—Wisdom disclaims the word,
nor holds society with those who own
it.—*Colton.*

PRODIGALITY.—The gains of prodigals are like fig-trees growing on a
precipice: for these, none are better but
kites and crows; for those, only harlots
and flatterers.—*Socrates.*

The prodigal robs his heir, the miser
robs himself. The middle way is, justice to ourselves and others.—*Bruyère.*

We never find the Scriptures commending any prodigal but one, and him
only for ceasing to be so.—His prodigality brought him to the swine and
their trough, and from imitating their
sensuality, by a natural consequence, to
take up with their diet too.—*South.*

Let us not be too prodigal when we
are young, nor too parsimonious when
we are old. Otherwise we shall fall into
the common error of those, who, when
they had the power to enjoy, had not
the prudence to acquire; and when they
had the prudence to acquire, had no
longer the power to enjoy.—*Colton.*

When I see a young profligate squandering his fortune in bagnios, or at the
gaming-table, I cannot help looking on
him as hastening his own death, and in
a manner digging his own grave.—*Goldsmith.*

The difference between the covetous
man and the prodigal, is, that the former never has money, and the latter
will have none shortly.—*Ben Jonson.*

Prodigality and dissipation, at last
bring a man to the want of the necessities of life; he falls into poverty, misery, and abject disgrace; so that even
his acquaintances, fearful of being
obliged to restore to him what he has
squandered, fly from him as a debtor

from his creditors, and he is left abandoned by all the world.—*Volney.*

The injury of prodigality leads to
this, that he that will not economize
will have to agonize.—*Confucius.*

Prodigality is the devil's steward and
purse-bearer, ministering to all sorts of
vice; and it is hard, if not impossible,
for a prodigal person to be guilty of no
other vice but prodigality. For men
generally are prodigal because they are
first intemperate, luxurious, or ambitious.
And these, we know, are vices too costly
to be kept and maintained at an easy
rate; they must have large pensions,
and be fed with both hands, though the
man that feeds them starves for his
pains.—*South.*

PROFANITY.—Of all the dark catalogue of sins, there is not one more vile
and execrable than profaneness. It commonly does, and loves to cluster with
other sins; and he who can look up and
insult his Maker to his face, needs but
little improvement in guilt to make
him a finished devil.—*S. H. Cox.*

It chills my blood to hear the blest
Supreme rudely appealed to on each
trifling theme.—Maintain your rank, vulgarity despise. — To swear is neither
brave, polite, nor wise.—*Cowper.*

Ill deeds are doubled with an evil
word.—*Shakespeare.*

Profanity is both an unreasonable
and an unmanly sin, a violation alike
of good taste and good morals; an offence against both man and God.—Some
sins are productive of temporary profit
or pleasure; but profaneness is productive of nothing unless it be shame on
earth, and damnation in hell. It is the
most gratuitous of all kinds of wickedness—a sort of pepper-corn acknowledgment of the sovereignty of the devil
over those who indulge it.—*Tryon Edwards.*

The foolish and wicked practice of
profane cursing and swearing is a vice
so mean and low, that every person of
sense and character detests and despises
it.—*Washington.*

The devil tempts men through their
ambition, their cupidity or their appetite, until he comes to the profane
swearer, whom he catches without any
bait or reward.—*Horace Mann.*

Profit or pleasure there is none in swearing, nor anything in men's natural tempers to incite them to it. For though some men pour out oaths so freely, as if they came naturally from them, yet surely no man is born of a swearing constitution.—*Tillotson.*

If you wish to fit yourself for the dark world of woe, it will be time enough to learn its language after you have prepared for it, by more decent sins than profaneness.—*John Todd.*

Blasphemous words betray the vain foolishness of the speaker.—*Sir P. Sidney.*

Common swearing, if it have any serious meaning at all, argues in man a perpetual distrust of his own reputation, and is an acknowledgment that he thinks his bare word not to be worthy of credit. And it is so far from adorning and filling a man's discourse, that it makes it look swollen and bloated, and more bold and blustering than becomes persons of genteel and good breeding.—*Tillotson.*

Nothing is a greater, or more fearful sacrilege than to prostitute the great name of God to the petulancy of an idle tongue.—*Jeremy Taylor.*

Swearing is properly a superfluity of naughtiness, and can only be considered as a sort of pepper-corn sent, in acknowledgment of the devil's right of superiority.—*Robert Hall.*

Profaneness is a brutal vice.—He who indulges in it is no gentleman.—I care not what his stamp may be in society, or what clothes he wears, or what culture he boasts.—Despite all his refinement, the light and habitual taking of God's name in vain, betrays a coarse and brutal will.—*E. H. Chapin.*

Profanity never did any man the least good. No man is the richer, or happier, or wiser, for it. It commends no one to any society. It is disgusting to the refined; abominable to the good; insulting to those with whom we associate; degrading to the mind; unprofitable, needless, and injurious to society.

PROGRESS.—All that is human must retrograde if it do not advance.—*Gibbon.*

A fresh mind keeps the body fresh. Take in the ideas of the day, drain off

those of yesterday. As to the morrow, time enough to consider it when it becomes to-day.—*Bulwer.*

The moral law of the universe is progress. Every generation that passes idly over the earth without adding to that progress remains uninscribed upon the register of humanity, and the succeeding generation tramples its ashes as dust.—*Mazzini.*

Progress is the activity of to-day and the assurance of to-morrow.—*Emerson.*

True conservatism is substantial progress; it holds fast what is true and good in order to advance in both.—To cast away the old is not of necessity to obtain the new.—To reject anything that is valuable, lessens the power of gaining more. That a thing is new does not of course commend; that it is old does not discredit. The test question is, "Is it true or good?"—*Tryon Edwards.*

The wisest man may be wiser to-day than he was yesterday, and to-morrow than he is to-day. Total freedom from change would imply total freedom from error; but this is the prerogative of Omniscience alone.—*Colton.*

That past which is so presumptuously brought forward as a precedent for the present, was itself founded on some past that went before it.—*Mad. de Staël.*

Two principles govern the moral and intellectual world. One is perpetual progress, the other the necessary limitations to that progress. If the former alone prevailed, there would be nothing steadfast and durable on earth, and the whole of social life would be the sport of winds and waves. If the latter had exclusive sway, or even if it obtained a mischievous preponderancy, every thing would petrify or rot. The best ages of the world are those in which these two principles are the most equally balanced. In such ages every enlightened man ought to adopt both principles, and with one hand develop what he can, with the other restrain and uphold what he ought.—*Gentz.*

Who are they that would have all mankind look backward instead of forward, and regulate their conduct by things that have been done? those who are the most ignorant as to all things that are doing. Bacon said, time is the greatest of innovators; he might also have said the greatest of improvers.—*Colton.*

Every age has its problem, by solving which, humanity is helped forward.—*H. Heine.*

Men of great genius and large heart sow the seeds of a new degree of progress in the world, but they bear fruit only after many years.—*Mazzini.*

It is curious to note the old sea-margins of human thought. Each subsiding century reveals some new mystery; we build where monsters used to hide themselves.—*Longfellow.*

The world is full of hopeful analogies and handsome dubious eggs called possibilities.—*George Eliot.*

Revolutions never go backwards.—*Emerson.*

We ought not to be over-anxious to encourage innovation, in cases of doubtful improvement, for an old system must ever have two advantages over a new one; it is established and it is understood.—*Colton.*

By the disposition of a stupendous wisdom, moulding together the great mysterious incorporation of the human race, the whole, at one time, is never old, or middle-aged, or young, but moves on through the varied tenor of perpetual decay, fall, renovation, and progression.—*Burke.*

The grandest of all laws is the law of progressive development.—Under it, in the wide sweep of things, men grow wiser as they grow older, and societies better.—*Bovee.*

He that is good, will infallibly become better, and he that is bad, will as certainly become worse; for vice, virtue, and time, are three things that never stand still.—*Colton.*

Intercourse is the soul of progress.—*Buxton.*

He is only advancing in life, whose heart is getting softer, his blood warmer, his brain quicker, and his spirit entering into living peace.—*Ruskin.*

The individual and the race are always moving; and as we drift into new latitudes new lights open in the heavens more immediately over us.—*E. H. Chapin.*

Every step of progress which the world has made has been from scaffold to scaffold, and from stake to state.—*Wendell Philips.*

Intellectually, as well as politically, the direction of all true progress is toward greater freedom, and along an endless succession of ideas.—*Bovee.*

The true law of the race is progress and development.—Whenever civilization pauses in the march of conquest, it is overthrown by the barbarian.—*Simms.*

If a man is not rising upward to be an angel, depend upon it, he is sinking downward to be a devil.—He cannot stop at the beast.—*Coleridge.*

I am suffocated and lost when I have not the bright feeling of progression.—*Margaret Fuller.*

If virtue promises happiness, prosperity and peace, then progress in virtue is progress in each of these; for to whatever point the perfection of anything brings us, progress is always an approach toward it.—*Epictetus.*

All our progress is an unfolding, like the vegetable bud.—You have first an instinct, then an opinion, then a knowledge, as the plant has root, bud, and fruit.—Trust the instinct to the end, though you can render no reason.—*Emerson.*

We are never present with, but always beyond ourselves.—Fear, desire, and hope are still pushing us on toward the future.—*Montaigne.*

Some falls are means the happier to rise.—*Shakespeare.*

Mankind never loses any good thing, physical, intellectual, or moral, till it finds a better, and then the loss is a gain. No steps backward, is the rule of human history. What is gained by one man is invested in all men, and is a permanent investment for all time.—*Theodore Parker.*

Society moves slowly toward civilization, but when we compare epochs half a century or even quarter of a century apart, we perceive many signs that progress is made.—*Mrs. L. M. Child.*

Westward the course of empire takes its way.—*Bp. Berkeley.*

"Can any good come out of Nazareth?"—This is always the question of the wiseacres and knowing ones.—But the good, the new, comes from exactly that quarter whence it is not looked for, and is always something different from what is expected.—Everything new is received with contempt, for it begins in obscurity. It becomes a power unobserved.—*Feuerbach.*

The art of nations is cumulative, just as science and history are; the work of living men not superseding but building itself on the work of the past.—*Ruskin.* By a peculiar prerogative, not only each individual is making daily advances in the sciences, and may make advances in morality, but all mankind together are making a continual progress in proportion as the universe grows older; so that the whole human race, during the course of so many ages, may be considered as one man, who never ceases to live and learn.—*Pascal.*

The world owes all its onward impulses to men ill at ease. The happy man inevitably confines himself within ancient limits.—*Hawthorne.*

Progress is the real cure for an overestimate of ourselves.—*G. Macdonald.*

Progress is the law of life; man is not man as yet.—*Robert Browning.*

Generations are as the days of toilsome mankind.—What the father has made, the son can make and enjoy, but he has also work of his own appointed to him.—Thus all things wax and roll onwards—arts, establishments, opinions; nothing is ever completed, but completing.—*Carlyle.*

Nature knows no pause in progress and development, and attaches her curse on all inaction.—*Goethe.*

Works of true merit are seldom very popular in their own day; for knowledge is on the march and men of genius are the videttes that are far in advance of their comrades. They are not with them, but before them; not in the camp, but beyond it.—*Colton.*

The mind naturally makes progress, and the will naturally clings to objects, so that for want of right objects, it will attach itself to wrong ones.—*Pascal.*

Progress—the onward stride of God.—*Victor Hugo.*

The books which once we valued more than the apple of the eye, we

have quite exhausted. What is that but saying that we have come up with the point of view which the universal mind took through the eyes of one scribe; we have been that man, and have passed on.—*Emerson.*

Let us labor for that larger comprehension of truth, and that more thorough repudiation of error, which shall make the history of mankind a series of ascending developments.—*H. Mann.*

All the grand agencies which the progress of mankind evolves are the aggregate result of countless wills, each of which, thinking merely of its own end, and perhaps fully gaining it, is at the same time enlisted by Providence in the secret service of the world.—*James Martineau.*

We should so live and labor in our time that what came to us as seed may go to the next generation as blossom, and what came to us as blossom may go to them as fruit.—This is what we mean by progress.—*H. W. Beecher.*

We cannot believe that the church of God is already possessed of all that light which God intends to give it; nor that all Satan's lurking-places have already been found out.—*Jonathan Edwards.*

If God reveal anything to you by any other instrument, be as ready to receive it as ever you were to receive any truth by my ministry; for I am verily persuaded the Lord has more truth yet to break forth out of his holy word.—*John Robinson.*

All growth that is not toward God, is growing to decay.—*G. Macdonald.*

I find the great thing in this world is not so much where we stand, as in what direction we are moving.—*Oliver Wendell Holmes.*

PROMISE.—He who promises runs in debt.—*Talmud.*

It is easy to promise, and alas! how easy to forget!—*A. de Musset.*

Unclaimed promises are like uncashed cheques; they will keep us from bankruptcy, but not from want.—*Havergal.*

I had rather do and not promise, than promise and not do.—*A. Warwick.*

We promise according to our hopes, but perform according to our selfishness and our fears.—*Rochefoucauld.*

He who is most slow in making a promise is the most faithful in its performance.—*Rousseau.*

An acre of performance is worth the whole world of promise.—*Howell.*

A mind conscious of integrity scorns to say more than it means to perform.—*Burns.*

Magnificent promises are always to be suspected.—*Theodore Parker.*

Every brave man is a man of his word.—*Corneille.*

Thou oughtest to be nice, even to superstition, in keeping thy promises, and therefore equally cautious in making them.—*Fuller.*

In religion not to do as thou sayest, is to unsay thy religion in thy deeds, and to undo thyself by doing.—*Venning.*

Every divine promise is built upon four pillars: God's justice or holiness, which will not suffer Him to deceive; His grace or goodness, which will not suffer him to forget; His truth, which will not suffer Him to change; and His power, which makes him able to accomplish.—*Salter.*

PROMPTNESS.—Promptness is the soul of business.—*Chesterfield.*

Deliberate with caution, but act with decision and promptness.—*Colton.*

The keen spirit seizes the prompt occasion; makes the thought start into instant action, and at once plans and performs, resolves, and executes!—*Hannah More.*

Let's take the instant by the forward top; for we are old, and on our quickest decrees, the inaudible and noiseless foot of time steals ere we can effect them.—*Shakespeare.*

"How," said one to Sir W. Raleigh, of whom it was said he "could toil terribly,"—"how do you accomplish so much, and in so short a time?" "When I have anything to do, I go and do it," was the reply.

Celerity is never more admired than by the negligent.—*Shakespeare.*

Promptitude is not only a duty, but is also a part of good manners; it is favorable to fortune, reputation, influence, and usefulness; a little attention and energy will form the habit, so as

to make it easy and delightful.—*C. Simmons.*

If it were done when it is done, then it were well it were done quickly.—*Shakespeare.*

Know the true value of time; snatch, seize, and enjoy every moment of it.—No idleness, no delay, no procrastination; never put off till to-morrow what you can do to-day.—*Chesterfield.*

PROPERTY.—Property is dear to men not only for the sensual pleasure it can afford, but also because it is the bulwark of all they hold dearest on earth, and above all else, because it is the safeguard of those they love most against misery and all physical distress.—*W. G. Sumner.*

A great object is always answered, whenever any property is transferred from hands that are not fit for that property to those that are.—*Burke.*

The accumulation of property is no guarantee of the development of character, but the development of character, or of any other good whatever, is impossible without property.—*W. G. Sumner.*

The invectives against capital in the hands of those who have it, are double-faced, and when turned about are nothing but demands for capital in the hands of those who have it not, in order that they may do with it just what those who have it are now doing with it.—*W. G. Sumner.*

Property left to a child may soon be lost; but the inheritance of virtue—a good name, an unblemished reputation—will abide forever. If those who are toiling for wealth to leave their children, would but take half the pains to secure for them virtuous habits, how much more serviceable would they be. The largest property may be wrested from a child, but virtue will stand by him to the last.

PROSPERITY.—All sunshine makes the desert.—*Arab Proverb.*

Everything in the world may be endured, except continual prosperity.—*Goethe.*

Prosperity is the touchstone of virtue; for it is less difficult to bear misfortunes, than to remain uncorrupted by pleasure.—*Tacitus.*

A smooth sea never made a skillful mariner; neither do uninterrupted prosperity and success qualify men for usefulness and happiness.

If adversity hath killed his thousands, prosperity hath killed his ten thousands; therefore adversity is to be preferred. The one deceives, the other instructs; the one is miserably happy, the other happily miserable; and therefore many philosophers have voluntarily sought adversity and commend it in their precepts.—*Burton.*

Take care to be an economist in prosperity: there is no fear of your being one in adversity.—*Zimmermann.*

Prosperity's right hand is industry, and her left hand is frugality.

That fortitude which has encountered no dangers, that prudence which has surmounted no difficulties, that integrity which has been attacked by no temptation, can at best be considered but as gold not yet brought to the test, of which therefore the true value cannot be assigned.—*Johnson.*

Oh, how portentous is prosperity! how, comet-like, it threatens while it shines.—*Young.*

Prosperity has this property, it puffs up narrow souls, makes them imagine themselves high and mighty, and looks down upon the world with contempt; but a truly noble and resolved spirit appears greatest in distress, and then becomes more bright and conspicuous.—*Plutarch.*

Who feels no ills, should, therefore, fear them; and when fortune smiles, be doubly cautious, lest destruction come remorseless on him, and he fall unpitied.—*Sophocles.*

Prosperity too often has the same effect on its possessor, that a calm at sea has on the Dutch mariner, who frequently, it is said, in these circumstances, ties up the rudder, gets drunk, and goes to sleep.—*Bp. Horne.*

In prosperity prepare for a change; in adversity hope for one.—*Burgh.*

The virtue of prosperity is temperance, but the virtue of adversity is fortitude; and the last is the more sublime attainment.—*Bacon.*

The good things which belong to prosperity may be wished; but the good things which belong to adversity are to be admired.—*Seneca.*

As full ears load and lay down corn, so does too much fortune bend and break the mind. It deserves to be considered, too, as another disadvantage, that affliction moves pity, and reconciles our very enemies, but prosperity provokes envy, and loses us our very friends.—*Charron.*

As riches and favor forsake a man, we discover him to be a fool but nobody could find it out in his prosperity.—*Bruyère.*

No man is prosperous whose immortality is forfeited.—No man is rich to whom the grave brings eternal bankruptcy.—No man is happy upon whose path there rests but a momentary glimmer of light, shining out between clouds that are closing over him in darkness forever.—*H. W. Beecher.*

A weak mind sinks under prosperity as well as under adversity.—A strong and deep one has two highest tides, when the moon is at full, and when there is no moon.—*Hare.*

To rejoice in the prosperity of another is to partake of it.—*W. Austin.*

Many are not able to suffer and endure prosperity; it is like the light of the sun to a weak eye, glorious, indeed, in itself, but not proportioned to such an instrument.—*Jeremy Taylor.*

There is a glare about worldly success which is very apt to dazzle men's eyes.—*Hare.*

Greatness stands upon a precipice, and if prosperity carries a man ever so little beyond his poise, it overbears and dashes him to pieces.—*Seneca.*

Watch lest prosperity destroy generosity.—*H. W. Beecher.*

What Anacharsis said of the vine may aptly enough be said of prosperity. She bears the three grapes of drunkenness, pleasure, and sorrow; and happy is it if the last can cure the mischief which the former work. When afflictions fail to have their due effect, the case is desperate.—*Bolingbroke.*

He that swells in prosperity will be sure to shrink in adversity.—*Colton.*

One is never more on trial than in the moment of excessive good fortune.—*Lew Wallace.*

So use prosperity, that adversity may not abuse thee: if in the one, security admits no fears, in the other, despair will afford no hopes; he that in prosperity can foretell a danger can in adversity foresee deliverance.—*Quarles.*

To bring the best human qualities to anything like perfection, to fill them with the sweet juices of courtesy and charity, prosperity, or, at all events, a moderate amount of it, is required,—just as sunshine is needed for the ripening of peaches and apricots.—*Alexander Smith.*

It is the bright day that brings forth the adder, and that craves wary walking.—*Shakespeare.*

Prosperity is the touchstone of virtue: it is less difficult to bear misfortunes than to remain uncorrupted by pleasure. —*Tacitus.*

Prosperity, alas! is often but another name for pride.—*Mrs. Sigourney.*

There is ever a certain languor attending the fulness of prosperity. When the heart has no more to wish, it yawns over its possessions, and the energy of the soul goes out like a flame that has no more to devour.—*Young.*

They who lie soft and warm in a rich estate seldom come to heat themselves at the altar.—*South.*

While prosperous you can number many friends; but when the storm comes you are left alone.—*Ovid.*

The mind that is much elevated and insolent with prosperity, and cast down by adversity, is generally abject and base.—*Epicurus.*

Nothing is harder to direct than a man in prosperity; nothing more easily managed than one in adversity.—*Plutarch.*

PROTESTANTISM. — Protestantism makes the relation of a man to the Church to depend upon his relation to Christ; Romanism makes the relation of a man to Christ to depend on his relation to the Church.—*Schleiermacher.*

There is no liberty in Romanism, for its principle is domination and subjection.—There is none in atheism, for it denies God and the world to come.— It leaves us with no faith except in ourselves, limited to earthly wants, and with no motives but our appetites and passions, whose slaves we thus become. —Protestantism is our only escape from Romanism; and it will be found to be our only escape from atheism.—Deliver us from both, for they are our worst enemies.—*Paul Bonchard.*

Some one quoting the hackneyed sarcasm, that "between Protestantism and Romanism there is but a paper wall," the reply was, "True, but the whole Bible is printed on it."

Protestantism is Christianity reasserting its simplicity and purity, divesting itself of the burdens and corruptions imposed by man, renouncing mere human authority, and asserting the supremacy of our Lord Jesus Christ.—It is Christianity discarding the traditions and commandments of men, declaring the paramount authority of the inspired word of God, and rejecting everything not enjoined by the sanctions of Christ himself.

Four centuries ago, Protestantism had not an existence as an organized power. To-day it leads the world. The intelligence, the wealth, the force of arms, the morality, the civilization is with the Protestant nations.—*H. L. Wayland.*

The German Protestant declared, "I have rights as against the church"; the Puritan Protestant, "I have rights as against the government"; the Independent, or American Protestant, "I have rights as against civil governments, church governments, and all mankind. These God gave me, and I will preserve." These were the three great strides which landed on Plymouth Rock. —*H. W. Beecher.*

PROVERBS.—The wisdom of many, and the wit of one.—*Lord John Russell.*

Jewels five words long, that on the stretched forefinger of all time sparkle forever.—*Tennyson.*

Proverbs are the literature of reason, or the statements of absolute truth, without qualification. Like the sacred books of each nation, they are the sanctuary of its intuitions.—*Emerson.*

Proverbs are somewhat analogous to those medical formulas which, being in frequent use, are kept ready made up in the chemists' shops, and which often save the framing of a distinct prescription.—*Whately.*

The genius, wit, and spirit of a nation are discovered in its proverbs.—*Bacon.*

Proverbs are but rules, and rules do not create character. — They prescribe conduct, but do not furnish a full and proper motive.—They are usually but half truths, and seldom contain the principle of the action they teach.—*T. T. Munger.*

Short sentences drawn from long experiences.—*Cervantes.*

Sense, brevity, and point are the elements of a good proverb.—*Tryon Edwards.*

The study of proverbs may be more instructive and comprehensive than the most elaborate scheme of philosophy.—*Motherwell.*

The proverbial wisdom of the populace in the street, on the roads, and in the markets, instructs the ear of him who studies man more fully than a thousand rules ostentatiously displayed.—*Lavater.*

We frequently fall into error and folly, not because the true principles of action are not known, but because for a time they are not remembered; he may, therefore, justly be numbered among the benefactors of mankind who contracts the great rules of life into short sentences that may early be impressed on the memory, and taught by frequent recollection to occur habitually to the mind.—*Johnson.*

Proverbs were anterior to books, and formed the wisdom of the vulgar, and in the earliest ages were the unwritten laws of morality.—*Disraeli.*

Proverbs are the condensed wisdom of long experience, in brief, epigrammatic form, easily remembered and always ready for use.—They are the alphabet of morals; and are commonly prudential watchwords and warnings, and so lean toward a selfish view of life.—*T. T. Munger.*

The wisdom of nations lies in their proverbs, which are brief and pithy. Collect and learn them; they are notable measures of directions for human life; you have much in little; they save time in speaking; and upon occasion may be the fullest and safest answers.—*Penn.*

Proverbs may be said to be the abridgments of wisdom.—*Joubert.*

The proverb condenses the meaning and power of a thousand words into one short and simple sentence, and it is the more effective because it carries so much force in so compact a form.—*D. March.*

If you hear a wise sentence or an apt phrase, commit it to your memory.—*Sir Henry Sidney.*

Few maxims are true from every point of view.—*Vauvenargues.*

Proverbs, it has well been said, should be sold in pairs, a single one being but half a truth.—*W. Mathews.*

I am of opinion that there are no proverbial sayings which are not true, because they are all sentences drawn from experience itself, who is the mother of all sciences.—*Cervantes.*

Simple words, short maxims, homely truths, old sayings, are the masters of the world. In them is the hiding of the power that forms the character, controls conduct, and makes individuals and nations what they are. Great reformations, great revolutions in society, great eras in human progress and improvement, start from good words, right words, sound words, spoken in the fitting time, and finding their way to human hearts as easily as the birds find their homes.—*D. March.*

Proverbs were bright shafts in the Greek and Latin quivers.—*Disraeli.*

The Scripture vouches Solomon for the wisest of men; and his proverbs prove him so. The seven wise men of Greece, so famous for their wisdom all the world over, acquired all that fame each of them by a single sentence, consisting of two or three words.—*South.*

The benefit of proverbs, or maxims, is that they separate those who act on principle from those who act on impulse; and they lead to promptness and decision in acting.—Their value depends on four things: do they embody correct principles; are they on important subjects; what is the extent, and what the ease of their application?—*Tryon Edwards.*

Books and proverbs receive their chief value from the stamp and esteem of ages through which they have passed.—*Sir W. Temple.*

Proverbs are in the world of thought what gold coin is in the world of business—great value in small compass, and equally current among all people. Sometimes the proverb may be false, the coin counterfeit, but in both cases the false proves the value of the true.—*D. March.*

Proverbs are the cream of a nation's thought.—*Anon.*

PROVIDENCE.—(See "ATHEISM.")

There's a divinity that shapes our ends, rough hew them how we will.—*Shakespeare.*

Providence is like a curious piece of arras, made up of thousands of shreds, which single we know not what to make of, but put together they present us with a beautiful history.—*Flavel.*

To doubt the providence of God is presently to wax impatient with his commands.—*Edward Garrett.*

To the dim and bewildered vision of humanity, God's care is more evident in some instances than in others; and upon such instances men seize, and call them providences. It is well that they can; but it would be gloriously better if they could believe that the whole matter is one grand providence.—*G. Macdonald.*

The longer I live, the more faith I have in Providence, and the less faith in my interpretation of Providence.—*J. Day.*

Everything that happens in the world is part of a great plan of God running through all time.—*H. W. Beecher.*

In the huge mass of evil as it rolls and swells, there is ever some good working toward deliverance and triumph. —*Carlyle.*

Every blade of grass in the field is measured; the green cups and the colored crowns of every flower are curiously counted; the stars of the firmament wheel in cunningly calculated orbits; even the storms have their laws.— *Blaikie.*

Resignation and faith behold God in the smallest hair that falls; and the happiest life is that of him who has bound together all the affairs of life, great and small, and intrusted them to God.—*J. W. Alexander.*

What mockeries are our most firm resolves.—To will is ours, but not to execute. We map our future like some unknown coast, and say here is a harbor, there a rock; the one we will attain; the

other shun, and we do neither; some chance gale springs up, and bears us far o'er some unfathomed sea.—*L. E. Landon.*

The longer I live, the more convincing proofs I see of this truth, that God governs in the affairs of man; and if a sparrow cannot fall to the ground without his notice, is it probable that an empire can rise without his aid?—*Franklin.*

By going a few minutes sooner or later, by stopping to speak with a friend on the corner, by meeting this man or that, or by turning down this street instead of the other, we may let slip some impending evil, by which the whole current of our lives would have been changed. There is no possible solution in the dark enigma but the one word, "Providence."—*Longfellow.*

Providence is a greater mystery than revelation. The state of the world is more humiliating to our reason than the doctrines of the Gospel. A reflecting Christian sees more to excite his astonishment, and to exercise his faith, in the state of things between Temple Bar and St. Paul's, than in what he reads from Genesis to Revelations.—*Cecil.*

Who finds not Providence all good and wise, alike in what it gives and what denies?—*Pope.*

I once asked a hermit in Italy how he could venture to live alone, in a single cottage, on the top of a mountain, a mile from any habitation? He replied, that Providence was his next-door neighbor.—*Sterne.*

All nature is but art, unknown to thee; all chance, direction which thou canst not see; all discord, harmony not understood; all partial evil, universal good.— *Pope.*

We are not to lead events, but follow them.—*Epictetus.*

Either all is chance, and being but chance is of no consequence, or God rules the world, and all is well.—Whatever befalls is just and right, and therefore not unendurable.—*Andrew Lang.*

Duties are ours; events are God's.— This removes an infinite burden from the shoulders of a miserable, tempted, dying creature.—On this consideration only can he securely lay down his head and close his eyes.—*Cecil.*

He that will watch providences, shall never want providences to watch.—*Flavel.*

Some one has said that in war providence is on the side of the strongest regiments. And I have noticed that providence is on the side of clear heads and honest hearts;—and wherever a man walks faithfully in the ways that God has marked out for him, providence, as the Christian says,—luck, as the heathen says,—will be on that man's side.—In the long run you will find that God's providence is in favor of those that keep his laws, and against those that break them.—*H. W. Beecher.*

A cockle-fish may as soon crowd the ocean into its narrow shell, as vain man ever comprehend the decrees of God.—*Bp. Beveridge.*

Happy the man who sees a God employed in all the good and ill that checker life.—*Cowper.*

He who is truly religious finds a providence not more truly in the history of the world, than in his own personal and family history.—The rainbow which hangs a splendid circle in the heights of heaven, is also formed by the same sun in the dew-drop of the lowly flower.—*Richter.*

God hangs the greatest weights upon the smallest wires.—*Bacon.*

To make our reliance upon providence both pious and rational, we should prepare all things with the same care, diligence, and activity, as if there were no such thing as providence for us to depend upon; and then, when we have done all this, we should as wholly and humbly rely upon it, as if we had made no preparation at all.—*South.*

We must follow, not force providence.—*Shakespeare.*

God tempers the wind to the shorn lamb.—*Sterne.*

God's plans, like lilies pure and white unfold.—We must not tear the close-shut leaves apart.—Time will reveal the calyxes of gold.—*M. R. Smith.*

The providence that watches over the affairs of men, works out of their mistakes, at times, a healthier issue than could have been accomplished by their own wisest forethought.—*Froude.*

Our Lord God doeth work like a printer, who setteth the letters backward; we see and feel well His setting, but we shall see the print yonder—in the life to come.—*Luther.*

PRUDENCE.—There is no amount of praise which is not heaped on prudence; yet there is not the most insignificant event of which it can make us sure.—*Rochefoucauld.*

Too many, through want of prudence, are golden apprentices, silver journeymen, and copper masters.—*Whitefield.*

Men of sense often learn from their enemies. Prudence is the best safeguard. This principle cannot be learned from a friend, but an enemy extorts it immediately. It is from their foes, not their friends, that cities learn the lesson of building high walls and ships of war. And this lesson saves their children, their homes, and their properties.—*Aristophanes.*

Franklin left behind him more maxims than any of his countrymen, and prudence is the pivot on which they turn.—*A. Rhodes.*

If the prudence of reserve and decorum dictates silence in some circumstances, in others prudence of a higher order, may justify us in speaking our thoughts.—*Burke.*

Let prudence always attend your pleasures; it is the way to enjoy the sweets of them, and not be afraid of the consequences.

Prudence is the necessary ingredient in all the virtues, without which they degenerate into folly and excess.—*Jeremy Collier.*

Want of prudence is too frequently the want of virtue; nor is there on earth a more powerful advocate for vice than poverty.—*Goldsmith.*

The one prudence in life is concentration; the one evil is dissipation.—*Emerson.*

There is nothing more imprudent than excessive prudence.—*Colton.*

No other protection is wanting, provided you are under the guidance of prudence.—*Juvenal.*

The bounds of a man's knowledge are easily concealed if he has but prudence.—*Goldsmith.*

The richest endowments of the mind are temperance, prudence, and fortitude. Prudence is a universal virtue, which enters into the composition of all the rest; and where she is not, fortitude loses its name and nature.—*Voltaire.*

Prudence is a quality incompatible with vice, and can never be effectively enlisted in its cause.—*Burke.*

The rules of prudence, in general, like the laws of the stone tables, are for the most part prohibitive.—Thou shalt not, is their characteristic formula; and it is an especial part of Christian prudence that it should be so.—*Coleridge.*

Prudence is a duty which we owe ourselves, and if we will be so much our own enemies as to neglect it, we are not to wonder if the world is deficient in discharging their duty to us; for when a man lays the foundation of his own ruin, others too often are apt to build upon it.—*Fielding.*

The prudence of the best heads is often defeated by the tenderness of the best of hearts.—*Fielding.*

Those who, in the confidence of superior capacities or attainments, neglect the common maxims of life, should be reminded that nothing will supply the want of prudence; but that negligence and irregularity, long continued, will make knowledge useless, wit ridiculous, and genius contemptible.—*Johnson.*

Prudent men lock up their motives, letting only their familiars have a key to their hearts as to their garden.—*Shenstone.*

Aristotle is praised for naming fortitude as the first of the virtues; but he might, with propriety, have placed prudence before it, since without prudence fortitude is madness.—*S. G. Goodrich.*

Prudence is a conformity to the rules of reason, truth, and decency, at all times and in all circumstances. It differs from wisdom only in degree; wisdom being nothing but a more consummate habit of prudence; and prudence a lower degree or weaker habit of wisdom.—*J. Mason.*

It is by the goodness of God that in our country we have those three unspeakably precious things: freedom of speech, freedom of conscience, and the prudence never to practice either.—*Mark Twain.*

That man is prudent who neither hopes nor fears anything from the uncertain events of the future.—*Anatole France.*

PUBLIC.—The public is wiser than the wisest critic.—*Bancroft.*

Individuals are occasionally guided by reason, crowds never.—*Dean W. R. Inge.*

There is no tyranny so despotic as that of public opinion among a free people.—*Donn Piatt.*

In a free and republican government, you cannot restrain the voice of the multitude. Every man will speak as he thinks, or, more properly, without thinking, and consequently will judge of effects without attending to their causes.—*Washington.*

The public wishes itself to be managed like a woman; one must say nothing to it except what it likes to hear.—*Goethe.*

Very few public men but look upon the public as their debtors and their prey; so much for their pride and honesty.—*Zimmermann.*

That is, in a great degree, true of all men, which was said of the Athenians, that they were like sheep, of which a flock is more easily driven than a single one.—*Whately.*

Zeal for the public good is the characteristic of a man of honor and a gentleman, and must take the place of pleasures, profits. and all other private gratifications.—*Steele.*

Each man in his sphere, however narrow or extended, will find that his fellow-men weigh his character and his abilities often, and unconsciously stamp him with their estimate: and that the average resultant of these frequent estimates is just.—*E. Pierrepont.*

The public, with its mob yearning to be instructed, edified and pulled by the nose, demands certainties; . . . but there are no certainties.—*Mencken.*

Let a man proclaim a new principle. Public sentiment will surely be on the other side.—*T. B. Reed.*

Every man who loves his country, or wishes well to the best interests of society, will show himself a decided friend not only of morality and the laws, but of religious institutions, and honorably bear his part in supporting them.—*J. Hawes.*

If it has to choose who is to be crucified, the crowd will always save Barabbas.—*Jean Cocteau.*

Public opinion, or public sentiment, is able to sustain, or to pull down any law of the commonwealth.—*C. Simmons.*

PUNCTUALITY.—I could never think well of a man's intellectual or moral character, if he was habitually unfaithful to his appointments.—*Emmons.*

Method is the very hinge of business; and there is no method without punctuality.—*Cecil.*

I have always been a quarter of an hour before my time, and it has made a man of me.—*Lord Nelson.*

Appointments once made, become debts. If I have made an appointment with you, I owe you punctuality; I have no right to throw away your time, if I do my own.—*Cecil.*

Want of punctuality is a want of virtue.—*J. M. Mason.*

I give it as my deliberate and solemn conviction that the individual who is habitually tardy in meeting an appointment, will never be respected or successful in life.—*W. Fisk.*

Every child should be taught to pay all his debts, and to fulfil all his contracts, exactly in manner, completely in value, punctually at the time. Everything he has borrowed, he should be obliged to return uninjured at the time specified, and everything belonging to others which he has lost, he should be required to replace.—*Dwight.*

Better be three hours too soon than one minute too late.—*Shakespeare.*

When a secretary of Washington, excusing himself for being late, said that his watch was too slow, the reply of Washington was, "You must get a new watch, or I must get a new secretary."

It is of no use running; to set out betimes is the main point.—*Fontaine.*

Strict punctuality is, perhaps, the cheapest virtue which can give force to an otherwise utterly insignificant character.—*J. F. Boyes.*

Nothing inspires confidence in a business man sooner than punctuality, nor is there any habit which sooner saps his reputation than that of being always behind time.—*W. Mathews.*

Punctuality is the stern virtue of men of business, and the graceful courtesy of princes.—*Bulwer.*

The most indispensable qualification of a cook is punctuality. The same must be said of guests.—*B. Savarin.*

"Better late than never," is not half so good a maxim as "Better never late."

PUNISHMENT.—The whole of life and experience goes to show, that right or wrong doing, whether as to the physical or the spiritual nature, is sure in the end to meet its appropriate reward or punishment.—Penalties may be delayed, but they are sure to come.—*H. W. Beecher.*

It is as expedient that a wicked man be punished as that a sick man be cured by a physician; for all chastisement is a kind of medicine.—*Plato.*

Punishment is lame, but it comes.—*Herbert.*

The certainty of punishment, even more than its severity, is the preventive of crime.—*Tryon Edwards.*

One man meets an infamous punishment for that crime which confers a diadem upon another.—*Juvenal.*

The work of eradicating crimes is not by making punishment familiar, but formidable.—*Goldsmith.*

Don't let us rejoice in punishment, even when the hand of God alone inflicts it. The best of us are but poor wretches just saved from shipwreck. Can we feel anything but awe and pity when we see a fellow-passenger · swallowed by the waves?—*George Eliot.*

If punishment makes not the will supple it hardens the offender.—*Locke.*

Wickedness, when properly punished, is disgraceful only to the offender; unpunished, it is disgraceful to the whole community.—*C. Simmons.*

The public have more interest in the punishment of an injury than he who receives it.—*Cato.*

The punishment of criminals should be of use; when a man is hanged he is good for nothing.—*Voltaire.*

We do not aim to correct the man we hang; we correct and warn others by him.—*Montaigne.*

The object of punishment is threefold: for just retribution; for the protection of society; for the reformation of the offender.—*Tryon Edwards.*

Jails and prisons are the complement

of schools; so many less as you have of the latter, so many more you must have of the former.—*Horace Mann.*

Punishment is justice for the unjust.—*Augustine.*

Even legal punishments lose all appearance of justice, when too strictly inflicted on men compelled by the last extremity of distress to incur them.—*Junius.*

There are dreadful punishments enacted against thieves; but it were much better to make such good provisions that every man might be put in a method how to live, and so be preserved from the fatal necessity of stealing and dying for it.—*Moore.*

The seeds of our punishment are sown at the same time we commit the sin.—*Hesiod.*

To make punishments efficacious, two things are necessary; they must never be disproportioned to the offence, and they must be certain.—*Simms.*

The very worst use to which you can put a man, says Wilkes, is to hang him; but the hanging is not to make the man useful, but to punish his crime and protect society.—*C. Simmons.*

We will not punish a man because he hath offended, but that he may offend no more; nor does punishment ever look to the past, but to the future; for it is not the result of passion, but that the same thing may be guarded against in time to come.—*Seneca.*

Faults of the head are punished in this world; those of the heart in another; but as most of our vices are compound, so is their punishment.—*Colton.*

There is no future pang can deal that justice on the self-condemned, that he deals on his own soul.—*Byron.*

God is on the side of virtue; for whoever dreads punishment suffers it, and whoever deserves it dreads it.—*Colton.*

It is hard, but it is excellent, to find the right knowledge of when correction is necessary, and when grace doth most avail.—*Sir P. Sidney.*

There is no greater punishment than that of being abandoned to one's self.—*Quesnel.*

Crime and punishment grow out of one stem. Punishment is a fruit that,

unsuspected, ripens within the flower of the pleasure that concealed it.—*Emerson.*

The object of punishment is the prevention of evil; it can never be made impulsive to good.—*Horace Mann.*

Never was the voice of conscience silenced without retribution.—*Mrs. Jameson.*

The exposition of future punishment in God's word is not to be regarded as a threat, but as a merciful declaration. —If in the ocean of life, over which we are bound to eternity, there are these rocks and shoals, it is no cruelty to chart them down; it is an eminent and prominent mercy.—*H. W. Beecher.*

The existence of future punishment and everlasting destruction is an evidence of the goodness, the justice, and the wisdom of God: of goodness, in that it is a motive to prevent sin and turn men from evil; of justice, in that it is the righteous doom of irreclaimable sinners; and of wisdom, in that God can thus make the penalty of sin a motive to deter from sin.—*J. B. Walker.*

PURITY.—I pray thee, O God, that I may be beautiful within.—*Socrates.*

The chaste mind, like a polished plane, may admit foul thoughts, without receiving their tincture.—*Sterne.*

There's nothing ill can dwell in such a temple; if the ill spirit have so fair a house, good things will starve to dwell with it.—*Shakespeare.*

Make my breast transparent as pure crystal, that the world, jealous of me, may see the foulest thought my heart does hold.—*Buckingham.*

Evil into the mind of God or man, may come and go, and yet, if unapproved, still without sin.—*Milton.*

By the ancients, courage was regarded as practically the main part of virtue: by us, though I hope we are not less brave, purity is so regarded now. Courage, however kindled, is fanned by the breath of man: purity lives and derives its life solely from the Spirit of God.—*Hare.*

PURPOSE.—(See "ENERGY.")

The secret of success is constancy to purpose.—*Disraeli.*

The flighty purpose never is o'ertook

unless the deed go with it.—*Shakespeare.*

Thy purpose firm is equal to the deed. —Who does the best his circumstance allows, does well, acts nobly; angels could no more.—*Young.*

Man proposes, but God disposes.— *Thomas à Kempis.*

It is better by a noble boldness to run the risk of being subject to half of the evils we anticipate, than to remain in cowardly listlessness for fear of what may happen.—*Herodotus.*

It is the old lesson—a worthy purpose, patient energy for its accomplishment, a resoluteness undaunted by difficulties, and then success.—*W. M. Punshon.*

There is no road to success but through a clear strong purpose.—Nothing can take its place.—A purpose underlies character, culture, position, attainment of every sort.—*T. T. Munger.*

A man with a half-volition goes backwards and forwards, and makes no way on the smoothest road; a man with a whole volition advances on the roughest, and will reach his purpose, if there be even a little wisdom in it.—*Carlyle.*

The man without a purpose is like a ship without a rudder—a waif, a nothing, a no man. Have a purpose in life, and, having it, throw such strength of mind and muscle into your work as God has given you.—*Carlyle.*

PURSUIT.—I take it to be a principal rule of life, not to be too much addicted to one thing.—*Terence.*

The fruit that can fall without shaking, indeed is too mellow for me.—*Lady Montague.*

There are many things that are thorns to our hopes until we have attained them, and envenomed arrows to our hearts when we have.—*Colton.*

The rapture of pursuing is the prize the vanquished gain.—*Longfellow.*

Q

QUACKERY.—Heroes have gone out, quacks have come in; the reign of quacks has not ended with the nineteenth century. The sceptre is held with a firmer grasp; the empire has a wider boundary. We are all the slaves of quackery in one shape or another.

One portion of our being is always playing the successful quack to the other.—*Carlyle.*

He who attempts to make others believe in means which he himself despises, is a puffer; he who makes use of more means than he knows to be necessary, is a quack; and he who ascribes to those means a greater efficacy than his own experience warrants, is an imposter.— *Lavater.*

Pettifoggers in law and quacks in medicine have held from time immemorial the fee simple of a vast estate, subject to no alienation, diminution, revolution, nor tax—the folly and ignorance of mankind.—*Colton.*

Nothing more strikingly betrays the credulity of mankind than medicine. Quackery is a thing universal, and universally successful. In this case it is literally true that no imposition is too great for the credulity of men.— *Thoreau.*

Out, you impostors; quack-salving, cheating mountebanks; your skill is to make sound men sick, and sick men to kill.—*Massinger.*

From powerful causes spring the empiric's gains.—Man's love of life, his weakness and his pains—these first induce him the vile trash to try, then lend his name that others too may buy.— *Crabbe.*

Quackery has no such friend as credulity.—*C. Simmons.*

That science is worse than useless which does not point to the great end of our being.—Therefore literary, scientific, and theological quacks have done immense mischief in human society.— *Thacher.*

Said a clever quack to an educated physician, "How many of the passing multitude, do you suppose, appreciate the value of science, or understand the impositions of quackery?"—"Not more than one in ten," was the answer.— "Well," said the quack, "you may have the one, and I'll have the nine."

We affect to laugh at the folly of those who put faith in nostrums, but are willing to try ourselves whether there is any truth in them.—*Hazlitt.*

QUALITIES.—Wood burns because it has the proper stuff in it; and a man becomes famous because he has the proper stuff in him.—*Goethe.*

We should not judge of a man's merits by his great qualities, but by the use he makes of them.—*Rochefoucauld.*

Our good qualities often expose us to hatred and persecution more than our bad actions. "Persecuted for righteousness' sake," describes the condition of at least some in this world.

Hearts may be attracted by assumed qualities, but the affections are only to be fixed by those which are real.—*De Moy.*

It is not enough to have great qualities, we must also have the management of them.—*Rochefoucauld.*

Good nature and evenness of temper, will give you an easy companion for life; virtue and good sense an agreeable friend; love and constancy a good wife or husband.—*Spectator.*

QUARRELS.—I consider your very testy and quarrelsome people as I do a loaded gun, which may, by accident, at any time, go off and kill people.—*Shenstone.*

Quarrels would never last long if the fault was only on one side.—*Rochefoucauld.*

Beware of entrance to a quarrel; but, being in, bear it that the opposer may beware of thee.—*Shakespeare.*

He that blows the coals in quarrels he has nothing to do with, has no right to complain if the sparks fly in his face.—*Franklin.*

In most quarrels there is a fault on both sides. A quarrel may be compared to a spark, which cannot be produced without a flint as well as steel. Either of them may hammer on wood forever; no fire will follow.—*Colton.*

Jars concealed are half reconciled; but if generally known, it is a double task to stop the breach at home and men's mouths abroad.—*Fuller.*

Coarse kindness is, at least, better than coarse anger; and in all private quarrels the duller nature is triumphant by reason of its dullness.—*George Eliot.*

The quarrels of lovers are like summer storms. Everything is more beauti-

ful when they have passed. — *Mad. Necker.*

The hatred of those who are the most nearly connected, is the most inveterate. —*Tacitus.*

If you cannot avoid a quarrel with a blackguard, let your lawyer manage it rather than yourself. No man sweeps his own chimney, but employs a chimney-sweeper who has no objection to dirty work because it is his trade.— *Colton.*

In a false quarrel there is no true valor.—*Shakespeare.*

Two things, well considered, would prevent many quarrels; first to have it well ascertained whether we are not disputing about terms rather than things; and secondly, to examine whether that on which we differ is worth contending about.—*Colton.*

One should not quarrel with a dog without a reason sufficient to vindicate one through all the courts of morality. —*Goldsmith.*

When worthy men fall out, only one of them may be faulty at first; but if the strife continue long, both commonly become guilty.—*Fuller.*

Thrice is he armed that hath his quarrel just, and he but naked, though locked up in steel, whose conscience with injustice is corrupted.—*Shakespeare.*

QUESTION.—Judge of a man by his questions rather than by his answers. —*Voltaire.*

How do you know so much about everything?—was asked of a very wise and intelligent man; and the answer was, "By never being afraid or ashamed to ask questions as to anything of which I was ignorant."

A child can ask a thousand questions that the wisest man cannot answer.— *J. Abbott.*

There are innumerable questions to which the inquisitive mind can, in this state, receive no answer: Why do you and I exist? Why was this world created? And, since it was to be created, why was it not created sooner?—*Johnson.*

QUIET.—What sweet delight a quiet life affords.—*Drummond.*

I pray you bear me henceforth from

the noise and rumor of the field, where I may think the remnant of my thoughts in peace, and part this body and my soul with contemplation and devout desires.—*Shakespeare.*

The heart that is to be filled to the brim with holy joy must be held still. —*Bowes.*

The grandest operations, both in nature and grace, are the most silent and imperceptible.—The shallow brook babbles in its passage and is heard by every one; but the coming on of the seasons is silent and unseen.—The storm rages and alarms, but its fury is soon exhausted, and its effects are but partial and soon remedied; but the dew, though gentle and unheard, is immense in quantity, and is the very life of large portions of the earth.—And these are pictures of the operations of grace in the church and in the soul.—*Cecil.*

My notions of life are much the same as they are about travelling; there is a good deal of amusement on the road, but, after all, one wants to be at rest.— *Southey.*

Stillness of person and steadiness of features are signal marks of good breeding.—Vulgar persons can't sit still, or, at least, they must work their limbs or features.—*O. W. Holmes.*

I have often said that all the misfortunes of men spring from their not knowing how to live quietly at home, in their own rooms.—*Pascal.*

QUOTATIONS.—Quotation, sir, is a good thing; there is a community of mind in it: classical quotation is the parole of literary men all over the world.—*Johnson.*

An apt quotation is as good as an original remark.—*Proverb.*

The obscurest sayings of the truly great are often those which contain the germ of the profoundest and most useful truths.—*Mazzini.*

Quotation is the highest compliment you can pay to an author.—*Johnson.*

In quoting of books, quote such authors as are usually read; others you may read for your own satisfaction, but do not name them.—*Selden.*

The man whose book is filled with quotations, has been said to creep along the shore of authors, as if he were afraid

to trust himself to the free compass of reasoning. I would rather defend such authors by a different allusion, and ask whether honey is the worse for being gathered from many flowers.

It is the beauty and independent worth of the citations, far more than their appropriateness, which have made Johnson's Dictionary popular even as a reading-book.—*Coleridge.*

If these little sparks of holy fire thus heaped up together do not give life to your prepared and already enkindled spirit, yet they will sometimes help to entertain a thought, to actuate a passion, to employ and hallow a fancy.— *Jeremy Taylor.*

Next to the originator of a good sentence is the first quoter of it.—*Emerson.*

To select well among old things is almost equal to inventing new ones.— *Trublet.*

Why are not more gems from our great authors scattered over the country? Great books are not in everybody's reach; and though it is better to know them thoroughly than to know them only here and there, yet it is a good work to give a little to those who have neither time nor means to get more. Let every bookworm, when in any fragrant, scarce old tome he discovers a sentence, a story, an illustration, that does his heart good, hasten to give it.—*Coleridge.*

A couplet of verse, a period of prose, may cling to the rock of ages as a shell that survives a deluge.—*Bulwer.*

Selected thoughts depend for their flavor upon the terseness of their expression, for thoughts are grains of sugar or salt, that must be melted in a drop of water.—*J. P. Senn.*

A verse may find him who a sermon flies.—*Herbert.*

The proverb answers where the sermon fails, as a well-charged pistol will do more execution than a whole barrel of gunpowder idly exploded in the air.—*Simms.*

Have at you with a proverb.—*Shakespeare.*

The wise men of old have sent most of their morality down the stream of time in the light skiff of apothegm or epigram.—*E. P. Whipple.*

A thing is never too often repeated which is never sufficiently learned.—*Seneca.*

He presents me with what is always an acceptable gift who brings me news of a great thought before unknown. He enriches me without impoverishing himself.—*Bovee.*

Full of wise saws and modern instances.—*Shakespeare.*

To appreciate and use correctly a valuable maxim, requires a genius, a vital appropriating exercise of mind closely allied to that which first created it.—*W. R. Alger.*

Abstracts, abridgments, summaries, etc., have the same use as burning glasses, to collect the diffused rays of wit and learning in authors, and make them point with warmth and quickness upon the reader's imagination.—*Swift.*

A great man quotes bravely, and will not draw on his invention when his memory serves him with a word as good.—What he quotes he fills with his own voice and humor, and the whole cyclopedia of his table-talk is presently believed to be his own.—*Emerson.*

The multiplicity of facts and writings is become so great that everything must soon be reduced to extracts.—*Voltaire.*

Particles of science are often very widely scattered, and writers of extensive comprehension have incidental remarks upon topics remote from the principal subject, which are often more valuable than former treatises, and which are not known because not promised in the title. He that collects these is very laudably employed, as he facilitates the progress of others, and by making that easy of attainment which is already written, may give some adventurous mind leisure for new thoughts and original designs.—*Johnson.*

I pluck up the goodlisome herbs of sentences by pruning, eat them by reading, digest them by musing, and lay them up at length in the high seat of memory by gathering them together; that so, having tasted their sweetness, I may the less perceive the bitterness of life.—*Queen Elizabeth.*

When we would prepare the mind by a forcible appeal, an opening quotation is a symphony preluding on the chords

those tones we are about to harmonize.—*Disraeli.*

He that recalls the attention of mankind to any part of learning which time has left behind it, may be truly said to advance the literature of his own age.—*Johnson.*

Whatever we may say against collections, which present authors in a disjointed form, they nevertheless bring about many excellent results. We are not always so composed, so full of wisdom, that we are able to take in at once the whole scope of a work according to its merits. Do we not mark in a book passages which seem to have a direct reference to ourselves? Young people especially, who have failed in acquiring a complete cultivation of mind, are roused in a praiseworthy way by brilliant passages.—*Goethe.*

I have somewhere seen it observed that we should make the same use of a book that the bee does of a flower; she steals sweets from it, but does not injure it.—*Colton.*

Luminous quotations atone, by their interest, for the dullness of an inferior book, and add to the value of a superior work by the variety which they lend to its style and treatment.—*Bovee.*

There is no less invention in aptly applying a thought found in a book, than in being the first author of the thought.—*Bayle.*

We ought never to be afraid to repeat an ancient truth, when we feel that we can make it more striking by a neater turn, or bring it alongside of another truth, which may make it clearer, and thereby accumulate evidence. It belongs to the inventive faculty to see clearly the relative state of things, and to be able to place them in connection; but the discoveries of ages gone by belong less to their first authors than to those who make them practically useful to the world.—*Vauvenargues.*

The art of quotation requires more delicacy in the practice than those conceive who can see nothing more in a quotation than an extract.—*Disraeli.*

The adventitious beauty of poetry may be felt in the greater delight with a verse given in happy quotation than in the poem.—*Emerson.*

I quote others only the better to express myself.—*Montaigne.*

Whoever reads only to transcribe or quote shining remarks without entering into the genius and spirit of the author, will be apt to be misled out of a regular way of thinking, and the product of all this will be found to be a manifest incoherent piece of patchwork.—*Swift.*

I am but a gatherer and disposer of other men's stuff.—*Wasson.*

A good thought is a great boon for which God is first to be thanked; next, he who is the first to utter it; and then in a lesser but still a considerable degree, the friend who is the first to quote it to us.—*Bovee.*

The wisdom of the wise and the experience of ages may be preserved by quotation.—*Disraeli.*

To quote copiously and well requires taste, judgment and erudition, a feeling for the beautiful, an appreciation of the noble, and a sense of the profound.—*Bovee.*

By necessity, by proclivity, and by delight, we quote.—We quote not only books and proverbs, but arts, sciences, religions, customs, and laws; nay, we quote temples and houses, tables and chairs by imitation.—*Emerson.*

With just enough of learning to misquote.—*Byron.*

Our best thoughts come from others.—*Emerson.*

In literature, quotation is good only when the writer whom I follow goes my way, and, being better mounted than I, gives me a cast, as we say; but if I like the gay equipage so well as to go out of my road, I had better have gone afoot.—*Emerson.*

Every quotation contributes something to the stability or enlargement of the language.—*Johnson.*

Fine words!—I wonder where you stole them.—*Swift.*

I have only made a nosegay of culled flowers, and have brought nothing of my own but the thread that ties them together.—*Montaigne*

R

RAGE.—(See "ANGER," and "PASSION.")

In rage deaf as the sea; hasty as fire.—*Shakespeare.*

When passion is on the throne, reason is out of doors.—*M. Henry.*

Oppose not rage while rage is in its force, but give it way a while and let it waste.—*Shakespeare.*

When transported by rage, it is best to observe its effects on those who deliver themselves up to the same passion.—*Plutarch.*

Rage is essentially vulgar, and never more vulgar than when it proceeds from mortified pride, disappointed ambition, or thwarted wilfulness.—*H. Coleridge.*

'Tis in my head; 'tis in my heart; 'tis everywhere; it rages like a madness, and I most wonder how my reason holds.—*Otway.*

RAILLERY.—(See "SARCASM.")

Raillery is sometimes more insupportable than wrong; because we have a right to resent injuries, but it is ridiculous to be angry at a jest.—*Rochefoucauld.*

As nothing is more provoking to some tempers than raillery, a prudent person will not always be satirically witty where he can, but only where he may without offence. For he will consider that the finest stroke of raillery is but a witticism; and that there is hardly any person so mean, whose good will is not preferable to the pleasure of a horse-laugh.—*Burgh.*

Raillery is a mode of speaking in favor of one's wit against one's good nature.—*Montesquieu.*

The raillery which is consistent with good breeding is a gentle animadversion on some foible, which, while it raises the laugh in the rest of the company, doth not put the person rallied out of countenance, or expose him to shame or contempt. On the contrary, the jest should be so delicate that the object of it should be capable of joining in the mirth it occasions.—*Fielding.*

Raillery and wit were never made to answer our inquiries after truth, and to determine a question of rational controversy, though they may be sometimes serviceable to expose to contempt those inconsistent follies which have been first abundantly refuted by argument: they serve indeed only to cover nonsense with shame, when reason has first proved it to be mere nonsense.—*Watts.*

Above all things, raillery decline; it is in ablest hands a dangerous tool, but never fails to wound the meddling fool. —*Stillingfleet.*

Good humor is the best shield against the darts of satirical raillery.—*C. Simmons.*

If nettled by severe raillery, conceal the sting if you would escape a repetition of the evil.

Good-natured raillery is the sauce of civil entertainment, and without some such tincture of urbanity, good humor falters.—*L'Estrange.*

We cannot learn raillery; that must be a gift of nature; and I esteem him happy who does not wish to acquire it. The character of sarcasm is dangerous; although this quality makes those laugh whom it does not wound, it, nevertheless, never procures esteem.—*Oxenstiern.*

RAIN.—How singular, and yet how simple, the philosophy of rain!—Who but the Omniscient one could have devised such an admirable arrangement for watering the earth!—*Ure.*

The kind refresher of the summer heats.—*Thomson.*

How beautiful is the rain! After the dust and heat, in the broad and fiery street, and in the narrow lane; how beautiful is the rain!—*Longfellow.*

Dashing in big drops on the narrow pane, and making mournful music for the mind, I hear the singing of the frequent rain.—*W. H. Burleigh.*

The daily showers rejoice the thirsty earth, and bless the flowery buds.—*Prior.*

The clouds consign their treasures to the fields, and softly shaking on the dimpled pool prelusive drops, let all their moisture flow, in large effusion, o'er the freshened world.—*Thomson.*

The rain is playing its soft pleasant tune fitfully on the skylight, and the shade of the fast-flying clouds passes with delicate change across my book.—*N. P. Willis.*

Clouds dissolved the thirsty ground supply.—*Roscommon.*

Vexed sailors curse the rain for which poor shepherds prayed in vain.—*Waller.*

RAINBOW.—That gracious thing, made up of tears and light.—*Coleridge.*

So shines the setting sun on adverse skies, and paints a rainbow on the storm. —*Watts.*

Look upon the rainbow and praise him that made it.—Very beautiful it is in the brightness thereof: it compasseth the heavens about with a glorious circle, and the hands of the Most High have bended it.—*Ecclesiasticus.*

Be thou the rainbow to the storms of life: the evening beam that smiles the clouds away, and tints to-morrow with prophetic ray.—*Byron.*

Lo! in the dark east, expanded high, the rainbow brightens to the setting sun. —*Beattie.*

O, beautiful rainbow, all woven of light! heaven surely is open when thou dost appear, and bending above thee the angels draw near, and sing " The rainbow—the rainbow; the smile of God is here! ".—*Mrs. Hale.*

Hung on the shower that fronts the golden west, the rainbow bursts, like magic, on mine eyes, in hues of ancient promise there imprest, frail in its date, eternal in its meaning.—*C. T. Turner.*

Faithful to its sacred page, heaven still rebuilds thy span, nor lets the type grow pale with age, that first spoke peace to man.—*Campbell.*

The arc of light, born of the shower and colored by the sun, which spans the heavens!—*J. C. Prince.*

That smiling daughter of the storm.—*Colton.*

RANK.—(See " NOBILITY.")

To be vain of one's rank or place, is to show that one is below it.—*Stanislaus.*

Distinction of rank is necessary for the economy of the world, and was never called in question, but by barbarians and enthusiasts.—*Rowe.*

There are no persons more solicitous about the preservation of rank, than those who have no rank at all.—*Shenstone.*

Quality and title have such allurements that hundreds are ready to give up all their own importance, to cringe, to flatter, to look little, and to pall every pleasure in constraint, merely to be among the great, though without the least hopes of improving by their understanding or sharing their generosity: they might be happy among their equals, but those are despised for company where they are despised in turn.—*Goldsmith.*

Every error of the mind is the more conspicuous, and culpable, in proportion to the rank of the person who commits it.—*Juvenal.*

Rank and riches are chains of gold, but still chains.—*Ruffini.*

The generality of princes, if stripped of their purple and cast naked on the world, would immediately sink to the lowest rank of society, without a hope of emerging from their obscurity.—*Gibbon.*

Rank is a great beautifier.—*Bulwer.*

If it were ever allowable to forget what is due to superiority of rank, it would be when the privileged themselves remembered it.—*Mad. Swetchine.*

Of the king's creation you may be; but he who makes a count ne'er made a man.—*Southern.*

I weigh the man, not his title; 'tis not the king's stamp can make the metal better.—*Wycherly.*

The rank is but the guinea's stamp; the man's the gold for all that.—*Burns.*

RASHNESS.—Some act first, think afterward, and then repent forever.—*C. Simmons.*

Rashness is the faithful but unhappy parent of misfortune.—*Fuller.*

None are rash when they are not seen by anybody.—*Stanislaus.*

As sloth seldom bringeth actions to good birth, so hasty rashness always makes them abortive ere they are well formed.—*A. Warwick.*

Haste and rashness are storms and tempests, breaking and wrecking business: but nimbleness is a full, fair wind, blowing it with speed to the haven.—*Fuller.*

Rashness is the characteristic of ardent youth, and prudence that of mellowed age.—*Cicero.*

Rashness and haste make all things insecure.—*Denham.*

We may outrun by violent swiftness that which we run at, and lose by overrunning.—*Shakespeare.*

Cotton Mather used to say there was a gentleman mentioned in the nineteenth chapter of Acts, to whom he was more deeply indebted than almost any other person. And that was the town clerk of Ephesus, whose counsel was to do nothing rashly. Upon any proposal of consequence it was usual with him to say, "Let us first consult with the town clerk of Ephesus." What mischief, trouble, and sorrow would be avoided in the world were the people more in the habit of consulting this gentleman.

READING.—(See "Books.")

Reading serves for delight, for ornament, for ability.—The crafty contemn it; the simple admire it; the wise use it.—*Bacon.*

Always have a book at hand, in the parlor, on the table, for the family; a book of condensed thought and striking anecdote, of sound maxims and truthful apothegms. It will impress on your own mind a thousand valuable suggestions, and teach your children a thousand lessons of truth and duty. Such a book is a casket of jewels for your household. —*Tryon Edwards.*

Get a habit, a passion for reading; not flying from book to book, with the squeamish caprice of a literary epicure; but read systematically, closely, thoughtfully, analyzing every subject as you go along, and laying it up carefully and safely in your memory. It is only by this mode that your information will be at the same time extensive, accurate, and useful.—*W. Wirt.*

You may glean knowledge by reading, but you must separate the chaff from the wheat by thinking.

Much reading, like a too great repletion, stops up, through a course of diverse, sometimes contrary opinions, the access of a nearer, newer, and quicker invention of your own.—*Osborn.*

The pleasure of reading without application is a dangerous pleasure. Useless books we should lay aside, and make all possible good use of those from which we may reap some fruit.—*Foster.*

When in reading we meet with any

maxim that may be of use, we should take it for our own, and make an immediate application of it, as we would of the advice of a friend whom we have purposely consulted.—*Colton.*

One of the amusements of idleness is reading without the fatigue of close attention, and the world, therefore, swarms with writers whose wish is not to be studied but to be read.—*Johnson.*

There are four kinds of readers. The first is like the hour-glass; and their reading being as the sand, it runs in and runs out, and leaves not a vestige behind. A second is like the sponge, which imbibes everything, and returns it in nearly the same state, only a little dirtier. A third is like a jelly-bag, allowing all that is pure to pass away, and retaining only the refuse and dregs. And the fourth is like the slaves in the diamond mines of Golconda, who, casting aside all that is worthless, retain only pure gems.—*Coleridge.*

No entertainment is so cheap as reading, nor any pleasure so lasting.—*Lady M. W. Montague.*

It is well to read everything of something, and something of everything.—*Brougham.*

If the riches of the Indies, or the crowns of all the kingdoms of Europe, were laid at my feet in exchange for my love of reading, I would spurn them all.—*Fénelon.*

The foundation of knowledge must be laid by reading. General principles must be had from books, which, however, must be brought to the test of real life. In conversation you never get a system. What is said upon a subject is to be gathered from a hundred people. The parts of a truth, which a man gets thus, are at such a distance from each other, that he never attains to a full view.—*Johnson.*

Happy is he who has laid up in his youth, and held fast in all fortune, a genuine and passionate love for reading. —*Rufus Choate.*

A man of ability, for the chief of his reading, should select such works as he feels are beyond his own power to have produced. What can other books do for him but waste his time or augment his vanity?—*J. Foster.*

Some read books only with a view to find fault, while others read only to be taught: the former are like venomous spiders, extracting a poisonous quality, where the latter, like the bees, sip out a sweet and profitable juice.— *L'Estrange.*

It is manifest that all government of action is to be gotten by knowledge, and knowledge, best, by gathering many knowledges, which is reading.—*Sir P. Sidney.*

Think as well as read, and when you read. Yield not your minds to the passive impressions which others may make upon them. Hear what they have to say; but examine it, weigh it, and judge for yourselves. This will enable you to make a right use of books—to use them as helpers, not as guides to your understanding; as counsellors, not as dictators of what you are to think and believe.—*Tryon Edwards.*

Reading maketh a full man; conference a ready man; and writing an exact man; and, therefore, if a man write little, he had need have a great memory; if he confer little, he had need have a present wit; and if he read little, he had need have much cunning, to seem to know that he doth not.—*Bacon.*

For general improvement, a man should read whatever his immediate inclination prompts him to; though if he has a science to learn, he must regularly and resolutely advance. What we read with inclination makes a stronger impression. If we read without inclination, half the mind is employed in fixing the attention, so there is but half to be employed on what we read. If a man begins to read in the middle of a book, and feels an inclination to go on, let him not quit it to go to the beginning. He may perhaps not feel again the inclination.—*Johnson.*

What blockheads are those wise persons, who think it necessary that a child should comprehend everything it reads.—*Southey.*

By reading, we enjoy the dead; by conversation, the living; and by contemplation, ourselves. Reading enriches the memory; conversation polishes the wit; and contemplation improves the judgment. Of these, reading is the most important, as it furnishes both the others.—*Colton.*

The love of reading enables a man to exchange the wearisome hours of life, which come to every one, for hours of delight.—*Montesquieu.*

Read, and refine your appetite; learn to live upon instruction; feast your mind and mortify your flesh; read, and take your nourishment in at your eyes, shut up your mouth, and chew the cud of understanding.—*Congreve.*

Deep versed in books, but shallow in himself.—*Milton.*

They that have read about everything are thought to understand everything too; but it is not always so. Reading furnishes the mind only with the materials of knowledge; it is thinking that makes what we read ours. We are of the ruminating kind, and it is not enough to cram ourselves with a great load of collections. Unless we chew them over again, they will not give us strength and nourishment.—*Channing.*

Force yourself to reflect on what you read, paragraph by paragraph.—*Coleridge.*

Read not to contradict and confute, nor to believe and take for granted, nor to find talk and discourse, but to weigh and consider. Some books are to be tasted, others to be swallowed, and some few to be chewed and digested; that is, some books are to be read only in parts; others to be read, but not curiously; and some few to be read wholly, and with diligence and attention.—*Bacon.*

We should accustom the mind to keep the best company by introducing it only to the best books.—*Sydney Smith.*

It is wholesome and bracing for the mind to have its faculties kept on the stretch. It is like the effect of a walk in Switzerland, upon the body. Reading an essay of Bacon's for instance, or a chapter of Aristotle, or of Butler, if it be well and thoughtfully read, is much like climbing up a hill, and may do one the same sort of good. Set the tortoise to run against the hare, and even if he does not overtake it, he will do more than ever he did previously—more than he would ever have thought himself capable of doing. Set the hare to

run with the tortoise, he falls asleep.— *Guesses at Truth.*

Exceedingly well read and profited in strange concealments.—*Shakespeare.*

He picked something valuable out of everything he read.—*Pliny.*

No man can read with profit that which he cannot learn to read with pleasure. If I do not find in a book something which I am looking for, or am ready to receive, then the book is no book for me however much it may be for another man.—*Noah Porter.*

Multifarious reading weakens the mind more than doing nothing, for it becomes a necessity, at last, like smoking: and is an excuse for the mind to lie dormant whilst thought is poured in, and runs through, a clear stream over unproductive gravel, on which not even mosses grow. It is the idlest of all idleness, and leaves more of impotency than any other.—*F. W. Robertson.*

Had I read as much as others, I had remained as ignorant as they.—*Hobbes.*

We may read, and read, and read again, and still find something new, something to please, and something to instruct.—*Hardis.*

If I were to pray for a taste which should stand me under every variety of circumstances, and be a source of happiness and cheerfulness to me through life, and a shield against its ills, however things might go amiss and the world frown upon me, it would be a taste for reading. Give a man this taste, and the means of gratifying it, and you can hardly fail of making him happy. You make him a denizen of all nations, a contemporary of all ages. —*Sir J. Herschel.*

A page digested is better than a volume hurriedly read.—*Macaulay.*

How well he is read to reason against reading.—*Shakespeare.*

In science, read, by preference, the newest works; in literature the oldest. The classic literature is always modern. New books revive and redecorate old ideas; old books suggest and invigorate new ideas.—*Bulwer.*

We should be as careful of the books we read, as of the company we keep. The dead very often have more power than the living.—*Tryon Edwards.*

Never read a book through merely because you have begun it.—*Witherspoon.*

There are three classes of readers: some enjoy without judgment; others judge without enjoyment; and some there are who judge while they enjoy, and enjoy while they judge. The latter class reproduces the work of art on which it is engaged.—Its numbers are very small.—*Goethe.*

Thou mayest as well expect to grow stronger by always eating as wiser by always reading. Too much overcharges nature, and turns more into disease than nourishment. It is thought and digestion which make books serviceable, and give health and vigor to the mind.—*Fuller.*

Leibnitz has obtained this fruit from his great reading, that he has a mind better exercised for receiving all sorts of ideas, more susceptible of all forms, more accessible to that which is new and even opposed to him, more indulgent to human weakness, more disposed to favorable interpretations, and more industrious to find them.—*Fontenelle.*

One ought to read just as inclination takes him, for what he reads as a task will do him little good.—*Johnson.*

The man whom neither riches nor luxury nor grandeur can render happy may, with a book in his hand, forget all his troubles under the friendly shade of every tree, and may experience pleasures as infinite as they are varied, as pure as they are lasting, as lively as they are unfading, and as compatible with every public duty as they are contributory to private happiness.—*Zimmermann.*

Resolve to edge in a little reading every day, if it is but a single sentence. —If you gain fifteen minutes a day, it will make itself felt at the end of the year.—*H. Mann.*

The mind should be accustomed to make wise reflections, and draw curious conclusions as it goes along; the habit of which made Pliny the Younger affirm that he never read a book so bad but he drew some profit from it.—*Sterne.*

There is a gentle, but perfectly irresistible coercion in a habit of reading well directed, over the whole tenor of

a man's character and conduct, which is not the least effectual because it works insensibly and because it is really the last thing he dreams of.—*Sir John Herschel.*

By reading a man does, as it were, antedate his life, and make himself contemporary with past ages.—*Jeremy Collier.*

Every reader if he has a strong mind, reads himself into the book, and amalgamates his thoughts with those of the author.—*Goethe.*

I read hard, or not at all; never skimming, and never turning aside to merely inviting books; and Plato, Aristotle, Butler, Thucydides, Jonathan Edwards, have passed, like the iron atoms of the blood, into my mental constitution.—*F. W. Robertson.*

One may as well be asleep as to read for anything but to improve his mind and morals, and regulate his conduct.—*Sterne.*

A discursive student is almost certain to fall into bad company. Homes of entertainment, scientific and romantic, are always open to a man who is trying to escape from his thoughts. But a shelter from the tempest is dearly bought in the house of the plague. Ten minutes with a French novel or a German rationalist have sent a reader away with a fever for life.—*Willmott.*

When I take up a book I have read before I know what to expect; and the satisfaction is not lessened by being anticipated, I shake hands with and look the old tried and valued friend in the face, compare notes, and chat the hour away.—*Hazlitt.*

One must be rich in thought and character to owe nothing to books, though preparation is necessary to profitable reading; and the less reading is better than more:—book-struck men are of all readers least wise, however knowing or learned.—*A. B. Alcott.*

Insist on reading the great books, on marking the great events of the world. Then the little books can take care of themselves, and the trivial incidents of passing politics and diplomacy may perish with the using.—*A. P. Stanley.*

Reading furnishes the mind only with materials of knowledge; it is thinking makes what we read ours. So far as we apprehend and see the connection of ideas, so far it is ours; without that it is so much loose matter floating in our brain.—*Locke.*

One must be an inventor to read well. —As the proverb says, " He that would bring home the wealth of the Indies must carry out the wealth of the Indies."—There is creative reading as well as creative writing.—When the mind is braced by labor and invention, the page of whatever book we read becomes luminous with manifold allusion. Every sentence is doubly significant, and the sense of our author is as broad as the world. —*Emerson.*

Imprint the beauties of authors upon your imagination, and their good morals upon your heart.—*C. Simmons.*

Reading without purpose is sauntering, not exercise. More is got from one book on which the thought settles for a definite end in knowledge, than from libraries skimmed over by a wandering eye. A cottage flower gives honey to the bee, a king's garden none to the butterfly.—*Bulwer.*

When there is no recreation or business for thee abroad, thou mayst then have a company of honest old fellows, in leathern jackets, in thy study, which may find thee excellent divertisement at home.—*Fuller.*

By conversing with the mighty dead we imbibe sentiment with knowledge. We become strongly attached to those who can no longer either hurt or serve us, except through the influence which they exert over the mind. We feel the presence of that power which gives immortality to human thoughts and actions, and catch the flame of enthusiasm from all nations and ages.—*Hazlitt.*

Read not books alone, but men, and amongst them chiefly thyself.—If thou find anything questionable there, use the commentary of a severe friend, rather than the gloss of a sweet-lipped flatterer; there is more profit in a distasteful truth than in deceitful sweetness.—*Quarles.*

What is twice read is commonly better remembered than what is transcribed.—*Johnson.*

Few are sufficiently sensible of the importance of that economy in reading which selects, almost exclusively, the very first order of books.—Why should a man, except for some special reason, read an inferior book at the very time he might be reading one of the highest order.—*John Foster.*

It is not what people eat, but what they digest, that makes them strong. It is not what they gain, but what they save, that makes them rich. It is not what they read, but what they remember, that makes them learned.

I read for three things: first, to know what the world has done during the last twenty-four hours, and is about to do today; second, for the knowledge that I specially want in my work; and third, for what will bring my mind into a proper mood.—*H. W. Beecher.*

The average person cannot overread without peril of mental plethora, any more than he can overfeed with impunity. Literary dissipation is as weakening in its effects as dissipation of any other kind.—*H. C. Trumbull.*

Read much, but not many works.— *Sir W. Hamilton.*

To read without reflecting, is like eating without digesting.—*Burke.*

The man who is fond of books is usually a man of lofty thought, and of elevated opinions.—*Dawson.*

If we encountered a man of rare intellect we should ask him what books he read.—*Emerson.*

The first time I read an excellent work, it is to me just as if I had gained a new friend; and when I read over a book I have perused before, it resembles the meeting with an old one.—*Goldsmith.*

Reading should be in proportion to thinking, and thinking in proportion to reading.—*Emmons.*

Some read to think, these are rare; some to write, these are common; some to talk, and these are the great majority. —The first page of an author not unfrequently suffices all the purposes of this latter class, of whom it has been said, they treat books, as some do lords, inform themselves of their titles, and then boast of an intimate acquaintance.— *Colton.*

Read, read, sirrah, and refine your appetite; learn to live upon instruction; feast your mind and mortify your flesh. —Read and take your nourishment in at your eyes; shut up your mouth, and chew the cud of understanding.—*Congreve.*

Every book salesman is an advance agent for culture and for better citizenship, for education and for the spread of intelligence.—*Dr. Frank Crane.*

Even with all the leisure in the world and an income large enough to gratify all desires, men will seldom read serious books at the rate of twenty a year.—*Walter B. Pitkin.*

It was from my own early experience that I decided there was no use to which money could be applied so productive of good to boys and girls who have good within them and ability and ambition to develop it as the founding of a public library.—*Andrew Carnegie.*

As you grow ready for it, somewhere or other, you will find what is needful for you in a book.—*George Macdonald.*

Reading is seeing by proxy.—*Herbert Spencer.*

If a book is dull, that is a matter between itself and its maker; but if it makes me duller than I should otherwise have been, I have a grievance.—*Samuel McChord Crothers.*

There was so much of splendor and of glory, there was so much of wonder and delight, that there can be no ending of our story although the book is closed and it is night.—*Margaret Sangster.*

REASON.—The authority of reason is far more imperious than that of a master; for he who disobeys the one is unhappy, but he who disobeys the other is a fool.—*Pascal.*

Never reason from what you do not know. If you do, you will soon believe what is utterly against reason.—*Ramsay.*

"Things of reason" or aids to thought, may be described as devices in the human mind for apprehending reality, but not as it really is in itself.—*A. Wolf.*

"Theirs not to make reply, theirs not to reason why," may be a good enough motto for men who are on their way to be shot. But from such men expect no empires to be builded, no inventions made, no great discoveries brought to light.—*Bruce Barton.*

Man is a creature of impulse, emotion, action rather than reason. Reason is a very late development in the world of living creatures, most of whom, as far as we know, get along admirably in daily life without it.—*James T. Adams.*

If we would guide by the light of reason, we must let our minds be bold.—*Justice Brandeis.*

To despise the animal basis of life, to seek value only at the level of conscious intelligence and rational effort, is ultimately to lose one's sense of cosmic relationships.—*Lewis Mumford.*

If you make people think they're thinking, they'll love you; but if you really make them think, they'll hate you.—*Don Marquis.*

We think so because other people all think so; or because—or because—after all, we do think so; or because we were told so, and think we must think so; or because we once thought so, and think we still think so; or because, having thought so, we think we will think so.—*Henry Sidgwick.*

It may well be doubted whether human ingenuity can construct an enigma of the kind which human ingenuity may not, by proper application, resolve.—*Edgar Allan Poe.*

In me past, present, future meet—to hold long chiding conference. My lusts usurp the present tense—and strangle Reason in his seat.—*Siegfried Sassoon.*

Reason clears and plants the wilderness of the imagination to harvest the wheat of art.—*Austin O'Malley.*

Real life is, to most men, a long second-best, a perpetual compromise between the ideal and the possible; but the world of pure reason knows no compromise, no practical limitations, no barrier to the creative activity.—*Bertrand Russell.*

Irrationally held truths may be more harmful than reasoned errors.—*Thomas H. Huxley.*

If we are entirely reasonable, we must live like brutes whose instincts are the result of experience well reasoned out.—*Corra Harris.*

It is useless to attempt to reason a man out of a thing he was never reasoned into.—*Swift.*

Philosophers have done wisely when they have told us to cultivate our reason rather than our feelings, for reason reconciles us to the daily things of existence; our feelings teach us to yearn after the far, the difficult, the unseen.—*Bulwer.*

He that will not reason is a bigot; he that cannot reason is a fool; and he that dares not reason is a slave.—*Sir W. Drummond.*

Sound and sufficient reason falls, after all, to the share of but few men, and those few men exert their influence in silence.—*Goethe.*

Reason can no more influence the will, and operate as a motive, than the eyes which show a man his road can enable him to move from place to place, or than a ship provided with a compass can sail without a wind.—*Whately.*

Reason is like the sun, of which the light is constant, uniform, and lasting; fancy, a meteor of bright, but transitory lustre, irregular in its motion, and delusive in its direction.—*Johnson.*

The soundest argument will produce no more conviction in an empty head, than the most superficial declamation; a feather and a guinea fall with equal velocity in a vacuum.—*Colton.*

There is not so much difference in men's ideas of elementary truth, as is generally thought. A greater difference lies in their power of reasoning from these truths.—*Emmons.*

It has been my object and unquenched desire, to kindle young minds, and to guard them against the temptations of scorners, by showing that the scheme of Christianity, though not discoverable by human reason, is yet in accordance with it; that link follows link by necessary consequence; that religion passes out of the ken of reason only where the eye of reason has reached its own horizon; and that faith is then but its continuation; even as the day softens away into the sweet twilight, and twilight, hushed and breathless, steals into the darkness. —*Coleridge.*

The province of reason in matters of religion, is the same as that of the eye in reference to the external world: not to create objects; nor to sit in judgment on the propriety of their existence, but simply to discern them just as they are.—*Tryon Edwards.*

No doctrine can be a proper object of our faith which it is not more reasonable to receive than to reject.—*A. Alexander.*

Revelation may not need the help of reason, but man does, even when in possession of revelation. Reason is the candle in the man's hand which enables him to see what revelation is.—*Simms.*

To reason correctly from a false principle, is the perfection of sophistry.—*Emmons.*

Revelation is a telescope kindly given us, through which reason should look up to the heavens.

Good reasons must, of force, give place to better.—*Shakespeare.*

The voice of reason is more to be regarded than the bent of any present inclination; since inclination will at length come over to reason, though we can never force reason to comply with inclination.—*Addison.*

Neither great poverty nor great riches will hear reason.—*Fielding.*

When a man has not a good reason for doing a thing, he has one good reason for letting it alone.—*Walter Scott.*

Wise men are instructed by reason; men of less understanding, by experience; the most ignorant, by necessity; and beasts by nature.—*Cicero.*

We are afraid to put men to live and trade each on his own private stock of reason; because we suspect that this stock in each man is small, and that the individuals would do better to avail themselves of the general bank and capital of nations and of ages.—*Burke.*

He is not a reasonable man who by chance stumbles upon reason, but he who derives it from knowledge, from discernment, and from taste.—*Rochefoucauld.*

Reason is our intellectual eye, and like the bodily eye it needs light to see; and to see clearly and far it needs the light of heaven.

Strong reasons make strong actions.—*Shakespeare.*

Wouldst thou subject all things to thyself?—Subject thyself to thy reason. —*Seneca.*

There are those who never reason on what they should do, but on what they have done; as if reason had her eyes behind, and could only see backward.—*Fielding.*

When my reason is afloat, my faith cannot long remain in suspense, and I believe in God as firmly as in any other truth whatever; in short, a thousand motives draw me to the consolatory side, and add the weight of hope to the equilibrium of reason.—*Rousseau.*

Reason is the director of man's will, discovering in action what is good, for the laws of well-doing are the dictates of right reason.—*Hooker.*

An idle reason lessens the weight of the good ones you gave before.—*Swift.*

He that speaketh against his own reason speaks against his own conscience, and therefore it is certain that no man serves God with a good conscience who serves him against his reason.—*Jeremy Taylor.*

Human reason is like a drunken man on horseback; set it up on one side, and it tumbles over on the other.—*Luther.*

How often do we contradict the right rules of reason in the course of our lives! Reason itself is true and just, but the reason of every particular man is weak and wavering, perpetually swayed and turned by his interests, his passions, and his vices.—*Swift.*

Your giving a reason for it will not make it right.—You may have a reason why two and two should make five, but they will still make but four.—*Johnson.*

The weakness of human reason appears more evidently in those who know it not, than in those who know it.—*Pascal.*

The heart has reasons that reason does not understand.—*Bossuet.*

There are few things reason can discover with so much certainty and ease as its own insufficiency.—*Collier.*

He is next to the gods whom reason and not passion impels.—*Claudian.*

Here is the manliness of manhood that a man has a good reason for what he does, and has a will in doing it.—*A. Maclaren.*

He that takes away reason to make way for revelation puts out the light of both, and does much the same as if he would persuade a man to put out his eyes the better to receive the remote light of an invisible star by a telescope. —*Locke.*

The way to subject all things to thyself is to subject thyself to reason. Thou shalt govern many if reason govern thee.—Wouldst thou be the monarch of a little world?—command thyself.— *Quarles.*

Faith evermore looks upward and descries objects remote; but reason can discover things only near, and sees nothing that is above her.—*Quarles.*

How can finite grasp infinity?—*Dryden.*

Let us not dream that reason can ever be popular. Passions, emotions, may be made popular, but reason remains ever the property of the few.—*Goethe.*

If reasons were as plenty as blackberries I would give no man a reason upon compulsion.—*Shakespeare.*

We can only reason from what is; we can reason on actualities, but not on possibilities.—*Bolingbroke.*

I have no other but a woman's reason; I think him so, because I think him so. —*Shakespeare.*

Reason is progressive; instinct is complete; swift instinct leaps; slow reason feebly climbs.—*Young.*

Sure He that made us with such large discourse, looking before and after, gave us not that capability and godlike reason to rust in us unused.—*Shakespeare.*

God, who has given the Bible, has also given us our reason with which to examine and understand it; and we are guilty before Him if we bury this talent in the earth and hide our Lord's money. —*J. F. Clarke.*

REBELLION.—Rebellion against tyrants is obedience to God.—*Franklin.*

There is little hope of equity where rebellion reigns.—*Sir P. Sidney.*

This word "rebellion"—it had froze them up, as fish are in a pond.—*Shakespeare.*

Men seldom, or rather never for a length of time, and deliberately, rebel against anything that does not deserve rebelling against.—*Carlyle.*

RECKLESSNESS.—Who falls from all he knows of bliss, cares little into what abyss.—*Byron.*

I am one whom the vile blows and buffets of the world have so incensed that I am reckless what I do to spite the world.—*Shakespeare.*

Beware of desperate steps; the darkest day, live till to-morrow, will have passed away.—*Cowper.*

RECOMPENSE.—Recompense injury with justice, and unkindness with kindness.—*Confucius.*

There never was a person who did anything worth doing that did not receive more than he gave.—*H. W. Beecher.*

Mercy to him that shows it, is the rule.—*Cowper.*

Forever from the hand that takes one blessing from us, others fall; and soon or late, our Father makes his perfect recompense to all.—*Whittier.*

RECREATION.—(See "Amusement," and "Mirth.")

The bow cannot possibly always bent, nor can human nature or human frailty subsist without some lawful recreation.—*Cervantes.*

Men cannot labor on always. They must have recreation. And if they have it not from healthful sources, they will be very likely to take it from poisoned fountains.—Or, if they have pleasures, which, though innocent, are forbidden by the maxims of public morality, their very pleasures are liable to become poisoned fountains.—*O. Dewey.*

Make thy recreation servant to thy business, lest thou become a slave to thy recreation.—*Quarles.*

Sweet recreation barred, what doth ensue but moody and dull melancholy, kinsman to grim and comfortless despair; and at their heels, a huge infectious troop of pale distemperatures and foes to life.—*Shakespeare.*

Recreation is not being idle; it is easing the wearied part by change of occupation.

To re-create strength, rest. To re-create mind, repose. To re-create cheerfulness, hope in God. or change the object of attention to one more elevated and worthy of thought.—*C. Simmons.*

He that will make a good use of any part of his life must allow a large part of it to recreation.—*Locke.*

Amusements are to virtue, like breezes of air to the flame; gentle ones will fan it, but strong ones will put it out.—*Thomas.*

Diversions are the most properly applied to ease and relieve those who are too much employed. Those that are idle

have no need of them, and yet they, above all others, give themselves up to them. To unbend our thoughts, when they are too much stretched by our cares, is not more natural than it is necessary; but to turn our whole life into a holiday, is not only ridiculous, but destroyeth pleasure instead of promoting it.—*Saville.*

Recreation is intended to the mind as whetting is to the scythe, to sharpen the edge of it, which otherwise would grow dull and blunt. He, therefore, that spends his whole time in recreation is ever whetting, never mowing; his grass may grow and his steed starve. As, contrarily, he that always toils and never recreates, is ever mowing, never whetting; laboring much to little purpose; as good no scythe as no edge.—*Bp. Hall.*

Recreation is not the highest kind of enjoyment, but in its time and place is quite as proper as prayer.—*S I. Prime.*

RECTITUDE.—The great high-road of human welfare lies along the highway of steadfast well-doing, and they who are the most persistent, and work in the truest spirit, will invariably be the most successful.—*S. Smiles.*

If you would convince a man that he does wrong, do right. Men will believe what they see. Let them see.—*Thoreau.*

No man can do right unless he is good, wise, and strong. What wonder we fail?—*Charles Buxton.*

Nothing more completely baffles one who is full of trick and duplicity, than straightforward and simple integrity in another.—*Colton.*

In all things preserve integrity, and the consciousness of thine own uprightness will alleviate the toil of business, soften the hardness of ill-success and disappointment, and give thee an humble confidence before God when the ingratitude of men, or the iniquity of the times may rob thee of other reward.—*Paley.*

A straight line is the shortest in morals as in mathematics.—*Maria Edgeworth.*

The man who is so conscious of the rectitude of his intentions as to be willing to open his bosom to the inspection of the world, is in possession of one of the strongest pillars of a decided character. The course of such a man will be firm and steady, because he has nothing to fear from the world, and is sure of the approbation and support of Heaven.—*W. Wirt.*

REDEMPTION.—Underneath all the arches of Bible history, throughout the whole grand temple of the Scriptures, these two voices ever echo, man is ruined; man is redeemed.—*C. D. Foss.*

The work of redemption is the most glorious of all the works of God; it will forever remain the grand mirror to reflect the brightest beams of the divine glory.—*Emmons.*

And now, without redemption, all mankind must have been lost, adjudged to death and hell by doom severe.—*Milton.*

Alas! alas! why, all the souls that were, were forfeit once; and He that might the vantage best have took, found out the remedy.—*Shakespeare.*

Redemption is the science and the song of all eternity. Archangels, day and night, into its glories look. The saints and elders round the throne, old in the years of heaven, examine it perpetually.—*Pollok.*

Christ is redemption to us, only as he actually redeems and delivers our nature from sin. If he is not the law and spring of a new spirit of life, he is nothing to us. "As many as are led by the Spirit of God, they are the sons of God,"—as many; no more.—*Horace Bushnell.*

By Christ's purchasing redemption, two things are intended: his satisfaction and his merit; the one pays our debt, and so satisfies; the other procures our title, and so merits. The satisfaction of Christ is to free us from misery; the merit of Christ is to purchase happiness for us.—*Jonathan Edwards.*

The whole system, the whole structure of man and of the world, is moulded to be the theatre of the redemption of the sinner. Not in Eden, but on Calvary and in heaven, which is the child of Calvary, we see realized the whole idea of God.—*I. B. Brown.*

REFINEMENT.— Refinement is the lifting of one's self upwards from the merely sensual, the effort of the soul to etherealize the common wants and uses of life.—*H. W. Beecher.*

That alone can be called true refinement which elevates the soul of man,

purifying the manners by improving the intellect.—*Coleridge.*

Too great refinement is false delicacy, and true delicacy is solid refinement.—*Rochefoucauld.*

If refined sense and exalted sense be not so useful as common sense, their rarity, their novelty, and the nobleness of their objects make some compensation, and render them the admiration of mankind; as gold, though less serviceable than iron, acquires from its scarcity a value which is much superior.—*Hume.*

Whenever education and refinement grow away from the common people, they are growing toward selfishness, which is the monster evil of the world. That is true cultivation which gives us sympathy with every form of human life, and enables us to work most successfully for its advancement. Refinement that carries us away from our fellow-men is not God's refinement.—*H. W. Beecher.*

There is no reason why the brown hand of labor should not hold Thomson as well as the sickle. Ornamental reading shelters and even strengthens the growth of what is merely useful. A cornfield never returns a poorer crop because a few wild-flowers bloom in the hedge. The refinement of the poor is the triumph of Christian civilization.—*Willmott.*

Far better, and more cheerfully, I could dispense with some part of the downright necessaries of life, than with certain circumstances of elegance and propriety in the daily habits of using them.—*De Quincey.*

Ages of ignorance and simplicity are thought to be ages of purity. But the direct contrary I believe to be the case. Rude periods have that grossness of manners which is as unfriendly to virtue as luxury itself. Men are less ashamed as they are less polished.—*Warton.*

It is in refinement and elegance that the civilized man differs from the savage.—*Johnson.*

Men who walk on tiptoe all through life, holding up their skirts for fear they shall touch their fellows—who are delicate and refined in feeling, and who ring all the bells of taste high up in their own belfry where no one else can hear them, these dainty fools are the greatest sinners of all, for they use their higher faculties to serve the devil with.—*H. W. Beecher.*

Refinement creates beauty everywhere. It is the grossness of the spectator that discovers anything like grossness in the object.—*Hazlitt.*

True delicacy, as true generosity, is more wounded by an act of offence from itself, than to itself.—*Gréville.*

REFLECTION.—He that will not reflect is a ruined man.—*Old Proverb.*

Knowledge is acquired by study and observation, but wisdom cometh by opportunity of leisure; the ripest thought comes from the mind which is not always on the stretch, but fed, at times, by a wise passiveness.—*W. Mathews.*

Reflection is a flower of the mind, giving out wholesome fragrance; but revery is the same flower, when rank and running to seed.—*Tupper.*

The advice of a scholar, whose piles of learning were set on fire by imagination, is never to be forgotten. Proportion an hour's reflection to an hour's reading, and so dispirit the book into the student.—*Willmott.*

The reflections on a day well spent furnish us with joys more pleasing than ten thousand triumphs.— *Thomas à Kempis.*

We are told, " Let not the sun go down on your wrath," but I would add, never act or write till it has done so. This rule has saved me from many an act of folly. It is wonderful what a different view we take of the same event four-and-twenty hours after it has happened.—*Sydney Smith.*

A soul without reflection, like a pile without inhabitant, to ruin runs.—*Young.*

They only babble who practise not reflection.—I shall think; and thought is silence.—*Sheridan.*

There is one art of which every man should be a master—the art of reflection. —If you are not a thinking man, to what purpose are you a man at all?— *Coleridge.*

Evil is wrought by want of thought as well as by want of heart.—*Hood.*

Sum up at night what thou hast done by day, and in the morning what

thou hast to do.—Dress and undress thy soul; mark the decay and growth of it.—If with thy watch, that too be down, then wind up both; since we shall be most surely judged, make thine accounts agree.—*Herbert.*

A wise man reflects before he speaks. —A fool speaks, and then reflects on what he has uttered.—*French Proverb.*

Think twice before you speak, or act once, and you will speak or act the more wisely for it.—*Franklin.*

Every man deeply engaged in business, if all regard to another state be not extinguished, must have the conviction, if not the resolution of one who, being asked whether he retired from the army in disgust, answered, " that he laid down his commission for no other reason, but because there ought to be some time for sober reflection between the life of a soldier and his death."—*Johnson.*

REFORM.—He who reforms himself, has done much toward reforming others; and one reason why the world is not reformed, is, because each would have others make a beginning, and never thinks of himself doing it.—*T. Adams.*

One vicious habit each year rooted out, in time might make the worst man good.—*Franklin.*

Necessity reforms the poor, and satiety the rich.—*Tacitus.*

It is easier to enrich ourselves with a thousand virtues, than to correct ourselves of a single fault.—*Bruyère.*

What you dislike in another, take care to correct in yourself.—*Sprat.*

The true reformer is the seminal reformer, not the radical. And this is the way the Sower, who went forth to sow his seed, did really reform the world, without making any open assault to uproot what was already existing.— *Guesses at Truth.*

Many hope the tree may be felled that they may gather chips by the fall. —*Fuller.*

Charles Fox said that restorations were the most bloody of all revolutions; and he might have added that reformations are the best mode of preventing the necessity of either.—*Colton.*

He who reforms himself, has done more toward reforming the public, than

a crowd of noisy, impotent patriots.—
Lavater.

Reform like charity must begin at
home.—Once well at home, it will radiate
outward, irrepressible, into all that we
touch and handle, speak and work, ever
kindling new light by incalculable contagion, spreading in geometric ratio, far
and wide, doing only good wherever it
spreads, and not evil.—*Carlyle.*

How important, often, is the pain of
guilt, as a stimulant to amendment and
reformation.—*J. Foster.*

He that has energy enough to root out
a vice, should go further, and try to
plant a virtue in its place; otherwise he
will have his labor to renew.—A strong
soil that has produced weeds may be
made to produce wheat.—*Colton.*

How dangerous to defer those momentous reformations which the conscience is solemnly preaching to the
heart. If they are neglected, the difficulty and indisposition are increasing
every month. The mind is receding,
degree after degree, from the warm and
hopeful zone; till at last, it enter the
arctic circle, and become fixed in re-
lentless and eternal ice.—*J. Foster.*

Long is the way and hard, that out
of hell leads up to light.—*Milton.*

The great fundamental principle of
the Reformation was the individual responsibility of the human soul to its
Maker and Judge.—*T. W. Chambers.*

We are reformers in spring and summer; in autumn and winter we stand
by the old—reformers in the morning,
conservatives at night. Reform is affirmative, conservatism is negative; conservatism goes for comfort, reform for
truth.—*Emerson.*

Conscious remorse and anguish must
be felt, to curb desire, to break the
stubborn will, and work a second nature
in the soul.—*Rowe.*

They say best men are moulded out of
faults, and, for the most, become much
more the better for being a little bad!
—*Shakespeare.*

Reformation is a work of time. A national taste, however wrong it may be,
cannot be totally changed at once; we
must yield a little to the prepossession
which has taken hold on the mind, and
we may then bring people to adopt what
would offend them, if endeavored to be

introduced by violence.—*Sir J. Reynolds*

It is well known what strange work
there has been in the world, under the
name and pretence of reformation; how
often it has turned out to be, in reality,
deformation; or, at best, a tinkering sort
of business, where, while one hole has
been mended, two have been made.—
Bp. Horne.

It has been the fate of all bold ad-
venturers and reformers, to be esteemed
insane.—*G. B. Cheever.*

There is a boldness, a spirit of daring, in religious reformers, not to be
measured by the general rules which control men's purposes and actions.—*Daniel
Webster.*

When error is confuted, vice reproved,
and hypocrisy exposed, some are sure
to complain of uncourteousness, uncharitableness, and an unchristian spirit.
Such men would have been loud in their
complaints, and bitter in their censure,
of the prophets and apostles, and would
have doubted the personal piety, and
ultimate salvation, of Luther, and Knox,
and Whitefield.—*Anon.*

Mere outward reformation differs as
much from regeneration as white-wash-
ing an old rotten house differs from
pulling it down and building a new one
in its place.—*Toplady.*

What lasting progress was ever made
in social reformation, except when every
step was ensured by appeals to the
understanding and the will? — *W.
Mathews.*

Public reformers had need first practice on their own hearts that which they
propose to try on others.—*Charles I.*

The true social reformer is the faithful preacher of the gospel, and the only
organization truly potent for the perfection of society is the Christian church.
—*Seelye.*

There was a time when it was not the
fashion for public men to say, "Show
me a proved abuse, and I will do my
best to correct it."—Times are changed.
—Men now say, "Show me a practical
improvement, and that improvement I
will do my best to realize."—*Palmerston.*

The true reformer will not only hate
evil, but will earnestly endeavor to fill
its place with good.—*C. Simmons.*

To reform a man, you must begin
with his grandmother.—*Victor Hugo.*

RELIGION.—Whatever definitions men have given of religion, I find none so accurately descriptive of it as this: that it is such a belief of the Bible as maintains a living influence on the heart and life.—*Cecil.*

Religion, in its purity, is not so much a pursuit as a temper; or rather it is a temper, leading to the pursuit of all that is high and holy. Its foundation is faith; its action, works; its temper, holiness; its aim, obedience to God in improvement of self and benevolence to men.—*Tryon Edwards.*

The religion of Christ reaches and changes the heart, which no other religion does.—*Howells.*

Love God, and he will dwell with you. Obey God, and he will reveal to you the truth of his deepest teachings.—*Robertson.*

Christianity is the good man's text; his life is the illustration. How admirable is that religion, which, while it seems to have in view only the felicity of another world, is at the same time the highest happiness of this.—*Montesquieu.*

Indisputably the believers in the gospel have a great advantage over all others, for this simple reason, that, if true, they will have their reward hereafter; and if there be no hereafter, they can but be with the infidel in his eternal sleep, having had the assistance of an exalted hope through life, without subsequent disappointment.—*Byron.*

The sum and substance of the preparation needed for a coming eternity is, that you believe what the Bible tells you, and do what the Bible bids you.—*Chalmers.*

Take away God and religion, and men live to no purpose, without proposing any worthy and considerable end of life to themselves.—*Tillotson.*

Those who make religion to consist in the contempt of this world and its enjoyments, are under a very fatal and dangerous mistake. As life is the gift of heaven, it is religion to enjoy it. He, therefore, who can be happy in himself, and who contributes all in his power toward the happiness of others, answers most effectually the ends of his creation, is an honor to his nature, and a pattern to mankind.—*Addison.*

The joy of religion is an exorcist to the mind; it expels the demons of carnal mirth and madness.—*Cecil.*

True religion and virtue give a cheerful and happy turn to the mind; admit of all true pleasures, and even procure for us the highest.—*Addison.*

The contemplation of the Divine Being, and the exercise of virtue, are in their nature so far from excluding all gladness of heart, that they are perpetual sources of it. In a word, the true spirit of religion cheers as well as composes the soul. It banishes, indeed, all levity of behavior, all vicious and dissolute mirth, but in exchange fills the mind with a perpetual serenity, uninterrupted cheerfulness, and an habitual inclination to please others as well as to be pleased in itself.—*Spectator.*

If we were to be hired to religion, it is able to outbid the corrupted world with all it can offer us, being so much richer of the two in everything where reason is admitted to be a judge of the value.—*Halifax.*

True religion shows its influence in every part of our conduct; it is like the sap of a living tree, which penetrates the most distant boughs.

What Dr. Arnold said about the class of young men who professed their sentimental admiration of virtue, applies well to older persons: ' Commend me to those who not only love God, but who also hate the devil."

All humble, meek, merciful, just, pious, and devout souls are everywhere of one religion, and when death has taken off the mask, they will know one another, though the divers liveries they wear make them strangers.—*Penn.*

The pious man and the atheist always talk of religion; the one of what he loves, and the other of what he fears.—*Montesquieu.*

A ritual religion is generally light and gay, not serious in its spirit; all religions being so, which cast responsibility into outward observances.—*Martineau.*

Whether religion be true or false, it must be necessarily granted to be the only wise principle and safe hypothesis for a man to live and die by.—*Tillotson.*

No sciences are better attested than the religion of the Bible.—*Sir Isaac Newton.*

If it were only the exercise of the body, the moving of the lips, the bending of the knee, men would as commonly step to heaven as they go to visit a friend: but to separate our thoughts and affections from the world, to draw forth all our graces, and engage each in its proper object, and to hold them to it till the work prospers in our hands, this, this is the difficulty.—*Baxter.*

Men will wrangle for religion; write for it; fight for it; die for it; anything but live for it.—*Colton.*

What a lovely bridge between old age and childhood is religion! How instinctively the world begins with prayer and worship on entering life, and how instinctively, on quitting life, the old man turns back to prayer and worship, putting himself again side by side with the little child.—*Bulwer.*

Religion is so far from barring men any innocent pleasure, or comfort of human life, that it purifies the pleasures of it, and renders them more grateful and generous; and besides this, it brings mighty pleasures of its own, those of a glorious hope, a serene mind, a calm and undisturbed conscience, which do far out-relish the most studied and artificial luxuries.—*Shirley.*

If you are not right toward God, you can never be so toward man; and this is forever true, whether wits and rakes allow it or not.—*Lord Chatham to his Nephew.*

Never trust anybody not of sound religion, for he that is false to God can never be true to man.—*Lord Burleigh.*

The religion of a sinner stands on two pillars; namely, what Christ did for us in the flesh, and what he performs in us by his Spirit. Most errors arise from an attempt to separate these two.—*Cecil.*

If it be the characteristic of a worldly man that he desecrates what is holy, it should be of the Christian to consecrate what is secular, and to recognize a present and presiding divinity in all things.—*Chalmers.*

If a man is not rising upward to be an angel, depend upon it, he is sinking downward to be a devil. He cannot stop at the beast. The most savage of men are not beasts; they are worse, a great deal worse.—*Coleridge.*

The faith that only reaches to the head, will never sanctify the heart. Knowledge, without experience, will no more sanctify, than painted fire will burn, or the sight of water cleanse. It may do good to others, as the knowledge of Noah's carpenters was useful to him, while they perished in the flood.—*S. H. Cox.*

Philosophy can do nothing which religion cannot do better than she; and religion can do a great many other things which philosophy cannot do at all.—*Rousseau.*

It is one thing to take God and heaven for your portion, as believers do, and another thing to be desirous of it as a reserve, when you can keep the world no longer. It is one thing to submit to heaven, as a lesser evil than hell; and another thing to desire it as a greater good than earth. It is one thing to lay up treasures and hopes in heaven, and seek it first; and another thing to be contented with it in our necessity, and to seek the world before it, and give God what the flesh can spare. Thus differeth the religion of serious Christians and of carnal, worldly hypocrites.—*Baxter.*

A man who puts aside his religion because he is going into society, is like one taking off his shoes because he is about to walk upon thorns.—*Cecil.*

Too many persons seem to use their religion as a diver does his bell, to venture down into the depths of worldliness with safety, and there grope for pearls, with just so much of heaven's air as will keep them from suffocating, and no more; and some, alas! as at times is the case with the diver, are suffocated in the experiment.—*G. B. Cheever.*

"Let them learn first," says Paul, "to show piety at home." Religion should begin in the family. The holiest sanctuary is home. The family altar is more venerable than that of the cathedral. The education of the soul for eternity should begin and be carried on at the fireside.

If family religion were duly attended to and properly discharged, I think the preaching of the Word would not be the common instrument of conversion.—*Baxter.*

The moral virtues, without religion, are but cold, lifeless, and insipid; it is only religion which opens the mind to great conceptions, fills it with the most sublime ideas, and warms the soul with more than sensual pleasures.—*Addison.*

I have lived long enough to know what I did not at one time believe—that no society can be upheld in happiness and honor without the sentiment of religion.—*Laplace.*

Political and professional fame cannot last forever, but a conscience void of offence before God and man is an inheritance for eternity. Religion, therefore, is a necessary, an indispensable element in any great human character. There is no living without it. Religion is the tie that connects man with his Creator, and holds him to his throne. If that tie is sundered or broken, he floats away a worthless atom in the universe, its proper attractions all gone, its destiny thwarted, and its whole future nothing but darkness, desolation and death. A man with no sense of religious duty is he whom the Scriptures describes in so terse but terrific a manner, as "living without hope and without God in the world." Such a man is out of his proper being, out of the circle of all his duties, out of the circle of all his happiness, and away, far, far away from the purposes of his creation.—*Daniel Webster.*

It was an admirable and true saying of Plutarch, "That a city may as well be built in the air, as a commonwealth or kingdom be either constituted or preserved without the support of religion."—*Porteus.*

Independent of its connection with human destiny hereafter, I believe the fate of a republican government is indissolubly bound up with the fate of the Christian religion, and that a people who reject its only faith will find themselves the slaves of their own evil passions or of arbitary power.—*Lewis Cass.*

The great comprehensive truths, written in letters of living light on every page of our history, are these: Human happiness has no perfect security but freedom; freedom, none but virtue; virtue, none but knowledge; and neither freedom nor virtue has any vigor or immortal hope except in the principles of the Christian faith, and in the sanctions of the Christian religion.—*Quincy.*

We know, and, what is better, we feel inwardly, that religion is the basis of

civil society, and the source of all good and of all comfort.—*Burke.*

The Christian religion is one that diffuses among the people a pure, benevolent, and universal system of ethics, adapted to every condition of life, and recommended as the will and reason of the Supreme Deity, and enforced by sanctions of eternal punishment. —*Gibbon.*

True religion is the foundation of society, the basis on which all true civil government rests, and from which power derives its authority, laws their efficacy, and both their sanction. If it is once shaken by contempt, the whole fabric cannot be stable or lasting.—*Burke.*

Religion is equally the basis of private virtue and public faith; of the happiness of the individual and the prosperity of the nation.—*W. Barrow.*

Of all the dispositions and habits which lead to political prosperity, religion and morality are indispensable supports. In vain would that man claim the tribute of patriotism, who should labor to subvert these great pillars of human happiness, these firmest props of the duties of men and citizens. And let us with caution indulge the supposition that morality can be maintained without religion. Whatever may be conceded to the influence of refined education on minds of peculiar structure, reason and experience both forbid us to expect that national morality can prevail in exclusion of religious principles.—*Washington.*

If religious books are not widely circulated among the masses in this country, and the people do not become religious, I do not know what is to become of us as a nation.—*Daniel Webster.*

The religion of the gospel has power, immense power, over mankind; direct and indirect, positive and negative, restraining and aggressive. Civilization, law, order, morality, the family, all that elevates woman, or blesses society, or gives peace to the nations, all these are the fruits of Christianity, the full power of which, even for this world, could never be appreciated till it should be taken away.—*Tryon Edwards.*

It was religion, which, by teaching men their near relation to God, awakened in them the consciousness of their importance as individuals. It was the struggle for religious rights, which opened their eyes to all their rights. It was resistance to religious usurpation which led men to withstand political oppression. It was religious discussion which roused the minds of all classes to free and vigorous thought. It was religion which armed the martyr and patriot in England against arbitrary power; which braced the spirits of our fathers against the perils of the ocean and wilderness, and sent them to found here the freest and most equal state on earth.—*Channing.*

We live in the midst of blessings till we are utterly insensible to their greatness, and of the source from whence they flow. We speak of our civilization, our arts, our freedom, our laws, and forget entirely how large a share is due to Christianity. Blot Christianity out of the page of man's history, and what would his laws have been—what his civilization? Christianity is mixed up with our very being and our daily life; there is not a familiar object around us which does not wear a different aspect because the light of Christian love is on it—not a law which does not owe its truth and gentleness to Christianity—not a custom which cannot be traced, in all its holy healthful parts, to the gospel. —*Sir A. Park.*

If I could choose what of all things would be at the same time the most delightful and useful to me, I should prefer a firm religious belief to every other blessing; for this makes life a discipline of goodness; creates new hopes when all earthly ones vanish; throws over the decay of existence the most gorgeous of all lights; awakens life even in death; makes even torture and shame the ladder of ascent to paradise; and far above all combinations of earthly hopes, calls up the most delightful visions of the future, the security of everlasting joys, where the sensualist and the sceptic view only gloom, decay, annihilation, and despair.—*Sir H. Davy.*

Should a man happen to err in supposing the Christian religion to be true, he could not be a loser by the mistake. But how irreparable is his loss, and how inexpressible his danger, who should err in supposing it to be false.—*Pascal.*

It is a great dishonor to religion to imagine that it is an enemy to mirth and cheerfulness, and a severe exacter of pensive looks and solemn faces.—*Walter Scott.*

It is no good reason for a man's religion that he was born and brought up in it; for then a Turk would have as much reason to be a Turk as a Christian a Christian.—*Chillingworth.*

I have known what the enjoyments and advantages of this life are, and what the more refined pleasures which learning and intellectual power can bestow; and with all the experience that more than threescore years can give, I, now, on the eve of my departure, declare to you that health is a great blessing,—competence, obtained by honorable industry, a great blessing,—and a great blessing it is to have kind, faithful, and loving friends and relatives; but that the greatest of all blessings, as it is the most ennobling of all privileges, is to be indeed a Christian.—*Coleridge.*

God to love and serve, with all our powers—with all our heart, and soul, and mind, and strength; and as ourselves, to love our neighbor, this is religion; this doth God demand, and only this can bear the test of conscience here —hereafter of the judgment.

The task and triumph of religion is to make men and nations true and just and upright in all their dealings, and to bring all law as well as all conduct into subjection and conformity to the law of God.—*H. J. Van Dyke.*

When religion is made a science there is nothing more intricate; when it is made a duty, there is nothing more easy.

If we make religion our business, God will make it our blessedness.—*H. G. J. Adam.*

As to Jesus of Nazareth, my opinion of whom you particularly desire, I think the system of morals and his religion, as he left them to us, is the best the world ever saw, or is likely to see.—*Franklin.*

Religion, cultivated to the absolute neglect of science, would produce a reign of superstition, tyranny, and barbarism like that which covered Europe in the dark ages of the church. Science, cultivated to the utter neglect of religion, would produce a reign of infidelity, impiety, and sensuality. The two interests united, correct and perfect each other. —*C. W. Shields.*

Religion would not have enemies, if it were not an enemy to their vices.—*Massillon.*

Religion presents few difficulties to the humble; many to the proud; insuperable ones to the vain.—*Hare.*

Religion cannot pass away. The burning of a little straw may hide the stars of the sky, but the stars are there, and will reappear.—*Carlyle.*

When men cease to be faithful to God, he who expects to find them so to each other will be much disappointed.—*Bp. Horne.*

It will cost something to be religious: it will cost more to be not so.—*J. Mason.*

Religion does what philosophy could never do.—It shows the equal dealings of heaven to the happy and the unhappy, and levels all human enjoyments to nearly the same standard.—It offers to both rich and poor the same happiness hereafter, and equal hopes to aspire after it.—*Goldsmith.*

The writers against religion, while they oppose every system, are wisely careful never to set up any of their own.—*Burke.*

True religion extends alike to the intellect and the heart. Intellect is in vain if it lead not to emotion, and emotion is vain if not enlightened by intellect; and both are vain if not guided by truth and leading to duty.—*Tryon Edwards.*

Place not thy amendment only in increasing thy devotion, but in bettering thy life. It is the damning hypocrisy of this age that it slights all good morality, and spends its zeal in matters of ceremony, and a form of godliness without the power of it.—*Fuller.*

Depend upon it religion is, in its essence, the most gentlemanly thing in the world. It will alone gentilize, if unmixed with cant; and I know nothing else that will, alone.—*Coleridge.*

The Christian is the highest style of man.—*Young.*

Culture of intellect, without religion in the heart, is only civilized barbarism and disguised animalism.—*Bunsen.*

He that is a good man is three-quarters of his way toward the being a good Christian, wheresoever he lives, or whatsoever he is called.—*South.*

Of all the dispositions and habits which lead to political prosperity, religion and morality are indispensable supporters.—A volume could not trace all their connections with private and public felicity.—*Washington.*

Measure not men by Sundays, without regarding what they do all the week after.—*Fuller.*

A life that will bear the inspection of men and of God, is the only certificate of true religion.—*Johnson.*

The loss of popular respect for religion is the dry rot of social institutions. The idea of God as the Creator and Father of all mankind is in the moral world, what gravitation is in the natural; it holds all together and causes them to revolve around a common center. Take this away, and men drop apart; there is no such thing as collective humanity, but only separate molecules, with no more cohesion than so many grains of sand.—*H. M. Field.*

Every condition of life has its perils and its advantages; and the office of religion is, not to change that in which Providence has placed us, but to strengthen and sanctify our hearts that we may resist the temptations, and improve the opportunities of blessings presented to us.—*G. W. Bethune.*

The head truly enlightened will presently have a wonderful influence in purifying the heart; and the heart really affected with goodness, will much conduce to the directing of the head.—*Sprat.*

Religion is the best armor in the world, but the worst cloak.—*John Newton.*

Let your religion be seen. Lamps do not talk, but they do shine. A lighthouse sounds no drum, it beats no gong; yet, far over the waters, its friendly light is seen by the mariner.—*T. L. Cuyler.*

If our religion is not true, we are bound to change it; if it is true, we are bound to propagate it.—*Whately.*

By living according to the rules of religion a man becomes the wisest, the best, and the happiest creature that he is capable of being.—Honesty, industry, the employing of time well, a constant sobriety, an undefiled purity, with continual serenity, are the best preservatives, too, of life and health.—*Bp. Burnet.*

No creed is final. Such a creed as mine must grow and change as knowledge grows and changes.—*Sir Arthur Keith.*

The future of religion is connected with the possibility of developing a faith in the possibilities of human experience and human relationships that will create a vital sense of the solidarity of human interests and inspire action to make that sense a reality.—*John Dewey.*

I conceive the essential task of religion to be "to develop the consciences, the ideals, and the aspirations of mankind."—*Robert Andrews Millikan.*

Spiritual anarchy is not likely to work either for the happiness of the individual or for the welfare of society.—*Irving Babbitt.*

Very religious people always shock slightly religious people by their blasphemous attitude to religion; and it was precisely for blasphemy that Jesus was crucified.—*R. G. Collingwood.*

It usually takes as many generations to make a religious convert as to make a gentleman.—*Austin O'Malley.*

Religion is the first thing and the last thing, and until a man has found God and been found by God, he begins at no beginning, he works to no end.—*H. G. Wells.*

There need not be in religion, or music, or art, or love, or goodness, anything that is against reason; but never while the sun shines will we get great religion, or music, or art, or love, or goodness, without going beyond reason.—*Rev. Dr. Harry Emerson Fosdick.*

From the voiceless lips of the unreplying dead there comes no word, but in the night of death hope sees a star and listening love can hear the rustle of a wing.—*Robert Ingersoll.*

Christianity is a spiritual dynamic which has very little to do with the mechanism of social life.—*Dean Inge.*

Creeds grow so thick along the way their boughs hide God.—*Lizette Woodworth Reese.*

Reason is the triumph of the intellect, faith of the heart; and whether the one or the other shall best illumine the dark mysteries of our being, they only are

to be despaired of who care not to explore.—*James Schouler.*

What I mean by a religious person is one who conceives himself or herself to be the instrument of some purpose in the universe which is a high purpose, and is the motive power of evolution—that is, of a continual ascent in organization and power and life, and extension of life.—*G. B. Shaw.*

All the naturalistic religions are founded upon the assumption that nature—which "never did betray the heart that loved her"—is discoverable and ready to serve as an infallible guide.—*Joseph Wood Krutch.*

If I did not feel ... and hope that some day—perhaps millions of years hence—the Kingdom of God would overspread the whole world ... then I would give my office over this morning to anyone who would take it.—*Stanley Baldwin.*

The submergence of self in the pursuit of an ideal, the readiness to spend oneself without measure, prodigally, almost ecstatically, for something intuitively apprehended as great and noble, spend oneself knowing not why—some of us like to believe that this is what religion means.—*Benjamin N. Cardozo.*

Faith was once almost universally thought to be acceptance of a definite body of intellectual propositions, acceptance being based upon authority—preferably that of revelation from on high. ... Of late there has developed another conception of faith. This is suggested by the words of an American thinker: "Faith is tendency toward action." According to such a view, faith is the matrix of formulated creeds and the inspiration of endeavor. ... Faith in its newer sense signifies that experience itself is the sole ultimate authority.—*John Dewey.*

Such as men themselves are, such will God appear to them to be; and such as God appears to them to be, such will they show themselves in their dealings with their fellow men.—*Dean Inge.*

The religions we count false, may, for a time, have had their use; being, in their origin, faint, though misunderstood echoes of an early divine revelation, and also as Emerson says, "affirmations of the conscience, correct-

ing the evil customs of their times."—
Tryon Edwards.

The noblest charities, the best fruits of learning, the richest discoveries, the best institutions of law and justice, every greatest thing the world has seen, represents, more or less directly, the fruitfulness and creativeness of religion. —*Horace Bushnell.*

It has been said that true religion will make a man a more thorough gentleman than all the courts in Europe. And it is true that you may see simple laboring men as thorough gentlemen as any duke, simply because they have learned to fear God; and, fearing him, to restrain themselves, which is the very root and essence of all good breeding.— *C. Kingsley.*

There is something in religion, when rightly apprehended, that is masculine and grand. It removes those little desires which are "the constant hectic of a fool."—*Cecil.*

There is only one religion, though there are a hundred versions of it.—*G. B. Shaw.*

All religions die of one disease, that of being found out.—*John Morley.*

I would give nothing for that man's religion, whose very dog and cat are not the better for it.—*Rowland Hill.*

While men believe in the possibilities of children being religious, they are largely failing to make them so, because they are offering them not a child's but a man's religion—men's forms of truth and men's forms of experience.—*Phillips Brooks.*

Religion is the final centre of repose; the goal to which all things tend; apart from which man is a shadow, his very existence a riddle, and the stupendous scenes of nature which surround him as unmeaning as the leaves which the sibyl scattered in the wind.—*Robert Hall.*

What I want is, not to possess religion, but to have a religion that shall possess me.—*Charles Kingsley.*

. Nothing exposes religion more to the reproach of its enemies than the worldliness and hard-heartedness of its professors.—*M. Henry.*

No priestcraft can longer make man content with misery here in the hope of compensation hereafter. — *G. Stanley Hall.*

If we think of religion only as a means of escaping what we call the wrath to come, we shall not escape it; we are under the burden of death, if we care only for ourselves.—*Froude.*

The only impregnable citadel of virtue is religion; for there is no bulwark of mere morality, which some temptation may not overtop or undermine and destroy.—*Jane Porter.*

Religious contention is the devil's harvest.—*Fontaine.*

No man's religion ever survives his morals.—*South.*

All belief that does not render us more happy, more free, more loving, more active, more calm, is, I fear, an erroneous and superstitious belief.—*Lavater.*

The best perfection of a religious man is to do common things in a perfect manner.—*Bonaventura.*

There are those to whom a sense of religion has come in storm and tempest; there are those whom it has summoned amid scenes of revelry and idle vanity; there are those, too, who have heard its "still small voice" amid rural leisure and placid retirement. But perhaps the knowledge which causeth not to err is most frequently impressed upon the mind during the season of affliction.— *Walter Scott.*

Religion finds the love of happiness and the principles of duty separated in us; and its mission—its masterpiece is, to reunite them.—*Vinet.*

Unless we place our religion and our treasure in the same thing religion will always be sacrificed.—*Epictetus.*

I would rather think of my religion as a gamble than to think of it as an insurance premium.—*S. S. Wise.*

Religion is not a dogma, not an emotion, but a service.—Our redemption is not of the head alone, nor of the heart alone, but pre-eminently of the life, as the only infallible criterion of what we really are.—Not belief, not emotion, but obedience is the test.—Mere belief would make religion a mere theology.— Mere emotion would make it a mere excitement.—While the true divine of it is a life, begotten of grace in the depths of the human soul, subduing to

Christ all the powers of the heart and life, and incarnating itself in patient, steady, sturdy service—doing the will of God.—*R. D. Hitchcock.*

The word of God proves the truth of religion; the corruption of man, its necessity; government, its advantages.—*Stanislaus.*

If men are so wicked with religion, what would they be without it!—*Franklin.*

Formal religion was organized for slaves: it offered them consolation which earth did not provide.—*E. Hubbard.*

It is, I think, an error to believe that there is any need of religion to make life seem worth living.—*S. Lewis.*

The religion that makes the purest and happiest homes will always be the best for any country.—If Christianity does that, it is the best of all religions.

Anything that makes religion a second object makes it no object.—He who offers to God a second place offers him no place.—*Ruskin.*

See how powerful religion is: it commands the heart, it commands the vitals. Morality comes with a pruning-knife, and cuts off all sproutings, all wild luxuriances; but religion lays the axe to the root of the tree. Morality looks that the skin of the apple be fair; but religion searcheth to the very core.—*Culverwell.*

The race of men, while sheep in credulity, are wolves for conformity.—*Carl Van Doren.*

Many people think they have religion when they are troubled with dyspepsia.—*R. G. Ingersoll.*

When I was young, I was sure of many things; now there are only two things of which I am sure: one is, that I am a miserable sinner; and the other, that Christ is an all-sufficient Saviour. —He is well taught who learns these two lessons.—*John Newton.*

Religion is as necessary to reason as reason is to religion. The one cannot exist without the other. A reasoning being would lose his reason, in attempting to account for the great phenomena of nature, had he not a Supreme Being to refer to; and well has it been said, that if there had been no God, man-

kind would have been obliged to imagine one.—*Washington.*

If we subject everything to reason, our religion will have nothing mysterious or supernatural; if we violate the principles of reason, our religion will be absurd and ridiculous.—*Pascal.*

Over all the movements of life religion scatters her favors, but reserves the choicest, her divine blessing, for the last hour.—*Logan.*

Nothing can be hostile to religion which is agreeable to justice.—*Gladstone.*

What we need in religion, is not new light, but new sight; not new paths, but new strength to walk in the old ones; not new duties, but new strength from on high to fulfill those that are plain before us.—*Tryon Edwards.*

I extend the circle of religion very widely.—Many men fear and love God, and have a sincere desire to serve him, whose views of religious truth are very imperfect, and in some points utterly false.—But may not many such persons have a state of heart acceptable before God?—*Cecil.*

Religion, if it be true, is central truth; and all knowledge which is not gathered round it, and quickened and illuminated by it, is hardly worthy the name.—*Channing.*

All the principles which religion teaches, and all the habits which it forms, are favorable to strength of mind. It will be found that whatever purifies, also fortifies the heart.—*Blair.*

True religion teaches us to reverence what is under us, to recognize humility, poverty, wretchedness, suffering, and death, as things divine.—*Goethe.*

The flower of youth never appears more beautiful than when it bends toward the sun of righteousness.—*M. Henry.*

Religion—a daughter of Hope and Fear, explaining to Ignorance the nature of the Unknowable.—Impiety—your irreverence toward my deity.—*Ambrose Bierce.*

God is for men and religion for women. —*Joseph Conrad.*

There are but two religions,—Christianity and paganism, the worship of God and idolatry. A third between these is not possible. Where idolatry ends, there Christianity begins; and where idolatry begins, there Christianity ends.—*Jacobi.*

Many would like religion as a sort of lightning rod to their houses, to ward off, by and by, the bolts of divine wrath.—*H. W. Beecher.*

The external part of religion is doubtless of little value in comparison with the internal; and so is the cask in comparison with the wine contained in it; but if the cask be staved in, the wine must perish.—*Bp. Horne.*

Where true religion has prevented one crime, false religions have afforded a pretext for a thousand.—*Colton.*

Religion is the fear and love of God; its demonstration is good works; and faith is the root of both, for without faith we cannot please God; nor can we fear and love what we do not believe.—*Penn.*

I have taken much pains to know everything that is esteemed worth knowing amongst men; but with all my reading, nothing now remains to comfort me at the close of this life but this passage of St. Paul: "It is a faithful saying, and worthy of all acceptation, that Jesus Christ came into the world to save sinners." To this I cleave, and herein do I find rest.—*Selden.*

Religion is the answer to that cry of reason which nothing can silence; that aspiration of the soul which no created thing can meet; of that want of the heart which all creation cannot supply.—*I. T. Hecker.*

A religion that never suffices to govern a man, will never suffice to save him.—That which does not distinguish him from a sinful world, will never distinguish him from a perishing world.—*John Howe.*

Know that without star or angel for their guide, they who worship God shall find him.—Humble love, and not proud reason keeps the door of heaven.—Love finds admission where proud science fails.—*Young.*

I have now disposed of all my property to my family.—There is one thing more I wish I could give them, and that is the Christian religion.—If they had that, and I had not given them one shilling, they would have been rich, and if they had not that, and I had given them all the world, they would be poor.—*Patrick Henry.*

The body of all true religion consists in obedience to the will of God, in a confidence in his declaration, and an imitation of his perfections.—*Burke.*

It is only religion, the great bond of love and duty to God, that makes any existence valuable or even tolerable.—*Horace Bushnell.*

The heathen mythology not only was not true, but was not even supported as true; it not only deserved no faith, but it demanded none.—The very pretension to truth, the very demand of faith, were characteristic distinctions of Christianity.—*Whately.*

You have no security for a man who has no religious principle.—*Cobden.*

Religion's home is in the conscience.—It's watchword is the word "ought."—It's highest joy is in doing God's will.—*T. L. Cuyler.*

The religion of some people is constrained, like the cold bath when used, not for pleasure, but from necessity for health, into which one goes with reluctance, and is glad when able to get out.—But religion to the true believer is like water to a fish; it is his element; he lives in it, and could not live out of it.—*John Newton.*

Religion consists not so much in joyous feelings as in constant devotedness to God, and laying ourselves out for the good of others.—*Stewart.*

Inward religion, without the outward show of it, is like a tree without fruit, useless; and the outward show of religion, without inward sincerity, is like a tree without heart, lifeless.—*Venning.*

There never was law, or sect, or opinion did so magnify goodness as the Christian religion doth.—*Bacon.*

None but God can satisfy the longings of the immortal soul; as the heart was made for him, he only can fill it.—*Trench.*

My principles in respect of religious interest are two,—one is, that the Church shall not meddle with politics, and the government shall not meddle with religion.—*Kossuth.*

If your whole life is guided by religion, the hearts of others may be touched by this mute language, and may open to the reception of that spirit which dwells in you.—*Schleiermacher.*

Recollection is the life of religion. The Christian wants to know no new thing, but to have his heart elevated more above the world by secluding himself from it as much as his duties will allow, that religion may effect its great end by bringing its sublime hopes and prospects into more steady action on the mind.—*Cecil.*

An every-day religion—one that loves the duties of our common walk; one that makes an honest man; one that accomplishes an intellectual and moral growth in the subject; one that works in all weather, and improves all opportunities, will best and most healthily promote the growth of a church and the power of the Gospel.—*Horace Bushnell.*

REMEMBRANCE.—(See "MEMORY.")

Remembrance is the only paradise out of which we cannot be driven away.—*Richter.*

Remembered joys are never past; at once the fountain, stream, and sea, they were, they are, they yet shall be.—*J. Montgomery.*

Sorrows remembered sweeten present joy.—*Pollok.*

The world does not require so much to be informed as reminded.—*Hannah More.*

Praising what is lost makes the remembrance dear.—*Shakespeare.*

Of joys departed, not to return, how painful the remembrance.—*Robert Blair.*

The sweet remembrance of the just shall flourish when he sleeps in dust.—*Tate and Brady.*

The greatest comfort of my old age, and that which gives me the highest satisfaction, is the pleasing remembrance of the many benefits and friendly offices I have done to others.—*Cato.*

Pleasure is the flower that fades; remembrance is the lasting perfume.—*Boufflers.*

Remembrances last longer than present realities; I have preserved blossoms for many years, but never fruits.—*Richter.*

Every one can remember that which has interested himself.—*Plautus.*

I cannot but remember such things were, that were most precious to me.—*Shakespeare.*

REMORSE.—(See "GUILT.")

Remorse is the echo of a lost virtue.—*Bulwer.*

Remorse is virtue's root; its fair increase are fruits of innocence and blessedness.—*Bryant.*

There is no future pang can deal that justice on the self-condemned, he deals on his own soul.—*Byron.*

Remorse is a man's dread prerogative, and is the natural accompaniment of his constitution as a knowing, voluntary agent, left in trust with his own welfare and that of others. Remorse, if we exclude the notion of responsibility, is an enigma in human nature never to be explained.—*Isaac Taylor.*

Conscious remorse and anguish must be felt, to curb desire, to break the stubborn will, and work a second nature in the soul, ere virtue can regain the place she lost.—*Rowe.*

The fruition of what is unlawful must be followed by remorse. The core sticks in the throat after the apple is eaten, and the sated appetite loathes the interdicted pleasure for which innocence was bartered.—*Jane Porter.*

I am afraid to think what I have done; look on it again I dare not.—*Shakespeare.*

Think not that guilt requires the burning torches of the furies to agitate and torment it.—Frauds, crimes, remembrances of the past and terrors of the future, these are the domestic furies that are ever present to the minds of the impious.—*Cicero.*

Remorse not only turns God against us, but turns us against ourselves, and makes the soul like the scorpion in the fire, which stings itself to death.—*Thomas.*

Remorse is the consciousness of doing wrong with no sense of love; penitence the same consciousness with the feeling of sorrow and tenderness added.—*F. W. Robertson.*

To be left alone, and face to face with my own crime, had been just retribution.—*Longfellow.*

This is the bitterest of all, to wear the yoke of our own wrong-doing.—*G. Eliot.*

There is no man that is to himself knowingly guilty and that carries guilt about him, but receives a sting into his soul.—*Tillotson.*

Not sharp revenge, nor hell itself can find a fiercer torment than a guilty mind.—*Dryden.*

It is not just when a villainous act has been committed that it torments us; it is when we think of it afterward, for the remembrance of it lasts forever.—*Rousseau.*

Remorse is beholding heaven and feeling hell.—*Moore.*

REPARTEE.—The impromptu reply is the touchstone of the man of wit.—*Molière.*

Repartee is perfect, when it effects its purpose with a double edge. Repartee is the highest order of wit, as it bespeaks the coolest yet quickest exercise of genius at a moment when the passions are roused.—*Colton.*

I think I never knew an instance of great quickness of parts being joined with great solidity. The most rapid rivers are seldom or never deep.—*Shenstone.*

REPENTANCE.—Of all acts of man repentance is the most divine.—The greatest of all faults is to be conscious of none.—*Carlyle.*

True repentance consists in the heart being broken for sin and broken from sin. Some often repent, yet never reform; they resemble a man travelling in a dangerous path, who frequently starts and stops, but never turns back.—*Thornton.*

To do so no more is the truest repentance.—*Luther.*

Mere sorrow, which weeps and sits still, is not repentance.—Repentance is sorrow converted into action; into a movement toward a new and better life.—*M. R. Vincent.*

True repentance is to cease from sinning.—*Ambrose.*

Repentance is not only grief on account of this or that particular act; it is a deep-seated sorrow on account of the discrepancy between the outward acts of the will and that ideal which is presented to the conscience in the new

Adam—the typical—the Christian man. —*Martensen.*

There are two kinds of repentance: one is that of Judas, the other that of Peter; the one is ice broken, the other ice melted. Repentance unto life will be repentance in the life.—*Wm. Nevins.*

The best part of repentance is little sinning.—*Arabian Proverb.*

Right actions for the future are the best apologies for wrong ones in the past —the best evidence of regret for them that we can offer, or the world receive. —*Tryon Edwards.*

Blest tears of soul-felt penitence, in whose benign, redeeming flow, is felt the first, the only sense of guiltless joy that guilt can know.—*Moore.*

Repentance is a hearty sorrow for our past misdeeds, and a sincere resolution and endeavor, to the utmost of our power, to conform all our actions to the law of God. It does not consist in one single act of sorrow, but in doing works meet for repentance; in a sincere obedience to the law of Christ for the remainder of our lives.—*Locke.*

Repentance, without amendment, is like continually pumping without mending the leak.—*Dilwyn.*

He that waits for repentance, waits for that which cannot be had as long as it is waited for. It is absurd for a man to wait for that which he himself has to do.—*Wm. Nevins.*

God hath promised pardon to him that repenteth, but he hath not promised repentance to him that sinneth.—*Anselm.*

There is a greater depravity in not repenting of sin when it has been committed, than in committing it at first. To deny, as Peter did, is bad; but not to weep bitterly, as he did, when we have denied, is worse.—*Payson.*

True repentance hates the sin, and not merely the penalty; and it hates the sin most of all because it has discovered and felt God's love.—*W. M. Taylor.*

It is one thing to mourn for sin because it exposes us to hell, and another to mourn for it because it is an infinite evil; one thing to mourn for it because it is injurious to ourselves, and another to mourn for it because it is wrong and offensive to God.—It is one thing to be terrified; another, to be humbled.—*G. Spring.*

Repentance may begin instantly, but reformation often requires a sphere of years.—*H. W. Beecher.*

Repentance, to be of any avail, must work a change of heart and conduct.—*T. L. Cuyler.*

The slightest sorrow for sin is sufficient if it produce amendment, and the greatest insufficient if it do not.—*Colton.*

Repentance hath a purifying power, and every tear is of a cleansing virtue; but these penitential clouds must be still kept reopping; one shower will not suffice; for repentance is not one single action, but a course.—*South.*

Late repentance is seldom true, but true repentance is never too late.—*R. Venning.*

A true repentance shuns the evil itself, more than the external suffering or the shame.—*Shakespeare.*

The golden key that opens the palace of eternity.—*Milton.*

Repentance is the heart's sorrow, and a clear life ensuing.—*Shakespeare.*

Our greatest glory consists not in never falling, but in rising every time we may fall.—*Goldsmith.*

True repentance has a double aspect; it looks upon things past with a weeping eye, and upon the future with a watchful eye.—*South.*

The vain regret that steals above the wreck of squandered hours.—*Whittier.*

All of us who are worth anything spend our manhood in unlearning the follies, or expiating the mistakes of our youth.—*Shelley.*

Before God can deliver us we must undeceive ourselves.—*Augustine.*

If you would be good, first believe you are bad.—*Epictetus.*

What is past is past.—There is a future left to all men who have the virtue to repent, and the energy to atone.—*Bulwer.*

You cannot repent too soon, because you do not know how soon it may be too late.—*Fuller.*

Place not thine amendment only in increasing thy devotion, but in bettering thy life.—*Fuller.*

As it is never too soon to be good, so

it is never too late to amend; I will, therefore, neither neglect the time present, nor despair of the time past. If I had been sooner good, I might perhaps have been better; if I am longer bad, I shall, I am sure, be worse.—*Arthur Warwick.*

It is never too late with us, so long as we are aware of our faults and bear them impatiently.—*Jacobi.*

He who seeks repentance for the past, should woo the angel virtue for the future.—*Bulwer.*

When the soul has laid down its faults at the feet of God, it feels as though it had wings.—*E. Guérin.*

Repentance is the relinquishment of any practice from the conviction that it has offended God.—Sorrow, fear, and anxiety are properly not parts, but adjuncts of repentance, yet they are too closely connected with it to be separated.—*Addison.*

It is the greatest and dearest blessing that ever God gave to men, that they may repent; and therefore to deny or to delay it is to refuse health when brought by the skill of the physician—to refuse liberty offered to us by our gracious Lord.—*Bp. Taylor.*

It is a common error, and the greater and more mischievous for being so common, to believe that repentance best becomes and most concerns dying men. Indeed, what is necessary every hour of our life is necessary in the hour of death too, and as long as one lives he will have need of repentance, and therefore it is necessary in the hour of death too; but he who hath constantly exercised himself in it in his health and vigor, will do it with less pain in his sickness and weakness; and he who hath practised it all his life, will do it with more ease and less perplexity in the hour of his death.—*Johnson.*

Whatever stress some may lay upon it, a death-bed repentance is but a weak and slender plank to trust our all upon.—*Sterne.*

Death-bed repentance is burning the candle of life in the service of the devil, then blowing the snuff in the face of heaven.—*Lorenzo Dow.*

There is one case of death-bed repentance recorded, that of the penitent thief, that none should despair; and only one that none should presume.—*Augustine.*

Great is the difference betwixt a man's being frightened at, and humbled for his sins.—*Fuller.*

Sorrow for having done amiss is fruitless if it issue not in doing so no more. —*Bp. Horne.*

REPOSE.—(See "REST.")

Our foster-nurse of nature is repose. —*Shakespeare.*

If we find not repose in ourselves, it is in vain to seek it elsewhere.—*From the French.*

Repose is agreeable to the human mind; and decision is repose. A man has made up his opinions; he does not choose to be disturbed; and he is much more thankful to the man who confirms him in his errors, and leaves him alone, than he is to the man who refutes him, or who instructs him at the expense of his tranquillity.—*Sydney Smith.*

These should be hours for necessities, not for delights; times to repair our nature with comforting repose, and not for us to waste.—*Shakespeare.*

There is no mortal truly wise and restless at once; wisdom is the repose of minds.—*Lavater.*

Repose and cheerfulness are the badge of the gentleman—repose in energy. The Greek battle pieces are calm; the heroes, in whatever violent actions engaged, retain a serene aspect.—*Emerson.*

Have you known how to compose your manners? You have done a great deal! more than he who has composed books. Have you known how to take repose? You have done more than he who has taken cities and empires.— *Montaigne.*

Repose without stagnation is the state most favorable to happiness. "The great felicity of life," says Seneca, "is to be without perturbations."—*Bovee.*

REPROOF.—Reproof should not exhaust its powers upon petty failings; let it watch diligently against the incursions of vice, and leave foppery and futility to die of themselves.

Rebuke not in anger, or with severity; hard words are like hailstones in summer, beating down and destroying what they would nourish were they melted into drops.

Reprove not, in their wrath, excited men; good counsel comes all out of season then; but when their fury is appeased and past, they will perceive their faults, and mend at last. When he is cool and calm, then utter it.—*Randolph.*

Confront improper conduct, not by retaliation, but by example.—*J. Foster.*

When the most insignificant person tells us we are in error, we should listen, and examine ourselves, and see if it is so. To believe it possible we may be in error, is the first step toward getting out of it.

He who, when called upon to speak a disagreeable truth, tells it boldly and has done, is both bolder and milder than he who nibbles in a low voice, and never ceases nibbling.—*Lavater.*

Before thou reprehend another, take heed thou art not culpable in what thou goest about to reprehend. He that cleanses a blot with blotted fingers makes a greater blur.—*Quarles.*

I never was fit to say a word to a sinner, except when I had a broken heart myself; when I was subdued and melted into penitence, and felt as though I had just received pardon for my own soul, and when my heart was full of tenderness and pity.—*Payson.*

Reproof is a medicine like mercury or opium; if it be improperly administered, it will do harm instead of good.—*Horace Mann.*

Ill deeds are doubled with an evil word; the sting of a reproach is the truth of it.—*Shakespeare.*

Whenever anything is spoken against you that is not true, do not pass by or despise it because it is false; but forthwith examine yourself, and consider what you have said or done that may administer a just occasion of reproof.— *Plutarch.*

No reproach is like that we clothe in a smile, and present with a bow.—*Bulwer.*

Reprove thy friend privately; commend him publicly.—*Solon.*

Aversion from reproof is not wise. It is a mark of a little mind. A great man can afford to lose; a little, insignificant fellow is afraid of being snuffed out.— *Cecil.*

Few love to hear the sins they love to act.—*Shakespeare.*

The silent upbraiding of the eye is the very poetry of reproach; it speaks at once to the imagination.—*Mrs. Balfour.*

Better a little chiding than a great deal of heartbreak.—*Shakespeare.*

He had such a gentle method of reproving their faults that they were not so much afraid as ashamed to repeat them.—*Atterbury.*

Chide him for faults, and do it reverently when you perceive his blood inclined to mirth.—*Shakespeare.*

The reproof of a good man resembles fuller's earth; it not only removes the spots from our character, but it rubs off when it is dry.—*Williamson.*

I will chide no breather in the world but myself, against whom I know most faults.—*Shakespeare.*

Many men are angry with them that tell them of their faults, when they should be angry only with the faults that are told them.—*Venning.*

The most difficult province in friendship is the letting a man see his faults and errors, which should if possible be so contrived that he may see our advice is given him, not so much to please ourselves as for his own advantage.— The reproofs, therefore, of a friend should always be strictly just, and not too frequent.—*Budgell.*

REPUBLIC.—At twenty, every one is republican.—*Lamartine.*

Though I admire republican principles in theory, yet I am afraid the practice may be too perfect for human nature. We tried a republic last century and it failed. Let our enemies try next. I hate political experiments.—*Walpole.*

Republics come to an end by luxurious habits; monarchies by poverty.—*Montesquieu.*

It is the weakness and danger of republics, that the vices as well as virtues of the people are represented in their legislation.—*Mrs. Mary H. Hunt.*

Republicanism is not the phantom of a deluded imagination.—On the contrary, under no form of government are laws better supported, liberty and property better secured, or happiness more effectually dispensed to mankind.—*Washington.*

Equal and exact justice to all: peace, commerce and honest friendship with all nations, and entangling alliances with none; the support of State governments in all their rights, as the most competent administration of our domestic concerns, are the surest bulwarks against anti-republican tendencies.—*Jefferson.*

REPUTATION.—(See " NAME.")

Reputation is what men and women think of us; character is what God and angels know of us.—*Paine.*

Regard your good name as the richest jewel you can possibly be possessed of —for credit is like fire; when once you have kindled it you may easily preserve it, but if you once extinguish it, you will find it an arduous task to rekindle it again.

The way to gain a good reputation, is, to endeavor to be what you desire to appear.—*Socrates.*

A proper self-regard becomes improper as soon as we begin to value reputation more than real character.—*Morning Star.*

The two most precious things this side the grave are our reputation and our life. But it is to be lamented that the most contemptible whisper may deprive us of the one, and the weakest weapon of the other. A wise man, therefore, will be more anxious to deserve a fair name than to possess it, and this will teach him so to live, as not to be afraid to die.—*Colton.*

See that your character is right, and in the long run your reputation will be right.

The purest treasure mortal times afford is spotless reputation; that away, men are but gilded loam or painted clay.—*Shakespeare.*

A fair reputation is a plant delicate in its nature, and by no means rapid in its growth.—It will not shoot up in a night, like the gourd of the prophet, but like that gourd, it may perish in a night. —*Jeremy Taylor.*

Reputation, reputation, reputation! Oh, I have lost my reputation! I have lost the immortal part of myself; and what remains is bestial.—*Shakespeare.*

The reputation of a man is like his shadow, gigantic when it precedes him, and pigmy in its proportions when it follows.—*Talleyrand.*

Whatever ignominy or disgrace we

have incurred, it is almost always in our power to re-establish our reputation.—*Rochefoucauld*.

A reputation for good judgment, fair dealing, truth, and rectitude, is itself a fortune.—*H. W. Beecher*.

Good will, like a good name, is got by many actions, and lost by one.—*Jeffrey*.

One may be better than his reputation, but never better than his principles.—*Latena*.

Reputation is but the synonym of popularity; dependent on suffrage, to be increased or diminished at the will of the voters.—*Washington Allston*.

The blaze of reputation cannot be blown out, but it often dies in the socket.—*Johnson*.

Who swerves from innocence, who makes divorce of that serene companion, a good name, recovers not his loss; but walks with shame, with doubt, with fear, and haply with remorse.—*Wordsworth*.

My name and memory I leave to men's charitable speeches, to foreign nations, and to the next age.—*Bacon*.

In all the affairs of this world, so much reputation is, in reality, so much power.—*Tillotson*.

We should be careful to deserve a good reputation by doing well; and when that care is once taken, not to be over-anxious about the success.—*Rochester*.

There are two modes of establishing our reputation: to be praised by honest men, and to be abused by rogues.—It is best, however, to secure the former, because it will invariably be accompanied by the latter.—*Colton*.

Reputation is sometimes as wide as the horizon, when character is but the point of a needle.—Character is what one really is; reputation what others believe him to be.—*H. W. Beecher*.

Nothing is so uncertain as general reputation.—A man injures me from humor, passion, or interest; hates me because he has injured me; and speaks ill of me because he hates me.—*Home*.

He that tears away a man's good name tears his flesh from his bones, and by letting him live gives him only a cruel opportunity of feeling his misery, of burying his better part and surviving himself.—*South*.

Some men's reputation seems like seed-wheat, which thrives best when brought from a distance.—*Whately*.

A man's reputation is not in his own keeping, but lies at the mercy of the profligacy of others.—Calumny requires no proof.—*Hazlitt*.

Reputation is an idle and most false imposition, oft got without merit, and lost without deserving.—*Shakespeare*.

No man was ever written out of reputation but by himself.—*Monk*.

Associate with men of good quality, if you esteem your own reputation; it is better to be alone than in bad company.—*Washington*.

A reputation once broken may possibly be repaired, but the world will always keep their eyes on the spot where the crack was.

Garments that have once one rent in them are subject to be torn on every nail, and glasses that are once cracked are soon broken.—Such is man's good name when once tainted with just reproach.—*Bp. Hall*.

There are few persons of greater worth than their reputation; but how many are there whose worth is far short of their reputation!—*Stanislaus*.

Reputation is rarely proportioned to virtue.—We have seen a thousand people esteemed, either for the merit they had not yet attained or for what they no longer possessed.—*Evremond*.

When a man has once forfeited the reputation of his integrity, he is set fast; nothing will then serve his turn, neither truth nor falsehood.—*Tillotson*.

A good name is properly that reputation of virtue which every man may challenge as his right and due in the opinion of others, till he has made forfeit of it by the viciousness of his actions.—*South*.

An honest reputation is within the reach of all; they obtain it by social virtues and doing their duty.—This kind of reputation, though neither brilliant nor startling, is often the most conducive to happiness.—*Duclos*.

O! reputation, dearer far than life, thou precious balsam, lovely, sweet of smell, whose cordial drops once spilt by some rash hand, not all thy owner's care, nor the repenting toil of the rude spiller, ever can collect to its first purity and native sweetness.—*Sir W. Raleigh.*

RESENTMENT.—Resentment is a union of sorrow with malignity; a combination of a passion which all endeavor to avoid with a passion which all concur to detest.—*Johnson.*

Resentment is, in every stage of the passion, painful, but it is not disagreeable, unless in excess.—*Home.*

There is a spirit of resistance implanted by the Deity in the breast of man, proportioned to the size of the wrongs he is destined to endure.—*C. J. Fox.*

Resentment seems to have been given us by nature for defence, and for defence only; it is the safeguard of justice, and the security of innocence.—*Adam Smith.*

RESERVE.—A reserved man is in continual conflict with the social part of his nature, and even grudges himself the laugh into which he is sometimes betrayed.—*Shenstone.*

Persons extremely reserved are like old enamelled watches, which had painted covers that hindered your seeing what o'clock it was.—*Walpole.*

Some reserve is a debt to prudence, as freedom and simplicity of conversation is a debt to good nature.—*Shenstone.*

Reserve may be pride fortified in ice; dignity is worth reposing on truth.—*W. R. Alger.*

Reserve is no more essentially connected with understanding, than a church organ with devotion, or wine with good nature.—*Shenstone.*

There is nothing more allied to the barbarous and savage character than sullenness, concealment, and reserve.—*Park Godwin.*

Reserve is the truest expression of respect toward those who are its objects.—*De Quincey.*

There would not be any absolute necessity for reserve if the world were honest; yet even then it would prove expedient. For, in order to attain any degree of deference, it seems necessary that people should imagine you have more accomplishments than you discover.—*Shenstone.*

RESIGNATION.—Resignation is putting God between ourselves and our troubles.—*Mad. Swetchine.*

Resignation is the courage of Christian sorrow.—*Vinet.*

"My will, not thine, be done," turned paradise into a desert. "Thy will, not mine, be done," turned the desert into a paradise, and made Gethsemane the gate of heaven.—*Pressense.*

Let God do with me what He will, anything He will; and, whatever it be, it will be either heaven itself, or some beginning of it.—*Mountford.*

O Lord, I do most cheerfully commit all unto Thee.—*Fénelon.*

Trust in God, as Moses did, let the way be ever so dark; and it shall come to pass that your life at last shall surpass even your longing. Not, it may be, in the line of that longing, that shall be as it pleaseth God; but the glory is as sure as the grace, and the most ancient heavens are not more sure than that.—*Robert Collyer.*

Vulgar minds refuse to crouch beneath their load; the brave bear theirs without repining.—*Thomson.*

All the precepts of Christianity agree to teach and command us to moderate our passions, to temper our affections toward all things below; to be thankful for the possession, and patient under the loss whenever he that gave shall see fit to take away.—*Sir W. Temple.*

How calmly do those glide through all, even the roughest events, who can but make a right estimate of the happiness as well as the virtue of a governable will, resigned to the will of God. —It was a philosophical maxim, that a wise moral man could not be injured, or miserable. But it is much more true of him who has that divine wisdom of Christian resignation, which twines and enwraps all his choices with God's; and is neither at the pains nor the hazards of his own election, but is secure, unless omniscience can be deceived and omnipotence defeated, that he shall have what is really best for him.—*Palmer.*

Remember you are but an actor in a drama of such sort as the author chooses.—If it be his pleasure that you should act a poor man, see that you act it well; or a cripple, or a ruler, or a private citizen. For this is your business, to act well the given part; but to choose it belongs to another.—*Epictetus*.

It is a higher exhibition of Christian manliness to be able to bear trouble than to get rid of it.—*H. W. Beecher*.

We cannot conquer fate and necessity, yet we can yield to them in such a manner as to be greater than if we could.—*Landor*.

It were no virtue to bear calamities if we do not feel them.—*Mad. Necker*.

No cloud can overshadow a true Christian but his faith will discern a rainbow upon it.—*Bp. Horne*.

It is not where we have gathered up our brighter hopes, that the dawn of happiness breaks. It is not where we have glanced our eye with affright, that we find the deadliest gloom. What should this teach us? To bow to the great and only source of light, and live humbly and with confiding resignation. —*Goethe*.

Submission to God is the only balm that can heal the wounds he gives.— *Emmons*.

Thy way, not mine, O Lord, however dark it be; lead me by thine own hand; choose out the path for me.—*H. Bonar*.

All we have is the Almighty's, and shall not God have his own when he calls for it?—*Penn*.

There is but one way to tranquillity of mind and happiness, and that is to account no external things thine own, but to commit all to God.—*Epictetus*.

Every man has his chain and clog, only it is looser and lighter to one than to another; and he is more at ease who takes it up and carries it than he who drags it.—*Seneca*.

Whate'er my doom, it cannot be unhappy, for God has given me the boon of resignation.—*Wilson*.

Demand not that events should happen as you wish, but wish them to happen as they do, and you will go on well.—*Epictetus*.

RESOLUTION.—(See "PURPOSE," "PERSEVERANCE," and "OPPOSITION.")

He who is firm and resolute in will moulds the world to himself.—*Goethe*.

Good resolutions are a pleasant crop to sow.—The seed springs up so readily, and the blossoms open so soon with such a brave show, especially at first. But when the time of flowers has passed, what as to the fruit?—*L. Malet*.

The block of granite which is an obstacle in the pathway of the weak, becomes a stepping-stone in the pathway of the strong.—*Carlyle*.

To think we are able is almost to be so; to determine upon attainment is frequently attainment itself; earnest resolution has often seemed to have about it almost a savor of omnipotence. —*S. Smiles*.

The nerve which never relaxes—the eye which never blanches—the thought which never wanders—the purpose that never wavers—these are the masters of victory.—*Anon*.

Experience teacheth that resolution is a sole help in need.—*Shakespeare*.

If we have need of a strong will in order to do good, it is still more necessary for us in order not to do evil.— *Mole*.

A good inclination is but the first rude draught of virtue, but the finishing strokes are from the will, which, if well disposed, will by degrees perfect it, or if ill disposed will quickly deface it.— *South*.

"Resolution," says John Foster, "is omnipotent."—He that resolves upon any great and good end, has, by that very resolution, scaled the chief barrier to it.—He will find such resolution removing difficulties, searching out or making means, giving courage for despondency, and strength for weakness, and like the star to the wise men of old, ever guiding him nearer and nearer to perfection.—*Tryon Edwards*.

But little is accomplished, because but little is vigorously attempted; and but little is attempted, because difficulties are magnified. A timorously cautious spirit, so far from acting with resolution, will never think itself in possession of the preliminaries for acting at all. Perhaps perseverance has been the radical principle of every truly great character.—*J. Foster*.

Do not, for one repulse, forego the purpose that you resolved to effect.— *Shakespeare*.

A good intention clothes itself with power.—*Emerson*.

If we are but fixed and resolute—bent

on high and holy ends, we shall find means to them on every side and at every moment; and even obstacles and opposition will but make us "like the fabled spectre-ships, which sail the fastest in the very teeth of the wind."—*Tryon Edwards.*

Be stirring as the time, be fire with fire, threaten the threatener, and outface the brow of bragging horror; so shall inferior eyes, that borrow their behaviors from the great, grow great by your example and put on the dauntless spirit of resolution.—*Shakespeare.*

You may be whatever you resolve to be.—Determine to be something in the world, and you will be something.—"I cannot," never accomplished anything; "I will try," has wrought wonders.—*J. Hawes.*

There is no impossibility to him who stands prepared to conquer every hazard.—The fearful are the failing.—*Sarah J. Hale.*

Either I will find a way, or I will make one.—*Sir P. Sidney.*

RESPONSIBILITY.—The most important thought I ever had was that of my individual responsibility to God.—*Daniel Webster.*

Responsibility educates. — *Wendell Phillips.*

All men, if they work not as in the great taskmaster's eye, will work wrong, and work unhappily for themselves and for you.—*Carlyle.*

Nothing keeps alive the sense of the unworthiness of a life going to waste like the thought of God's watchful eye. Nor is there anything to tone up the honesty of men like the remembrance of personal accountability. — *Monday Club Sermons.*

The feeling of a direct responsibility of the individual to God is almost wholly a creation of Protestantism.—*John Stuart Mill.*

If the master takes no account of his servants, they will make small account of him, and care not what they spend, who are never brought to an audit.—*Fuller.*

Every human being has a work to carry on within, duties to perform abroad, influences to exert, which are peculiarly his, and which no conscience but his own can teach.—*Channing.*

Much misconstruction and bitterness are spared to him who thinks naturally upon what he owes to others rather than what he ought to expect from them.—*Mad. Guizot.*

Responsibility walks hand in hand with capacity and power.—*J. G. Holland.*

Responsibility is measured, not by the amount of injury resulting from wrong action, but by the distinctness with which conscience has the opportunity of distinguishing between the right and the wrong.—*F. W. Robertson.*

Sin with the multitude, and your responsibility and guilt are as great and as truly personal, as if you alone had done the wrong.—*Tryon Edwards.*

The assurance that this is a state of probation, should give vigor to virtue and solemnity to truth. Every hour assumes a fearful responsibility when we view it as the culturer of an immortal harvest.—*Mrs. Sigourney.*

REST.—Rest is the sweet sauce of labor.—*Plutarch.*

Absence of occupation is not rest; a mind quite vacant is a mind distressed.—*Cowper.*

True rest is not that of torpor, but that of harmony; it is not refusing the struggle, but conquering in it; not resting from duty, but finding rest in it.—*F. W. Robertson.*

Some seek bread; and some seek wealth and ease; and some seek fame, but all are seeking rest.—*Langbridge.*

Certainly work is not always required of a man. There is such a thing as a sacred idleness—the cultivation of which is now fearfully neglected.—*G. Macdonald.*

Rest is valuable only so far as it is a contrast. Pursued as an end, it becomes a most pitiable condition.—*D. Swing.*

Too much rest itself becomes a pain.—*Homer.*

All work and no rest takes the spring and bound out of the most vigorous life.—Time spent in judicious resting is not time wasted, but time gained.—*M. B. Grier.*

Rest is not quitting the busy career; rest is the fitting of self to its sphere.—*J. Dwight.*

Alternate rest and labor long endure.
—*Ovid.*

There are pauses amidst study, and even pauses of seeming idleness, in which a process goes on which may be likened to the digestion of food. In those seasons of repose, the powers are gathering their strength for new efforts; as land which lies fallow recovers itself for tillage.—*J. W. Alexander.*

Rest unto our souls!—'tis all we want —the end of all our wishes and pursuits: we seek for it in titles, in riches and pleasures—climb up after it by ambition,—come down again and stoop for it by avarice,—try all extremes; nor is it till after many miserable experiments, that we are convinced, at last, we have been seeking everywhere for it but where there is a prospect of finding it; and that is, within ourselves, in a meek and lowly disposition of heart.—*Sterne.*

To will what God doth will, is the only science that gives us rest.—*Longfellow.*

RESTLESSNESS.—'Tis plain there is not in nature a point of stability to be found; everything either ascends or declines: when wars are ended abroad, sedition begins at home; and when men are freed from fighting for necessity, they quarrel through ambition.

The mind is found most acute and most uneasy in the morning. Uneasiness is, indeed, a species of sagacity—a passive sagacity. Fools are never uneasy.—*Goethe.*

A restless mind, like a rolling stone, gathers nothing but dirt and mire. Little or no good will cleave to it; and it is sure to leave peace and quietness behind it.—*Balguy.*

Always driven toward new shores, or carried hence without hope of return, shall we never, on the ocean of age, cast anchor for even a day?—*Lamartine.*

RESURRECTION.—Our Lord has written the promise of the resurrection, not in books alone, but in every leaf in spring-time.—*Luther.*

The diamond that shines in the Saviour's crown shall beam in unquenched beauty, at last, on the forehead of every human soul, risen through grace to the immortality of heaven.

RETIREMENT.—To judge rightly of our own worth we should retire from the world so as to see both its pleasures and pains in their proper light and dimensions—thus taking the heart from off this world and its allurements, which so dishonor the understanding as to turn the wisest of men into fools and children.—*Sterne.*

He whom God hath gifted with the love of retirement, possesses, as it were, an extra sense.—*Bulwer.*

Our life, exempt from public haunt, finds tongues in trees, books in the running brooks, sermons in stones, and good in everything.—*Shakespeare.*

Let me often to these solitudes retire, and in their presence reassure my feeble virtue.—*Bryant.*

A man who can retire from the world to seek entertainment in his closet, has a thousand advantages of which other people have no idea.—He is master of his own company and pleasures, and can command either the one or the other according to his circumstances or temper. All nature is ready for his view, and all ages appear at his call. He can transport himself to the most distant regions, and enjoy the best and politest company that ever the world afforded.—*Hibernicus's Letters.*

Depart from the highway, and transplant thyself in some enclosed ground, for it is hard for a tree that stands by the wayside to keep its fruit until it be ripe.—*Chrysostom.*

Nature I'll court in her sequestered haunts, by mountain, meadow, streamlet, grove, or cell; where the poised lark his evening ditty chaunts, and health, and peace, and contemplation dwell.—*Smollett.*

Before you think of retiring from the world, be sure you are fit for retirement; in order to which it is necessary that you have a mind so composed by prudence, reason, and religion, that it may bear being looked into; a turn to rural life, and a love for study.—*Burgh.*

Don't think of retiring from the world until the world will be sorry that you retire. I hate a fellow whom pride or cowardice or laziness drive into a corner, and who does nothing when he is there but sit and growl. Let him come out as I do, and bark.—*Johnson.*

A foundation of good sense, and a cultivation of learning, are required to give a seasoning to retirement, and make us taste its blessings.—*Dryden*.

How use doth breed a habit in a man! this shadowy desert, unfrequented woods, I better brook than flourishing peopled towns.—*Shakespeare*.

RETRIBUTION.—Retribution is one of the grand principles in the divine administration of human affairs; a requital is imperceptible only to the wilfully unobservant. There is everywhere the working of the everlasting law of requital: man always gets as he gives. —*J. Foster*.

God is a sure paymaster. He may not pay at the end of every week, or month, or year, but remember He pays in the end.—*Anne of Austria*.

Life resembles the banquet of Damocles; the sword is ever suspended.— *Voltaire*.

Old age seizes upon an ill-spent youth, like fire upon a rotten house.— It was rotten before, and must have fallen of itself, so that it is only one ruin anticipating another.—*South*.

The more pure and righteous a moral being is, the more squarely must he antagonize, the more intensely must he hate, the more surely must he punish impurity and unrighteousness. Volcanic fire inside the globe, and forked lightning outside of it, are faint emblems of holy wrath.—When a thoroughly bad man stands revealed only lightning is logical.—He that sows the wind ought to reap the whirlwind.—*R. D. Hitchcock*.

Man never fastened one end of a chain around the neck of his brother, that God did not fasten the other end round the neck of the oppressor.— *Lamartine*.

" One soweth and another reapeth " is a verity that applies to evil as well as good.—*George Eliot*.

Nemesis is lame, but she is of colossal stature; and sometimes, while her sword is not yet unsheathed, she stretches out her huge left arm and grasps her victim. The mighty hand is invisible, but the victim totters under the dire clutch. —*George Eliot*.

God's mill grinds slow but sure.— *Herbert*.

The blind and cowardly spirit of evil is forever telling you that evil things are pardonable, and you shall not die for them; and that good things are impossible, and you need not live for them. And, if you believe these things, you will find some day, to your cost, that they are untrue.—*Ruskin*.

RETROSPECTION.—Often a retrospect delights the mind.—*Dante*.

The thought of our past years in me doth breed perpetual benediction.— *Wordsworth*.

A man advanced in years, who thinks fit to look back upon his former life, and call that only life which was passed with satisfaction and enjoyment, will find himself very young, if not in his infancy.—*Steele*.

From the sad years of life we sometimes do short hours, yea, minutes strike, keen, blissful, bright, never to be forgotten; which, through the dreary gloom of time o'erpast, shine like fair sunny spots on a wild waste.—*Joanna Baillie*.

Of no day can the retrospect cause pain to a good man, nor has one passed away which he is unwilling to remember: the period of his life seems prolonged by his good acts; and we may be said to live twice, when we can reflect with pleasure on the days that are gone.—*Martial*.

He possesses dominion over himself, and is happy, who can every day say, " I have lived." To-morrow the heavenly Father may either involve the world in dark clouds, or cheer it with clear sunshine; he will not, however, render ineffectual the things which have already taken place.—*Horace*.

To look back to antiquity is one thing; to go back to it another. If we look back to it, it should be as those who are running a race, only to press forward the faster, and to leave the beaten way still further behind.—*Colton*.

REVENGE.—(See "Injury," and " Forgiveness.")

Revenge is a common passion; it is the sin of the uninstructed.—The savage deems it noble; but the religion of Christ, which is the sublime civilizer, emphatically condemns it. Why? Because religion ever seeks to ennoble man; and nothing so debases him as revenge.—*Bulwer.*

Revenge is the abject pleasure of an abject mind.—*Juvenal.*

It is a work of prudence to prevent injury, and of a great mind, when done, not to revenge it. He that hath revenge in his power, and does not use it, is the great man; it is for low and vulgar spirits to transport themselves with vengeance. To endure injuries with a brave mind is one half the conquest.

By taking revenge, a man is but even with his enemy; but in passing over it, he is superior.—*Bacon.*

Revenge is like a boomerang. Although for a time it flies in the direction in which it is hurled, it takes a sudden curve, and, returning, hits your own head the heaviest blow of all.

A spirit of revenge is the very spirit of the devil; than which nothing makes a man more like him, and nothing can be more opposite to the temper Christianity was designed to promote. If your revenge be not satisfied, it will give you torment now; if it be, it will give you greater hereafter. None is a greater self-tormentor than a malicious and revengeful man, who turns the poison of his own temper in upon himself. —*J. M. Mason.*

He that studieth revenge keepeth his own wounds green, which otherwise would heal and do well.—*Bacon.*

Revenge, at first, though sweet, bitter, ere long, back on itself recoils.—*Milton.*

Dare not usurp thy maker's place by giving way to wrath—wrath that goes forth in vengeance; "vengeance is mine, I will repay, saith the Lord."—*C. Simmons.*

The best manner of avenging ourselves is by not resembling him who has injured us.—*Jane Porter.*

Revenge has ears more deaf than adders to the voice of any true decision. —*Shakespeare.*

If you are affronted it is better to pass it by in silence, or with a jest, though with some dishonor, than to endeavor revenge.—If you can keep reason above passion, that and watchfulness will be your best defenders.—*Newton.*

Revenge is a kind of wild justice, which, the more a man's nature runs to, the more ought law to weed it out. —*Bacon.*

Revenge is barren of itself; itself is the dreadful food it feeds on; its delight is murder; its satiety despair.—*Schiller.*

Revenge is an act of passion; vengeance of justice.—Injuries are revenged; crimes are avenged.—*Joubert.*

In revenge a man is but even with his enemies; but it is a princely thing to pardon, for Solomon saith, "It is the glory of a man to pass over a transgression."—*Bacon.*

To revenge is no valor, but to bear. —*Shakespeare.*

Hath any wronged thee? Be bravely revenged.—Slight it, and the work is begun; forgive it, and it is finished.—He is below himself that is not above any injury.—*Quarles.*

Heat not a furnace for your foe so hot that it do singe thyself.—*Shakespeare.*

REVERENCE.—The majesty of God revere; fear him, and you have nothing else to fear.—*Fordyce.*

Reverence is the very first element of religion; it cannot but be felt by every one who has right views of the divine greatness and holiness, and of his own character in the sight of God.—*C. Simmons.*

The Turks carefully collect every scrap of paper that comes in their way, because the name of God may be written thereon.—*Richter.*

We treat God with irreverence by banishing him from our thoughts, not by referring to his will on slight occasions.—*Ruskin.*

The soul of the Christian religion is reverence.—*Goethe.*

Reverence is an ennobling sentiment; it is felt to be degrading only by the vulgar mind, which would escape the sense of its own littleness by elevating itself into an antagonist of what is above it. He that has no pleasure in looking up is not fit so much as to look down. —*Washington Allston.*

Rather let my head stoop to the block, than these knees bow to any save to the God of heaven.—*Shakespeare.*

Boyle, it is said, never mentioned the name of God without a visible and reverent pause in his discourse.

While it is undesirable that any man should receive what he has not examined, a far more frequent danger is that of flippant irreverence.—*Goethe.*

Reverence is one of the signs of strength; irreverence one of the surest indications of weakness.—No man will rise high who jeers at sacred things.—The fine loyalties of life must be reverenced or they will be foresworn in the day of trial.

REVERIE.—Reverie is when ideas float in our mind without reflection or regard of the understanding.—*Locke.*

Reverie, which is thought in its nebulous state, borders closely upon the land of sleep, by which it is bounded as by a natural frontier.—*Victor Hugo.*

Sit in reverie, and watch the changing color of the waves that break upon the idle seashore of the mind.—*Longfellow.*

Do anything innocent rather than give yourself up to reverie. I can speak on this point from experience; for at one period of my life, I was a dreamer and castle-builder. Visions of the distant and future took the place of present duty and activity. I spent hours in reverie. The body suffered as much as the mind. The imagination threatened to inflame the passions, and I found, if I meant to be virtuous, I must dismiss my musings. The conflict was a hard one; but I resolved, prayed, resisted, sought refuge in occupation, and at length triumphed.—*Channing.*

To lose one's self in reverie, one must be either very happy, or very unhappy. —Reverie is the child of extremes.—*Rivarol.*

Both mind and heart, when given up to reverie and dreaminess, have a thousand avenues open for the entrance of evil.—*C. Simmons.*

Few habits are more injurious than musing, which differs from thinking as pacing one's chamber does from walking abroad. The mind learns nothing, and is not strengthened, but weakened, returning perpetually over the same barren track. Where the thoughts are

sombre, the evil is doubly great, and not only time and vigor are squandered, but melancholy becomes fixed. It is really a disease, and the question how it should be treated is one of the most important in anthropology.—*J. W. Alexander.*

In that sweet mood when pleasant thoughts bring sad thoughts to the mind.—*Wordsworth.*

There is no self-delusion more fatal than that which makes the conscience dreamy with the anodyne of lofty sentiments, while the life is groveling and sensual.—*J. R. Lowell.*

REVOLUTION.—Revolution is the larva of civilization.—*Victor Hugo.*

Political convulsions, like geological upheavings, usher in new epochs of the world's progress.—*Wendell Phillips.*

Great revolutions are the work rather of principles than of bayonets, and are achieved first in the moral, and afterwards in the material sphere.—*Mazzini.*

Revolutions begin in the best heads, and run steadily down to the populace. —*Metternich.*

Too long denial of guaranteed right is sure to lead to revolution—bloody revolution, where suffering must fall upon the innocent as well as the guilty. —*U. S. Grant.*

Nothing has ever remained of any revolution but what was ripe in the conscience of the masses.—*Ledru Rollin.*

All experience hath shown that mankind are more disposed to suffer, while evils are sufferable, than to right themselves by abolishing the forms to which they are accustomed.—*Jefferson.*

We deplore the outrages which accompany revolutions. But the more violent the outrages, the more assured we feel that a revolution was necessary! The violence of these outrages will always be proportioned to the ferocity and ignorance of the people: and the ferocity and ignorance of the people will be proportioned to the oppression and degradation under which they have been accustomed to live.—*Macaulay.*

Revolutions are not made, they come. A revolution is as natural a growth as an oak. It comes out of the past. Its foundations are laid far back.—*Wendell Phillips.*

Times and occasions and provocations will teach their own lessons. But with or without right, a revolution will be the very last resource of the thinking and the good.—*Burke.*

Let them call it mischief; when it's past and prospered, it will be virtue.—*Ben Jonson.*

The working of revolutions misleads me no more; it is as necessary to our race as its waves to the stream, that it may not be a stagnant marsh. Ever renewed in its forms, the genius of humanity blossoms.—*Herder.*

It is far more easy to pull down than to build up, and to destroy than to preserve. Revolutions have on this account been falsely supposed to be fertile of great talent; as the dregs rise to the top during a fermentation, and the lightest things are carried highest by the whirlwind.—*Colton.*

The best security against revolution is in constant correction of abuses and the introduction of needed improvements. It is the neglect of timely repair that makes rebuilding necessary.—*Whately.*

The surest way to prevent seditions is to take away the matter of them; for if there be fuel prepared, it is hard to tell whence the spark shall come that shall set it on fire.—*Bacon.*

Revolutions are like the most noxious dung-heaps, which bring into life the noblest vegetables.—*Napoleon.*

Those who give the first shock to a state are naturally the first to be overwhelmed in its ruin. The fruits of public commotion are seldom enjoyed by the man who was the first to set it a-going; he only troubles the water for another's net.—*Montaigne.*

Who does more earnestly long for a change than he who is uneasy in his present circumstances? And who run to create confusions with so desperate a boldness, as those who having nothing to lose, hope to gain by them?—*Sir T. More.*

The whirlpool of the hour engulfs the growth of centuries!—Pause ere ye rive with strength of fever, things embedded long in social being.—You will uproot no form, with which the thoughts and habits of weak mortals have long been twined, without the bleeding rent of thousand ties which to the common heart of nature link it.—Wrenched, perchance you'll mock a clumsy relic of forgotten days, while you have scattered in the dust, unseen, a thousand living crystals.—*Talfourd.*

REWARD.—He who wishes to secure the good of others has already secured his own.—*Confucius.*

Every duty brings its peculiar delight, every denial its appropriate compensation, every thought its recompense, every cross its crown; pay goes with performance as effect with cause. Meanness overreaches itself; vice vitiates whoever indulges in it; the wicked wrong their own souls; generosity greatens; virtue exalts; charity transfigures; and holiness is the essence of angelhood. God does not require us to live on credit; he pays us what we earn as we earn it, good or evil, heaven or hell, according to our choice.—*Charles Mildmay.*

Blessings ever wait on virtuous deeds, and though a late, a sure reward succeeds.—*Congreve.*

He who sows, even with tears, the precious seed of faith, hope, and love, shall doubtless come again with joy, bringing his sheaves with him, because it is the very nature of that seed to yield a joyful harvest.—*Cecil.*

It is the amends of a short and troublesome life, that doing good and suffering ill entitles man to a longer and better.—*Penn.*

No man, who continues to add something to the material, intellectual, and moral well being of the place in which he lives, is left long without proper reward.—*Booker T. Washington.*

RHETORIC.—Rhetoric is nothing but reason well dressed, and argument put in order.—*Jeremy Collier.*

The best rules of rhetoric are, to speak intelligently; speak from the heart; have something to say; say it; and stop when you've done.—*Tryon Edwards.*

There is truth and beauty in rhetoric; but it oftener serves ill turns than good ones.—*Penn.*

Mere rhetoric, in serious discourses, is like flowers in corn, pleasing to those who look only for amusement, but prejudical to him who would reap profit from it.—*Swift.*

Rhetoric without logic, is like a tree with leaves and blossoms, but no root; yet more are taken with rhetoric than logic, because they are caught with fine expressions when they understand not reason.—*Selden.*

All a rhetorician's rules teach nothing but to name his tools.—*Samuel Butler.*

The florid, elevated, and figurative way is for the passions; for love and hatred, fear and anger, are begotten in the soul by showing their objects out of their true proportion, either greater than the life, or less; but instruction is to be given by showing them what they naturally are. A man is to be cheated into passion, but reasoned into truth.—*Dryden.*

All the arts of rhetoric, besides order and clearness, are for nothing else but to insinuate wrong ideas, move the passions, and thereby mislead the judgment.—*Locke.*

RICHES.—(See "WEALTH.")

He is rich whose income is more than his expenses; and he is poor whose expenses exceed his income.—*Bruyère.*

Riches are not an end of life, but an instrument of life.—*H. W. Beecher.*

I cannot call riches by a better name than the "baggage" of virtue; the Roman word is better, "impediment." For as the baggage is to an army, so are riches to virtue. It cannot be spared or left behind, and yet it hindereth the march; yea, and the care of it sometimes loseth or disturbeth the victory. Of great riches there is no real use, except in the distribution; the rest is but conceit.—*Bacon.*

My riches consist not in the extent of my possessions, but in the fewness of my wants.—*J. Brotherton.*

Riches exclude only one inconvenience, and that is poverty.—*Johnson.*

The pride of dying rich raises the loudest laugh in hell.—*John Foster.*

He hath riches sufficient, who hath enough to be charitable.—*Sir T. Browne.*

Agur said, "Give me neither poverty nor riches"; and this will ever be the prayer of the wise. Our incomes should be like our shoes: if too small, they will gall and pinch us, but if too large,
they will cause us to stumble and to trip. But wealth, after all, is a relative thing, since he that has little, and wants less, is richer than he that has much, but wants more. True contentment depends not upon what we have; a tub was large enough for Diogenes, but a world was too little for Alexander.—*Colton.*

Plenty and indigence depend upon the opinion every one has of them; and riches, like glory or health, have no more beauty or pleasure, than their possessor is pleased to lend them.—*Montaigne.*

The larger the income, the harder it is to live within it.—*Whately.*

Believe not much them that seem to despise riches, for they despise them who despair of them; and none are worse than they when riches come to them.—*Bacon.*

A man that hoards up riches and enjoys them not, is like an ass that carries gold and eats thistles.—*Burton.*

Misery assails riches, as lightning does the highest towers; or as a tree that is heavy laden with fruit breaks its own boughs, so do riches destroy the virtue of their possessor.—*Burton.*

If thou art rich, then show the greatness of thy fortune; or what is better, the greatness of thy soul, in the meekness of thy conversation; condescend to men of low estate, support the distressed, and patronize the neglected. Be great.—*Sterne.*

Of all the riches that we hug, of all the pleasures we enjoy, we can carry no more out of this world than out of a dream.—*Bonnell.*

Be not penny-wise; riches have wings; sometimes they fly away of themselves, and sometimes they must be set flying to bring in more.—*Bacon.*

To value riches is not to be covetous. They are the gift of God, and, like every gift of his, good in themselves, and capable of a good use. But to overvalue riches, to give them a place in the heart which God did not design them to fill, this is covetousness.—*H. L. Wayland.*

To have what we want is riches, but to be able to do without is power.—*G. Macdonald.*

Riches, though they may reward virtue, cannot cause it.—He is much more noble who deserves a benefit than he who bestows one.—*Feltham.*

Public sentiment will come to be, that the man who dies rich dies disgraced.—*Andrew Carnegie.*

Riches are valuable at all times and to all men, because they always purchase pleasures such as men are accustomed to and desire: nor can anything restrain or regulate the love of money but a sense of honor and virtue, which, if not equal at all times, will naturally abound most in ages of knowledge and refinement.—*Hume.*

Every man is rich or poor, according to the proportion between his desires and enjoyments. Of riches as of everything else, the hope is more than the enjoyment. While we consider them as the means to be used at some future time for the attainment of felicity, ardor after them secures us from weariness of ourselves; but no sooner do we sit down to enjoy our acquisitions than we find them insufficient to fill up the vacuities of life.—*Johnson.*

The rich are the real outcasts of society, and special missions should be organized for them.—*Norman Macleod.*

A man who succeeds to his father's reputation must be greater than him, to be considered as great; but he that succeeds to his father's riches, will have to encounter no such deduction. The popular opinion adds to our means, but diminishes our merits; and it is not an unsafe rule to believe less than you hear with respect to a man's fortune, and more than you hear with respect to his fame.—*Colton.*

There are two things needed in these days; first, for rich men to find out how poor men live; and second, for poor men to know how rich men work.—*E. Atkinson.*

The sons of the rich, the educated darlings of wealthy families, are nowhere.—All their gifts were only so many fatal temptations, and they themselves are forgotten, like bad copies of good pictures.—*J. W. Forney.*

A fortune is usually the greatest of misfortunes to children. It takes the muscles out of the limbs, the brain out of the head, and virtue out of the heart.

In this world, it is not what we take up, but what we give up, that makes us rich.—*H. W. Beecher.*

If I have but enough for myself and family, I am steward only for myself and them; if I have more, I am but a steward of that abundance for others.—*Herbert.*

I have a rich neighbor that is always so busy that he has no leisure to laugh; the whole business of his life is to get money, more money, that he may still get more. He considers not that it is not in the power of riches to make a man happy; for it was wisely said that "there be as many miseries beyond riches as on this side of them."—*Izaak Walton.*

One cause, which is not always observed, of the insufficiency of riches, is that they very seldom make their owner rich.—*Johnson.*

Riches without charity are nothing worth. They are a blessing only to him who makes them a blessing to others.—*Fielding.*

If the search for riches were sure to be successful, though I should become a groom with a whip in my hand to get them, I will do so. As the search may not be successful, I will follow after that which I love.—*Confucius.*

He is richest who is content with the least, for content is the wealth of nature.—*Socrates.*

Wealth is not his that has it, but his that enjoys it.—*Franklin.*

No man can tell whether he is rich or poor by turning to his ledger.—It is the heart that makes a man rich.—He is rich according to what he is, not according to what he has.—*H. W. Beecher.*

"If I were rich," says one, "I would—" Illusion!—We often hold firmer to the last crown we have amassed than to the first which we gained.—*J. P. Senn.*

Man was born to be rich, or grows rich by the use of his faculties, by the union of thought with nature. Property is an intellectual production. The game requires coolness, right reasoning, promptness, and patience in the players. Cultivated labor drives out brute labor. —*Emerson.*

An eager pursuit of fortune is inconsistent with a severe devotion to truth. The heart must grow tranquil before the thought can become searching.—*Bovee.*

Riches are apt to betray a man into arrogance.—*Addison.*

Satiety comes of riches, and contumaciousness of satiety.—*Solon.*

The use we make of our fortune determines as to its sufficiency.—A little is enough if used wisely, and too much if expended foolishly.—*Bovee.*

Riches are the pettiest and least worthy gifts which God can give a man. What are they to God's Word, to bodily gifts, such as beauty and health; or to the gifts of the mind, such as understanding, skill, wisdom! Yet men toil for them day and night, and take no rest. Therefore God commonly gives riches to foolish people to whom he gives nothing else.—*Luther.*

Worldly riches are like nuts; many clothes are torn in getting them, many a tooth broke in cracking them, but never a belly filled with eating them.—*Venning.*

If thou art rich, thou art poor; for, like an ass, whose back with ingots bows, thou bearest thy heavy riches but a journey, and death unloads thee.—*Shakespeare.*

There is no less merit in keeping what we have got, than in first acquiring it. Chance has something to do with the one, while the other will always be the effect of skill.—*Ovid.*

Much learning shows how little mortals know; much wealth, how little worldlings can enjoy.—*Young.*

Riches do not delight us so much with their possession, as torment us with their loss.—*Gregory.*

Some of God's noblest sons, I think, will be selected from those that know how to take wealth, with all its temptations, and maintain godliness therewith. It is hard to be a saint standing in a golden niche.—*H. W. Beecher.*

Never respect men merely for their riches, but rather for their philanthropy; we do not value the sun for its height, but for its use.—*Bailey.*

The greatest and the most amiable privilege which the rich enjoy over the poor is that which they exercise the least,—the privilege of making others happy.—*Colton.*

Riches should be admitted into our houses, but not into our hearts; we may take them into our possession, but not into our affections.—*Charron.*

Riches, honors, and pleasures are the sweets which destroy the mind's appetite for heavenly food; poverty, disgrace, and pain are the bitters which restore it.—*Bp. Horne.*

Every man is rich or poor according to the proportion between his desires and his enjoyments.—*Johnson.*

Wouldst thou multiply thy riches?—diminish them wisely.—Or wouldst thou make thine estate entire?—divide it charitably.—Seeds that are scattered increase, but hoarded up they perish.—*Quarles.*

Riches amassed in haste will diminish, but those collected by little and little will multiply.—*Goethe.*

I take him to be the only rich man that lives upon what he has, owes nothing, and is contented; for there is no determinate sum of money, nor quantity of estate that can denote a man rich, since no man is truly rich that has not so much as perfectly satiates his desire of having more; for the desire of more is want, and want is poverty.—*Howe.*

We see how much a man has, and therefore we envy him; did we see how little he enjoys, we should rather pity him.—*Seed.*

A great estate is a great disadvantage to those who do not know how to use it, for nothing is more common than to see wealthy persons live scandalously and miserably; riches do them no service in order to virtue and happiness; it is precept and principle, not an estate, that makes a man good for something.—*Marcus Antoninus.*

If a rich man is proud of his wealth, he should not be praised until it is known how he employs it.—*Socrates.*

There is a burden of care in getting riches; fear in keeping them; temptation in using them; guilt in abusing them; sorrow in losing them; and a burden of account at last to be given concerning them.—*M. Henry.*

As riches and favor forsake a man we discover him to be a fool, but nobody could find it out in his prosperity.—*Bruyère.*

Nothing is so hard for those who abound in riches as to conceive how others can be in want.—*Swift.*

A rich man, of cultivated tastes, with every right to gratify them, knowing enough of sorrow to humble his heart toward God, and soften it toward his neighbor—gifted with not only the power but will to do good, and having lived long enough to reap the fruits of an honorable youth in a calm old age—such a man, in spite of his riches, is not unlikely to enter the kingdom of heaven.—*Mulock.*

We are so vain as to set the highest value upon those things to which nature has assigned the lowest place. What can be more coarse and rude in the mine than the precious metals, or more slavish and dirty than the people that dig and work them? And yet they defile our minds more than our bodies, and make the possessor fouler than the artificer of them. Rich men, in fine, are only the greater slaves.—*Seneca.*

He who recognizes no higher logic than that of the shilling may become a very rich man, and yet remain a very poor creature, for riches are no proof of moral worth, and their glitter often serves only to draw attention to the worthlessness of their possessor, as the glowworm's light reveals the grub.—*S. Smiles.*

RIDICULE.—Ridicule is the first and last argument of fools.—*C. Simmons.*

The talent of turning men into ridicule, and exposing to laughter those one converses with, is the gratification of little minds and ungenerous tempers. A young man with this cast of mind cuts himself off from all manner of improvement.—*Addison.*

Your sayer of smart things has a bad heart.—*Pascal.*

Ridicule may be the evidence of wit or bitterness and may gratify a little mind, or an ungenerous temper, but it is no test of reason or truth.—*Tryon Edwards.*

Man learns more readily and remembers more willingly what excites his ridicule than what deserves esteem and respect.—*Horace.*

He who brings ridicule to bear against truth finds in his hand a blade without a hilt. The most sparkling and pointed flame of wit flickers and expires against the incombustible walls of her sanctuary.—*Landor.*

It has been said that ridicule is the best test of truth, for that it will not stick where it is not just. I deny it. A truth viewed in a certain light, and attacked in certain words, by men of wit and humor, may, and often doth, become ridiculous, at least so far that the truth is only remembered and repeated for the sake of the ridicule.—*Chesterfield.*

Ridicule is the weapon most feared by enthusiasts of every description; from its predominance over such minds it often checks what is absurd, but fully as often smothers that which is noble.—*Walter Scott.*

Ridicule, which chiefly arises from pride, a selfish passion, is but at best a gross pleasure, too rough an entertainment for those who are highly polished and refined.—*Home.*

Reason is the test of ridicule—not ridicule the test of truth.—*Bp. Warburton.*

Ridicule is a weak weapon when levelled at strong minds, but common men are cowards and dread an empty laugh.—*Tupper.*

If there be any one habit which more than another is the dry-rot of all that is high and generous in youth, it is the habit of ridicule.—*L. E. Landon.*

Ridicule is generally made use of to laugh men out of virtue and good sense, by attaching everything praiseworthy in human life.—*Addison.*

Betray mean terror of ridicule, thou shalt find fools enough to mock thee; but answer thou their language with contempt, and the scoffers will lick thy feet.—*Tupper.*

Learn from the earliest days to inure your principles against the perils of ridicule: you can no more exercise your reason if you live in the constant dread of laughter, than you can enjoy your life if you are in the constant terror of death.—*Sydney Smith.*

Cervantes smiled Spain's chivalry away.—*Byron.*

It is said that ridicule is the test of truth; but it is never applied except when we wish to deceive ourselves—when if we cannot exclude the light, we would fain draw the curtain before it. The sneer springs out of the wish to deny; and wretched must that state of mind be, that wishes to take refuge in doubt.—*L. E. Landon.*

It was the saying of an ancient sage that humor was the only test of gravity, and gravity of humor; for a subject that would not bear raillery was suspicious, and a jest that would not bear a serious examination was certainly false wit.—*Shaftesbury.*

Vices, when ridiculed, first lose the horror they ought to raise, grow by degrees approved, and almost aim at praise.—*Whitehead.*

RIGHT.—Whatever is physiologically right, is morally right; and whatever is physiologically wrong is morally wrong. —*Mark Hopkins.*

Let a man try faithfully, manfully to be right, he will daily grow more and more right. It is at the bottom of the condition on which all men have to cultivate themselves.—*Carlyle.*

I would rather be right than be president.—*Henry Clay.*

Let us have faith that right makes might, and in that faith, let us to the end, dare to do our duty, as we understand it.—*Lincoln.*

Nothing but the right can ever be expedient, since that can never be true expediency which would sacrifice a greater good to a less.—*Whately.*

No man has a right to do as he pleases, except when he pleases to do right.—*C. Simmons.*

There is no right without a parallel duty, no liberty without the supremacy of the law, no high destiny without earnest perseverance, no greatness without self-denial.—*Lieber.*

The fears of one class of men are not the measure of the rights of another.— *Bancroft.*

Would you be exempt from uneasiness; do nothing you know or even suspect is wrong. Would you enjoy the purest pleasure; do everything in your power which you believe is right. —*Rules of Life.*

All men are endowed by their Creator with inalienable rights; among these are life, liberty, and the pursuit of happiness.—*Jefferson.*

One of the grandest things in having rights is, that though they are your rights you may give them up.—*G. Macdonald.*

There is no credit in knowing how to spell, but positive disgrace in being ignorant on that point. So there can be no credit in doing right, while it is infamous to do wrong.—*G. F. Train.*

Right is might, and ever was, and ever shall be so.—*Holiness, meekness, patience, humility, self-denial, and self-sacrifice, faith, love,—each is might, and every gift of the spirit is might.—*Hare.*

Never, with the Bible in our hands, can we deny rights to another, which, under the same circumstances, we would claim for ourselves.—*G. Spring.*

RIVALRY.—Two stars keep not their motion in one sphere.—*Shakespeare.*

Nothing is ever done beautifully which is done in rivalship; or nobly, which is done in pride.—*Ruskin.*

It is the privilege of posterity to set matters right between those antagonists who, by their rivalry for greatness, divided a whole age.—*Addison.*

In ambition, as in love, the successful can afford to be indulgent toward their rivals. The prize our own, it is graceful to recognize the merit that vainly aspired to it.—*Bovee.*

ROGUERY.—After long experience of the world, I affirm before God, that I never knew a rogue who was not unhappy.—*Junius.*

Rogues are always found out in some way.—Whoever is a wolf will act as a wolf; that is the most certain of all things.—*Fontaine.*

Make yourself an honest man, and then you may be sure that there is one rascal less in the world.—*Carlyle.*

A rogue is a roundabout fool.—*Coleridge.*

ROMANCE.—(See "NOVELS.")

Romance is the poetry of literature.— *Mad. Necker.*

Lessons of wisdom have never such

power over us as when they are wrought into the heart through the groundwork of a story which engages the passions. —*Sterne.*

The habitual indulgence in such reading is a silent, ruining mischief.—*Hannah More.*

In this commonplace world every one is said to be romantic who either admires a fine thing or does one.—*Pope.*

Romance has been elegantly defined as the offspring of fiction and love.—*Disraeli.*

In the meanest hut is a romance, if you but knew the hearts there.—*Van Ense.*

I despair of ever receiving the same degree of pleasure from the most exalted performances of genius which I felt in childhood from pieces which my present judgment regards as trifling and contemptible.—*Burke.*

To the romance writers, and comparatively decorous dramatists of his own time, Nicolé gave the title of public poisoners.

Fiction may be more instructive than real history; but the vast rout of romances and novels, as they are, do incalculable mischief. I wish we could collect all together, and make one vast fire of them. I should exult to see the smoke of them ascend, like that of Sodom and Gomorrah: the judgment would be as just.—*J. Foster.*

RUINS.—The legendary tablets of the past.—*Walter Scott.*

Black-letter record of the ages.—*Diderot.*

I do love these ancient ruins.—We never tread upon them but we set our foot upon some reverend history.—*John Webster.*

Cicero was not so eloquent as thou, thou nameless column with the buried base.—*Byron.*

Mile-stones on the road of time.—*Chamfort.*

Historic records of the past, but each, also, an index of the world's progress.

RUMOR.—He that easily believes rumors has the principle within him to augment rumors.—It is strange to see the ravenous appetite with which some devourers of character and happiness

fix upon the sides of the innocent and unfortunate.—*Jane Porter.*

Stuffing the ears of men with false reports.—*Shakespeare.*

Rumor was the messenger of defamation, and so swift, that none could be first to tell an evil tale.—*Pollok.*

Curse the tongue whence slanderous rumor, like the adder's drop, distils her venom, withering friendship's faith, turning love's favor.—*Hillhouse.*

The flying rumors gathered as they rolled, and all who told it added something new, and all who heard it made enlargement too; in every ear it spreads, on every tongue it grew.—*Pope.*

On rumor's tongues continual slanders ride.—*Shakespeare.*

How violently do rumors blow the sails of popular judgments!—How can one discern between the truth and truth-likeness, between shows and substance.—*Sir P. Sidney.*

Rumor is a pipe blown by surmises, jealousies, conjectures, and of so easy and plain a stop, that the blunt monster with uncounted heads, the still discordant wavering multitude can play upon it.—*Shakespeare.*

S

SABBATH.—Perpetual memory of the Maker's rest.—*Bp. Mant.*

The Sunday is the core of our civilization, dedicated to thought and reverence.—It invites to the noblest solitude and to the noblest society.—*Emerson.*

He who ordained the Sabbath loves the poor.—*J. R. Lowell.*

The Sabbath is the link between the paradise which has passed away, and the paradise which is yet to come.—*Wylie.*

Sunday is the golden clasp that binds together the volume of the week.—*Longfellow.*

He that remembers not to keep the Christian Sabbath at the beginning of the week, will be in danger of forgetting, before the end of the week, that he is a Christian.—*E. Turner.*

Where there is no Christian Sabbath, there is no Christian morality; and without this, free institutions cannot long be sustained.—*McLean.*

The longer I live the more highly do I estimate the Christian Sabbath, and the more grateful do I feel to those who impress its importance on the community.—*Daniel Webster.*

I never knew one man or woman who steadily avoided the house of prayer and public worship on the Lord's day, who did not come to grief, and bring other people to grief.—*Bellows.*

I am no fanatic, I hope, as to Sunday; but as I look abroad over the map of popular freedom in the world, it does not seem to me accidental that Switzerland, Scotland, England, and the United States—the countries which best observe Sunday—constitute almost the entire map of safe popular government.—*Joseph Cook.*

The streams of religion run deeper or shallower, as the banks of the Sabbath are kept up or neglected. A preacher in Holland called the Sabbath "God's dyke, shutting out an ocean of evils."—*Calcott.*

To say nothing of the divine law, on mere worldly grounds it is plain that nothing is more conducive to the health, intelligence, comfort, and independence of the working classes, and to our prosperity as a people, than our Christian American Sabbath.—*Tryon Edwards.*

A world without a Sabbath would be like a man without a smile, like a summer without flowers, and like a homestead without a garden. It is the joyous day of the whole week.—*H. W. Beecher.*

Sunday, that day so tedious to the triflers of earth, so full of beautiful repose, of calmness and strength for the earnest and heavenly-minded.—*Maria McIntosh.*

Sunday is the common people's great Liberty day, and they are bound to see to it that work does not come into it.—*H. W. Beecher.*

Without a Sabbath, no worship; without worship, no religion; and without religion, no permanent freedom.—*Montalembert.*

O what a blessing is Sunday, interposed between the waves of worldly business like the divine path of the Israelites through the sea! There is nothing in which I would advise you to be more strictly conscientious than in keeping the Sabbath day holy. I can truly declare that to me the Sabbath has been invaluable.—*Wilberforce.*

The green oasis, the little grassy meadow in the wilderness, where, after the week-day's journey, the pilgrim halts for refreshment and repose.—*C. Reade.*

Break down Sunday, close the churches, open the bars and the theatres on that day, and where would values be?—What was real estate worth in Sodom?—*H. L. Wayland.*

To that in men which is secular and animal, Sunday says, "Rest"; to that which is intellectual, moral, and social, "Grow."—*H. W. Beecher.*

The keeping of one day in seven holy, as a time of relaxation and refreshment as well as public worship, is of inestimable benefit to a state, considered merely as a civil institution.—*Blackstone.*

A holiday Sabbath is the ally of despotism.—*Hallam.*

I have found, by long and sound experience, that the due observance of the Sabbath day, and of the duties of it, have been of singular comfort and advantage to me. The observance of the day hath ever had joined to it a blessing on the rest of my time; and the week so begun hath been blessed and prosperous to me.—*Sir M. Hale.*

I feel as if God had, by giving the Sabbath, given fifty-two springs in every year.—*S. T. Coleridge.*

It would be as difficult to take an inventory of the benefits the world receives from the sunshine as to enumerate the blessings we derive from the Christian Sabbath.—*H. D. Ganse.*

I think the world of to-day would go mad, just frenzied with strain and pressure, but for the blessed institution of Sunday.—*Brooke Herford.*

He that would prepare for heaven must honor the Sabbath upon earth.—*D. Wilson.*

Sunday is like a stile between the fields of toil, where we can kneel and pray, or sit and meditate.—*Longfellow.*

There is a Sunday conscience, as well as a Sunday coat; and those who make religion a secondary concern put the coat and conscience carefully by to put on only once a week.—*Dickens*.

A corruption of morals usually follows a profanation of the Sabbath.—*Blackstone*.

There are many persons who look on Sunday as a sponge to wipe out the sins of the week.—*H. W. Beecher*.

The law of the Sabbath is the keystone of the arch of public morals; take it away, and the whole fabric falls.

The Sabbath is God's special present to the workingman, and one of its chief objects is to prolong his life, and preserve efficient his working tone.—The savings bank of human existence is the weekly Sabbath.—*Blaikie*.

I never knew a man escape failures, in either mind or body, who worked seven days in a week.—*Sir Robert Peel*.

Through the week we go down into the valleys of care and shadow.—Our Sabbaths should be hills of light and joy in God's presence; and so as time rolls by we shall go on from mountain top to mountain top, till at last we catch the glory of the gate, and enter in to go no more out forever.—*H. W. Beecher*.

If the Sunday had not been observed as a day of rest during the last three centuries, I have not the slightest doubt that we should have been at this moment a poorer people and less civilized. —*Macaulay*.

Hail, hallowed day, that binds a yoke on vice, gives rest to toil, proclaims God's holy truth, blesses the family, secures the state, prospers communities, nations exalts, pours life and light on earth, and points the way to heaven!—*Tryon Edwards*.

God's altar stands from Sunday to Sunday, and the seventh day is no more for religion than any other—it is for rest.—The whole seven are for religion, and one of them for rest, for instruction, for social worship, for gaining strength for the other six.—*H. W. Beecher*.

SACRIFICE.—We can offer up much in the large, but to make sacrifices in little things is what we are seldom equal to.—*Goethe*.

Our virtues are dearer to us the more we have had to suffer for them. It is the same with our children. All profound affection admits a sacrifice.—*Vauvenargues*.

Self-preservation is the first law of nature; self-sacrifice the highest rule of grace.

SADNESS.—What signifies sadness; a man grows lean upon it.—*Mackenzie*.

A feeling of sadness that is not akin to pain, resembles sorrow only as the mist resembles rain.—*Longfellow*.

It was a saying of Aristotle, that all noble-minded men are inclined to sadness. It is not merely the feeling that their lot is a hard one which oppresses them; it is something more—it is their inward sympathy and consciousness of participation in the sufferings of the human race to which they belong.—*Guesses at Truth*.

He whose days in wilful woe are worn, the grace of his Creator doth despise, that will not use his gifts for thankless niggardise.—*Spenser*.

By sadness you destroy the divine image in your soul. God is joy. All nature rejoices in him, and would you be sad? A true joy makes the heart fear God.—*Lombez*.

We ask God to forgive us for our evil thoughts and evil temper, but rarely, if ever, ask him to forgive us for our sadness. Joy is regarded as a happy accident of the Christian life, an ornament and a luxury rather than a duty.—*R. W. Dale*.

Ah, this beautiful world! Indeed, I know not what to think of it. Sometimes it is all gladness and sunshine, and heaven itself lies not far off; and then it suddenly changes and is dark and sorrowful, and the clouds shut out the day. In the lives of the saddest of us there are bright days when we feel as if we could take the great world in our arms. Then come the gloomy hours, when all without and within is dismal, cold, and dark. Believe me, every heart has its secret sorrows, which the world knows not; and oftentimes we call a man cold when he is only sad.—*Longfellow*.

The deep undertone of the world is sadness—a solemn bass, occurring at measured intervals and heard through all other tones. Ultimately, all the strains of this world's music resolve themselves into that tone; and I believe that, rightly felt, the cross, and the cross alone, interprets the mournful mystery of life, the sorrow of the Highest—the Lord of

Life,—the result of error and sin, but ultimately remedial, purifying and exalting.—*F. W. Robertson.*

Take my word for it, the saddest thing under the sky is a soul incapable of sadness.—*Countess de Gasparin.*

"Keep aloof from sadness," says an Icelandic writer, "for sadness is a sickness of the soul." Life has, indeed, many ills, but the mind that views every object in its most cheering aspect, and every doubtful dispensation as replete with latent good, bears within itself a powerful and perpetual antidote. The gloomy soul aggravates misfortune, while a cheerful smile often dispels those mists that portend a storm.—*Mrs. Sigourney.*

I wonder many times that ever a child of God should have a sad heart, considering what the Lord is preparing for him.—*Rutherford.*

It is quite deplorable to see how many rational creatures mistake suffering for sanctity, and think a sad face and a gloomy habit of mind propitious offerings to that Deity whose works are all light and lustre and harmony and loveliness.—*Lady Morgan.*

'Tis impious in a good man to be sad.—*Young.*

Of all the sad words of tongue or pen, the saddest are these: "It might have been."—*Whittier.*

Gloom and sadness are poison to us, the origin of hysterics, which is a disease of the imagination caused by vexation, and supported by fear.—*Sévigné.*

SAINTS.—A true saint is a divine landscape or picture, where all the rare beauties of Christ are lively portrayed and drawn forth.—He hath the same spirit, the same judgment, the same will with Christ.—*T. Watson.*

Some rivers, as historians tell us, pass through others without mingling with them; just so should a saint pass through this world.—*Venning.*

When we think of saints we are apt to think of very pale, still persons, who are all the while wishing they weren't alive, and all that. My ideal of a saint is a brown woman, with red arms, who gets up early in the morning and goes to work for others—who stands the brunt of household work, and who bears with children that she did not bear. That is my saint. Rather a busy, bustling saint, but she is a saint. People say of her, "What a homely, good creature she is." To my mind that is more complimentary than to have the pope put her in the calendar.—*H. W. Beecher.*

A saint is a man of convictions, who has been dead a hundred years, canonized now, but cannonaded while living.—*H. L. Wayland.*

The saints are God's jewels, highly esteemed by and dear to him; they are a royal diadem in his hand.—*M. Henry.*

The elect are whosoever will, and the nonelect, whosoever won't.—*H. W. Beecher.*

SARCASM.—Sarcasm is the language of the devil; for which reason I have long since as good as renounced it.—*Carlyle.*

Sarcasm poisons reproof.—*E. Wigglesworth.*

A sneer is the weapon of the weak. Like other devil's weapons, it is always cunningly ready to our hand, and there is more poison in the handle than in the point.—*J. R. Lowell.*

At the best, sarcasms, bitter irony, scathing wit, are a sort of sword-play of the mind. You pink your adversary, and he is forthwith dead; and then you deserve to be hung for it.—*Bovee.*

He that cometh to seek after knowledge with a mind to scorn and censure shall be sure to find matter for his humor, but none for his instruction.—*Bacon.*

The arrows of sarcasm are barbed with contempt.—It is the sneer in the satire or ridicule that galls and wounds.—*W. Gladden.*

A true sarcasm is like a swordstick—it appears, at first sight, to be much more innocent than it really is, till, all of a sudden, there leaps something out of it—sharp and deadly and incisive—which makes you tremble and recoil.—*Sydney Smith.*

SATIETY.—Satiety comes of too frequent repetition; and he who will not give himself leisure to be thirsty can never find the true pleasure of drinking.—*Montaigne.*

The sweetest honey is loathsome in its own deliciousness, and in the taste confounds the appetite.—*Shakespeare.*

With much we surfeit; plenty makes us poor.—*Drayton.*

Some are cursed with the fulness of satiety; and how can they bear the ills of life, when its very pleasures fatigue them?—*Colton.*

The flower that we do not pluck is the only one that never loses its beauty or its fragrance.—*W. R. Alger.*

The most voluptuous and loose person breathing, were he tied to follow his hawks and his hounds, his dice and his courtships every day, would find it the greatest torment and calamity that could befall him; he would fly to the mines and galleys for his recreation.—*South.*

A surfeit of the sweetest things the deepest loathing to the stomach brings. —*Shakespeare.*

To loathe the taste of sweetness, whereof little more than a little is by much too much.—*Shakespeare.*

Attainment is followed by neglect, possession by disgust, and the malicious remark of the Greek epigrammatist on marriage, may be applied to many another course of life, that its two days of happiness are the first and the last.— *Johnson.*

With pleasure drugged, he almost longed for woe.—*Byron.*

There is no sense of weariness like that which closes a day of eager and unintermitted pursuit of pleasure.—The apple is eaten and the core sticks in the throat.—Expectation has given way to ennui, and appetite to satiety.—*Bovee.*

Pleasure, when it is a man's chief purpose, disappoints itself; and constant application to it palls the faculty of enjoying it, and leaves the sense of our inability for what we wish, with a disrelish of everything else. The intermediate seasons of the man of pleasure are more heavy than one would impose upon the vilest criminal.—*Steele.*

SATIRE.—Satire is a sort of glass, wherein beholders generally discover everybody's face but their own; which is the chief reason for the reception it meets in the world, and that so very few are offended with it.—*Swift.*

Satire should not be like a saw, but a sword; it should cut, and not mangle.

Satire is a composition of salt and mercury; and it depends upon the different mixture and preparation of those ingredients, that it comes out a noble medicine, or a rank poison.—*Jeffrey.*

Lampoons and satires, that are written with wit and spirit, are like poisoned darts, which not only inflict a wound, but make it incurable.—*Addison.*

Satires and lampoons on particular people circulate more by giving copies in confidence to the friends of the parties, than by printing them.—*Sheridan.*

A satirist of true genius, who is warmed by a generous indignation of vice, and whose censures are conducted by candor and truth, merits the applause of every friend to virtue. He is a sort of supplement to the legislative authority of his country, assisting the unavoidable defects of all legal institutions for the regulation of manners, and striking terror, even where the divine prohibitions themselves are held in contempt.— *Crousaz.*

Satire should, like a polished razor, keen, wound with a touch that is scarcely felt or seen.—*Lady M. W. Montague.*

No sword bites so fiercely as an evil tongue.—*Sir P. Sidney.*

A satire should expose nothing but what is corrigible, and should make a due discrimination between those that are, and those that are not the proper objects of it.—*Addison.*

In fashionable circles, satire which attacks the fault, rather than the person, is unwelcome; while that which attacks the person and spares the fault is always acceptable.—*Richter.*

A little wit and a great deal of ill nature will furnish a man for satire; but the greatest instance and value of wit is to commend well.—*Tillotson.*

Satire! thou shining supplement of public laws.—*Young.*

By satire kept in awe, they shrink from ridicule, though not from law.— *Byron.*

To lash the vices of a guilty age.— *Churchill.*

Of a bitter satirist—Swift, for instance —it might be said, that the person or thing on which his satire fell shrivelled up as if the devil had spit on it.—*Hawthorne.*

It is as hard to satirize well a man of distinguished vices, as to praise well a man of distinguished virtues.—*Swift.*

Satirical writers and talkers are not half so clever as they think themselves, or as they are thought to be.—They do winnow the corn, it is true, but it is to feed on the chaff.—It requires talent and generosity to find out talent and generosity in others, but only self-conceit and malice are needed to discover or imagine faults.—*Sharpe.*

Arrows of satire, feathered with wit, and wielded with sense, fly home to their mark.—*C. Simmons.*

Of satires I think as Epictetus did: "If evil be said of thee, and if it be true, correct thyself; if it be a lie, laugh at it." By dint of time and experience I have learned to be a good post-horse; I go through my appointed daily stage, and care not for the curs who bark at me along the road.—*Frederick the Great.*

It is much easier for an ill-natured, than for a good-natured man to be witty; but the most gifted men are the least addicted to depreciate either friends or foes.—Your shrewd, sly, wit-speaking fellow is generally a shallow personage, and frequently he is as venomous and false when he flatters as when he reviles. —*Sharp.*

As men neither fear nor respect what has been made contemptible, all honor to him who makes oppression laughable as well as detestable.—Armies cannot protect it then; and walls that have remained impenetrable to cannon have fallen before a roar of laughter or a hiss of contempt.—*E. P. Whipple.*

We smile at the satire expended upon the follies of others, but we forget to weep at our own.—*Mad. Necker.*

In the present state of the world it is difficult not to write lampoons.—*Juvenal.*

The most annoying of all public reformers is the personal satirist. Though he may be considered by some few as a useful member of society, yet he is only ranked with the hangmen, whom we tolerate because he executes the judgment we abhor to do ourselves, and avoid with a natural detestation of his office. The pen of the one and the cord of the other are inseparable in our minds. —*Jane Porter.*

Viewed in its happiest form satire has one defect which seems to be incurable, —its uniformity of censure. Bitterness scarcely admits those fine transitions which make the harmony of a composition. Aquafortis bites a plate all over alike. The satirist is met by the difficulty of the etcher.—*Willmott.*

Curst be the verse how well so'er it flow, that tends to make one worthy man my foe, gives virtue scandal, innocence a fear, or from the soft-eyed virgin steals a tear.—*Pope.*

The end of satire is the amendment of vices by correction, and he who writes honestly is no more an enemy to the offender, than the physician is to the patient when he prescribes harsh remedies.—*Dryden.*

SAVING. — (See "ECONOMY," "THRIFT," "FRUGALITY," etc.)

SCANDAL.—(See "SLANDER.")

Believe that story false that ought not to be true.—*Sheridan.*

Number among your worst enemies the hawker of malicious rumors and unexplored anecdote.—*Lavater.*

Scandal is a never-failing vehicle for dulness. The true-born Englishman had died silently among the grocers and trunk-makers, if the libeller had not helped off the poet.—*I. B. Brown.*

"No one," says Jerome, "loves to tell a tale of scandal except to him who loves to hear it." Learn, then, to rebuke and check the detracting tongue by showing that you do not listen to it with pleasure. Never make your ear the grave of another's good name.

Many a wretch had rid on a hurdle who has done much less mischief than utterers of forged tales, coiners of scandal, and clippers of reputation.—*Sheridan.*

Without the consent of the world, a scandal doth not go deep; it is only a slight stroke upon the injured party, and returneth with the greater force upon those that gave it.—*Saville.*

How large a portion of chastity is sent out of the world by distant hints,—nodded away and cruelly winked into suspicion, by the envy of those who are past all temptation of it themselves. How often does the reputation of a helpless creature bleed by a report which the party propagating it beholds with pity, and is sorry for it, and hopes it may not be true, but in the meantime gives it her pass, that at least it may have fair play in the world,—to be believed or not, according to the charity of those into whose hands it shall happen to fall.—*Sterne.*

The tale-bearer and the tale-hearer should be both hanged up, back to back, one by the tongue, the other by the ear.—*South.*

If there is any person to whom you feel dislike, that is the person of whom you ought never to speak.—*Cecil.*

Great numbers of moderately good people think it fine to talk scandal; they regard it as a sort of evidence of their own goodness.—*F. W. Faber.*

The improbability of a malicious story serves to help forward the currency of it, because it increases the scandal. So that, in such instances, the world is like the one who said he believed some things because they were absurd and impossible. —*Sterne.*

Scandal breeds hatred; hatred begets division; division makes faction, and faction brings ruin.—*Quarles.*

If hours did not hang heavy what would become of scandal?—*Bancroft.*

I never listen to calumnies, because, if they are untrue, I run the risk of being deceived, and if they are true, of hating persons not worth thinking about.—*Montesquieu.*

There are a set of malicious, prating, prudent gossips, both male and female, who murder characters to kill time; and will rob a young fellow of his good name before he has years to know the value of it.—*Sheridan.*

Scandal is the sport of its authors, the dread of fools, and the contempt of the wise.—*W. B. Clulow.*

In scandal, as is robbery, the receiver is always as bad as the thief.—*Chesterfield.*

There is a lust in a man, no charm can tame, of loudly publishing his neighbor's shame; on eagle's wings immortal scandals fly, while virtuous actions are but born and die.—*Harvey.*

A cruel story runs on wheels, and every hand oils the wheels as they run. —*George Eliot.*

As to people saying a few idle words about us, we must not mind that, any

more than the old church steeple minds the rooks cawing about it.—*George Eliot.*

Praise undeserved is scandal in disguise.—*Pope.*

The greatest scandal waits on greatest state.—*Shakespeare.*

SCEPTICISM.—Scepticism is slow suicide.—*Emerson.*

The great trouble with the scepticism of the age is, that it is not thorough enough.—It questions everything but its own foundations.—*J. M. Gibson.*

Free thinkers are generally those who never think at all.—*Sterne.*

Sceptics are generally ready to believe anything provided it is only sufficiently improbable; it is at matters of fact that such people stumble.—*Von Knebel.*

I know not any crime so great a man could contrive to commit, as poisoning the sources of eternal truth.—*Johnson.*

I would rather dwell in the dim fog of superstition, than in air rarified to nothing by the air-pump of unbelief; in which the panting breast expires, vainly and convulsively gasping for breath.—*Richter.*

Men are ready to believe everything when they believe nothing.—They have diviners when they cease to have prophets; witchcraft when they cease to have religious ceremonies; and they open the caves of sorcery when they shut the temples of the Lord.—*Chateaubriand.*

The sceptic, in a vain attempt to be wise beyond what is permitted to man, plunges into a darkness more deplorable, and a blindness more incurable than that of the common herd, whom he despises, and would fain instruct. When he plunges into the depths of infidelity, like the miser who leaps from the shipwreck, he will find that the treasures he bears about him will only sink him the deeper in the abyss.—*Colton.*

Imperfect knowledge is the parent of doubt: thorough and honest research dispels it.—*Tryon Edwards.*

Scepticism has never founded empires, established principles, or changed the world's heart.—The great doers in history have always been men of faith.— *E. H. Chapin.*

The sceptical writers are a set whose

business it is to prick holes in the fabric of knowledge wherever it is weak and faulty; and when these places are properly repaired, the whole building becomes more firm and solid than it was before.—*Reid.*

Skepticism becomes the mark and even the pose of the educated mind. It is no longer directed against this and that article of the older creeds but is rather a bias against any kind of far-reaching ideas, and a denial of systematic participation on the part of such ideas in the intelligent direction of affairs.—*John Dewey.*

Every persón who has mastered a profession is a sceptic concerning it.— *G. Bernard Shaw.*

SCIENCE.—Science is the topography of ignorance.—*O. W. Holmes.*

I have come to have very profound and deep-rooted doubts whether Science, as practiced at present by the human race, will ever do anything to make the world a better and happier place to live in, or will ever stop contributing to our general misery.—*Hendrik Van Loon.*

A single mind can acquire a fair knowledge of the whole field of science, and find plenty of time to spare for ordinary human affairs. Not many people take the trouble to do so. But without a knowledge of science one cannot understand current events. That is why our modern literature and art are mostly so unreal.—*J. B. S. Haldane.*

Physical science reads through its sense of touch like a blind man, and the supply of books in braille type on the spiritual life is very small.—*Austin O'Malley.*

Those who speak of the incompatibility of science and religion either make science say that which it never said or make religion say that which it never taught.—*Pope Pius XI.*

Men sometimes speak as though the progress of science must necessarily be a boon to mankind, but that, I fear, is one of the comfortable nineteenth century delusions which our more disillusioned age must discard.—*Bertrand Russell.*

The Sciences are beneficent. They prevent men from thinking.—*Anatole France.*

If a man hasn't got plenty of good common sense, the more science he has the worse for his patient.—*O. W. Holmes.*

The intellectual content of religions has always finally adapted itself to scientific and social conditions after they have become clear. . . . For this reason I do not think that those who are concerned · about the future of a religious attitude should trouble themselves about the conflict of science with traditional doctrines.—*John Dewey.*

In the scientific world I find just that disinterested devotion to great ends that I hope will spread at last through the entire range of human activity.—*H. G. Wells.*

If rational men cooperated and used their scientific knowledge to the full, they could now secure the economic welfare of all.—*Bertrand Russell.*

The most beautiful thing we can experience is the mysterious. It is the source of all true art and science. He to whom this emotion is a stranger, who can no longer pause to wonder and stand rapt in awe, is as good as dead: his eyes are closed. . . . To know that what is impenetrable to us really exists, manifesting itself as the highest wisdom and the most radiant beauty which our dull faculties can comprehend only in their most primitive forms—this knowledge, this feeling, is at the center of true religiousness. In this sense, and in this sense only, I belong in the ranks of devoutly religious men.—*Albert Einstein.*

In praising science, it does not follow that we must adopt the very poor philosophies which scientific men have constructed. In philosophy they have much more to learn than to teach.—*Dean Inge.*

Science is organized knowledge.— *Herbert Spencer.*

Great discoveries and improvements invariably involve the co-operation of many minds. I may be given credit for having blazed the trail but when I look at the subsequent developments I feel the credit is due to others rather than to myself.—*Alexander Graham Bell.*

Let us not fear that the issues of natural science shall be scepticism or anarchy.—Through all God's works there runs a beautiful harmony.—The remotest truth in his universe is linked to that which lies nearest the throne.—*E. H. Chapin.*

As knowledge advances, science ceases to scoff at religion; and religion ceases to frown on science. The hour of mockery by the one, and of reproof by the other, is passing away. Henceforth, they will dwell together in unity and good-will. They will mutually illustrate the wisdom, power, and grace of God. Science will adorn and enrich religion; and religion will ennoble and sanctify science.

Science—in other words, knowledge—is not the enemy of religion; for, if so, then religion would mean ignorance; but it is often the antagonist of school-divinity.—*O. W. Holmes.*

Science ever has been, and ever must be, the safeguard of religion.—*Sir David Brewster.*

Human science is an uncertain guess. —*Prior.*

It has been said that science is opposed to, and in conflict with revelation. But the history of the former shows that the greater its progress, and the more accurate its investigations and results, the more plainly it is seen not only not to clash with the latter, but in all things to confirm it. The very sciences from which objections have been brought against religion have, by their own progress, removed those objections, and in the end furnished full confirmation of the inspired Word of God.—*Tryon Edwards.*

Twin-sister of natural and revealed religion, and of heavenly birth, science will never belie her celestial origin, nor cease to sympathize with all that emanates from the same pure home. Human ignorance and prejudice may for a time seem to have divorced what God has joined together; but human ignorance and prejudice shall at length pass away, and then science and religion shall be seen blending their particolored rays into one beautiful bow of light, linking heaven to earth and earth to heaven.—*R. D. Hitchcock.*

It was an admirable reply of a converted astronomer, who, when interrogated concerning his comparative estimate of religion and the science he had formely idolized, answered, "I am now bound for heaven, and I take the stars in my way."

Science when well-digested is nothing but good sense and reason.—*Stanislaus.*

Learning is the dictionary, but sense the grammar of science.—*Sterne.*

The sciences are of sociable disposition, and flourish best in the neighborhood of each other; nor is there any branch of learning but may be helped and improved by assistance drawn from other arts.—*Blackstone.*

Science surpasses the old miracles of mythology.—*Emerson.*

Art and science have their meeting point in method.—*Bulwer.*

In my investigation of natural science, I have always found that whenever I can meet with anything in the Bible on my subject, it always affords me a firm platform on which to stand.—*Lieut. Maury.*

I will frankly tell you that my experience in prolonged scientific investigations convinces me that a belief in God—a God who is behind and within the chaos of vanishing points of human knowledge—adds a wonderful stimulus to the man who attempts to penetrate into the regions of the unknown.—*Agassiz.*

The person who thinks there can be any real conflict between science and religion must be either very young in science or very ignorant in religion.—*Prof. Henry.*

Science is but a mere heap of facts, not a golden chain of truths, if we refuse to link it to the throne of God.—*F. P. Cobbe.*

Every great scientific truth goes through three stages.—First, people say it conflicts with the Bible.—Next they say it had been discovered before.—Lastly, they say they always believed it.—*Agassiz.*

There are hosts of men, of the profoundest thought, who find nothing in the disclosures of science to shake their faith in the eternal virtues of reason and religion.—*George Ripley.*

God pity the man of science who believes in nothing but what he can prove by scientific methods; for if ever a human being needed divine pity he does.—*Dr. J. G. Holland.*

The study of science teaches young men to think, while study of the classics teaches them to express thought.—*J. S. Mill.*

What is the true end and aim of science but the discovery of the ultimate power—a seeking after God through the study of his ways?—*W. H. Furness.*

Science cannot determine origin, and so cannot determine destiny. As it presents only a sectional view of creation, it gives only a sectional view of everything in creation.—*T. T. Munger.*

Nothing tends so much to the corruption of science as to suffer it to stagnate; these waters must be troubled before they can exert their virtues.—*Burke.*

It is certain that a serious attention to the sciences and liberal arts softens and humanizes the temper, and cherishes those fine emotions in which true virtue and honor consist. It very rarely happens that a man of taste and learning is not, at least, an honest man, whatever frailties may attend him.—*Hume.*

When man seized the loadstone of science, the loadstar of superstition vanished in the clouds.—*W. R. Alger.*

Science is nothing but trained and organized common sense, differing from the latter only as a veteran may from a raw recruit, and its methods differ from those of common sense, only as the guardsman's cut and thrust differ from the manner in which a savage wields his club.—*Huxley.*

What are the sciences but maps of universal laws; and universal laws but the channels of universal power; and universal power but the outgoings of a supreme universal mind?—*E. Thomson.*

Our abiding belief is, that just as the workmen in the tunnel of St. Gothard, working from either end, met at last, to shake hands, in the very central root of the mountain, so the students of nature and the students of Christianity will yet join hands in the unity of reason and faith, in the heart of their deepest mysteries.—*L. Moss.*

Believe in God, and bid all knowledge God-speed; sooner or later the full harmony will reveal itself, and the

discords and contradictions disappear.

There can be no real conflict between science and the Bible—between nature and the Scriptures—the two books of the Great Author. Both are revelations made by him to man; the earlier telling of God-made harmonies coming up from the deep past, and rising to their height when man appeared; the later teaching man's relations to his Maker, and speaking of loftier harmonies in the eternal future.—*Prof. Dana.*

Science is but the statement of truth found out.

Godless science reads nature only as Milton's daughters did Hebrew, rightly syllabling the sentences, but utterly ignorant of the meaning.—*Coley.*

If the God of revelation is most appropriately worshipped in the temple of religion, the God of nature may be equally honored in the temple of science. Even from its lofty minarets the philosopher may summon the faithful to prayer, and the priest and sage exchange altars without the compromise of faith or knowledge.—*Sir David Brewster.*

Science corrects the old creeds, sweeps away, with every new perception, our infantile catechisms, and necessitates a faith commensurate with the grander orbits and universal laws which it discloses.—*Emerson.*

SCRIPTURES.—(See " BIBLE.")

SEA.—Praise the sea, but keep on the land.—*Herbert.*

Roll on, thou deep and dark blue ocean—roll, ten thousand fleets sweep over thee in vain; man marks the earth with ruin—his control stops with the shore; upon the watery plain the wrecks are all thy deed, nor doth remain a shadow of man's ravage, save his own, when, for a moment like a drop of rain, he sinks into thy depths with bubbling groan, without a grave, unknell'd, uncoffin'd, and unknown.—*Byron.*

The sea has been called deceitful and treacherous, but there lies in this trait only the character of a great natural power, which renews its strength, and, without reference to joy or sorrow, follows eternal laws which are imposed by a higher power.—*W. Humboldt.*

Surely oak and threefold brass surrounded his heart who first trusted a frail vessel to the merciless ocean. —*Horace.*

He that will learn to pray, let him go to sea.—*Herbert.*

The ocean's surfy, slow, deep, mellow voice is full of mystery and awe, moaning over the dead it holds in its bosom, or lulling them to unbroken slumbers in the chambers of its vasty depths. —*Haliburton.*

There is society where none intrudes, by the deep sea, and music in its roar. —*Byron.*

Whoever commands the sea, commands the trade, whoever commands the trade of the world, commands the riches of the world, and consequently the world itself.—*Sir W. Raleigh.*

Thou glorious mirror, where the Almighty's form glasses itself in tempests: in all time, calm or convulsed—in breeze, or gale, or storm, icing the pole, or in the torrid clime dark-heaving;—boundless, endless, and sublime—the image of eternity—the throne of the invisible; even from out thy slime the monsters of the deep are made; each zone obeys thee; thou goest forth, dread, fathomless, alone.—*Byron.*

Mystery of waters, never slumbering sea! impassioned orator, with lips sublime, whose waves are arguments to prove a God.—*R. Montgomery.*

SECRECY.—Secrecy has been well termed the soul of all great designs. Perhaps more has been effected by concealing our own intentions, than by discovering those of our enemy. But great men succeed in both.—*Colton.*

A proper secrecy is only the mystery of able men; mystery is the only secrecy of weak and cunning ones. —*Chesterfield.*

What is mine, even to my life, is hers I love; but the secret of my friend is not mine.—*Sir P. Sidney.*

Two may keep counsel, putting one away.—*Shakespeare.*

Talkers and futile persons, are commonly vain and credulous withal; for he that talketh what he knoweth will also talk what he knoweth not; therefore set it down, that a habit of secrecy is both politic and moral.—*Bacon.*

Secrets are so seldom kept, that it may be with some reason doubted, whether the quality of retention be generally bestowed, and whether a secret has not some subtile volatility by which it escapes imperceptibility, at the smallest vent, or some power of fermentation, by which it expands itself, so as to burst the heart that will not give it way.—*Johnson.*

If a fool knows a secret, he tells it because he is a fool: if a knave knows one, he tells it whenever it is his interest to tell it. But women and young men are very apt to tell what secrets they know, from the vanity of having been trusted. Trust none of these whenever you can help it.—*Chesterfield.*

He who trusts secrets to a servant makes him his master.—*Dryden.*

To tell our own secrets is generally folly, but that folly is without guilt; to communicate those with which we are intrusted is always treachery, and treachery for the most part combined with folly.—*Johnson.*

Trust no secrets to a friend, which, if reported, would bring infamy.—*Thales.*

Washington, having been asked by an officer on the morning of a battle, what were his plans for the day, replied in a whisper, Can you keep a secret? On being answered in the affirmative, the general added—so can I.

He deserves small trust who is not privy counsellor to himself.—*Ford.*

I have play'd the fool, the gross fool, to believe the bosom of a friend would hold a secret mine own could not contain.—*Massinger.*

How can we expect another to keep our secret if we cannot keep it ourselves?—*Rochefoucauld.*

The truly wise man should have no keeper of his secret but himself. —*Guizot.*

Who shall be true to us, when we are so unsecret to ourselves?—*Shakespeare.*

Three may keep a secret, if two of them are dead.—*Franklin.*

It is said that he or she who admits

the possession of a secret, has already half revealed it.—It is a great deal gained toward the acquisition of a treasure, to know exactly where it is.—*Simms.*

Secrecy is the chastity of friendship.—*Jeremy Taylor.*

Nothing is so oppressive as a secret.—It is difficult for ladies to keep it long; and I know, in this matter, a good number of men who are women.—*Fontaine.*

When a secret is revealed, it is the fault of the man who has intrusted it.—*Bruyère.*

A secret is too little for one, enough for two, and too much for three.—*Howell.*

Secrecy is best taught by commencing with ourselves.—*Chamfort.*

He that discovers himself till he hath made himself master of his desires, lays himself open to his own ruin, and makes himself a prisoner to his own tongue.—*Quarles.*

I will govern my life and my thoughts as if all the world were to see the one and to read the other; for what does it signify to make anything a secret to my neighbor, when to God all our privacies are open?—*Seneca.*

A resolution that is communicated is no longer within thy power; thy intentions become now the plaything of chance; he who would have his commands certainly carried out must take men by surprise.—*Goethe.*

A secret in his mouth is like a wild bird put into a cage; whose door no sooner opens, but it is out.—*Ben Jonson.*

He was a wise fellow, and had good discretion, that, being bid to ask what he would of the king, desired he might know none of his secrets.—*Shakespeare.*

To keep your secret is wisdom; but to expect others to keep it is folly.—*O. W. Holmes.*

A man is more faithful to the secret of another man than to his own; a woman, on the contrary, preserves her own secret better than that of another.—*Bruyère.*

Where secrecy or mystery begins, vice or roguery is not far off.—*Johnson.*

Fire that is closest kept burns most of all.—*Shakespeare.*

Secrecy is for the happy; misery, hopeless misery needs no veil; under a thousand suns it dares act openly.—*Schiller.*

People addicted to secrecy are so without knowing why; they are not so for cause, but for secrecy's sake.—*Hazlitt.*

Secrets with girls, like guns with boys, are never valued till they make a noise.—*Crabbe.*

Never confide your secrets to paper; it is like throwing a stone in the air, you do not know where it may fall.—*Calderon.*

Thou hast betrayed thy secret as a bird betrays her nest, by striving to conceal it.—*Longfellow.*

What thou seest speak of with caution.—*Solon.*

'Tis in my memory locked, and you yourself shall keep the key of it.—*Shakespeare.*

I vow and protest there's more plague than pleasure with a secret.—*Colman.*

Trust him not with your secrets, who, when left alone in your room, turns over your papers.—*Lavater.*

Conceal thy domestic ills.—*Thales.*

When two friends part they should lock up one another's secrets, and interchange their keys.—*Feltham.*

There is as much responsibility in imparting your own secrets, as in keeping those of your neighbor.—*Darley.*

None are so fond of secrets as those who do not mean to keep them. Such persons covet secrets as spendthrifts do money, for the purpose of circulation.—*Colton.*

SECTS.—Sects and Christians that desire to be known by the undue prominence of doing some single feature of Christianity, are imperfect just in proportion to the distinctness of their peculiarities. The power of Christian truth is in its unity and sympathy, and not in the saliency or brilliancy of any of its special doctrines. The spirit of Christ is the great essential truth.—*H. W. Beecher.*

The effective strength of sects is not

to be ascertained merely by counting heads.—*Macaulay.*

It is written, that the coat of our Saviour was without seam; whence some would infer, that there should be no division in the church of Christ. It should be so indeed; yet seams in the same cloth neither hurt the garment, nor misbecome it; and not only seams, but schisms will be while men are fallible.—*Milton.*

I do not want the walls of separation between different orders of Christians to be destroyed, but only lowered, that we may shake hands a little easier over them.—*Rowland Hill.*

SELF-APPROBATION.—We follow the world in approving others; we go far before it in approving ourselves.—*Colton.*

A man's first care should be to avoid the reproaches of his own heart; his next, to escape the censures of the world. If the last interferes with the former, it ought to be entirely neglected; but otherwise there cannot be a greater satisfaction to an honest mind, than to see those approbations which it gives itself, seconded by the applauses of the public. A man is more sure of his conduct, when the verdict which he passes upon his own behavior is thus warranted and confirmed by the opinion of all that know him.—*Addison.*

One self-approving hour whole years outweighs of stupid starers, and of loud huzzas.—*Pope.*

Self-approbation, when founded in truth and a good conscience, is a source of some of the purest joys known to man.—*C. Simmons.*

Be displeased with what thou art, if thou desirest to attain to what thou art not; for where thou hast pleased thyself, there thou abidest, and if thou sayest I have enough, thou perishest.—*Augustine.*

SELF-CONCEIT.—He who gives himself airs of importance, exhibits the credentials of impotence.—*Lavater.*

The sluggard is wiser in his own conceit than seven men who can render a reason. He who has no inclination to learn more will be very apt to think that he knows enough. Nor is it wonderful that he should pride himself in the abundance of his wisdom, with whom

every wavering thought, every half-formed imagination, passes for a fixed and substantial truth. Obstinacy also, which makes him unable to discover his mistakes, makes him believe himself unable to commit them.—*Powell.*

There are few people who are more often in the wrong than those who cannot endure to be thought so.—*Rochefoucauld.*

All men who know not where to look for truth save in the narrow well of self, will find their own image at the bottom and mistake it for what they are seeking.—*J. R. Lowell.*

The weakest spot in every man is where he thinks himself to be the wisest. —*Emmons.*

Conceited men are a harmless kind of creatures, who, by their overweening self-respect, relieve others from the duty of respecting them at all.—*H. W. Beecher.*

Of all the follies incident to youth, there are none which blast their prospects, or render them more contemptible, than self-conceit, presumption, and obstinacy. By checking progress in improvement, they fix one in long immaturity, and produce irreparable mischief.—*Blair.*

He that fancies himself very enlightened, because he sees the deficiencies of others, may be very ignorant, because he has not studied his own.—*Bulwer.*

I look upon the too good opinion that man has of himself, as the nursing mother of all false opinions, both public and private.—*Montaigne.*

When a person feels disposed to overestimate his own importance, let him remember that mankind got along very well before his birth, and that in all probability they will get along very well after his death.

A wise man knows his own ignorance; a fool thinks he knows everything.—*C. Simmons.*

The proportion of those who think is extremely small; yet every individual flatters himself that he is one of the number.—*Colton.*

We are very apt to be full of ourselves, instead of Him that made what we so much value, and but for whom we have no reason to value ourselves. For we have nothing that we can call our own, no, not ourselves; for we are all but tenants, and at will too, of the great Lord of ourselves, and of this great farm, the world that we live upon.—*Penn.*

In one thing men of all ages are alike: they have believed obstinately in themselves.—*Jacobi.*

Self-conceit is a weighty quality, and will sometimes bring down the scale when there is nothing else in it. It magnifies a fault beyond proportion, and swells every omission into an outrage.—*Jeremy Collier.*

The less a man thinks or knows about his virtues the better we like him.—*Emerson.*

Prize not thyself by what thou hast, but by what thou art; he that values a jewel by its golden frame, or a book by its silver clasps, or a man by his vast estate, errs.—*Quarles.*

Many men spend their lives in gazing at their own shadows, and so dwindle away into shadows thereof.—*Hare.*

Even dress is apt to inflame a man's opinion of himself.—*Home.*

Whenever nature leaves a hole in a person's mind, she generally plasters it over with a thick coat of self-conceit. —*Longfellow.*

In the same degree that we overrate ourselves, we shall underrate others; for injustice allowed at home is not likely to be corrected abroad.—*Washington Allston.*

Wouldest thou not be thought a fool in another's conceit, be not wise in thy own: he that trusts to his own wisdom, proclaims his own folly: he is truly wise, and shall appear so, that hath folly enough to be thought not worldly wise, or wisdom enough to see his own folly. —*Quarles.*

He who is always his own counsellor will often have a fool for his client. —*Hunter.*

Oftentimes nothing profits more than self-esteem, grounded on what is just and right.—*Milton.*

SELF-CONTROL.—If you would learn self-mastery, begin by yielding yourself to the One Great Master.—*Lobstein.*

Conquer thyself. Till thou hast done this, thou art but a slave; for it is almost as well to be subjected to another's appetite as to thine own.—*Burton.*

The command of one's self is the greatest empire a man can aspire unto, and consequently, to be subject to our own passions is the most grievous slavery. He who best governs himself is best fitted to govern others.

He who reigns within himself and rules his passions, desires and fears is more than a king.—*Milton.*

For want of self-restraint many men are engaged all their lives in fighting with difficulties of their own making, and rendering success impossible by their own cross-grained ungentleness; whilst others, it may be much less gifted, make their way and achieve success by simple patience, equanimity, and self-control.—*Smiles.*

Self-government is, indeed, the noblest rule on earth; the object of a loftier ambition than the possession of crowns or sceptres. The truest conquest is where the soul is bringing every thought into captivity to the obedience of Christ. The monarch of his own mind is the only real potentate.—*Caird.*

The man whom Heaven appoints to govern others, should himself first learn to bend his passions to the sway of reason.—*Thomson.*

To rule self and subdue our passions is the more praiseworthy because so few know how to do it.—*Guiccardini.*

Every temptation that is resisted, every noble aspiration that is encouraged, every sinful thought that is repressed, every bitter word that is withheld, adds its little item to the impetus of that great movement which is bearing humanity onward toward a richer life and higher character.—*Fiske.*

Most powerful is he who has himself in his own power.—*Seneca.*

A father inquires whether his boy can construe Homer, or understand Horace; but how seldom does he ask, or examine, or think whether he can restrain his passions,—whether he is grateful, generous, humane, compassionate, just, and benevolent.—*Lady Hervey.*

What is the best government? — That which teaches us to govern ourselves. —*Goethe.*

He that lays down precepts for governing our lives and moderating our passions, obliges humanity not only in the present, but for all future generations.—*Seneca*.

Those who can command themselves, command others.—*Hazlitt*.

More dear in the sight of God and His angels than any other conquest is the conquest of self.—*A. P. Stanley*.

Let not any one say that he cannot govern his passions, nor hinder them from breaking out and carrying him to action; for what he can do before a prince or a great man, he can do alone, or in the presence of God if he will. —*Locke*.

Self-control is promoted by humility. Pride is a fruitful source of uneasiness. It keeps the mind in disquiet. Humility is the antidote to this evil.—*Mrs. Sigourney*.

I will have a care of being a slave to myself, for it is a perpetual, a shameful, and the heaviest of all servitudes; and this may be done by uncontrolled desires.—*Seneca*.

The constancy of sages is nothing but the art of locking up their agitation in their hearts.—*Rochefoucauld*.

One of the most important, but one of the most difficult things for a powerful mind is, to be its own master. A pond may lie quiet in a plain; but a lake wants mountains to compass and hold it in.—*Addison*.

He who would govern others should first be master of himself.—*Massinger*.

He is a fool who cannot be angry; but he is a wise man who will not. —*Old Proverb*.

A man must first govern himself, ere he be fit to govern a family; and his family, ere he be fit to bear the government in the commonwealth.—*Sir W. Raleigh*.

Real glory springs from the silent conquest of ourselves; without that the conqueror is only the first slave. —*Thomson*.

No conflict is so severe as his who labors to subdue himself.—*Thomas à Kempis*.

Do you want to know the man against whom you have most reason to guard yourself? Your looking-glass will give you a very fair likeness of his face.—*Whately*.

Over the times thou hast no power.— To redeem a world sunk in dishonesty has not been given thee. Solely over one man therein thou hast a quite absolute, uncontrollable power.—Him redeem and make honest.—*Carlyle*.

No man is free who cannot command himself.—*Pythagoras*.

It is the man who is cool and collected, who is master of his countenance, his voice, his actions, his gestures, of every part, who can work upon others at his pleasure.—*Diderot*.

Wouldst thou have thy flesh obey thy spirit? Then let thy spirit obey thy God. Thou must be governed, that thou may'st govern.—*Augustine*.

Better conquest never canst thou make, than warn thy constant and thy nobler parts against giddy, loose suggestions.—*Shakespeare*.

Who to himself is law, no law doth need.—*Chapman*.

When Alexander had subdued the world, and wept that none were left to dispute his arms, his tears were an involuntary tribute to a monarchy that he knew not, man's empire over himself. —*Jane Porter*.

No one who cannot master himself is worthy to rule, and only he can rule. —*Goethe*.

May I govern my passions with absolute sway, and grow wiser and better as life wears away.—*Watts*.

The most precious of all possessions, is power over ourselves; power to withstand trial, to bear suffering, to front danger; power over pleasure and pain; power to follow our convictions, however resisted by menace and scorn; the power of calm reliance in scenes of darkness and storms. He that has not a mastery over his inclinations; he that knows not how to resist the importunity of present pleasure or pain, for the sake of what reason tells him is fit to be done, wants the true principle of virtue and industry, and is in danger of never being good for anything.—*Locke*.

SELF-DECEPTION.—No man was ever so much deceived by another, as by himself.—*Gréville*.

It many times falls out, that we deem ourselves much deceived in others, because we first deceived ourselves.—*Sir P. Sidney.*

Nothing is so easy as to deceive one's self, for what we wish we readily believe; but such expectations are often inconsistent with the reality of things.—*Demosthenes.*

The coward reckons himself cautious; the miser thinks himself frugal.—*Home.*

Every man is his own greatest dupe.—*W. R. Alger.*

Who has deceived thee so often as thyself?—*Franklin.*

The greatest of fools is he who imposes on himself, and in his greatest concerns thinks he knows that which he has least studied, and of which he is profoundly ignorant.—*Shaftesbury.*

The first and worst of all frauds is to cheat one's self. All sin is easy after that.—*Bailey.*

From the beginning of the world to this day there never was any great villainy acted by men but it was in the strength of some great fallacy put upon their minds by a false representation of evil for good, or good for evil.—*South.*

To be deceived by our enemies or betrayed by our friends is insupportable; yet by ourselves we are often content to be so treated.—*Rochefoucauld.*

We cheat ourselves in order to enjoy a quiet conscience, without possessing virtue.—*Lambert.*

Many a man has a kind of kaleidoscope, where the broken bits of glass are his own merits and fortunes; and they fall into harmonious arrangements and delight him, often most mischievously, and to his ultimate detriment; but they are a present pleasure.—*A. Helps.*

SELF-DENIAL.—The worst education which teaches self-denial, is better than the best which teaches everything else and not that.—*Sterling.*

Every personal consideration that we allow, costs us heavenly state. We sell the thrones of angels for a short and turbulent pleasure.—*Emerson.*

Teach self-denial, and make its practice pleasurable, and you can create for the world a destiny more sublime than

ever issued from the brain of the wildest dreamer.—*Walter Scott.*

Shall we call ourselves benevolent, when the gifts we bestow do not cost us a single privation?—*Degerando.*

The secret of all success is to know how to deny yourself.—Prove that you can control yourself, and you are an educated man; and without this all other education is good for nothing.

To you self-denial may only mean weariness, restraint, ennui; but it means, also, love, perfection, sanctification.

Of all sorts of earthly good the price is self-denial.—The lower must be sacrificed for the greater; the coarser give place to the finer.—Every step of our progress toward success is a sacrifice.—We gain by losing; grow by dwindling; live by dying.—*R. D. Hitchcock.*

'Tis much the doctrine of the times that men should not please themselves, but deny themselves everything they take delight in; not look upon beauty, wear no good clothes, eat no good meat, etc., which seems the greatest accusation that can be upon the Maker of all good things. If they are not to be used, why did God make them?—*Selden.*

The more a man denies himself, the more he shall obtain from God.—*Horace.*

There never did, and never will exist anything permanently noble and excellent in the character which is a stranger to the exercise of resolute self-denial.—*Walter Scott.*

When you give, take to yourself no credit for generosity, unless you deny yourself something in order that you may give.—*Henry Taylor.*

Self-abnegation, that rare virtue, that good men preach and good women practice.—*O. W. Holmes.*

In vain do they talk of happiness who never subdued an impulse in obedience to a principle.—He who never sacrificed a present to a future good, or a personal to a general one, can speak of happiness only as the blind speak of color.—*H. Mann.*

Self-denial is an excellent guard of virtue, for it is safer and wiser to abate somewhat of our lawful enjoyments than to gratify our desires to the utmost of what is permitted, lest the bent of nature toward pleasure hurry us further.—*Townson.*

He is one of the noblest conquerors who carries on a successful warfare against his own appetites and passions, and has them under wise and full control.—*Tryon Edwards.*

One secret act of self-denial, one sacrifice of inclination to duty, is worth all the mere good thoughts, warm feelings, passionate prayers in which idle people indulge themselves.—*J. H. Newman.*

Self-denial does not belong to religion as characteristic of it; it belongs to human life.—The lower nature must always be denied when you are trying to rise to a higher sphere.—It is no more necessary to be self-denying to be a Christian, than it is to be an artist, or an honest man, or a man at all in distinction from a brute.—Of all joyous experiences there are none like those which spring from true religion.—*H. W. Beecher.*

Whoever will labor to get rid of self, to deny himself according to the instructions of Christ, strikes at once at the root of every evil, and finds the germ of every good.—*Fénelon.*

They that deny themselves for Christ, shall enjoy themselves in Christ.—*J. M. Mason.*

One never knows himself till he has denied himself.—The altar of sacrifice is the touchstone of character.—*O. P. Gifford.*

Sacrifice alone, bare and unrelieved, is ghastly, unnatural, and dead; but self-sacrifice, illuminated by love, is warm and life; it is the death of Christ, the life of God, and the blessedness and only proper life of man.—*F. W. Robertson.*

Contempt of all outward things that come in competition with duty fulfils the ideal of human greatness.—It is sanctioned by conscience, that universal and eternal lawgiver, whose chief principle is, that everything must be yielded up for right.—*Channing.*

That which especially distinguishes a high order of man from a lower, and which constitutes human goodness and nobleness, is self-forgetfulness, self-sacrifice, the disregard of personal pleas-

ure, personal indulgence, personal advantage, remote or present, because some other line of conduct is more right.—*J. A. Froude.*

The first lesson in Christ's school is self-denial.—*M. Henry.*

Self-denial is the result of a calm, deliberate, invincible attachment to the highest good, flowing forth in the voluntary renunciation of everything inconsistent with the glory of God or the good of our fellow-men.—*G. Spring.*

The very act of faith by which we receive Christ is an act of utter renunciation of self and all its works, as a ground of salvation.—It is really a denial of self, and a grounding of arms in the last citadel into which it can be driven, and is, in its principle, inclusive of every subsequent act of self-denial by which sin is forsaken or overcome.—*Mark Hopkins.*

Self-denial is indispensable to a strong character, and the loftiest kind thereof comes only of a religious stock—from consciousness of obligation and dependence on God.—*Theodore Parker.*

Brave conquerors! for so you are, that war against your own affections and the huge army of the world's desires.—*Shakespeare.*

Self-denial is a kind of holy association with God; and by making him your partner interests him in all your happiness.—*Boyle.*

SELF-EXAMINATION. — Observe thyself as thy greatest enemy would do, so shalt thou be thy greatest friend.—*Jeremy Taylor.*

The superior man will watch over himself when he is alone. He examines his heart that there may be nothing wrong there, and that he may have no cause of dissatisfaction with himself.—*Confucius.*

We should every night call ourselves to an account: What infirmity have I mastered to-day? what passions opposed? what temptation resisted? what virtue acquired? Our vices will abate of themselves if they be brought every day to the shrift.—*Seneca.*

Think not rightly to examine yourself by looking only to your own inner motives and feelings, which are the hardest of all things to analyze if looked at in the abstract, and apart from outward actions. But ask, "Do I believe all that God teaches, and endeavor to do all that God commands?" For in this is the evidence of true love to him.—*Tryon Edwards.*

It belongs to every large nature, when it is not under the immediate power of some strong unquestioning emotion, to suspect itself, and doubt the truth of its own impressions, conscious of possibilities beyond its own horizon.—*George Eliot.*

In self-examination, take no account of yourself by your thoughts and resolutions in the days of religion and solemnity, but examine how it is with you in the days of ordinary conversation and in the circumstances of secular employment.—*Jeremy Taylor.*

Let not sleep fall upon thy eyes till thou hast thrice reviewed the transactions of the past day. Where have I turned aside from rectitude? What have I been doing? What have I left undone, which I ought to have done? Begin thus from the first act, and proceed; and, in conclusion, at the ill which thou hast done, be troubled, and rejoice for the good.—*Pythagoras.*

If any speak ill of thee, fly home to thy own conscience and examine thy heart. If thou art guilty, it is a just correction; if not guilty, it is a fair instruction.—*Herbert.*

Never lose sight of this important truth, that no one can be truly great until he has gained a knowledge of himself, a knowledge which can only be acquired by occasional retirement.—*Zimmermann.*

If thou seest anything in thyself which may make thee proud, look a little further and thou shalt find enough to humble thee; if thou be wise, view the peacock's feathers with his feet, and weigh thy best parts with thy imperfections.—*Quarles.*

I will chide no breather in the world but myself, against whom I know most faults.—*Shakespeare.*

When you descant on the faults of others, consider whether you be not guilty of the same. To gain knowledge of ourselves, the best way is to convert the imperfections of others into a mirror for discovering our own.—*Home.*

I study myself more than any other subject; it is my metaphysic, and my physic.—*Montaigne.*

Inspect the neighborhood of thy life; every shelf, every nook of thine abode. —*Richter.*

Never let us be discouraged with ourselves. It is not when we are conscious of our faults that we are the most wicked; on the contrary, we are less so. We see by a brighter light; and let us remember for our consolation, that we never perceive our sins till we begin to cure them.—*Fénelon.*

Though not always called upon to condemn ourselves, it is always safe to suspect ourselves.—*Whately.*

It is pretty safe to presume that about all the glaring effects or petty weaknesses which we are looking for in others may be found in ourselves, with a little careful investigation.

Go to your bosom, knock there and ask your heart what it doth know that is like my brother's fault; if it confess a natural guiltiness, such as his is, let it not sound a thought upon your tongue against my brother.—*Shakespeare.*

How shall we learn to know ourselves? By reflection? Never; but only through action. Strive to do thy duty; then shalt thou know what is in thee.—*Goethe.*

In order to judge of the inside of others, study your own; for men in general are very much alike, and though one has one prevailing passion, and another has another, yet their operations are much the same; and whatever engages or disgusts, pleases, or offends you in others will engage, disgust, please or offend others in you.—*Chesterfield.*

Of all exercises there are none of so much importance, or so immediately our concern, as those which let us into the knowledge of our own nature. Others may exercise the understanding or amuse the imagination; but these only can improve the heart and form the human mind to wisdom.—*Bp. Warburton.*

SELF-IMPROVEMENT.—That discipline which corrects the eagerness of worldly passions, which fortifies the heart with virtuous principles, which enlightens the mind with useful knowledge, and furnishes to it matter of enjoyment from within itself, is of more consequence to real felicity than all the provisions which we can make of the goods of fortune.—*Blair.*

The best rules to form a young man, are, to talk little, to hear much, to reflect alone upon what has passed in company, to distrust one's own opinions, and value others that deserve it. —*Sir W. Temple.*

Self-inspection—the best cure for self-esteem.

By all means sometimes be alone; salute thyself; see what thy soul doth wear; dare to look in thy chest, and tumble up and down what thou findest there.—*Wordsworth.*

You will find that the mere resolve not to be useless, and the honest desire to help other people, will, in the quickest and delicatest ways, improve yourself.—*Ruskin.*

Is it asked, how can the laboring man find time for self-culture? I answer, that an earnest purpose finds time, or makes it. It seizes on spare moments, and turns fragments to golden account. A man who follows his calling with industry and spirit, and uses his earnings economically, will always have some portion of the day at command. And it is astonishing how fruitful of improvement a short season becomes, when eagerly seized and faithfully used. It has often been observed, that those who have the most time at their disposal profit by it the least. A single hour in the day, steadily given to the study of some interesting subject, brings unexpected accumulations of knowledge.—*Channing.*

"Know thyself," said the old philosophy.—"Improve thyself," saith the new. —Our great object in time is not to waste our passions and gifts on the things external that we must leave behind, but that we cultivate within us all that we can carry into the eternal progress beyond.—*Bulwer.*

Be always displeased at what thou art, if thou desire to attain to what thou art not; for where thou hast pleased thyself there thou abidest.—*Quarles.*

It is a very serious duty, perhaps of all duties the most serious, to look into one's own character and conduct, and accurately read one's own heart. It is virtually looking into eternity, and all its vast and solemn realities, which must appear delightful or awful, according as the heart appears to be conformed or not conformed to God.—*Emmons.*

People seldom improve, when they have no other model but themselves to copy after.—*Goldsmith.*

Each year, one vicious habit rooted out in time ought to make the worst man good.—*Franklin.*

By these things examine thyself. By whose rules am I acting; in whose name; in whose strength; in whose glory? What faith, humility, self-denial, and love of God and to man have there been in all my actions?—*J. Mason.*

By undue and overstrained self-inspection the mind is apt to become morbid and depressed, and to breed scruples, which tease and harass without producing any real fruit. The man becomes a valetudinarian in religion, full of himself, his symptoms, his ailments, the delicacy of his moral health; and valetudinarians are always a plague, not only to themselves, but to everybody connected with them.—*Gouldburn.*

When a tradesman is about to weigh his goods, he first of all looks to his scales and sees that his weights are right. And so for all wise, or safe, or profitable self-examination, we are not to look to frames, or feelings, or to the conduct of others, but to God's word, which is the only true standard of decision.—*Tryon Edwards.*

SELFISHNESS.—Selfishness is that detestable vice which no one will forgive in others, and no one is without in himself.—*H. W. Beecher.*

One thing is clear to me, that no indulgence of passion destroys the spiritual nature so much as respectable selfishness.—*G. Macdonald.*

A man is called selfish, not for pursuing his own good, but for neglecting his neighbor's.—*Whately.*

He who lives only to benefit himself confers on the world a benefit when he dies.—*Tertullian.*

Show me the man who would go to heaven alone, and I will show you one who will never be admitted there.—*Feltham.*

How much that the world calls selfishness is only generosity with narrow walls—a too exclusive solicitude to maintain a wife in luxury, or make one's children rich.—*T. W. Higginson.*

Our infinite obligations to God do not fill our hearts half as much as a petty uneasiness of our own; nor his infinite perfections as much as our smallest wants.—*Hannah More.*

The essence of true nobility is neglect of self. Let the thought of self pass in, and the beauty of a great action is gone like the bloom from a soiled flower.—*J. A. Froude.*

The virtues are lost in self-interest as rivers are in the sea.—*Rochefoucauld.*

There are some tempers wrought up by habitual selfishness to an utter insensibility of what becomes of the fortunes of their fellow-creatures, as if they were not partakers of the same nature or had no lot or connection at all with the species.—*Sterne.*

He who makes an idol of his self-interest, will often make a martyr of his integrity.

Those who are most disinterested, and have the least of selfishness, have best materials for being happy.—*Mrs. Sigourney.*

There are too many who reverse both the principles and the practice of the apostle; they become all things to all men, not to serve others, but themselves; and they try all things only to hold fast that which is bad.—*Colton.*

So long as we are full of self we are shocked at the faults of others. Let us think often of our own sin, and we shall be lenient to the sins of others.—*Fénelon.*

It is astonishing how well men wear when they think of no one but themselves.—*Bulwer.*

Our gifts and attainments are not only to be light and warmth in our own dwellings, but are to shine through the window, into the dark night, to guide and cheer bewildered travellers on the road.—*H. W. Beecher.*

The selfish man suffers more from his selfishness than he from whom that selfishness withholds some important benefit.—*Emerson.*

Sordid selfishness doth contract and narrow our benevolence, and cause us,

like serpents, to infold ourselves within ourselves, and to turn out our stings to all the world besides.—*Walter Scott.*

Whenever education and refinement grow away from the common people, they are growing toward selfishness, which is the monster evil of the world.—*H. W. Beecher.*

Selfishness is the root and source of all natural and moral evils.—*Emmons.*

Supreme and abiding self-love is a very dwarfish affection, but a giant evil.

The very heart and root of sin is an independent spirit.—We erect the idol self, and not only wish others to worship, but worship it ourselves.—*Cecil.*

Heroism, magnanimity, and self-denial, in all instances in which they do not spring from a principle of religion, are but splendid altars on which we sacrifice one kind of self-love to another.—*Colton.*

It is very natural for a young friend and a young lover to think the persons they love have nothing to do but to please them.—*Pope.*

It is not truth, justice, liberty, that men seek; they seek only themselves.—And oh, that they knew how to seek themselves aright!—*Jacobi.*

That household god, a man's own self.—*Flavel.*

Some people think that all the world should share their misfortunes, though they do not share in the sufferings of any one else.—*A. Poincelot.*

The world is governed only by self-interest.—*Schiller.*

Milton has carefully marked, in his Satan, the intense selfishness which would rather reign in hell than serve in heaven.—*Coleridge.*

Self-interest, that leprosy of the age, attacks us from infancy, and we are startled to observe little heads calculate before knowing how to reflect.—*Mad. Girardin.*

As a man goes down in self, he goes up in God.—*G. B. Cheever.*

Beware of no man more than of yourself; we carry our worst enemies within us.—*Spurgeon.*

We are too much haunted by ourselves, projecting the central shadow of self on everything around us.—And then comes the Gospel to rescue us from this selfishness.—Redemption is this, to forget self in God.—*F. W. Robertson.*

Deliver me, O Lord, from that evil man, myself.—*T. Brooks.*

Think about yourself, about what you want, what you like, what respect people ought to pay you, what people think of you, and then to you nothing will be pure. May God keep our hearts pure from that selfishness which is the root of all sin.—*C. Kingsley.*

Selfishness is a vice utterly at variance with the happiness of him who harbors it, and as such, condemned by self-love. —*Sir J. Mackintosh.*

Where all are selfish, the sage is no better than the fool, and only rather more dangerous.—*Froude.*

Though selfishness hath defiled the whole man, yet sensual pleasure is the chief part of its interest, and, therefore, by the senses it commonly works; and these are the doors and windows by which iniquity entereth into the soul.— *Baxter.*

Did any man, at his death, ever regret his conflicts with himself, his victories over appetite, his scorn of impure pleasure, or his sufferings for righteousness' sake?—*Channing.*

I would tear out my own heart if it had no better disposition than to love only myself, and laugh at all my neighbors.—*Pope.*

SELF-KNOWLEDGE. — Self-knowledge is that acquaintance with ourselves which shows us what we are, and what we ought to be, in order to our living comfortably and usefully here, and happily hereafter.—*J. Mason.*

Of all knowledge the wise and good seek most to know themselves.—*Shakespeare.*

The first step to self-knowledge is self-distrust. Nor can we attain to any kind of knowledge, except by a like process.

"Know thyself," was counted one of the oracles of the Greeks. It was inscribed as one of their three great precepts, in letters of gold, on the temple at Delphos, and regarded as divine.

To reach perfection, we must be made sensible of our failings, either by the admonitions of friends, or the invectives of enemies.—*Diogenes.*

There is one knowledge which it is every man's duty and interest to acquire, namely, self-knowledge. Else to what end was man alone, of all animals, endued by the Creator with the faculty of self-consciousness?

The precept, "Know yourself," was not solely intended to obviate the pride of mankind; but likewise that we might understand our own worth.—*Cicero.*

He that knows himself, knows others; and he that is ignorant of himself, could not write a very profound lecture on other men's heads.—*Colton.*

No one who has not a complete knowledge of himself will ever have a true understanding of another.—*Novalis.*

The highest and most profitable learning is the knowledge of ourselves. To have a low opinion of our own merits, and to think highly of others, is an evidence of wisdom. All men are frail, but thou shouldst reckon none so frail as thyself.—*Thomas à Kempis.*

Absalom, who was a fool, wished himself a judge; Solomon, who was a wise man, trembles at the undertaking, and suspects his own fitness for it. The more knowing and considerate men are, the better they are acquainted with their own weakness, and the more jealous of themselves.—*M. Henry.*

Self-knowledge is best learned, not by contemplation, but action.—Strive to do your duty, and you will soon discover of what stuff you are made.—*Goethe.*

Common and lamentable is our mental self-ignorance, that men ignore their intellectual faculties, their only self-culture consisting in the care of their bodies. —Like the rich fool in the parable, they think only of the stomach, even when they address their words to the soul.— *C. Wadsworth.*

The first step to improvement, whether mental, moral, or religious, is to know ourselves—our weaknesses, errors, deficiencies, and sins, that, by divine grace, we may overcome and turn from them all.—*Tryon Edwards.*

An humble knowledge of thyself is a surer way to God than a deep search after learning.—*Thomas à Kempis.*

The height of all philosophy is to know thyself; and the end of this knowledge is to know God. Know thyself, that thou mayest know God; and know God, that thou mayest love him and be like him. In the one thou art initiated into wisdom; and in the other perfected in it.—*Quarles.*

Nothing will make us so charitable and tender to the faults of others, as, by self-examination, thoroughly to know our own.—*Fénelon.*

'Tis greatly wise to talk with our own hearts, and ask them how we stand toward God and heaven; where we have failed; and how we may avoid failure in future; how grow wise and good; how others, bless, and be ourselves approved, by God, and conscience, and our fellowmen.

Man, know thyself; all wisdom centres there.—*Young.*

Sum up at night what thou hast done by day, and in the morning what thou hast to do; dress and undress thy soul; mark the decay or growth of it. If with thy watch, that too be down, then wind up both. Since thou shalt be most surely judged, make thine accounts agree.—*Herbert.*

Trust not yourself, but your defects to know, make use of every friend and every foe.—*Pope.*

Other men's sins are before our eyes; our own are behind our back.—*Seneca.*

No man ever made an ill figure who understood his own talents, nor a good one, who mistook them.—*Swift.*

Learn God, and thou shalt know thyself.—*Tupper.*

The most difficult thing in life is to know yourself.—*Thales.*

Our own opinion of ourselves should be lower than that formed by others, for we have a better chance at our imperfections.—*Thomas à Kempis.*

SELF-LOVE.—Of all mankind each loves himself the best.—*Terence.*

There are different kinds of self-love. As an instinct, it is desirable and important. As a modification of true benevolence, it is commendable. But as an idolatrous affection, it is censurable. —*C. Simmons.*

The greatest of all flatterers is self-love.—*Rochefoucauld.*

Self-love is the most delicate and the most tenacious of our sentiments: a mere nothing will wound it, but nothing can kill it.

The shadow of the sun is largest, when his beams are lowest. On the contrary, we are always least when we make ourselves the greatest.

In all time self-love has blinded the wisest.—*Villefre.*

The most amiable people are those who least wound the self-love of others. —*Bruyère.*

A man who loves only himself and his pleasures is vain, presumptuous, and wicked even from principle.—*Vauvenargues.*

All other love is extinguished by self-love; beneficence, humanity, justice, and philosophy sink under it.—*Epicurus.*

By a happy contradiction, no system of philosophy gives such a base view of human nature as that which is founded on self-love. So sure is self-love to degrade whatever it touches.—*Hare.*

Those who have affirmed self-love to be the basis of all our sentiments and actions are much in the right. There is no occasion to demonstrate that men have a face; as little need is there of proving to them that they are actuated by self-love.—*Voltaire.*

It is this unquiet self-love that renders us so sensitive. The sick man, who sleeps ill, thinks the night long. We exaggerate, from cowardice, all the evils which we encounter; they are great, but our sensibility increases them.—*Fénelon.*

Self-love is an instrument useful but dangerous: it often wounds the hand which makes use of it, and seldom does good without doing harm.—*Rousseau.*

Our self-love is ever ready to revolt from our better judgment, and join the enemy within.—*Steele.*

Self-love is not so vile a sin as self-neglecting.—*Shakespeare.*

The cause of all the blunders committed by man arises from excessive self-love.—He who intends to be a great man ought to love neither himself nor his own things, but only what is just, whether it happens to be done by himself or by another.—*Plato.*

Love thyself last.—*Shakespeare.*

Most actions, good or bad, may be resolved into the love of ourselves; but the self-love of some men inclines them to please others, and the self-love of others is wholly employed in pleasing themselves. This makes the great distinction between virtue and vice.—*Swift.*

Offended self-love never forgives.—*Vigée.*

It is falling in love with our own mistaken ideas that makes fools and beggars of half mankind.—*Young.*

Self-love leads men of narrow minds to measure all mankind by their own capacity.—*Jane Porter.*

There are wounds of self-love which one does not confess to one's dearest friends.—*J. P. Senn.*

Self-love is, in almost all men, such an over-weight that they are incredulous of a man's habitual preference of the general good to his own; but when they see it proved by sacrifices of ease, wealth, rank, and of life itself, there is no limit to their admiration.—*Emerson.*

Self-love, as it happens to be well or ill conducted, constitutes virtue and vice.—*Rochefoucauld.*

Self-love is a cup without any bottom; you might pour all the great lakes into it, and never fill it up.—*O. W. Holmes.*

Self-love is too apt to draw some consolation even from so bitter a source as the calamities of others.—The sting of our pains is diminished by the assurance that they are common to all; and from feelings equally egotistical, it unfortunately happens that the zest and relish of our pleasures is heightened by the contrary consideration, namely, that they are confined to ourselves. This conviction it is that tickles the palate of the epicure, that inflames the ardor of the lover, that lends to ambition her ladder, and extracts the thorns from a crown.—*Colton.*

Self-love is the instrument of our preservation; it resembles the provision for the perpetuity of mankind—it is necessary, it is dear to us, it gives us pleasure, and we must possess it.—*Voltaire.*

SELF-PRAISE.—There is not one wise man among twenty will praise himself.—*Shakespeare.*

Say nothing of yourself, either good, bad, or indifferent; nothing good, for that is vanity; nothing bad, for that is affectation; nothing indifferent, for that is silly.

It is equally a mistake to hold one's

self too high, or to rate one's self too cheap.—*Goethe.*

We acknowledge that we should not talk of our wives; but we seem not to know that we should talk still less of ourselves.—*Rochefoucauld.*

A man's praises have very musical and charming accents in the mouth of another, but sound very flat and untunable in his own.—*Xenophon.*

Self-praise occasionally succeeds with ignorant and credulous persons; very seldom with those who have much knowledge of the world. He who can make a discerning mind think more highly of him for what he says of himself, must be a person of unusual ability and address.—*G. W. Hervey.*

A man's accusations of himself are always believed; his praises of self never.—*Montaigne.*

SELF-RELIANCE.—Help thyself, and God will help thee.—*Herbert.*

If you would have a faithful servant, and one that you like, serve yourself.—*Franklin.*

Men throw themselves on foreign assistances to spare their own, which, after all, are the only certain and sufficient ones.—*Montaigne.*

They can conquer who believe they can.—*Virgil.*

Great is the strength of an individual soul, true to its high trust; mighty is it, even to the redemption of a world.—*Mrs. L. M. Child.*

Let every eye negotiate for itself, and trust no agent.—*Shakespeare.*

Look well into thyself; there is a source of strength which will always spring up if thou wilt always look there.—*M. Antoninus.*

Our remedies oft in ourselves do lie, which we ascribe to Heaven.—*Shakespeare.*

No external advantages can supply the place of self-reliance.—The force of one's being, if it has any force, must come from within.—No one can safely imitate another; nor by following in the footsteps of another can he ever gain distinction or enjoy prosperity.—*R. W. Clark.*

I have ever held it a maxim, never to do through another what it was possible for me to do myself.—*Montesquieu.*

God gives every bird its food, but he does not throw it into the nest.—*J. G. Holland.*

Self-distrust is the cause of most of our failures.—In the assurance of strength there is strength; and they are the weakest, however strong, who have no faith in themselves or their powers.—*Bovee.*

Time and I against any two.—*Philip II.*

The best lightning-rod for your protection is your own spine.—*Emerson.*

The spirit of self-help is the root of all genuine growth in the individual; and, exhibited in the lives of many, it constitutes the true source of national vigor and strength. Help from without is often enfeebling in its effects, but help from within invariably invigorates. —*S. Smiles.*

Doubt whom you will, but never doubt yourself.—*Bovee.*

A person under the firm persuasion that he can command resources virtually has them.—*Livy.*

The supreme fall of falls is this, the first doubt of one's self.—*Countess de Gasparin.*

Trust in God, but keep your powder dry.—*Cromwell.*

"Give me a standing place," said Archimedes, "and I will move the world."—Goethe has changed the postulate into the precept. "Make good thy standing place, and move the world."—*S. Smiles.*

Men seem neither to understand their riches nor their strength.—Of the former they believe greater things than they should; of the latter, less.—*Bacon.*

We must not calculate on the weather, or on fortune, but upon God and ourselves.—He may fail us in the gratification of our wishes, but never in the encounter with our exigencies.—*Simms.*

The man who cannot enjoy his own natural gifts in silence, and find his reward in the exercise of them, will generally find himself badly off.—*Goethe.*

The man who makes everything that leads to happiness depend upon himself, and not upon other men, has adopted the very best plan for living happily. This is the man of moderation, the man of manly character and of wisdom.—*Plato.*

Welcome evermore to gods and men is the self-helping man.—*Emerson.*

Providence has done, and I am persuaded is disposed to do, a great deal for us; but we are not to forget the fable of Jupiter and the countryman.—*Washington.*

In life, as in whist, hope nothing from the way cards may be dealt to you. Play the cards, whatever they be, to the best of your skill.—*Bulwer.*

The human mind, in proportion as it is deprived of external resources, sedulously labors to find within itself the means of happiness. learns to rely with confidence on its own exertions, and gains with greater certainty the power of being happy.—*Zimmermann.*

It is impossible you should take true root but by the fair weather that you make yourself; it is needful that you frame the season for your own harvest. —*Shakespeare.*

God helps those that help themselves. —*Franklin.*

A man that only translates, shall never be a poet; nor a painter, that only copies; nor a swimmer, that swims always with bladders; so people that trust wholly to others' charity, and without industry of their own, will always be poor.—*Sir W. Temple.*

SELF-RESPECT.—When thou hast profited so much that thou respectest thyself, thou mayest let go thy tutor.—*Seneca.*

Every one stamps his own value on himself.—The price we challenge for ourselves is given us.—Man is made great or little by his own will.—*Schiller.*

Have not too low thoughts of thyself. The confidence a man hath of his being pleasant in his demeanor is a means whereby he infallibly cometh to be such.—*Burton.*

It has been said that self-respect is the gate of heaven, and the most cursory observation shows that a degree of reserve adds vastly to the latent force of character.—*Tuckerman.*

Who will adhere to him that abandons himself?—*Sir P. Sidney.*

The pious and just honoring of ourselves may be thought the fountainhead from whence every laudable and worthy enterprise issues forth.—*Milton.*

It may be no less dangerous to claim, on certain occasions, too little than too much. There is something captivating in spirit and intrepidity, to which we often yield as to a resistless power; nor can he reasonably expect the confidence of others who too apparently distrusts himself.—*Johnson.*

Above all things, reverence yourself. —*Pythagoras.*

Be noble-minded! Our own heart, and not other men's opinions of us, forms our true honor.—*Schiller.*

To have a respect for ourselves guides our morals; and to have a deference for others governs our manners.—*Sterne.*

I care not so much what I am in the opinion of others as what I am in my own; I would be rich of myself and not by borrowing.—*Montaigne.*

Self-respect,—that corner-stone of all virtue.—*Sir John Herschel.*

Self-respect is the noblest garment with which a man may clothe himself, —the most elevating feeling with which the mind can be inspired. One of Pythagoras's wisest maxims is that in which he enjoins the pupil to " reverence himself."—*S. Smiles.*

No more important duty can be urged upon those who are entering the great theatre of life than simple loyalty to their best convictions.—*E. H. Chapin.*

The reverence of man's self, is, next to religion, the chiefest bridle of all vices. —*Bacon.*

Self-reverence, self-knowledge, self-control, these three alone lead life to sovereign power.—*Tennyson.*

One self-approving hour whole years outweigh.—*Pope.*

SELF-RIGHTEOUSNESS.—Let us pray God that he would root out of our hearts everything of our own planting and set out there, with his own hand, the tree of life bearing all manner of fruits.—*Fénelon.*

Regret not that which is past; and trust not to thine own righteousness.— *St. Anthony.*

No man can quench his thirst with sand, or with water from the Dead Sea; so no man can find rest from his own character, however good, or from his own acts, however religious.—*Bonar.*

You can always tell when a man is a

great way from God—when he is always talking about himself, how good he is.— *D. L. Moody.*

If there be ground for you to trust in your own righteousness, then, all that Christ did to purchase salvation, and all that God did to prepare the way for it is in vain.—*Jonathan Edwards.*

Self-righteousness is the devil's masterpiece to make us think well of ourselves. —*T. Adam.*

While a man rests on his own merits for acceptance with God, it is of little consequence whether he be a pagan idolater, or a proud, ignorant Pharisee. —I know not which of the two is most distant from the kingdom of God.—*J. Milner.*

That which of all things unfits man for the reception of Christ as a Saviour, is not gross profligacy and outward, vehement transgression, but it is self-complacency, fatal self-righteousness and self-sufficiency.—*A. Maclaren.*

To trust one's own righteousness, is like seeking shelter under one's own shadow.—We may stoop to the ground, and the lower we bend, the shadow is beneath us still.—But if we flee to the shadow of a great rock, or a wide-spreading tree, then we find shelter from the noon-day sun.—*Chinese Preacher.*

SELF-RULE.—(See " WILL," " SELF-CONTROL.")

SELF-WILL.—Self-will is so ardent and active, that it will break a world to pieces, to make a stool to sit on.—*Cecil.*

Self-will is the source and spring of all that envy, malice, bitterness of spirit, malcontentedness and impatience, and of all those dark passions, those inordinate desires and lusts, that reign in the hearts and lives of wicked men.—*J. Smith.*

Lawless are they that make their wills their law.—*Shakespeare.*

An obstinate, ungovernable self-sufficiency plainly points out to us that state of imperfect maturity at which the graceful levity of youth is lost and the solidity of experience not yet acquired.—*Junius.*

SENSE.—(See " COMMON SENSE.")

Of plain, sound sense, life's current coin is made.—*Young.*

I have long thought, that the different abilities of men, which we call wisdom or prudence for the conduct of public affairs or private life, grow directly out of that little grain of good sense which they bring with them into the world; and that the defect of it in men comes from some want in their conception or birth.—*Sir W. Temple.*

Success in business is due to administration; and capacity in administration is due to that faculty, power, or quality called common sense.

Good sense, which only is the gift of Heaven, and though no science, fairly worth the seven.—*Pope.*

Nothing is useless to the man of sense; he turns everything to account.—*La Fontaine.*

SENSIBILITY.—(See "FEELINGS.")

Too much sensibility creates unhappiness; too much insensibility leads to crime.—*Talleyrand.*

Fine sensibilities are like woodbines, delightful luxuries of beauty to twine round a solid, upright stem of understanding; but very poor things, if, unsustained by strength, they are left to creep along the ground.—*John Foster.*

The heart that is soonest awake to the flowers, is always the first to be touched with the thorns.—*Moore.*

Sensibility would be a good portress, if she had but one hand; with her right she opens the door to pleasure, but with her left to pain.—*Colton.*

Where virtue is, sensibility is its ornament and becoming attire; but it, and all the amiable qualities may become, and too often have become the panders of vice, and the instruments of seduction.—*Coleridge.*

Sensibility is the power of woman.—*Lavater.*

Dearly bought the hidden treasure, finer feelings can bestow; chords that vibrate sweetest pleasure, thrill the deepest notes of woe.—*Burns.*

Men's feelings are always purest and most glowing in the hour of meeting and of farewell; like the glaciers, which are transparent and rosy-hued only at sunrise and sunset, but throughout the day are gray and cold.—*Richter.*

Laughter and tears are meant to turn the wheels of the same machinery of sensibility; one is wind-power, and the other water-power; that is all.—*O. W. Holmes.*

It is with feeling as with religion, if a man really have any, he will have none to speak of.—*H. N. Hudson.*

The period of tender sensibilities looks to a period of active character, for the formation of which the sensibilities are given and the requisite excitements provided, after which they pass from the form of mere sensibilities into habits and fixtures of feeling and action. —Character is made up, first of passive, afterward of active emotions.—*G. B. Cheever.*

Sensibility is neither good nor evil in itself, but in its application.—Under the influence of Christian principle it makes saints and martyrs; ill-directed, or uncontrolled, it is a snare, and the source of every temptation.—*H. More.*

SENSITIVENESS.—Sensitiveness is closely allied to egotism.—Indeed excessive sensitiveness is only another name for morbid self-consciousness.— The cure for it is to make more of our objects, and less of ourselves.—*Bovee.*

There are moments when petty slights are harder to bear than even a serious injury. Men have died of the festering of a gnat-bite.—*Cecil Danby.*

Quick sensitiveness is inseparable from a ready understanding.—*Addison.*

That chastity of honor which felt a stain like a wound.—*Burke.*

SENSUALITY.—Sensuality is the grave of the soul.—*Channing.*

He that lives in the kingdom of sense, shall die in the kingdom of sorrow.— *Baxter.*

If sensuality were happiness, beasts were happier than men; but human felicity is lodged in the soul, not in the flesh.—*Seneca.*

If sensuality be our only happiness, we ought to envy the brutes; for instinct is a surer, shorter, safer guide to such happiness than reason.—*Colton.*

Though selfishness hath defiled the whole man, yet sensual pleasure is the chief part of its interest, and therefore by the senses it commonly works, and these are the doors and the windows by which iniquity entereth into the soul.— *Baxter.*

I have never known a man who was sensual in his youth, who was high-minded when old.—*Charles Sumner.*

Those wretches who never have experienced the sweets of wisdom and virtue, but spend all their time in revels and debauches, sink downward day after day, and make their whole life one continued series of errors. They taste no real or substantial pleasure; but, resembling so many brutes, with eyes always fixed on the earth, and intent upon their loaden tables, they pamper themselves in luxury and excess.—*Plato.*

What is a man, if his chief good, and market of his time, be but to sleep, and feed? a beast, no more.—*Shakespeare.*

What if one might have all the pleasures of the world for the asking?—Who would so unman himself as by accepting them to desert his soul and become a perpetual slave to his senses?—*Seneca.*

Sordid and infamous sensuality, the most dreadful evil that issued from the box of Pandora, corrupts the entire heart and eradicates every virtue.—*Fénelon.*

The body of a sensualist is the coffin of a dead soul.—*Bovee.*

All sensuality is one, though it takes many forms, as all purity is one. It is the same whether a man eat, or drink, or cohabit, or sleep sensually. They are but one appetite, and we only need to see a person do any one of these things to know how great a sensualist he is.—*Thoreau.*

Sin the mother, and shame the daughter of lewdness.—*Sir P. Sidney.*

A youth of sensuality and intemperance delivers over a worn-out body to old age.—*Cicero.*

When the cup of any sensual pleasure is drained to the bottom, there is always poison in the dregs.—*Jane Porter.*

SENTIMENT.—Sentiment is intellectualized emotion; emotion precipitated, as it were, in pretty crystals by the fancy.—*J. R. Lowell.*

Sentiment has a kind of divine alchemy, rendering grief itself the source of tenderest thoughts and far-reaching desires, which the sufferer cherishes as sacred treasures.—*Talfourd.*

Sentiment and principle are often mistaken for each other, though, in fact, they widely differ.—Sentiment is the virtue of ideas; principle the virtue of action.—Sentiment has its seat in the head; principle, in the heart. Sentiment suggests fine harangues and subtle

distinctions; principle conceives just notions, and performs good actions in consequence of them. Sentiment refines away the simplicity of truth, and the plainness of piety; and "gives us virtue in words, and vice in deeds." Sentiment may be called the Athenian who knew what was right; and principle, the Lacedemonian who practised it.—*Blair.*

A general loftiness of sentiment, independence of men, consciousness of good intentions, self-oblivion in great objects, clear views of futurity, thoughts of the blessed companionship of saints and angels, trust in God as the friend of truth and virtue—these are the states of mind in which I should live.—*Channing.*

Cure the drunkard, heal the insane, mollify the homicide, civilize the Pawnee, but what lessons can be devised for the debaucher of sentiment?—*Emerson.*

SERVANTS.—If the master takes no account of his servants, they will make small account of him, and care not what they spend, as they are never brought to an audit.—*Fuller.*

Be not too familiar with thy servants; at first it may beget love, but in the end 'twill breed contempt.—*Fuller.*

Command thy servant advisably with few plain words, fully, freely, and positively, with a grave countenance, and settled carriage: These will procure obedience, gain respect, and maintain authority.—*Fuller.*

Be not served with kinsmen, or friends, or men entreated to stay; for they expect much, and do little; nor with such as are amorous, for their heads are intoxicated; and keep rather too few, than one too many.—*Lord Burleigh.*

Let thy servants be such as thou mayest command, and entertain none about thee but those to whom thou givest wages; for those that will serve thee without thy hire will cost thee treble as much as they that know thy fare.—*Sir Walter Raleigh.*

If thou employest plain men, and canst find such as are commonly honest, they will work faithfully, and report fairly. Cunning men will, for their own credit, adventure without command; and from thy business derive credit to themselves.—*Fuller.*

I have been formerly so silly as to hope that every servant I had might be made a friend; but I am now convinced that the nature of servitude generally bears a contrary tendency.—*People's* characters are to be chiefly collected from their education and place in life; birth itself does but little.—*Shenstone.*

'Tis better that thou be rather something sparing, than very liberal, to even a good servant; for as he grows full, he inclines either to be idle, or to leave thee: and if he should at any time murmur, thou mayest govern him by a seasonable reward.—*Fuller.*

We become willing servants to the good by the bonds their virtues lay upon us.—*Sir P. Sidney.*

If thou hast a loitering servant, send him of thy errand just before his dinner.—*Fuller.*

Expect not more from servants than is just; reward them well if they observe their trust; nor with them pride or cruelty invade, since God and nature them our brothers made.—*Denham.*

Reward a good servant well, and rather get quit of a bad one than disquiet thyself with him.—*Fuller.*

If you treat with courtesy your equal who is privileged to resent an impertinence, how much more cautious should you be to your dependants, from whom you demand a respectful demeanor.—*Chambers.*

SEXES.—No improvement that takes place in either of the sexes, can be confined to itself; each is a universal mirror to each; and the respective refinement of the one, will be in reciprocal proportion to the polish of the other.—*Colton.*

A person who despises or undervalues, or neglects the opposite sex, will soon need humanizing. What God hath joined together, let no man put asunder.—*C. Simmons.*

The sexes were made for each other, and only in the wise and loving union of the two is the fulness of health and duty and happiness to be expected.—*W. Hall.*

For contemplation he, and valor formed; for softness she, and sweet attractive grace; he for God only, she for God in him.—*Milton.*

SHAME.—While shame keeps watch virtue is not wholly extinguished from the heart, nor will moderation be utterly exiled from the mind of tyrants.—*Burke.*

I regard that man as lost, who has lost his sense of shame.—*Plautus.*

Nothing is truly infamous but that which is wicked, and therefore shame can never disturb an innocent and virtuous mind.—*Sherlock.*

It is the guilt, not the scaffold, which constitutes the shame.—*Corneille.*

Blush not now, said a distinguished Italian to his young relative whom he met coming out of a haunt of vice; the time to have blushed was when you went in.

Shame may restrain what law does not prohibit.—*Seneca.*

Shame is a great restraint upon sinners at first; but that soon falls off: and when men have once lost their innocence, their modesty is not like to be long troublesome to them. For impudence comes on with vice, and grows up with it. Lesser vices do not banish all shame and modesty; but great and abominable crimes harden men's foreheads, and make them shameless. When men have the heart to do a very bad thing, they seldom want the face to bear it out.—*Tillotson.*

Those who fear not guilt, yet start at shame.—*Churchill.*

I never wonder to see men wicked, but I often wonder to see them not ashamed.—*Swift.*

Of all evils to the generous, shame is the most deadly pang.—*Thomson.*

Honor and shame from no condition rise; act well your part—there all the honor lies.—*Pope.*

Shame is nature's hasty conscience.—*Maria Edgeworth.*

Be assured that when once a woman begins to be ashamed of what she ought not to be ashamed of, she will not be ashamed of what she ought.—*Livy.*

Mortifications are often more painful than real calamities.—*Oliver Goldsmith.*

WILLIAM SHAKESPEARE
(1564–1616)

FAMILIAR PHRASES *from* SHAKESPEARE

Arranged Alphabetically According to Key Words

Complete expressions of thought will be found under subjects throughout the book. Familiar phrases which, though much used by Shakespeare, are found in the works of his predecessors, will be found in the general section of familiar phrases beginning on page 735.

A

Melted . . . into thin air.—*Tempest, IV, i, 148.*

I would applaud thee to the very echo.—*Macbeth, V, iii, 53.*

A goodly apple rotten at the heart.—*Merchant of Venice, I, iii, 102.*

Make assurance double sure.—*Macbeth, IV, i, 83.*

B

Chronicle small beer.—*Othello, II, i, 160.*

It beggar'd all description.—*Anthony and Cleopatra, II, ii, 203.*

Beggars mounted run their horse to death.—*III Henry VI, I, iv, 127.*

The true beginning of our end.—*Midsummer Night's Dream, V, i, 111.*

I see, lady, the gentleman is not in your books.—*Much Ado About Nothing, I, i, 79.*

With all appliances and means to boot.—*II Henry IV, III, i, 29.*

Brevity is the soul of wit.—*Hamlet, II, ii, 90.*

C

Must I hold a candle to my shames?—*Merchant of Venice, II, vi, 41.*

Cares of state.—*King Lear, I, i, 51.*

A harmless necessary cat.—*Merchant of Venice, IV, i, 55.*

As vigilant as a cat to steal cream.—*I Henry IV, IV, ii, 64.*

'Twas caviar to the general.—*Hamlet, II, ii, 457.*

Cheek by jole.—*Midsummer Night's Dream, III, ii, 338.*

You Banbury cheese.—*Merry Wives of Windsor, I, i, 130.*

When we have shuffled off this mortal coil.—*Hamlet, III, i, 67.*

As cold as any stone.—*Henry V, II, iii, 27.*

Cold comfort.—*King John, V, vii, 42.*

That it should come to this.—*Hamlet, I, ii, 137.*

Comparisons are odorous.—*Much Ado About Nothing, III, v, 18.*

Screw your courage to the sticking place.—*Macbeth, I, vii, 60.*

The crack of doom.—*Macbeth, IV, i, 117.*

Shall I seem crest-fall'n . . . ?—*Richard II, I, i, 188.*

The most unkindest cut of all.—*Julius Caesar, III, ii, 187.*

I can cut a caper.—*Twelfth Night, I, iii, 129.*

D

To dance attendance on their lordships' pleasures.—*Henry VIII, V, ii, 31.*

It was so dark, Hal, that thou couldst not see thy hand.—*I Henry IV, II, iv, 247.*

We've seen better days.—*Timon of Athens, IV, ii, 27.*

A man can die but once; we owe God a death.—*II Henry IV, III, ii, 250.*

Cowards die many times before their deaths.—*Julius Caesar, II, ii, 32.*

He will give the devil his due.—*I Henry IV, I, ii, 132.*

The winter of our discontent.—*Richard III, I, i, 1.*

O, understand my drift.—*Merry Wives of Windsor, II, ii, 123.*

A dry jest, sir.—*Twelfth Night, I, iii, 80.*

E

Tear a passion to tatters . . . to split the ears of the groundlings.—*Hamlet, III, ii, 11.*

Friends, Romans, countrymen, lend me your ears.—*Julius Caesar, III, ii, 78.*

He hath eaten me out of house and home.—*II Henry IV, II, i, 80.*

What, you egg! Young fry of treachery.—*Macbeth, IV, ii, 83.*

Lack-lustre eye.—*As You Like It, II, vii, 21.*

Thou tell'st me there is murder in mine eye.—*As You Like It, III, v, 10.*

Make thy two eyes, like stars, start from their spheres.—*Hamlet, I, v, 15.*

An eye-sore to our solemn festival.—*Taming of the Shrew, III, ii, 102.*

A woeful ballad made to his mistress' eyebrow.—*As You Like It, II, vii, 147.*

F

The whining schoolboy, with his satchel and shining morning face.—*As You Like It, II, vii, 145.*

In maiden meditation, fancy-free.—*Midsummer Night's Dream, II, i, 163.*

Play fast and loose with faith.—*King John, III, i, 242.*

A fig for Peter.—*II Henry VI, II, iii, 67.*

I have them at my fingers' ends.—*Twelfth Night, I, iii, 82.*

Nay, I will, that's flat.—*I Henry IV, I, iii, 218.*

Pound of flesh.—*Merchant of Venice, IV, i, 307.*

As willingly as one would kill a fly.—*Titus Andronicus, V, i, 142.*

Make haste; the better foot before.—*King John, IV, ii, 170.*

We are for you.—*As You Like It, V, iii, 10.*

For ever and a day.—*As You Like It, IV, i, 143.*

The slings and arrows of outrageous fortune.—*Hamlet, III, i, 56.*

O, I am fortune's fool.—*Romeo and Juliet, III, i, 141.*

I doubt some foul play.—*Hamlet, I, ii, 255.*

G

The glass of fashion and the mould of form.—*Hamlet, III, i, 161.*

It will go hard with poor Antonio.—*Merchant of Venice, III, ii, 293.*

If he fall in, good night.—*I Henry IV, I, iii, 194.*

Nay, if thy wits run the wild-goose chase, I have done.—*Romeo and Juliet, II, iv, 75.*

I'll never be such a gosling to obey instinct.—*Coriolanus, V, iii, 34.*

It was Greek to me.—*Julius Caesar, I, ii, 281.*

My salad days when I was green in judgement.—*Antony and Cleopatra, I, v, 73.*

The green sickness [envy].—*Antony and Cleopatra, III, ii, 6.*

H

I'll cavil on the ninth part of a hair.—*I Henry IV, III, i, 140.*

A hand open as day.—*II Henry IV, IV, iv, 31.*

Is it not as this mouth should tear this hand for lifting food to't?—*King Lear, III, iv, 14.*

In my heart's core, ay, in my heart of heart.—*Hamlet, III, ii, 78.*

Heart with strings of steel.—*Hamlet, III, iii, 69.*

My old heart is crack'd.—*King Lear, II, i, 92.*

Let me wring your heart.—*Hamlet, III, iv, 36.*

I'll warrant him heart-whole.—*As You Like It, IV, i, 49.*

But I will wear my heart upon my sleeve for daws to peck at.—*Othello, I, i, 64.*

Show it a fair pair of heels and run for it.—*I Henry IV, II, iv, 53.*

'Tis neither here nor there.—*Othello, IV, iii, 59.*

It out-herods Herod.—*Hamlet, III, ii, 16.*

I have you on the hip.—*Merchant of Venice, IV, i, 334.*

I am in a holiday humour.—*As You Like It, IV, i, 69.*

He speaks home, madam.—*Othello, II, i, 166.*

More honour'd in the breach than the observance.—*Hamlet, I, iv, 15.*

A high hope for a low heaven.—*Love's Labour's Lost, I, i, 197.*

A horse! a horse! my kingdom for a horse.—*Richard III, V, iv, 7.*

My purpose is, indeed, a horse of that colour.—*Twelfth Night, II, iii, 181.*

K

A man of my kidney.—*Merry Wives of Windsor, III, v, 117.*

This is the way to kill a wife with kindness.—*Taming of the Shrew, IV, i, 211* (Lyly used "kill it by cullyng it" in "Euphues," p. 215, in 1579).

A little more than kin, and less than kind.—*Hamlet, I, ii, 65.*

Every inch a king.—*King Lear, IV, vi, 109.*

Seal the bargain with a holy kiss.—*Two Gentlemen of Verona, II, ii, 6.*

Pale as his shirt, his knees knocking each other.—*Hamlet, II, i, 81.*

He's very knowing.—*Antony and Cleopatra, III, iii, 26.*

L

Let us not be laughing-stocks to other men's humours.—*Merry Wives of Windsor, III, i, 88.*

Lay on, Macduff.—*Macbeth, V, viii, 33.*

Thou liest in thy throat.—*Twelfth Night, III, iv, 172.*

I bear a charmed life.—*Macbeth, V, viii, 12.*

After life's fitful fever, he sleeps well.—*Macbeth, III, ii, 23.*

The livelong day.—*Julius Caesar, I, i, 46.*

A lily-livered, action-taking knave.—*King Lear, II, ii, 18.*

Livers white as milk.—*Merchant of Venice III, ii, 83.*

I am pigeon-liver'd and lack gall.—*Hamlet, II, ii, 604.*

This is the short and long of it.—*Merry Wives of Windsor, II, ii, 60.*

How many fathom deep I am in love.—*As You Like It, IV, i, 210.*

The course of true love never did run smooth.—*Midsummer Night's Dream, I, i, 132.*

One that loved not wisely but too well.—*Othello, V, ii, 343.*

M

It makes us, or it mars us.—*Othello, V, i, 4.*

To the manner born.—*Hamlet, I, iv, 15.*

It is meat and drink to me.—*As You Like It, V, i, 11.*

As merry as the day is long.—*Much Ado About Nothing, II, i, 52.*

The milk of human kindness.—*Macbeth, I, v, 17.*

In my mind's eye.—*Hamlet, I, ii, 185.*

That would hang us, every mother's son.—*Midsummer Night's Dream, I, ii, 80.*

N

What's in a name? That which we call a rose by any other name would smell as sweet.—*Romeo and Juliet, II, ii, 43.*

Nay, I have ta'en you napping, gentle love.—*Taming of the Shrew, IV, ii, 46.*

May's new-fangled mirth.—*Love's Labour's Lost, I, i, 106.*

O

And thus I clothe my naked villainy with old odd ends, stol'n out of holy writ.—*Richard III, I, iii, 336.*

P

An itching palm.—*Julius Caesar, IV, iii, 9.*

Thou art in a parlous state.—*As You Like It, III, ii, 45.*

Base is the slave that pays.—*Henry V, II, i, 100.*

How camest thou in this pickle?—*Tempest, V, i, 281.*

The law, whereof you are a well deserving pillar.—*Merchant of Venice, IV, i, 238.*

I am the very pink of courtesy.—*Romeo and Juliet, II, iv, 61.*

A plague o' both your houses.—*Romeo and Juliet, III, i, 94.*

The play's the thing.—*Hamlet, II, ii, 633.*

That's past praying for.—*I Henry IV, II, iv, 211.*

The primrose path of dalliance.—*Hamlet, I, iii, 50.*

The lady doth protest too much.—*Hamlet, III, ii, 240.*

R

And thus the native hue of resolution is sicklied o'er with the pale cast of thought.—*Hamlet, III, i, 84.*

This was the noblest Roman of them all.—*Julius Caesar, V, v, 68.*

Something is rotten in the state of Denmark.—*Hamlet, I, iv, 90.*

S

Like a drunken sailor on a mast; ready, with every nod, to tumble down. —*Richard III, III, iv, 101.*

Now our sands are almost run.—*Pericles, V, ii, 1.*

Full of wise saws and modern instances.—*As You Like It, II, vii, 156.*

How sharper than a serpent's tooth it is to have a thankless child.—*King Lear, I, iv, 310.*

Single blessedness.—*Midsummer Night's Dream, I, i, 74.*

More sinn'd against than sinning.—*King Lear, III, ii, 146.*

Your skins are whole.—*Merry Wives of Windsor, III, i, 111.*

Sleep that knits up the ravell'd sleave of care.—*Macbeth, II, ii, 35.*

I have not slept one wink.—*Cymbeline, III, iv, 103.*

O, my offence is rank, it smells to heaven.—*Hamlet, III, iii, 36.*

From the smoke into the smother.—*As You Like It, I, ii, 299.*

So so.—*As You Like It, V, i, 29:*

I know a man . . . sold a goodly manor for a song.—*All's Well that Ends Well, III, ii, 10.*

Sweets to the sweet.—*Hamlet, V, i, 266.*

As swift as meditation, or the thoughts of love.—*Hamlet, I, v, 29.*

Swifter than arrow from the Tartar's bow.—*Midsummer Night's Dream, III, ii, 101.*

At one fell swoop.—*Macbeth, IV, iii, 219.*

T

Thereby hangs a tale.—*Othello, III, i, 8.*

Your tale, sir, would cure deafness.—*Tempest, I, ii, 106.*

Let me tell the world.—*I Henry IV, V, ii, 66.*

The dark backward and abysm of time.—*Tempest, I, ii, 50.*

The whips and scorns of time.—*Hamlet, III, i, 70.*

The time is out of joint.—*Hamlet I, v, 189.*

Can one desire too much of a good thing?—*As You Like It, IV, i, 124.*

To tread a measure with you on this grass.—*Love's Labour's Lost, V, ii, 186.*

Well said: that was laid on with a trowel.—*As You Like It, I, ii, 112.*

Like to a pair of loving turtle-doves. —*I Henry VI, II, ii, 30.*

V

Thou art an elm, my husband, I, a vine.—*Comedy of Errors, II, ii, 175.*

W

Shall we wag?—*Merry Wives of Windsor, II, i, 238.*

The dogs of war.—*Julius Caesar, III, i, 270.*

Men's evil manners live in brass; their virtues we write in water.—*Henry VIII, IV, ii, 45.*

Westward-ho.—*Twelfth Night, III, i, 146.*

Little better than one of the wicked. —*I Henry IV, I, ii, 100.*

The wine of life is drawn, and the mere lees is left this vault to brag of.—*Macbeth, II, iii, 96.*

Thy wish was father, Harry, to that thought.—*II Henry IV, IV, v, 93.*

'Tis now the very witching time of night.—*Hamlet, III, ii, 406.*

Frailty, thy name is woman.—*Hamlet, I, ii, 146.*

A poor lone woman.—*II Henry IV, II, i, 35.*

Answer me in one word.—*As You Like It, III, ii, 237.*

How every fool can play upon the word!—*Merchant of Venice, III, v, 43.*

O, how full of briers is this working-day world!—*As You Like It, I, iii, 12.*

Y

It did me yeoman's service.—*Hamlet, V, ii, 36.*

SICKNESS.—(See "DISEASE" and "PAIN.")

Sickness and disease are in weak minds the sources of melancholy; but that which is painful to the body, may be profitable to the soul. Sickness, the mother of modesty, puts us in mind of our mortality, and while we drive on heedlessly in the full career of worldly pomp and jollity, kindly brings us to a proper sense of our duty and destiny.—Burton.

In sickness let me not so much say, am I getting better of my pain? as am I getting better for it?—Shakespeare.

Of all the know-nothing persons in this world, commend us to the man who has "never known a day's illness." He is a moral dunce, one who has lost the greatest lesson of life; who has skipped the finest lecture in that great school of humanity, the sick-chamber.—Hood.

Few spirits are made better by the pain and languor of sickness; as few great pilgrims become eminent saints. —Thomas à Kempis.

It is in sickness that we most feel the need of that sympathy which shows how much we are dependent upon one another for our comfort, and even necessities. Thus disease, opening our eyes to the realities of life, is an indirect blessing.—H. Ballou.

In sickness the soul begins to dress herself for immortality. And first she unties the strings of vanity that made her upper garments cleave to the world and sit uneasy.—Jeremy Taylor.

When a man is laboring under the pain of any distemper, it is then that he recollects there is a God, and that he himself is but a man. No mortal is then the object of his envy, his admiration, or his contempt; and, having no malice to gratify, the tales of slander excite him not.—Pliny.

Sickness is a sort of early old age; it teaches us a diffidence in our earthly state.—Pope.

As in the body, so in the soul; they are oft most desperately sick who are least sensible of their disease, while he that fears each wound as mortal, seeks a timely cure, and is healed.—A. Warwick.

SILENCE.—(See "TONGUE," and "SPEECH.")

He can never speak well, who knows not how to hold his peace.—Plutarch.

True silence is the rest of the mind, and is to the spirit what sleep is to the body, nourishment and refreshment. It is a great virtue; it covers folly, keeps secrets, avoids disputes, and prevents sin.—Penn.

Some men envelop themselves in such an impenetrable cloak of silence, that the tongue will afford us no symptoms of the mind. Such taciturnity, indeed, is wise if they are fools, but foolish if they are wise; and the only method to form a judgment of these mutes, is narrowly to observe when, where, and how they smile.

Silence is the safest course for any man to adopt who distrusts himself.—Rochefoucauld.

Euripides was wont to say that silence was an answer to a wise man; but we seem to have greater occasion for it in our dealing with fools and unreasonable persons; for men of breeding and sense will be satisfied with reason and fair words.—Plutarch.

Silence is the understanding of fools, and one of the virtues of the wise.—Boileau.

Of all virtues, Zeno made choice of silence; for by it, said he, I hear other men's imperfections, and conceal my own.—Rule of Life.

A man's profundity may keep him from opening on a first interview, and his caution on a second; but I should suspect his emptiness, if he carried on his reserve to a third.—Colton.

I do know of those that therefore only are reputed wise, for saying nothing.—Shakespeare.

Silence is a virtue in those who are deficient in understanding.—Bouhours.

If the prudence of reserve and decorum dictates silence in some circumstances, in others prudence of a higher order may justify us in speaking our thoughts.—Burke.

The silence, often, of pure innocence, persuades when speaking fails.—Shakespeare.

Silence is the highest wisdom of a fool as speech is the greatest trial of a wise man.—If thou wouldst be known as wise, let thy words show thee so; if thou doubt thy words, let thy silence feign thee so.—It is not a greater point of wisdom to discover knowledge than to hide ignorance.—*Quarles*.

Silence, when nothing need be said, is the eloquence of discretion.—*Bovee*.

Speech is great, but silence is greater. —*Carlyle*.

The silence of the place was like a sleep, so full of rest it seemed.—*Longfellow*.

Silence is the perfectest herald of joy; I were but little happy if I could say how much.—*Shakespeare*.

He who, silent, loves to be with us, and who loves us in our silence, has touched one of the keys that ravish hearts.—*Lavater*.

A good word is an easy obligation; but not to speak ill requires only our silence, which costs us nothing.—*Tillotson*.

The temple of our purest thoughts is silence.—*Mrs. S. J. Hale*.

Let us be silent that we may hear the whispers of the gods.—*Emerson*.

It is the wise head that makes the still tongue.—*W. J. Lucas*.

This is such a serious world that we should never speak at all unless we have something to say.—*Carlyle*.

Silence in woman is like speech in men; deny it who can.—*Ben Jonson*.

Most men speak when they do not know how to be silent. He is wise who knows when to hold his peace. Tie your tongue, lest it be wanton and luxuriate; keep it within the banks; a rapidly flowing river soon collects mud.—*Ambrose*.

Fellows who have no tongues are often all eyes and ears.—*Haliburton*.

There are three kinds of silence. Silence from words is good, because inordinate speaking tends to evil. Silence, or rest from desires and passions is still better, because it promotes quietness of spirit. But the best of all is silence from unnecessary and wandering thoughts, because that is essential to internal recollection, and because it lays a foundation for a proper reputation

and for silence in other respects.—*Mad. Guyon*.

A silent man is easily reputed wise. The unknown is always wonderful. A man who suffers none to see him in the common jostle and undress of life easily gathers round him a mysterious veil of unknown sanctity, and men honor him for a saint.—*F. W. Robertson*.

What a strange power there is in silence! How many resolutions are formed, how many sublime conquests effected, during that pause when lips are closed, and the soul secretly feels the eye of her Maker upon her!—They are the strong ones of earth who know how to keep silence when it is a pain and grief unto them, and who give time to their own souls to wax strong against temptation.—*Emerson*.

Silence is the ornament and safeguard of the ignorant.

Silence is the safest respondent for all the contradiction that arises from impertinence, vulgarity, or envy.—*Zimmermann*.

The main reason why silence is so efficacious an element of repute is, first, because of that magnification which proverbially belongs to the unknown; and, secondly, because silence provokes no man's envy, and wounds no man's self-love.—*Bulwer*.

Silence in times of suffering is the best.—*Dryden*.

Speech is often barren; but silence also does not necessarily brood over a full nest. Your still fowl, blinking at you without remark, may all the while be sitting on one addled nest-egg; and when it takes to cackling, will have nothing to announce but that addled delusion.—*George Eliot*.

The unspoken word never does harm. —*Kossuth*.

Silence and reserve suggest latent power. What some men think has more effect than what others say.—*Chesterfield*.

Nothing is so good for an ignorant man as silence; if he were sensible of this he would not be ignorant.—*Saadi*.

If you would pass for more than your value, say little.—It is easier to look wise than to talk wisely.

Learn to hold thy tongue.—Five words cost Zacharias forty weeks of silence.—*Fuller.*

As we must render an account of every idle word, so we must of our idle silence.—*Ambrose.*

Silence is the ecstatic bliss of souls, that by intelligence converse.—*Otway.*

I spake no word; inferior joys live but by utterance; rapture is born dumb. —*H. Neele.*

Silence is the element in which great things fashion themselves together; that at length they may emerge, full-formed and majestic, into the delights of life, which they are thenceforth to rule.—*Carlyle.*

The more a man desirous to pass at a value above his worth, and can, by dignified silence, contrast with the garrulity of trivial minds, the more will the world give him credit for the wealth he does not possess.—*Bulwer.*

A judicious silence is always better than truth spoken without charity.— *De Sales.*

Silence is a figure of speech, unanswerable, short, cold, but terribly severe.—*Theodore Parker.*

A judicious reticence is hard to learn, but it is one of the great lessons of life. —*Chesterfield.*

If thou desire to be held wise, be so wise as to hold thy tongue.—*Quarles.*

There is a silence, the child of love, which expresses everything, and proclaims more loudly than the tongue is able to do.—*Alfieri.*

A person that would secure to himself great deference will, perhaps, gain his point by silence as effectually as by anything he can say.—*Shenstone.*

He knows not how to speak who cannot be silent; still less how to act with vigor and decision. Who hastens to the end is silent; loudness is impotence.—*Lavater.*

I like better for one to say some foolish thing upon important matters than to be silent. That becomes the subject of discussion and dispute, and the truth is discovered.—*Diderot.*

As men of sense and genius say much in few words, so on the other hand the weak and foolish speak much and say little.—*Rochefoucauld.*

Talkers and futile persons are commonly vain and credulous withal, for he that talketh what he knoweth will also talk what he knoweth not; therefore set it down that a habit of secrecy is both politic and moral.—*Bacon.*

Blessed is the man who, having nothing to say, abstains from giving wordy evidence of the fact.—*George Eliot.*

If any man think it a small matter to bridle his tongue, he is much mistaken; for it is a point to be silent when occasion requires, and better than to speak, though never so well.—*Plutarch.*

Of a distinguished general it was said that "he could hold his tongue in ten languages."

It is only reason that teaches silence; the heart teaches us to speak.—*Richter.*

It is better either to be silent, or to say things of more value than silence. Sooner throw a pearl at hazard than an idle or useless word; and do not say a little in many words, but a great deal in a few.—*Pythagoras.*

None preaches better than the ant, and she says nothing.—*Franklin.*

I think the first virtue is to restrain the tongue; he approaches nearest to the gods who knows how to be silent, even though he is in the right.—*Cato.*

If a word be worth one shekel, silence is worth two.—*Rabbi Ben Azai.*

Silence is one of the great arts of conversation, as allowed by Cicero himself, who says "there is not only an art, but an eloquence in it." A well-bred woman may easily and effectually promote the most useful and elegant conversation without speaking a word.—The modes of speech are scarcely more variable than the modes of silence.—*Blair.*

Silence never shows itself to so great an advantage as when it is made the reply to calumny and defamation.—*Addison.*

SIMPLICITY.—In character, in manners, in style, in all things, the supreme excellence is simplicity.—*Longfellow.*

When a man is made wholly of the dove, without the least grain of the serpent in his composition, he becomes ridiculous in many circumstances, and often discredits his best actions.—*Addison.*

Simplicity, of all things, is the hardest to be copied.—*Steele.*

He is of a free and open nature that thinks all men honest who but seem to be so, and will as tenderly be led by the nose as asses are.—*Shakespeare.*

Goodness and simplicity are indissolubly united.—The bad are the most sophisticated, all the world over, and the good the least.—*H. Martineau.*

Nothing is more simple than greatness; indeed, to be simple is to be great.—*Emerson.*

Whose nature is so far from doing harms that he suspects none.—*Shakespeare.*

Simplicity of character is the natural result of profound thought.—*Hazlitt.*

The most agreeable of all companions is a simple, frank man, without any high pretensions to an oppressive greatness—one who loves life, and understands the use of it; obliging alike at all hours; above all, of a golden temper, and steadfast as an anchor. For such an one we gladly exchange the greatest genius, the most brilliant wit, the profoundest thinker.—*Lessing.*

Purity and simplicity are the two wings with which man soars above the earth and all temporary nature.—Simplicity is in the intention; purity in the affection: simplicity turns to God; purity unites with and enjoys him.—*Thomas à Kempis.*

When thought is too weak to be simply expressed, it is a clear proof that it should be rejected.—*Vauvanargues.*

The greatest truths are the simplest; and so are the greatest men.—*Hare.*

A childlike mind, in its simplicity, practices that science of good to which the wise may be blind.—*Schiller.*

If our love were but more simple, we should take Him at his word, and our lives would be all sunshine in the sweetness of the Lord.—*Faber.*

Elegance of language may not be in the power of all of us; but simplicity and straightforwardness are. Write much as you would speak; speak as you think. If with your inferiors, speak no coarser than usual; if with your superiors, no finer. Be what you say; and, within the rules of prudence, say what you are.—*Alford.*

Upright simplicity is the deepest wisdom, and perverse craft the merest shallowness.—*Barrow.*

Simplicity is Nature's first step, and the last of Art.—*P. J. Bailey.*

There is a majesty in simplicity which is far above the quaintness of wit.—*Pope.*

SIN.—Sin is, essentially, a departure from God.—*Luther.*

Sin is any want of conformity unto, or transgression of the law of God.—*Shorter Catechism.*

He that falls into sin is a man, that grieves at it is a saint, that boasteth of it is a devil; yet some glory in that shame, counting the stains of sin the best complexion of their souls.—*Fuller.*

The recognition of sin is the beginning of salvation.—*Luther.*

Sin is first pleasing, then it grows easy, then delightful, then frequent, then habitual, then confirmed; then the man is impenitent, then he is obstinate, then he is resolved never to repent, and then he is ruined.—*Leighton.*

All the sin that has darkened human life and saddened human history began in believing a falsehood: all the power of Christianity to make men holy is associated with believing truth.—*J. A. Broadus.*

If thou wouldst conquer thy weakness thou must never gratify it.—No man is compelled to evil; only his consent makes it his.—It is no sin to be tempted; it is to yield and be overcome.—*Penn.*

He who sins against men may fear discovery, but he who sins against God is sure of it.—*Jones.*

Few love to hear the sins they love to act.—*Shakespeare.*

The worst effect of sin is within, and is manifest not in poverty, and pain, and bodily defacement, but in the discrowned faculties, the unworthy love, the low ideal, the brutalized and enslaved spirit.—*E. H. Chapin.*

Our sins, like our shadows when day is in its glory, scarce appear; toward evening, how great and monstrous they are!—*Suckling.*

Sin is never at a stay; if we do not retreat from it, we shall advance in it; and the further on we go, the more we have to come back.—*Barrow.*

Use sin as it will use you; spare it not, for it will not spare you; it is your murderer, and the murderer of the world: use it, therefore, as a murderer should be used. Kill it before it kills you. You love not death; love not the cause of death.—*Baxter.*

Respectable sin is, in principle, the mother of all basest crime.—Follow it to the bitter end, and there is ignominy as well as guilt eternal.—*Horace Bushnell.*

If you would be free from sin, fly temptation: he that does not endeavor to avoid the one cannot expect Providence to protect him from the other. If the first sparks of ill were quenched, there would be no flame, for how can he kill, that dares not be angry; or be an adulterer in act, who does not transgress in thought; or be perjured, that fears an oath; or defraud, that does not allow himself to covet?—*Palmer.*

The deadliest sin were the consciousness of no sin.—*Carlyle.*

Most sins begin at the eyes; by them commonly, Satan creeps into the heart: that man can never be in safety that hath not covenanted with his eyes.

The wages that sin bargains for with the sinner, are life, pleasure, and profit; but the wages it pays him, are death, torment, and destruction. To understand the falsehood and deceit of sin, we must compare its promises and payments together.—*South.*

When we think of death, a thousand sins, which we have trodden as worms beneath our feet, rise up against us as flaming serpents.—*Walter Scott.*

I fear nothing but doing wrong.—*Sterne.*

As sins proceed they ever multiply; and like figures in arithmetic, the last stands for more than all that went before it.—*Sir T. Browne.*

Guilt, though it may attain temporal splendor, can never confer real happiness. The evident consequences of our crimes long survive their commission,

and, like the ghosts of the murdered, forever haunt the steps of the malefactor.—*Walter Scott.*

It is as supreme a folly to talk of a little sin as it would be to talk of a small decalogue that forbids it, or a diminutive God that hates it, or a shallow hell that will punish it.—*C. S. Robinson.*

No man becomes fully evil at once; but suggestion bringeth on indulgence; indulgence, delight; delight, consent; consent, endeavor; endeavor, practice; practice, custom; custom, excuse; excuse, defence; defence, obstinacy; obstinacy, boasting; boasting, a seared conscience and a reprobate mind.

Sin may open bright as the morning, but it will end dark as night.—*Talmage.*

Bad men hate sin through fear of punishment; good men hate sin through their love of virtue.—*Juvenal.*

What is human sin but the abuse of human appetites, of human passions, of human faculties, in themselves all innocent?—*R. D. Hitchcock.*

The course of evil begins so slowly, and from such slight source, an infant's hand might stem the breach with clay; but let the stream get deeper, and philosophy, aye, and religion too, shall strive in vain, to turn the headlong current.

There are some sins which are more justly to be denominated surprises than infidelities. To such the world should be lenient, as, doubtless, Heaven is forgiving.—*Massillon.*

There is no sin we can be tempted to commit, but we shall find a greater satisfaction in resisting than in committing.

We are saved from nothing if we are not saved from sin. Little sins are pioneers of hell.—*Howell.*

There are three things which the true Christian desires in respect to sin: Justification, that it may not condemn; sanctification, that it may not reign; and glorification, that it may not be.—*Cecil.*

He that hath slight thought of sin never had great thoughts of God.—*Owen.*

There is a vast difference between sins of infirmity and those of presumption, as vast as between inadvertency and deliberation.—*South.*

Every gross act of sin is much the same thing to the conscience that a great blow is to the head; it stuns and bereaves it of all use of its senses for a time.—*South.*

Whatever disunites man from God disunites man from man.—*Burke.*

It is not only what we do, but also what we do not do, for which we are accountable.—*Molière.*

No sin is small.—It is against an infinite God, and may have consequences immeasurable.—No grain of sand is small in the mechanism of a watch.—*Jeremy Taylor.*

Every sin is a mistake, as well as a wrong; and the epitaph for the sinner is, "Thou fool!"—*A. Maclaren.*

If I were sure God would pardon me, and men would not know my sin, yet I should be ashamed to sin, because of its essential baseness.—*Plato.*

The sin that now rises to your memory as your bosom sin, let this be first of all withstood and mastered.—Oppose it instantly by a detestation of it, by a firm will to conquer it, by reflection, by reason, by prayer.—*Channing.*

How immense appear to us the sins that we have not committed.—*Mad. Necker.*

Sin is to be overcome, not so much by direct opposition to it as by cultivating opposite principles. Would you kill the weeds in your garden, plant it with good seed; if the ground be well occupied there will be less need of the hoe. —*A. Fuller.*

There is more bitterness in sin's ending than there ever was sweetness in its acting.—If you see nothing but good in its commission, you will suffer only woe in its conclusion.—*Dyer.*

Sins are like circles in the water when a stone is thrown into it; one produces another.—When anger was in Cain's heart, murder was not far off.—*Philip Henry.*

If I grapple with sin in my own strength, the devil knows he may go to sleep.—*H. G. J. Adams.*

I could not live in peace if I put the shadow of a wilful sin between myself and God.—*George Eliot.*

Man-like it is, to fall into sin; fiend-like it is, to dwell therein; Christ-like it is, for sin to grieve; God-like it is, all sin to leave.—*Longfellow.*

There is no fool equal to the sinner, who every moment ventures his soul.—*Tillotson.*

Sins of the mind have less infamy than those of the body, but not less malignity.—*Whichcote.*

It is not true that there are no enjoyments in the ways of sin; there are, many and various.—But the great and radical defect of them all is, that they are transitory and unsubstantial, at war with reason and conscience, and always leave a sting behind. We are hungry, and they offer us bread; but it is poisoned bread. We are thirsty, and they offer us drink; but it is from deadly fountains. They may and often do satisfy us for the moment; but it is death in the end. It is only the bread of heaven and the water of life that can so satisfy that we shall hunger no more and thirst no more forever.—*Tryon Edwards.*

SINCERITY.—Sincerity is to speak as we think, to do as we pretend and profess, to perform what we promise, and really to be what we would seem and appear to be.—*Tillotson.*

Sincerity is the face of the soul, as dissimulation is the mask.—*S. Dubay.*

Sincerity, a deep, genuine, heart-felt sincerity is, a trait of true and noble manhood.

Inward sincerity will of course influence the outward deportment; where the one is wanting, there is great reason to suspect the absence of the other.—*Sterne.*

Sincerity is the indispensable ground of all conscientiousness, and by consequence of all heartfelt religion.—*Kant.*

Sincerity is no test of truth—no evidence of correctness of conduct.—You may take poison sincerely believing it the needed medicine, but will it save your life?—*Tryon Edwards.*

Sincerity, thou first of virtues, let no mortal leave thy onward path, although the earth should gape, and from the gulf of hell destruction rise, to take dissimulation's winding way.—*Home.*

The shortest and surest way to live with honor in the world, is to be in reality what we would appear to be; all human virtues increase and strengthen themselves by the practice and experience of them.—*Socrates.*

Sincerity is like traveling on a plain, beaten road, which commonly brings a man sooner to his journey's end than by-ways, in which men often lose themselves.—*Tillotson.*

The whole faculties of man must be exerted in order to call forth noble energies; and he who is not earnestly sincere lives in but half his being, self-mutilated, self-paralyzed.—*Coleridge.*

His words are bonds, his oaths are oracles; his love sincere, his thoughts immaculate; his tears, pure messengers sent from his heart; his heart as far from fraud, as heaven from earth.—*Shakespeare.*

Sincerity and truth are the basis of every virtue.—*Confucius.*

It is often said it is no matter what a man believes if he is only sincere. But let a man sincerely believe that seed planted without ploughing is as good as with; that January is as favorable for seed-sowing as April; and that cockle seed will produce as good a harvest as wheat, and is it so?—*H. W. Beecher.*

You know I say just what I think, and nothing more nor less.—I cannot say one thing and mean another.—*Longfellow.*

SINGULARITY.—Let those who would affect singularity with success, first determine to be very virtuous, and they will be sure to be very singular. —*Colton.*

He who would be singular in his apparel had need have something superlative to balance that affectation.— *Feltham.*

Singularity is laudable, when in contradiction to a multitude, it adheres to the dictates of morality and honor. In concerns of this kind it is to be looked upon as heroic bravery, in which a man leaves the species only as he soars above it.—*Addison.*

SLANDER.—(See "SCANDAL," "REPUTATION.")

Slander is a vice that strikes a double blow, wounding both him that commits, and him against whom it is committed. —*Saurin.*

Believe nothing against another, but on good authority; nor report what may hurt another, unless it be a greater hurt to some other to conceal it.—*Penn.*

The worthiest people are the most injured by slander, as it is the best fruit which the birds have been pecking at. —*Swift.*

Slander is the revenge of a coward, and dissimulation his defence.—*Johnson.*

When will talkers refrain from evil-speaking? When listeners refrain from evil-hearing.—*Hare.*

Diogenes being asked, "What is that beast, the bite of which is the most dangerous?" replied, "Of wild beasts, the bite of a slanderer; and of tame beasts, that of the flatterer."

Plato, hearing that some asserted he was a very bad man, said, "I shall take care so to live that nobody will believe them."—*Guardian.*

Slander as often comes from vanity as from malice.

Slanderers are like flies, that pass all over a man's good parts to light only on his sores.—*Rule of Life.*

No one is safe from slander. The best way is to pay no attention to it, but live in innocence and let the world talk.—*Molière.*

Who stabs my name would stab my person, too, did not the hangman's axe lie in the way.—*Crown.*

The slanderer inflicts wrong by calumniating the absent; and he who gives credit to the calumny before he knows its truth, is equally guilty.—*Herodotus.*

No might nor greatness can censure escape; back-wounding calumny the whitest virtue strikes; what king so strong, can tie the gall up in the slanderous tongue?—*Shakespeare.*

The slanderer and the assassin differ only in the weapon they use; with the one it is the dagger, with the other the tongue.—The former is worse than the latter, for the last only kills the body, while the other murders the reputation and peace.—*Tryon Edwards.*

Slander, whose edge is sharper than

the sword; whose tongue outvenoms all the worms of Nile; whose breath rides on the posting winds, and doth belie all corners of the world.—*Shakespeare*.

Divines do rightly infer from the sixth commandment, that scandalizing one's neighbor with false and malicious reports, whereby I vex his spirit, and consequently impair his health, is a degree of murder.—*Sir W. Raleigh*.

Slugs crawl and crawl over our cabbages, like the world's slander over a good name. You may kill them, it is true, but there is the slime.—*Douglas Jerrold*.

A slanderer felt an adder bite his side: What followed from the bite? The serpent died.

Curst be the tongue, whence slanderous rumor, like the adder's drop distils her venom, withering friendship's faith, turning love's favor.—*Hillhouse*.

Slander meets no regard from noble minds; only the base believe what the base only utter.—*Bellers*.

There would not be so many open mouths if there were not so many open ears.—*Bp. Hall*.

The man that dares traduce because he can with safety to himself, is not a man.—*Cowper*.

He, who would free from malice pass his days, must live obscure, and never merit praise.—*Gay*.

Oh! many a shaft, at random sent, finds mark the archer little meant; and many a word, at random spoken, may soothe or wound a heart that's broken. —*Walter Scott*.

Done to death by slanderous tongues. —*Shakespeare*.

It is commonly unnecessary to refute slander and calumny, except by perseverance in well doing; they are sparks, which, if you do not fan them, will soon go out.

If evil be said of thee, and it is true, correct it; if it be a lie, laugh at it.

That thou art blamed, shall not be thy defect; for slander's mark was ever yet the fair; so thou be good, slander doth but approve thy worth the greater. —*Shakespeare*.

Next to the slanderer, we detest the bearer of the slander to our ears.—*M. H. Catherwood*.

Life would be a perpetual flea-hunt if a man were obliged to run down all the innuendoes, inveracities, insinuations, and suspicions which are uttered against him.—*H. W. Beecher*.

The surest method against scandal is to live it down by perseverance in well-doing.—*Boerhaave*.

If slander be a snake, it is a winged one. It flies as well as creeps.—*Douglas Jerrold*.

How frequently are the honesty and integrity of a man disposed of by a smile or shrug! How many good and generous actions have been sunk into oblivion by a distrustful look, or stamped with the imputation of bad motives, by a mysterious and seasonable whisper!—*Sterne*.

There is nothing which wings its flight so swiftly as calumny, nothing which is uttered with more ease; nothing is listened to with more readiness, nothing dispersed more widely.—*Cicero*.

The slander of some people is as great a recommendation as the praise of others.—*Fielding*.

Listen not to a tale-bearer or slanderer, for he tells thee nothing out of good will; but as he discovereth of the secrets of others, so he will of thine in turn.—*Socrates*.

Calumny would soon starve and die of itself if nobody took it in and gave it lodging.—*Leighton*.

If any speak ill of thee, flee home to thy own conscience, and examine thy heart: if thou be guilty, it is a just correction; if not guilty, it is a fair instruction: make use of both; so shalt thou distil honey out of gall, and out of an open enemy create a secret friend. —*Quarles*.

When the tongue of slander stings thee, let this be thy comfort,—they are not the worst fruits on which the wasps alight.—*Burger*.

Close thine ear against him that shall open his mouth secretly against another. If thou receivest not his words, they fly back and wound the reporter. If thou dost receive them, they fly forward, and wound the receiver.—*Lavater*.

The way to check slander is to despise it; attempt to overtake and refute it, and it will outrun you.—*A. Dumas.*

If any one tells you a person speaks ill of you, do not make excuse about what is said, but answer: "He was ignorant of my other faults else he would not have mentioned these alone."—*Epictetus.*

There is nobody so weak of invention that he cannot make up some little stories to vilify his enemy.—*Addison.*

Have patience awhile; slanders are not long-lived.—Truth is the child of time; ere long she shall appear to vindicate thee.—*Kant.*

Slander cannot make the subject of it either better or worse.—It may represent us in a false light, or place a likeness of us in a bad one, but we are always the same.—Not so the slanderer, for calumny always makes the calumniator worse, but the calumniated never. —*Colton.*

We cannot control the evil tongues of others, but a good life enables us to despise them.—*Cato.*

SLAVERY.—Whatever makes man a slave takes half his worth away.—*Pope.*

Disguise thyself as thou wilt, still, slavery, thou art a bitter draught.—*Sterne.*

That execrable sum of all villainies commonly called the slave-trade.—*J. Wesley.*

Corrupted freemen are the worst of slaves.—*Garrick.*

Here lies the evil of slavery: Its whips, imprisonments, and even the horrors of the middle passage, are not to be named, in comparison with the extinction of the proper consciousness of a human being—with the degradation of a man into a brute.—*Channing.*

There is a law above all human enactments, written upon the heart by the finger of God; and while men despise fraud, and loathe rapine, and abhor blood, they shall reject with indignation the wild and guilty phantasy, that man can hold property in man.—*Brougham.*

Slavery is a system of the most complete injustice.—*Plato.*

Every man has a property in his own

person; this nobody has a right to but himself.—*Locke.*

Natural liberty is the gift of the beneficent Creator of the whole human race.—*Alexander Hamilton.*

Slavery is a system of outrage and robbery.—*Socrates.*

Slavery is an atrocious debasement of human nature.—*Franklin.*

Slavery is a state so improper, so degrading, so ruinous to the feelings and capacities of human nature, that it ought not to be suffered to exist.—*Burke.*

Slavery is not only opposed to all the principles of morality, but, as it appears to me, is pregnant with appalling and inevitable danger to the Republic.—*Humboldt.*

I envy neither the heart nor the head of that man from the North, who rises here in Congress to defend slavery from principle.—*John Randolph.*

We have found that this evil, slavery, has preyed upon the very vitals of the Union, and has been prejudicial to all the States in which it has existed.—*James Monroe.*

The abolition of domestic slavery is the greatest object of desire in these colonies, where it was unhappily introduced in their infant state.—*Thos. Jefferson.*

I can only say that there is not a man living who wishes more sincerely than I do to see a plan adopted for the abolition of slavery.—*Washington.*

Not only does the Christian religion, but Nature herself, cry out against the state of slavery.—*Pope Leo X.*

It is injustice to permit slavery to remain for a single hour.—*William Pitt.*

Slavery is contrary to the fundamental law of all societies.—*Montesquieu.*

Slavery in all its forms, in all its degrees, is a violation of divine law, and a degradation of human nature.—*Brissot.*

Those are men-stealers who abduct, keep, sell, or buy slaves or freemen.—*Grotius.*

Where slavery is, there liberty cannot be; and where liberty is, there slavery cannot be.—*Charles Sumner.*

It is observed by Homer that a man loses half his virtue the day he becomes a slave; he might have added, with truth, that he is likely to lose more than half when he becomes a slave-master. —*Whately.*

We can apply to slavery no worse name than its own. Men have always shrunk instinctively from this state, as the most degraded. No punishment, save death, has been more dreaded; and, to avoid it, death has often been endured. Slavery virtually dissolves the domestic relations. It ruptures the most sacred ties upon earth. It violates home. It lacerates best affections; produces and gives license to cruelty; compels the master systematically to degrade the mind of the slave; and to resist that improvement which is the design and end of the Creator.—Millions may rise up and tell me that the slave suffers little from cruelty. I know too much of human nature, human history, and human passion, to believe them.— *Channing.*

Englishmen will never be slaves; they are free to do whatever the Government and public opinion allow them to do. —*George Bernard Shaw.*

The man who gives me employment, which I must have or suffer, that man is my master, let me call him what I will.—*Henry George.*

The whole commerce between master and slave is a perpetual exercise of the most boisterous passions; the most unremitting despotism on the one part, and degrading submission on the other. The man must be a prodigy who can retain his manners and morals undepraved by such circumstances. The hour of emancipation must come; but whether it will be brought on by the generous energies of our own minds, or by the bloody scenes of St. Domingo, is a leaf of our history not yet turned over. The Almighty has no attribute which can take sides with us in such a contest. —*Jefferson.*

From my earliest youth I have regarded slavery as a great moral and political evil.—I think it unjust, repugnant to the natural equality of mankind, founded only in superior power; a standing and permanent conquest by the stronger over the weaker.—All pretence of defending it on the ground of different races, I have ever condemned, and have even said that if the black race is weaker, that is a reason against and not for its subjection and oppression.—In a religious point of view, I have ever regarded and spoken of it, not as subject to any express denunciation, either in the Old Testament or the New, but as opposed to the whole spirit of the gospel, and to the teachings of Jesus Christ.—The religion of Christ is a religion of kindness, justice, and brotherly love:—but slavery is not kindly affectionate; it does not seek another's and not its own; it does not let the oppressed go free; it is but a continual act of oppression.—*Daniel Webster.*

No one is a slave whose will is free. —*Tyrius Maximus.*

SLEEP.—(See " BED.")

Our foster-nurse of nature is repose.— *Shakespeare.*

Blessings on him who first invented sleep.—It covers a man all over, thoughts and all, like a cloak.—It is meat for the hungry, drink for the thirsty, heat for the cold, and cold for the hot.—It makes the shepherd equal to the monarch, and the fool to the wise.—There is but one evil in it, and that is that it resembles death, since between a dead man and a sleeping man there is but little difference.— *Cervantes.*

"Sleep is so like death," says Sir Thomas Browne, "that I dare not trust myself to it without prayer." They both, when they seize the body, leave the soul at liberty; and wise is he that remembers of both, that they can be made safe and happy only by virtue.— *Sir W. Temple.*

Sleep, to the homeless thou art home; the friendless find in thee a friend.— *Ebenezer Elliott.*

Sleep, that knits up the ravell'd sleeve of care; the death of each day's life, sore labor's bath; balm of hurt minds; great nature's second course; chief nourisher in life's feast.—*Shakespeare.*

Sleep is pain's easiest salve, and doth

fulfil all offices of death, except to kill.
—*Donne.*

Tired nature's sweet restorer, balmy
sleep; he, like the world, his ready
visit pays where fortune smiles—the
wretched he forsakes.—*Young.*

When tir'd with vain rotations of the
day, sleep winds us up for the succeeding dawn.—*Young.*

In thee oppressors soothe their angry
brow; in thee, th' oppress'd forget tyran-
nic pow'r; in thee, the wretch condemn'd
is equal to his judge; and the sad lover
to his cruel fair; nay, all the shining
glories men pursue, when thou art
wanted, are but empty noise.—*Steele.*

Sleep, the antechamber of the grave.
—*Richter.*

One hour's sleep before midnight, is
worth two after.—*Fielding.*

Downy sleep, death's counterfeit.—
Shakespeare.

Put off thy cares with thy clothes; so
shall thy rest strengthen thy labor; and
and so shall thy labor sweeten thy rest.
—*Quarles.*

God gives sleep to the bad, in order
that the good may be undisturbed.—
Saadi.

When one turns over in bed, it is
time to turn out.—*Wellington.*

Weariness can snore upon the flint,
when restive sloth finds the down pillow
hard.—*Shakespeare.*

Leave your bed upon the first desertion of sleep; it being ill for the eyes
to read lying, and worse for the mind
to be idle; since the head during that
laziness is commonly a cage for unclean
thoughts.—*F. Osborn.*

It is a shame when the church itself
is a cemetery, where the living sleep
above the ground, as the dead do beneath.—*Fuller.*

Sleep, the type of death, is also, like
that which it typifies, restricted to the
earth.—It flies from hell, and is excluded
from heaven.—*Colton.*

Sleep, thou repose of all things; thou
gentlest of the duties; thou peace of
the mind, from which care flies; who
dost soothe the hearts of men wearied
with the toils of the day, and refittest
them for labor.—*Ovid.*

It is a delicious moment, certainly,
that of being well nestled in bed and
feeling that you shall drop gently to
sleep. The good is to come, not past;
the limbs are tired enough to render the
remaining in one posture delightful; the
labor of the day is gone. A gentle failure of the perceptions creeps over you;
the spirit of consciousness disengages itself once more, and with slow and hush-
ing degrees, like a mother detaching her
hand from that of a sleeping child, the
mind seems to have a balmy lid closing
over it, like the eye—it is closed—the
mysterious spirit has gone to take its
airy rounds.—*Leigh Hunt.*

SLOTH. — Sloth, like rust, consumes
faster than labor wears, while the key
often used is always bright.—*Franklin.*

Sloth, if it has prevented many crimes,
has also smothered many virtues.—
Colton.

Flee sloth, for the indolence of the
soul is the decay of the body.—*Cato.*

Sloth makes all things difficult, but
industry all easy; and he that riseth
late must trot all day, and shall scarce
overtake his business at night; while
laziness travels so slowly that poverty
soon overtakes him.—*Franklin.*

Sloth is torpidity of the mental
faculties; the sluggard is a living insensible.—*Zimmermann.*

Many are idly busy.—Domitian was
busy, but then it was in catching flies.—
Jeremy Taylor.

Excess is not the only thing that
breaks up both health and enjoyment;
many are brought into a very ill and
languishing habit of body by mere sloth,
which is both a great sin, and the cause
of many more.—*South.*

Sloth never arrived at the attainment
of a good wish.—*Cervantes.*

SMILES.—A smile is the whisper of
a laugh.—*Child's Definition.*

A face that cannot smile is never
good.—*Martial.*

Smiles from reason flow, to brute denied, and are of love the food.—*Milton.*

A woman has two smiles that an angel
might envy—the smile that accepts a
lover before words are uttered, and the
smile that lights on the first-born babe,
and assures it of a mother's love.—
Haliburton.

Those happiest smiles that played on her ripe lips seemed not to know what guests were in her eyes, which parted thence as pearls from diamonds dropped. —*Shakespeare*.

Wrinkles should merely indicate where smiles have been.—*Mark Twain*.

Eternal smiles his emptiness betray, as shallow streams run dimpling all the way.—*Pope*.

What a sight there is in that word "smile!" it changes like a chameleon. There is a vacant smile, a cold smile, a smile of hate, a satiric smile, an affected smile; but, above all, a smile of love.— *Haliburton*.

A beautiful smile is to the female countenance what the sunbeam is to the landscape: it embellishes an inferior face, and redeems an ugly one.—*Lavater*.

Something of a person's character may be discovered by observing how he smiles.—Some people never smile; they only grin.—*Bovee*.

There are many kinds of smiles, each having a distinct character. Some announce goodness and sweetness, others betray sarcasm, bitterness, and pride; some soften the countenance by their languishing tenderness, others brighten by their spiritual vivacity.—*Lavater*.

Loud laughter is the mirth of the mob, who are only pleased with silly things; for true wit or good sense never excited a laugh since the creation of the world. —A man of parts and fashion, therefore, is only seen to smile, but never heard to laugh.—*Chesterfield*.

The odor is the rose; the smile, the woman.—*R. U. Johnson*.

A disagreeable smile distorts the lines of beauty, and is more repulsive than a frown.—*Lavater*.

SNEERING.—The habit of sneering marks the egotist, the fool, or the knave, or all three.—*Lavater*.

I fancy that it is just as hard to do your duty when men are sneering at you as when they are shooting at you.— *Woodrow Wilson*.

Who can refute a sneer?—*William Paley*.

There was a laughing devil in his sneer, which raised emotions both of rage and fear; and where his frown of hatred darkly fell, hope withering fled, and mercy sighed farewell.—*Byron*.

The most insignificant people are the most apt to sneer at others. They are safe from reprisals, and have no hope of rising in their own esteem but by lowering their neighbors.—*Hazlitt*.

What would the nightingale care if the toad despised her singing? She would still sing on, and leave the cold toad to his dark shadows. And what care I for the sneers of men who grovel upon earth? I will still sing on in the ear and bosom of God.—*H. W. Beecher*.

A sneer is often the sign of heartless malignity.—*Lavater*.

SNOBS.—He who forgets his own friends meanly to follow after those of a higher degree is a snob.—*Thackeray*.

Snobs in high places assume great airs, and are pretentious in all they do, and the higher their elevation, the more conspicuous is the incongruity of their position.—*S. Smiles*.

A snob is one who is always pretending to be something better—especially richer or more fashionable than others —*Thackeray*.

SOBRIETY.—Modesty and humility are the sobriety of the mind; temperance and chastity are the sobriety of the body.—*Winchcote*.

SOCIETY.—Man is a social animal, formed to please and enjoy in society.— *Montesquieu*.

Society is the offspring of leisure; and to acquire this forms the only rational motive for accumulating wealth, notwithstanding the cant that prevails on the subject of labor.—*Tuckerman*.

Man, in society, is like a flower blown in its native bud. It is there only that his faculties, expanded in full bloom, shine out, there only reach their proper use.—*Cowper*.

We take our colors, chameleon-like, from each other.—*Chamfort*.

There are four varieties in society; the lovers, the ambitious, observers, and fools. The fools are the happiest.— *Taine*.

Society is a wall of very strong masonry, as it now stands; it may be sapped in the course of a thousand years, but stormed in a day—no! You dash your head against it—you scatter your brains, and you dislodge a stone. Society smiles in scorn, effaces the stain, and replaces the stone.—*Bulwer.*

The code of society is stronger with some persons than that of Sinai; and many a man who would not scruple to thrust his fingers in his neighbor's pocket, would forego peas rather than use his knife as a shovel.—*J. R. Lowell.*

Society is composed of two great classes: those who have more dinners than appetite, and those who have more appetite than dinners.—*Chamfort.*

Society is now one polished horde, formed of two mighty tribes, the bores and bored.—*Byron.*

Society undergoes continual changes; it is barbarous, it is civilized, it is Christianized, it is rich, it is scientific; but this change is not amelioration. For everything that is given something is taken. Society acquires new arts, and loses old instincts. The civilized man has built a coach, but has lost the use of his feet; he has a fine Geneva watch, but cannot tell the hour by the sun.—*Emerson.*

We are more sociable, and get on better with people by the heart than the intellect.—*Bruyère.*

Men would not live long in society if they were not the dupes of each other.—*Rochefoucauld.*

Society is like a lawn, where every roughness is smoothed, every bramble eradicated, and where the eye is delighted by the smiling verdure of a velvet surface. He, however, who would study nature in its wildness and variety, must plunge into the forest, must explore the glen, must stem the torrent, and dare the precipice.—*Washington Irving.*

Society is the atmosphere of souls; and we necessarily imbibe from it something which is either infectious or healthful.—*Bp. Hall.*

Besides the general infusion of wit to heighten civility, the direct splendor of intellectual power is ever welcome in fine society, as the costliest addition to its rule and its credit.—*Emerson.*

There is a sort of economy in Providence that one shall excel where another is defective. in order to make them more useful to each other, and mix them in society.—*Addison.*

It is certain that either wise bearing or ignorant carriage is caught, as men take diseases, one from another: therefore, let all take heed as to the society in which they mingle, for in a little while they will be like it.—*Rule of Life.*

We are a kind of chameleons, taking our hue—the hue of our moral character, from those who are about us.—*Locke.*

To attain excellence in society, an assemblage of qualifications is requisite: disciplined intellect, to think clearly, and to clothe thought with propriety and elegance; knowledge of human nature, to suit subject to character; true politeness, to prevent giving pain; a deep sense of morality, to preserve the dignity of speech; and a spirit of benevolence, to neutralize its asperities, and sanctify its powers.—*Mrs. Sigourney.*

Hail, social life! into thy pleasing bounds I come to pay the common stock, my share of service, and, in glad return, to taste thy comforts, thy protected joys.—*Thomson.*

Disagreeing in little things and agreeing in great ones is what forms and keeps up a commerce of society and friendship among reasonable men, and among unreasonable men breaks it.

The history of any private family, however humble, could it be fully related for five or six generations, would illustrate the state and progress of society better than the most elaborate dissertation.—*Southey.*

There exists a strict relation between the class of power and the exclusive and polished circles. The last are always filled, or filling from the first. Fashion, though in a strange way, represents all manly virtue. It is virtue gone to seed; a kind of posthumous honor; a hall of the past. Great men are not commonly in its halls: they are absent in the field: they are working, not triumphing. Fashion is made up of their children.—*Emerson.*

Society is no comfort to one not sociable.—*Shakespeare.*

From social intercourse are derived some of the highest enjoyments of life; where there is a free interchange of sentiments the mind acquires new ideas, and by a frequent exercise of its powers, the understanding gains fresh vigor.—*Addison.*

The secret of success in society is a certain heartiness and sympathy. A man who is not happy in company, cannot find any word in his memory that will fit the occasion; all his information is a little impertinent. A man who is happy there, finds in every turn of the conversation occasions for the introduction of what he has to say. The favorites of society are able men, and of more spirit than wit, who have no uncomfortable egotism, but who exactly fill the hour and the company, contented and contenting.—*Emerson.*

Without good company all dainties lose their true relish, and like painted grapes, are only seen, not tasted.—*Massinger.*

No company is preferable to bad, because we are more apt to catch the vices of others than their virtues, as disease is far more contagious than health.—*Colton.*

Too elevated qualities often unfit a man for society. We do not go to market with ingots, but with silver and small change.—*Chamfort.*

The uprooting of human beings from the land, the concentration in cities, the breakdown of the authority of the family, of tradition, and of moral conventions, the complexity and the novelty of modern life, and finally the economic insecurity of our industrial system have called into being the modern social worker. They perform a function in modern society which is not a luxury but an absolute necessity.—*Walter Lippmann.*

The change from the individual life of the animal to the group life of civilized man, which becomes a life of ever-expanding complexity as our scientific civilization advances, would obviously be impossible unless the individual learned in ever-increasing measure to subordinate his impulses and interests to the furtherance of the group life.—*Robert Andrews Millikan.*

In the pioneer days of our history it was easy to love one's neighbor and respect his rights, when possibly the neighbor lived at a distance of four or five miles and the relations were not intimate enough to occasion a clash of interests. Now one finds that society rather than another individual is his neighbor.—*Dr. John Grier Hibben.*

Society—the only field where the sexes have ever met on terms of equality, the arena where character is formed and studied, the cradle and the realm of public opinion, the crucible of ideas, the world's university, at once a school and a theatre, the spur and the crown of ambition, the tribunal which unmasks pretension and stamps real merit, the power that gives government leave to be, and outruns the lazy church in fixing the moral sense.—*Wendell Phillips.*

Society has only one law, and that is custom.—Even religion is socially powerful only so far as it has custom on its side.—*Hamerton.*

We must have the press of the crowd to draw virtue from us.—*Angelo Patri.*

Social problems can no longer be solved by class warfare any more than international problems can be solved by wars between nations. Warfare is negative and will sooner or later lead to destruction, while good will and cooperation are positive and supply the only safe basis for building a better future.—*Fridtjof Nansen.*

You may live in the fashionable quarter of town, but there is a dark slum somewhere on your property.—*Austin O'Malley.*

I believe that we already have a science of society—a very young and very incomplete science, but one that is steadily growing and that is capable of indefinite extension.—*Beatrice Webb.*

Half of the secret of getting along with people is consideration of their views; the other half is tolerance in one's own views.—*Daniel Frohman.*

Other people are quite dreadful. The only possible society is oneself.—*Oscar Wilde.*

The only worthwhile achievements of man are those which are socially useful.—*Dr. Alfred Adler.*

The ideal society would enable every man and woman to develop along their individual lines, and not attempt to force all into one mould, however admirable.—*J. B. S. Haldane.*

What an argument in favor of social connections is the observation that, by communicating our grief we have less, and by communicating our pleasures we have more.—*Greville.*

Let him who expects one class of society to prosper in the highest degree, while the other is in distress, try whether one side of his face can smile while the other is pinched.—*Fuller.*

Socialism is only a blind yearning after liberty and equality. It is the unsteady and brilliant dream of an earthly republic which can be realized only in the true Church of God.—*F. D. Huntington.*

SOLDIER.—A soldier seeking the bubble reputation even in the cannon's mouth.—*Shakespeare.*

Policy goes beyond strength, and contrivance before action; hence it is that direction is left to the commander, and execution to the soldier, who is not to ask Why? but to do what he is commanded.—*Xenophon.*

Soldiers are the only carnivorous animals that live in a gregarious state.—*Zimmermann.*

Soldiers that carry their lives in their hands, should carry the grace of God in their hearts.—*Baxter.*

A soldier, a mere tool, a kind of human sword in a fiend's hand; the other is master-mover of this warlike puppet.—*Byron.*

Ignorance, poverty, and vanity make many soldiers.—*Zimmermann.*

Dost thou know the fate of soldiers? —They are but ambition's tools, to cut a way to her unlawful ends.—And when they are worn, hacked, hewn with constant service, thrown aside, to rust in peace and rot in hospitals.—*Southern.*

Without a home must the soldier go, a changeful wanderer, and can warm himself at no home-lit hearth.—*Schiller.*

Soldiers looked at as they ought to be are to the world as poppies to cornfields.—*Douglas Jerrold.*

SOLITUDE.—A wise man is never less alone than when he is alone.—*Swift.*

If the mind loves solitude, it has thereby acquired a loftier character, and it becomes still more noble when the taste is indulged in.—*W. Humboldt.*

It had been hard to have put more truth and untruth together in a few words than in that speech, "Whosoever is delighted with solitude is either a wild beast or a god."—*Bacon.*

It has been said that he who retires to solitude is either a beast or an angel; the censure is too severe, and the praise unmerited: the discontented being, who retires from society, is generally some good-natured man, who has begun his life without experience, and knew not how to gain it in his intercourse with mankind.—*Goldsmith.*

Those beings only are fit for solitude, who like nobody, and are liked by nobody.—*Zimmermann.*

That which happens to the soil when it ceases to be cultivated, happens to man himself when he foolishly forsakes society for solitude; the brambles grow up in his desert heart.—*Rivarol.*

In solitude the mind gains strength, and learns to lean upon itself; in the world it seeks or accepts of a few treacherous supports—the feigned compassions of one, the flattery of a second, the civilities of a third, the friendship of a fourth; they all deceive, and bring the mind back to retirement, reflection, and books.—*Sterne.*

No doubt solitude is wholesome, but so is abstinence after a surfeit.—*The true life of man is in society.—Simms.*

Conversation enriches the understanding, but solitude is the school of genius.—*Gibbon.*

Living a good deal alone will, I believe, correct me of my faults; for a man can do without his own approbation in society, but he must make great exertions to gain it when he lives alone. Without it I am convinced solitude is not to be endured.—*Sydney Smith.*

An entire life of solitude contradicts the purpose of our being, since death itself is scarcely an idea of more terror.—*Burke.*

Half the pleasure of solitude comes from having with us some friend to whom we can say how sweet solitude is. —*W. Jay.*

Solitude is a good school, but the world is the best theatre; the institution is best there, but the practice here; the wilderness hath the advantage of discipline, and society opportunities of perfection.—*Jeremy Taylor.*

Leisure and solitude are the best effect of riches, because mother of thought. Both are avoided by most rich men, who seek company and business; which are signs of their being weary of themselves.—*Sir. W. Temple.*

If from society we learn to live, it is solitude should teach us how to die.—*Byron.*

One hour of thoughtful solitude may nerve the heart for days of conflict—girding up its armor to meet the most insidious foe.—*Percival.*

Solitude, seeming a sanctuary, proves a grave; a sepulchre in which the living lie, where all good qualities grow sick and die.—*Cowper.*

Amid the crowd, the hum, the shock of men, to hear, to see, to feel, and to possess, and roam along, the world's tired denizen, with none to bless us, none whom we can bless; this is to be alone; this, this is solitude.—*Byron.*

To be exempt from the passions with which others are tormented, is the only pleasing solitude.—*Addison.*

Solitude has but one disadvantage; it is apt to give one too high an opinion of one's self. In the world we are sure to be often reminded of every known or supposed defect we may have.—*Byron.*

It is easy, in the world, to live after the world's opinion; it is easy, in solitude, to live after your own; but the great man is he who, in the midst of the crowd, keeps with perfect sweetness the independence of solitude.—*Emerson.*

The love of retirement has in all ages adhered closely to those minds which have been most enlarged by knowledge, or elevated by genius. Those who enjoyed everything generally supposed to confer happiness have been forced to seek it in the shades of privacy.—*Johnson.*

Solitude is one of the highest enjoyments of which our nature is susceptible. It is also, when too long continued, capable of being made the most severe, indescribable, unendurable source of anguish.—*Deloreine.*

Solitude is sometimes best society, and short retirement urges sweet return.—*Milton.*

Oh! lost to virtue, lost to manly thought, lost to the noble sallies of the soul, who think it solitude to be alone.—*Young.*

How sweet, how passing sweet, is solitude! but grant me still a friend in my retreat, whom I may whisper, solitude is sweet.—*Cowper.*

O sacred solitude! divine retreat! choice of the prudent! envy of the great! by thy pure stream, or in thy waving shade, we count fair wisdom.—*Young.*

Solitude shows us what we should be; society shows us what we are.—*Cecil.*

We ought not to isolate ourselves, for we cannot remain in a state of isolation. Social intercourse makes us the more able to bear with ourselves and with others.—*Goethe.*

Alone, man—weak, tottering—yet with God this handful of dust made to be unmade, moulded to be molding, grasps the ungraspable, utters the ineffable, and when what seems too profound for human intelligence sweeps into the horizon, solitude is no more and misery has departed.—*Emil G. Hirsch.*

It would do the world good if every man in it would compel himself occasionally to be absolutely alone. Most of the world's progress has come out of such loneliness.—*Bruce Barton.*

Get away from the crowd when you can. Keep yourself to yourself, if only for a few hours daily.—*Arthur Brisbane.*

It is the mark of a superior man that, left to himself, he is able endlessly to amuse, interest and entertain himself out of his personal stock of meditations, ideas, criticisms, memories, philosophy, humor and what not.—*George Nathan.*

You cannot build up a character in a solitude; you need a formed character to stand a solitude.—*Austin O'Malley.*

I really only have Perfect Fun with myself. Other people won't stop and look at the things I want to look at or, if they do, they stop to please me or to humor me or to keep the peace.—*Katherine Mansfield.*

The strongest man in the world is he who stands most alone.—*Ibsen.*

There is a pleasure in the pathless woods; there is a rapture on the lonely shore; there is society, where none intrudes, by the deep sea, and music in its roar.—*Byron*.

Solitude, the safeguard of mediocrity, is to genius the stern friend, the cold, obscure shelter where moult the wings which will bear it farther than suns and stars. He who would inspire and lead his race must be defended from traveling with the souls of other men, from living, breathing, reading, and writing in the daily, time-worn yoke of their opinions.—*Emerson*.

Solitude cherishes great virtues and destroys little ones.—*Sydney Smith*.

In solitude, where we are least alone. —*Byron*.

What would a man do if he were compelled to live always in the sultry heat of society, and could never better himself in cool solitude?—*Hawthorne*.

Unsociable humors are contracted in solitude, which will, in the end, not fail of corrupting the understanding as well as the manners, and of utterly disqualifying a man for the satisfactions and duties of life. Men must be taken as they are, and we neither make them nor ourselves better by flying from or quarreling with them.—*Burke*.

In the world a man lives in his own age; in solitude in all ages.—*W. Mathews*.

Converse with men makes sharp the glittering wit, but God to man doth speak in solitude.—*J. S. Blackie*.

Until I truly loved I was alone.—*Mrs. Norton*.

This sacred shade and solitude, what is it? It is the felt presence of the Deity.—Few are the faults we flatter when alone.—By night an atheist half believes a God.—*Young*.

Solitude and company may be allowed to take their turns: the one creates in us the love of mankind, the other that of ourselves; solitude relieves us when we are sick of company, and conversation when we are weary of being alone, so that the one cures the other. There is no man so miserable as he that is at a loss how to use his time.—*Seneca*.

SONG.—(See "BALLADS.")

A careless song, with a little nonsense in it now and then, does not misbecome a monarch.—*Horace Walpole*.

A song will outlive all sermons in the memory.—*H. Giles*.

Little dew-drops of celestial melody. —*Carlyle*.

It was his nature to blossom into song, as it is a tree's to leaf itself in April.— *Alexander Smith*.

The best days of the church have always been its singing days.—*T. L. Cuyler*.

SOPHISTRY.—The age of chivalry is gone; that of sophisters, economists, and calculators has succeeded.—*Burke*.

Sophistry is like a window curtain— it pleases as an ornament, but its true use is to keep out the light.

Sophistry, like poison, is at once detected and nauseated, when presented to us in a concentrated form; but a fallacy which, when stated barely in a few sentences, would not deceive a child, may deceive half the world, if diluted in a quarto volume.—*Whately*.

Some men weave their sophistry till their own reason is entangled.—*Johnson*.

To reason justly from a false principle is the perfection of sophistry, which it is more difficult to expose than to refute false reasoning.—The proper way to expose its errors is to show that just and conclusive reasonings have been built on some false or absurd principle. —*Emmons*.

The juggle of sophistry consists, for the most part, in using a word in one sense in the premises, and in another sense in the conclusion.—*Coleridge*.

SORROW.—On the sands of life sorrow treads heavily, and leaves a print time cannot wash away.—*H. Neele*.

Sorrow is a kind of rust of the soul which every new idea contributes in its passage to scour away. It is the putrefaction of stagnant life, and is remedied by exercise and motion.—*Johnson*.

Sorrow breaks season, and reposing hours; makes the night morning, and the noontide night.—*Shakespeare*.

Never morning wore to evening, but some heart did break.—*Tennyson*.

The deeper the sorrow the less tongue it has.—*Talmud*.

To forecast our sorrows is only to increase the suffering without increasing our strength to bear them.—Many of life's noblest enterprises might never have been undertaken if all the difficulties and defects could be foreseen.—*T. L. Cuyler.*

The happiest, sweetest, tenderest homes are not those where there has been no sorrow, but those which have been overshadowed with grief, and where Christ's comfort was accepted. The very memory of the sorrow is a gentle benediction that broods ever over the household, like the silence that comes after prayer. There is a blessing sent from God in every burden of sorrow.—*J. R. Miller.*

Sorrows are our best educators. A man can see further through a tear than a telescope.

Grief should be the instructor of the wise: sorrow is knowledge; they who know the most must mourn the deepest o'er the fatal truth,—the tree of knowledge is not that of life.—*Byron.*

With sorrow comes experience, and that cruel knowledge of life which teaches us to guard against our hopes. —*E. Gaboriau.*

It is the veiled angel of sorrow who plucks away one thing and another that bound us here in ease and security, and, in the vanishing of these dear objects, indicates the true home of our affections and our peace.—*E. H. Chapin.*

The path of sorrow, and that path alone, leads to the land where sorrow is unknown; no traveller ever reached that blessed abode who found not thorns and briers in his road.—*Cowper.*

Wherever souls are being tried and ripened, in whatever commonplace and homely way, there God is hewing out the pillars for His temple.—*Phillips Brooks.*

Earth hath no sorrow that heaven cannot heal.—*Moore.*

The mind profits by the wreck of every passion, and we may measure our road to wisdom by the sorrows we have undergone.—*Bulwer.*

Sorrow preys upon its solitude, and nothing more diverts it from its sad visions of the other world, than calling it at moments back to this. The busy have no time for tears.—*Byron.*

Give sorrow words: the grief, that does not speak, whispers the o'erfraught heart, and bids it break.—*Shakespeare.*

He that hath so many and great causes of joy, and yet is in love with sorrow and peevishness, deserves to starve in the midst of plenty, and to want comfort while he is encircled with blessings.—*Jeremy Taylor.*

Sorrow is the handmaid of God, not of Satan.—She would lead us, as she did the Psalmist, to say, "Who will show us any good?" that after having said this we may also say with him, "Lord, lift thou the light of thy countenance upon us."—*A. S. Hardy.*

Short time seems long in sorrow's sharp sustaining; though woe be heavy, yet it seldom sleeps, and they who watch, see time how slow it creeps.—*Shakespeare.*

He that hath pity on another man's sorrow shall be free from it himself; and he that delighteth in, and scorneth the misery of another shall one time or other fall into it himself.—*Sir W. Raleigh.*

The man who has learned to triumph over sorrow wears his miseries as though they were sacred fillets upon his brow, and nothing is so admirable as a man bravely wretched.—*Seneca.*

The violence of sorrow is not at the first to be striven withal; being, like a mighty beast, sooner tamed with following than overthrown by withstanding.—*Sir P. Sidney.*

Sorrows remembered sweeten present joy.—*Pollok.*

One can never be the judge of another's grief. That which is a sorrow to one, to another is joy. Let us not dispute with any one concerning the reality of his sufferings; it is with sorrows as with countries—each man has his own.—*Chateaubriand.*

Whole years of joy glide unperceived away, while sorrow counts the minutes as they pass.—*Havard.*

Sorrow was made for man, not for beasts; yet if men encourage melancholy too much, they become no better than beasts.—*Cervantes.*

An excess of sorrow is as foolish as

profuse laughter; while, on the other hand, not to mourn at all is insensibility.—*Seneca.*

Our sorrows are like thunder-clouds, which seem black in the distance, but grow lighter as they approach.—*Richter.*

One sorrow never comes but brings an heir that may succeed as his inheritor.—*Shakespeare.*

Out of suffering have emerged the strongest souls; the most massive characters are seamed with scars; martyrs have put on their coronation robes glittering with fire, and through their tears have the sorrowful first seen the gates of heaven.—*E. H. Chapin.*

The deeper the sorrow the less tongue it hath.—*Talmud.*

Social sorrow loses half its pain.—*Johnson.*

The sorrow which calls for help and comfort is not the greatest, nor does it come from the depths of the heart.—*W. Humboldt.*

The capacity of sorrow belongs to our grandeur; and the loftiest of our race are those who have had the profoundest griefs because they have had the profoundest sympathies.—*Henry Giles.*

Life, with all its sorrows, cares, perplexities and heartbreaks, is more interesting than bovine placidity, hence more desirable. The more interesting it is, the happier it is.—*William Lyon Phelps.*

Sorrow is the source of literature, joy is the source of virtue.—*Austin O'Malley.*

The soul would have no rainbow had the eyes no tears.—*John Vance Cheney.*

Where there is sorrow, there is holy ground.—*Oscar Wilde.*

We come to learn that it does not pay to grieve too much over our errors. Ordinarily we try to do the best we can.—*T. L. Masson.*

She would have made a splendid wife, for crying only made her eyes more bright and tender.—*O. Henry.*

Never a tear bedims the eye that time and patience will not dry.—*Bret Harte.*

To withhold from a child some knowledge—apportioned to his understanding—of the world's sorrows and wrongs is

to cheat him of his kinship with humanity.—*Agnes Repplier.*

This world is so full of care and sorrow that it is a gracious debt we owe to one another to discover the bright crystals of delight hidden in somber circumstances and irksome tasks.—*Helen Keller.*

Those touches of manhood, of nature, of sorrow, of pride, of generosity and pity, which make the whole world kin, tell us specifically and with emphasis that we are of one family, and should be of one household forever.—*Henry Watterson.*

A coal fire softens iron, and sorrow softens a man's heart, but both revert to the original hardness.—*Austin O'Malley.*

I shall not let a sorrow die until I find the heart of it, nor let a wordless joy go by until it talks to me a bit.—*Sara Teasdale.*

Sorrows gather around great souls as storms do around mountains; but, like them, they break the storm and purify the air of the plain beneath them.—*Richter.*

We may learn from children how large a part of our grievances is imaginary. But the pain is just as real.—*Bovee.*

Sorrows humanize our race; tears are the showers that fertilize the world.—*Owen Meredith.*

Light griefs do speak, while sorrow's tongue is bound.—*Seneca.*

A small sorrow distracts; a great one makes us collected.—*Richter.*

Sorrow is only one of the lower notes in the oratorio of our blessedness.—*A. J. Gordon.*

Has it never occurred to us, when surrounded by sorrows, that they may be sent to us only for our instruction, as we darken the eyes of birds when we wish them to sing?—*Richter.*

Sorrow is our John the Baptist, clad in grim garments, with rough arms, a son of the wilderness, baptizing us with bitter tears, preaching repentance; and behind him comes the gracious, affectionate, healing Lord, speaking peace and joy to the soul.—*F. D. Huntington.*

Alas! by some degree of woe, we

every bliss must gain; the heart can ne'er a transport know that never feels a pain.—*Lyttleton.*

The sorrows of a noble soul are as May frosts, which precede the milder seasons; but the sorrows of a hardened, lost soul, are as the autumn frosts, which foretell but the coming of winter. —*Richter.*

SOUL.—(See " IMMORTALITY.")

What is mind? No matter. What is matter? Never mind. What is the soul? It is immaterial.—*Hood.*

Whatever that be which thinks, which understands, which wills, which acts, it is something celestial and divine, and on that account must necessarily be eternal.—*Cicero.*

Either we have an immortal soul, or we have not. If we have not, we are beasts; the first and wisest of beasts it may be; but still beasts. We only differ in degree, and not in kind; just as the elephant differs from the slug. But by the concession of the materialists, we are not of the same kind as beasts; and this also we say from our own consciousness. Therefore, methinks, it must be the possession of a soul within us that makes the difference.—*Coleridge.*

The problem of restoring to the world original and eternal beauty is solved by the redemption of the soul.—*Emerson.*

The soul, of origin divine, God's glorious image, freed from clay, in heaven's eternal sphere shall shine, a star of day! —The sun is but a spark of fire, a transient meteor in the sky; the soul immortal as its sire, shall never die.— *Montgomery.*

The soul on earth is an immortal guest, compelled to starve at an unreal feast; a pilgrim panting for the rest to come; an exile, anxious for his native home.—*H. More.*

The intellect of man sits visibly enthroned upon his forehead and in his eye, and the heart of man is written upon his countenance. But the soul reveals itself in the voice only, as God revealed Himself to the prophet of old in the still small voice, and in the voice from the burning bush.—*Longfellow.*

The soul, considered with its Creator, is like one of those mathematical lines that may draw nearer to another for all eternity without a possibility of touch-

ing it; and can there be a thought so transporting as to consider ourselves in these perpetual approaches to Him, who is not only the standard of perfection, but of happiness?—*Addison.*

I consider the soul of man as the ruin of a glorious pile of buildings; where, amidst great heaps of rubbish, you meet with noble fragments of sculpture, broken pillars and obelisks, and a magnificence in confusion.—*Steele.*

The human soul is like a bird that is born in a cage. Nothing can deprive it of its natural longings, or obliterate the mysterious remembrance of its heritage.—*Epes Sargent.*

The wealth of a soul is measured by how much it can feel; its poverty by how little.—*W. R. Alger.*

Heaven-born, the soul a heavenward course must hold; beyond the world she soars; the wise man, I affirm, can find no rest in that which perishes, nor will he lend his heart to aught that doth on time depend.—*Michael Angelo.*

Had I no other proof of the immortality of the soul than the oppression of the just and the triumph of the wicked in this world, this alone would prevent my having the least doubt of it. So shocking a discord amidst a general harmony of things would make me naturally look for a cause; I should say to myself we do not cease to exist with this life; everything reassumes its order after death.—*Rousseau.*

Little, indeed, does it concern us in this our mortal stage, to inquire whence the spirit hath come; but of what infinite concern is the consideration whither it is going. Surely such consideration demands the study of a life.—*Southey.*

The body, that is but dust; the soul, it is a bud of eternity.—*N. Culverwell.*

Where are Shakespeare's imagination, Bacon's learning, Galileo's dream? Where is the sweet fancy of Sidney, the airy spirit of Fletcher, and Milton's thought severe? Methinks such things should not die and dissipate, when a hair can live for centuries, and a brick of Egypt will last three thousand years. I am content to believe that the mind of man survives, somehow or other, his clay.—*Barry Cornwall.*

It seems to me as if not only the form but the soul of man was made to

walk erect and look upon the stars.—
Bulwer.

To look upon the soul as going on
from strength to strength, to consider
that she is to shine forever with new
accessions of glory, and brighten to all
eternity; that she will be still adding
virtue to virtue, and knowledge to
knowledge,—carries in it something wonderfully agreeable to that ambition
which is natural to the mind of man.—
Addison.

The mind is never right but when it
is at peace within itself; the soul is in
heaven even while it is in the flesh,
if it be purged of its natural corruptions, and taken up with divine thoughts
and contemplations.—*Seneca.*

I am fully convinced that the soul is
indestructible, and that its activity will
continue through eternity. It is like
the sun, which, to our eyes, seems to
set in night; but it has in reality only
gone to diffuse its light elsewhere.—
Goethe.

Everything here, but the soul of man,
is a passing shadow.—The only enduring
substance is within.—When shall we
awake to the sublime greatness, the
perils, the accountableness, and the
glorious destinies of the immortal soul?
—*Channing.*

The saddest of all failures is that of a
soul, with its capabilities and possibilities, failing of life everlasting, and entering on that night of death upon which
no morning ever dawns.—*Herrick Johnson.*

Life is the soul's nursery—its training
place for the destinies of eternity.—
Thackeray.

SOUND.—There is in souls a sympathy with sounds, and as the wind is
pitched the ear is pleased with melting
airs or martial, brisk or grave; some
chord in unison with what we hear is
touched within us, and the heart replies.
—*Cowper.*

Undescribed sounds, that come a-
swooning over hollow grounds, and
wither drearily on barren moors.—*Keats.*

How deep is the magic of sound may
be learned by breaking some sweet
verses into prose. The operation has
been compared to gathering dew-drops,
which shine like jewels upon the flower,
but run into water in the hand. The

elements remain, but the sparkle is gone.
—*Willmott.*

Stern winter loves a dirge-like sound.
—*Wordsworth.*

Not rural sights alone, but rural
sounds exhilarate the spirits, and restore
the tone of languid nature. Mighty
winds, that sweep the skirts of some
far-spreading wood· of ancient growth,
make music not unlike the dash of ocean
on his winding shore, and lull the spirit
while they fill the mind.—*Cowper.*

Verse sweetens toil, however rude the
sound.—*Gifford.*

The sound must seem an echo to the
sense.—*Pope.*

SPECIALTY.—A man is like a bit of
Labrador spar, which has no lustre as
you turn it in your hand until you come
to a particular angle; then it shows
deep and beautiful colors.—There is no
adaptation or universal applicability in
men, but each has his special talent, and
the mastery of successful men consists
in adroitly keeping themselves where
and when that turn shall be oftenest
to be practised.—*Emerson.*

No one can exist in society without
some specialty. Eighty years ago it was
only necessary to be well dressed and
amiable; to-day a man of this kind
would be too much like the garçons at
the cafés.—*Taine.*

Let every one ascertain his special
business or calling, and then stick to it,
if he would be successful.—*Franklin.*

SPECULATION.—Many brilliant
speculations are but shining soap bubbles, which turn to nothing as you gaze
at them.

The besetting evil of our age is the
temptation to squander and dilute
thought on a thousand different lines of
inquiry.—*Sir John Herschel.*

The practices of good men are more
subject to error than their theories and
speculations.—I will then honor good
examples, but I will live by good precepts.

A wise man was he who counselled
that speculation should have free course,
and look fearlessly toward all the thirty-
two points of the compass, whithersoever and howsoever it listed.—*Carlyle.*

Conjecture as to things useful is
good; but conjecture as to what it

would be useless to know, such as whether men ever went upon all-fours, is very idle.—*Johnson.*

SPEECH.—(See "TONGUE" and "TALKING.")

Speech is a faculty given to man to conceal his thoughts.—*Talleyrand.*

A superior man is modest in his speech, but exceeds in his actions.—*Confucius.*

According to Solomon, life and death are in the power of the tongue; and as Euripides truly affirmeth, every unbridled tongue in the end shall find itself unfortunate; in all that ever I observed I ever found that men's fortunes are oftener made by their tongues than by their virtues, and more men's fortunes overthrown thereby, also, than by their vices.—*Sir Walter Raleigh.*

Speeches cannot be made long enough for the speakers, nor short enough for the hearers.—*Perry.*

It is usually said by grammarians, that the use of language is to express our wants and desires; but men who know the world hold that he who best knows how to keep his necessities private, is the most likely person to have them redressed; and that the true use of speech is not so much to express our wants as to conceal them.—*Goldsmith.*

There is a wide difference between speaking to deceive, and being silent to be impenetrable.—*Voltaire.*

Never is the deep, strong voice of man, or the low, sweet voice of woman, finer than in the earnest but mellow tones of familiar speech, richer than the richest music, which are a delight while they are heard, which linger still upon the ear in softened echoes, and which, when they have ceased, come, long after, back to memory, like the murmurs of a distant hymn.—*Henry Giles.*

Half the sorrows of women would be averted if they could repress the speech they know to be useless—nay, the speech they have resolved not to utter.—*George Eliot.*

The common fluency of speech in many men, and most women, is owing to a scarcity of matter and a scarcity of words; for whoever is a master of language and has a mind full of ideas, will be apt in speaking to hesitate upon the choice of both; whereas common speakers have only one set of ideas, and one set of words to clothe them in; and these are always ready at the mouth; so people come faster out of a church when it is almost empty, than when a crowd is at the door.—*Swift.*

It was justly said by Themistocles that speech is like tapestry unfolded, where the imagery appears distinct; but thoughts, like tapestry in the bale, where the figures are rolled up together.—*Bacon.*

Sheridan once said of some speech, in his acute, sarcastic way, that "it contained a great deal both of what was new and what was true; but that what was new was not true, and what was true was not new."—*Hazlitt.*

There are three things that ought to be considered before some things are spoken,—the manner, the place, and the time.—*Southey.*

Nothing is more silly than the pleasure some people take in "speaking their minds." A man of this make will say a rude thing, for the mere pleasure of saying it, when an opposite behavior, full as innocent, might have preserved his friend, or made his fortune.—*Steele.*

A printed speech is like a dried flower: the substance, indeed, is there, but the color is faded and the perfume gone.—*Lorain.*

A sentence well couched takes both the sense and the understanding.—I love not those cart-rope speeches that are longer than the memory of man can measure.—*Feltham.*

Never rise to speak till you have something to say; and when you have said it, cease.—*Witherspoon.*

We seldom repent of speaking little, very often of speaking too much; a vulgar and trite maxim, which all the world knows, but which all the world does not practise.—*Bruyère.*

Such as thy words are, such will thine affections be esteemed; and such as thine affections, will be thy deeds; and such as thy deeds will be thy life.—*Socrates.*

A constant governance of our speech, according to duty and reason, is a high instance and a special argument of a thoroughly sincere and solid goodness.—*Barrow.*

Think all you speak, but speak not all you think.—Thoughts are your own; your words are so no more.—*Delany.*

Speech is silvern, silence is golden; speech is human, silence is divine.— *German Proverb.*

Discretion of speech is more than eloquence; and to speak agreeably to him with whom we deal is more than to speak in good words, or in good order. —*Bacon.*

Speak but little and well if you would be esteemed a man of merit.—*Trench.*

As a vessel is known by the sound, whether it be cracked or not, so men are proved by their speeches whether they be wise or foolish.—*Demosthenes.*

There are three things to aim at in public speaking; first to get into your subject, then to get your subject into yourself, and lastly, to get your subject into your hearers.—*Bp. Gregg.*

A good speech is a good thing, but the verdict is the thing.—*Daniel O'Connell.*

SPIRIT.—Spirit is now a very fashionable word; to act with spirit, to speak with spirit, means only to act rashly, and to talk indiscreetly. An able man shows his spirit by gentle words and resolute actions; he is neither hot nor timid.— *Chesterfield.*

He that loseth wealth, loseth much; he that loseth friends, loseth more; but he that loseth his spirits loseth all.— *Spanish Maxim.*

A man of a right spirit is not a man of narrow and private views, but is greatly interested and concerned for the good of the community to which he belongs, and particularly of the city or village in which he resides, and for the true welfare of the society of which he is a member.—*Jonathan Edwards.*

It is impossible that an ill-natured man can have a public spirit; for how should he love ten thousand men, who never loved one?

High spirit in man is like a sword, which, though worn to annoy his enemies, yet is often troublesome to his friends: he can hardly wear it so inoffensively but it is apt to incommode one or other of the company: it is more properly a loaded pistol, which accident alone may fire and kill one.—*Shenstone.*

He hath a poor spirit who is not planted above petty wrongs.—*Feltham.*

SPRING.—Winter, lingering, chills the lap of May.—*Goldsmith.*

Spring unlocks the flowers to paint the laughing soil.—*Heber.*

So then the year is repeating its old story again. We are come once more, thank God! to its most charming chapter. The violets and the May flowers are as its inscriptions or vignettes. It always makes a pleasant impression on us, when we open again at these pages of the book of life.—*Goethe.*

Stately spring! whose robe-folds are valleys, whose breast-bouquet is gardens, and whose blush is a vernal evening.— *Richter.*

If spring came but once in a century, instead of once a year, or burst forth with the sound of an earthquake, and not in silence, what wonder and expectation there would be in all hearts to behold the miraculous change! But now the silent succession suggests nothing but necessity. To most men only the cessation of the miracle would be miraculous, and the perpetual exercise of God's power seems less wonderful than its withdrawal would be.—*Longfellow.*

Sweet spring, full of sweet days and roses, a box where sweets compacted lie. —*Herbert.*

Wide flush the fields; the softening air is balm; echo the mountains round; the forest smiles; and every sense, and every heart is joy.—*Thomson.*

Sweet daughter of a rough and stormy sire, hoar winter's blooming child, delightful spring.—*Mrs. Barbauld.*

Ye may trace my step o'er the wakening earth, by the winds which tell of the violet's birth.—*Mrs. Hemans.*

Fair-handed spring unbosoms every grace.—*Thomson.*

Spring hangs her infant blossoms on the trees, rocked in the cradle of the western breeze.—*Cowper.*

STARS.—Ye stars, that are the poetry of heaven!—*Byron.*

When I gaze into the stars, they look down upon me with pity from their serene and silent spaces, like eyes glistening with tears over the little lot of man. Thousands of generations, all as noisy as our own, have been swallowed up by time, and there remains no record of them any more. Yet Arcturus and Orion, Sirius and Pleiades, are still shining in their courses, clear and young, as when the shepherd first noted them in the plain of Shinar!—*Carlyle.*

If the stars should appear one night in a thousand years, how would men believe and adore; and preserve for many generations the remembrance of the city of God which had been shown! But every night come out these envoys of beauty, and light the universe with their admonishing smile.—*Emerson.*

Silent, one by one, in the infinite meadows of heaven, blossomed the lovely stars, the forget-me-nots of angels.—*Longfellow.*

The gems of heaven, that gild night's sable throne.—*Dryden.*

What are ye orbs? The words of God? the Scriptures of the skies?—*Bailey.*

Look up, and behold the eternal fields of light that lie round about the throne of God. Had no star ever appeared in the heavens, to man there would have been no heavens; and he would have laid himself down to his last sleep, in a spirit of anguish, as upon a gloomy earth vaulted over by a material arch—solid and impervious.—*Carlyle.*

The stars are mansions built by nature's hand, and, haply, there the spirits of the blest dwell, clothed in radiance, their immortal rest.—*Wordsworth.*

The stars hang bright above, silent, as if they watched the sleeping earth.—*Coleridge.*

A star is beautiful; it affords pleasure, not from what it is to do, or to give, but simply by being what it is. It befits the heavens; it has congruity with the mighty space in which it dwells. It has repose; no force disturbs its eternal peace. It has freedom; no obstruction lies between it and infinity.—*Carlyle.*

The sentinel stars set their watch in the sky.—*Campbell.*

O powers illimitable! it is but the outer hem of God's great mantle, our poor stars do gem.—*Ruskin.*

There they stand, the innumerable stars, shining in order like a living hymn, written in light.—*N. P. Willis.*

One sun by day; by night ten thousand shine, and light us deep into the deity.—How boundless in magnificence and might!—Stars teach as well as shine, and every student of the night inspire; the elder scripture writ by God's own hand, authentic, uncorrupt by man.—*Young.*

The evening star, love's harbinger, appeared.—*Milton.*

I am as constant as the northern star; of whose true, fixed, and resting quality there is no fellow in the firmament.—*Shakespeare.*

These preachers of beauty, which light the world with their admonishing smile.—*Emerson.*

STATE.—That state is best ordered where the wicked have no command, and the good have.—*Pittacus.*

What constitutes a state? Not high raised battlement, or labored mound, thick wall, or moated gate; not cities, proud with spires and turrets crowned, nor bays and broad-armed ports, where, laughing at the storm, rich navies ride, nor starred and spangled courts.—No!—men, high-minded men, with powers as far above all brutes endowed as beasts excel cold rocks and brambles; men, who their duties know, but know their rights, and knowing dare maintain—these constitute a state.—*Sir W. Jones.*

In a free country there is much clamor with little suffering: in a despotic state there is little complaint but much suffering.—*Caruot.*

A state to prosper, must be built on foundations of a moral character, and this character is the principal element of its strength, and the only guaranty of its permanence and prosperity.—*J. L. M. Curry.*

STATESMANSHIP. — True statesmanship is the art of changing a nation from what it is into what it ought to be.—*W. R. Alger.*

The worth of a state, in the long run, is the worth of the individuals composing it.—*J. Stuart Mill.*

Honest statesmanship is the wise employment of individual meannesses for the public good.—*Lincoln.*

The great difference between the real statesman and the pretender is, that the one sees into the future, while the other regards only the present; the one lives by the day, and acts on expediency; the other acts on enduring principles and for immortality.—*Burke.*

The true genius that conducts a state is he, who doing nothing himself, causes everything to be done; he contrives, he invents, he foresees the future; he reflects on what is past; he distributes and proportions things; he makes early preparations; he incessantly arms himself to struggle against fortune, as a swimmer against a rapid stream of water; he is attentive night and day, that he may leave nothing to chance.—*Fénelon.*

If I had wished to raise up a race of statesmen higher than politicians, animated not by greed or selfishness, by policy or party, I would familiarize the boys of the land with the characters of the Bible.—*John Hall.*

What morality requires, true statesmanship should accept.—*Burke.*

Statesman, yet friend to truth! of soul sincere, in action faithful, and in honor clear, who broke no promise, served no private end, who gain'd no title, and who lost no friend; ennobled by himself, by all approved, praised, wept, and honored.—*Pope.*

The three great ends for a statesman are, security to possessors, facility to acquirers, and liberty and hope to the people.—*Coleridge.*

A statesman, we are told, should follow public opinion; doubtless—as a coachman follows his horses, having firm hold on the reins, and guiding them.—*Hare.*

It is curious that we pay statesmen for what they say, not for what they do, and judge them from what they do, not from what they say.—Hence they have one code of maxims for professions, and another for practice, and make up their consciences as the Neapolitans do their beds, with one set of furniture for show, and another for use.—*Colton.*

STATION.—Our distinctions do not lie in the places we occupy, but in the grace and dignity with which we fill them.—*Simms.*

Eminent stations make great men more great, and little ones less.—*Bruyère.*

They that stand high have many blasts to shake them.—*Shakespeare.*

Bacon has compared those who move in higher spheres to those heavenly bodies in the firmament, which have much admiration, but little rest; and it is not necessary to invest a wise man with power, to convince him that it is a garment bedizzened with gold, which dazzles the beholder by its splendor, but oppresses the wearer by its weight.—*Colton.*

Men and statues that are admired in an elevated situation, have a very different effect on us when we approach them; the first appear less than we imagined them, the last bigger.—*Greville.*

How happy the station which every moment furnishes opportunities of doing good to thousands!—How dangerous that which every moment exposes to the injuring of millions!—*Bruyère.*

He who thinks his place below him will certainly be below his place.—*Saville.*

Whatever the place allotted us by providence, that is for us the post of honor and duty.—God estimates us not by the position we are in, but by the way in which we fill it.—*Tryon Edwards.*

The place should not honor the man, but the man the place.—*Agesilaus.*

If God, says Cecil, were to send two angels, one to rule an empire, and the other to sweep its streets, each would feel that his place was the place of duty and honor, and would be satisfied with it.

A true man never frets about his place in the world, but just slides into it by the gravitation of his nature, and swings there as easily as a star.—*E. H. Chapin.*

Men in great places are thrice servants: servants of the sovereign or state, servants of fame, and servants of business; so as they have no freedom, neither in their persons, in their actions, or in their times.—*Bacon.*

True dignity is never gained by place, and never lost when honors are withdrawn.—*Massinger.*

If any man is rich and powerful he comes under the law of God by which the higher branches must take the burnings of the sun, and shade those that are lower; by which the tall trees must protect the weak plants beneath them.—*H. W. Beecher.*

Whom the grandeur of his office elevates over other men will soon find that the first hour of his new dignity is the last of his independence.—*Aguesseau.*

Every man whom chance alone has, by some accident, made a public character, hardly ever fails of becoming, in a short time, a ridiculous private one.—*Cardinal de Retz.*

STEWARDSHIP.—It is a dark sign when the owner is seen to be growing poor, and his steward is found to be growing rich.—*Spencer.*

Our children, relations, friends, honors, houses, lands, and endowments, the goods of nature and fortune, nay, even of grace itself, are only lent. It is our misfortune, and our sin, to fancy they are given. We start, therefore, and are angry when the loan is called in. We think ourselves masters, when we are only stewards, and forget that to each of us it will one day be said, "Give an account of thy stewardship."—*Bp. Horne.*

As to all that we have and are, we are but stewards of the Most High God.—On all our possessions, on our time, and talents, and influence, and property, he has written, "Occupy for me, and till I shall come."—To obey his instructions and serve him faithfully, is the true test of obedience and discipleship.—*C. Simmons.*

There is no portion of our time that is our time, and the rest God's; there is no portion of money that is our money, and the rest God's money. It is all His; He made it all, gives it all, and He has simply trusted it to us for His service. A servant has two purses, the master's and his own, but we have only one.—*Monod.*

STOICISM.—There are two ways of escaping from suffering; the one by rising above the causes of conflict, the other by sinking below them.—The one is the religious method; the other is the vulgar, worldly method.—The one is Christian elevation; the other is stoicism.—*H. W. Beecher.*

'Tis pride, rank pride, and haughtiness of soul; I think the Romans call it stoicism.—*Addison.*

To feel for none is the true social art of the world's stoics—men without a heart.—*Byron.*

A soul that pity touched but never

shook; trained, from his cradle, the fierce extremes of good and ill to brook; impassive, fearing but the shame of fear, a stoic of the woods, a man without a fear.—*Campbell.*

STORY-TELLING.—Story-telling is subject to two unavoidable defects—frequent repetition and being soon exhausted; so that whoever values this gift in himself, has need of a good memory, and ought frequently to shift his company.—*Swift.*

Stories now, to suit a public taste, must be half epigram, half pleasant vice.—*J. R. Lowell.*

No story is the same to us after the lapse of time: or rather we who read it are no longer the same interpreters.—*George Eliot.*

I cannot tell how the truth may be; I say the tale as it was said to me.—*Walter Scott.*

A story should, to please, at least seem true, be apropos, well told, concise, and new; and whensoe'er it deviates from these rules, the wise will sleep, and leave applause to fools.—*Stillingfleet.*

STRENGTH.—Oh! it is excellent to have a giant's strength; but it is tyrannous to use it like a giant.—*Shakespeare.*

Strength, wanting judgment and policy to rule, overturneth itself.—*Horace.*

The exhibition of real strength is never grotesque. Distortion is the agony of weakness. It is the dislocated mind whose movements are spasmodic.—*Willmott.*

Strength alone knows conflict; weakness is below even defeat, and is born vanquished.—*Mad. Swetchine.*

Although men are accused of not knowing their own weakness, yet perhaps a few know their own strength. It is in men as in soils, where sometimes there is a vein of gold which the owner knows not of.—*Swift.*

Strength is born in the deep silence of long-suffering hearts; not amidst joy.—*Mrs. Hemans.*

What is strength without a double share of wisdom? Vast, unwieldy, burthensome, proudly secure, yet liable to fall by weakest subtleties; strength's not made to rule, but to subserve, where wisdom bears command.—*Milton.*

STUDY.—(See "Knowledge.")

There are more men ennobled by study than by nature.—*Cicero.*

The love of study, a passion which derives great vigor from enjoyment, supplies each day, each hour, with a perpetual round of independent and rational pleasure.—*Gibbon.*

He that studies only men, will get the body of knowledge without the soul; and he that studies only books, the soul without the body. He that to what he sees, adds observation, and to what he reads, reflection, is in the right road to knowledge, provided that in scrutinizing the hearts of others, he neglects not his own.—*Colton.*

A few books, well studied, and thoroughly digested, nourish the understanding more than hundreds but gargled in the mouth, as ordinary students use.—*F. Osborn.*

As there is a partiality to opinions, which is apt to mislead the understanding, so there is also a partiality to studies, which is prejudicial to knowledge.—*Locke.*

When a king asked Euclid whether he could not explain his art to him in a more compendious manner? he was answered, that there was no royal way to geometry. Other things may be seized by might, or purchased with money, but knowledge is to be gained only by study, and study to be prosecuted only in retirement.—*Johnson.*

Our delight in any particular study, art, or science rises and improves in proportion to the application which we bestow upon it. Thus, what was at first an exercise becomes at length an entertainment.—*Addison.*

As land is improved by sowing it with various seeds, so is the mind by exercising it with different studies.—*Melmoth.*

You are to come to your study as to the table, with a sharp appetite, whereby that which you read may the better digest. He that has no stomach to his book will very hardly thrive upon it.—*Earl of Bedford.*

Mankind have a great aversion to intellectual labor, but, even supposing knowledge to be easily attainable, more people would be content to be ignorant than would take even a little trouble to acquire it.—*Johnson.*

Studies teach not their own use; that is a wisdom without them and above them, won by observation.—*Bacon.*

If you devote your time to study, you will avoid all the irksomeness of this life, nor will you long for the approach of night, being tired of the day; nor will you be a burden to yourself, nor your society insupportable to others.—*Seneca.*

There is no study that is not capable of delighting us after a little application to it.—*Pope.*

They are not the best students who are most dependent on books. What can be got out of them is at best only material; a man must build his house for himself.—*G. Macdonald.*

Desultory studies are erased from the mind as easily as pencil marks; classified studies are retained like durable ink.—*Cooper.*

The man who has acquired the habit of study, though for only one hour every day in the year, and keeps to the one thing studied till it is mastered, will be startled to see the progress he has made at the end of a twelvemonth.—*Bulwer.*

Since I began to ask God's blessing on my studies, I have done more in one week than I have done in a whole year before.—*Payson.*

Whatever study tends neither directly nor indirectly to make us better men and citizens is at best but a specious and ingenious sort of idleness, and the knowledge we acquire by it only a creditable kind of ignorance, nothing more.—*Bolingbroke.*

As the turning of logs will make a dull fire burn, so change of studies will a dull brain.—*Longfellow.*

I study much, and the more I study the oftener I go back to those first principles which are so simple that childhood itself can lisp them.—*Mad. Swetchine.*

A boy will learn more true wisdom in a public school in a year than by a private education in five.—It is not from masters, but from their equals that youth learn a knowledge of the world.—*Goldsmith.*

Shun no toil to make yourself remarkable by some one talent.—Yet do rot devote yourself to one branch exclusively.—Strive to get clear notions about all.—Give up no science entirely, for all science is one.—*Seneca.*

The understanding is more relieved by change of study than by total inactivity. —*W. B. Clulow.*

There is an unspeakable pleasure attending the life of a voluntary student. —*Goldsmith.*

The love of study, a passion which derives fresh vigor from enjoyment, supplies each day and hour with a perpetual source of independent and rational pleasure.—*Gibbon.*

The more we study the more we discover our ignorance.—*Shelley.*

Studies serve for delight, for ornament, and for ability. Their chief use for delight is in privateness and retiring; for ornament is in discourse; and ability is in the judgment and disposition of business. For expert men can execute, and, perhaps, judge of particulars, one by one; but the general counsels and the plots and marshalling of affairs come best from those that are learned.—*Bacon.*

To the man who studies to gain a thorough insight into science, books and study are merely the steps of the ladder by which he climbs to the summit; as soon as a step has been advanced he leaves it behind.—The majority of mankind, however, who study to fill their memory with facts do not use the steps of the ladder to mount upward, but take them off and lay them on their shoulders in order that they may take them along, delighting in the weight of the burden they are carrying.—They ever remain below because they carry what should carry them.—*Schopenhauer.*

It is a great mistake of many ardent students that they trust too much to their books, and do not draw from their own resources—forgetting that of all sophists our own reason is that which abuses us least.—*Rousseau.*

Impatience of study is the mental disease of the present generation.—*Johnson.*

STYLE.—Style may be defined, " proper words in proper places."—*Swift.*

Style is the dress of thoughts; let them be ever so just, if your style is homely, coarse, and vulgar, they will appear to as much disadvantage, and be as ill received, as your person, though ever so well proportioned, would be if dressed in rags, dirt, and tatters.—*Chesterfield.*

The style shows the man. Whether in speaking or writing, a gentleman is always known by his style.—*From the Latin.*

Style is only the frame to hold our thoughts. It is like the sash of a window, if heavy it will obscure the light. The object is to have as little sash as will hold the light, that we may not think of the former, but have the latter. —*Emmons.*

Obscurity in writing is commonly a proof of darkness in the mind; the greatest learning is to be seen in the greatest plainness.—*Wilkins.*

A sentence well couched takes both the sense and the understanding.—*Feltham.*

If a man really has an idea he can communicate it; and if he has a clear one, he will communicate it clearly.— *Emmons.*

With many readers, brilliancy of style passes for affluence of thought; they mistake buttercups in the grass for immeasurable gold mines under ground.— *Longfellow.*

Generally speaking, an author's style is a faithful copy of his mind. If you would write a lucid style, let there first be light in your own mind; and if you would write a grand style, you ought to have a grand character.—*Goethe.*

If I am ever obscure in my expressions, do not fancy that therefore I am deep. If I were really deep, all the world would understand, though they might not appreciate. The perfectly popular style is the perfectly scientific one. To me an obscurity is a reason for suspecting a fallacy.—*Charles Kingsley.*

Style is the gossamer on which the seeds of truth float through the world. —*Bancroft.*

The lively phraseology of Montesquieu was the result of long meditation. His words, as light as wings, bear on them grave reflections.—*Joubert.*

Style is a man's own; it is a part of his nature.—*Buffon.*

Intense study of the Bible will keep any man from being vulgar in point of style.—*Coleridge.*

Style is the intimate and inseparable fact of the personality of the writer—it is the verbal body of the man's moral and mental life—it holds his emotions and experiences, is charged with his sensations, and is, in simplest words, his manifestations refined and polished by his artistic faculty. Only men of peculiar or strong personality attain a style which distinguishes them, and imposes itself as a model upon the groping and undecided or formless writers whose work does not make models, but only imitates them.

Any style formed in imitation of some model must be affected and straight-laced.—*E. P. Whipple.*

A man's style is nearly as much a part of himself as his face, or figure, or the throbbing of his pulse; in short, as any part of his being which is subjected to the action of his will.—*Fénelon.*

A pure style in writing results from the rejection of everything superfluous.—*Mad. Necker.*

He who thinks much says but little in proportion to his thoughts. He selects that language which will convey his ideas in the most explicit and direct manner. He tries to compress as much thought as possible into a few words. On the contrary, the man who talks everlastingly and promiscuously, who seems to have an exhaustless magazine of sound, crowds so many words into his thoughts that he always obscures, and very frequently conceals them.—*Washington Irving.*

Whoever wishes to attain an English style, familiar but not coarse, and elegant but not ostentatious, must give his days and nights to the volumes of Addison.—*Johnson.*

The least degree of ambiguity, which leaves the mind in suspense as to the meaning, ought to be avoided with the greatest care.—*Blair.*

In composing, think much more of your matter than your manner. Spirit, grace, and dignity of manner are of great importance, both to the speaker and writer; but of infinitely more importance are the weight and worth of matter.—*W. Wirt.*

The obscurity of a writer is generally in proportion to his incapacity.—*Quint_ian.*

The unaffected of every country nearly resemble each other, and a page of Confucius and Tillotson have scarce any material difference. Paltry affectation, strained allusions, and disgusting finery are easily attained by those who choose to wear them; they are but too frequently the badges of ignorance or of stupidity whenever it would endeavor to please.—*Goldsmith.*

A copious manner of expression gives strength and weight to our ideas, which frequently make impression upon the mind, as iron does upon solid bodies, rather by repeated strokes than a single blow.—*Melmoth.*

Those who make antitheses by forcing the sense are like men who make false windows for the sake of symmetry. Their rule is not to speak justly, but to make accurate figures.—*Pascal.*

Whatever is pure is also simple; it does not keep the eye on itself.—The observer forgets the window in the landscape it displays.—A fine style gives the view of fancy—of its figures, its trees, its palaces without a spot.—*Willmot.*

Clear writers, like clear fountains, do not seem so deep as they are; the turbid looks most profound.—*Landor.*

An era is fast approaching when no writer will be read by the majority, except those that can effect that for bales of manuscript that the hydrostatic screw performs for bales of cotton, by condensing into a period what before occupied a page.—*Cotta.*

A great writer possesses, so to speak, an individual and unchangeable style, which does not permit him easily to preserve the anonymous.—*Voltaire.*

There is a certain majesty in plainness; as the proclamation of a prince never frisks it in tropes or fine conceits, in numerous and well-turned periods, but commands in sober natural expressions.—*South.*

To have good sense and ability to express it are the most essential and necessary qualities in companions. When thoughts rise in us fit to utter among familiar friends, there needs but very little care in clothing them.—*Steele.*

Propriety of thought and propriety of diction are commonly found together. Obscurity and affectation are the two greatest faults of style.—*Macaulay.*

He who would reproach an author for

obscurity should look into his own mind to see whether it is quite clear there. In the dusk the plainest writing is illegible.—*Goethe*.

Words in prose ought to express the intended meaning; if they attract attention to themselves, it is a fault; in the very best styles you read page after page without noticing the medium.—*Coleridge*.

Long sentences in a short composition are like large rooms in a little house.—*Shenstone*.

In what he leaves unsaid I discover a master of style.—*Schiller*.

Perspicuity is the frame-work of profound thoughts.—*Vauvenargues*.

When we meet with a natural style we are surprised and delighted, for we expected to find an author, and have found a man.—*Pascal*.

When you doubt between words, use the plainest, the commonest, the most idiomatic.—*Eschew* fine words as you would rouge, and love simple ones as you would native roses on your cheek.—*Hare*.

Every good writer has much idiom; it is the life and spirit of language.—*Landor*.

I hate a style that is wholly flat and regular, that slides along like an eel, and never rises to what one can call an inequality.—*Shenstone*.

The old prose writers wrote as if they were speaking to an audience; among us, prose is invariably written for the eye alone.—*Niebuhr*.

Nothing is so difficult as the apparent ease of a clear and flowing style.—Those graces which, from their presumed facility, encourage all to attempt to imitate them, are usually the most inimitable.—*Colton*.

Antithesis may be the blossom of wit, but it will never arrive at maturity unless sound sense be the trunk, and truth the root.—*Colton*.

If the way in which men express their thoughts is slipshod and mean, it will be very difficult for their thoughts themselves to escape being th> same.—*Alford*.

To write in a genuine familiar or truly English style is to write as any one would speak in common conversation, who had a thorough command and

choice of words, or who could discourse with ease, force, and perspicuity, setting aside all pedantic and oratorical flourishes.—*Hazlitt*.

It is equally true of the pen as the pencil, that what is drawn from life and the heart alone bears the impress of immortality.—*Tuckerman*.

Obscurity and affectation are the two great faults of style. Obscurity of expression generally springs from confusion of ideas; and the same wish to dazzle, at any cost, which produces affectation in the manner of a writer, is likely to produce sophistry in his reasoning.—*Macaulay*.

Perhaps that is nearly the perfection of good writing which effects that for knowledge which the lens effects for the sunbea when it condenses its brightness in order to increase its force.—*Colton*.

SUBLIMITY.—Sublimity is Hebrew by birth.—*Coleridge*.

The sublime and the ridiculous are often so nearly related that it is difficult to class them separately. One step above the sublime makes the ridiculous, and one step above the ridiculous makes the sublime again.—*Thomas Paine*.

The sublimest thoughts are conceived by the intellect when it is excited by pious emotion.—*W. Nevins*.

One source of sublimity is infinity.—*Burke*.

The sublime is the temple-step of religion, as the stars are of immeasurable space. When what is mighty appears in nature,—a storm, thunder, the starry firmament, death,—then utter the word "God" before the child. A great misfortune, a great blessing, a great crime, a noble action are building sites for a child's church.—*Richter*.

From the sublime to the ridiculous there is but one step.—*Napoleon*.

"The sublime," says Longinus, "is often nothing but the echo or image of magnanimity"; and where this quality appears in any one, even though a syllable be not uttered, it excites our applause and admiration.—*Hume*.

Nothing so effectually deadens the taste of the sublime as that which is light and radiant.—*Burke*.

The sublime, when it is introduced at

a seasonable moment, has often carried all before it with the rapidity of lightning, and shown at a glance the mighty power of genius.—*Longinus.*

The truly sublime is always easy, and always natural.—*Burke.*

SUBMISSION.—To will what God doth will, that is the only science that gives us any rest.—*Malesherbes.*

As thou wilt; what thou wilt; when thou wilt.—*Thomas à Kempis.*

Submission is the footprint of faith in the pathway of sorrow.

To-morrow!—I dare not ask; I know not what is best: God hath already said what shall betide.—*Longfellow.*

Study the singular benefits and advantages of a will resigned and melted into the will of God. Such a spirit hath a continual Sabbath within itself, and its thoughts are established and at rest.—*Flavel.*

That is best which God sends; it was his will; it is mine.—*O. Meredith.*

Give what thou canst, without thee we are poor, and with thee rich, take what thou wilt away.—*Cowper.*

God of the just, Thou gav'st the bitter cup. I bow to thy behest, and drink it up.—*H. K. White.*

To do or not to do; to have, or not to have, I leave to thee; thy only will be done in me; all my requests are lost in one, "Father, thy will be done!"—*C. Wesley.*

In the many adversities and trials of life it is often hard to say "Thy will be done." But why not say it? God ever does only what is right and wise and best; what is prompted by a father's love, and what to his children will work out their highest good.—*Payson.*

"O father! not my will, but thine be done"; be this our charm, mellowing earth's griefs and joys, that we may cling forever to thy heart, in perfect rest.—*Keble.*

God is too great to be withstood, too just to do wrong, too good to delight in any one's misery.—We ought, therefore, quietly to submit to his dispensations as the very best.—*Bp. Wilson.*

The strength of a man consists in finding out the way God is going, and going in that way too.—*H. W. Beecher.*

But peace! I must not quarrel with the will of highest dispensation, which, haply, hath ends above my reach to know.—*Milton.*

Submission to God is the only balm that can heal the wounds he gives us.—*Emmons.*

The highest attainment, as well as enjoyment of the spiritual life, is to be able at all times and in all things to say, "Thy will be done."—*Tryon Edwards.*

Patience, says another, is an excellent remedy for grief, but submission to the hand of him that sends it is a far better. —*C. Simmons.*

SUBTLETY.—(See "CUNNING.")

Subtlety may deceive you; integrity never will.—*Cromwell.*

Subtlety will sometimes give safety, no less than strength; and minuteness has sometimes escaped, where magnitude would have been crushed. The little animal that kills the boa is formidable chiefly from its insignificance, which is incompressible by the folds of its antagonist.—*Colton.*

This is the fruit of craft, that he that shoots up high, looks for the shaft, and finds it in his own forehead.—*Middleton.*

Cunning is the dwarf of wisdom.—*W. R. Alger.*

Cunning pays no regard to virtue, and is but the low mimic of wisdom.—*Bolingbroke.*

SUCCESS.—Success in life is a matter not so much of talent or opportunity as of concentration and perseverance.—*C. W. Wendte.*

Mere success is one of the worst arguments in the world of a good cause, and the most improper to satisfy conscience: and yet in the issue it is the most successful of all other arguments, and does in a very odd, but effectual, way, satisfy the consciences of a great many men, by showing them their interest.—*Tillotson.*

Moderation is commonly firm, and firmness is commonly successful.—*Johnson.*

The road to success is not to be run upon by seven-leagued boots. Step by step, little by little, bit by bit—that is the way to wealth, that is the way to wisdom, that is the way to glory. Pounds are the sons, not of pounds, but of pence.—*Charles Buxton.*

He that would make sure of success should keep his passion cool, and his expectation low.—*Jeremy Collier.*

The man who succeeds above his fellows is the one who, early in life, clearly discerns his object, and towards that object habitually directs his powers. Even genius itself is but fine observation strengthened by fixity of purpose. Every man who observes vigilantly and resolves steadfastly grows unconsciously into genius.—*Bulwer.*

Nothing can seem foul to those that win.—*Shakespeare.*

All the proud virtue of this vaunting world fawns on success and power, however acquired.—*Thomson.*

Success is full of promise till men get it, and, then it is as a last year's nest, from which the bird has flown.—*H. W. Beecher.*

In most things success depends on knowing how long it takes to succeed.—*Montesquieu.*

Everybody finds out, sooner or later, that all success worth having is founded on Christian rules of conduct.—*H. M. Field.*

Success soon palls. The joyous time is when the breeze first strikes your sails, and the waters rustle under your bows.—*Charles Buxton.*

Success at first doth many times undo men at last.—*Venning.*

Success has a great tendency to conceal and throw a veil over the evil deeds of men.—*Demosthenes.*

The greatest results in life are usually attained by simple means and the exercise of ordinary qualities. These may for the most part be summed in these two—common sense and perseverance.—*Feltham.*

To know a man, observe how he wins his object, rather than how he loses it; for when we fail, our pride supports; when we succeed, it betrays us.—*Colton.*

The surest way not to fail is to determine to succeed.—*Sheridan.*

To become an able and successful man in any profession, three things are necessary, nature, study, and practice.

Not what men do worthily, but what they do successfully, is what history makes haste to record.—*H. W. Beecher.*

The great high-road of human welfare lies along the old highway of steadfast well-doing; and they who are the most persistent, and work in the truest spirit, will invariably be the most successful; success treads on the heels of every right effort.—*S. Smiles.*

He that has never known adversity, is but half acquainted with others, or with himself. Constant success shows us but one side of the world. For, as it surrounds us with friends, who will tell us only our merits, so it silences those enemies from whom alone we can learn our defects.—*Colton.*

It is success that colors all in life: success makes fools admired, makes villains honest: all the proud virtue of this vaunting world fawns on success and power, howe'er acquired.—*Thomson.*

People judge, for the most part, by the success. Let a man show all the good conduct that is possible, if the event does not answer, ill fortune passes for a fault, and is justified by a very few persons.—*Evremond.*

Success serves men as a pedestal; it makes them look larger, if reflection does not measure them.—*Joubert.*

Had I miscarried, I had been a villain; for men judge actions always by events; but when we manage by a just foresight, success is prudence, and possession right.—*Higgons.*

Nothing succeeds so well as success.—*Talleyrand.*

Success produces confidence; confidence relaxes industry, and negligence ruins the reputation which accuracy had raised.—*Jonson.*

Let them call it mischief; when it is past and prospered, it will be virtue.—*Ben Jonson.*

It is not in mortals to command success, but we will do more, we will deserve it.—*Addison.*

Had I succeeded well, I had been reckoned among the wise; our minds are so disposed to judge from the event.—*Euripides.*

Few things are impracticable in themselves, and it is for want of application, rather than of means, that men fail of success.—*Rochefoucauld.*

If you wish success in life, make perseverance your bosom friend, experience your wise counsellor, caution your elder

brother, and hope your guardian genius.
—*Addison.*

I believe the true road to preeminent success in any line is to make yourself master of that line.—*Andrew Carnegie.*

From above we can hear the crowd below growling and grumbling and taking it easy.—*Robert Dollar.*

Never one thing and seldom one person can make for a success. It takes a number of them merging into one perfect whole.—*Marie Dressler.*

Like the British Constitution, she owes her success in practice to her inconsistencies in principle.—*Thos. Hardy.*

'Tis the golfer who cannot hole his putts that pays and pays and pays. 'Tis the golfer who holes them that plays and plays and plays.—*Kerr N. Petrie.*

Success is counted sweetest by those who ne'er succeed.—*Emily Dickinson.*

Nothing can stand against success and yet keep fresh. Nations as well as individuals feel its vulgarizing power.—*R. B. Cunninghame Graham.*

We can do anything we want to do if we stick to it long enough.—*Helen Keller.*

Man cannot be satisfied with mere success. He is concerned with the terms upon which success comes to him. And very often the terms seem more important than the success.—*Charles A. Bennett.*

In history as in life it is success that counts. Start a political upheaval and let yourself be caught, and you will hang as a traitor. But place yourself at the head of a rebellion and gain your point, and all future generations will worship you as the Father of their Country.—*Hendrik Van Loon.*

How shall we pass most swiftly from point to point, and be present always at the focus where the greatest number of vital forces unite in their purest energy? To maintain this ecstasy is success in life.—*Walter Pater.*

We do not know, in most cases, how far social failure and success are due to heredity, and how far to environment. But environment is the easier of the two to improve.—*J. B. S. Haldane.*

If a man can write a better book, preach a better sermon, or make a better mouse-trap than his neighbor, though he build his house in the woods, the world will make a beaten path to his door.—*Generally attributed to Emerson, also claimed by Elbert Hubbard.*

Possessions, outward success, publicity, luxury—to me these have always been contemptible. I believe that a simple and unassuming manner of life is best for everyone, best both for the body and the mind.—*Albert Einstein.*

Put all good eggs in one basket and then watch that basket.—*Andrew Carnegie.*

Somebody said it couldn't be done, but he with a chuckle replied that "maybe it couldn't," but he would be one who wouldn't say so till he'd tried.—*Edgar A. Guest.*

One never learns by success. Success is the plateau that one rests upon to take breath and look down from upon the straight and difficult path, but one does not climb upon a plateau.—*Josephine Preston Peabody.*

The difference between failure and success is doing a thing nearly right and doing it exactly right.—*Edward C. Simmons.*

Life has a way of overgrowing its achievements as well as its ruins.—*Edith Wharton.*

The eminently successful man should beware of the tendency of wealth to chill and isolate.—*Otto H. Kahn.*

Character is the real foundation of all worth-while success.—*John Hays Hammond.*

The simple virtues of willingness, readiness, alertness and courtesy will carry a young man farther than mere smartness.—*Henry P. Davison.*

SUFFERING.—(See "AFFLICTION," "SORROW.")

To be born is to suffer: to grow old is to suffer: to die is to suffer: to lose what is loved is to suffer: to be tied to what is not loved is to suffer: to endure what is distasteful is to suffer. In short, all the results of individuality, of separate self-hood, necessarily involve pain or suffering.—*Subhadra Bhikshu.*

Humanity either makes, or breeds, or tolerates all its afflictions, great or small.—*H. G. Wells.*

To love all mankind a cheerful state

of being is required; but to see into mankind, into life, and still more into ourselves, suffering is requisite.—*Richter.*

Know how sublime a thing it is to suffer and be strong.—*Longfellow.*

Suffering is the surest means of making us truthful to ourselves.—*Sismondi.*

God washes the eyes by tears until they can behold the invisible land where tears shall come no more.—*H. W. Beecher.*

Night brings out stars, as sorrow shows us truths.—*Bailey.*

We need to suffer that we may learn to pity.—*L. E. Landon.*

Forgiveness is rarely perfect except in the breasts of those who have suffered.

SUICIDE.—When all the blandishments of life are gone the coward sneaks to death; the brave lives on.—*Martial.*

Against self-slaughter there is a prohibition so divine that cravens my weak hand.—*Shakespeare.*

Self-murder, that infernal crime, which all the gods level their thunder at!—*Fane.*

O deaf to nature and to Heaven's command, against thyself to lift the murdering hand!—Oh, damned despair, to shun the living light, and plunge thy guilty soul in endless night!—*Lucretius.*

There are some vile and contemptible men who, allowing themselves to be conquered by misfortune, seek a refuge in death.—*Agathon.*

Suicide is a crime the most revolting to the feelings; nor does any reason suggest itself to our understanding by which it can be justified. It certainly originates in that species of fear which we denominate poltroonery. For what claim can that man have to courage who trembles at the frowns of fortunes? True heroism consists in being superior to the ills of life in whatever shape they may challenge him to combat.—*Napoleon.*

He is not valiant that dares to die; but he that boldly bears calamity.—*Massinger.*

Suicide sometimes proceeds from cowardice, but not always; for cowardice sometimes prevents it; since as many live because they are afraid to die, as die because they are afraid to live.—*Colton.*

I look upon indolence as a sort of suicide; for the man is efficiently destroyed, though the appetite of the brute may survive.—*Chesterfield.*

The miserablest day we live there is many a better thing to do than die.—*Darley.*

What a folly it is to dread the thought of throwing away life at once, and yet have no regard to throwing it away by parcels and piecemeal?—*John Howe.*

Men would not be so hasty to abandon the world either as monks or as suicides, did they but see the jewels of wisdom and faith which are scattered so plentifully along its paths; and lacking which no soul can come again from beyond the grave to gather.—*Mountford.*

Those men who destroy a healthful constitution of body by intemperance as manifestly kill themselves as those who hang, or poison, or drown themselves.—*Sherlock.*

The dread of something after death puzzles the will, and makes us rather bear the ills we have, than fly to others that we know not of.—*Shakespeare.*

To die in order to avoid anything that is evil and disagreeable, is not the part of a brave man, but of a coward; for it is cowardice to shun the trials and crosses of life, not undergoing death because it is honorable, but to avoid evil.—*Aristotle.*

SUNDAY.—(See " SABBATH.")

SUN.—That orbed continent, the fire that severs day from night.—*Shakespeare.*

The glorious sun,—the centre and soul of our system,—the lamp that lights it,—the fire that heats it,—the magnet that guides and controls it;—the fountain of color, which gives its azure to the sky, its verdure to the fields, its rainbow-hues to the gay world of flowers, and the purple light of love to the marble cheek of youth and beauty.—*Sir David Brewster.*

The sun-god's crest upon his azure shield, the heavens.—*Bailey.*

The sun does not shine for a few trees and flowers, but for the wide world's joy.—So God sits, effulgent, in heaven, not for a favored few, but for the universe of life, and there is no creature so poor or low that he may not look up with childlike confidence, and say, " My father! thou art mine."—*H. W. Beecher.*

The golden sun, in splendor likest heaven, dispenses light from far; days, months, and years, toward his all-cheering lamp turn their swift motions, or are turned by his magnetic beam that warms the universe.—*Milton.*

Fairest of lights above! thou sun whose beams adorn the spheres, and with unwearied swiftness move, to form the circle of our years.—*Watts.*

Thou earliest minister of the Almighty, who chose thee for his shadow; thou chief star, centre of many stars, thou dost rise, and shine, and set in glory!—*Byron.*

Sunbeam of summer, what is like thee, hope of the wilderness, joy of the sea! —One thing like thee to mortals is given, the faith touching all things with hues of heaven!—*Mrs. Hemans.*

SUNRISE.—Yonder comes the powerful King of day, rejoicing in the East.—*Thomson.*

And lo! in a flash of crimson splendor, with blazing, scarlet clouds running before his chariot and heralding his majestic approach, God's sun rises upon the world.—*Thackeray.*

See! the sun himself! on wings of glory up the East he springs.—Angel of light, who from the time the heavens began their march sublime, hath, first of all the starry choir, trod in his maker's steps of fire.—*Moore.*

As a giant strong, a bridegroom gay, the sun comes through the gates of day, and hurls his beams o'er the proud hills —a stream of glory and a flood of day. —*Broome.*

SUNSET.—The sun, when he from noon declines, and with abated heat less fiercely shines; seems to grow milder as he goes away.—*Dryden.*

The zenith spreads its canopy of sapphire, and the West has a magnificent array of clouds, and as the breeze plays on them they assume the forms of mountains, castled cliffs and hills, and shadowy glens, and groves, and beetling rocks, and some in golden masses float, and others have edges of burning crimson.—Never from the birth of time were

scattered o'er the glowing sky more splendid colorings.—*Carrington.*

The death-bed of a day, how beautiful!—*Bailey.*

The West is crimson with retiring day, and the North gleams with its own native light.—*J. H. Bryant.*

His rays are all gold, and his beauties are best, as painting the skies he sinks down in the West, and foretells a bright rising again.—*Watts.*

Sunsets in themselves are generally superior to sunrises; and with the sunset we appreciate images drawn from departed peace, and faded glory.—*Hillard.*

More joyful eyes look at the setting, than at the rising sun.—Burdens are laid down by the poor, whom the sun consoles more than the rich.—I yearn toward him when he sets, not when he rises.—*Richter.*

The weary sun hath made a golden set; and by the light track of his fiery car, gives token of a goodly day tomorrow.—*Shakespeare.*

SUPERFLUITIES.—What man in his right senses, that has wherewithal to live free, would make himself a slave for superfluities? What does that man want who has enough? Or what is he the better for abundance that can never be satisfied?—*L'Estrange.*

Were the superfluities of a nation valued, and made a perpetual tax or benevolence, there would be more almshouses than poor, more schools than scholars, and enough to spare for government beside.—*Penn.*

Our superfluities should give way to our brother's conveniences. and our conveniences, to our brother's necessities; yea, even our necessities should give way to their extremity for the supplying of them.—*Venning.*

Superfluity creates necessity, and necessity superfluity. Take care to be an economist in prosperity: there is no fear of your being one in adversity.—*Zimmermann.*

There are, while human miseries abound, a thousand ways to waste superfluous wealth, without one fool or flatterer at your board, without one hour of sickness or disgust.—*Armstrong.*

Manage as we may, misery and suffering will always' cleave to the border of superfluity.—*Jacobi.*

Wherever desirable superfluities are imported, industry is excited, and thereby plenty is produced. Were only necessaries permitted to be purchased, men would work no more than was necessary for that purpose.—*Franklin.*

He who accustoms himself to buy superfluities, may be obliged, ere long, to sell his necessities.—*C. Simmons.*

SUPERSTITION.—Superstitions are, for the most part, but the shadows of great truths.—*Tryon Edwards.*

Religion worships God, while superstition profanes that worship.—*Seneca.*

By superstitions I mean all hypocritical arts of appeasing God and procuring his favor without obeying his laws, or reforming our sins: infinite such superstitions have been invented by heathens, by Jews, by Christians themselves, especially by the Church of Rome, which abounds with them.—*Sherlock.*

Superstition is but the fear of belief, religion is the confidence and trust.

The greatest burden in the world is superstition, not only of ceremonies in the church, but of imaginary and scarecrow sins at home.—*Milton.*

Superstition always inspires bitterness; religion, grandeur of mind.—The superstitious man raises beings inferior to himself to deities.—*Lavater.*

Superstition is a senseless fear of God; religion the intelligent and pious worship of the deity.—*Cicero.*

Superstition is the only religion of which base souls are capable.—*Joubert.*

We are all tattooed in our cradles with the beliefs of our tribe; the record may seem superficial, but it is indelible. You cannot educate a man wholly out of the superstitious fears which were implanted in his imagination, no matter how utterly his reason may reject them. —*O. W. Holmes.*

The child taught to believe any occurrence a good or evil omen, or any day of the week lucky, hath a wide inroad made upon the soundness of his understanding.—*Watts.*

The less we know as to things that can be done, the less sceptical are we as to things that cannot. Hence it is that sailors and gamblers, though not re-

markable for their devotion, are even proverbial for their superstition; the solution of this phenomenon is, that both these descriptions of men have so much to do with things beyond all possibility of being reduced either to rule or to reason,—the winds and the waves,—and the decisions of the dice-box.

They that are against superstition, oftentimes run into it on the wrong side. If I wear all colors but black, then I am superstitious in not wearing black. —*Selden.*

Open biographical volumes wherever you please, and the man who has no faith in religion is the one who hath faith in a nightmare and ghosts.—*Bulwer.*

It is of such stuff that superstitions are commonly made; an intense feeling about ourselves which makes the evening star shine at us with a threat, and the blessing of a beggar encourage us. And superstitions carry consequences which often verify their hope or their foreboding.—*George Eliot.*

It were better to have no opinion of God at all than such an opinion as is unworthy of him, for the one is unbelief, and the other is contumely.—Superstition is the reproach of the deity.

A peasant can no more help believing in a traditional superstition than a horse can help trembling when he sees a camel.—*George Eliot.*

Superstition is the poetry of life. It is inherent in man's nature; and when we think it is wholly eradicated, it takes refuge in the strangest holes and corners, whence it peeps out all at once, as soon as it can do it with safety.—*Goethe.*

Superstition is not, as has been defined, an excess of religious feeling, but a misdirection of it, an exhausting of it on vanities of man's devising.—*Whately.*

Superstition renders a man a fool, and scepticism makes him mad.—*Fielding.*

There is a superstition in avoiding superstition, when men think they do best if they go farthest from the superstition, — by which means they often take away the good as well as the bad. —*Bacon.*

Look how the world's poor people are amazed at apparitions, signs, and prodigies!—*Shakespeare.*

Liberal minds are open to conviction

Liberal doctrines are capable of improvement. There are proselytes from atheism; but none from superstition.—*Junius.*

As it addeth deformity to an ape to be so like a man, so the similitude of superstition to religion makes it the more deformed.—*Bacon.*

That the corruption of the best thing produces the worst, is grown into a maxim, and is commonly proved, among other instances, by the pernicious effects of superstition and enthusiasm, the corruptions of true religion.—*Hume.*

I think we cannot too strongly attack superstition, which is the disturber of society; nor too highly respect genuine religion, which is the support of it.—*Rousseau.*

Weakness, fear, melancholy, together with ignorance, are the true sources of superstition. Hope, pride, presumption, a warm indignation, together with ignorance, are the true sources of enthusiasm. —*Hume.*

The master of superstition is the people, and in all superstition wise men follow fools.—*Bacon.*

SURETYSHIP.—He that would be master of his own, must not be bound for another.—*Franklin.*

Beware of suretyship for thy best friend. He that payeth another man's debt seeketh his own decay. But if thou canst not otherwise choose, rather lend thy money thyself upon good bonds, although thou borrow it; so shalt thou secure thyself, and pleasure thy friend. —*Burleigh.*

If thou be bound for a stranger, thou art a fool; if for a merchant, thou puttest thy estate to learn to swim; if for a lawyer, he will find an evasion by a syllable or a word; if for a poor man, thou must pay it thyself; if for a rich man, he needs not; therefore, from suretyship, as from a manslayer or enchanter, bless thyself; for the best return will be this—if thou force him for whom thou art bound to pay it himself he will become thy enemy; if thou pay it thyself, thou wilt become a beggar.— *Sir W. Raleigh.*

He who is surety is never sure himself. Take advice, and never be security for more than you are quite willing to lose. Remember the word of the wise man: "He that is surety for a stranger shall smart for it; and he that hateth suretyship is sure."—*Spurgeon.*

Endorsing character is hazardous; endorsing credit, presumptuous.—*C. Simmons.*

Such as are betrayed by their easy nature to be ordinary security for their friends leave so little to themselves, as their liberty remains ever after arbitrary at the will of others; experience having recorded of many, whom their fathers had left elbow-room enough, that by suretyship they have expired in a dungeon.—*F. Osborn.*

If any friend desire thee to be his surety, give him a part of what thou hast to spare; if he press thee further, he is not thy friend at all, for friendship rather chooseth harm to itself than offereth it.—*Sir W. Raleigh.*

SUSPENSE.—Of all the conditions to which the heart is subject, suspense is one that most gnaws and cankers into the frame. One little month of suspense, when it involves death, we are told by an eye-witness, is sufficient to plough fixed lines and furrows in a convict of five-and-twenty,—sufficient to dash the brown hair with gray, and to bleach the gray to white.—*Bulwer.*

It is a miserable thing to live in suspense: it is the life of a spider.—*Swift.*

But not long; for in the tedious minutes' exquisite interval—I'm on the rack; for sure the greatest evil man can know bears no proportion to this dread suspense.—*Froude.*

The suspense—the fearful, acute suspense, of standing idly by while the life of one we dearly love is trembling in the balance; the racking thoughts that crowd upon the mind, and make the heart beat violently, and the breath come thick; the desperate anxiety "to be doing something" to relieve the pain or lessen the danger which we have no power to alleviate; and the sinking of soul which the sad sense of our helplessness produces,—what tortures can equal these, and what reflections or efforts can, in the full tide and fever of the time, allay them.—*Dickens.*

Uncertainty! fell demon of our fears! The human soul that can support despair, supports not thee.—*Mallet.*

SUSPICION.—Always to think the worst, I have ever found to be the mark of a mean spirit and a base soul.—*Boling-broke.*

Suspicion is no less an enemy to virtue than to happiness. He that is already corrupt is naturally suspicious, and he that becomes suspicious will quickly be corrupt.—*Johnson.*

To be suspicious is to invite treachery.—*Voltaire.*

There is no rule more invariable than that we are paid for our suspicions by finding what we suspect.—*Thoreau.*

Don't seem to be on the lookout for crows, else you'll set other people watching.—*George Eliot.*

Discreet and well-founded suspicion avoids a multitude of evils, which credulity brings upon itself. We ought always to be suspicious enough to avoid all improper and forbidden trust in man, or in our own hearts.—*C. Simmons.*

Never put much confidence in such as put no confidence in others. A man prone to suspect evil is mostly looking in his neighbor for what he sees in himself. As to the pure all things are pure, even so to the impure all things are impure.—*Hare.*

Suspicion always haunts the guilty mind: the thief doth fear each bush an officer.—*Shakespeare.*

Suspicion is far more apt to be wrong than right; oftener unjust than just. It is no friend to virtue, and always an enemy to happiness.—*H. Ballou.*

At the gate which suspicion enters, love and confidence go out.

He that lives in perpetual suspicion lives the life of a sentinel never relieved, whose business it is to look out for and expect an enemy, which is an evil not very far short of perishing by him.—*Young.*

The virtue of a coward is suspicion.—*Herbert.*

Ignorance is the mother of suspicion.—*W. R. Alger.*

Suspicion is the poison of true friendship.—*Augustine.*

There is nothing makes a man suspect much, more than to know little, and therefore men should remedy suspicion by procuring to know more, and not keep their suspicions in smother.—*Bacon.*

One of the principal ingredients in the happiness of childhood is freedom from suspicion—why may it not be combined with a more extensive intercourse with mankind? A disposition to dwell on the bright side of character is like gold to its possessor; but to imagine more evil than meets the eye, betrays affinity for it.—*Mrs. Sigourney.*

Whose own hard dealings teach them, suspect the thoughts of others.—*Shakespeare.*

Surmise is the gossamer that malice blows on fair reputations, the corroding dew that destroys the choice blossoms. Surmise is primarily the squint of suspicion, and suspicion is established before it is confirmed.—*Zimmermann.*

Open suspecting of others comes of secretly condemning ourselves.—*Sir P. Sidney.*

Suspicions amongst thoughts are like the bats amongst birds, they ever fly by twilight: certainly they are to be repressed, or at least well guarded, for they cloud the mind, lose friends, check business, dispose kings to tyranny, husbands to jealousy, and wise men to irresolution and melancholy; they are defects, not in the heart, but in the brain.—*Bacon.*

Undue suspicion is more abject baseness even than the guilt suspected.—*A. Hill.*

It is hardly possible to suspect another without having in one's self the seeds of the baseness the other is accused of.—*Stanislaus.*

A noble brother, whose nature is so far from doing harms, that he suspects none.—*Shakespeare.*

SWEARING.—(See " PROFANITY.")

SYMPATHY.—Next to love, sympathy is the divinest passion of the human heart.—*Burke.*

To rejoice in another's prosperity, is to give content to your own lot; to mitigate another's grief, is to alleviate or dispel your own.—*Tryon Edwards.*

One of the greatest of all mental pleasures is to have our thoughts often divined; ever entered into with sympathy.—*L. E. Landon.*

Shame on those hearts of stone, that cannot melt in soft adoption of another's sorrow!—*A. Hill.*

No radiant pearl, which crested fortune wears, no gem, that twinkling hangs from beauty's ears; not the bright stars, which night's blue arch adorn; nor rising sun, that gilds the vernal morn; shine with such lustre as the tear that flows down virtue's manly cheek for others' woes.—*Darwin.*

More helpful than all wisdom or counsel is one draught of simple human pity that will not forsake us.—*George Eliot.*

The generous heart should scorn a pleasure which gives others pain.—*Thomson.*

There is a kind of sympathy in souls that fits them for each other; and we may be assured when we see two persons engaged in the warmths of a mutual affection, that there are certain qualities in both their minds which bear a resemblance to one another.—*Steele.*

To commiserate is sometimes more than to give, for money is external to a man's self, but he who bestows compassion communicates his own soul.—*Mountford.*

The only true knowledge of our fellowman is that which enables us to feel with him—which gives us a fine ear for the heart-pulses that are beating under the mere clothes of circumstance and opinion.—*George Eliot.*

With a soul that ever felt the sting of sorrow, sorrow is a sacred thing.—*Cowper.*

Sympathy is the first great lesson which man should learn. It will be ill for him if he proceeds no farther; if his emotions are but excited to roll back on his heart, and to be fostered in luxurious quiet. But unless he learns to feel for things in which he has no personal interest, he can achieve nothing generous or noble.—*Talfourd.*

Our sympathy is never very deep unless founded on our own feelings.—We pity, but do not enter into the grief which we have never felt.—*L. E. Landon.*

Open your hearts to sympathy, but close them to despondency. The flower which opens to receive the light of day shuts against rain.

Let us cherish sympathy. It prepares the mind for receiving the impressions of virtue; and without it there can be no true politeness. Nothing is more odious than that insensibility which wraps a man up in himself and his own concerns, and prevents his being moved with either the joys or the sorrows of another.—*Beattie.*

All sympathy not consistent with acknowledged virtue is but disguised selfishness.—*Coleridge.*

Sympathy wanting, all is wanting.—Personal magnetism is the conductor of the sacred spark that puts us in human communion, and gives us to company, conversation, and ourselves.—*A. B. Alcott.*

It is a lively spark of nobleness to descend in most favor to one when he is lowest in affliction.—*Sir P. Sidney.*

It is an eternal truth in the political as well as the mystical body, that "where one member suffers, all the members suffer with it."—*Junius.*

Our sympathy is cold to the relation of distant misery.—*Gibbon.*

A helping word to one in trouble is often like a switch on a railroad-track—an inch between wreck and smooth-rolling prosperity.—*H. W. Beecher.*

Public feeling now is apt to side with the persecuted, and our modern martyr is full as likely to be smothered with roses as with coals.—*E. H. Chapin.*

It may, indeed, be said that sympathy exists in all minds, as Faraday has discovered that magnetism exists in all metals; but a certain temperature is required to develop the hidden property, whether in the metal or the mind.—*Bulwer.*

Every man rejoices twice when he has a partner of his joy; a friend shares my sorrow and makes it but a moiety, but he swells my joy and makes it double.—*Jeremy Taylor.*

The more sympathies we gain or awaken for what is beautiful, by so much deeper will be our sympathy for that which is most beautiful, the human soul.—*J. R. Lowell.*

It is certain my belief gains quite infinitely the very moment I can convince another mind thereof.—*Novalis.*

The capacity of sorrow belongs to our grandeur, and the loftiest of our race are those who have had the profoundest sympathies, because they have had the profoundest sorrows.—*Henry Giles.*

Happy is the man who has that in his

soul which acts upon the dejected as April airs upon violet roots. Gifts from the hand are silver and gold, but the heart gives that which neither silver nor gold can buy. To be full of goodness, full of cheerfulness, full of sympathy, full of helpful hope, causes a man to carry blessings of which he is himself as unconscious as a lamp is of its own shining. Such a one moves on human life as stars move on dark seas to bewildered mariners; as the sun wheels, bringing all the season with him from the south.— *H. W. Beecher.*

The world has no sympathy with any but positive griefs; it will pity you for what you lose, but never for what you lack.—*Mad. Swetchine.*

He that sympathizes in all the happiness of others, perhaps himself enjoys the safest happiness; and he that is warned by the folly of others has perhaps attained the soundest wisdom.— *Colton.*

Grief is a stone that bears one down, but two bear it lightly.—*W. Hauff.*

T

TACT.—A little tact and wise management may often evade resistance, and carry a point, where direct force might be in vain.—*Anon.*

A tact which surpassed the tact of her sex as much as the tact of her sex surpasses the tact of ours.—*Macaulay.*

Never join with your friend when he abuses his horse or his wife, unless the one is to be sold, and the other to be buried.—*Colton.*

Tact comes as much from goodness of heart as from fineness of taste.—*Endymion.*

A quick and sound judgment, good common sense, kind feeling, and an instinctive perception of character, in these are the elements of what is called tact, which has so much to do with acceptability and success in life.—*C. Simmons.*

Talent is power; tact is skill.

Talent is wealth; tact is ready money. —Talent makes the world wonder that it gets on no faster; tact excites astonishment that it gets on so fast.—And the secret is that it makes no false steps, loses no time; takes all hints, and, by

keeping its eye on the weathercock, it is able to take advantage of every wind that blows.—*W. P. Scargill.*

I have known some men possessed of good qualities which were very serviceable to others, but useless to themselves, like a sundial on the front of a house, to inform the neighbors and passengers, but not the owner within.— *Swift.*

Men may have the gifts both of talent and of wit, but unless they have also prudence and judgment to dictate when, where, and the how those gifts are to be exerted, the possessors of them will conquer only where nothing is to be gained, and be defeated where everything is to be lost; they will be outdone by men of less brilliant, but more convertible qualifications, and whose strength, in one point, is not counterbalanced by any disproportion in another.—*Colton.*

Tact is one of the first mental virtues, the absence of which is often fatal to the best of talents; it supplies the place of many talents.—*Simms.*

Talent is something, but tact is everything. Talent is serious, sober, grave, and respectable; tact is all that, and more too. It is not a seventh sense, but is the life of all the five. It is the open eye, the quick ear, the judging taste, the keen smell, and the lively touch; it is the interpreter of all riddles, the surmounter of all difficulties, the remover of all obstacles.—*W. P. Scargill.*

TALENT.—(See "CHARACTER.")

Men of talent are men for occasions.

Talent is the capacity of doing anything that depends on application and industry; it is a voluntary power, while genius is involuntary.—*Hazlitt.*

As to great and commanding talents, they are the gift of Providence in some way unknown to us. They rise where they are least expected. They fail when everything seems disposed to produce them, or at least to call them forth.— *Burke.*

Talent, lying in the understanding, is often inherited; genius, being the action of reason or imagination, rarely or never. —*Coleridge.*

Whatever you are from nature, keep to it; never desert your own line of talent. Be what nature intended you for, and you will succeed; be anything else, and you will be ten thousand times worse than nothing!—*Sydney Smith.*

Great talents, such as honor, virtue, learning, and parts, are above the generality of the world, who neither possess them themselves, nor judge of them rightly in others; but all people are judges of the lesser talents, such as civility, affability, and an obliging, agreeable address and manner, because they feel the good effects of them, as making society easy and pleasing.—*Chesterfield.*

Nature has concealed at the bottom of our minds talents and abilities of which we are not aware. The passions alone have the privilege of bringing them to light, and of giving us sometimes views more certain and more perfect than art could possibly produce.—*Rochefoucauld.*

Great offices will have great talents, and God gives to every man the virtue, temper, understanding, taste, that lifts him into life, and lets him fall just in the niche he was ordained to fill.—*Cowper.*

It always seemed to me a sort of clever stupidity only to have one sort of talent—like a carrier-pigeon.—*George Eliot.*

Talents, angel bright, if wanting worth, are shining instruments in false ambition's hand, to render faults illustrious, and give infamy renown.—*Young.*

Talent, like beauty, to be pardoned, must be obscure and unostentatious.—*Lady Blessington.*

Talent for talent's sake is a bauble and a show. Talent working with joy in the cause of universal truth lifts the possessor to new power as a benefactor.—*Emerson.*

Talents, to strike the eye of posterity, should be concentrated. Rays, powerless while they are scattered, burn in a point.—*Willmott.*

Talents of the highest order, and such as are calculated to command universal admiration, may exist apart from wisdom.—*Robert Hall.*

TALKING.—(See "LOQUACITY" and "SPEECH.")

It has been well observed, that the tongue discovers the state of the mind no less than that of the body; but, in either case, before the philosopher or the physician can judge, the patient must open his mouth.—*Colton.*

The tongue of a fool is the key of his counsel, which, in a wise man, wisdom hath in keeping.—*Socrates.*

As it is the characteristic of great wits to say much in few words, so it is of small wits to talk much and say nothing.—*Rochefoucauld.*

Never hold any one by the button, or the hand, in order to be heard out; for if people are unwilling to hear you, you had better hold your tongue than them.—*Chesterfield.*

The lover and physician are both popular from the same cause. We talk to them only of ourselves. That, I daresay, was the origin of confession-egotism under the name of religion.—*L. E. Landon.*

He that cannot refrain from much speaking is like a city without walls; therefore if thou observest this rule in all assemblies thou shalt seldom err; restrain thy choler, hearken much, and speak little, for the tongue is the instrument of the greatest good and greatest evil that is done in the world.—*Sir W. Raleigh.*

A man should be careful never to tell tales of himself to his own disadvantage; people may be amused, and laugh at the time, but they will be remembered, and brought up against him upon some subsequent occasion.—*Johnson.*

I know a lady that loves talking so incessantly, she won't give an echo fair play; she has that everlasting rotation of tongue that an echo must wait till she dies before it can catch her last words!—*Congreve.*

They think too little who talk too much.—*Dryden.*

When I think of talking, it is of course with a woman. For talking at its best being an inspiration, it wants a corresponding divine quality of receptiveness, and where will you find this but in a woman?—*O. W. Holmes.*

Such as thy words are, such will thy affections be esteemed; and such will thy deeds as thy affections, and such thy life as thy deeds.—*Socrates.*

Talkers are no good doers.—*Shakespeare.*

They talk most who have the least to say.—*Prior.*

Those who have but little business to

attend to, are great talkers. The less men think, the more they talk.—*Montesquieu.*

If you light upon an impertinent talker, that sticks to you like a burr, deal freely with him, break off the discourse, and pursue your business.—*Plutarch.*

Words learned by rote a parrot may rehearse; but talking is not always to converse; not more distinct from harmony divine, the constant creaking of a country sign.—*Cowper.*

Speaking much is a sign of vanity; for he that is lavish in words, is a niggard in deed.—*Sir W. Raleigh.*

There are braying men in the world as well as braying asses; for, what's loud and senseless talking and swearing, any other than braying.—*L'Estrange.*

A wise man reflects before he speaks; a fool speaks, and then reflects on what he has uttered.—*Delile.*

Talkative people who wish to be loved are hated; when they desire to please, they bore; when they think they are admired, they are laughed at; they injure their friends, benefit their enemies, and ruin themselves.—*Plutarch.*

Great talkers are like leaky vessels; everything runs out of them.—*C. Simmons.*

A civil guest will no more talk all, than eat all the feast.—*Herbert.*

Wise men talk because they have something to say; fools, because they would like to say something.

As empty vessels make the loudest sound, so they that have least wit are the greatest babblers.—*Plato.*

The talkative listen to no one, for they are ever speaking.—And the first evil that attends those who know not how to be silent, is, that they hear nothing.—*Plutarch.*

A talkative person runs himself into great inconveniences by babbling out his own and other's secrets.—*Ray.*

Many a man's tongue shakes out his master's undoing.—*Shakespeare.*

We often say things because we can say them well, rather than because they are sound and reasonable.—*Landor.*

There are many who talk on from ignorance rather than from knowledge, and who find the former an inexhaustible fund of conversation.—*Hazlitt.*

Let your words be few, especially when your betters, or strangers, or men of more experience, or understanding, are in the place, for in so doing you do yourself at once two great mischiefs: first, you betray, and discover your own weakness and folly; and next, you rob yourself of that opportunity which you might otherwise have to gain wisdom and experience, by hearing those that you silence by your impertinent talking. —*Sir M. Hale.*

Does a man speak foolishly?—suffer him gladly, for you are wise. Does he speak erroneously?—stop such a man's mouth with sound words that cannot be gainsaid. Does he speak truly?—rejoice in the truth.—*Cromwell.*

Brisk talkers are usually slow thinkers. There is, indeed, no wild beast more to be dreaded than a communicative man having nothing to communicate. If you are civil to the voluble they will abuse your patience; if brusque, your character.—*Swift.*

There is the same difference between the tongues of some, as between the hour and the minute hand; one goes ten times as fast, and the other signifies ten times as much.—*Sydney Smith.*

The common fluency of speech in many men, and most women, is owing to a scarcity of matter and a scarcity of words, for whoever is a master of language and has a mind full of ideas, will be apt, in speaking, to hesitate upon the choice of his words.—*Swift.*

If thy words be too luxuriant, confine them, lest they confine thee.—He that thinks he can never speak enough, may easily speak too much.—A full tongue and an empty brain are seldom parted. —*Quarles.*

What a spendthrift he is of his tongue. —*Shakespeare.*

Cautiously avoid speaking of the domestic affairs either of yourself, or of other people.—Yours are nothing to them but tedious gossip; and theirs are nothing to you.—*Chesterfield.*

One learns tacturnity best among those who have none, and loquacity among the taciturn.—*Richter.*

The man who talks everlastingly and promiscuously, and who seems to have an exhaustless magazine of sound, crowds so many words into his thoughts, that he always obscures, and very frequently conceals them.—*Washington Irving.*

It is a sad thing when men have neither the wit to speak well, nor judgment to hold their tongues.—*Bruyère.*

Great knowledge, if it be without vanity, is the most severe bridle of the tongue. For so have I heard, that all the noises and prating of the pool, the croaking of frogs and toads, are hushed and appeased upon the bringing upon them the light of a candle or torch. Every beam of reason and ray of knowledge checks the dissolution of the tongue.—*Jeremy Taylor.*

It has been said in praise of some men, that they could talk whole hours together upon anything; but it must be owned to the honor of the other sex, that there are many among them who can talk whole hours together upon nothing.—*Addison.*

The more ideas a man has the fewer words he takes to express them. Wise men never talk to make time; they talk to save it.—*Uncle Esek.*

TASTE.—May not taste be compared to that exquisite sense of the bee, which instantly discovers and extracts the quintessence of every flower, and disregards all the rest of it?—*Gréville.*

Taste, if it mean anything but a paltry connoisseurship, must mean a general susceptibility to truth and nobleness, a sense to discern, and a heart to love and reverence all beauty, order, goodness, wheresoever, or in whatsoever forms and accompaniments, they are to be seen. This surely implies, as its chief condition, a finely-gifted mind, purified into harmony with itself, into keenness and justness of vision; above all, kindled into love and generous admiration.—*Carlyle.*

Taste and elegance, though they are reckoned only among the smaller and secondary morals, yet are of no mean importance in the regulation of life. A moral taste is not of force to turn vice into virtue: but it recommends virtue, with something like the blandishments of pleasure.—*Burke.*

When the taste is purified, the morals are not easily corrupted.

Whatever injures the body, the morals, or the mind, will lessen or vitiate taste; thus, disorders of the body and violent passions of the mind, will do this, and so will also excessive care or covetousness; but above all, a habit of intemperance and keeping low company will greatly deprave that which was once a good taste.—*Osborne.*

Delicacy of taste has the same effect as delicacy of passion; it enlarges the sphere both of our happiness and misery, and makes us sensible to pain as well as pleasures, which escape the rest of mankind.—*Hume.*

It is for the most part in our skill in manners, and in the observances of time and place and of decency in general, that what is called taste consists; and which is in reality no other than a more refined judgment. The cause of a wrong taste is a defect of judgment.—*Burke.*

Talk what you will of taste, you will find two of a face as soon as two of a mind.—*Pope.*

Good taste is the flower of good sense.—*A. Poincelot.*

Delicacy of taste is favorable to love and friendship, by confining our choice to few people, and making us indifferent to the company and conversation of the greater part of men.—*Hume.*

A truly elegant taste is generally accompanied with excellency of heart.—*Fielding.*

Bad taste is a species of bad morals.—*Bovee.*

A fastidious taste is like a squeamish appetite; the one has its origin in some disease of the mind, as the other has in some ailment of the stomach.—*Southey.*

Taste is often one of the aspects of fashion. Folly borrows its mask, and walks out with wisdom arm in arm. Like virtues of greater dignity, it is assumed.—*Willmott.*

Taste is not stationary. It grows every day, and is improved by cultivation, as a good temper is refined by religion.—*Willmott.*

Taste is, so to speak, the microscope of the judgment.—*Rousseau.*

Taste depends upon those finer emotions which make the organization of the soul.—*Sir J. Reynolds.*

I think I may define taste to be that faculty of the soul which discerns the beauties of an author with pleasure, and the imperfections with dislike.—*Addison.*

TATTLING.—(See "GOSSIP.")

I have ever heard it said that spies and tale-bearers have done more mischief in this world than poisoned bowl or the assassin's dagger.—*Schiller.*

Be careful that you believe not hastily strange news and strange stories; and be much more careful that you do not report them, though at the second hand; for if it prove an untruth it brings an imputation of levity upon him that reports it, and possibly some disadvantage to others.—*Sir Matthew Hale.*

The tongue is the worst part of a bad servant.—*Juvenal.*

Fire and sword are but slow engines of destruction in comparison with the babbler.—*Steele.*

Said Plautus, who was one of the wits of his time, "I would have tale-bearers and tale-hearers punished—the one hanging by the tongue, the other by the ears." Were his will a law, many a tattling gossip would have her vowels turned to mutes, and be justly tongue-tied.—*A. Warwick.*

Gossip is always a personal confession either of malice or imbecility; it is a low, frivolous, and too often a dirty business.—There are neighborhoods where it rages like a pest; churches are split in pieces by it, and neighbors made enemies for life.—Let the young avoid or cure it while they may.—*J. G. Holland.*

The thoughtless tattling tongue often murders the peace, and blights the good name of others, as surely and wickedly as if inflamed by malice.—*C. Simmons.*

The excessive pleasure we feel in talking of ourselves, ought to make us apprehensive that we afford little to our hearers.—*Rochefoucauld.*

I may hear a tale with delight, and perhaps smile at an innocent jest, but I will not jest, nor joy at a tale disgracing an innocent person.—*A. Warwick.*

TAXES.—Taxes are the sinews of the state.—*Cicero.*

Millions for defence; not a cent for tribute.—*C. C. Pinckney.*

The taxes are indeed very heavy, and if those laid by the government were the only ones we had to pay, we might more easily discharge them; but we have many others, and much more grievous to some of us. We are taxed twice as much by our idleness, three times as much by our pride, and four times as much by our folly; and from these taxes the commissioners cannot ease or deliver us by allowing an abatement.—*Franklin.*

What a benefit would the government render to itself, and to every city, village, and hamlet in the States, if it would tax whiskey and rum almost to the point of prohibition! Was it Bonaparte who said that he found vices very good patriots? "He got five millions from the love of brandy, and he should be glad to know which of the virtues would pay him as much." Tobacco and opium have broad backs, and will cheerfully carry the load of armies, if you choose to make them pay high for such joy as they give, and such harm as they do.—*Emerson.*

Taxation without representation is injustice and oppression.—It brought on the American Revolution, and gave birth to a free and mighty nation.

Taxing is an easy business.—Any projector can contrive new impositions; any bungler can add to the old; but is it altogether wise to have no other bounds to your impositions than the patience of those who are to bear them?—*Burke.*

Kings ought to shear, not skin their sheep.—*Herrick.*

As the general rule in constitutional states liberty is a compensation for the heaviness of taxation, and in despotic states the equivalent for liberty is the lightness of taxation.—*Montesquieu.*

TEACHING.—(See "EDUCATION.")

I am indebted to my father for living, but to my teacher for living well.—*Alexander of Macedon.*

Scratch the green rind of a sapling, or wantonly twist it in the soil, and a scarred or crooked oak will tell of the act for centuries to come. So it is with the teachings of youth, which make impressions on the mind and heart that are to last forever.

The highest function of the teacher consists not so much in imparting knowledge as in stimulating the pupil in its love and pursuit.

To know how to suggest is the art of teaching.—*Amiel.*

The true aim of every one who aspires to be a teacher should be, not to impart his own opinions, but to kindle minds.—*F. W. Robertson.*

Of what unspeakable importance is her education who pre-occupies the unwritten page of being; who produces impressions which only death can obliterate, and mingles with the cradle-dream what shall be read in eternity!—*Mrs. Sigourney.*

In the education of children there is nothing like alluring the interest and affection; otherwise you only make so many asses laden with books.—*Montaigne.*

Whatever you would have your children become, strive to exhibit in your own lives and conversation.—*Mrs. Sigourney.*

A wisely chosen illustration is almost essential to fasten the truth upon the ordinary mind, and no teacher can afford to neglect this part of his preparation. —*Howard Crosby.*

Thoroughly to teach another is the best way to learn for yourself.—*Tryon Edwards.*

Teachers should be held in the highest honor. They are the allies of legislators; they have agency in the prevention of crime; they aid in regulating the atmosphere, whose incessant action and pressure cause the life-blood to circulate, and to return pure and healthful to the heart of the nation.—*Mrs. Sigourney.*

The one exclusive sign of a thorough knowledge is the power of teaching.—*Aristotle.*

Delightful task, to rear the tender thought, to teach the young idea how to shoot, to pour fresh instruction over the mind, to breathe the enlivening spirit, and to fix the generous purpose in the glowing heart.—*Thomson.*

The secret of successful teaching is to teach accurately, thoroughly, and earnestly; this will impart interest to instructions, and awaken attention to them. All sciences, in their nature or connections, are replete with interest, if teachers properly illustrate and impress their truths in a pleasing, earnest manner.—*C. Simmons.*

The teacher who is attempting to teach without inspiring the pupil with a desire to learn is hammering on cold iron.—*H. Mann.*

Those who educate children well are more to be honored than even their parents, for these only give them life, those the art of living well.—*Aristotle.*

Be understood in thy teaching, and instruct to the measure of capacity.— Precepts and rules are repulsive to a child, but happy illustration wins him.— *Tupper.*

Do not train boys to learning by force and harshness; but direct them to it by what amuses their minds, so that you may be the better able to discover with accuracy the peculiar bent of the genius of each.—*Plato.*

The best teacher is the one who suggests rather than dogmatizes, and inspires his listener with the wish to teach himself.—*Bulwer.*

The method of teaching which approaches most nearly to the method of investigation, is incomparably the best; since, not content with serving up a few barren and lifeless truths, it leads to the stock on which they grew.—*Burke.*

If ever I am a teacher, it will be to learn more than to teach.—*Mad. Deluzy.*

If, in instructing a child, you are vexed with it for want of adroitness, try, if you have never tried before, to write with your left hand, and then remember that a child is all left hand.— *J. F. Boyse.*

To waken interest and kindle enthusiasm is the sure way to teach easily and successfully.—*Tryon Edwards.*

A good schoolmaster minces his precepts for children to swallow, hanging clogs on the nimbleness of his own soul, that his scholars may go along with him. —*Fuller.*

Improvement depends far less upon length of tasks and hours of application than is supposed. Children can take in but a little each day; they are like vases with a narrow neck; you may pour little or pour much, but much will not enter at a time.—*Michelet.*

A tutor should not be continually thundering instruction into the ears of his pupil, as if he were pouring it through a funnel, but induce him to think, to distinguish, and to find out things for himself; sometimes opening the way, at other times leaving it for him to open; and so accommodate his precepts to the capacity of his pupil.—*Montaigne.*

It would be a great advantage to some schoolmasters if they would steal two hours a day from their pupils, and give their own minds the benefit of the robbery.—*J. F. Boyse.*

He that governs well, leads the blind; but he that teaches, gives him eyes; and it is glorious to be a sub-worker to grace, in freeing it from some of the inconveniences of original sin.—*South.*

Let our teaching be full of ideas. Hitherto it has been stuffed only with facts.—*Anatole France.*

The fear of losing one's job has kept education in America fifty years behind its possible improvement.—*Dr. Eliot.*

The most potent of all indirect influences in the development of our citizenry is the influence of a good teacher.—*Armand J. Gerson.*

I cannot think but that the world would be better and brighter if our teachers would dwell on the Duty of Happiness as well as the Happiness of Duty.—*J. Lubbock.*

During the Middle Ages Europe was far too much influenced by celibate men. Today much too big a part in public life is played by celibate women, and too little by mothers. I find no new ideas more genuinely disgusting than that held by many educated authorities that a woman ceases to be suitable as a teacher when she becomes a mother.—*J. B. S. Haldane.*

Many earnest persons, who have found direct education for themselves fruitless and unprofitable, declare that they first began to learn when they began to teach, and that in the education of others they discovered the secret of their own.—*Gamaliel Bradford.*

Instruction in things moral is most necessary to the making of the highest type of citizenship.—*Theodore Roosevelt.*

TEARS.—There is a sacredness in tears. They are not the mark of weakness, but of power. They speak more eloquently than ten thousand tongues. They are the messengers of overwhelming grief, of deep contrition, and of unspeakable love.—*Washington Irving.*

Tears are the safety-valves of the heart when too much pressure is laid on it.—*Albert Smith.*

Only they have to weep bitter tears who know what has come to them is the result of their foolish conduct, their ignorant way, their want of proper understanding of life and what love means. —*Emil G. Hirsch.*

When I consider life and its few years —a wisp of fog between us and the sun; a call to battle and the battle done ere the last echo dies within our ears, I wonder at the idleness of tears.—*Lizette Woodworth Reese.*

Love is loveliest when embalmed in tears.—*Walter Scott.*

I would hardly change the sorrowful words of the poets for their glad ones. —Tears dampen the strings of the lyre, but they grow the more tender for it, and ring even the clearer and more ravishingly for it.—*J. R. Lowell.*

A smile is ever the most bright and beautiful with a tear upon it.—What is the dawn without its dew?—The tear, by the smile, is made precious above the smile itself.—*Landor.*

Tears, idle tears, I know not what they mean,—tears from the depth of some divine despair rise in the heart, and gather in the eyes, in looking on the happy autumn fields, and thinking of days that are no more.—*Alfred Lord Tennyson.*

Weep for love, but not for anger; a cold rain will never bring flowers.—*Duncan.*

Tearless grief bleeds inwardly.—*Bovee.*

O, banish the tears of children! Continual rains upon the blossoms are hurtful.—*Richter.*

The young man who has not wept is a savage, and the old man who will not laugh is a fool.—*George Santayana.*

My plenteous joys, wanton in fullness, seek to hide themselves in drops of sorrow.—*Shakespeare.*

Beauty's tears are lovelier than her smiles.—*Campbell.*

God made both tears and laughter, and both for kind purposes; for as laughter enables mirth and surprise to breathe freely, so tears enable sorrow to vent itself patiently. Tears hinder sorrow from becoming despair and madness; and laughter is one of the very privileges of reason, being confined to the human species.—*Leigh Hunt.*

All the rarest hues of human life take radiance and are rainbowed out in tears. —*Massey.*

There ought to be more tears of penitence over our neglects of Christ, more tears of sympathy with the afflicted, and more tears of joy over the infinite good things which Jesus brings to us.—*T. L. Cuyler.*

Of all the portions of life it is in the two twilights, childhood and age, that tears fall with the most frequency; like the dew at dawn and eve.—*W. R. Alger.*

Scorn the proud man that is ashamed to weep.—*Young.*

Tears hinder sorrow from becoming despair.—*Leigh Hunt.*

Those tender tears that humanize the soul.—*Thomson.*

Heaven and God are best discerned through tears; scarcely perhaps are discerned at all without them. The constant association of prayer with the hour of bereavement and the scenes of death suffice to show this.—*James Martineau.*

The tear of joy is a pearl of the first water; the mourning tear, only of the second.—*Richter.*

Tears are often the telescope through which men see far into heaven.—*H. W. Beecher.*

Some tears belong to us because we are unfortunate: others because we are humane: many because we are mortal. —But most are caused by our being unwise.—It is these last, only, that of necessity produce more.—*Leigh Hunt.*

What would women do if they could not cry?—What poor, defenceless creatures they would be.—*Jerrold.*

Tears are the softening showers which cause the seed of heaven to spring up in the human heart.—*Walter Scott.*

Shame on those breasts of stone that cannot melt in soft adoption of another's sorrow.—*A. Hill.*

Every tear of sorrow sown by the righteous springs up a pearl.—*M. Henry.*

What a hell of witchcraft lies in the small orb of one particular tear!— *Shakespeare.*

Pride dries the tears of anger and

vexation; humility, those of grief. The one is indignant that we should suffer: the other calms us by the reminder that we deserve nothing else.—*Mad. Swetchine.*

Repentance hath a purifying power, and every tear is of a cleansing virtue; but these penitential clouds must be still kept dropping; one shower will not suffice; for repentance is not one single action but a course.—*South.*

TEMPER,—(See "Good Nature.")

Good temper, like a sunny day, sheds a brightness over everything; it is the sweetener of toil and the soother of disquietude.—*Washington Irving.*

The happiness and misery of men depend no less on temper than fortune.— *Rochefoucauld.*

Through certain humors or passions, and from temper merely, a man may be completely miserable, let his outward circumstances be ever so fortunate.— *Shaftesbury.*

Inviolable fidelity, good-humor, and complacency of temper, outlive all the charms of a fine face, and make the decays of it invisible.—*Tatler.*

If a man has a quarrelsome temper, let him alone. The world will soon find him employment. He will soon meet with some one stronger than himself, who will repay him better than you can. A man may fight duels all his life, if he is disposed to quarrel.—*Cecil.*

Men who have had a great deal of experience learn not to lose their tempers.—*V. Cherbuliez.*

Those who are surly and imperious to their inferiors are generally humble, flattering, and cringing to their superiors. —*Fuller.*

Courtesy of temper, when it is used to veil churlishness of deed, is but a knight's girdle around the breast of a base clown. —*Walter Scott.*

It is an unhappy, and yet I fear a true reflection, that they who have uncommon easiness and softness of temper have seldom very noble and nice sensations of soul.—*Greville.*

A tart temper never mellows with age; and a sharp tongue is the only edged tool that grows keener with constant use. —*Washington Irving.*

A noble heart, like the sun, showeth

its greatest countenance in its lowest estate.—*Sir P. Sidney.*

I have often thought that it required as much grace to keep the apostle Peter from knocking a man down in the street as to make the apostle John look like an angel.—*J. M. Mason.*

Too many have no idea of the subjection of their temper to the influence of religion, and yet what is changed if the temper is not? If a man is as passionate, malicious, resentful, sullen, moody, or morose after his conversion as before it, what is he converted from or to?—*John Angell James.*

The perverse temper of children is too often corrected with the rod, when the cause lies in fact in a diseased state of body.

More than half the difficulties of the world would be allayed or removed by the exhibition of good temper.—*Arthur Helps.*

Temper, if ungoverned, governs the whole man.—*Shaftesbury.*

A cheerful temper, joined with innocence, will make beauty attractive, knowledge delightful, and wit good-natured. It will lighten sickness, poverty, and affliction; convert ignorance into an amiable simplicity, and render deformity itself agreeable.—*Addison.*

The difficult part of good temper consists in forbearance, and accommodation to the ill-humor of others.—*Empson.*

Of all bad things by which mankind are curst, their own bad tempers surely are the worst.—*Cumberland.*

An attribute so precious, that it becomes a virtue, is a gentle and constant equality of temper. What an unutterable charm does it give to the society of the man who possesses it! How is it possible to avoid loving him whom we always find with serenity on his brow, and a smile on his countenance!—*Bp. Stanley.*

A man who cannot command his temper should not think of being a man of business.—*Chesterfield.*

Good temper is the most contented, the most comfortable state of the soul; the greatest happiness both for those who possess it, and for those who feel its influence. With "gentleness" in his own character, "comfort" in his house, and

"good temper" in his wife, the earthly felicity of man is complete.

Bad temper is its own scourge. Few things are more bitter than to feel bitter. A man's venom poisons himself more than his victim.—*Charles Buxton.*

If religion does nothing for your temper it has done nothing for your soul.—*Clayton.*

Unsociable tempers are contracted in solitude, which will in the end not fail of corrupting the understanding as well as the manners, and of utterly disqualifying a man for the satisfactions and duties of life. Men must be taken as they are, and we neither make them nor ourselves better by flying from or quarrelling with them.—*Burke.*

Temperament is but the atmosphere of character, while its groundwork in nature is fixed and unchangeable.—*Arthur Helps.*

TEMPERANCE.—(See "DRINKING" and "DRUNKENNESS.")

Temperance is the lawful gratification of a natural and healthy appetite.—*J. B. Gough.*

I have four good reasons for being an abstainer—my head is clearer, my health is better, my heart is lighter, and my purse is heavier.—*Guthrie.*

I dare not drink for my own sake, I ought not to drink for my neighbor's sake.—*T. L. Cuyler.*

The temperate are the most truly luxurious. By abstaining from most things, it is surprising how many things we enjoy.—*Simms.*

Temperance puts wood on the fire, meal in the barrel, flour in the tub, money in the purse, credit in the country, contentment in the house, clothes on the children, vigor in the body, intelligence in the brain, and spirit in the whole constitution.—*Franklin.*

Temperance and labor are the two best physicians; the one sharpens the appetite—the other prevents indulgence to excess.—*Rousseau.*

Temperance is a bridle of gold, and he that can use it aright is liker a God than a man; for as it will transform a beast to a man again, so it will make a man a God.—*Burton.*

Temperance, that virtue without pride, and fortune without envy, that gives vigor of frame and tranquillity of mind; the best guardian of youth and support of old age, the precept of reason as well as religion, the physician of the soul as well as the body, the tutelar goddess of health, and universal medicine of life.— *Sir W. Temple.*

Physic is of little use to a temperate person, for a man's own observation on what he finds does him good, and what hurts him, is the best physic to preserve health.—*Bacon.*

Except thou desire to hasten thine end, take this for a general rule, that thou never add any artificial heat to thy body by wine or spice, until thou find that time hath decayed thy natural heat; and the sooner thou beginnest to help Nature, the sooner she will forsake thee, and leave thee to trust altogether to Art.—*Sir W. Raleigh.*

'Tis to thy rules, O temperance, that we owe all pleasures that from health and strength can flow, vigor of body, purity of mind, unclouded reason, sentiment refined.—*Chandler.*

Temperance to be a virtue must be free and not forced. Virtue may be defended, as vice may be withstood by a statute, but no virtue is or can be created by a law, any more than by a battering ram a temple or obelisk can be reared.—*Bartol.*

He who would keep himself to himself should imitate the dumb animals, and drink water.—*Bulwer.*

If you wish to keep the mind clear and the body healthy, abstain from all fermented liquors.—*Sydney Smith.*

I consider the temperance cause the foundation of all social and political reform.—*Cobden.*

If temperance prevails, then education can prevail; if temperance fails, then education must fail.—*Horace Mann.*

Fools! not to know how health and temperance bless the rustic swain, while luxury destroys her pampered train.—*Hesiod.*

Against diseases here, the strongest fence is the defensive virtue, abstinence.

Drinking water neither makes a man sick nor in debt nor his wife a widow.— *John Neal.*

Though I look old yet I am strong and lusty, for in my youth I never did apply hot and rebellious liquors in my blood.—*Shakespeare.*

Every inordinate cup is unblessed, and the ingredient is the devil.—*Shakespeare.*

Temperance keeps the senses clear and unembarrassed. It appears with life in the face, and decorum in the person; it gives you the command of your head, secures your health, and preserves you in a condition for business.—*Jeremy Collier.*

Oh, temperance, thou fortune without envy; thou universal medicine of life, that clears the head and cleanses the blood, eases the stomach, strengthens the nerves, and perfects digestion.—*Sir W. Temple.*

Above all, let the poor hang up the amulet of temperance in their homes.— *Horace Mann.*

If thou well observe the rule of not too much, by temperance taught, in what thou eatest and drinkest, seeking from thence due nourishment, not gluttonous delight, till many years over thy head return, so mayst thou live, till, like ripe fruit, thou drop into thy mother's lap, or be with ease gathered, not harshly plucked, in death mature.—*Milton.*

Great men should drink with harness on their throats.—*Shakespeare.*

The receipts of cookery are swelled to a volume, but a good stomach excels them all; to which nothing contributes more than industry and temperance.— *Penn.*

Temperance is reason's girdle, and passion's bride, the strength of the soul, and the foundation of virtue.—*Jeremy Taylor.*

If it is a small sacrifice to you to discontinue the use of wine, do it for the sake of others; if a great sacrifice, do it for your own.—*S. J. May.*

Temperance is to the body what religion is to the soul, the foundation and source of health and strength and peace. —*Tryon Edwards.*

The smaller the drink the clearer the head and the cooler the blood, which are great benefits in temper and business. —*Penn.*

Temperance gives nature her full play, and enables her to exert herself in all her force and vigor.—*Addison.*

Temperance is corporal piety; it is

the preservation of divine order in the body.—*Theodore Parker.*

TEMPTATION.—Temptations are a file which rub off much of the rust of our self-confidence.—*Fénelon.*

If we keep ourselves from opportunities, God will keep us from sin.

No man is matriculated to the art of life till he has been well tempted.—*George Eliot.*

To pray against temptations, and yet to rush into occasions, is to thrust your fingers into the fire, and then pray they might not be burnt.—*Secker.*

It is one thing to be tempted, another thing to fall.—*Shakespeare.*

God is better served in resisting a temptation to evil than in many formal prayers.—*Penn.*

Do all that you can to stand, and then fear lest you may fall, and by the grace of God you are safe.—*Tryon Edwards.*

Temptation is the fire that brings up the scum of the heart.—*Boston.*

If there were no evil in ourselves there could be no temptation from without, for nothing evil could seem pleasant.—*F. M. Crawford.*

Bearing up against temptations and prevailing over them is the very thing wherein the whole life of religion consists. It is the trial which God puts upon us in this world, by which we are to make evidence of our love and obedience to him, and of our fitness to be made members of his kingdom.—*Samuel Clarke.*

Every temptation is great or small according as the man is.—*Jeremy Taylor.*

The devil tempts us not. It is we tempt him, beckoning his skill with opportunity.—*George Eliot.*

To resist temptation once is not a sufficient proof of honesty. If a servant, indeed, were to resist the continued temptation of silver lying in a window, when he is sure his master does not know how much there is of it, he would give a strong proof of honesty. But this is a proof to which you have no right to put a man. You know there is a certain degree of temptation which will overcome any virtue. Now, in so far as you approach temptation to a man, you do him an injury; and, if he is overcome, you share his guilt.—*Johnson.*

After listening to thousands of prayers for pardon to offenders, I can hardly recall a case where I did not feel that I might have fallen as my fellow-man has done, if I had been subjected to the same demoralizing influences and pressed by the same temptations.—*Horatio Seymour.*

Opportunity often makes the thief.

Lie in the lap of sin, and not mean harm? It is hypocrisy against the devil: They that mean virtuously, and yet do so, the devil their virtue tempts, and they tempt heaven.—*Shakespeare.*

Learn to say "No"; it will be of more use to you than to be able to read Latin.—*Spurgeon.*

Temptations, when we meet them at first, are as the lion that roared upon Samson; but if we overcome them, the next time we see them we shall find a nest of honey within them.—*Bunyan.*

Every moment of resistance to temptation is a victory.—*Faber.*

To realize God's presence is the one sovereign remedy against temptation.—*Fénelon.*

Occasions of adversity best discover how great virtue or strength each one hath.—For occasions do not make a man frail, but show what he is.—*Thomas à Kempis.*

Temptation is a fearful word. It indicates the beginning of a possible series of infinite evils. It is the ringing of an alarm bell, whose melancholy sounds may reverberate through eternity. Like the sudden, sharp cry of "Fire!" under our windows by night, it should rouse us to instantaneous action, and rouse every muscle to its highest tension.—*Horace Mann.*

Most confidence has still most cause to doubt.—*Dryden.*

Temptation in the line of duty God has provided for; but for temptation sought and coveted, God has no provision.—*G. E. Rees.*

It is a most fearful fact to think of, that in every heart there is some secret spring that would be weak at the touch of temptation, and that is liable to be assailed. Fearful, and yet salutary to think of, for the thought may serve to keep our moral nature braced. It warns us that we can never stand at ease, or lie down in the field of life, without sentinels of watchfulness and camp-fires of prayer.—*E. H. Chapin.*

When devils will their blackest sins put on, they do suggest at first with heavenly shows.—*Shakespeare.*

Temptations without imply desires within; men ought not to say, "How powerfully the devil tempts," but "How strongly I am tempted."—*H. W. Beecher.*

Better shun the bait than struggle in the snare.—*Dryden.*

To be like Christ in this world we must, more or less, be the subjects of temptation. But He instantly and successfully resisted temptation, so that though tempted, He was "without sin." We also, to carry out the Christian character, must resist, to complete victory, all the temptations with which we may be assailed.—*J. Bate.*

He who has no mind to trade with the devil, should be so wise as to keep away from his shop.—*South.*

As the Sandwich Islander believes that the strength and valor of the enemy he kills passes into himself, so we gain the strength of the temptations we resist.—*Emerson.*

I see the devil's hook, and yet cannot help nibbling at his bait.—*M. Adams.*

Some temptations come to the industrious, but all temptations attack the idle.—*Spurgeon.*

The time for reasoning is before we have approached near enough to the forbidden fruit to look at it and admire.—*Margaret Percival.*

When a man resists sin on human motives only, he will not hold out long.—*Bp. Wilson.*

To attempt to resist temptation, to abandon our bad habits, and to control our dominant passions in our own unaided strength, is like attempting to check by a spider's thread the progress of a ship borne along before wind and tide.—*Waugh.*

It is the bright day that brings forth the adder, and that craves wary walking.—*Shakespeare.*

That fortitude which has encountered no dangers, that prudence which has surmounted no difficulties, that integrity which has been attacked by no temptation, can at best be considered but as gold not yet brought to the test, of

which, therefore, the true value cannot be assigned.—*Johnson.*

When the flesh presents thee with delights, then present thyself with dangers; where the world possesses thee with vain hopes, there possess thyself with true fear; when the devil brings thee oil, bring thou vinegar. The way to be safe is never to be secure.—*Quarles.*

If you take temptations into account, who is to say that he is better than his neighbor?—*Thackeray.*

St. Augustine teaches that there is in each man a Serpent, an Eve, and an Adam. Our senses and natural propensities are the Serpent; the excitable desire is Eve; and the reason is the Adam. Our nature tempts us perpetually; criminal desire is often excited; but sin is not completed till reason consents.—*Pascal.*

How oft the sight of means to do ill deeds makes deeds ill done!—*Shakespeare.*

No one can ask honestly or hope fully to be delivered from temptation unless he has himself honestly and firmly determined to do the best he can to keep out of it.—*Ruskin.*

A vacant mind invites dangerous inmates, as a deserted mansion tempts wandering outcasts to enter and take up their abode in its desolate apartments.—*Hilliard.*

Few men have virtue to withstand the highest bidder.—*Washington.*

Sometimes we are devils ourselves, when we will tempt the frailty of our powers, presuming on their changeful potency.—*Shakespeare.*

The temptation is not here, where you are reading about it or praying about it. It is down in your shop, among bales and boxes, ten-penny nails, and sand-paper.—*E. H. Chapin.*

No place, no company, no age, no person is temptation-free; let no man boast that he was never tempted, let him not be high-minded, but fear, for he may be surprised in that very instance wherein he boasteth that he was never tempted at all.—*Spenser.*

God chooses that men should be tried, but let a man beware of tempting his neighbor. God knows how and how much, and where and when. Man is his brother's keeper, and must keep him acoording to his knowledge.—*G. Macdonald.*

Do not give dalliance too much the rein; the strongest oaths are straw to the fire in the blood.—*Shakespeare.*

No degree of temptation justifies any degree of sin.—*N. P. Willis.*

The difference between those whom the world esteems as good and those whom it condemns as bad, is in many cases little else than that the former have been better sheltered from temptation.—*Hare.*

Most dangerous is that temptation that doth goad us on to sin in loving virtue.—*Shakespeare.*

When I cannot be forced, I am fooled out of my integrity. He cannot constrain if I do not consent. If I do but keep possession, all the posse of hell cannot violently eject me; but I am cast out when I cowardly surrender to his summons. Thus there needs no more to be my undoing but myself.—*Fuller.*

The absence of temptation is the absence of virtue.—*Goethe.*

TENDERNESS. — A tender-hearted and compassionate disposition, which inclines men to pity and feel for the misfortunes of others, and which is, even for its own sake, incapable of involving any man in ruin and misery, is of all tempers of mind the most amiable; and though it seldom receives much honor, is worthy of the highest.—*Fielding.*

Tenderness, without a capacity of relieving, only makes the man who feels it more wretched than the object which sues for assistance.—*Goldsmith.*

When death, the great reconciler, has come, it is never our tenderness that we repent of, but our severity.—*George Eliot.*

Tenderness is the repose of love.—*Rivarol.*

The less tenderness a man has in his nature the more he requires of others.—*Rahel.*

There never was any heart truly great and generous that was not also tender and compassionate.—*South.*

Tenderness is the repose of passion.—*Joubert.*

The quiet tenderness of Chaucer— where you almost seem to hear the hot tears falling, and the simple choking words sobbed out.—*J. R. Lowell.*

Speak the truth by all means; be bold and fearless in your rebuke of error, and in your keener rebuke of wrong doing; but be human, and loving, and gentle, and brotherly the while.—*W. M. Punshon.*

TERROR.—(See " SUPERSTITION.")

THANKFULNESS. — (See " GRATITUDE.")

God has two dwellings: one in heaven, and the other in a meek and thankful heart.—*Izaak Walton.*

Many favors which God gives us ravel out for want of hemming through our unthankfulness; for though prayer purchases blessings, giving praise keeps the quiet possession of them.—*Fuller.*

The worship most acceptable to God, comes from a thankful and cheerful heart.—*Plutarch.*

God's goodness hath been great to thee.—Let never day nor night unhallowed pass but still remember what the Lord hath done.—*Shakespeare.*

Wouldst thou first pause to thank thy God for every pleasure, for mourning over griefs thou wouldst not find the leisure.—*Ruckert.*

The private and personal blessings we enjoy, the blessings of immunity, safeguard, liberty, and integrity, deserve the thanksgiving of a whole life.—*Jeremy Taylor.*

Pride slays thanksgiving, but an humble mind is the soil out of which thanks naturally grow.—A proud man is seldom a grateful man, for he never thinks he gets as much as he deserves.—*H. W. Beecher.*

If one should give me a dish of sand, and tell me there were particles of iron in it, I might look for them with my eyes, and search for them with my clumsy fingers, and be unable to detect them; but let me take a magnet and sweep through it, and how would it draw to itself the almost invisible particles by the mere power of attraction. —The unthankful heart, like my finger in the sand, discovers no mercies; but let the thankful heart sweep through the day, and as the magnet finds the iron, so it will find, in every hour, some heavenly blessings, only the iron in God's sand is gold!—*H. W. Beecher.*

When thankfulness o'erflows the swelling heart, and breathes in free and uncorrupted praise for benefits received, propitious Heaven takes such acknowledgment as fragrant incense, and doubles all its blessings.—*Lillo.*

Or any ill escaped, or good attained, let us remember still Heaven chalked the way that brought us thither.—*Shakespeare.*

Best of all is it to preserve everything in a pure, still heart, and let there be for every pulse a thanksgiving, and for every breath a song.—*Gesner.*

THEFT.—(See "Dishonesty.")

THEATRES.—Although it is said of plays that they teach morality, and of the stage that it is the mirror of human life, these assertions are mere declamations, and have no foundation in truth and experience.—*Sir John Hawkins.*

The idea that the theatre is managed in accordance with pure morals is a vain imagination. Those who build and manage theatres do so with the view of a good investment and profitable employment. They know the taste of their customers. They must either conform to these tastes, or lose money by opposing them. A theatre conducted on such principles as would make it safe to the morals of youth would not pay its proprietor.—*W. Arnot.*

The threatre was, from the very first, the favorite haunt of sin, though honest men — some very honest, wise, and worthy men—maintained it might be turned to good account; and so, perhaps, it might, but never was; from first to last it was an evil place.—*Pollok.*

There should be one theatre where we might take our young daughters without tainting their fresh souls by images of wickedness, or worse, putting it in such pleasant and pathetic shape that they mistake it for virtue.—*Miss Mulock.*

I do not hesitate for a moment to pronounce the theatre to be one of the broadest avenues that lead to destruction: fascinating, no doubt it is, but on that account the more delusive and the more dangerous. Vice in every form lives, and moves, and has its being in the purlieus of the theatre. Light and darkness are not more opposed to each other than the Bible and the play-book.

If the one be good, the other must be evil. The only way to justify the stage, as it is, as it has ever been, as it is ever likely to be, is to condemn the Bible—the same individual cannot defend both.—*Hannah More.*

If the theatre is ever to be a school of morals, we may well say of it what Hamlet says of its acting, "Reform it altogether."

Coming away from a modern play, as out of the reeking, noxious theatre where it is acted, is, to many, like quitting a moral hell—a very ingenious, elegant, amusing, but nevertheless as black as Avernus, and into which the descent is quite as easy.—*Miss Mulock.*

It is remarkable how virtuous and generously disposed every one is at a play. We uniformly applaud what is right, and condemn what is wrong, when it costs us nothing but the sentiment.—*Hazlitt.*

There is so much of the glare and grief of life connected with the stage, that it fills me with most solemn thoughts.—*Henry Giles.*

There is that in theatrical representation which awakens whatever romance belongs to our character.—The magic lights, the pomp of scene, the fair, false, exciting life that is detailed before us, crowding into some three short hours all our most busy ambition could desire— all these appeals to our senses are not made in vain.—Our taste for castle-building and visions deepens upon us, and we chew a mental opium which stagnates the other faculties, but wakes that of the ideal.—*Bulwer.*

How much is it to be wished that the celebration of nature and of God were intrusted to none but men of noble minds.—*Goethe.*

Aside from the moral contamination incident to the average theatre, the influence intellectually is degrading. Its lessons are morbid, distorted, and superficial; they do not mirror life.—*T. T. Munger.*

The claim of the theatre as a school of morals is false; not because it is immoral, but because it cannot, from its own nature, be a teacher of morals.— The abuses that have clustered about it are enormous.—In evil days it sinks to the bottom of the scale of decency, and in best days it hardly rises to the average.—*T. T. Munger.*

THEOLOGY.—The theological systems of men and schools are always determined by the character of their ideal of Christ, the great central fact of the Christian system.—*J. G. Holland.*

All my theology is reduced to this narrow compass, " Jesus Christ came into the world to save sinners."—*Archibald Alexander.*

None but a theology that came out of eternity can carry you and me safely to and through eternity.—*T. L. Cuyler.*

Theology is but the science of mind applied to God. As schools change, theology must necessarily change. Truth is everlasting, but our ideas of truth are not. Theology is but our ideas of truth classified and arranged.—*H. W. Beecher.*

We can no more have exact religious thinking without theology, than exact mensuration and astronomy without mathematics, or exact iron-making without chemistry.—*John Hall.*

What makes a Christian is not the theology we have in our heads, but the faith and love we have in our hearts.— We must, indeed, have a clear statement of truth in orderly propositions, that is, a system of dogmas, to have anything to trust to at all. There can be no faith in an unseen person but through the medium of thoughts concerning him, and these thoughts put into words are a creed.

A theology at war with the laws of physical nature would be a battle of no doubtful issue. The laws of our spiritual nature give still less chance of success to the system which would thwart or stay them.—*Channing.*

The way to begin a Christian life is not to study theology.—Piety before theology. Right living will produce right thinking.—Theologies are well in their place, but repentance and love must come before all other experiences. —*H. W. Beecher.*

The best theology is rather a divine life than a divine knowledge.—*Jeremy Taylor.*

Of all the qualities a theologian must possess, a devotional spirit is the chief.— For the soul is larger than the mind, and the religious emotions lay hold on the truths to which they are related; on many sides at once.—A powerful understanding, on the other hand, seizes on single points, and however enlarged in its own sphere, is never safe from its narrowness of view.

As the grave grows nearer my theology is growing strangely simple, and it begins and ends with Christ as the only Saviour of the lost.—*Bp. Whipple.*

THEORIES.—To despise theory is to have the excessively vain pretension to do without knowing what one does, and to speak without knowing what one says.—*Fontenelle.*

Thoughts are but dreams till their effects be tried.—*Shakespeare.*

Conjecture as to things useful, is good; but conjecture as to what it would be useless to know, is very idle.—*Johnson.*

Theory is the guide to practice, and practice the ratification and life of theory.

The theory that can absorb the greatest number of facts, and persist in doing so, generation after generation, through all changes of opinion and detail, is the one that must rule all observation.—*John Weiss.*

It is much easier to design than to perform. A man proposes his schemes of life in a state of abstraction and disengagement, exempt from the enticements of hope, the solicitations of affection, the importunities of appetite, or the depressions of fear, and is in the same state with him that teaches upon land the art of navigation, to whom the sea is always smooth, and the wind always prosperous.—*Johnson*

Most men take least notice of what is plain, as if that were of no use; but puzzle their thoughts, and lose themselves in those vast depths and abysses which no human understanding can fathom.—*Sherlock.*

THOUGHT.—In the end, thought rules the world. There are times when impulses and passions are more powerful, but they soon expend themselves; while mind, acting constantly, is ever ready to drive them back and work when their energy is exhausted.—*J. McCosh.*

Thinking is the talking of the soul with itself.—*Plato.*

All grand thoughts come from the heart.—*Vauvenargues.*

The great thinker is seldom a disputant. He answers other men's arguments by stating the truth as he sees it.—*D. March.*

They are never alone who are accompanied by noble thoughts.—*Sir P. Sidney.*

Garner up pleasant thoughts in your mind, for pleasant thoughts make pleasant lives.—*Wilkins.*

The greatest events of an age are its best thoughts. Thought finds its way into action.—*Boice.*

Those who have finished by making all others think with them, have usually been those who began by daring to think for themselves.—*Colton.*

In matters of conscience first thoughts are best; in matters of prudence last thoughts are best.—*Robert Hall.*

Spiritual force is stronger than material; thoughts rule the world.—*Emerson.*

The pleasantest things in the world are pleasant thoughts, and the greatest art in life is to have as many of them as possible.

To have thought far too little, we shall find in the review of life, among our capital faults.—*J. Foster.*

Temples have their sacred images; and we see what influence they have always had over a great part of mankind; but, in truth, the ideas and images in men's minds are the invisible powers that constantly govern them; and to these they all pay universally a ready submission.—*Jonathan Edwards.*

Thinking, not growth, makes manhood. Accustom yourself, therefore, to thinking. Set yourself to understand whatever you see or read. To join thinking with reading is one of the first maxims, and one of the easiest operations.—*Isaac Taylor.*

Thought is the property of those only who can entertain it.—*Emerson.*

There are very few original thinkers in the world, or ever have been; the greatest part of those who are called philosophers, have adopted the opinions of some who went before them, and so having chosen their respective guides, they maintain with zeal what they have thus imbibed.—*Dugald Stewart.*

Thinkers are scarce as gold; but he, whose thoughts embrace all their subject, who pursues it uninterruptedly and fearless of consequences, is a diamond of enormous size.—*Lavater.*

We may divide thinkers into those who think for themselves, and those who think through others.—The latter are the rule, and the former the exception.—The first are original thinkers in a double sense, and egotists in the noblest meaning of the word.—It is from them only that the world learns wisdom. —For only the light which we have kindled in ourselves can illuminate others.—*Schopenhauer.*

The key to every man is his thought. Sturdy and defying though he look, he has a helm which he obeys, which is the idea after which all his facts are classified. He can only be reformed by showing him a new idea which commands his own.—*Emerson.*

The sober second thought of the people is seldom wrong.—*M. Van Buren.*

The happiness of your life depends upon the quality of your thoughts, therefore guard accordingly; and take care that you entertain no notions unsuitable to virtue and reasonable nature. —*Marcus Antoninus.*

If, instead of a gem or even a flower, we could cast the gift of a lovely thought into the heart of a friend, that would be giving as the angels give.— *G. Macdonald.*

The rich are too indolent, the poor too weak, to bear the insupportable fatigue of thinking.—*Cowper.*

What we are afraid to do before men, we should be afraid to think before God.

Bad thoughts are worse enemies than lions and tigers; for we can keep out of the way of wild beasts, but bad thoughts win their way everywhere. The cup that is full will hold no more; keep your hearts full of good thoughts, that bad thoughts may find no room to enter.

Every one must see and feel, that bad thoughts quickly ripen into bad actions; and that, if the latter only are forbidden, and the former left free, all morality will soon be at an end.—*Bp. Porteus.*

Man being made a reasonable, and so a thinking creature, there is nothing more worthy of his being, than the right direction and employment of his thoughts, since upon this depend both his usefulness to the public, and his own present and future benefit in all respects. —*Penn.*

Thought engenders thought. Place one idea upon paper, another will follow it, and still another, until you have written a page. You cannot fathom your mind. It is a well of thought which has no bottom. The more you draw from it, the more clear and fruitful will it be. If you neglect to think yourself, and use other people's thoughts, giving them utterance only, you will never know what you are capable of. At first your ideas may come out in lumps, homely and shapeless; but no matter; time and perseverance will arrange and polish them. Learn to think, and you will learn to write; the more you think, the better you will express your ideas. —*G. A. Sala.*

Great men are they who see that spiritual is stronger than any material force—that thoughts rule the world.— *Emerson.*

All truly wise thoughts have been thought already thousands of times; but to make them truly ours, we must think them over again honestly, till they take root in our personal experience.— *Goethe.*

Second thoughts they say are best.— *Shakespeare.*

Our thoughts are ours, their ends none of our own.—*Shakespeare.*

Thoughts come into our minds by avenues which are left open, and thoughts go out of our minds through avenues which we never voluntarily opened.—*Emerson.*

Guard well thy thoughts; our thoughts are heard in Heaven.—*Young.*

A thought is often original, though you have uttered it a hundred times.— It has come to you over a new route, by a new and express train of association.—*O. W. Holmes.*

A thinking man is the worst enemy the Prince of Darkness can have; every time such an one announces himself, I doubt not there runs a shudder through the nether empire; and new emissaries are trained with new tactics, to, if possible, entrap and hoodwink and handcuff him.—*Carlyle.*

A man might frame, and let loose a star, to roll in its orbit, and yet not have done so memorable a thing before God, as he who lets go a golden-orbed thought to roll through the generations of time.—*H. W. Beecher.*

Thoughts that do often lie too deep for tears.—*Wordsworth.*

All that a man does outwardly is but the expression and completion of his inward thought. To work effectually, he must think clearly; to act nobly, he must think nobly. Intellectual force is a principal element of the soul's life, and should be proposed by every man as the principal end of his being.— *Channing.*

The greatest events of an age are its best thoughts. It is the nature of thought to find its way into action.— *Bovee.*

Learning without thought is labor lost; thought without learning is perilous.—*Confucius.*

Mankind have a great aversion to intellectual labor; but even supposing knowledge to be easily attainable, more people would be content to be ignorant than would take even a little trouble to acquire it.—*Johnson.*

Fully to understand a grand and beautiful thought requires, perhaps, as much time as to conceive it.—*Joubert.*

Though an inheritance of acres may be bequeathed, an inheritance of knowledge and wisdom cannot. The wealthy man may pay others for doing his work for him, but it is impossible to get his thinking done for him by another, or to purchase any kind of self-culture.— *S. Smiles.*

Earnest men never think in vain though their thoughts may be errors.— *Bulwer.*

I have asked several men what passes in their minds when they are thinking, and I could never find any man who could think for two minutes together. Everybody has seemed to admit that it was a perpetual deviation from a particular path, and a perpetual return to it; which, imperfect as the operation is, is the only method in which we can operate with our minds to carry on any process of thought.—*Sydney Smith.*

Thoughts, even more than overt acts, reveal character.—*W. S. Plumer.*

A vivid thought brings the power to paint it; and in proportion to the depth of its source is the force of its projection.—*Emerson.*

Good thoughts are blessed guests, and should be heartily welcomed, well fed, and much sought after. Like rose leaves, they give out a sweet smell if laid up in the jar of memory.—*Spurgeon.*

"Give me," said Herder to his son, as he lay in the parched weariness of his last illness, "give me a great thought, that I may quicken myself with it."—*Richter.*

Our thoughts are epochs in our lives; all else is but as a journal of the winds that blow while we are here.—*Thoreau.*

The busiest of living agents are certain dead men's thoughts; they are forever influencing the opinions and destinies of men.—*Bovee.*

Secret study, silent thought, is, after all, the mightiest agent in human affairs.—*Channing.*

When God lets loose a great thinker on this planet, then all things are at risk.—There is not a piece of science, but its flank may be turned to-morrow; nor any literary reputation, nor the so-called eternal names of fame, that may not be revised and condemned.—*Emerson.*

Nurture your mind with great thoughts; to believe in the heroic makes heroes.—*Disraeli.*

It is the hardest thing in the world to be a good thinker without being a good self-examiner.—*Shaftesbury.*

The walls of rude minds are scrawled all over with facts, with thoughts. They shall one day bring a lantern and read the inscriptions.—*Emerson.*

Thought means life, since those who do not think do not live in any high or real sense. Thinking makes the man.—*A. B. Alcott.*

Thought is the seed of action; but action is as much its second form as thought is its first. It rises in thought, to the end that it may be uttered and acted. Always in proportion to the depth of its sense does it knock importunately at the gates of the soul, to be spoken, to be done.—*Emerson.*

A thought embodied and embrained

in fit words walks the earth a living being.—*E. P. Whipple.*

It is the habitual thought that frames itself into our life. It affects us even more than our intimate social relations do. Our confidential friends have not so much to do in shaping our lives as thoughts have which we harbor.—*J. W. Teal.*

Unless a man can link his written thoughts with the everlasting wants of men, so that they shall draw from them as from wells, there is no more immortality to the thoughts and feelings of the soul than to the muscles and the bones.—*H. W. Beecher.*

There is no thought in any mind, but it quickly tends to convert itself into a power, and organizes a huge instrumentality of means.—*Emerson.*

Every great originating mind produces in some way a change in society; every great originating mind, whose exercise is controlled by duty, effects a beneficial change. This effect may be immediate, may be remote. A nation may be in a tumult to-day for a thought which the timid Erasmus placidly penned in his study more than two centuries ago.—*E. P. Whipple.*

It is thought that has aroused my intellect from its slumbers, and which has given lustre to virtue, and dignity to truth; and it is by those examples which have inflamed my soul with the love of goodness, and not by means of sculptured marble, that I hold communion with Shakespeare and Milton, with Johnson and Burke, with Howard and Wilberforce.—*F. Wayland.*

A man would do well to carry a pencil in his pocket, and write down the thoughts of the moment. Those that come unsought for are commonly the most valuable, and should be secured, because they seldom return.—*Bacon.*

Alas, we make a ladder of our thoughts, where angels step, but sleep ourselves at the foot; our high resolves look down upon our slumbering acts.—*L. E. Landon.*

Thinking leads man to knowledge. He may see and hear, and read and learn whatever he pleases, and as much as he pleases; he will never know anything of it, except that which he has thought over, that which by thinking he has made the property of his own mind. Is it then saying too much if I say that man, by thinking only, becomes truly man? Take away thought from man's life, and what remains?—*Pestalozzi.*

An arrow may fly through the air and leave no trace; but an ill thought leaves a trail like a serpent.

The old thoughts never die; immortal dreams outlive their dreamers and are ours for aye; no thought once formed and uttered ever can expire.—*Mackay.*

Be able to command the thoughts of others, as well as your own; the more you know, the more you may both know and do.

When a nation gives birth to a man who is able to produce a great thought, another is born who is able to understand and admire it.—*Joubert.*

Some people study all their life, and at their death they have learned everything except to think.—*Domergue.*

It is much easier to think right without doing right, than to do right without thinking right. Just thoughts may, and often do, fail of producing just deeds; but just deeds are sure to beget just thoughts. The clearest understanding can do little in purifying an impure heart, the strongest little in straightening a crooked one. You cannot reason or talk an Augean stable into cleanliness. A single day's work would make more progress in such a task than a century's words.—*Hare.*

Nothing is so practical as thought; our view of life moulds our life; our view of God moulds our souls; and the clearer and richer the spiritual world to us, the more spiritual and heavenly, that is the more practical and loving, the more full of high aims and lowly services will our lives be.

There are soft moments even to desperadoes. God does not, all at once, abandon even them.—*Cecil.*

Some people pass through life soberly and religiously enough, without knowing why, or reasoning about it, but, from force of habit merely, go to heaven like fools.—*Sterne.*

Thought is deeper than speech; feeling deeper than thought; souls to souls can never teach what to themselves was taught.—*Cranch.*

The men of action are, after all, only the unconscious instruments of the men of thought.—*Heine.*

Nothing is comparable to the pleasure of an active and prevailing thought —a thought prevailing over the difficulty and obscurity of the object, and refreshing the soul with new discoveries and images of things; and thereby extending the bounds of apprehension, and as it were enlarging the territories of reason. —*South.*

THREATS.—The man who threatens the world is always ridiculous; for the world can easily go on without him, and, in a short time, will cease to miss him.—*Johnson.*

I consider it a mark of great prudence in a man to abstain from threats or any contemptuous expressions, for neither of these weaken the enemy, but the one makes him more cautious, and the other excites his hatred, and a desire to revenge himself.—*Machiavelli.*

Those that are the loudest in their threats are the weakest in the execution of them.—*Colton.*

TIME.—(See "OCCUPATION.")

As every thread of gold is valuable, so is every moment of time.—*J. Mason.*

Time is the chrysalis of eternity.—*Richter.*

To choose time is to save time.—*Bacon.*

If time be of all things the most precious, wasting time must be the greatest prodigality, since lost time is never found again; and what we call time enough always proves little enough. Let us then up and be doing, and doing to the purpose; so by diligence shall we do more with less perplexity.—*Franklin.*

The great rule of moral conduct is, next to God, to respect time.—*Lavater.*

Spend your time in nothing which you know must be repented of; in nothing on which you might not pray for the blessing of God; in nothing which you could not review with a quiet conscience on your dying bed; in nothing which you might not safely and properly be found doing if death should surprise you in the act.—*Baxter.*

No preacher is listened to but time; which gives us the same train and turn of thought that elder people have tried in vain to put into our heads.—*Swift.*

Youth is not rich in time, it may be poor; part with it as with money, sparing; pay no moment, but in purchase of its worth; and what it's worth, ask death-beds; they can tell.—*Young.*

Time! the corrector where our judgments err; the test of truth, and love; the sole philosopher, for all beside are sophists.—*Byron.*

Time will bring to light whatever is hidden; it will conceal and cover up what is now shining with the greatest splendor.—*Horace.*

Time will discover everything to posterity; it is a babbler, and speaks even when no question is put.—*Euripides.*

Make use of time if thou lovest eternity; yesterday cannot be recalled; tomorrow cannot be assured; only to-day is thine, which if thou procrastinate, thou losest; and which lost is lost forever. One to-day is worth two to-morrows.—*Quarles.*

Time is painted with a lock before, and bald behind, signifying thereby that we must take time by the forelock, for when it is once passed there is no recalling it.—*Swift.*

Keep forever in view the momentous value of life; aim at its worthiest use—its sublimest end; spurn, with disdain, those foolish trifles and frivolous vanities, which so often consume life, as the locusts did Egypt; and devote yourself, with the ardor of a passion, to attain the most divine improvements of the human soul. In short, hold yourself in preparation to make the transition to another life, whenever you shall be claimed by the Lord of the world.—*J. Foster.*

There is a time to be born, and a time to die, says Solomon, and it is the memento of a truly wise man; but there is an interval between these two times of infinite importance.—*Richmond.*

Our yesterdays follow us; they constitute our life, and they give character and force and meaning to our present deeds.—*Joseph Parker.*

The bell strikes one. We take no note of time, but from its loss. To give it then a tongue is wise in man. As if an angel spoke, I feel the solemn sound. If heard aright, it is the knell of my departed hours. Where are they? With

the years beyond the flood. It is the signal that demands despatch; how much is to be done!—*Young.*

Time is lent us to be laid out in God's service, and we cannot be too diligent in it, if we consider that time is precious, short, passing, uncertain, irrevocable when gone, and that for which we must be accountable.

There is no saying shocks me so much as that which I hear very often, "that a man does not know how to pass his time." It would have been but ill-spoken by Methusaleh in the nine hundred and sixty-ninth year of his life.—*Cowley.*

Time is the greatest of all tyrants. As we go on toward age, he taxes our health, limbs, faculties, strength, and features.—*J. Foster.*

The hours of a wise man are lengthened by his ideas, as those of a fool are by his passions. The time of the one is long, because he does not know what to do with it; so is that of the other, because he distinguishes every moment of it with useful or amusing thoughts; or, in other words, because the one is always wishing it away, and the other always enjoying it.—*Addison.*

Much may be done in those little shreds and patches of time, which every day produces, and which most men throw away, but which nevertheless will make at the end of it no small deduction from the life of man.—*Colton.*

Hours have wings and fly up to the author of time and carry news of our usage. All our prayers cannot entreat one of them either to return or slacken its pace. The misspents of every minute are a new record against us in heaven. Sure if we thought thus we would dismiss them with better reports, and not suffer them to fly away empty, or laden with dangerous intelligence. How happy is it when they carry up not only the message but the fruits of good, and stay with the Ancient of Days to speak for us before his glorious throne. —*Milton.*

"Improve your opportunities," said Bonaparte to a school of young men, "every hour lost now is a chance of future misfortune."

Remember that time is money. He that can earn ten shillings a day by his labor, and goes abroad or sits idle one half of that day, though he spends but sixpence during his diversion or idleness, ought not to reckon that the only expense; he has really spent, or rather thrown away, five shillings besides.—*Franklin.*

Time hurries on with a resistless, unremitting stream, yet treads more soft than e'er did midnight thief that slides his hand under the miser's pillow, and carries off his prize.—*Blair.*

An Italian philosopher said that "time was his estate"; an estate indeed which will produce nothing without cultivation, but will always abundantly repay the labors of industry, and generally satisfy the most extensive desires, if no part of it be suffered to lie waste by negligence, to be overrun with noxious plants, or laid out for show rather than for use. —*Johnson.*

There can be no persevering industry without a deep sense of the value of time.—*Mrs. Sigourney.*

Time, with all its celerity, moves slowly on to him whose whole employment is to watch its flight.—*Johnson.*

Time is the measure of business as money is of wares; and business is bought at a dear hand where there is small despatch. The Spartans and Spaniards have been noted to be of small despatch, and hence the maxim, "Let my death come from Spain"; for then it will be long in coming.—*Sir Francis Bacon.*

Wherever anything lives, there is, open somewhere, a register in which time is being inscribed.—*Henri Bergson.*

Whatever comes, this too shall pass away.—*Ella Wheeler Wilcox.*

Time, like a flurry of wild rain, shall drift across the darkened plane.—*Charles G. D. Roberts.*

The lifeless boughs of time.—*Edgar Lee Masters.*

You'll find as you grow older that you weren't born such a very great while ago after all. The time shortens up.—*William Dean Howells.*

Time is so fleeting that if we do not remember God in our youth, age may find us incapable of thinking about him. —*Hans Christian Andersen.*

Measure, time and number are noth-ing but modes of thought or rather of imagination.—*Benedict Spinoza.*

The race is not to the swift, nor the battle to the strong, neither yet bread to the wise, nor yet riches to men of understanding, nor yet favor to men of skill, but time and chance happeneth to them all.—*Elbert Hubbard.*

New time always! Old time we cannot keep. Time does not become sacred to us until we have lived it, until it has passed over us and taken with it a part of ourselves.—*John Burroughs.*

Regret for time wasted can become a power for good in the time that remains. And the time that remains is time enough, if we will only stop the waste and the idle, useless regretting.—*Arthur Brisbane.*

Time's horses gallop down the lessening hill.—*Richard Le Gallienne.*

Time, whose tooth gnaws away everything else, is powerless against truth.—*Thomas H. Huxley.*

The end crowns all; and that old common arbitrator, time, will one day end it.—*Shakespeare.*

Time, the cradle of hope, but the grave of ambition, is the stern corrector of fools, but the salutary counsellor of the wise, bringing all they dread to the one, and all they desire to the other; it warns us with a voice that even the sagest discredit too long, and the silliest believe too late. Wisdom walks before it, opportunity with it, and repentance behind it; he that has made it his friend will have little to fear from his enemies, but he that has made it his enemy will have little to hope from his friends.—*Colton.*

It is notorious that joy and grief can hasten and delay time. Locke is of opinion that a man in great misery may so far lose his measure as to think a minute an hour; or in joy make an hour a minute.—*Tatler.*

Nay, dally not with time, the wise man's treasure though fools are lavish of it.—The fatal fisher hooks our souls, while we waste moments.—*Old Play.*

The laboring man and the artificer knows what every hour of his time is worth, and parts not with it but for the full value: they are only noblemen and gentlemen, who should know best how

to use it, that think it only fit to be
cast away; and their not knowing how
to set a true value upon this, is the true
cause of the wrong estimate they make
of all other things.—*Clarendon.*

What a folly to dread the thought of
throwing away life at once, and yet
have no regard to throwing it away by
parcels and piecemeal.—*John Howe.*

The same object seen from the three
different points of view—the past, the
present, and the future—often exhibits
three different faces to us; like those
sign-boards over shop doors, which represent the face of a lion as we approach,
of a man when we are in front, and of
an ass when we have passed.—*Longfellow.*

It is better to be doing the most insignificant thing than to reckon even a
half-hour insignificant.—*Goethe.*

He lives long that lives well, and time
misspent is not lived, but lost.—*Fuller.*

We always have time enough, if we
will but use it aright.—*Goethe.*

A man that is young in years may be
old in hours, if he has lost no time.—
Bacon.

Be avaricious of time; do not give
any moment without receiving it in
value; only allow the hours to go from
you with as much regret as you give to
your gold; do not allow a single day
to pass without increasing the treasure
of your knowledge and virtue.—*Letour-
neux.*

Time well employed is Satan's deadliest foe; it leaves no opening for the
lurking fiend.—*C. Wilcox.*

There are no fragments so precious
as those of time, and none are so heedlessly lost by people who cannot make
a moment, and yet can waste years.—
Montgomery.

As if you could kill time without injuring eternity!—*Thoreau.*

Lost, yesterday, somewhere between
sunrise and sunset, two golden hours,
each set with sixty diamond minutes.
No reward is offered, for they are gone
forever!—*Mrs. Sigourney.*

Nothing lies on our hands with such
uneasiness as time. Wretched and
thoughtless creatures! In the only
place where covetousness were a virtue
we turn prodigals.—*Addison.*

Oh, time! the beautifier of the dead;
adorner of the ruin; comforter and only
healer when the heart hath bled.

Time is the most undefinable yet
paradoxical of things; the past is gone,
the future has not come, and the present becomes the past even while we
attempt to define it, and, like the flash
of the lightning, at once exists and expires.—*Colton.*

God, who is liberal in all his other
gifts, shows us, by the wise economy of
his providence, how circumspect we
ought to be in the management of our
time, for he never gives us two moments together.—*Fénelon.*

All my possessions for a moment of
time. Last words of—*Queen Elizabeth.*

What a solemn and striking admonition to youth is that inscribed on the
dial at All Souls, Oxford,—periunt et
imputantur,—the hours perish, and are
laid to our charge; for time, like life,
can never be recalled.—*S. Smiles.*

I wasted time, and now doth time
waste me.—*Shakespeare.*

Lost wealth may be replaced by industry, lost knowledge by study, lost
health by temperance or medicine, but
lost time is gone forever.—*S. Smiles.*

Each moment, as it passes, is the
meeting place of two eternities.

What I most value next to eternity,
is time.—*Mad. Swetchine.*

There is not a single moment in life
that we can afford to lose.—*Goulburn.*

Pastime is a word that should never
be used but in a bad sense; it is vile
to say a thing is agreeable, because it
helps to pass the time away.—*Shenstone.*

What is time?—The shadow on the
dial, the striking of the clock, the running of the sand, day and night, summer and winter, months, years, centuries—these are but the arbitrary and
outward signs—the measure of time, not
time itself. Time is the life of the soul.
—*Longfellow.*

Spare moments are the gold dust of
time;—of all the portions of our life,
the spare minutes are the most fruitful
in good or evil. They are gaps through
which temptations find easiest access to
the garden of the soul.

Those that dare lose a day, are dangerously prodigal; those that dare misspend it, are desperate.—*Bp. Hall.*

Dost thou love life? then do not squander time, for that is the stuff life is made of.—*Franklin.*

Time was, is past; thou canst not it recall: time is, thou hast; employ the portion small; time future, is not; and may never be: time present, is the only time for thee.

Lost wealth may be restored by industry,—the wreck of health regained by temperance,—forgotten knowledge restored by study,—alienated friendship smoothed into forgetfulness,—even forfeited reputation won by penitence and virtue. But who ever looked upon his vanished hours,—recalled his slighted years,—stamped them with wisdom,—or effaced from Heaven's record the fearful blot of wasted time?—*Mrs. Sigourney.*

We sleep, but the loom of life never stops, and the pattern which was weaving when the sun went down is weaving when it comes up in the morning.—*H. W. Beecher.*

The greatest loss of time is delay and expectation, which depend upon the future. We let go the present, which we have in our power, and look forward to that which depends upon chance,—and so relinquish a certainty for an uncertainty.—*Seneca.*

Time is what we want most, but what alas! we use worst.—*Penn.*

A man's time, when well husbanded, is like a cultivated field, of which a few acres produces more of what is useful to life, than extensive provinces, even of the richest soil, when overrun with weeds and brambles.—*Hume.*

All that time is lost which might be better employed.—*Rousseau.*

Time is cried out upon as a great thief; it is people's own fault. Use him well, and you will get from his hand more than he will ever take from yours.—*Miss Wetherell.*

Well arranged time is the surest mark of a well arranged mind.—*Pitman.*

Observe a method in the distribution of your time. Every hour will then know its proper employment, and no time will be lost. Idleness will be shut out at every avenue, and with her, that

numerous body of vices, that make up her train.—*Bp. Horne.*

Count that day lost, whose slow descending sun views from thine hand no worthy action done.—*Young.*

Know the true value of time; snatch, seize, and enjoy every moment of it.—No idleness; no laziness; no procrastination;—never put off till to-morrow what you can do to-day.—*Chesterfield.*

TIMIDITY.—(See "DIFFIDENCE.")

TITLES.—Titles, instead of exalting, debase those who act not up to them.—*Rochefoucauld.*

The wise sometimes condescend to accept of titles; but none but a fool would imagine them of any real importance. We ought to depend upon intrinsic merit, and not on the slender helps of a title.—*Goldsmith.*

The three highest titles that can be given a man are those of a martyr, hero, saint.—*Gladstone.*

Titles, indeed, may be purchased; but virtue is the only coin that makes the bargain valid.—*Burton.*

Titles of honor are like the impressions on coin, which add no value to gold and silver, but only render brass current.—*Sterne.*

It is not titles that reflect honor on men, but men on their titles.—*Machiavelli.*

Title and ancestry render a good man more illustrious, but an ill one more contemptible. Vice is infamous, though in a prince; and virtue honorable, though in a peasant.—*Addison.*

Of the king's creation you may be; but he who makes a count never made a man.—*Southern.*

Titles of honor add not to his worth, who is himself an honor to his title.—*John Ford.*

Virtue is the first title of nobility.—*Molière.*

How impious is the title of "sacred majesty" applied to a worm, who, in the midst of his splendor, is crumbling into dust!—*Thomas Paine.*

Where there is no difference in men's worths, titles are all jests.—*Beaumont and Fletcher.*

A fool, indeed, has great need of title, it teaches men to call him count and duke, and to forget his proper name of fool.—*J. Crown.*

"Man" is a name of honor for a king; additions take away from each chief thing.—*Chapman.*

TOIL.—(See "LABOR.")

TOLERATION.—The tolerance of all religions is a law of nature, stamped on the hearts of all men.—*Voltaire.*

Be thankful that your lot has fallen on times when, though there may be many evil tongues and exasperated spirits, there are none who have fire and fagot at command.—*Southey.*

Toleration is a good thing in its place; but you cannot tolerate what will not tolerate you, and is trying to cut your throat.—*Froude.*

There are those who believe something, and therefore will tolerate nothing; and on the other hand, those who tolerate everything, because they believe nothing.—*R. Browning.*

Among the best men are diversities of opinion, which should no more, in true reason, breed hatred, than one that loves black should be angry with him that is clothed in white; for thoughts are the very apparel of the mind.—*Sir P. Sidney.*

How it is possible to imagine that a religion breathing the spirit of mercy and benevolence, teaching the forgiveness of injuries, the exercise of charity, and the return of good for evil, can be so perverted as to breathe the spirit of slaughter and persecution, of discord and vengeance, for differences of opinion, is a most unaccountable and extraordinary phenomenon. Still more extraordinary, that it should be the doctrine, not of base and wicked men merely, seeking to cover up their own misdeeds, but of good men, seeking the way of salvation with uprightness of heart and purpose. It affords a melancholy proof of the infirmity of human judgment, and teaches a lesson of humility from which spiritual pride may learn meekness, and spiritual zeal a moderating wisdom.—*Story.*

We anticipate a time when the love of truth shall have come up to our love of liberty, and men shall be cordially tolerant and earnest believers both at once.—*Phillips Brooks.*

Tolerance comes with age; I see no fault committed that I myself could not have committed at some time or other. —*Goethe.*

Religious liberty, according to both Locke and Montesquieu, may and does require intolerance of an intolerant religion; and the very spirit of peace and gentleness may require war to be waged by the state against an aggressive religion.—*Connelly.*

It is not a merit to tolerate, but rather a crime to be intolerant.—*Shelley.*

Error tolerates, truth condemns.—*Caballero.*

The responsibility of tolerance lies with those who have the wider vision.— *George Eliot.*

It is the natural feeling of most persons that charity is founded upon the uncertainty of truth. I believe it is founded on the certainty of truth.— *Maurice.*

TO-MORROW.—(See "DELAY.")

TONGUE.—(See "SILENCE," and "SPEECH.")

The tongue is, at the same time, the best part of man, and his worst: with good government, none is more useful; without it, none is more mischievous.— *Anacharsis.*

The chameleon, who is said to feed upon nothing but air, has of all animals the nimblest tongue.—*Swift.*

When we advance a little into life, we find that the tongue of man creates nearly all the mischief of the world.— *Paxton Hood.*

The cure of an evil tongue must be done at the heart. The weights and wheels are there, and the clock strikes according to their motion. A guileful heart makes a guileful tongue and lips. It is the work-house where is the forge of deceits and slanders; and the tongue is only the outer shop where they are vended, and the door of it. Such ware as is made within, such, and no other, can come out.—*Leighton.*

The Chinese have a saying, that an unlucky word dropped from the tongue, cannot be brought back again by a coach and six horses.—*Goldsmith.*

There are but ten precepts of the law of God, and two of them, so far as concerns the outward organ and vent of the sins there forbidden, are bestowed on the tongue, as though it was ready to fly out both against God and man, if not thus bridled.—*Leighton.*

The tongue of a fool is the key of his counsel which, in a wise man, wisdom hath in keeping.—*Socrates.*

It is observed in the course of worldly things, that men's fortunes are oftener made by their tongues than by their virtues; and more men's fortunes overthrown thereby than by their vices.—*Sir W. Raleigh.*

Give not thy tongue too great liberty, lest it take thee prisoner. A word unspoken is, like the sword in the scabbard, thine. If vented, thy sword is in another's hand. If thou desire to be held wise, be so wise as to hold thy tongue.—*Quarles.*

Open your mouth and purse cautiously; and your stock of wealth and reputation shall, at least in repute, be great.—*Zimmermann.*

A wound from a tongue is worse than a wound from a sword; for the latter affects only the body, the former the spirit.—*Pythagoras.*

Scholars are men of peace; they bear no arms, but their tongues are sharper than a razor; their pens carry further, and give a louder report than thunder. I had rather stand in the shock of a basilisk, than in the fury of a merciless pen.—*Sir T. Browne.*

The tongue is but three inches long, yet it can kill a man six feet high.—*Japanese Proverb.*

A tart temper never mellows with age; and a sharp tongue is the only edged tool that grows keener and sharper with constant use.—*Washington Irving.*

There are many men whose tongues might govern multitudes if they could govern their tongues.—*G. D. Prentice.*

If thou desire to be wise, be so wise as to hold thy tongue.—*Lavater.*

A fool's heart is in his tongue; but a wise man's tongue is in his heart.—*Quarles.*

By examining the tongue, physicians find out the diseases of the body; and philosophers, the diseases of the mind and heart.—*Justin.*

In the use of the tongue God hath distinguished us from beasts, and by the well or ill using it we are distinguished from one another; and there-

fore, though silence be innocent as death, yet it is rather the state of death than life.—*Jeremy Taylor.*

No sword bites so fiercely as an evil tongue.—*Sir P. Sidney.*

No one will tell a tale of scandal, except to him who loves to hear it. Learn, then, to check and rebuke the detracting tongue, by showing that you do not listen to it but with displeasure.—*Jerome.*

We cannot control the evil tongues of others; but a good life enables us to disregard them.—*Cato.*

It is a great misfortune, not to have sense enough to speak well, and judgment enough to speak little.

Of a learned and distinguished, but very cautious general, it was said, "that he could be silent in ten languages."

This I always religiously observed, as a rule, says one, never to chide my husband before company, nor to prattle abroad of miscarriages at home. What passes between two people is much easier made up than when once it has taken air.—*Erasmus.*

If wisdom's ways you widely seek, five things observe with care: of whom you speak, to whom you speak, and how, and when, and where.

Beware the tongue that's set on fire of hell, and flames in slander, falsehood, perjury, in malice, idle-talking, thoughtless tales; speak not too much, nor without thought; let truth in all things small or great, dwell on thy lips. Remember, God hath said, "He that in word offends not, is a perfect man; while he that bridles not his tongue deceives himself and shows his faith in vain!"

TRADE.—He that hath a trade hath an estate; and he that hath a calling hath a place of profit and honor. A ploughman on his legs is higher than a gentleman on his knees.—*Franklin.*

There is nothing so useful to man in general, nor so beneficial to particular societies and individuals, as trade. This is that alma mater, at whose plentiful breast all mankind are nourished.—*Fielding.*

Two of a trade seldom agree.—*Ray's Proverbs.*

In transactions of trade it is not to be supposed that, as in gaming, what one party gains the other must necessarily lose. The gain to each may be equal. If A. has more corn than he can consume, but wants cattle; and B. has more cattle, but wants corn; exchange is gain to each; thereby the common stock of comforts in life is increased.—*Franklin.*

There is a Spanish proverb, that one who would grow rich must buy of those who go to be executed, as not caring how cheap they sell; and sell to those who go to be married, as not caring how dear they buy.—*Fuller.*

TRADITION.—What an enormous magnifier is tradition! How a thing grows in the human memory and in the human imagination, when love, worship, and all that lies in the human heart, is there to encourage it.—*Carlyle.*

Tradition, as held by the Romanists, is subordinate to Scripture and dependent on it, about as some parasite plants are on the tree that supports them. The former cling to the latter, and rest upon it; then gradually overspread it with their own foliage, till, by little and little, they weaken, and then smother it.—*Whately.*

Tradition is an important help to history, but its statements should be carefully scrutinized before we rely on them.—*Addison.*

To follow imperfect, uncertain, or corrupted traditions, in order to avoid erring in our own judgment, is but to exchange one danger for another.—*Whately.*

I am well satisfied that if you let in but one little finger of tradition, you will have in the whole monster—horns and tail and all.—*T. Arnold.*

TRAGEDY.—Tragedy has the great moral defect of giving too much importance to life and death.—*Chamfort.*

Tragedy warms the soul, elevates the heart, and can and ought to create heroes. In this sense, perhaps, France owes a part of her great actions to Corneille.—*Napoleon.*

The world is a comedy to those who think; a tragedy to those who feel.—*Horace Walpole.*

The pleasure arising from an extraordinary agitation of the mind is frequently so great as to stifle humanity;

hence arises the entertainment of the common people at executions, and of the better sort at tragedies.—*DuBois.*

TRAVEL.—All travel has its advantages. If the traveller visits better countries, he may learn to improve his own; and if fortune carries him to worse, he may learn to enjoy his own.—*Johnson.*

Travel is the frivolous part of serious lives, and the serious part of frivolous ones.—*Mad. Swetchine.*

Only that travelling is good which reveals to me the value of home, and enables me to enjoy it better.—*Thoreau.*

It is not fit that every man should travel; it makes a wise man better, and a fool worse.—*Feltham.*

As the Spanish proverb says, "He who would bring home the wealth of the Indies, must carry the wealth of the Indies with him"—so it is in travelling; a man must carry knowledge with him, if he would bring home knowledge.—*Johnson.*

Some are found to travel with no other intent than that of understanding and collecting pictures, studying seals, and describing statues; on they travel from this cabinet of curiosities to that gallery of pictures; waste the prime of life in wonder; skilful in pictures; ignorant in men; yet impossible to be reclaimed, because their follies take shelter under the names of delicacy and taste.—*Goldsmith.*

One telling Socrates that such an one was nothing improved by his travels, "I very well believe it," said he, "for he took himself along with him."—*Montaigne.*

Men may change their climate, but they cannot change their nature.—A man that goes out a fool cannot ride or sail himself into common sense.—*Addison.*

Usually speaking, the worst bred person in company is a young traveller just returned from abroad.—*Swift.*

To be a good traveller argues one no ordinary philosopher.—A sweet landscape must sometimes atone for an indifferent supper, and an interesting ruin charm away the remembrance of a hard bed.—*Tuckerman.*

Those who visit foreign nations, but associate only with their own countrymen, change their climate, but not their customs.—They see new meridians, but the same men; and with heads as empty as their pockets, return home with travelled bodies, but untravelled minds. —*Colton.*

Travel gives a character of experience to our knowledge, and brings the figures on the tablet of memory into strong relief.—*Tuckerman.*

The use of travelling is to regulate imagination by reality, and, instead of thinking how things may be, to see them as they are.—*Johnson.*

Of dead kingdoms I recall the soul, sitting amid their ruins.—*N. P. Willis.*

The bee, though it finds every rose has a thorn, comes back loaded with honey from his rambles, and why should not other tourists do the same.—*Haliburton.*

To see the world is to judge the judges.—*Joubert.*

Rather see the wonders of the world abroad than, living dully sluggardized at home, wear out thy youth with shapeless idleness.—*Shakespeare.*

The proper means of increasing the love we bear to our native country is to reside some time in a foreign one.—*Shenstone.*

Know most of the rooms of thy native country before thou goest over the threshold thereof.—*Fuller.*

The travelled mind is the catholic mind, educated out of exclusiveness and egotism.—*A. B. Alcott.*

He travels safe, and not unpleasantly, who is guarded by poverty, and guided by love.—*Sir P. Sidney.*

He who never leaves his own country is full of prejudices.—*Goldoni.*

The world is a great book, of which they who never stir from home read only a page.—*Augustine.*

A pilgrimage is an admirable remedy for over-fastidiousness and sickly refinement.—*Tuckerman.*

They, and they only, advantage themselves by travel, who, well fraught with the experience of what their own country affords, carry ever with them large and thriving talents, and careful observation. —*F. Osborn.*

A traveller without observation is a bird without wings.—*Saadi.*

Railway travelling is not travelling at all; it is merely being sent to a place, and very little different from becoming a parcel.—*Ruskin.*

Nothing tends so much to enlarge the mind as travelling, that is, making visits to other towns, cities, or countries beside those in which we were born and educated.—*Watts.*

Peregrinations charm our senses with such unspeakable and sweet variety, that some count him unhappy that never travelled—a kind of prisoner, and pity his case, that, from his cradle to his old age, he beholds the same, and still the same.—*Burton.*

It is but to be able to say that they have been to such a place, or have seen such a thing, that, more than any real taste for it, induces the majority of the world to incur the trouble and fatigue of travelling.—*Marryatt.*

Our object in travelling should be, not to gratify curiosity, and seek mere temporary amusement, but to learn, and to venerate, to improve the understanding and the heart.—*Gresley.*

There is nothing that a man can less afford to leave at home than his conscience or his good habits; for it is not to be denied that travel is, in its immediate circumstances, unfavorable to habits of self-discipline, regulation of thought, sobriety of conduct, and dignity of character. Indeed, one of the great lessons of travel is the discovery how much our virtues owe to the support of constant occupation, to the influence of public opinion, and to the force of habit; a discovery very dangerous, if it proceed from an actual yielding to temptations resisted at home, and not from a consciousness of increased power put forth in withstanding them. —*Packe.*

TREACHERY.—It is time to fear when tyrants seem to kiss.—*Shakespeare.*

Of all the vices to which human nature is subject, treachery is the most infamous and detestable, being compounded of fraud, cowardice, and revenge. The greatest wrongs will not justify it, as it destroys those principles of mutual confidence and security by which only society can subsist.—*L. M. Stretch.*

There is no traitor like him whose

domestic treason plants the poniard within the breast that trusted to his truth.—*Byron.*

TREASON.—Treason pleases, but not the traitor.—*Cervantes.*

The man was noble; but with his last attempt he wiped it out; betrayed his country; and his name remains to the ensuing age abhorred.—*Shakespeare.*

Treason doth never prosper; for if it prosper, none dare call it treason.—*Sir J. Harrington.*

In the clear mind of virtue treason can find no hiding place.—*Sir P. Sidney.*

Fellowship in treason is a bad ground of confidence.—*Burke.*

Though those who are betrayed do feel the treason sharply, yet the traitor stands in worse case of woe.—*Shakespeare.*

Is there not some chosen curse, some hidden thunder in the stores of heaven, red with uncommon wrath, to blast the man who owes his greatness to his country's ruin!—*Addison.*

Cæsar had his Brutus; Charles the First, his Cromwell; and George the Third—("Treason!" cried the Speaker) —may profit by their example. If this be treason, make the most of it.—*Patrick Henry.*

A traitor is good fruit to hang from the boughs of the tree of liberty.—*H. W. Beecher.*

Where trust is greatest, there treason is in its most horrid shape.—*Dryden.*

TREES.—This is the forest primeval. The murmuring pines and the hemlocks, bearded with moss and in garments green, indistinct in the twilight, stand like Druids of eld, with voices sad and prophetic, stand like harpers hoar, with beards that rest on their bosoms.—*Longfellow.*

I think that I shall never see
A poem lovely as a tree.

*   *   *   *   *

Poems are made by fools like me,
But only God can make a tree.
    —*Joyce Kilmer.*

The groves were God's first temples. Ere man learned to hew the shaft, and lay the architrave, and spread the roof above them,—ere he framed the lofty vault, to gather and roll back the sound of anthems; in the darkling wood, amidst the cool and silence, he knelt

down and offered to the Mightiest solemn thanks and supplication.—*Bryant.*

Stranger, if thou hast learned a truth which needs no school of long experience, that the world is full of guilt and misery, and hast seen enough of all its sorrows, crimes and cares to tire thee of it, enter this wild wood and view the haunts of Nature. The calm shade shall bring a kindred calm, and the sweet breeze that makes the green leaves dance shall waft a balm to thy sick heart.—*Bryant.*

TRIALS.—(See "AFFLICTION.")

The best people need afflictions for trial of their virtue. How can we exercise the grace of contentment, if all things succeed well; or that of forgiveness, if we have no enemies?—*Tillotson.*

It was a beautiful and striking reply, given by one in affliction, who, when asked how it was that he bore it so well, replied,—"It lightens the stroke, I find, to draw near to Him who handles the rod."—*Tryon Edwards.*

We are always in the forge, or on the anvil; by trials God is shaping us for higher things.—*H. W. Beecher.*

There is a sanctity in suffering when meekly born. Our duty, though set about by thorns, may still be made a staff, supporting even while it tortures. Cast it away, and, like the prophet's rod, it changes to a snake.—*Jerrold.*

Reckon any matter of trial to thee among thy gains.—*T. Adams.*

Trials are medicines which our gracious and wise physician prescribes, because we need them; and he proportions the frequency and weight of them to what the case requires. Let us trust in his skill, and thank him for his prescription.—*John Newton.*

Prosperity tries the fortunate, adversity the great.—*Pliny the Younger.*

God hath many sharp-cutting instruments and rough files for the polishing of his jewels; and those he especially loves, and means to make the most resplendent, he hath oftenest his tools upon.—*Leighton.*

When a founder has cast a bell he does not presently fix it in the steeple, but tries it with his hammer, and beats it on every side to see if there be any flaw in it. So Christ doth not, presently after he has converted a man, convey him to heaven; but suffers him first to be beaten upon by many temptations, and then exalts him to his crown.—*Cecil*.

The hardest trial of the heart is, whether it can bear a rival's failure without triumph.—*Aikin*.

The cloud which appeared to the prophet Ezekiel carried with it winds and storms, but it was environed with a golden circle; so the storms of affliction which happen to God's children, are encompassed with brightness and smiling felicity.—*N. Caussin*.

God often lays the sum of his amazing providences in very dismal afflictions; as the limner first puts on the dusky colors, on which he intends to draw the portraiture of some illustrious beauty.—*Charnock*.

A truly virtuous person is like good metal,—the more he is fired, the more he is fined; the more he is opposed, the more he is approved. Wrongs may well try him and touch him, but they cannot imprint on him any false stamp.—*Richelieu*.

Every man will have his own criterion in forming his judgment of others. I depend very much on the effect of affliction. I consider how a man comes out of the furnace; gold will lie for a month in the furnace without losing a grain.—*Cecil*.

As the musician straineth his strings, and yet he breaketh none of them but maketh thereby a sweeter melody and better concord; so God, through affliction, makes his own better unto the fruition and enjoying of the life to come.—*Cawdrey*.

God had one Son on earth without sin, but never one without suffering.—*Augustine*.

The brightest crowns that are worn in heaven have been tried, and smelted, and polished, and glorified through the furnaces of tribulation.—*E. H. Chapin*.

God often afflicts his people to bring them nearer and keep them nearer to himself, to make earth less attractive and heaven more desirable.

Under the shadow of earthly disappointment, all unconsciously to ourselves, our Divine Redeemer is walking by our side.—*E. H. Chapin*.

Blessed be the discipline that makes me reach out to a closer union with Jesus!—Blessed be the dews of the spirit that keep my leaf ever green!—Blessed be the trials which shake down the ripe golden fruits from the branches.—*T. L. Cuyler*.

Great trials seem to be a necessary preparation for great duties.—*E. Thomson*.

In the time of Jesus, the mount of transfiguration was on the way to the cross.—In our day the cross is on the way to the mount of transfiguration.—If you would be on the mountain, you must consent to pass over the road to it.—*H. C. Trumbull*.

It is the easiest thing in the world to obey God when he commands us to do what we like, and to trust him when the path is all sunshine. The real victory of faith is to trust God in the dark, and through the dark.—*T. L. Cuyler*.

Life has no smooth road for any of us; and in the bracing atmosphere of a high aim the very roughness stimulates the climber to steadier steps, till the legend, "over steep ways to the stars" fulfils itself.—*W. C. Doane*.

There are many trials in life which do not seem to come from unwisdom or folly; they are silver arrows shot from the bow of God, and fixed inextricably in the quivering heart.—They are to be borne.—They were not meant, like snow or water, to melt as soon as they strike; but the moment an ill can be patiently borne it is disarmed of its poison, though not of its pain.—*H. W. Beecher*.

As in nature, and in the arts, so in grace; it is rough treatment that gives souls, as well as stones, their lustre.—The more the diamond is cut the brighter it sparkles, and in what seems hard dealing God has no end in view but to perfect our graces.—He sends tribulations, but tells us their purpose, that "tribulation worketh patience, and patience experience, and experience hope."—*Guthrie*.

Outward attacks and troubles rather fix than unsettle the Christian, as tempests from without only serve to root the oak more firmly in the ground.—*H. More*.

The surest way to know our gold is to look upon it and examine it in God's furnace, where he tries it that we may see what it is. If we have a mind to know whether a building stands strong or no, we must look upon it when the wind blows. If we would know whether a staff be strong, or a rotten, broken reed, we must observe it when it is leaned on and weight is borne upon it. If we would weigh ourselves justly we must weigh ourselves in God's scales that he makes use of to weigh us.—*Jonathan Edwards*.

It is trial that proves one thing weak and another strong.—A house built on the sand is in fair weather just as good as if builded on a rock.—A cobweb is as good as the mightiest cable when there is no strain upon it.—*H. W. Beecher*.

As sure as ever God puts his children in the furnace, he will be in the furnace with them.—*Spurgeon*.

Among my list of blessings infinite stands this the foremost, that my heart has bled.—*Young*.

There are no crown-wearers in heaven that were not cross-bearers here below. —*Spurgeon*.

TRIFLES.—(See "LITTLE THINGS.")

Trifles make perfection, but perfection itself is no trifle.—*Michael Angelo*.

There is nothing insignificant—nothing.—*Coleridge*.

Nothing is more unworthy of a wise man, or ought to trouble him more, than to have allowed more time for trifling, and useless things, than they deserved.—*Plato*.

He that has "a spirit of detail" will do better in life than many who figured beyond him in the university.—Such an one is minute and particular.—He adjusts trifles; and these trifles compose most of the business and happiness of life.—Great events happen seldom, and affect few; trifles happen every moment to everybody; and though one occurrence of them adds little to the happiness or misery of life, yet the sum total of their continual repetition is of the highest consequence.—*Daniel Webster*.

There are no trifles in the moral universe of God. Speak but one true word to-day, and it shall go ringing on through the ages.—*W. M. Punshon*.

It is in those acts which we call tri-

vialities that the seeds of joy are forever wasted.—*George Eliot*.

He who esteems trifles for themselves is a trifler; he who esteems them for the conclusions to be drawn from them, or the advantage to which they can be put, is a philosopher.—*Bulwer*.

One kernel is felt in a hogshead; one drop of water helps to swell the ocean; a spark of fire helps to give light to the world. None are too small, too feeble, too poor to be of service. Think of this and act. Life is no trifle.

A life devoted to trifles, not only takes away the inclination, but the capacity for higher pursuits. The truths of Christianity have scarcely more influence on a frivolous than on a profligate character.—*Hannah More*.

Think naught a trifle, though it small appear; sands make the mountain, moments make the year, and trifles, life. Your care to trifles give, else you may die ere you have learned to live.—*Young*.

Johnson well says, "He who waits to do a great deal of good at once will never do anything." *Life* is made up of little things. It is very rarely that an occasion is offered for doing a great deal at once. True greatness consists in being great in little things.—*C. Simmons*.

There is a kind of latent omniscience not only in every man, but in every particle.—*Emerson*.

Delude not yourself with the notion that you may be untrue and uncertain in trifles and in important things the contrary. Trifles make up existence, and give the measure by which to try us; and the fearful power of habit, after a time, suffers not the best will to ripen into action.—*C. M. von Weber*.

The chains which cramp us most are those which weigh on us least.—*Mad. Swetchine*.

Trifles make the sum of human things, and half our misery from our foibles springs.—*H. More*.

Trifles discover character more than actions of seeming importance; what one is in little things he is also in great.

Small causes are sufficient to make a man uneasy when great ones are not in the way. For want of a block he will stumble at a straw.—*Swift*.

The great moments of life are but moments like the others. Your doom is spoken in a word or two. A single look from the eyes, a mere pressure of the hand, may decide it; or of the lips, though they cannot speak.—*Thackeray*.

Those who give too much attention to trifling things become generally incapable of great ones.—*Rochefoucauld*.

Trifles we should let not plague us only, but also gratify us; we should seize not their poison-bags only, but their honey-bags also.—*Richter*.

Those who place their affections at first on trifles for amusement, will find these become at last their most serious concerns.—*Goldsmith*.

As it would be great folly to shoe horses, as Nero did, with gold, so it is to spend time in trifles.—*J. Mason*.

Whoever shall review his life will find that the whole tenor of his conduct has been determined by some accident of no apparent moment.—*Johnson*.

The power of duly appreciating little things belongs to a great mind; a narrow-minded man has it not, for to him they are great things.—*Whately*.

Trifles discover a character more than actions of importance. In regard to the former, a person is off his guard, and thinks it not material to use disguise. It is no imperfect hint toward the discovery of a man's character to say he looks as though you might be certain of finding a pin upon his sleeve.—*Shenstone*.

There is no real elevation of mind in a contempt of little things. It is, on the contrary, from too narrow views that we consider those things of little importance, which have, in fact, such extensive consequences.—*Fénelon*.

There is a care for trifles which proceeds from love of conscience, and is most holy; and a care for trifles which comes of idleness and frivolity, and is most base.—*Ruskin*.

Great merit, or great failings, will make you respected or despised; but trifles, little attentions, mere nothings, either done or neglected, will make you either liked or disliked in the general run of the world.—*Chesterfield*.

A stray hair, by its continued irrita-tion, may give more annoyance than a smart blow.—*J. R. Lowell*.

If the nose of Cleopatra had been a little shorter it would have changed the history of the world.—*Pascal*.

Men are led by trifles.—*Napoleon*.

A grain of sand leads to the fall of a mountain when the moment has come for the mountain to fall.—*Ernest Renan*.

Frivolous curiosity about trifles, and laborious attentions to little objects which neither require nor deserve a moment's thought, lower a man, who from thence is thought, and not unjustly, incapable of greater matters.—*Chesterfield*.

The creation of a thousand forests is in one acorn.—*Emerson*.

The mind of the greatest man on earth is not so independent of circumstances as not to feel inconvenienced by the merest buzzing noise about him; it does not need the report of a cannon to disturb his thoughts. The creaking of a vane or a pully is quite enough. Do not wonder that he reasons ill just now; a fly is buzzing by his ear; it is quite enough to unfit him for giving good counsel.—*Pascal*.

A little and a little, collected together, become a great deal; the heap in the barn consists of single grains, and drop and drop make the inundation.—*Saadi*.

Think nothing too little; seek for the cross in the daily incidents of life, look for the cross in everything. Nothing is too little which relates to man's salvation, nor is there anything too little in which either to please God or to serve Satan.—*Pusey*.

TROUBLE.—(See "ANXIETY," "AFFLICTION," and "TRIALS.")

Men are born to trouble at first, and are exercised in it all their days.—There is a cry at the beginning of life and a groan at the end of it.—*Arnot*.

When troubles come from God, then naught behoves like patience; but for troubles wrought of men, patience is hard—I tell you it is hard.—*Jean Ingelow*.

Would you touch a nettle without being stung by it; take hold of it stoutly. Do the same to other annoyances, and hardly will anything annoy you.—*Hare*.

If all men were to bring their miseries together in one place, most would be glad to take each his own home again rather than take a portion out of the common stock.—*Solon.*

It is a kind and wise arrangement of Providence that weaves our sorrows into the elements of character; and that all the disappointments, and conflicts, and afflictions of life may, if rightly used, become the means of improvement, and create in us the sinews of strength.— Trouble is a marvellous mortifier of pride, and an effectual restrainer of self-will. Difficulties string up the energies to loftier effort, and intensity is gained from repression. By sorrow the temper is mellowed and the feeling is refined. When suffering has broken up the soil, and made the furrows soft, there can be implanted the hardy virtues which outbrave the storm. In short, trial is God's glorious alchemy, by which the dross is left in the crucible, the baser metals are transmuted, and the character is enriched with gold.—*W. M. Punshon.*

The little troubles and worries of life, so many of which we meet, may be as stumbling blocks in our way, or we may make them stepping-stones to a noble character and to Heaven.

Troubles are often the tools by which God fashions us for better things.—*H. W. Beecher.*

If the sun of God's countenance shine upon me, I may well be content to be wet with the rain of affliction.—*Bp. Hall.*

Never borrow trouble. If the evil is not to come, it is useless, and so much waste; if it is to come, best keep all your strength to meet it.—*Tryon Edwards.*

When thou hast truly thanked the Lord for every blessing sent, but little time will then remain for murmur or lament.

Outward attacks and troubles rather fix than unsettle the Christian, as tempests from without only serve to root the oak faster; while an inward canker will gradually rot and decay it.—*Hannah More.*

Tribulation will not hurt you, unless it does—what, alas! it too often does—unless it hardens you, and makes you sour and narrow and sceptical.—*E. H. Chapin.*

It is not the will of God to give us more troubles than will bring us to live by faith on him; he loves us too well to give us a moment of uneasiness but for our good.—*Romaine.*

Troubles are usually the brooms and shovels that smoothe the road to a good man's fortune; and many a man curses the rain that falls upon his head, and knows not that it brings abundance to drive away hunger.—*Basil.*

Men's happiness springs mainly from moderate troubles, which afford the mind a healthful stimulus, and are followed by a reaction which produces a cheerful flow of spirits.—*E. Wigglesworth.*

If you tell your troubles to God, you put them into the grave; they will never rise again when you have committed them to him. If you roll your burden anywhere else, it will roll back again, like the stone of Sisyphus.—*Charles H. Spurgeon.*

I have had many troubles in my life, but the worst of them never came.—*James A. Garfield.*

Women like to sit down with trouble as if it were knitting.—*Ellen Glasgow.*

It is distrust of God, to be troubled about what is to come; impatience against God, to be troubled with what is present; and anger at God, to be troubled for what is past.—*Bp. Patrick.*

The wise man thinks about his troubles only when there is some purpose in doing so; at other times he thinks about other things.—*Bertrand Russell.*

Trouble is the next best thing to enjoyment; there is no fate in the world so horrible as to have no share in either its joys or sorrows.—*Longfellow.*

When Anaxagoras was told of the death of his son, he only said—"I knew he was mortal." So we in all casualties of life should say, I knew my riches were uncertain; that my friend was but a man. Such considerations would soon pacify us, because all our troubles proceed from their being unexpected.—*Plutarch.*

Set about doing good to somebody. Put on your hat, and go and visit the sick and poor of your neighborhood; inquire into their circumstances, and minister to their wants. Seek out the desolate, and afflicted, and oppressed, and tell them of the consolations of religion. I have often tried this method, and have always found it the best medicine for a heavy heart.—*Howard.*

There are many troubles which you cannot cure by the Bible and the hymn book, but which you can cure by a good perspiration and a breath of fresh air.—*H. W. Beecher.*

Sorrow comes soon enough without despondency; it does a man no good to carry around a lightning-rod to attract trouble.—*Anon.*

Perhaps when the light of heaven shows us clearly the pitfalls and dangers of the earth road that led to the heavenly city, our sweetest songs of gratitude will be not for the troubles we have conquered, but for those we have escaped.—*Barr.*

The true way of softening one's troubles is to solace those of others.—*Mad. de Maintenon.*

In all troublous events we may find comfort, though it be only in the negative admission that things might have been worse.—*Barr.*

TRUISMS.—Half the noblest passages in poetry are truisms; but these truisms are the great truths of humanity; and he is the true poet who draws them from their fountains in elemental purity, and gives us to drink.—*L. E. Landon.*

Deny first-truths, and reasoning is void. If an opponent denies them, we can only add: "Be not as the horse and the mule, who have no understanding."—*C. Simmons.*

Never reason from what you do not know.—*Ramsay.*

Fundamental truths should be both clear and familiar truths; self-evident truths are a solid foundation for reasoning.—*C. Simmons.*

TRUST.—To be trusted is a greater compliment than to be loved.—*J. Macdonald.*

The soul and spirit that animates and keeps up society is mutual trust.—*South.*

I think that we may safely trust a good deal more than we do. We may waive just so much care of ourselves as we honestly bestow elsewhere.—*Thoreau.*

The man who trusts men will make fewer mistakes than he who distrusts them.—*Cavour.*

Trust God where you cannot trace him. Do not try to penetrate the cloud he brings over you; rather look to the bow that is on it. The mystery is God's; the promise is yours.—*Macduff.*

Trust not any man with thy life, credit, or estate. For it is mere folly for a man to enthrall himself to his friend, as though, occasion being offered, he might not become an enemy.—*Burleigh.*

Trust him little who praises all, him less who censures all, and him least who is indifferent about all.—*Lavater.*

If thou be subject to any great vanity or ill, then therein trust no man; for every man's folly ought to be his greatest secret.—*Sir W. Raleigh.*

Take special care that thou never trust any friend or servant with any matter that may endanger thine estate; for so shalt thou make thyself a bond-slave to him that thou trustest, and leave thyself always to his mercy.—*Sir W. Raleigh.*

We trust as we love, and where we love.—If we love Christ much, surely we shall trust him much.—*T. Brooks.*

Trust in God does not supersede the employment of prudent means on our part. To expect God's protection while we do nothing is not to honor but to tempt providence.—*Quesnel.*

Look at that beautiful butterfly, and learn from it to trust in God. One might wonder where it could live in tempestuous nights, in the whirlwind, or in the stormy day; but I have noticed it is safe and dry under the broad leaf when rivers have been flooded, and the mountain oaks torn up from their roots.—*Jeremy Taylor.*

How calmly may we commit ourselves to the hands of him who bears up the world.—*Richter.*

I have never committed the least matter to God, that I have not had reason for infinite praise.—*Anna Shipton.*

An undivided heart, which worships God alone, and trusts him as it should, is raised above all anxiety for earthly wants.—*Geikie.*

Trust God for great things; with your five loaves and two fishes, he will show you a way to feed thousands.—*Horace Bushnell.*

To trust God when we have securities in our iron chest is easy, but not thankworthy; but to depend on him for what we cannot see, as it is more hard for man to do, so it is more acceptable to God.—*Feltham.*

We do not trust God, but tempt him, when our expectations slacken our exertions.—*M. Henry.*

He that taketh his own cares upon himself loads himself in vain with an uneasy burden. I will cast all my cares on God; he hath bidden me; they cannot burden him.—*Bp. Hall.*

TRUTH.—(See "ERROR.")

Truth is the foundation of all knowledge and the cement of all societies.—*Dryden.*

There is no fit search after truth which does not, first of all, begin to live the truth which it knows.—*Horace Bushnell.*

Statistics—I can prove anything by statistics—except the truth.—*George Canning.*

The proselyting spirit is inseparable from the love of truth, for it is only the effort to win others to our way of thinking.—*G. Forster.*

One of the sublimest things in the world is plain truth.—*Bulwer.*

What we have in us of the image of God is the love of truth and justice.—*Demosthenes.*

Truth is the object of our understanding, as good is of our will; and the understanding can no more be delighted with a lie than the will can choose an apparent evil.—*Dryden.*

General, abstract truth is the most precious of all blessings; without it man is blind, it is the eye of reason.—*Rousseau.*

Every one wishes to have truth on his side, but it is not every one that sincerely wishes to be on the side of truth.—*Whately.*

Truth, whether in or out of fashion, is the measure of knowledge, and the business of the understanding; whatsoever is beside that, however authorized by consent, or recommended by rarity, is nothing but ignorance, or something worse.—*Locke.*

The greatest homage we can pay to truth is to use it.—*Emerson.*

All truth undone becomes unreal; "he that doeth his will shall know," says Jesus.—*F. W. Roberston.*

Truth can hardly be expected to adapt herself to the crooked policy and wily sinuosities of worldly affairs; for truth, like light, travels only in straight lines.—*Colton.*

Truth and love are two of the most powerful things in the world; and when they both go together they cannot easily be withstood.—*Cudworth.*

Every violation of truth is a stab at the health of human society.—*Emerson.*

There is no progress in fundamental truth.—We may grow in knowledge of its meaning, and in the modes of its application, but its great principles will forever be the same.—*W. Radcliffe.*

Truth lies in character. Christ did not simply speak the truth; he was truth; truth, through and through; for truth is a thing not of words, but of life and being.—*Robertson.*

We must not let go manifest truths because we cannot answer all questions about them.—*Jeremy Collier.*

Christianity knows no truth which is not the child of love and the parent of duty.—*Phillips Brooks.*

Truth without charity is often intolerant and even persecuting, as charity without truth is weak in concession and untrustworthy in judgment.—But charity, loyal to truth and rejoicing in it, has the wisdom of the serpent with the harmlessness of the dove.—*J. Swartz.*

Much of the glory and sublimity of truth is connected with its mystery.—To understand everything we must be as God.—*Tryon Edwards.*

The grand character of truth is its capability of enduring the test of universal experience, and coming unchanged out of every possible form of fair discussion.—*Sir John Herschel.*

Religious truth, touch what points of it you will, has always to do with the being and government of God, and is, of course, illimitable in its reach.—*R. D. Hitchcock.*

In the discovery of truth, in the development of man's mental powers and privileges, each generation has its assigned part; and it is for us to endeavour to perform our portion of this perpetual task of our species.—*Whewell.*

To restore a common-place truth to its first uncomomn lustre you need only translate it into action. But to do this you must have reflected on its truth.—*Coleridge.*

The finest and noblest ground on which people can live is truth; the real with the real; a ground on which nothing is assumed.—*Emerson.*

A truth that one does not understand becomes an error.—*Desbarolles.*

What a man sees only in his best moments as truth is truth in all moments. —*Joseph Cook.*

Keep one thing forever in view—the truth; and if you do this, though it may seem to lead you away from the opinions of men, it will assuredly conduct you to the throne of God.—*Horace Mann.*

A charitable untruth, an uncharitable truth, and an unwise management of truth or love, are all to be carefully avoided of him that would go with a right foot in the narrow way.—*Bp. Hall.*

If a thousand old beliefs were ruined in our march to truth we must still march on.—*Stopford A. Brooke.*

It is the special privilege of truth always to grow on candid minds.—*Scrivener.*

Falsehood is in a hurry; it may be at any moment detected and punished; truth is calm, serene; its judgment is on high; its king cometh out of the chambers of eternity.—*Joseph Parker.*

Our recognition and apprehension of the highest truth is essentially an affair of the heart, far more than of the head. —*J. S. Kieffer.*

You need not tell all the truth, unless to those who have a right to know it all. But let all you tell be truth.—*Horace Mann.*

It is wondrous how, the truer we become, the more unerringly we know the ring of truth, can discern whether a man be true or not, and can fasten at once upon the rising lie in word and look and dissembling act—wondrous how the charity of Christ in the heart perceives every aberration from charity in others, in ungentle thought or slanderous tone. —*F. W. Robertson.*

It is easier to find a score of men wise

enough to discover the truth than to find one intrepid enough, in the face of opposition, to stand up for it.

No one truth is rightly held till it is clearly conceived and stated, and no single truth is adequately comprehended till it is viewed in harmonious relations to all the other truths of the system of which Christ is the centre.—*A. A. Hodge.*

It is not so difficult a task to plant new truths as to root out old errors, for there is this paradox in men: they run after that which is new, but are prejudiced in favor of that which is old.

A truth that is merely acquired from others only clings to us as a limb added to the body, or as a false tooth, or a wax nose. A truth we have acquired by our own mental exertions, is like our natural limbs, which really belong to us. —This is exactly the difference between an original thinker and the mere learned man.—*Schopenhauer.*

Truth spoken before its time may be not only hurtful, but even unlawful.—*Jukes.*

The withholding of truth is sometimes a worse deception than a direct misstatement.

There is an idiom in truth which falsehood never can imitate.—*Lord Napier.*

It is easier to perceive error than to find truth, for the former lies on the surface and is easily seen, while the latter lies in the depth, where few are willing to search for it.—*Goethe.*

Truth does not do as much good in the world, as its counterfeit does mischief.—*Rochefoucauld.*

When two truths seem directly opposed to each other, we must not question either, but remember there is a third —God—who reserves to himself the right to harmonize them.—*Mad. Swetchine.*

Truth comes to us with a slow and doubtful step; measuring the ground she treads on, and forever turning her curious eye, to see that all is right behind; and with a keen survey choosing her onward path.—*Percival.*

Truth is not only violated by falsehood; it may be equally outraged by silence.—*Amien.*

No truth so sublime but it may be seen to be trivial to-morrow in the light of new thoughts.—*Emersrn.*

If the world goes against truth, then Athanasius goes against the world.—*Athanasius.*

Truth is the gravitation principle of the universe, by which it is supported, and in which it inheres.—*W. M. Evarts.*

Truth is by its very nature intolerant, exclusive, for every truth is the denial of its opposing error.—*Luthardt.*

The deepest truths are the simplest and the most common.—*F. W. Robertson.*

Without seeking, truth cannot be known at all. It can neither be declared from pulpits, nor set down in articles, nor in any wise prepared and sold in packages ready for use. Truth must be ground for every man by himself out of its husk, with such help as he can get, indeed, but not without stern labor of his own.—*Ruskin.*

If it is the truth what does it matter who says it.—*Anon.*

Truth is as much a matter of experience as of speculation.—An honest man will generally find it.—To know it, one must feel it; above all, must live in it.—Then it becomes vital to his spirit—a part of his being.—*R. Turnbull.*

There are two peculiarities in the truths of religion: a divine beauty which renders them lovely, and a holy majesty which makes them venerable.—And there are two peculiarities in errors: an impiety which renders them horrible, and an impertinence which renders them ridiculous.—*Pascal.*

Truth is always consistent with itself, and needs nothing to help it out; it is always near at hand and sits upon our lips, and is ready to drop out before we are aware; whereas a lie is troublesome, and sets a man's invention on the rack, and one trick needs a great many more of the same kind to make it good.—*Tillotson.*

Fear is not in the habit of speaking truth; when perfect sincerity is expected, perfect freedom must be allowed; nor has any one who is apt to be angry when he hears the truth, any cause to wonder that he does not hear it.—*Tacitus.*

Truth, like beauty, varies in its fashions, and is best recommended by different dresses to different minds; and he that recalls the attention of mankind to any part of learning which time has left

behind it, may be truly said to advance the literature of his own age.—*Johnson.*

When a man has no design but to speak plain truth, he may say a great deal in a very narrow compass.—*Steele.*

"There is nothing," says Plato, "so delightful as the hearing or the speaking of truth"—for this reason there is no conversation so agreeable as that of the man of integrity, who hears without any intention to betray, and speaks without any intention to deceive.—*Sherlock.*

It is not enough that we swallow truth: we must feed upon it, as insects do on the leaf, till the whole heart be colored by its qualities, and show its food in every fibre.—*Coleridge.*

The most natural beauty in the world is honesty and moral truth; for all beauty is truth. True features make the beauty of a face; and true proportions the beauty of architecture; as true measures that of harmony and music. In poetry, which is all fable, truth still is the perfection.—*Shaftesbury.*

Some modern zealots appear to have no better knowledge of truth, nor better manner of judging it, than by counting noses.—*Swift.*

He that finds truth, without loving her, is like a bat; which, though it have eyes to discern that there is a sun, yet hath so evil eyes, that it cannot delight in the sun.—*Sir P. Sidney.*

It is curious to observe how the nature of truth may be changed by the garb it wears; softened to the admonition of friendship, or soured into the severity of reproof; yet this severity may be useful to some tempers: it somewhat resembles a file, disagreeable in its operation, but hard metal may be the brighter for it.—*Mackenzie.*

All extremes are error. The reverse of error is not truth, but error still. Truth lies between extremes.—*Cecil.*

"Truth," it has been well said, "is the property of no individual, but is the treasure of all men. The nobler the truth or sentiment, the less import the question of authorship." The larger and deeper the historical basis of our religious conception, the less will it be exposed to ruin "when the rain descends, and the floods come, and the winds blow."—*A. P. Stanley.*

As Thales measured the pyramids from

their shadows, so we may measure the height and antiquity of the truth, by the extent of its corruptions.—*Stilling-fleet.*

I believe that it is better to tell the truth than a lie. I believe it is better to be free than to be a slave. And I believe it is better to know than be ignorant.—*H. L. Mencken.*

To seek for the truth, for the sake of knowing the truth, is one of the noblest objects a man can live for.—*Dean Inge.*

Honesty of thought and speech and written word is a jewel, and they who curb prejudice and seek honorably to know and speak the truth are the only builders of a better life.—*John Galsworthy.*

A truth that disheartens because it is true is of far more value than the most stimulating of falsehoods.—*Maeterlinck.*

Perfect truth is possible only with knowledge, and in knowledge the whole essence of the thing operates on the soul and is joined essentially to it.—*Benedict Spinoza.*

My way of joking is to tell the truth. It's the funniest joke in the world.—*G. Bernard Shaw.*

Whatever has a mystery thrown round it causes the truth to appear more grand and awful.—*Francis Thompson.*

To all appearances, fiction is the native dialect of mankind, and the truth an esoteric language as yet but imperfectly learned and little loved.—*Carl Van Doren.*

Evil thoughts, lusts, and malicious purposes cannot go forth, like wandering pollen, from one human mind to another, finding unsuspected lodgment, if virtue and truth build a strong defence.—*Mary Baker Eddy.*

The most striking contradiction of our civilization is the fundamental reverence for truth which we profess and the thorough-going disregard for it which we practice.—*Vilhjalmur Stefansson.*

One day Soshi was walking on the bank of a river with a friend. "How delightfully the fishes are enjoying themselves in the water!" exclaimed Soshi. His friend spake to him thus: "You are not a fish; how do you know that the fishes are enjoying themselves?" "You

are not myself," returned Soshi; "how do you know that I do not know that the fishes are enjoying themselves?"—*Okakura Kakuzo.*

Truths turn into dogmas the moment they are disputed.—*G. K. Chesterton.*

It is twice as hard to crush a half-truth as a whole lie.—*Austin O'Malley.*

Some persons profit by lying convincingly; I, by telling the truth unconvincingly. It is not so difficult as you might suppose, for in this world, where actually nothing is commonplace, people believe only in the commonplace, that which they are accustomed to see.—*Robert L. Ripley.*

Ultimately, our troubles are due to dogma and deduction; we find no new truth because we take some venerable but questionable proposition as the indubitable starting point, and never think of putting this assumption itself to a test of observation or experiment.—*Will Durant.*

The only atheism is the denial of truth.—*Arthur Lynch.*

Still rule those minds on earth at whom sage Milton's wormwood words were hurled: *Truth like a bastard comes into the world never without ill-fame to him who gives her birth.*—*Thomas Hardy.*

Unless there is a recovery of the true dualism or, what amounts to the same thing, a reaffirmation of the truths of the inner life in some form—traditional or critical, religious or humanistic—civilization in any sense that has been attached to that term hitherto is threatened at its base.—*Irving Babbitt.*

Funny how people despise platitudes, when they are usually the truest thing going. A thing has to be pretty true before it gets to be a platitude.—*Katharine Fullerton Gerould.*

The old faiths light their candles all about, but burly Truth comes by and blows them out.—*Lizette Woodworth Reese.*

Man with his burning soul has but an hour of breath to build a ship of truth in which his soul may sail—sail on the sea of death, for death takes toll of beauty, courage, youth, of all but truth.—*John Masefield.*

It is strange but true; for truth is al-

ways strange, stranger than fiction.—
Byron.

Truth does not consist in minute accuracy of detail, but in conveying a right impression; and there are vague ways of speaking that are truer than strict facts would be. When the Psalmist said, " Rivers of water run down mine eyes, because men keep not thy law," he did not state the fact, but he stated a truth deeper than fact, and truer.—*Alford.*

Truth is only developed in the hour of need; time, and not man, discovers it.—*Bonald.*

The interests of society often render it expedient not to utter the whole truth, the interests of science never: for in this field we have much more to fear from the deficiency of truth, than from its abundance.—*Colton.*

I have seldom known any one who deserted truth in trifles, that could be trusted in matters of importance.—*Paley.*

Accustom your children to a strict attention to truth, even in the most minute particulars. If a thing happened at one window, and they, when relating it, say that it happened at another, do not let it pass, but instantly check them; you do not know where deviations from truth will end.—*Johnson.*

We find but few historians who have been diligent enough in their search for truth; it is their common method to take on trust what they distribute to the public; by which means a falsehood once received from a famed writer becomes traditional to posterity.—*Dryden.*

The greatest friend of truth is time; her greatest enemy is prejudice; and her constant companion is humility.—*Colton.*

No bad man ever wished that his breast was made of glass, or that others could read his thoughts. But the misery is, that the duplicities, the temptations, and the infirmities that surround us, have rendered the truth, and nothing but the truth, as hazardous and contraband a commodity as a man can possibly deal in.—*Colton.*

Truth is established by investigation and delay; falsehood prospers by precipitancy.—*Tacitus.*

Receiving a new truth is adding a new sense.—*Liebig.*

Seven years of silent inquiry are needful for a man to learn the truth, but fourteen in order to learn how to make it known to his fellowmen.—*Plato.*

Of all duties, the love of truth, with faith and constancy in it, ranks first and highest. To love God and to love truth are one and the same.—*Silvio Pellico.*

As has been finely expressed, " Principle is a passion for truth," And as an earlier and homelier writer hath it, " The truths we believe in are the pillars of our world."—*Bulwer.*

He who seeks truth should be of no country.—*Voltaire.*

He that opposes his own judgment against the consent of the times ought to be backed with unanswerable truths; and he that has truth on his side is a fool, as well as a coward, if he is afraid to own it because of other men's opinions.—*De Foe.*

Truth is the most powerful thing in the world, since even fiction itself must be governed by it, and can only please by its resemblance.—*Shaftesbury.*

The confusion and undesigned inaccuracy so often to be observed in conversation, especially in that of uneducated persons, proves that truth needs to be cultivated as a talent, as well as recommended as a virtue.—*Mrs. Fry.*

Truths of all others the most awful and interesting are too often considered as so true that they lose all the power of truth, and lie bed-ridden in the dormitory of the soul, side by side with the most despised and exploded errors.—*Coleridge.*

Truth is so great a perfection, that if God would render himself visible to men, he would choose light for his body and truth for his soul.—*Pythagoras.*

As one may bring himself to believe almost anything he is inclined to believe, it makes all the difference whether we begin or end with inquiry, " What is truth? "—*Whately.*

Peace if possible, but truth at any rate.—*Luther.*

Dare to be true; nothing can need a lie; a fault which needs it most grows two thereby.—*Herbert.*

It is perilous to separate thinking rightly, from acting rightly.—He is already half false who speculates on truth

and does not do it.—The penalty paid
by him who speculates on truth without
doing it, is, that by degrees the very
truth he holds becomes a falsehood.—
F. W. Roberston.

Truth is always congruous and agrees
with itself; every truth in the universe
agrees with all others.—*Daniel Webster.*

Error always addresses the passions
and prejudices: truth scorns such mean
intrigue, and only addresses the understanding and the conscience.—*Azel
Backus.*

We must never throw away a bushel
of truth because it happens to contain
a few grains of chaff; on the contrary,
we may sometimes profitably receive a
bushel of chaff for the few grains of
truth it may contain.—*A. P. Stanley.*

The way of truth is like a great road.
It is not difficult to know it. The evil is
only that men will not seek it.—*Meneius.*

I have always found that the honest
truth of our own mind has a certain attraction for every other mind that loves
truth honestly.—*Carlyle.*

Men must love the truth before they
thoroughly believe it.—*South.*

There are three parts in truth: first,
the inquiry, which is the wooing of it;
secondly, the knowledge of it, which is
the presence of it; and thirdly, the belief, which is the enjoyment of it.—
Bacon.

According to Democritus, truth lies at
the bottom of a well, the water of which
serves as a mirror in which objects may
be reflected.—I have heard, however,
that some philosophers, in seeking for
truth, to pay homage to her, have seen
their own image and adored it instead.—
Richter.

While you live, tell truth and shame
the devil.—*Shakespeare.*

Search for the truth is the noblest occupation of man; its publication is a
duty.—*Mad. de Staël.*

Truth crushed to earth will rise again;
the eternal years of God are hers; but
error wounded writhes in pain, and dies
amid her worshippers.—*Bryant.*

We must not let go manifest truths
because we cannot answer all questions
about them.—*Jeremy Collier.*

Stick to the old truths and the old paths,
and learn their divineness by sick beds,

and in every-day work, and do not
darken your mind with intellectual puzzles, which may breed disbelief, but can
never breed vital religion or practical
usefulness.—*C. Kingsley.*

Seize upon truth, wherever it is found,
amongst your friends, amongst your foes,
on Christian or on heathen ground; the
flower's divine where'er it grows.—*Watts.*

TWILIGHT.—The day is done; and
slowly from the scene the stooping sun
upgathers his spent shafts, and puts
them back into his golden quiver!—
Longfellow.

Softly the evening came. The sun
from the western horizon, like a magician, extended his golden wand o'er the
landscape.—*Longfellow.*

The weary sun hath made a golden
set, and, by the bright track of his fiery
car, gives token of a goodly day to-
morrow.—*Shakespeare.*

Oh, how beautiful is the summer night,
which is not night, but a sunless, yet
unclouded, day, descending upon earth
with dews, and shadows, and refreshing
coolness! How beautiful the long mild
twilight, which, like a silver clasp, unites
to-day with yesterday! How beautiful
the silent hour, when morning and evening thus sit together, hand in hand, beneath the starless sky of midnight!—
Longfellow.

Twilight gray hath in her sober livery
all things clad.—*Milton.*

What heart has not acknowledged the
influence of this hour, the sweet and
soothing hour of twilight—the hour of
love—the hour of adoration—the hour
of rest—when we think of those we love,
only to regret that we have not loved
them more dearly; when we remember
our enemies only to forgive them.—
Longfellow.

Nature hath appointed the twilight,
as a bridge, to pass us out of night into
day.—*Fuller.*

Twilight hour! whose mantle is the
drapery of dreams, and who hast ever
been in poetry life's holy time; thou
wert wont to steal upon us, as thy san-
dals were of dew! how sadly comes the
rustle of thy step in the decaying
seasons of the year!—*N. P. Willis.*

How lovely are the portals of the
night, when stars come out to watch the
daylight die!—*T. Cole.*

Parting day dies like the dolphin, whom each pang imbues with a new color as it gasps away, the last still loveliest, till 'tis gone, and all is gray.—*Byron.*

TYRANNY.—Tyranny and anarchy are never far asunder.—*J. Bentham.*

Free governments have committed more flagrant acts of tyranny than the most perfectly despotic governments we have ever known.—*Burke.*

Every wanton and causeless restraint of the will of the subject, whether practised by a monarch, a nobility, or a popular assembly, is a degree of tyranny. —*Blackstone.*

Bad laws are the worst sort of tyranny.—*Burke.*

Hardness ever of hardness is the mother.—*Shakespeare.*

Power, unless managed with gentleness and discretion, does but make a man the more hated; no intervals of good humor, no starts of bounty, will atone for tyranny and oppression.—*Jeremy Collier.*

Tyranny is always weakness.—*J. R. Lowell.*

Hateful is the power, and pitiable is the life, of those who wish to be feared rather than to be loved.—*Cornelius Nepos.*

There is a natural and necessary progression, from the extreme of anarchy to the extreme of tyranny; and arbitrary power is most easily established on the ruins of liberty abused to licentiousness. —*Washington.*

Tyranny sways, not as it hath power, but as it is suffered.—*Shakespeare.*

It is worthy of observation that the most imperious masters over their own servants are at the same time the most abject slaves to the servants of other masters.—*Seneca.*

Tyrants and oppressors, when living, are the terror of mankind; but when dead, they are the objects of general contempt and scorn. The death of Nero was celebrated by the Romans with bonfires and plays; birds ate the naked flesh of Pompey; Alexander lay unburied thirty days; but a useful and holy life is generally closed by an honorable and lamented death.—*Anon.*

A tyrant never tasteth of true friendship, nor of perfect liberty.—*Diogenes.*

Tyrants forego all respect for humanity in proportion as they are sunk beneath it. Taught to believe themselves of a different species, they really become so, lose their participation with their kind, and in mimicking the god dwindle into the brute.—*Hazlitt.*

A king ruleth as he ought; a tyrant as he lists; a king to the profit of all, a tyrant only to please a few.—*Aristotle.*

Tyranny absolves all faith; and who invades our rights can never be but an usurper.—*Brooke.*

Kings will be tyrants from policy, when subjects are rebels from principle. —*Burke.*

Tyranny is far the worst of treasons. —The prince who neglects or violates his trust is more a brigand than the robber-chief.—*Byron.*

Of all the evils that infest a state, a tyrant is the greatest; his sole will commands the laws, and lords it over them. —*Euripides.*

And with necessity, the tyrant's plea, excused his devilish deeds.—*Milton.*

That sovereign is a tyrant who knows no law but his own caprice.—*Voltaire.*

Where law ends, tyranny begins.—*William Pitt, the Elder.*

Rebellion to tyrants is obedience to God.—*Franklin.*

Necessity is the argument of tyrants; it is the creed of slaves.—*William Pitt, the Younger.*

U

UNBELIEF.—(See "Infidelity.")

Narrowness is the mother of unbelief. Obtain a broad outlook if you would agree with God in your philosophy and be able to transmit God's own thought into your life.—*Joseph Cook.*

All unbelief is the belief of a lie.—*H. Bonar.*

No man is an unbeliever, but because he will be so; and every man is not an unbeliever, because the grace of God conquers some, changes their wills, and binds them to Christ.—*Charnock.*

Disbelief in futurity loosens in a great measure the ties of morality, and may be for that reason pernicious to the peace of civil society.—*Hume.*

One day when D'Alembert and Condorçet were dining with Voltaire, they proposed to converse on atheism; but Voltaire stopped them at once.. " Wait," said he, " till my servants have withdrawn; I do not wish to have my throat cut to-night."—*G. B. Cheever.*

In all unbelief there are these two things: a good opinion of one's self, and a bad opinion of God.—*H. Bonar.*

There is but one thing without honor, smitten with eternal barrenness, inability to do or to be, and that is unbelief. He who believes nothing, who believes only the shows of things, is not in relation with nature and fact at all.—*Carlyle.*

How deeply rooted must unbelief be in our hearts, when we are surprised to find our prayers answered, instead of feeling sure that they will be so, if they are only offered up in faith, and in accordance with the will of God!—*Hare.*

When Dr. Johnson was asked why so many literary men were infidels, he replied, " Because they are ignorant of the Bible." Were they truly acquainted with its contents, they must acknowledge it to be from God. And the truth of the remark is confirmed by the fact that some of the most distinguished advocates of Christianity took up the Bible to oppose, but ended by believing and defending it.—*W. R. Williams.*

Unbelief, in distinction from disbelief, is a confession of ignorance where honest inquiry might easily find the truth.—" Agnostic " is but the Greek for " ignoramus."—*Tryon Edwards.*

In the hands of unbelief half-truths are made to do the work of whole falsehoods.—The sowing of doubts is the sowing of dragon's teeth, which ere long will sprout up into armed and hostile men.—*E. F. Burr.*

You think you are too intelligent to believe in God.—I am not like you.—Not every one who wishes to be is an atheist.—*Napoleon.*

It is intelligence that discovers intelligence in the universe; and a great mind is better capable than a small one of seeing God in his works.—*Thiers.*

Unbelief does nothing but darken and destroy. It makes the world a moral desert, where no divine footsteps are heard, where no angels ascend and descend, where no living hand adorns the fields, feeds the birds of heaven, or regulates events.—*Krummacher.*

" I seem," says Hume, " affrighted and confounded with the solitude in which I am placed by my philosophy. When I look abroad, on every side I see dispute, contradiction, distraction. When I turn my eye inward, I find nothing but doubt and ignorance. Where am I? or what am I? From what cause do I derive my existence? To what condition shall I return? I am confounded with questions. I begin to fancy myself in a most deplorable condition, environed with darkness on every side." —What a confession of the wretchedness of unbelief!—*C. Simmons.*

Profound minds are the most likely to think lightly of the resources of human reason, and it is the superficial thinker who is generally strongest in every kind of unbelief.—*Sir H. Davy.*

I know of no condition worse than that of the man who has little or no light on the supreme religious questions, and who, at the same time, is making no effort to come to the light.—*E. F. Burr.*

Unbelief is criminal because it is a moral act, an act of the whole nature.—Belief or unbelief is a test of a man's whole spiritual condition, because it is the whole being, affections, will, conscience, as well as the understanding, which are concerned in it.—*A. Maclaren.*

Oh, ye infidel philosophers, teach me how to find joy in sorrow, strength in weakness, and light in darkest days; how to bear buffeting and scorn; how to welcome death, and to pass through it into the sphere of life, and this not for me only, but for the whole world that groans and travails in pain; and till you can do this, speak not to me of a better revelation than the Bible.—*H. W. Beecher.*

Better that they had ne'er been born who read to doubt, or read to scorn.—*Walter Scott.*

There is no strength in unbelief.—Even the unbelief of what is false is no source of might.—It is the truth shining from behind that gives the strength to disbelieve.—*G. Macdonald.*

UNCERTAINTY.—All that lies between the cradle and the grave is uncertain.—*Seneca.*

Uncertainty! fell demon of our fears! The human soul, that can support despair, supports not thee.—*Mallet.*

A bitter and perplexed, "What shall I do?" is worse to man than worst necessity.—*Coleridge.*

The torment of suspense is very great; and as soon as the wavering, perplexed mind begins to determine, be the determination which way soever, it will find itself at ease.—*South.*

What Shakespeare says of doubts is equally true of vacillation and uncertainty of purpose, "that they make us lose the good we oft might win by fearing to attempt."—*C. Simmons.*

UNDERSTANDING.—It is a common fault never to be satisfied with our fortune, nor dissatisfied with our understanding.—*Rochefoucauld.*

The eye of the understanding is like the eye of the sense; for as you may see great objects through small crannies or holes, so you may see great axioms of nature through small and contemptible instances.—*Bacon.*

True fortitude of understanding consists in not suffering what we do know to be disturbed by what we do not know.—*Paley.*

The defects of the understanding, like those of the face, grow worse as we grow old.—*Rochefoucauld.*

It is the same with understanding as with eyes; to a certain size and make just so much light is necessary, and no more. Whatever is beyond, brings darkness and confusion.—*Shaftesbury.*

The improvement of the understanding is for two ends; first, our own increase of knowledge; secondly, to enable us to deliver that knowledge to others.—*Locke.*

A man of understanding finds less difficulty in submitting to a wrong-headed fellow, than in attempting to set him right.—*Rochefoucauld.*

It is not the eye that sees the beauty of the heaven, nor the ear that hears the sweetness of music or the glad tidings of a prosperous occurrence, but the soul, that perceives all the relishes of sensual and intellectual perfections; and the more noble and excellent the soul is, the greater and more savory are its perceptions.—*Jeremy Taylor.*

The light of the understanding humility kindleth, and pride covereth.—*Quarles.*

He who calls in the aid of an equal understanding doubles his own; and he who profits of a superior understanding raises his powers to a level with the height of the superior understanding he unites with.—*Burke.*

I know no evil so great as the abuse of the understanding, and yet there is no one vice more common.—*Steele.*

I hold myself indebted to any one from whose enlightened understanding another ray of knowledge communicates to mine.—Really to inform the mind is to correct and enlarge the heart.—*Junius.*

No one knows what strength of parts he has till he has tried them.—And of the understanding one may most truly say, that its force is generally greater than it thinks till it is put to it.—Therefore the proper remedy is, to set the mind to work, and apply the thoughts vigorously to the business, for it holds in the struggles of the mind, as in those of war, that to think we shall conquer is to conquer.—*Locke.*

UNHAPPINESS.— (See " HAPPINESS.")

It is better not to be than to be unhappy.—*Dryden.*

They who have never known prosperity can hardly be said to be unhappy; it is from the remembrance of joys we have lost, that the arrows of affliction are pointed.—*Mackenzie.*

We degrade life by our follies and vices, and then complain that the unhappiness which is only their accompaniment is inherent in the constitution of things.—*Bovee.*

The most unhappy of all men is he who believes himself to be so.—*Hume.*

A perverse temper, and a discontented, fretful disposition, wherever they prevail, render any state of life unhappy.—*Cicero.*

Man's unhappiness comes of his greatness; it is because there is an infinite in him, which, with all his cunning, he cannot quite bury under the finite.—*Carlyle.*

If we cannot live so as to be happy, let us at least live so as to deserve it.—*Fitche.*

In this world of resemblances, we are content with personating happiness; to feel it is in art beyond us.—*Mackenzie.*

Oh, how bitter a thing it is to look into happiness through another man's eyes!—*Shakespeare.*

As the ivy twines around the oak, so do misery and misfortune encompass the happiness of man. Felicity, pure and unalloyed, is not a plant of earthly growth; her gardens are the skies.—*Burton.*

Hardly a man, whatever his circumstances and situation, but if you get his confidence, will tell you that he is not happy. It is however certain that all men are not unhappy in the same degree, though by these accounts we might almost be tempted to think so. Is not this to be accounted for, by supposing that all men measure the happiness they possess by the happiness they desire, or think they deserve?—*Greville.*

What is earthly happiness? that phantom of which we hear so much and see so little; whose promises are constantly given and constantly broken, but as constantly believed; that cheats us with the sound instead of the substance, and with the blossom instead of the fruit.—*Colton.*

Perfect happiness, I believe, was never intended by the Deity to be the lot of one of his creatures in this world; but that he has very much put in our power the nearness of our approaches to it is what I have steadfastly believed.—*Jefferson.*

We never enjoy perfect happiness; our most fortunate successes are mingled with sadness; some anxieties always perplex the reality of our satisfaction.—*Corneille.*

UNION, AND UNITY.—Men's hearts ought not to be set against one another, but set with one another, and all against evil only.—*Carlyle.*

By uniting we stand; by dividing we fall.—*John Dickinson.*

Union does everything when it is perfect.—It satisfies desires, simplifies needs, foresees the wishes, and becomes a constant fortune.—*Senancour.*

The number two hath, by the heathen, been accounted accurst, because it was the first departure from unity.—*J. Trapp.*

The multitude which does not reduce itself to unity is confusion; the unity which does not depend upon the multitude, is tyranny.—*Pascal.*

The union of Christians to Christ, their common head, and by means of the influence they derive from him, one to another, may be illustrated by the loadstone. It not only attracts the particles of iron to itself by the magnetic virtue, but by this virtue it unites them one to another.—*Cecil.*

The great unity which true science seeks is found only by beginning with our knowledge of God, and coming down from him along the stream of causation to every fact and event that affects us.—*Howard Crosby.*

What science calls the unity and uniformity of nature, truth calls the fidelity of God.—*Martineau.*

UNKINDNESS.—More hearts pine away in secret anguish for unkindness from those who should be their comforters, than for any other calamity in life.—*Young.*

Hard unkindness mocks the tear it forced to flow.—*Gray.*

Unkind language is sure to produce the fruits of unkindness, that is, suffering in the bosom of others.—*Bentham.*

Rich gifts wax poor when givers prove unkind.—*Shakespeare.*

He who has once stood beside the grave, to look back upon the companionship which has been forever closed, feeling how impotent there is the wild love, or the keen sorrow, to give one instant's pleasure to the pulseless heart, or atone in the lowest measure to the departed spirit for the hour of unkindness, will scarcely for the future incur that debt to the heart which can only be discharged to the dust.—*Ruskin.*

As unkindness has no remedy at law, let its avoidance be with you a point of honor.—*H. Ballou.*

She hath tied sharp-toothed unkindness, a vulture here.—*Shakespeare.*

USEFULNESS.— (See "BENEVOLENCE"; and "GOODNESS.")

Nothing in this world is so good as

usefulness. It binds your fellow creatures to you, and you to them; it tends to the improvement of your own character and gives you a real importance in society, much beyond what any artificial station can bestow.—*B. C. Brodie.*

The world's idea of greatness has been that he is greatest who best succeeds in using his fellow-men for the furtherance of his own ends.—Christianity holds him the greatest who is himself most useful to others.—*P. H. Hoge.*

There is but one virtue—the eternal sacrifice of self.—*George Sand.*

Have I done anything for society? I have then done more for myself. Let that question and truth be always present to thy mind, and work without cessation.—*Simms.*

Think that day lost, whose low descending sun views from thy hand no worthy action done.—*Anon.*

In the school of Pythagoras it was a point of discipline, that if among the probationers, there were any who grew weary of studying to be useful, and returned to an idle life, they were to regard them as dead; and, upon their departing, to perform their obsequies, and raise them tombs with inscriptions, to warn others of the like mortality, and quicken them to refine their souls above that wretched state.—*Addison.*

The useful and the beautiful are never separated.—*Periander.*

Doing good is the only certainly happy action of a man's life.—*Sir P. Sidney.*

All the good things of this world are no further good than as they are of use; and whatever we may heap up to give to others, we enjoy only as much as we can make useful to ourselves and others, and no more.—*Defoe.*

Knowest thou not, thou canst not move a step on this earth without finding some duty to be done, and that every man is useful to his kind, by the very fact of his existence?—*Carlyle.*

The maelstrom attracts more notice than the quiet fountain; a comet draws more attention than the steady star. But it is better to be the fountain than the maelstrom, and the star than comet, following out the sphere and orbit of

quiet usefulness in which God places us. —*John Hall.*

On the day of his death, in his eightieth year, Elliot, " the Apostle of the Indians," was found teaching an Indian child at his bedside. " Why not rest from your labors now? " asked a friend. " Because," replied the venerable man, " I have prayed God to render me useful in my sphere, and he has heard 'my prayers; for now that I can no longer preach, he leaves me strength enough to teach this poor child the alphabet."— *J. Chaplin.*

We live in a world which is full of misery and ignorance, and the plain duty of each and all of us is to try to make the little corner he can influence somewhat less miserable and somewhat less ignorant than it was before he entered it.—*Huxley.*

How often do we sigh for opportunities of doing good, while we neglect the openings of Providence in little things, which would frequently lead to the accomplishment of most important usefulness. Good is done by degrees. However small in proportion the benefit which follows individual attempts to do good, a great deal may thus be accomplished by perseverance, even in the midst of discouragements and disappointments.—*Crabbe.*

Thousands of men breathe, move, and live; pass off the stage of life and are heard of no more. Why? They did not a particle of good in the world; none were blest by them, none could point to them as the instrument of their redemption; their light went out in darkness, and they were not remembered more than the insects of yesterday. Will you thus live and die, O man immortal? Live for something.— *Chalmers.*

Amid life's quests there seems but worthy one, to do men good.—*Bailey.*

I never knew a man that was bad, fit for any service that was good. There was always some disqualifying ingredient mixing with the compound, and spoiling it. The accomplishment of anything good is a physical impossibility in such a man. He could not if he would, and it is not more certain that he would not if he could, do a good and virtuous action.—*Burke.*

Try to make at least one person happy every day, and then in ten years you may have made three thousand, six hundred and fifty persons happy, or brightened a small town by your co tribution to the fund of general enjoyment.—*Sydney Smith.*

Of the Earl of Shaftesbury it was said, that "his long and perfect life had no day misspent, and no hour without some deed of loving-kindness to others."

USURER.—A money-lender. He serves you in the present tense; he lends you in the conditional mood; keeps you in the subjunctive; and ruins you in the future!—*Addison.*

He was a man versed in the world, as pilot in his compass; the needle pointed ever to that interest which was his loadstar; and he spread his sails with vantage to the gale of others' passions.—*Ben Johnson.*

Go not to a covetous old man, with any request, too soon in the morning, before he hath taken in that day's prey; for his covetousness is up before him, and he before thee, and he is in ill humor; but stay till the afternoon, till he be satiated upon some borrower.—*Fuller.*

V

VAGRANT.—Beware of those who are homeless by choice! You have no hold on a human being whose affections are without a taproot!—*Southey.*

He that has a home, and a family, has given hostages to the community for good citizenship, but he that has no such connecting interests, is exposed to temptation, to idleness, and in danger of becoming useless, if not a burden and a nuisance in society.—*Johnson.*

VAIN-GLORY.—Vain-glorious men are the scorn of the wise, the admiration of fools, the idols of parasites, and the slaves of their own vaunts.—*Bacon.*

The vain-glory of this world is a deceitful sweetness, a fruitless labor, a perpetual fear, a dangerous honor; her beginning is without Providence, and her end not without repentance.—*Quarles.*

That tumor of a man, the vain-glorious Alexander, used to make his boast that never any man went beyond him

in benefits; and yet he lived to see a poor fellow in a tub, to whom there was nothing that he could give, and from whom there was nothing that he could take away.—*Seneca.*

Some intermixture of vain-glorious tempers puts life into business, and makes a fit composition in grand enterprises and hazardous undertakings. For men of solid and sober natures have more of the ballast than the sail.—*Bacon.*

VALENTINE.—Hail to thy returning festival, old Bishop Valentine! Great is thy name in the rubric. Like unto thee, assuredly, there is no other mitred father in the calendar.—*Lamb.*

The fourteenth of February is a day sacred to St. Valentine! It was a very odd notion, alluded to by Shakespeare, that on this day birds begin to couple; hence, perhaps, arose the custom of sending on this day letters containing professions of love and affection.—*Noah Webster.*

VALOR.—The truly valiant dare everything except doing any other body an injury.—*Sir P. Sidney.*

Valor gives awe, and promises protection to those who want heart or strength to defend themselves. This makes the authority of men among women, and that of a master buck in a numerous herd.—*Sir W. Temple.*

How strangely high endeavors may be blessed, where piety and valor jointly go.—*Dryden.*

No man can answer for his own valor or courage, till he has been in danger.—*Rochefoucauld.*

The better part of valor is discretion.—*Shakespeare.*

Those who believe that the praises which arise from valor are superior to those which proceed from any other virtues have not considered.—*Dryden.*

Dare to do your duty always; this is the height of true valor.—*C. Simmons.*

If thou desire to be truly valiant, fear to do any injury; he that fears to do evil is always afraid to suffer evil; he that never fears is desperate; he that fears always is a coward: he is the true valiant man that dares nothing but what he may, and fears nothing but what he ought.—*Quarles.*

Fear to do base and unworthy things is valor; if they be done to us, to suffer them is also valor.—*Ben Jonson.*

I love the man that is modestly valiant, that stirs not till he most needs, and then to purpose.—A continued patience I commend not.—*Feltham.*

There is no love-broker in the world can more prevail in man's commendation with woman, than report of valor. —*Shakespeare.*

The mean of true valor lies between the extremes of cowardice and rashness. —*Cervantes.*

When valor preys on reason, it eats the sword it fights with.—*Shakespeare.*

The estimate and valor of a man consists in the heart and in the will; there his true honor lies. Valor is stability, not of arms and legs, but of courage and the soul; it does not lie in the valor of our horse, nor of our arms, but in ourselves. He that falls obstinate in his courage, if his legs fail him, fights upon his knees.—*Montaigne.*

True valor, on virtue founded strong, meets all events alike.—*Mallet.*

Valor employ'd in an ill quarrel, turns to cowardice; and virtue then puts on foul vice's vizor.—*Massinger.*

True valor lies in the mind, the never-yielding purpose; nor owns the blind award of giddy fortune.—*Thomson.*

Valor would cease to be a virtue if there were no injustice.—*Agesilaus.*

The love of glory, the fear of shame, the design of making a fortune, the desire of rendering life easy and agreeable, and the humor of pulling down other people are often the causes of that valor so celebrated among men.—*Rochefoucauld.*

It is said of untrue valors, that some men's valors are in the eyes of them that look on.—*Bacon.*

It is a brave act of valor to contemn death; but where life is more terrible than death it is then the truest valor to dare to live.—*Sir Thomas Browne.*

Whatever comes out of despair cannot bear the title of valor, which should be lifted up to such a height, that holding all things under itself, it should be able to maintain its greatness, even in the midst of miseries.—*Sir P. Sidney.*

Valor hath its bounds, as well as other virtues, which once transgressed, the next step is into the territories of vice, so that, by having too large a proportion of this heroic virtue, unless a man be very perfect in its limits, which, on the confines, are very hard to discern, he may, unawares, run into temerity, obstinacy, and folly.—*Montaigne.*

VANITY.—Every man has just as much vanity as he wants understanding. —*Pope.*

The most violent passions have their intermissions; vanity alone gives us no respite.—*Rochefoucauld.*

Extinguish vanity in the mind, and you naturally retrench the little superfluities of garniture and equipage. The blossoms will fall of themselves when the root that nourishes them is destroyed.—*Steele.*

Vanity is the poison of agreeableness; yet as poison, when properly applied, has a salutary effect in medicine, so has vanity in the commerce and society of the world.—*Greville.*

Take away from mankind their vanity and their ambition, and there would be but few claiming to be heroes or patriots.—*Seneca.*

The general cry is against ingratitude, but the complaint is misplaced, it should be against vanity; none but direct villains are capable of wilful ingratitude; but almost everybody is capable of thinking he hath done more than another deserves, while the other thinks he hath received less than he deserves. —*Pope.*

An egotist will always speak of himself, either in praise or in censure; but a modest man ever shuns making himself the subject of his conversation.— *Bruyère.*

Nothing is so credulous as vanity, or so ignorant of what becomes itself.— *Shakespeare.*

I will not call vanity and affectation twins, because, more properly, vanity is the mother, and affectation is the darling daughter; vanity is the sin, and affectation is the punishment; the first may be called the root of self-love, the other the fruit. Vanity is never at its full growth till it spreadeth into affectation, and then it is complete.—*Saville.*

It is our own vanity that makes the vanity of others intolerable to us.—*Rochefoucauld.*

Pride and vanity are forever spoken of side by side; and many suppose that they are merely different shades of the same feeling. Yet, so far are they from being akin, they can hardly find room in the same breast. A proud man will not stoop to be vain; a vain man is so busy in bowing and wriggling to catch fair words from others, that he can never lift up his head into pride.—*Anon.*

The strongest passions allow us some rest, but vanity keeps us perpetually in motion. What a dust do I raise! says the fly upon a coach-wheel. And at what a rate do I drive! says the fly upon the horse's back.—*Swift.*

When men will not be reasoned out of a vanity, they must be ridiculed out of it.—*L'Estrange.*

Vanity makes us do more things against inclination than reason.—*Rochefoucauld.*

They who do speak ill of themselves, do so mostly as the surest way of proving how modest and candid they are.—*Anon.*

Vanity keeps persons in favor with themselves, who are out of favor with all others.—*Shakespeare.*

Of all our infirmities, vanity is the dearest to us; a man will starve his other vices to keep that alive.—*Franklin.*

Ladies of fashion starve their happiness to feed their vanity, and their love to feed their pride.—*Colton.*

Offended vanity is the great separator in social life.—*A. Helps.*

Pride is never more offensive than when it condescends to be civil; whereas vanity, whenever it forgets itself, naturally assumes good humor.—*Cumberland.*

If you cannot inspire a woman with love of you, fill her above the brim with love of herself; all that runs over will be yours.—*Colton.*

The vainest woman is never thoroughly conscious of her beauty till she is loved by the man who sets her own passion vibrating in return.—*George Eliot.*

Vanity is the quicksand of reason.—*George Sand.*

It is vanity which makes the rake at twenty, the worldly man at forty, and the retired man at sixty. We are apt to think that best in general for which we find ourselves best fitted in particular.—*Pope.*

Our vanities differ as our noses do; all conceit is not the same conceit, but varies in correspondence with the mental make in which one of us differs from another.—*George Eliot.*

Great mischiefs happen more often from folly, meanness, and vanity, than from the greater sins of avarice and ambition.—*Burke.*

Light vanity, insatiate cormorant, consuming means soon preys upon itself.—*Shakespeare.*

O Vanity, how little is thy force acknowledged, or thy operations discerned! How wantonly dost thou deceive mankind, under different disguises!—Sometimes thou dost wear the face of pity; sometimes of generosity; nay, thou hast the assurance to put on those glorious ornaments which belong only to heroic virtue.—*Fielding.*

In a vain man, the smallest spark may kindle into the greatest flame, because the materials are always prepared for it.—*Hume.*

It is difficult to divest one's self of vanity; because impossible to divest one's self of self-love.—*Horace Walpole.*

Vanity is the foundation of the most ridiculous and contemptible vices—the vices of affectation and common lying.—*Adam Smith.*

Guard against that vanity which courts a compliment, or is fed by it.—*Chalmers.*

Vanity is the fruit of ignorance. It thrives most in subterranean places, never reached by the air of heaven and the light of the sun.—*Ross.*

I give vanity fair quarter wherever I meet with it, being persuaded that it is often productive of good to its possessor and to others within the sphere of its action; and therefore in many cases it would not be altogether absurd if a man were to thank God for his vanity, among the other comforts of his life.—*Franklin.*

A golden mind stoops not to shows of dross.—*Shakespeare.*

People who are very vain are usually equally susceptible; and they who feel one thing acutely, will so feel another.—*Bulwer.*

Vanity is so anchored in the heart of man that a soldier, sutler, cook, street porter, vapor and wish to have their admirers; and philosophers even wish the same. Those who write against it wish to have the glory of having written well; and those who read it wish to have the glory of having read well; and I, who write this, have perhaps this desire; and perhaps those who will read this.—*Pascal.*

Virtue would not go far if vanity did not keep it company.—*Rochefoucauld.*

Vanity, indeed, is the very antidote to conceit; for while the former makes us all nerve to the opinion of others, the latter is perfectly satisfied with its opinion of itself.—*Bulwer.*

Alas for human nature, that the wounds of vanity should smart and bleed so much longer than the wounds of affection!—*Macaulay.*

It was prettily devised of Æsop that the fly sat upon the axletree of the chariot-wheel, and said, "What a dust do I raise!" So are there some vain persons that, whatsoever goeth alone or moveth upon greater means, if they have never so little hand in it, they think it is they that carry it.—*Bacon.*

Vanity indeed is a venial error; for it usually carries its own punishment with it.—*Junius.*

There is no vice or folly that requires so much nicety and skill to manage as vanity; nor any which by ill management makes so contemptible a figure.—*Swift.*

Every man's vanity ought to be his greatest shame, and every man's folly ought to be his greatest secret.—*Quarles.*

Charms which, like flowers, lie on the surface and always glitter, easily produce vanity; hence women, wits, players, soldiers, are vain, owing to their presence, figure, and dress. On the contrary, other excellences, which lie down deep like gold, and are discovered with difficulty—strength, profoundness of intellect, morality—leave their possessors modest and proud.—*Richter.*

Every occasion will catch the senses of the vain man, and with that bridle and saddle you may ride him.—*Sir P. Sidney.*

We are so presumptuous that we wish to be known to all the world, even to those who come after us; and we are so vain that the esteem of five or six persons immediately around us is enough to amuse and satisfy us.—*Pascal.*

When we are conscious of the least comparative merit in ourselves, we should take as much care to conceal the value we set upon it as if it were a real defect; to be elated or vain upon it is showing your money before people in want.—*Cibber.*

Scarcely have I ever heard or read the introductory phrase, "I may say without vanity," but some striking and characteristic instance of vanity has immediately followed.—*Franklin.*

There is more jealousy between rival wits than rival beauties, for vanity has no sex. But in both cases there must be pretensions, or there will be no jealousy.—*Colton.*

Vanity may be likened to the smooth-skinned and velvet-footed mouse, nibbling about forever in expectation of a crumb; while self-esteem is too apt to take the likeness of the huge butcher's dog, who carries off your steaks, and growls at you as he goes.—*Simms.*

There is much money given to be laughed at, though the purchasers don't know it; witness A.'s fine horse, and B.'s fine house.—*Franklin.*

Vanity is a strong temptation to lying; it makes people magnify their merit, over-flourish their family, and tell strange stories of their interest and acquaintance.—*Jeremy Collier.*

Every one at the bottom of his heart cherishes vanity; even the toad thinks himself good-looking—"rather tawny perhaps, but look at his eye!"—*Wilson.*

Vanity makes men ridiculous, pride odious, and ambition terrible.—*Steele.*

Tell me not of the pain of falsehood to the slandered! There is nothing so agonizing to the fine skin of vanity as the application of a rough truth.—*Bulwer.*

To be a man's own fool is bad enough; but the vain man is everybody's.—*Penn.*

Were not vanity a principle of absolute levity, some men would carry enough with them, every day, to crush an elephant.—*Whelpley.*

He whose ruling passion is the love of praise is a slave to every one who has a tongue for flattery or calumny.

Vanity is as ill at ease under indifference, as tenderness is under the love which it cannot return.—*George Eliot.*

Those who live on vanity must, not unreasonably, expect to die of mortification.—*Mrs. Ellis.*

Pride makes us esteem ourselves; vanity to desire the esteem of others.—It is just to say as Swift has done, that a proud man is too proud to be vain.—*Blair.*

There is no folly of which a man who is not a fool cannot get rid except vanity; of this nothing cures a man except experience of its bad consequences, if indeed anything can cure it.—*Rousseau.*

Vanity is the weakness of the ambitious man, which exposes him to the secret scorn and derision of those he converses with, and ruins the character he is so industrious to advance by it.—*Addison.*

A vain man can never be altogether rude.—Desirous as he is of pleasing, he fashions his manners after those of others.—*Goethe.*

When a man has no longer any conception of excellence above his own, his voyage is done; he is dead; dead in the trespasses and sins of blear-eyed vanity.—*H. W. Beecher.*

She neglects her heart who studies her glass.—*Lavater.*

Vanity is as advantageous to a government, as pride is dangerous.—*Montesquieu.*

There is no restraining men's tongues or pens when charged with a little vanity.—*Washington.*

Never expect justice from a vain man; if he has the negative magnanimity not to disparage you, it is the most you can expect.—*Washington Allston.*

Vanity is so closely allied to virtue, and to love the fame of laudable actions approaches so near the love of laudable actions for their own sake, that these passions are more capable of mix-

ture than any other kinds of affection; and it is almost impossible to have the latter without some degree of the former.—*Hume.*

If vanity does not entirely overthrow the virtues, at least it makes them all totter.—*Rochefoucauld.*

There is no arena in which vanity displays itself under such a variety of forms as in conversation.—*Pascal.*

There's none so homely but loves a looking-glass.—*South.*

VARIETY.—Variety is the very spice of life, that gives it all its flavor.—*Cowper.*

I take it to be a principal rule of life, not to be too much addicted to any one thing.—*Terence.*

Order in variety we see; though all things differ, all agree.—*Pope.*

The most delightful pleasures cloy without variety.—*Publius Syrus.*

The earth was made so various, that the mind of desultory man, studious of change, and pleased with novelty, might be indulged.—*Cowper.*

As land is improved by sowing it with various seeds so is the mind by exercising it with different studies.—*Pliny.*

Variety's the source of joy below, from which still fresh revolving pleasures flow; in books and love, the mind one end pursues, and only change the expiring flame renews.—*Gay.*

How nature delights and amuses us by varying even the character of insects; the ill-nature of the wasp, the sluggishness of the drone, the volatility of the butterfly, the slyness of the bug!—*Sydney Smith.*

Variety alone gives joy; the sweetest meats the soonest cloy.—*Prior.*

Countless the various species of mankind; countless the shades that separate mind from mind; no general object of desire is known; each has his will, and each pursues his own.—*Gifford.*

Nothing is pleasant that is not spiced with variety.—*Bacon.*

Variety of mere nothings gives more pleasure than uniformity of something.—*Richter.*

VENGEANCE.—(See "Revenge.")

If you have committed iniquity, you must expect to suffer; for vengeance

with its sacred light shines upon you.—
Sophocles.

Deep vengeance is the daughter of
deep silence.—*Alfieri.*

Is it to be thought unreasonable that
the people, in atonement for the wrongs
of a century, demanded the vengeance
of a single day?—*Robespierre.*

Vengeance has no foresight.—*Napoleon.*

VERBOSITY.—(See "Talking"; and
"Language.")

Words, words, mere words; no matter
from the heart.—*Shakespeare.*

Redundancy of language is never
found with deep reflection. Verbiage
may indicate observation, but not thinking. He who thinks much, says but
little in proportion to his thoughts. He
selects that language which will convey
his ideas in the most explicit and direct manner. He tries to compress as
much thought as possible into a few
words. On the contrary, the man who
talks everlastingly and promiscuously,
who seems to have an exhaustless magazine of sound, crowds so many words
into his thoughts that he always obscures, and very frequently conceals
them.—*Washington Irving.*

He draweth out the thread of his verbosity finer than the staple of his argument.—*Shakespeare.*

An era is fast approaching, when no
writer will be read by the majority, except those that can effect that for bales
of manuscript that the hydrostatic screw
performs for bales of cotton, by condensing that matter into a period that
before occupied a page.—*Cotta.*

VICE.—No vassalage is so ignoble, no
servitude so miserable, as that of vice;
mines and galleys, mills and dungeons,
are words of ease compared to the service of sin; therefore, the bringing sinners
to repentance is so noble, so tempting
a design, that it drew even God himself
from heaven to prosecute it.—*Baxter.*

Vice stings us even in our pleasures,
but virtue consoles us even in our pains.
—*Colton.*

This is the essential evil of vice, that
it debases a man.—*E. H. Chapin.*

I lay it down as a sacred maxim, that
every man is wretched in proportion to
his vices; and affirm that the noblest

ornament of a young, generous mind,
and the surest source of pleasure, profit,
and reputation, in life, is an unreserved
acceptance of virtue.

The willing contemplation of vice is
vice.—*Arabian Proverb.*

He that has energy enough in his constitution to root out a vice should go a
little farther, and try to plant a virtue
in its place, otherwise he will have his
labor to renew; a strong soil that has
produced weeds, may be made to produce wheat with far less difficulty than
it would cost to make it produce nothing.—*Colton.*

The martyrs to vice far exceed the
martyrs to virtue, both in endurance
and in number. So blinded are we to
our passions, that we suffer more to insure perdition than salvation. Religion
does not forbid the rational enjoyments
of life as sternly as avarice forbids them.
She does not require such sacrifices of
ease as ambition; or such renunciation
of quiet as pride. She does not murder
sleep like dissipation; or health like intemperance; or scatter wealth like extravagance or gambling. She does not
embitter life like discord; or shorten it
like duelling; or harrow it like revenge.
She does not impose more vigilance than
suspicion; more anxiety than selfishness;
or half as many mortifications as vanity!—*Hannah More.*

The good make a better bargain, and
the bad a worse, than is usually supposed; for the rewards of the one, and
the punishments of the other not unfrequently begin on this side of the grave;
for vice has more martyrs than virtue;
and it often happens that men suffer
more to be damned than to be saved.—
Colton.

One vice worn out makes us wiser than
fifty tutors.—*Bulwer.*

It is only in some corner of the brain
which we leave empty that vice cannot
obtain a lodging. When she knocks at
your door be able to say: "No room
for your ladyship; pass on."—*Bulwer.*

The only safety is to fear and be
ashamed of vice in its beginnings, and
for its own sake, not because our indulgence is made public. "Blush not now,"
said an Italian nobleman to his young
relative, whom he met issuing from a
haunt of vice; "you should have blushed
when you went in."

As to the general design of providence, the two extremes of vice may serve to keep up the balance of things. When we speak against one capital vice, we ought to speak against its opposite; the middle betwixt both is the point for virtue.—*Pope.*

In actions of life, who seeth not the filthiness of evil wanteth a great foil to perceive the beauty of virtue.—*Sir P. Sidney.*

Virtue will catch as well as vice by contact; and the public stock of honest, manly principle will daily accumulate. We are not too nicely to scrutinize motives as long as action is irreproachable. It is enough to deal out its infamy to convicted guilt and declared apostasy.—*Burke.*

We do not despise all those who have vices, but we do despise all those who have not a single virtue.—*Rochefoucauld.*

Great examples to virtue, or to vice, are not so productive of imitation as might at first sight be supposed. There are hundreds that want energy, for one that wants ambition; and sloth has prevented as many vices in some minds as virtue in others. Idleness is the grand Pacific Ocean of life, and in that stagnant abyss, the most salutary things produce no good, the most noxious no evil. Vice, indeed, abstractedly considered, may be, and often is, engendered in idleness, but the moment it becomes efficiently vice, it must quit its cradle and cease to be idle.—*Colton.*

Vice repeated is like the wandering wind; blows dust in others' eyes, to spread itself.—*Shakespeare.*

Bad passions become more odious in proportion as the motives to them are weakened; and gratuitous vice cannot be too indignantly exposed to reprehension.

No man ever arrived suddenly at the summit of vice.—*Juvenal.*

Wise men will apply their remedies to vices, not to names; to the causes of evil which are permanent, not the occasional organs by which they act, and the transitory modes in which they appear.—*Burke.*

Why is there no man who confesses his vices? It is because he has not yet laid them aside. It is a waking man only who can tell his dreams.—*Seneca.*

Experience tells us that each man most keenly and unerringly detects in others the vice with which he is most familiar himself.—*F. W. Robertson.*

Society is the atmosphere of souls; and we necessarily imbibe from it something which is either infectious or salubrious. The society of virtuous persons is enjoyed beyond their company, while vice carries a sting into solitude. The society or company you keep is both the indication of your character and the former of it. In vicious society you will feel your reverence for the dictates of conscience wear off, and that name at which angels bow and devils tremble, you will hear contemned and abused. The Bible will supply materials for unmeaning jest or impious buffoonery; the consequence of this will be a practical deviation from virtue, the principles will become sapped, the fences of conscience broken down; and when debauchery has corrupted the character a total inversion will take place, and the sinner will glory in his shame.—*Robert Hall.*

What maintains one vice would bring up two children.—*Franklin.*

When Mandeville maintained that private vices were public benefits, he did not calculate the widely destructive influence of bad example. To affirm that a vicious man is only his own enemy is about as wise as to affirm that a virtuous man is only his own friend.—*Colton.*

When our vices have left us we flatter ourselves that we have left them.—*Rochefoucauld.*

A society composed of none but the wicked could not exist; it contains within itself the seeds of its own destruction, and, without a flood, would be swept away from the earth by the deluge of its own iniquity. The moral cement of all society is virtue; it unites and preserves, while vice separates and destroys. The good may well be termed the salt of the earth, for where there is no integrity there can be no confidence; and where there is no confidence there can be no unanimity.—*Colton.*

The vicious man lives at random, and acts by chance, for he that walks by no rule can carry on no settled or steady design.—*Tillotson.*

Vice is a monster of so frightful mien as to be hated needs but to be seen;

yet seen too oft, familiar with her face, we first endure, then pity, then embrace. —*Pope.*

One sin doth provoke another.— *Shakespeare.*

Many a man's vices have at first been nothing worse than good qualities run wild.—*Hare.*

The hatred of the vicious will do you less harm than their conversation.— *Bentley.*

But when to mischief mortals bend their will, how soon they find fit instruments of ill!—*Pope.*

I know no friends more faithful and more inseparable than hard-heartedness and pride, humility and love, lies and impudence.—*Lavater.*

Men often abstain from the grosser vices as too coarse and common for their appetites, while the vices that are frosted and ornamented are served up to them as delicacies.—*H. W. Beecher.*

Vice is the bane of a republic, and saps the foundations of liberty.—If our industry, economy, temperance, justice, and public faith, are once extinguished by the opposite vices, our boasted constitution which is built on the pillars of virtue, must necessarily fall.—*Emmons.*

Vice loses half its evil by losing all its grossness.—*Burke.*

The gods are just, and of our pleasant vices make instruments to plague us.—*Shakespeare.*

Vice can deceive under the shadow and guise of virtue.—*Juvenal.*

Vice incapacitates a man from all public duty; it withers the powers of his understanding, and makes his mind paralytic.—*Burke.*

There is no vice so simple but assumes some mark of virtue on its outwards parts.—*Shakespeare.*

Vice always leads, however fair at first, to wilds of woe.—*Thomson.*

Beware of the beginnings of vice.— Do not delude yourself with the belief that it can be argued against in the presence of the exciting cause.—Nothing but actual flight can save you.—*B. R. Haydon.*

The end of a dissolute life is, most commonly, a desperate death.—*Bion.*

Our pleasant vices are made the whip to scourge us.—*Shakespeare.*

Vices and frailties correct each other, like acids and alkalies. If each vicious man had but one vice, I do not know how the world could go on.—*Whately.*

People do not persist in their vices because they are not weary of them, but because they cannot leave them off. It is the nature of vice to leave us no resource but in itself.—*Hazlitt.*

Crimes sometimes shock us too much; vices almost always too little.—*Hare.*

Virtue seems to be nothing more than a motion consonant to the system of things; were a planet to fly from its orbit it would represent a vicious man. —*Shenstone.*

What we call vice in our neighbor may be nothing less than a crude virtue. To him who knows nothing more of precious stones than he can learn from a daily contemplation of his breastpin, a diamond in the mine must be a very uncompromising sort of stone.—*Simms.*

The vicious obey their passions as slaves do their masters.—*Diogenes.*

A few vices are sufficient to darken many virtues.—*Plutarch.*

Vice is but a nurse of agonies.—*Sir P. Sidney.*

To attack vices in the abstract, without touching persons, may be safe fighting, but it is fighting with shadows.— *Junius.*

Vices are as truly contrary to each other as to virtue.—*Fuller.*

Vices that are familiar we pardon, and only new ones do we reprehend.— *Publius Syrus.*

The martyrs to vice far exceed the martyrs to virtue, both in endurance and in number. So blinded are we by our passions that we suffer more to be damned than to be saved.—*Colton.*

The most fearful characteristic of vice is its irresistible fascination—the ease with which it sweeps away resolution, and wins a man to forget his momentary outlook, and his throb of penitence, in the embrace of indulgence.—*E. H. Chapin.*

Vices are contagious, and there is no trusting the well and sick together.— *Seneca.*

Let thy vices die before thee.—*Franklin.*

Vices are often habits rather than passions.—*Rivarol.*

Say everything for vice which you can, magnify any pleasures as much as you please, but don't believe you have any secret for sending on quicker the sluggish blood, and for refreshing the faded nerve.—*Sydney Smith.*

Vice—that digs her own voluptuous tomb.—*Byron.*

The vices operate like age; bringing on disease before its time, and in the prime of youth they leave the character broken and exhausted.—*Junius.*

There are vices which have no hold upon us, but in connection with others, and which, when you cut down the trunk, fall like the branches.—*Pascal.*

Every age and nation has certain characteristic vices, which prevail almost universally, which scarcely any person scruples to avow, and which even rigid moralists but faintly censure. Succeeding generations change the fashion of their morals with the fashion of their hats and their coaches; take some other kind of wickedness under their patronage, and wonder at the depravity of their ancestors.—*Macaulay.*

VICISSITUDES. — Misfortune does not always wait on vice, nor is success the constant guest of virtue.—*Hazard.*

Such are the vicissitudes of the world, through all its parts, that day and night, labor and rest, hurry and retirement, endear each other. Such are the changes that keep the mind in action; we desire, we pursue, we obtain, we are satiated; we desire something else, and begin a new pursuit.—*Johnson.*

But yesterday the word of Cæsar might have stood against the world; now lies he there, and none so poor to do him reverence.—*Shakespeare.*

The most affluent may be stripped of all, and find his worldly comforts, like so many withered leaves, dropping from him.—*Sterne.*

Happy the man who can endure the highest and the lowest fortune.—He who has endured such vicissitudes with equanimity has deprived misfortune of its power.—*Seneca.*

Vicissitude of fortune which spares neither man nor the proudest of his works, but buries empires and cities in a common grave.—*Gibbon.*

Sometimes the brightest day hath a cloud, and summer evermore succeeds barren winter with its wrathful, nipping cold.—So cares and joys abound, as seasons fleet.—*Shakespeare.*

VICTORY.—Victories that are easy are cheap.—Those only are worth having which come as the result of hard fighting.—*H. W. Beecher.*

The smile of God is victory.—*Whittier.*

Pursue not a victory too far. He hath conquered well that hath made his enemy fly; thou mayest beat him to a desperate resistance, which may ruin thee.—*Herbert.*

In victory the hero seeks the glory, not the prey.—*Sir P. Sidney.*

It is the contest that delights us, not the victory. We are pleased with the combat of animals, but not with the victor tearing the vanquished. What is sought for is the crisis of victory, and the instant it comes, it brings satiety.—*Pascal.*

A victory is twice itself when the achiever brings home full numbers.—*Shakespeare.*

Who overcomes by force hath overcome but half his foe.—*Milton.*

He who surpasses or subdues mankind must look down on the hate of those below.—*Byron.*

Victory or Westminster Abbey.—*Nelson.*

Victory may be honorable to the arms, but shameful to the counsels of the nation.—*Bolingbroke.*

VIGILANCE.—It is the enemy who keeps the sentinel watchful.—*Mad. Swetchine.*

Better three hours too soon, than one minute too late.—*Shakespeare.*

He is most free from danger, who, even when safe, is on his guard.—*Publius Syrus.*

Eternal vigilance is the price of liberty.—*Jefferson.*

VILLAINY.—The most stormy ebullitions of passion, from blasphemy to murder, are less terrific than one single act of cool villainy; a still rabies is more dangerous than the paroxysms of a fever. Fear the boisterous savage of passion less than the sedately grinning villain.—*Lavater.*

It is the masterpiece of villainy to smoothe the brow, and so outface suspicion.—*Howard.*

The evil you teach me I will execute, and it shall go hard but I will better the instruction.—*Shakespeare.*

Villainy, when detected, never gives up, but boldly adds impudence to imposture.—*Goldsmith.*

Villainy that is vigilant will be an over-match for virtue, if she slumber at her post.—*Colton.*

One murder made the villain; millions the hero.—Princes were privileged to kill, and numbers sanctified the crime.—*Bp. Porteus.*

VIOLENCE.—Violent fires soon burn out themselves, small showers last long, but sudden storms are short; he tires betimes that spurs too fast.—*Shakespeare.*

Violence ever defeats its own ends. Where you cannot drive you can always persuade. A gentle word, a kind look, a god-natured smile can work wonders and accomplish miracles. There is a secret pride in every human heart that revolts at tyranny. You may order and drive an individual, but you cannot make him respect you.—*Hazlitt.*

Nothing good ever comes of violence.—*Luther.*

Violent delights have violent ends.—*Shakespeare.*

The violence done us by others is often less painful than that which we do to ourselves.—*Rochefoucauld.*

Nothing violent, oft have I heard tell, can be permanent.—*Marlowe.*

Vehemence without feeling is but rant.—*H. Lewes.*

VIRTUE.—To be innocent is to be not guilty; but to be virtuous is to overcome our evil feelings and intentions.—*Penn.*

It is the edge and temper of the blade that make a good sword, not the richness of the scabbard; and so it is not money or possessions that make man considerable, but his virtue.—*Seneca.*

There is a nobility without heraldry. Though I want the advantage of a no-

ble birth, said Marius, yet my actions afford me a greater one; and they who upbraid me with it are guilty of an extreme injustice in not permitting me to value myself upon my own virtue, as much as they value themselves upon the virtue of others.—*Sallust.*

That virtue which requires to be ever guarded is scarce worth the sentinel.—*Goldsmith.*

A great deal of virtue, at least the outward appearance of it, is not so much from any fixed principle, as the terror of what the world will say, and the liberty it will take upon the occasions we shall give.—*Sterne.*

Virtue is its own reward, and brings with it the truest and highest pleasure; but if we cultivate it only for pleasure's sake, we are selfish, not religious, and will never gain the pleasure, because we can never have the virtue.—*Newman.*

Virtue is an angel; but she is a blind one and must ask of knowledge to show her the pathway that leads to her goal. Mere knowledge, on the other hand, like a Swiss mercenary, is ready to combat either in the ranks of sin or under the banners of righteousness—ready to forge cannon-balls or to print New Testaments, to navigate a corsair's vessel or a missionary ship.—*Horace Mann.*

All bow to virtue, and then walk away.—*De Finod.*

Virtue I love, without austerity; pleasure, without effeminacy; and life, without fearing its end.—*St. Everemond*

Were there but one virtuous man in the world, he would hold up his head with confidence and honor; he would shame the world, and not the world him.—*South.*

There is but one pursuit in life which it is in the power of all to follow, and of all to attain. It is subject to no disappointments, since he that perseveres makes every difficulty an advancement, and every conquest a victory; and this is the pursuit of virtue. Sincerely to aspire after virtue is to gain her; and zealously to labor after her ways is to receive them.—*Colton.*

To be able under all circumstances to practise five things constitutes perfect virtue; these five are gravity, generosity of soul, sincerity, earnestness, and kindness.—*Confucius*.

The great slight the men of wit who have nothing but wit; the men of wit despise the great who have nothing but greatness; the good man pities them both, if with greatness or wit, they have not virtue.—*Bruyère*.

I willingly confess that it likes me better when I find virtue in a fair lodging than when I am bound to seek it in an ill-favored creature.—*Sir P. Sidney*.

We rarely like the virtues we have not.—*Shakespeare*.

Virtue without talent is a coat of mail without a sword; it may indeed defend the wearer, but will not enable him to protect his friend.—*Colton*.

Nothing is more unjust, however common, than to charge with hypocrisy him that expresses zeal for those virtues which he neglects to practise; since he may be sincerely convinced of the advantages of conquering his passions without having yet obtained the victory, as a man may be confident of the advantages of a voyage or a journey, without having courage or industry to undertake it, and may honestly recommend to others those attempts which he neglects himself.—*Johnson*.

It would not be easy, even for an unbeliever, to find a better translation of the rule of virtue from the abstract into the concrete, than to endeavor so to live that Christ would approve our life.—*John Stuart Mill*.

Wealth is a weak anchor, and glory cannot support a man; this is the law of God, that virtue only is firm, and cannot be shaken by a tempest.—*Pythagoras*.

No man can purchase his virtue too dear, for it is the only thing whose value must ever increase with the price it has cost us. Our integrity is never worth so much as when we have parted with our all to keep it.—*Colton*.

Every man is ready to give in a long catalogue of those virtues and good qualities he expects to find in the person of a friend; but very few of us are careful to cultivate them in ourselves.—*Addison*.

I am no herald to inquire of men's pedigrees; it sufficeth me if I know their virtues.—*Sir P. Sidney*.

Every condition of life, if attended with virtue, is undisturbed and delightful; but when vice is intermixed, it renders even things that appear sumptuous and magnificent, distasteful and uneasy to the possessor.—*Plutarch*.

He that is good will infallibly become better, and he that is bad will as certainly become worse; for vice, virtue, and time are three things that never stand still.—*Colton*.

He who thinks no man above him but for his virtue, and none below him but for his vice, can never be obsequious or assuming in a wrong place, but will frequently emulate men in rank below him, and pity those above him.—*Tatler*.

Never expecting to find perfection in men, in my commerce with my contemporaries I have found much human virtue. I have seen not a little public spirit; a real subordination of interest to duty; and a decent and regulated sensibility to honest fame and reputation. The age unquestionably produces daring profligates and insidious hypocrites. What then? Am I not to avail myself of whatever good is to be found in the world because of the mixture of evil that will always be in it? The smallness of the quantity in currency only heightens the value. They who raise suspicions on the good, on account of the behavior of ill men, are of the party of the latter.—*Burke*.

The most virtuous of all men, says Plato, is he that contents himself with being virtuous without seeking to appear so.—*Fénelon*.

Many who have tasted all the pleasures of sin have forsaken it and come over to virtue; but there are few, if any, who having tried the sweets of virtue could ever be drawn off from it, or find in their hearts to fall back to their former course.—*Jeffrey*.

Every virtue gives a man a degree of fecility in some kind: honesty gives a man a good report; justice, estimation; prudence, respect; courtesy and liberality, affection; temperance gives health; fortitude, a quiet mind, not to be moved by any adversity.—*Walsingham*.

Virtue is so delightful, whenever it is

perceived, that men have found it their interest to cultivate manners, which are, in fact, the appearances of certain virtues; and now we are come to love the sign better than the thing signified, and to prefer manners without virtue, to virtue without manners.—*Sydney Smith*.

By what causes has so inconsiderable a beginning, as that of the colonies of New England, under such formidable, and apparently almost insurmountable difficulties, resulted, in so brief a period, in such mighty consequences? They are to be found in the high moral and intellectual qualities of the pilgrims: their faith, piety, and confident trust in a superintending Providence; their stern virtues; their patriotic love of liberty and order; their devotion to learning; and their indomitable courage and perseverance. These are the causes which surmounted every obstacle, and which have led to such mighty results.—*John C. Calhoun*.

The virtue of a man ought to be measured not by his extraordinary exertions, but by his every-day conduct.—*Pascal*.

What the world calls virtue is a name and a dream without Christ. The foundation of all human excellence must be laid deep in the blood of the Redeemer's cross and in the power of his resurrection.—*F. W. Robertson*.

Virtue consists in doing our duty in the various relations we sustain to ourselves, to our fellow-men, and to God, as it is made known by reason, revelation, and Providence.—*A. Alexander*.

We are apt to mistake our vocation in looking out of the way for occasions to exercise great and rare virtues, and stepping over the ordinary ones which lie directly in the road before us. When we read we fancy we could be martyrs; when we come to act we find we cannot bear a provoking word.—*H. More*.

I cannot praise a fugitive and cloistered virtue, unexercised and unbreathed, that never sallies out and sees her adversary. The virtue that knows not the utmost that vice promises to her followers, and rejects it, is but a blank virtue, not a pure.—*Milton*.

Virtue is the dictate of reason, or the remains of the divine light, by which men are made beneficent and beneficial to each other. Religion proceeds from the same end, and the good of mankind so entirely depends upon these two, that no people ever enjoyed anything worth desiring that was not the product of them.—*Algernon Sidney*.

There are two things that declare, as with a voice from heaven, that he that fills that eternal throne must be on the side of virtue, and that which he befriends must finally prosper and prevail. The first is that the bad are never completely happy and at ease, although possessed of everything that this world can bestow; and that the good are never completely miserable, although deprived of everything that this world can take away. The second is that we are so framed and constituted that the most vicious cannot but pay a secret though unwilling homage to virtue, inasmuch as the worst men cannot bring themselves thoroughly to esteem a bad man, although he may be their dearest friend, nor can they thoroughly despise a good man, although he may be their bitterest enemy.—*Colton*.

Virtue is certainly the most noble and secure possession a man can have. Beauty is worn out by time or impaired by sickness—riches lead youth rather to destruction than welfare, and without prudence are soon lavished away; while virtue alone, the only good that is ever durable, always remains with the person that has once entertained her. She is preferable both to wealth and a noble extraction.—*Savage*.

Keep thy spirit pure from worldly taint by the repellent strength of virtue.—*Bailey*.

If he does really think there is no distinction between virtue and vice, why, sir, when he leaves our house let us count our spoons.—*Johnson*.

Virtue by calculation is the virtue of vice.—*Joubert*.

If you can be well without health, you may be happy without virtue.—*Burke*.

Our virtues would be proud if our faults whipped them not; and our crimes would despair if they were not cherished by our virtues.—*Shakespeare*.

When men grow virtuous in old age they are merely making an offering to God of the devil's leavings.—*Swift*.

Guilt, though it may attain temporal

splendor, can never confer real happiness; the evil consequences of our crimes long survive their commission, and, like the ghosts of the murdered, forever haunt the steps of the malefactor; while the paths of virtue, though seldom those of worldly greatness, are always those of pleasantness and peace.—*Walter Scott.*

The only impregnable citadel of virtue is religion; for there is no bulwark of mere morality which some temptation may not overtop, or undermine and destroy.—*Sir P. Sidney.*

Virtue is not to be considered in the light of mere innocence, or abstaining from harm; but as the exertion of our faculties in doing good.—*Bp. Butler.*

No virtue can be real that has not been tried. The gold in the crucible alone is perfect; the loadstone tests the steel, and the diamond is tried by the diamond, while metals gleam the brighter in the furnace.—*Calderon.*

The virtues, like the Muses, are always seen in groups. A good principle was never found solitary in any breast. —*Jane Porter.*

On every occasion in which virtue is exercised, if something is not added to happiness, something is taken away from anxiety.—*Bentham.*

Content not thyself that thou art virtuous in the general; for one link being wanting, the chain is defective. Perhaps thou art rather innocent than virtuous, and owest more to thy constitution than to thy religion.—*Penn.*

I would be virtuous for my own sake, though nobody were to know it; as I would be clean for my own sake, though nobody were to see me.—*Shaftesbury.*

Virtue has many preachers, but few martyrs.—*Helvetius.*

Do not be troubled because you have not great virtues. God made a million spears of grass where he made one tree. The earth is fringed and carpeted, not with forests, but with grasses. Only have enough of little virtues and common fidelities, and you need not mourn because you are neither a hero nor a saint.—*H. W. Beecher.*

They who disbelieve in virtue because man has never been found perfect, might as reasonably deny the sun because it is not always noon.—*Hare.*

Beware of making your moral staples consist of the negative virtues.—It is good to abstain, and to teach others to abstain, from all that is sinful or hurtful.—But making a business of it leads to emaciation of character unless one feeds largely on the more nutritious diet of active benevolence.—*O. W. Holmes.*

It is not virtue, but a deceptive copy and imitation of virtue, when we are led to the performance of duty by pleasure as its recompense.—*Cicero.*

A large part of virtue consists in good habits.—*Paley.*

The virtue of Paganism was strength; the virtue of Christianity is obedience. —*Hare.*

Many new years you may see, but happy ones you cannot see without deserving them. These virtue, honor, and knowledge alone can merit, alone can produce.—*Chesterfield.*

Virtue is uniform and fixed, because she looks for approbation only from Him who is the same yesterday, to-day, and forever.—*Colton.*

Virtues go ever in troops; so thick that sometimes some are hid in the crowd, which yet are virtues though they appear not.—*Bp. Hall.*

Certainly, virtue is like precious odors, most fragrant when they are incensed or crushed; for prosperity doth best discover vice, but adversity doth best discover virtue.—*Bacon.*

Live virtuously, and you cannot die too soon, nor live too long.—*Lady Russell.*

Blessed is the memory of those who have kept themselves unspotted from the world! Yet more blessed and more dear the memory of those who have kept themselves unspotted in the world! —*Mrs Jameson.*

Virtue is a state of war, and to live in it we have always to combat with ourselves.—*Rousseau.*

Hast thou virtue? Acquire also the graces and beauties of virtue.—*Franklin.*

Virtue is that perfect good which is the complement of a happy life; the only immortal thing that belongs to mortality.—*Seneca.*

While shame keeps its watch virtue is

not wholly extinguished in the heart.—*Burke.*

Good company and good discourse are the very sinews of virtue.—*Izaak Walton.*

No state of virtue is complete save as it is won by a conflict with evil, and fortified by the struggles of a resolute and even bitter experience.—*Horace Bushnell.*

Perfect virtue is to do unwitnessed what we should be capable of doing before all the world.—*Rochefoucauld.*

Virtue is the habitual sense of right, and the habitual courage to act up to that sense of right, combined with benevolent sympathies, and the charity which thinketh no evil. The union of the highest conscience and highest sympathy fulfils my notion of virtue.—*Mrs. Jameson.*

Our life is short, but to expand that span to vast eternity is virtue's work.—*Shakespeare.*

It has ever been my experience that folks who have no vices have very few virtues.—*Lincoln.*

Virtue, not rolling suns, the mind matures; that life is long which answers life's great end.—*Young.*

This is the law of God, that virtue only is firm, and cannot be shaken by a tempest.—*Pythagoras.*

VISITORS.—Visits are for the most part neither more nor less than inventions for discharging upon our neighbors somewhat of our own unendurable weight.—*Nicole.*

Visitors are insatiable devourers of time, and fit only for those who, if they did not visit, would do nothing.—*Cowper.*

Unwelcome are the loiterer, who makes appointments he never keeps; the consulter, who asks advice he never follows; the boaster, who seeks for praise he does not merit; the complainer, who whines only to be pitied; the talker, who talks only because he loves to talk always; the profane and obscene jester, whose words defile; the drunkard, whose insanity has got the better of his reason; and the tobacco-chewer and smoker, who poisons the atmosphere and nauseates others.

VIVACITY.—I do not dislike extreme vivacity in children; but would see enough of it to make an animated character, when the violence of animal spirits shall subside in time. It is easier to restrain excess than to quicken stupidity. Gravity in childhood may become stupidity in old age.—*Mrs. Sigourney.*

Vivacity in youth is often mistaken for genius, and solidity for dulness.

Extreme volatile and sprightly tempers seem inconsistent with any great enjoyment. There is too much time wasted in the mere transition from one object to another. No room for those deep impressions which are made only by the duration of an idea, and are quite requisite to any strong sensation, either of pleasure or of pain. The bee to collect honey, or the spider to gather poison, must abide some time upon the weed or flower. They whose fluids are mere sal volatile seem rather cheerful than happy men.—*Shenstone.*

The vivacity which augments with years is not far from folly.—*Rochefoucauld.*

VOICE.—How wonderful is the human voice!—It is indeed the organ of the soul. The intellect of man sits enthroned, visibly, on his forehead and in his eye, and the heart of man is written on his countenance, but the soul reveals itself in the voice only.—*Longfellow.*

Her voice was ever soft, gentle, and low, an excellent thing in woman.—*Shakespeare.*

His voice attention still as midnight draws—his voice more gentle than the summer's breeze.—*Dryden.*

The sweetest of all sounds is that of the voice of the woman we love.—*Bruyère.*

How often the spell of beauty is rudely broken by coarse, loud talking! How often you are irresistibly drawn to a plain, unassuming woman, whose soft, silvery tones render her positively attractive. In the social circle how pleasant it is to hear a woman talk in that low key which always characterizes the true lady. In the sanctuary of home how such a voice soothes the fretful child and cheers the weary husband!—*Lamb.*

The influence of temper upon tone deserves much consideration.—In the voice there is no deception; it is, to many, the index of the mind, denoting moral qualities; and it may be remarked that the low, soft tones of gentle and amiable beings, whatever their musical endowments may be, seldom fail to please; besides which the singing of ladies indicates the cultivation of their taste.—*Mordaunt*.

There is no index of character so sure as the voice.—*Tancred*.

When those we have loved have long vanished from the earth, then will the beloved voice come back and bring with it all our old tears and the disconsolate heart that sheds them.—*Richter*.

Her voice is soft; not shrill and like the lark's, but tenderer, graver, almost hoarse at times! As though the earnestness of love prevailed and quelled all shriller music.—*Barry Cornwall*.

A lovely countenance is the fairest of all sights, and the sweetest harmony is the sound of the voice of her whom we love.—*Bruyère*.

To a nice ear the quality of a voice is singularly affecting. Its depth seems to be allied to feeling; at least the contralto notes alone give an adequate sense of pathos. They are born near the heart.—*Tuckerman*.

The tones of human voices are mightier than strings or brass to move the soul.—*Klopstock*.

There is in the voice of a menaced man, who calls you, something imperious which subdues and commands.—*M. de Martignac*.

How sweetly sounds the voice of a good woman! When it speaks it ravishes all senses.—*Massinger*.

Thy voice is celestial melody.—*Longfellow*.

VOLUPTUOUSNESS.—The voluptuous and effeminate are never brave; they have no courage in time of danger.—*Fénelon*.

Voluptuousness, like justice, is blind; but that is the only resemblance between them.—*Pascal*.

The rich and luxurious may claim an exclusive right to those pleasures which are capable of being purchased by pelf, in which the mind has no enjoyment, and which only afford a temporary relief to languor by steeping the senses in

forgetfulness; but in the precious pleasures of the intellect, so easily accessible by all mankind, the great have no exclusive privilege;. for such enjoyments are only to be procured by our own industry.—*Zimmermann*.

VOWS.—Make no vows to perform this or that; it shows no great strength, and makes thee ride behind thyself.—*Fuller*.

The gods are deaf to hot and peevish vows; they are polluted offerings, more abhorred than spotted livers in the sacrifice.—*Shakespeare*.

Lovers' vows seem sweet in every whispered word.—*Byron*.

Unheedful vows may heedfully be broken.—*Shakespeare*.

Hasty resolutions are of the nature of vows, and to be equally avoided.—*Penn*.

Men's vows are women's traitors.—*Shakespeare*.

The vows that woman makes to her fond lover are only fit to be written on air, or on the swiftly passing stream.—*Catullus*.

Those mouth-made vows which break themselves in swearing.—*Shakespeare*.

VULGARITY.—To endeavor to work upon the vulgar with fine sense is like attempting to hew blocks with a razor.—*Pope*.

Be true to your own highest convictions. Intimations from our own souls of something more perfect than others teach, if faithfully followed, give us a consciousness of spiritual force and progress never experienced by the vulgar of high life, or low life, who march as they are drilled to the step of their times.—*Channing*.

The vulgarity of inanimate things requires time to get accustomed to; but living, breathing, bustling, plotting, planning, human vulgarity is a species of moral ipecacuanha enough to destroy any comfort.—*Carlyle*.

Disorder in a drawing-room is vulgar; in an antiquary's study, not; the black battle-stain on a soldier's face is not vulgar, but the dirty face of a housemaid is.—*Ruskin*.

Be thou familiar, but by no means vulgar.—*Shakespeare*.

W

WAG.—A wag is in the last order even of pretenders to wit and humor.—Generally he has his mind prepared to receive some occasion of merriment, but is of himself too empty to draw any out of his own thoughts, and therefore he laughs at the next thing he meets, not because it is ridiculous, but because he is under the necessity of laughing.—*Steele.*

One of the most silly and contemptible of men is the professed wag, whose great aim in life is to raise a laugh which might better be against himself than at his ill-timed jokes.

WAGERS.—Fools for arguments use wagers.—*Butler.*

Most men, until by losing rendered sager, will back their opinions by a wager.—*Byron.*

WAITING.—They also serve who only stand and wait.—*Milton.*

Wayworn, pressed with toils and strife, we are waiting, hoping, watching, praying, till we reach the gates of life.—*Ray Palmer.*

Beautiful is the activity that works for good, and the stillness that waits for good; blessed the self-sacrifice of the one, and the self-forgetfulness of the other.—*R. Collyer.*

It is the slowest pulsation which is the most vital. The hero will then know how to wait as well as to make haste. All good abides with him who waiteth wisely.—*Thoreau.*

WALKING.—The art of walking is at once suggestive of the dignity of man. —Progressive motion alone implies power, but in almost every other instance it seems a power gained at the expense of self-possession.—*Tuckerman.*

If you are for a merry jaunt I will try for once who can foot it farthest.—*Dryden.*

The sum of the whole is this: walk and be happy; walk and be healthy.—The best way to lengthen out our days is to walk steadily and with a purpose. —The wandering man knows of certain ancients, far gone in years, who have staved off infirmities and dissolution by earnest walking—hale fellows, close upon ninety, but brisk as boys.—*Dickens.*

WANTS.—It is not from nature, but from education and habits, that our wants are chiefly derived.—*Fielding.*

We are ruined, not by what we really want, but by what we think we do; therefore, never go abroad in search of your wants: for if they be real wants they will come in search of you. He that buys what he does not want, will soon want what he cannot buy.—*Colton.*

Hundreds would never have known want if they had not at first known waste.—*Spurgeon.*

I do not understand those to be poor and in want, who are vagabonds and beggars, but such as are old and cannot travel, such poor widows and fatherless children as are ordered to be relieved, and the poor tenants that travail to pay their rents and are driven to poverty by mischance, and not by riot or careless expenses; on such have thou compassion, and God will bless thee for it.—*Sir W. Raleigh.*

Wants awaken intellect. To gratify them disciplines intellect. The keener the want, the lustier the growth.—*Wendell Phillips.*

Great wants proceed from great wealth, but they are undutiful children, for they sink wealth down to poverty.—*Home.*

The fewer our wants, the nearer we resemble the gods.—*Socrates.*

The wants of women are an unknown quantity.—*A. Rhodes.*

Of all the enemies of idleness, want is the most formidable. Want always struggles against idleness; but want herself is often overcome, and every hour shows some who had rather live in ease than in plenty.—*Johnson.*

How few are our real wants!—How easy it is to satisfy them!—Our imaginary ones are boundless and insatiable.

He can feel no little wants who is in pursuit of grandeur.—*Lavater.*

To men pressed by their wants all change is ever welcome.—*Ben Jonson.*

If any one say that he has seen a just man in want of bread, I answer that it was in some place where there was no other just man.—*S. Clement.*

The relief that is afforded to mere want, as want, tends to increase that want.—*Whately.*

Choose rather to want less, than to have more.—*Thomas à Kempis.*

Human life is a constant want and ought to be a constant prayer.—*S. Osgood.*

Every one is poorer in proportion as he has more wants, and counts not what he has, but wishes only for what he has not.—*Manilius.*

The stoical scheme of supplying our wants by lopping off our desires, is like cutting off our feet when we want shoes. —*Swift.*

WAR.—War! that mad game the world so loves to play.—*Swift.*

He who makes war his profession cannot be otherwise than vicious.—War makes thieves, and peace brings them to the gallows.—*Machiavelli.*

There never was a good war, or a bad peace.—*Franklin.*

When wars do come, they fall upon the many, the producing class, who are the sufferers.—*U. S. Grant.*

A great war leaves the country with three armies—an army of cripples, an army of mourners, and an army of thieves.—*German Proverb.*

If war has its chivalry and its pageantry, it has also its hideousness and its demoniac woe. Bullets respect not beauty. They tear out the eye, and shatter the jaw, and rend the cheek.—*J. S. C. Abbott.*

The practices of war are so hateful to God, that were not his mercies infinite, it were in vain for those of that profession to hope for any portion of them. —*Sir W. Raleigh.*

War is the business of barbarians.—*Napoleon.*

Men who have nice notions of religion have no business to be soldiers.—*Wellington.*

War is a profession by which a man cannot live honorably; an employment by which the soldier, if he would reap any profit, is obliged to be false, rapacious, and cruel.—*Machiavelli.*

I am of opinion that, unless you could bray Christianity in a mortar, and mould it into a new paste, there is no possibility of a holy war.—*Bacon.*

All the talk of history is of nothing almost but fighting and killing, and the honor and renown which are bestowed on conquerors, who, for the most part, are mere butchers of mankind, mislead growing youth, who, by these means, come to think slaughter the most laudable business of mankind, and the most heroic of virtues.—*Locke.*

The greatest curse that can be entailed on mankind is a state of war. All the atrocious crimes committed in years of peace, all that is spent in peace by the secret corruptions, or by the thoughtless extravagance of nations, are mere trifles compared with the gigantic evils which stalk over this world in a state of war. God is forgotten in war; every principle of Christianity is trampled upon.—*Sydney Smith.*

War is nothing less than a temporary repeal of the principles of virtue. It is a system out of which almost all the virtues are excluded, and in which nearly all the vices are included.—*Robert Hall.*

The chief evil of war is more evil. War is the concentration of all human crimes. Here is its distinguishing, accursed brand. Under its standard gather violence, malignity, rage, fraud, perfidy, rapacity, and lust. If it only slew man, it would do little. It turns man into a beast of prey.—*Channing.*

Who has ever told the evils and the curses and the crimes of war? Who can describe the horrors of the carnage of battle? Who can portray the fiendish passions which reign there! If there is anything in which earth, more than any other, resembles hell, it is its wars.—*Albert Barnes.*

We cannot make a more lively representation and emblem to ourselves of hell, than by the view of a kingdom in war.—*Clarendon.*

War is an instrument entirely inefficient toward redressing wrong; and multiplies, instead of indemnifying losses. —*Jefferson.*

Of all the evils to public liberty, war is perhaps the most to be dreaded, because it comprises and develops every other. War is the parent of armies; from these proceed debts and taxes. And armies, and debts, and taxes, are the known instruments for bringing the many under the dominion of the few. In war, too, the discretionary power of the executive is extended; its influenc in dealing out offices, honors, and emoluments is multiplied; and all the means of seducing the minds are added to those of subduing the force of the people! No nation could preserve its freedom in the midst of continual warfare.—*Madison.*

Rash, fruitless war, from wanton glory waged, is only splendid murder.—*Thomson.*

The next dreadful thing to a battle lost is a battle won.—*Wellington.*

Let the gulled fool the toils of war pursue, where bleed the many to enrich the few.—*Shenstone.*

A book glorifying war may be quite as anti-social, and to my mind quite as obscene, as one glorifying illicit love, but it is never suppressed, and seldom publicly denounced.—*J. B. S. Haldane.*

One of the most remarkable things about war, as Thucydides has remarked, is that it takes away your freedom and puts you in a region of necessity. You may choose whether or not to fight, but once fighting, your power of choice is gone.—*Gilbert Murray.*

For Sale—Croix de Guerre, $6.— Classified advertisement in a Sunday paper, October, 1920.

War hath no fury like a non-combatant.—*C. E. Montague.*

We Americans cannot conceive of a war without a moral background. . . . It may now be accepted as a principle that any weak saddle-colored nation that happens to be situated near us and also happens to possess a lot of mahogany or hemp or cocoanuts or gold mines had better look out. We have our moral eye on such people and are likely to introduce American morality at any moment. —*W. E. Woodward.*

If the intellectual has any function in society, it is to preserve a cool and unbiased judgment in the face of all solicitations to passion. . . . During the war, the ordinary virtues, such as thrift, industry, and public spirit, were used to swell the magnitude of the disaster by producing a greater energy in the work of mutual extermination.—*Bertrand Russell.*

If nations could overcome the mutual fear and distrust whose somber shadow is now thrown over the world, and could

meet with confidence and good will to settle their possible differences, they would easily be able to establish a lasting peace.—*Fridtjof Nansen.*

Moral disarmament is to safe-guard the future; material disarmament is to save the present, that there may be a future to safeguard.—*Elihu Root.*

The man who enjoys marching in line and file to the strains of music falls below my contempt; he received his great brain by mistake—the spinal cord would have been amply sufficient.— *Albert Einstein.*

War will disappear, like the dinosaur, when changes in world conditions have destroyed its survival value.—*Robert Andrews Millikan.*

We wake up to find the whole world building competitive trade barriers, just as we found it a few years ago building competitive armaments. We are trying to reduce armaments to preserve the world's solvency. We shall have to reduce competitive trade barriers to preserve the world's sanity. As between the two, trade barriers are more destructive than armaments and more threatening to the peace of the world.—*Owen D. Young.*

It seems perfectly clear to me that we can never make any real progress toward permanent peace so long as we recognize the institution of war as legitimate and clothe it with glory.—*William E. Borah.*

O snap the fife and still the drums and show the monster as she is.— *Richard Le Gallienne.*

Universal peace will be realized, not because man will become better, but because a new order of things, a new science, new economic necessities, will impose peace.—*Anatole France.*

Yes; quaint and curious a war is! You shoot a fellow down you'd treat if met where any bar is, or help to half a crown.—*Thomas Hardy.*

The monk that invented gunpowder did as much to stop war as did all the sermons of his brethren.—*Austin O'Malley.*

There is only one virtue, pugnacity; only one vice, pacifism. That is an essential condition of war.—*G. Bernard Shaw.*

The one distinctive advance in civil society achieved by the Anglo-Saxon world is fairly betokened by the passing away of this notion of a peculiar possession in the way of honor which had to be guarded by arms.—*Norman Angell.*

It is a puzzling fact that international conduct is so often judged by far lower standards than are the acts of individuals. . . . Men who would not think of assaulting another to gain an end—who would indeed suffer great loss, and be proud to suffer it, rather than obtain their rights by such a method—feel that a nation should be ever ready to assert its claims by blows.—*George M. Stratton.*

War comes today as the result of one of three causes: either actual or threatened wrong by one country to another, or suspicion by one country that another intends to do it wrong . . . or, from bitterness of feeling, dependent in no degree whatever upon substantial questions of difference. . . . The least of these three causes of war is actual injustice.—*Elihu Root.*

It is perhaps significant that the adherents of war are more and more justifying it by its past record and reminding us of its ancient origin. . . . The little lad who stoutly defends himself on the school ground may be worthy of much admiration, but if we find him, a dozen years later, the bullying leader of a street-gang . . . our admiration cools amazingly.—*Jane Addams.*

Even toy soldiers should be abolished. We must disarm the nursery!—*Dr. Paulina Luisi.*

It is the business of the church to make my business impossible.—*Earl Haig.*

The war against war is going to be no holiday excursion or camping party. The military feelings are too deeply grounded to abdicate their place among our ideals until better substitutes are offered .than the glory and shame that come to nations as well as individuals from the ups and downs of politics and the vicissitudes of trade.—*William James.*

The difficulty about arguing is that when you get before an audience everybody is in favor of peace. . . . But when it comes to an election the issue as to international peace does not play any part at all.—*William Howard Taft.*

Let us pity and forgive those who urge increased armaments, for "they know not what they do."—*Andrew Carnegie.*

In Flanders fields the poppies blow between the crosses, row on row, that mark our place; and in the sky the larks, still bravely singing, fly scarce heard amid the guns below.—*John McRae.*

I am for anything in this world that keeps the problem of finding a substitute for war in people's minds.—*Ida Tarbell.*

I now know that wars do not end wars.—*Henry Ford.*

What? you have voted a war with such rapidity and such indifference?

Oh! it is a war of no importance, it will cost only eight million dollars.

And men?

The men are included in the eight million dollars.—*Anatole France.*

It is a fearful thing to lead this great peaceful people into war, into the most terrible and disastrous of all wars, civilization itself seeming to be in the balance. But the right is more precious than peace, and we shall fight for the things which we have always carried nearest our hearts—for democracy, for the right of those who submit to authority to have a voice in their own governments, for the rights and liberties of small nations, for a universal dominion of right by such a concert of free peoples as shall bring peace and safety to all nations and make the world itself at last free.—*Woodrow Wilson.*

The old proverb that Beelzebub has to be driven out by Beelzebub is a dangerous one: the use of evil will create more evil, war more hostile feelings, and the use of force more need of force.—*Fridtjof Nansen.*

Militarism and warfare are childish things, if they are not more horrible than anything childish can be. They must become things of the past.—*H. G. Wells.*

As long as war is regarded as wicked it will always have its fascinations. When it is looked upon as vulgar, it will cease to be popular.—*Oscar Wilde.*

To be prepared for war is one of the most effectual ways of preserving peace.—*Washington.*

Success in war, like charity in religion, covers a multitude of sins.—*Napier.*

Dress it as we may, feather it, daub it with gold, huzza it, and sing swaggering songs about it, what is war, nine times out of ten, but murder in uniform?—*Douglas Jerrold.*

Laws are commanded to hold their tongues among arms, and tribunals fall to the ground with the peace they are no longer able to uphold.—*Burke.*

War, which society draws upon itself, is but organized barbarism, an inheritance of the savage state, however disguised or ornamented.—*Louis Napoleon.*

I abominate war as unchristian. I hold it to be the greatest of human crimes, and to involve all others—violence, blood, rapine, fraud—everything that can deform the character, alter the nature, and debase the name of man.—*Lord Brougham.*

Peace is the happy natural state of man; war is corruption and disgrace.—*Thomson.*

War, even in the best state of an army, with all the alleviations of courtesy and honor, with all the correctives of morality and religion, is nevertheless so great an evil, that to engage in it without a clear necessity is a crime of the blackest dye. When the necessity is clear, it then becomes a crime to shrink from it.—*Southey.*

It is only necessary to make war with five things: with the maladies of the body, the ignorances of the mind, with the passions of the body, with the seditions of the city, and the discords of families.—*Pythagoras.*

The life of states is like that of men. The latter have the right of killing in self-defence; the former to make wars for their own preservation.—*Montesquieu.*

WASTE.—Waste not the smallest thing created, for grains of sand make mountains, and atomies infinity. Waste not the smallest time in imbecile infirmity, for well thou knowest that seconds form eternity.—*E. Knight.*

Waste cannot be accurately told, though we are sensible how destructive it is. Economy, on the one hand, by which a certain income is made to maintain a man genteelly; and waste, on the other, by which on the same income another man lives shabbily, cannot be defined. It is a very nice thing; as one man wears his coat out much sooner than another, we cannot tell how.—*Johnson.*

Waste not, want not. Wilful waste makes woful want.

It has always been more difficult for a man to keep than to get; for, in the one case, fortune aids, but in the other, sense is required. Therefore, we often see a person deficient in cleverness rise to wealth; and then, from want of sense, roll head over heels to the bottom.—*Basil.*

WATCHFULNESS.—Wise distrust and constant watchfulness are the parents of safety.

A soul without watchfulness is, like a city without walls, exposed to the inroads of all its enemies.—*Secker.*

We ought not to be careless and indifferent about the future. But as there are goods in life possible to be obtained, and evils capable of being avoided, so we should provide ourselves with proper means to obtain the one and escape the other. Watchfulness and industry are natural virtues, and recommended to us by the conduct even of brute creatures. If we neglect our own interest, we deserve the calamities which come upon us; and have no reason to hope for the compassion of others, when we take no care of ourselves.—*Bp. Conybeare.*

WEAKNESS.—The weakest spot with mankind is where they fancy themselves most wise.—*C. Simmons.*

To excuse our faults on the ground of our weakness is to quiet our fears at the expense of our hopes.

To be weak is miserable, doing or suffering.—*Milton.*

Few men have done more harm than those who have been thought to be able to do the least; and there cannot be a greater error than to believe a man whom we see qualified with too mean parts to do good, to be, therefore, incapable of doing hurt. There is a supply of malice, of pride, of industry, and even of folly, in the weakest, when he sets his heart upon it, that makes a strange progress in wickedness.—*Clarendon.*

The strength of man sinks in the hour

of trial: but there doth live a power that to the battle girdeth the weak.—*Joanna Baillie.*

Weakness is thy excuse, and I believe it; weakness to resist Philistian gold, what murderer, what traitor, parricide, incestuous, sacrilegious, but may plead it? All wickedness is weakness.—*Milton.*

Never mind what a man's virtues are; waste no time in learning them. Fasten at once on his infirmities.—*Bulwer.*

The weak may be joked out of anything but their weakness.—*Zimmermann.*

In all our weaknesses we have one element of strength if we recognize it.— Here, as in other things, knowledge of danger is often the best means of safety. —*E. P. Roe.*

Some of our weaknesses are born in us, others are the result of education; it is a question which of the two gives us most trouble.—*Goethe.*

Men are in general so tricky, so envious, and so cruel, that when we find one who is only weak, we are happy.—*Voltaire.*

Delusion and weakness produce not one mischief the less, because they are universal.—*Burke.*

The more weakness, the more falsehood; strength goes straight; every cannon-ball that has in it hollows and holes goes crooked. Weaklings must lie.—*Richter.*

Weaknesses, so called, are nothing more nor less than vice in disguise!—*Lavater.*

Weakness has its hidden resources, as well as strength. There is a degree of folly and meanness, which we cannot calculate upon, and by which we are as much liable to be foiled as by the greatest ability or courage.—*Hazlitt.*

The weak soul, within itself unblest, leans for all pleasure on another's breast. —*Goldsmith.*

WEALTH.—(See " RICHES.")

The wealth of man is the number of things which he loves and blesses, which he is loved and blessed by.—*Carlyle.*

Worldly wealth is the devil's bait; and those whose minds feed upon riches, recede in general from real happiness, in proportion as their stores increase; as the moon, when she is fullest of light, is farthest from the sun.—*Burton.*

Seek not proud wealth; but such as thou mayest get justly, use soberly, distribute cheerfully, and leave contentedly, yet have not any abstract or friarly contempt of it.—*Bacon.*

Wealth is like a viper, which is harmless if a man knows how to take hold of it; but if he does not, it will twine round his hand and bite him.—*St. Clement.*

The way to wealth is as plain as the way to market. It depends chiefly on two words, industry and frugality; that is, waste neither time nor money, but make the best use of both. Without industry and frugality, nothing will do; and with them, everything.—*Franklin.*

Wealth is not of necessity a curse, nor poverty a blessing.—Wholesome and easy abundance is better than either extreme; better for our manhood that we have enough for daily comfort; enough for culture, for hospitality, for Christian charity.—More than this may or may not be a blessing.—Certainly it can be a blessing only by being accepted as a trust.—*R. D. Hitchcock.*

In the age of acorns, a single barleycorn had been of more value to mankind than all the diamonds in the mines of India.

Our wealth is often a snare to ourselves, and always a temptation to others.—*Colton.*

The million covet wealth, but how few dream of its perils! Few are aware of the extent to which it ministers to the baser passions of our nature; of the selfishness it engenders; the arrogance which it feeds; the self-security which it inspires; the damage which it does to all the nobler feelings and holier aspirations of the heart!—*Neale.*

The greatest humbug in the world is the idea that money can make a man happy. I never had any satisfaction with mine until I began to do good with it.—*C. Pratt.*

Prefer loss to the wealth of dishonest gain; the former vexes you for a time; the latter will bring you lasting remorse. —*Chilo.*

Barring some piece of luck I have seen but few men get rich rapidly except by means that would make them writhe to have known in public.—*Warner.*

Men pursue riches under the idea that

their possession will set them at ease and above the world. But the law of association often makes those who begin by loving gold as a servant, finish by becoming its slaves; and independence without wealth is at least as common as wealth without independence.—Colton.

The acquisition of wealth is a work of great labor; its possession a source of continual fear; its loss, of excessive grief. —From the Latin.

The pulpit and the press have many commonplaces denouncing the thirst for wealth; but if men should take these moralists at their word, and leave off aiming to be rich, the moralists would rush to rekindle, at all hazards, this love of power in the people lest civilization should be undone.—Emerson.

An accession of wealth is a dangerous predicament for a man. At first he is stunned if the accession be sudden, and is very humble and very grateful. Then he begins to speak a little louder, people think him more sensible, and soon he thinks himself so.—Cecil.

There are not a few who believe in no God but Mammon, no devil but the absence of gold, no damnation but being poor, and no hell but an empty purse; and not a few of their descendants are living still.—South.

Those who obtain riches by labor, care, and watching, know their value. Those who impart them to sustain and extend knowledge, virtue, and religion, know their use. Those who lose them by accident or fraud know their vanity. And those who experience the difficulties and dangers of preserving them know their perplexities.—C. Simmons.

Gold is worse poison to men's souls, doing more murders in this loathsome world, than any mortal drug.—Shakespeare.

He is richest who is content with the least, for content is the wealth of nature. —Socrates.

People who are arrogant on account of their wealth are about equal to the Laplanders, who measure a man's worth by the number of his reindeer.—Frederika Bremer.

Abundance is a blessing to the wise; the use of riches in discretion lies; learn this, ye men of wealth—a heavy purse in a fool's pocket is a heavy curse.—Cumberland.

There is no security against the perils of wealth except in becoming rich toward God.—C. Simmons.

If you would take your possessions into the life to come, convert them into good deeds.

He that will not permit his wealth to do any good to others while he is living, prevents it from doing any good to himself when he is dead; and by an egotism that is suicidal and has a double edge, cuts himself off from the truest pleasure here and the highest happiness hereafter.—Colton.

As riches and favor forsake a man we discover him to be a fool, but nobody could find it out in his prosperity.— Bruyère.

The gratification of wealth is not found in mere possession or in lavish expenditure, but in its wise application.—Cervantes.

Wealth is not his that has it, but his that enjoys it.—Franklin.

Money and time are the heaviest burdens of life, and the unhappiest of all mortals are those who have more of either than they know how to use.— Johnson.

That plenty should produce either covetousness or prodigality is a perversion of providence; and yet the generality of men are the worse for their riches.—Penn.

To whom can riches give repute, or trust, content, or pleasure, but the good and just?—Pope.

Many a beggar at the cross-way, or gray-haired shepherd on the plain, hath more of the end of all wealth than hundreds who multiply the means.— Tupper.

Wealth may be an excellent thing, for it means power, leisure, and liberty.— J. R. Lowell.

Can wealth give happiness? look round and see—what gay distress! what splendid misery! — whatever fortune lavishly can pour, the mind annihilates, and calls for more.

What real good does an addition to a fortune, already sufficient, procure? Not any. Could the great man, by having his fortune increased, increase also his appetites, then precedence might be attended with real enjoyment.—*Goldsmith.*

Leisure and solitude are the best effect of riches, because the mother of thought. Both are avoided by most rich men, who seek company and business, which are signs of being weary of themselves.— *Sir W. Temple.*

If thou art rich thou art poor; for, like an ass, whose back with ingots bows, thou bearest thy heavy riches but a journey, and death unloads thee. — *Shakespeare.*

There is no society, however free and democratic, where wealth will not create an aristocracy.—*Bulwer.*

In proportion as nations become more corrupt, more disgrace will attach to poverty and more respect to wealth.— *Colton.*

Though hereditary wealth, and the rank which goes with it, are too much idolized by creeping sycophants and the blind abject admirers of power, they are too rashly slighted in shallow speculations of the petulant, assuming, short-sighted coxcombs of philosophy. Some decent regulated pre-eminence, some preference given to birth, is neither unnatural, unjust, nor impolitic.

Riches are gotten with pain, kept with care, and lost with grief. The cares of riches lie heavier upon a good man than the inconveniences of an honest poverty. —*L'Estrange.*

Wealth, after all, is a relative thing, since he that has little, and wants less, is richer than he that has much, and wants more.—*Colton.*

The greatest and the most amiable privilege which the rich enjoy over the poor is that which they exercise the least—the privilege of making them happy.—*Colton.*

Wealth is nothing in itself; it is not useful but when it departs from us; its value is found only in that which it can purchase. As to corporeal enjoyment, money can neither open new avenues of pleasure, nor block up the passages of anguish. Disease and infirmity still continue to torture and enfeeble, perhaps exasperated by luxury, or promoted by softness. With respect to the mind, it has rarely been observed that wealth contributes much to quicken the discernment or elevate the imagination, but

may, by hiring flattery, or laying diligence asleep, confirm error and harden stupidity.—*Johnson.*

When I caution you against becoming a miser, I do not therefore advise you to become a prodigal or a spendthrift.— *Horace.*

It is poor encouragement to toil through life to amass a fortune to ruin your children. In nine cases out of ten, a large fortune is the greatest curse which could be bequeathed to the young and inexperienced.

Let us not envy some men their accumulated riches; their burden would be too heavy for us; we could not sacrifice, as they do, health, quiet, honor, and conscience, to obtain them: it is to pay so dear for them that the bargain is a loss.—*Bruyère.*

The secret of making money is saving it. It is not what a man earns—not the amount of his income, but the relation of his expenditures to his receipts, that determines his poverty or wealth.

It is only when the rich are sick that they fully feel the impotence of wealth. —*Colton.*

The consideration of the small addition often made by wealth to the happiness of the possessor may check the desire and prevent the insatiability which sometimes attends it.

Gross and vulgar minds will always pay a higher respect to wealth than to talent; for wealth, although it be a far less efficient source of power than talent, happens to be far more intelligible.— *Colton.*

He is a great simpleton who imagines that the chief power of wealth is to supply wants. In ninety-nine cases out of a hundred it creates more wants than it supplies.

Excessive wealth is neither glory nor happiness. There is in a fortune a golden mean which is the appropriate region of virtue and intelligence. Be content with that; and if the horn of plenty overflow, let its droppings fall upon your fellow-men; let them fall like the droppings of honey in the wilderness to cheer the faint and weary pilgrim.—*W. Wirt.*

Whosoever shall look heedfully upon those who are eminent for their riches will not think their condition such as that he should hazard his quiet, and much less his virtue, to obtain it; for all that great wealth generally gives above a moderate fortune is more room for the freaks of caprice, and more privilege for ignorance and vice, a quicker succession of flatterers, and a larger circle of voluptuousness.

It is far more easy to acquire a fortune like a knave than to expend it like a gentleman.—*Colton.*

The wealth of a state consists not in great treasures, solid walls, fair palaces, weapons, and armor; but its best and noblest wealth, and its truest safety, is in having learned, wise, honorable, and well-educated citizens.

Wealth consists not in having great possessions, but in having few wants.—*Epicurus.*

The most brilliant fortunes are often not worth the littleness required to gain them.—*Rochefoucauld.*

Very few men acquire wealth in such a manner as to receive pleasure from it. —As long as there is the enthusiasm of the chase they enjoy it.—But when they begin to look around and think of settling down, they find that that part by which joy enters in, is dead in them.— They have spent their lives in heaping up colossal piles of treasure, which stand at the end, like the pyramids in the desert, holding only the dust of things. —*H. W. Beecher.*

Less coin, less care; to know how to dispense with wealth is to possess it.— *Reynolds.*

Wealth is not acquired, as many persons suppose, by fortunate speculations and splendid enterprises, but by the daily practice of industry, frugality, and economy. He who relies upon these means will rarely be found destitute, and he who relies upon any other, will generally become bankrupt.— *Francis Wayland.*

It requires a great deal of boldness and a great deal of caution to make a great fortune; and when you have got it, it requires ten times as much wit to keep it.—*Rothschild.*

To acquire wealth is difficult, to preserve it more difficult, but to spend it wisely most difficult of all.—*E. P. Day.*

A great fortune is a great servitude.— *Seneca.*

When a man dies, the people ask, "what property has he left behind him?" But the angels, as they bend over his grave, inquire, "what good deeds hast thou sent on before thee?" —*Mahomet.*

Wherever there is excessive wealth, there is also in its train excessive poverty, as where the sun is highest, the shade is deepest.—*Landor.*

A statistician says a man stands sixteen chances to be killed by lightning to one of being worth a million of money.

Wealth hath never given happiness, but often hastened misery; enough hath never caused misery, but often quickened happiness.—*Tupper.*

If thou desire to purchase honor with thy wealth, consider first how that wealth became thine; if thy labor got it, let thy wisdom keep it; if oppression found it, let repentance restore it; if thy parent left it, let thy virtues deserve it; so shall thy honor be safer, better, and cheaper.—*Quarles.*

Wealth has seldom been the portion and never the mark to discover good people; but God, who disposeth of all things wisely, hath denied it to many whose minds he has enriched with the greater blessings of knowledge and virtue, as the fairer testimonies of his love to mankind.—*Izaak Walton.*

What a man does with his wealth depends upon his idea of happiness. Those who draw prizes in life are apt to spend tastelessly, if not viciously; not knowing that it requires as much talent to spend as to make.—*E. P. Whipple.*

Wealth has now all the respect paid to it which is due only to virtue and to talent, but we can see what estimate God places upon it, since he often bestows it on the meanest and most unworthy of all his creatures.—*Swift.*

Many men want wealth, not a competence merely, but a five-story competence, and religion they would like as a sort of lightning-rod to their houses, to ward off, by and by, the bolts of divine wrath.—*H. W. Beecher.*

Excess of wealth is cause of covetousness.—*Marlowe.*

Much learning shows how little mortals know; much wealth, how little worldlings can enjoy.—*Young.*

The world is coming, more and more, to the belief that superfluous wealth is a public trust.—*Hewitt.*

A man who possesses wealth possesses power, but it is a power to do evil as well as good.—*A. S. Roe.*

WELCOME.—A tableful of welcome makes scarce one dainty dish.—*Shakespeare.*

'Tis sweet to know there is an eye will mark our coming, and look brighter when we come.—*Byron.*

Small cheer and great welcome make a merry feast.—*Shakespeare.*

Welcome as happy tidings after fears. —*Otway.*

Welcome ever smiles, and farewell goes out sighing.—*Shakespeare.*

Welcome as kindly showers to the long parched earth.—*Dryden.*

Welcome the coming, speed the going guest.—*Pope.*

WELL-DOING.—It is not so much matter what is done, as how it is done, that God minds.—Not how much, but how well.—It is the well-doing that meets with the well-done.—*Venning.*

Work, every hour, paid or unpaid; see only that thou work and thou canst not escape thy reward. Whether thy work be fine or coarse, planting corn, or writing epics, so only it be honest work, done to thine own approbation, it shall earn a reward to the senses, as well as to the thought. The reward of a thing well done, is to have done it.—*Emerson.*

Let no man be sorry he has done good, because others have done evil! If a man has acted right, he has done well, though alone; if wrong, the sanction of all mankind will not justify him. —*Fielding.*

Constant activity in doing good, and endeavoring to make others happy, is one of the surest ways of making ourselves so.

WICKEDNESS.—(See "SIN.")

The disposition to do an evil deed is, of itself, a terrible punishment of the deed it does.—*C. Mildmay.*

Wickedness may well be compared to a bottomless pit, into which it is easier to keep one's self from falling, than, being fallen, to give one's self any stay from falling infinitely.—*Sir P. Sidney.*

They are the same beams that shine and enlighten which are apt to scorch too; and it is impossible for a man engaged in any wicked way, to have a clear understanding of it, and a quiet mind in it altogether.—*South.*

Wickedness is a wonderfully diligent architect of misery, and shame, accompanied with terror, commotion, remorse, and endless perturbation.—*Plutarch.*

To those persons who have vomited out of their souls all remnants of goodness, there rests a certain pride in evil; and having else no shadow of glory left them, they glory to be constant in iniquity.—*Sir P. Sidney.*

Bias, one of the seven wise men, being in a storm with wicked men, who cried mightily to God, "Hold your tongues," said he, "it were better he knew not you were here."

The happiness of the wicked passes away like a torrent.—*Racine.*

The hatred of the wicked is only roused the more from the impossibility of finding any just grounds on which it can rest; and the very consciousness of their own injustice is only a grievance the more against him who is the object of it.—*Rousseau.*

It is a man's own dishonesty, his crimes, his wickedness, and barefaced assurance, that takes away from him soundness of mind; these are the furies, these the flames and firebrands, of the wicked.—*Cicero.*

To see and listen to the wicked is already the beginning of wickedness.— *Confucius.*

What rein can hold licentious wickedness, when down the hill he holds his fierce career?—*Shakespeare.*

Well does Heaven take care that no man secures happiness by crime.—*Alfieri.*

There is no man suddenly either excellently good or extremely wicked; but grows so, either as he holds himself up in virtue, or, lets himself slide to viciousness.—*Sir P. Sidney.*

Combinations of wickedness would overwhelm the world, by the advantage which licentious principles afford, did not those who have long practised perfidy grow faithless to each other.— *Johnson.*

If weakness may excuse, what murderer, what traitor, parricide, incestuous, sacrilegious, but may plead it? All wickedness is weakness; that plea, therefore, with God or man will gain thee no remission.—*Milton.*

If the wicked flourish, and thou suffer, be not discouraged; they are fatted for destruction, thou art dieted for health.—*Fuller.*

Was ever any wicked man free from the stings of a guilty conscience—from a secret dread of the divine displeasure, and of the vengeance of another world?—*Tillotson.*

Wickedness may prosper for a while, but in the long run he that sets all knaves at work will pay them.—*L'Estrange.*

No wickedness proceeds on any grounds of reason.—*Livy.*

There is a method in man's wickedness; it grows up by degrees.—*Beaumont and Fletcher.*

The sure way to wickedness is always through wickedness.—*Seneca.*

There is wickedness in the intention of wickedness, even though it be not perpetrated in the act.—*Cicero.*

I will undertake to explain to any one the final condemnation of the wicked, if he will explain to me the existence of the wicked—if he will explain why God does not cause all those to die in the cradle of whom he foresees that, when they grow up, they will lead a sinful life.—*Whately.*

WIFE.—(See " MARRIAGE.")

A good wife is heaven's last, best gift to man,—his gem of many virtues, his casket of jewels; her voice is sweet music, her smiles his brightest day, her kiss the guardian of his innocence, her arms the pale of his safety, her industry his surest wealth, her economy his safest steward, her lips his faithful counsellors, her bosom the softest pillow of his cares. —*Jeremy Taylor.*

There is one name which I can never utter without a reverence due to the religion which binds earth to heaven—a name cheered, beautified, exalted and hallowed—and that is the name of wife. —*Bulwer.*

Sole partner, and sole part of all my 'oys, dearer thyself than all.—*Milton.*

A faithful wife becomes the truest and tenderest friend, the balm of comfort, and the source of joy; through every various turn of life the same.—*Savage.*

There is nothing upon this earth that can be compared with the faithful attachment of a wife; no creature who, for the object of her love, is so indomitable, so persevering, so ready to suffer and die. Under the most depressing circumstances, woman's weaknesses become a mighty power; her timidity becomes fearless courage; all her shrinking and sinking passes away; and her spirit acquires the firmness of marble—adamantine firmness—when circumstances drive her to put forth all her energy and the inspiration of her affections.—*Daniel Webster.*

A wife's a man's best piece; who till he marries, wants making up: she is the shrine to which nature doth send us forth on pilgrimage; she is the good man's paradise, and the bad's first step to heaven, a treasure which, who wants, cannot be trusted to posterity, nor pay his own debts; she's a golden sentence writ by our Maker, which the angels may discourse of, only men know how to use, and none but devils violate.—*Shirley.*

A light wife doth make a heavy husband.—*Shakespeare.*

It very seldom happens that a man is slow enough in assuming the character of a husband, or a woman quick enough in condescending to that of a wife.—*Addison.*

When a young woman behaves to her parents in a manner particularly tender and respectful, from principle as well as nature, there is nothing good and gentle that may not be expected from her in whatever condition she is placed. Of this I am so thoroughly persuaded, that, were I to advise any friend of mine as to his choice of a wife, I know not whether my first counsel would be, " Look out for one distinguished by her attention and sweetness to her parents." —*Fordyce.*

She is adorned amply, that in her husband's eye looks lovely—the truest mirror that an honest wife can see her beauty in.—*J. Tobin.*

First get an absolute conquest over thyself, and then thou wilt easily govern thy wife.—*Fuller.*

No man knows what the wife of his bosom is—what a ministering angel she is, until he has gone with her through the fiery trials of this world.—*Washington Irving.*

Her pleasures are in the happiness of her family.—*Rousseau.*

A good wife makes the cares of the world sit easy, and adds a sweetness to its pleasures: she is a man's best companion in prosperity, and his best if not only friend in adversity; the most careful preserver of his health, and the kindest attendant on his sickness; a faithful adviser in distress, a comforter in affliction, and a discreet manager of all his domestic affairs.—*L. M. Stretch.*

A wife is essential to great longevity; she is the receptacle of half a man's cares, and two-thirds of his ill-humor.—*Chas. Reade.*

If you would have a good wife marry one who has been a good daughter.

The good wife is none of our dainty dames, who love to appear in a variety of suits every day new; as if a gown, like a stratagem in war, were to be used but once. But our good wife sets up a sail according to the keel of her husband's estate; and, if of high parentage, she doth not so remember what she was by birth, that she forgets what she is by match.—*Fuller.*

Unhappy is the man for whom his own wife has not made all other women sacred.

You are my true and honorable wife, as dear to me, as are the ruddy drops that visit my sad heart.—*Shakespeare.*

O woman! when the good man of the house may return, when the heat and burden of the day is past, do not let him at such time, when he is weary with toil and jaded by discouragement, find upon his coming that the foot which should hasten to meet him is wandering at a distance, that the soft hand which should wipe the sweat from his brow is knocking at the door of other houses. —*Washington Irving.*

Hanging and wiving go by destiny.— *Shakespeare.*

Without our hopes, without our fears, without the home that plighted love endears, without the smiles from plighted beauty won, oh! what were man?—a world without a sun.—*Campbell.*

When it shall please God to bring thee to man's estate, use great providence and circumspection in choosing thy wife. For from thence will spring all thy future good or evil, and it is an action of life like unto a stratagem of war, wherein a man can err but once.— *Sir P. Sidney.*

The wife when danger or dishonor lurks, safest and seemliest by her husband stays, who guards her, or with her the worst endures.—*Milton.*

Nothing can be more touching than to behold a soft and tender female, who has been all weakness and dependence, and alive to every trivial roughness while treading the prosperous paths of life, suddenly rising in mental force to be the comforter and supporter of her husband under misfortune, and abiding with unshrinking firmness the bitterest blast of adversity.—*Washington Irving.*

A woman in a single state may be happy, or may be miserable, but most happy, and most miserable, these are epithets applicable only to the wife.— *Coleridge.*

In the election of a wife, as in a project of war, to err but once is to be undone forever.—*Middleton.*

Why man, she is mine own; and I as rich in having such a jewel, as twenty seas if all their sands were pearl, the water nectar, and the rocks pure gold.— *Shakespeare.*

Of earthly goods, the best is a good wife; a bad, the bitterest curse of human life.—*Simonides.*

Be thou the rainbow to the storms of life; the evening beam that smiles the clouds away, and tints to-morrow with prophetic ray.—*Byron.*

The sum of all that makes a just man happy consists in the well choosing of his wife.—*Massinger.*

I chose my wife, as she did her wedding-gown, for qualities that would wear well.—*Goldsmith.*

For a wife take the daughter of a good mother.—*Fuller.*

To be a man in a true sense is, in the first place and above all things to have a wife.—*Michelet.*

My dear, my better half.—*Sir P. Sidney.*

The highest gift and favor of God is a

pious, kind, godly, and domestic wife, with whom thou mayest live peaceably, and to whom thou mayest intrust all thy possessions, yea, thy body and thy life.—*Luther.*

No man can live piously or die righteously without a wife.—*Richter.*

The death of a man's wife is like cutting down an ancient oak that has long shaded the family mansion. Henceforth the glare of the world, with its cares and vicissitudes, falls upon the widower's heart, and there is nothing to break their force, or shield him from the full weight of misfortune. It is as if his right hand were withered; as if one wing of his angel was broken, and every movement that he made brought him to the ground. His eyes are dimmed and glassy, and when the film of death falls over him, he misses those accustomed tones which might have smoothed his passage to the grave.—*Lamartine.*

Across the threshold led, and every tear kissed off as soon as shed, his house she enters, there to be a light shining within when all without is night; a guardian-angel o'er his life presiding, doubling his pleasure, and his cares dividing!—*Rogers.*

Heaven will not be heaven to me if I do not meet my wife there.—*Andrew Jackson.*

Even in the happiest choice, where favoring heaven has equal love and easy fortune given, think not, the husband gained, that all is done; the prize of happiness must still be won; and, oft, the careless find it to their cost, the lover in the husband may be lost; the graces might, alone, his heart allure; they and the virtues, meeting, must secure.—*Lyttleton.*

The good wife commandeth her husband, in any equal matter, by constantly obeying him.

WILL.—(See "SELF-WILL.")

He wants wit who wants resolved will.—*Shakespeare.*

Great souls have wills; feeble ones have only wishes.—*Chinese Proverb.*

At twenty years of age the will reigns; at thirty, the wit; and at forty, the judgment.—*Gratian.*

The highest obedience in the spiritual life is to be able always, and in all

things, to say, "Not my will, but thine be done."—*Tryon Edwards.*

Remember that your will is likely to be crossed every day, and be prepared for it by asking only for God's will.

Prescribe no positive laws to thy will; for thou mayest be forced to-morrow to drink the same water thou despisest to-day.—*Fuller.*

No action will be considered blameless, unless the will was so, for by the will the act was dictated.—*Seneca.*

In the schools of the wrestling master, when a boy falls he is bidden to get up again, and to go on wrestling day by day till he has acquired strength; and we must do the same, and not after one failure suffer ourselves to be swept along as by a torrent. You need but will, and it is done; but if you relax your efforts you will be ruined; for ruin and recovery are both from within.—*Epictetus.*

The will of man is by his reason swayed.—*Shakespeare.*

God made thee perfect, not immutable! and good he made thee, but to persevere he left it in thy power; ordained thy will by nature free, not overruled by fate inextricable, or strict necessity.—*Milton.*

To commit the execution of a purpose to one who disapproves of the plan of it is to employ but one-third of the man; his heart and his head are against you, you have commanded only his hands.—*Colton.*

We have more power than will; and it is only to exculpate ourselves that we often say that things are impracticable.—*Rochefoucauld.*

Whatever the will commands the whole man must do; the empire of the will over all the faculties being absolutely over-ruling and despotic.—*South.*

There is nothing good or evil save in the will.—*Epictetus.*

In the moral world there is nothing impossible if we can bring a thorough will to do it.—Man can do everything with himself, but he must not attempt to do too much with others.—*W. Humboldt.*

He who has a firm will molds the world to himself.—*Goethe.*

Calmness of will is a sign of grandeur. The vulgar, far from hiding their will, blab their wishes. A single spark of occasion discharges the child of passion into a thousand crackers of desire.—*Lavater.*

The saddest failures in life are those that come from not putting forth the power and will to succeed.—*E. P. Whipple.*

The general of a large army may be defeated, but you cannot defeat the determined mind of a peasant.—*Confucius.*

It is the will that makes the action good or bad.—*Herrick.*

We cannot be held to what is beyond our strength and means; for at times the accomplishment and execution may not be in our power, and indeed there is nothing really in our own power except the will: on this are necessarily based and founded all the principles that regulate the duty of man.—*Montaigne.*

Every man stamps his value on himself. The price we challenge for ourselves is given us by others.—Man is made great or little by his own will.—*Schiller.*

Study the singular benefits and advantages of a will resigned and melted into the will of God.—Such a spirit hath a continual sabbath within itself, and the thoughts are established and at rest.—*Flavel.*

People do not lack strength; they lack will.—*Victor Hugo.*

A good inclination is but the first rude draft of virtue; the finishing strokes are from the will, which, if well-disposed, will by degrees perfect, or if ill-disposed will by the superinduction of evil habits quickly deface it.—*South.*

The despotism of will in ideas is styled plan, project, character, obstinacy; its despotism in desires is called passion.—*Rivarol.*

If the will, which is the law of our nature, were withdrawn from our memory, fancy, understanding, and reason, no other hell for a spiritual being could equal what we should then feel from the anarchy of our powers. It would be conscious madness—a horrid thought!—*Milton.*

To deny the freedom of the will is to make morality impossible.—*Froude.*

In idle wishes fools supinely stay; be

there a will and wisdom finds a way.—*Crabbe.*

" My will, and not thine be done," turned paradise into a desert.—" Not my will, but thine be done," turned the desert into paradise, and made Gethsemane the gate of heaven.—*Pressense.*

If we make God's will our law, then God's promise shall be our support and comfort, and we shall find every burden light, and every duty a joy.—*Tryon Edwards.*

All the grand agencies which the progress of mankind evolves are the aggregate result of countless wills, each of which, thinking merely of its own end, and perhaps fully gaining it, is at the same time enlisted by Providence in the secret service of the world.—*James Martineau.*

" I will " is no word for man.—There is a far diviner one, " I ought."—Bow passion to reason, reason to conscience, and conscience to God, and then be as resolute and determined as you choose.—*Maclaren.*

Do God's will as if it were thy will, and he will accomplish thy will as if it were his own.—*Rabbi Gamaliel.*

To will what God wills is the only science that gives us rest.—*Longfellow.*

Let a man begin with an earnest " I ought," and if he perseveres, by God's grace he will end in the free blessedness of " I will." Let him force himself to abound in small acts of duty, and he will, by and by, find them the joyous habit of his soul.—*F. W. Robertson.*

WILLS.—There are two things in which men, in other things wise enough, do usually miscarry; in putting off the making of their wills and their repentance till it be too late.—*Tillotson.*

He that defers his charity until he is dead is, if a man weighs it rightly, rather liberal of another man's goods than his own.—*Bacon.*

Those who give not till they die show that they would not then if they could keep it any longer.—*Bp. Hall.*

What you leave at your death let it be without controversy, else the lawyers will be your heirs.—*F. Osborn.*

Generosity during life is a very different thing from generosity in the hour of death; one proceeds from genuine liberality and benevolence; the other from pride or fear, or from the fact that you cannot take your money with you to the other world.

You give me nothing during your life, but you promise to provide for me at your death. If you are not a fool, you know what you make me wish for.—*Martial.*

What thou givest after thy death, remember that thou givest it to a stranger, and most times to an enemy; for he that shall marry thy wife will despise thee, thy memory and thine, and shall possess the quiet of thy labors, the fruit which thou hast planted, enjoy thy love, and spend with joy and ease what thou hast spared and gotten with care and travail.—*Sir W. Raleigh.*

Posthumous charities are the very essence of selfishness, when bequeathed by those who, when alive, would part with nothing.—*Colton.*

If rich men would remember that shrouds have no pockets, they would, while living, share their wealth with their children, and give for the good of others, and so know the highest pleasure wealth can give.—*Tryon Edwards.*

It is but a mean and miserly spirit that for a lifetime keeps wealth only to self, and so leaves children to the struggles of the world without the help that might aid them to comfort and success.

WIND.—The gentle wind, a sweet and passionate wooer, kisses the blushing leaf.—*Longfellow.*

A wailing, rushing sound, which shook the walls as though a giant's hand were on them; then a hoarse roar, as if the sea had risen; then such a whirl and tumult that the air seemed mad; and then, with a lengthened howl, the waves of wind swept on.—*Dickens.*

Perhaps the wind wails so in winter for the summer's dead; and all sad sounds are nature's funeral cries for what has been and is not.—*George Eliot.*

God tempers the wind to the shorn lamb.—*Sterne.*

Ill blows the wind that profits nobody. —*Shakespeare.*

Thou wind! which art the unseen similitude of God the Spirit, his most sweet and mightiest sign.—*Bailey.*

There's a strange music in the stirring wind.—*Bowles.*

The sobbing wind is fierce and strong; its cry is like a human wail.—*Susan Coolidge.*

Seas are the fields of combat for the winds, but when they sweep along some flowery coast, their wings move mildly, and their rage is lost.—*Dryden.*

WINE.—(See "DRINKING.")

A vine bears three grapes, the first of pleasure, the second of drunkenness, and the third of repentance.—*Anacharsis.*

Wine heightens indifference into love, love into jealousy, and jealousy into madness. It often turns the good-natured man into an idiot, and the choleric into an assassin. It gives bitterness to resentment, it makes vanity insupportable, and displays every little spot of the soul in its utmost deformity.—*Addison.*

Wine and youth are fire upon fire.—*Fielding.*

As fermenting in a vessel works up to the top whatever it has in the bottom, so wine, in those who have drunk beyond measure, vents the most inward secrets. —*Montaigne.*

There is a devil in every berry of the grape.—*Koran.*

The first glass for myself; the second for my friends; the third for good humor; and the fourth for mine enemies. —*Sir W. Temple.*

What stores of sentiment in that butt of raciest Sherry! What a fund of pensive thought! What suggestions for delicious remembrance! What "aids to reflection" in that Hock of a century old! What sparkling fancies, whirling and foaming, from a stout body of thought in that full and ripe Champagne! What mild and serene philosophy in that Burgundy, ready to shed "its sunset glow" on society and nature! —*Talfourd.*

Wine maketh the hand quivering, the eye watery, the night unquiet, lewd dreams, a stinking breath in the morning, and an utter forgetfulness of all things.—*Pliny.*

Wine has drowned more than the sea. —*Publius Syrus.*

Polished brass is the mirror of the body and wine of the mind.—*Æschylus.*

Wine is a turn-coat; first, a friend; then, a deceiver; then, an enemy.—*Old Proverb.*

Wine is a noble, generous liquor, and we should be humbly thankful for it; but, as I remember, water was made before it.—*John Eliot.*

O thou invisible spirit of wine, if thou hast no name to be known by, let us call thee—Devil! Oh, that men should put an enemy to their mouths, to steal away their brains! that we should, with joy, revel, pleasure, and applause, transform ourselves into beasts!—*Shakespeare.*

The conscious water saw its God, and blushed.—*Crashaw.*

Wine is like anger, for it makes us strong, blind and impatient, and it leads us wrong; the strength is quickly lost; we feel the error long.—*Crabb.*

Wine invents nothing; it only tattles. It lets out all secrets.—*Schiller.*

Ah! sly deceiver; handed o'er and o'er, yet still believed; exulting o'er the wreck of sober vows!—*Armstrong.*

WISDOM.—(See " KNOWLEDGE.")

Common-sense in an uncommon degree is what the world calls wisdom.—*Coleridge.*

What we call wisdom is the result of all the wisdom of past ages.—Our best institutions are like young trees growing upon the roots of the old trunks that have crumbled away.—*H. W. Beecher.*

Wisdom is the name God gives to religion, so telling the world what it will hardly believe, that the two great things which so engross the desire and designs of both the nobler and ignobler sort of mankind, are to be found in religion, viz.: wisdom and pleasure, and that the former is the direct way to the latter, as religion is to both.—*South.*

The Delphic oracle said I was the wisest of all the Greeks. It is because that I alone, of all the Greeks, know that I know nothing.—*Socrates.*

He is wise who knows the sources of knowledge—who knows who has written and where it is to be found.—*A. A. Hodge.*

There is one person that is wiser than anybody, and that is everybody.—*Talleyrand.*

Wisdom for a man's self is, in many branches thereof, a depraved thing; it is the wisdom of rats, that will be sure to leave a house some time before it fall; it is the wisdom of the fox, that thrusts out the badger who digged and made room for him; it is the wisdom of the crocodiles, that shed tears when they would devour.—*Bacon.*

Very few men are wise by their own counsel, or learned by their own teaching; for he that was only taught by himself had a fool to his master.—*Ben Jonson.*

You read of but one wise man, and all that he knew was—that he knew nothing.—*Congreve.*

What is it to be wise?—'Tis but to know how little can be known—to see all others' faults and feel our own.—*Pope.*

Much wisdom often goes with fewest words.—*Sophocles.*

Wisdom is the right use of knowledge. To know is not to be wise. Many men know a great deal, and are all the greater fools for it. There is no fool so great a fool as a knowing fool. But to know how to use knowledge is to have wisdom.—*Spurgeon.*

The wise man is but a clever infant, spelling letters from a hieroglyphical prophetic book, the lexicon of which lies in eternity.—*Carlyle.*

It may be said, almost without qualification, that true wisdom consists in the ready and accurate perception of analogies. Without the former quality, knowledge of the past is uninstructive; without the latter, it is deceptive.—*Whately.*

Wisdom is to the mind what health is to the body.—*Rochefoucauld.*

In an active life is sown the seed of wisdom; but he who reflects not, never reaps; has no harvest from it, but carries the burden of age without the wages of experience; nor knows himself old, but from his infirmities, the parish register, and the contempt of mankind. And age, if it has not esteem, has nothing.—*Young.*

Our chief wisdom consists in knowing our follies and faults, that we may correct them.

True wisdom is a thing very extraordinary. Happy are they that have it: and next to them, not the many that think they have it, but the few that are sensible of their own defects and imperfections, and know that they have it not.—*Tillotson.*

It is as great a point of wisdom to hide ignorance as to discover knowledge, to know what we do not know, as what we do.

God gives men wisdom as he gives them gold; his treasure house is not the mint, but the mine.

A wise man's day is worth a fool's life.—*Arabic.*

The wise man has his foibles, as well as the fool. But the difference between them is, that the foibles of the one are known to himself and concealed from the world; and the foibles of the other are known to the world and concealed from himself.—*J. Mason.*

It is too often seen, that the wiser men are about the things of this world, the less wise they are about the things of the next.—*Gibson.*

No man can be wise on an empty stomach.—*George Eliot.*

Among mortals second thoughts are wisest.—*Euripides.*

Human wisdom makes as ill use of her talent when she exercises it in rescinding from the number and sweetness of those pleasures that are naturally our due, as she employs it favorably and well in artificially disguising and tricking out the ills of life to alleviate the sense of them.—*Montaigne.*

The first consideration a wise man fixeth upon is the great end of his creation; what it is, and wherein it consists; the next is of the most proper means to that end.—*Walker.*

The wise man endeavors to shine in himself; the fool to outshine others. The first is humbled by the sense of his own infirmities, the last is lifted up by the discovery of those which he observes in other men. The wise man considers what he wants, and the fool what he abounds in. The wise man is happy when he gains his own approbation, and the fool when he recommends himself to the applause of those about him.—*Addison.*

A wise man looks upon men as he does on horses; all their caparisons of title, wealth, and place, he considers but as harness.—*Cecil.*

The wisdom of the ignorant somewhat resembles the instinct of animals; it is diffused only in a very narrow sphere, but within the circle it acts with vigor, uniformity, and success.—*Goldsmith.*

The proverbial wisdom of the populace at gates, on roads, and in markets, instructs him who studies man more fully than a thousand rules ostentatiously arranged.—*Lavater.*

There are but two classes of the wise; the men who serve God because they have found him, and the men who seek him because they have found him not. All others may say, "Is there not a lie in my right hand?"—*Cecil.*

The wise man does three things: he abandons the world before it abandons him; prepares his sepulchre before entering it; and does all with the design of pleasing God before entering into his presence.

When a man is made up wholly of the dove, without the least grain of the serpent in his composition, he becomes ridiculous in many circumstances of life, and very often discredits his best actions.—*Addison.*

Wisdom allows nothing to be good that will not be so forever; no man to be happy but he that needs no other happiness than what he has within himself; no man to be great or powerful that is not master of himself.—*Seneca.*

We ought not to judge of men's merits by their qualifications, but by the use they make of them.—*Charron.*

Wisdom prepares for the worst, but folly leaves the worst for the day when it comes.—*Cecil.*

No man is the wiser for his learning; it may administer matter to work in, or objects to work upon; but wit and wisdom are born with a man.—*Selden.*

The wisest man is generally he who thinks himself the least so.—*Boileau.*

He that thinks himself the wisest is generally the greatest fool.—*Colton.*

It is more easy to be wise for others than for ourselves.—*Rochefoucauld.*

The intellect of the wise is like glass; it admits the light of heaven and reflects it.—*Hare.*

Living in an age of extraordinary events and revolutions, I have learned from thence this truth, which I desire might be communicated to posterity: that all is vanity which is not honest, and that there is no solid wisdom but in real piety.—*Evelyn.*

The strongest symptom of wisdom in man is his being sensible of his own follies.—*Rochefoucauld.*

Wisdom does not show itself so much in precept as in life—in firmness of mind and a mastery of appetite. It teaches us to do as well as to talk; and to make our words and actions all of a color.—*Seneca.*

The wise man walks with God, surveys far on the endless line of life; values his soul, thinks of eternity; both worlds considers, and provides for both; with reason's eye his passions guards; abstains from evil; lives on hope—on hope, the fruit of faith; looks upward, purifies his soul, expands his wings, and mounts into the sky; passes the sun, and gains his Father's house, and drinks with angels from the fount of bliss.—*Pollok.*

Perfect wisdom hath four parts, viz., wisdom, the principle of doing things aright; justice, the principle of doing things equally in public and private; fortitude, the principle of not flying danger, but meeting it; and temperance, the principle of subduing desires and living moderately.—*Plato.*

True wisdom is to know what is best worth knowing, and to do what is best worth doing.—*Humphrey.*

Wisdom teaches us to do, as well as talk, and to make our words and actions all of a color.—*Seneca.*

He who learns the rules of wisdom without conforming to them in his life is like a man who ploughs in his field but does not sow.—*Saadi.*

Wisdom without innocency is knavery; innocence without wisdom is foolery; be therefore as wise as serpents and innocent as doves. The subtilty of the serpent instructs the innocency of the dove; the innocency of the dove corrects the subtilty of the serpent. What God hath joined together let not man separate.—*Quarles.*

The wisdom of one generation will be the folly of the next.—*Priestley.*

The wise man is also the just, the pious, the upright, the man who walks in the way of truth. The fear of the Lord, which is the beginning of wisdom, consists in a complete devotion to God.—*Zochler.*

The two powers which in my opinion constitute a wise man are those of bearing and forbearing.—*Epictetus.*

If wisdom were conferred with this proviso, that I must keep it to myself and not communicate it to others, I would have none of it.—*Seneca.*

The first point of wisdom is to discern that which is false; the second, to know that which is true.—*Lactantius.*

Wisdom is ofttimes nearer when we stoop than when we soar.—*Wordsworth.*

The sublimity of wisdom is to do those things living which are to be desired when dying.—*Jeremy Taylor.*

A man's wisdom is his best friend; folly his worst enemy.—*Sir W. Temple.*

In seeking wisdom thou art wise; in imagining that thou hast attained it thou art a fool.—*Rabbi Ben-Azai.*

Human wisdom is the aggregate of all human experience, constantly accumulating, selecting, and reorganizing its own materials.—*Story.*

To know that which before us lies in daily life is the prime wisdom.—*Milton.*

Let me be ignorant, and in nothing good, but graciously to know I am no better; thus wisdom wishes to appear most bright when it doth tax itself.—*Shakespeare.*

WISHES.—(See "DESIRE.")

Wishing—the constant hectic of the fool.—*Young.*

The apparently irreconcilable dissimilarity between our wishes and our means, between our hearts and this world, remains a riddle.—*Richter.*

I respect the man who knows distinctly what he wishes. The greater part of all the mischief in the world arises from the fact that men do not sufficiently understand their own aims. They have undertaken to build a tower, and spend no more labor on the foundation than would be necessary to erect a hut.—*Goethe.*

Wishes run over in loquacious impotence; will presses on with laconic energy.—*Lavater.*

Every wish is like a prayer with God. —*E. B. Browning.*

It is a fearful mistake to believe that because our wishes are not accomplished they can do no harm.—*Gertrude.*

Wishes are, at least, the easy pleasures of the poor.

To a resolute mind, wishing to do is the first step toward doing.—But if we do not wish to do a thing it becomes impossible.

It is probable that God punishes the wrong wish as truly as he does the actual performance; for what is performance but a wish perfected with power; and what is a wish but a desire wanting opportunity of action; a desire sticking in the birth, and miscarrying for lack of strength and favorable circumstances to bring it into the world.—*South.*

There is nothing more properly the language of the heart than a wish. It is the thirst and egress of it, after some wanted, but desired object.—*South.*

I could write down twenty cases wherein I wished that God had done otherwise than he did, but which I now see, if I had had my own way, would have led to extensive mischief.—*Cecil.*

Happy the man who early learns the wide chasm that lies between his wishes and his powers!—*Goethe.*

Wishes are the parents of large families, but the children are generally inefficient and useless.—They are the source of idle and vain dreams, and of air castles which have no solid foundation.—The idle wish sends one on a vain journey from which he gains nothing but mental emptiness and discontent with his lot, and it may be, some rebukes of conscience, if it is sharp enough to see his folly.—*Anon.*

What we ardently wish we soon believe.—*Young.*

Men's thoughts are much according to their inclination.—*Bacon.*

Why wish for more?—Wishing of all employments is the worst.—*Young.*

Our wishes are the true touchstone of our estate; such as we wish to be we are. Worldly hearts affect earthly things; spiritual, divine. We cannot better know what we are than by what we would be.—*Bp. Hall.*

WIT.—(See "HUMOR.")

Wit consists in assembling, and putting together with quickness, ideas in which can be found resemblance and congruity, by which to make up pleasant pictures and agreeable visions in the fancy.—*Locke.*

Wit is not leveled so much at the muscles as at the heart; and the latter will sometimes smile when there is not a single wrinkle on the cheek.—*Lyttleton.*

Wit is brushwood; judgment, timber; the one gives the greatest flame, and the other yields the most durable heat; and both meeting make the best fire.—*Overlung.*

Wit is proper and commendable when it enlightens the intellect by good sense, conveyed in jocular expression; when it infringes neither on religion, charity, and justice, nor on peace; when it maintains good humor, sweetens conversation, and makes the endearments of society more captivating; when it exposes what is vile and base to contempt; when it reclaims the vicious, and laughs them into virtue; when it answers what is below refutation; when it replies to obloquy; when it counterbalances the fashion of error and vice, playing off their own weapons of ridicule against them; when it adorns truth; when it follows great examples; when it is not used upon subjects, improper for it, or in a manner unbecoming, in measure intemperate, at an undue season or to a dangerous end.—*Barrow.*

Less judgment than wit, is more sail than ballast. Yet it must be confessed, that wit gives an edge to sense, and recommends it extremely.—*Penn.*

Let your wit rather serve you for a buckler to defend yourself, by a handsome reply, than the sword to wound others, though with never so facetious a reproach, remembering that a word cuts deeper than a sharper weapon, and the wound it makes is longer curing.—*Osborn.*

Be rather wise than witty, for much wit hath commonly much froth, and it is hard to jest and not sometimes jeer too, which many times sinks deeper than was intended or expected, and what was designed for mirth ends in sadness.—*C. Trenchild.*

Where judgment has wit to express it, there is the best orator.—*Penn.*

Some people seem born with a head in which the thin partition that divides

great wit from folly is wanting.—
Southey.

Wit loses its respect with the good,
when seen in company with malice; and
to smile at the jest which places a thorn
in another's breast, is to become a principal in the mischief.—*Sheridan.*

To place wit above sense is to place
superfluity above utility.—*Mad. de
Maintenon.*

Punning is a conceit arising from the
use of two words that agree in the
sound, but differ in the sense. The only
way, therefore, to try a piece of wit, is
to translate it into a different language;
if it bears the test, you may pronounce
it true; but if it vanishes in the experiment, you may conclude it to have been
a pun.—*Addison.*

Wit should be used as a shield for defence rather than as a sword to wound
others.—*Fuller.*

Witticisms are never agreeable when
they are injurious to others.

Wit is the most rascally, contemptible,
beggarly thing on the face of the earth.
—*Murphy.*

When wit transgresses decency, it degenerates into insolence and impiety.—
Tillotson.

Great wits to madness sure are near
allied, and thin partitions do their
bounds divide.—*Dryden.*

As it is the characteristic of great wits
to say much in few words, so small wits
seem to have the gift of speaking much
and saying nothing.—*Rochefoucauld.*

Wit is the salt of conversation, not
the food.—*Hazlitt.*

The impromptu reply is precisely the
touchstone of the man of wit.—*Molière.*

Genuine and innocent wit is surely the
flavor of the mind. Man could not direct his way by plain reason, and support his life by tasteless food; but God
has given us wit, and flavor, and brightness, and laughter, and perfumes, to enliven the days of man's pilgrimage, and
to charm his pained steps over the burning marl.—*Sydney Smith.*

It is by vivacity and wit that man
shines in company; but trite jokes and
loud laughter reduce him to a buffoon.
—*Chesterfield.*

Perpetual aiming at wit is a very bad
part of conversation. It is done to
support a character; it generally fails;
it is a sort of insult to the company, and
a restraint upon the speaker.—*Swift.*

Though wit be very useful, yet unless
a wise man has the keeping of it, that
knows when, where, and how to apply
it, it is like wild-fire, that runs hissing
about, and blows up everything that
comes in its way.—*Walter Scott.*

I like that wit whose fittest symbol
is the playful pinch which a father gives
to the cheek of his roguish boy or the
pretended bite which a mother prints
upon the tempting, snowy shoulder of
her babe.—*D. G. Mitchell.*

He who has provoked the shaft of
wit, cannot complain that he smarts
from it.—*Johnson.*

There are heads sometimes so little,
that there is no room for wit, sometimes
so long that there is no wit for so much
room.—*Fuller.*

WOMAN.—A beautiful and chaste
woman is the perfect workmanship of
God, the true glory of angels, the rare
mircle of earth, and the sole wonder of
the world.—*Hermes.*

The finest compliment that can be
paid to a woman of sense is to address
her as such.

Next to God we are indebted to
women, first for life itself, and then for
making it worth having.—*Bovee.*

Contact with a high-minded woman is
good for the life of any man.—*Henry
Vincent.*

Women have more strength in their
looks, than we have in our laws; and
more power by their tears, than we have
by our arguments.—*Saville.*

Kindness in women, not their beauteous looks, shall win my love.—*Shakespeare.*

O woman! in our hours of ease, uncertain, coy, and hard to please, and
variable as the shade, by the light
quivering aspen made; when pain and
anguish wring the brow, a ministering
angel thou.—*Walter Scott.*

There is nothing by which I have
through life more profited, than by the
just observations, the good opinions, and
sincere and gentle encouragement of
amiable and sensible women.—*Sir S.
Romilly.*

He is no true man who ever treats

women with anything but the profoundest respect. She is no true woman who cannot inspire and does not take care to enforce this. Any real rivalry of the sexes is the sheerest folly and most unnatural nonsense.

God has placed the genius of women in their hearts; because the works of this genius are always works of love.—*Lamartine.*

There is one in the world who feels for him who is sad a keener pang than he feels for himself; there is one to whom reflected joy is better than that which comes direct; there is one who rejoices in another's honor, more than in any which is one's own; there is one on whom another's transcendent excellence sheds no beam but that of delight; there is one who hides another's infirmities more faithfully than one's own; there is one who loses all sense of self in the sentiment of kindness, tenderness, and devotion to another; that one is woman.—*Washington Irving.*

There is a woman at the beginning of all great things.—*Lamartine.*

There is something still more to be dreaded than a Jesuit and that is a Jesuitess.—*Eugène Sue.*

Women never truly command, till they have given their promise to obey; and they are never in more danger of being made slaves, than when the men are at their feet.—*Farquhar.*

Men at most differ as heaven and earth; but women, worst and best, as heaven and hell.—*Tennyson.*

To the disgrace of men it is seen, that there are women both more wise to judge what evil is expected, and more constant to bear it when it is happened. —*Sir P. Sidney.*

The buckling on of the knight's armor by his lady's hand was not a mere caprice of romantic fashion. It is the type of an eternal truth that the soul's armor is never well set to the heart unless a woman's hand has braced it, and it is only when she braces it loosely that the honor of manhood fails.—*Ruskin.*

A good and true woman is said to resemble a Cremona fiddle—age but increases its worth and sweetens its tone.— *O. W. Holmes.*

The single woman's part in life may be a noble one; she may elevate herself and help others, but her's must always be a second place.—She is never fulfilling the part nature intended her to fulfil; but the wife and mother is the crowned queen.—*Mrs. H. R. Haweis.*

The most dangerous acquaintance a married woman can make is the female confidante.—*Mad. Deluzy.*

Contact with a high-minded woman is good for the life of any man.—*Henry Vincent.*

A handsome woman is a jewel; a good woman is a treasure.—*Saadi.*

Nearly every folly committed by woman is born of the stupidity or evil influence of man.—*Michelet.*

The dignity of woman consists in being unknown to the world.—Her glory is the esteem of her husband; her pleasure the happiness of her family.—*Rousseau.*

Christianity has lifted woman to a new place in the world.—And just in proportion as Christianity has sway, will she rise to a higher dignity in human life.—What she has now, and all she shall have of privileges and true honor, she owes to that gospel which took those qualities which had been counted weak and unworthy, and gave them a divine glory in Christ.—*Herrick Johnson.*

There are three classes into which all old women are divided: first, that dear old soul: second, that old woman; and third, that old witch.—*Coleridge.*

"Woman!" With that word, life's dearest hopes and memories come. Truth, beauty, love, in her adored, and earth's lost paradise restored, in the green bower of home.—*Halleck.*

The greater part of what women write about women is mere sycophancy to man.—*Mad. de Staël.*

The world is the book of women. Whatever knowledge they may possess is more commonly acquired by observation than by reading.—*Rousseau.*

A woman's greatest glory is to be little talked about by men, whether for good or ill.—*Pericles.*

A woman's heart, like the moon, is always changing, but there is always a man in it.—*Punch.*

Woman is quick to recognize genius, and to listen when wisdom speaks.—She may chatter in the presence of fools, but knows and appreciates the value of earnest, sensible men.—*C. H. Dall.*

The intuitions of women are better and readier than those of men; her quick decisions without conscious reasons, are frequently far superior to a man's most careful deductions.—*W. Aikman.*

The deepest tenderness a woman can show to a man, is to help him to do his duty.—*Mulock.*

It is only the nature of their education that puts a woman at such disadvantage, and keeps up the notion that they are our inferiors in ability.—The best sources of knowledge are shut off from them, and the surprise is that they manage to keep so abreast of us as they do.—*Story.*

All men who avoid female society have dull perceptions and are stupid, or else have gross tastes, and revolt against what is pure.—*Thackeray.*

No one knows like a woman how to say things which are at once gentle and deep.—*Victor Hugo.*

There can be no higher ambition for a Christian woman than to be a faithful wife and a happy and influential mother. It is the place which God has given woman, and she who fills it well, is as honorable and honored as the most illustrious man can be.—*C. A. Stoddard.*

A woman has this quality in common with the angels, that those who suffer belong to her.—*Balzac.*

Women famed for their valor, their skill in politics, or their learning, leave the duties of their own sex, in order to invade the privileges of ours. I can no more pardon a fair one for endeavoring to wield the club of Hercules, than I could a man for endeavoring to twirl her distaff.—*Goldsmith.*

Women for the most part do not love us. They do not choose a man because they love him, but because it pleases them to be loved by him. They love love of all things in the world, but there are very few men whom they love personally.—*Alphonse Karr.*

Women are the poetry of the world in the same sense as the stars are the poetry of heaven.—Clear, light-giving, harmonious, they are the terrestrial planets that rule the destinies of mankind.—*Hargrave.*

Women are ever in extremes; they are

either better or worse than men.—*Bruyère.*

One reason why women are forbidden to preach the gospel, is, that they would persuade without argument and reprove without giving offence.—*J. Newton.*

O, what makes women lovely? Virtue, faith, and gentleness in suffering; an endurance through scorn or trial; these call beauty forth, give it the stamp celestial, and admit it to sisterhood with angels.—*Brent.*

Woman is like the reed which bends to every breeze, but breaks not in the tempest.—*Whately.*

Woman was taken out of man; not out of his head to top him, nor out of his feet to be trampled underfoot; but out of his side to be equal to him, under his arm to be protected, and near his heart to be loved.—*M. Henry.*

Women are the books, the arts, the academies, that show, contain, and nourish all the world.—*Shakespeare.*

I have often had occasion to remark the fortitude with which women sustain the most overwhelming reverses of fortune. Those disasters which break down the spirit of a man and prostrate him in the dust seem to call forth all the energies of the softer sex, and give such intrepidity and elevation to their character, that at times it approaches to sublimity.—*Washington Irving.*

'Tis beauty, that doth oft make women proud; 'tis virtue, that doth make them most admired; 'tis modesty, that makes them seem divine.—*Shakespeare.*

Women govern us; let us try to render them more perfect. The more they are enlightened, so much the more we shall be. On the cultivation of the minds of women, depends the wisdom of man.—*Sheridan.*

Virtue, modesty, and truth are the guardian angels of woman.

Women that are the least bashful are not unfrequently the most modest; and we are never more deceived than when we would infer any laxity of principle from that freedom of demeanor which often arises from a total ignorance of vice.—*Colton.*

Men are women's playthings; woman is the devil's.—*Victor Hugo.*

For a silence and a chaste reserve is

woman's genuine praise, and to remain quiet within the house.—*Euripides.*

The best woman has always somewhat of a man's strength; and the noblest man of a woman's gentleness.—*Miss Mulock.*

The happiest women, like the happiest nations, have no history.—*George Eliot.*

Modern woman can not get away from love. She is no new woman.—*Mussolini.*

The thing needed . . . to raise women (and to raise men too) is these friendships without love between men and women. And if between married men and married women, all the better.—*Florence Nightingale.*

A woman is never too old to be touched by the faithfulness of an old lover.—*Evelyn Schuyler Schaeffer.*

They often say woman cannot keep a secret, but every woman in the world, like every man, has a hundred secrets in her own soul which she hides from even herself. The more respectable she is, the more certain it is the secrets exist.—*Austin O'Malley.*

The female of the species is more deadly than the male.—*Rudyard Kipling.*

Woman's love is writ in water, woman's faith is traced in sand.—*Aytoun.*

Of all the men I have known, I cannot recall one whose mother did her level best for him when he was little who did not turn out well when he grew up.—*Frances Parkinson Keyes.*

The position of women has no fixed relation to the general level of culture. It has been higher in the remote past than in recent times, and amongst savages it is by no means uniformly low.—*L. T. Hobhouse.*

I am a woman—therefore I may not call to him, cry to him, fly to him, bid him delay not!—*R. W. Gilder.*

Woman reduces us all to a common denominator.—*G. Bernard Shaw.*

Women are like dogs really. They love like dogs, a little insistently. And they like to fetch and carry and come back wistfully after hard words, and learn rather easily to carry a basket.—*Mary Roberts Rinehart.*

Women are doormats and have been— the years these mats applaud—they keep the men from going in with muddy feet to God.—*Mary Carolyn Davies.*

There are only two kinds of women, the plain and the colored.—*Oscar Wilde.*

The great weakness of women (who seek careers) is that they have never been trained to work like men. I mean trained so from infancy. Men are brought up in the tradition that men must work.—*John B. Watson.*

O Woman, you are not merely the handiwork of God, but also of men; these are ever endowing you with beauty from their own hearts. . . . You are one-half woman and one-half dream.—*Rabindranath Tagore.*

Even if we conclude that women are not innately better than men, yet because woman is fundamentally different from man in some respects, she may continue to do more than her part for the welfare of future generations, though she still retain many of her hardly won liberties.—*E. B. Bourland.*

Modern invention has banished the spinning wheel, and the same law of progress makes the woman of today a different woman from her grandmother. —*Susan B. Anthony.*

'Til we are built like angels, with hammer, and chisel, and pen, we will work for ourselves and a woman, for ever and ever, Amen.—*Rudyard Kipling.*

Women do about all the reading and play-going that is done in America; at least they are responsible for most of the play-going, since men mostly "go along" under their influence. They keep up most of our music, they maintain most of our painting and sculpture, they are the mainstay of our churches, our educational, cultural, and social institutions, they are the arbiters of taste and style for both sexes and in all particulars.—*Henry A. Beers.*

Somebody must be longsuffering and meek. With all their follies and vanities and limitations, it has been the women who have always practiced this negative but essential virtue.—*Corra Harris.*

It is the law of eternal justice that man cannot degrade women without himself falling into degradation; and he cannot raise them without himself becoming better.—*A. Marten.*

Discretion and good nature have been always looked upon as the distinguishing ornaments of female conversation. The woman whose price is above rubies, has no particular in the character given of her by the wise man, more endearing than that " she openeth her mouth with wisdom, and in her tongue is the law of kindness."—*Freeholder.*

Most females will forgive a liberty, rather than a slight; and if any woman were to hang a man for stealing her picture, although it were set in gold, it would be a new case in law; but if he carried off the setting, and left the portrait, I would not answer for his safety. —*Colton.*

A woman too often reasons from her heart; hence two-thirds of her mistakes and her troubles.—*Bulwer.*

Recreation or pleasure is to a woman what the sun is to the flower; if moderately enjoyed, it beautifies, it refreshes, and improves; if immoderately, it withers, deteriorates, and destroys. But the duties of domestic life, exercised, as they must be, in retirement, and calling forth all the sensibilities of the female, are, perhaps, as necessary to the full development of her charms, as the shades and shadows are to the rose; confirming its beauty, and increasing its fragrance. —*Colton.*

The society of women is the element of good manners.—*Goethe.*

As the vine which has long twined its graceful foliage about the oak, and been lifted by it in sunshine, will, when the hardy plant is rifted by the thunderbolt, cling round it with its caressing tendrils, and bind up its shattered boughs, so is it beautifully ordered by Providence that woman, who is the mere dependent and ornament of man in his happier hours, should be his stay and solace when smitten with sudden calamity; winding herself into the rugged recesses of his nature, tenderly supporting the drooping head and binding up the broken heart.—*Washington Irving.*

The foundation of domestic happiness is faith in the virtue of woman.—*Landor.*

Oh, if the loving, closed heart of a good woman should open before a man, how much controlled tenderness, how

many veiled sacrifices and dumb virtues, would he see reposing therein!—*Richter.*

All a woman has to do in this world is contained within the duties of a daughter, a sister, a wife, and a mother. —*Steele.*

The brain women never interest us like the heart women; white roses please less than red.—*O. W. Holmes.*

When I see the elaborate study and ingenuity displayed by women in the pursuit of trifles, I feel no doubt of their capacity for the most herculean undertakings.—*Julia Ward Howe.*

How many women are born too finely organized in sense and soul for the highway they must walk with feet unshod! Life is adjusted to the wants of the stronger sex. There are plenty of torrents to be crossed in its journey; but their stepping-stones are measured by the strides of men, and not of women.— *O. W. Holmes.*

O woman! in ordinary cases so mere a mortal, how in the great and rare events of life dost thou swell into the angel!—*Bulwer.*

Woman's honor is nice as ermine, will not bear a soil.—*Dryden.*

No amount of preaching, exhortation, sympathy, benevolence, will render the condition of our working-women what it should be so long as the kitchen and the needle are subtsantially their only resources.—*Horace Greeley.*

To feel, to love, to suffer, to devote herself will always be the text of the life of a woman.—*Balzac.*

Most men like in women what is most opposite their own characters.—*Fielding.*

I have often thought that the nature of women was inferior to that of men in general, but superior in particular.— *Lord Greville.*

Let a woman once give you a task, and you are hers, heart and soul; all your care and trouble lend new charms to her, for whose sake they were taken. To rescue, to revenge, to instruct or protect a woman is all the same as to love her.—*Richter.*

If thou wouldst please the ladies, thou must endeavor to make them pleased with themselves.—*Fuller.*

Women do act their part when they

do make their ordered houses know them.—*Sheridan Knowles.*

Woman—last at the cross, and earliest at the grave.—*E. S. Barrett.*

Women have more heart and more imagination than men.—*Lamartine.*

O woman! lovely woman! Nature made thee to temper man; we had been brutes without you. Angels are painted fair, to look like you; there is in you all that we believe of heaven—amazing brightness, purity, and truth, eternal joy, and everlasting love.—*Otway.*

She is not made to be the admiration of all, but the happiness of one.—*Burke.*

Even the most refined and polished of men seldom conceal any of the sacrifices they make, or what it costs to make them. This is reserved for women, and is one of the many proofs they give of their superiority in all matters of affection and delicacy.—*Willmott.*

The errors of women spring, almost always, from their faith in the good, or their confidence in the true.—*Balzac.*

Win and wear her if you can.—She is the most delightful of God's creatures—Heaven's best gift—man's joy and pride in prosperity, and his support and comfort in affliction.—*Shelley.*

Women wish to be loved without a why or a wherefore—not because they are pretty or good, or well-bred, or graceful, or intelligent, but because they are themselves.—*Amiel.*

Women are self-denying and uncandid; men are self-indulgent and outspoken; and this is the key to a thousand double misunderstandings, for good women are just as stupid in misunderstanding men as good men are in misunderstanding women.—*Charles Reade.*

Women do not transgress the bounds of decorum so often as men; but when they do they go greater lengths.—*Colton.*

All the reasonings of men are not worth one sentiment of women.—*Voltaire.*

A handsome woman who has the qualities of an agreeable man is the most delicious society in the world. She unites the merit of both sexes. Caprice is in the women the antidote to beauty.—*Bruyère.*

Women's thoughts are ever turned upon appearing amiable to the other sex; they talk and move and smile with a design upon us; every feature of their faces, every part of their dress, is filled with snares and allurements. There would be no such animals as prudes or coquettes in the world were there not such an animal as man.—*Addison.*

The surest way to win the regard of a sensible woman is to treat her intellect with deferential respect—to talk to her as a thinking being.

A woman may be ugly, ill-shaped, wicked, ignorant, silly, and stupid, but hardly ever ridiculous.—*Louis Desnoyers.*

Let men say what they will; according to the experience I have learned, I require in married women the economical virtue above all other virtues.—*Fuller.*

If we would know the political and moral condition of a state, we must ask what rank women hold in it.—Their influence embraces the whole of life.—*A. Marten.*

A man without religion is to be pitied, but a Godless woman is a horror above all things.—*Miss Evans.*

Women have more good sense than men. They have fewer pretensions, are less implicated in theories, and judge of objects more from their immediate and involuntary impressions on the mind, and therefore more truly and naturally.—*Hazlitt.*

A woman's lot is made for her by the love she accepts.—*George Eliot.*

Maids must be wives and mothers to fulfil the entire and holiest end of woman's being.—*Mrs. Kemble.*

He is a fool who thinks by force or skill to turn the current of a woman's will.—*Samuel Tuke.*

Men have sight; women insight.—*Victor Hugo.*

A man only begins to know women as he grows old; and for my part, my idea of their cleverness rises every day.—*Thackeray.*

The future of society is in the hands of mothers; if the world was lost through woman she alone can save it.—*Beaufort.*

Earth has nothing more tender than a woman's heart when it is the abode of piety.—*Luther.*

Most of their faults women owe to us, while we are indebted to them for most of our better qualities.—*C. Lemesle.*

She is no true woman for whom every man may find it in his heart to have a certain gracious and holy and honorable love; and she is not a woman who returns no love, and asks no protection.—*Bartol.*

The test of civilization is the estimate of woman.—*G. W. Curtis.*

The Christian religion alone contemplates the conjugal union in the order of nature; it is the only religion which presents woman to man as a companion; every other abandons, her to him as a slave. To religion alone do women owe the liberty they enjoy; and from the liberty of women that of nations has flowed, accompanied with the proscription of many inhuman usages diffused over other parts of the world; such as slavery, seraglios, and eunuchs.—*Pierre.*

Some are so uncharitable as to think all women bad, and others are so credulous as to believe they are all good. All will grant her corporeal frame more wonderful and more beautiful than man's. And can we think God would put a worse soul into her better body?—*Feltham.*

Honor to women! they twine and weave the roses of heaven into the life of man; it is they that unite us in the fascinating bonds of love; and, concealed in the modest veil of the graces, they cherish carefully the external fire of delicate feeling with holy hands.—*Schiller.*

Purity of heart is the noblest inheritance, and love the fairest ornament of women.—*M. Claudius.*

Love, which is only an episode in the life of a man, is the entire history of woman's life.—*Mad. de Staël.*

Frequently, when doubtful how to act in matters of importance, I have received more useful advice from women than from men.—Women have the understanding of the heart, which is better than that of the head.—*Rogers.*

WONDER.—All wonder is the effect of novelty on ignorance.—*Johnson.*

The man who cannot wonder, who does not habitually wonder and worship, is but a pair of spectacles behind which there is no eye.—*Carlyle.*

It was through the feeling of wonder that men now and at first began to philosophize.—*Aristotle.*

In wonder all philosophy began, in wonder it ends, and admiration fills up the interspace; but the first wonder is the offspring of ignorance, the last is the parent of adoration.—*Coleridge.*

Wonder is involuntary praise.—*Young.*

Wonder, connected with a principle of rational curiosity, is the source of all knowledge and discovery, and it is a principle even of piety; but wonder which ends in wonder, and is satisfied with wonder, is the quality of an idiot.—*Horsley.*

"Wonder," says Aristotle, "is the first cause of philosophy." This is quite as true in the progress of the individual as in that of the concrete mind; and the constant aim of philosophy is to destroy its parent.—*Bulwer.*

WORDS.—Words are the counters of wise men, and the money of fools.—*Hobbes.*

Words should be employed as the means, not as the end; language is the instrument, conviction is the work.—*Sir J. Reynolds.*

Volatility of words is carelessness in actions; words are the wings of actions.—*Lavater.*

The knowledge of words is the gate of scholarship.—*Wilson.*

What you keep by you, you may change and mend; but words, once spoken, can never be recalled.—*Roscommon.*

Words are both better and worse than thoughts; they express them, and add to them; they give them power for good or evil; they start them on an endless flight, for instruction and comfort and blessing, or for injury and sorrow and ruin.—*Tryon Edwards.*

No man has a prosperity so high or firm, but that two or three words can dishearten it; and there is no calamity which right words will not begin to redress.—*Emerson.*

Not in books only, nor yet in oral discourse, but often also in words there are boundless stores of moral and historic truth, and no less of passion and imagination laid up, from which lessons of infinite worth may be derived.—*Whately.*

Seest thou a man that is hasty in his words? there is more hope of a fool than of him.—*Solomon.*

I would rather speak the truth to ten men than blandishments and lying to a million.—Try it, ye who think there is nothing in it; try what it is to speak with God behind you—to speak so as to be only the arrow in the bow which the Almighty draws.—*H. W. Beecher.*

Words are like leaves; and where they most abound, much fruit of sense beneath is rarely found.—*Pope.*

Bad words are as influential as the plague and the pestilence. They have wrought more evil than battle, murder, and sudden death. They creep through the ear into the heart, call up all its bad passions, and tempt it to break God's commandments. A few bad words got into the ear of the mother of mankind, and they led her on to eat the forbidden fruit, and thus to bring death into the world.—*G. Mogridge.*

A good word is an easy obligation; but not to speak ill requires only our silence, which costs us nothing.—*Tillotson.*

You may tame the wild beast; the conflagration of the forest will cease when all the timber and the dry wood are consumed; but you cannot arrest the progress of that cruel word which you uttered carelessly yesterday or this morning.—*F. W. Roberston.*

When words are scarce they're seldom spent in vain.—*Shakespeare.*

Words may be either servants or masters. If the former they may safely guide us in the way of truth.—If the latter they intoxicate the brain and lead into swamps of thought where there is no solid footing.

Among the sources of those innumerable calamities which from age to age have overwhelmed mankind, may be reckoned as one of the principal, the abuse of words.—*Bp. Horne.*

"The last word" is the most dangerous of infernal machines; and husband and wife should no more fight to get it than they would struggle for the possession of a lighted bomb-shell.—*Douglas Jerrold.*

Good words do more than hard speeches, as the sunbeams without any noise will make the traveller cast off his cloak, which all the blustering winds could not do, but only make him bind it closer to him.—*Leighton.*

Words are but the signs and counters of knowledge, and their currency should be strictly regulated by the capital which they represent.—*Colton.*

There are words which sever hearts more than sharp swords; there are words the point of which sting the heart through the course of a whole life.—*Frederika Bremer.*

He who seldom speaks, and with one calm well-timed word can strike dumb the loquacious, is a genius or a hero.—*Lavater.*

Some so speak in exaggerations and superlatives that we need to make a large discount from their statements before we can come at their real meaning.—*Tryon Edwards.*

Such as thy words are, such will thy affections be esteemed; and such will thy deeds be as thy affections; and such thy life as thy deeds.—*Socrates.*

Learn the value of a man's words and expressions, and you know him. Each man has a measure of his own for everything; this he offers you inadvertently in his words. He who has a superlative for everything wants a measure for the great or small.—*Lavater.*

Words, when written, crystallize history; their very structure gives permanence to the unchangeable past.

Men suppose their reason has command over their words; still it happens that words in return exercise authority on reason.—*Bacon.*

A man cannot speak but he judges and reveals himself.—With his will, or against his will, he draws his portrait to the eye of others by every word.—Every opinion reacts on him who utters it.—*Emerson.*

It makes a great difference in the force of a sentence whether a man be behind it or no.—*Emerson.*

It is with a word as with an arrow—once let it loose and it does not return.—*Abd-el-Kader.*

It is a kind of good deed to say well; and yet words are no deeds.—*Shakespeare.*

If you do not wish a man to do a

thing, you had better get him to talk about it; for the more men talk, the more likely they are to do nothing else. —*Carlyle.*

The finest words in the world are only vain sounds, if you cannot comprehend them.—*Anatole France.*

Such little, puny things are words in rhyme: poor feeble loops and strokes as frail as hairs.—*Christopher Morley.*

Don't confound the language of the nation with long-tailed words in *osity* and *ation.*—*J. Hookham Frere.*

A thousand words will not leave so deep an impression as one deed.—*Ibsen.*

He that uses many words for explaining any subject, doth, like the cuttlefish, hide himself in his own ink.—*Ray.*

WORK.—(See "LABOR.")

Concentration is my motto—first honesty, then industry, then concentration. —*Andrew Carnegie.*

I never did anything worth doing by accident, nor did any of my inventions come by accident.—*Thomas A. Edison.*

All one's work might have been better done; but this is the sort of reflection a worker must put aside courageously if he doesn't mean every one of his conceptions to remain for ever a private vision, an evanescent reverie.—*Joseph Conrad.*

There is no truer and more abiding happiness than the knowledge that one is free to go on doing, day by day, the best work one can do, in the kind one likes best, and that this work is absorbed by a steady market and thus supports one's own life. Perfect freedom is reserved for the man who lives by his own work and in that work does what he wants to do.—*R. G. Collingwood.*

Give me love and work—these two only.—*William Morris.*

If a man love the labor of any trade, apart from any question of success or fame, the Gods have called him.— *Robert Louis Stevenson.*

A man is a worker. If he is not that he is nothing.—*Joseph Conrad.*

We are coming to see that there should be no stifling of Labor by Capital, or of Capital by Labor; and also that there should be no stifling of Labor by Labor, or of Capital by Capital.— *John D. Rockefeller, Jr.*

Folks who never do any more than they get paid for, never get paid for any more than they do.—*Elbert Hubbard.*

The greatest asset of any nation is the spirit of its people, and the greatest danger that can menace any nation is the breakdown of that spirit—the will to win and the courage to work.—*George B. Cortelyou.*

I believe in the inherent right of every citizen to employment at a living wage and I pledge my support to whatever measures I may deem necessary for inaugurating self-liquidating public works . . . to provide employment for all surplus labor at all times.—*Franklin D. Roosevelt.*

I believe in work, hard work and long hours of work. Men do not break down from overwork, but from worry and dissipation.—*Charles E. Hughes.*

We have too many people who live without working, and we have altogether too many who work without living.— *Dean Charles R. Brown.*

There are at all times in America about a million men who are without work because they are not able to work, unwilling to take the work offered them or don't want to work. They go to an office or factory seeking work, but secretly hoping and praying that they will not be able to get it.—*James J. Davis.*

He was in love with his work, and he felt the enthusiasm for it which nothing but the work we can do well inspires in us.—*William Dean Howells.*

I like work; it fascinates me. I can sit and look at it for hours.—*Jerome K. Jerome.*

He who would really benefit mankind must reach them through their work.— *Henry Ford.*

The man who does not work for the love of work but only for money is not likely to make money nor to find much fun in life.—*Charles M. Schwab.*

All growth depends upon activity. There is no development physically or intellectually without effort, and effort means work. Work is not a curse; it is the prerogative of intelligence, the only means to manhood, and the measure of civilization.—*Calvin Coolidge.*

St. Edmund of Canterbury was right when he said to somebody, "Work as though you would live forever; but live as though you would die to-day."

Man must work. That is certain as the sun. But he may work grudgingly or he may work gratefully; he may work as a man, or he may work as a machine. There is no work so rude, that he may not exalt it; no work so impassive, that he may not breathe a soul into it; no work so dull that he may not enliven it.—*Henry Giles.*

The force, the mass of character, mind, heart or soul that a man can put into any work, is the most important factor in that work.—*A. P. Peabody.*

The moment a man can really do his work, he becomes speechless about it; all words are idle to him; all theories. Does a bird need to theorize about building its nest, or boast of it when built? All good work is essentially done that way; without hesitation; without difficulty; without boasting.—*Ruskin.*

All men, if they work not as in the great taskmaster's eye, will work wrong, work unhappily for themselves and you. —*Carlyle.*

Work is as much a necessity to man as eating and sleeping.—Even those who do nothing that can be called work still imagine they are doing something. —The world has not a man who is an idler in his own eyes.—*W. Humboldt.*

A nation's welfare depends on its ability to master the world; that on its power of work; and that on its power of thought.—*Theodore Parker.*

Not alone to know, but to act according to thy knowledge, is thy destination, proclaims the voice of thy inmost soul. Not for indolent contemplation and study of thyself, nor for brooding over emotions of piety—no, for action was existence given thee; thy actions, and thy actions alone, determine thy worth.—*Fichte.*

WORLD.—That one vast thought of God which we call the world.—*Bulwer.*

The only true method of action in this world is to be in it, but not of it.—*Mad. Swetchine.*

He that will often place this world and the next before him, and look steadfastly at both, will find the latter constantly growing greater, and the former less to his view.

Knowledge of the world is dearly bought if at the price of moral purity. —*E. Wigglesworth.*

This world is a dream within a dream; and as we grow older, each step is an awakening. The youth awakes, as he thinks, from childhood; the full-grown man despises the pursuits of youth as visionary; and the old man looks on manhood as a feverish dream. Death the last sleep? No! it is the last and final awakening!—*Walter Scott.*

It is a beautiful and a blessed world we live in, and while life lasts, to lose the enjoyment of it is a sin.—*A. W. Chambers.*

The heavens and the earth alike speak of God, and the great natural world is but another Bible, which clasps and binds the written one; for nature and grace are one—grace the heart of the flower, and nature its surrounding petals. —*H. W. Beecher.*

The world is God's epistle to mankind —his thoughts are flashing upon us from every direction.—*Plato.*

Trust not the world, for it never payeth what it promiseth.—*Augustine.*

"The world," is a conventional phrase, which being interpreted, signifies all the rascality in it.—*Dickens.*

The only fence against the world is a thorough knowledge of it.—*Locke.*

A soul disengaged from the world is a heavenly one; and then are we ready for heaven when our heart is there before us.—*John Newton.*

There are many that despise half the world; but if there be any that despise the whole of it, it is because the other half despises them.—*Colton.*

The gratitude of the world is but the expectation of future favors; its happiness, a hard heart and good digestion.— *Walpole.*

All the world's ends, arrangements, changes, disappointments, hopes, and fears, are without meaning, if not seen and estimated by eternity!—*Tryon Edwards.*

Hell is God's justice; heaven is his love; earth, his long-suffering.

We may despise the world, but w̄

cannot do without it.—*Baron Wesenberg.*

The great see the world at one end by flattery, the little at the other end by neglect; the meanness which both discover is the same; but how different, alas! are the mediums through which it is seen?—*Greville.*

You have too much respect upon the world: they lose it that do buy it with much care.—*Shakespeare.*

The world is seldom what it seems; to man, who dimly sees, realities appear as dreams, and dreams realities.—*Moore.*

Thou must content thyself to see the world imperfect as it is. Thou wilt never have any quiet if thou vexest thyself because thou canst not bring mankind to that exact notion of things and rule of life which thou hast formed in thy own mind.—*Fuller.*

The world is a comedy to those who think, a tragedy to those who feel.—*Horace Walpole.*

The world is made up, for the most part, of fools or knaves, both irreconcilable foes to truth: the first being slaves to a blind credulity, which we may properly call bigotry: the last too jealous of that power they have usurped over the folly and ignorance of the others, which the establishment of the empire of reason would destroy.—*Buckingham.*

Contact with the world either breaks or hardens the heart.—*Chamfort.*

We may be pretty certain that persons whom all the world treats ill deserve the treatment they get. The world is a looking-glass, and gives back to every man the reflection of his own face. Frown at it, and it will in turn look sourly upon you; laugh at it and with it, and it is a jolly, kind companion; and so let all young persons take their choice.—*Thackeray.*

The life of the mere votary of the world is, of all others, the most uncomfortable; for that which is his god doth not always favor him, and that which should be, never.

The unrest of this weary world is its unvoiced cry after God.—*Munger.*

I have run the silly rounds of pleasure, and have done with them all. I have enjoyed all the pleasures of the world, and I appraise them at their real worth, which is in truth very low; those who have only seen their outside always overrate them, but I have been behind the scenes, I have seen all the coarse pulleys and dirty ropes which move the gaudy machines, and I have seen and smelt the tallow candles which illuminate the whole decoration, to the astonishment and admiration of the ignorant audience. When I reflect on what I have seen, what I have heard, and what I have done, I can hardly persuade myself that all that frivolous hurry and bustle of pleasure in the world had any reality; but I look upon all that is passed as one of those romantic dreams which opium commonly occasions, and I do by no means desire to repeat the nauseous dose.—*Chesterfield.*

A clear stream reflects all the objects on its shore, but is unsullied by them; so it should be with our hearts; they should show the effect of all earthly objects, but remain unstained by any.

All worldly things are so much without us, and so subject to variety and uncertainty, that they do not make us when they come, nor mend us while they stay, nor undo us when they are taken away.

To understand the world is wiser than to condemn it. To study the world is better than to shun it. To use the world is nobler than to abuse it. To make the world better, lovelier, and happier, is the noblest work of man or woman.

He who imagines he can do without the world deceives himself much; but he who fancies the world cannot do without him is still more mistaken.—*Rochefoucauld.*

The world is a country which nobody ever yet knew by description; one must travel through it one's self to be acquainted with it. The scholar, who in the dust of his closet talks or writes of the world, knows no more of it than that orator did of war, who endeavored to instruct Hannibal in it.—*Chesterfield.*

A good man and a wise man may at times be angry with the world, at times grieved for it; but be sure no man was ever discontented with the world who did his duty in it.—*Southey.*

Crates threw his gold into the sea, saying, "I will destroy thee, lest thou destroy me." If men do not put the love of the world to death, the love of the world will put them to death.—*Venning.*

Oh, what a glory doth this world put on, for him who with a fervent heart goes forth under the bright and glorious sky, and looks on duties well performed, and days well spent.—*Longfellow.*

The created world is but a small parenthesis in eternity, and a short interposition for a time, between such a state of duration as was before it, and may be after it.—*Sir Thomas Browne.*

A man that depends on the riches and honors of this world, forgetting God and the welfare of his soul, is like a little child that holds a fair apple in the hand, of agreeable exterior, promising goodness, but that within is rotten and full of worms.

What is meant by a " knowledge of the world " is simply an acquaintance with the infirmities of men.—*Dickens.*

The world is God's workshop for making men.—*H. W. Beecher.*

God hath not taken all that pains in forming, framing, furnishing, and adorning this world, that they who were made by him to live in it, should despise it; it will be well enough if they do not love it so immoderately as to prefer it before him who made it.—*Clarendon.*

It would be most lamentable if the good things of this world were rendered either more valuable or more lasting; for, despicable as they already are, too many are found eager to purchase them, even at the price of their souls!—*Colton.*

It is not this earth, nor the men who inhabit it, nor the sphere of our legitimate activity, that we may not love; but the way in which the love is given, which constitutes worldliness.—*F. W. Robertson.*

There is such a thing as a worldly, and such a thing as an unworldly spirit. —And according as we partake of the one or the other, the savor of our lives is ordinary, commonplace, poor, and base, or elevating, invigorating, useful, noble, holy.—*A. P. Stanley.*

Buying, possessing, accumulating, this is not worldliness.—But doing this in the love of it, with no love to God para-

mount—doing it so that thoughts of God and eternity are an intrusion—doing it so that one's spirit is secularized in doing it—this is worldliness.—*Herrick Johnson.*

Supposing men were to live forever in this world, I cannot see how it is possible for them to do more toward their establishment here than they do now.—*Bruyère.*

WORSHIP.—We should worship as though the Deity were present. If my mind is not engaged in my worship, it is as though I worshipped not.—*Confucius.*

The tongue blessing God without the heart is but a tinkling cymbal; the heart blessing God without the tongue is sweet but still music; both in concert make their harmony, which fills and delights heaven and earth.—*Venning.*

I have never known a man, who habitually and on principle absented himself from the public worship of God, who did not sooner or later bring sorrow upon himself or his family.—*Bellows.*

The dullest observer must be sensible of the order and serenity prevalent in those households where the occasional exercise of a beautiful form of worship in the morning gives, as it were, the keynote to every temper for the day, and attunes every spirit to harmony.—*Washington Irving.*

A church-going people are apt to be a law-abiding people.—*E. A. Park.*

It is for the sake of man, not of God, that worship and prayers are required; that man may be made better—that he may be confirmed in a proper sense of his dependent state, and acquire those pious and virtuous dispositions in which his highest improvement consists.—*Blair.*

First worship God; he that forgets to pray, bids not himself good-morrow or good-day.—*T. Randolph.*

What greater calamity can fall upon a nation than the loss of worship.—*Carlyle.*

My words fly up, my thoughts remain below: words, without thoughts, never to heaven go.—*Shakespeare.*

It is an axiom of the Christian faith that the mode of worship must correspond to the essence of God, which is spiritual; and the feeling of the worshipper must correspond to the character of God, which is paternal.—*J. P. Thompson.*

Man is a religious being; the heart instinctively seeks for a God. Whether he worships on the banks of the Ganges, prays with his face upturned to the sun, kneels toward Mecca or, regarding all space as a temple, communes with the Heavenly Father according to the Christian creed, man is essentially devout.— *Wm. Jennings Bryan.*

Ritual will always mean throwing away something; *destroying* our corn or wine upon the altar of our gods.—*G. K. Chesterton.*

As the skull of a man grows broader, so do his creeds. And his gods they are shaped in his image and mirror his needs. And he clothes them with thunders and beauty, he clothes them with music and fire, seeing not, as he bows by their altars, that he worships his own desire.—*Don Marquis.*

WORTH.—Worth begets in base minds, envy; in great souls, emulation. —*Fielding.*

Many a man who now lacks shoeleather would wear golden spurs if knighthood were the reward of worth.— *Jerrold.*

One of the most important truths in the world is that there is worth enough in any rascal to cost the spilling of the Precious Blood.—*Austin O'Malley.*

. . . I am not sure that God always knows who are His great men; He is so very careless of what happens to them while they live.—*Mary Austin.*

WRITING.—A writer is dear and necessary for us only in the measure in which he reveals to us the inner working of his soul.—*Leo Tolstoi.*

If I were authorized to address any word directly to our novelists, I should say: Do not trouble yourself about standards or ideals, but try to be faithful and natural. . . .—*William Dean Howells.*

The artist (in literature) appeals to that part of our being which is not dependent on wisdom; to that in us which is a gift and not an acquisition—and, therefore, more permanently enduring. He speaks to our capacity for delight and wonder, to the sense of mystery surrounding our lives; to our sense of pity, and beauty, and pain.—*Joseph Conrad.*

A poem or story, though published in the biggest United States magazine of the newsstand type is not published at all; the fight has to begin all over again if it is to win any place as a "classic," even for a year!—*Vachel Lindsay.*

Art (literature) is not a branch of pedagogy.—*James Branch Cabell.*

For myself I live, live intensely and am fed by life, and my value, whatever it be, is in my own kind of expression of that.—*Henry James.*

Everything which I have created as a poet has had its origin in a frame of mind and a situation in life; I never wrote because I had, as they say, found a good subject.—*Henrik Ibsen.*

The most poignantly personal autobiography of a biographer is the biography he has written of another man. —*George Jean Nathan.*

Of all that is written, I love only what a person hath written with his blood. —*Friedrich Nietzsche.*

It has taken me years of struggle, hard work and research to learn to make one simple gesture, and I know enough about the art of writing to realize that it would take as many years of concentrated effort to write one simple, beautiful sentence.—*Isadora Duncan.*

The psychologist knows that what makes for supreme greatness in writing fiction is not intelligence nearly so much as half a dozen other traits.—*Walter B. Pitkin.*

There seems to be no physical handicap or chance of environment that can hold a real writer down, and there is no luck, no influence, no money that will keep a writer going when she is written out.—*Kathleen Norris.*

Any man who will look into his heart and honestly write what he sees there, will find plenty of readers.—*Ed Howe.*

The writer does the most who gives his reader the most knowledge, and takes from him the least time.—*Sydney Smith.*

Writing is like religion. Every man who feels the call must work out his own salvation.—*George Horace Lorimer.*

WRONG.—No fallacy can hide wrong, no subterfuge cover it so shrewdly but that the All-Seeing One will discover and punish it.—*Rivarol.*

A noble part of every true life is to learn to undo what has been wrongly done.

A man should never be ashamed to own he has been in the wrong, which is but saying in other words that he is wiser to-day than he was yesterday.—*Pope.*

There is no sort of wrong deed of which a man can bear the punishment alone; you can't isolate yourself and say that the evil that is in you shall not spread. Men's lives are as thoroughly blended with each other as the air they breathe; evil spreads as necessarily as disease.—*George Eliot.*

We make ourselves more injuries than are offered to us; they many times pass for wrongs in our own thoughts, that were never meant so by the heart of him that speaketh. The apprehension of wrong hurts more than the sharpest part of the wrong done.—*Feltham.*

Be not familiar with the idea of wrong, for sin in fancy mothers many an ugly fact.

To revenge a wrong is easy, usual, and natural, and, as the world thinks, savors of nobleness of mind; but religion teaches the contrary, and tells us it is better to neglect than to require it.—*J. Beaumont.*

It is vain to trust in wrong; as much of evil, so much of loss, is the formula of human history.—*Theodore Parker.*

To persist in doing wrong extenuates not the wrong, but makes it much more heavy.—*Shakespeare.*

My soul is sick with every day's report of wrong and outrage with which earth is filled.—*Cowper.*

There are few people who are more often in the wrong than those who cannot endure to be so.—*Rochefoucauld.*

Wrong is but falsehood put in practice.—*Landor.*

It is better to suffer wrong than to do it, and happier to be sometimes cheated than not to trust.—*Johnson.*

Y

YEARNINGS.—Ere yet we yearn for what is out of our reach, we are still in the cradle. When wearied out with our yearnings, desire again falls asleep—we are on the death-bed.—*Bulwer.*

So it is that men sigh on, not knowing what the soul wants, but only that it needs something.—Our yearnings are homesicknesses for heaven.—Our sighings are sighings for God, just as children that cry themselves asleep away from home, and sob in their slumber, not knowing that they sob for their parents.—The soul's inarticulate moanings are the affections yearning for the Infinite, and having no one to tell them what it is that ails them.—*H. W. Beecher.*

There is a time in the lives of most of us when, despondent of all joy in an earthly future, and tortured by conflicts between inclination and duty, we transfer all the passion and fervor of our troubled souls to enthusiastic yearnings for the divine love, looking to its mercy, and taking thence the only hopes that can cheer—the only strength that can sustain us.—*Bulwer.*

YOUTH.—Youth is the gay and pleasant spring of life, when joy is stirring in the dancing blood, and nature calls us with a thousand songs to share her general feast.—*Ridgeway.*

Youth is the period of building up in habits, and hopes, and faiths. Not an hour but is trembling with destinies; not a moment, once passed, of which the appointed work can ever be done again, or the neglected blow struck on the cold iron.—*Ruskin.*

Youth is the opportunity to do something and to become somebody.—*T. T. Munger.*

Youth is the season of hope, enterprise, and energy, to a nation as well as an individual.—*W. R. Williams.*

Tell me what are the prevailing sentiments that occupy the minds of your young men, and I will tell you what is to be the character of the next generation.—*Burke.*

Youth, with swift feet, walks onward in the way; the land of joy lies all before his eyes.—*Bulwer.*

Consider what heavy responsibility lies upon you in your youth, to determine, among realities, by what you will be delighted, and, among imaginations, by whose you will be led.—*Ruskin.*

Young men are as apt to think themselves wise enough, as drunken men are to think themselves sober enough. They look upon spirit to be a much better thing than experience, which they call coldness. They are but half mistaken; for though spirit without experience is dangerous, experience without spirit is languid and ineffective.—*Chesterfield.*

The strength and safety of a community consist in the virtue and intelligence of its youth, especially of its young men.—*J. Hawes.*

The follies of youth become the vices of manhood and the disgrace of old age.

The retrospect of youth is often like visiting the grave of a friend whom we have injured, and are prevented by his death from the possibility of making reparation.—*L. E. Landon.*

The greatest part of mankind employ their first years to make their last miserable.—*Bruyère.*

Sad, indeed, is the spectacle of the youth idling away the spring-time of his existence, and not only losing the sweet benefit of time, but wasting, in the formation of evil habits, those hours in which he might clothe himself with angel-like perfection.

Reckless youth makes rueful age.—*Moore.*

Bestow thy youth so that thou mayest have comfort to remember it when it hath forsaken thee, and not sigh and grieve at the account thereof. While thou art young thou wilt think it will never have an end; but the longest day hath its evening, and thou shalt enjoy it but once; it never turns again; use it therefore as the spring-time, which soon departeth, and wherein thou oughtest to plant and sow all provisions for a long and happy life.—*Sir W. Raleigh.*

The excesses of our youth are drafts upon our old age, payable with interest, about thirty years after date.—*Colton.*

He who cares only for himself in youth will be a very niggard in man-

hood, and a wretched miser in old age —*J. Hawes.*

Youth changes its inclinations through heat of blood; old age perseveres in them through the power of habit.—*Rochefoucauld.*

Youthful rashness skips like a hare over the meshes of good counsel.—*Shakespeare.*

If a young man is loose in his principles and habits; if he lives without plan and without object, spending his time in idleness and pleasure, there is more hope of a fool than of him.—*J. Hawes.*

He who spends his younger days in dissipation is mortgaging himself to disease, and poverty, two inexorable creditors, who are certain to foreclose at last and take possession of the premises.

Youth is beautiful. Its friendship is precious. The intercourse with it is a purifying release from the worn and stained hardness of older life.—*N. P. Willis.*

In the morning of our days, when the senses are unworn and tender, when the whole man is awake in every part, and the gloss of novelty is fresh upon all the objects that surround us, how lively at that time are our sensations, but how false and inaccurate the judgments we form of things!—*Burke.*

Youth is a continual intoxication; it is the fever of reason.—*Rochefoucauld.*

As I approve of a youth that has something of the old man in him, so I am no less pleased with an old man that has something of the youth. He that follows this rule may be old in body, but can never be so in mind.—*Cicero.*

Keep true to the dreams of thy youth. —*Schiller.*

Every period of life has its peculiar temptations and dangers. But youth is the time when we are the most likely to be ensnared. This, pre-eminently, is the forming, fixing period, the spring season of disposition and habit; and it is during this season, more than any other, that the character assumes its permanent shape and color, and the young are wont to take their course for time and for eternity.—*J. Hawes.*

Youth no less becomes the light and

careless livery that it wears, than settled age his sables and his weeds, importing health and graveness.—*Shakespeare.*

In general, a man in his younger years does not easily cast off a certain complacent self-conceit, which principally shows itself in despising what he has himself been a little time before.—*Goethe.*

Unless a tree has borne blossoms in spring, you will vainly look for fruit on it in autumn.—*Hare.*

The best rules to form a young man are, to talk little, to hear much, to reflect alone upon what has passed in company, to distrust one's own opinions, and value others' that deserve it.—*Sir W. Temple.*

The heart of youth is reached through the senses; the senses of age are reached through the heart.—*Bretonne.*

It is not easy to surround life with any circumstances in which youth will not be delightful; and I am afraid that, whether married or unmarried, we shall find the vesture of terrestrial existence more heavy and cumbrous the longer it is worn.—*Steele.*

The golden age never leaves the world; it exists still, and shall exist, till love, health, and poetry, are no more—but only for the young.—*Bulwer.*

I love the acquaintance of young people; because, in the first place, I do not like to think myself growing old. In the next place, young acquaintances must last longest, if they do last; and then young men have more virtue than old men; they have more generous sentiments in every respect.—*Johnson.*

Youth, enthusiasm, and tenderness are like the days of spring. Instead of complaining, oh, my heart, of their brief duration, try to enjoy them.—*Ruckert.*

My salad days, when I was green in judgment.—*Shakespeare.*

At almost every step in life we meet with young men from whom we anticipate wonderful things, but of whom, after careful inquiry, we never hear another word. Like certain chintzes, calicoes, and ginghams, they show finely on their first newness, but cannot stand the sun and rain, and assume a very sober aspect after washing-day.—*Hawthorne.*

It is a truth but too well known, that rashness attends youth, as prudence does old age.—*Cicero.*

In the species with which we are best acquainted, namely, our own, I am far, even as an observer of human life, from thinking that youth is its happiest season, much less the only happy one.—*Paley.*

Youth, when thought is speech and speech is truth.—*Walter Scott.*

Youth is not the age of pleasure; we then expect too much, and we are therefore exposed to daily disappointments and mortifications. When we are a little older, and have brought down our wishes to our experience, then we become calm and begin to enjoy ourselves.—*Lord Liverpool.*

Like virgin parchment, capable of any inscription.—*Massinger.*

Oh, the joy of young ideas painted on the mind, in the warm, glowing colors fancy spreads on objects not yet known, when all is new and all is lovely!—*Hannah More.*

The fairest flower in the garden of creation is a young mind, offering and unfolding itself to the influence of divine wisdom, as the heliotrope turns its sweet blossoms to the sun.—*J. E. Smith.*

The self-conceit of the young is the great source of those dangers to which they are exposed.—*Blair.*

The youth of the soul is everlasting, and eternity is youth.—*Richter.*

The morning of life is like the dawn of day, full of purity, of imagery, and harmony.—*Chateaubriand.*

Which of us that is thirty years old has not had his Pompeii? Deep under ashes lies the life of youth—the careless sport, the pleasure and passion, the darling joy.—*Thackeray.*

Hard are life's early steps; and but that youth is buoyant, confident, and strong in hope, men would behold its threshold and despair.—*L. E. Landon.*

Girls we love for what they are; young men for what they promise to be.—*Goethe.*

It is with youth as with plants, from the first fruits they bear we learn what may be expected in future.—*Demophilus.*

Youth ever thinks that good whose goodness or evil he sees not.—*Sir P. Sidney.*

There are no more pitiable objects in the world—and we see them too often in our large cities—than youths who are men only in the follies and vices of manhood. They know everything that is not worth knowing, but of learning, culture, true art, and pure religion they know nothing.—*C. A. Stoddard.*

Youth is not like a new garment, which we can keep fresh and fair by wearing sparingly. Youth, while we have it, we must wear daily, and it will fast wear away.—*J. Foster.*

Youths will never live to age unless they keep themselves in breath by exercise, and in heart by joyfulness. Too much thinking doth consume the spirits; and oft it falls out, that while one thinks too much of doing, he fails to do the effect of his thinking.—*Sir P. Sidney.*

Youth is not rich in time; it may be poor; part with it, as with money, sparingly; pay no moment of it but in purchase of its worth; and what its worth ask deathbeds—they can tell.—*Young.*

The destiny of any nation, at any given time, depends on the opinions of its young men under five-and-twenty.—*Goethe.*

There is no funeral so sad to follow as the funeral of our own youth, which we have been pampering with fond desires, ambitious hopes, and all the bright berries that hang in poisonous clusters over the path of life.—*Landor.*

No one should make a statement like "youth is the happiest time of life" without being prepared to accept its intellectual consequences.—*William Lyon Phelps.*

Adolescence is certainly far from a uniformly pleasant period. Early manhood might be the most glorious time of all were it not that the sheer excess of life and vigor gets a fellow into continual scrapes.—*Don Marquis.*

There is as close a connection between youth and faith as between age and compromise.—*Austin O'Malley.*

The red sweet wine of youth.—*Rupert Brooke.*

For God's sake give me the young man who has brains enough to make a fool of himself.—*Robert Louis Stevenson.*

When we are out of sympathy with the young, then I think our work in this world is over.—*G. Macdonald.*

When will young and inexperienced men learn caution and distrust of themselves.—*Burke.*

It must be an industrious youth that provides against age; he that fools away the one, must either beg or starve in the other.—*Estrange.*

Youth is to all the glad season of life, but often only by what it hopes, not by what it attains or escapes.—*Carlyle.*

I would not waste my spring of youth in idle dalliance; I would plant rich seeds, to blossom in my manhood, and bear fruit when I am old.—*Hillhouse.*

Over the trackless past, somewhere, lie the lost days of our tropic youth.—*Bret Harte.*

What could be more charming than a boy before he has begun to cultivate his intellect? He is beautiful to look at; he gives himself no airs; he understands the meaning of art and literature instinctively; he goes about enjoying his life and making other people enjoy theirs.—*Virginia Woolf.*

Z

ZEAL.—Nothing can be fairer or more noble than the holy fervor of true zeal.—*Molière.*

Zeal is the fire of love, active for duty—burning as it flies.—*Williams.*

Zeal and duty are not slow; but on occasion's firelock watchful wait.—*Milton.*

If our zeal were true and genuine, we should be more angry with a sinner than with a heretic.—*Addison.*

Experience shows that success is due less to ability than to zeal. The winner is he who gives himself to his work, body and soul.—*Charles Buxton.*

People give the name of zeal to their propensity to mischief and violence, though it is not the cause, but their interest that inflames them.—*Montaigne.*

The frenzy of nations is the statesmanship of fate.—*Bulwer.*

I like men who are temperate and moderate in everything. An excessive zeal for that which is good, though it may not be offensive to me, at all events raises my wonder, and leaves me in a difficulty how I should call it.—*Montaigne.*

Zeal is very blind, or badly regulated, when it encroaches upon the rights of others.—*Quesnel.*

All true zeal for God is a zeal also for love, mercy, and goodness.—*R. E. Thompson.*

A zealous soul without meekness, is like a ship in a storm, in danger of wrecks. A meek soul without zeal, is like a ship in a calm, that moves not so fast as it ought.—*J. M. Mason.*

Zeal without knowledge is like expedition to a man in the dark.—*John Newton.*

Zeal for the public good is the characteristic of a man of honor and a gentleman, and must take place of pleasures, profits, and all other private gratifications. Whoever wants this motive, is an open enemy, or an inglorious neuter to mankind, in proportion to the misapplied advantages with which nature and fortune have blessed him.—*Steele.*

Zeal without knowledge is like fire without a grate to contain it; like a sword without a hilt to wield it by; like a high-bred horse without a bridle to guide him. It speaks without thinking, acts without planning, seeks to accomplish a good end without the adoption of becoming means.—*Bate.*

False zeal may rise as high as true, and indeed much higher; because it is extremely apt to estimate its object above its intrinsic and comparative importance. Besides, when a totally selfish heart is awakened into zeal, there is nothing in it to stem the tide of affections, which all unite and harmonize in the ardent pursuit of a selfish end.

True zeal is a strong, steady, uniform, benevolent affection; but false zeal is a strong, desultory, boisterous, selfish passion.—*Emmons.*

Whether zeal or moderation be the point we aim at, let us keep fire out of the one, and frost out of the other.—*Addison.*

Zealous men are ever displaying to you the strength of their belief, while judicious men are showing you the grounds of it.—*Shenstone.*

It is the living, present apprehension of God that makes the Christian zealot, as it made the Jewish.—It is the admixture of ignoble, selfish, narrow or confused notions with that apprehension, which degrades and debases that zeal, and in the end destroys it.—*R. E. Thompson.*

When we see an eager assailant of wrongs, a special reformer, we feel like asking him, What right have you, sir, to your one virtue? Is virtue piecemeal? —*Emerson.*

I have never known a trader in philanthropy who was not wrong in his head or heart, somewhere or other.—*Coleridge.*

'Tis a zealot's faith that blasts the shrines of the false god, but builds no temple to the true.—*Sydney Dobell.*

Zealots have an idol, to which they consecrate themselves high-priests, and deem it holy work to offer sacrifices of whatever is most precious.—*Hawthorne.*

For virtue's self may too much zeal be had; the worst of madness is a saint run mad.—*Pope.*

Violent zeal even for truth has a hundred to one odds to be either petulancy, ambition, or pride.—*Swift.*

Nothing hath wrought more prejudice to religion, or brought more disparagement upon truth, than boisterous and unseasonable zeal.—*Barrow.*

To be furious in religion is to be irreligiously religious.—*Penn.*

RECENT THOUGHT

NOTE: *Many other quotations from recent writers will be found in the body of the work.*

ADVENTURE.—Adventures are an indication of inefficiency. Good explorers don't have them.—*Herbert Spencer Dickey.*

AGE.—You take all the experience and judgment of men over fifty out of the world and there wouldn't be enough left to run it.—*Henry Ford.*

At sixty a man has passed most of the reefs and whirlpools. Excepting only death, he has no enemies left to meet. . . . That man has awakened to a new youth. . . . Ergo, he is young.—*George Luks.*

AMERICA.—The educated American is profoundly skeptical about machines, inclined to regard every invention as obsolescent as soon as it has been made, but naïvely trustful about political platitudes or philosophical half-truths.—*Lord Eustace Percy.*

In America you must live life with a smile, even before your toothbrush has had time to reach your mouth.—*Prince William of Sweden.*

The reason American cities are prosperous is that there is no place to sit down.—*Alfred J. Talley.*

Joy is a fruit that Americans eat green.—*Amando Zegri.*

Americans invent everything, but don't profit by them. They invented the League of Nations but are not in it and cocktails but do not drink them.—*Aristide Briand.*

One of the things that is wrong with America is that everybody who has done anything at all in his own field is expected to be an authority on every subject under the sun.—*Elmer Davis.*

The American may not be a materialist but he has certainly hallowed commercialism, and made of it both a romantic and a moral adventure.—*Agnes Repplier.*

ANARCHISTS.—Every anarchist is a baffled dictator.—*Benito Mussolini.*

ARGUMENT.—Debate is the death of conversation.—*Emil Ludwig.*

People generally quarrel because they cannot argue.—*G. K. Chesterton.*

ART.—Art and life ought to be hurriedly remarried and brought to live together.—*Hugh Walpole.*

There is no such thing as modern art. There is art—and there is advertising.—*Albert Sterner.*

Art, like morality, consists in drawing the line somewhere.—*G. K. Chesterton.*

BEAUTY.—It's a sort of bloom on a woman. If you have it you don't need to have anything else; and if you don't have it, it doesn't much matter what else you have.—*Sir James M. Barrie.*

Who can explain the secret pathos of Nature's loveliness? It is a touch of melancholy inherited from our mother Eve. It is an unconscious memory of the lost Paradise. It is the sense that even if we should find another Eden, we would not be fit to enjoy it perfectly nor stay in it forever.—*Henry Van Dyke.*

BOOKS.—A dose of poison can do its work only once, but a bad book can go on poisoning people's minds for any length of time.—*John Murray.*

Truly each new book is as a ship that bears us away from the fixity of our limitations into the movement and splendor of life's infinite ocean.—*Helen Keller.*

BROADMINDEDNESS. — Broadmindedness is the result of flattening highmindedness out.—*George Saintsbury.*

BUILDING.—Something men have that half-gods never know, the power to sensitize cold, lifeless things; to make stones breathe, and out of metal grow escarpments that deny the need of wings.—*Virginia McCormick.*

BUSINESS.—Business is a combination of war and sport.—*André Maurois.*

A criminal is a person with predatory instincts who has not sufficient capital to form a corporation.—*Howard Scott.*

The "tired business man" is one whose business is usually not a successful one. —*Senator Joseph R. Grundy.*

CAPITAL PUNISHMENT.—The worst use you can put a man to is to kill him.—*Dr. A. D. Rockwell.*

CENSORSHIP.—So many new ideas are at first strange and horrible though ultimately · valuable that a very heavy responsibility rests upon those who would prevent their dissemination.— *J. B. S. Haldane.*

CHARM.—Charm is almost as poor a butter for parsnips as good intentions. —*Heywood Broun.*

CHRISTIANITY.—The modern Christian differs from his grandparents, even from his parents, perhaps, in being a Christian from choice.—*Hanford Henderson.*

CHURCH.—On the boat coming from America a man said to me: "My church is *The* Church." I replied: "Go fill your bath tub with salt water and say, 'This is the ocean.'"—*Gipsy Smith.*

CIVILIZATION.—The origin of civilization is man's determination to do nothing for himself which he can get done for him.—*H. C. Bailey.*

COMMITTEES.—If you want to kill any idea in the world today, get a committee working on it.—*C. F. Kettering.*

COMPLAINING.—We have no more right to put our discordant states of mind into the lives of those around us and rob them of their sunshine and brightness than we have to enter their houses and steal their silver-ware.—*Julia Seton.*

CONCEIT.—Conceit is God's gift to little men.—*Bruce Barton.*

CONTENTMENT.—Contentment is a warm sty for eaters and sleepers.— *Eugene O'Neill.*

CONVERSATION.—Americans cannot realize how many chances for mental improvement they lose by their inveterate habit of keeping up six conversations when there are twelve in the room.—*Ernest Dimnet.*

COOKING.—The intention of every other piece of prose may be discussed and even mistrusted; but the purpose of a cookery book is one and unmistakable. Its object can conceivably be no other than to increase the happiness of mankind.—*Joseph Conrad.*

COST.—Sometimes one pays most for the things one gets for nothing.—*Alfred Einstein.*

COURAGE.—The bravest thing you can do when you are not brave is to profess courage and act accordingly.— *Corra Harris.*

CRIME.—Physical deformity calls forth our charity. But the infinite misfortune of moral deformity calls forth nothing but hatred and vengeance.— *Clarence Darrow.*

CRITICISM.—Half of the secular unrest and dismal, profane sadness of modern society comes from the vain idea that every man is bound to be a critic of life.—*Henry Van Dyke.*

Criticism surprises the soul in the arms of convention.—*George Santayana.*

There are some literary critics . . . who remind me of a gong at a grade crossing clanging loudly and vainly as the train roars by.—*Christopher Morley.*

The good critic is he who recounts the adventures of his soul in the milieu of masterpieces.—*Anatole France.*

The proper function of a critic is to save the tale from the artist who created it.—*D. H. Lawrence.*

DEATH.—Death is not a foe, but an inevitable adventure.—*Sir Oliver Lodge.*

Some people are so afraid to die that they never begin to live.—*Henry van Dyke.*

DEMOCRACY.—The essential problem is how to govern a large-scale world with small-scale local minds.—*Dr. Alfred Zimmern.*

Parliaments, which were originally set up to limit the profligacy of the ruling powers, have by evolution become less apt to limit than to increase expenditures.—*André Tardieu.*

The country still has faith in the rule of the people it's going to elect next. —*Ted Cook.*

Democracy is ever eager for rapid progress, and the only progress which can be rapid is progress down hill.—*Sir James Jeans.*

Democracy has not failed; the intelligence of the race has failed before the problems the race has raised.—*Robert M. Hutchins.*

DEPRESSION.—Depressions may bring people closer to the church—but so do funerals.—*Clarence Darrow.*

The times are not so bad as they seem; they couldn't be.—*Jay Franklin.*

A too exclusive concern with the ideas of little men has brought statesmanship virtually to a standstill. A too exclusive concern with the interests of big men has stalled the economic machine.—*Glenn Frank.*

DICTATORSHIP.—Dictatorship is always merely an aria, never an opera.—*Emil Ludwig.*

DISCIPLINE.—Of course it is essential that the authority of officers in the military service be preserved. That's the reason they have set rules for the method of communication between privates and higher officers. For, believe me, if there were too much rubbing of elbows between officers and men it would soon be discovered that there were many captains who should be in shirt sleeves and many men in shirt sleeves who should be captains.—*Charles G. Dawes.*

DISILLUSIONMENT.—Wisdom comes by disillusionment.—*George Santayana.*

DOLE.—The dole is utterly demoralizing; its chief effect is to turn the unemployed into the unemployable.—*Dean Inge.*

DOUBT.—The heart-breaking hesitation of Lincoln, the troublesome doubts and perplexed questionings, reveal as nothing else could the simple integrity of his nature.—*Vernon Louis Parrington.*

DREAMS.—Never a ship sails out of the bay but carries my heart as a stowaway.—*Roselle Mercier Montgomery.*

So I have nothing? Ah, you're wrong. Why, I have all my dreams—priceless are my riches when my brain with fancy teems.—*Dorothy Snowden.*

DUTY.—Duty has nothing to do with what somebody else conceives to be for the common good—that is, with morality in the derivative sense of the mores of a people.—*Robert Andrews Millikan.*

ECONOMISTS.—Economists have not yet earned the right to be listened to attentively.—*John Maynard Keynes.*

ECONOMY.—Economy is going without something you do want in case you should, some day, want something which you probably won't want.—*Anthony Hope Hawkins.*

EDUCATION.—There is nothing like education for bringing to light, and assessing, the essential inequality between one mind and another.—*Lord Hewart.*

The first thing education teaches you is to walk alone.—*Trader Horn.*

There are obviously two educations. One should teach us how to make a living and the other how to live.—*James Truslow Adams.*

In some small field each child should . . . attain, within the limited range of its experience and observation, the power to draw a justly limited inference from observed facts.—*Charles W. Eliot.*

Science teaching (for children) should begin, not with the mythical body in rest or uniform motion, but with the human body.—*J. B. S. Haldane.*

EFFICIENCY.—It is more than probable that the average man could, with no injury to his health, increase his efficiency fifty per cent.—*Walter Dill Scott.*

EMOTION.—Ride your emotions as the shallop rides the waves; don't get upset among them. There are people who enjoy getting swamped emotionally just as, incredibly, there are people who enjoy getting drunk.—*Mary Austin.*

By starving emotions we become humorless, rigid and stereotyped; by repressing them we become literal, reformatory and holier-than-thou; encouraged, they perfume life; discouraged, they poison it.—*Dr. Joseph Collins.*

EMPLOYEES.—It is an article of faith in my creed to pick the man who does not take himself seriously, but does take his work seriously.—*Michael C. Cahill.*

The employer generally gets the employees he deserves.—*Sir Walter Gilbey.*

ENGLISHMEN.—The typical Englishman is a strong being who takes a cold bath in the morning and talks about it for the rest of the day.—*Ellen Wilkinson.*

ENVIRONMENT.—Complete adaptation to environment means death. The essential point in all response is the desire to control environment.—*John Dewey.*

EUGENICS.—Eugenics is supported by politically-minded scientists and scientifically-minded politicians as an antidote to democracy.—*Bertrand Russell.*

EXECUTIVES.—Executive ability is deciding quickly and getting somebody else to do the work.—*J. G. Pollard.*

EXPERIENCE.—In youth we learn how little we can do for ourselves; in age how little we can do for others. The wisdom of experience is incommunicable.—*Isabel Paterson.*

A prudent person profits from personal experience, a wise one from the experience of others.—*Dr. Joseph Collins.*

FAILURE.—Never give a man up until he has failed at something he likes.—*Lewis E. Lawes.*

FAITH.—You may be deceived if you trust too much, but you will live in torment if you do not trust enough.—*Dr. Frank Crane.*

FAME.—Battles nor song can from oblivion save, but fame upon a white deed loves to build. From out a cup of water Sidney gave not one drop has been spilled.—*Lizette Woodworth Reese.*

FANATICISM.—Fanaticism harkens only to its own counsel, which it believes to be inspired.—*Francis Wilson.*

FARMING.—One of the surpluses that has given us the most trouble has been that of farm leaders.—*Alexander Legge.*

The farther we get away from the land, the greater our insecurity.—*Henry Ford.*

FEAR.—Our instinctive emotions are those that we have inherited from a much more dangerous world, and contain, therefore, a larger proportion of fear than they should.—*Bertrand Russell.*

FREEDOM.—Freedom is not worth having if it does not connote freedom to err.—*Mahatma Gandhi.*

GENERALIZATION.—The narrower the mind, the broader the statement. —*Ted Cook.*

GENIUS.—If we are to have genius we must put up with the inconvenience of genius, a thing the world will never do; it wants geniuses, but would like them just like other people.—*George Moore.*

Genius is one per cent inspiration and ninety-nine per cent perspiration.—*Thomas A. Edison.*

GOVERNMENT.—You can't run a government solely on a business basis. . . . Government should be human. It should have a heart.—*Herbert H. Lehman.*

GREATNESS.—Greatness is so often a courteous synonym for great success. —*Philip Guedalla.*

For he, to whom we had applied our shopman's test of age and worth, was elemental when he died, as he was ancient at his birth: the saddest among kings of earth, bowed with a galling crown, this man met rancor with a cryptic mirth, laconic and Olympian.— *Edwin Arlington Robinson.*

HAPPINESS.—You never see the stock called Happiness quoted on the exchange.—*Henry Van Dyke.*

There is no record in history of a happy philosopher: they exist only in romantic legends.—*H. L. Mencken.*

It is better to desire the things we have than to have the things we desire. —*Henry Van Dyke.*

HATE.—Hate is ravening vulture beaks descending on a place of skulls. —*Amy Lowell.*

Hating people is like burning down your own house to get rid of a rat.— *Rev. Harry Emerson Fosdick.*

HOLLYWOOD.—What I like about Hollywood is that one can get along quite well by knowing two words of English—swell and lousy.—*Vicki Baum.*

HUMOR.—A man isn't poor if he can still laugh.—*Raymond Hitchcock.*

HUSBANDS.—Husbands are awkward things to deal with; even keeping them in hot water will not make them tender.—*Mary Buckley.*

IDEALISM.—Words without actions are the assassins of idealism.—*Herbert Hoover.*

The attainment of an ideal is often the beginning of a disillusion.—*Stanley Baldwin.*

No folly is more costly than the folly of intolerant idealism.—*Winston Churchill.*

No ideal is as good as a fact.—*Dr. Richard C. Cabot.*

IDEAS.—New ideas can be good or bad, just the same as old ones.—*Franklin D. Roosevelt.*

Hang ideas. They are tramps, vagabonds, knocking at the back door of your mind, each taking a little of your substance, each carrying away some crumb of that belief in a few simple notions you must cling to if you want to live decently and would like to die easy.—*Joseph Conrad.*

IGNORANCE.—Any frontal attack on ignorance is bound to fail because the masses are always ready to defend their most precious possession—their ignorance.—*Hendrik Van Loon.*

It is not the crook in modern business that we fear, but the honest man who doesn't know what he is doing.—*Owen D. Young.*

INDIVIDUALITY.—Individuality is either the mark of genius or the reverse. Mediocrity finds safety in standardization.—*Judge Frederick E. Crane.*

IRELAND.—The cup of Ireland's misfortunes has been overflowing for centuries and it is not full yet.—*Sir Boyle Roche.*

JAZZ.—Jazz will endure as long as people hear it through their feet instead of their brains.—*John Philip Sousa.*

KNOWLEDGE.—Knowledge is the eye of desire and can become the pilot of the soul.—*Will Durant.*

I had six honest serving men—They taught me all I knew: Their names were Where and What and When—and Why and How and Who.—*Rudyard Kipling.*

LAW.—In spite of all the cynics say, the infallible way of inducing a sense of wrongdoing is by making laws.—*William Bolitho.*

Laws should be like clothes. They should be made to fit the people they are meant to serve.—*Clarence Darrow.*

The moment you step into the world of facts, you step into the world of limits. You can free things from alien or accidental laws, but not from the laws of their own nature.—*G. K. Chesterton.*

The trouble with law and government is lawyers.—*Clarence Darrow.*

LEISURE.—If the world were not so full of people, and most of them did not have to work so hard, there would be more time for them to get out and lie on the grass, and there would be more grass for them to lie on.—*Don Marquis.*

Leisure, itself the creation of wealth, is incessantly engaged in transmuting wealth into beauty by secreting the surplus energy which flowers in great architecture, great painting and great literature. Only in the atmosphere thus engendered floats that impalpable dust of ideas which is the real culture. A colony of ants or bees will never create a Parthenon.—*Edith Wharton.*

LIBERTY.—Liberty has restraints but no frontiers.—*Lloyd George.*

Liberty is not merely a privilege to be conferred; it is a habit to be acquired. —*Lloyd George.*

LIFE.—One does not expect in this world; one hopes and pays car-fares.—*Josephine Preston Peabody.*

From the point of view of morals, life seems to be divided into two periods: in the first we indulge, in the second we preach.—*Will Durant.*

I don't know a better preparation for life than a love of poetry and a good digestion.—*Zona Gale.*

LITERATURE.—The reason we constantly discover new truth in Shakespeare is that his complete understanding of the particular includes the universal. —*Austin O'Malley.*

I crave for nothing more than to be powerless against the power of your Word.—*Lodewijk van Deijssel.*

Many dead books remain unburied and offend the air simply because we dishonestly pretend that they are alive and kicking.—*Arnold Bennett.*

LONELINESS.—Loneliness is only an opportunity to cut adrift and find yourself.—*Anna Shannon Monroe.*

LOVE.—We owe to the Middle Ages the two worst inventions of humanity—romantic love and gunpowder.—*André Maurois.*

By the time you swear you're his, shivering and sighing, and he vows his passion is infinite, undying—lady, make a note of this: one of you is lying.—*Dorothy Parker.*

MAN.—We either light up with cold, piercing rays of intellect or we burn with passionate flame of emotion. Sometimes, like a coastguard signal, our lamps alternate red and white.—*Grace Thompson Seton.*

Human affairs inspire in noble hearts only two feelings—admiration or pity.—*Anatole France.*

MARRIAGE.—God help the man who won't marry until he finds a perfect woman, and God help him still more if he finds her.—*Ben Tillett.*

In America, England and some other countries, marriage is often delayed for economic reasons. The repression sends thousands of young people to theaters and to the moving picture shows.—*Sergei M. Eisenstein.*

MEMORY.—Memory is a capricious and arbitrary creature. You never can tell what pebble she will pick up from the shore of life to keep among her treasures, or what inconspicuous flower of the field she will preserve as the symbol of "thoughts that do often lie too deep for tears.". . . And yet I do not doubt that the most important things are always the best remembered.—*Henry Van Dyke.*

The past is hidden somewhere outside the realm, beyond the reach of intellect in some material object (in the sensation which that material object will give us) which we do not suspect, and as for that object, it depends upon chance whether we come upon it or not before we ourselves die.—*Marcel Proust.*

MIDDLE AGE.—Of middle age the best that can be said is that a middle-

aged person has likely learned to have a little fun in spite of his troubles.—*Don Marquis.*

MIND.—A man's mind is wont to tell him more than seven watchmen sitting in a tower.—*Rudyard Kipling.*

MISSIONARIES.—I can never have done with my apologies to the Chinese people that in the name of a gentle Christ we have sent such people to them. Preachers who would have bored you beyond endurance you sent cheerfully to the foreign field.—*Pearl S. Buck.*

MODERNITY.—We are in sight of a generation . . . of omniscient babies.—*Bishop of Durham.*

MONEY.—What this country needs is a good five-cent nickel.—*Ed Wynn.*

It's good to have money and the things that money can buy, but it's good, too, to check up once in a while and make sure that you haven't lost the things that money can't buy.—*George Horace Lorimer.*

I see nothing in the life of a rich man which the workman need envy, outside the regularity and security of his existence.—*St. John Ervine.*

MONOTONY.—Monotony is the awful reward of the careful.—*A. G. Buckham.*

MORALITY.—Moral vanity is the snare of good people.—*Margaret Deland.*

The super-businessmen have to a large extent failed to see that the need for morality in the people they practically govern is greater than ever, because social relations are infinitely more delicate and complex in adjustment than heretofore.—*James T. Adams.*

Two points of danger beset mankind; namely, making sin seem either too large or too small.—*Mary Baker Eddy.*

Virtue knows that it is impossible to get on without compromise, and tunes herself, as it were, a trifle sharp to allow for an inevitable fall in playing.—*Samuel Butler.*

NORMALITY.—The only glory most of us have to hope for is the glory of being normal.—*Katherine Fullerton Gerould.*

OPENMINDEDNESS.—Minds are like parachutes. They only function when they are open.—*Lord Thomas Dewar.*

An open mind is all very well in its way, but it ought not to be so open that there is no keeping anything in or out of it. It should be capable of shutting its doors sometimes, or it may be found a little draughty.—*Samuel Butler.*

ORATORY.—All epoch-making revolutionary events have been produced not by the written but by the spoken word. —*Adolf Hitler.*

A hundred years ago our affairs for good or evil were wielded triumphantly by rhetoricians. Now our affairs are hopelessly muddled by strong, silent men.—*G. K. Chesterton.*

PATRIOTISM.—Patriotism is the willingness to kill and be killed for trivial reasons.—*Bertrand Russell.*

PEACE.—Peace is the golden wisp that binds the sheaf of blessings.—*Katherine Lee Bates.*

PESSIMISM.—A pessimist is a man who thinks everybody as nasty as himself, and hates them for it.—*George Bernard Shaw.*

PHILOSOPHY.—Philosophy recovers itself when it ceases to be the device for dealing with the problems of philosophers and becomes the method, cultivated by philosophers, for dealing with the problems of men.—*John Dewey.*

POLITICS.—Bad officials are elected by good citizens who do not vote.—*Chicago Government Poster.*

If you wish the sympathy of broad masses then you must tell them the crudest and most stupid things.—*Adolf Hitler.*

Politics is like a race horse. A good jockey must know how to fall with the least possible damage.—*Edouard Herriot.*

Most statesmen have long noses. But I suppose that is very lucky, because most of them cannot see further than the length of them, so that a statesman with a short nose is handicapped by nature.—*Paul Claudel.*

How a minority, reaching majority, seizing authority, hates a minority.—*L. H. Robbins.*

No quarrel ought ever to be converted into a policy.—*Lloyd George.*

There is no more independence in politics than there is in jail.—*Will Rogers.*

PRIDE.—We can believe almost anything if it be necessary to protect our pride.—*Dr. Douglas A. Thom.*

PROGRESS.—What we call Progress is the exchange of one Nuisance for another Nuisance.—*Havelock Ellis.*

There is no law of progress. Our future is in our own hands, to make or to mar. It will be an uphill fight to the end, and would we have it otherwise? Let no one suppose that evolution will ever exempt us from struggles. "You forget," said the Devil, with a chuckle, "that I have been evolving too."—*Dean Inge.*

PROSPERITY.—Prosperity is only an instrument to be used, not a deity to be worshipped.—*Calvin Coolidge.*

PSYCHOANALYSIS.—A wonderful discovery—psychoanalysis. Makes quite simple people feel they're complex.—*S. N. Behrman.*

PSYCHOLOGY.—Psychology is a rubber stamp pressed upon a slippery, dodging ghost.—*Maxwell Bodenheim.*

PUBLICITY.—I have often wondered if newspaper publicity would not have had thirteen original colonies fighting among themselves if we had been present at their conference at the time of the Revolution.—*William Hard.*

All dead to Shame, and moribund to Mind, Science and Art turn mountebanks and shriek "This way for Beauty! Truth is cheap this week!"—*Lee Wilson Dodd.*

REALISM.—Boys like romantic tales; but babies like realistic tales—because they find them romantic. In fact, a baby is about the only person, I should think, to whom a modern realistic novel could be read without boring him.—*G. K. Chesterton.*

REASON.—The three most important events of human life are equally devoid of reason—birth, marriage and death.—*Austin O'Malley.*

REFORMERS.—Most reformers, like a pair of trousers on a windy clothesline, go through a vast deal of vehement motion, but stay in the same place.—*Austin O'Malley.*

REGRET.—Regret is like a mountain-top from which we survey our dead life, a mountaintop on which we pause and ponder, and very often looking into the twilight we ask ourselves whether it would be well to send a letter or some token.—*George Moore.*

RELIGION.—Religion is the sum of the expansive impulses of a being.—*Havelock Ellis.*

Man will never be entirely willing to give up this world for the next nor the next world for this.—*Dean Inge.*

Religion may be the most immoral thing in the world. It is, when it is a religion which brings comfort without rebuke, when it gives satisfaction without conviction of sin.—*Halford E. Luccock.*

The service of the Christian religion and my own faith in essential Christianity would not be diminished one iota if it should in some way be discovered that no such individual as Jesus existed.—*Dr. Robert A. Millikan.*

To swallow and follow, whether old doctrine or new propaganda, is a weakness still dominating the human mind.—*Charlotte Perkins Gilman.*

Science and religion no more contradict each other than light and electricity.—*Rev. William Hiram Foulkes.*

REMORSE.—Remorse is surgical in action; it cuts away foul tissues of the mind.—*Christopher Morley.*

SALESMEN.—The book salesman should be honored because he brings to our attention, as a rule, the very books we need most and neglect most.—*Dr. Frank Crane.*

SATIRE.—Satire is a lonely and introspective occupation, for nobody can describe a fool to the life without much patient self-inspection.—*Frank Moore Colby.*

SCIENCE.—In war it serves that we may poison and mutilate each other. In peace it has made our lives hurried and uncertain. Instead of freeing us in great measure from spiritually exhausting labor, it has made men into slaves of machinery, who for the most part complete their monotonous long day's work with disgust and must continually tremble for their poor rations.—*Albert Einstein.*

Biologists can be just as sensitive to heresy as theologians.—*H. G. Wells.*

Science is always wrong. It never solves a problem without creating ten more.—*George Bernard Shaw.*

Have we not all felt the shrinkage of the much vaunted miracles of science into the veriest kitchen utensils of comfort-worshipping society?—*Henry Van Dyke.*

There was once a golden age because golden hearts beat in it. If it comes again, it will scarcely be through scientific progress.—*Louise Imogen Guiney.*

Science is for the most part agnostic about the existence of a personal God, but it is positive in rejecting much that has been falsely taught and believed about God.—*Dean Inge.*

Physical science is truth with her wings clipped.—*Austin O'Malley.*

SECRETS.—I usually get my stuff from people who promised somebody else that they would keep it a secret.—*Walter Winchell.*

SELF-RELIANCE.—There is no man so low down that the cure for his condition does not lie strictly within himself.—*T. L. Masson.*

SHOWMANSHIP.—The showmanship idea of yesterday was to give the public what it wanted. This is a fallacy. You don't know what they want and they don't know what they want.—*S. L. Rothafel.*

SINCERITY.—To be sincere with ourselves is better and harder than to be painstakingly accurate with others.—*Agnes Repplier.*

SKEPTICISM.—I prefer credulity to skepticism and cynicism, for there is more promise in almost anything than in nothing at all.—*Ralph Barton Perry.*

The skeptic—and this is fortunate for him—is not obliged to explain how human dilemma arose. It is indeed one of the advantages of his position that it enables him to shirk that obligation which others seem to feel—that of accounting for all phenomena by some explanation, however improbable.—*Joseph Wood Krutch.*

SLANG.—Slang is just sport-model language stripped down to get more speed with less horsepower.—*Buffalo "Evening News."*

SORROW.—Sorrow, like rain, makes roses and mud.—*Austin O'Malley.*

Sorrows are like tall angels with starcrowns in their hair.—*Margery Eldredge Howell.*

SPECULATION.—A man cannot administer great corporations which employ armies of men and serve large communities if his judgment is diluted and distracted by huge speculative transactions. . . . A man cannot be a good doctor and keep telephoning to his broker between visits to his patients, nor a good lawyer with one eye on the ticker.—*Walter Lippmann.*

Artificial inflation of stocks must be considered a crime as serious as counterfeiting, which it closely resembles.—*André Maurois.*

STANDARDIZATION.—If you think of "standardization" as the best that you know today, but which is to be improved tomorrow—you get somewhere.—*Henry Ford.*

STATISTICS.—Statistics are no substitute for judgment.—*Henry Clay.*

There are three kinds of lies—lies, damnable lies, and statistics.—*Commander Holloway H. Frost.*

SUCCESS.—Success is little more than a chemical compound of man with moment.—*Philip Guedalla.*

Who wants to get on? . . . It is only changing what you are for something no better.—*Anthony Hope Hawkins.*

All our triumphs are but shadows at noon whereby we measure failure.—*Anna Hempstead Branch.*

TALK.—If men who did things talked half as much as men who know how things ought to be done, life would not be worth living.—*Prince of Wales.*

The silent bear no witness against themselves.—*Aldous Huxley.*

TASTE.—Good taste is better than bad taste, but bad taste is better than no taste.—*Arnold Bennett.*

TECHNOCRACY.—Technocracy is just communism with spats.—*John C. Stevens.*

Nothing you can't spell will ever work.—*Will Rogers.*

TEMPER.—Though we speak with the tongues of men and angels and give our bodies to be burned, if we are irritable or hard to live with, it all counts for nothing.—*Margaret Widdemer.*

We must interpret a bad temper as the sign of an inferiority complex.—*Dr. Alfred Adler.*

TEMPERAMENT.—The most beautiful thing in the world . . . is a creature with the genius of temperament, which is a far different thing from the temperament of genius.—*Frances Hodgson Burnett.*

TEMPERANCE.—The only way you can fight booze is by ceasing to make life chronically painful for the masses.—*George Bernard Shaw.*

Temperance is the control of all the functions of our bodies. The man who refuses liquor, goes in for apple pie and develops a paunch is no ethical leader for me.—*John Erskine.*

Many a man has won glory for lifelong temperance through a queasy stomach.—*Austin O'Malley.*

TEMPTATION.—A new variety of temptation is, as we grow older, unusual.—*E. V. Lucas.*

THOUGHT.—Thinking is the hardest work there is, which is the probable reason why so few engage in it.—*Henry Ford.*

Life has taught me to think, but thinking has not taught me how to live.—*Herzen.*

It is thought, and thought only, that divides right from wrong; it is thought, and thought only, that elevates or degrades human deeds and desires.—*George Moore.*

THRIFT.—The doctrine of thrift for the poor is dumb and cruel, like advising them to try and lift themselves by their bootstraps.—*Norman Thomas.*

TRUTH.—I am not struck so much by the diversity of testimony as by the many-sidedness of truth.—*Stanley Baldwin.*

Truth lives in the cellar, error on the doorstep.—*Austin O'Malley*.

Facts that are not frankly faced have a habit of stabbing us in the back.—*Sir Harold Bowden*.

Truth is beautiful and divine no matter how humble its origin.—*Michael Idvorsky Pupin*.

Truth, like a bird, is ever poised for flight at man's approach.—*Jean Brown*.

Treat kindly every miserable truth that knocks begging at your door, otherwise you will some day fail to recognize Truth Himself when He comes in rags.—*Austin O'Malley*.

VEGETARIANISM. — Vegetarianism is harmless enough, although it is apt to fill a man with wind and self-righteousness.—*Dr. Robert Hutchinson*.

VIRTUE.—Every vice was once a virtue, and may become respectable again, just as hatred becomes respectable in wartime.—*Will Durant*.

WAR.—The tendency is to be broadminded about other people's security.—*Aristide Briand*.

As men of reason we scoff at war; as men of business we fear it; as men of religion and good-will we loathe it; and as artists we love it.—*Ernest Raymond*.

You are not going to get peace with millions of armed men. The chariot of peace cannot advance over a road littered with cannon.—*Lloyd George*.

WILL.—Will is character in action.—*William McDougall*.

WISDOM.—The wise man is he who knows the relative value of things—*Dean Inge*.

Any fool can carry on, but only the wise man knows how to shorten sail.—*Joseph Conrad*.

One fool can ask more questions in a minute than twelve wise men can answer in an hour.—*Lenin*.

WOMAN.—There are a few things that never go out of style, and a feminine woman is one of them.—*Jobyna Ralston*.

It is not education which makes women less domestic, but wealth.—*Dr. Katharine Jeanne Gallagher*.

Men are like the earth and we are like the moon; we turn always one side to them and they think there is no other.—*Olive Schreiner*.

Being a woman is a terribly difficult task, since it consists principally in dealing with men.—*Joseph Conrad*.

A capacity for self-pity is one of the last things that any woman surrenders.—*Irvin S. Cobb*.

As any psychologist will tell you, the worst thing you can possibly do to a woman is to deprive her of a grievance.—*Beverly Nichols*.

WORDS.—Many a treasure besides Ali Baba's is unlocked with a verbal key.—*Henry Van Dyke*.

God wove a web of loveliness, of clouds and stars and birds, but made not anything at all so beautiful as words.—*Anna Hempstead Branch*.

Although words exist for the most part for the transmission of ideas, there are some which produce such violent disturbance in our feelings that the rôle they play in the transmission of ideas is lost in the background.—*Albert Einstein*.

WORK.—Nothing is really work unless you would rather be doing something else.—*Sir James M. Barrie*.

As a cure for worrying, work is better than whiskey.—*Thomas A. Edison*.

WORRY.—It ain't no use putting up your umbrella till it rains.—*Alice Hegan Rice*.

Worry is interest paid on trouble before it becomes due.—*Dean Inge*.

YOUTH.—Youth is always too serious, and just now it is too serious about frivolity.—*G. K. Chesterton*.

Youth, though it may lack knowledge, is certainly not devoid of intelligence; it sees through shams with sharp and terrible eyes.—*H. L. Mencken*.

Youth is like cordite, quite innocuous in free air but highly explosive in confinement.—*A. Saywell*.

FAMILIAR PHRASES

FAMILIAR PHRASES

Alphabetically Arranged According to Key Words

Familiar phrases from the Bible will be found on page 48b ff., and from Shakespeare, on page 589b ff.

A

"He must be a first rater . . ." "A-1." —*Dickens, Pickwick Papers, xli.*

All his dealings are square, and above the board.—*Joseph Hall, Virtues and Vices, 15 (1608).*

Brutus and Cassius shone by their absence.—*André de Chénier, Tiberius I, i.*

Accidents will occur in the best regulated families.—*Dickens, David Copperfield, xxviii.*

The old Adam.—*Book of Common Prayer: Baptism of Those of Riper Years.*

Afraid of his own shadow.—*John Baret, An Alvearie, Vol. V, l. 92 (1574).*

All is well that ends well.—*John Heywood, Proverbs, I, x (1546).*

All is for the best.—*Chaucer, Frankeleyns Tale, l. 159 (c 1386).*

All is for the best in the best of possible worlds.—*Voltaire, Candide, i.*

God's in his heaven—all's right with the world!—*R. Browning, Pippa Passes, I.*

Almighty gold.—*Jonson, Epistle to Elizabeth, Countess of Rutland.*

Almighty dollar.—*W. Irving, Wolfert's Roost: The Creole Village (1836).*

When angry, count ten before you speak.—*Jefferson, Writings, XVI, p. 111.*

No other sauce . . . except appetite. —*John Barbour, Bruce, III, 540 (c 1375).*

I have upset my apple-cart; I am done for.—*Lucian, Pseudolus, l. 32.*

To hold by the apron strings.—*Ray, English Proverbs (1678).*

Art for art's sake.—*Cousin, Lecture XXII, Sorbonne, 1818.*

It's clever, but is it Art?—*Kipling, Conundrum of the Workshops.*

Love's great artillery.—*Crashaw, Prayer, l. 18.*

B

The balance of Europe.—*Unknown, A German Diet, subtitle (1653).*

To make the best of a bad bargain.— *Sir Walter Scott, Quentin Durward, Ch. 36.*

His bark is worse than his bite.—*G. Herbert, Jacula Prudentum.*

Barkis is willin'!—*Dickens, David Copperfield, i.*

Bats in the belfry.—*Phillpotts, Peacock House, p. 219.*

To beard the lion in his den.—*Sir Walter Scott, Marmion, IV, xiv.*

And so to bed.—*Samuel Pepys, Diary, 2 Jan., 1659.*

You rose on the wrong side of the bed today.—*Richard Brome, Court Beggar, II, (1653).*

He that makes his bed, lies there.— *G. Herbert, Jacula Prudentum.*

Between you and me and the bed-post. —*Bulwer-Lytton, Eugene Aram, IV, i.*

A good bedside manner.—*Du Maurier, caption under cartoon in Punch, 15 March, 1884.*

A bee in his bonnet.—*Ray, English Proverbs (1678).*

Life isn't all beer and skittles.—*T. Hughes, Tom Brown's Schooldays, Ch. 2 (1857).*

To beg the question.—*Aristotle, Topica, VIII, 13.*

Beggars should be no choosers.—*John Heywood, Proverbs, I, x (1546).*

Benedick.—*Thomas Kyd, Spanish Tragedy, II, (1594).*

Without benefit of clergy [unmarried]. —*Kipling, title of short story.*

Better half [wife].—*P. Sidney, Arcadia, III.*

Big butter-and-egg man.—*Texas Guinan, 1924.*

The bigger they come the harder they fall.—*Robert Fitzsimmons (1902).*

Birds of a feather flock together.— *Aristotle, Rhetoric, I, xi, 25.* Quoted as a proverb.

The birds are flown.—*John Heywood, Three Hundred Epigrams, 280.*

I should kill two birds with one stone, as that excellent thrifty proverb says.— *Thomas Shadwell, Miser, II.*

I have it here in black and white.— *Jonson, Every Man in His Humour, IV, iii.*

He could make white of black and black of white.—*Ovid, Metamorphoses, XI, l. 313.*

Devils are not so black as they are painted.—*Thomas Lodge, A Margarite of America, p. 57 (1596).*

As blind as a bat at noon.—*John Clarke, Paraemiologia, 52 (1639).*

Blood is thicker than water.—*Ray, English Proverbs (1678).*

There's no getting blood out of a turnip.—*Marryat, Japhet, Ch. 4.*

Waving the bloody shirt [as applied to Republicans' denunciation of Democrats for bringing on the Civil War].— *U. S. Senator Oliver P. Morton (?).*

Blowing the trumpet of my own praise.—*Thomas Knight, Turnpike Gate, I, i (1799).*

In the same boat.—*Herodas, Sententiae, VI, 12.*

Boloney.—*Alfred E. Smith.*

A bone for you to pick on.—*James Calfhill, Answer to Martial, 277 (1565).*

Bred in the bone.—*Pilpay, Two Fishermen, Fable XIV.*

They have made no bones at it.—*Richard Shacklock, Hatcher of Heresies.*

Brain trust.—*James M. Kieran (Lindley, The Roosevelt Revolution).*

As bold as brass.—*George Parker, Life's Painter, 162.*

None but the brave deserves the fair.—*Dryden, Alexander's Feast, i.*

I know which side my bread is buttered.—*John Heywood, Proverbs, II, viii (1546).*

I won't quarrel with my bread and butter.—*Swift, Polite Conversation, I.*

And now, Madam, . . . we shall try who shall get the breeches.—*Antonius Musa Brassavolus, My Wife and I (1540)—William Belos tr.*

As brown as a berry.—*Chaucer, Canterbury Tales: Prologue, l. 207 (c 1386).*

Brown study.—*John Lyly, Euphues, p. 80 (1579).*

You too, Brutus (Et tu, Brute)!—*Julius Caesar, as Brutus stabbed him.*

He told those who remained [in Congress] that . . . he was only talking for Buncombe [a county in North Carolina].—*John H. Wheeler, Hist. North Carolina, 18.*

Beat about the bush.—*Plautus, Mercator, III, iv.*

Business is business.—*Octave Mirbeau, title of play.*

That which is everybody's business is nobody's business.—*Walton, Compleat Angler, I, ii.* Quoting a friend.

As busy as bees.—*Chaucer, Marchantes Tale: Epilogue, l. 4 (c 1386).*

She looketh as butter would not melt in her mouth.—*John Heywood, Proverbs, I, x (1546).*

He did not care a button for it.—*Rabelais, Works, II, xvi.*

Let bygans be bygans.—*Francis Nethersole, Parables, 5.*

C

Would ye both eat your cake and have your cake?—*John Heywood, Proverbs, I, ix (1546).*

The game is not worth the candle.—*Montaigne, Essays, II, xxvii.*

He is consuming just like a candle on both ends.—*Richard Flecknoe, Enigmatic Characters, p. 64.*

Paddle your own canoe.—*Marryat, Settlers in Canada, Ch. 8 (1840).*

Set the cart before the horse.—*John Heywood, Proverbs, II, vii (1546).*

Castles in the air.—*William Painter, The Palace of Pleasure, i, 266.*

Castles . . . in Spain.—*Chaucer, Romaunt of the Rose, l. 2573* (first known use in English—used in French literature in the thirteenth century).

To see how the cat jumps.—*Sir Walter Scott, Journal, 7 Oct., 1826.*

It would make a cat laugh.—*J. R. Planché, Extravaganza, IV, 148.*

There are more ways of killing a cat than choking her with cream.—*Kingsley, Westward Ho, Ch. 20.*

When the cat is abroad the mice play.—*John Florio, First Fruites, Fo. 33.*

A cat may look on a king.—*John Heywood, Proverbs, II, v (1546).*

The devil playeth oft . . . . as doth the cat with the mouse.—*Unkn., Ayenbite, 179.*

She watches him as a cat would watch a mouse.—*Swift, Polite Conversation, III.*

It has been the providence of Nature to give this creature nine lives.—*Pilpay, The Greedy Cat, Fable III.*

He's like a cat; fling him which way you will, he'll light on his legs.—*Ray, English Proverbs, 109.*

Catch who that catch might.—*John Gower, Confessio Amantis, VII, l. 4422 (c 1390).*

Chestnut [stale joke].—*William Dimond, The Broken Sword.*

To pull chestnuts from the fire with the cat's paw.—*Molière, L'Etourdi, III, vi.* Based on story told by Geoffrey Whitney in "Choice of Emblems," p. 53.

Cherchez la femme (Find the woman).—*Alexandre Dumas, père, Les Mohicans de Paris, III, x.*

I swear she's no chicken; she's on the wrong side of thirty, if she be a day.—*Swift, Polite Conversation, I.*

You reckon your chickens before they are hatched.—*Erasmus, Colloquies, 39 (Bailey tr.).*

A chip o' the old block.—*William Rowley, A Match at Midnight, I.*

Cleanliness is, indeed, next to godliness.—*J. Wesley, Sermons, XCIII.* Quoted but without indication of source.

Human clothes-horses.—*Carlyle, Latter-Day Pamphlets, No. III.*

Did a sable cloud turn forth her silver lining on the night?—*Milton, Comus, l. 221.*

To be in clover.—*Ray, English Proverbs, 57.*

Coals to Newcastle.—*James Melville, Autobiography, I, 163 (1583).*

The coast was clear.—*Drayton, Nymphidia (1627).*

Cut my coat after my cloth.—*Unkn., Godly Queen Hester: Interlude.*

Let not the cobbler go above his last.—*Appelles (Pliny the Elder, Historia Naturalis, XXXV, x, 36).*

I can look sharp as well as another, and let me alone to keep the cobwebs out of my eyes.—*Cervantes, Don Quixote, II, xxviii.*

What a tale of a cock and a bull he told.—*John Day, Law Trickes, IV, ii (1608).*

Care to our coffin adds a nail.—*Wolcot, Expostulatory Odes, Ode 15.*

In cold blood.—*Horace, Ars Poetica, l. 465.*

Two is company, three is a crowd.—*T. Fuller, Gnomologia.*

Comparisons are odious.—*John Fortescue, De Laudibus Legum Angliae, Ch. 19.*

To return the compliment.—*W. Gilbert, H. M. S. Pinafore, Act I.*

Confusion worse confounded.—*Milton, Paradise Lost, II, 996.*

She stoops to conquer.—*Goldsmith, title of comedy.*

I came, I saw, I conquered (Veni, vidi, vici).—*Julius Caesar.*

Too many cooks spoil the broth.—*Balthazar Gerbier, Discourse of Building (1662).*

From the four corners of the world.—*G. S. Du Bartas, Devine Weekes and Workes, Week 1, Day 2 (Sylvester tr.).*

Kiss till the cow comes home.—*Beaumont and Fletcher, Scornful Lady, III, i.*

The cream of the jest.—*Ray, English Proverbs, 69 (1678).*

Crocodiles, that shed tears when they would devour.—*F. Bacon, Essays: Of Wisdom for a Man's Self.*

Thou hast a crooked tongue, holding with the hound and running with the hare.—*Unkn., Jacob's Well, 263 (c 1440).*

Till crows' feet be grown under your eyes.—*Chaucer, Troilus and Criseyde, II, 403.*

I shall cry my eyes out.—*Cervantes, Don Quixote, I, xi.*

To cut the earth from under my feet. —*Geoffrey Fenton, Bandello, II, 10 (1567).*

D

Daisies won't tell.—*Anita Owen, Sweet Bunch of Daisies (1894).*

As fresh as a daisy.—*Eaton Stannard Barrett, Heroine, III, 155 (1815).*

With faint praises one another damn. —*Wycherley, Plain Dealer: Prologue, l. 6.*

On with the dance! let joy be unconfin'd.—*Byron, Childe Harold, III, xxii.*

Dark as pitch.—*Bunyan, Pilgrim's Progress, I.*

A dark brown taste.—*George Ade, Remorse.*

Dark horse.—*Disraeli, The Young Duke, I, v (1831).*

Deaf as a door.—*Nicholas Breton, Works, II, 49.*

Dumb and deaf as a post.—*Thomas Churchyard, Chippes, p. 136.*

Dead as dishwater.—*Garrick, Correspondence, I, p. 465.*

Dead as a door nail.—*William Langland, Piers Plowman, II, l. 183.*

The dead do tell no tales.—*John Wilson, Andronicus Commenius, I, iv (1664).*

The jaws of death.—*G. S. Du Bartas, Devine Weekes and Workes, II, i (Sylvester tr.).*

Nothing is certain but death and taxes. —*Franklin, Letter to M. Leroy (1789).*

Defining night by darkness, death by dust.—*P. J. Bailey, Festus: Water and Wood.*

The devil to pay.—*Unkn., (Reliq. Antiquae, I, 257 – 1400).*

Talk of the devil and he'll appear.—*Erasmus, Adagia, No. 17.*

The devil take the hindmost.—*Beaumont and Fletcher, Philaster, V (1610).*

Betwixt the devil and the deep sea.—*Erasmus, Adagia, p. 94.* Quoted from the Greek.

Speak the truth and shame the devil. —*Rabelais, Works, V, Author's Prologue.*

The die is cast.—*Julius Caesar, (Suetonius, Twelve Caesars: Julius, Sec. 32).*

Never say die.—*R. H. Barham, Merchant of Venice.*

Dirty work at the crossroads.—*Walter Melville, No Wedding Bells for Him.*

Divine discontent.—*Kingsley, Health and Education.*

An ounce of discretion is worth a pound of wit.—*Ray, English Proverbs.*

Distance lends enchantment to the view.—*T. Campbell, Pleasures of Hope, I, 7.*

Distinction without a difference.— *Fielding, Tom Jones, VI, xiii.*

I will die in the last ditch.—*William of Orange (Hume, History of England, Ch. 43).*

Dull as ditch water.—*Dickens, Our Mutual Friend, III, x.*

Who loves me will love my dog also.— *St. Bernard, In Festo Sancti Michaelis: Sermo Primus (c 1150).*

It is hard to teach an old dog tricks.— *William Camden, Remains, p. 326 (1605).*

A dog hath a day.—*John Heywood, Proverbs, I, xi (1546).*

'Twould make a dog laugh.—*J. P. Collier, Roxburghe Ballads, 158 (c 1603).*

Dog in the manger.—*Tusser, Hundreth Good Pointes of Husbandrie, 69 (1580).* Based on an old fable of a dog who keeps an ox from the hay.

Dumb's a sly dog.—*Cibber, Love Makes the Man, IV.*

It is bad to awaken a sleeping dog.— *Le Roux de Lincy, Tresor de Jehan de Meung (13th Century ms.).* Quoted as a proverb.

Dollar diplomacy.—*Unkn., Harper's Weekly, 23 April, 1910, p. 8.*

No . . . . shadow of doubt.—*W. Gilbert, Gondoliers, I.*

Drink like a fish.—*James Shirley, Works, VI, p. 321 (1646).*

To drown the eyes in tears.—*Sophocles, Antigone, l. 803.*

As drunk as a lord.—*Unkn., Somers Tracts, VII, 184 (1659).*

Drunk as owls.—*Stevenson, Treasure Island, Ch. 24.*

I deem it all but ducks and drakes.—
Unkn., Careless Content.

E

I was all ear.—*Milton, Comus, l. 560.*

Turn the deaf ear.—*Swift, Dingley and Brent.*

In at one ear and out at the other.—
Quintilian, De Institutione Oratoria, II, v, Sec. 13.

If your ear burns, some one is talking about you.—*Pliny the Elder, Historia Naturalis, XXVIII, Sec. 2.*

They stand with ears pricked up.—
Vergil, Aeneid, I, l. 152.

Set folks together by the ears.—*Samuel Butler the Elder, Hudibras, I, i, 1.*

The early bird catches the worm.—
William Camden, Remains, p. 333 (1605).

Early to bed and early to rise, makes a man healthy and wealthy and wise.—
Ray, English Proverbs, 38.

Lightly [easy] come, lightly go.—
Unkn., Time's Whistle, l. 2828 (1614).

Other men live to eat, while I eat to live.—*Socrates (Diogenes Laertius, Socrates, II, Sec. 34).*

Not to venture all his eggs in one basket.—*Cervantes, Don Quixote, III, ix.*

Going as if he trod upon eggs.—*Robert Burton, Anatomy of Melancholy, III, ii, 3.*

Elbow grease.—*Unkn., New Dict. Canting Crew (1690).*

He had an elephant on his hands.—
J. Cheever Goodwin, Wang: Elephant Song (1891).

The king's English.—*Thomas Wilson, Rhetorique, 162 (1560).*

English as she is spoke.—*Andrew White Tuer, title of reprint of a guide to English for Portuguese students (1883).*

The Eternal Feminine.—*Goethe, Faust, II, v.*

Every day, in every way, I am getting better and better.—*Émile Coué.*

Every man for himself and God for us all.—*John Heywood, Proverbs, II, ix (1546).*

The exception proves the rule.—*John Wilson, The Cheats: To the Reader (1664).*

Better a bad excuse, than none at all.
—*William Camden, Remains, p. 293 (1605).*

She hath an eye behind her.—*John Still, Gammer Gurton's Needle, II, ii (c 1565).*

All looks yellow to the jaundic'd eye.
—*Pope, Essay on Criticism, II, p. 359.*

With affection beaming in one eye and calculation out of the other.—*Dickens, Martin Chuzzlewit, Ch. 8.*

Don't fire until you see the white of their eyes.—*Col. William Prescott.*

F

My face is my fortune.—*Unkn., old nursery rhyme.*

Two faces under one hood.—*Thomas Fuller, Gnomologia.*

Faint hearts fair ladies never win.—
Unkn., A Proper Ballad in Praise of My Lady Marquess (1569).

Change [a fair exchange] be no robbery.—*John Heywood, Proverbs, II, ii (1546).*

Faithful Achates (fidus Achates).—
Vergil, Aeneid, VI, l. 158.

Familiarity breeds contempt.—*Publilius Syrus, Sententiae, No. 640.*

A far cry to Lochow.—*Sir Walter Scott, Rob Roy, Ch. 29.*

Fat, fair and forty.—*John O'Keeffe, Irish Minnie, II, iii.*

Nobody loves a fat man.—*Maclyn Arbuckle.*

The fat is in the fire.—*John Heywood, Proverbs, I, iii (1546).*

A man must take the fat with the lean.—*Dickens, David Copperfield, Ch. 51.*

Clever to a fault.—*R. Browning, Bishop Blougram's Apology.*

Feather my nest.—*Unkn., Respublica, i, 1 (1553).*

To show the number of his slain enemies by the number of feathers in his cap.—*Richard Hansard, A Description of Hungary (1599).*

A brain of feathers and a heart of lead.—*Pope, Dunciad, II, l. 44.*

The fair feathers still make the fair fowls.—*John Davies, School of Folly, 46 (1611).*

On a fence [undecided].—*J. R. Lowell, Biglow Papers, II, iii.*

Figures won't lie, but liars will figure.
—*Gen. Charles H. Grosvenor.*

A finger in every pie.—*Cervantes, Don Quixote, II, xxii.*

She has more goodness in her little finger than he has in his whole body.—
Swift, Polite Conversation, II.

They say fingers were made before forks.—*Swift, Polite Conversation, II.*

Out of the frying-pan into the fire.—
Tertullian, De Carne Christi, vi.

Brent child fire dreadeth.—*Unkn., Reliq. Antiquae, I, 113 (c 1300).*

First come, first served.—*Henry Brinkelow, Complaint of Roderick Mors, Ch. 17 (c 1540).*

Neither flesh nor fish.—*Unkn., Rede Me and Be Not Wrothe, I, 3 (1528).*

Neither fish, nor flesh, nor good red herring.—*John Heywood, Proverbs, I, x (1546).*

Like a fish out of water.—*Sozomen, Ecclesiastical History, I, xiii.*

There are as good fish in the sea as ever came out of it.—*Sir Walter Scott, Fortunes of Nigel, Ch. 35.*

We have other fish to fry.—*Rabelais, Works, VI, xii (1552).*

All is fish that cometh to net.—*John Heywood, Proverbs, I, ii (1546).*

The whales, you see, eat up the little fish.—*Thomas Churchyard, Chippes, 145 (1575).*

As fit as a fiddle.—*William Haughton, English-Men for My Money, IV, i (1616).*

As flat as pancakes.—*T. Middleton, Roaring Girl, II, i (1611).*

They'd skin a flea for his hide and tallow.—*Henry Mayhew, London Labour, I, l. 134.*

Fleas in mine ears.—*Unkn., Pilgr. Lyf. Manhode, II, xxxix, 91 (c 1430).*

To make your flesh creep.—*Dickens, Pickwick Papers, Ch. 8.*

A close mouth catches no flies.—*Cervantes, Don Quixote, I, xi.*

I'll have a fling.—*John Fletcher, Rule a Wife and Have a Wife, III, v (1624).*

As welcome as the flowers in May.—*James Howell, Letters, I, 60 (1645).*

The flowing bowl.—*Horace, Epistles, I, v. 19.*

No fool like an old fool.—*John Heywood, Proverbs, II, ii (1546).*

A fool and his money be soon at debate.—*Tusser, Hundreth Good Pointes of Husbandrie, 19 (1580).*

Fools rush in where angels fear to tread.—*Pope, Essay on Criticism, III, 66.*

A fool's paradise.—*Unkn., Paston Letters, II, p. 109 (1462).*

Forgiven and forgotten.—*John Heywood, Proverbs, II, iii (1546).*

Forgotten man.—*William Graham Sumner, The Forgotten Man and Other Essays (1883).*

There are only about four hundred people in New York Society.—*Ward McAllister.*

Fourth estate [the press].—*Macaulay, Essays: Hallam's Constitutional History (1828).*

French leave.—*John Trusler, Chesterfield's Principles and Politeness (1760).*

Friend in court.—*Chaucer, Romaunt of the Rose, l. 5541.*

A friend in need is a friend indeed.—*Richard Graves, Spiritual Quixote, VII, xxii, heading (1772).* The idea was expressed by Plautus.

Enough to fright you out of your seven senses.—*Rabelais, Works, V, xv.*

In his own grease I made him fry.—*Chaucer, Wife of Bath's Prologue, l. 487 (c 1386).*

Full of years and honors.—*Pliny the Younger, Epistles, II, i, 2.*

Make the fur fly.—*Samuel Butler the Elder, Hudibras, I, iii, 278.*

G

Gay Lothario.—*Rowe, Fair Penitent, V, i.*

Gentlemen's gentlemen.—*Sheridan, Rivals, II, ii.*

Never examine the teeth of a gift horse.—*St. Jerome, Epistulae ad Ephesus: Proem.* Quoted as a proverb.

Whose house is of glass must not throw stones.—*G. Herbert, Jacula Prudentum (1640).*

Glittering generalities.—*F. J. Dickman, Providence Journal, 14 Dec., 1849.*

This story will never go down.—*Fielding, Tumble-Down Dick, Air 1.*

You may go farther and fare worse.—*Plautus, Trinummus, l. 63.*

God helps them who help themselves.—*Proverb in all languages.*

These things lie on the knees of the gods.—*Homer, Iliad, XVII, 514.*

Worth thy weight in gold.—*Henry Medwall, Nature, l. 936 (c 1500).*

As good as gold.—*Dickens, Christmas Carol, Stave 3.*

All is not gold that glisters.—*John Heywood, Proverbs, I, x (1546).*

Golden mean.—*Horace, Odes, II, x, 5.*

Golden rule.—*Isaac Watts, Logick (1725).*

Gone glimmering.—*Byron, Childe Harold, II, ii.*

Gone to the demnition bow-wows.—*Dickens, Nicholas Nickleby, II, xxxvi.*

If you can't be good, be careful.—*Harrington Tate, refrain of song (1907).*

Put himself upon his good behaviour.—*Byron, Don Juan, V, xlvii.*

To kill the goose that laid the golden eggs.—*Aesop, Fables, II.*

Not able to say bo to a goose.—*Unkn., Mar-Prelate's Epistle, 60 (1588).*

What was sauce for the goose was sauce for the gander.—*R. Head and F. Kirkman, English Rogue, II, 120 (1671).*

This . . . cutting of throats . . . goes . . . against the grain—*Dryden, Amboyna, I, i (1673).*

Grand Panjandrum—*S. Foote, An Incoherent Story.*

The grapes are sour.—*Aesop, Fables: The Fox and the Grapes.*

I have not let the grass grow under my feet.—*Unkn., Spanish Bawd, IV, iii.*

Go to grass.—*Beaumont and Fletcher, Little French Lawyer, IV, vii.*

One foot in the grave.—*Plutarch, Morals: On the Training of Children.*

As secret as the grave.—*Cervantes, Don Quixote, II, lxii.*

I fear the Greeks, even when bringing gifts.—*Vergil, Aeneid, II, 49.*

When Greeks joined Greeks, then was the tug of war.—*Nathaniel Lee, Alexander the Great, IV, ii.*

Mrs. Grundy.—*Thomas Morton, Speed the Plough (1798).*

H

Hail fellow well-met.—*Thomas Becon, Chatechism, 561 (c 1550).*

Living from hand to mouth.—*G. S. Du Bartas, Devine Weekes and Workes, II, i, l. 122 (Sylvester tr.—1605).*

There is nothing . . . but what you can turn your hand to.—*Cervantes, Don Quixote, I, xxv.*

They two are hand in glove.—*Ray, English Proverbs, 347 (1678).*

He is handsome that handsome does. —*Gay, Wife of Bath, III, i (1713)*.

Where do you hang out?—*Dickens, Pickwick Papers, Ch. 30*.

Yes, we must, indeed, all hang together, or, most assuredly, we shall all hang separately.—*Franklin*.

As good be hanged for a sheep as a lamb.—*Ray, English Proverbs*.

Hard as nails.—*Dickens, Oliver Twist, Ch. 9*.

A harper is laughed at who plays always on the same string.—*Horace, Ars Poetica, l. 355*.

One of the has beens.—*Wm. Hone, Every-Day Book, II, 820 (1826)*.

Earls as go mad in their castles, and females what settles their hash.— *George R. Sims, Dagonet Ballads: Polly*.

Make haste slowly.—*Caesar Augustus (Suetonius, Twelve Caesars: Augustus, XXV, iv)*.

Haste makes waste.—*John Heywood, Proverbs, I, ii (1546)*.

I'd eat my hat.—*Dickens, Pickwick Papers, Ch. 13*.

Here's your hat, what's your hurry? —*Bartley C. Costello, title of song (1904)*.

Buried was the bloody hatchet.— *Longfellow, Hiawatha, XIII, l. 7*.

To have and to hold from this day forward, for better, for worse, for richer, for poorer, in sickness, and in health, to love and to cherish, till death do us part.—*Book of Common Prayer: Solemnization of Matrimony*.

Make hay while the sun shines.— *Cervantes, Don Quixote, I, xi*.

His head was turned by too great success.—*Seneca, Epistulae ad Lucilium, cxiv, 8*.

Over head and heels.—*Catullus, Carmina, Ode XVII, l. 9*.

Two heads are better than one.— *Homer, Iliad, X, 225*.

Heads I win, tails you lose.—*Unkn., Croker Papers, III, 59*.

His heart runs away with his head.— *George Colman the Younger, Who Wants a Guinea, I, i*.

It terrifies the cockles of my heart.— *Samuel Wesley, Maggots, p. 126 (1685)*.

From the bottom of the heart.—*Vergil, Aeneid, XI, 377*.

His heart was in his work.—*Longfellow, The Building of the Ship, l. 7*.

Thy heart is in thy hose.—*Unkn., Townely Plays, 113 (c 1410)*.

My heart was in my mouth.—*Petronius, Satyricon, Sec. 62*.

Eat not thy heart.—*Pythagoras (Diogenes Laertius: Pythagoras, Sec. 17)*.

Their hearts are in the right place.— *Disraeli, Infernal Marriage, I, i*.

Hearts of oak.—*Rabelais, Works, V, Prologue (1562)*.

Two souls with but a single thought, two hearts that beat as one.—*Von Munch Bellinghausen, Ingomar the Barbarian (Lovell tr.)*.

I took to my heels.—*Terence, Eunuchus, V, ii*.

Hell is paved with good intentions.— *Ray, English Proverbs (1670)*.

They would say . . . hell were broken loose.—*Jonson, Every Man in His Humour, IV, i*.

Hen-pecked.—*Richard Steele, Spectator 479 (1712)*.

He will hew to the line of right, let the chips fly where they may.—*Roscoe Conkling, speech, 1880*.

High brow.—*Epictetus, Encheiridion, xxii*.

Have ye him on the hip.—*John Heywood, Proverbs, II, v (1546)*.

Hobson's choice.—*Thomas Ward, England's Reformation, iv (1630)*. Thomas Hobson (1544–1631) was a stable keeper who, according to Steele, gave his customers no choice at all.

Go the whole hog.—*Marryat, Japhet, liv*. Quoted as an Americanism, but believed to be of Irish origin, hog meaning shilling *(Notes and Queries, 27 Sept., 1851)*.

Made honest by an act of parliament. —*Jonson, Devil Is an Ass, IV, i*.

Who think honesty the best policy.— *Edwin Sandys, Europae Speculum, 102 (1599)*.

By hook or crook.—*John Wycliffe, Controversial Tracts (c 1380)*. Based on custom of allowing tenants as much timber as could be gathered by hook and crook.

Hope springs eternal in the human breast.—*Pope, Essay on Man, I, 95*.

While there's life, there's hope.— *Cicero, Epistolae ad Atticum, IX, x*. Quoted as common saying.

He who lives on hope.—*Wodroephe, Spared Houres, 302 (1623)*.

You are poking up a hornet's nest.— *Plautus, Amphitruo, l. 707*.

A man may well bring a horse to the water, but he cannot make him drink without he will.—*John Heywood, Proverbs, I, xi (1546)*.

Altogether upon the high horse.— *Garrick, Correspondence, I, p. 205*.

Horse-laugh.—*Steele, Guardian 29*.

Whosoever reckoneth without his host, he reckoneth twice.—*Wm. Caxton, Blanchardyn, 202 (c 1489)*.

My house is to me as my castle.—*Wm. Staunford, Plees del Coron (1567)*.

One half of the world knoweth not how the other half liveth.—*Rabelais, Works, II, xxxii (1532)*. Quoted as common saying.

More hungry than any wolf.—*John Palsgrave, Acolastus, Sig. L 1 (1540)*.

I

Skating over thin ice.—*R. Emerson, Essays, First Series: Prudence*.

To break the ice.—*F. Bacon, Essays: Of Cunning*.

Where ignorance is bliss, 'tis folly to be wise.—*T. Gray, Ode on a Distant Prospect of Eton College.*

Give an inch and you'll take an ell.—*John Heywood, Proverbs, II, ix (1546).*

Die by inches.—*Amiel, Journal, 1 Sept., 1874.*

Innocent as the child unborn.—*Unkn, (Somers Tracts, VIII, 131 [1679]).*

Add insult to injury.—*Phaedrus, Fables, V, iii, 5.*

Strike while the iron is hot.—*Addaeus, Epigram (Greek Anthology, X, xx).*

Two irons in the fire.—*Beaumont and Fletcher, Faithful Friends, I, ii.*

J

Jack-of-all-trades.—*Geffray Minshull, Essays, 50 (1618).*

I'd do it as soon as say Jack Robinson.—*F. Burney, Evelina, Let. 82 (1778).*

That she, this maiden, which that May is highte . . . should wedded be unto this January.—*Chaucer, Marchantes Tale, 449 (c 1386).*

John Bull.—*Arbuthnot, History of John Bull (1712).*

The yellow eye of Journalism.—*Carlyle, French Revolution, II, iii, Ch. 3.*

Grave as a judge.—*Samuel Wesley, Maggots (1685).*

K

With all our most holy illusions knocked higher than Gilderoy's kite.—*Kipling, The Lesson.*

L

My Lady Bountiful.—*Farquhar, Beaux' Stratagem, I, i.*

Land of Nod.—*Swift, Polite Conversation, II (1738).*

It's a long lane that has no turning.—*Samuel Richardson, Clarissa Harlowe, IV, 237.*

As large as life, and twice as natural.—*Carroll, Through the Looking Glass, vii.*

The last, but not the least.—*John Lyly, Euphues, p. 343 (1580).*

Better late than never.—*Livy, History, IV, Sec. 23.*

Amends may never come too late.—*Thomas Lodge and Robert Greene, A Looking Glass for London (c 1590).*

Laugh in your sleeve.—*Cicero, De Finibus, II, xviii, 76.*

Laugh and the world laughs with you.—*E. Wilcox, Solitude.*

Now you can laugh but on one side of your mouth.—*Torriano, Piazza Universale, p. 173 (1666).*

He laughs best that laughs last.—*Vanbrugh, Country House, II, v (1706).* Quoted as old proverb.

A little learning is a dangerous thing.—*Pope, Essay on Criticism, II, 15.*

When they saw the Englishmen at the weakest, they turned the leaf and sang another song.—*Edward Hall, Chronicle, 180 (1548).*

Right as an aspes leaf she 'gan to shake.—*Chaucer, Troilus and Criseyde, III, 1200.*

My last voyage, a leap in the dark.—*Hobbes, 1679 (Watkins, Anecdotes of Men of Learning).*

Then I shall be able to pull the leg of that chap.—*Thomas Churchyard, Blackbirding, 216 (1563).*

I'll laugh an' sing, an' shake my leg.—*Burns, Second Epistle to J. Lapraik.*

On his last legs.—*T. Middleton, Old Law, V, i.*

Let well alone, as the saying is.—*Terence, Phormio, l. 419.*

Their [bear cubs'] mother . . . licks them into proper shape.—*Pliny the Elder, Historia Naturalis, VIII, Sec. 36.*

Unlicked cubs.—*Congreve, Old Batchelor, IV, viii.*

As we journey through life let us live by the way.—*Walter Watson, Sit Down, My Crony.*

Life is short and art is long.—*Hippocrates, Aphorisms, 1.*

A merry life and a short.—*Edmund Gayton, Festivous Notes on Don Quixote, 101 (1654).*

Such is life.—*Dickens, Great Expectations, Ch. 15.*

The light that never was, on sea or land.—*Wordsworth, Elegiac Stanzas, Suggested by a Picture of Peele Castle in a Storm, l. 15.*

Come, and trip it as ye go, on the light fantastic toe.—*Milton, L'Allegro, 33.*

It must be done like lightning.—*Jonson, Every Man in His Humour, IV, v.*

Looking as like . . . as one pea does like another.—*Rabelais, Works, V, ii.*

I carry off the chief share because I am called the Lion.—*Phaedrus, Fables, I, v, 7.*

Keep a stiff upper lip.—*P. Cary, title.*

Little said is soon amended.—*Wright, Songs: Philip and Mary (c 1555).*

Little Tin Gods on Wheels.—*Kipling, Public Waste. Also attributed to Robert Grant.*

Live and learn.—*Unkn., Roxburghe Ballads, I, 80 (1620).*

Live and let live.—*L'Estrange, Fables of Aesop, 127.*

Long-winded tale.—*Beattie, Minstrel, I, 44.*

Look ere thou leap.—*Tyndale, Obedience of a Christian Man, 304 (1528).*

Neither for love nor money.—*Unkn., Pedlar's Prophecy, 578 (1595).*

Love me little, love me long.—*John Heywood, Proverbs, II, ii (1546).*

It's love that makes the world go round.—*Unkn. (Chansons Nationales et Populaires de France, II, 180).*

Love will find out the way.—*Unkn., title (Percy, Reliques).*

All is fair in love and war.—*F. E. Smedley, Frank Fairlegh, i (1850).* A suggestion that such a saying was common occurs in Beaumont and Fletcher, The Lovers' Progress (1630).

There is no love lost between us.—*Cervantes, Don Quixote, IV, xxiii.*

All mankind love a lover.—*R. Emerson, Essays, First Series: Of Love.*

M

Mad were as an hare.—*Chaucer, Freres Tale, 29 (c 1386).*

Mad as a hatter.—*Thackeray, Pendennis, x.*

To go mad with fixed rule and method.—*Horace, Satires, II, iii, 271.*

If the hill will not come to Mahomet, Mahomet will go to the hill.—*F. Bacon, Essays: Of Boldness.*

Make both ends meet.—*T. Fuller, Worthies of England (1662).*

Mere man.—*Book of Common Prayer: Shorter Catechism.*

Man higher up.—*O. Henry, Man About Town.*

Man of destiny.—*Schiller, Wallenstein's Tod, III, xv, 171.*

Man of the world.—*E. Young, Night Thoughts, VIII, 8.*

Man proposes, but God disposes.—*Thomas à Kempis, De Imitatione Christi, I, xix.*

The hood makes not the monk, nor the apparel the man.—*Robert Greene, Works, IX, p. 19.*

Thou wilt scarce be a man before thy mother.—*Beaumont and Fletcher, Love's Cure, II ii.*

Henceforth, whenever we cast doubt upon a tale . . . we will tell it to the marines. If they believe it, it is safe to say it is true.—*Charles II (Pepys, Diary).*

Lest in making hasty choice [marriage], leisure for repentance should follow.—*Wm. Painter, Palace of Pleasure, 115 (1566).*

Needles and pins, needles and pins, when a man marries his trouble begins.—*Unkn. (Halliwell, Nursery Rhymes, p. 122).*

Men must work, and women must weep.—*Kingsley, Three Fishers, i.*

Midnight oil.—*Gay, Fables: Introduction, 15.*

Oh, Mirth and Innocence! Oh, Milk and Water.—*Byron, Beppo, lxxx.*

Crying for shed milk.—*Andrew Yarranton, England's Improvement, II, p. 107.*

Bring grist to the mill.—*Arthur Golding, Calvin on Deuteronomy, 755 (1583).*

The water that's past cannot make the mill go.—*Thomas Draxe, Bibliotheca Scholastica Instructissima, p. 151 (1633).*

God's mill grinds slow but sure.—*Proverbiae Cod. Coisl. 396 (Gaisford, Paraemiologia Graeca, 164).*

Not to mince the matter.—*Cervantes, Don Quixote: Author's Preface.*

Misery loves company.—*Ray, English Proverbs (1670).* The same thought was expressed in different words by Publilius Syrus, Sententiae, 995.

An inch in a miss is as good as an ell.—*Wm. Camden, Remains.*

I'm from Missouri; you've got to show me.—*W. D. Vandiver, Representative from Missouri (Literary Digest, 28. Jan., 1922).*

Give me the mitten [reject me].—*Sam Slick, Human Nature, p. 90.*

Money talks.—*Unkn., Baudoin de Sebourc, XXIV, 443.*

Wanton money, which burned out the bottom of his purse.—*T. More, Works, p. 195 (c 1530).*

Don't throw a monkey-wrench into the machinery.—*Philander Johnson (Everybody's Magazine, May, 1920, p. 36).*

The more the merrier, the fewer the better fare.—*John Palsgrave, Lesclarissement de la Langue Françoyse, 885 (1530).*

They make . . . of a molehill a mountain.—*Thomas Becon, Catechism (c 1560).*

Mum is counsel.—*John Palsgrave, Acolastus, Sig. B 2 (1540).*

Murder will out.—*Chaucer, Prioresses Tale, 124 (c 1386).* Thought expressed in other words in an anonymous poem written a century earlier.

Music has charms to soothe a savage breast.—*Congreve, Mourning Bride, I, i, 1 (1697).*

N

Thou hittest the nail on the head.—*John Stanbridge, Vulgaria, V. (c 1520).*

Nature fakirs.—*Edward B. Clark, Roosevelt on the Nature-Fakirs, Everybody's Magazine, June, 1907.*

Necessity the mother of invention.—*Latin proverb.*

We give necessity the praise of virtue.—*Quintilian, De Institutione Oratoria, I, viii, 14 (c 90).*

Neck or nothing.—*Swift, Polite Conversation, I, and Cibber, Lady's Last Stake, III.*

Grope out a needle in a load of hay.—*Jeremy Taylor, Kicksey Winsey, VII.*

A new man; an upstart.—*Cicero, De Officiis, I, xxxix, 138.*

Nick of time.—*Suckling, Goblins, V.*

No better than she should be.—*Unkn., Pasquils Jests, 35 (1604).*

No man's land.—*Unkn., Chronicles of Edward I, Rolls, i, 291 (1320).*

Noblesse oblige.—*Duc de Levis, Maxims, 73.*

A little nonsense now and then is relished by the wisest men.—*Unkn., old nursery rhyme.*

Follow thy nose.—*John Heywood, Royal King, I.*

To cut off one's nose to spite one's face.—*Publilius Syrus, Sententiae, 611.*

Paying through the nose.—*Origin uncertain—believed to be based on tax known as nose tax levied by Odin in Sweden (Grimm, Deutsche Rechts Alterthümer).*

To be led by the noses like brute beasts.—*Arthur Golding, Calvin on Deuteronomy, CXXI (1583)*.

As plain as the nose on your face.—*Erasmus, Praise of Folly, 25 (1516)*.

Turn up his nose.—*G. Eliot, Mill on the Floss, III, v.*

Hold their noses to the grindstone.—*John Heywood, Proverbs, I, v (1546)*.

Nought lay down, nought take up.—*John Heywood, Proverbs, I, vi (1546)*.

We always took good care of number one.—*Marryat, Frank Mildmay, xix.*

O

Off agin, on agin, gone agin.—*Finnigin.—Strickland Gillilan, Finnigin to Flannigan.*

To throw oil on the fire.—*Horace, Satires, II, iii, 21.*

O. K.—*Archives of Sumner County, Tenn., 6 Oct., 1790.* May be a mistake for O. R. (Order Recorded).

One-horse town.—*Twain, Undertaker's Story.*

Solitary as an oyster.—*Dickens, Christmas Carol, I.*

P

Mind your P's and Q's.—*Hannah Cowley, Who's the Dupe?, I, ii (1779)*. Possibly pints and quarts.

We are paid in our own coin.—*Pliny the Younger, Epistles, III, ix.*

He who pays the piper can call the tune.—*Ray, English Proverbs.*

Fine words butter no parsnips.—*Arthur Murphy, Citizen, I, ii.*

You're not the only pebble on the beach.—*Henry Braistead, title of song (1896)*.

Take her down a peg or so.—*Mrs. Frances Sheridan, Dupe, IV, iv.*

Run a moist pen slick through everything and start afresh.—*Dickens, Martin Chuzzlewit, xvii.*

A penny for your thought.—*John Heywood, Proverbs, II, iv (1546)*.

A penny well sav'd is as good as one earned.—*Unkn., Roxburghe Ballads, VI, 349 (c 1686)*.

Penny wise and pound foolish.—*Wm. Camden, Remains, p. 330 (1605)*.

To buy the pig in the poke.—*John Heywood, Proverbs, I, ix (1546)*.

Gild the pill.—*Molière, Amphitryon, III, x, 24.*

Fill your pipe with that 'ere reflection.—*Dickens, Pickwick Papers, Ch. 16 (1836)*.

The pitcher that goes too often to the well leaves behind either the handle or the spout.—*Cervantes, Don Quixote, I, xxx.*

Avoid your children: small pitchers have wide ears.—*John Heywood, Proverbs, II, v.*

A place for everything, and everything in its place.—*Smiles, Thrift, p. 66.*

As plain as a pike-staff.—*Wm. Sherlocks, Hatcher of Her es (1565)*.

As pleased as Punch.—*Dickens, Hard Times, I, vi.*

Not to put too fine a point upon it.—*Dickens, Bleak House, xi.*

One man's meat is another man's poison.—*Lucretius, De Rerum Natura, IV, 637.*

As poor as church mice.—*John Ozell, Molière, IV, 33.*

Any port in a storm, they say.—*James Cobb, First Floor, II, ii.*

Possession is nine points of the law.—*T. Fuller, Holy War, V, xxix.*

Said the pot to the kettle, "Get away, blackface."—*Cervantes, Don Quixote, II, lxvii.*

I think this piece will help to boil thy pot.—*Wolcot, The Bard Complimenteth Mr. West (c 1790)*. Probably the origin of "pot-boiler".

Practice makes perfect.—*Periander (Diogenes Laertius, Periander, vi)*.

Present company excepted.—*John O'Keeffe, London Hermit.*

No time like the present.—*Mary Manley, Lost Lover, IV, i (1696)*.

No more privacy than a goldfish.—*Attributed to both H. H. Munro and Irvin S. Cobb.*

He's my prize-packet.—*Arthur W. Pinero, Preserving Mr. Panmure, II.*

The proof of the pudding is the eating.—*Cervantes, Don Quixote, II, xxiv.*

Proud as Lucifer.—*Unkn. (Wright, Political Poems, i, 315 [c 1394])*:

Proud as a peacock.—*Henry Bradshaw, St. Werburga, 69 (1513)*.

You've done yourselves proud.—*Twain, Innocents at Home, v.*

Purple cow.—*G. Burgess, title.*

Another such [Pyrrhic] victory . . . and we are undone.—*Pyrrhus (Plutarch, Lives: Pyrrhus, xxi, 9)*.

Q

On the Q. T.—*Unkn., Talkative Man from Poplar (1870)*.

Pop the question.—*Samuel Richardson, Sir Charles Grandison, VI, xx, 101.*

Burning questions of the day.—*Karl R. Hagenbach, Grundlinien der Liturgik und Homiletik (1803)*.

Ask me no questions, and I'll tell you no fibs.—*Goldsmith, She Stoops to Conquer, III, i.*

R

Racking the brains.—*Charles Churchill, Gotham, II, 13.*

A rag and a bone and a hank of hair.—*Kipling, Vampire, i.*

Rain dogs and polecats.—*Richard Brome, City Wit, IV, i (1653)*.

It cannot rain but it pours.—*Swift, Prose Miscellanies: Title.*

Keep somewhat till a rainy day.—*Nicholas Breton, Works, I, p. 39 (1582)*.

As rare a bird (rara avis) upon the earth as a black swan.—*Juvenal, Satires, VI, 165.*

I begin to smell a rat.—*Cervantes, Don Quixote, I, x.*

Red tape.—*Sydney Smith (Lady Holland, Memoir, p. 245).*

Women's reasons; they would not because they would not.—*John Lyly, Love's Metamorphosis, IV, i.*

Neither rhyme nor reason.—*T. More (F. Bacon, Apothegms, 287).*

When they asked who was dead, he stammered and said, "I don't know—I just came for the ride."—*Unkn., The Young Fellow of Clyde.*

Let her rip.—*Benjamin, Hard Times.*

All roads lead to Rome.—*La Fontaine, Fables, XII.*

To rob Peter, and give it Paul.—*Unkn., Jacob's Well, 138 (c 1440).*

Rome was not built in a day.—*P. A. Manzolli, Zodiacus Vitae, XII, 460.*

When you are in Rome, live in the Roman style.—*St. Ambrose (J. Taylor, Ductor Dubitantium, I, i, 5).*

Rope of sand.—*Bacon, Promus, 778.*

They were suffered to have rope enough till they had haltered themselves.—*T. Fuller, Holy War, V, vii (1639).*

Under the rose (sub rosa).—*Robert Dymoke, Letter to Stephen Vaughan, 1546 (State Papers, Henry VIII, II, 200).* In ancient times a rose was hung above the table when the host did not wish the guests to carry tales, and in the middle ages it was carved on the ceilings of confessionals and council chambers.

There is no royal road to geometry.—*Euclid (Proclus, Commentaria in Euclidem, II, iv).*

I had passed the Rubicon.—*John Adams, Works, IV, p. 8.* Referring to Caesar's great decision.

The wife rules the roast.—*Juvenal, Satires, VI, 149.*

S

Attic salt.—*Pliny, Historia Naturalis, XXXI, vii, 41.*

Not worth his salt.—*Petronius, Satyricon, Sec. 57.*

A grain of salt being added.—*Pliny, Historia Naturalis, XXIII, 8.*

Up to scratch.—*Hazlitt, Fight.*

Scratch my back, and I'll scratch yours.—*Petronius, Satyricon, Sec. 44.*

Scylla guards the right side; insatiate Charybdis the left.—*Vergil, Aeneid, III, 420.*

Play the second fiddle.—*C. H. Spurgeon, Salt-Cellars.*

Custom becomes a sort of second nature.—*Cicero, De Finibus, V, xxv, 74.*

On whom he many a sheepish eye did cast.—*John Grange, Golden Aphroditis, D 1 (1577).*

Where my shoe pinches.—*Plutarch, Lives: Aemilius Paulus, v, 2.*

Sick as a dog.—*Gabriel Harvey, Works, I, 161 (1592).*

The real Simon Pure.—*Centlivre, Bold Stroke for a Wife, V, i (1710).*

Live or die, sink or swim.—*George Peele, Edward I (c 1586).*

Six of one and half-a-dozen of the other.—*Marryat, Pirate, iv.*

It burst in six or in seven.—*Unkn., Avowyne of Arthur, lxv (c 1340).*

He would ask a flint.—*J. Berthelson, English-Danish Dictionary, skin.*

Sleep like a top.—*D'Avenant, Rivals, III (1668).*

Sleep of the just.—*Racine, Abrégé de l'Histoire de Port Royal, IV, 517.*

There's many a slip 'twixt the cup and the lip.—*Palladas (Greek Anthology, X, 32).*

The name of the Slough was Despond.—*Bunyan, Pilgrim's Progress, I.*

A sort of chit-chat, or small talk.—*Chesterfield, Letters, June 20, 1791.*

There is no smoke without a fire.—*Plautus, Curculio, l. 53.*

A chill snake lurks in the grass.—*Vergil, Eclogues, II, 93.*

Snug as a bug in a rug.—*Franklin, Letter to Miss Georgiana Shipley, Sept., 1772.*

Good for sore eyes.—*Swift, Polite Conversation, I.*

Savage as a bear with a sore head.—*Marryat, King's Own, xxvi.*

Call a spade a spade.—*Philip of Macedon (Plutarch, Apothegms of Kings and Great Commanders: Philip).*

Speed the parting guest.—*Homer, Odyssey, XV, 81 (Pope tr.).*

Spell-binders.—*William Cassius Goodloe (1888).*

Born wi' a silver spoon in his mouth.—*John Wilson, Noctes Ambrosianae.* Quoted as proverb.

In the spring a young man's fancy lightly turns to thoughts of love.—*Tennyson, Locksley Hall, 19.*

To hitch his wagon to a star.—*R. Emerson, Society and Solitude: Civilization.*

True as steel.—*Chaucer, Legend of Good Women, IX, 21 (1385).*

Let them stew in their own juice.—*Bismarck (Labouchere, Diary of a Besieged Resident).*

Wrong end of the stick.—*Gabriel Harvey, Letter-Book, p. 5 (1573).*

A stitch in time may save nine.—*T. Fuller, Gnomologia, 6291 (1732).*

The way to a man's heart is through his stomach.—*Fanny Fern, Willis Parton.*

Leave no stone unturned.—*Euripides, Heracleidae, 1002.*

The rolling stone never gathereth moss.—*John Heywood, Proverbs, I, xi (1546).*

Within a stone's throw of it.—*Cervantes, Don Quixote, I, ix.*

Driven into a desperate strait.—*Massinger, Great Duke of Florence, III, i.*

Strait laced.—*John Heywood, Proverbs, I, ix (1546).*

I did not care one straw.—*Terence, Eunuchus, l. 411.*

We catch hold of hopes . . . as drowning men do upon thorns, or straws. —*L'Estrange, Seneca's Epistles, XVIII (c 1680).*

The last straw breaks the camel's back.—*T. Fuller, Gnomologia, 5129.*

Two strings to my bow.—*Terence, Phormio, l. 603.*

To strive against the stream.—*Juvenal, Satires, IV, 89.*

Stuffed shirt.—*Attributed to Fay Templeton, who used it in 1899.*

Survival of the fittest.—*H. Spencer, Principles of Biology, III, xii, 165.*

Swan song.—*Plato, Phaedo, 84.*

Swear like a fish-wife.—*Edmund Gayton, Festivous Notes on Don Quixote, p. 60 (not exact words).*

Sweet tooth.—*John Lyly, Euphues and His England, p. 308.*

Matters go swimmingly.—*Cervantes, Don Quixote, II, xxxvi.*

T

Performed to a T.—*Rabelais, Works, IV, xli.*

Teach the young idea how to shoot. —*J. Thomson, Seasons: Spring, 1152.*

They have digged their grave with their teeth.—*T. Adams, Works, p. 108 (1630).*

Telling tales out of school.—*Tyndale, Practice of Prelates, 249 (1530).*

A storm in a wine-ladle.—*Cicero, De Legibus, III, xvi, 36.* Quoted as proverb. Several variations lead from this to "Tempest in a teapot."

Through thick and through thin.— *Chaucer, Reeves Tale, 148 (c 1386).*

A thief of venison . . . can keep a forest best of any man.—*Chaucer, Phisiciens Tale, 83.*

Even thieves have a code of laws.— *Cicero, De Officiis, II, xi, 40.*

Considering [thinking] cap.—*Robert Armin, Foole upon Foole, p. 40 (1605).*

He that goes barefoot must not plant thorns.—*G. Herbert, Jacula Prudentum (1640).*

Wrapt in thought as in a veil.—*J. Thomson, City of Dreadful Night, II.*

Three sheets in the wind.—*R. H. Dana, Two Years Before the Mast, xx.* Quoted. No source given.

My voice stuck in my throat.—*Vergil, Aeneid, II, 774.*

With thumb turned.—*Juvenal, Satires, III, 36.* Sign of condemnation in Roman arena.

When he should get aught, each finger is a thumb.—*John Heywood, Proverbs, II, v.*

They steal my [stage] thunder.—*John Dennis (Biographia Britannica, V, 103).*

Kill time.—*Rabelais, Works, IV, lxiii.*

Time and tide stayeth for no man.— *R. Brathwaite, English Gentleman, 189 (1630).*

Time is money.—*Franklin, Advice to a Young Tradesman.*

The big toad in the little puddle.— *T. Fuller, Gnomologia.*

Horny-handed sons of toil.—*Denis Kearney, speech, San Francisco, c 1878.*

Tom, Dick, and Harry.—*John Adams, Works, X, 351 (c 1800).*

Tommy Atkins.—*Used in 1815 on sample forms sent out by British war office.*

Not to be handled with a pair of tongs.—*John Clarke, Paraemiologia, 34 (1639).*

Better the feet slip than the tongue. —*G. Herbert, Jacula Prudentum.*

Hold your tongue.—*Horace, Odes, III, i, 2.*

Their secrets lay at their tongues' end.—*Richard Tarlton, News Out of Purgatory, 69 (1590).*

With tooth and nail.—*James Calfhill, Answer to Martial, 228 (1565).*

Tough customer.—*Dickens, Barnaby Rudge, i.*

I had her . . . up a tree, as the Americans say.—*Thackeray, Major Gahagan, v.*

This peck of troubles.—*Cervantes, Don Quixote, II, liii.*

The naked truth.—*Horace, Odes, I, xxiv, 7.*

Truth is in a well.—*Democritus (Diogenes Laertius, Pyrrho, IX, 72).*

Truth is . . . stranger than fiction.— *Byron, Don Juan, XIV, ci.*

The truth may stretch but will not break.—*Cervantes, Don Quixote, II, xvii.*

One good turn deserves another.— *Petronius, Satyricon, 45.*

I suppose, to use our national motto, something will turn up.—*Disraeli, Popanilla, vii (1828).*

Strange all this difference should be twixt Tweedledum and Tweedledee.— *John Byrom, On the Feud Between Handel and Bononcini.* Also attributed to Swift and Pope.

I care not two-pence.—*Beaumont and Fletcher, Coxcomb, V, i.*

Not worth a two-penny dam.—*Duke of Wellington, Letter to His Brother (Dispatches, I).*

U

Uncle Sam.—*Unkn., editorial, Troy, N. Y., Post, 7 Sept., 1813.*

Unmentionables.—*Dickens, Sketches by Boz.*

They are all upper-crust here.—*T. C. Haliburton, Sam Slick in England, xxiv (1843).*

On our uppers.—*Guy W. Carryl, How a Cat Was Annoyed and a Poet Was Booted.*

V

Variety's the very spice of life.— *Cowper, Task, II, 606.*

Shrinking as violets do in summer's ray.—*T. Moore, Lalla Rookh: Veiled Prophet of Khorassan, 294.*

W

All will come out in the washing.— *Cervantes, Don Quixote, I, xx.*

The king has sent me some of his dirty linen to wash.—*Voltaire, Reply to General Manstein.*

Waste not, want not.—*T. Hardy, Under the Greenwood Tree, viii.*

Trouble runs off him like water off a duck's back.—*G. Herbert, Jacula Prudentum.*

This business will never hold water.—*Cibber, She Wou'd and She Wou'd Not, IV.*

The way of all flesh.—*J. Webster, Westward Ho! II, ii (1603).*

Under the weather.—*Stevenson, Wrecker, iv.*

Life on life downstricken goes . . . to the land of the western god.—*Sophocles, Oedipus Tyrannus, 176.*

I wist not what was what.—*Unkn., Ywaine and Gavin, 432 (c 1400).*

Whatever is is right.—*Democritus (Diogenes Laertius, Democritus, IX, 45).*

Put his shoulder to the wheel.—*Robert Burton, Anatomy of Melancholy, II, i, 2.*

I want to see the wheels go round.—*John Habberton, Helen's Babies, 11.*

Let us wet our whistles.—*Petronius, Satyricon, 34.*

Whistling to keep myself from being afraid.—*Dryden, Amphitryon, II, i.*

Sow . . . wild oats.—*Plautus, Trinummus, IV, iv, 128.*

To him that will, ways are not wanting.—*G. Herbert, Jacula Prudentum (1640).*

An ill wind that bloweth no man good.—*John Heywood, Song Against Idleness (c 1540).*

Wind bag.—*Sophocles (Plato, Theaetetus, 160).*

To attack windmills.—*Cervantes, Don Quixote, I, viii.*

These lovely lamps, these windows of the soul.—*G. S. Du Bartas, Devine Weekes and Workes, I, vi (Sylvester tr.).*

A wink's as good as a nod with some folks.—*Dorothy Wordsworth, Journal, I, 129 (1802).*

Neither with thee, nor without thee, can I live.—*Ovid, Amores, III, xi, 39.*

The wolf from the door.—*John Skelton, Colyn Cloute, 1531 (c 1500).*

Who's afraid of the big bad wolf?—*Ann Ronell, title of song (1933).*

A wolf in his belly.—*Beaumont and Fletcher, Women Pleased, I, ii.*

On account of that wonderful event, a nine days' solemn feast was celebrated by the Romans.—*Livy, History, I, 31.*

Don't shout till you are out of the wood.—*Sophocles (Cicero, Epistolae ad Atticum, IV, viii).*

Ye cannot see the wood for the trees.—*John Heywood, Proverbs, II, iv (1546).*

The woods are full of them.—*A. Wilson, American Ornithology: Preface (1808).*

Her word . . . was found as true as any bond.—*Chaucer, Book of the Duchesse, 935.*

A word to the wise is sufficient.—*Plautus, Persa, 729.*

Yet will the woman have the last word.—*Unkn., School House of Women, 76 (1542).*

You actually snatch the words from my mouth.—*Plautus, Mercator, 176.*

Before I eat these words, I will make thee eat a piece of my blade.—*Richard Stanyhurst, Description of Ireland, Fo. 20 (1577).*

Winged words.—*Homer, Iliad, XX, 331.*

It will go all in your day's work.—*Swift, Polite Conversation, I.*

Man's work lasts till set of sun; woman's work is never done.—*Unkn., Roxburghe Ballads, III, 302 (c 1655).*

All work and no play makes Jack a dull boy.—*James Howell, Proverbs, 12 (1659).*

It takes all sorts of people to make a world.—*Douglas Jerrold, Story of a Feather (Punch, V, 55).*

All the world and his wife.—*Swift, Polite Conversation, III (1738).*

The world, the flesh, and the devil.—*Book of Common Prayer: Litany.*

This world surely is wide enough to hold both thee and me.—*Sterne, Tristram Shandy, II, xii.*

Be wisely worldly, but not worldly wise.—*Quarles, Emblems, II, 2.*

Tread on a worm and it will turn.—*Robert Greene, The Worth of Wit.*

The worse for wearing.—*John Heywood, Proverbs, II, i (1546).*

Let the worst come to the worst.—*Cervantes, Don Quixote, I, v.*

Y

Yankee Doodle.—*Edward Bangs, Yankee's Return to Camp.* Also attributed to Dr. Richard Shuckburg, British officer stationed at Albany in 1758.

You know me Al.—*Ring Lardner, title.*

Bloom of youth.—*Terence, Andria, 74.*

AUTHORS' REFERENCE INDEX

www.ingramcontent.com/pod-product-compliance
Lightning Source LLC
Chambersburg PA
CBHW020237290326
41929CB00044B/37